HIPPOCRENE STANDARD DICTIONARY

## Revised Edition

# POLISH-ENGLISH
# ENGLISH-POLISH

## with Complete Phonetics

# HIPPOCRENE STANDARD DICTIONARY

# POLISH-ENGLISH ENGLISH-POLISH

## DICTIONARY

### with Complete Phonetics

## IWO CYPRIAN POGONOWSKI

### Revised Edition

**HIPPOCRENE BOOKS**
*New York, 1991*

Second Revised Edition, 1990
Sixth Printing, 1991

Hippocrene Books, Inc.
171 Madison Avenue
New York, New York 10016

Printed in the United States or America


Library of Congress Cataloging in Publication Data

Pogonowski, Iwo Cyprian, 1921–
    Dictionary, Polish-English, English-Polish

    1. Polish language—Dictionaries—English.
2. English language—Dictionaries—Polish.
I. Title.
PG6640.P54   1982        491.8'5321        82-9211
ISBN 0-87052-908-0 (hb)    AACR2
ISBN 0-87052-882-3 (pbk)

To my wife, Magdalena

# CONTENTS
# SPIS TRESCI

# Introduction

The Polish-English part of this dictionary contains about 16,000 entries. The unique feature of the work is the way in which ordinary English pronunciation is used to convey the approximate sound of the Polish word. There is no need, therefore, to learn the complicated phonetic symbols which are often a stumbling block in the everyday use of dictionaries by non-scholars.

Unlike English, the Polish language has an abundance of grammatical forms. Changes in endings of nouns, adjectives and verbs correspond to their function in a sentence, their gender, their number and their tense. Thus Polish declensions call for seven different endings, for each gender, in the singular and in the plural. The number of Polish words is further increased by the multitude of augmentatives and diminutives.

Unlike English, Polish pronunciation is consistent and clear. Polish achieves the size of its vocabulary by use of prefixes and suffixes to a greater extent than the English language. Thus English has some 120,000 root words, about double the 60,000 root words in Polish. Yet the many variants in the Polish language provide a vocabulary of half a million words, about the same as in English.

Spoken by over 50 million people today, the Polish language, with its logic, finery and elegance will continue to serve well abstract thinkers such as mathematicians and philosophers, as well as novelists and poets, thus contributing to the pluralistic culture of the world.

<u>EXAMPLE OF NOUN AND ADJECTIVE DECLENSION IN POLISH LANGUAGE</u>

DOBRY DOM = GOOD HOME, GOOD HOUSE

SINGULAR:

| | | | |
|---|---|---|---|
| NOMINATIVUS | = MIANOWNIK | DOBRY DOM | GOOD HOME |
| GENETIVUS | = DOPEŁNIACZ | DOBREGO DOMU | OF A GOOD HOME |
| DATIVUS | = CELOWNIK | DOBREMU DOMOWI | FOR A GOOD HOME |
| ACCUSATIVUS | = BIERNIK | DOBRY DOM | A GOOD HOME |
| INSTRUMENTALIS=NARZĘDNIK | | DOBRYM DOMEM | BY A GOOD HOME |
| LOCATIVUS | = MIEJSCOWNIK | W DOBRYM DOMU | IN A GOOD HOME |
| VOCATIVUS | = WOŁACZ | O DOBRY DOMU! | OH! GOOD HOME |

PLURAL:

| | | | |
|---|---|---|---|
| NOMINATIVUS | = MIANOWNIK | DOBRE DOMY (2,3,4) | GOOD HOMES |
| | | DOBRYCH DOMÓW (5...) | GOOD HOMES |
| GENETIVUS | = DOPEŁNIACZ | DOBRYCH DOMÓW | OF GOOD HOMES |
| DATIVUS | = CELOWNIK | DOBRYM DOMOM | FOR GOOD HOMES |
| ACCUSATIVUS | = BIERNIK | DOBRE DOMY (2,3,4) | GOOD HOMES |
| | | DOBRYCH DOMÓW (5...) | GOOD HOMES |
| INSTRUMENTALIS=NARZĘDNIK | | DOBRYMI DOMAMI | BY GOOD HOMES |
| LOCATIVUS | = MIEJSCOWNIK | W DOBRYCH DOMACH | IN GOOD HOMES |
| VOCATIVUS | = WOŁACZ | O DOBRE DOMY!(2,3,4) | OH!GOOD HOMES |
| | | O (PIĘC) DOBRYCH | OH! (FIVE) |
| | | DOMÓW! (5...) | GOOD HOMES |

<u>NOTE:</u> (2,3,4) = Small Polish plural of two, three and four.
    ( 5...) = Large Polish plural of five and more.

<u>DIMINUTIVES:</u>    <u>SING.</u>: DOBRY DOMEK - <u>PLUR.</u>: DOBRE DOMKI (2,3,4)
                                        DOBRYCH DOMKÓW (5...)
                    DOBRY DOMECZEK        DOBRE DOMECZKI (2,3,4)
                                        DOBRYCH DOMECZKÓW (5...)
<u>AUGMENTATIVES:</u>   <u>SING.</u>:DOBRE DOMISKO   <u>PLUR.</u>:DOBRE DOMISKA(2,3,4)
                                        DOBRYCH DOMISK (5...)

XII

<u>EXAMPLE OF CONJUGATION OF A VERB IN THE POLISH LANGUAGE</u>

CZYTAC (chi-tach) = TO READ

- PAST TENSE -

PERFECT FORM = SINGLE TIME COMPLETED OCCURENCE

| | | | | |
|---|---|---|---|---|
| MASCULINE | "I" | (JA) | CZYTAŁEM | I READ |
| FEMININE | "I" | (JA) | CZYTAŁAM | |
| MASCULINE | "YOU" | (TY) | CZYTAŁES | YOU READ |
| FEMININE | "YOU" | (TY) | CZYTAŁAS | |
| | | (ON) | CZYTAŁ | HE READ |
| | | (ONA) | CZYTAŁA | SHE READ |
| | | (ONO) | CZYTAŁO | IT READ |
| MASCULINE | "WE" | (MY) | CZYTALISMY | WE READ |
| FEMININE | "WE" | (MY) | CZYTAŁYSMY | |
| MASC.PLUR. | "YOU" | (WY) | CZYTALISCIE | YOU READ |
| FEM. PLUR. | "YOU" | (WY) | CZYTAŁYSCIE | |
| | | (ONI) | CZYTALI | THEY READ |
| FEM.& NEUTER | | (ONE) | CZYTAŁY | |

CZYTYWAC (chi-ti-vach)=TO READ (OFTEN)

IMPERFECT FORM = MULTIPLE INCOMPLETE OCCURENCE IN THE PAST

| | | | | |
|---|---|---|---|---|
| MASCULINE | "I" | (JA) | CZYTYWAŁEM | I USED TO READ |
| FEMININE | "I" | (JA) | CZYTYWAŁAM | |
| MASCULINE | "YOU" | (TY) | CZYTYWAŁES | YOU USED TO READ |
| FEMININE | "YOU" | (TY) | CZYTYWAŁAS | |
| | | (ON) | CZYTYWAŁ | HE USED TO READ |
| | | (ONA) | CZYTYWAŁA | SHE USED TO READ |
| | | (ONO) | CZYTYWAŁO | IT USED TO READ |
| MASCULINE | "WE" | (MY) | CZYTYWALISMY | WE USED TO READ |
| FEMININE | "WE" | (MY) | CZYTYWAŁYSMY | |
| MASC.PLUR. | "YOU" | (WY) | CZYTYWALISCIE | YOU USED TO READ |
| FEM. PLUR. | "YOU" | (WY) | CZYTYWAŁYSCIE | |
| | | (ONI) | CZYTYWALI | THEY USED TO READ |
| FEM.& NEUTER | | (ONE) | CZYTYWAŁY | |

<u>EXAMPLES</u> OF WORDS DERIVED FROM THE VERB "CZYTAC"= TO READ

DOCZYTAC, DOCZYTAC SIE, DOCZYTYWAC, DOCZYTYWAC SIE,
NACZYTAC SIE, NACZYTYWAC SIE, OCZYTAC SIE, ODCZYTAC,
ODCZYTYWAC, POCZYTAC, POCZYTAC SOBIE, POCZYTYWAC, POCZY-
TYWAC SOBIE, PRZECZYTAC, ROZCZYTAC SIE, ROZCZYTYWAC SIE,
WCZYTAC SIE, WCZYTYWAC SIE, WYCZYTAC, WYCZYTYWAC, ZACZY-
TYWAC, SIE, ZACZYTAC SIE describe all the possible ways
and conditions of reading with the exception of "reread-
ing" which can not be translated into Polish in one word.
Besides the twenty three verbs are nouns: CZYTANKA, CZY-
TELNICTWO, CZYTELNIK, CZYTELNIA, CZYTELNOSC, ODCZYT, POCZY-
TALNOSC, NIEPOCZYTALNOSC, POCZYTNOSC, and adjectives as:
CZYTELNY, NIECZYTELNY, OCZYTANY, NIEOCZYTANY, POCZYTALNY,
NIEPOCZYTALNY, POCZYTNY etc.

XIII

# Przedmowa

Angielsko-polska część słownika zawiera około 20,000 haseł. Wymowę słów angielskich podano w języku polskim, a nie w symbolach fonetycznych, które często przysparzają trudności w codziennym użyciu słowników.

Bogactwo polskich form gramatycznych nie ma odpowiednika w angielskim. Język angielski bogatszy jest w wyrażenia zwyczajowo-idiomatyczne; więcej też jest w nim przyimków i zaimków. Ogólnie biorąc język polski ma więcej form rzeczownikowych, przymiotnikowych oraz czasownikowych. W angielskim natomiast prawie każdy rzeczownik bez zmiany pisowni może być użyty jako czasownik, a nieraz także jako przymiotnik. Polskie zasady gramatyczne i fonetyczne można wyrazić słowami "zawsze z kilkoma wyjątkami," angielskie zasady gramatyczne i fonetyczne są bardziej płynne — mówi się w nich "często," "czasem" i "nieraz." W angielskim przewazają wyrazenia i fonetyka zwyczajowe.

Hasła wybrano z uwzględnieniem słownictwa używanego obecnie w Polsce i Ameryce; są wśrod nich ważniejsze wyrażenia potoczne. Język angielski, bogaty, energiczny i stosunkowo nieskomplikowany gramatycznie, jest obecnie językiem swiatowego przemysłu, handlu i wiedzy scisłej, i liczebnie na świecie dominuje.

Język polski, oparty na pięknych tradycjach, elegancki i logiczny, dobrze służy myśli abstrakcyjnej i literaturze pięknej, wnosząc znaczne walory do pluralistycznej kultury świata.

# POLISH-ENGLISH

a (a)(as"a" in car) conj. and;
or; but; then: at that time
a to (a to) conj. and so
abażur (a-bá-zhoor) m. lamp
shade; a device to screen light
abdykować (ab-di-kó-vaćh) v.
abdicate, abdicate the throne
abecadło (a-be-tsá-dwo) n.
A.B.C., alphabet
abonament (a-bo-ná-ment) m.
subscription, season ticket
abonent (a-bó-nent) m.subscrib-
er, holder of a season ticket
abonować (a-bo-nó-vaćh) v.
subscribe to a periodical etc.
absencja (ab-sén-tsya) f.
absence, non-attendance
abstrakcja(ab-strák-tsya) f.
abstraction; abstract
absurd (áb-soord) m. absurdity
aby (á-bi) conj. to; in order
to, in order that, only to
ach ! (akh) excl.:oh ! ah!
aczkolwiek (ach-kól-vyek) conj.
though; although, albeit, tho
adapter (a-dáp-ter) m. record
player, adapter; pick-up
administracja (ad-mee-ñees-
tráts-ya) f.administration;
(management) authorities
admirał (ad-mée-raw) m.admiral
adres (ád-res) m.address
adwokat (ad-vó-kat) m. lawyer
afera (a-fé-ra) f. swindle
aferzysta (a-fe-zhís-ta) m.
swindler; confidence man
afisz (á-feesh) m. poster
afiszować (a-fee-shó-vaćh) v.
advertise; flaunt: parade
agrafka (a-gráf-ka) f. safety
pin; hist.: buckle; brooch
agrest (ág-rest) m.gooseberry
aha ! (ákh-a!) excl.:oh yes...
a jakże ! (a-yák-zhe) excl.
oh yes...: yes indeed!
akacja (a-káts-ya) f. acacia;
locust tree: black locust
akcja (ák-tsya) f. action;
share; plot; campain
akord (ák-ort) m. chord; piece
work; contract work
AK (a-ká) f. Polish Home Army
(W.W.II) (Armia Krajowa)

akowiec (a-kóv-yets) m. soldier
of the Polish Home Army (W.W.II)
aksamit (ak-sá-meet) m. velvet
akt (akt) m. deed; act; certificate; painting of a nude
akta (ák-ta) pl. documents;
deeds; dossier; files; records
aktualny (ak-too-ál-ni) m.
timely; current; up to date
akumulator (a-koo-moo-lá-tor)m.
battery: storage battery
akuszerka (a-koo-shér-ka) f.
midwife: accoucheuse
akwarela (ak-va-ré-la) f. watercolor; painting in water color
albo (á-lbo) conj. or; else
albowiem (al-bó-vyem) conj. for;
as; since;because; on account of
ale (á-le) conj. however; but;
still; yet; not at all; n.defect
aleja (a-le-ya) f. avenue: alley
ależ (á-lesh) conj. why (yes)
alfa (ál-fa) f. alpha
alfabet (al-fá-bet) m. alphabet
alfons (ál-fons) m. pimp; cadet
alimenty (a-lee-mén-ti) pl.
alimony for separated wife
alkohol (al-kó-khol) m. alcohol
alpejski (al-pey-skee) adj. m.
Alpine: of the Alps
aluzja (a-looz-ya) f. hint:
allusion; insinuation: dig
ałun (á-woon) m. alum
amant (á-mant) m. lover: beau
ambasada (am-ba-sá-da) f.
embassy; ambassador and his staff
ambicja (am-beéts-ya) f. ambition: aspiration: self esteem
ambona (am-bó-na) f. pulpit
Amerykanin (A-me-ri-ká-ñeen) m.
American: man native of America
Amerykanka (A-me-ri-kán-ka) f.
American: American women
amerykański (a-me-ri-kañ-skee)
adj. m. American: of America
amnestia (am-nést-ya) f.amnesty
amory (a-mó-ri) pl. flirtation;
courting; love affairs
amortyzacja (a-mor-ti-záts-ya)
f. depreciation; amortization
amperomierz (am-pe-ró-myesh) m.
ammeter: meter of amperes

amputować (am-poo-tó-vaćh) v. amputate ; to cut off

amunicja (a-moo-ńeéts-ya) f. ammunition; munitions

analfabeta (a-nal-fa-bé-ta) m. illiterate; an ignorant

analiza (a-na-leé-za) f. analysis ; parsing

analogia (a-na-ló-g-ya) f. analogy; parallelism; parity

ananas (a-ná-nas) m. pineapple; rascal; rogue; blighter

andrus (an-droos) m. rough kid

andrut (ánd-root) m. wafer

anegdota (a-neg-dó-ta) f. anecdote; story; theme

aneksja (a-néks-ya) f. annexation; rape of a country

anemia (a-ném-ya) f. anemia

angażować (an-ga-zhó-vaćh) v. engage; undertake; hire;bind

angielski (an—gél-skee) adj. m. English; English language

ani (á-ńee) conj. neither; nor; no; not; or; not even

anielski (a-ńél-skee) adj. m. angelic; cherubic; angelical

animusz (a-ńeé-moosh) m. courage; verve; vigor; zest

anioł (á-ńow) m. angel

aniżeli (a-ńee-zhé-lee) part. rather; than; rather than

ankieta (an—ḱé-ta) f. poll; inquiry; questionnaire

anons (á-nons) m. advertisement in a newspaper; ad

antybiotyki (an-ti-bee-yó-tikee) pl. antibiotics

antyk (án-tik) antique

antypatyczny (an-ti-pa-tichni) adj. m. repugnant

apartament (a-par-tá-ment) m. residence; suite of rooms

aparat (a-pa-rat) m. apparatus; appliance; camera; gadget;gear

apel (áp-el) m. appeal; rollcall; appeal; muster; parade

apetyt (a-pé-tit) m. appetite

apostolski (a-pos-tól-skee) adj. m. apostolic; missionary

aprobować (a-pro-bó-vaćh) v. approve; endorse; sanction

aprowizacja (a-pro-vee-záts-ya) f. food supply; provisions

apteczka (ap-téch-ka) f. first aid kit; medicine chest

apteka (ap-té-ka) f. pharmacy

arbiter (ar-bée-ter) m. umpire; arbitrator; moderator; mediator

arbuz (ár-boos) m. watermelon

architekt (ar-khee-tekt) m. architect

arcydzieło (ar-tsi-dżhé-wo) n. masterpiece

arena (a-ré-na) f. arena; stage

areszt (á-resht) m. arrest; jail

argument (ar-goó-ment) m. argument; reason; contention

arkusz (ar-koosh) m. sheet

armata (ar-má-ta) f. cannon

armator (ar-má-tor) m. shipowner; skipper; charterer

armia (árm-ya) f. army; array

arogancja (a-ro-gán-tsya) f. arrogance; insolence; conceit

arteria(ar-tér-ya) f. artery

artykuł (ar-ti-koow) m. article

artretyzm (ar-tré-tizm) m. arthritis; gout

artyleria (ar-ti-lér-ya) f. artillery; gunnery; ordnance

artysta (ar-ti-sta) m. artist

arytmetyka (a-rit-mé-ti-ka) f. arithmetic

as (as) m. ace ; A flat

asceta (as-tsé-ta) m. ascetic

asekuracja (a-se-koo-ráts-ya) f. insurance; assurance

aspiryna (as-pee-rí-na) f. aspirin

astma (ást-ma) f. asthma

asygnata (a-sig-ná-ta) f. order (of payment)

asymilować (a-si-mee-ló-vaćh) v. assimilate; absorb; liken

asystować (a-sis-tó-vaćh) v. accompany; attend; court; assist

atak (á-tak) m. attack; charge (fit); spasm; offensive

atlas (át-las) m. atlas

atleta (at-lé-ta) m. athlete

atłas (át-was) m. satin

atmosfera (at-mos-fé-ra) f. atmosphere; air; climate; tone

atom (á-tom) m. atom
atol (á-tol) m. atoll
atomowy (a-to-mó-vi) adj. m.
  atomic
atrakcja (a-trák-tsya) f.
  attraction; high light
atrament (a-trá-ment) m. ink
atut (á-toot) m. trump
audycja (aw-díts-ya)f. broadcast; program; pop
aukcja (áwk-tsya) f. auction
autentyczny (aw-ten-tích-ni)
  adj. m. authentic; genuine
auto (áw-to) n. motor car
autor (áw-tor) m. author
autostrada (aw-to-strá-da) f.
  superhighway; freeway
awans (á-vans) m. promotion;
  advancement; preferment
awantura (a-van-tóo-ra) f.
  brawl; fuss; row; scandal
azot (á-zot) m, nitrogen
aż (ásh) part. as much; up to;
  'til ; until; as far as
ażeby (a-zhé-bi) conj. that;
  in order that; so that
ażurowy (a-zhoo-ró-vi) adj. m.
  lace-like; transparent
ba (bá) excl.: hey ?; nay;
  indeed..; and even; what more
baba (bá-ba) f. woman (old,
  simple); grandmother; rammer
babiarz (báb-yash) m. lady
  chaser; ladies' man
babie lato (bá-bye lá-to) n.
  Indian Summer; lass;chick;cake
babka (báb-ka) f. grandmother;
babrać (báb-rach) v. smear;
  stain; dabble; soil; fumble
bachor (bá-khor) m. kid; brat
baczność (bách-noshch) f.
  attention; care
bać się (bach sháń) v. fear
badacz (bá-dach) m. researcher
badać (bá-dach) v. investigate;
  examine; research ; explore
badyl (bá-dil) m. stem; weed
badylarz (ba-dí-lash) m.
  marketing gardener (slang)
bagatela (ba-ga-té-la) f.
  trifle ; easy matter
bagaż (bá-gash) m. luggage

bagażowy (ba-ga-zhó-vi) m. porter; adj.m. baggage-; luggage-
bagnet (bág-net) m. bayonet
bagno (bág-no) m. swamp; morass
bajka (báy-ka) f. fairy-tale;
  gossip; scandal; story; fable
bajoro (ba-yó-ro) n. muddy pool
bak (bak) m. gasoline tank;
  side whisker ⌡bacteria;
bakterie ( bak-tér-ye) pl.germs
bal (bal) m. ball; bale; log
balet (bá-let) m. ballet
balia (bál-ya) f. wash tub
balkon (bál-kon) m. balcony
balustrada (ba-loos-trá-da) f.
  railing; hand rail; guard rail
bałagan (ba-wá-gan) m. mess;
  disorder; disarray; confusion
bałamucić (ba-wa-móo-tseech) v.
  lead astray; loiter; flirt; coax
bałwan (báw-van) m. snowman; ass;
  breaking wave crest; blockhead;
  fool; nitwit; fetish; idol; lump
banał (bá-naw) m. stock phrase;
  tag; banality; truism; triviality
banan (bá-nan) m. banana
banda (bán-da) f. band; gang
bandaż (bán-dash) m. bandage
bandera (ban-dé-ra) f. flag
bandyta (ban-dí-ta) m. bandit
bank (bank) m. bank; pool
bankiet (bán-ket ) m. banquet
banknot (bánk-not) m. banknote
bankrut (bánk-root) m. bankrupt
babtysta (bap-tís-ta) m. baptist
bar (bar) m. bar; barium
barman (bár-man) m. barman
barak (bá-rak) m. barrack
baran (bá-ran) m. ram;tup; idiot
baraszkować (ba-rash-kó-vach)
  v. frolic; gambol; romp; caper
barbarzyńca (bar-ba-zhiń-tsa)
  m. barbarian; savage; vandal
barczysty (bar-chís-ti) m.
  broad-shouldered; square built
bardziej (bár-dzhey)adv.more;
  (emphatic "bardzo"); worse
bardzo (bár-dzo) adv. very
bariera (bar-yé-ra) f. rail;
  barrier; hand rail; obstacle
barki (bár-kee) pl. shoulders
barłóg (bár-woog) m. litter bed

barszcz (barshch) m. beet soup
barwa (bár-va) f. color; hue
bary (bá-ri) pl. large
shoulders ; parallel bars
barykada (ba-ri-ká-da) f.
barricade ; barrier
baryłka (ba-riw-ka) f. barrel
basen (bá-sen) m. pool; tank
bastard (bás-tard) m. bastard
baśń (baśhń) f. fable; myth
bat (bat) m. whip; lash
bateria (ba-tér-ya) f. battery
bawełna (ba-véw-na) f. cotton
bawialnia (ba-vyál-ña) f.
sitting room; parlor
bawić (bá-veech) v. amuse;
entertain ; recreate; stay
bawidamek (ba-vee-dá-mek) m.
ladies man ; gallant
bawoł (bá-voow) m. buffalo
baza (bá-za) f. base ; basis
bazgrać (báz-grach) v. scribble;
scrawl; scratch; daub; splotch
bażant (bá-zhant) m. pheasant
bąbel (bówn-bel) m. blister
bądź (bownch) v. be this
bądź (bownch) conj. either-or
bąk (bównk) m. horse fly;
blunder; vulg. : fart
bąkać(bówn-kach) v. mumble;
hint ; mutter; hum
bebechy (be-bé-khi) pl. guts
beczka (béch-ka) f. barrel
bednarz (béd-nash) m. cooper
befsztyk (béf-shtik) m. beefsteak
beksa (bék-sa) f. cry baby
beletrystyka (be-le-tris-ti-
ka) f. fiction ; letters
belka (bél-ka) f. beam; bar
bełkot (béw-kot) m. mumbling
benzyna (ben-zína) f. gasoline
berbeć (bér-bech) m. small kid;
toddler ; brat; dot
berek (be-rek) m. tag play
beret (bé-ret) m. beret ; cap
besztać (bésh-tach) v. scold;
rebuke ; chide; rebuke:trounce
bestia (bés-tya) f. beast
beton (bé-ton) m. concrete
bety (bé-ti) pl. bedding
bez (bes) prep. without

bez (bes) m. lilac;prep.without
bez-(bes) prefix = suffix less
beza (bé-za) f. meringue
bezbarwny (bez-bárw-ni) adj.
m. colorless; plain; drab; dull
bezbłędny (bez-bwáñd-ni) adj.
m. faultless; correct; perfect
bezbolesny (bez-bo-lés-ni) adj.
m. painless
bezbronny (bez-brón-ni) adj.
m. defenseless: helpless;unarmed
bezcelowy (bez-tse-ló-vi) adj.
m. aimless; pointless; useless
bezcenny (bez-tsén-ni) adj.m.
priceless; invluable; inestimable
bezchmurny (bez-khmóo-rni)
adj. m. cloudless; serene; clear
bezdomny (bez-dóm-ni) adj. m.
homeless; houseless; shelterless
bezdzietny (bez-dzhét-ni) adj
m. childless; without offspring
bezdźwięczny (bez-dzhváñch-ni)
adj. m. soundless; voiceless
bezecny (be-zéts-ni) adj. m.
wicked; infamous; ignominious
bezgotówkowy (bez-go-toov-kó-
vi) adj. m. without cash
bezgrzeszny (bez-gzhésh-ni)
adj. m. sinless;inocent; chaste
bezkonkurencyjny (bez-kon-koo-
ren-tsíy-ni) adj. m. unrivaled
bezkrwawy (bez-krva-vi) adj.
m. bloodless; free of bloodshed
bezkształtny (bez-kshtáwt-ni)
adj. m. shapeless; formless
bezład (béz-wat) m. disorder
bezmiar (béz-myar) m. immen-
sity ; boundlessness; vastness
bezmyślnosć (bez-miśhl-noshch)
f. thoughtlessness ; wantonness
beznadziejny (bez-na-dzhéy-ni)
adj. m. hopeless; desperate
bez ogródek (bez o-gróo-dek)
adv. bluntly; unequivocally
bezokolicznik (bez-o-ko-leech-
ñeek) m. infinitive (mood)
bezowocny (bez-o-vóts-ni) m.
fruitless; vain; unsuccessful
bezpieczeństwo (bez-pye-cheñ-
stvo) m. security; safety
bezpłatnie (bez-pwát-ñe) adv.
free of charge ; gratuitously

bezpłciowy (bez-pwchó-vi) adj.
m. sexless; neutral; insipid
bezpodstawny (bez-pod-stáv-ny)
adj. m. groundless; baseless
bezpośrednio (bez-po-shred-ño)
adv. directly; directly
bezprawny (bez-práv-ni) adj.
m. lawless; illegal; illicit
bezprzedmiotowy (bez-przed-myo-
tó-vi) adj. m.        aimless
bezprzykładny (bez-pzhi-kwád-
ni) adj. m. unprecedented
bezradny (bez-rád-ni) adj. m.
helpless; baffled; at a loss
bezręki (bez-rán-kee) adj.m.
armless; handless (cripple)
bezrobotny (bez-ro-bó-tni)
adj. m. unemployed
bezrolny (bez-ról-ni) adj.m.
landless; with no land
bezsenny (bez-sén-ni) adj. m.
sleepless; restless; wakeful
bezsens (béz-sens) m. nonsense
bezsilny (bez-shéel-ni) adj.
m. powerless; weak; helpless
bezskuteczny (bez-skoo-téch-
ni) adj. m. to no avail;
futile; ineffective; nugatory
bezsporny (bez-spór-ni) adj.
m. incontestable; undebatable
bezsprzeczny (bez-spzhech-ni)
adj. m. indisputable; evident
bezstronność (bez-stron-noshch)
f. impartiality; fairness
beztroski (bez-trós-kee) adj.
m. carefree; careless;jaunty
bezustanny (bez-oos-tán-ni)
adj. m. ceaseless; endless
bezużyteczny (bez-oo-zhi-téch-
ni) adj. m. useless; idle
bezwartościowy (bez-var-tosh-
chó-vi) adj. m. worthless
bezwarunkowy (bez-va-roon-kó-vi)
adj. m. unconditional: utter
bezwładność (bez-vwád-noshch)
f. inertia; torpor; decline
bezwstydny (bez-vstid-ni) adj.
m. shameless; lewd; flagrant
bezwyznaniowy (bez-viz-na-ño-
vi) adj. m. nonsectarian
bezwzględny (bez-vzglánd-ni)
adj. m. ruthless; despotic
bezzębny (bez-zánb-ni) adj. m.
toothless; edentate

bezzwłoczny (bez-zvwóch-ni)
adj. m. immediate; prompt
bezzwrotny (bez-zvrót-ni) adj.
m. not to be refunded
beż (besh) m. beige
bęben ( bán-ben) m. drum; kid;
brat; barrel; cylinder;tumbler
bęcwał (bánts-vaw) m. nincompoop; dullard; chickle head
bękart (bán-kart) m. bastard
biadać (byá-dać) v. moan
białaczka (bya-wách-ka) f.
leukemia
białko (byá-wko) n. egg white;
protein; white of the eye
biały (byá-wi) adj. m. white
biba (bee-ba) f. drinking spree
biblia (béeb-lya) f. Bible
biblioteka (beeb-lyo-té-ka) f.
library: bookcase; book series
bibuła (bee-boó-wa) f. blotting
paper; illegal political
publication; literary trash
bicz (béech) m. whip; whiplash
bić (béech) v. beat; defeat(etc)
biec (byets) v. run; trot; flow
bieda (bye-da) f. poverty; want;
trouble; distress; evil days
biedny (byéd-ni) adj. m. poor
bieg (byeg) m. run; race; course
biegle (byé-gle) adv. fluently
biegun (bye-goon) m. pole;
rocker; spindle; trunnion
biegunka (bye-góon-ka) f.
diarrhea; dysentery
biel (byel) f.whiteness; white
bielizna (bye-leéz-na) f. linen
bielmo (byél-mo) n. cataract
bierny (byér-ni) adj. m. passive
bieżący (bye-zhówn-tsi) adj. m.
current; flowing; running
bieżnia (byézh-ña) f. runway;
track; racecourse; tyre tread
bigos (bee-gos) m. hashed meat
and cabbage (Polish style)
bijatyka (bee-ya-tí-ka) f.
fight; brawl; tussle; scrimmage
bila (bee-la) f. billiard ball
bilans (bee-lans) m. balance
sheet; balance; rest; outcome
bilet (bee-let) m. note; ticket
biodro (byód-ro) n. hip; huckle
biszkopt (beésh-kopt) m.
biscuit; sponge cake; cracer

bitny (beet-ni) adj. m. valiant
bitwa (beet-va) f. battle;fight
biuro (byoo-ro) n. office
biust (byoost) m. bust; breast
biustonosz (byoos-to-nosh) m.
brassiere; bra; bust bodice
biżuteria (bee-zhoo-ter-ya) f.
jewelry: jewels
blacha (bla-kha) f. sheet
metal; cook top; tinware
blady (bla-di) adj. m. pale
blaga (bla-ga) f. lie; bluff
blankiet (blan-ket ) m. blank
form; printed form: blank
blask (blask) m. flush; luster
bliski (blees-kee) adj. m.
near; imminent; near by;close
blizna (bleez-na) f. scar
bliźni (bleezh-nee)m. fellow
man; twin: identical; neighbor
blokować (blo-ko-vach) v.block;
blockade; obstruct; stall
blondynka (blon-din-ka) f.
blonde (girl); fair haired girl
bluzka (blooz-ka) f. blouse
bluźnić (bloozh-neech) v. curse;
blaspheme; talk nonsense
błahość (bwa-khoshch) f. trifle
błagać (bwa-gach) v. beseech
błazen (bwa-zen) m. clown;
buffoon  ⌠mistake; lapse
błąd (bwownt) m. error; slip-up;
błąkać się (bwown-kach shan)v.
wander; stray; roam; rove
błękit (bwan-keet) m. blue;
azure; blue pigment: sky
błocić (bwo-cheech) v. get
muddy: soil with mud; spatter
błogi (bwo-gee) adj. m.bliss-
ful; delightful; sweet
błogosławić (bwo-go-swa-veech)
v. bless; praise; exalt; thank
błona (bwona) f. membrane; coat;
film; tunic; velum; web
błonie (bwo-ñe) n. meadow;
plain; public grassy land
błotnik (bwot-ñeek) m.(car)
fender; mudguard; splash board
błoto (bwo-to) n. mud: muck
błysk (bwisk) m. flash; flare
bo (bo) conj. because; for; or;
as; since; or else; but then

bochenek (bo-khe-nek) m. loaf
bocian (bo-chan) m. stork
boczny (boch-ny) adj. m. lateral; side ; collateral (line)
boczyć się (bo-chych shan) v.
sulk; be angry; look askance
bodaj (bo-day) part. may be;
should be...; would be...;
bodziec (bo-dzhets) m. stimulus
bogactwo (bo-gats-tvo) n.riches;
wealth; means; fortune; plenty
bogaty (bo-ga-ti) adj. m. rich
bogobojny (bo-go-boy-ni) adj.
m. pious; devout; church going
bohater (bo-kha-ter) m. hero
boisko (bo-ees-ko) n. stadium;
field; threshing floor;gridiron
bojaźń (bo-yazhñ) f. fear; fright
boja (bo-ya) f. buoy ; beacon
bojkot (boy-kot) m. boycott
bojownik (bo-yov-ñeek) m.
fighter; militant; champion
bok (bok) m. side; flank
boks (boks) m. boxing; stall
boleć (bo-lech) v. pain; ache
bolesny (bo-les-ni) adj. m. sore;
painful; sad; woeful; dismal
bomba (bom-ba) f. bomb; sphere
bombowiec (bom-bo-vyets) m.
bomber ; bombing plane
borykać się (bo-ri-kach shan)
v. cope; struggle; wrestle
bosak (bo-sak) m. boat hook
boso (bo-so) adv. barefoot
bosy (bo-si) adj. m. barefoot
bowiem (bo-vyem) conj. for;
because; since; as; hence
boży (bo-zhi) adj. m. God's
Bóg (book)m. God
bój (booy) m. fight; battle
ból (bool) m. pain; ache; sore
bór (boor) m. forest; wood
bóść (booshch) v. gore; sting
bóżnica (boozh-ñee-tsa) f.
synagogue: house of prayer
bractwo (brats-tvo) n. fraternity; brotherhood; guild
brać (brach) v. take; hold etc.
brak (brak) m. lack; need;want;
scarcity; shortage;absence;fault
brama (bra-ma) f. gate; gateway;
front door; wicket

bransoletka (bran-so-lét-ka) f.
  bracelet; wristlet; bangle
brat (brat) m. brother; mate
bratać (brá-tać) v. unite;
  fraternize; chum up
bratanek (bra-tá-nek) m. nephew
bratanica (bra-ta-née-tsa) f.
  niece
brednie (bréd-ne) n. nonsense
brew (brev) f. eyebrow
brewerie (bre-vér-ye) n. brawl
brezent (bré-zent) m. tarpau-
  lin; canvas
brnąć (brnównch) v. wade
broczyć (bró-chich) v. bleed
broda (broda) f. beard; chin
brodzić (bró-dźheech)v. wade
broić (bró-eech) v. make
  mischief; frolic; romp;gambol
brom (brom) m. bromine
brona (bró-na) f. harrow
bronić (bró-neech) v. defend
bronz (brons) m. bronze
broń (broń) f. weapon; arms
broszka (brósh-ka) f. brooch
broszura (bro-shóo-ra) f.
  pamphlet; folder; booklet
browar (bró-var) m. brewery
bród (broot) m. ford
brud (broot) m. dirt; filth
bruk (brook) m. pavement
brukiew (bróo-kęv) f. turnip
brulion (bróol-yon) m. rough
  draft; notebook; exercise book
brunatny (broo-ná-tni) adj. m.
  brown; tawny; tan colored
brunetka (broo-nét-ka) f.
  brunette
brutal (bróo-tal) m. brute
bruzda (broóz-da) f. furrow;
  groove; deep wrinkle; streak
brwi (brvee) pl. eye brows
brykać (brí-kach) v. prance
bryła (brí-wa) f. lump; mass
bryzg (brizk) m. splash
bryzgać (bríz-gach) v. splash
brzeg (bzhek) m. shore; margin
brzemię (bzhe-myęn) n. burden
brzęk (bzhęnk) m. clink; chink;
  rattle; ping; buzz; hum;drone
brzuch (bzhookh) m. belly; abdomen; stomach; tummy; guts

brzydki (bzhíd-kee) adj. m.
  ugly; unsightly; hideous; foul
brzydzić się (bzhi-dźheech śhän)
  v. feel disgust; loathe; abhor
brzytwa (bzhít-va) f. razor
buchać (bóo-khach) v. squirt;
  spout;burst forth; flare; blaze
bucik (bóo-cheek) m. shoe; boot
buda (bóo-da) f. shed (stall)
budowa (boo-dó-va) f. construction; erection; framework
budowla (boo-dóv-la) f. building (large); edifice;structure
budynek (boo-dí-nek) m. building; edifice; house
budzić (bóo-dźheech)v. wake up
budzik (bóo-dźheek)m. alarm
  clock; alarum clock
budżet (bóo-jet) m. budget
bujać (boó-yach) v. rock; lie
bufor (bóo-for) m. buffer
bułka (boów-ka) f. roll (breakfast); bread roll; loaf
bunt (boont) m. mutiny
bura (boó-ra)f . reprimand
burak (bóo-rak) m. beet
burda (bóo-r-da) f. scuffle;row;
  brawl; disturbance; rough neck
burmistrz (boor-meestsh) m.
  mayor
bursztyn (boor-shtin) m. amber
burta (bçor-ta) f. ship's side
bury (boo-ri)adj. m. dark gray
burza (bóo-zha) f. tempest;
  storm; wind storm; rain storm
burżuazja (boor-zhoo-áz-ya) f.
  bourgeoisie; middle class
busola (boo-só-la) f. compass
but (boot) m. boot; shoe; sabot
buta (bóo-ta) f. arrogance
butelka (boo-tél-ka) f. bottle
butny (bóot-ni) adj. m. arrogant; insolent; overbearing
buzia (boó-zha) f. face; mouth
by (bi) conj. in order that;
  (conditional)as if; at least
byczy (bí-chi) adj. m. 1. bull's
  2. very good; glorious
być (bich) v. be; exist; live
bydlę (bíd-län) n. beast; brute
byle (bi-le) conj. in order to;
  so as to; pron. any; slap-dash

byży (bí-wi) adj. m. former
bynajmniej (bi-náy-mñey) adv.
  by no means; not at all
bystrość (bíst-roshch) f.
  swiftness; shrewdness
byt (bit) m. existence
bytność (bít-noshch) f. stay
bywać (bí-vach) v. frequent
bywalec (bi-vá-lets) m.patron
  frequenter; man of the world
bzdura (bzdoó-ra) f. nonsense
bzik (bżheek)adj. m. crank;
  loony; crazy; m. fad; craze
bzykać (bzí-kach) v. buzz
cackać się (tsáts-kach sháñ)v.
  fondle; pamper; humor;coddle
cacko (tsáts-ko) n. jewel;
  trinket; plaything;toy;beauty
cal (tsal) m. inch
całka (tsáw-ka) f. integral
całkiem (tsáw-kem) adv.quite;
  entirely; completely; totally
całkowity (tsaw-ko-vée-ti)
  adj. m. total; complete
cało (tsá-wo) adv. (in one
  piece) safely; safe and sound
całować (tsa-wó-vach) v. kiss;
  embrace; give a kiss
całus (tsá-woos) m. kiss
cap (tsap) m. billy goat
cąber (tsówn-ber) m. rump;
  fillet
cążki (tsównzh-kee) pl. small
  tongs; pliers; pincers
ceber (tsé-ber) m. bucket
cebula (tse-bóo-la) f. onion
cech (tsekh) m. trade; guild
cecha (tsé-kha) f. feature;
  mark; trait; stamp; character
cechować (tse-khó-vach) v.
  mark; characterize; calibrate
cedr (tsedr) m. cedar
cedzić (tsé-dzheech)v. strain;
  filter; percolate;sip;trickle
cegielnia (tse- gél-ña) f.
  brickyard; brick factory
cegła (tség-wa) f. brick
cel (tsel) m. purpose; aim
cela (tsé-la) f. cell
celnik (tsél-ñeek) m. customs
  inspector; customs officer
celować (tse-lo-vach) v. aim;
  excel; exceed

celuloza (tse-loo-ló-za) f.
  cellulose
cembrować (tsem-bró-vach) v.
  case(well); timber (a shaft)
cement (tsé-ment) m. cement
cena (tsé-na) f. price; value
cenić (tsé-ñeech) v. value;rate;
  esteem; prize; evaluate
cennik (tsén-ñeek) m. price
  list; price catalogue
centnar (tsént-nar) m. hundredweight
centrala (tsen-trá-la) f. head
  office ; main office ; exchange
centrum (tsént-room) n. center
centryfuga (tsen-tri-foo-ga) f.
  centrifuge; separator
centymetr (tsen-tí-metr) m.
  centimeter ___ blockhead
cep (tsep) m. flail; darn; mend
cera (tsé-ra) f. complexion
ceramiczny (tse-ra-méech-ni)
  adj. m. ceramic; earthenware
cerata (tse-rá-ta) f. oilcloth
ceregiele (tse-re-ge-le) n.
  fuss; petty formalities
certować sie(tser-to-vach shan)v.
  pretend;stand on ceremony;fuss
cewka (tsév-ka) f. spool
cęgi (tsáñ-gee) pl. tongs
cętka (tsáñt-ka) f. dot
chałat (khá-wat) m. lab.coat
chałastra (kha-wás-tra) f. mob
chałupa (kha-woo-pa) f. hut
cham (kham) m. roughneck; boor
charakter (kha-rák-ter) m.
  disposition; character
charczeć (khár-chech) v.
  wheese; snort; be hoarse
chata (khá-ta) f. hut; cabin
chcieć (khchech) v. want
chciwiec (khchée-vyets) m.
  greedy man; grasping man
chełpić się (khew-peech sháñ)
  v. boast; brag; bluster;vaunt
chemia (khém-ya) f. chemistry
chemiczny (khe-méech-ni) adj.m.
  chemical
cherlak (khér-lak) m. weakling
chęć (kháñch) f. wish; desire
chędogi (kháñ-do-gi) adj. m.
  neat; clean; tidy; orderly

chichot (khée-khot) m. giggle;
laughter ; chuckle; titter
chimera (khee-mé-ra) f. whim
chinina (khee-ńée-na) f. quinine
chiński (kheeń-skee) adj.m.
Chinese
chirurg (khée-roorg) m. surgeon ; sawbones (slang)
chlapać (khlá-pach) v. splash
chleb (khleb) m. bread
chlew (khlev) m. pigsty;pigpen
chlor (khlor) m. chlorine
chluba (khlóo-bą) f.glory,pride
chlubić się (khlóo-beech śháń)
v. boast; flatter oneself
chlusnąć (khlóos-nówńch) v.
splash; fling; spout; spurt
chłeptać (khwép-tach) v. lap up
chłodzić (khwó-dźheech)v. cool
chłonąć (khwó-nówńch) v. absorb;
devour; drink in; inhale
chłop (khwop) m. peasant; man
chłosta (khwós-ta) f. lashing
chłód (khwoot) m. cold; freshness ; coolnes̨s; iciness;shiver
chłystek (khwis-tek) m. squirt
chmara (khmá-ra) f. swarm
chmiel (khmyel) m. hop; hops
chmura (khmoó-ra) f. cloud
chociaż (khó-chash) conj.albeit;
even if; though, tho'; while
chociaż = chocby = chociażby
choc (khoch) conj. at least
chodnik (khód-ńeek) m. sidewalk; pathway; stair carpet
chodzić (khó-dźheech) v. go;
walk; move; creep; pace;attend
choina (kho-eé-na) f. fir
cholera (kho-lé-ra) f. cholera
excl.:damn ! hell! the devil!
cholewa (kho-lé-va) f. boot
chorągiew (kho-rówń-gev) f.
flag; standard; ensign
choroba (kho-ro-ba) f. sickness
chory (khó-ri) adj. m. sick;
ill; ailing; infirm; unwell
chowac (khó-vach) v. hide
chód (khoot) m. gait; walk
chór (khoor) m. choir
chów (khoof) m. breeding
chrabąszcz (khrá-bówshch) m.
beetle;May —bug

chrapać (khrá-pach) v. snore
chroniczny (khro-ńéech-ni) adj.
m. chronic
chronic (khró-ńeech) v. shelter;
protect; quard; shield; fence
chropowaty (khro-po-vá-ti) adj.
m. rough; callous; coarse;harsh
chrust (khroost) m. kindling
chrupać (khroó-pach) v. crunch
chrypka (khríp-ka) f. hoarseness; sore throat
Chrystus (khris-toos) m. Christ
chrzan (khzhan) m. horseradish
chrząstka (khzhównst-ka) f.
cartilage; gristle; copula
chrząszcz (khshównshch) m.
May bug; beetle; cockchafer
chrzcić (khzhcheech) v. baptize
chrzest (khzhest) m. baptism
chrześcijanin (khzhe-śhchee-yá-ńeen) m. Christian
chrzęst (khzháńst) m. clatter
chrzęścić (khzháń-śhcheech) v.
clank; jangle; grate; crunch
chuchać (khoó-khach) v. puff
chuchro (khóokh-ro) m. weakling
chuć (khooch) f. lust
chudnąć (khood-nówńch) v.lose
weight; grow thin; lose flesh
chuligan (khoo-leé-gan) m.
hoodlum; ruffian; roughneck
chustka (khoóst-ka) f. handkerchief; kerchief; scarf
chwacki (khvats-kee) adj. m.
brave; plucky; gallant; rakish
chwalić (khvá-leech) v. praise
chwała (khvá-wa) f. praise;
glory; splendor; pride
chwast (khvast) m. weed
chwiac (khvyach) v. waver
chwila (khvee-la) f. moment
chwycić (khvi-cheech) v. grasp
chwyt (khvit) m. grasp; grip
chyba (khí-ba) part. maybe
chybotać (khi-bó-tach) v. rock
chybić (khi-beech) v. miss
chylić (khí-leech) v. bow
chyłkiem (khiw-kem) adj.
stealthily; on the sly
chytry (khit-ri) adj. m. sly
chyży (khi-zhi) adj. m. swift
ci (chee) pron. these; they;
part.: for you

ciało (ćha-wo) n. body; substance ; frame; anatomy;corpse
ciarki (ćhar-kee) pl. shudder
ciasnota (ćhas-nó-ta) f. tightness;,narrow-mindedness
ciastko (ćhast-ko) n . cake;pie
ciasto (ćhás-to) n, dough
ciąć (ćhównćh) v. cut; clip
ciagnąc (ćhówng-nównćh)v.pull
ciągnik (ćhówng-ńeek) m. tractor ; agrimotor; crawler
ciąża (ćhówn-zha) f. pregnancy
ciążenie (ćhówn-zhe-ńe) v. gravitation ;tendency
cichaczem (ćhee-kha-chem) adv. stealthily ;, on the quiet
cichnąć (ćheekh-nównćh) v. quiet down; subside ; abate
cicho (ćhee-kho) adv. silently; noiselessly ; softly;privately
cichy (ćheé-khi) adj. m. quiet; still; low;gentle; calm; serene
ciec (ćhets) v. leak; flow
ciecz (ćhech) f. liquid
ciekawy (ćhé-kav) adj. m. cute; curious ;interesting;prying
cielak (ćhé-lak) m. calf
cielesny (ćhe-lés-ni) adj. m. carnal; bodily; sexual
ciemię (ćhe-myáń) n. crown of the head ; septum of the skull
ciemiężenie (ćhe-myáń-zhe-ńe) n. oppression ; subjugation
ciemnia (ćhém-ńa) f. dark room
ciemno (ćhém-no) adv. darkly
ciemny (ćhém-ni) adj. m. dark
cieniować (ćhe-ńo-vaćh) v. shade ; modulate; grade
cienisty (ćhe-ńees-ti) adj. m. shady ; shade giving
cienki (ćhen-kee) adj. m. thin
cień (ćheń) m. shade ; shadow
cieplarnia (ćhe-plár-ńa) f. greenhouse,; hothouse; stove
ciepło (ćhe-pwo) adv. warm
ciepławy (ćhe-pwá-vi) adj. m. lukewarm ; tepid
ciepły (ćhep-wi) adj. m. warm
cierń (ćherń) m. thorn; pricle
cierpiący (ćher-pyówn-tsi) adj. m., suffering ; ailing;ill
cierpieć (ćhér-pyećh) v.suffer; anguish; be troubled; endure

cierpki (ćherp-kee) adj. m. tart; acid;surly;acrid;sour
cierpliwość (ćher-pleé-voshćh) f. patience; endurance
cierpliwy (ćher-pleé-vi) adj.
m. enduring; patient; forbearing
cierpnąć (ćhérp-nównćh) v. grow numb; creep; go to sleep
ciesielstwo (ćhe-shél-stvo) n. carpentry (in construction)
cieszyć (ćhé-shićh) v. cheer
cieśla (ćheśh-la) m. carpenter (constr.);wood worker;shipwright
cietrzew (ćhe-tzhev) m. black- cock; black grouse; grey hen
cieśnina (ćheśh-ńeé-na) f. strait
cięcie (ćhań-che) n. cut; gash
cięciwa (ćhan-cheé-va) f. chord; bow string; string; subtense
cięgi (ćhań-gee) pl. lashing
cięty (ćháń-ti) adj. m. sharp- tongued; biting;dogged;incisive
ciężar (ćháń-zhar) m. weight; burden; gravity; onus; duty;task
ciężec (ćháń-zhećh) v. grow heavy ; become a burden;encumber
ciężki (ćháńzh-kee) adj. m. heavy ; weighty; bulky; oppressive
ciężko (ćháńzh-ko) adv. heavily
ciocia (ćhó-ćha) f. auntie;aunt
cios (ćhos) m. blow; stroke; hit ; shok; ashlar; block; joint
cioteczny brat (ćho-téch-ni brat) m. cousin
ciotka (ćhót-ka) f. aunt
ciosać (ćhó-saćh) v. hew; chop out
cis (ćhees) m. yew
cisawy (ćhees-ávi) adj. m. chesnut (horse)
ciskać (ćhees-kaćh) v. fling;cast; throw,; hurl: sling; plunk;let fly
cisnąc (ćhées-nównćh) v. press; squeeze; bear; urge; pinch;crowd
cisza (ćhee-sha) f. calm ; silence
ciśnienie (ćheesh-ńé-ńe) n. pressure ; blood pressure; thrust
ciuch (ćhookh) m. used clothing
ciułać (ćhoo-waćh) v. hoard
ciurkiem (ćhoór-ḱem) adv. in a trickle,; with big drops
ciupa (ćhoo-pa) f. jail; clink
ciupasem (ćhoo-pá-sem) adv. under convoy under armed convoy

ciżba (čhéezh-ba) f. crowd
ckliwy (tsklée-vi) adj. m.
qualmy ; sickly; faint;sloppy
clić (tsleéch) v. collect
custom duty ;lay a custom duty
cło (tswo) n. customs
cmentarz (tsmén-tash) m. cemetery ; burjal ground
cmokać (tsmo-kach) v. smack
cnota (tsnó-ta) f. virtue
co (tso) pron. part. what ;which
codzień (tsó-dzheń)adv. daily
cofać się (tsó-fach shań) v.
back up ; remove; withdraw
cokolwiek (tso-kól-vyek) pron.
anything ; whatever; somewhat
comber (tsóm-ber) m. saddle
(of mutton);rump;loin; haunch
coraz (tsó-raz) adv. ever
cos (tsośh) pron. something
córka (tsóor-ka) f. daughter
cóż (tsoosh) pron. what then
cuchnąć (tsóokh-nówńch) v.
stink foul ; smell foul
cucić (tsóo-cheéch) v. revive
cud (tsoot) m. wonder; miracle
cudzołożyć (tsoo-dzo-wó-zhich)
v. commit adultery
cudzoziemiec (tsoo-dzo-zhe-
myets) m. alien; foreigner
cudzy (tsóo-dzi) adj. m.
someone else's ; alien;foreign
cudzysłów (tsoo-dzi-swoof)m.
quotation marks
cukier (tsóo-ker) m. sugar
cuma (tsóo-ma) f. mooring
cwał (tsvaw) m. full gallop
cwaniak (tsvá-ńak) m. city
slicker; sly dog;crafty guy
cwany (tsvá-ni) adj. m. sly;
cunning; crafty; artful
cyc (tsits) m. nipple (vulg.)
cyfra (tsíf-ra) f. number
cygan (tsí-gan) m. gipsy;
cheat; Gypsy;swindler; liar
cykl (tsikl) m. cycle
cylinder (tsi-leén-der) m.
cylinder; barrel; top hat
cyna (tsi-na) f. tin
cynamon (tsi-ná-mon)m.cinnamon
cynober (tsi-nó-ber) m.vermil-
ion

cyngiel (tsin-gel) m. trigger
cynik (tsi-ńeek) m. cynic
cynk (tsink) m. zinc; tutenag
cypel (tsi-pel) m. cape; tip
cyprys (tsí-pris) m. cypress
cyrk (tsirk) m. circus
cyrkiel (tsír-kel) m. compass
cysterna (tsis-tér-na) f.
cistern; tank car; vat
cytadela (tsi-ta-dé-la) f.
citadel; fortress
cytata (tsi-ta-ta) f. quotation
cytryna (tsi-trí-na) f. lemon
cywil (tsi-veel) m. civilian
cyzelować (tsi-ze-ló-vach) v.
engrave; carve; elaborate
czad (chat) m. carbon monoxide
czaić się (cha-eéch shań) v.
lie in wait; lurk; stalk;crouch
czajnik (chá y-ńeek) m. tea-pot
czajka (chá y-ka) f. gull
czako (chá-ko) f. shako
czapka (cháp-ka) f. cap; pileus
czapla (cháp-la) f. heron
czaprak (cháp-rak) m. horse
blanket; caparison; trappings
czar (char) m. spell; charm
czarno (chár-no) adv. blackly
czart (chárt) m. devil; deuce
czas (chas) m. time; duration
czaszka (chásh-ka) f. skull
czaty (chá-ti) pl. watch;
lookout; wait; ambush
cząstka (chowńst-ka) f. particle
czcić (chcheéch) v. adore;
worship; idolize; venerate
czcigodny (chchee-god-ni) adj.
m. honorable; revered; venerable
czcionka (chchyoń-ka) f. type;
character; letter in print
czczo (chcho) adv. empty (stomach) ; emptily; vainly; idly
czego (che-go) conj. why? what?
czek (chek) m. check (in banking)
czekać (che-kach) v. wait;
expect; waste time; be in store
czekanie (che-ka-ńe) n. wait
czekan (ché-kan) f. pickhammer
czekolada (che-ko-lá-da) f.
chocolate; slab of chocolate
czeladnik (che-lád-ńeek) m.
apprentice; journeyman

czelność (chél-noshćh) f. impudence ; effrontery; nerve
czelusć (ché-looshćh) f. abyss; gulf; precipice; depths [to what?
czemu (ché-moo) part. why ?what
czepek (ché-pek) m. bonnet; hood ; night cap; caul;calyptra
czepiać się (chép-yach shán) v. cling; hang on; peck at
czereda (che-ré-da) f. gang; throng ; crowd; swarm; pack
czerep (ché-rep) m. shell; skull; fragment; splinter;shard
czereśnia (che-résh-ña) f. cherry ; cherry tree; gean
czernić (chér-ñeećh) v, blacken ; black; paint black
czerń (cherñ) f. black color
czerpać (chér-pach) v. scoop; draw; ladle; derive (benefit)
czerstwy (chérs-tvi) adj. m. stale; robust(man); firm
czerw (chejv) m. worm ; grub
czerwienić się (cher-vyé-ñeech sháñ) v. blush (redden)
czerwony (cher-vó-ni) adj. m. red ; scrlet; crimson; ruddy
czesać (ché-sach) v. comb ;brush
czeski (chés-kee) adj. m. Czech
czesne (chés-ne) n. tuition
cześć (cheshćh) f. honor; cult; respect ; adoration;good name
często (cháñs-to) adv. often
częstokroć (chañ-stó-kroch) adv. often ; repeatedly
częstość (cháñs-toshćh) f. frequency ; recurrence
częstotliwosć (chañ-sto-tleé-woshćh) f. frequency ;recurrence
częstować (cháñ-stó-vach) v. treat to something : regale
częsty (cháñs-ty) adj. m. frequent : repeated often
częściowy (chán-shchó-vi) adj. m. partial ; fragmentary
część (cháñshćh) f. part :share
czkawka (chkáv-ka) f. hiccups
człon (chwon) m. element; segment ; link ; member; clause
członek (chwo-nek) m. limb; member; man's sex organ
człowiek (chwó-vyek) m. man ; individual; chap; somebody

czmychnąć (chmíkh-nówñćh) v. bolt; steal out; whisk away
czochrać (chókh-rach) v. tousle; ripple; hackle ;scratch
czołg (chowg) m. tank (military) ; reptile
czołgać (chów-gach) v. crawl
czoło (chó-wo) n. forehead
czop (chop) m. peg. plug; pin
czosnek (chós-nek) m. garlic
czterdzieści (chter-dżhésh-ćhee) num. forty
czternaście (chter-nash-ćhe) num. fourteen
czteropiętrowy (chte-ro-pyáñ-tró-vi) adj. m. four stories high ; four storeyed
cztery (chté-ri) num. four
czub (choop) m. tuft; crest
czucie (choó-ćhe) n. feeling; smelling ; sense perception
czuc (chooćh) v. feel; smell
czujka (choóy-ka) f. sentry
czułość (choó-woshćh) f. tenderness ; affection; caress
czuły (choó-wi) adj. m. tender; affectionate; sensitive;keen
czupurny (choo-poór-ni) adj. m. pugnacious; boastful;defiant
czuwać (choó-vach) v. watch; nurse ; look-out ; stay up;tend
czwartek (chvár-tek) m. Thursday
czwarty (chvár-ti) num. fourth
czworobok (chvo-ró-bok) m. quadrilateral; square;tetragon
czworokąt (chvo-ró-kownt) m. quadrangle; quad; tetragon
czwórka (chvoór-ka) f. four-some; crew of four; good mark
czy (chi) conj. if; whether
czychać (chí-khach) v. lurk
czyj (chiy) pron. whose
czyjs (chiysh) pron. somebody's anybody's; someone else's
czyli (chi-lee) conj. or; otherwise; that is to say
czym...tym (chim...tim) adv. the sooner... the; the more the...; the less... the...
czyn (chin) m. act. deed
czynsz (chinsh) m. rent
czynić (chi-ñeećh) v. do; render ; act; amount;cause

czyrak (chi-rak) m. boil; furuncle; boil; anbury; rising
czynnik (chin-ñeek) m. factor
czysto (chi-sto) adv. clean
czysty (chis-ti) adj. m. clean
czyszczenie (chish-che-ñe) n. cleaning; brushing;diarrhoea
czyscic (chish-cheech) v. clean; scour; brush; rub;purge
czysciec (chish-chets) m. purgatory; woundwort
czytac (chi-tach) v. read
czytelnia (chi-tel-ña) f. reading room;lending library
czytelnik (chi-tel-ñeek) m. reader; reading individual
czytelny (chi-tel-ni) adj. m. legible; readable
czyz (chish) part. if; whether
cma (chma) f. obscurity; swarm; night butterfly ;night moth
cmic (chmeech) v. obscure; dim; darken; eclipse; smoke; sicken
cwiartka (chvyart-ka) f. one quarter; one fourth of a liter
cwierc (chwyerch) f. one fourth (of a liter etc.)
cwiczenie (chvee-che-ñe) n. exercise; instruction; drill
cwiek (chvyek) m. nail; stud
cwikła (chvee'k-wa) f. beetroot with horseradish (salad)
dach (dakh) m. roof; shelter
dac (dach) v. give; pay;result
daktyl (dak-til) m. date
dal (dal) f. distance; remote - ness; far away; aloof
dalece (da-le-tse) adv. further; by far; so far;(so)much so
dalej (da-ley) adv. further; moreover; further on; so on
dalmierz (dal-myesh) m. range finder; telemeter
dalszy (dal-shi) adj. m. further; farther; later; another
dama (da-ma) f. lady; partner
dana (da-na) adj.f.given (data)
danie (da-ñe) m. serving; dish; course
danser (dan-ser) m. dancer
dane (da-ne) pl. data
dar (dar) m. gift; present
daremnie (da-rem-ñe) adv. in vain; without success

daremny (da-rem-ni) adj. m. futile; vain; idle; ineffective
darmo (dar-mo) adv. free; gratuitously; to no avail
darowac (da-ro-vach) v. give; forgive; overlook; spare
data (da-ta) f. date
datek (da-tek) n. small gift
dawac (da-vach) v. give (often)
dawno (dav-no) adv. long ago
dąb (domp) m. oak tree (wood)
dąc (downch) y. blow; resound
dąsac się (down-sach sham) v. sulk; be in the pouts; mump
dążyc (down-zhich) v. aspire; tend; aim; be bound; trend
dbac (dbach) v. care;set store
dech (dekh) m. breath; gust
decydowac (de-tsi-do-vach) v. decide; resolve; determine
decyzja (de-tsis-ya) f. decision; ruling; resolve
delikatnosc (de-lee-kat-noshch) f. delicacy; gentleness; tact
defekt (de-fekt) m. defect
demaskowac (de-mas-ko-vach) v. unmask; uncover; denounce
demokracja (de-mo-krats-ya) f. democracy
denerwowac (de-ner-vo-vach) v. bother; make nervous; irritate
dentysta (den-tis-ta) m. dentist
depesza (de-pe-sha) f. wire; telegram; cable; dispatch
deponowac (de-po-no-vach) v. deposit; put in safe keeping
depozyt (de-po-zit) m. deposit
deptac (dep-tach) v. trample; tread; pace up and down;stain
derka (der-ka) f. rug; blanket
desen (de-señ) m. pattern; design; decorative design
deska (des-ka) f. plank; board
desperacja (des-pe-rats-ya) f. desperation; despair
deszcz (deshch) m. rain
detal (de-tal) m. retail; detail; trifling matter
determinacja (de-ter-mee-nats-ya) f. determination
dewiza (de-vee-za) f. foreign money; motto; slogan; device

dębina (dȧn-bee-na) f. oak
wood; oak bark
dętka (dȧnt-ka) f. pneumatic
tire; tube; air chamber
diabeł (dyȧ-bew) m. devil
dieta (dye-ta) f. diet;regimen
dla (dla) prep. for; to;towards
dlaczego (dla—che-go)prep. why;
what for
dlatego (dla—te-go)prep.
because; this is why; and so
dławić (dwa-veech) v. choke;
squash; throttle; strangle
dłoń (dwoń) f. palm of the
hand; hand; metacarpus; quart
dłubać (dwoo-bach)v. groove;
poke; tinker; pick one's teeth
dług (dwoog) m. debt; obligation
długi (dwoo-gee) adj. m. long
długo (dwoo-go) adv. a long
time; a long way; long before
dłuto (dwoo-to) n. chisel
dłutować (dwoo-to-vach) v.
chisel; cut with chisel
dłuźnik (dwoozh-ňeek) m. debtor
dmuchać (dmoo-khach)v. blow
dniówka (dňoóv-ka) f. day's
work; work by day; time work
dno (dno) n. bottom; utterness
do (do) prep. to; into; up;till
doba (do-ba) f. 24 hours
dobić (do-beech) v. deal
a death blow; drive home
dobierać (do-bye-rach) v.
match; take more; select
dobitny (do-beet-ni) adj. m.
expressive; emphatic; distinct
doborowy (do-bo-ro-vi) adj. m.
choice; select; picked
dobosz (do-bosh) m. drummer
dobór (do-boor) m. selection;
assortment; choice;assortment
dobra (do-bra) n. riches
dobranoc (do-bra-nots)(indecl.)
good-night
dobrany (do-bra-ni) adj. m.
matching; becoming;accordant
dobre (do-bre) adj. n. good
dobro (do-bro) n. good; right
dobrobyt (do-bro-bit) m. well-
being; prosperity; welfare
dobroczynność (do-bro-chin-
noshch) f. charity; works of
mercy; philanthropy

dobroć (do—roch) f. kindness
dobroduszny (do-bro-doósh-ni)
adj. m. kindhearted; kindly
dobrodziej (do-bro-dźhey) m.
benefactor ; his reverence
dobrotliwy (do-bro-tlee-vi)
adj. m. kind; good natured
dobrowolny (do-bro-wól-ni)
adj. m. voluntary; gratuitus
dobry (do-bri) adj. m. good;
kind; right; hearty; retentive
dobrze (do-rze) adv. well;
O K; rightly; properly ;okay
dobudówka (do-boo-doóv-ka) f.
building extension
dobyć (do-bich) v. pullout
dobytek (do-bi-tek) m. belongings; effects; livestock
doceniać (do-tse-ňach) v.
duly appreciate; value
docent (do-tsent) m. associate
professor ; lecturer
dochodzenie (do-kho-dze-ňe) n
investigation; inquiry
dochodzić (do-kho-dźheech)v.
draw near; investigate; reach
dochód (do-khoot) m. income;
revenue; profit; returns
dociąć (do-chownch) c. sting;
taunt; fit by cutting off
dociec (do-chets) v. find out
dociekać (do-che-kach) v.
search; investigate; find out
docierać (do-chye-rach) v.
draw near; reach; reduce
friction ; rub up; get at
docinek (do-chee-nek) m. taunt
doczekać (do-che-kach) v. wait;
live to see; wait 'til
doczepiać (do-chep-yach) v. fix
append; attach; hitch; link
doczesny (do-ches-ni) adj. m.
temporal; worldly; mundane
dodać (do-dach) v. add; sum up
dodatek (do-da-tek) m. supplement; addition; fixture; extra
dodatni (do-dat-ňee) adj. m.
positive; advantageous; active
dodawanie (do-da-va-ňe) n.
addition
dogadać się (do-ga-dach shȧň)v.
come to terms;communicate well
dogadzać (do-ga-dzach) v.
please; accommodate; satisfy

doglądać (do-glown-dach) v.
supervise; tend; oversee
dogmat (dóg-mat) m. dogma
dogodny (do-gód-ni) adj. m.
convenient; suitable; handy
dogonić (do-go-ñeech) v. catch
up ; overtake; be in hot pursuit
dogryzać (do-gri-zach) v. vex;
tease ; finish munching;disturb
doić (do-eech) v. milk; fleece
dojarka (do-yar-ka) f. milk
maid; milking machine
dojazd (do-yazt) m. access;drive;
approach; means of transport
dojechać (do-yé-khach) v. reach;
arrive; approach; bang; hit
dojeżdżać (do-yezh-jach) v.
commute; be coming; pull in
dojmujący (doy-moo-yówn-tsi) adj.
m. acute; piercing; sharp;keen
dojrzały (doy-zha-wi) adj. m.
ripe; mellow; mature; adult
dojrzeć (doy-zhech) v. glimpse;
notice;;ripen; be ripe;mellow
dojście (doy-shche) n. approach
dok (dok) m. dock
dokarmić (do-kar-meech) v.
nourish additionally
dokazać (do-ká-zach) v. prove;
achieve; accomplish;do the trick
dokazywać (do-ka-zí-vach) v.
frolic; gambol; romp and play
dokąd (do-kównt) adv. where;till
whither; where to ? how far?till
dokładać (do-kwa-dach) v. add;
throw in; pay more; give moore
dokładny (do-kwad-ni) adj. m.
accurate; exact; precise
dokoła (do-ko-wa) adv. round;
round about; all round
dokonać (do-kó-nach) v. achieve;
accomplish; carry out;fulfil;do
dokończenie (do-koñ-che-ñe) n.
conclusion; completion; end
doktor (dók-tor) m. doctor
dokręcać (do-kráñ-tsach) v.
tighten; screw tight; turn off
dokuczać (do-koo-chach) v. vex;
annoy; nag; bully; sting;trouble
dola (do-la) f. fortune; lot
dolar (dó-lar) m. dollar
doliczyć (do-lee-chich) v.
count up ; add; charge more

dolina (do-lee-na) f. valley;
dale; glen; coomb; pocket
dolny (dól-ny) adj. m. lower
dołączyć (do-wówn-chich) v.add;
join; enclose; affix; tack on
dołek (do-wek) m. dimple; pit
dom (dom) m. house ⌐v. demand
domagać się (do-ma-gach sháñ)
domiar (do-myar) m. additional
assessment; surtax;on top of it
domniemany (do-mñe-ma-ni) adj.
m. supposed; assumed; alleged
domostwo (do-mós-tvo) n. household; homestead; farmstead
domownik (do-mów-ñeek) m.
inmate ; housemate
domowy (do-mó-vi) adj. m.
domestic; homemade; private
domysł (do-misw) m. guess
doniesienie (do-ñe-she-ñe) m.
denunciation; report; news
doniosły (do-ño-swi) adj. m.
significant; far reaching
donosiciel (do-no-shee-chel)
m. denunciator; informer
donosny (do-nósh-ni) adj. m.
resounding; renging; loud
dookoła(do-o-ko-wa) adv. round;
round about; all around; around
dopasć (dó-pashch) v. catch up;
overtake; reach at a run;seize
dopalać (do-pa-lach) v. after-
burn; finish burning; burn up
dopasowac (do-pa-só-vach) v.
fit; adapt; adjust; match;tone
dopatrywac (do-pa-tri-vach) v.
see to it; find out; keep an eye
dopełnic (do-pew-ñeech) v.fulfil;
fill up; complete ; make up
dopędzic (do-páñ-dzheech) v.
catch up with; overtake;gain on
dopiąc (do-pyównch) v. attain;
buckle up; button up; obtain
dopiero (do-pye-ro) adv. only;
just; hardly; barely ; not till
dopilnowac (do-peel-no-vach) v.
see something done ;supervise
dopisek (do-pee-sek) m. postscript; foot note
dopłata (do-pwa-ta) f. extra
payment; surcharge;extra fare
dopływ (do-pwif) m. tributary

dopomagać (do-po-má-gać) v.
help; be of assistance
dopominać się (do-po-meé-nach
shän)v. put in claim; demand
dopóki (do-pooki) conj. as
long; as far; while; until;till
dopóty (do-pob-ti) conj. til ;
until ; so far; up to here
dopraszać się (do-pra-shach
shän) v. solicit; beg; insist
doprawdy (do-práv-di) adv.
truly; indeed; really
doprawiać (do-práv-yach) v.
add (to taste); replace
doprowadzić (do-pro-va-dźheech)
v. lead to; cause; provoke
dopust Boży (dó-poost Bo-zhi)
m. calamity; scourge;act of God
dopuszczać (do-poosh-chach) v.
admit; allow; permit; be open
dopytać się (do-pi-tach shän)
v. find out; inquire; question
dorabiać (do-ráb-yach) v. make
additionally; replace; finish
doradca (do-rád-tsa) m. adviser; counselor ; guide
dorastać (do-rás-tach) v.
mature; grow; grow up; reach
doraźnie (do-ráźh-ñe) adv.
(immediately) on the spot
doręczyć (do-rán-chich) v.
hand in; deliver; transmit
dorobek (do-ró-bek) m. acquisition; rise to affluence
dorobkiewicz (do-rob-ke-veech)
m. upstart; parvenu
doroczny (do-róch-ni) adj. m.
yearly; annual; recurring yearly
dorodny (do-ród-ni) adj. m.
handsome; fine-looking; shapely
dorosły (do-rós-wy) adj. m.
adult; grown up; mature ;grown
dorożka (do-rozh-ka) f. cab
dorównywać (do-roov-ni-vach) v.
match; equal; catch up with
dorsz (dorsh) m. cod (fish)
dorywczy (do-riv-chi) v.
occasional; improvised; fitful; off-and-on; hit-and-run
dorzecze (do-zhe-che) n.
river basin; drainage area
dorzeczny (do-zhéch-ni) adj. m.
reasonable; sensible; efficient;
adequate;acceptable;logical

dorzucać (do-zhoó-tsach) v.
throw in; add; throw as far as
dosadny (do-sád-ni) adj. m.
forceful ; expressive ; crisp
dosiadać (do-sha-dach) v.
mount (horse); bestride
dosięgać (do-shäñ-gach) v.
reach; attain; catch up with
doskonalić (dos-ko-na-leech)
v. perfect; improve ; cultivate
doskwierać (do-skvye-rach) v.
pinch; gripe ; trouble; worry
dosłowny (do-swóv-ni) adj. m.
literal ; verbal; textual
dosłyszeć (do-swi-shech) v.
hear well ; catch a sound
dostać (dos-tach) v. get;
obtain ; reach; take out
dostarczyć (dos-tar-chich) v.
provide; supply ; deliver
dostateczny (do-sta-tech-ni)
adj. m. sufficient ; adequate
dostatek (do-stá-tek) m. abundance; wealth; affluence
dostawca (do-stáw-tsa) m.
supplier ; provider
dostawa (do-stá-va) f. delivery
dostawać (do-stá-vach) v. reach;
receive ; be attended to
dostęp (do-stäñp) m. access
dostojnik (do-stóy-ñeek) m.
dignitary ; notable of high rank
dostosować (do-sto-so-vach) v.
accommodate; subordinate;fit
dostroić (do-stró-yeech) v.
tune up ; conform; adapt
dostrzec (dó-stzhets) v. notice;
behold ; perceive; spot; spy;see
dostudzić (do-stoo-dźheech) v.
cool off ; plenty; sufficient
dosyć (do-sich) adv. enough;
dosztukować (do-shtoo-kó-vach)
v. piece on; eke out; sew on
dość (doshch) adv. enough
dośrodkowy (do-shrod-kó-vi)
adj. m. centripetal;concentric
doświadczyć (do-shvyád-chich) v.
experience ; sustain; feel
dotarcie (do-tar-che) n. reaching; overcoming friction
dotąd (dó-tównt) adv. up till
now; here to fore ; hitherto;
thus far; so far; yet; by then;
till then;still;not...as yet

dotkliwy (dot-klee-vi) adj. m.
painful ; keen; intense; severe
dotknąć (dot-known'ch) v. touch
dotknięcie (dot-kñá'n—che) n.
touch; contact; feeling;stroke
dotrzec (do-tzhech) v. reach;
overcome friction ; rub up
dotrzymac (do-tzhi-mach) v.
keep; stick to one's
commitment ; adhere;redeem
dotychczas (do-tikh-chas) adv.
up to now; hitherto; to date
dotyczyc (do-ti-chich) v.
concern; relate; regard; affect
dotyk (do-tik) m. touch;feel
dowcip (dov-cheep) m. wit;
joke; jest; gag; quip; sally
dowiedziec się (do-vye-dzhech
śhań) v. get to know; learn
dowidzenia (do-vee-dze-ña)
good bye,; see you later
dowierzac (do-vye-zhach) v.
trust; have confidence in
dowieśc (do-vyeshch) v. prove
dowiezc (do-vyezhch) v.
1. supply 2. drive to
dowodzic (do-vo-dzheech)v.
conduct;keep proving
dowolnie (do-vol-ñe) adv. at
will; optionally; freely
dowolny (do-vol-ni) adj. m.
optional; any; whichever
dowod (do-voot) m. proof;
evidence ; record; token
dowodca (do-vood-tsa) m.
commander        ⌐delivery
dowoz (do-voos) m. supply;
doza (do-za) f. dose
dozbroic (do-zbro-eech) v.
rearm; supplement weapons
dozgonny (do-zgon-ni) adj. m.
lifelong; lasting 'til death
doznac (do-znach) v. go through;
undergo ; endure; feel;suffer
dozorca (do-zor-tsa) m. caretaker; watchman; overseer
dozorowac (do-zo-ro-vach) v.
oversee; supervise; attend
dozor (do-zoor) m. surveillance
dozwolic (do-zvo-leech) v.
allow to happen; let happen
dożynki (do-zhin-kee) pl.
harvest festivities

dożywocie (do-zhi-vo-che)n.
life estate; life pension
doł (doow) m. pit; bottom part
drab (drap) m. ruffian; scamp
drabina (dra-bee-na) f. ladder
dramat (dra-mat) m. drama
drań (drań) m. scoundrel; crumb
drapacz (dra-pach) m. scraper
drapac (dra-pach) v. scratch)
drapieznik (dra-pyezh-ñeek) m.
beast of prey; plunderer
drastyczny (dra-stich-ni) adj.
m. drastic; rough; violent
dratwa (drat-va) f. pitched-
thread; shoemaker's twine
drażliwy (drazh-lee-vi) adj.
m. touchy; irritable; ticklish
draznic (drazh-ñeech) v. tease;
irritate; whet; vex; annoy; jar
drąg (drownk) m. pole; bar
drążyc (drown-zhich) v. hollow
out; bore; torment ; fret;gnaw
drelich (dre-leekh) m. denim
dren (dren) n. drain (pipe)
dreptac (drep-tach) v. trip-
trot; toddle; totter; patter
dreszcz (dreshch) m. chill;
shudder; thrill; flutter; shiver
dreszczowiec (dresh-cho-vyets)
m. thriller (novel or movie)
drewno (drev-no) n. piece of
wood; timber ; log; xylem
dręczyc (drań-chich) v. torment
dretwiec (drań-tvyech) v. grow
numb; grow stiff; stiffen
drgac (drgach) v. tremble;
vibrate; quiver; throb; wobble
drobiazg (drob-yazk) m. trifle;
detail; trinket; small fry
drobina (dro-bee-na) f. particle
drobne (drob-ne) n. small
change; petty cash ; small coin
drobnica (drob-ñee-tsa) f.
small goods; packages
drobnostka (drob-nost-ka) f.
trifle; small matter; trinket
drobny (dro-bni) adj. m. small;
tiny ; trivial; petty; slight
droga (dro-ga) f. 1. road;
2.journey; 3.adj.f. dear
drogeria (dro-ger-ya) f. drugstore ; drysaltery

drogi (dró-gee) adj. m. dear;
expensive ; costly; beloved
drogowskaz (dro-góv-skas) m.
road sign ; signpost
drozd (drozt) m. thrush
drożdże (dróżh-je) pl. yeast
drożeć (dró-zhech) v. grow
dear ; rise in price ;appreciate
drożyzna (dro-zhiz-na) f. high
cost of living ; high prices
drób (droop) pl. paltry
dróżka (droo̅zh-ka) f. path
druciany (droo-cha̅-ni) adj. m.
of wire; made out of wire
drugi (droo-gee) num. second;
other ; the other one; latter
druh (drookh) m. buddy;
companion; friend; boy scout
druk (drook) m. print; printing
drut (droot) m. wire
druzgotać (drooz-go-tach) v.
smash ; shatter; crush to pieces
drużba (droozh-ba) m. best man
drużyna (droo-zhi-na) f. team
drwal (drval) m. lumber jack
drwić (drveech) v. mock;deride
drwiny (drvee-ny) pl. mockery
dryg (drik) m.knack; flair for
drzazga (dzha̅z-ga) f. splinter
drzeć (dzhech) v. tear; pull
drzemka (dshem-ka) f. nap
drzewo (dshe-vo) n. tree
drzeworyt (dshe-vo-rit) m.
woodcut; wood engraving
drzwi (dzhvee) n. door
drżeć (drzhech) v. shiver;shake
dubeltówka (doo-bel-toov-ka) f.
double barrel gun; shotgun
duch (dookh) m. spirit; ghost;
state of mind ; intent; life
duchowieństwo (doo-khov-yeń-stvo)
pl. clergy ; priesthood
dudek (doo-dek) m. 1. hoopoe;
2. dupe; fool; dolt; booby
dudnić (dood-ńeech) v. resound
dudy (doo-di) pl. bagpipe
dukat (doo-kat) m. ducat
dulka (dool-ka) f. oarlock
duma (doo-ma) f. pride : epic
dumać (doo-mach) v. meditate
dumny (doom-ni) adj. m. proud
dupa (doo-pa) f. ass (vulg.)
dur (door) m. typhoid fever

dureń (doo-reń) m. fool; ass
durzyć (doo-zhich) v. fool;
infatuate; bewilder; dupe
dusić (doo-sheech) v. strangle
dusigrosz (doo-shee-grosh) m.
penny pincher; niggard
dusza (doo-sha) f. soul;psyche
dużo (doo-zho) adv. much; many
duży (doo-zhi) adj. m. big;
large; great; fair-sized
dwa (dva) num. two
dwakroć (dva-kroch) num. twice
dwanaście (dva-na̅sh-che) num.
twelve
dwieście (dvyesh-che) num. 200
dwoić (dvo-eech) v. double
dwojaczki (dvo-yach-kee) pl.
twins ; double pot [the two;
dwoje (dvo-ye) num. two;in two;
couple ;two(fold);two(ways)
dwór (dvoor) m. country manor
dworski (dvor-skee) adj. m.
courtly; manorial; of court
dworzec (dvo-zhets) m. (railway) station ; depot
dwukrotnie (dvoo-krot-ńe) adv.
twice ; twice over
dwunastka (dvoo-nast-ka) f.
twelve ;(team)of twelve
dwustronny (dvoo-stron-ni)adj.
m. two-sided; bilateral
dyg (dik) m. curtsy ; bob
dygnitarz (dig-ńee-tash) m.
dignitary; high-ranking man
dygotać (di-go-tach) v. tremble
dykta (dik-ta) f. plywood
dyktator (dik-ta-tor) m.
dictator ;absolute ruler
dylemat (di-le-mat) m. dilem-
ma; perplexity; fix
dym (dim) m. smoke; fumes
dymić (di-meech) v. smoke
dynamit (di-na-meet) m. dynamite; W.W, II German ersatz bread
dyndać (din-dach) v. dangle
dynia (di-ńa) f. pumpkin
dyplom (di-plom) m. diploma
dyplomacja (di-plo-mats-ya) f.
diplomacy; policy; tact
dyrekcja (di-rek-tsya) f.
management ; headquarters
dyrygent (di-ri-gent) m.
orchestra conductor

dyscyplina (dis-tsi-plee-na) f.
discipline; branch; line
dysk (disk) m. disc; discus
dyskrecja (dis-krets-ya) f.
discretion; management
dyskusja (dis-koos-ya) f.
discussion; debate
dysponowac (dis-po-no-vach) v.
dispose; control; order
dysputa (dis-poo-ta) f. dispute; debate; controversy
dystans (dis-tans) m. distance
dystyngowany (dis-tin-go-va-
ni) adj. m. distinguished
dysza (di-sha) f. nozzle;
blast pipe; snout; twyer
dyszec (di-shech) v. gasp;pant
dywan (di-van) m. carpet; rug
dywidenda (di-vee-den-da) f.
dividend
dywizja (di-veez-ya) f. division
dyżurny (di-zhoor-ny) adj. m.
on call; on duty; orderly
dzban (dzban) m. jug; pitcher
dziac się (dzhach shan) v.
occur; happen; take place
dziadek (dzha-dek) m. grandfather; nut cracer
dział (dzhaw) m. section
działacz (dzha-wach) m. acti-
vist(in politics, religion etc)
działać (dzha-wach) v. act;
work; be active; be effective
działka (dzhaw-ka) f. parcel
działo (dzha-wo) n. cannon
dziarski (dzhar-skee) adj. m.
brisk; lively; swinging; rakish
dziąsło (dzhown swo)n. gum
dzicz (dzheech)pl. savages
dzida (dzhee-da) f. spear ;pike
dzieci (dzhe-chee) pl. children
dzieciństwo (dzhe-cheen-stvo)
n. childhood; boyhood;infancy
dziecko (dzhets-ko) n. child;
baby; trot; brat; kiddie; kid
dziedziczyć (dzhe-dzhee-chich)
v. inherit (property,features)
dziedzina (dzhe-dzhee-na) f.
realm; area;sphere ; domain
dziedziniec (dzhe-dzhee-nets)m.
yard; court; backyard

dziegieć (dzhe-gech) m. tar
dzieje (dzhe-ye) pl. history
dziejowy (dzhe-yo-vi) adj. m.
historical; historic
dziekan (dzhe-kan) m. dean
dzielić (dzhe-leech) v. divide;
share; split; distribute
dzielnica (dzhel-nee-tsa) f.
province; quarter; section
dzielny (dzhel-ni) adj. m.
brave; resourceful; efficient
dzieło (dzhe-wo) n. achieve-
ment; work; composition
dziennik (dzhen-neek)m. daily-
news; daily; journal; diary
dzienny (dzhen-ni) adj. m.
daily; diurnal; day's
dzień (dzheń)m. day; daylight
dzień dobry(dzheń dob-ri)good morn-
dzierżawa (dzher-zha-va) f. ___ing
lease; rental; holding
dzierżyć (dzher-zhich) v.
wield (power); hold ; grip
dziesiątka (dzhe-shownt-ka) f.
ten;(team of)ten
dziesięć (dzhe-shańch) num.
ten
dziewczyna (dzhev-chi-na) f.
girl; lass; wench; maid
dziewica (dzhe-vee-tsa) f.
virgin; maiden
dziewięć (dzhe-vyańch) num.
nine
dziewiętnaście (dzhe-vyańt-
nashche) num. nineteen
dzieciol (dzhań-chow) m.
woodpecker
dziękczynienie (dzhańk-chi-
ńe-ńe)n. thanks-giving
dziękować (dzhań-ko-vach) v.
thank ; give thanks
dzik (dzheek) m. boar; tusker
dziobac (dzho-bach)v. peck
dziob (dzh-oob) m. beak; bill
dzisiejszy (dzhee-shey-shi)
adj. m. today's ; modern
dziś (dzheesh) adv. today
dziupla (dzhoop-la) f. (tree)
hollow (in a trnk)
dziura (dzhoo-ra) f. hole
dziurawy (dzhoo-ra-vi) adj. m.
leaky; full of holes
dziw (dzheef) m. wonder

dziwactwo (dżhee-vats-tvo) n.
crank; fad; craze; peculiarity
dziwić (dżhee-veech) v. astonish
dziwny (dżheev-ni)adj.m.strange;
dzwon (dzvon) m. bell; chime
dźwięczeć (dżhvyań-chech) v.
ring; sound; jingle; clang
dźwięk (dżhvyańk) m. sound
dźwig (dżhveek) n. crane
dźwigać (dżhvee-gach)v. lift;
hoist; raise; heave; erect;carry
dżdżysty (j-jis-ti) adj. m. wet;
rainy ; drizzly (weather)
dżem (jem) m. jam; fruit jam
dżet (jet) m. jet
dżinsy (jeen-si) pl. blue
jeans (pants)
dżokey (jo-key) m. jockey
dżudo (joo-do) m. judo (sport)
dżuma (joo-ma) f. plague
dżungla (joon-gla) f. jungle
echo (ekho) n. echo; response
edukacja (e-doo-kats-ya) f.
education; schooling;instruction
efekt (e-fekt) m. effect
efektowny (e-fek-tov-ni) adj.
m. showy ; striking; attractive
efektywny (e-fek-tiv-ni) adj.
m. efficient ; effective; real
egida (e-gee-da) f. protection;
auspices ; protectorate
egoista (e-go-ees-ta) m.egotist
egoistyczny (e-go-ees-tich-ni)
adj. m. selfish; self seeking
egzamin (eg-za-meen) m. examination; exam ; standing a test
egzekucja (eg-ze-koots-ya) f.
execution ; seizure; flogging
egzemplarz (eg-zem-plash) m.
copy (sample); specimen
egzystencja (eg-zis-ten-tsya)
f. existence; livelihood
ekierka (e-ker—ka) f. set
square ;draftsman's triangle
ekipa (e-kee-pa) f. team;crew
ekonomia (e-ko-nom-ya) f.
economics; thrift; economy
ekran (ek-ran) m. screen;shield
ekspedient (ex-pe-dyent) m.
salesperson ; clerk;salesman
ekspedycja (ex-pe-dits-ya) f.
1. dispatch 2. expedition

ekspert (ex-pert) m. expert
eksploatować (ex-plo-a-to-vach)
v. exploit; sweat; utilize
eksponat (ex-po-nat) m. exhibit
ekspozytura (ex-po-zy-too-ra)
f. agency; branch office
ekwipować (ek-vee-po-vach) v.
equip; fit out; provide with
elaborat (e-la-bo-rat) m. study (elaboration)
elastyczność (e-las-tich-noshch)
elasticity; resilience;flexibility
elegancja (e-le-gants-ya) f.
elegance; fashion; style
elektrociepłownia (e-lek-tro-
chep-wov-ña) f. steamplant
elektryczność (e-lek-trich-
noshch) f. electricity
element (e-le-ment) m. element
elementarny (e-le-men-tar-ni)
adj. m. fundamental; primary
elewator (e-le-va-tor) m.
elevator ; hoist
emalia (e-mal-ya) f. enamel
emeryt (e-me-rit) m. retired
person; pensioner; pensionary
emigracja (e-mee-grats-ya) f.
emigration; exile; emigrants
emisja (e-mees-ya) f. emission
emocja (e-mo-tsya) f. thrill
entuzjazm (en-tooz-yazm) m.
enthusiasm; rapture
energia (e-nerg-ya) f. energy
energiczny (e-ner-geech-ni)
adj. m. energetic; vigorous
epoka (e-po-ka) f. epoch
epitet (e-pee-tet) m. epithet
era (era) f. era; epoch
erotyczny (e-ro-tich-ni) adj.
m. erotic; sexual
eskadra (es-kad-ra) f. squad-
ron; aerial fleet: flight
eskorta (es-kor-ta) f. escort
estetyczny (es-te-tich-ni)
adj. m.esthetic; in good taste
etap (e-tap) m. stage (of development) ; halting place
etatowy (e-ta-to-vi) adj. m.
permanent (job); full time
eter (e-ter) m. ether
etyczny (e-tich-ni) adj. m.
ethical; moral

etykieta (e-ti-ke—ta) f. label;
etiquette; formality;ceremonial
ewakuacja (e-va-koo-a-tsya) f.
evacuation
ewangielia (e-van-gél--ya) f.
gospel; gospel truth
ewangielik (e-van-ge—leek) m.
protestant; Lutheran
ewentualnosc (e-ven-too-al-
nośhćh) f. possibility
ewentualnie (e-ven-too-al-ñe)
adv. possibly; if need be
ewidencja (e-vee-dén-tsya) f.
records; list; files ; roll
ewolucja (e-vo-loo-tsya) f.
evolution; development
fabryczny (fa-brich-ni) adj.
m. manufactured
fabryka (fa-bri-ka) f. factory
fabuła (fa-boo-wa) f. fable;
plot of a novel etc.; story
facet (fá-tset) m. guy
fachowiec (fa-kho-vyets) m.
expert; specialist;connoisseur
fajdać (fay-dach) v. shit (vulg.)
fajans (fáy-ans) m. earthenware
fajerka (fa-yér-ka) f.cook-top
unit; stove lid
fajka (fáy-ka)f. pipe (for
smoking); wild boar's tusk
fajtłapa (fayt-wa-pa) m. all
thumbs guy( awkward,clumsy man)
fakt (fakt) m. fact
faktor (fák-tor) m. broker;
agent; factor; intermediary
faktycznie (fak-tich-ñe) adv.
in fact;actually; indeed; truly
fala (fa-la) f. wave; tide;surge
falisty (fa-lees-ti) adj. m.
wavy; rolling; corrugated
falochron (fa-ló-khron) m.
breakwater : pier; jetty; mole
falsyfikat (fal-si-fée-kat) m.
forgery; counterfeit; fake
fałd (fawt) m. fold (wrinkle)
fałsz (fawsh) m. falsehood
fałszować (faw-shó-vach) v.
falsify; fake; forge; sing flat
fama (fa-ma) f. fame; rumor
fanaberie (fa-na-bér-ye) pl.
whims; fads; frills; ostentation
fanatyk (fa-ná-tik) m. fanatic;
enthusiast; bigot; maniac

fanfaron (fan-fá-ron) m.
braggart; coxcomb; swaggerer
fantastyczny (fan-tas-tich-ni)
adj. m. fantastic; wild; odd
fantazja (fan-taz-ya) f. dash;
imagination; fiction; whim
fara (fá-ra) f. parish church
farba (fár-ba) f. paint; dye
color; dyeing; blood
farbowac (far-bó-vach) v. dye
farsa (far-sa) f. farce;mockery
farsz (farsh) m. stuffing
fartuch (fár-tookh)m. apron
fasola (fa-só-la) f. bean
fasonowac (fa-so-no-vach) v.
fashion; shape; mold model
fatalny (fa-tal-ni) adj. m.
fatal; ill-fated; awful;fateful
fastryga (fas-tri-ga) f. tack;
basting; baste; tacks
faszyzm (fa-shizm) m. fascism
fatyga (fa-ti-ga) f. trouble;
fatigue; trouble; bother;pains
fatałaszki (fa-ta-wash-kee) pl.
knik-knacks; frippery; trinkets
febra (féb-ra) fever;the shakes
faworyzować (fa-vo-ri-zo-vach)
v. favor; play favorites
felczer (fél-cher) m. male
nurse ; medical assistant
federacja (fe-de-rats-ya) f.
federation ; union
feralny (fe-rál-ni) adj. m.
unlucky; ill fated; hapless
ferie (fér-ye) pl. holidays
ferma (fér-ma) f. farm ; ranch
ferment (fér-ment) m. ferment
festyn (fes-tin) m. festival
fetor (fé-tor) m. stench
figa (feé-ga) f. fig ; nix
figiel (fee-gel) m. practical
joke ; prank; trick; ill turn
figura (fee-góo-ra) f. figure;
shape ; form; image; big wig
fikcja (feek-tsya) f. fiction
filar (fee-lar) m. pillar
filatelista (fee-la-te-lees-ta)
m. stamp-collector
filc (feelts) m. felt
filia (feél-ya) f. branch
( store ); branch-office
filiżanka (fee-lee-zhán-ka) f.
cup ; cupful; coffee-cup

film (feelm) m. film

filolog (fee-lo-lok) m. philologist; linguist

filozof (fee-lo-zof) m. philosopher

filtr (feeltr) m. filter

filut (fee-loot) m. jester;
rogue; sly boots; joker

finanse (fee-nan-se) pl.
finances; finance; funds

finisz (fee-neesh) m. end (of
a run); the finish

fiołek (fyo-wek) m. violet

fiołkowy (fyow-ko-vi) adj. m.
purple; violet; of the violet

firanka (fee-ran-ka) f.
curtain; drapery

firma (feer-ma) f. business;
firm; name of a firm

fisharmonia (fees-har-mon-ya)
f. harmonium

fizjognomia (feez-yo-gnom-ya)
f. face; external aspect

fizjonomia (feez-yo-nom-ya) f.
face; physiognomy

fizjolog (feez-yo-lok) m.
physiologist

fizyczny (feez-ich-ni) adj. m.
physical; bodily; manual

fizyk (fee-zik) m. physicist

flaczki (flach-kee) pl. tripe

flaga (fla-ga) f. banner;
flag; ensign; standard

flaki (fla-kee) pl. bowels

flakon (fla-kon) m. vase

flanela (fla-ne-la) f. flannel

flaszka (flash-ka) bottle

flama (fla-ma) f, lady-love

flądra (flown-dra) f. flounder

flegma (fleg-ma) f. phlegm

flejtuch (fley-tookh) m. slut

flet (flet) m. flute

flirt (fleert) m. flirt

flisak (flee-sak) m. raftsman

flora (flo-ra) f. flora

floret (flo-ret) m. foil

flota (flo-ta) f. navy; fleet

fluksja (flooks-ya) f. tooth-
infection swelling

fluid (floo-eet) m. fluid

fochy (fo-khi) pl. blues;
whims; sulks; pouts

foka (fo-ka) f. seal

folgować (fol-go-vach) v.
slacken; relax; indulge; abate

folklor (folk-lor) m. folklore

folusz (fo-loosh)m.fulling mill

folwark (fol-vark) m. farm

fonetyczny (fo-ne-tich-ni) adj.
phonetic

fontanna (fon-tan-na) f.
fountain ; spurt ; waterworks

foremny (fo-rem-ni) adj. m.
shapely ;handsome; symmetrical

forma (for-ma) f. shape; mold

format (for-mat) m. size

formularz (for-moo-lash) m.
(application) form ; blank

formuła (for-moo-wa) f. formula

fornir (for-neer) m. veneer

forsa (for-sa) f. (money);
dough; bread; tin; chink

forsować (forso-vach) v. force;
strain ; urge; exhort;overcome

fort (fort) m. fort; stronghold

forteca (for-te-tsa) f. for -
tress; citadel ; stronghold

fortel (for-tel) m. stratagem;
trick ; ruse; subterfuge

fortepian (for-te-pyan) m.
grand piano; piano

fortuna (for-too-na) f. fortune

fosa (fo-sa) f. moat

fosfat (fos-fat) m. phosphate

fosfor (fos-foor)m. phosphorus

fotel (fo-tel) m. armchair

fotograf (fo-to-graf) m.
photographer

fotografia (fo-to-graf-ya) f.
photograph ; snap shot; picture

fracht (frakht) m. freight

fragment (frag-ment) m. fragment ; episode; excerpt;scrap

frak (frak) m. evening formal

framuga (fra-moo-ga) f. recess
(structure); bay; embrasure

frant (frant) m. sly dog; knave

frasunek (fra-soo-nek) m. worry;
grief; sorrow; care; trouble

fraszka (frasz-ka) f. trifle

frazes (fra-zes) m. platitude

frekwencja (fre-kven-tsya) f.
attendance; turnout; frequency

fredzla (frandz-la) f. fringe

fresk (fresk) m. fresco
front (front) m. front ;face,etc
froterować (fro-te-ro-vach) v.
  rub ; polish ; wax (floors)
frunąć (froo-nownch) v. fly
  away ; fly about; flee
frymarczyć (fri-mar-chich) v.
  barter ; trade; traffic
fryzjer (friz-yer) m. barber;
  hairdresser ; beautician
fujara (foo-ya-ra) m. & f. all-
  thumbs; nincompoop; pan-pipe
fukać (foo-kach) v. scold
fundacja (foon-dats-ya) f.
  foundation ; endowment
fundament (foon-da-ment) m.
  foundation; substructure
fundusz (foon-doosh) m. fund
funkcja (foonk-tsya) f.
  function; office ; duties
funt (foont) m. pound
fura (foo-ra) f. cart; wagon
furgon (foor-gon) m. truck
furia (foor-ya) f. fury; rage
furiat (foor-yat) m. madman
furman (foor-man) m. carter
furora (foo-ro-ra) f. sensation
furtka (foort-ka) f. gate
fusy (foo-si) pl. grounds
fuszer (foo-sher) m. bungler
futerał (foo-te-raw) m.
  (gun)case; holster
futro (foo-tro) n. fur
futryna (foo-tri-na) f. doorframe ; window-frame
futrzarz (foot-zhash) m. furrier
fuzja (fooz-ya) f. fusion;
  rifle ; shotgun
gabardyna (ga-bar-di-na) f.
  gabardine
gabinet (ga-bee-net) m. study;
  (ruling)cabinet; office
gablotka (ga-blot-ka) f. showcase
gad (gat) m. reptile ;mean guy
gadać (ga-dach) v. talk; yak;
  prattle ; talk nonsense
gaduła (ga-doo-wa) m. clapper
gaj (gay) m. grove
gala (ga-la) f. gala
galanteria (ga-lan-ter-ya) f.
  haberdashery
galareta (ga-la-re-ta) f. jelly

galeria (ga-ler-ya) f. gallery
galimatias (ga-lee-mat-yas) m.
  gibberish; hotchpotch; mess
galon (ga-lon) m. gallon
galop (ga-lop) m. gallop; run
galwaniczny (gal-va-neech-ni)
  adj. m. galvanic ; voltaic
gałąź (ga-wownzh) f. branch
gałgan (gaw-gan) m. rag; rascal; good-for-nothing;scamp
gałganiarz (gaw-ga-nash) m.
  ragtagman; ragpicker
gałka (gaw-ka) f. knob
gama (ga-ma) f. scale
gamoń (ga-moń) m. lout; oaf
ganek (ga-nek) m. balcony
gangrena (gan-gre-na) f.
  gangrene; depravity; corruption
ganić (ga-neech) v. blame
gapa (ga-pa) f. sucker
gapić się (ga-peech shań) v.
  gape; star-gaze ; moon; stare
gapie (ga-pye) pl. gapers
garaż (ga-rash) m. garage
garb (garb) m. hunch; hump
garbarnia (gar-bar-ña) f.
  tannery ; tan-yard
garbować (gar-bo-vach) v. tan
garbaty (gar-ba-ti) adj. m.
  hunch-backed; humpy; uneven
garbus (gar-boos) m.=garbaty
garbić (gar-beech) v. stoop
garderoba (gar-de-ro-ba) f.
  wardrobe; dressing-room
gardło (gard-wo) n. throat
gardłować (gard-wo-vach) v.
  v. talk big; clamor; cry for
gardłowy (gard-wo-vi) adj. m.
  guttural; punishable by death
gardzić (gar-dźheech)v. scorn;
  despise ; have in contempt
gardziel (gar-dźhel) f. throat;
  fauces; choke; gorge; jaws
garnąć (gar-nownch) v. gather
garncarz (garn-tsash) m. potter
garnek (gar-nek) m. pot; potful
garnirować (gar-ñee-ro-vach) v.
  garnish; trim (a dress etc.)
garnitur (gar-ñee-toor) m. set;
  suit; suite; assortment
garnizon (gar-ñee-zon) m.
  garrison

garnuszek (gar-noo-shek) m. cup
garstka (garst-ka) f. handful
garsc (garshch) f. handful
gasic (ga-sheech) v. extinguish; quench ; put out;eclipse
gasnąc (gas-nownch) v. die out
gaśnica (gash-nee-tsa) f.
fire-extinguisher
gastronomiczny (gas-tro-no-
meech-ni) adj. m. gastronomic
gastryczny (gas-trich-ni)
adj. m. gastric
gatunek (ga-too-nek) m. kind;
quality; sort; class; species
gawęda (ga-van-da) f. chat
gawiedz (ga-vyedzh ) f. mob;
rabble ; populace; gaping crowd
gawron (ga-vron) m. rook
gaz (gas) m. gas; open throttle
gaza (ga-za) f. gauze
gazeciarz (ga-ze-chash) m.
newspaperboy; newsstand
gazeta (ga-ze-ta) f. newspaper
gazolina (ga-zo-lee-na) f.
gasoline; gasolene: petrol
gazomierz (ga-zo-myesh) m.
gas-meter
gazownia (ga-zov-na) f. gas-
plant; gas works
gaznik (gazh-neek) m. carburet-
or
gaza (ga-zha) f. wage; salary
gąbczasty (gownb-cha-sti) adj.
m. spongy; squashy; mushy
gąbka (gownb-ka) f. sponge
gąsienica (gown-she-nee-tsa)
f. caterpillar; band; track
gąsior (gown-shor) m. gander;
jar; demijohn; ridge tile
gąszcz (gownshch) m. thicket
gbur (gboor) m. rude; boor
gburowaty (gboo-ro-va-ti) adj.
m. boorish; rude ; churlish
gdakac (gda-kach) v. cackle;
yak
gderac (dge-rach) v. grumble
gdy (gdi) conj. when; as; that
gdyby (gdi-bi) conj. if
gdyz (gdish) conj. for; because
gdzie (gdzhe) adv. conj. where
gdzie indziej(gdzhe-een-dzhey)
adv. elsewhere

gdziekolwiek (gdzhe-kol-vyek)
adv. anywhere; wherever
gdzie niegdzie (gdzhe-neg-dzhe)
adv. here and there; in places
gdzies (gdzhesh) adv. somewhere ; somewhere round
gejzer (gey-zer) m. geyser
gen (gen) m. (biol) gene
genealogia (ge-ne-a-log-ya) f.
genealogy; origin
generacja (ge-ne-rats-ya) f.
generation
generalny (ge-ne-ral-ni) adj.
m. general ; widespread
general (ge-ne-raw) m. general
genetyczny (ge-ne-tich-ni)
adj. m. genetic
geneza (ge-ne-za) f. origin;
genesis ; birth
genialny (ge-nal-ni) adj. m.
ingenious; genial ; great
geniusz (ge-nyoosh) m. genius
geodezja (ge-o-dez-ya) f.
geodesy
geografia (ge-o-graf-ya) f.
geography
geologia (ge-o-log-ya) f.
geology
geometra (ge-o-met-ra) m.
surveyor ; land surveyor
geometria (ge-o-metr-ya) f.
geometry ; geometry book
georginia (ge-or-gee-na) f.
dahlia
germański (ger-man-skee) adj.
m. Germanic
gest (gest) m. gesture ;motion
gestykulowac (ges-ti-koo-lo-
vach) v. gesticulate
getto (get-to) n. ghetto
gęba (gan-ba) f. mug; mouth;
puss ; snout; muzzle; face
gęgac (gan-gach) v. cackle
gęs (gansh) f. goose
gęsl (ganshl) f. lute
gęstosc (gan-stoshch) f. density; thickness; closeness
gęstwina (gan-stvee-na) f.
thicket; array; accumulation
giąc (gyownch)v. bow; bend
gibki (geeb-kee) adj. m.
pliant; flexible; limber

giełda (ǵew-da) f. stock-
exchange; money-market
giez (ǵes) m. gadfly; breeze
giętki (ǵ ańt-kee) adj. m.
flexible; nimble; elastic
gigant (gee-gant) m. giant
gilza (geel-za) f. (cartridge)
case; shell; cigarette tube
gimnastyczny (geem-nas-tích-
ni) adj. m. gymnastic
gimnazjum (geem-náz-yoom) n.
high-school; middle-school
ginąć (gee-nównch) v. perish
ginekolog (gee-ne-kó-log) m.
gynecologist
gips (geeps) m. gypsum
gitara (gee-tá-ra) f. guitar
glazura (gla-zoó-ra) f. glaze
gleba (glé-ba) f. soil
glejt (gleyt) m. safe-conduct
ględzic (glań-dźheéch)v. talk-
through one's hat; talk-
nonsense;twaddle; blather
gliceryna (glee-ce-ri-na) f.
glycerin
glin (gleen) m. aluminum
glina (gleé-na) f. clay; loam
glista (gleés-ta) f. earthworm; ascaris; nema
glob (glop) m. globe; sphere
gładki (gwad-kee) adj. m. plain;
smooth; sleek;even; level;glib
gładzic (gwa-dźheéch)v. smooth;
(put to death);mangle; stroke
głaskac (gwás-kach) v. caress;
fondle; stroke;pet; tickle
głaz (gwas) m. boulder; rock
głąb (gwownp) f, depth
głąb (gwównp) m. stalk
głębia (gwánb-ya) f. depth;
deep; interior; intensity
głęboki (gwań-bó-kee) adj. m.
deep; distant; remote; intense
głębokosć (gwań-bó-koshch) f.
depth; profundity; keenness
głodny (gwód-ni) adj. m. hungry
głodowac (gwo-do-vach) v.
starve; hunger; lay off food
głodzic (gwo-dźheéch)v. starve
(somone); underfeed; deprive
głos (gwos) m. voice; sound;tone
głosowac (gwo-só-vach) v. vote

głosnik (gwosh-ńeek) m. loudspeaker;public-address system
głosno (gwósh-no) adv. loud
głosny (gwósh-ni) adj. m. loud
głowa (gwó-va) f. head; chief
głowic się (gwo-veéch shań) v.
beat one's brains out;puzzle
głod (gwoot) m. hunger; famine
głog (gwook) m. hawthorn
główka (gwoó-vka) f. pinhead;
knob; tip; top; boss; heading
głownodowodzący (gwoov-no-do-
vo-dzówn-tsi) m. commander-
in-chief
główny (gwoóv-ni) adj. m.
main; predominant; foremost
głuchy (gwoó-khi) adj. m. deaf
głupi (gwoó-pee) adj. m. silly;
stupid; foolish; asinine
głupiec (gwoop-yets) m. dumb-
head; fool; idiot;loony; goof
głupota (gwoo-pó-ta) f. stupidity;imbecility; foolishness
głupstwo (gwoop-stwo) n.
nonsense; trifle; blunder
głuszec (gwoó-shets) m. grouse
gmach (gmakh) m. large building
gmatwac (gma-tvach) v. tangle;
embroil; mix up; complicate
gmerac (gme-rach) v. rummage
gmin (gmeen) m. populace
gmina (gmeé-na) f. county
subdivision ; parish
gnat (gnat) m. bone (slang)
gnębic (gnáń-beech) v. oppress
gniady (gńa-di) adj. m. bay
(horse); dark brown horse
gniazdo (gńaz-do) n. nest
gnic (gńeech) v. rot; decay
gnida (gńeéda) f. nit
gniesć (gńeshch) v. squeeze
gniew (gńev) m. anger; wrath
gniezdzic się (gńéźh-dźheech
shań) v. nestle ; cluster
gnilny (gńeel-ni) adj. m.
putrid; of rot; septic
gnoic (gno-eech) v. putrefy
gnojówka (gno-yoóv-ka) f.
liquid manure; manure pit
gnój (gnooy) m. manure; dung;
stinker (vulg.); lousy bum
gnuśny (gnoósh-ni) adj. m.
sluggish; lazy; idle; listless

godło (gód-wo) n. emblem
godność (gód-noshch) f. dignity; name; pride; self-esteem
godny (gód-ni) adj. m. worthy
gody (go-di) n. nuptials; mating
godzić (go-dżheech) v. reconcile; hire; square; engage
godzien (go-dżhen) adj. m.
deserving ; worth; worthy
godzina (go-dżhee-na) f. hour
godziwy (go-dżhee-vi) adj. m.
proper; suitable; just; fair
goić (go-eech) v. heal; cure
goleń (go-leń) m. shin-bone
golić (go-leech) v. shave
golonka (go-loń-ka) f. pig's
feet dish ; knuckle
gołąb (go-wównp) m. pigeon
gołoledź (go-wo-ledźh) f.
glazed frost ;frozen dew
gołosłowny (go-wo-swóv-ni) adj.
m. unfounded; proofless; vain
goły (go-wi) adj. m. naked
gonić (go-ńeech) v. chase; hunt
goniec (go-ńets) m. messenger
gonitwa (go-ńeet-va) f. chase
gont (gont) m. shingle
gorąco (go-rówń-tso) n. heat
gorący (go-rówń-tsi) adj. m.
hot; sultry; warm; hearty;lively
gorączka (go-rovńch-ka) f. fever; shakes; excitement; heat
gorczyca (gor-chí-tsa) f.
mustard; charlock
gorętszy (go-rańt-shi) adj.
m.hotter; fervent; intense
gorliwiec (gor-lee-vyets) m.
zealot; ardent supporter
gorliwy (gor-lee-vi) adj. m.
zealous; keen; eager; devout
gorset (gor-set) m. girdle
gorszy (gor-shi) adj. m. worse
gorszyć (gor-shich) v. demoralize; scandalize; shock;deprave
gorycz (go-rich) f. bitterness
goryl (go-ril) m. gorilla
gorzałka (go-zhaw-ka) f. brandy spirits ; booze; spirit
gorzec (go-zhech) v. be ablaze
gorzej (go-zhey) adv. worse
gorzelnia (go-zhel-ńa) f.
distillery ; still
gorzki (gózh-kee) adj. n.bitter

gospoda (gos-pó-da) f. inn
gospodarczy (gos-po-dar-chi)
adj. n. economic;farm; charring
gospodarka (gos-po-dar-ka) f.
economy;housekeeping; farming
gospodarny (gos-po-dar-ni) adj.
m. economical; thrifty
gospodarstwo (gos-po-dar-stvo)
n. household; farm; possessions
gospodarz (gos-po-dash) m.
landlord; host ; farmer;manager
gospodyni (gos-po-di-ńee) f.
landlady; hostess; manageress
gosposia (gos-po-śha) f.
housekeeper; maid; servant
gościć (góśh-cheech) v. receive; entertain; treat; stay at
gościna (gośh-chée-na) f.
visit; stay at sb house
gościnność (gosh-chéen-noshch)
f. hospitality
gość (góshch) m. guest;caller
gościec (góśh-chets) m. gout;
arthritis
gotować (go-tó-vach) v. cook;
boil; get ready; prepare
gotowość (go-tó-voshch) f.
readiness ; willingness
gotowy (go-tó-vi) adj. m.
ready ; done; complete;willing
gotówka (go-tóov-ka) f. cash
gotyk (gó-tik) m. Gothic
goździk (góźh-dżheek)m. carnation ; clove; gilly-flower
góra (goo-ra) f. mountain
góral (goo-ral) m. mountaineer
górnictwo (goor-ńeets-tvo) n.
mining ; mining industry
górnik (goor-ńeek) m. miner
górnolotny (goor-no-lót-ni)
adj. m. lofty ; soaring;gaudy
górny (goor-ni) adj. m. upper
górować (goo-ro-vach) v. prevail; excel; dominate ; rise
górski (goor-skee) adj. m.
mountainous ; mountain
górzysty (goo-zhís-ti) adj.
m. hilly ; mountainous
gówniarz (goov-ńash) m.
(vulg.): shitass; whipster
gówno (góov-no) m. shit (vulg.)
gra (gra) f. game;sham; acting
grab (grap) m. hornbeam; hardbeam

grabarz (gra-bash) m. grave-digger;sexton; burying beetle
grabić (gra-beech) v. rake; plunder ; rob; sack; rake up
grabie (gra-bye) n. rake
grabież (gra-byesh) f. plunder
graca (gra-tsa) f. scraper
gracja (grats-ya) f. grace
gracować (gra-tsó-vaćh) v. scrape; rake; mix mortar
gracz (grach) m. player; gambler; double-dealer; sly fox
grać (graćh) v. play; act; gamble ; pretend; pulsate
grad (grad) m. hail; volley
grafika (fra-feé-ka) f. graphic art ; graphics; art of writing
gram (gram) m. gram
gramatyka (gra-má-ti-ka) f. grammar; grammar book
gramofon (gra-mo-fon) m. record player; phonograph
gramolić się (gra-mo-leećh shán) v. clamber;climb
granat (gra-nat) m. grenade
granatnik (gra-nát-ńeek) m. mortar ; howitzer
granatowy (gra-na-to-vi) adj. m. navy blue ; of grenades
granda (grán-da) f. swindle
graniastosłup (gra-ńa-stó-swoop) m. prism
granica (gra-ńee-tsa) f. boundary; limit; border; range
granit (gra-ńeet) m. granite
granulować (gra-noo-ló-vaćh) v. granulate
grań (grań) f. (mountain) ridge; crest; edge; razor's edge
grasować (gra-so-vaćh) v. roam about; prowl; maraud; stalk
grat (grat) m. run down furniture (or man); crock; trash
gratis (gra-tees) adv. free of charge; something given free
gratka (grat-ka) f. windfall
gratulacja (gra-too-láts-ya) f. congratulations ;felicitation
grawer (gra-ver) m. engraver
grawitacja (gra-vee-táts-ya) f. gravitation
grdyka (grdí-ka) f. Adam's apple

grecki (greéts-kee) adj. m. Greek
gremialnie (grem-yál-ńe) adv. in-a-mass; completely;altogether
grobla (grob-la) f. dike; dam
grobowiec (gro-bóv-yets) m. tomb ; sepulchre ;family vault
grobowy (gro-bo-vi) adj. m. grave ; deathly; gloomy;dismal
groch (grokh) m. pea; pea plant
grom (grom) m. thunderclap
gromada (gro-má-da) f. crowd; throng; community; team
gromadzić (gro-má-dźheećh) v. amass; hoard; gather;attract
gromić (gro-meećh) v. storm; rout ; reprimand; defeat
grono (gro-no) n. bunch of grapes ; cluster; group;body
gronostaj (gro-no-stay) m. ermine
grosz (grosh) m. penny (copper)
groszek (gro-shek) m, green pea(s) ; spotted pattern
grot (grot) m. dart; spike
grota (gro-ta) f. grotto; care
groza (gro-za) f. dread; horror
grozić (gro-źheećh)v. threaten
groźba (groźh-ba) f. threat
grób (groop) m. grave ; tomb
gród (groot) m. (fortified)town
gródż (groodźh)f. bulkhead
grubiański (groob-yáń-skee) adj. m. rude ; coarse; obscene
grubość (groo-boshćh) f. thickness ; girth; size; grist
gruby (groo-by) adj. m. thick; fat; stout; big;low-pitched
gruchotać (groo-kchó-taćh) v. shatter; batter; rattle;crash
gruczoł (groo-chow) m. gland
gruda (groo-da) f. lump; clod
grudzień (groo-dźheń) m. December
grunt (groont) m. ground; soil
grupa (groo-pa) f. group ; class
grusza (groo-sha) f. pear-tree
gruz (groos) m. rubble ; ruins
gruzeł (groo-zew) m. clot
gruzy (groo-zi) pl. debris
gruźlica (groozh-leé-tsa) f. tuberculosis; consumption

gryka (gri-ka) f. buckwheat
grymas (gri-mas) m. grimace
grypa (gri-pa) f. flu;influenza
grysik (gri-sheek) m. grits
gryzoń (gri-zoń) m. rodent
gryzc (grizhch) v. bite;torment
grzac (gzhach) v. warm;fire; thrash
grządka (gzhównd-ka) f. flower
bed ; patch ; (hen-)roost
grząsc (gzhównshch) v. wade
grząski (gzhówn-skee) adj. m.
quaggy; slimy; slushy; miry
grzbiet (gzhbyet) m. back;
spine ; ridge; butt; edge;rib
grzebac (gzhe-bach) v. bury;
rummage; dig;rake up; fumble
grzebień (gzhe-byeń) m. comb;
crest of a wave; ridge;teaser
grzech (gzhekh) m. sin; fault
grzechotka (gzhe-khot-ka) f.
rattle; flapper; clapper
grzechotnik (gzhe-khot-ńeek)
m. rattlesnake
grzecznosc (gzhech-noshch) f.
politeness; favor; attentions
grzęznąc (gzhańz-nównch) v.
get stuck;wade; flounder;sink
grzmiący (gzhmyówn-tsi) adj. m.
thundering; booming;fulminatory
grzmot (gzhmot) m. thunder; hag
grzyb (gzhip) m. mushroom;
fungus; snuff
grzywa (gzhi-va) f. mane
grzywna (gzhiv-na) f. fine
gubernator (goo-ber-na-tor) m.
governor(general)
gubic (goo-beech) v. loose;ruin
gula (goo-la) f. knob; bump
gulasz (goo-lash) m. meat soup
gulgotac (gool-go-tach) v.
gurgle; bubble; gobble
guma (goo-ma) f. rubber
gumno (goom-no) n. barn (yard)
gust (goost) m. taste; palate
guz (goos) m. bump; tumor
guzdrac się (gooz-drach shań) v.
dawdle; dally; waste time;lag
gwałcic (gvaw-cheech) v. rape;
violate; compel; coerce;force
gwałt (gvawt) m. rape; outrage
gwałtowny (gvaw-tov-ni) adj.
m. 1. outrageous 2. urgent

gwar (gvar) m. hum; noise
gwara (gva-ra) f. dialect;
slang ; jargon; lingo; cant;
patter ; colloquial language
gwarancja (gva-ran-tsya) f.
warranty; guarantee; pledge
gwardia (gvar-dya) f. guard
gwarny (gvar-ni) adj. m. noisy
gwarzyc (gva-zhich) v. chat
gwiazda (gvyaz-da) f. star
gwint (gveent)m.thread (mech.)
gwintowac (gveen-to-vach) v.
cut thread ; tap; rifle
gwizd (gveezt) m. whistle
gwoli (gvo-lee) conj. for the
sake of ; because of;in order
gwozdz (gwoozhdzh) m. nail to
gzyms (gzims) m. molding
cornice; mantelpiece
habit (kha-bit) m. monk's
frock ; habit ; nun's frock
haczyk (kha-chik) m. small
hook ; barb; snag; catch
hafciarka (haf-char-ka) f.
embroideress
haft (khaft) m. embroidery
haftka (khaft-ka) f. clasp
hak (khak) m. hook ; clamp
hala (kha-la) f. (sports) hall
halka (khal-ka) f. petticoat
halny wiatr (hal-ni vyatr)
Tatra wind ( foehn )
halucynacja (kha-loo-tsi-nats-
ya) f. hallucination
hałas (kha-was) m. noise; din
hałasowac (kha-wa-so-vach) v.
make noise ; be noisy
hałastra (kha-was-tra) f. mob;
rabble; riff-raff; ragtag mob
hałaśliwy (kha-wash-lee-vi)
adj. m. noisy ; loud; rowdy
hamak (kha-mak) m. hammock
hamowac (kha-mo-vach) v.apply
brakes; restrain; hamper;curb
hamulec (kha-moo-lets) m. brake
hamulec ręczny (kha-moo-lets
rańch-ni) handbrake
handel (khandel) m. commerce
handlarz (khand-lash) m. merchant;shopkeeper; peddler
handlowac (khan-dlo-vach) v.
trade; deal; be in business

hangar (khan-gar) m. hangar
haniebny (kha-neb-ni) adj. m.
disgraceful; dirty; foul; vile
hanba (khan-ba) f. disgrace
hanbic (khan-beech) v. disgrace
haracz (kha-rach) m. tribute
harcerstwo (khar-tser-stvo) n.
scouting
harcerz (khar-tsesh) m. boy
scout
hardy (kha-rdy) adj. m. haughty
harfa (khar-fa) f. harp
harmider (khar-mee-der) m.
hullabaloo; clatter; din; row
harmonia (khar-mon-ya) f. harmony; accordion; harmonics
harowac (kha-ro-vach) v. toil
harpun (khar-poon) m. harpoon
hart (khart) m. fortitude;
hardness; sternness;temper;grit
hartowac (khar-to-vach) v.
temper; harden; anneal;quench
hasac (kha-sach) v. frisk;
frolic; romp;gambol; dance
haslo (kha-swo) n. password
haubica (khau-bee-tsa) f.
howitzer
haust (khaust) m. gulp; swig
hazard (kha-zard) m. risk;
hazard; the gaming table
heban (khe-ban) m. ebony
hebel (khe-bel) m. plane
hebrajski (kheb-ray-skee) adj.
m. Hebrew
heca (khe-tsa) f. fun; fuss
hegemonia (khe-ge-mon-ya) f.
hegemony
hej (khey) excl.: hey! ho!
hejnal (khey-naw) m. trumpet-
call; bugle-call; reveille
hektar (khek-tar) m. hectare
helm (khewm) m. helmet; dome
hemoroidy (khe-mo-roy-di) pl.
piles;hemorrhoids
hen (khen) adv. far; away
herb (kherp) m. coat-of-arms
herbaciarnia (kher-ba-char-na)
f. teahouse
herbata (kher-ba-ta) f. tea
herbatnik (kher-bat-neek) m.
biscuit
heretyk (khe-re-tik) m. heretic

herezja (khe-rez-ya) f. heresy
hermetyczny (kher-me-tich-ni)
adj. m. air-tight; hermetic
heroiczny (khe-ro-eech-ni) adj.
m. heroic
heroizm (khe-ro-eezm) m. heroism
herszt (khersht) m. ringleader
het (khet) adv. far; away
hetman (khet-man) m. commander
hiacynt (khya-tsint) m.hyacinth
hiena (khee-e-na) f. hyena
hierarchia (khye-rar-khya) f.
hierarchy
hieroglif (khye-ro-gleef) m.
hieroglyph; illegible writing
higiena (khee-ge-na) f. hygiene;
sanitation; hygienics
hinduski (kheen-doos-kee) adj.
m. Hindu
hiperbola (khee-per-bo-la) f.
hyperbola ; hyperbole
hipnotyczny (kheep-no-tich-ni)
adj. m. hypnotic ; mesmeric
hipochondryk(khee-po-khon-drik)
m. hypochondriac
hipokryta (khee-po-kri-ta) m.
hypocrite ; pretender;dissembler
hipopotam (khee-po-po-tam) m.
hippopotamus
hipoteka (khee-po-teka) f. title;
mortgage ; records office
hipoteza (khee-po-te-za) f.
hypothesis ; assumption
histeria (khees-ter-ya) f.
hysteria ; hysterical fit
historia (khees-tor-ya) f. story; history ; affair; show;fuss
hiszpanski (kheesh-pan-skee)
adj. m. Spanish
hitlerowiec (kheet-le-ro-vyets)
m. hitlerite
hodowac (kho-do-vach) v. breed
hodowca (kho-dov-tsa) m. breeder; grower ; farmer;cultivator
hojny (khoy-ni) adj. m. generous; lavish; liberal; profuse
hokej (kho-key) m. hockey
holenderski (kho-len-der-skee)
adj. m. Dutch
holowac (kho-lo-vach) v. tow;
haul; drag; tug; haul; truck

hołd (khowd) m. tribute
hołota (kho-wó-ta) f. riffraff
honor (kho-nor) m. honor
honorarium (kho-no-rar-yoom)
 n. fee; honorarium
horda (khor-da) f. horde; throng
horrendalny (kho-ren-dal-ni)
 adj. m. awful; horrible
hormon (khor-mon) m. hormone
horoskop (kho-ros-kop) m.
 horoscope ; prophesy ;prospect
horyzont (kho-ri-zont) m.hor-
 izon; vistas; prospects
hotel (kho-tel) m. hotel
hoży (kho-zhi) adj. m. brisk;
 handsome; comely; fresh
hrabia (khrab-ya) m. count
hrabina (khra-bee-na) f.
 countess
hrabianka (khra-byan-ka) f.
 countess (miss)
hrabstwo (khrab-stwo) n. county
hreczka (khrech-ka) f. buckwheat
hreczkosiej (khrech-ko-shey)
 m.country bumpkin
hubka (khoob-ka) f. tinder
huczeć (khoo-chech) v. roar
hufnal (khoof-nal) m. horse-
 shoe nail
huk (khook) m. bang; roar
hulać (khoo-lach) v. carouse;
 riot; make merry; run wild
hulajnoga (khoo-lay-no-ga) f.
 scooter (without motor)
hulaka (khoo-la-ka) m. carous-
 er; debaucher; rioter; rake
hulanka (khoo-lan-ka) f. riot;
 debauch ; junket; carouse;revel
hultaj (khool-tay) m. libertine;
 rascal; rogue
humanista (khoo-ma-ñees-ta) m.
 humanist ; classical scholar
humanitarny (khoo-ma-ñee-tar-
 ni) m. humane; humanitarian
humor (khoo-mor) m. humor
hura (khoo-ra) f. hurrah !
 cheers ! long live !
huragan (khoo-ra-gan) m. hurricane ; cyclone
hurmem (khoor-mem) adv. in
 swarms ; in a mass; altogether

hurt (khoort) m. wholesale
humus (khoo-moos) m. humus
husarz (khoo-sash) m. Polish
 winged-armor cavalryman (hist.)
hustać (khoosh-tach) v. swing;
 rock; dandle; toss up and down
huśtawka (khoosh-tav-ka) f.
 swing ; seesaw ; swing boat
huta (khoo-ta) f. metal or
 glass mill ; smelting works
hutnik (khoot-ñeek) m. metal
 or glass(man)worker ;metalurgist
hycel (khi-tsel) m. dogcatcher;
 rascal ; good for nothing
hydrant (khid-rant) m. hydrant
hydraulika (khi-drau-lee-ka)
 f. hydraulics ; plumbing
hymn (himn) m.anthem; hymn
i (ee) conj. and; also; too
ichtiologia (eekh-tyo-log-ya)
 f. ichthyology
idea (ee-de-a) f. idea ; aim
idealista (ee-de-a-lees-ta) m.
 idealist ; dreamer; visionary
idealny (ee-de-al-ni) adj. m.
 ideal ; perfect; visionary
identyczny (ee-den-tich-ni)
 adj. m. identical ; similar
ideologia (ee-de-o-log-ya) f.
 ideology ; world view
idiosynkrazja (ee-dyo-sin-kraz-
 ya) f. idiosyncrasy
idiota (ee-d-yó-ta) m. idiot
idiotka (eed-yot-ka) f. idiot
iglaste drzewo (ee-glas-te
 dzhe-vo) m. coniferous tree
iglica (eeg-lee-tsa) f. spire
igła (eeg-wa) f. needle
ignorancja (eeg-no-ran-tsya) f.
 ignorance; lack of knowledge
igrać (eeg-rach) v. play; trifle
igrzysko (ee-gzhis-ko) n.
 spectacle (games); contest
ikra (eek-ra) f. spawn; roe
ile (ee-le) adv. how much
ilekroć (ee-le-kroch) adv.
 every time; whenever ; when
iloczas (ee-lo-chas) m. quantity (of a vowel or syllable)
iloczyn (ee-lo-chin) m. (multiplication) product
iloraz (ee-lo-raz) m. (division)
 quotient

ilościowy (ee-losh-cho-vi)adj.
m. quantitative; numerical
ilość (ee-loshch) f. quantity
iluminacja (ee-loo-mee-nats-ya)
f. illumination; floodlight
ilustracja (ee-loos-trats-ya)
f. illustration; figure;picture
iluzja (ee-looz-ya) f. illusion
ił (eew) m. loam
im (eem) conj. the more...
imać (ee-mach) v. size upon
imadło (ee-mad-wo) n . (shop)
vice ; chuck; holder ; vise
imaginacja (ee-ma-gee-nats-ya)
f. imagination; empty fancy
imbir (eem-beer) m. ginger
imbryk (eem-brik) m. teapot
imieniny (ee-mye-nee-ni) n.
name-day; name-day party
imiennie (ee-myen-ne) adv. by
name; personally; individually
imiennik (ee-myen-neek) m.
namesake
imiesłów (ee-mye-swoov) m.
participle
imię (ee-myan) n. name (given)
imigracja (ee-mee-grats-ya) f.
immigration; the immigrants
imigrant (ee-mee-grant) m.
immigrant;foreign settler
imigrować (ee-mee-gro-vach) v.
immigrate;settle in a new land
imitacja (ee-mee-tats-ya) f.
imitation; counterfeit; fake
imitować (ee-mee-to-vach) v.
imitate; mimic; simulate
impas (eem-pas) m. deadlock
imperialista (eem-per-ya-lees-
ta) m. imperialist
imperium (eem-per-yoom) n.
empire
impertynent (eem-per-ti-nent) m.
arrogant; pert,impertinent man
impet (eem-pet) m. impetus
imponować (eem-po-no-vach) v.
impress; impose on sb; dazzle
import (eem-port) m. import
impregnować (eem-preg-no-vach)
v. impregnate; make waterproof
impreza (eem-pre-za) f. enterprise; spectacle; show; stunt
improwizować (eem-pro-vee-zo-
vach) v. improvise; extemporize

impuls (eem-pools) m. impulse
inaczej (ee-na-chey) adv. otherwise; differently; unlike
inauguracja (ee-na-goo-rats-ya)
f. inauguration; opening
inaugurować (ee-na-goo-ro-vach)
v. inaugurate; initiate
in blanko (een-blan-ko) adv.
in blank ; blank check
incydent (een-tsi-dent) m.
incident; happening; event
indagacja (een-da-gats-ya) f.
investigation; questioning
indeks (een-deks) m. index
indemnizacja (een-dem-nee-
zats-ya) f. indemnity
indukcja (een-dook-tsya) f.
induction; generalized reasoning
indyk (een-dik) m. turkey
indyczka (een-dich-ka) f.
turkey-hen
indywidualny (een-di-vee-doo-
al-ni) adj. m. individual
inercja (een-erts-ya) f. inertia ; inaction; inertness
infekcja (een-fekts-ya) f.
infection; contamination
infiltracja (een-feel-trats-ya)
f. infiltration
inflacja (een-flats-ya) f.
inflation
influenza (een-floo-en-za) f.
influenza ; flu ; grippe
informacja (een-for-mats-ya) f.
information ; intelligence;news
informacyjny (een-for-ma-tsiy-
ni) adj. m. information (office)
informować (een-for-mo-vach) v.
inform ; instruct; post up
ingerencja (een-ge-ren-tsya) f.
interference; meddling
inhalacja (een-kha-lats-ya) f.
inhalation; breathing in
inicjał (ee-neets-yaw) m. initial (letter); ornate letter
inicjator (ee-neets-ya-tor) m.
originator ; mover ; founder
inicjatywa (ee-neets-ya-ti-va)
f. initiative; enterprise
inkasować (een-ka-so-vach) v.
collect (money); get a blow
inklinacja (een-klee-nats-ya)
f. inclination ; liking

inkwizycja (een-kvee-zíts-ya)
f. inquisition ; investigation
innowacja (een-no-vats-ya) f.
innovation ; novelty ,
innowierca (een-no-vyer-tsa)
m.dissenter; heretic
inny (eén-ni) adj. m. other;
different; another (one)
inscenizacja (een-stse-ñee-záts-
ya) f. putting on stage
inspekcja (een-spék-tsya) f.
inspection; review; inspectorate
inspekty (een-spék-ti) n. hotbed ; glass covered frame
inspiracja (een-spee-ráts-ya)
f. inspiration ; breathing in
instalacja (een-sta-láts-ya) f.
installation ; plumbing, etc
instalator (een-sta-la-tor) m.
plumber; fitter; electrician
instrukcja (een-strook-tsya)
f. instruction ; order;training
instrument (een-stroo-ment) m.
instrument; tool; deed;appliance
instynkt (eén-stinkt) m. instinct ; aptitude; knack
instytucja (een-sti-toots-ya) f.
institution ; establishment
insynuacja (een-si-noo-áts-ya)
f. insinuation; innuendo
integralny (een-te-grál-ni)
adj. m. integral; whole; entire
intelekt (een-te-lekt) m. intellect; intelligence; mind
intelektualista (een-te-lek-
too-a-lees-ta) m. intellectual
inteligencja (een-te-lee-gén-
tsya) f.intelligensia ; intelligence;(quick)understanding
inteligentny (een-te-lee-gen-
tni) adj. m. intelligent
intencja (een-tén-tsya) f. intention ; purpose; view;finality
intensywny (een-ten-siv-ni)
adj. m. intensive; strenuous
interes (een-té-res) m. inte r-
est; business;store; matter
interesowny (een-te-re-sów-ni)
adj. m. selfish; greedy
interesujący (een-te-re-soo-
yown-tsi) adj. m. interesting
internat (een-tér-nat) m. boarding school

interpretacja (een-ter-pre-
táts-ya) f. interpretation
interwencja (een-ter-vén-tsya)
f. intervention.interference
intratny (een-trát-ni) adj. m.
lucrative; profitable ;paying
introligator (een-tro-lee-gá-
tor) m. bookbinder
intruz (eén-troos) m. intruder
intryga (een-trí-ga)f. plot;
intrigue ; machination
intuicja (een-too-eéts-ya) f.
intuition ; insight; feeling
intuicyjny (een-too-ee-tsiy-ni)
adj. m. intuitive
inwalida (een-va-leé-da) m.
invalid; disabled (soldier)
inwazja (een-váz-ya) f. invasion
inwencja (een-vén-tsya) f. in-
ventiveness; invention
inwentarz (een-vén-tash) m.
inventory; stock; list
inwestycja (een-ves-tits-ya)
f. investment ; capital outlay
inżynier (een-zhi-ñer) m.
engineer (with college degree)
inżynieria (een-zhi-ñér-ya) f.
engineering
ircha (eér-kha) f. suede-
leather; chamois ; shammy
irlandzki(eer-lándz-kee) adj.
Irish ,
irys (ee-ris) m. iris
ironia (ee-ro-ñya) f. irony
irygacja (ee-ri-gáts-ya) f.
irrigation ; watering
irytacja (ee-ri-táts-ya) f.
irritation ; vexation; chafe
iskać (eesk-ach) v. v. seek
lice; cleanse of vermin
iskra (ees-kra) f. spark
istnieć (eest-ñech) v. exist
istnienie (eest-ñé-ñe) n.
existence;being; entity
istny (eest-ni) adj. m. real;
veritable ;downright; sheer
istota (ees-tó-ta) f. being;
essence ; gist; sum; entity
istotny (ees-tót-ni) adj. m.
real; substantial ; vital
istotnie (ees-tót-ñe) adv.
indeed; truly ; really;in fact
iscie (eésh-che) adv. indeed;
truly ; really; in truth

iść (ééshch) v. go; walk
izba (éez-ba) f. room; chamber
izba handlowa (éez-ba khan-
dló-va) f. Chamber of Commerce
izolacja (ee-zo-láts-ya) f.
isolation; insulation; seal
izolator (ee-zo-lá-tor) m. insu-
lator; non-conductor
izolacyjna taśma (ee-zo-la-tsiy-
na tásh-ma) f. insulating tape
izoterma (ee-zo-ter-ma) f. iso-
therm;line of equal temperature
izotop (ee-zo-top) m. isotope
izraelicki (eez-ra-e-léets-kee)
adj. m. Israeli; of Israel
izraelita (eez-ra-e-lee-ta) m.
Israelite; citizen of Izrael
iż (eezh) conj. that(literary)
iżby (éezh-bi) conj.m. in order
that; in order to; lest
ja (ya) pron. I;(indecl.):self
jabłecznik (yab-wech-ńeek) m.
apple cider; apple pie
jabłko (yáp -ko) n. apple
jabłoń (yá-bwoń) f. apple tree
jacht (yakht) m. yacht
jachtklub (yákht-kloob) m.
yacht club
jad (yat) m. venom; poison
jadalnia (ya-dál-ńa) f. dining-
room; mess; mess-hall
jadalny (ya-dál-ni) adj. m.
eatable; edible; dining-
jadło (yád-wo) n. food;edibles
jadłodajnia (ya-dwo-dáy-na) f.
restaurant; eating house
jadłospis (yad-wo-spees) m.
menu; bill of fare
jaglana kasza (yag-lá-na ká-
sha) f. millet-groats
jaglica (yag-lee-tsa) f.
trachoma; viral eye infection
jagnię (yág-ńań) n. lamb
jagoda (ya-gó-da)f. berry
jajko (yáy-ko) n. egg( small)
jajo (yá-yo) n. egg; ovum
jajko na twardo(yáy-ko na twár
do) hard-boiled egg
jajko na miękko(yáy-ko na myáń-
ko) soft-boiled egg
jajecznica (ya-yech-ńee-tsa) f.
scrambled eggs

jajnik (yáy-ńeek) m. ovary
jak (yak) adv. how;as;if; than
jakby (yák-bi) adv. as if; if
jakgdyby (yak-gdí-bi) adv.
as if; seemingly; sort of
jaka (yá-ka) pron. f. what;
which; f. jacket
jaki (yá-kee) pron. m. what;
which one? that;some; like
jakie (yá-ke) pron. n. what;
which=jaki(fem.& neuter)
jakiś (yak-eesh) pron. some
jakkolwiek (yak-kól-vyek) conj.
though; pron. somehow;anyhow
jakkolwiek (yak-kól-vyek) adv.
somehow; anyhow; however
jako (yá-ko) adv. as;by way of
jako tako(yá-ko tá-ko) adv.
so-so; tolerably well
jakoś (yá-kosh) adv. somehow
jakość (ya-kóshch) f. quality
jakościowo (ya-kosh-chó-vo)
adv. m. qualitatively
jakże (yák-zhe) pron. how;sure
jałmużna (yaw-moozh-na) f.
alms; charity;(hist.endowment)
jałowcówka (ya-wov-tsóov-ka) f.
gin; juniper-flavored vodka
jałowiec (ya-wo-vyets) m. juni-
per(Juniperus);
jałowieć (ya-wo-vyech) v. grow-
sterile; grow unproductive
jałowy (ya-wo-vi) adj. m.
barren;sterile;arid;aseptic
jałówka (ya-woov-ka) f. heifer
jama (yá-ma) f. pit; hole; den;
cavity; cave; burrow; hollow
jamnik (yám-ńeek) f. dachshund
jankes (yán-kes) m. Yankee
Japończyk (ya-póń-chik) m.
Japanese
japoński (ya-póń-skee) adj. m.
Japanese; of Japan
jar (yar) m. canyon; ravine
jarmark (yár-mark) m. fair
jarosz (yá-rosh) m. vegetarian
jarski (yár-skee) adj. m.
vegetarian; meatless
jary (yá-ri) adj. robust; vigorous; hale; spring-
jarzębiak (ya-zháń-byak) m.
sorb brandy; rowan-berry vodka

jarzębina (ya-zhań-bée-na) f.
sorb tree; rowan;rowan berry
jarzmo (yázh-mo) n. yoke
jarzyć (ya-zhích) v. sparkle;
glitter; glow; shimmer
jarzyna (ya-shi-na) f. vegetable ; dish of vegetables
jasełka (ya-séw-ka) pl. crib;
Nativity play; créche
jasiek (ya-śhek) m. little
pillow ; bean; beans
jaskinia (yas-kée-ña) f. cave
jaskiniowiec (yas-kee-ñó-vyets)
m. cave dweller; cave man
jaskółka (yas-koów-ka) f.
swallow; martin; harbinger
jaskrawy (yas-kra-vi) adj. m.
glowing ; showy ; vivid;extreme
jasno (yás-no) adv. clearly;
brightly ; cheerfully;plainly
jasny (yás-ny) adj. m. clear;
, bright ; light; shining;noble
jasnowidz (yas-no-veets) m.
clairvoyant ; cristal gazer;seer
jastrząb (yas-tzhoẃnp) m. fal-
kon; hawk; goshawk
jaszczyk (yash-chik) m. muni-
tion box; ammunition trailer
jaśmin (yaśh-meen) m. jasmine
jaśnieć (yaśh-ńech) v. shine;
sparkle; radiate; gleam; pale
jatka (yat-ka) f. shambles;
butcher's shop ; massacre
jatki (yát-kee) pl. shambles
jaw (yav) m. reality;v.expose
jawić (yą-veech) v. appear;show
jawny (yav-ni) adj. m. evident;
public ; open; notorious;sheer
jawor (ya-vor) m. plane tree;
maple; sycamore;sycamore wood
jaz (yas:) m. weir ; milldam
jazda (yáz-da) f. ride ;driving
jaźń (yaźhń) f. ego; self;
the I ; the inner man ; psyche
jąć (yowńch) v. seize; begin
jądro (yown-dro) n. nucleus;
testicle; kernel; core
jąkać (yowń-kach) v. stutter
jątrzyć (yown-tzhích) v. irritate; fester ;vex; embitter
jechać (yé-khaćh) v. ride;drive
jeden (yé-den) num. one; some

jedenaście (ye-de-naśh-ćhe)
num. eleven
jedlina (yed-lee-na) f. fir
grove; fir and spruce branches
jednać (yéd-naćh) v. conciliate
jednak (yéd-nak) conj. however;
yet; still;but; after all;though
jednaki (yed-ná-kee) adj. m.
identical; similar; equal;alike
jedno (yéd-no) n. num. one; one-
jednocześnie (yed-no-cheśh-ñe)
adv. simultaneously; also
jednoczyć (yed-no-chich) v.
unify; merge; join; unite
jednogłośnie (yed-no-gwośh-ñe)
adv. unanimously; in chorus
jednokrotnie (yed-no-krot-ñe)
adv. one time; once
jednostka (yed-nost-ka)f. unit;
individual;entity;measure;digit
jedność (yéd-noshćh) f. unity
jedwab (yéd-vab) m. silk
jedynaczka (ye-di-nách-ka) f.
only daughter
jedynak (ye-dí-nak) m. only son
jedynie (ye-dí-ñe) adv. only;
merely ; solely; nothing but
jedyny (ye-di-ni) adj. m. the
only one ; the sole; unique
jedzenie (ye-dze-ñe) n. meat;
food; victuals; feed; eats
jemioła (ye-myó-wa) mistletoe
jeleń (ye-leń) m. stag; deer
jelito (ye-lee-to) n. intestine;
bowel; gut
jełczeć (yew-chech) v. grow-
rancid :become rancid
jeniec (ye-ńets) m. captive
jerzyna (ye-zhi-na) f. blackberry
jesień (ye-śheń) f. autumn;
fall; the fall of the leaf
jesienny (ye-shen-ni) adj. m.
autumnal; of automn
jesion (ye-shon) m. ash tree
jesionka (ye-śhón-ka) f. fall
overcoat; light overcoat
jesiotr (ye-śhotr) m. sturgeon
jestestwo (yes-tes-tvo) m.
being ; nature; creature
jeszcze (yesh-che) adv. still;
besides; more; yet ; way back

jeść (yeshch) v. eat; feed sb
jeśli (yesh-lee) conj. if
jezdnia (yezd-ña) f. roadwav
jezuita (ye-zoo-ée-ta) m. Jesuit; member of Jesuit Order
jeździec (yeźh-dzhets) m.
horseman; rider; equestrian
jeż (yesh) m. porcupine
jeżdżenie (yezh-dzhé-ñe) n.
riding; driving; tyrannizing
jeżeli (ye-zhé-lee) conj. if
jeżyć się (ye-zhich shañ) v.
bristle up; stand on end
jeżyna (ye-zhi-na) f. blackberry; blackberry bush;bramble
jęczeć (yañ-chech) v. moan;
groan; wail; whine;complain
jęczmień (yañch-myeñ) m. barley
jędrny (yañdr-ni) adj. m. firm;
robust; strong; terse; pithy
jędza (yañ-dza) f. witch; shrew
jęk (yañk) m. groan; moan; wail
jęknąć (yañk-nownch) v. moan;
groan; whine; bellyache(once)
język (yañ-zik) m. tongue
jod (yod) m. iodine
jodła (yód-wa)f.fir tree; spruce
jodyna (yo-dí-na) f. tincture
of iodine; iodine
jon (yon) m. ion
jowialny (yo-vyál-ni) adj. m.
jovial; debonair; genial
jubiler (yoo-bee-ler) m. jeweler (store or profession)
jubileusz (yoo-bee-lé-oosh) m.
jubilee; anniversary
jucht (yoo-kht) m. Russian
leather; water-proof leather
juczny koń (yooch-ni koñ) adj.
m. pack-horse; beast of burden
judzić (yoo-dzheech)v.instigate
juki (yoo-kee) pl. packsaddle
junak (yoo-nak) m. brave; swaggerer; dashing fellow
jurysdykcja (yoo-ris-dik-tsya)
f. jurisdiction;legal authority
juta (yoo-ta) f. jute; jute plant
jutro (yoo-tro) adv. tomorrow
jutrzejszy (yoo-tshéy-shi) adj.
m. tomorrow's; future
jutrzenka (yoo-tzhén-ka) f.
day-break; morning star; dawn

już (yoozh) conj. already;
at any moment; by now;no more
jużci (yoozh-chee) conj. of
course; certainly;sure thing!
kabalarka (ka-ba-lar-ka) f.
fortune teller (by cards)
kabała (ka-bá-wa) f. cabbala
kabaret (ka-bá-ret) m. cabaret
kabel (ká-bel) m. cable
kabestan (ka-be-stan) m. cap-
stan; winch; windlass
kabina (ka-bee-na) f. cabin
kabłąk (kab-wownk) m. bow;hoop
kabotyn (ka-bo-tin) m. poser;
buffoon; second-rate actor
kabriolet (ka-bryó-let) m.
convertible car; gig
kabza (kab-za) m. purse
kac (kats) m. hangover
kacerz (ká-tsesh) m. heretic
kacet (ká-tset) m. Nazi concentration camp
kaczka (kách-ka) f. duck
kaczor (ká-chor) m. drake
kadłub (kád-woop) m. trunk;
hull; fuselage; framework
kadra (kád-ra) f. staff; cadre
kadzić (ká-dzheech)v. incense;
flatter; fart (vulg.)
kadzidło (ka-dzhéed-wo)n.
incense; fragrance;frankincense
kadź (kadźh) f. tub; tubful
kafar (ká-far) m. piledriver
kafel (ká-fel) m. tile (ceramic)
kaftan (káf-tan) m. jacket
kaftan bezpieczeństwa (káf-tan
bez-pye-cheñ-stva) m. straight
jacket;"waistcoat"
kaftanik (kaf-tá-ñeek) m. bodice; vest;jacket; caftan
kaganiec (ka-gá-ñets) m. muzzle;
torch ; oil lamp; lamp; cresset
kajać się (káy-ach shañ) v.
repent; confess with contrition
kajak (ká-yak) m. kayak;canoe
kajdany (kay-dá-ni) pl. hand-
cuffs;shackles; chains; bonds
kajuta (ka-yoo-ta) f. ship-
cabin; living qyarter at sea
kajzerka (kay-zer-ka) f. fancy
roll of bread ; kaiser roll
kakao (ka-ká-o) n. cacao

kaktus (kák-toos) m. cactus
kalać (ká-lach) v. pollute;
foul up; stain;befoul; sully
kalafior (ka-lá-fyor) m. cauliflower ; form of snow
kalarepa (ka-la-ré-pa) f.
turnip-cabbage; kohlrabi
kalectwo (ka-léts-tvo) n. disability; lameness; cripplehood
kaleczyć (ka-le-chich) v. wound;
mutilate; hurt; injure;cripple
kalejdoskop (ka-ley-dos-kop) m.
kaleidoscope; medley;miscellany
kaleka (ka-le-ka) m; f. cripple
kalendarz (ka-len-dash) m.
calendar; almanach
kalesony (ka-le-só-ni) pl.
underware;drawers;under pants
kalina (ka-lee-na) f. guelder-
rose; cranberry shrub (tree)
kalka (kál-ka) f. carbon paper
kalkulacja (kal-koo-láts-ya) f.
calculation; computation
kalkulować (kal-koo-ló-vach) v.
calculate; compute; work out
kaloria (ka-lór-ya), f. calorie
kaloryfer (ka-lo-rí-fer) m.
radiator; steam heater; heater
kalosz (ká-losh) m. rubber
overshoe; galosh; rubber boot
kalumnia (ka-loom-ña) f.
calumny; slander; aspersion
kalwin (kál-veen) m. Calvinist
kał (kaw) m. excrement; stool
kałamarz (ka-wá-mash) m. ink-
stand; ink bottle; ink pot
kałuża (ka-woo-zha) f. puddle
kamelia (ka-mél-ya) f. camellia
kameralna muzyka (ka-me-rál-na
moo-zi-ka) chamber music
kamerdyner (ka-mer-dí-ner) m.
butler ; valet (de chambre)
kamerton (ka-mér-ton) m.
tuning-fork"U", shaped
kamfora (kam-fó-ra) f. camphor
kamgarn (kám-garn) m. worsted
kamienica (ka-mye-ñée-tsa) f.
apartment house; tenants
kamieniec (ka-myé-ñech) v.
petrify; turn into stone
kamieniołom (ka-mye-ño-wom) f.
quarry; stone pit

kamień (ká-myeň) m. stone
kamizelka (ka-mee-zél-ka) f.
waistcoat; vest; camisole
kampania (kam-pá-ña) f. campaign ; drive(promotional)
kamrat (kám-rat) m. chum
kamyk (kám-ik) m. pebble
kanadyjski (ka-na-diý-skee) adj.
m. Canadian ; of Canada
kanalia (ka-nál-ya) f. scoundrel
kanalizacja (ka-na-lee-záts-ya)
f. sewers ;sanitation; drainage
kanał (ká-naw) m. channel; dyke;
sewer; duct; ditch; conduit;tube
kanapa (ka-ná-pa) f. sofa
kanapka (ka-náp-ka) f. sandwich; small size sofa
kanarek (ka-ná-rek) m. canary
kancelaria (kan-tse-lár-ya) f,
office: chancellery; archives
kancerować (Kan-tse-ró-vach) v.
damage: mangle; lacerate; hack
kanciarz (kán-chash) m. swindler; trickster ; con man
kanciasty (kan-chá-sti) adj.
m. angular; awkward: stiff
kanclerz (kán-tslesh) m.
chancellor(chief of government)
kandelabr (kan-dé-labr) m.
chandelier; street lamp
kandydat (kan-di-dat) m. candidate; applicant; aspirant
kangur (kán-goor) m. kangaroo
kanon (ká-non) m. canon (priest)
kanonierka (ka-no-ñér-ka) f.
gunboat; patrol boat
kanonik (ka-nó-ñeek) m. canon
(priest); monsignor; prelate
kanonizować (ka-no-ñee-zó-vach)
v. canonize ; glorify
kant (kant) m. edge; crease;
swindle; trick; racket; chant
kantar (kan-tar) m. halter
kantor (kán-tor) m. office;
counter; counting office
kantyna (kan-tí-na) f. canteen
kanwa (kán-va) f. canvas
kapa (ká-pa) f. bedspread;cover
kapać (ká-pach) v. dribble;
trickle; drip;fall drop by drop
kapela (ka-pé-la) f. (music)
band; choir

kapelan (ka-pé-lan) m. chaplain(in armed forces, hospital)
kapelusz (ka-pé-loosh) m. hat
kapilarny (ka-pee-lár-ni) adj. m. capillary
kapiszon (ka-pée-shon) m. hood
kapitalista (ka-pee-ta-leés-ta) m. capitalist
kapitalizm (ka-pee-tá-leezm) m. capitalism
kapitał (ka-pée-taw) m. capital
kapitan (ka-pée-tan) m. captain
kapitulacja (ka-pee-too-lá-tsya) f. surrender; capitulation ; giving up
kapitulować (ka-pee-too-ló-vach) v. surrender; give up
kaplica (kap-leé-tsa) f. chapel
kapliczka (kap-leéch-ka) f. shrine; wayside shrine
kapłan (ká-pwan) m. priest
kapłon (ká-pwon) m. capon
kapota (ką-pó-ta) f. long coat
kapral (káp-ral) m. corporal
kaprys (káp-ris) m. caprice; fad; whim; fency; freak;vagary
kaptować (kap-tó-vach) v. win over; bring over; canvas
kaptur (káp-toor) m. hood
kapturowy sąd (kap-too-ró-vi soẃnd) kangaroo court
kapusta (ka-poós-ta) f. cabbage ; a dish of cabbage
kapuś (ká-poośh) m. stool-pigeon ; informer; police spy
kapuśniak (ka-poośh-ñak) m. cabbage soup; drizzle;mizzle
kara (ká-ra) f. penalty; fine; punishment; correction;nuisance
karabin (ka-rá-been) m. rifle
karać (ká-rach) v. punish
karafka (ka-ráf-ka) f. serving-bottle; water bottle; flagon
karakuły (ka-ra-koó-wi) pl. astrakhan sheep fur
karalny (ka-rál-ni) adj. m. punishable ;deserving a fine
karaluch (ka-rá-lookh) m. cockroach ; black beetle
karambol (ka-rám-bol) m. collision ; cannon; carom
karaś (ká-rash) m. crucian

karat (ká-rat) m. carat
karawaniarz (ka-ra-vá-ñash) m. undertaker; coffin bearer
karb (karb) m. notch; score; crease; fold; nick; tally;curl
karbid (kár-beed) m. carbide
karbol (kár-bol) m. carbolic acid ; phenol
karbować (kar-bó-vach) v. notch; curl; tally; crimp;fold
karbunkuł (kar-boón-koow) m. ulcer ; carbuncle
karburator (kar-boo-rá-tor) m. carburetor
karcer (kár-tser) m. prison; dark cell; detention
karciarz (kár-chash) m. (cards) gambler; card player; gamester
karcić (kár-cheéch) v. reproof; admonish; scold; castigate
karczemny (kar-chém-ni) adj. m. rude ; vulgar; coarse
karczma (kárch-ma) f. tavern
karczoch (kár-chokh) m. artichoke (thistlelike plant)
karczować (kar-chóv-ach) v. dig up (stumps); clear land
kardiografia (kar-dyo-gráf-ya) f. cardiography
kardynalny (kar-di-nál-ni) adj. m. fundamental; essential
kardynał (kar-di-naw) m. cardinal; prince(Catholic Church)
karetka (ka-rét-ka) f. ambulance; (prison or mail) van; chaise
kariera (kar-yé-ra) f. career
kark (kark) m. neck ; nape
karkołomny (kar-ko-wóm-ni) adj. m. neckbreaking ; breakneck
karłowaty (kar-wo-vá-ti) adj. m. dwarfish ; undersized
karamel (ka-rá-mel) m. caramel
karmić (kár-meéch) v. feed; nourish ; nurse; suckle;nurture
karmin (kár-meen) m. carmine
karnawał (kar-ná-vaw) m. carnival ꭍpenally
karnie (kár-ñe) adv. in order;
karność (kár-noshch) f. discipline ; orderly conduct
karny (kar-ni) adj. m. disciplined; penal ; punitive

karo (ka-ro) n. diamonds (in
cards); square cut, décolleré
karoseria (ka-ro-sér-ya) f.
car body ; truck body
karp (karp) m. carp (fish)
karta (kar-ta) f. card; page;
note; sheet; ticket; charter
kartel (kar-tel) m.(industrial)
trust ; cartel; combine; pool
kartofel (kar-to-fel) m. potato
kartoflanka (kar-to-flan-ka) f.
potato soup; type of onion
kartograf (kar-to-graf) m.
cartographer ; map maker
karton (kar-ton) m. cardboard
kartoteka (kar-to-te-ka) f.
card index ; file
karuzela (ka-roo-ze-la) f.
merry-go-round ; carousel
kary koń (ka-ri koń)m.black
horse; horse of black color
karygodny (ka-ri-god-ni) adj.
m. unpardonable ; guilty;gross
karykatura (ka-ri-ka-too-ra)
f. cartoon ; caricature;parody
karykaturzysta (ka-ri-ka-too-
zhís-ta) m. cartoonist
karzeł (ka-zhew) m. dwarf
kasa (ka-sa) f. cashier's desk;
cash register; ticket office
kasjer (kas-yer) m. cashier
kask (kask) m. helmet ; tin hat
kaskada (kas-ka-da) f. cascade
kasować (ka-so-vach) v. cancel
kasta (kas-ta) f. caste
kastrować (kas-tro-vach) v.
castrate; geld
kasyno (ka-si-no) n. casino;
club ; mess-hall; mess room
kasza (ka-sha) f. grits; groats;
cereals ; gruel; porridge;mess
kaszel (ka-shel) m. cough
kaszkiet (kash-ket ) m. cap
kasztan (kash-tan) m. chestnut
kat (kat) m. executioner
katafalk (ka-ta-falk) m. bier
kataklizm (ka-tak-leezm) m.
cataclysm ; disaster; calamity
katalizator (ka-ta-lee-za-tor)
m. catalyst
katalog (ka-ta-lok) m. catalog
katar (ka-tar) m. headcold ;
running nose ; catarrh

katarakta (ka-ta-rak-ta) f.
cataract: opaque eye/lens
kataryniarz (ka-ta-ri-nash) m.
organ grinder
katarynka (ka-ta-rin-ka) f.
barrel organ; street organ
katastrofa (ka-tas-tro-fa) f.
catastrophe; disaster; crash
katecheta (ka-te-khe-ta) m.
teacher of catechism
katedra (ka-te-dra) f. pulpit;
univ. dept. chair; cathedral
kategoria (ka-te-gor-ya) f.
category; division; class
kategoryczny (ka-te-go-rich-ni)
adj. m. absolute; categorical
katoda (ka-to-da) f. cathode
katolicki (ka-to-leets-kee)
adj. m. Catholic
katować (ka-to-vach) v. torture; beat cruelly; hack
kaucja (kaw-tsya) f. bail; deposit; security; recognizance
kauczuk (kaw-chook) f. India
natural rubber; caoutchouc
kaukaski (kaw-kas-kee) adj. m.
Caucasian; of Caucasus
kawa (ka-va) f. coffee
kawaler (ka-va-ler) m. bachelor; suitor; beau; cavalier
kawaleria (ka-va-ler-ya) f.
cavalry ; young folks
kawalkada (ka-val-ka-da) f.
cavalcade
kawał (ka-vaw) m. piece; joke;
cheat ; lump; funny business
kawałek (ka-va-wek) m. bit;
morsel; scrap; chunk;1000zł.
kawiarnia (kav-yar-ña) f. café
kawior (kav-yor) m. caviar
kawka (kav-ka) f. jackdaw
kawon (ka-von) m. watermelon
kawowy (ka-vo-vi) adj. m. (of)
coffee; coffee-
kazać (ka-zach) v. order;tell;
preach ; make sb. do something
kazanie (ka-za-ñe) n. sermon
kazić (ka-żheech)v. pollute;
corrupt; blemish;contaminate
kazirodztwo (ka-żhee-ródz-tvo)
n. incest
kaznodzieja (kaz-no-dżhe-ya) m.
preacher; evangelist

kaźń (kaźhń) f. execution,
każdorazowy (kazh-do-ra-zo-vi)
adj.m.every;each;every single
każdy (kázh-di) pron. every;
each; respective; any; all
kącik (kown-cheek) m. nook
kąkol (kown-kol) m. cockle-
weed; corn cockle
kąpać (kown-pach) v. bathe;soak
kąpiel (kown-pyel) f. bath
kąpielisko (kown-pye-lees-ko)
n. resort;spa; public bath
kąsać (kown-sach) v. bite
kąsek (kown-sek) m. bit; nip
kąt (kownt) m. corner; angle
kątomierz (kown-to-myesh) m.
protractor ; dial-sight
kciuk (kchook) m. thumb
kelner (kel-ner) m. waiter
kelnerka (kel-ner-ka) f.
waitress; bar maid
keson (ke-son) m. caisson
kędzierzawy (kań-dzhe-zha-vi)
adj. m. curly; curled; fuzzy
kędzior (kań-dzhor) m. curl;
lock; ringlet
kępa (kań-pa) f. cluster;
holm ; hurst; clump; tuft
kęs (kańs) m. bit; mouthful
kibic (kee-beets) m. kibitzer
kibić (kee-beech) f. figure;
waist ; middle
kichać (kee-khach) v. sneeze
kiecka (kets-ka) f. frock;
skirt; petticoat (inelegant)
kiedy (ke-di) conj. when; as;
ever; how soon?;while; since
kiedy indziej ( ke-di een-dzhey)
adj. some other time
kiedykolwiek ( ke-di-kol-vyek)
adv. whenever; at any time
kiedyś ( ke-dish) adv. someday; in the past; once;one day
kiedyż ? ( ke-dish) adv. when-
then ? when on earth?
kielich ( ke-leekh) m. goblet;
chalice; cup; cupful; glassful
kielnia ( kel-ńa) f. trowel
kieł ( kew) m. tusk; canine-
tooth; fang;cutting bit
kiełbasa ( kew-ba-sa) f. sau.-
sage

kiełek ( ke-wek) m. sprout
kiełkować ( kew-ko-vach) v.
sprout. germinate; spring up
kiełzać (k ew-zach) v. bridle
kiep ( kep) m. oaf; fool; gull
kiepski (kep-skee) adj. m.
mean; bad; poor; second-rate
kier ( ker) m. (cards) hearts
kierat ( ke-rat) m. thrasher
kiermasz ( ker-mash) m. fair
kierować ( ke-ró-vach) v.steer;
manage; run; show the way
kierownik ( ke-rov-ńeek) m.
manager; director ;supervisor
kierunek ( ke-roo-nek) m.
direction ; course; trend;line
kiesa ( ke-sa) m. purse
kieszeń ( ke-sheń) f. pocket
kij (keey) m. stick cane; staff
kijanka (kee-yan-ka) f. tadpole
kikut (kee-koot) m. stump ;stub
kilim (kee-leem) m. rug ;carpet
kilka (keel-ka) num. a few;some
kilkakroć (keel-ka-kroch) adv.
repeatedly ;again and again
kilkakrotny (keel-ka-krot-ni)
adj. m. repeated ;recurring
kilkudniowy (keel-koo-dno-vi)
adj. m. of several days
kilkoro (keel-ko-ro) num. some;
several ; one or two; a number
kilof (kee-lof) m. pick ; hack
kilogram (kee-lo-gram) m. kilogram ; 2.2 pounds
kilometr (kee-lo-metr) m. kilometer: 3,280.8 feet
kiła (kee-wa) f. syphilis
kinetyka (kee-ne-ti-ka) f.
kinetics; science of motion
kino (kee-no) n. cinema;movies
kiosk (kyosk) m. kiosk; booth
kipieć (kee-pyech) v. boil
kisić (kee-sheech) v. ferment
kisnąć (kees-nownch) v. turn
sour ; ferment; pickle; fug
kiszka (keesh-ka) f. intestine
kiść (keeshch) f. bunch; wrist
kit (keet) m. putty ; mastic
kiwać (kee-vach) v. rock; nod;
wag; dangle;fool dodge; jink
klacz (klach) f. mare
klajster (klay-ster) m. glue;
paste ; water base glue

klakson (klák-son) m. car horn
klamka (klám-ka) f. door knob
klamra (klám-ra) f. buckle;
clasp ; bracket; fastener;staple
klapa (klá-pa) f. lapel: valve
klapsy (kláp-si) pl. spanking
klarować (kla-ró-vach) v. clarify ; filter;clear; purify
klarnet (klár-net) m. clarinet
klasa (klá-sa) f. class; classroom ; rank; order; division
klaskać (klás-kach) v. clap
klasowy (kla-só-vi) adj. m.
class ; of classes; class-
klasyczny (kla-sich-ni) adj. m.
classic ; standard;conventional
klasyfikować (kla-si-fee-kó-
vach) v. classify;sort; grade
klasztor (klásh-tor) m. monastery ; convent; cloister
klatka (klát-ka) f. cage ; crate
klatka schodowa (klát-ka skho-
dó-va) staircase ; stairway
klatka piersiowa (klát-ka
pyer-shó-va) ribcage; chest
klauzula (klaw-zóo-la) f.
clause ; proviso; reservation
klawisz (klá-veesh) m. (piano)
key;stool pigeon; jailer
kląć (klównch) v. curse; swear
klątwa (klównt-va) f. curse;
ban; excommunication; anathema
klecić (kle-cheech) v. botch
kleic (klé--eech) v. glue;
stick together; fudge; shape
kleik (klé—eek) m. gruel
klej (kley) m. glue ; cement
klejnot (kléy-not) m. jewel
klekotać (kle-kó-tach) v. clatter; rattle; chatter; prate
kleks (kleks) m. blot;ink-spot
klepać (kle-pach) v. hammer;
flatten ; prattle; pat;blab;clap
klepka (klép-ka) f. stave
klepsydra (klep-síd-ra) f. hour-
glass; obituary notice
kleptomania (klep-to-ma-ña) f.
kleptomania: impulse to steal
kler (kler) m. clergy;priesthood
kleszcz (kleshch) m. tick
kleszcze (klésh-che) n. pliers;
tongs ; claws; pincers; nippers

klękać (klán-kach) v. kneel
down; bend the knee; kneel
klęska (kláns-ka) f. defeat;
disaster; calamity
klęsnąć (kláns-nównch) v.
shrink; subside; go down
klient (klée—ent) m. customer
klika (klée-ka) f. clique
klimat (klée-mat) m. climate
klin (kléen) m. wedge;cotter
klinga (kléen-ga) f. (sword)
blade; sabre-blade
kliniczny (klee-néech-ni) adj.
clinic ; clinic-
klinika (klee-ñee-ka) f. clinic
klisza (klée-sha) f. (photo)
plate; printing plate
klitka (kléet-ka) f. cell
kloc (klots) m. log; block
klomb (klomp) m. flower bed
klon (klon) m. maple
klops (klops) m. meat loaf
klosz (klosh) m. glass cover;
lamp shade; dish cover
klozet (kló-zet) m. toilet
klub (kloob) m. club; union
klucz (klooch) m. key; wrench
kluska (kloós-ka) f. boiled
dough strip; dumpling
kładka (kwád-ka) f. foot-
bridge; gangway; brow
kłaki (kwá-kee) pl. oakum;
shaggy hair; matted hair
kłam (kwam) m. lie; falsehood
kłamac (kwá-mach) v. lie
kłamca (kwám-tsa) m. liar
kłaniac się (kwá-ñach shan) v.
salute; bow; greet; worship
kłaśc (kwashch) v. lay; put
dawn; place; set; deposit
kłąb (kwównp) m. clew; ball
kłąbek (kwówn-bek) m. ball
(of thread); hunk of yarn
kłębic się (kwán-beech shań) v.
whirl; swirl; surge; billow
kłoda (kwo-da) f. log; clog
kłopot (kwo-pot) m. trouble
kłopotac (kwo-pó-tach) v.
trouble; disturb; worry
kłopotliwy (kwo-pot-lée-vi) adj.
troublesome; baffling
kłos (kwos) m. (corn) ear

kłócić (kwoó-cheećh) v. quarrel
kłódka (kwoód-ka) f. padlock
kłotliwy (kwoot-lée-vi) adj.
m., quarrelsome; cantankerous
kłótnia (kwoó-tňa) f. quarrel
kłuć (kwoóćh) v. stab; prick
kłus (kwoós) m. trot;jog· trot
kłusownik (kwoo-sóv-ňeek) m.
poacher; trespassing hunter
kmieć (kmyećh) m. peasant
kminek (kmeé-nek) m. cumin
knajpa (knáy-pa) f. tavern
knebel (kné-bel) m. gag
knocić (knó-cheećh) v. bungle
knot (knot) m. wick;fuse;bungle
knuć (knoóćh) v. plot; scheme
koalicja (ko-a-leéts-ya) f.
coalition; temporary union
kobiałka (ko-byáw-ka) f.
wicker-basket; chip basket
kobieciarz (ko-byé-ćhash) m.
ladychaser; lady's man
kobiecość (ko-byé-tsooshćh) f.
womanhood; femininity
kobiecy (ko-byé-tsi) adj. m.
female; womanish; feminine
kobierzec (ko-byé-zhets) m.
carpet; anything like a carpet
kobieta (ko-byé-ta) f. woman
kobyła (ko-bi-wa) f. mare
kobza (kób-za) f. bagpipe
koc (kóts) m. blanket; coverlet
kochać (kó-khaćh) v. love
kochanie (ko-khá-ňe) n. love;
darling; sweetheart; affection
kochany (ko-khá-ni) adj. m.
beloved; loving; affectionate
kochliwy (kokh-leé-vi) adj. m.
easily in love; amorous
koci (kó-ćhee)adj. m. catlike
kociak (kó-ćhak) m. kitty;
lassie; lass; pinup. girl
kocioł (kó-ćhow) m. kettle;
boiler; pot; encirclement
kocur (ko-tsoor) m. tomcat
koczować (ko-chó-vaćh) v. nomad-
ize; wander about;be encamped
koczownik (ko-chóv-ňeek) m.
nomad; wanderer; vagrant
kodeks (kó-deks) m. (legal)code
koedukacja (ko-e-doo-káts-ya)
f. coeducation

koegzystencja (ko-eg-zis-tén-
tzya) f. coexistence
kofeina (ko-fε—eé-na) f.
caffeine; alkaloid in coffee
kogut (ko-goot) m. cock ;rooster
koić (kó—eećh) v. soothe
kojarzenie (ko-ya-zhé-ňe) n.
matching ; association; union
kojarzyć (ko-yá-zhićh) v. unite;
bind; join; link; connect
kojący (ko-yówn-tsi) adj. m.
soothing;comforting; balmy
kojec (kó-yets) m. coop ; pen
kokaina (ko-ka-eé-na) f.' co-
caine; an alkaloid drug
kokarda (ko-kár-da) f. rosette;
bow ; slip-knot; knot
kokietka (ko-k ét-ka), f. flirt
kokietować (ko-ke —to-vaćh) v.
flirt ; court; woo; coquet
koklusz (kók-loosh) m.
whooping-cough
kokos (kó-kos) m. l. coconut
2. good business ; a grand thing
kokoszka (ko-kósh-ka) f. brood-
hen; laying hen
koks (koks) m. coke; gas coke
koksownia (kok-sóv-ňa) f. cok-
ing plant ; cokery
kolaboracja (ko-la-bo-ráts-ya)
f.collaboration ; collaborators
kolacja (ko-láts-ya) f. supper
kolano (ko-lá-no) m. knee
kolarstwo (ko-lár-stvo) n.
cycling ; bicycle sport
kolarz (kó-lash) m. cyclist
kolący (ko-lówn-tsi) adj. m.
prickly; thorny; spiked
kolba (kól-ba) f. (rifle) butt
kolczasty (kol-chás-ti) adj. m.
barbed ; thorny; spiny
kolczyk (kól-chik) m. earring;
earmark; ear tag; eardrop
kolebka (ko-léb-ka) f. cradle
kolec (kó-lets) m. thorn
kolega (ko-lé-ga) m. buddy;
colleague; fellow worker
koleina (ko-le-eé-na) f. truck;
rut; groove; wheel trace
kolej (kó-ley) f. railroad
kolejka (ko-léy-ka) f. (waiting)
line;narrow-gage railroad; turn

kolejno (ko-léy-no) adv. by
turns; one after the other
kolejny (ko-léy-ni) adj. m.
next; successive; following
kolekcja (ko-lék-tsya) f. collection ; things collected
kolektywizacja (ko-lek-ti-vee-
záts-ya) f. collectivization
koleżeństwo (ko-le-zhéń-stvo)
n. fellowship; comradeship
kolęda (ko-láň-da) f. Christmas
carol; song of joy or praise
kolędować (ko-laň-dó-vach) v.
sing carols; wait a long time
koliber (ko-lee-ber) m. hum-
mingbird
kolia (kól-ya) f. necklace
kolidować (ko-lee-dó-vach) v.
collide ; interfere
koligacja (ko-lee-gáts-ya) f.
(family) relationship
kolisty (ko-leés-ti) adj. m.
circular ; round
kolizja (ko-leéz-ya) f. collision; clash; interference
kolka (kól-ka) f. colic
kolokwium (ko-lók-vyoom) m.
oral examination; test
kolonia (ko-lóń-ya) f. colony
kolonista (ko-lo-neés-ta) m.
settler; colonist; colonial
kolońska woda (ko-lóń-ska vo-
da) cologne water
kolor (kó-lor) m.color;tint;hue
koloryt (ko-ló-rit) m. coloring
kolosalny (ko-lo-sál-ni) adj.
m. colossal; vast;tremendous
kolportaż (kol-pór-tash) m.
(paper) distribution
kolumna (ko-lóom-na) f. column
kołatać (ko-wá-tach) v. knock;
rattle; beg; throb; bang;
kołczan (ków-chan) m. quiver
kołdra (ków-dra) f. quilter-
cover; quilt; coverlet
kolek (kó-wek) m. peg ;stake
kołnierz (ków-ñesh) m. collar
koło (kó-wo) n. wheel; circle
koło (kó-wo) prep. around;
near; about; by; in vicinity
kołodziej (ko-wo-dżhey) m.
wheelwright

kołowacizna (ko-wo-va-cheéz-
na) f. dizziness
kołować (ko-wó-vach) v. revolve;
confuse ; circle; stray; whirl
kołowrotek (ko-wo-vró-tek) m.
spinning-wheel; reel; winch
kołowrót (ko-wó-vroot) m. windlass ; hoist; gin; whip;turnpike
kołowy ruch (ko-wó-vi rookh)
vehicular traffic
kołpak (ków-pak) m. pointed
fur cap ; calpack
kołtun (ków-toon) m. hair.snarl;
bigot; moron; obscurant
kołysać (ko-wí-sach) v. rock;
sway ; toss to and fro; roll
kołysanka (ko-wi-sán-ka) f.
lullaby ; cradle song;berceuse
kołyska (ko-wís-ka) f. cradle
komar (kó-mar) m. mosquito
kombajn (kóm-bayn) m. combine
kombinacja (kom-bee-náts-ya) f.
combination ;union; scheme;slip
kombinować (kom-bee-nó-vach) v.
combine; speculate ; scheme
komedia (ko-méd-ya) f. comedy
komenda (ko-mén-da) f. command ; headquarters ; an order
komentarz (ko-mén-tash) m. commentary ; glossary; remark
kometa (ko-mé-ta) f. comet
komfort (kóm-fort) m. comfort
komiczny (ko-meéch-ni) adj. m.
comic ; amusing; funny;droll
komin (ko-meen) m. chimney
kominek (ko-mée-nek) m. fireplace ; hearth; open fire
kominiarz (ko-mee-ñash) m.
chimney-sweep
komis (kó-mees) m. (on) commission sale; commission shop
komisariat (ko-mee-sár-yat) m.
police station: commissariat
komisja (ko-meés-ya) f. commission; board (of inquiry etc.)
komitet (ko-mée-tet) m. committee ; board
komitywa (ko-mee-ti-va) f.
intimacy ; good friendly terms
komiwojażer (ko-mee-vo-ya-zher)
m. traveling salesman
komnata (kom-ná-ta) f. chamber

komoda (ko-mó-da) f. chest of
drawers ; low-boy;commode
komora (ko-mó-ra) f. chamber
komora celna (ko-mó-ra tsél-na)
customs office; custom house
komorne (ko-mór-ne) n. (appartment) rent ; rental
komórka (ko-moó-rka) f. cell
kompan (kóm-pan) m. chum ;pal
kompania (kom-páń-ya) f. company ; stock company; society
kompas (kóm-pas) m. compass
kompensata (kom-pen-sá-ta) f.
compensation; indemnity
kompetentny (kom-pe-tén-tni)
adj. m. competent; qualified
kompleks (kóm-pleks) m. complex; group;(inferiority)complex
komplement (kom-ple-ment) m.
compliment ;complement
komplet (kóm-plet) m. set
kompozytor (kom-po-zí-tor) m.
composer ( of music)
kompot (kóm-pot) m. compote
kompres (kóm-pres) m. compress
kompromis (kom-pró-mees) m.
compromise ;accomodation
kompromitacja (kom-pro-mee-tá-
tsya) f disgrace; loss of face
komuna (ko-moó-na) f. commune
komunał (ko-moó-naw) m. platitude; banality; commonplace
komunia (ko-moóń-ya) f. communion;part of Catholic mass
komunikacja (ko-moo-ńee-káts-
ya) f. communication ;contact
komunikat (ko-moo-ńée-kat) m.
bulletin ; communiqué; report
komunikować (ko-moo-ńee-ko-vać)
v. inform; give news; report
komunista (ko-moo-ńées-ta) m.
communist(advocate or supporter)
konać (ko-nać) v. agonize;
expire; be dying;die(with greed)
konar (ko-nar) m. limb; branch
koncentryczny (kon-tsen-trích-
ni) adj. m. concentric
koncept (kón-tsept) m. concept;
idea; joke; plan ;brain wave
koncert (kón-tsert) m. concert
koncesja (kon-tsés-ya) f. concession; license; license to do...

koncha (kón-kha) f. shell;
lobe
kondensator (kon-den-sá-or) m.
condenser ; capacitor
kondolencja (kon-do-lén-tsya)
f. condolence ;words of sympathy
kondukt (kón-dookt) m. funeral
procession ;funeral service
konduktor (kon-doók-tor) m.
conductor (train-ticket inspector in charge of passengers
kondycja (kon-dits-ya) f.
condition; form ; status
konewka (ko-név-ka) f.
(watering) can; pot;jug;pewter
konfederacja (kon-fe-de-ráts-
ya) f. confederation; confederacy
konfekcja (kon-fék-tsya) f.
ready-made clothes (pl.)
konferencja (kon-fe-rén-tsya)
f. conference ; meeting (official)
konferować (kon-fe-ró-vać) v.
confer ;hold a conference
konfesjonał (kon-fes-yo-naw)
m. confessional
konfiskata (kon-fees-ká-ta) f.
seizure ; confiscation
konfitura (kon-fee-too-ra) f.
jam ; preserve; candied fruits
konfrontować (kon-fron-tó-vać)
v. confront ;bring face to face
kongres (kón-gres) m. congress
koniak (kó-ńak) m. brandy;cognac
koniczyna (ko-ńee-chi-na) f.
clover ; trefoil; shamrock
koniec (kó-ńets) m. end;
conclusion; tip; point ;close
koniecznie (ko-ńech-ńe) adv.
absolutely; necessarily
konieczny (ko-ńéch-ni) adj. m.
indispensable ;vital;necessary
konik (kó-ńeek) m. pony
konik polny (kó-ńeek pól-ni)
grasshopper; cricket (Locusta)
konina (ko-ńee-na) f. horsemeat; horseflesh
koniunktura (koń-yoonk-too-ra)
f. market condition ;situation
konkluzja (kon-klooz-ya) f.
conclusion ; inference
konkretny (kon-krét-ni) adj. m.
concrete; definite ;real

konkurencja (kon-koo-rén-tsya)
f. competition; rivalry;contest
konkurs (kón-koors) m. contest
konnica (kon-ñee-tsa) f. cavalry ; cavalry unit; horse
konno (kón-no) adv. on horseback ; sit astraddle ;mounted
konny (kón-ni) adj. m. mounted
konopie (ko-nóp-ye) n. hemp
konował (ko-nó-vaw) m. farrier;
quack doctor ; sawbones
konserwa (kon-sér-va) f. preserve; conservatists
konserwatorium (kon-ser-va-tór-
yoom) n. conservatory
konsola (kon-só-la) f. console
konspirować (kon-spee-ró-vach)
v. plot ; conspire; keep secret
konstatować (kon-sta-tó-vách)
v. state; ascertain ; find
konsternacja (kon-ster-náts-ya)
f. consternation ; dismay
konstrukcja (kon-strook-tsya)
f. construction ;design; plan
konstruować (kon-stroo-ó-vách)
v. construct ;build; make
konstytucja (kon-sti-toóts-ya)
f. constitution; physique
konsulat (kon-soó-lat) m. consulate (office or term of office)
konsumować (kon-soo-mó-vách) v.
consume ; eat; drink; use up
konsylium (kon-sil-yoom) n.
consultation (usually medical)
konszachty (kon-shakh-ti) pl.
collusion ; scheming
kontakt (kón-takt) m. contact
kontaktować się (kon-tak-tó-
vach śhăn) v. contact :touch
konto (kón-to) n. account
kontrabanda (kon-tra-bán-da)
f. smuggling ;contraband
kontrakt (kón-trakt) m. contract enforcable by law
kontraktować (kon-trak-tó-vách)
v. contract; hire; engage
kontrast (kón-trast) m. contrast (pointing the differences)
kontrastować (kon-tras-tó-vach)
v. contrast ;stand in contrast
kontratak (kontr-a-tak) m.
counter-attack

kontrola (kon-tró-la) f. control; checking; check up
kontrolny (kon-tról-ni) adj.
m. of control;of supervision
kontrolować (kon-tro-ló-vach)
v. control; check; verify
kontrpropozycja (kontr-pro-po-
zíts-ya) f. counterproposal
kontrrewolucja (kontr-re-vo-
loóts-ya)f.counterrevolution
kontrowersja(kon-tro-vérs-ya)
f. controversy; a quarrel
kontuar (kon-too-ar) m. counter
kontur (kón-toor) m. outline
kontusz (kón-toosh) m. split-
sleeve Polish overcoat (of old)
kontuzja (kon-tooz-ya) f. shock
kontynent (kon-ti-nent) m.
continent; mainland ;land mass
konwalia (kon-vál-ya) f. lily
of the valley ; convallaria
konwikt (kón-veekt) m. boarding school (for boys or girls)
konwój (kón-vooy) m. convoy
konwulsja (kon-voóls-ya) f.
convulsion; a fit ; a spasm
koń (koń) m. horse ; steed
koń mechaniczny (koń me-kha-
ñeéch-ni) mechanical horsepower; horsepower
końcowy (koń-tso-vi) adj. m.
final; terminal;/last; late
końcówka (koń-tsoov-ka) f.
ending; remainder;tail-piece
kończyć (kón-chićh) v. end;
finish; quit; be dying; stop
kończyna (koń-chi-na) f. extremity; limb; member ; leg
kooperacja (ko-o-pe-ráts-ya)
f. cooperation ; acting together
koordynacja (ko-or-di-náts-ya)
f. coordination (mental&phys.)
kopa (kó-pa) threescore (60);
pile; dozens; stack
kopa siana (kó-pa śhá-na) haystack ; hayrick
kopać (kó-pach) v. dig; kick
kopalnia (ko-pál-ña) f. mine
koparka (ko-pár-ka) f. excava-
tor; mechanical shovel
kopcić (kop-ćheéćh) v. soot;
smoke; blacken with smoke

kopciuszek (kop-choo-shek) m.
Cinderella; drudge
kopec (ko-pech) m. soot
koper (ko-per) m. dill; fennel
koperta (ko-per-ta) f. envelope; quilt-case;(watch-)case
kopiasty (kop-yas-ti) adj. m.
heaped; piled up;heaped(plate)
kopiec (kop-yets) m. mound;
barrow ; mound;heap; knoll
kopiowac (kop-yo-vach) v. copy
kopula (ko-poo-wa) f. dome
kopyto (ko-pi-to) n. hoof
kora (ko-ra) f. bark; cortex
koral (ko-ral) m. coral (red)
korale (ko-ra-le) pl. bead
necklace; coral beads; gills
korba (kor-ba) f. crank; winch
kordon (kor-don) m. cordon
korek (ko-rek) m. cork; fuse;
stopper; traffic jam; tie-up
korekta (ko-rek-ta) f. proof
korepetycja (ko-re-pe-tits-ya)
f. tutoring; private lessons
korespondencja (ko-res-pon-den-
tsya) f. correspondence;letters
korespondent wojenny (ko-res-
pon-dent vo-yen-ni) war correspondent; war reporter
korkociag (kor-ko-chownk) m.
cork-screw; tail-spin; twist
korniszon (kor-nee-shon) m.
pickled cucumber; gherkin
korny (kor-ni) adj. m. humble
korona (ko-ro-na) f. crown
koronacja (ko-ro-nats-ya) f.
coronation; crowning
koronka (ko-ron-ka) f. lace
koronowac (ko-ro-no-vach) v.
crown ; be crowned
korowod (ko-ro-vood) m. procession; pageant; train;difficulty
korporacja (kor-po-rats-ya) f.
corporation ; association;guild
korpulentny (kor-poo-len-tni)
adj. m. fat; corpulent; obese
korpus (kor-poos) m. body;
staff. (army) corps, etc
korsarz (kor-sash) m. pirate
kort tenisowy (kort te-nee-so-
vi) tennis court
korupcja (ko-roop-tsya) f. corruption; venality; bribery

korygowac (ko-ri-go-vach) v.
correct; rectify; put right
korytarz (ko-ri-tash) m. corridor; passage-way; lobby
koryto (ko-ri-to) n. through;
river-bed ; channel; chute
korzec (ko-zhets) m. bushel
korzen (ko-zhen) m. root; spice
korzyc (ko-zhich)v. humble;
humiliate ; prostrate
korzystac (ko-zhis-tach) v.
profit; gain;enjoy a right
korzystny (ko-zhist-ni) adj.
m. profitable; favorable
korzysc (ko-shishch) f. profit
kos (kos) m. blackbird
kosa (ko-sa) f. scythe; tress
kosiarka (ko-shar-ka) f. mower
kosic (ko-sheech) v. mow; scythe
kosmaty (kos-ma-ti) adj. m.
shaggy ; hairy; fleecy
kosmetyczka (kos-me-tich-ka) f.
vanity bag ; beautician
kosmetyk (kos-me-tik) m. cosmetic : makeup(skin and hair)
kosmiczny (kos-meech-ni) adj.
m. cosmic ; outer space
kosmopolita (kos-mo-po-lee-ta)
m. cosmopolite ;cosmopolitan
kosmyk (kos-mik) m. wisp ; strand
kosodrzewina (ko-so-dzhe-vee-
na) f. dwarf mountain pine
kosooki (ko-so-o-ki) adj. m.
with slanting eyes; with scowl-
ing eyes ; cross-eyed
kostium(kos-tyoom) m. suit;dress
kostka (kost-ka) f. small bone;
ankle; knuckle; die; lump
kostnica (kost-nee-tsa) f.
morgue ; mortuary ;dead house
kostniec (kost-nech) v. grow
stiff ; ossify; freeze
kosy (ko-si) adj. m. slanting
kosz (kosh) m. basket ;Tartar camp
koszary (ko-sha-ry) pl. barracks ( military); caserns
koszenie (ko-she-ne) n. mowing
koszerny (ko-sher-ni) adj. m.
kosher (clean or fit to eat)
koszmar (kosh-mar) m. nightmare ; frightening experience
koszt (kosht) m. cost ; price;
expense; charge; economic costs

kosztorys (kosh-tó-ris) m.
estimate (of cost),
kosztowny (kosh-tóv-ni) adj.
m. expensive ; costly;precious
koszula (ko-shoo-la) f. shirt
koszyk (kó-shik) f. small
basket,; grab bag; hilt guard
koszykówka (ko-shi-koov-ka) f.
basketball
kościany (kosh-cha-ni) adj. m.
bone ; osseous;made out of bone
kościec (kósh-chets) m. skeleton ; framework ; frame
kościelny (kosh-chel-ni) adj.
m, of church ; ecclesiastical
kościotrup (kosh-cho-troop) m.
skeleton (vulg.)
kościół (kósh-choow), m. church
kościsty (kosh-chee-sti) adj.
m. bony; angular ; rawboned
kość (kóshch) f. bone ; spine
koślawić (ko-shla-veech) v.
deform ; distort; crook
koślawy (ko-shla-vi) adj. m.
crooked; lame ; lopsided
kot (kot) m. cat; pussy cat;puss
kotara (ko-tá-ra) f. curtain
kotek (kó-tek) m. kitten ;puss
kotlet (kót-let) m. cutlet
kotlina (kot-lee-na) f. dale
kotłować (kot-wó-vach) v.whirl;
seethe; surge; drive crazy
kotłownia (kot-wov-ña) f.
boiler room ;boiler house
kotwica (kot-vee-tsa) f. anchor
kotwiczyć (kot-vee-chich) v.
anchor ; lie at anchor
kowadło (ko-vád-wo) m. anvil
kowal (kó-val), m. blacksmith
kowalny (ko-vál-ni) adj. m.
malleable ; ductile; forgeable
koza (kó-za)f. goat; jail
kozioł (kó-zhow) m. buck;gambol
koźlę (kóźh-ań) n. kid ;goatling
kożuch (ko-zhookh) m. sheepskin
furcoat ;coating on hot milk
kół (koow) m. stake; post
kółko (kow-ko) m. small wheel;
small circle: (soc.) circle
kpiarz (kpyash) m. scoffer
kpić (kpeech) v. jeer; sneer
kpiny (kpee-ni) n. mockery ;
this is preposterous ! (exp.)

kra (kra) f. ice floe
krach (krakh ) m. crash
kraciasty (kra-chás-ti) adj.
m. checquered ; grated;checkered
kradzież (krá-dżhesh) f. theft
kradziony (kra-dżho-ni) adj.
m. stolen ; robbed
kraina (kra-ee-na) f. land;
region ; province ;country
kraj (kray) m. country; verge;
edge; hem of a garment; land
krajać (krá-yach) v. cut;slice;
carve; operate; hack; saw
krajobraz (kray-ob-ras) m.
landscape; scenery painting
krajowy (kra-yo-vi) adj. m.
native; nationally made,
krajoznawczy (kra-yo-znáv-chi)
adj. m. hiking, touring
krakać (krá-kach) v. croak
kram (krám) m. booth; mess;
trouble; stall; odds and ends
kramarz (krá-mash) m. huckster
kran (kran) m. tap; faucet
kraniec (kra-ñets) m. border;
edge; end; extremity; margin
krańcowy (krań-tsó-vi) adj. m.
extreme ; marginal; excessive
krasa (krá-sa) f. grace;
beauty; loveliness ; splendor
krasić (kra-sheech) v. decorate
krasomówca (kra-so-moov-tsa) m.
orator(very eloquent)
kraść (kráshch) v. steal; rob
kraśnieć (krásh-ñech) v. blush;
grow beautiful; redden
krata (krá-ta) f. grate
krater (krá-ter) m. crater
krawat (krá-vat) m. (neck) tie
krawcowa (krav-tsó-va) f.
seamstress ;tailor's wife
krawędź (kra-vándźh) f. edge
krawęznik (kra-vańzh-ñeek) m.
curb(stone); roof-hip
krawiec (kráv-yets) m. tailor
krąg (krownk) m. ring ; ver-
tebre; disk; range; sphere
krążek (krówń-zhek) m. small
disk; potter's wheel;pulley
krążyć (krówń-zhich) v. circulate; rotate; wander; stray
kreacja (kre-áts-ya) f. (dress)
creation; theatre part

kreda (kré-da) f. chalk
kredens (kré-dens) m. china
cabinet ; cupboard; buffet
kredka (kréd-ka) f. crayon;
lipstick; chalk for writing
kredowy (kre-dó-vi) adj. m.
cretaceous;chalky;made of chalk
kredyt (kré-dit) m. credit
krem (krém) m. cream;custard
krematorium (kre-ma-tór-yoom)
n. crematorium ; crematory
kremowy (kre-mó-vi) adj. m.
creamcolored; cream yellow
kreować (kre-o-vach) v. create;
act; set up; institute; appoint
krepa (kré-pa) f. crape
kres (krés) m. end; limit;term
kreska (krés-ka) f. dash(line);
stroke; hatch; scar; accent
kreślić (kresh-leech) v. draw;
trace; sketch; cross out
kret (kret) m. mole ; schemer
kretowisko (kre-to-vees-ko) n.
krew (krev) f. blood ⌐molehill
krewetka (kre-vét-ka) f. shrimp
krewki (krév-kee) adj. m. rash;
quick-tempered; impetuous
krewny (krév-ni) m. relative
kręcić (krán-cheech) v. twist;
turn; shoot film;fuss; boss
kręcony (krán-tsó-ni) adj. m.
twisted; curled;winding;spiral
kręgle (kráng-le) n. bowling
(ninepin)game of bowles;tenpins
kręgosłup (kran-gós-woop) m.
spine; vertebral column
kręgowiec (kran-go-vyets) m.
vertebrate ;animal with spine
krępować (krán-pó-vach) v. bind;
embarrass; hamper; hinder
krępy (kran-pi) adj. m. stocky;
thickset; sturdy; short
krętactwo (kran-tats-tvo) n.
cheat; foul dealing; shuffle
krętacz (krán-tach) m. double-
dealer; dodger; quibbler;cheat
kręty (kran-ti) adj. m. curved;
curly; winding; tortuous
krnąbrny (krnownbr-ni) adj. m.
stubborn; unruly; restive;balky
krochmal (krókh-mal) m. starch
krochmalić (krokh-má-leech) v.
starch ; beat up; stiffen

krocie (kró-che) pl. thousands
kroczyć (kró-chich) v. stride
kroić (kró-eech) v. cut; slice
krok (krók) m. step ;pace;march
krokiew (kró-kev) f. rafter
krokodyl (kro-kó-dil) m. crocodile ; split flap (aviation)
kromka (króm-ka) f. slice
kronika (kro-née-ka) f.chronicle
kropić (kró-peech) v. sprinkle
kropka (króp-ka) f. dot ; point
kropkować (krop-kó-vach) v. dot
kropla (króp-la) f. drop
krosno (krós-no) n. loom
krosta (krós-ta) f. pimple
krotochwila (kro-to-khvée-la)
f. joke; burlesque; farce
krowa (kró-va) f. cow; mine
krój (krooy) m. cut; fashion
król (krool) m. king; rabbit
królestwo (kroo-lés-tvo) n.
kingdom; the realms; sphere
królewicz (kroo-le-veech) m.
crown prince ; king's son
królewski (kroo-lev-skee) adj.
m. royal; king's; queen's
królik (krool-eek) m. rabbit
królikarnia (kroo-lee-kár-ña)
f. warren ; rabbit warren
królowa (kroo-ló-va) f. queen
krótki (króot-kee) adj. m.
short; brief ;terse; concise
krótko (króo-tko) adv. briefly;
shortly; tersely;(hold) tightly
krtań (krtań) f. larynx
kruchy (kroó-khi) adj. m. brittle;
frail; tender; crisp; crusty
krucjata (kroots-ya-ta) f. crusade ; action for some cause
krucyfiks (kroo-tsi-feeks) m.
crucifix ; cross of Jesus
kruczek (kroó-chek) m. trick
kruczy (kroó-chi) adj. m. jet-
black; raven's (color)
kruk (krook) m. raven
krupy (kroó-pi) pl. groats
kruszec (kroo-shets) m. (metal)
ore ; metal; gold; silver
kruszec (kroo-shech) v. crumble;
grow brittle; repent
kruszyć (kroo-shich) v. crush;
crumb; destroy; shatter;disrupt

kruszyna (kroo-shi-na) f. crumb
kruźganek (kroozh-gán-ek) m.
portico ; gallery;ambulatory
krwawica (krva-vee-tsa) f. hard-
won money; toil ; labor
krwawić (krvá-veech) v. bleed
krwawy (krvá-vi) adj. m. bloody;
bloodthirsty; bloodstained
krwiobieg (krvee-ó-byeg) m.
blood circulation
krwisty (krvées-ti) adj. m.
sanguineous; blood-red
krwotok (krvó-tok) m. hemorrhage : bleeding
kryć (krich) v. hide; conceal;
cover ;roof over;shield; mask
kryjówka (kri-yoov-ka) f.
hiding-place ; hide-out
kryminalista (kri-mee-na-lees-
ta) m. criminal, crime;thriller
kryminał (kri-mée-naw) m. prison;
krynica (kri-ńee-tsa) f. spring
krystalizować (kris-ta-lee-zó-
vach) v. crystallize ; shape
kryształ (krish-taw) m. crystal
kryterium (kri-ter-yoom) n.
criterion; touchstone; test
kryty (kri-ti) adj. m. covered
krytyczny (kri-tich-ni) adj. m.
critical; decisive; crucial
krytyk (kri-tik) m. critic
krytyka (kri-ti-ka) f. criticism; review; censure
kryzys (kri-zis) m. crisis
krzaczasty (kzha-chás-ti) adj.
m. bushy; shaggy; beetle
krzak (kzhak) m. bush
krzątać (kzhówn-tach)v. bustle
krzątanina (kzhown-ta-ńee-na)
f. bustle ; comings and goings
krzem (kzhem) m. silicone
krzemień (kzhe-myeń) f. flint
krzepić (kzhe-peech) v. brace
up; refresh; invigorate;fortify
krzepki (kzhep-kee) adj. vigorous; lusty; robust; husky
krzepnąć (kzhep-nownch) v. coagulate; gather strength
krzesać (kzhe-sach) v. strike
fire ; strike sparks
krzesiwo (kzhe-shee-vo) n.
tinder-box ; flint

krzesło (kzhes-wo) n. chair
krzew (kzhev) m. shrub
krzewić (kzhe-veech) v. spread;
propagate; teach; graft
krzta (kzhta) f. whit; bit
krztusiec (kzhtoo-shets) m.
whooping-cough
krztusić się (kzhtoo-sheech
shań) v. choke; stifle
krzyczeć (kzhí-chech) v. shout;
cry ; scream; yell; clamor
krzyk (kzhik) m. cry; scream;
shriek ; yell; outcry; call
krzykacz (kzhi-kach) m. bawler;
crier ; shouter; agitator
krzykliwy (kzhik-lee-vi) adj.
m. noisy ; clamorous; loud
krzywa (kzhi-va) f. curve
krzywda (kzhiv-da) f. harm;
wrong ; a sense of wrong
krzywdzący (kzhiv-dzówn-tsi)
adj. m. harmful; injurious
krzywdzić (kzhiw-dźheech)v.
harm; wrong ;damage;be unfair
krzywica (kzhi-vee-tsa) f.
rickets ;rachitis;sweep saw
krzywić (kzhi-veech) v. bend
krzywić się (kzhi-veech shań)
v. make faces; bend ; warp
krzywo (kzhi-vo) adv. crooked
krzywy (kzhi-vi) adj. m. crooked; skew; distorted;slanting
krzyż (kzhish) m. cross
krzyżować (kzhi-zhó-vach) v.
cross; thwart; crucify
krzyżówka (kzhi-zhoov-ka) f.
crossword puzzle
ksiądz (kshównts) m. priest
książę (kshown-zhan) m. prince;
duke; ruler of a duchy
książka (kshównzh-ka) f. book
księga (kshan-ga) f. register;
large book: volume; tome
księgarnia (kshan-gar-ńa) f.
bookstore ; bookshop
księgarz (kshan-gash) m. bookseller; owner of a bookstore
księgować (kshań-go-vach) v.
keep-books ;enter in the books
księgowy (kshan-gó-vi) m. bookkeeper ; accountant
księgozbiór (kshań-gó-zbyoor)
m. book collection; library

księstwo (kshañ-stvo) n. duchy
księżna (kshàñzh-na) f. princess ; wife of a prince
księży (kshań-zhi) adj. m.
priestly ;belonging to a priest
księżyc (kshań-zhits) m. moon
kształcić (kshtaw-cheech) v.
educate ; train; form;school
kształt (kshtawt) m. form;
shape ; configuration; figure
kształtny (kshtawt-ni) adj. m.
shapely ; neat; nicely made
kształtować (kshtaw-to-vach) v.
shape ; form; mold ; fashion
kto (kto) pron. who ; all;those
kto inny (kto eén-ni) pron.
somebody else ; someone else
kto bądź (kto bōwńdch) pron.
anybody ; nayone;just anyone
ktoś (ktosh) pron. somebody
ktorędy (ktoo-rañ-di) adv.
which way; how to get there?
który (ktoo-ri) pron. who;
which; that ; any; whichever
któż (ktoosh) pron. whichever
ku (koo) prep. towards; to
kubatura (koo-ba-too-ra) f.
(building) volume ;cubature
kubek (koó-bek) m. cup: mug
kubeł (koó-bew) m. pail;bucket
kucharka (koo-khár-ka) f. cook
kucharz (koo-khash)m. cook
kuchenka gazowa (koo-khén-ka
ga-zó-va)f.(gas) hotplate
kuchnia (kookh-ña) f. kitchen
stove; cooking range; kitchen
kucnąć (koóts-nōwńch)v. squat
kucyk (koó-tsik) m. small pony
kuć (kooch) v. hammer; shoe a
horse; cram lessons: peck;coin
kudłaty (kood-wá-ti) adj. m.
shaggy; hairy ; hirsute
kudły (koód-wi) pl. shaggy hair
kufel (koó-fel) m. beer mug
kufer (koo-fer) m. trunk
kuglarz (koóg-lash) m. juggler
kukiełkowy teatr (koo- kew -kó-
vi teatr) puppet-show
kukła (kook-wa) f. puppet
kukułka (koo-koów-ka) f. cuckoo
bird; cuckoo clock
kukurydza (koo-koo-rí-dza) f.
maize; corn; Indian corn

kula (koó-la) f. sphere; bullet
crutch; ball; globe; shot
kulawy (koo-lá-vi) adj. m. lame
kulbaczyć (kool-ba-chich) v.
saddle (a horse)
kulec (koó-lech) v. limp
kulić się (koó-leech shañ) v.
snuggle; crouch; cringe;nestle
kulinarny (koo-lee-nár-ni) adj.
m. culinary ; of cooking
kulisy (koo-leé-si) pl. theatre
scenes ; the inner facts; links
kulisty (koo-leé-sti) adj. m.
spherical; ball-shaped
kulminacyjny (kool-mee-na-tsiy-
ni) adj. m. culminant; climactic
kult (koólt) m. cult ;worship
kultura (kool-too-ra) f. culture ; good manners;cultivation
kuluar (koo-loó-ar) m. lobby
kułak (koó-wak) m. fist;punch
kum (koom) m. godfather; crony
kumoterstwo (koo-mo-te-r-stvo)
n. favoritism; log rolling
kumulacja (koo-moo-láts-ya) f.
cumulation; merger; fusion
kuna (koó-na) f. marten
kundel (koón-del) m. mongrel
kunszt (koonsht) m. art;skill
kunsztowny (koon-shtóv-ni) adj.
m. artistic; artful;ingenious
kupa (koó-pa) f. heep; pile;
lot; excrement; assemblage
kupczyc (koóp-chich) v. bargain;
trade ; influence peddling
kupić (koó-peech) v. buy
kupiec (koó-pyets) m. shopkeeper ; merchant; dealer
kupno (koóp-no) n. purchase
kupon (koó-pon) m. coupon
kur (koor) m. cock; cock crow
kura (koó-ra) f. hen; hen bird
kuracja (koo-ráts-ya) f. cure
kuratorium (koo-ra-tór-yum) n.
board of trustees (of schools)
kurcz (koorch) m. cramp;shrinking
kurczę (koor-chañ) n. chicken
kurczyć (koór-chich) v. shrink
kurek (koó-rek) m. tap; cock
kurier (koór-yer) m. courier
kurnik (koór-ñeek) m. chicken
house; hen house; hen roost
poultry house; hen cote

kuropatwa (koo-ro-pát-va) f.
partridge (game bird)
kurowac (koo-ró-vach) v. heal;
cure ; treat for an illness
kurs (koors) m. course;rate;fare
kursowac (koor-só-vach)v.
circulate; ferry; run; ply
kurtka (koór-tka) f. jacket
kurtyna (koor-ti-na)f. curtain
kurwa (koór-va) f. whore (vulg.)
kurz (koosh) m. dust
kurza ślepota (koózha shle-po-
ta) night blindness
kusic (koo-sheech) v. tempt
kustosz (koós-tosh) m. custo-
dian; curator ; conservator
kusy (koosi) adj. m. short
kusza (koó-sha) f. crossbow
kuśnierz (koósh-nesh) m. furrier
kuter (koó-ter) m. cutter
kutwa (koót-va) f. miser
kuty (koo-ti) adj. m. forged;
shod; cunning; sly; shrewd
kuzyn (koó-zin) m. cousin
kuzynka (koo-zin-ka) f. cousin
kuznia (koózh-na) f. forge
kwadra (kvád-ra)f.quarter moon
kwadrans (kvád-rans) m. quarter
of an hour; fiftee minutes
kwadrat (kvád-rat) m. square
kwakac (kvá-kach) v. quack
kwalifikacja (kva-lee-fee-káts-
ya) f. qualification;evaluation
kwalifikowac (kva-lee-fee-kó-
vach) qualify ; class;appraise
kwapic się (kva-peech shan) v.
be eager; be in a hurry
kwarantanna (kva-ran-tán-na) f,
quarantine; period of isolation
kwarc (kvárts) m. quartz
kwarta (kvár-ta) f. quart
kwartalny (kvar-tál-ni) adj. m.
quarterly;occuring quarterly
kwas (kvas) m.acid; pl.discord
kwasic (kva-sheech) v. sour;
ferment; pickle;embitter;be idle
kwaskowaty (kvas-ko-va-ti) adj.
m. sourish ; acidulous
kwasy (kva-si) pl. fusses; bad-
blood; ill humor; dissent
kwaśny (kvash-ni) adj. m. sour
kwatera (kva-té-ra) f. quarters;
lodging; living accommodation

kwaterka (kva-tér-ka) f. quarter
of a liter; quarter liter bottle
kwesta (kves-ta) f. collection
(for); passing the hat around
kwestia (kvést-ya) f. question
kwestionariusz (kves-tio-nár-
yoosh) m. questionnaire
kwękac (kvan-kach) v. complain
kwiaciarka (kvya-chár-ka) f.
florist; flower girl
kwiaciarnia (kvya-chár-na) f.
flower shop; florist's
kwiat (kvyat) m. flower
kwiczec (kvee-chech) v. squeak
kwiczoł (kvee-chow) m. field-
fare (Turdus pilavis)
kwiecien (kvye-chen) m. April
kwiecisty (kvye-chees-ti) adj.
m. flowery; colorful; ornate
kwietnik (kvyet-neek) m. flower-
bed; carpet bed
kwik (kveek) m. squeal; squeak
kwit (kveet) m. receipt
kwitnąc (kveet-nownch)v. blossom ;grow moldy; look healthy
kwitowac (kvee-tó-vach) v. give
receipt; relinquish; forgo
kwoka (kvó-ka) f. sitting hen
kwota (kvó-ta) f. amount (of
money); amount ; allocation
kynologiczny związek (ki-no-lo-
geéch-ni zvyówn-zek) kennel
club ; kennel association
labirynt (la-bée-rint) m. la-
byrinth; maze
laborant (la-bó-rant) m. lab.
technician; assistant chemist
laboratorium (la-bo-ra-tór-
yoom) m. laboratory ; lab
lac (lach) v. pour; shed; (spill)
lada (lá-da) f. counter; chest
lada (lá-da) part. any; whatever; the least; paltry
lada kto (lá-da kto) anybody
ladacznica (la-dach-nee-tsa) f.
harlot; prostitute; strumpet
laik (lá-eek) m. layman
lak (lak) m. sealing wax
lakier (la-ker) m. varnish
lakmus (lák-moos) m. litmus
lakoniczny (la-ko-neéch-ni) adj.
m. terse; brief; curt; laconic
stating much in few words

lakować (la-ko-vach) v. seal
lalka (lál-ka) f. doll ;puppet
laktoza (lak-to-za) f. lactose
lament (la-ment) m. lament
lamować (la-mo-vach) v. laminate
lamówka (la-moóv-ka) f. trim;
border ; edge; trimming; piping
lampa (lám-pa) f. lamp
lampart (lám-part) m. leopard
lampas (lám-pas) m.stripe;lampas
lampion (lám-pyon) m. lampion
lamus (la-moos) m. storeroom
lanca (lán-tsa) f. lance; spear
lancet (lán-tset) m. lancet ;fleam
landara (lan-da-ra) f. jalopy;
old crate ; rumble-tumble
lanie (la-ñe) n. pouring; cast-
ing; beating ;thrashing; licking
lanolina (la-no-lee-na) f. lanolin ; wool-fat (in ointments)
lansady (lan-sa-di) pl. pranc-
ing gait ; skips; leaps; bounds
lansować (lan-so-vach) v. launch
lapidarny (la-pee-dár-ni) adj.
m. terse; concise ;curt; crisp
lapis (la-pees) m. silver nitrate ; lunar caustic
lapsus (lap-soos) m. lapse(slip)
laryngologia (la-rin-go-lóg-ya)
f. laryngology
las (las) m. wood; forest ;thicket
lasek (la-sek) m. grove
laska (lás-ka) f. cane ; stick
laskowy orzech (las-ko-vi
o-zhekh)m.hazelnut
lasować (la-so-vach) v. slake
lata (la-ta) pl. years
latać (la-tach)v.fly;be running
latarka (la-tár-ka) f. flashlight ; torch : small lamp
latarnia (la-tár-ña) f. street-
light ; lantern; beacon
latarnia morska (la-tár-ña mór-
ska) lighthouse
latarnik (la-tár-ñeek) m. lighthouse keeper
latawiec (la-táv-yets) m. kite
lato (la-to) n. Summer
latorośl (la-to-roshl) f. shoot;
offspring: scion; sprig; sprout
laubzega (lawb-ze-ga) f. fret-
saw; jigsaw; scroll saw

laufer (law-fer) m. runner;
(chess)bishop
laury (law-ri) pl. laurels
laureat (law-ré-at) m. laure-
ate ; prize-winner
lawa (la-va) f vulcanic lava
lawenda (la-ven-da) f. lavender ; lavender water
laweta (la-ve-ta) f. gun-
carriage; heavy gun base
lawina (la-vee-na) f. avalanche ; shower(of words)
lawirować (la-vee-ro-vach) v.
veer; tack; intrigue
lazaret (la-za-ret) m. field
hospital(for infections)
lazur (la-zoor) m. azure; sky
blue; blue pigment
ląd (lownd) m. 1. land;
2. mainland; 3. continent
lądować (lown-do-vach) v. land;
disembark; go ashore; alight
lecieć (le-chech) v. fly; run;
hurry;wing; drift; drop; fall
leciutko (le-choot-ko) adv.
bearly touching;very lightly
leciwy (le-chee-vi) adj. m.
up in years;advanced in years
lecz (lech) conj. but;however
leczenie (le-che-ñe) n. healing ; cure; treatment
lecznica (lech-ñee-tsa) f. hospital; clinic;nursing home
leczyć (le-chich) v. heal;
treat; nurse;practice medicine
ledwie (led-vye) adv. hardly;
scarcely; barely;almost;nearly
ledwo że nie (le-dvo zhe ñe)
adv. almost; nearly; hardly
legacja (le-gáts-ya) f. legation; legacy; bequest
legalizować (le-ga-lee-zo-vach)
legalize; certify; attest
legalny (le-gál-ni) adj. m.
legal; lawful;allowed by law
legat (le-gat) m. bequest;
papal muncio
legawiec (le-ga-vyets) m.
pointer ; setter
legenda (le-gen-da) f. legend
legendarny (le-gen-dár-ni) adj.
m. legendary ; fabulous;storied

legia (leg-ya) f. legion
legion (leg-yon) m. legion
legitymacja (le-gee-ti-máts-ya)
f. i-d card; identification
papers; membership card etc
legitymować się (le-gee-ti-mo-
vačh śhań) v. prove one's
identity; identify oneself
lęgnąć (leg-nównch) v. fall
in battle; perish; lie down
legowisko (le-go-veé-sko) n.
berth; bedding;encampment;den
legumina (le-goo-meé-na) f.
dessert; sweet dish;legumin
lej (ley) m. crater; funnel
lejce (ley-tse) pl. reins
lejek (le-yek) m. small funnel
lek (lek) m. medicine; drug
lekarski (le-kár-skee) adj. m.
medical ; medicinal
lekarz (le-kash) m. physician
lekceważący (lek-tse-va-zhown-
tsi) adj. m. disrespectful
lekceważenie (lek-tse-va-zhe-
ńe) n. disdain;disrespect
lekceważyć (lek-tse-vá-zhich)
v. slight; scorn; neglect
lekcja (lek-tsya) f. lesson
lekki (lek-kee) adj. m. light;
light-hearted;graceful; slight
lekko (lek-ko) adv. easily
lekkoatleta (lek-ko-at-le-ta) m.
field&track man
lekkomyślny (lek-ko-mishl-ni)
adj. m. careless; thoughtless;
reckless; rash; fickle
lektura (lek-too-ra) f. reading
matter ; reading list; reading
lemiesz (le-myesh) m. plough-
share : blade; vomer
lemoniada (le-mo-ńá-da) f. lemonade; lemon squash
len (len) m. flax ;linen;
lenić się (le-ńeech śhań) v.
be idle; be lazy; shed hair
leniec (le-ńech) v. shed hair
leninizm (le-ńee-ńeezm) m. Le-
ninism ;Lenin's interpretation
lenistwo (le-ńees-tvo) n. laziness : idleness; sluggishness
leniwy (le-ńee-vi) adj. m. lazy
lennik (len-ńeek) m. vassal
pledging fealty to overlord

lenno (len-no) n. fief
leń (leń) m. lazy-bones; idler;
lazy bum ; sluggard
lep (lep) m. glue ; flypaper
lepianka (lep-yán-ka) f. adobe;
mud hut; mud cabin
lepić (le-peech) v. stick; glue
lepiej (lep-yey) adv. better;
rather ;(feel) better
lepki (lep-kee) adj. m. sticky
lepszy (lep-shi) adj. m. better
lesbijka (les-beéy-ka) f. les-
bian ;homosexual women
lesisty (le-shees-ti) adj. m.
wooded; woody; forest-
leszcz (leshch) m. bream
leszczyna (lesh-chi-na) f.
hazelnut tree ; hazel grove
leśnictwo (leśh-ńeets-tvo) n.
forestry ; forest-range
leśniczówka (leśh-ńee-choov-ka)
f. ranger's house (forester's)
leśniczy (leśh-ńee-chi) m. ranger ; forest-ranger ;forester
leśnik (leśh-ńeek) m. forester
leśny (leśh-ni) adj. m. of
forest; of forestry ;forest-
letarg (le-targ) m. lethargy
letni (let-ńee) adj. m. lukewarm; half-hearted; summer
letnik (let-ńeek) m. vacationer
letnisko (let-ńees-ko) n. summer
resort ;summer vacation spot
lew (lev) m. lion; lady's man
lewa (le-ya) f. left (side)
lewar (le-var) m. lever; jack
lewatywa (le-ya-ti-va) f. enema
lewica (le-veé-tsa) f. the left
(polit.) ; left-hand side
lewo (le-vo) adv. to the left
lewy (le-vi) adj. m. left; false
lezć (leżhch) v. crowl; creep-
along; plod along; climb;jostle
leżak (le-zhak) m. folding
(canvas) chair;deck-chair
leżeć (le-zhech) v. lie; (fit)
lędźwie (lańdźh-vye) pl. loins
lęgnąć (lańg-nównch) v. hatch
lęk (lańk) m. fear;anxiety;dread
lękać się (lań-kach śhań) v.
be afraid; dread;stand in awe
lękliwy (lańk-lee-vi) adj. m.
timid ;faint-hearted;apprehensive

lgnąć (lgnownch) v. adhere;sink; stick; be partial; feel attracted
libacja (lee-báts-ya) f. drinking party; drinking bout
liberalny (lee-be-rál-ni) adj. m.liberal; broad-minded
liberał (lee-bé-raw) m. liberal
libertyn (lee-bér-tin) m. libertine; free thinker
lice (lee-tse) n. face; cheek; the right side; evidence
licencja (lee-tsén-tsya) f. license (ermission to practice)
licho (lee-kho) adv. poorly
licho (lee-kho) n. evil; devil
lichota (lee-kho-ta) f. rubbish
lichtarz (leekh-tash) m. candlestick ; candelabrum;candelabra
lichwa (leekh-va) f. usury
lichwiarz (leekh-vyash) m. usurer; loan shark; money lender
lichy (lee-khi) adj. m. shoddy; shabby; poor; mean;rotten;petty
lico (lee-tsom.face; cheek; surface; front; outer part
licować (lee-tsó-vach) v. fit for... ; comport ;veneer; face
licytacja (lee-tsi-táts-ya) f. auction ; bidding; the bid
licytować (lee-tsi-tó-vach) v. auction; bid ; offer; call
liczba (leech-ba) f. number; figure ; integer; group; class
liczbowy (leech-bó-vi) adj. m. numerical ;numeral
licznik (leech-neek) m. counter; numerator; gasmeter; electrometer, etc.;taximeter; register
liczny (leech-ni) adj. m.numerous ; large; abundant;plentiful
liczyć (lee-chich) v. count ; reckon;compute;calculate
liczydło (lee-chid-wo) n. abacus; counter; register
liga (lee-ga) f. league ;alliance
lik (leek) m. lot ;countless
lignina (leeg-nee-na) f. lignin
likier (lee-k̉er) m. liquor
likwidacja (leek-vee-dáts-ya) f. liquidation ;closing down
likwidować (leek-vee-do-vach) v. liquidate ;do away with

lila (lee-la) adj. m. (color) pale-violet; lily-
lilia (leél-ya) f. lily
liliowy (leel-yó-vi) adj. m. lilac (color) ; lily-
liliput (lee-leé-poot) m. little dwarf ; midget; pygmy
limfa (leém-fa) f. lymph
limit (lee-meet) m. limit
limuzyna (lee-moo-zi-na) f. limousine; pilot's enclosure
lin (leen) m. tench
lina (lee-na) f. line; rope
lincz (leénch) m. lynch
linczować (leen-chó-vach) v. lynch; kill by mob action
lingwista (leen-gveés-ta) m. linguist (specialist)
linia (leén-ya) f. line; lane
linijka (lee-neéy-ka) f. ruler
liniować (lee-ñyó-vach) v. rule; line (paper)
liniowy okręt (leeñ-yó-vi okrańt) liner (ship);battleship
linoleum (lee-no-lé-oom) n. linoleum (floor covering)
linoskoczek (lee-no-skó-chek) m. tightrope artist
linotyp (lee-nó-tip) m. linotype (typesetting machine)
linowa kolejka (lee-nó-va koley-ka) cable car
lipa (lee-pa) f.1.linden tree 2. fake; cheat; fraud
lipiec (leép-yets) m. July
lira (lee-ra) f. lyre
liryczny (lee-rich-ni) adj. m. lyric; lyrical
liryk (lee-rik) m. lyrist;lyric
liryka (lee-ri-ka) f. lyric poetry ; lyricism
lis (lees) m. fox; sly man
list (leest) m. letter;note
lista (lees-ta) f. list;roll
listonosz (lees-to-nosh) m. postman
listopad (lees-tó-pad) m. November
listownie (lees-tóv-ñe) adv. by letter ; by mail
listwa (lees-tva) f. trim
liszaj (lee-shay) m. herpes

liszka (leesh-ka) f. caterpillar ; vixen; sly fox
liściasty (leesh-chas-ti) odj.
m. leafy ; leafed; foliaceous
liść (leeshch) m. leaf ; frond
litania (lee-tań-ya) f. litany
litera (lee-te-ra) f. letter
literacki (lee-te-ráts-kee)
adj. m. literary ; of letters
literat (lee-te-rat) m. writer
literatura (lee-te-ra-too-ra)
f. literature ; writings
litewski (lee-tev-skee) adj. m.
Lithuanian ;Lithuanian language
litograf (lee-to-graf) m.
lithographer
litościwy (lee-tosh-chee-vi)
adj. m. merciful; compassionate
litość (lee-toshch) f. pity;
mercy ; compassion
litować się (lee-to-vach shań)
v. have pity ;feel pity
litr (leetr) m. liter
liturgia (lee-toor-gya) f.
liturgy; religious ritual
lity (lee-ti) adj. m. massive
solid; cast; pure-
lizać (lee-zach) v. lick
lizol (lee-zol) m. lysol
lizus (lee-zoos) m. bootlicker
lniany (lna-ni) adj. m. linen;
flaxen; linseed
loch (lokh) m. dungeon; cellar
lodołamacz (lo-do-wa-mach) m.
icebreaker : ice shield
lodowaty (lo-do-va-ti) adj. m.
icy ; ice-cold; chilling;frigid
lodowiec (lo-do-vyets) m. glacier;mass of ice and snow
lodowisko (lo-do-vees-ko) n.
skating-rink ; ice rink
lodownia (lo-dov-na) f. ice-
chamber ; ice-cellar; icy cold
lodowy (lo-do-yy) adj. m. of ice
lodówka (lo-dov-ka) f. refrige r-
ator; ice box; ice chest
lody (lo-di) pl. ice cream
logarytm (lo-ga-ritm) m. loga-
rithm
logiczny (lo-geech-ni) adj. m.
logical ;consistent; sound
logik (lo-geek) m. logician:
expert in logic

logika (lo-gee-ka) f. logic
lojalność (lp-yal-noshch) f.
loyalty ;straightforwardness
lojalny (lo-yal-ni) adj. m.
loyal; staunch; low-abiding
lok (lok) m. curl; coil
lokaj (lo-kay) m. lackey
lokal (lo-kal) m. premises
lokalizować (lo-ka-lee-zo-vach)
lo calize ; locate; range
lokalny (lo-kal-ni) adj. m.
local; regional;of a place
lokata (lo-ka-ta) f. investment
lokator (lo-ka-tor) m. tenant
lokomocja (lo-ko-mots-ya) f.
locomotion ; communication
lokomotywa (lo-ko-mo-ti-va) f.
train engine; locomotive
lokować (lo-ko-vach) v. place
lombard (lom-bard) m. pawnshop
lont (lont) m. fuse ;slow-match
lornetka (lor-net-ka) f. field
glasses; opera glasses
los (los) m. lot; fate; chance;
lottery-ticket; destiny;hazard
losować (lo-so-vach) v. draw
lots ; raffle ; draw cuts
lot (lot) m. flight ; speed
loteria (lo-ter-ya) f. lottery
lotnia (lot-na) f. hang glider
lotnictwo (lot-neets-tvo) n.
aviation; aeronautics;air force
lotnik (lot-neek) m. aviator
lotnisko (lot-nees-ko) n. airport; airfield; aerodrome
lotniskowiec (lot-nees-kov-
yets) m. aircraft carrier
lotny (lot-ni) adj. m. bright;
quick; swift;sharp; subtle
lotos (lo-tos) m. lotus
loża masońska (lo-zha ma-sońs-
ka) shriner's lodge
lód (loot) m. ice; pl.ice cream
lśniacy (lshnown-tsi)adj. m.
shining; bright;glossy; sleek
lśnić (lshneech) v. glitter;
shine ;gleam; glimmer; shimmer
lub (loop) conj. or;or else
luba (loo-ba) f. sweetheart
lubić (loo-beech) v. like;
be fond; enjoy; be partial
lubieżny (loo-byezh-ni) adj.
m. lustful; voluptuous; lewd

lubość (loo-boshch) f. delight
lubować się (loo-bó-vach śháń)
v. take delight ; find pleasure
lud (loot) m. people; nation
ludność (loód-noshch) f. population (of a given territory)
ludny (loód-ni) adj. m. populous ; teeming; crowded
ludobójstwo (loo-do-bóoy-stvo)
n. genocide;killing of a nation
ludowy (loo-do-vi) adj. m. pop-
ulist; popular; country
ludożerca (loo-do-zhér-tsa) m.
cannibal ; man man-eater
ludzie (loo-dzhe) pl. people
ludzkość (loódz-koshch) f.
mankind; humaneness; humanity
lufa (loo-fa) f. gunbarrel
luk (look) m. hatch ;skylight
luka (loo-ka) f. gap;blank;break
lukier (loo—ker) m. sugar-
icing ; frosting
lukratywny (look-ra-tiv-ni) adj.
m. lucrative ; profitable
luksus (look-soos) m. luxury
lunatyk (loo-na-tik) l. sleepwalker; 2. loony
lunąć (loo-nównch) v. rain in
torrents;slap ;lash down;whack
luneta (loo-ne-ta) f. field-
glass ;spy-glass; telescope
lupa (loo-pa) f. magnifying
glass ; jeweler's glass (loop)
lusterko (loos-ter-ko) n. hand-
glass ; rear-view mirror(in a car)
lustro (loos-tro) n. mirror
lustrować (loos-tró-vach) v.
inspect; review ; check; audit
lut (loot) m. solder
luteranin (loo-te-ra-ńeen) m.
Lutheran
lutnia (loot-ńa) f. flute
lutować (loo-to-vach) v. solder
luty (loo-ti) m. February
luty (loo-ty) adj. m. bleak;
grim ; severe; bleak
luz (loos) m. clearance; play
luzak (loo-zak) m. loose (replacement) horse
luzować (loo-zó-vach) v. replace;
relieve ; loosen;slacken;ease off)
luźny (loozh-ni) adj. m. loose

lwi (lvee) adj. m. lion's
lżej (lzhey) adv. lighter;
easier ; with less weight
lżenie (lzhé-ńe) n. abuse; insults;vituperation
lżyć (lzhich) v. abuse; insult
Łabędź (wa-bańdźh)m. swan
łach (wakh) m. rag ; clout
łacha (wa-kha) f. sandbank
łachman (wákh-man) m. rag
łachudra (wa-khoód-ra) m.
ragtagman; ragamuffin
łaciarz (wa-chash) m. patcher
łaciaty (wa-chá-ti) adj. m.
in patches ; pinto(horse)
łacina (wa-chee-na) f. Latin
łaciński (wa-cheéń-skee) adj.
m. Latin; of Latin
Ład (wad) m. order;orderliness
ładnie (wád-ńe) adv. nicely
ładnieć (wad-ńech) v. grow
pretty ; grow prettier
ładny (wád-ny) adj. m. nice
ładować (wa-do-vach) v. load;
charge ; cram; fill
ładownica (wa-dow-ńee-tsa) f.
cartridge pouch (or box)
ładunek (wa-doó-nek) m. load;
cargo; charge ; shipload;burden
łagodność (wa-gód-noshch) f.
gentleness ; kindliness;suavity
łagodny (wa-gód-ni) adj. m.
gentle ;mild;soft;meek;easy
łagodzący (wa-go-dzówń-tsi) adj.
m. alleviating; extenuating
łagodzić (wa-gó-dźheech)v.
soothe; relieve; alleviate
attenuate; mitigate; smooth
łajać (wa-yach) v. scold; chide
łajdactwo (way-dáts-tvo) n.
mean trick;scoundrels ;rabble
łajdak (wáy-dak) m. scoundrel
łajno (wáy-no) n. dung; shit
łaknąć (wak-nównch) v. hunger
for; thirst for ;crave for
łakocie (wa-kó-che) pl. deli-
cacies ; sweets;tidbits;candy
łakomić się (wa-ko-meéch śháń)
v. covet; lust;be tempted
łakomy (wa-kó-mi) adj. m.
greedy; covetous; avid
Łakomstwo (wa-kóm-stvo) n.
greed; gluttony;greediness

Łamać (wa-mach) v. break;crush; quarry;shatter; crack; snap
Łamigłowka (wa-mee-gwoow-ka) f. riddle; puzzle;jig-saw puzzle
Łamistrajk (wa-mee-strayk) m. scab; strikebreaker
Łamliwy (wam-lee-vi) adj. m. fragile;frail;brittle;breakable
Łan (wan) m. stand of wheat
Łania (wa-ña) f. hind; doe
Łańcuch (wań-tsookh) m. chain; range; series; train;succession
Łańcuchowa reakcja (wań-tsoo-khó-va re-ák-tsya) chain reaction
Łapa (wa-pa) f. paw ;claw;arm
Łapać (wa-pać) v. catch;snatch
Łapanka (wa-pan-ka) f. roundup
Łapcie (wap-će) n. bast sandals ; moccasins
Łapczywość (wap-chi-voshch) f. greed; greediness; avidity
Łapczywy (wap-chi-vi) adj. m. greedy; money-grubbing
Łapka (wap-ka) f. (mouse) trap
Łapówka (wa-poov-ka) f. bribe
Łapserdak (wap-ser-dak) m. rogue; ragamuffin;scoundrel
Łasica (wa-shee-tsa) f. weasel
Łasić się (wa-sheech shañ) v. fawn on sb.; toady
Łaska (was-ka) f. grace ; clemency; favor; generosity;mercy
Łaskawy (was-ka-vi) adj. m. gracious; kind; generous
Łaskotać (was-ko-tać) v. tickle; titillate
Łaskotliwy (was-kot-lee-vi) adj. m. ticklish; titillating
Łasy (wa-si) adj. m. greedy
Łaszczyć się (wash-chich shañ) v. covet; lust
Łata (wa-ta) f. patch
Łatać (wa-tać) v. patch up
Łatanina (wa-ta-nee-na) f. patch work; bungling
Łatwo (wat-vo) adv. easily
Łatwopalny (wat-vo-pál-ni) adj. m. inflammable ; combustible
Łatwość (wat-voshch) f. ease; facility ;aptitude; fluency
Łatwowierny (wat-vo-vyér-ni) adj. m. credulous ;gullible

Łatwy (wat-vi) adj. m. easy
Ława (wa-va) f. bench ;footing
Ławica (wa-vee-tsa) f. (fish) shoal ; sandbank; shelf; layer
Ławka (waf-ka) f. pew; bench
Ławnik (wav-ñeek) m. juror; alderman ; assessor
Łazić (wa-żheech)v. crawl; loiter ; slouch about;creep
Łazienka (wa-żhén-ka) f. bathroom; toilet; bath
Łazik (wa-żheek) m. tramp; jeep
Łaźnia (ważh-ña) f. bath
Łażący (wa-zhówn-tsi) adj. m. dragging; crawling;scansorial
Łączący (wówn-chówn-tsy) adj. m. uniting; joining; unitive
Łącznica (wównch-ñeé-tsa) f. junction ;switchboard
Łącznie (wówn-chñe) adv. together; including; inclusive of
Łącznik (wównch-ñeek) m. hyphen; liaisonman ;link; tie; bond
Łączność (wównch-noshch) f. contact; communication; unity; signal service; connection
Łączny (wównch-ni) adj. m. joint; combined;total; global
Łączyć (wówn-chich) v. join; unite ;merge;link;bind;weld
Łąka (wówn-ka) f. meadow
Łeb (wep) m. head; pate
Łechtać (wékh-tać) v. tickle; flatter ; titillate; lure
Łęk (wańk) m. saddlebow; syncline; arch; bow; pommel
Łgać (wgać) v. lie;brag;boast
Łgarstwo (wgár-stvo) n. lie
Łgarz (wgash) m. liar; braggart
Łkać (wkać) v. sob
Łobuz (wo-boos) m. rogue; rascal; scamp; scoundrel
Łodyga (wo-dí-ga) f. stem
Łoić (wo-eech) v. tallow; beat up; wallop; curry
Łokieć (wo—kech) m. elbow
Łom (wom) m.crowbar;scrap;junk
Łomot (wo-mot) m. crash; crack
Łono (wo-no) n. lap; bosom;womb
Łopata (wo-pa-ta) f. spade
Łopot (wo-pot) m. (sail)flutter
Łoskot (wos-kot) n. clatter; bang; din; rumble;racket;boom

Łosoś (wo-sośh) m. salmon
Łoś (wośh) m. elk; moose
Łotewski (wo-tev-skee) adj. m.
 Latvian ; Latvian language
Łotr (wotr) m, vicious scoun—
 drel; knave; rascal; rogue
Łowczy (wóv-chi) adj. m. hunting; huntsman's; hunter's
Łowić (wóv-eećh) v. trap;
 fish; catch; hunt; chase
Łowiectwo (wov-yéts-tvo) n.
 hunting; game shooting
Łowy (wó-vi) pl. hunt; chase
Łozina (wo-żhee-na) f. wicker;
 sallow; osier; osier-bed
łoże (wo-żhe) n. bed; cradle
łożyć (wo-zhićh) v. spend
łożysko (wo-zhis-ko) n.(river)
 bed; (ball) bearing
łódka (woód-ka) f. small boat
łódź (woódżh) f. boat;craft
łój (wooy) m. tallow;suet;sebum
łów (woov) m. hunt; chase
łóżeczko (woo-zhéch-ko) n.
 (child's) bed; small bed
łóżko (woóżh-ko) n. bed;bunk
łubin (woó-been) m. lupin
łucznik (woóch-ńeek) n. archer
łuczywo (woo-chi-vo) n. resin-
 ous kindling;resinous chips
łudzący (woo-dzówn-tsi) adj.
 m. delusive; deceptive
łudzić (woó-dżheećh)v. delude;
 deceive; give false hope
Ług (woog) m. lye
Ługować (woo-gó-vaćh) v. leach;
 lixiviate
Łuk (wook) m. bow; arch; bent;
 vault
Łuna (woó-na) f. glow (of sun
 or fire)
Łup (woop) m. booty; spoils
łupać (woó-paćh) v. cleave;
 split; ache; give shooting pain
Łupek (woó-pek) m, slate
łupić (woó-peećh) v. plunder
Łupież (woó-pyezh) f. dandruff
Łupieżca (woo-pyeżh-tsa) m.
 plunderer; looter; pillager
Łupina (woo-pee-na) f. husk;
 shell; peel; skin; hull;rind
łuska (woós-ka) f. scale; husk;
 shell; pod; flake; rind

Łuskać (woós-kaćh) v. scale;
 husk; peel; pod; hull (rice)
Łuszczyć (woósh-chićh) v. peel;
 pare; flake off ; shell off
Łuza (woo-za) f. billiard
 pocket
Łydka (wit-ka) f. calf(leg-shank)
Łyk (wik) m. gulp; sip; draft
Łykać (wi-kaćh) v. swallow;
 gulp; sip; bolt; gorge; drink
Łyko (wi-ko) n. bast; phoem
łykowaty (wi-ko-vá-ti) adj. m.
 wiry; tough; fibrous
Łypać (wi-paćh) v. blink
Łysek (wi-sek) m. (boldhead)
 boldy; bold-faced animal
Łysieć (wi-śhećh) v. become
 bold; grow bold; lose hair
Łysina (wi-śhée-na) f. pate
Łyskać (wís-kaćh) v. flash
Łysy (wi-si) adj. m. bold
Łyżeczka (wi-zhéch-ka) f. tea-
 spoon; dessert spoon; curette
Łyżka (wízh-ka) f. spoon;spoonful
Łyżwa (wizh-va) f. skate
Łyżwiarz (wízh-vyash) m.skater
łyżwowy (wiżh-vo-vi)adj.of skates
Łza (wza) f. tear
Łzawy (wzá-vi) adj. m. tearful
Łzowy kanał (wzó-vi ká-naw)
 tear canal; tear duct
maca (má-tsa) f. matzos
macać (má-tsaćh) v. feel; grope
machać (má-khaćh) v. wave;whisk;
 swing; wag; lash; flap;brandish
macher (má-kher) m. trickster
machina (ma-khée-na) f. (large)
 machine; bureaucratic machine
machinacja (ma-khee-náts-ya) f.
 machination; dodge; intrigue
machlojka (ma-khlóy-ka) f.
 swindle; defraudation
macica (ma-ćhee-tsa) f. uterus;
 womb; screw nut; tap root
macierz (má-ćhesh) f. mother
 country; matrix; mother
macierzanka (ma-ćhe-zhán-ka) f.
 thyme ; wild thyme
macierzyński (ma-ćhe-zhiń-ski)
 adj. m. maternal; mother's
macierzyństwo (ma-ćhe-zhiń-stvo)
 n. maternity; motherhood

macierzysty (ma-che-zhis-ti)
adj. m. maternal; (parental)
maciora (ma-chó-ra) f. sow
macka (máts-ka) f. tentacle;
feeler; antenna; horn
macocha (ma-tsó-kha) f. stepmother; not as good as mother
maczac (má-chach) v. dip; soak
maczuga (ma-choó-ga) f. bat;
club; bludgeon; cudgel
magazyn (ma-gá-zin) m. store;
warehouse; repository; store
magazynier (ma-ga-zi-ner) m.
warehouseman; storekeeper
magia (mág-ya) f. sorcery
magiczny (ma-geéch-ni) adj. m.
magic; conjuring tricks
magiel (má-gel) m. mangle
magik (ma-geek) m. magician
magister (ma-geés-ter) m.mas-
ter (diplomat); chemist
magisterium (ma-gees-tér-yoom)
n. master's degree
magistrat (ma-geés-trat) m.
city hall; municipality
maglowac (mag-ló-vach) v, mangle; calender; bother; crush
magnat (mág-nat) m. magnate
magnes (mág-nes) m. magnet
magnetofon (mag-ne-tó-fon) m.
tape-recorder
magnetyczny (ma-gne-tich-ni)
adj. m. magnetic;magnetical
magnetyzm (mag-ne-tizm) m.
magnetism;personal charm
magnez (mág-nes) m. magnesium
magnezja (mag-néz-ya) f. mag-
nesia; magnesium
magnolia (mag-nól-ya) f. magnolia (Magnolia)
mahometanin (ma-kho-me-tá-neen)
m. Mohammedan; Moslem
mahon (ma-khon) m. mahogany
maic (ma-eech) v. decorate
with green leaves
maj (may) m. May
majaczyc (ma-yá-chich) v. rave;
loom ; be delirious
majatek (ma-yown-tek) m. fortune; estate; property;wealth
majdan (máy-dan) m. parade-
ground; personal junk; traps

majeranek (ma-ye-rá-nek) m.
marjoram; fragrant mint(cooking)
majestat (ma-yés-tat) m. majesty; kingship; stateliness
majetnosc (ma-yant-noshch) f.
wealth; fortune; property
majetny (ma-yant-ni) adj. m.
well to do ;wealthy; affluent
majonez (ma-yo-nes) m. mayon-
naise ; egg yoke dressing
major (ma-yor) m. major
majówka (ma-yoov-ka) f. May-
outing ; picnic; junket
majster (máy-ster) m. qualified
craftman; boss; master;foreman
majstersztyk (may-ster-shtik) m.
masterpiece;greatest work
majstrowac (may-stró-vach) v.
tinker ; make (an object)
majtek (máy-tek) m. deckhand
majtki (máyt-kee) pl. panties
mak (mák) m. poppy seed
makaron (ma-ká-ron) m. macaroni
makata (ma-ká-ta) f. tapestry
makler (mák-ler) m. broker
makolagwa (ma-ko-lówng-va) f.
linnet; lass; lassie
makrela (ma-kre-la) f. mackerel
maksyma (ma-ksí-ma) f. axiom;
maxim ; adage ;rule of conduct
maksymalny (ma-ksi-mál-ni) adj.
m. maximum ;top-;peak-;most-
makulatura (ma-koo-la-too-ra) f.
waste-paper;spoilage; rubbish
makuch (má-kookh) m. oilcake
malaria (ma-lár-ya) f. malaria
malarstwo (ma-lár-stvo) m.
painting (art); house painting
malarz (ma-lash) m. painter
malec (má-lets) m. youngster
malec (má-lech) v. shrink;dwindle
malenki (ma-len-kee) adj. m.
very small; tiny; insignificant
malenstwo (ma-len-stvo) n. tiny
thing; little one; little mite
malina (ma-lee-na) f. raspberry
malowac (ma-ló-vach) v. paint;
stain; color; make up;depict
malowidło (ma-lo-veed-wo) m.
painting; picture (painted)
malowniczy (ma-lov-nee-chi)
adj. m. picturesque; vivid

maltretować (mal-tre-to-vach)
v. abuse; mistreat; il_-treat
malwersacja (mal-ver-sáts-ya)
f. embezzlement; peculation
mało (má-wo) adv. little; few;
seldom; lack; not enough
małoduszny (ma-wo-doosh-ni)
adj. m.small-minded; narrow-
minded; cheap ;fainthearted
małoletni (ma-wo-lét-ñee)adj.
m. minor; under age ;juvenile
małomówny (ma-wo-moov-ni) adj.
m. reticent; laconic;taciturn
małostkowy (ma-wost-kó-vi) adj.
m. fussy; petty; mean
małpa (maw-pa) f. ape; monkey
małpować (maw-po-vach) v. ape
mały (má-wi) adj. m. little;
small,size; low; modest;slight
małżeński (maw-zheñ-skee) adj.
m. matrimonial ;conjugal
małżeństwo (maw-sheñ-stwo) n.
married couple; wedlock
małżonek (maw-zho-nek) m. husband ; spouse; consort; mate
małżonka (maw-zhon-ka) f. wife
mama (má-ma) f. mamma ; mother
mamałyga (ma-ma-wi-ga) f.
maize gruel ; hominy
mamić (má-meech) v. deceive;
delude ;beguile; lure;tempt
mamidło (ma-meéd-wo) n. illusion ; delusion;lure;seduction
mamona (ma-mó-na) f. mammon
mamlać (mám-ró-tach) v. mumble
mamrotać (mam-ró-tach) v. mutter ; mumble; gibber
mamut (má-moot) m. mammoth
manatki (ma-nát-kee) pl.person-
al belongings; traps
mandaryn (man-dá-rin) n. man-
darin; Chinese dignnitary.
mandat (man-dat) m. mandate;
traffic ticket ; fine
mandolina (man-do-lée-na) f.
mandolin with 8 to 10 strings
manekin (ma-ne-keen)m.mannequin
manewr (má-nevr) m. maneuver
manewrować (ma-nev-ró-vach) v.
maneuver; steer;handle; switch
maneż (má-nesh) m. riding-
school; horse-driven thrasher

mangan (mán-gan) m. manganese
mania (má-ñya) f. mania ;fad
maniak (má-ñyak) m. maniac;crank
manicure (ma-ñee-keer) m.
manicure;doing one's fingernails
manic (má-ñeech) v. deceive;tempt
maniera (ma-ñe-ra) f. manner
manierka (ma-ñer-ka) f. canteen
manifest (ma-ñee-fest) m. man-
ifesto; a public declaration
manifestacja (ma-ñee-fes-táts-ya)
f. manifestation; demonstration
manifestować (ma-ñee-fes-tó-
vach) v. demonstrate; display
manipulacja (ma-ñee-poo-láts-ya)
f. manipulation; handling
manipulować (ma-ñee-poo-ló-vach)
v. manipulate;handle; tinker
mankiet (mán-ket) m. cuff;turn-up
mankament (man-ká-ment) m. defect; shortcoming; fault
manko (mán-ko) n. (acc.) shortage; allowance for cash errors
manna (mán-na) f. cream of
wheat; a godsend manna
manometr (ma-nó-metr) m. pressure gauge; steam gauge
manowce (ma-nóv-tse) pl. road-
less area; misguided direction
manufaktura (ma-noo-fak-toó-ra)
f. fabrics; manufacture; shop
manuskrypt (ma-noós-kript) m.
manuscript(hand or typewritten)
mankuctwo (mañ-koots-tvo) n.
left-handedness;
mapa (má-pa) f. map; chart
mara (má-ra) f. ghost; apparition; nightmare; dream; vision
marazm (ma-razm) m. sluggishness
marchew (mar-khev) f. carrot
marcepan (mar-tse-pan) m. mar-
zipan; marchpane
margaryna (mar-ga-ri-na) f.
margarine ; marge (slang)
margines (mar-gée-nes) m. margin; edge; border;minor thing
mariaż (mar-yazh) m. marriage
marionetka (mar-yo-nét-ka) f.
puppet;dummy ; figurehead
marka (már-ka) f. mark; brand;
stamp; trade mark; reputation
markotno (mar-kót-no) adv. sad

markotny (mar-kót-ni) adj. m.
peevish; moody; sullen; sad
marksistowski (mark-shees-tóvs-
kee) adj. m. Marxist: of Marx
marksizm (márk-sheezm) m.
Marxism; Marxist believes
marmolada (mar-mo-lá-da) f.
marmalade; jam; shambles
marmur (már-moor) m. marble
marniec (már-ñech) v. deteriorate; waste; decline; perish
marnosć (már-noshch) f. futil-
ity; flimsiness; vanity
marnotrawny (mar-no-tráv-ni)
adj. m. wasteful; prodigal
marnowac (mar-nó-vach) v. waste
marny (már-ni) adj. m. poor;
meagre: sorry; of no value
marsz(marsh) m. march; walk
marsz ! (marsh) excl.: (command)
forward march; split ! get
out !          off you go !
marszałek (mar-shá-wek) m.
marshal; Polish Seym speaker
marszczyc (mársh-chich) v.
wrinkle; frown; crease; ripple
marszruta (marsh-róo-ta) f.
route ; itinerary
martwica (mart-vée-tsa) f.
necrosis ; sinter; travertine
martwic (márt-veech) v. distress;grieve; vex; worry;afflict
martwy (márt-vi) adj. m. dead
martyr (már-tir) m. martyr
maruder (ma-róo-der) m. maraud-
er; straggler; loiterer
marudzic (ma-róo-dźheech)v.
loiter; grumble; lag behind
mary (má-ri) pl. mar; bier
marynarka (ma-ri-nár-ka) f.
jacket; sportscoat; navy
marynarz (ma-rí-nash) m. mariner; sailor; seaman;jack(tar)
marynata (ma-ri-ná-ta) f. pickle
marynowac (ma-ri-nó-vach) v.
pickle; marinade; side-track
marzec (ma-zhets) m. March
marzenie (ma-zhé-ñe) n. dream;
reverie; day dream; pensiveness
marznąć (márzh-nówñch) v. freeze
marzyciel (ma-zhí-chel) m.
dreamer; fantast; visionary

marzyc (má-zhich) v. dream
masa (má-sa) f. bulk; mass
masa perłowa (má-sa per-wó-va)
f. mother of pearl
masakra (ma-sák-ra) f. massacre; carnage; butchery
masakrowac (ma-sak-ró-vach) v.
massacre; slaughter;butcher;
masarnia (ma-sár-ña) f. pork·
meat shop; pork butcher's shop
masarz (má-sash) m. pork-
butcher; pork meat worler
masaz (má-sash) m. massage
masazysta (ma-sa-zhis-ta) m.
masseur ; rubber
maselniczka (ma-sel-ñéech-ka)
f. butter-dish; small churn
maska (más-ka) f. mask; hood
maskowac (mas-kó-vach) v.
disguise; mask;hide; screen
masło (más-wo) n. butter
masonski (ma-són-skee) adj. m.
masonic; freemason's
masowac (ma-só-vach) v. massage
masowo (ma-só-vo) adv. wholesale; in a mass; in masses
masywnosc (ma-siv-noshch) f.
massiveness ; solidity
masywny (ma-siv-ni) adj. m.
massive ; solid; bulky; massy
maszerowac (ma-she-ró-vach) v.
march ; march on; keep marching
maszkara (mash-ká-ra) f. monster; scarecrow; eyesore
maszt (masht) m. mast;flagstaff
maszyna (ma-shí-na) f. machine
maszynka do golenia (ma-shin-
ka do go-lé-ña) safety razor
maszyneria (ma-shi-nér-ya) f.
machinery ; mechanism
maszynista (ma-shi-ñées-ta) m.
railroad engineer
maszynistka (ma-shi-ñéest-ka)
f. typist
maszynopis (ma-shi-nó-pees) m.
typescript; typewritten copy
masć (máshch) f. ointment;
horse color; unguent
maslanka (ma-shlán-ka) f.
buttermilk; product of churning
mat (mat) m. flat color; checkmate (one's opponent)

mata (ma-ta) f. mat; matting
matactwo (ma-táts-tvo) n. legal
trickery; fraudulence; deceit
matczyny (mat-chi-ni) adj. m.
maternal ; mother's
matematyczny (ma-te-ma-tich-ni)
adj. m. mathematical
matematyk (ma-te-ma-tik) m.
mathematician (also student)
matematyka (ma-te-ma-ti-ka) f.
mathematics ;science of numbers
materac (ma-te-rats) m. mattress
materia (ma-ter-ya) f. matter;
stuff; subject ;point;puss;cloth
materialista (ma-ter-ya-lees-ta)
m. materialist
materialistyczny (ma-ter-ya-
lees-tich-ni) adj. m. materia-
listic (opposite to spiritual)
materiał (ma-ter-yaw) m. material; substance; stuff ; cloth
matka (mat-ka) f. mother
matnia (mat-ña) f. snare; trap
matowy (ma-to-vi) adj. m. flat
color ; dull; without luster
matrona (ma-tro-na) f. matron
matryca (ma-tri-tsa) f. matrix;
die ; type;mold ; stencil;swage
matrykuła (ma-tri-koo-wa) f.
register of university students
matrymonialny (ma-tri-mo-nál-ni)
adj. m. matrimonial;marital
matura (ma-too-ra) f. final
highschool examination
maur etański (maw- re-tañ-skee)
adj. m. Moorish ; of Moors
mazać (ma-zach) v. smear; daub
mazgaj (maz-gay) m. crybaby
mazur (ma-zoor) m. mazurka
rythm; Mazurian ; Mazovian
maż (mażh) f. grease;tallow
mącić (mown-cheech) v. blur;
ruffle ; muddy; cloud;confuse
mączka (mownch-ka) f. fine
flour;powder; dust; starch
mądrość (mown-droshch) f. wisdom; intelligence; sagacity
mądry (mown-dri) adj. m. sage
mąka (mown-ka) f. flour; meal
mąż (mownsh) m. husband; man
mąż stanu (mownsh sta-noo)
statesman ; outstanding politician; outstanding diplomat

mdlec (mdlech) v. faint ;weaken
mdlić (mdleech) v. nauseate
mdłosc (mdwoshch) f. nausea
mdło (mdwo) adv. dull; nauseating; sickening; faintly;dimly
meble (meb-le) pl. furniture
mecenas (me-tse-nas) m. lawyer
mech (mekh) m. moss ; down
mechaniczny (me-kha-ñeech-ni)
adj. m. mechanical;automatic
mechanik (me-kha-ñeek) m. mechanic; Jack of all trades
mechanika (me-kha-ñee-ka) f.
mechanics ;practical mechanics
mechanizm (me-kha-ñeesm) m.
mechanism;gear ; device
mecz (mech) m. sport match
meczet (me-chet) m. mosque
medal (me-dal) m. medal
mediacja (med-yáts-ya) f. me-
diation; settling of differences
meduza (me-doo-za) f. jellyfish
medycyna (me-di-tsí-na) f. medicine; art of healing
medyczny (me-dich-ni) adj. m.
medical; medicinal
medyk (me-dik) m. medical student; medic(hist.:physician)
medykament (me-di-ka-ment) m.
drug; medicine (hist. expr.)
medytacja (me-di-táts-ya) f.
meditation; thinking deeply
megafon (me-ga-fon) m. loudspeaker; megaphone,
megaloman (me-ga-lo-man) m. meg-
alomaniac;self appointed boss
melancholia (me-lan-khól-ya) f.
melancholy; the blues;dejection
melasa (me-la-sa) f. molasses
meldować (mel-do-vach) v. report; register; announce
meldunek (mel-doo-nek) m. report; announcement; notification
melioracja (mel-yo-ráts-ya) f.
reclamation of land; drainage
melodia (me-lód-ya) f. melody
meloman (me-lo-man) m. music
lover; music enthusiast
melon (me-lon) m. melon
melonik (me-lo-ñeek) m. bowler
hat; derby; bowler;billycock
memoriał (me-mor-yaw) m. memorial;minutes' journal (commercial)

menażeria (me-na-zhér-ya) f.
menagerie ;animal collection
menażka (me-nazh-ka) f-mess kit
mennica (men-née-tsa) f. mint
menstruacja (men-stroo-áts-ya)
f. menstruation ;,menses
mentalność (men-tál-noshćh) f.
mentality ; a way of thinking
menu (mé-noo) m. menu ;bill of
mer (mer) m. mayor　　ｆare
merdać (mér-daćh) v. wag tail
merytoryczny (me-ri-to-rích-ni)
adj. m. of substance ;essential
meszek (mé-shek) m. down; nap
meta (mé-ta) f. goal; hang-out
metafizyka (me-ta-feé-zi-ka) f.
metaphysics (speculative phil.)
metal (mé-tal) m. metal
metalowy (me-ta-ló-vi) adj. m.
metallic[luster, sound etc)
metalurgia (me-ta-lúr-gya) f.
metallurgy : science of metals
metamorfoza (me-ta-mor-fo-za)
f. metamorphosis ;metamorphism
meteor (me-té-or) m. meteor
meteorologia (me-te-o-ro-lóg-
ya) f. meteorology[system
metoda (me-tó-da) f. method;
metodyczny (me-to-dích-ni) adj.
m. methodical ;systematic
metr (metr) m. meter : 39.37in.
metro (mét-ro) n. subway
metropolia (me-tro-pól-ya) f.
metropolis ; main large city
metryczny (me-trich-ni) adj. m.
metric ; metrical
metryka (me-trí-ka) f. birth-
certificate;the public register
metys (mé-tis) m. metis
mewa (mé-va) f. sea -gull
mezalians (me-zál-yans) m. mis-
alliance ; improper alliance
mezanin (me-zá-ńeen) m. mezzanine
męczarnia (mań-chár-ńa) f. torture; torment; anguish; agony
męczennik (mań-chen-ńeek) m.
martyr : sufferer for faith etc.
męczyć (man-chićh) v. bother;
torment; oppress;tire; exhaust
mędrek (man-drek) m. smart
aleck;know-all; wiseacre
mędrzec (mań-dzhets) m. sage

męka (mań-ka) f. fatigue; torment ;pain;distress; nuisance
męski (mańs-kee) adj. m. masculine; manly ; man's; virile;male
męskość (mańs-koshćh) f. manhood ; virility; manliness
męstwo (mańs-tvo) n. bravery
mętny (mańt-ni) adj. m. turbid;
dull ;dim; blurred;vague; fishy
męty (mań-ti) n. dregs; scum of
society ; underworld; raffle
mężatka (mań-zhát-ka) f. married woman; femme covert (legal.)
mężczyzna (mańzh-chiz-na) m. man
mężnieć (mańzh-ńećh) v. grow
manly ; muster courage;take heart
mężny (mańzh-ni) adj. m. brave
mglisty (mgleés-ti) adj. m.
foggy; misty; dim;nebulous;vague
mgła (mgwa) f. fog; mist ; cloud
mgławica (mgwa-veé-tsa) f, neb-
ula ; cloud;,hazy idea; haze
mgnienie (mgńe-ńe) n. blink;
twinkle ; wink; flash;jiffy;trice
miał (myaw) m. dust; powder
miałki (myaw-kee) adj. m. fine
( sugar ; sand etc.); powdered
miano (myá-no) n. name ;designation
mianować (mya-nó-vaćh) v. appoint ; promote; give a title
mianowicie (mya-no-veé-će)
adv. namely ; to wit ; that is ...
mianownik (mya-nóv-ńeek) m.
denominator; nominative
miara (myá-ra) f. measure; gauge
yard-stick;foot-rule;amount;limit
miarkować (myar-ko-vaćh) v.
guess; note; mitigate one's self
miarodajny (mya-ro-dáy-ni) adj.
m. authoritative; competent
miarowy (mya-ró-vi) adj. m.
rhythmic ; steady; regular
miasteczko (myas-tech-ko) n.
borough ;country town
miasto (myas-to) n. town
miałczeć (myaw-chech) v. mew
miazga (myáz-ga) f. pulp ; squash
miażdżyć (myázh-dzhićh) v. crush;
squash ; smash; grind;lacerate
miąć (myownćh) v. crumple ;wrinkle
miąższ (myównzhsh) m. pulp;
flesh of fruit; pomace; squash

miech 63 międzyplanetarny

miech (myekh) m. bellows
miecz (myech) m. sword
mieć (myeć) v. have;hold; run
miednica (myed-née-tsa) f. hand
washtub ; pelvis;wash basin
miedza (myé-dza) f. farm boundary strip ; bounds; balk
miedź (myedźh) f. copper
miedziak (myé-dźhak) m. copper
penny; copper coin
miedziany (mye-dźhá-ni) adj. m.
of copper; of brass
miedzioryt (mye-dźhó-rit) m.
copper engraving
miejsce (myejs-tse) n. place;
location; spot; room; space;
seat;employment;berth; scene
miejscowość (myey-stso-voshćh)
f. locality ; place;town;village
miejscowy (myeys-tso-vi) adj.
m. local; native; indigenous
miejski (myéys-kee) adj. m. of
town; of city ;urban
mielizna (mye-leéz-na) f. shoal;
shallow water ; sandbank; shelf
mielenie (mye-lé-ñe) n. grinding;
milling; mincing; jabber;prattling;
mielony (mye-ló-ni) adj. m.
ground ; milled; minced;chewed up
mieniać (mye-ñać) v. change;
swap; exchange; convert
mienić (mye-ñeećh) v. call; glitter; shimmer; change color
mienić sie (mye-ñeech shäñ) v.
change one's color; glitter
mienie (mye-ñe) n. property;
belongings ;estate; effects
miernictwo (myer-ñeets-tvo) m.
surveying; land measuring
mierniczy (myer-née-chi) m. surveyor; adj. m. geodetic
miernosc (myer-noshćh)f.medioc-
rity ; average range
miernota (myer-no-ta) f. average
intelligence; mediocrity
mierny (myer-ny) adj. m. mediocre; mean; moderate;indifferent
mierzeja (mye-zhe-ya) f. sand-bar
mierzić(myer-źheećh) v. be disgusting; sicken;make unbearable
mierznąć (myezh-nównćh) v. become disgusting; pall on sb

mierzwa (myesh-va) f. litter
mierzwić (myézh-veećh) v. tousle
mierzyć (mye-zhićh) v. measure;
judge; try on; aim;tend towards
miesiąc (mye-shownts) m. month;
moon ; lunar month _massage
miesic(mye-sheećh)v. knead;
miesięcznie (mye-shäñch-ñe)
adv. monthly ; every month
miesięcznik (mye-shäñch-ñeek)
m. monthly paper ; monthly
mieszać (mye-shaćh) v. mix;
mingle; shuffle; confuse
mieszać się (mye-shach shäñ)
v. meddle; become confused
mieszanina (mye-sha-née-na) f.
mixture; compound ; medley
mieszanka (mye-shan-ka) f.
blend ;mix; mixture;miscellany
mieszczanin (myesh-chá-ñeen) m.
burgher ; townsman; citizen
mieszczaństwo (myesh-chañ-stvo)
n. middle class ;narrow-minded-
mieszek (mye-shek) m.small ness
bellows; bag ; money-bag
mieszkać (myesh-kaćh) v. dwell;
live; stay ;have a flat; lodge
mieszkalny (myesh-kál-ny) adj.
m. inhabitable; habitable
mieszkanie (myesh-ká-ñe) n.
apartment; rooms; lodgings
mieszkaniec (myesh-ká-ñets) m.
inhabitant; lodger; resident
mieść (myeshćh) v. sweep; fling
mieścić (myésh-ćheećh) v. contain; fit ;hold; store; place
mieścina (myesh-ćhee-na) f.
small town, out-of-the-way
miewać (mye-vaćh) v. have
occasionally; feel sometimes
mięczak (myäñ-chak) m. mollusk
mlędlić (myänd-leećh) v. bruise;
hackle; crush; hold forth
między (myäñ-dzi) prep. between;
among; in the midst
międzymorze (myäñ-dzi-mo-zhe) n.
isthmus : narrow strip between sea
międzynarodowy (myañ-dzi-na-ro-
dó-vi) adj. m. international
międzyplanetarny (myañ-dzi-pla-
ne-tár-ni) adj. m. interplane-
tary ; of cosmic space

miękczyc (myáňk-chich) v. soft-
en; move; touch; palatalize
miękisz (myáň-keesh) m. pulp
miękki (myáňk-kee) adj. m.
soft ; flabby; limp; supple
miękko (myáňk-ko) adv. softly
miękkosc (myáňk-koshch) f.
softness ; irresolution;pliancy
mięknąc (myáňk-nównch) v.
soften, up ;relax; relent
miesien (myáň-sheň) m. muscle
mięsisty (myáň-shees-ti) adj.
m. fleshy ;meaty; pulpous
mięsiwo (myáň-shee-vo) n. meat
mięso (myáň-so) n. flesh; meat
mięsozerny (myáň-so-zhér-ni)
adj. m. carnivorous;meat eating
mięta (myáň-ta) f. mint ;trifle
miętosic (myáň-to-sheech) v.
crumble; knead ; crush up
mig (meeg) m. split second;
twinkle; sign language
migac (mee-gach) v. twinkle
migawka (mee-gáv-ka) f. camera
shutter; news in brief
migdał (meeg-daw) m. almond;
tonsil ; good and tasty thing
migi (mee-gee) pl. sign language; speaking by signs
migotac (mee-go-tach) v. twinkle; flicker; waver;whisk;flit
migracja (mee-gráts-ya) f. mi-
gration; migrating (of groups)
migrena (mee-gre-na) f. mi-
graine; sick headache
mijac (mee-yach) v. go past;
pass, by; pass away; go by
mijac się z prawdą (mee-yach
sháň z práv-dówn) swerve from
the truth; to be untrue
mika (mee-ka) f. mica
mikrob (mee-krob) m. microbe
mikrofon (mee-kró-fon) m. microphone ;transmitter
mikroskop (mee-krós-kop) m. microscope
mikroskopijny (m ee-kros-ko-
peéy-ni) adj. m. microscopic
mikstura (meeks-too-ra) f. mixture; concoction; medicine
mila (mee-la) f. mile (1609,35m)
mila morska (mee-la mór-ska) f.
nautical mile ( 1853,2 meters)

milczący (meel-chówn-tsi) adj.
m. silent; reticent ; mum;tacit
milczec (meel-chech) v. be silent; quit talking; be quiet
milczenie (meel-che-ňe) n. silence; keeping still; stillness
milczkiem (meelch-kem) adv.
secretly; stealthily;on the sly
mile (mee-le) adv. pleasantly;
kindly ; warmly; courteously
miliard (meel-yard) m. thousand
million; billion
milicja (mee-leets-ya) f. mi-
litia; police; constabulary
milicjant (mee-leets-yant) m.
policeman; constable
miligram (mee-lee-gram) m. mil-
ligram ; 1/1,000 of a gram
milimetr (mee-leé-metr) m. millimeter: 1/1,000 of a meter
milion (meel-yon) m. million
milioner (meel-yo-ner) m. mil-
lionaire; a very wealthy man
milionowe miasto (meel-yo-no-ve
mya-sto) city of million people
militarny (mee-lee-tár-ni) adj.
m. military; of soldiers
militaryzowac (mee-lee-ta-ri-
zo-vach) v. militarize
milknąc (meelk-nównch) v. abate;
guit talking; die away;subside
miło (mee-wo) adv. nicely;
pleasantly; agreeably
miło poznac (mee-wo poz-nach)
glad to meet ; nice to meet
miłosierdzie (mee-wo-sher-dzhe)
m. charity; mercy;compassion
miłosierny (mee-wo-shér-ni) adj.
m. merciful; charitable
miłosny list (mee-wós-ni leest)
love letter
miłostka (mee-wost-ka) f. little
love affair
miłosc (mee-woshch) f. love
miłosnik (mee-wosh-ňeek) m.
fancier; amateur ; fan
miłowac (mee-wo-vach) v. love
miły (mee-wy) adj. m. pleasant;
beloved; likable;nice;enjoyable
mimiczny (mee-meéch-ni) adj. m.
mimic; imitative:make-believe
mimo (mee-mo) prep. in spite of;
notwithstanding ; (al)though

mimo (mee-mo) adv. past; by
mimochodem (mee-mo-khó-dem) adv.
by the way; incidentally
mimo woli (mee-mo vo-lee) adv.
involuntarily: unintentional
mimowolny (mee-mo-vól-nĭ) adj.
m. involuntary; unintentional
mimo wszystko (mee-mo vshist-ko)
after all; in spite of all
mina (mee-na) f. 1. facial
expression; 2. mine ; air
minaret (mee-na-ret) m. minaret
minąc (mee-nównch) v. pass by
mineralny (mee-ne-rál-ni) adj.
m. mineral;containing minerals
mineralogia (mee-ne-ra-lóg-ya)
f. mineralogy
minerał (mee-né-raw) m. mineral
minia (meeń-ya) f. minium; red
lead base; red lead
miniatura (meeń-ya-too-ra) f.
miniature; miniature copy
minimalny (mee-ńee-mál-ny) adj.
m. minimal;the least possible
minimum (mee-ńee-moom) m. minimum;adv. at the very least
miniony (mee-ńo-ni) adj. m. bygone; of long ago; olden
minister (mee-ńees-ter) m. minister; cabinet member
ministerialny (mee-ńees-ter-
yál-ni) adj. m. ministerial
ministerstwo (mee-ńees-tér-stvo)
n. ministry;department of state
minorowy (mee-no-ró-vi) adj. m.
in minor key; low-spirited
minuta (mee-noo-ta) f. minute
minutowy (mee-noo-tó-vi) adj.
m. of one minute
miodownik (myo-dóv-ńeek) m.
gingerbread
miodowy miesiąc (myo-do-vi mye-
shównts) honeymoon
miodosytnia (myo-do-sit-ńa) f.
meadbar
miot (myot) m. throw; cast; lit-
ler; brood ;animal birth; fling
miotacz (myo-tach) m. thrower
miotacz ognia (myo-tach óg-ńa)
m. firethrower
miotac (myó-tach) v. throw; fling;
toss ;hurl; stir; rave; storm
miotła (myót-wa) f. broom

mióð (myoot) m. honey ; mead
mir (meer) m. esteem ;respect
miriady (meer-ya-di) pl. myr-
iads : large numbers
mirra (meer-ra) f. myrrh
mirt (meert) m. myrtle
misa (mee-sa) f. platter; bowl
misja (mees-ya) f. mission
misjonarz (mees-yo-nash) m.
missionary
miska (mees-ka) f. dish; pan
misterny (mees-tér-ni) adj. m.
fine; delicate; subtle;clever
mistrz (meestsh) m. master;
maestro; champion; expert
mistrzostwo (mees-tzhós-tvo)
m. championship; mastery
mistrzowski ruch (mees-tzhóvs-
kee rookh) masterstroke
mistycyzm (mees-ti-cizm) m.
mysticism ;intuitive knowledge
mistyczny (mees-tich-ni) adj.
m. mystic ; mystical: occult
mistyfikacja (mees-ti-fee-
káts-ya)f.mystification
mistyfikowac (mees-ti-fee-kó-
vach) v. mystify; hoax;deceive
mistyk (mees-tik) m. mystic
misyjny (mee-síy-ni) adj. m.
missionary; mission-
miś (meesh) m. teddy bear;
nylon fur coat or jacket
mit (meet) m. myth; mythology
mitologia (mee-to-lóg-ya) f.
mythology : study of myths
mitologiczny (mee-to-lo-geéch-
ni) adj. m. mythologic
mitra (mee-tra) f. mitre
mitręga (mee-trán-ga) f. delay;
waste of time ; delay; dawdler
mitręzyc (mee-trán-zhych) v.
loiter; waste time;dally; lag
mityczny (mee-tích-ni) adj. m.
mythical; mythic ; fictitious
mitygowac (mee-ti-gó-vach) v.
quiet; appease ;check;restrain
mityng (mee-ting) m. (mass)
meeting : a gathering of people
mizantrop (mee-zán-trop) m.
misanthrope ; hater of people
mizdrzyc się (meez-dzhich shań)
v. ogle; wheedle ;make eyes

mizerak (mee-zé-rak) m. poor
soul; weakling; poor devil
mizeria (mee-zér-ya) f. cucumber salad ; shabby possessions
mizerny (mee-zér-ni) adj. m.
meager; ill-looking; mean;paltry
mknąć (mknównch) v. fleet;rush
mlaskać (mlás-kach)v.lap; smack
mlecz (mlech) m. marrow ;milt
mleczarnia (mle-chár-ña) f.
dairy ; creamery : milk bar
mleczny (mlech-ni) adj. m. milk;
milky; dairy; lactic;milk-white
mleć (mlech) v. grind; mill
mleko (mlé-ko) n. milk
młocarnia (mwo-tsár-ña) f.
thresher ;threshing-machine
młocka (mwóts-ka) f. threshing
młoda (mwó-da) adj. f. young
młode (mwó-de) adj. pl. young
n.pl. the young; litter
młodociany (mwo-do-chá-ni) adj.
m. juvenile; youthful
młodosc (mwo-doshch) f. youth
młody (mwo-di) adj. m. young
młodzian (mwo-dzhan) m. young
man ; lad ; youth
młodzieniaszek (mwo-dżhe-ña-
shek) m. sprig; stripling;lad
młodzieniec (mwo-dżhé-ñets) m.
young man ; lad: youth
młodzieńczy (mwo-dżheñ-chi)
adj. m. youthful
młodzież (mwo-dzhesh) f. youth;
young generation
młodzik (mwo-dzheek)m. youngster; teenager; youngling
młokos (mwó-kos) m. kid
młot (mwot) m. sledge; hammer
młotek (mwo-tek) m. hammer;
tack-hammer ;clapper
młócić (mwoó-cheech) v. thrash
młyn (mwin) m. mill; grinder
młynarz (mwi-nash) m. miller
młynek (mwi-nek) m. handgrinder
młyński (mwiñ-skee) adj. m.
mill-; of a mill
mnich (mñeekh) m. monk; friar
mniej (mñey) adv. less; fewer
mniej wiecej (mñey vyañ-tsey)
more or less ; about; round
mniejsza o to '(mñey-sha o to)
never mind that (exp.)

mniejszosc (mñey-shoshch) f.
minority; the lesser part
mniejszy (mñey-shi) adj. m.
smaller; lesser ;less; minor
mniemać (mñe-mach) v. suppose;
deem ; imagine;think; consider
mniemanie (mñe-ma-ñe) n. opinion ;notion;conviction
mniszka (mñeesh-ka) f. nun
mnoga (mnó-ga) num. plural
mnogi (mnó-gee) adj. m. numerous ; of the plural
mnogosc (mnó-goshch) f. abundance; plurality; multitude
mnożenie (mno-zhé-ñe) n. multiplication ;increase; breeding
mnożyć (mnó-zhich) v. multiply
mnóstwo (mnoós-tvo) n. very
many; multitude; swarm; loads
mobilizacja (mo-bee-lee-záts-
ya) f. mobilization ;call-up
mobilizować (mo-bee-lee-zó-
vach) v. mobilize; call up
moc (mots)f. might; great-
deal; power;vigor;strength
mocarstwo (mo-tsár-stvo) n.
strong country;(world)power
mocarz (mó-tsash) m. strong
man; potentate; powerful man
mocny (móts-ni) adj. m. strong
mocować się (mo-tsó-vach shañ)
v. wrestle; exert oneself
mocz (moch) m. urine
moczar (mo-char) m. bog; marsh
moczopędny (mo-cho-pañd-ni)
adj. m. diuretic
moczowy (mo-chó-vi) adj. m.
uric; urinary; of urine
moczyć (mo-chich) v. wet;
drench; steep; soak;urinate
moda (mó-da) f. fashion
model (mó-del) m. model
modelować (mo-de-ló-vach) v.
model; shape; mold; fashion
modernizować (mo-der-ni-zó-vach)
v. modernize;bring up to date
modlić się (mód-leech shañ) v.
pray; say one's prayers
modlitewnik (mod-lee-tév-ñeek)
m. prayer-book
modlitwa (mod-leét-va) f.
prayer ; grace(at meal time)

modła (mod-wa) f. mold; standard; fashion; model; pattern
modniarka (mod-ńár-ka) f. milliner; modiste; hat maker
modny (mod-ni) adj. m. fashionable; in fashion;in vogue
modry (mod-ri) adj. m. azure-blue; deep blue;cerulean blue
modrzew (mod-zhev) m. larch
modulacja (mo-doo-láts-ya) f.
modulation ;inflection
modulować (mo-doo-ló-vaćh) v.
modulate; inflect; regulate
modyfikacja (mo-di-fee-káts-ya)
f. modification; alteration
modyfikować (mo-di-fee-kó-vaćh)
v. modify; alter; qualify
modystka (mo-dist-ka) f. modiste; milliner; hat maker
mogący (mo-gown-tsi) adj. m.
able; capable; competent
mogiła (mo-gee-wa) f. tomb
mojżeszowy (moy-zhe-sho-vi)
adj. m. Mosaic : of Moses
mokka (mok-ka) f. natural coffee :, mocha: Mocha coffee
moknąć (mok-nownćh) v. get wet;
get soaked, drenched ;be soaked
mokradło (mo-krád-wo) n. bog
mokry (mok-ri) adj. m. wet;
moist ; watery;rainy; sweaty
molekularny (mo-le-koo-lár-ni)
adj. m. molecular; of molecule
molekuła (mo-le-koó-wa) f. molecule ; smallest particle
molestować (mo-les-tó-vaćh) v.
molest;, annoy; vex; trouble
molo (mó-lo) n. pier; mole;
jetty; breakwater ; quay
moment (mo-ment) m. moment
momentalny (mo-men-tál-ni) adj.
m. instantaneous ;immediate
monarcha (mo-nár-kha) m. monarch ; sovereign: king
monarchista (mo-nar-khees-ta)
m. monarchist ; royalist
moneta (mo-né-ta) f. coin ;chink
moneta brzecząca (mo-ne-ta
bzhań-chówn-tsa) cash; coins
mongolski (mon-gól-skee) adj. m.
Mongol ; of Mongolia
monitor (mo-ńee-tor) m. monitor

monitować (mo-ńee-tó-waćh) v.
admonish ; monitor : check on
monogram (mo-nó-gram) m. monogram; initials in a design
monokl (mó-nokl) m. eye-glass
monolog (mo-nó-log) m. monologue; soliloquy of one actor
monopol (mo-nó-pol), m. monopoly
monoteizm (mo-no-té-eezm) m.
monotheism; belief in one god
monotonia (mo-no-tóń-ya) f. monotony; sameness; no variety
monotonny (mo-no-toń-ni) adj.
m. monotonous ;drab; dull
monstrualny (mon-stroo-ál-ni)
adj. m. monstrous ; horrible
monstrum (mon-stroom) n. monster ; monstrosity
montaż (mon-tazh) m. mounting;
assembling ;installation; set-up
monter (mon-ter), m. installator
montować (mon-tó-vaćh) v. install; put together; put up
monumentalny (mo-noo-men-tál-ni) adj. m. monumental
mops (mops) m. pug-dog
moralizator (mo-ra-lee-zá-tor)
m. moralizer
moralizować (mo-ra-lee-zó-vaćh)
v. moralize; discuss morality
moralność (mo-rál-noshćh) f.
morals ; morality; ethics
moralny (mo-rál-ni) adj. m.
moral; ethical;of good conduct
morał (mó-raw) m. moral lesson
moratorium (mo-ra-tó-ryoom) n.
moratorium; legalized delay
mord (mord) m. murder; slaughter
morda (mór-da) f. snout; muzzle;
vulg: mug; kisser; puss; phiz
morderca (mor-der-tsa) m. murderer; assassin; cutthroat
morderczy (mor-der-chi) adj. m.
murderous; cutthroat; deadly
morderstwo (mor-der-stvo) n.
murder; assassination
mordęga (mor-dań-ga) f. toil;
drudge;, moil;fag; strain
mordować (mor-dó-vaćh) v. kill;
torment;harass;toil;sweat;worry
mordować się (mor-dó-vaćh shań)
v. toil; kill oneself with work

morela (mo-ré-la) f. apricot
morena (mo-ré-na) f. moraine
morfina (mor-fée-na) f. morphine (derivative of opium)
morfologia (mor-fo-lóg-ya) f. morphology: science of forms
morga (mór-ga) f. acre
morowy (mo-ró-vi) adj. m. pestilential; clever; good buddy; fine fellow; first-rate
mors (mors) m. walrus
morska choroba (mórs-ka kho-ró-ba) seasickness; dizziness
morski (mórs-kee) adj. m. maritime; sea; nautical; naval
morwa (mór-va) f. mulberry
morze (mozhe) n. sea ; ocean
morzyć (mo-zhich) v. starve
mosiądz (mo-shównts) m. brass
moskit (mos-keet) m. mosquito
most (most) m. bridge
mościc (mósh-cheech) v. pad (nest); make a bed of straw
motać (mo-tach) v. reel; embroil; entangle; intrigue; spool
motek (mo-tek) m. reel ; ball
motłoch (mot-wokh) m. mob
motocykl (mo-to-tsikl) m. motorcycle (a two-wheeled vehicle)
motor (mo-tor) m. motor
motorówka (mo-to-róov-ka) f. motorboat
motoryzacja (mo-to-ri-záts-ya) f. motorization;mechanization
motoryzować (mo-to-ri-zo-vach) v. motorize; mechanize
motyka (mo-ti-ka) f. hoe
motyl (mo-til) m. butterfly
motyw (mo-tiv) m. motif; motive
motywować (mo-ti-vó-vach) v. give reasons; explain;justify
mowa (mo-va) f. speech; language
mozaika (mo-záy-ka) f. mosaic
mozolić (mo-zó-leech) v. toil; take pains; exert oneself
mozolny (mo-zol-ni) adj. m. toilsome;strenuous arduous
mozół (mo-zoow) m. exertion
moździerz (mózh-dżhesh) m. mortar ; mine thrower
może (mo-zhe) adv. perhaps; maybe; very likely; how about?

możliwość (mozh-lee-voshch) f. possibility; chance; contigency
możliwości (mozh-lee-vosh-chee) pl. scope ;vistas; capabilities
możliwy (mozh-lee-vi) adj. possible ; fairly good; passable
można (mozh-na) v. imp. it is possible; one may; one can
możność (mozh-noshch) f. power; freedom to; free choice to
możny (mózh-ni) adj. m. potent; powerful; mighty
móc (moots) v. (potentially) to be able ; be capable
mój (mooy) pron. my; mine
mol (mool) m. moth
mól książkowy (mool kshównzh-kó-vi) bookworm
mor (moor) m. pestilence; epidemic ;plague ; pest
mórg (moorg) m. acre
mówca (móov-tsa) m. speaker
mówić (moo-veech) v. speak; talk; say; tell ;say things
mównica (moov-nee-tsa) f. (pulpit); speaker's platform
mózg (moozk) m. brain
mózgowy (mooz-gó-vi) adj. m. cerebral ; of the brain
mroczny (mroch-ni) adj. m. dusky; gloomy ;obscure;dark
mrok (mrok) m. dusk; twilight
mrowić się (mró-veech shań) v. swarm ; teem; be alive
mrowie (mrov-ye) n. swarm; tingle ;gooseflesh;creeps
mrowisko (mro-vées-ko) n. anthill ; ants'nest
mrozić (mro-żheech) v. freeze; congeal; refrigerate ; chill
mroźny (mróżh-ni) adj. m.frosty; icy ; freezing
mrówka (mróov-ka) f. ant ;emmet
mróz (mroos) m. frost ;the cold
mruczeć (mroo-chech) v. mumble; mutter ; purr; murmur; grumble
mrugać (mroo-gach) v. twinkle; blink; wink ; flicker; flinch
mruk (mrook) m. mumbler; grumbler; man of few words;growler
mrukliwy (mrook-lee-vi) adj. m. mumbling; sulky; gruff;taciturn

mrużyć (mroo-zhich) v. blink; wink ; squint; half-shut(eyes)
mrzonka (mzhón-ka) f. illusion
msza (msha) f. mass (in church)
mszalny (mshál-ni) adj. m. for mass; of mass (in the church)
mszał (mshaw) m. missal
mściciel (mshchee-chel) m. avenger ; retaliator
mścić (mshcheech) v. avenge
mściwy (mshchee-vi) adj. m. vindictive; vengeful
mszczenie (mshche-ne) n. vengeance ; retaliation
mszyca (mshi-tsa) f. mite
mszysty (mshis-ti) adj. m. mossy
mucha (moo-kha) f. fly
mufka (moof-ka) f. muff
mularz (moo-lash) m. mason
mulat (moo-lat) m. mulatto
mulisty (moo-lees-ty) adj. m. muddy; oozy; slimy ; sludgy
muł (moow) m. ooze; slime
muł (moow) m. mule
mumia (moom-ya) f. mummy
mundur (moon-door) m. uniform
municypalny (moo-nee-tsi-pál-ni) adj. m. municipal
munsztuk (moon-shtook) m. (bridle) bit; mouthpiece
mur (moor) m. brick wall
murarz (moo-rash) m. bricklayer
murawa (moo-ra-va) f. lawn
murować (moo-ró-vach) v. lay-bricks ; build in brick(in stone)
murowany (moo-ro-vá-ni) adj. m. of bricks; of stone ; certain
murzyn (moo-zhin) m. negro
mus 1, (moos) m. necessity; compulsion ; constraint
mus 2., (moos) m. froth ;mousse
musiec (moo-shech) v. be obliged to; have to ;be forced; must
muskać (moos-kach) v. touch lightly ; skim; stroke
muskularny (moos-koo-lár-ni) adj. m. muscular ; strong;hefty;beefy
muskuł (moos-koow) m. muscle
musować (moo-so-vach) v. foam; froth ; bubble; fizz; sparkle
muszka (moosh-ka) f. fly; gunbead; face skin-spot ;bow-tie; midge; dry-fly; patch (on skin)

muszkat (moosh-kat) m. nutmeg
muszkiet (moosh-ket) m. musket ; smooth bore firearm
muszla (moosh-la) f. shell;conch
musztarda (moosh-tar-da) f. mustard seasoning
musztra (moosh-tra) f. (drill) training; exercise
muslin (moosh-leen) m. muslin
mutacja (moo-táts-ya) f. mutation; change; variation
muterka (moo-ter-ka) f. (bolt) nut; female screw
muza (moo-za) f. Muse
muzealny (moo-ze-ál-ni) adj. m. of museum
muzeum (moo-ze-oom) n. museum
muzułmanin (moo-zoow-ma-neen) m. Moslem (Mussulman)
muzyczny (moo-zich-ni) adj. m. musical; set to music
muzyk (moo-zik) m. musician
muzyka (moo-zi-ka) f. music
muzykalnosc (moo-zi-kál-noshch) f. ear for music
muzykalny (moo-zi-kál-ni) adj. m. having ear for music
muzykant (moo-zi-kant) m. low class musician ; bandsman
my (mi) pron. we ; us
myc (mich) v. wash
mycka (mits-ka) f. skull-cap
mydlarnia (mid-lár-na) f. soap-store; soap-works; perfumery
mydlarstwo (mid-lar-stvo) n. soap-making; soap-boiling
mydlarz (mid-lash) m. soap-maker
mydlic (mid-leech) v. soap; froth; dress someone down
mydlic oczy (mid-leech o-chi) v. pull wool over eyes
mydliny (mid-lee-ni) pl. soapsuds; lather
mydło (mid-wo) n. soap; soft soap
mylic (mi-leech) v. mislead; misguide;confuse; deceive
mylny (mil-ni) adj. m. wrong.
mysz (mish) f. mouse
myszkować (mish-kó-vach) v. covertly explore; trace scent
mysl (mishl) f. thought; idea
myslący (mish-lown-tsi) adj. m. thoughtful; reflective

myśleć (mish-lech) v. think
myśliciel (mish-lee-chel) m.
thinker ;one who thinks a lot
myśliwiec (mish-leev-yets) m.
fighter plane ; fighter pilot
myśliwy (mish-lee-vi) m. hunter
myślnik (mishl-ñeek) m. dash
(mark); hyphen
myślowy (mish-lo-vi) adj. m.
mental;, reflective; intellectual
myto, (mi-to) n. toll; tollgate
mżyc (mzhich) v. drizzle
na (na) prep. on; upon; at;
for; by; in;
NOTE: verbs with prefix na
NOT INCLUDED HERE: CHECK WITH-
OUT THE PREFIX"na"
nabawic się (na-ba-veech shañ)
v. bring upon oneself; incur
nabawic strachu (na-ba-veech
stra-khoo)v.frighten
nabiał (na-byaw) m. dairy
products including eggs
nabiegac się (na-bye-gach shañ)v.
have, run a lot; exert oneself
nabic (na-beech) v. load weapon;
beat up(somebody); whack
nabiegły krwią (na-byeg-wi
krvyown) adj.m. bloodshot
nabierac (na-bye-rach) v. take;
take in; tease; cheat; amass
nabijac (na-bee-yach) v. stud;
(repeatedly) load gun
nabijac się (na-bee-yach shañ)
v. make fun of (somebody)
nabożeństwo (na-bo-zheñ-stvo)
n. church service
nabożny (na-bozh-ni) adj. m.
pious; religious; godly;devoutly
nabrac (na-brach) v. take; take
in; tease; cheat; gather;swell
nabój (na-booy) m. charge; car-
trige; round of ammunition
nabrzeże (na-bzhe-zhe) n. wharf;
embankment; landing-pier
nabrzmiały (na-bzhmya-wi) adj.
m. swollen : distended
nabytek (na-bi-tek) m. acquisition; purchase;new recruit
nabrzmiewac (na-bzhmye-vach) v.
swell ;plump up; plump out
nabywac (na-bi-vach) v. acquire;
obtain; gain; buy; purchase

nabywca (na-biv-tsa) m. buyer
nacechowany (na-tse-kho-va-ni)
adj. m. marked; characterized
nachodzic (na-kho-dzheech)v.
intrude; (abstr.) haunt
nachylac (na-khi-lach) v. stoop;
bend; incline; lean ;tilt;slant
nachylenie (na-khi-le-ñe) n.tilt
slope; inclination ;batter;slant
nacięcie (na-chañ-che) n. incision; notch; cut ;nick;score
naciągac (na-chown-gach) v.
streach; draw; strain; pull
one's leg;take sb in; infuse
naciek (na-chek) m. infiltration; leak ; swelling
nacierac (na-che-rach) v. rub;
attack; harass ; demand
nacinac (na-chee-nach) v. notch;
cut; score; nick;hoax;dupe
nacisk (na-cheesk) m. pressure;
stress; accent;thrust; push
naciskac (na-chees-kach) v.
press; urge ;bear on; push
nacjonalista (na-tsyo-na-lees-
ta) m. nationalist
nacjonalizacja (na-tsyo-na-lee-
zats-ya) f. nationalization
nacjonalizm (na-tsyo-na-leezm)
m. nationalism
nacjonalizowac (na-tsyo-na-lee-
zo-vach) v. nationalize
naczekac się (na-che-kach shañ)
v. wait too long:tire of waiting
na czczo (na chcho) adv. on an
empty stomach : unfed; fasting
naczelnik (na-chel-ñeek) m.
manager; chief; head; master
naczelny (na-chel-ni) adj. m.
chief; head; paramount; primate; principal;main;paramount
naczerpac (na- cher-pach) v.
dip up; draw (fluid);scoop up
naczynie (na-chi-ñe) n. vessel
nad (nad) prep. over; above; on
upon; beyond; at; of;for
nadajnik (na-day-ñeek) m.
transmitter : feeder
nadal (na-dal) adv. still; in
future; continue (to do)
nadaremnie (na-da-rém-ñe) adv.
in vain; unsuccessfully; to no
purpose; without result

nadaremny (na-da-rém-ni) adj.
m. fruitless; vain;unsuccessful
nadarzać się (na-da-zhach shán)
v. happen; occur; turn up
nadawać (na-da-vach) v. confer
bestow ;grant; endow; christen
nadawca (na-dav-tsa) m. sender
nadąć (na-downch) v. puff up
nadąsany (na-down-sa-ni) adj.
m. sulky; sullen; stuffy
nadążać (na-down-zhach) v. keep
up with; cope with ;keep pace
nadbałtycki (nad-baw-tits-kee)
adj. m. on the Baltic ;Baltic
nadbiec (nad-byets) v. come
running up; hasten up ;run up
nadbrzeże (nad-bzhe-zhe) n.
shore; coast; littoral
nadbrzeżny (nad-bzhézh-ni) adj.
m. coastal; sea-shore
nadbudowa (nad-boo-do-va) f.
superstructure ;added floor
nadbudować (nad-boo-do-vach)
v. build on ;add an upper floor
nadchodzić (nad-khó-dzheech)v.
approach; arrive; come
nadciągać (nad-chown-gach) v.
draw near; be nearing; come
nadciśnienie (nad-cheesh-ńe-ńe)
n. excess pressure;hypertension
nadczłowiek (nad-chwo-vyek) m.
superman ; superhuman man
nadejście (na-dey-shche) v.
coming; arrival; oncoming
nadepnąć (na-dep-nownch) v.
step on ; tread on (crushing)
nader (na-der) adv. greatly;
excessively; highly; most
nadesłać (na-de-swach) v. send
in; forward; remit
nade wszystko (na-de vshist-ko)
adv. above all (else)
nadęty (nad-án-ti) adj. m.
puffed up; inflated; superior
nadgraniczny (nad-gra-ńeech-ni)
adj. m. near-border ;frontier-
nadjechać (nad-yé-khach) v.
drive up; come up; arrive
nadlecieć (nad-le-chech) v. fly
in ; arrive in a hurry
nadleśniczy (nad-leśh-ńee-chi)
m. chief ranger; forest inspector: head of rangers

nadliczbowy (nad-leech-bó-vi)
adj. m. overtime; additional
nadludzki (nad-loodz-ki) adj.
m. superhuman ; divine
nadmiar (nád-myar) m. excess
nadłamać (nad-wa-mach) v. break
slightly; cause a slight break
nadmienić (nad-myé-ńeech) v.
mention ; allude;hint; add
nadmierny (nad-myér-ni) adj.
m. excessive; extravagant;undue
nadmorski (nad-mor-skee) adj.
m. seaside-;maritime
nadmuchać (na-dmoo-khach) v.
inflate; blow up with air
nadobny (na-dob-ny) adj. m.
handsome; comely; pretty
nadobowiązkowy (nad-o-bo-vyownz-
kó-vi) adj. m. optional
na doł (na doow) down; down
stairs; downwards
nadpic (nád-peech) v. take a
sip; start overfilled drink
nadpływać (nad-pwi-nównch) v.
sail in; swim in; arrive
nadprodukcja (nad-pro-dook-
tsya) f. excess production
nadprogramowy (nad-pro-gra-mo-
vi) adj. m. extra; additional
nadprzyrodzony (nad-pzhy-ro-dzó-
ni) adj. m. supernatural
nadpsuty (nad-psóo-ti) adj. m.
partly spoiled; impaired
nadrabiać (nad-ráb-yach) v.
catch up with; make up; work
ahead of schedule:compensate for
nadruk (na-drook) m. overprint
nadrzędny (nad-zhánd-ni) adj.
m. superior; primary;precedent
nadskakiwać (nad-ska-kee-vach)
v. try to ingratiate oneself
nadsłuchiwać (nad-swoo-khee-
vach) v. strain to listen
nadspodziewany (nad-spo-dżhe-vá-
ni) adj. m. unexpected
nadstawiać (nad-stáv-yach) v.
expose; risk; hold out; cock
nadto (nád-to) adv. moreover;
besides; too much; too many
nadużycie (nad-oo-zhi-che) n.
abuse; excess; misuse
nadużywać (nad-oo-zhi-vach) v.
abuse; take advantage ;strain

nadwaga (nad-vá-ga) f. overweight;allowed extra weight
nadwartość (nad-vár-toshch) f.
overvalue in economics
nadwątlic (nad-vownt-leech) v.
weaken; impair; damage
nadwiślański (nad-veesh-lań-
skee) adj. m. on the Vistula
nadwodny (nad-vód-ni) adj. m.
near water; riverside; aquatic
nadwozie (nad-vó-zhe) m. car-
body; body of a car or truck
nadwyrężac (nad-vi-rán-zhach)
v. impair; strain; weaken
nadwyżka (nad-vízh-ka) f. surplus; excess amount
nadymac (na-di-mach) v. puff up
nadymic (na-di-meech) v. fill
with smoke;make a lot of smoke
nadzieja (na-dźhe-ya) f. hope
nadziemski (nad-żhem-skee) adj.
m. celestial; heavenly;divine
nadzienie (na-dźhe-ne) n.
stuffing ; filling; forcemeat
nadziewac (na-dżhe-vach) v.
stuff;pierce with;put on; fill
nadzorca (nad-zór-tsa) m. overseer; superintendent;supervisor
nadzór (nád-zoor) m. supervision
nadzwyczaj (nad-zvi-chay) adv.
unusually; extremely; most
nadzwyczajny (nad-zvi-chay-ni)
adj. m. extraordinary; extreme
nafta (náf-ta) f. petroleum
naftalina (naf-ta-lée-na) f,
naphthalene; naphthaline
nagabywac (na-ga-bi-vach) v.
annoy; accost; trouble;molest
nagana (na-gá-na) f. blame
nagi (ná-gi) adj. m. naked;
bare ; nude; bald; empty
naginac (na-gee-nach) v. bend
down; submit to; adapt; bow
nagle (nág-le) adv. suddenly
naglic (nág-leech) v. urge
nagłość (nág-woshch) f. urgency
nagłówek (na-gwoó-vek) m. heading; caption; title; headline
nagły (nág-wi) adj. m. sudden;
urgent;instant;abrupt; pressing
nagminny (na-gmeen-ni) adj. m.
universal;usual;current;general

nagniotek (na-gnó-tek) m.
(skin) corn; callus on the skin
nagonka (na-gón-ka) f. campaign
against; hue and cry against
nagosc (ná-goshch) f. nudity
nagradzac (na-grá-dzach) v.
reward; give prize;recompense
nagrobek (na-gró-bek) m. tomb
nagroda (na-gro-da) f. reward
nagrodzic (na-gró-dźheech)v.
reward; requite; recompense
nagromadzic (na-gro-má-dźheech)
v. accumulate; amass; heap up
nagrzewac (na-gzhé-vach) v.
warm up ; heat up; preheat
naigrawac (na-ee-gra-vach) v.
mock; scoff; deride;ridicule
naiwny (na-eev-ni) adj. m. naive
najazd (ná-yazt) m. invasion
najbardziej (nay-bár-dźhey)
adv. most(of all)
najechac (na-ye-khach)v.overrun;
invade; run into;ram; crowd
najedzony (na-ye-dzó-ni) adj.
m. full (of food); satiated
najem (ná-yem) m. hire
najemnik (na-yém-neek) m.
hireling; mercenary;free lance;
soldier of fortune;wage earner
najemny (na-yém-ni) adj. m.venal;
mercenary; hired labor
najesc się (ná-yeshch shań) v.
eat plenty of; eat a lot
najeźdźca (na-yeźhdźh-tsa) m.
invader; assailant; violator
najeżdżac (na-yezh-dzhach) v.
invade; run into; attack; ram
najeżony (na-ye-zho-ni) adj. m.
bristling; bristly ; beset
najgorszy (nay-gor-shi) adj. m.
worst; the worst of all
najgorzej (nay-go-zhey) adv.
worst of all : worst possible
najlepiej (nay-lép-yey) adv.
best ; best of all
najlepszy (nay-lép-shi) adj. m.
best; best of all; best possible
najmniej (náy-mney) adv. least
najmniejszy (nay-mney-shi) adj.
m. least; smallest; least of all
najmowac (nay-mó-vach) v. rent;
hire; engage; lease

najpierw (náy-pyerv) adv. first
of all.in the first place
najście (naysh-che) n. intrusion; inroad; invasion;incursion
najsc (nayshch) v., intrude
najwięcej (nay-vyań-tsey) adv.
most of all (worst, of all)
najwiekszy (nay-vyań-shi) adj.
m. biggest; largest; extreme
najwyżej (nay-vi-zhey) adv.
highest; at the very most
najwyższy (nay-vizh-shi) adj.
m. highest; top; utmost
nakarmic (na-kár-meech) v. feed
nakaz (na-kas) m. order ;writ
nakazywac (na-ka-zi-vach) v.
order; demand; command
nakleic (na-klé—eech) v. stick
on ; pastę up; mount; post
nakład (na-kwad), m. outlay
nakładac (na-kwa-dach) v. lay
on; put on; plaçe; set;spread
nakładca (na-kwád-tsa) m. publisher (of printed work )
nakłaniac (na-kwa-nach) v. persuade ;induce; bring;get;urge
na koniec (na kó-nets) adv.
finally ; at the end
nakreslac (na-krésh-lach) v.
delineate ; sketch;draft;write
nakręcac (na-krań-tsach) v. wind
up; shoot (movie);turn ;direct
nakrętka (na-krańt-ka) f.(screw)
nut; female screw; jam nut
nakrycie, (na-kri-che) n. cover
nakrywac (na-kri-vach) v. cover
nakrywka (na-kriv-ka) f. lid
na kształt (na kshtawt) in form
of...;in shape of; a kind of...
nalac (na-lach) v. pour in; pour
on (liquid only,no sand etc.)
nalegac (na-lé-gach) v. insist
naleganie (na-le-gá-ne) n. insistence ;urgent demand
nalepiac (na-lép-yach) v. stick
on; paste on; mount; glue on
nalepka (na-lép-ka) f. label
naleśnik (na-lésh-neek) m. pancake wrap around stuffing
nalewac (na-le-vach) v. pour in
należec (na-lé-zhech) v. belong
należnosc (na-lézh-noshch) f.
due; ration ; charge; fee

należny (na-lézh-ni) adj. m.
due. owing; rightful; proper
nalezycie (na-le-zhi-che) adv.
properly; duly; suitably
nalezyty (na-le-zhi-ti) adj.
m. proper; right; appropriate
nalot (na-lot) m. air raid;
(skin) rush ; coating
naładowac (na-wa-do-vach) v.
load; charge; cram
nałogowiec (na-wo-go-vyets) m.
addict; chain-smoker
nałogowy (na-wo-gó-vi) adj. m.
addicted ; inveterate;habitual
nałogowy pijak (na-wo-go-vi
pee-yak) alcoholic
nałóg (na-woog) m. addiction
namacalny (na-ma-tsál-ni) adj.
m. tangible; substantial
namaszczac (na-másh-chach)v.
anoint ; grease; smear
namaszczenie (na-mash-che-ne)
n. unction ;anointing
namawiac (na-máv-yach) v.
persuade ; prompt; urge;egg on
namazac (na-má-zach) v. daubover; anoint ; scrawl(scribble)
namiastka (na-myást-ka) f.
substitute; ersatz; stopgap
namiernik (na-myér-neek) m.
direction finder; pelorus
namiestnik (na-myést-neek) m.
regent; governor; viceroy
namiętnosc (na-myańt-noshch) f.
passion ; infatuation; fervor
namiętny (na-myańt-ni) adj. m.
passionate ; keen; ardent;lusty
namiot (na-myot) m. tent
namoczyc (na-mo-chich) v. wet;
soak ; soak; steep; drench
namoknąc (na-mók-nownch) v. get
soaked ; become saturated
namowa (na-mó-va) f. persuasion
namulic (na-moó-leech) v. slime
up ; silt up; mud up; ooze up
namydlic (na-mid-leech) v.
soap up ; put soap lather on
namysł (na-misw) m. reflection
namyslac się(na-mish-lach shan)v.
ponder; reflect ; think over
nanosic (na-nó-sheech) v.bring;
deposit; plot; track (mud)
na nowo (na nó-vo) adv. anew

naocznie (na-óch-ńe) adv. by
eye; visually ; clearly
naoczny świadek (na-óch-ni
shvyá-dek) eyewitness;bystander
na odwrót (na ód-vroot) adv.
inversely;the other way round
na ogół (na ó-goow) adv. (in
general) generally; on the whole
na około (na o-kó-wo) adv. all
around; about;right round
naokoło (na-o-kó-wo) prep. round
naonczas (na-ón-chas) adv. at
that time; then;in those days
naoliwić (na-o-lee-veech) v. oil;
lubricate : grease;make slippery
na opak (na ó-pak) adv. backward; perversely; the wrong way
na ostatek (na o-stá-tek) adv.
finally; in the end; at last
naostrzyć (na-os-tzhich) v.
sharpen up ; become sharp
na ościez (na ósh-chesh) adv.
wide open; opened all the way
na oślep (na ósh-lep) adv. blind-
ly; full tilt; headlong
na ówczas (na oóv-chas) adv. at
that time ;then; in those days
napad (ná-pad) m. assault;attempt
napadac (na-pá-dach) v. assail
napar (ná-par) m. infusion;
brew ; a beverage brewed
naparstek (na-pár-stek) m. thimble: dram; thimble full
naparzyć (na-pa-zhich) v. infuse
napaskudzić (na-pas-koo-dźheech)
v. soil up; make a mess; dirty
napastliwy (na-past-lee-vi) adj.
m. aggressive ;malicious;bitter
napastnik (na-pást-ńeek) m. aggressor; forward center (sport)
napastowac (na-pas-to-vach) v.
pester; attack; wax molest;worry
napaśc (ná-pashch) f. assault
napawać (na-pá-vach) v. fill up
(with feelings .panic, wander)
napatrzyć się (na-pát-shich sháń)
v, see enough ;have a good look
napełniac (na-péw-ńach) v. fill
up ; inspire; imbue; pervade
napewno (na-pév-no) adv. surely;
certainly; for sure ;without fail
naped (ná-paňd) m. propulsion:
drive;force; driving gear

napędowy (na-pań-dó-vi) adj.
m. motive ;driving; impulsive
napędzac (na-páń-dzach) v. chase
in; propel ;round up;drift in
napic się (ná-peech sháń) v.
have a drink ; quench one's thirst
napierac (na-pye-rach) v. press
forward; insist,; advance
napięcie (na-pyáń-che) n. tension; strain; voltage;intensity
napiętek (na-pyáń-tek) m. heel
napiętnowac (na-pyáňt-no-vach)
v. brand; stigmatize;censure
condemn as being very bad;stamp
napięty (na-pyáń-ty) adj. m.
tense; taut; strained; tight
napinac (na-pée-nach) v. strain
napis (ná-pees) m. inscription
napitek (na-pée-tek) m. drink
napiwek (na-pée-vek) m. tip
napluć (ná-plooch) v. spit on
napływ (ná-pwiv), m. influx
napływac (na-pwi-vach) v. inflow; flow in; flock;pour in
napływowy (na-pwi-vo-vi) adj.
m. alluvial; immigrant; allien
napoczynac (na-po-chi-nach) v.
start up; open; broach
napominac (na-po-mée-nach) v.
admonish; reprimand: rebuke
napomknąc (na-pom-knównch) v.
mention; hint at: allude to
napomnienie (na-pom-ńe-ńe) n.
admonition; reprimand;rebuke
na pomoc ! (na po-mots) excl:
help ! give help! please,help!
napotny (na-pót-ni) adj. m.
sudatory; perspiratory
napotykac (na-po-ti-kach) v.
run in; come across:be faced with
napowietrzny (na-po-vyétzh-ni)
adj. m. aerial; overhead-
na powrót (na póv-root) adv.
return; again; on the way back
na pozór (na pó-zoor) adv. ap-
parently; on the face of it
napój (ná-pooy) m. drink
na pół (na poow) adv. in half
napor (ná-poor) m. pressure
naprawa (na-prá-va) f. repair;
redress: renovation: reform
naprawdę (na-práv-daň) adv. indeed; really: truly; positively

naprawiać (na-praw-yach) v. repair: fix; mend; rectify;reform
naprędce (na-pránd-tse) adv.
hastily: in a hurry;slapdash
naprężenie (na-pran-zhe-ne) n.
tension; strain; tautness
naprężyć (na-pran-zhich) v.
tauten; stretch;strain
naprowadzać (na-pro-vá-dzach)
v. lead in; direct to;advise
na próżno (na proozh-no) adv.
in vain: uselessly;to no avail
naprzeciw (na-pzhe-cheev) adv.
opposite: vis-a-vis
naprzec (na-pzhech) v. press;
urge : press hard; insist on
na przekor (na pzhe-koor) adv.
in despite: just to spite
na przełaj (na pzhe-way) adv.
shortcut (across obstacles)
na przemian (na pzhé-myan) adv.
alternately : by turns
naprzód (ná-pzhoot) adv. forwards;first;in the first place
na przykład (na pzhík-wat) adv.
for instance; for example
naprzykrzac się(na-pshík-shach
shán)v bother;molest:pester
napuchnąć (na-pookh-nównch)v.
swell ; become swollen
napuchły (na-pookh-wi) adj. m.
swollen;bulging; distended
napuścic (na-poosh-cheech) v.
set up ; impregnate; let in
napuszony (na-poo-shó-ni) adj.
m. puffed up bristling;ruffled
napychac (na-pi-khach) v. stuff;
cram;cram;fill;pack:crowd,stow
narada (na-rá-da) f. consultation ; council;. conference
naradzac się (na-rá-dzach shán)v.
consult; confer with;deliberate
naramiennik (na-ra-myén-neek)
m. epaulet; shoulder-strap
narastac (na-ras-tach) v. grow
on ;increase; accumulate;accrue
naraz (ná-ras) adv. suddenly
na razie (na rá-zhe) adv. for
the time being ;for the present
narażac (na-rá-zhach) v. expose
to endanger
narciarstwo (nar-char-stvo) n.
skiing

narciarz (nár-chash) m. skier
narcyz (nár-tsis) m. narcissus
nareszcie (na-résh-che) adv.
at last : finally;at long last
narecze (na-ran-che) n. armful
narkotyczny (nar-ko-tích-ni)
adj. m. narcotic;causing numbness
narkotyk (nar-kó-tik) m.narcot-
ic :drug for sleep and relief
narkoza (nar-kó-za) f. anesthe-
sia ; anaesthetization
narobić (na-ró-beech) v.mess up;
cause nuisance; make a mess
narodowość (na-ro-dó-voshch) f.
nationality;national status
narodowy (na-ro-dó-vi) adj. m.
national;of national character
narodzenie (na-ro-dzé-ne) n.
birth; a being born;the beginning
narodzić się (na-ró-dzheech shán)
v. be born; originate; arise
narodziny (na-ro-dzhee-ni) n.
birth; origin; the beginning
narosl (ná-roshl) f. tumor;
growth;excrescence; wart;knar
narowisty (na-ro-vees-ti) adj.
m. restive;vicious:skittish
narożnik (na-rózh-neek) m. corner;angle; cross-roads;gusset
narożny (na-rózh-ni) adj. m.
corner-; at the street corner
naród (ná-root) m. nation;people
narów (ná-roof) m. vice ( res-
tivness); bad habit; fault
narta (nár-ta) f. ski; sleigh
naruszac (na-roo-shach) v. disturb; violate; injure; harm
naruszenie (na-roo-shé-ne) n.
offense; disturbance; breach
narwany (na-rvá-ni) adj. m.
hot-head; reckless; rash
narybek (na-ri-bek) m. small
fry; coming generation
narząd (na-zhównt) m. organ
narzecze (na-zhé-che) n. ( primitive)dialect
narzeczona (na-zhe-chó-na) f.
fiancée: an engaged woman
narzeczony (na-zhe-chó-ni) m.
fiance
narzekać (na-zhe-kach) v. complain: grumble: lament

narzekanie (na-zhe-ká-ñe) n.
complaints;kick; bitching
narzędzie (na-zháń-dzhe) n.
tool; utensil; implement
narzucać (na-zhoo-tsaćh) v.
throw over; impose;shovel on
nasada (na-sá-da) f. base
nasenna pigułka (na-sén-na pi-
góow-ka) sleeping-pill
nasiadówka (na-śha-doóv-ka) f.
sitzbath; hip-bath
nasiąkać (na-śhówń-kaćh) v.
soak up;become saturated;imbibe
nasienie (na-śhe-ñe) m. seed;
sperm; semen; posterity
nasilenie (na-śhee-le-ñe) n.
intensification; intensity
naskórek (na-skoó-rek) m. outer
skin; epidermis; cuticle
naskarżyć (na-skár-zhićh) v.
denounce; lodge a complain
nasłuchać się (na-swoo-khaćh
śhăn) v. hear plenty
nasłuchiwać (na-swoo-khee-vaćh)
v. monitor (radio);listen
nasmarować (na-sma-ro-vaćh) v.
smear over; grease; lubricate
nastać (ná-staćh) v. set in;
enter; occur; come about
nastanie (na-stá-ñe) n. arrival;
setting-in; advent; coming
nastarczyć (na-stár-chićh) v.
supply enough; keep pace; cope
nastawać (na-stá-yaćh) v. insist
nastawiać (na-stáv-yaćh) v. set
up; set right; tune in; point
nastawienie (na-sta-vyé-ñe) n.
attitude; bias; disposition
następca (na-stáńp-tsa) m. successor ; heir
następnie (na-stáńp-ñe) adv.
next; then; subsequently
następny (na-stáńp-ni) adj. m.
next; the next; the following
następować (na-stáń-po-vaćh) v.
follow; tread; come after;ensue
następstwo (na-stáńp-stvo) n.
result; succession; upshot
następujacy (na-stáń-poo-yown-
tsi) adj. m. successive; following; the following
nastraszyć (na-stra-shićh) v.
frighten; intimidate

nastręczać (na-stráń-chaćh) v.
afford; present; offer; procure
nastroić (na-stró-eećh) v. at-
tune; tune up ; dispose to
nastroszyć (na-stro-shićh) v.
bristle up; perk up; heap up
nastrój (ná-strooy) m. mood
nasturcja (na-stoór-tsya) f.
nasturtia ; lark-heel
nasuwać (na-soó-vaćh) v. shove
up ; draw over; afford;overthrust
nasycać (na-si-tsaćh) v. satiate; satisfy ; sate; saturate
nasycenie (na-si-tsé-ñe) n. sa-
tiation; saturation ;satisfaction
nasycony (na-si-tsó-ni) adj. m.
satiate; saturated ; replete
nasyłać (na-si-waćh) v. send on
nasyp (ná-sip) m. embankment
nasypać (na-sí-paćh) v. pour in;
spread up (dry powder etc)
nasz (nash) pron. our; ours
naszyć (na-shićh) v. sew on;
trim with; trim
naszkicować (na-shkee-tsó-vaćh)
v. sketch ; make a sketch
naszyjnik (na-shiy-ñeek) m.
necklace ; neck jewelry
naśladować (na-śhla-dó-vaćh) v.
imitate ; mimic; reproduce
naśladowanie (na-śhla-do-vá-ñe)
n. imitation; copy
naśladowca (na-śhla-dóv-tsa)
m. imitator
naśmiewać się (na-śhmyé-vaćh
śhăn) v. laugh at; deride
naświetlać (na-śhvyet-laćh) v.
explain; irradiate; expose
natarcie (na-tár-ćhe) n.
1. rubbing; 2. onslaught; attack; offensive; advance
natarczywość (na-tar-chi-voshćh)
n. insistency ; obtrusiveness
natarczywy (na-tar-chi-vi) adj;
n. insistent; pressing;urgent
natchnąć (nát-khnown'ćh) v. inspire; infuse; penetrate
natchnienie (nat-khńe-ñe) n.
inspiration; brain wave;impulse
natenczas (na-ten-chas) adv.
then; at that time; as
natężać (na-tán-zhaćh) v. strain;
intensify; strenghten; exert

natężenie (na-tan-zhe-ne) n.
tension;strain; effort;pitch
natężony (na-tan-zho-ni) adj.
m. intense, : strained
natknąć (nat-knownch) v. come
across ;butt; stick; stud
natłoczony (na-two-cho-ni) adj.
m. crowded; packed; huddled
natłoczyć (na-two-chich) v.
cram: pack: crowd; huddle
natłok (na-twok) m. crowd;
throng; pressure accumulation
natomiast (na-to-myast) adv.
however: yet; on the contrary
natłuścić (na-twoosh-cheech) v.
oil; grease; lubricate
natrafic (na-tra-feech) v. encounter;. come across
natręctwo (na-trańts-tvo) n.
intrusiveness;importunity
natręt (na-trańt) m. intruder
natrętny (na-trańt-ni) adj. m.
intrusive; bothersome
natrysk (na-trisk) m. shower-
bath: shower; sprying
natrząsać się (na-tzhown-sach
shań)v.scoff at: sneer;poke fun
natrzeć (na-tzhech) v. rub;
attack; harass: scold; rate
natura (na-too-ra) f. nature
naturalizacja (na-too-ra-lee-
záts-ya) f. naturalization
naturalizować (na-too-ra-lee-zo-
vach) v. naturalize
naturalny (na-too-rál-ni) adj.
m. natural; true to life
natychmiast (na-tikh-myast) adv.
at once;instantly; right away
natychmiastowy (na-tikh-myas-
to-vi), adj. m. instantaneous
nauczać (na-oo-chach) v. teach;
instruct; tutor; train
nauczanie (na-oo-cha-ne) n.
teaching; instruction
nauczka (na-ooch-ka) f. (pointed) lesson (unpleasant)
nauczyciel (na-oo-chi-chel) m.
teacher: instructor
nauczyć się (na-oo-chich shań)
v. learn: come to know
nauka (na-oo-ka) f. science;
learning; study; teaching

naukowiec (na-oo-kóv-yets) m.
scientist; scholar: researcher
naukowość (na-oo-kó-voshch) f.
erudition; scholarship;learning
naukowy (na-oo-kó-vi) adj. m.
scientific; scholarly;academic
naumyślnie (na-oo-mishl-ne)
adv. on purpose; of set purpose
nawa (ná-va) f. nave; aisle
nawadniać (na-vád-nach) v.
irrigate: saturate with water
nawalić (na-vá-leech) v. pile
up; fail; bungle;break down
nawał (ná-vaw) m. no end of
nawała (na-vá-wa)f. overwhelm-
ing mass; swarms; onslaught
nawałnica (na-vaw-nee-tsa) f.
tempest; storm; hurricane
nawarstwienie (na-var-stvye-ne)
n. stratification
nawarzyć (na-vá-zhich) v. brew;
cook; concoct; get in trouble
nawet (ná-vet) adv. even
nawet gdyby (na-vét gdí-bi)
adv. even if; even though
nawias (ná-vyas), m. parenthesis
nawiasem (na-vyá-sem) adv. incidentally; by way of digression
nawiasowy (na-vya-só-vi) adj.
m. parenthetical; incidental
nawiązać (na-vyówn-zach) v.
tie to; refer to; enter in
nawiazanie (na-vyówn-zá-ne) n.
connection; reference to
nawiedzać (na-vyé-dzach) v.
visit; haunt; afflict; obsess
nawierzchnia (na-vyezh-khna) f.
surface (finish); pavement
nawijać (na-vee-yach) v. wind
up;reel; roll up; spool: coil
nawlekać (na-vlé-kach) v. thread;
string; slip on
nawodnienie (na-vod-ne-ne) n.
irrigation; saturation with water
nawoływać (na-vo-wi-vach) v.
call; hail; exhort to halloo
nawozić (na-vó-zheech) v. fertilize; manure ;truck;cart; fill
nawóz (ná-voos) m. manure ;dung
na wpół (na vpoow) adv. half;
semi-: half-(finished, boiled)
nawracać (na-vra-tsach) v. turn
around; convert ; turn back

nawrócenie (na-vroo-tsé-ñe) n.
conversion; being converted
nawrót (ná-vroot) m. return;
relapse; recurrence; set-back
na wskroś (na vskrosh) adv.
throughout; from end to end
nawyk (ná-vik) m. habit; wont
nawykać ( na-vi-kach) v. accustom; fall into a habit
nawykły (na-vik-wi) adj. m.
accustomed; get used to...
na wylot (na vi-lot) adv. through
and through; right through
nawymyślać (na-vi-mish-lach) v.
revile; abuse;insult; invent
na wyrywki (na vi-riv-kee) adv.
at random;at haphazard
nawzajem (na-vzá-yem) adv. mu-
tually; same to you
na wznak (ná vznak) adv. on
one's back; on one's supine
nazad (ná-zat) adv. back (wards)
nazajutrz (na-zá-jootsh) adv.
next morning; next day
nazbierać (na-zbyé-rach) v.
gather up; collect;assemble
nazbyt (ná-zbit) adv. too much
na zewnątrz (na zév-nówntsh)
adv. out; outwards; outside
naznaczyć (na-zna-chich) v.
mark;fix; appoint;outline;scar
nazwa ( náz-va) f. designation;
name; appellation; title
nazwisko (naz-vee-sko) m. family name; surname;reputation
nazywać (na-zi-vach) v. call;
name;term; denominate; christen
nażarty (na-zhar-ti) adj. m.
gorged; stuffed(greedily)
nażreć się (ná-zhreth sháñ) v.
gorge; stuff oneself (vulg.)
negacja (ne-gáts-ya) f. negation; opposite of positive
negatyw (ne-gá-tiv) m. negative
negatywny (ne-ga-tív-ni) adj.
m. negative; saying "no"
negliż (nég-leesh) m. undress;
morning dress; dishabille
negocjacje (ne-go-tsyáts-ye) pl.
negotiations;settling a treaty
negować (ne-gó-vach) v. deny
nekrolog (ne-kró-log) m. obituary notice : obituary

nektar (nék-tar) m. nectar
neofita (ne-o-fée-ta) m. convert; neophyte; proselyte
neologizm (ne-o-ló-geezm) m.
neologism; new word;new meanning
neon (né-on) m. neon light
nepotyzm (ne-pó-tizm) m. nepo-
tizm; favoritism to relatives
nerka (ner-ka) f. kidney
nerw (nerv) m. nerve;vigor;ardor
nerwica (ner-vée-tsa) f. neurosis; nervous disturbance
nerwoból (ner-vo-bool) m. neuralgia; severe pain,along a nerve
nerwowość (ner-vo-voshch) f.
nervosity; irritability; fidgets
nerwowy (ner-vo-vi) adj. m. nervous;made up of nerves; fearful
neseser (ne-sé-ser) m. dressing
case; make-up case; toilet case
netto (nét-to) adv. net (cost)
neutralizować (ne-oo-tra-lee-
zó-vach) v. neutralize
neutralność (ne-oo-trál-noshch)
f. neutrality; neutral status
neutralny (ne-oo-trál-ni) adj.
m. neutral; indifferent
neutron (né-oo-tron) m. neutron
newralgia (ne-vrál-gya) f.
neuralgia; pain along a nerve
newroza (ne-vró-za) f. neurosis
nęcić (náñ-cheech) v. entice;
court; allure; tempt;be seductive
nędza (náñ-dza) f. misery
nędzarz (náñ-dzash) m. destitute
wretch; beggar; pauper
nędznik (náñdz-ñeek) m. villain
nędzny (náñdz-ni) adj. m. wretched;miserable ; shabby; sorry
nękać (náñ-kach) v. molest; hurry;
torment; harass; annoy; worry
ni to ni owo (ñee to ñee o-vo)
adv. neither this nor that
ni stąd ni zowąd (ñee stównt
ñee zo-vównt) without reason;
suddenly ; for no reason whatever
niania (ná-ña) f. (baby's)
nurse ; nanny; dry nurse
niańczyć (ñań-cheech) v. nurse
niańka (ñáñ-ka) f. nurse
niby (ñee-bi) adv. as if; pre-
tending ;as it were; like
nic (ñeets) pron. nothing; nought

nic nie szkodzi (ńeets ńe shko-
dźhee)expr.: does not matter
nic z tego (ńeets z té-go)
expr.: no use: to no purpose;
nicość (ńeé-tsoshch) f. nothing-
ness; oblivion; nonentity
nicpoń (ńéts-poń) m. good-for-
nothing;"ńogoodnik"; scamp
niczyj (ńeé-chiy) adj. m. no-
man's: ńobody's; no one's
nici (ńeé-ćhee) pl. l. threads
2. nothing: nothing of it
nić (ńeećh) f. thread
nie (ńe) part. no : not(any)
nie jeszcze (ńe yesh-che)not-
yet; not for a long time
nieagresja (ńe-a-gres-ya) f.
nonaggression (treaty)
niebaczny (ńe-bach-ni) adj. m.
imprudent; rush; inconsiderate
niebawem (ńe-ba-vem) adv. soon
niebezpieczeństwo (ńe-bez-pye-
cheń-stvo) m. danger ;peril
niebezpieczny (ńe-bez-pyéch-ni)
adj. m. dangerous; risky;tricky
niebiański (ńe-byan-skee) adj.
m. heavenly ; divine
niebieskawy (ńe-byes-ka-vi) adj.
m. bluish
niebieski (ńe-byes-kee) adj. m.
blue; heavenly; of the sky
niebieskooki (ńe-byes-ko-ó-kee)
adj. m. blue-eyed
niebiosa (ńe-byó-sa) pl. Hea-
vens: the visible sky
niebo (ńe-bo) n. sky
nieborak (ńe-bo-rak) m. poor
soul; poor soul;poor devil
nieboszczyk (ńe-bósh-chik) m.
deceased; dead person
niebosiężny (ńe-bo-shańzh-ni)
adj. m. sky-high; towering
niebotyczny (ńe-bo-tich-ni) adj.
m. sky-high ; sky reaching
niebożę (ńe-bo-zhań) n. poor
soul; poor thing; poor devil
nie byle jak (ńe bi.-le yak)expr:
not just any way;not carelessly
niebyły (ńe-bi-vi) adj. m. null
and void ; unexisting
niebywale (ńe-bi-vá-le) adv.
unusually; exceptionally
niebywały (ńe-bi-va-wi) adj. m.
unheard-of ; unusual; uncommon

niecały (ńe-tsá-wi) adj. m.
incomplete :defective; less than
niecenzuralny (ńe-tsen-zoo-
rál-ni) adj. m. indecent; un-
printable : obscene; suggestive
niech (ńekh) part. let :suppose
niechcący (ńe-khtsówn-tsi) adv.
unintentionally ; unawares
niechęć (ńe-khańćh) f. disincli-
nation; aversion; ill-will
niechętny (ńe-khańt-ni) adj. m.
unwilling; reluctant : averse
niechluj (ńé-khlooy) m. grub;
sloppy ; slut: dirty: sloven
niechybny (ńe-khib-ni) adj. m.
without fail :certain:unerring
niechże (ńekh-zhe) part. let
niecić (ńe-ćheećh) v. kindle;
stir up ; light (a fire)
nieciekawy (ńe-ćhe-ka-vi) adj.
m. blank; void of interest
niecierpliwić się (ńe-ćher-pleé-
veech shań) v. be impatient
niecierpliwy (ńe-ćher-pleé-vi)
adj. m. impatient; restless
niecnota (ńe-tsnó-ta) m. scamp;
rogue: rascal: scoundrel
niecny (ńéts-ni) adj. m. vile
nieco (ńé-tso) adv. somewhat;
a little : a trifle; slightly
niecodzienny (ńe-tso-dźhén-ni)
adj. m. uncommon : unusual
nieczesany (ńe-che-sá-ni) adj.
m. unkempt : disorderly
nieczęsty (ńe-chań-sti) adj. m.
infrequent : not frequent
nieczuły (ńe-choó-wi) adj. m.
callous : heartless: insensible
nieczynny (ńe-chin-ni) adj. m.
inert; inactive:put of order
nieczysty (ńe-chis-ti) adj. m.
unclean :polluted: dirty; shady
nieczytelny (ńe-chi-tel-ni) adj.
m. illegible; cramped:crabbed
niedaleki (ńe-da-lé-kee) adj. m.
near; not distant;at hand
niedaleko (ńe-da-lé-ko) adv.
near; not far; a short way off
niedawno (ńe-dáv-no) adv. recently; not long ago;newly
niedbale (ńe-dbá-le) adv. carelessly; casually: nonchalantly
niedbalstwo (ńe-dbál-stvo) n.
negligence : laxity;carelessness

niedbały (ñe-dba-wi) adj. m.
negligent;untidy;lax;careless
niedługi (ñe-dwoo-gee) adj. m.
short; not long
niedługo (ñe-dwoo-go) adv. soon;
not long; before long;by and by
niedobitki (ñe-do-beet-kee) pl.
survivors; routed soldiers
niedobór (ñe-do-boor) m. deficit; shortage; scarcity; loss
niedobrany (ñe-do-bra-ni) adj.
m. ill-suited; ill-matched
niedobry (ñe-dob-ri) adj. m.
no-good; bad; wicked; nasty
niedobrze (ñe-dob-zhe) adv. not
well; badly;wrong;improperly
nie doceniać(ñe-do-tse-ñach) v.
underestimate; estimate too low
niedociągnięcie (ñe-do-chown-
gnań-che) n. shortcoming
niedogodność (ñe-do-god-noshch)
f. inconvenience; drawback
niedogodny (ñe-do-god-ni) adj.
m. inconvenient: undesirable
nie dogotowany(ñe-do-go-to-va-
ni) adj. m. underdone; half-
cooked; half-raw: under done
nie dojadać(ñe-do-ya-dach) v.
not eat enough;starve
niedojda (ñe-doy-da) m. nitwit;
bungler; fumbler; lout
niedojrzały (ñe-doy-zha-wi) adj.
m. unripe; immature; under age
niedokładny (ñe-do-kwad-ni) adj.
m. inaccurate; inexact
niedokończony (ñe-do-koń-cho-ni)
adj. m. unfinished;incomplete
niedokrwisty (ñe-do-krvees-ti)
adj. m. anemic; anaemic
niedola (ñe-do-la) f. adversity
niedołęga (ñe-do-wañ-ga) m.
blunderer; cripple;duffer
niedołęstwo (ñe-do-wań-stvo) m.
inefficiency; clumsiness
niedomagać (ñe-do-ma-gach) v.
be unwell; be ailing
nie domknięty(ñe-do-mknañ-ti)
adj. m. ajar; slightly open
niedomówienie (ñe-do-moo-vye-ñe)
n. vague hint; insinuation
niedomyślny (ñe-do-miśhl-ni)
adj. m. slow thinking

niedopałek (ñe-do-pa-wek) m.
(cigarette) butt: stub;ember
niedopatrzenie (ñe-do-pa-tzhe-
ñe) n. oversight; neglect
niedopuszczalny (ñe-do-poosh-
chál-ni) adj. m. inadmissible
niedorozwinięty (ñe-do-roz-
vee-ñañ-ti) adj. m. underdeveloped; mentally retarded
niedorzeczny (ñe-do-zhech-ni)
adj. m. absurd; ridiculous
niedoskonały (ñe-dos-ko-na-wi)
adj. m. imperfect;deficient
niedosłyszalny (ñe-do-swi-shál-
ni) adj. m. inaudible
niedosmażony (ñe-do-sma-zho-ni)
adj. m. underdone; half-raw
nie dospać(ñe-dos-pach) v.
sleep too short time; not sleep
enough; not to have enough sleep
niedostateczny (ñe-dos-ta-tech-
ni) adj. m. insufficient
niedostatek (ñe-dos-ta-tek) m.
shortage; indigence; poverty
niedostępny (ñe-do-stáñp-ni)
adj. m. inaccessible;out of reach
niedostosowanie (ñe-dos-to-so-
va-ñe)n. maladjustment
niedostrzegalny (ñe-do-stzhe-
gál-ni) adj. m. imperceptible
niedościgły (ñe-do-shcheeg-wi)
adj. m. matchless; inimitable
niedoświadczenie (ñe-do-shvyad-
ché-ñe) n. inexperience
niedouczony (ñe-do-oo-cho-ni)
adj. n. half-educated
nie dowarzony (ñe do-va-zho-ni)
adj. m. half-boiled; rough
niedowarzony (ñe-do-va-zho-ni)
adj. m. immature;undereducated
niedowiarek (ñe-do-vya-rek) m.
unbeliever; atheist; skeptic
niedowidzieć (ñe-do-vee-dźech)
v. be short-sighted
nie dowierzać(ñe-do-vye-zhach)
v. distrust; disbelieve
niedowład (ñe-do-vwat) m. pare-
sis: partial paralysis
niedozwolony (ñe-doz-vo-ló-ni)
adj. m. not allowed;illicit
niedrogi (ñe-dro-gee) adj. m.
cheap; inexpensive

nieduży (ńe-doo-zhi) adj. m.
small; little;not big;not tall
niedwuznaczny (ńe-dvoo-znach-ni)
adj. m. unequivocal; clear
niedyskrecja (ńe-dis-krets-ya)
f. indiscretion;indelicacy,
niedyspozycja (ńe-dis-po-zits-
ya) f. indisposition
niedziela (ńe-dżhé-la)f. Sunday
niedźwiadek (ńe-dżhvyá-dek) m.
bear cub ; Teddy bear,
niedźwiedzica (ńe-dzhvye-dżheé-
tsa) f. female bear:she-bear
niedźwiedź (ńe-dżhvyedżh) m.
bear : bearskin; clumsy man
nieelastyczny (ńe-e-las-tich-
ni) adj. m. inelastic
nieestetyczny (ńe-es-te-tich-
ni) adj. m. unesthetic
nieetyczny (ńe-e-tich-ni) adj.
m. unethical; immoral
niefachowy (ńe-fa-khó-vi) adj.
m. incompetent; inexpert
nieforemny (ńe-fo-rém-ni) adj.
m. shapeless; deformed
nieformalnie (ńe-for-mál-ńe)
adv. informally; illegally
niefortunny (ńe-for-tóon-ni)
adj. m. unlucky; regrettable
niefrasobliwy (ńe-fra-sob-leé-
vi) adj. m. care-free;jaunty
niegdyś (ńég-dish) adv. formerly; once; at one time
niegodny (ńe-gód-ni) adj. m.
unworthy;undignified;vile;base
niegodziwy (ńe-go-dżheé-vi)adj.
m. wicked;vile;base;mean;foul
niegościnny (ńe-gosh-cheén-ni)
adj. m. inhospitable;desolate
niegrzeczny (ńe-gzhéch-ni) adj.
m. rude; impolite;unkind: bad
niegustowny (ńe-goos-tóv-ni)
adj. m. tasteless;in bad taste
niehigieniczny (ńe-khee-ge-
ńeéch-ni) adj. m. unsanitary
niehonorowy (ńe-kho-no-ró-vi)
adj. m. dishonorable; unfair
nieistotny (ńe-ees-tó-tni) adj.
m. inessential; immaterial
niejaki (ńe-yá-kee) adj. m. a;
one; certain;some;slight
niejasno (ńe-yás-no) adv. dimly:
vaguely;ambiguously;obscurely

niejasny (ńe-yás-ni) adj. m.dim;
unclear;indistinct;vague;obscure
niejeden (ńe-yé-den) adj. m.
many a; quite a number
niejednokrotnie (ńe-yed-no-krót-
ńe) adv. repeatedly;recurrently
nie karany (ńe ka-rá-ni) adj. m.
with a clean record; not con-
victed before
niekiedy (ńe-kyé-di) adv. now
and then; sometimes; at times
niekonsekwentny (ńe-kon-se-kvént-
ni) adj. m. inconsistent
niekorzystny (ńe-ko-zhíst-ni)
adj. m. disadvantageous
niekorzyść (ńe-kó-zhishch) f.
disadvantage; detriment
niekształtny (ńe-kshtáwt-ni)
adj. m. unshapely; formless
niektóry (ńe-ktoó-ry) adj. m.
some;one here and there
nieledwie (ńe-léd-vye) adv. all
but; almost;practically
nielegalny (ńe-le-gál-ni) adj.
m. illegal;unlawful:illicit
nieletni (ńe-lét-ńee) adj. m.
under age;juvenile; minor
nieliczny (ńe-leéch-ni) adj. m.
not numerous; scarce;rare;small
nielitościwy (ńe-lee-tosh-cheé-
vi) adj. m. unmerciful
nielogiczny (ńe-lo-geéch-ni)
adj. m. illogical; nonsensical
nieludzki (ńe-loódz-kee) adj.
inhuman: atrocious;ruthless
nieład (ńe-wat) m. disorder;
disarray; confusion:mess
nieładnie (ńe-wád-ńe) adv. not
nicely: unattractively;wrongly
niełaska (ńe-wás-ka) f. disgrace;
disfavor;loss of respect
niemal (ńe-mal) adv. almost;
nearly ;pretty nearly;well-nigh
niemało (ńe-má-wo) adv. not a
few; pretty much ;not a little
niemały (ńe-má-wi) adj. m. pretty big ;fair-sized;goodly;no mean
niemądry (ńe-mownd-ri) adj. unwise; ill-judged ;silly;stupid
niemczyć (ńem-chich) v.Germanize
niemęski (ńe-mań-kee)adj.m.unmanly
niemiecki (ńem-yéts-kee) adj. m.
German ; German language

niemiły (ńe-mee-wi) adj. m. unpleasant;unsightly;harsh;surly
niemniej jednak (ńe-mney yednak) nevertheless; all the same;none the less; however
niemoc (ńe-mots) f. impotence
niemodny (ńe-mód-ni) adj. m. outmoded; out of fashion
niemoralny (ńe-mo-rál-ni) adj. m. immoral; dishonest
niemowa (ńe-mó-ya) m.∝ f. mute
niemowlę (ńe-móv-lań) n. baby
niemożliwy (ńe-mozh-lee-vi) adj. m. impossible
niemrawy (ńe-mra-vi) adj. m. sluggish; tardy; indolent
niemy (ńie-mi) adj. m. dumb
nienaganny (ńe-na-gáń-ni) adj. m. blameless; faultless
nienaruszalny (ńe-na-roo-shál-ni) adj. m. inviolable
nienaruszony (ńe-na-roo-shó-ni) adj. m. intact·undisturbed
nienasycony (ńe-na-si-tso-ni) adj. m. insatiable; (chem. unsaturated); voracious
nienaturalny (ńe-na-too-rál-ni) adj. m. unnatural; insincere
nienawistny (ńe-na-veest-ni) adj. m. hateful;full of hatred
nienawisc (ńe-ná-veeshćh) f. hate; abomination;detestation
nie nazwany (ńe naz-vá-ni) adj. m. unnamed; not maned
nienormalny (ńe nor-mál-ni) adj. m. abnormal; insane
nieobecnosc (ńe-o-béts-noshćh) f. absence; non-attendance
nieobecny (ńe-o-béts-ni) adj. m. absent; not present;not in
nieobez nany (ńe-o-bez-na-ni) adj. m. uninformed; ignorant
nieobliczalny (ńe-o-blee-chál-ni) adj. m. unreliable; incalculable;irresponsible
nieobyczajny (ńe-o-bi-cháy-ni) adj. m. immoral;ill-mannered
nieoceniony (ńe-o-tse-ńo-ni) adj. m. inestimable
nieoczekiwany (ńe-oche-kee-vá-ni) adj. m. unexpected
nieodłączny (ńe-od-wowńch-ni) adj. m. inseparable

nieodmienny (ńe-od-myén-ni) adj. m. invariable;undeclinable
nieodparty (ńe-od-pár-ti) adj. m. irrefutable; compelling
nieodpowiedni (ńe-od-po-vyéd-ńee) adj. m. inadequate; wrong
nieodpowiedzialny (ńe-od-po-vyedżhál-ni) adj. m. irresponsible
nieodstępny (ńe-od-stáńp-ni) adj. m. inseparable;ever present
nieodwołalny (ńe-od-vo-wál-ni) adj. m. irrevocable; final
nieodzownie (ńe-od-zóv-ńe) adv. inevitably; absolutely
nieodzowny (ńe-od-zóv-ni) adj. m. indispensable;irrevocable
nieodżałowany (ńe-od-zha-wo-vá-ni) adj. m. never enough regretted; much regretted
nieoględny (ńe-o-glánd-ni) adj. m. inconsiderate;reckless;rash
nieograniczony (ńe-o-gra-ńee-chó ni) adj. m. infinite; boundless
nieokiełzany (ńe-o-ḱew-za-ni) adj. m. unbridled; uncontrollable
nieokreslony (ńe-o-kresh-ló-ni) adj. m. indefinite;undetermined
nieokrzesany (ńe-o-kzhe-sá-ni) adj. m. rude;crude;ill-mannered
nieomal (ńe-o-mal) adv. almost; nearly; pretty nearly;practically
nieomylny (ńe-o-mil-ni) adj. m. infallible;unerring;sure
nieopatrzny (ńe-o-pátzh-ni) adj. m. unguarded;inconsiderate
nieopisany (ńe-o-pee-sá-ni) adj. m. indescribable;excessive;extreme
nieopłacalny (ńe-o-pwa-tsál-ni) adj. m. unprofitable
nieopłacony (ńe-o-pwa-tso-ni) adj. m. unpaid;not paid for
nieopodal (ńe-o-pó-dal) adv. near by; close at hand;next door
nieorganiczny (ńe-or-ga-ńeech-ni) adj. m. inorganic;inanimate
nieosobowy (ńe-o-so-bó-vi) adj. m. inpersonal; not personal
nieostrożny (ńe-os-trozh-ni) adj. m. careless; imprudent
nieoswojony (ńe-os-vo-yo-ni) adj. m. untamed; unfamiliar
nieoświecony (ńe-ośh-vye-tso-ni) adj. m. dark; ignorant

nieoznaczony (ňe-oz-na-chó-ni)
adj. m. indefinite;unmarked
niepalący (ňe-pa-lówn-tsi) adj.
m. not smoking; non smoking
niepalność(ně-pál-noshćh)f.in-
combustibility;non-inflammability
niepalny (ňe-pál-ni) adj. m.
incombustible;uninflammable
niepamięc (ne-pá-myañćh) f.
oblivion; forgetfulness
niepamiętny (ne-pa-myañt-ni)
adj. m. forgetful; immemorial
nieparlamentarny (ne-par-la-
men-tár-ni) adj. unparliamen-
tary rough (language)
nieparzysty (ňe-pa-zhís-ti)
adj. m. odd;uneven; unpaired
niepełnoletni (ňe-pew-no-let-
ňee) adj. m. minor; underage
niepewnosc (ňe-pév-noshćh) f.
uncertainty; incertitude
niepewny (ne-pév-ni) adj. m.
uncertain ;insecure; unsafe
niepisany (ňe-pee-sá-ni) adj.
m. unwritten; not in writing
niepiśmienny (ňe-peesh-myén-ni)
adj. m. illiterate;unlettered
niepłacący (ňe-pwa-tsówn-tsi)
adj. m. non-paying
niepłodny (ňe-pwód-ni) adj. m.
sterile; barren; infertile
niepłonny (ne-pwon-ni) adj. m.
well-founded ; motivated
niepochlebny (ňe-po-khléb-ni)
adj. m. unfavorable
niepocieszony (ne-po-čhe-sho-
ni) adj. m. desolate
niepoczciwy (ňe-poch-cheé-vi)
adj. m. wicked; unkind
niepoczytalny (ňe-po-chi-tál-ni)
adj. m. irresponsible ;insane
niepodejrzany (ňe-po-dey-zha-ni)
adj. m. unsuspected
niepodległość (ňe-pod-lég-woshćh)
f. independence ;sovereignty
niepodległy (ňe-pod-lég-wi) adj.
m. independent; sovereign
niepodobieństwo (ne-po-do-byeń-
stvo) n. impossibility
niepodobna (ňe-po-dób-na) adv.
it's impossible ;there is no way
niepodobny (ňe-po-dób-ni) adj.
m. unlike; unlikely ;dissimilar

niepodzielny (ňe-podżhél-ni)
adj. m. indivisible;undivided
niepogoda (ňe-po-gó-da) f. bad
weather; foul weather
niepogwałcony (ňe-po-gvaw-tso-
ni) adj. m. inviolate
niepohamowany (ňe-po-ha-mo-
vá-ni) adj. m. unrestrained
niepojętny (ňe-po-yánt-ni)
adj. m. dull(man);stupid
niepojęty (ňe-po-yáń-ti) adj.
m. inconceivable; incomprehensible; unimaginable
niepokalany (ňe-po-ka-lá-ni)
adj. m. immaculate;faultless
niepokaźny (ňe-po-káżh-ni) adj.
m. inconspicuous;modest;shabby
niepokoić (ňe-po-kó-eećh) v.
disturb; trouble; annoy;pester
niepokonany (ňe-po-ko-ná-ni)
adj. m. invincible;irresistible
niepokój (ňe-pó-kooy) m. anxiety; unrest;trouble;agitation
niepolityczny (ňe-po-lee-tich-
ni) adj. m. impolitical; in-
expedient; improper;impolitic
niepomierny (ňe-po-myér-ni)
adj. m. excessive ; extreme
niepomny (ňe-póm-ni) adj. m.
forgetful; oblivious
niepomyślny (ňe-po-míshl-ni)
adj. m. adverse ; unlucky
niepopłatny (ňe-po-pwát-ni)
adj. m. unprofitable
niepoprawny (ňe-po-práv-ni)
adj. m. incorrigible
niepopularny (ňe-po-poo-lár-ni)
adj. m. unpopular
nieporadny (ňe-po-rád-ni) adj.
m. awkward ;helpless
nieporęczny (ňe-po-rańch-ni)
adj. m. cumbersome ;unhandy
nieporozumienie (ňe-po-ro-zoo-
myé-ňe) n. misunderstanding
nieporównany (ňe-po-roov-ná-
ni) adj. m. incomparable
nieporuszony (ňe-po-roo-shó-ni)
adj. m. immovable; firm
nieporządek (ňe-po-zhówň-dek)
adj. m. disorder; mess
nieporządny (ňe-po-zhównd-ni)
adj. m. disorderly; untidy;
messy;slipshod;chaotic

nieposłuszeństwo (ńe-po-swoo-sheń-stvo) ·n. disobedience
niepospolity (ńe-po-swoósh-ni) adj. m. disobedient:unruly
niepospolity (ńe-pos-po-leé-ti) adj. m. uncommon: rare
niepostrzeżenie(ńe-po-stshe-zhé-ńe)adv.imperceptibly;unnoticeably
niepotrzebny (ńe-po-tzhéb-ni) adj. m. unnecessary; useless
niepowetowany (ńe-po-ve-to-va-ni) adj. m. irreparable
niepowodzenie (ńe-po-vo-dzhé-ńe) n. failure; adversity
niepowołany (ńe-po-vo-wá-ni) adj. m. uncalled for; incompetent; unfit; undesirable
niepowrotny (ńe-pov-rót-ni) adj. m. irrevocable; irrecoverable; beyond recall
niepowstrzymany (ńe-pov-stzhi-má-ni) adj. m. irresistible
niepowszedni (ńe-pov-shéd-ńee) adj. m. uncommon: exceptional
niepowściągliwy (ńe-pov-shchówng-leé-vi) adj. m. intemperate
niepozorny (ńe-po-zór-ni) adj. m. inconspicuous; modest
niepożądany (ńe-po-zhówn-da-ni) adj. m. undesirable; undesired
niepożyteczny (ńe-po-zhi-téch-ni) adj. m. useless;unprofitable
niepraktyczny (ńe-prak-tích-ni) adj. m. impractical;unwieldy
niepraktykujący (ńe-prak-ti-koo-yówn-tsi)adj. m. noncommunicant ; retired (professional)
nieprawda (ńe-práv-da) f. untruth; falsehood; lie
nieprawdopodobny (ńe-prav-do-po-dób-ni) adj. m. improbable
nieprawdziwy (ńe-prav-dzheé-vi) adj. m. untrue; false ;faked
nieprawidłowość (ńe-pra-vee-dwó-voshćh) f. anomaly; irregularity; falsity;incorrectness
nieprawidłowy (ńe-pra-vee-dwó-vi) adj. m. anomalous; irregular; contrary to the rules
nieprawny (ńe-práv-ni) adj. m. illegal; unlawful; invalid
nieprawomyślny (ńe-pra-vo-mishl-ni) adj. m. unorthodox;disloyal

nieprawy (ńe-prá-vi) adj. m. unrighteous; adulterous; bastard; unlawful; illegitimate
nieproporcjonalny (ńe-pro-por-tsyo-nál-ni) adj. m. disproportional;out of proportion
nieproszony (ńe-pro-shó-ni) adj. m. uncalled for; self-invited; unwelcome (guest)
nieprzebaczalny (ńe-pzhe-ba-chál-ni) adj. m. unpardonable
nieprzebłagany (ńe-pzhe-bwa-ga-ni) adj. m. implacable
nieprzebrany (ńe-pzhe-bra-ni) adj. m. inexhaustible;countless
nieprzebyty (ńe-pzhe-bi-ti) adj. m. impassable; unfordable
nieprzejednany (ńe-pzhe-yed-ná-ni) adj. m. irreconcilable
nieprzejrzysty (ńe-pzhey-zhís-ti) adj. m. not clear
nieprzekupny (ńe-pzhe-koóp-ni) adj. m. unbribable;incorruptible
nieprzemakalny (ńe-pzhe-ma-kál-ni) adj. m. waterproof
nieprzenikniony (ńe-pzhe-ńeek-ńó-ni) adj. m. impenetrable
nieprzepuszczalny (ńe-pzhe-poosh-chál-ni) adj. m. impervious ;impenetrable
nieprzerwany (ńe-pzher-vá-ni) adj. m. continuous ;ceaseless
nieprześcigniony (ńe-pzhesh-cheeg-ńó-ni) adj. m. unsurpassable ; unexcelled
nieprzewidziany (ńe-pzhe-vee-dżhá-ni) adj. m. unforeseen
nieprzezorny (ńe-pzhe-zór-ni) adj. m. improvident; unforseeing ;wanting of foresight
nieprzezroczysty (ńe-pzheżh-ro-chiś-ti) adj. m. opaque
nieprzezwyciężony (ńe-pzhez-vi-chàn-zho-ni) adj. m. invincible ;insurmountable
nieprzychylny (ńe-pzhi-khil-ni) adj. m. unfriendly ;prejudiced
nieprzydatny (ńe-pzhi-dát-ni) adj. m. useless ; unserviceable
nie przygotowany(ńe-pzhi-go-to-va-ni) adj. m. unprepared
nieprzyjaciel (ńe-pzhi-ya-chel) m. enemy; foe ;ill-wisher

nieprzyjacielski (ńe-pzhi-ya-
chél-skee) adj. m. enemy; hostile; enemy's; enemy-
nieprzyjazny (ńe-pzhi-yaz-ni)
adj. m.unfriendly; inimical
nieprzyjaźń (ńe-pzhi-yazń) f.
hostility; unfriendliness
nieprzyjemnosc (ńe-pzhi-yém-
nośhćh) f. unpleasantness
nieprzyjemny (ńe-pzhi-yém-ni)
adj. unpleasant; disagreeable
nie;:..vmuszony (ńe-pzhi-moo-
shó-ni) adj. m. free; uncon-
strained ; voluntary
nieprzystępny (ńe-pzhis-tánp-
ni) adj. m. inaccessible
nieprzytomność (ńe-pzhi-tóm-
nośhćh) f. unconsciousness;
absentmindedness
nieprzytomny (ńe-pzhi-tóm-ni)
adj. m. unconscious; absent-
minded ;frantic;mad; wild
nieprzyzwoitosc (ńe-pzhi-zvo-
eé-toshćh) f. indecency
nieprzyzwoity (ńe-pzhiz-vo-eé-
ti) adj. m. indecent; obscene
nieprzyzwyczajony (ńe-pzhi-zvi-
cha-yó-ni) adj. m. unaccustomed; lacking of habit
niepunktualny (ńe-poon-ktoo-ál-
ni) adj. m. unpunctual; late
nierad (ńé-rad) adj. m. unwilling; discontent ; annoyed
nieraz (ńé-ras) adv. often;
again and again ;many a time
nierdzewny (ńe-rdzév-ni) adj.
m. rustproof ;stainless
nierealny (ńe-re-ál-ni) adj. m.
imaginary; unreal; unrealizable
nieregularnosć (ńe-re-goo-lár-
nośhćh) f. irregularity
nieregularny (ńe-re-goo-lár-ni)
adj. m. irregular ; erratic
niereligijny (ńe-re-lee-geéy-
ni) adj. m. irreligious
nierogacizna (ńe-ro-ga-cheéz-
na) f. pl. swines pl.
nierozdzielny (ńe-roz-dźhél-ni)
adj. m. inseparable
nierozerwalny (ńe-ro-zer-vál-ni)
adj. m. indissoluble
nierozgarnięty (ńe-roz-gar-ńáń-
ti) adj. m. dull; (dim-witted)

nierozłączny (ńe-roz-woẃnch-ni)
adj. m. inseparable
nierozmyslny (ńe-roz-mishl-ni)
adj. m. unintentional
nierozpuszczalny (ńe-roz-poosh-
chál-ni) adj. m. indissoluble
nierozsądny (ńe-roz-sóẃnd-ni)
adj. m. unwise; unreasonable
nierozwaga (ńe-roz-vá-ga) f.
inconsideration; rashness
nierozważny (ńe-roz-vázh-ni)
adj. m. imprudent; inconsiderate; thoughtless; rush; hasty
nierównosć (ńe-roov-nośhćh) f.
inequality ;unevenness
nierówny (ńe-roóv-ni) adj. m.
unequal; crooked; uneven
nieruchliwy (ńe-rookh-leé-vi)
adj. m. slow ; unwieldy
nieruchomosć (ńe-roo-khó-mośhćh)
f. real estate; immobility
nieruchomy (ńe-roo-khó-mi) adj.
m. immobile; fixed ;still;at rest
nierychło (ńe-rikh-wo) adv. not
soon; slowly; not forthcoming
nierzadko ńe-zhád-ko) adv. often; now and then; not seldom
nierząd (ńe-zhoẃnt) m. prostitution; anarchy; debauchery
nierzeczowy (ńe-zhe-chó-vi) adj.
m. pointless; futile
nierzeczywisty (ńe-zhe-chi-veés-
ti) adj. m. unreal ;fictitious
nierzetelny (ńe-zhe-tél-ni) adj.
m. dishonest; unreliable
niesamowity (ńe-sa-mo-veé-ti)
adj. m. weird; uncanny; unearthy
niesforny (ńe-sfór-ni) adj. m.
unruly; disorderly ;turbulent
nieskalany (ńe-ska-lá-ni) adj.
m. immaculate; spotless; pure
nieskazitelny (ńe-ska-źhee-tél-
ni) adj. m. unblemished; upright; spotless; moral
nieskładny (ńe-skwád-ni) adj.
m. awkward ;discordant;clumsy
nieskończonosc (ńe-skoń-cho-
nośhćh) f. infinity
nieskończony (ńe-skoń-chó-ni)
adj. m. unfinished; infinite
nieskromny (ńe-skróm-ni) adj.
m. indecent; immodest;morally
offensive; improper

nieskuteczny (ńe-skoo-tech-ni) adj. m. ineffective: futile
niesłabnący (ńe-swab-nown-tsi) adj. m. unabated;unflagging
niesława (ńe-swá-va) f. infamy
niesławny (ńeswáv-ni) adj. m. infamous ;inglorious:disgraceful
niesłowny (ńe-swóv-ni) adj. m. unreliable; undependable
niesłusznosć (ńe-swoósh-noshćh) f. injustice :groundlessness
niesłuszny (ńe-swoósh-ni) adj. m. unjust; wrong :groundless
niesłychany (ńe-swi-khá-ni) adj. m. unheard of; unprecedented
niesmaczny (ńe-smách-ni)adj. m. tasteless: unsavory; unseemly
niesmak (ńes-mak) m. bad taste; disgust: repugnance;nasty taste
niesnaski (ńes-nás-kee) pl. dissension ;discord; quarrels
niespełna (ńes-péw-na) adv. nearly; not all;not quite: about
niespodzianka (ńe-spo-dźhán-ka) f. surprise : surprise gift
niespodziewany (ńe-spo-dźhe-vá-ni) adj. m. unexpected ;unlooked for
niespokojny (ńe-spo-kóy-ni) adj. m. restless; fussy :upset;fretful
niesporo (ńe-spo-ro) adv. slowly
nie sposób (ńe spó-soop) adv. it's impossible :by no means
niespożyty (ńe-spo-zhi-ti) adj. m. durable; indefatigable
niesprawiedliwość (ńe-spra-vyed-leé-voshćh) f. injustice
niesprawiedliwy (ńe-spra-vyed-leé-vi) adj. m. unjust;unfair
niesprawny (ńe-správ-ni) adj. m. ineffective; inefficient
nie sprzyjający (ńe spzhi-ya-yówn-tsi) adj. m. adverse
niestały (ńe-sta-wi) adj. m. unsteady; inconsistent;variable
niestaranny (ńe-sta-ran-ni) adj. m. careless;sloppy: dowdy
niestateczny (ńe-sta-tech-ni) adj. m. unstable; fickle: flighty
niestety (ńe-sté-ti) adv. alas; unfortunately: I am sorry
niestosowny (ńe-sto-sóv-ni) adj. m. improper; unsuitable;unfit: inappropriate; out of place

niestrawnosć (ńe-strav-noshćh) f. indigestion: dyspepsia
niestrawny (ńe-stráv-ni) adj. m. indigestible: stodgy; dull
niestrudzony (ńe-stroo-dzó-ni) adj. m. indefatigable; uptiring
niestworzony (ńe-stvo-zhó-ni) adj. m. unreal; nonsense
niesumienny (ńe-soo-myeń-ni) adj. m. unscrupulous ;unreliable
nieswojo (ńe-svó-yo) adv. uneasily;strangely: qualmishly
nieswój (ńe-svooy) adj. m. ill at ease; uncomfortable;seedy; strange : off color
niesymetryczny (ńe-si-me-trich-ni) adj. m. asymmetrical
niesympatyczny (ńe-sim-pa-tich-ni) adj. m. unpleasant
nieszczególny (ńe-shche-goól-ni) adj. m. mediocre ; so-so
nieszczelny (ńe-shchél-ni) adj. m. leaky; not shut tight
nieszczery (ńe-shche-ri) adj. m. insincere; double dealing
nieszczęsny (ńe-shcháns-ni) adj. m. miserable; ill-fated
nieszczęście (ńe-shchań-śhćhe) n. misfortune; disaster
nieszczęśliwy (ńe-śhćhań-śhlee-vi) adj. m. unhappy;ill-starred
nieszkodliwy (ńe-shkod-lee-vi) adj. m. harmless; not grave
nieszlachcic (ńe-shlákh-tseets) m. commoner; man not of gentry
nieszpetny (ńe-shpet-ni) adj. m. fairly good-looking
nieszpory (ńe-shpó-ri) pl. vespers; evening prayers
niescisły (ńe-śhćhees-wi) adj. m. inexact: inaccurate; faulty
niescisliwy (ńe-śhćheesh-lee-vi) adj. m. incompressible
nieść (ńeshćh) v. carry; bring; bear; lay; afford; drive;waft
nieslubny (ńe-shloob-ni) adj. m. illegitimate; out of wedlock
niesmiały (ńe-śhmyá-wi) adj. m. coy; shy; timid; bashful
niesmiertelny (ńe-śhmyer-tél-ni) adj. m. immortal: everlasting
nieświadomy (ńe-śhvya-dó-mi) adj. m. ignorant; unaware :involuntary

nietakt (ñe-takt) m. lack of
tact; slip; taktlessness
nietaktowny (ñe-tak-tóv-ni) adj.
m. tactless; indelicate
nietknięty (ñe-tknáñ-ti) adj. m.
intact;virgin;untouched
nietolerancja (ñe-to-le-ránts-ya)
f. intolerance
nietoperz (ñe-tó-pesh) m. bat
nietowarzystki (ñe-to-va-zhís-
kee) adj. n. unsociable
nietrafny (ñe-tráf-ni) adj. m.
wrong; missing the mark
nietrzeźwy (ñe-tzheźh-vi) adj.
m. drank; tipsy;unsound
nietutejszy (ñe-too-téy-shi) adj.
m. stranger; non-resident
nietykalny (ñe-ti-kál-ni) adj.
m. immune; inviolable
nie tyle (ñe tí-le) adv.not so
much : not exactly; but;rather
nie tylko (ñe tíl-ko) adv. not
only ; anything but
nieubłagalny (ñe-oo-bwa-gál-ni)
adj. m. implacable;irrevocable
nieuchronny (ñe-oo-khrón-ni) adj.
inevitable ; inescapable
nieuchwytny (ñe-oo-khvít-ni) adj.
m. elusive;evasive;inaudible
nieuctwo (ñe-oóts-tvo) n. lack
of education : ignorance
nieuczciwy (ñe-ooch-chée-vi) adj.
m. dishonest ; foul;unfair
nieuczynny (ñe-oo-chín-ni) adj.
m. unobliging ; disobliging
nieudolny (ñe-oo-dól-ni) adj. m.
awkward; clumsy; decrepit
nieufny (ñe-oóf-ni) adj. m. dis-
trustful : suspicious
nieugaszony (ñe-oo-ga-shó-ni)
adj. m. unextinguished; un-
quenchable; unsuppressible
nieugięty (ñe-oo-gyáñ-ti) adj.
m. inflexible;unyielding
nieuk (ñe-ook) m. know-nothing
nieukojony (ñe-oo-ko-yó-ni) adj.
m. inconsolable
nieuleczalny (ñe-oo-le-chál-ni)
adj. m. incurable
nieumiarkowany (ñe-oo-myar-ko-
vá-ni) adj. m. intemperate
nieumiejętny (ñe-oo-mee-yáñt-
ni) adj. m. inexpert; unskilled

nieumyślny (ñe-oo-míshl-ni)
adj. m. unintentional
nieunikniony (ñe-oo-ñeek-ñó-ni)
adj. m. unavoidable:inevitable
nieuprzedzony (ñe-oo-pzhe-dzó-
ni) adj. m. unbiased; not
forwarned; not prejudiced
nieuprzejmy (ñe-oo-pzhéy-mi)
adj. m. impolite; discourteous
nieurodzaj (ñe-oo-ró-dzay) m.
bad harvest; bad crops;scarcity
nie usprawiedliwiony (ñe-oos-pra-
vyed-lee-vyó-ni) adj. m. un-
excused;unjustified; wantom
nieustanny (ñe-oos-tán-ni) adj.
m. constant; perpetual;unceasing
nieustraszony (ñe-oos-tra-sho-
ni) adj. m. fearless; intrepid
nieusuwalny (ñe-oo-soo-vál-ni)
adj. m. immovable: irremovable
nie uszkodzony (ñe oosh-ko-dzó-
ni) adj. m. unhurt; undamaged
nieuwaga (ñe-oo-vá-ga) f. inat-
tention; absentmindedness
nieuważny (ñe-oo-vázh-ni) adj.
m. inattentive;careless
nieuzasadniony (ñe-oo-za-sad-ñó-
ni) adj. m. unfounded;unjustified
nieuzbrojony (ñe-ooz-bro-yó-ni)
adj. m. unarmed: disarmed
nieużyteczny (ñe-oo-zhi-téch-
ni) adj. m. useless; superfluous
nieużyty (ñe-oozhí-ti) adj. m.
unused; uncooperative;disobliging
niewart (ñe-vart) adj. m. not
worth: unworthy; not deserving
nie warto (ñe vár-to) adv. not
worth (talking):not worth while
nieważny (ñe-vázh-ni) adj. m.
invalid; trivial;null and void
niewątpliwy (ñe-vówñt-plée-vi)
adj. m. sure; doubtless
niewczesny (ñe-vchés-ni) adj.
m. untimely; late; inopportune
niewdzięczny (ñe-vdzháñch-ni)
adj. m. ungrateful; thankless
niewesoły (ñe-ve-só-wi) adj.
m. sad; joyless; pretty bad
niewiadomy (ñe-vya-dó-mi) adj.
m. unknown(direction, origin etc.)
niewiara (ñe-vyá-ra) f. disbelief; mistrust; unbelief
niewiasta (ñe-vyás-ta) f. woman

niewidomy (ñe-vee-do-mi) adj.
m. blind;lacking insight
niewidzialny (ñe-vee-dzhal-ni)
adj. m. invisible
niewiedza(ñe-vye-dza) adj. m.
ignorance: unawarness
niewiele (ñe-vye-le) adv. not
much; not many: little: few
niewielki (ñe-vyel-kee) adj. m.
small; little: unimportant
niewierny (ñe-vyer-ni) adj. m.
disloyal; infidel; unfaithful
niewieści (ñe-vyesh-chee) adj.
m. womanly: feminine
niewinność (ñe-veen-noshch) f.
innocence: purity: chastity
niewinny (ñe-veen-ni) adj. m.
not guilty: innocent;harmless
niewłaściwy (ñe-vwash-chee-vi)
adj. m. improper: unsuitable
niewola (ñe-vo-la) f. captivity;
slavery; bondage:servitude
niewolić (ñe-vo-leech) v. enslave; compel: oppress
niewolnica (ñe-vol-ñee-tsa) f.
slave: serf: prisoner of war
niewolnik (ñe-vol-ñeek) m. slave
nie wolno (ñe vol-no) v. not
allowed ; not permitted
niewód (ñe-voot) m. dragnet
niewprawny (ñe-vprav-ni) adj.
m. unversed; unskilled; inexpert: incompetent: inefficient
niewspołmierny (ñe-wspoow-myer-
ni) adj. m. incommensurable
nie wtajemniczony(ñe-vta-yem-
nee-cho-ni) adj. m. uninitiat-
ed; outsider: not privy
niewyczerpany (ñe-vi-cher-pa-ni)
adj. m. inexhaustible
niewygoda (ñe-vi-go-da) f. discomfort: trouble: hardship
niewygodny (ñe-vi-god-ni) adj.
m. uncomfortable: awkward
niewykonalny (ñe-vi-ko-nal-ni)
adj. m. unfeasible: unworkable
niewykształcony (ñe-vi-kshtaw-
tso-ni) adj. m. uneducated
niewymierny (ñe-vi-myer-ni) adj.
m. irrational; surd
niewymowny (ñe-vi-mov-ni) adj.
m. unspeakable:inexpressible

niewymuszony (ñe-vi-moo-sho-ni)
adj. m. free (and easy)
niewymyślny (ñe-vi-mishl-ni)
adj. m. unsophisticated
niewypał (ñe-vi-paw) m. dud
niewypłacalny (ñe-vi-pwa-tsal-
ni) adj. m. insolvent
niewypowiedziany (ñe-vi-po-vye-
dżhá-ni) adj. m. untold
niewyraźnie (ñe-vi-rażh-ñe) adv.
indistinctly : seedily
niewyraźny (ñe-vi-rażh-ni) adj.
m. queer; indistinct
niewyrobiony (ñe-vi-ro-byo-ni)
adj. m. raw; inexperienced
niewyrozumiały (ñe-vi-ro-zoo-
myá-wi) adj. m. intolerant
niewysłowiony (ñe-vi-swo-vyo-
ni) adj. m. ineffable
niewyspany (ñe-vis-pa-ni) adj.
m. sleepy; not slept enough
niewystarczający (ñe-vis-tar-
cha-yown-tsi) adj. m. insufficient : inadequate
niewystawny (ñe-vis-tav-ni) adj.
m. frugal; modest; simple
niewytłumaczony (ñe-vi-twoo-ma-
cho-ni) adj. m. inexplicable
niewytrwały (ñe-vi-trva-wi)
adj. m. not persistent
niewytrzymały (ñe-vi-tzhi-ma-wi)
adj. m. not enduring
niewzruszony (ñe-vzroo-sho-ni)
adj. m. unmoved ;rigid
niezachwiany (ñe-za-khvya-ni)
adj. m. unshaken ;undeterred
niezadowolenie (ñe-za-do-vo-le-
ñe) n . discontent :displeasure
niezadowolony (ñe-za-do-vo-lo-ni)
adj. m. dissatisfied :displeased
niezakłócony (ñe-za-kwoo-tso-ni)
adj. m. undisturbed :upmarred
niezależność (ñe-za-lezh-noshch)
f. independence :self-sufficiency
niezależny (ñe-za-lezh-ni) adj.
m. independent; self contained
niezamężna (ñe-za-mañzh-na) adj.
f. unmarried :single woman
niezamożny (ñe-za-mozh-ni) adj.
m. rather poor: indigent
niezapominajka (ñe-za-po-mee-
náy-ka) f. forget-me-not

niezapomniany (ně-za-pom-ňá-ni)
adj. m. not-to-be-forgotten
niezaprzeczalny (ňe-za-pzhe-
chál-ni) adj. m. undeniable
niezaradny (ně-za-rád-ni) adj.
m. helpless ' resourceless
niezasłużony (ňe-za-swoo-zhó-
ni) adj. m. undeserved
niezawisły (ňe-za-veés-wi) adj.
m. independent:self-dependent
niezawodnie (ňe-za-vód-ňe) adv.
surely; without fail:infallibly
niezawodny (ňe-za-vód-ni) adj.
m. sure: never failing: safe
niezbadany (ňe-zba-dá-ni) adj.
m. unexplorable:,inscrutable
niezbędny (ňe-zbáňd-ni) adj.
m, indispensable: essential
niezbity (ňe-zbée-ti) adj. m.
irrefutable; uncontrovertible
niezbyt (ňe-zbít) adv. not very
(much) : none too; not too
niezdarny (ňe-zdár-ni) adj. m.
clumsy: awkward;,bungled
niezdatny (ňe-zdát-ni) adj. m.
unfit: unqulified:unserviceable
niezdecydowany (ňe-zde-tsi-do-
vá-ni) adj. m. undecided
niezdolność (ňe-zdól-noshch)
f. inability; unfitness
niezdolny (ňe-zdol-ni) adj. m.
incapable; unable;unfit: dull
niezdrowy (ňe-zdro-vi) adj. m.
unhealthy: unwell:ill;sickly
niezdyscyplinowany (ňe-zdis-tsi-
plee-no-vá-ni) adj. m. un-
disciplined : unruly
niezgłębiony (ňe-zgwáňb-yó-ni)
adj. m. inscrutable: abyssal
niezgoda (ňe-zgó-da) f. discord;
disagreement: dissension
niezgodność (ňe-zgód-noshch)
f. inconsistency,; clash
niezgodny (ňe-zgód-ni) adj. m.
discordant; incompatible
niezgrabny (ňe-zgráb-ni) adj.
m. unhandy; clumsy;shapeless
nieziszczalny (ňe-zeesh-chál-
ni) adj. m. unattainable
niezliczony (ňe-zlee-chó-ni)
adj. m. uncountable:countless
niezłomny (ňe-zwóm-ni) adj. m.
inflexible; firm: steadfast

niezmącony (ňe-zmówň-tsó-ni)
adj. m. unruffled:undisturbed
niezmienny (ňe-zmyeň-ni) adj.
m. invariable: constant;fixed
niezmierny (ňe-zmyér-ni) adj.
m. immense: vast: boundless
niezmordowany (ňe-zmor-do-vá-ni)
adj. m. indefatigable;tireless
nieznaczny (ňe-znách-ni) adj.
m. trivial; insignificant
nieznajomość (ňe-zna-yo-moshch)
f. ignorance: unawareness
nieznajomy (ňe-zna-yó-mi) adj.
m. unknown; strange (faces etc.)
nieznany (ňe-zná-ni) adj. m.
unknown: unfamiliar: obscure
nieznośny (ňe-znósh-ni) adj. m.
unbearable: annoying:nasty;pesky
niezręczny (ňe-zráňch-ni) adj.
m. awkward: clumsy;tactless
niezrozumiały (ňe-zro-zoo-mya-
wi) adj. m. unintelligible
niezrównany (ňe-zroov-ná-ni)
adj. m. matchless; incomparable;peerless: unique; grand
niezwłoczny (ňe-zvwóch-ni) adj.
m. instant:prompt: immediate
niezwyciężony (ňe-zvi-cháň-zhó-
ni) adj. m. invincible
niezwykły (ňe-zvík-wi) adj. m.
unusual;extreme: rare: odd
nieżonaty (ňe-zho-ná-ti) adj.
m. unmarried: single: bachelor
nieżyczliwy (ňe-zhich-lee-vi)
adj. m. unfriendly;ill-disposed
nieżyt (ňe-zhit) m. inflamma-
tion:catarrh; hay fever:colitis
nieżywy (ňe-zhi-vi) adj. m.
dead; lifeless: inanimate
nigdy (ňeeg-di) adv. never
nigdzie (ňeeg-dzhe) adv. nowhere: anywhere(after negation)
nijaki (ňee-ya-kee) adj. m.
none; neuter (gender)
nikczemnik (ňeek-chém-ňeek) m.
villain: scoundrel; wretch
nikczemny (ňeek-chém-ni) adj.
vile:abject; despicable: base
nikel (ňee-kel) m. nickel
nikły (ňéek-wi) adj. m. scanty
niknąć (ňéek-nówňch) v. vanish
nikotyna (ňee-ko-tí-na) f. nicotine: poisonous tabacco extract

nikt (ñeekt) pron. nobody
nim (ñeem) conj. before:till
nimb (ñeemp) m. halo:aureole
niniejszy (ñee-ñey-shi) adj. m.
this; present: the present
niski (ñees-kee) adj. m. low
nisko (ñees-ko) adv. low
nisza (ñee-sha) f. niche;recess
niszczący (ñeesh-chown-tsi) adj.
m. destructive: disruptive
niszczeć (ñeesh-chech) v. waste
away: deteriorate: decay:waste
niszczyciel (ñeesh-chi-chel)
m. devastator: destrover:waster
niszczyć (ñeesh-chich) v. destroy;spoil:ruin: wreck;damage
nit (ñeet) m. rivet
nitka (ñeet-ka) f. thread
nitować (nee-to-vach) v. rivet
niwa (ñee-va) f. field:soil
niweczyc (ñee-vé-chich) v. destroy: annihilate: lay waste
niwelacja (ñee-ve-láts-ya) f.
leveling; survey: surveying
niwelować (nee-ve-lo-vach) v.
level: survey
nizina (ñee-żhee-na) f. lowland
niż (ñeezh) m. lowland;atmospher-
ic low
niż (ñeesh) conj. than
niżej (ñee-zhey) adv. lower;
below; down: further down
niższość (ñeesh-shoshch) f.
inferiority
niższy (neezh-shi) adj. m. lower; inferior: shorter
no (no) part. why; well; now;
then: just: there· there now!
noc (nots) f. night
nocleg (nots-leg) m. place to
sleep : night's lodging
nocny (nots-ni) adj. m. noctur-
nal; night-
nocować (no-tso-vach) v. spend
night· stay overnight; sleep
noga (no-ga) f. leg : foot
nogawica (no-ga-vee-tsa) f.
legging : trouser leg
nomenklatura (no-men-kla-too-
ra) f. nomenclature
nominacja (no-mee-nats-ya) f.
appointment : nomination
nominalny (no-mee-nál-ni) adj.
m. nominal : face(value)

nonsens (non-sens) m. nonsense
nora (no-ra) f. burrow
norma (nor-ma) f. standard;
norm: rule: general principle
normalizacja (nor-ma-lee-zats-
ya) f. normalization;standard
normalizować (nor-ma-lee-zo-vach)
v. normalize: standardize
normalny (nor-mal-ni) adj. m.
normal: standard: ordinary
normowac (nor-mo-vach) v. regulate: standardize;normalize
nos (nos) m. nose : snout
nosic (no-sheech) v. carry;
wear: bear :have about one
nosorożec (no-so-ro-shets) m.
rhinoceros (with horn )
nostalgia (nos-tál-gya) f. nostalgia: homesickness
nosze (no-she) pl. stretchers
nota (no-ta) f. note; grade
notariusz (no-tár-yoosh) m. notary public
notatka (no-tát-ka) f. note
notatnik (no-tát-ñeek) m. note-
book· diary: notes
notes (no-tes) m. pocket note-
book· notebook
notoryczny (no-to-rich-ni) adj.
m. notorious : flagrant:arrant
notować (no-to-vach) v. make
notes; take notes: write down
notowanie (no-to-va-ñe) n.
quotation : record
nowela (no-ve-la) f. short
story : amendment
nowelista (no-ve-lees-ta) m.
short story writer
nowicjat (no-veéts-yat) m. novitiate : novitiate
nowicjusz (no-veéts-yoosh) m.
novice : beginner: tiro
nowina (no-vee-na) f. news
nowinka (no-veen-ka) f. fad
nowiutki (no-vyoot-kee) adj. m.
brand-new; spick-and-span
nowoczesny (no-vo-ches-ni) adj.
m. modern :up to date:newest
noworoczny (no-vo-roch-ni) adj.
m. New Year's : of New Year
nowość (no-voshch) f. novelty
nowotwór (no-vo-tvoor) m. tumor : new coined word

nowożytny (nu-vo-zhit-ni) adj.
m. (of) modern (perio
nowy (no-vi) adj. m. new
nozdrze (nóz-dzhe) n. nostril
nożownik (no-zhov-neek) m.
knifer; knife-fighter
nożyce (no-zhi-tse) pl. shears;
clippers ! large shears
nożyczki (no-zhich-kee) pl.
scissors; small scissors
nożyk (no-zhik) m.pocketknife
nów (noov) m. new moon
nóż (noosh) m. knife ;cutter
nucić (noo-cheech) v. hum
nuda (noo-da) f. boredom
nudności(nood-nosh-chee) pl.
nausea : impulse to vomit
nudny (nood-ni) adj. m. boring;
nauseating :dull: sickening
nudysta (noo-dis-ta) m. nudist
nudziarz (noo-dzhash) m. bore
nudzić (noo-dzheech) v. bore
numer (noo-mer) m. number
numerować (noo-me-ro-vach) v.
number : give a number to
numerowy (noo-me-ro-vi) adj. m.
porter; bell-boy: hotel waiter
numizmatyka (noo-meez-ma-ti-ka)
f. numismatics ;study of coins
nuncjusz (noon-tsyoosh) m. nun-
cio ; papal ambassador
nurek (noo-rek) m. diver
nurkować (noor-ko-vach) v. dive
nurt (noort) m. current (flowing): stream: trend; wake
nurtować (noor-to-vach) v. fret;
penetrate ; pervade: ferment
nurzać (noo-zhach) v. dip; welter in; plunge :immerse:steep
nuta (noo-ta) f. (sound) note
nuty (noo-ti) pl. written music: printed music: score
nuż (noozh) adv. if; and if
nużący (noo-zhown-tsi) adj. m.
tiring :tiresome: wearisome
nużyć (noo-zhich) v. tire :weary
nygus (ni-goos) m. lazybones
nygusować (ni-goo-so-vach) v.
lounge about; loiter ; loaf
nylon (ne-lon) m. nylon
nyża (ni-zha) f. niche; alcove

o (o) prep. of; for; at; by;
about; against; with; to: over
oaza (o-a-za) f. oasis
oba (o-ba) pron. both
obabrać (o-ba-brach) v. besmear
obaj (o-bay) pron. both
obalenie (o-ba-le-ne) n. overthrow: subversion; abolition
obalić (o-ba-leech) v. overthrow :knock down: fell;refute
obarczyć (o-bar-chich) v. encumber; saddle :load: burden
obarzanek (o-ba-zha-nek) m.
round cracknel torus shaped
obawa (o-ba-va) f. fear; apprehension ; phobia;anxiety
obawiać się (o-bav-yach shań) v.
be anxious ; fear: dread
obcas (ob-tsac) m. heel
obcążki (ob-tsownzh-kee) pl.
(small) tongs : pincers:pliers
obcesowo (ob-tse-so-vo) adv.
headlong; outright :abruptly
obcęgi (ob-tsań-gee) pl. tongs
obchodzic (ob-kho-dzheech) v.
go around; evade; elude;
celebrate :inspect:by-pass
obchód (ob-khoot) m. (daily)
beat; celebration ;circuit
obciągać (ob-chown-gach) v.
pull down; cover; pull tight
obciążać (ob-chown-zhach) v.
burden; charge (account)
obcierać (ob-chę-rach) v. wipe
obcinać (ob-chee-nach) v. cut
off; clip :crop;chop off
obcisły (ob-chees-wi) adj. m.
tight : close fitting:clinging
obcokrajowiec (ob-tso-kra-yo-
vyets) m. foreigner : alien
obcokrajowy (ob-tso-kra-yo-vi)
adj. m. foreign : alien
obcować (ob-tso-vach) v. associate :have an intercourse
obcowanie (ob-tso-va-ne) n. intercourse; association
obcy (ob-tsi) adj. m. strange;
foreign :unfamiliar: unrelated
obczyzna (ob-chiz-na) f.foreign
country ; exile: foreign land
obdarować (ob-da-ro-vach) v.
bestow :lavish gifts on ...

obdarty (ob-dar-ti) adj. m. ragged;in rags: tattered

obdarzyć (ob-da-zhich) v. bestow: lavish gifts on ...

obdzielić (ob-dzhe-leech)v. divide; distribute ;deal;endow

obdzierać (ob-dzhe-rach)v. rip off; skin off ;strip; fleece

obecnie (o-bets-ñe) adv. at present ;just ɲow;to-day

obecnosc (o-bets-noshch) f. presence : attendaɲce

obejmowac (o-bey-mo-vach) v. embrace; enfold; span; include; take over; take in; grasp

obejrzeć (o-bey-zhech) v. inspect ; glancę at; see

obejście (o-bey-shche) n. bypass; farmyard ; manner

obejść (o-beyshch) v. go around

obelga (o-bel-ga) f. insult; outrage; abuse: affront

obelżywy (o-bel-zhi-vi) adj. m. insulting; abusive:opprobrious

oberwac (o-ber-vach) v. tear off; cop it; pluck:get a knock

oberża (o-ber-zha) f. inn

oberżysta (o-ber-zhis-ta) m. innkeeper:owner of an inn

oberżnąć (o-ber-zhnównch) v. cut off; trim; clip

obeschnąć (o-bes-khnównch) v. dry up: get dry: dry

obetrzec (o-be-tzhech) v. wipe out: dust: rub sore: skin

obezwładnic (o-bez-vwad-ñeech) v. overpower:subdue: disable

obeznany (o-bez-na-ni) adj. m. familiar: acquainted;conversant

obfitosc (ob-fee-toshch) f. plenty: abundance:profusion

obfity (ob-fee-ti) adj. m. abundant: ample: profuse:liberal

obgadywac (ob-ga-di-vach) v. talk ill; talk over: crab

obgryzac (ob-gri-zach) v. nibble bare: gnaw: pick a bone: bite

obiad (ob-yat) m. dinner

obicie (o-bee-che) n. upholstery; padding; chip; beating ;drubbing

obiecywac (o-bye-tsi-vach) v. promise: look forward to

obieg (o-byek) m. circulation

obiegac (o-bye-gach) v. runaround; circulate;revolve

obiekcja (o-byek-tsya) f. objection: demur

obiekt (ob-yekt) m. object; target: subject: building

obiektyw (o-byek-tiv) m.object-lens: object-glass; ɟbjective

obiektywny (o-byek-tiv-ni) adj. m. objective;impartial

obierac (o-bye-rach) v. choose; elect; peel: pick: strip

obierzyny (o-bye-zhi-ni) pl. peelings; parings

obieralny (o-bye-ral-ni) adj. m. elective: eligibɭe

obietnica (o-byet-ñee-tsa) f. promise: engagement

obijac (o-bee-yach) v. chip; hoop; loaf ;hurt: injure

objadac się (ob-ya-dach shañ) v. gorge; overeat : cram

objasniac (ob-yash-ñach) v. explain ; make clear: gloss

objaw (ɟb-yav) m. symptom

objawic (ob-ya-veech) v. reveal

objazd (ɟb-yazt) m. tour; circuit ;detour:diversion:by-pass

objąc (ɟb-yównch) v. embrace; assume: grasp: encompass:span

objeżdżac (ob-yezh-dzhach) v. ride; around;break in a horse

objętosc (ob-yañ-toshch) f. volume; bulk:capacity: content

obkładac (ob-kwa-dach) v. wrap; cover: line: impose:hit:buffet

oblegac (ob-le-gach) v. besiege

oblac (ɟb-lach) v. pour on(water)

oblekac (ob-le-kach) v. clothe; put on; cover; encase: don

oblepiac (ob-le-pyach) v. paste over: stick: post:plaster over

oblewac (ob-le-vach) v. pour on: drench: bathe; sprinkle·wash

oblężenie (ob-lañ-zhe-ñe) m. siege: state of siege

obliczac (ob-lee-chach) v. count: reckon; figure out: mean

oblicze (ob-lee-che) n. face

obliczenie (ob-lee-che-ñe) n. calculation: evaluation: count

obligacja (ob-lee-gáts-ya) f.
obligation; bond ; share
oblizać (ob-lee-zach) v. lick
obładować (ob-wa-do-vach) v.
load down;heap; burden
obława (ob-wá-va) f. roundup;
posse ; man hunt: chase: raid
obłąkany (ob-wown-ká-ni) adj.
m. insane; loony; madman
obłęd (ób-waht) m. insanity
obłędny (ob-wand-ni) adj. m.
mad; wild ; insane: crazy
obłok (ób-wok) m. cloud
obłowić się (ob-wo-veech shan)
v. pick up a lot;make a pile
obłożnie (ob-wózh-ne) adv. bedridden; severely (ill)
obłożyc (ob-wo-zhich) v. cover;
wrap: line:impose: hit;buffet
obłuda (ob-woo-da) f. hypocrisy
obłudnik (ob-wood-neek) m.hyp-
ocrite:snuffler:dissembler
obłudny (ob-wood-ni) adj. m.
hypocritical;false: canting
obłupać (ob-woo-pach) v. shell;
peel :bark: flay: skin
obłuszczać (ob-woosh-chach) v.
scale; shell: husk; flay: skin
obły (ob-wi) adj.oval;tapering;
terete; cylindrical: oval
obmacać (ob-ma-tsach) v. feel
about; explore with fingers
obmawiac (ob-maw-yach) v. slander; backbite; gossip:speak ill
obmierznąć (ob-myerzh-nownch) v.
get sick of (something)
obmowa (ob-mo-va) f. slander;
detraction: backbiting
obmurować (ob-moo-ró-vach) v.
brick in; brick veneer
obmyślać (ob-mish-lach) v. design; contrive; reflect
obmywac (ob-mi-vach) v. wash-
up :sponge·down·give a wash
obnażac (ob-na-zhach) v. denude;
bare ; unclothe:strip;uncover
obniżac (ob-nee-zhach) v. lower;
sink; drop; abate; level down
obniżenie (ob-nee-zhé-ne) n.
decrease; reduction; lowering
obniżka (ob-neezh-ka) f. reduction; depreciation:drop:fall

obojczyk (o-bóy-chik) m. collar
bone;clavicle: amice:gorget
obnosic (ob-nó-sheech) v. take
around; flaunt ; parade
obojętnie (o-bo-yaht-ne) adv.
indifferently;slapg:no matter
obojętność (o-bo-yaht-noshch)
f. indifference: neutrality
obojętny (o-bo-yant-ni) adj. m.
indifferent; neutral
obok (ó-bok) adv. prep. beside;
next; about:close by:by:close
obopólny (o-bo-pool-ni) adj. m.
common; mutual:reciprocal
obora (o-bó-ra) f. cowbarn
obosieczny (o-bo-shéch-ni) adj.
m.two-edged: double edged
obowiązek (o-bo-vyówn-zek) m.
duty; obligation: responsibility
obowiązkowy (o-bo-vyownz-ko-vi)
adj. m. dutiful; compulsory
obowiązany (o-bo-wyówn-za-ni)
adj. m. obligated;compelled
obowiązujący (o-bo-vyówn-zoo-
yown-tsi) adj. m. obligatory
obowiązywac (o-bo-vyówn-zi-vach)
v. be in force (law etc)
obozować (o-bo-zó-vach) v. camp;
camp out: tent:encamp;bivouac
obój (o-booy) m. oboe, (horn)
obóz (o-boos) m. camp
obrabiać (ob-ra-byach) v. machine (metal, wood etc.); work-
over; fashion; shape;till:hem
obrabiarka (ob-rab-yar-ka) f.
machine tool: lathe
obrabowac (ob-ra-bo-vach) v. rob
obracac (ob-ra-tsach) v. turnover; rotate: crank
obrachowac (ob-ra-khó-vach) v.
compute: figure out: calculate
obrachunek (ob-ra-khoo-nek) m.
settlement; bill;"day of reckoning":count: reckoning
obrada (ob-ra-da) f. conference
obradować (ob-ra-do-vach) v.
confer: deliberate: debate: sit
obradzać (ob-ra-dzach) v. bear
crops: yield a crop:be plentiful
obramowac (ob-ra-mó-vach) v.
frame:encircle; encase:hem:edge
obrastac (ob-ras-tach) v. overgrow: grow ;grow all over

obraz (ob-raz) m. picture;
image : painting:drawing
obraza (ob-ra-za) f. affront;
offense ;insult:outrage:offence
obrazek (ob-ra-zek) m. illustration; small picture
obrazić (ob-ra-źheećh) v. offend : affront; insult:sting
obrazowy (ob-ra-zó-vi) adj. m.
pictorial ; picturesque:vivd
obrażenie (ob-ra-zhé-ńe) n.
offense; injury: insults
obraźliwy (ob-rażh-leé-vi) adj.
m. offensive; touchy:resentful
obrażać (ob-ra-zhaćh) v. offend;
(repeatedly) insult: affront
obrąb (ob-równb) m. cutoff
obrąbek (ob-równ-bek) m. hem
obrączka (ob-równch-ka) f. ring
obręb (ob-rańb) m. compass;
area:reach:extent:precincts
obrębiać (ob-rańb-yaćh) v. hem
obręcz (ob-rańch) f. hoop; tire;
rim: band: gridle: ring:circle
obrobić (ob-ro-beećh) v. machine
obrok (ob-rok) m. feed;fodder
obrona (ob-ro-na) f. defense
obronność (ob-ron-noshćh) f.
defense capability;defences
obronny (ob-ron-ni) adj. m. de-
fensive:fortified:protective
obrońca (ob-roń-tsa) m. defender
guard; barrister:advocate
obrośnięty (ob-rosh-ńań-ti) adj.
m. overgrown;, unshaven
obrotny (ob-rot-ni) adj. m.
active; skillful; nimble:agile
obrotowy (ob-ro-tó-vi) adj. m.
turnover (tax);rotary;revolving
obroża (ob-ro-zha) f. (dog) collar: neck band
obrócić (ob-roo-ćheećh) v. rotate ;revolve :turn: go
obrót (ob-root) m. turn; turnover: revolution: slew: sales
obrus (ob-roos) m. tablecloth
obruszać (ob-roo-shaćh) v. loos-
en up: irritate; bring down
obrywać (ob-ri-vaćh) v. tear
off: tear away:pluck;wrench off
obryzgiwać (ob-riz-gee-vaćh) v.
splash; spatter

obrzęd (ob-zhańd) m. rite; ceremony . custom
obrzęk (ob-zhańk) m. swelling
obrzękły (ob-zhańk-wi) adj. m.
swollen : oedemous: tumid
obrzmiały (obzh-mya-wi) adj.
m. swollen : oedemous: tumid
obrzucać (ob-zhoo-tsaćh) v.
throw upon : hurl:pelt; fell
obrzydliwy (ob-zhid-leé-vi)
adj. m. revolting; disgusting
obrzydzenie (ob-zhi-dzé-ńe) n.
aversion: nausea: disgust
obrzynać (ob-zhi-naćh) v. clip;
cut: cut off; edge: trim;cheat
obsada (ob-sá-da) f. cast; crew;
garrison; staff: mounting
obsadka (on-sad-ka) f. penholder: small mounting
obsadzać (ob-sá-dzaćh) v. plant;
staff: set: fix: occupy;stock
obserwacja (ob-ser-váts-ya) f.
observation: remark
obserwator (ob-ser-vá-tor) m.
observer: look out man:witness
obserwatorium (ob-ser-va-tor-
yoom) m. observatory
obserwować (ob-ser-vo-vaćh) v.
watch; observe; take stock
obsługa (ob-swoo-ga) f. attendance; service: staff
obsługiwać (ob-swoo-geé-vaćh)
v. wait-upon; service
obstalować (ob-sta-lo-vaćh) v.
order (a suit of clothes etc.)
obstalunek (ob-sta-loó-nek) m.
order; a request to supply
obstawać (ob-sta-vaćh) v. insist on; hold to; stand by;
persist in; abide by
obstąpić (ob-stówn-peećh) v.
surround: form a circle;cluster
obstrzał (ob-stzhaw) m. gunfire: scope of fire: firing
obstrukcja (ob-strook-tsya) f.
obstruction; constipation
obsuwać (ob-soo-vaćh) v. slide
down; creep: lower:bring down
obsuwisko (ob-soo-veés-ko) n.
landslide : landslip
obsychać (ob-si-khaćh) v. dry
up : get parched: run dry;go dry

obsyłać (ob-si-wach) v. send around (messengers,etc.)
obsypywac (ob-si-pi-vach) v. strew: sprinkle: shower:heap
obszar (ob-shar) m. area; range
obszarnik (ob-shár-ñeek) m. landowner:large,scale farmer
obszerny (ob-sher-ni) adj. m. spacious: extensive:vast:broad
obsztorcowac (ob-shtor-tso-vach) v. snub; give hard time
obszukac (ob-shoo-kach) v. search: ransack:make a search
obszyc (ob-shich) v. sew around
obuch (o-bookh) m. back of axe; sledge: head,of an axe
obudzic (o-boo-dźheech)v. wake up;awaken; excite; stir up
obumarły (o-boo-mar-wi) adj. m. deadened; half dead:decaying
obumierac (o-boo-myé-rach)v. wither; atrophy:decay: shrink
oburącz (o-boo-rownch) adv. with both hands:with both arms
oburzac (o-boo-zhach) v. revolt; shock· provoke indignation
oburzony (o-boo-zhó-ni) adj. m. indignant: resentful
obustronny (o-boo-strón-ni) adj. m. bilateral;mutual:reciprocal
obuwie (o-boo-vye) n. footwear
obwarowywac (ob-va-ro-vi-vach) v. fortify; entrench: secure
obwąchiwac (ob-vown-khee-vach) v. sniff around:smell around
obowiązywac (ob-vyown-zi-vach) v. bind up; bandage; tie
obwieszczac (ob-vyesh-chach) v. announce; proclaim: notify
obwieszczenie (ob-vyesh-che-ñe) n. proclamation· notice
obwiniac (ob-vee-ñach) v. accuse
obwisac (ob-vee-sach) v. sag; droop: hang loosely: flag
obwodowy (ob-vo-do-vi) adj. m. circumferential; district
obwoluta (ob-vo-loo-ta) f. wrapper; book-jacket: file cover
obwołać (ob-vó-wach) v. acclaim; proclaim· call names
obwód (ob-voot) f. perimeter
oby (obi) part. may...:may you

obycie (o-bi-che) n. good manners: experience;familiarity
obyczaj (o-bi-chay) m. custom
obyczajnosć (o-bi-cháy-noshch) f. decency; morality: morals
obyczajny (o-bi-cháy-ni) adj. m. decent; moral
obydwaj (o-bi-dvay) num. both
obyty (o-bi-ti) adj. m. familiar; easy·mannered:polished
obywac sie (o-bi-vach shań) v. do without: dispense with
obywatel (o-bi-va-tel) m. citizen; squire:inhabitant
obywatelka (o-bi-va-tel-ka) f. citizen: inhabitant: citizeness
obywatelstwo (o-bi-va-tel-stvo) m. citizenship;nationality
obznajomic (ob-zna-yo-meech)v. familiarize: acquaint:inform
obżarstwo (ob-zhar-stvo) n. gluttony: stuffing oneself
ocalec (o-tsá-lech) v.survive (danger)·rescue: save
ocalenie (o-tsa-lé-ñe) n. rescue: salvation: escape
ocalic (o-tsá-leech) v. rescue
ocean (o-tsé-an) m. ocean
ocena (o-tsé-na) f. grade; estimate; appraisal
ocet (o-tset) m. vinegar
och!(okh !) excl.: oh,!
ochędożyc (o-khań-do-zhich) v. clean: put in order
ochlapac (o-khla-pach) v. splash: splatter/with mud)
ochładzac (o-khwá-dzach) v. cool; chill: refresh
ochłap (ó-khwap) m. offal; trash; scrap of meat
ochłonąc (o-khwo-nownch) v. calm down: get cooler: cool
ochoczo (o-khó-cho) adv.eagerly; cheerfully: gladly;gaily
ochota (o-khó-ta) f. eagerness; forwardness; willingness
ochotnik (o-khót-ñeek) n. volunteer· serving of free will
ochraniac (o-khra-ñach) v. protect; preserve: shield
ochrona (o-khró-na) f. (shelter) protection; conservation

ochronny (o-khroń-ni) adj. m.
protective; preventive
ochrypły (o-khrip-wi) adj. m.
hoarse; husky: raucous
ochrypnąć (o-khrip-nównch) v.
hoarsen; grow hoarse
ochrzcić (okh-zhcheéch) v. baptize; christen; name: dub
ociągać się(o-chówn-gach shań)
v. linger: delay:put off
ociec (ó-chets) v. drain; drip
ociekać (o-che-kach) v. drain;
drip: stream; overflow: dry
ociemniały (o-chem-ńa-wi) adj.
m. blind: blind man
ocieniać (o-che-ńach) v. shade
over: protect from the sun
ocieplać (o-chép-lach) v. warm
up: make warmer: get warm
ocierać (o-che-rach) v. wipe
off: rub sore: gall; abrade
ociężały (o-chań-zha-wi) adj.
m. inert; (lazy) heavy; tardy;
dull: ponderous: languid:bovine
ociosać (o-cho-sach) v. hew
ocknąć się (óts-knównch shań)
v. wake up (from a nap) awake
oclić (óts-leech) v. assess custom duty; levy duty;pay duty
oczarować (o-cha-ro-vach) v.
charm; enchant;fascinate:ravish
oczekiwać (o-che-kee-vach) v.
wait for; await; expect;hope
oczekiwanie (o-che-kee-va-ńe)
n. expectation: prospect
oczerniać (o-cher-ńach) v.
slander; malign; defame; vilify
oczko (óch-ko) n. (needle) eye-
let; little eye:mesh:stitch
oczny (óch-ni) adj. m. optic
oczyszczać (o-chish-chach) v.
clean; purify; dust: clear
oczytany (o-chi-ta-ni) adj. m.
well-read: of wide reading
oczywisty (o-chi-vees-ti) adj.
m. obvious; self-evident;plain
oczywiście (o-chi-veésh-che)
adv. obviously; of course
od (od) prep. from; off; of;
for; since; out of; with; per;
by; then (idiomatic)
odbarwić (od-bár-veech) v.
bleach; decolorize

odbicie (od-bee-che) n. reflection; bounce; ricochet; beating
back; deflection: repercussion
odbic (od-beech) v. bounce back;
rescue; recover: reflect:print
odbiegać (od-byé-gach) v. desert; deviate; stray; digress
odbijać (od-bée-yach) v. reflect; print; put off; fend
off; recapture: leave a trace
odbiorca (od-byór-tsa) m. receiver; customer; addressee
odbiornik (od-byór-ńeek) m.
(radio) receiver: collector
odbiór (od-byoor) m. receipt;
reception; collection
odbitka (od-beét-ka) f. copy;
reprint: impression: proof:slip
odblask (ód-blask) m. reflection
of light: gleam: irradiation
odbudowa (od-boo-dó-va) f. reconstruction: restoration
odbudować (od-boo-do-vach) v.
rebuild: restore: reconstruct
odbyt (ód-bit) m. 1. sale
2. anus: end of alimentary tract
odbywać (od-bí-vach) v. do;
perform; be in progress
odcedzić (od-tsé-dżeech) v.
strain: strain out: drain away
odchodzić (od-khó-dżheech)v.
go away; leave; walk off;
split;sail; retire; withdraw
odchudzać (od-khoo-dzach) v.
reduce (weight); slim:slenderize
odchylać (od-khi-lach) v. deflect; slant; slope:bend back
odchylenie (od-khi-lé-ńe) n.
deviation: declination:variation
odciągać (od-chówn-gach) v.
draw aside: retract:divert:delay
odciążać (od-chówn-zhach) v.
relieve;unburden; lighten:ease
odcień (ód-cheń) m. shade; tint;
undertone; tinge:hue:cast: tone
odcierpieć (od-cher-pyech) v.
suffer for; expiate; atone
odcinać (od-chee-nach) v. cut
off; sever; amputate; detach
odcinek (od-chée-nek) m. sector;
segment; space; period; receipt
odcisk (ód-cheesk) m. imprint;
skin-corn: stamp:trace: squeeze

odcyfrować (od-tsi-fró-vach) v.
decipher; make out
odczekać (od-che-kach) v. wait
out: wait for the right moment
odczepić (od-che-peech) v. detach; unhook; get rid:clear out
odczuć (od-choóch) v. feel;
notice; resent; smart from
odczyn (ód-chin) m. (chem) reaction: chemical change
odczynnik (od-chin-ńeek) m.
reagent; reacting substance
odczyt (ód-chit) m. lecture
odczytać (od-chi-tach) v. read
over; take the reading; call
oddać (od-dach) v. give back;
pay back; render; deliver
oddalać (od-da-lach) v. remove;
send away; drive away
oddalony (od-da-lo-ni) adj. m.
distant; remote ;far away
oddany (od-dá-ni) adj. m. given
up; devoted ;loving; intent
oddawać (od-dá-vach) v. give
back; pay back; return:repay
od dawna (od dáv-na) since a
long time :long since
oddech (ód-dekh) m. breath
oddychać (od-di-khach) v.
breathe; take breath; respire
oddział (od-dźhaw) m. division;
section; ward; branch; detail
oddziaływać (od-dzha-wi-vach)
v. influence; affect
oddzielać (od-dźhé-lach) v. separate; divorce; split
oddzielny (od-dźhél-ni) adj. m.
separate ;individual;discrete
oddzierać (od-dźhé-rach) v.
tear off; pull off;null away
oddźwięk (od-dźhvyáńk) m. echo;
resonance; repercussion
odebrać (o-dé-brach) v. take
away; receive; withdraw;regain
odechcieć sic (o-dekh-chech shan)
v. lose interest:cease liking
odegnać (o-dég-nach) v. chase
away; drive away; drive off
odegrać się (o-dé-grach shań) v.
win back; recover;take place
odejmować (o-dey-mo-vach) v.
subtract; deduct; take away
diminish;withdraw; deprive

odejście (o-déy-shche) n. departure ; withdrawal;deviation
odejść (o-deyshch) v. depart;
go away; leave; abandon
odemknąć (o-dem-knównch) v.
open ; half open;set ajar:unbolt
odepchnąć (o-dép-khnównch) v.
shove away; beat back;reject
odeprzeć (o-dep-zhech) v. repel;
repulse; fight off; retort
oderwać (o-dér-vach) v. tear
off; break off; detach;sever
odesłać (o-dés-wach) v. send
back: return;refer; direct
odetchnać (o-dét-knównch) v.
breathe (freely) ; respire
odetkać (o-dét-kach) v. unstop;
open; uncork: unchoke: fall out
odezwa (o-déz-va) f. proclamation; appeal;urgent request
odgadywać (od-ga-di-vach) v.
guess : surmise; solve a riddle
odgałęziac (od-ga-wań-żhach) v.
branch away; fork off; ramify
odganiać (od-ga-ńach) v. chase
away: drive off; dismiss
odgarniać (od-gar-ńach) v. shove
away: rake aside: push aside
odginać (od-gée-nach) v. unbend;
fold back; straighten· curve
odgłos (ód-gwos) m. echo; resonance : sound; noise; thud
odgniatac (od-gńa-tach) v. bruise ; wrinkle; crease (the skin)
odgrażać się (od-gra-zhach sháń)
v.talk big; threaten
odgradzać (od-gra-dzach) v.
fence off; separate; shut out
odgrodzić (od-gro-dźheech) v. divide off; fence off; shut off
odgruzować (od-groo-zó-vach) v.
clear off rubbish from a space
odgrywać (od-gri-vach) v. play
off; perform; act; make believe
odgryzać (od-gri-zach) v. bite
off; snap off; gnaw off
odgrzebywać (od-gzhe-bí-vach) v.
dig up; rake up;unearth: turn up
odgrzewać (od-gzhe-vach) v. re-
warm; rehash; warm up (food)
odjazd (ód-yazt) m. departure
odjeżdżać (od-yézh-dżhach) v.
depart; be off; abandon;start

odjęcie (od-yáñ-che) n. deduction; amputation; weaning
odkazić (od-ka-źheéch) v. disinfect; sterilize
odkażać (od-ka-zhach) v. disinfect (repeatedly); sterilize
odkażenie (od-ka-zhe-ñe) n. disinfection: sterilization
odkąd (od-kównt) adv. since; since when ? ever since;from
odkleić (od-kle-eech) v. unglue; unstick; detach; ungum
odkładać (od-kwa-dach) v. put aside; save; put back;put off
odkłonic się (od-kwo-ñeech śháñ) v. greet back
odkopać (od-ko-pach) v. dig up
odkorkować (od-kor-kó-wach) v. uncork; unjam·(the traffic)
odkręcić (od-kráñ-cheech) v. unscrew; turn around
odkroic (od-kró-yeech) v. cut — off; carve off; slice off
odkryc (od-krich) v. discover; uncover: lay bare;expose;notice
odkrycie (od-kri-che) n. discovery;exploration; exposure
odkupić(od-kóo-peech) v. repurchase; redeem; buy ;replace
odkupienie (od-koo-pye-ñe) n. redemption ; repurchase
odkurzacz (od-koo-zhach) m. vacuum cleaner; carpet sweeper
odkuwać się (od-koo-vach śháñ) v. recoup losses;forge;knock off
odlać (od-lach) v.pour off;cast
odlatywać (od-la-ti-vach) v. fly away; fly off· take off
odległość (od-leg-woshch) f. distance: remotness; interval
odległy (od-leg-wi) adj. m. distant; remote; far away:long ago
odlepiac (od-lep-yach) v. unglue; unstick; detach; ungum
odlew (od-lev) m. cast; pour
odlewać (od-lé-vach) v. pour off; cast; mould; pour out
odlewacz (od-le-vach) m. founder
odlewnia (od-lev-ña) f. foundry
odliczać (od-lee-chach) v. deduct; count;reckon off;allow
odliczenie (od-lee-che-ñe) n. deduction; allowance

odlot (od-lot) m. departure (by plane): take-off; start
odludek (od-loo-dek) m. recluse
odludny (od-lood-ni) adj. m. solitary; lonely; secluded
odłam (od-wam) m. fraction
odłamać (od-wá-mach) v. break off; sever; snap off
odłamek (od-wá-mek) m. chip; splinter; fragment;chip;stub
odłazić (od-wá-źheech) v. crawl away; get unstuck; come off
odłączyc (od-woñ-chich) v. sever; disconnect; separate
odłożyc (od-wó-zhich) v. set aside; put off; put back
odłóg (od-wook) m. fallow
odłupać (od-woo-pach) v. split off; chip off; break off
odma płucna (od-ma pwoots-na) f. pneumothorax; pneumatosis
odmarznąc (od -már-znówñch) v. thaw; melt; get warm;unfreeze
odmawiać (od-máv-yach) v.refuse; say prayers; decline;recite
odmeldowac (od-mel-do-vach) v. take a formal leave
odmęt (od-máñt) m. chaotic whirlpool; confusion; depths
odmiana (od-mýa-na) f. change; alteration;modification
odmieniać (od-mye-ñach) v. change; alter; decline ; conjugate
odmienny (od-myén-ni) adj. m. mutable; different; unlike
odmierzac (od-myé-zhach) v. measure off ;mark off
odmłodzic (od-mwo-dźheech) v. rejuvenate;make (look) younger
odmowa (od-mó-va) f. refusal; denial; saving "no"
odmówic (od-moo-veech) v.refuse; say prayers,: say "no"
odmrozic (od-mro-źheech) v. get frostbite ; get frozen: thaw
odmrożenie (od-mro-zhe-ñe) n. frostbite ; kibe
odmruknąc (od-mrook-nówñch) v. mutter back; grunt out
odnajać (od-ná-yowñch) v. sublet
odnawiać (od-náv-yach) v. renew; renovate ; restore;reform

odnajdywać (od-nay-di-vach) v.
recover; find ; discover
od niechcenia (od ne-khtse-na)
adv. carelessly; willy-nilly
odniemczać (od-nem-chach) v.
de-Germanize (language etc.)
odniesienie (od-ne-she-ne) n.
carrying back; reference (line)
odnieść (od-neshch) v. bring
back; take back ;sustain
odnoga (od-no-ga) f. spur;
branch ; offshoot; river pass
odnosić (od-no-sheech) v. take
back; carry back (repeatedly)
odnośnie (od-nosh-ne) prep.
concerning ; in comparison
odnośnik (od-nosh-neek) m. reference; footnote(in a text)
odnośny (od-nosh-ni) adj. m.
relative; respectiye ;proper
odnotować (od-no-to-vach) v.
check off ; note down; state
odnowa (od-no-va) f. renewal;
restoration ; regeneration
odnowić (od-no-veech) v. renew; renovate :reform;revive
odosobnić (od-o-sob-neech) v.
isolate; confine ;stand alone
odosobnienie (od-o-sob-ne-ne)
n. isolation ;privacy;seclusion
odór (o-door) m. reek; smell
odpad (od-pat) m. refuse; dropout ; waste; muck; scraps
odpadać (od-pa-dach)v. drop off;
fall off ; peel off; come off
odpadki (od-pad-kee) pl. waste
odparcie (od-par-che) n. repulsion; rejection ; refutation
odparować (od-pa-ro-vach) v.
parry; repel; evaporate
odparzenie (od-pa-zhe-ne) n.
gall; scald ; chafe (skin)
odparzyć (od-pa-zhich) v. blister ; chafe one's skin
odpędzać (od-pań-dzach) v. chase-
away; repel: expel;banish
odpiąć (od-pyownch) v. unfasten;
unbutton ;unbuckle; unclasp
odpieczętować (od-pye-chań-to-
vach) v. unseal ;open(a letter)
odpinać (od-pee-nach) v. unbutton; disconnect; undo;unclasp

odpierać (od-pye-rach) v. repel;
refute ; force back; disprove
odpiłowac (od-pee-wo-vach) v.
saw off; file off; cut off
odpis (od-pees) m. copy
odpisać (odpee-sach) v. copy;
write back; answer· deduct
odpłacić (od-pwa-cheech) v.
repay; reciprocate;get back at
odpłata (od-pwa-ta) f. retribution ; repayment; retaliation
odpłynąć (od-pwi-nownch) v.
float away; sail away; swim
away; put to sea  low tide
odpływ (od-pwif) m. ebb; outflow;
odpoczynek (od-po-chi-nek) m.
rest; repose; relax from work
odpoczywać (od-po-chi-vach) v.
rest; have a rest;take a rest
odpokutować (od-po-koo-to-vach)
v. expiate; atone; pay dearly
odporność (od-por-noshch) f.
immunity;resistance:hardiness
odpowiadać (od-po-vya-dach) v.
answer to; correspond to
odpowiedni (od-po-vyed-nee) adj.
m. respective; adequate; suitable; fit; right;due;opportune
odpowiedzialność (od-po-vye-
dzhal-noshch) f. responsibility;
liability: civil liability
odpowiedzialny (od-po-vye-dzhal-
ni) adj. m. responsible; liable;
accountable; trustworthy
odpór (od-poor) m. opposition;
resistance; opposition
odprasować (od-pra-so-vach) v.
press; iron; press out;express
odprawa (od-pra-va) f. dispatch;
rebuff;briefing; debriefing
odprawiać (od-prav-yach) v.dis-
patch; dismiss; celebrate
(mass); order away; send away
odprężać (od-pran-zhach) v. relax; slacken; let down;recoil
odprężenie (od-pran-zhe-ne) m.
relax; easing of tension;détente
odprowadzać (od-pro-va-dzach)
v. divert; drain off; escort
odpruwać (od-proo-vach) v.
rip off (buttons);rip away
odprzedać (od-pzhe-dach)v. resell

odprzedaż (od-pzhé-dash) f. re- sale;sale at second hand
odpust (od-poost) m. indulgence
odpuszczenie (od-poosh-che-ńe) n. foregiveness; remission
odpychać (od-pí-khach) v. repel
odpychanie (od-pi-khá-ńe) n. repulsion; repelling
odra (ód-ra) f. measles pl. rubeola (high fever&skin eruption)
odrabiać (od-ráb-yach) v. work off; work out; get done;undo
odraczać (od-ra-chach) v. put off; postpone; defer; delay
odradzać (od-ra-dzach) v. advise against; regenerate; revive
odrapać (o-dra-pach) v. scratch up; dilapidate; scrape off
odrastać (od-rás-tach) v. grow back; sprout again; shoot again
odraza (od-ra-za) f. aversion
odrazu (od-ra-zoo) adv. at once
odrażający (od-ra-zha-yówn-tsi) adj. m. repulsive; hideus
odrąbać (od-równ-bach) v. chop off; hew away; cut off
odrębność (od-ránb-noshch) n. distinction; individuality
odrębny (od-ránb-ni) adj. m. distinct; individual:separate
odręczny (od-ránch-ni) adj. m. freehand; personal; longhand
odrętwiały (od-ránt-vya-wi) adj. m. numbed; torpid : stiff
odrobić (od-ro-beech) v. work off; work out; get done: do
odrobina (od-ro-bee-na) f. small bit; particle· shred; a dash
odroczenie (od-ro-che-ńe) n. adjournment; postponment
odroczyć (od-ro-chich) v. put off; delay; defer; postpone
odrodzenie (od-ro-dze-ńe) m. rebirth; renaissance
odrodzić (od-ro-dźheech) v. regenerate ;renew; revive
odróżniać (od-roozh-ńach) v. distinquish; differentiate
odróżniać się (od-roozh-ńach shań) v. differ :be different
odruch (ód-rookh) m. reflex
odrywać (od-ri-vach) v. tear off; sever;separate;break off

odrzec (ód-zhech) v. reply
odrzucać (od-zhoó-tsach) v. reject; repulse; cast away
odrzutowiec (od-zhoo-tóv-yets) m. jet (plane)
odrzwia (ód-zhvya) pl. doorframe: mine prop set
odrzynać (od-zhi-nach) v. cut off; cut away; detach: sever
odsądzać (od-sówn-dzach) v. deny; infamize;deprive of merit
odsetka (od-sét-ka) f. interest point; percentage; proportion
odsiadywać (od-śha-di-vach) v. sit out; serve (sentence)
odsiecz (ód-shech) f. rescue
odskoczyć (od-sko-chich) v. jump off; spring back:dart away
odsłonić (od-swó-ńeech) v. unveil;expose; display: show
odsprzedać (od-spzhe-dach) v. resell; sale at second hand
odstawać (od-sta-vach) v. hangloose; not fit; come off
odstawić (od-sta-veech) v. put aside ; deliver; play(dumb)
odstąpić (od-stówn-peech) v. step back; secede; cede
odstęp (ód-stánp) m. margin; space; interval; lapse (of time)
odstępca (od-stánp-tsa) m. renegade; deserter; turncoat
odstępne (od-stánp-ne) n. payment for giving up a lease
odstraszyć (od-stra-shich) v. deter; frighten away;scare
odstręczyć (od-strán-chich) v. dissuade; turn away;repel;deter
odstrzał (ód-stzhaw) m. shooting off; firing (game, mine)
odsunąć (od-soó-nównch) v. push away; shove away; brush aside
odsyłacz (od-si-wach) m. reference mark; footnote mark
odsyłać (od-sí-wach) v. send back; refer ;return; direct
odsypać (od-si-pach) v. pour off (not liquid);alluviate
odsypiać (od-síp-yach) v. catch up on sleep ; sleep off
odszkodowanie (od-shko-do-vá-ńe) n. indemnity : compensation

odszukać (od-shoo-kać) v. retrieve; run down;seek out:find
odśrodkowy (od-śhrod-ko-vi)
adj. m. centrifugal
odświeżyć (od-śhvye-zhićh) v.
refresh; recondition·restore
odświętny (od-śhvyańt-ni) adj.
m. festive;ceremonial·showy
odtąd (od-tównt) adv. henceforth; from now on; from here
odtłuścić (od-twoósh-ćheećh)
v. degrease; reduce weight
odtrącać (od-trówn-tsaćh) v.
repel; jostle; knock off; deduct (charges);thrust aside
odtrutka (od-troót-ka) f.anti-
dote! counterpoison
odtwarzać (od-tva-zhaćh) v.
reproduce; reconstitute
odtwórca (od-tvoór-tsa) m. re-
producer; performer
oduczać (od-oó-chaćh) v. un-
teach; unlearn; break a habit
odurzać (o-doó-zhaćh) v. stun;
make dopey; stupefy;daze;dizzy
odurzenie (o-doo-zhe-ńe) n.
stupor; giddiness;intoxication
odwadniać (od-vad-ńaćh) v.
drain; dehvdrate: dewater
odwaga (od-va-ga) f. courage
odwalić (od-va-leećh) v. push
away; beat it; copy; get over
with; roll aside;remove:sham
odwar (od-var) m. decoction
odważnik (od-vázh-ńeek) n.
scale— weight
odważny (od-vázh-ni) adj. m.
brave; courageous;bold;daring
odważyć (od-va-zhićh) v. weigh
odważyć się (od-va-zhich śhań)
v. dare;have the courage:risk
odwdzięczyć się(od-vdźh ań-chich
śhań) v. repay (with gratitude; return; requite:repay
odwet (od-vet) m. retaliation;
retort; revenge; requital
odwiązać (od-vyówn-zaćh) v.
untie: unfasten; unbuckle;undo
odwieczny (od-vyéch-ni) adj. m.
eternal; immemorial·age long
odwiedzać (odvye-dzaćh) v.vis-
it; call on; nav a visit;
pav a call; come to see

odwiedziny (od-vye-dżheé-ni)n.
visit; call; coming to see
odwijać (od-veé-yaćh) v. unwrap
odwilż (od-veelzh) f. thaw
odwlekać (od-vlé-kaćh) v. put
off; postpone;delay;drag away
odwodnic (od-vód-ńeećh) v. drain
odwodzić (od-vó-dźheećh)v. draw
off;draw aside;dissuade
odwołać (od-vo-waćh) v. take
back; appeal; refer; recall
odwołanie (od-vo-wa-ńe) n. recall; appeal;repeal;cancellation
odwozić (od-vo-źheećh) v. take
back (by car); drive back
odwód (od-voot) m. reserve
odwracać (od-vrá-tsaćh) v. reverse; turn around;invert
odwrotny (od-vrót-ni) adj. m.
reverse;opposite;converse
odwrót (od-vroot) m. retreat;
reverse; withdrawal
odwykać (od-vi-kaćh) v. break
a habit; loose the habit
odwzajemniać (od-vza-yem-ńaćh)
v. reciprocate;repay;return
odyniec (o-di-ńets) m. boar
odzew (od-zev) m. echo; reply
odziedziczyć(o-dżhe-dżheé-chich)
v. inherit; succeed(to a title)
odzienie (o-dżhe-ńe) n. clothing
odzież (o-dżhezh) f. clothes
odznaczać (od-zna-chaćh) v.
distinguish; decorate;mark off
odznaczenie (od-zna-che-ńe) n.
distinction;award;decoration
odznaka (od-zna-ka) f. badge
odzwierciadlać (od-zvyer-ćhad-
lach) v. reflect (something)
odzwyczajać (od-zvi-chá-yaćh)
v. break a habit;make loose a
habit
odzyskać (od-zis-kaćh) v. retrieve;regain;recover:win back
odzywać się (od-zi-vaćh śhań) v.
speak up;drop a line:respond
odźwierny (od-dżhvyer-ni) m.
doorman;janitor;caretaker
odżyć (od-zhićh) v. come back to
life; revive;be reborn:reappear
odżywczy (od-zhiv-chi) adj. m.
nutritious;nourishing;alimentary
odżywiać (od-zhiv-yaćh) v.nour-
ish; feed ;supply with food

odżywienie (od-zhiv-yé-ńe) n. food ; nourishment; diet

ofensywa (o-fen-si-va) f. offensive ; push; attack

oferma (o-fér-ma) f. sad sack

oferta (o-fér-ta) f. offer

ofiara (o-fyá-ra) f. victim; offering;sacrifice; dupe

oficer (o-fée-tser) m. (military) officer

oficjalny (o-feets-yál-ni) adj. m. official;formal;reserved

oficyna (o-fee-tsi-na) f. backhouse; printing shop;annex

ofuknąć (o-fook-nównch) v. rebuke; reprimand;trounce;rate

ogar (ó-gar) m. bloodhound

ogarek (o-ga-rek) m. candleend; stump; stub:cigarette end

ogarniac (o-gár-ńaćh) v. seize; comprehend;take in;grasp

ogien (o-geń) m. fire; flame

ogier (o-ger) m. stallion

ogladać (o-glówn-daćh) v. inspect; consider; see

oględny (o-glánd-ni) adj. circumspect;moderate;cautious

ogłada (o-gwá-da) f. good manners; refinement;urbanity:polish

ogłaszac (o-gwa-shaćh)v. advertize; declare; publish

ogłuchnąć (o-gwookh-nównch) v. become deaf; be hushed

oglupiec (o-gwoop-yećh) v. become stupid;grow silly

ognie sztuczne (óg-ńe shtoóchne) pl. fireworks

ogniotrwały (o-gño-trva-wi) adj. fireproof;incombustible·

ognisko (od-ńees-ko) n. hearth; focus; camp fire·fire place

ognisty (og-ńees-ti) adj. m. fiery;flaming; passionate

ogniwo (og-ńee-vo) n. link

ogolic (o-gó-leech) v. shave

ogon (ó-gon) m. tail;trail;scut

ogonek (o-gó-nek) m. waiting line;queue;diacritical mark

ogorzały (o-go-zhá-wi) adj. m. sunburnt;tanned;weather beaten

ogólnie (o-goól-ńe) adv. generally;as a rule;universally

ogólny (o-goól-ni) adj. m. general;prevailing; global; total

ogół (ó-goow) m. people; public

ogółem (o-goo-wem) adv. on the whole; as a whole; altogether

ogórek (o-goó-rek) m. cucumber

ogórkowy sezon (o-goor-kó-vi se-zon) slack time(season)

ograbic (o-grá-beech) v. rob

ograniczony (o-gra-ńee-chó-ni) adj. m. narrow-minded; limited

ogrodnik (o-gród-ńeek) m. gardener; horticulturist

ogrodzic (o-gró-dźheećh)v. fence in; enclose;wall in; rail in

ogromny (o-grom-ni) adj. m. huge

ogród (ó-good) m. garden

ogryzac (o-grí-zaćh) v. gnaw away; nimble at; pick(a bone)

ogrzewac (o-gzhé-vaćh) v. heat

ohydny (o-khíd-ni) adj. m. hideous; gastlv;abonimable:vile

o ile (o eé-le) conj. as far as

ojciec (óy-ćhets) m. father

ojciec chrzestny (oy-ćhyets khzhést-ni) godfather

ojczym (óy-chim) m. stepfather

ojczysty język (oy-chís-ti yáńzik) native tongue

ojczyzna (oy-chíz-na) f. native country; motherland;homeland

okaleczyc (o-ka-le-chićh) v. maim;crinnle:lame;mutilate

oka mgnienie (ó-ka mgńe-ńe) n. eye blink; split second

okap (ó-kap) m. eaves;overlap

okaz (ó-kas) m. specimen;type

okazac (o-ka-zaćh) v. show; demonstrate; evidence;exhibit

okazały (o-ka-zá-wi) adj. m. magnificent;stately:grand

okaziciel (o-ka-żhee-ćhel) m. bearer (of a check etc.)

okazja (o-káz-ya) f. opportunity

okazyjny (o-ka-zíy-ni) adj. m. occasional; chance(acquaintance)

okazywac (o-ka-zí-vaćh) v. demonstrate; show ;manifest;disnlav

oklaski (o-klás-kee) pl. applause;clapping; acclamations

oklaskiwac (o-klas-kee-vaćh) v. applaud ; clap (one's hands)

okleić (o-kle-eech) v. paste-
over;stick over; smear over
oklepany (o-kle-pá-ni) adj. m.
commonplace; (well) worn
okład (ó-kwat) m. compress;
hotpad ; lining;wrapping
okładka (o-kwád-ka) f. (book)
cover; book binding
okłamać (o-kwa-mach) v. deceive; tell a lie; delude
okno (ók-no) n. window
oko (ó-ko) n. eye; eye sight
okolica (o-ko-lee-tsa) f. region; surroundings;vicinity
okoliczność (o-ko-leech-noshch)
f. circumstance; fact;occasion
około (o-ko-wo) prep. near;
about; more or less;at;on;or so
okoń (ó-koń) m. perch; bass
okop (ó-kop) m. trench
okopcić (o-kóp-cheech) v. soot
okostna (o-kost-na) f. perios-
teum; lining of the bones
okólnik (o-kool-neek) m. circular; corral;poultry yard
okpić (ó-kpeech) v. pool wool
over eyes; deceive;cheat;gull
okradać (o-krá-dach) v. pickpocket; burglarize ; rob
okrakiem (o-krá-kem) adv.
astraddle;with legs wide apart
okrasa (o-kra-sa) f. fat; ornament ; seasoning ;gravy;lard
okrasić (o-krá-sheech) v. adorn;
season ;add a condiment
okratować (o-kra-tó-vach) v.
grate; bar (a window)
okratowanie (o-kra-to-va-ńe)
m. grating; railings; bars
okrąg (o-krownk) m. district
okrągły (o-krówng-wi) adj. m.
round; spherical:full(month etc)
dkrążać (o-krówn-zhach) v. encircle; circle;revolve:detour
okres (ó-kres) m. period;phase
okreslać (o-kresh-lach) v.
define; qualify;fix;appoint
okręcać (o-krań-tsach) v. coil
around;wrap; turn around
okręt (ó-krańt) m. ship:boat
okrężny (o-krańzh-ni) adj. m.
roundabout;indirect;devious
circuitous; circular:travelling-
pedlar's(trade etc.)

okropność (o-króp-noshch) f.
horror; atrocity;outrage
okropny (o-króp-ni) adj. m.
horrible;fearful;awful;extreme
okruch (ó-krookh) m. crumb
okrucieństwo (o-kroo-chyeń-
stvo) n. cruelty;atrocities
okrutny (o-króot-ni) adj. m.
cruel;savage;excessive; sore
okrycie (o-kri-che) n. covering; wrap;garment;overcoat
okrywać (o-kri-vach) v. cover
okrzyczany (o-kzhi-chá-ni) adj.
m. notorious;famous;renowned
okrzyk (ó-kzhik) m. outcry
okrzyknąć (o-kzhik-nownch) v.
proclaim;declare; brand
oktawa (ok-ta-va) f. octave
okucie (o-koó-che) n. hardware; ferrule; fitting
okuć (ó-kooch) v. shoe a horse;
shackle; fit a lock and hinges
okular (o-koo-lar) m. eyeglass
okularnik (o-koo-lár-ńeek) m.
cobra;poisonous snake of Asia
okulista (o-koo-lees-ta) m.
eye doctor;eye surgeon;oculist
okultyzm (o-kool-tizm) m. oc-
cultism; hidden knowledge
okup (ó-koop) m. ransom
okupacja (o-koo-páts-ya) f.
occupation; occupancy
okupować (o-koo-pó-vach) v.
occupy;invade a territory
okupywać (o-koo-pi-vach) v. pay
ransom; compensate;redeem;atone
olbrzym (ól-bzhim) m. giant
olbrzymi (ol-bzhi-mee) adj. m.
gigantic;huge;cllossal;excessive
olcha (ól-kha) f. alder tree
oleander (o-le-án-der) m. oleander (an evergreen shrub)
olej (ó-ley) m. oil; oil paint
olej lniany (ó-ley lńa-ni) adj.
m. linseed-oil
oligarchia (o-lee-gár-khya) m.
oligarchy;the ruling persons
óliwa (o-lee-va) f. olive; oil
oliwić (o-lee-veech) v. oil
oliwka (o-leev-ka) f. olive-tree
olszyna (ol-shi-na) f. alder-
tree stand; alder wood
olśniewać (ol-shńe-vach) v.
dazzle; ravish;enchant·

ołów (owoof) m. lead;lead shot
ołówek (o-woo-vek) m. lead
pencil;drawing in pencil
ołtarz (ow-tash) m. altar
omackiem (o-máts-'kem) adv.
gropingly ; blindfold
omal (ó-mal) adv. nearly
omamic (o-má-meech) v. deceive
omaścic (o-másh-cheech) v. add
fat; add butter(on bread etc.)
omawiac (o-máv-yach) v. discuss
omdlały (om-dlá-wi) adj. m.
fainted; faint; languid
omdlec (om-dlech) v. faint
omen (ó-men) m. omen
omieszkac (o-myésh-kach) v.
fail;omit;neglect·
omijac (o-mée-yach) v. pass
omlet (óm-let) m. omelet
omłócic (o-mwóo-cheech) v.
thresh out; give a thrashing
omotac (o-mó-tach) v. entangle
omówic (o-móo-veech) v. discuss
omylic (o-mí-leech) v. mislead
omylny (o-míl-ni) adj. m. fal-
lible;misleading;deceitful
omyłka (o-miw-ka) f. error
on; ona; ono (on; o-na; ó-no)
pron. he; she; it
oni (o-ñee) m. pl. they;
one (ó-ne) f. pl. they
ondulacja (on-doo-láts-ya) f.
(hair) wave;permanent wave
ondulacja trwała (on-dóo-lats-
ya trvá-wa) permanent (wave)
onegdaj (o-nég-day) adv. the
other day;two days ago
ongiś (ón-geesh) adv. (arch)
at one time;once upon a time
oniemiały (o-ñe-myá-wi) adj.
m. mute; dumb; speechless
oniesmielac (o-ñe-shmye-lach)
v. intimidate;browbeat;cow
opactwo (o-páts-tvo) n. abbey
opaczny (o-pách-ni) adj. m.
wrong; mistaken;improper
opad (ó-pat) m. (rain) fall
opadac(o-pá-dach) v. subside
(na)opak (na o-pak) adv. up-
side down; reverse;wrong way
opakowanie (o-pa-ko-va-ñe) n.
wrapping ; packing

opal (ó-pal) m. opal
opalac się (o-pá-lach shañ) v.
suntan; tan;bronze;lie on the sun
opalanie (o-pa-la-ñe) n. heating (house etc.);fire marking
opalenizna (o-pa-le-ñeez-na) f.
suntan; tan; scorched remains
opał (ó-paw) m. fuel for heating
opamiętac (o-pa-myáñ-tach) v.
sober down; bring to reason
opanowac (o-pa-nó-vach) v.
master;conquer;seize; learn
opanowany (o-pa-no-vá-ni) adj.
m. cool-headed;composed;calm
opary (o-pá-ri) pl. fumes
oparcie (o-pár-che) n. support
oparzyc (o-pá-zhich) v. scald
opasac (o-pá-sach) v. belt;
girdle;grid;encircle;surround
opaska (o-pás-ka) f. band
opasły (o-pás-wi) adj. m. obese
opasc (o-pashch) v. drop; sink;
hang loose;settle;collapse;slope
opatentowac (o-pa-ten-tó-vach)
v. patent ;take out a patent
opatrunek (o-pa-troo-nek) m.
dressing; bandage; field dressing
opatrywac (o-pa-tri-vach) v.
fix; dress; provide;prepare
opera (o-pé-ra) f. opera; opera
house; no end of a joke
operacja (o-pe-ráts-ya) f. surgery; operation; action;process
operowac (o-pe-ró-vach) v.oper-
ate; manipulate; act; handle
opętanie (o-páñ-tá-ñe) n. obsession;demonical possession
opieczętowac (o-pye-cháñ-tó-
vach) v. seal up; seal
opieka (o-pye-ka) f. care
opiekowac (o-pye-kó-vach) v.
take care; care for;have charge
opiekun (o-pye-koon) m. guardian; curator; foster-parent
opierac się (o-pye-rach shañ)
v. lean; base; relay;rest;defy
opieszały (o-pye-shá-wi) adj.
m. slow; tardy; lazy; inert
opinia (o-peéñ-ya) f. opinion;
view; reputation; sentiment
opis (ó-pees) m. description
oplątać (o-plówn-tach) v. ensnare; entangle; entwine

opluwać (o-ploo-vach) v. spit
on ;spit at; slander; defame
opłacać (o-pwa-tsach) v. pay;
bribe ;cover the cost;reward
opłakany (o-pwa-ka-ni) adj. m.
deplorable ;sad; pitiful
opłakiwać (o-pwa-kee-vach) v.
lament; deplore ;mourn
opłata (o-pwa-ta) f. fee
opłatek (o-pwa-tek) m. wafer
opłucna (o-pwoots-na) f. pleu-
ra ;membrane around the lungs
opłukiwać (o-pwoo-kee-vach) v.
rinse; wash with water
opływać (o-pwi-vach) v. sail
around; abound ;encircle;roll
opływowy (o-pwi-vo-vi) adj. m.
streamlined; streamline
opodal (o-po-dal) adv. near by
opodatkować (o-po-dat-ko-vach)
v. tax ; impose a tax
opona (o-po-na) f. tire
oponować (o-po-no-vach) v.
oppose ; take exception
opornie (o-por-ńe) adv. with
difficulty ; arduosly
oporny (o-por-ni) adj. m. balky;
recalcitrant ; refractory
opowiadać (o-pov-ya-dach) v.
tell —. tale ;relate;record
opozycja (o-po-zits-ya) f. opposition ; resistance
opór (o-poor) m. resistance
opoźniać (o-poozh-ńach) v. delay ; retard;slow down defer
opóźnienie (o-poozh-ńe-ńe) n.
delay ;deferment;tardiness
opracować (o-pra-tso-vach) v.
work up : elaborate:compile
oprawa (o-pra-va) f. frame;
binding ;framework:handle
oprawca (o-prav-tsa) m. skinner;
executioner :torturer;assassin
opresja (o-pres-ya)f.oppression
oprocentowanie (o-pro-tsen-to-
wa-ńe) n. interest(on money)
oprowadzać (o-pro-va-dzach) v.
show around : act as a guide
oprócz (o-rooch) prep.: except;
besides : apart from:but:save
opróżniać (o-proozh-ńach) v.
empty ;clear:evacuate·unload

opryskliwy (o-prisk-lee-vi)
adj. m. peevish;gruff;harsh
opryszek (o-pri-shek) m. hood-
lum:hooligan:rowdy:rough-neck
oprzeć (op- zhech) v. lean; base;
resist:become inffamed;inflame
oprzytomnieć (o-pzhi-tom-ńech)
v. recover; collect oneself
optyk (op-tik) m. optician
optymista (op-ti-mees-ta) m.
optimist: one of cheerful views
opublikować (o-poo-blee-ko-
vach) v. publish:make public
opuchły (o-pookh-wi) adj. m.
swollen; dilated
opuchlina (o-pookh-lee-na) f.
swelling, :dilatation
opuszczać (o-poosh-chach) v.
leave; omit; abandon· lower
opustoszały (o-poos-to-sha-vi)
adj. m. deserted·desolate;empty
opuszczenie (o-poosh-che-ńe) n.
omission:lowering:reduction
orać (o-rach) v. till; plough
oranżeria (o-ran-zher-ya) f.
greenhouse: hothouse:orangery
oraz (o-raz) conj. as well as
orbita (or-bee-ta) f. orbit
order (or-der) m. decoration;
order(for service rendered etc.)
ordynarny (or-di-nar-ni) adj.
m. gross; coarse:vulgar:trashy
orędzie (o-rań-dźhe) n. (official) message;proclamation
oręż (o-rańsh) m. weapon
organiczny (or-ga-ńeech-ni)
adj. m. organic:constitutional
organista (or-ga-ńees-ta) m.
organist :organ player
organizacja (or-ga-ńee-zats-
ya)f.organization:organized group
organizm (or-ga-ńeezm) m. organism: any living thing
orgia (org-ya) f. orgy
orka (or-ka) f. tillage
orkiestra (or—k'es-tra) f. orchestra: orchestra pit
orny (or-ni) adj. m. arable
orszak (or-shak) m. retinue
ortodoksja (or-to-doks-ya) f.
orthodoxy: conventionality

ortografia (or-to-gra-fya) f.
orthography;correct spelling
oryginalny (o-ri-gee-nál-ni)
adj. m. original;inventive;new
orzech (o-zhekh) m. nut;walnut
orzeczenie (o-zhe-che-ńe) m.
decision; sentence; ruling
orzeł (o-zhew) m, eagle;genius
orzeźwiac (o-zhéźh-vyać) v.
refresh; brace up; invigorate
osa (o-sa) f. wasp; vixen;shrew
osad (o-sat) m. sediment; dregs
osada (o-sa-da) f. settlement
osadnik (o-sád-ńeek) m. settler
osadzać (o-sa-dzać) v. plant;
seat; settle; place;fix;steady
osamotnienie (o-sa-mot-ńe-ńe)
n. isolation;loneliness
osądzać (o-sown-dzách) v.
sentence ; judge;prejudge
oschły (óskh-wi) adj. m. arid;
dry; cold; stiff; stand-offish
osełka (o-sew-ka) f. whetstone
oset (o-set) m. thistle,teasel
osiadać (o-shá-dach) v. settle;
subside; make a settlement
osiągnąć (o-showng-nownch) v.
attain;achieve;gain;reach
osiedlać (o-shed-lách) v.
settle;make a settlement
osiem (o-shem) num. eight
osiemdziesiąt (o-shem-dzhe-
shownt) num. eighty
osiemnaście (o-shem-násh-che)
num. eighteen
osiemset (o-shem-set) num.
eight hundred v. be orphaned
osierocić (o-she-ró-cheech)
osika (o-shee-ka) f. aspen
osikać (o-shee-kach) v. sprinkle; piss on (vulg.)
osiodłać (o-shod-wach) v. saddle ; reduce to subiugation
osioł (o-shyow) m. donkey; ass
oskarżać (o-skár-zhach) v.
accuse ;charge with;indict
oskrzela (o-skzhé-la) pl. n.
bronchia ;main part of windpine
oskrzydlac (o-skzhid-lach) v.
outflank ;go beyond; cut off
oskubac (o-skoo-bach) v. fleece;
feather;pluck;skin; soak
osłabiać (o-swáb-yach) v. weak-
en ;reduce; lessen;diminish

osłabienie (o-swa-byé-ńe) n.
weakness ; diminuation;debilitation
osłona (o-swó-na) f. shield;
cover ; protection; defense
osładzać (o-swa-dzách) v. sweet-
en ; put sugar; cheer up
osłupiały (o-swoo-pyá-wi) adj.
m. amazed; aghast ; astounded
osmarować (o-sma-ró-vach) v.
besmear; libel ; run down; soil
osoba (o-só-ba) f. person
osobisty (o-so-bees-ti) adj.
m. personal; private ;particular
osobiście (o-so-beésh-che) adv.
personally ; in person
osobnik (o-sób-ńeek) m. individual ; specimen; person
osobny (o-sób-ni) adj. m.sep-
arate; private ; individual
osobowosc (o-so-bo-voshch) f.
personality ; individuality
osowiały (o-so-vyá-wi) adj. m.
depressed; dejected;glum:monish
ospa (ós-pa) f. smallpox
ospały (os-pá-wy) adj. m.
drowsy; sleepy; sluggish; dull
ostatecznie (o-sta-téch-ńe) adv.
finally; after all; at last
ostateczny (o-sta-téch-ni) adj.
m. final ;ultimate; eventual
ostatek (o-stá-tek) m. reminder ; rest; remains; scrap
ostatni (o-stát-ńee) adj. m.
last; late; end;closing; parting
ostatnio (o-stát-ńo) adv. of late;
lately; not long ago ; recently
ostoja (o-stó-ya) f. mainstay
ostroga (o-stró-ga) f. spur
ostrokątny (o-stro-kównt-ni)
adj. m. sharp-angled
ostrożnosc (o-stróżh-noshch)
f. caution; prudence; care
ostrożny (o-stroźh-ni) adj. m.
careful; prudent;cautious; wary
ostry (ó-stri) adj. m. sharp
ostryga (o-stri-ga) f. oyster
ostrze (ó-stzhe) n. cutting
edge; spike ;blade; point;prong
ostrzegać (o-stzhé-gach) v.
warn of: warn against;admonish
ostrzeliwać (o-stzhe-lée-vach)
v. shoot at; strafe ; fire at;
accustom to gun fire

ostrzeżenie (o-stzhe-zhe-ńe)
n. warning ;danger sign:notice
ostrzyc (o-stzhich) v. sharp-
en : whet;grind;put an edge
ostrzygac (o-stzhi-gach) v.
cut (hair) ; shear sheep;trim
ostudzac (o-stoo-dzach) v. cool
ostygac (o-stí-gach) v. cool
down ; chill; cool off: abate
osuszac (o-soo-shach) v. dry;
drain : dehumidify;wipe; mop
oswobodzic (o-svo-bo-dżheech)
v. free ; liberate:rescue:rid
oswoic (o-svo-eech) v. tame;
familiarize; tame;domesticate
oszacowac (o-sha-tso-vach) v.
evaluate; estimate;appraise
oszczep (osh-chep) m. javelin
oszczerstwo (osh-cher-stvo) n.
calumny; libel; defamation
oszczędnosci (osh-chańd-nosh-
chee) pl. savings(money)
oszklenie (o-shkle-ńe) n. glaz-
ing (of windows)
oszołomic (o-sho-wo-meech) v.
stun: daze:stunefy;bewilder
oszpecic (o-shpe-cheech) v. deface; disfigure;deform; mar
oszukac (o-shoo-kach) v. cheat
oszust (o-shoost) m. cheater
oś (osh) f. axle (axis)
oscienny (o-shchen-ni) adj. m.
bordering: adjoining: adjacent
ość (oshch) f. (fish) bone
oslepiac (o-shle-pyach) v.
blind; dazzle; strike blind
osmieszac (o-shmye-shach) v.
ridicule;deride;make fun of
osrodek (o-shro-dek) m. center
oswiadczenie (o-shviad-che-ńe)
n. declaration; pronouncement
oswiadczyny (c-shvyad-chi-ni)
pl. marriage proposal
oswiata (o-shvya-ta) f. education; learning
oswiecac (o-shvye-tsach) v.
light up; enlighten; educate
oswietlenie (o-shvyet-le-ńe) n.
lighting ;light: illumination
otaczac (o-ta-chach) v. surround;enclose;turn on a lathe
otchłan (ot-khwań) f. abyss

otępienie (o-tań-pye-ńe) n.
dullness ;stupor:stupefaction
oto (o-to) part. here; there
otoczenie (o-to-che-ńe) n. environment ;setting; associates
otoczyc (o-to-chich) v. surround; enclose;turn on a lathe
otomana (o-to-ma-na) f. couch
otoż (o-toosh) conj. now
otruc (o-trooch) v. poison
otrucie (o-troo-che) n. poisoning
otrzaskac (o-tshas-kach)v.acquaint
otrząsac (o-tzhown-sach) v.
shake loose; shudder; strew
otrzewna (o-tzhev-na) f. peri-
toneum; lining of abdomen
otrzezwiec (o-tzhezh-vyech) v.
sober up;be disillusioned;brisk up
otrzymac(o-tzhi-mach) v. receive ; get; be given;acquire
otulic (o-too-leech) v. tuck in;
wrap;wrap up: shroud:enfold: lag
otwarcie (o-tvar-che) adv.openly;
frankly; in plain words;outright
otwarty (o-tvar-ti) adj. m.
open; frank:overt;professed
otwierac (ot-vye-rach) v. open
otwor (ot-voor) m. opening
otyły (o-ti-wi) adj. m. obese
owacja (o-vats-ya) f. ovation
owad (o-vad) m. insect
owal (o-val) m. oval
owca (ov-tsa) f. sheep
owczarek (ov-cha-rek) m. sheep-dog
owczarnia(ov-char-ńa)f. sheep-fold
owdowiały (ov-do-vya-wi) adj.
m. widowed ; one who lost wife
owies (o-vyes) m. oats
owiewac (o-vye-vach) v. blow
upon;sweep over· encompass:inspire
owijac (o-vee-yach) y. wrap up
owłosiony (o-vwo-sho-ni) adj.
m. hairy; hirsute; shaggy; pilose
owo (o-vo) pron. that : that thing
owoc (o-vots) m. fruit ;fruitage
owrzodzenie (o-vzho-dze-ńe) n.
ulceration : sore: sores
owsianka (ov-shan-ka) f. oatmeal; kasha; porridge
owszem (ov-shem) part. yes;
certainly; on the contrary
ozdabiac (o-zdab-yach) v. dec-
:orate; adorn :trim: garnish

ozdoba (oz-dó-ba) f. decoration
oziębiać (o-żhán-byach) v. cool
off; chill; cool down; damp
oziębły (o-żhánb-wi) adj. m.
frigid ; cold; reserved; dry
oznaczać (o-zna-chach) v. mark;
signify ; indicate; fix; spell
oznajmiać (o-znay-myach) v.
announce ;inform; notify;state
oznaka (o-zna-ka) f. sign;
symptom; badge; mark
ozór (o-zoor) m. (bull's)
tongue; gossiping tongue
ożenić (o-zhe-ñeech) v. marry
ożywiać (o-zhiv-yach) v. bring
to life; animate;brisk up
ożywienie (o-zhi-vye-ñe) n.
animation ;liveliness: stir
ożywiony (o-zhiv-yo-ni) adj. m.
animated; lively; brisk,
ósemka (oo-sém-ka) f. eight
ósma godzina (oós-ma go-dżhee-
na) eight o'clock
ósmak (oós-mak) m. eighth grad-
er; eighth grade pupil
ów (oof) m. pron. that
owa (ó-va)f. pron. that
owo (ó-vo)n. pron. that
owi (ó-vee)pl. m. pron. that
owe (ó-ve)pl. f. pron. that
ówczesny (oov-chés-ni) adj. m.
the then;of those days
ówdzie (oóv-dżhe) adv. elsewhere; there
pa ! (pa) excl.: bye-bye !
pacha (pá-kha) f. armpit
pachnąć (pákh-nównch) v. smell
(good) ;have a fragrance
pachołek (pa-kho-wek) m. boy;
page ;servant:menial; flunkey
pachwina (pakh-vee-na) f. groin
pacierz (pá-chesh) m. prayer
pacierzowy stos (pa-che-zhó-vi
stos) spinal column; spine
paciorki (pa-chór-kee) pl.
string of beads ;short prayer
pacjent (páts-yent) m. patient
pacyfista (pa-tsi-feés-ta) m.
pacifist ;believer in peace
pacyfizm (pa-tsi-feezm) m.
pacifism; ideology of peace
paczka (pách-ka) f. parcel

paczyć (pá-chich) v. warp
padać (pá-dach) v. fall down
padalec (pa-dá-lets) m. blind-
worm; slow warm
padlina (pad-lée-na) f. carrion
pagórek (pa-goó-rek) m. hill
pająk (pá-yównk) m. spider
pajęczyna (pa-yáñ-chi-na) f.
cobweb ; spider web;gossamer
paka (pá-ka) f. crate ;lock-up
pakować (pa-kó-vach) v. pack;
cram; wrap ; pack off; pack up
pakunek (pa-koó-nek) m. baggage
pal (pál) m. pile ; stake:picket
palący (pa-lówn-tsi) m. smoker
palec (pá-lets) m. finger : toe
palenie (pa-le-ñe) n. smoking
palenisko (pa-le-ñées-ko) n.
hearth ; fireplace; grate
paleta (pa-lé-ta) f. palette
palić (pá-leech) v. burn; smoke
cigarette; heat;scorch;shoot
paliwo (pa-leé-vo) n. fuel
palma (pál-ma) f. palm-tree
palnik (pál-ñeek) m. burner
palto (pál-to) n. overcoat
pałac (pá-wats) m. palace
pałka (páw-ka) f. stick; club
pamflet (pám-flet) m. pamphlet
pamiątka (pa-myównt-ka) f.
souvenir; token of remembrance
pamięć (pá-myáñch) f. memory
pamiętać (pa-myáñ-tach) v. remember; recall:be careful
pamiętnik (pa-myáñt-ñeek) m.
diary; memoirs; album
pan (pan) m. lord ; master;
mister; you ;gentleman: squire
pan młody (pan mwo-di) m. bridegroom; man about to be married
pani (pa-ñee) f. lady; you;
madam ; mistress(in school etc.)
panika (pa-ñee-ka) f. panic' scare
panna (pán-na) f. miss; girl:lass
panna młoda (pán-na mwó-da) f,
bride; woman about to be married
panoszyć się (pa-nó-shich śháñ)
v. domineer ; boss : run the show
panować (pa-nó-vach) v. rule;
reign; be master of; command;rife
panteizm (pan-té-eezm) m. pan-
theism

pantera (pan-té-ra) f. panther
pantoflarz (pan-tó-flash) m.
henpecked husband·
pantofel (pan-tó-fel) m. slipper;
shoe; light low shoe
pantomima (pan-to-mée-ma) f.
pantomime; gestures no words
panujący (pa-noo-yówn-tsi) adj.
m. prevailing; ruling
pański (pań-skee) adj. m.
lord's; your's
państwo (pań-stvo) n. state;
married, couple
papa (pá-pa) f. feltpaper
papier (pá-pyer), m. paper
papieros (pa-pyé-ros) m. cigarette;tabacco rolled in paper
papieski (pa-pyés-kee) adj. m.
papal; of the Pope
papież (pá-pyesh) m. pope
papka (páp-ka) f. pulp; mash;
pap; gruel; paste; slurry
paplać (páp-lach) v. prattle
paproc (pá-proch) f. fern
papryka (pa-prí-ka) f. red-
pepper; paprica· paprika
papuga (pa-póo-ga) f. parrot
para 1. (pá-ra) f. couple
para 2. (pá-ra) f. steam
parabola (pa-ra-bó-la) f. parabola,
parada (pa-rá-da) f. parade
paradoks (pa-rá-doks) m. para-
dox; apparent contradiction
parafia (pa-ráf-ya) f. parish
parafina (pa-ra-fée-na) f.
paraffin(waxy petroleum)
paragraf (pa-ra-graf) m. para-
graph(a distinct section)
paraliż (pa-rá-leesh) m. paralysis;crippling of activities
parametr (pa-rá-metr) m. para-
meter;element, of an orbit
parapet (pa-rá-pet) m. window-
sill; stool· rail; breastwork
parasol (pa-rá-sol) m. umbrella
parawan (pa-ra-van) n. screen
parcelować (par-tse-ló-vach) v.
parcel out(land);cut up
parcie (pár-che) n. thrust
park (párk) m. park
parkan (pár-kan) m. fence; net;
hoarding

parlament (par-lá-ment) m.
parliament; national legislature
parny (pár-ni) adj. m. sultry
parobek (pa-ró-bek) m. farmhand; plough man; rustic
parodia (pa-ród-ya) f. parody
parokrotnie (pa-ro-krót-ñe) adv.
repeatedly; a couple of times
parostatek (pa-ro-stá-tek) m.
steamboat; steamer; steamship
parować (pa-ró-vach) v. evaporate; vaporize; cook by steam
parowiec (pa-ró-vyets) m. steamboat; steamer; steamship
parowóz (pa-ró-voos) m. steam
locomotive : railroad engine
parów (pa-roov) m. ravine
parówki (pa-róov-kee) pl. hot
dogs; sausages; frankfurters
parszywy (par-shi-vi) adj. m.
mangy; scabby; lousy; horrid
partacki (par-táts-kee) adj. m.
bungled up; botched;fudged
partacz (pár-tach) m. bungler
parter (pár-ter) m. ground
floor; first floor; parterre
partia (párt-ya) f. party; card
game; political party; game
partner (párt-ner) m. partner
partyjny (par-tíy-ni) adj. m.
party(member); party member
partykuła (par-ti-koó-wa) f.
particle;
partyzantka (par-ti-zánt-ka)
f. guerrilla; partisan war
parytet (pa-ri-tet) m. parity
parzyć (pá-zhich) v. scald;
steam; burn; percolate; couple
parzysty numer (pa-zhis-ti noó-
mer) even number
pas (pas), m. belt; traffic lane
pasat (pá-sat), m. trade wind
pasażer (pa-sá-zher) m. passenger : chap; fellow; liner
pasek (pá-sek) m. belt; band
pasieka (pa-shé-ka) f. apiary
pasierb (pá-sherb) m. stepson
pasierbica (pa-sher-bée-tsa) f.
stepdaughter
pasja (pás-ya) f. passion
paskarz (pás-kash) m. profiteer
pasmo (pás-mo) n. streak; tract;
range; traffic lane

pasożyt (pa-só-zhit) m. parasite ; sponger

pasta (pás-ta) f. paste

pasterka (pas-tér-ka) f. midnight mass; shepherdess

pasterz (pás-tesh) m. shepherd

pastwa (pás-tva) f. prey

pastwisko (pas-tveés-ko) n. pasture ; grass, land

pastylka (pas-til-ka) f. tablet

pasywny (pa-sív-ni) adj. m. passive; acted upon

pasza (pá-sha) f. fodder

paszcza (pásh-cha) f. jaw

paszport (pásh-port) m. passport ; certificate

paść (pashch) v. fall down; graze ; tend cattle; feed

patelnia (pa-tél-ña) f. frying-pan with a handle

patent (pá-tent) m. patent

patetyczny (pa-te-tích-ni) adj. m. pathetic ; pompous; turgid

patolog (pa-to-lok) m. pathologist ; specialist in pathology

patriarcha (pa-tree-ár-kha) m. patriarch

patriota (pa-tree-ó-ta) m. patriot

patron (pá-tron) m. sponsor; stencil; pattern ; protector

patronat (pa-tró-nat) m.patronage :power to grant favors

patroszyc (pa-tro-shich) v. disembowel; gut ; draw (a fowl)

patrzec (pá-tzhech) v. look

patyk (pá-tik) m. stick

patyna (pa-tí-na) f. patina

pauza (páw-za) f. pause

paw (pav) m. peacock

paznokieć (paz-nó-kyech) m. (finger) nail ; toe nail

pazur (pá-zoor) m. claw

paź (pash) m. page

październik (pazh-dzhér-ñeek)m. October

pączek (pówn-chek) m. bud

pąsowy (pówn-só-vi) adj. m. red; crimson : bright red·poppy red

pchać (pkhach) v. push; thrust

pchła (pkhwa) f. flea

pchnięcie (pkhñań-che) n. push; thrust; jostle : shove: lunge

pech (pekh) m. bad luck

pechowiec (pe-khó-vyets) m. unlucky fellow; lackless chap

pedagog (pe-dá-gok) m. pedagogue; educator: educationist

pedał (pé-daw) m. 1. pedal; 2. gay; homosexual ; pansy boy

pedant (pé-dant) m. pedant

pejcz (peych) m. horsewhip

pejzaż (péy-zash) m. landscape

peleryna (pe-le-rí-na) f. cape

pelikan (pe-leé-kan) m. pelican

pełnia (péw-ña) f. fullness

pełnić (péw-ñeech) v. fulfill

pełno (péw-no) adv. plenty

pełnoletni (pew-no-lét-ñee) adj. m. adult; of age

pełnomocnictwo (pew-no-mots-ñeets-tvo) n. power of attorney; full powers (legal)

pełhy (péw-ni) adj. m. full

pełzać (péw-zach) v. creep; crawl ; fawn; drag: cringe

penicylina (pe-ñee-tsi-leé-na) f. penicillin

pensja (pén-sya) f. salary; pension; allowance; wages

pensjonat (pen-syó-nat) m. boarding house

perfidny (per-feéd-ni) adj. m. perfidious ; double dealing

perfumy (per-foo-mi) pl. scent; perfume ; perfumes

pergamin (per-gá-meen) m. parchment: sheep skin

period (pér-yod) m. period

perkal (pér-kal) m. calico

perła (pér-wa) f. pearl

peron (pé-ron) m. train- platform at railroad station

perski (pér-skee) adj. m. Persian; Iranian; of Iran

personalny (per-so-nál-ni) adj. m. personal; personnel officer

personel (per-só-nel) m. staff; personnel; employees

perspektywa (per-spek-tí-va) f. perspective;sense of proportion

perswazja (per-svaz-ya) f. persuasion; power of persuading

pertraktacja (per-trak-táts-ya) f. negotiation; parley

peruka (pe-róo-ka) f. wig

peruwiański (pe-roo-vyań-skee) adj. m. Peruvian; of Peru

peryskop (pe-rís-kop) m.periscope

pestka (pést-ka) f. kernel;pip; drupe; stone; trifle

pesymista (pe-si-mees-ta) m. pessimist

petent (pé-tent) m. petitioner

pewien (pé-vyen) adj. m. certain; one,; a; an; some; sure

pewnik (pév-ńeek) m. axiom

pewniak (pév-ńak) m. cinch; surefooted man; certainty

pewny (pév-ni) adj. m. sure; secure; dependable· safe

pęcak (pań-tsak) m. peeled barley; hulled barley

pęcherz (pań-khesh) m. bladder

pęcznieć (páńch-ńech) v. swell

pęd (pańd) m. rush; dash; run; speed;impetus;urge;shoot;sprout

pędzel (pań-dzel) m. (paint) brush; tuft of hair

pędzic (pań-dźeech) v. drive; run; lead; distill;hurry

pęk (pańk) m. bunch

pękać (pań-kach) v. burst;split; crack;go,off; burst; snap

pępek, (pań-pek) m. navel

pętac (pań-tach) v. shackle; hobble;knock about

pętak (pań-tak) m. squirt

pętelka (pań-tél-ka) f. loop; noose; knot

piać (pyach) v. crow ; sing

piana (pya-na) f. foam

pianino (pya-ńee-no) n. piano

piasek (pya-sek) m. sand

piasta (pyas-ta) f. hub; nave

piastować (pyas-tó-vach) v. nurse; tend; hold

piąc się(pyównch śhań)v.climb

piątek (pyówn-tek) m. Friday

piątka (pyównt-ka) f. five

piąty (pyówn-ti) num. fifth

picie (peé-che) n. drinking

pic (peech) v. drink; booze

picuś (peé-tsoośh) m. dandy

piec (pyets) m. stove; oven; furnace; kitchen stove; kiln

piec (pyets) v. bake; roast ; burn; scorch; sting; smart

piechota (pye-khó-ta) m. infantry ;a variety of beans

piechotą (pye-khó-tówn) adv. on foot; (go) on foot

piecza (pyé-cha) f. care; charge

pieczarka (pye-chár-ka) f. meadow mushroom

pieczątka (pye-chównt-ka) f. seal; stamp; signet

pieczeń wołowa (pyé-cheń vo-wó-va) f. roast beef,

pieczyste (pye-chis-te) n. roast meat; meat course; joint; roast

pieczywo (pye-chi-vo) n. bakerygoods; bread; baking

pieg (pyeg) m. freckle ;enhelis

piegowaty (pye-go-vá-ti) adj. m. freckled

piekarnia (pye-kár-ńa) f. bakery; baker's shop

piekarz (pyé-kash) m. baker

piekielny (pye-kél-ni) adj. m. infernal; of hell; hellish

piekło (pyék-wo) n. hell,

pielęgniarka (pye-lang-ńár-ka) f. nurse; hospital nurse

pielęgnować (pye-lang-nó-vach) v. nurse; tend; care;cultivate

pielgrzym (pyél-gzhim) m. pilgrim ;wanderer to holy place

pielucha (pye-loo-kha) f. diaper; baby's napkin

pieniądz (pye-ńównts) m. money; coin; currency; funds

pienić (pye-ńeech) v. foam; sparkle; cover with foam

pieniężny (pye-ńánzh-ni) adj. m. monetary; pecuniary;moneyed

pień (pyeń) m. trunk; stem; stump ; snag; stock; root

pieprz (pyepsh) m. pepper

pierdzieć (pyér-dzhech) v. fart (vulg.); stink,up

pierdzioch (pyér-dżhokh)m. old fart (vulg.); old stinker

piernat (pyér-nat) m. featherbed ; bedding

piernik (pyér-ńeek) m. gingerbread; duffer

pierś, (pyersh), f. breast; chest

pierścień (pyersh-cheń) m. ring

pierścionek (pyersh-chó-nek) m. ring (small)

pierwej (pyer-vey) adv. of
first; sooner; before; first
pierwiastek (pyer-vyás-tek) m.
root; element; radical,
pierworodny (pyer-vo-ród-ni)
adj. m. firstborn,
pierwotny (pyer-vót-ni) adj.
m. primitive; primarv;original
pierwszenstwo (pyerv-sheń-stvo)
n. priority; precedence
pierwszy (pyer-vshi) num. first
pierzchać (pyézh-khach) v. run
away; flv;flee; disperse;scutter
pierze (pye-zhe) n. feathers
pierzyna (pye-zhí-na) f.feather-
bed; eider down; quilt
pies (pyes) m. dog
pieszczota (pyesh-chó-ta) f.
caress; endearment
pieszo (pye-sho) adv. on foot
pieścic (pyésh-čheećh) v. fondle;caress;pet;hug; babble
piesn (pyeśhń) f. song
pietruszka (pyet-roósh-ka) f.
parsley,
pięciobój (pyań-chó-booy) m.
pentathlon
pięcioletni (pyan-cho-lét-ńee)
adj. m. five year old
pięć (pyańch) num. five
piędź (pyandźh) m. palm; span
pięćdziesiąt (pyań-dzhe-shównt)
num. fifty
pięćset (pyánch-set) num. five-
hundred
pięknosć (pyank-noshćh) f.
beauty; good looks; loveliness
piękny (pyan-kni) adj. m.beau-
tiful; lovely; fine:handsome
pieściarz (pyańsh-ćhash) m.
boxer ; pugilist
pięść (pyáńshćh) f. fist,
pięsciarstwo (pyansh-čhár-stvo)
m. box; boxing; pugilism
pięta (pyan-ta) f. heel
piętnastoletni (pyańt-nas-to-
lét-ńi) adj. m. fifteen years
old
piętnasty (pyańt-násti) num.
fifteenth
piętnaście (pyańt-nash-che) num.
fifteen
piętno (pyańt-no) n. mark;stig-
ma; brand; stamp; impress

piętro (pyańt-ro) n. story;
floor ;storey
piętrzyc (pyańt-zhićh) v. pile
up ; bank up;heap; accumulate
pigułka (pee-goów-ka) f. pill
pijak (pee-yak) m. drunk
pijany (pee-yá-ni) adj. m.
drunk ; tipsv; intoxicated;elated
pijawka (pee-yáv-ka) f. leech
pikantny (pee-kánt-ni) adj. m.
spicy; piquant; pungent; sharp
piknik (peek-ńeek) m. picnic
pilnik (peel-ńeek) m. file
pilnosć (peel-noshćh) f. diligence; urgencv;industry: care
pilny (peel-ni) adj. m. diligent; urgent; industrious:careful
pilot (peé-lot) m. pilot
pilsń (peélshń) f. felt
piła (pee-wa) f. saw; bore
piłka (peew-ka) f. ball; hand-
saw : football; socker; shot
piłowac (pee-wo-vačh) v. file;
saw : bore; rasp
pingwin (peen-gveen) m. penguin
piołunówka (pyo-woo-noóv-ka) f.
absinth flavored liqueur
pion (pyon) m. plumb (line)
pionek (pyo-ńek) m. pawn
pionier (pyo-ńer) m. pioneer
pionowy (pyo-nó-vi) adj. m.
vertical; upright; plumb
piorun (pyo-roon) m. thunder-
bolt; lightning shaft
piorunochron (pyo-roo-no-khron)
m. lightning-rod
piosenka (pyo-sén-ka) f. song
piórko (pyoór-ko) n. (small)
feather; pen ; plumelet
pióro (pyoó-ro) n. feather; pen
piramida (pee-ra-meé-da) f.
pyramid
pirat (peé-rat) m. pirate
pirotechnika (pee-ro-tekh-ńee-
ka) f. pyrotechnics
pisać (pee-saćh) v. write
pisarz (peé-sash) m. writer
pisemnie (pee-sem-ńe) adv. in
writing; in black and white
pisk (peesk) m. squeal
piskliwy (peesk-leé-vi) adj. m.
shrill; squeaky; thin; strident;
piping; reedv

pisklę (peesk-lań) n. chicken;
nestling; squealer
piskorz (pees-kosh) m.loach;eel
pismo (pees-mo) n. writing;
letter; newspaper; scripture;
alphabet; type; print
pisownia (pee-sov-ña) f. spelling; orthography
pistolet (pees-to-let) m. pistol; handgun ; gun ; spray gun
pisuar (pee-soo-ar) m. urinal
piszczeć (peesh-chech) v.creak:
squeak; screech; squeal;peep
piszczel (peesh-chel) m. shin-
bone; tibia; blow pipe
piśmiennictwo (peesh-myen-ñeets-
tvo) n. literature
piśmiennie (peesh-myén-ñe) adv.
in writing;in black and white
piwiarnia (pee-vyár-ña) f.
beer hall;beer house;saloon
piwnica (peev-ñee-tsa) f. cellar; basement; coal cellar
piwny (peev-ni) adj. m. brown
(color); hazel; beer-
piwo (pee-vo) n. beer
piwonia (pee-vó-ña) f. peony
piwowar (pee-vó-var) m. brewer
piżama (pee-zhá-ma) f. pyjamas
plac (plats) m. square; area;
ground;building site; field
plac boju (pláts bó-yoo) battle
field; field of battle
placek (plá-tsek) m. cake; pie
placówka (pla-tsoov-ka) f.
sentry; post; outpost;agency
plaga (plá-ga) f. plague
plagiator (plag-ya-tor) m.
plagiarist
plakat (plá-kat) m. poster
plama (plá-ma) f. blot; stain
plamić (plá-meech) v. blot;
stain; soil; tarnish; defile
plan (plan) m. plan; design;map
planeta (pla-né-ta) f. planet
planować (pla-nó-vach) v. plan
planowo (pla-nó-vo) adv. according to plan; systematically
plantacja (plan-táts-ya) f.
plantation
plaster (plás-ter) m. plaster;
patch; tape; adhesive; slice

plastyczne sztuki (plas-tich-ne
shtoo-kee) fine arts
plastyczny (plas-tich-ni) adj.
m. plastic; artistic; vivid
plastyk (plás-tik) m. artist;
plastic (substance)
platerować (pla-te-ró-vach) v.
plate (with an other metal)
platforma (plat-fór-ma) f. platform :truck; lorry; shelf
platoniczny (pla-to-ñeech-ni)
adj. m. Platonic;unsubstantial
platyna (pla-tí-na) f. platinum
plazma (pláz-ma) f. plasma
plaża (plá-zha) f. beach
plażować (pla-zho-vach)v.sun-bathe
plądrowac (plown-dró-vach) v.
plunder; ransack
pląsy (plown-si) pl. dance
plątac (plown-tach) v. entangle
plebania (ple-bá-ña) f. rectory
plebiscyt (ple-bees-cit) m. pleb-
iscite; people's direct vote
plecak (plé-tsak) m. rucksack
plecionka (ple-chón-ka) f. plaid
braid; wattle; basket work
plecy (ple-tsi) pl. back;backing
pleć (plech) v. weed (a garden)
plemienny (ple-myén-ni) adj. m.
tribal; of a trbe
plemię (ple-myań) n. tribe
plemnik (plém-ñeek) m. sperm
plenum (ple-noom) n. plenary
session; plenary assembly
pleść (pleshch) v. twist; blab;
weave;interlace; talk nonsense
pleśnieć (plésh-ñech) v. mold
pletwa (plét-va) f. fin;dovetail
plewic (ple-veech) v. weed
plik (pleek) m. bundle; sheaf
plisa (plee-sa) f. pleat
plomba (plom-ba) f. lead seal;
tooth filling; stopping
plon (plon) m. crop;yield
plotka (plót-ka) f. gossip; rumor; piece of gossip
pluc (plooch) v. spit; abuse
plugawy (ploo-gá-vi) adj. m.
filthy; squalid;foul;obscene
plus (ploos) m. plus; asset
plusk (ploosk) m. splash
pluskać (ploos-kach) v. splash

pluskiewka (ploos-kév-ka) f.
thumbtack;drawing pin
pluskwa (ploós-kva) f. bedbug
plusz (ploosh) m. plush
plutokracja (ploo-to-kráts-ya)
f. plutocracy
pluton (ploó-ton) m. platoon
plwocina (plvo-chee-na) f.
spittle;expectoration; spit
płaca (pwa-tsa) f. wage;salary
płachta (pwákh-ta) f. sheet
płacić (pwá-cheech) v. pay
płacz (pwach) m. cry; weep
płakać (pwá-kach) v. cry; weep
płaski (pwás-kee) adj. m. flat
płaskorzeźba (pwas-ko-zhéźh-ba)
f. (bas) relief; bas-relief
płaskowyż (pwas-kóvish) m. pla-
teau; table land
płaszcz (pwashch) m. overcoat
płaszczyć (pwásh-chich) v. flatten; become flat;fall, flat
płaszczyzna (pwash-chiz-na) f.
plane;surface;area;sheet;plain
płat (pwat) m. slice; lobe
płatać (pwá-tach) v. cut; play
(tricks);slice;split;fell
płatek (pwa-tek) m. flake
płatność (pwát-noshch) f. payment ; remittance
pławić (pwa-veech) v. float;
wallow : duck; drown;soak
płaz (pwas) m. reptile
płaz (pwas) m. flat of sabre
płciowy (pwcho-vi) adj. m.
sexual: genital; sex-(urge etc.)
płeć (pwech) f. sex; complexion
płetwa (pwet-va) f. fin
płochliwy (pwo-khlee-vi) adj.
m. timid ; shy; skittish
płochy (pwo-khi) adj. m. fri-
volous ;shy;timid;fickle
płodny (pwód-ni) adj. m. fertile ;productive; prolific
płodzić (pwo-dźheech)v. beget
płomień (pwo-myeń) m. flame
płonąć (pwo-nównch) v.be on
fire ;blaze;be inflamed;glow
płonny (pwon-ni) adj. m. sterile ;useless;vain;of no avail
płoszyć (pwo-shich) v. frighten
płot (pwot) m. fence ;hoarding

płowieć (pwo-vyech) v. fade
płowy (pwó-vi) adj. m. flaxen;
fair; buff; fallow; fawn
płód (pwoot) m. fetus; fruit
płócienny (pwoo-chen-ni) adj.
m. linen; canvas-(sail,shoes etc.)
płotno (pwoót-no) n. linen;canvas
płuco (pwoo-tso) n. lung
płucny (pwoots-ni) adj. m. pul-
monary
pług (pwook) m. plough; plow
płukać (pwoo-kach) v. rinse;
wash; gargle
płyn (pwin) m. liquid: fluid
płynąć (pwi-nównch) v. flow;
swim; sail; drift; go by;come
płynny (pwin-ni) adj. m. liquid;
fluent: fluid;smooth;graceful
płyta (pwi-ta) f, plate; slab;
disk; sheet: board;record
płyta gramofonowa (pwi-ta gra-
mofo-nó-va) f. (musical) record ; disk
płytki (pwit-kee) adj. m. shallow; flat; trivial; poinless
pływac (pwi-vach) v. swim; float;
navigate; be afloat; be evasive
pływak (pwi-vak) m. swimmer;
float; quibler; buoy
pniak (pńak) m. stump; trunk
po (po) prep. after; to; up to;
till; upon; for; at; in; up;
of; next; along; about; over;
past; behind ; as far as
pobicie (po-bee-che) n. battery
pobić (po-beech) v. beat up;
defeat ; beat in; thrash; spank
pobielac (po-bye-lach) v. whiten;
tin : make white; paint white
pobierac (po-bye-rach) v. take;
collect ; receive;get;draw;charge
pobliski (pob-lees-kee) adj. m.
nearby ; neighboring
pobłażac (po-bwa-zhach) v. indulge; forbear ; be tolerant
pobłażliwy (po-bwazh-lee-vi)
adj. m. lenient; forgiving
poboczny (po-boch-ni) adj. m.
lateral; secondary ; accessory
poborca (po-bór-tsa) m. (tax)
collector : tax gatherer
poborowy (po-bo-ró-vi) m. recruit ; recruiting

pobory (po-bo-ri) pl. salary
pobrać (po-brach) v. receive;
collect; get: draw; gather
pobudka (po-bood-ka) f. incentive; motive; reveille
pobudliwy (po-bood-lee-vi) adj.
m. excitable: ebullient
pobyt (po-bit) m. stay: visit
pocałować (po-tsa-wo-vach) v.
kiss: give a kiss
pocałunek (po-tsa-woo-nek) m.
kiss: caress with the lips
pochlebiać (po-khle-byach) v.
flatter: adulate: expect:fawn
pochlebny (po-khleb-ni) adj. m.
flattering: complimentary
pochłaniać (po-khwa-nach) v.
absorb: swallow up:engulf
pochmurny (po-khmoor-ni) adj.
m. gloomy; cloudy: overcast
pochodnia (po-khod-na) f. torch
pochodny (po-khod-ni) adj. m.
derivative: derived
pochodzenie (po-kho-dze-ne) n.
origin; descent; source
pochopny (po-khop-ni) adj. m.
hasty; eager; rush: ready
pochować (po-kho-vach) v. bury
pochód (po-khoot) m. march;
procession; parade Jvagina
pochwa (pokh-va) f. sheath;
pochwała (po-khva-wa) f. praise;
eulogy: approval: applouse
pochylić (po-khi-leech) v. incline; slope: slant: droop
pochyły (po-khi-wi) adj. m. inclined; stooped: sloping:oblique
pociąć (po-chownch) v. cut up;
slash; sting; saw up:intersect
pociąg (poch-ownk) m. train;
affinity: inclination
pociągać (po-chown-gach) v.pull:
draw; attract;tug: attract:coat
pociągnięcie (po-chowng-nan-che)
n. pull; move: stroke: pluck
po cichu (po chee-khoo) adv.
secretly; silently; softly
pocić (po-cheech) v. sweat
pociecha (po-che-kha) f. comfort; joy:solace:satisfaction
po ciemku (po chem-koo) adv.
in the dark:while in the dark
pocierać (po-che-rach) v. rub

pocieszać (po-che-shach) v. console; comfort;cheer up; solace
pocieszenie (po-che-she-ne) n.
consolation: comfort; solace
pocieszny (po-chesh-ni) adj. m.
funny; amusing;droll; comic
pocisk (po-cheesk) m. missile;
bullet; projectile
po co ? (po tso) what for ?
począć (po-chownch) v. begin;
conceive: become pregnant
początek (po-chown-tek) m. beginning; start:outset;fore-part
początkujący (po-chownt-koo-yown-tsi) m. beginner
poczciwy (poch-chee-vi) adj. m.
good-hearted ; friendly ;kindly
poczekać (po-che-kach) v. wait
poczekalnia (po-che-kal-na) f.
waiting room
poczęstować (po-chan-sto-vach)
v. treat: entertain; serve
poczęstunek (po-chan-stoo-nek)
m. treat; drinks; entertainment
poczta (poch-ta) f. post; mail
pocztówka (poch-toov-ka) f.
postcard: picture postcard
poczucie (po-choo-che) n. feeling; sense; consciousness
poczwórny (po-chvoor-ni) adj.
m. fourfold;four times as large,
as tall;as long, as strong,as big
poczynać (po-chi-nach) v. begin
(aggressively); conceive
poczytalny (po-chi-tal-ni) adj.
m. accountable; sane
poczytny (po-chit-ni) adj. m.
popular (book):widely read
pod (pod) prep. under; below;
towards; on; in ; underneath
podać (po-dach) v. give; hand;
pass ;serve: shake (hand)
podanie (po-da-ne) n. application : request; legend
podarek (po-da-rek) m. gift
podarty (po-dar-ti) adj. m. torn
podatek (po-da-tek) m. tax :duty
podatnik (po-dat-neek) m. taxpayer; rate payer
podaż (po-dazh) f. supply
podążać (po-down-zhach) v. make
for; draw to: make ons's way
podbicie (pod-bee-che) n. conquest; instep; lining ;ceiling

podbiec (pód-byets) v. run up
podbiegunowy (pod-bye-goo-nó-vi) adj. m. polar;near pole
podbój (pód-booy) m. conquest
podbudowa (pod-boo-dó-va) f. substructure; base course
podbródek (pod-broó-dek) m. chin; bib; feeder
podburzać (pod-boó-zhach) v. stir up; incite to revolt
podchmielony (pod-khmye-ló-ni) adj. m. tipsy; in drink
podchodzić (pod-kho-dźheech)v. approach; assume an attitude
podchwycić (pod-khvi-cheech) v. catch up; snatch up; spot
podchwytliwy (pod-khvit-lee-vi) adj. m. captious (question etc.)
podciągać (pod-chówn-gach) v. draw up;pull up;improve;class
podczas (pod-chas) prep. during; while;when; whereas
podczerwony (pod-cher-vó-ni) adj. m. infrared
poddac (pód-dach) v. surrender; suggest;submit; expose
pod dostatkiem (pod dos-tát-kyem) adv. plenty; enough
podejmować (po-dey-mó-vach) v. take up; entertain;pick up
podejrzany (po-dey-zha-ni) adj. m. suspect;suspicious; shady
podejrzliwy (po-dey-zhlee-vi) adj. m. suspicious;distrustful
podeptac (po-dep-tach) v. tramp (under foot);bustle about
poderwac (po-der-vach) v. jerk up; pick up; weaken;rouse
podeszwa (po-desh-va) f. sole
podginac (pod-gée-nach) v. tuck up; cock;turn up; bend(a knee)
podglądac (pod-glówn-dach) v. spy; peep; pry; snoop
podgorski (pod-goor-skee) adj. m. foot-hill;piedmont
podjechac (pod-ye-khach) v. drive up;ride uphill; come up
podgrzewac (pod-gzhé-vach) v. warm up; heat up;
podjudzać (pod-yoo-dzach) v. stir up; incite (to evil)
podkasac (pod-ká-sach) v. tuck up; turn up; rise

podkład (pód-kwat) m. base; railroad tie;undercurrent;bedding
podkładac (pod-kwá-dach) v. lay under; put under;plant as evidence
podkop (pód-kop) m. mine; sap
podkowa (pod-kó-va) f. horse-shoe; semicircle
podkradac (pod-krá-dach) v.thieve; pilfer; creep up
podkreslac (pod-kresh-lach) v.stress underline; emphasize; accentuate
podkuwac (pod-koó-vach) v. shoe(horse);hoppail a shoe; cram
podlegac (pod-le-gach) v. be subject; be liable;succomb;undergo
podleglosc (pod-leg-woshch) f. dependence; subjection;subordination
podlewac (pod-le-vach) v. water
podlizywac się (pod-lee-zi-vach shań) v. suck up to;make up to
podlotek (pod-ló-tek) f. fledgling; flapper;girl in her teens
podłoga (pod-wo-ga) f. floor
podłosc (pod-woshch) f. meanness
podług (pód-woo)) prep. : according to;in conformity with
podłużny (pod-woozh-ni) adj. m. oblong; longitudinal; elongated
podły (pód-wi) adj. m. mean
podmiejski (pod-myéy-skee) adj. m. suburban
podminowac (pod-mee-nó-vach) v. undermine; sap
podmiot (pód-myot) m. subject
podmuch (pód-mookh) m. gust; blow; puff; waft; breath;blast
podmywac (pod-mi-vach) v. wash under; sap; undermine;wash away
podniebienie (pod-ne-bye-ne) n. palate;roof of the mouth
podniecac (pod-ne-tsach) v.flurry excite;agitate;rouse;egg on
podniesc (pod-neshch) v. lift; hoist;rise;elevate;rear;incerease
podnieta (pod-ne-ta) f. stimulus;impulse;spur;stimulant
podniosły (pod-nos-wi) adj. m. sublime; ;elevated; lofty
podnosic (pod-no-sheech) v.hoist; raise; lift; take up; elevate
podnóżek (pod-noó-zhek) m. footstool; ottoman ;leg rest

podobać się (po-do-bach shän)
v. please; be attractive;like
podobny (po-dob-ni) adj. m.
similar; like; congenial
podoficer (pod-o-fee-tser) m.
noncommissioned officer
podołać (po-do-wach) v. be up
to;be equal to;cope;manage
podomka (po-dom-ka) f. house-
robe; dressing gown
podówczas (pod-oov-chas) adv.
at that time;at the time;then
podpadać (pod-pá-dach) v. be
spotted; fall under a category
podpalenie (pod-pa-le-ñe) n.
arson; setting of fire
podpatrzyć (pod-pá-tzhich) v.
spy; peep; find out; pry
podpierać (pod-pye-rach) v.
prop up; support; bolster
podpinać (pod-pee-nach) v.pin;
buckle up; strap;fasten;gird
podpis (pod-pees) m. signature
podpływać (pod-pwi-vach) v.
swim up; sail up; row up
podpora (pod-po-ra) f. prop
podporucznik (pod-po-rooch-
ñeek) m. second lieutenant
podporządkować (pod-po-zhöwnt-
ko-vach) v. subordinate
podprowadzic (pod-pro-va-
dżheech) v. bring near
podpułkownik (pod-poow-kov-
ñeek) m. lieutenant colonel
podrażnic (pod-rázh-ñeech) v.
displease; irritate;vex;gall
podręcznik (pod-rañch-ñeek) m.
handbook; textbook; manual
podrozeć (pod-ró-zhech) v. go
up; grow dear; rise in price
podróż (pód-roozh) f. travel;
voyage; journey; passage
podróżnik (pod-roozh-ñeek) m.
traveler; voyager; wayfarer
po drugie (po droo-ge) adv.
in the second place; second
podrzec (pód-zhech) v. tear up
podrzędny (pod-zhänd-ni) adj.
m. subordinate; secondary
podsądny (pod-sownd-ni) m. defendant; the person sued
podskakiwać (pod-ska-kee-vach)
v. leap; jump up;hop;skip

podsłuch (pód-swookh) m. eavesdropping; wire tapping;listen in
podstawa (pod-stá-va) f. base;
basis;footing;mount;principle
podstawic (pod-stá-veech) v.
substitute;put under;bring round
podstęp (pod-stänp) m.trick;ruse;
guile; deceit;piece of deceit
podstępny (pod-stänp-ni) adj. m.
deceitful; tricky; crafty;insidious
podstrzygać (pod-stzhi-gach) v.
trim the hair; shorten the hair
podsuwać (pod-soo-vach) v. push
near; plant; suggest; slip under
podsycac (pod-si-tsach) v. foment; feed; fan (a quarrel etc.)
podsypywać (pod-si-pi-vach) v.
pour (sand etc.);strew; sprinkle
podszept (pod-shept) m. suggestion: prompting; insinuation
podszeptywac (pod-shep-ti-vach)
v. prompt; suggest;hint;insinuate
podszewka (pod-shév-ka) f. lining ; inside information
podswiadomy (pod-shvya-do-mi)
adj. m. subconscious(mental process)
podupadac (pod-oo-pá-dach) v.
decline; deteriorate;fall into decay
poduszka (po-doosh-ka) f. pillow;
pad; cushion; ball (of the thumb)
podwajac (pod-va-yach) v. double;
duplicate; increase twofold
podważyć (pod-va-zhich) v. lever
up; pry up; shake(an opinion)
podwiązka (pod-vyówns-ka) f.
garter; suspender; ligature
podwieczorek (pod-vye-cho-rek)
m. afternoon tea; afternoon snack
podwiezc (pód-vyeżhch) v. give
a ride; give a lift(in one's car)
podwładny (pod-vwad-ni) adj. m.
subordinate (to somebody);inferior
podwodna łódz (pod-vod-na woodżh)
f. submarine (under water warship)
podwoic (pod-vo-eech)v. double
podwozie (pod-vo-żhe) n. chassis
podworko (pod-voor-ko) n. backyard ;farmyard:court;courtyard
podwyżka (pod-vizh-ka) f. raise
podzelowac (pod-ze-lo-vach) v.
resole (shoes, boots, foot ware)
podziac (po-dżhach) v. loose
podział (po-dżhaw) m. division

podziałka (po-dżhaw-ka) f.
scale; graduation; division
podzielać (po-dżhe-lach) v.
share; participate; concur
podzielić (po-dżhe-leech) v.
divide (into parts)
podzielny (po-dżhél-ni) adj. m.
adj. m. divisible (easily)
podziemie (pod-żhém-ye) n.base-
ment; underworld
podziemny (pod-żhém-ni) adj. m.
underground; secret
podziękować (po-dżhań-ko-vach)
v. thank; decline with thanks
podziewać (po-dżhe-vach) v.
loose; mislay;leave somewhere
podziw (po-dżheef) m. admiration; wander
podzwrotnikowy (pod-zvrot-nee-
ko-vi) adj. m. tropical
podżegacz (pod-zhe-gach) m. instigator; warmonger; abettor
poemat (po-e-mat) m. poem
poeta (po-e-ta) m. poet
poetka (po-ét-ka) f. poet
poezja (po-éz-ya) f. poetry
pogadanka (po-ga-dán-ka) f,
talk; chat; chatty lecture
poganiac (po-ga-nach) v. drive;
egg on; urge on; prod on;hustle
poganin (po-ga-neen) m. pagan
pogarda (po-gár-da) f. contempt
pogarszać (po-gár-shach) v.
make worse; aggravate;worsen
pogawędka (po-ga-vánd-ka) f.
chat; chit-chat
pogląd (po-glównd) m. opinion
pogłębiać (po-gwánb-yach) v.
deepen; dig deeper; dredge
pogłoska (po-gwos-ka) f. rumor
pogniewać się (po-gne-vach shań)
v. get angry; be angry
pogoda (po-gó-da) f. weather;
cheerfulness; fine weather
pogodny (po-gód-ni) adj. m.
serene; cheerful; sunny
pogodzic (po-gó-dzheech) v.
reconcile; square (things)
pogoń (po-goń) f. pursuit;
chase; hunt; quest; pursuers
pogorszenie (po-gor-she-ne) n.
worsening; deterioration

pogorszyc (po-gór-shich) v.
make worse; aggravate
pogorzelisko (po-go-zhe-lees-
ko) n. after fire ruins
pogotowie (po-go-tó-vye) n.
ambulance service; readiness
pogranicze (po-gra-ñee-che) n.
borderland; border line
pogrom (pó-grom) m. rout
pogromca (po-gróm-tsa) m.tam-
er; conqueror
pogrożka (po-groozh-ka) f.
threat;threatening expression
pogrzeb (pó-gzhep) m. funeral
pogrzebacz (po-gzhe-bach) m.
poker (for stirring a fire)
pogwałcic (po-gvaw-cheech) v.
violate; outrage;transgress
poic (pó-eech) v. water; ply
pojawic się (po-ya-veech shań)
v. appear; emerge; occur;arise
pojazd (pó-yazt) m. car;vehicle
pojąć (po-yównch) v. grasp;
marry; comprehend;understand
pojechac (po-ye-khach) v. go;
leave; take (train, boat etc.)
pojednac (po-yéd-nach) v. reconcile (two or more parties)
pojednawczy (po-yed-náv-chi)
adj. m. conciliatory
pojedynczy (po-ye-dín-chi) adj.
m. single; individual; onefold
pojedynek (po-ye-di-nek) m.
duel; encounter; single combat
pojemnik (po-yém-neek) m. container; vessel; receptacle
pojemnosc (po-yém-noshch) f.
capacity; cubic content
pojezierze (po-ye-żhe-zhe) n.
lake land ; lake district
pojęcie (po-yáñ-che) n. notion;
idea; concept; comprehension
pojętny (po-yáñt-ni) adj. m.
intelligent; sharp; teachable
pojmować (poy-mó-vach) v.grasp;
comprehend; conceive;imagine
pojutrze (po-joot-zhe) adv. day
after tomorrow
pokarm (pó-karm) m. food; feed
pokaz (pó-kas) m. display; shaw
pokazywać (po-ka-zi-vach) v.
show; point; exhibit; let see

pokaźny (po-kaźh-ni) adj. m.
respectable; appreciable
pokład (pók-wad) m. deck; layer
pokątny (po-kównt-ni) adj. m.
underhanded; secret; illegal
pokłon (pók-won) m. bow; homage
pokłócić się (po-kwoó-cheech
śhań)v. fall out with;quarrel
pokochać (po-kó-khach) v. fall
in love; become fond of
pokoik (po-kó-eek) m. little
room; little cozy room
pokojówka (po-ko-yóov-ka) f.
maid; housemaid; chamber maid
pokolenie (po-kole-ñe) n. generation; about 30 years
pokonać (po-kó-nach) v. defeat
pokorny (po-kor-ni) adj. m.
humble; meek; submissive
pokost (pó-kost) m. varnish
pokrajać (po-kra-yach) v. cut
up; carve up; slice; slash
pokój (pó-kooy) m. room; peace
pokrapiać (po-krá-pyach) v.
sprinkle; wash down (a meal)
pokrewieństwo (po-krev-yeń-stvo)
n. kinship; kindred;relation
pokrewny (po-krev-ni) m. related; kindred; akin; cognate
pokrótce (po-króot-tse) adv.
in short; in brief;concisely
pokrycie (po-kri-che) n. cover
pokryć (pó-krich) v. cover
po kryjomu (po-kri-yó-moo) adv.
secretly; on the sly; in secret
pokrywa (po-kri-va) f. lid
pokrywać (pokri-vach) v. cover;
upholster; serve (mare)
pokrzepić (po-kzhé-peech) v.
invigorate; refresh; fortify
pokrzywa (po-kzhee-va) f. nettle
pokrzyżować (po-kzhi-zhó-vach)
v. cross up; confound ;tangle
pokup (pó-koop) m. demand
pokupny (po-koóp-ni) adj. m.
in demand ; selable
pokusa (po-koó-sa) f. temptation
pokuta (po-koó-ta) f. penance
pokwitować (po-kvee-tó-vach) v.
receipt ; acknowledge receipt
pokwitowanie (po-kvee-to-va-ñe)
n. receipt ⌡(liquid)
polać (pó-lach)v. pour over

Polak (pó-lak) m. Polonian;
Pole; Polonius; vulg.:polack
polana (po-lá-na) f. glade
polano (po-lá-no) n. billet; log
polarny (po-lar-ni) adj. m. polar ; of the polar axis
pole (po-le) n. field
polec (pó-lets) v. fall; be
killed (in battle)
polecać (po-le-tsach) v. recommend; commend; instruct; order
polegać (po-le-gach) v. rely
polemika (po-le-mee-ka) f. po-
lemics; controversy
polepszać (po-lep-shach) v. improve; ameliorate; mend; better
polerować (po-le-ró-vach) v.
polish; furbish; burnish;refine
polewać (po-le-vach) v. water;
glaze; glaze; enamel; ice
polewka (po-lev-ka) f. broth
polędwica (po-länd-vee-tsa) f.
sirloin; loin; fillet(of beef)
policja (po-leets-ya) f. police
policzek (po-lee-chek) m. cheek
politechnika (po-lee-tekh-ñee-
ka) f. polytechnic college
politowanie (po-lee-to-va-ñe)
n. pity; compassion
polityk (po-lee-tik) m. politician; statesman
polka (pól-ka) f. polka; Polish
girl; Polish woman; Pole
polny (pól-ni) adj. m. field
polon (pó-lon) m. polonium
(chem.)
polonez (po-ló-nez) m.polonaise
(dance)
Polonia (po-lon-ya) f. Polish
colony ; Polish emigrants
Polonus (po-ló-noos) m. Pole of
old ;typical Pole of the past
polot (pó-lot) m. elan ;imagination
polować (po-ló-vach) v. hunt
polski (pól-skee) adj. m. Polish ; Polish language
polszczyć (polsh-chich) v.Polo-
nize ;invest with Polish traits
polszczyzna (pol-shchiz-na) f.
Polish language ; Polish traits
polubić (po-loó-beech)v. get to
like ; become fond;take a fancy

polubownie (po-loo-bov-ñe) adv.
amicably; by compromise
połamać (po-wá-mach) v. break
połączenie (po-wówn-che-ñe) n.
connection; linkage;contact
połknąć (pów-knówñch) v. swallow;gulp down; drink down
połowa (po-wó-va) f. half
położenie (po-wo-zhe-ñe) n.
position; situation; site
położna (po-wózh-na) f. midwife
położnica (po-wozh-ñee-tsa) f,
woman in childbed
położyc (po-wo-zhich) v. lay
down; place;deposit;fell;ruin
połóg (po-wook) m. childbirth
połów ryb (pó-woov rib) fish
catch; fishing; fish haul
południe (po-wood-ñe) n. noon;
south; midday; the South
południk (po-wood-ñeek) m. meridian; the line of longitude
południowo-wschodni (po-wood-
ñó-vo wskhód-ñee) south-east
południowo-zachodni (po-wood-
ñó-vo za-khod-ñee) south-west
południowy (po-wood-ñó-vi) adj.
m. south; midday; southerly
połykac (po-wi-kach) v. swallow
połysk (pó-wisk) m. glitter;
gloss ; luster; sheen; sparkle
pomadka (po-mád-ka) f. lipstick
pomagac (po-má-gach) v. help
pomalenku (po-ma-leñ-koo) adv.
little by little; very slowly
pomału (po-má-woo) adv. little
by little; slowly; leisurely
pomarancza (po-ma-rañ-cha) f.
orange ; orange tree
pomarszczony (po-marsh-chó-ni)
adj. m. wrinkled; creased
pomazac (po-má-zach) v. smear-
over; anoint; soil; scrawl
pomawiać (po-máv-yach) v. accuse; impute ; charge with
pomiar (po-myar) m. measurement;
survey ; surveying;mensuration
pomiatac (po-myá-tach) v. push
around; spurn; hold in contempt
pomidor (po-mee-dor) m. tomato
pomieszać (po-myé-shach) v. mix
up ; mingle; blend;stir;tangle;
muddle up;embroil;mistake

pomieszanie zmysłów (po-mye-sha-
ñe zmís-wooy) insanity; madness
pomieszczac (po-myesh-chach) v.
admit; contain; accomodate
pomiędzy (po-myán-dzi) prep.
between; among; in the midst
pomijac (po-mee-yach) v. pass
over; omit; overlook; leave out
pomimo (po-mee-mo) prep. in
spite of; notwithstanding
pomnażać (po-mna-zhach) v. multiply; increase; intensify
pomniejszac (po-mñey-shach) v.
diminish; lessen;reduce;belittle
pomnik (póm-ñeek) m. monument
pomoc (po-mots) f. help ; aid
pomocnik (po-móts-ñeek) m. helper; assistant: helpmate; aid
pomocny (po-móts-ni) adj. m.
helpful; instrumental
pomorski (po-mór-skee) adj. m.
Pomeranian; of Pomerania
pomost (pó-most) m. platform
pomóc (pó-moots) v. help; assist
pompa (póm-pa) f. pump; pomp
pompowac (pom-pó-vach) v. pump
pomsta (pó-msta) f. vengeance
pomruk (póm-rook) m. murmur;
grumble; growl;purr; rumble
pomstowac (pom-stó-vach) v.
curse; swear; revile;vituperate
pomyje (po-mí-ye) pl. dish-
water; hog-wash; swill; lap
pomylic (po-mi-leech) v. confound; be mistaken; mislead
pomyłka (po-miw-ka) f. error
pomysł (pó-misw) m. idea
pomyslnosc (po-mishl-noshch) f.
prosperity; success; happiness
pomyslny (po-mishl-ni) adj. m.
successful; favorable; good
pomywaczka (po-mi-vách-ka) f.
dishwasher; scullery maid
ponad (po-nat) prep. above;
over; beyond;upwards of;super-;
more than;over and above;besides
ponadto (po-nád-to) prep. moreover; besides; furthermore;also
ponaglac (po-nág-lach) v. rush;
urge; remind;press; urge on
ponaglenie (po-nag-le-ñe) n.
reminder; pressure
ponawiać (po-náv-yach) v. renew

ponętny (po-nant-ni) adj. m.
seductive; attractive;alluring
poniechać (po-ńe-khać) v.give
up ;relinquish; renounce;desist
poniedziałek (po-ńe-dźha-wek)
m. Monday
poniekąd (po-ńe-kównt) adv.
partly;in a way; in a sense
poniesc (po-ńeshch) v. sustain;
carry ;bear; suffer;incur;push
ponieważ (po-ńe-vash) conj. because; as; since; for
poniewczasie (po-ńev-cha-she)
adv. too late ;after the event
poniewierac (po-ńe-vye-rach) v.
kick around;slight;mishandle
poniżej (po-ńee-zhey) adv. below; beneath ;hereunder;under
poniżyc (po-ńee-zhich) v. degrade; humble;tread down
ponosic (po-no-sheech) v. bear;
carry (away) ;suffer;incur
ponowic (po-no-veech) v. renew
ponownie (po-nov-ńe) adv. anew;
again ; afresh; a second time
ponowny (po-nov-ni) adj. m. repeated; renewed;reiterated
ponton (pon-ton) m. pontoon
ponury (po-noo-ri) adj m.gloomy
dismal; sullen; dreary; sullen
pończocha (pon-cho-kha) f.
stocking
popadac (po-pa-dach) v. fall in
poparcie (po-par-che) n. support; backing; promotion;push
popasc (po-pa-shch) v. fall in
popatrzec (po-pa-tzhech) v. look
popelina (po-pe-lee-na) f.
poplin;a ribbed cloth
popchnąć (pop-khnownch) v. push;
shove;hastle; jostle;steer
popełniac (po-pew-nach) v. commit;perpetrate
popęd (po-pant) m. impulse
popędliwy (po-pand-lee-vi) adj.
impetuous; rush;hot headed
popędzac (po-pan-dzach) v. drive
on; urge; push on; prod;spur
popielaty (po-pye-la-ti) adj. m.
charcoal-grey; ashen; gray
popielec (po-pye-lets) m. Ash
Wednesday

popielniczka (po-pyel-ńeech-
ka) f. ash-tray; ash pan
popierac (po-pye-rach) v. support; back;promote;favor;uphold
popiersie (po-pyer-she) n. bust
popic (po-peech) v. rinse down
popioł (po-pyoow) m. ashes;ash;
cinders; slag
popis (po-pees) m. show; parade
popisywac się (po-pee-si-vach
shań)v.show off;flaunt;parade
poplecznik (po-plech-ńeek) m.
backer; upholder; partisan
popłatny (po-pwat-ni) adj. m.
profitable; lucrative
popłoch (po-pwokh) m. panic
popołudnie (po-po-wood-ńe) n.
afternoon
po południu (po po-wood-ńoo) in
the afternoon
poprawa (po-pra-va) f.improve-
ment;change for the better
poprawka (po-prav-ka) f. correction;amendment; alteration
poprawny (po-prav-ni) adj. m.
correct;faultless;proper
po prostu (po pros-too) adv.
simply;openly;uncremoniously
poprzeczka (po-pzhech-ka) f.
crossbar; crossbeam;the bar
poprzedni (po-pzhed-ńee) adj.
m. previous; preceding;former
poprzedzac (po-pzhe-dzach) v.
precede;orelude;go before
poprzestac (po-pzhes-tach) v.
settle for; be satisfied
popularny (po-poo-lar-ni) adj.
m. popular; prevalent
popychac (po-pi-khach) v. push;
shove; ill treat; hustle; jostle
popychadło (po-pi-khad-wo) n.
drudge; scapegrace
popyt (po-pit) m. demand
pora (po-ra) f. time; season
porachunek (po-ra-khoo-nek) m.
reckoning; a bone to pick
porada (po-ra-da) f. advice
poradnia (po-rad-ńa) f. information bureau;dispensary;clinic
poradnik (po-rad-ńeek) m. guide;
handbook; reference book
poradzic (po-ra-dżhech) v. advise

poranek (po-rá-nek) m. morning
porastać (po-rás-tach) v. overgrow; grow; become overgrown
poratować (po-ra-tó-vach) v. help in distress; recuperate
porażenie (po-ra-zhé-ne) n. stroke; shock; paralysis
porażka (po-rázh-ka) f. defeat; set back; reverse
porcelana (por-tse-lá-na) f. china; porcelain
porcja (pór-tsya) f. portion
poręcz (pór-anch) f. banister
poręczenie (po-ran-che-ne) n. guarantee; bail;warranty;pledge
poręka (po-ran-ka) f. guaranty; pledge;sponsorship; surety
poronić (po-ro-neech) v. abort; miscarry; have a miscarriage
porost (po-rost) m. growth
porowaty (po-ro-vá-ti) adj. m. porous; full of pores
porozdawać (po-roz-dá-vach) v. give away; pass around
porozumienie (po-ro-zoo-mye-ne) m. understanding;agreement
poród (pó-root) m. child delivery; childbirth; partitution
porównać (po-roóv-nach) v. compare; draw a comparison; liken
porównanie (po-roov-ná-ne) n. comparison;equalization
poróżnić (po-roózh-neech) v. disunite; divide; embroil
port (port) m. port; harbor
portfel (pórt-fel) m. wallet
portier (pórt-yer) m. doorman
portki (pórt-kee) pl. pants (vulg.) ;breeches; trousers
portmonetka (port-mo-nét-ka) f. purse ; billfold; wallet
porto (por-to) n. postage
portret (pór-tret) m. portrait
portugalski (por-too-gál-skee) adj. m. Portuguese
poruczać (po-roó-chach) v. entrust; charge with
porucznik (po-roóch-neek) m. lieutenant
poruszać (po-roó-shach) v. move: touch ; sway; set in motion
poruszenie (po-roo-she-ne) n. agitation ;movement; stir;touch

poryw (pó-riv) m. impulse; rapture; gust; onrush; elation
porywać (po-ri-vach) v. snatch; carry off; whisk away;grab;thrill
porywacz (po-ri-vach) m. kidnaper; abductor; ravisher
porywczy (po-riv-chi) adj. m. rash;irritable;impetuous;hasty
porządek (po-zhówn-dek) n. order;tidiness;regularity;system
porządny (po-zhównd-ni) adj. m. neat; decent; accurate;reliable
porzucać (po-zhoo-tsach) v. abandon; desert;forsake; leave
porzucić (po-zhoo-cheech) v. abandon; give up; cast away
posada (po-sá-da) f. employment
posadzka (po-sádz-ka) f. parquet floor; tile floor
posąg (pó-sównk) m. statue
poselstwo (po-sél-stvo) n. legation; deputation; envoys
poseł (pó-sew) m. envoy; congressman; deputy; legate
posępny (po-sánp-ni) adj. m. gloomy; dismal; dreary; dark
posiadacz (po-sha-dach) m. bearer; holder; possessor;owner
posiadać (po-sha-dach) v. hold; own; possess; acquire;dominate
posiadłość (po-shád-woshch) f. estate; property; dominion
posiedzenie (po-she-dze-ne) n. session; conference; meeting
posilać (po-shee-lach) v. refresh; nourish; feed
posiłek (po-shee-wek) m. meal; refreshment; reinforcement
posłać (po-swach) f. send; make a bed; dispatch somewhere
posłanie (po-swa-ne) n. bed; bedding; message;dispatch
posłaniec (po-swa-nets) m. messenger; commissionaire
posłuchać (po-swoo-khach) v. listen; obey; take advice
posługa (po-swoo-ga) f. service
posługacz (po-swoo-gach) m. servant; attendant; commissionaire
posłuszny (po-swoosh-ni) adj. m. obedient; submissive;docile
pospolity (pos-po-lee-ti) adj. m. vulgar; common;commonplace

posrebrzać (po-sréb-zhaćh) v.
silver (plate);silver foil
post (post) m. fast; fast day
postać (pó-staćh) f. form;shape;
figure;human shape;personage
postanowić (po-sta-nó-veećh) v.
decide; enact;resolve;determine
postanowienie (po-sta-no-vye-ńe)
n. decision; resolve; provision
postarać się (po-stá-raćh śháń)
v. procure; obtain;get;try;find
postawa (po-stá-va) f. attitude;
posture; pose;bearing; position
postawny (po-stáw-ni) adj. m.
portly;handsome;well made
postawić (po-stá-veećh) v. set
up; put up;set;on;put on;raise
postąpić (po-stówn-peećh) v.
proceed; act; deal;follow;treat
posterunek (po-ste-roo-nek) m.
outpost; sentry; police station
postęp (pó-stáńp) m. progress;
advance;march;headway
postępowanie (postáń-po-va-ńe)
n. behavior; advance;procedure
postojowe (po-sto-yó-ve) n.
demurrage;adj.n.parking
postój (pó-stooy) m. halt;stop;
stand; parking;stopping place
postrach (pó-strakh) m. terror;
dread;scare;fright;bugaboo
postrzał (pó-stzhaw) m. gunshot;
wound;shot;rifle shot;lumbago
postrzelony (po-stzhe-ló-ni)
adj. m. wounded; crazy;cracked
postulat (po-stóo-lat) m. demand; claim; requirement
postument (po-stóo-ment) m.
pedestal; socle
posucha (po-sóo-kha) f. drought
posuw (pó-soov) m. feed (of a
drill); feed of a lathe
posuwać (po-sóo-vaćh) v. move;
shove; push on;carry;dash;speed
posyłać (po-sí-waćh) v.send over
posyłka (po-síw-ka) f. errand
posypywać (po-si-pi-vaćh) v.
dust; pour; sprinkle (dry)
poszanowanie (po-sha-no-va-ńe)
n. respect; observance(of a law)
poszarpać (po-shár-paćh) v.maul;
tear up; jag up;mangle;rend

poszczególny (po-shche-góól-
ni) adj. m. individual
poszerzać (po-shé-zhaćh) v.
widen;broaden;extend;ream;spread
poszewka (po-shév-ka) f. pil-
low-case ; pillow slip
poszkodowany (po-shko-do-vá-
ni) adj. m. victim ;sufferer
poszlaka (po-shlá-ka) f.trace:
circumstantial evidence; sign
poszukiwać (po-shoo-kée-vaćh)
v. search;look for;inquire;claim
poszukiwanie (po-shoo-kee-va-
ńe) n. search;quest;research
poście (póśh-ćheećh) v. fast
pościel (póśh-ćhel) f. bedclothes sheets and blankets
pościg (póśh-ćheeg) m. chase
pośladek (po-śhlá-dek) m. but-
tock; rump; bum
pośliznąć się (po-śhleéz-nównch
śháń) v. slip ;make a slip
poślubić (po-śhloó-beećh) v.
marry; take in marriage
pośmiertny (po-śhmyért-ni) adj.
m. posthumous (child, works etc.)
pośmiewisko (po-śhmye-veés-ko)
n.laughingstock;butt of ridicule
pośpiech (póśh-pyekh) m. haste;
hurry; dispatch
pośredni (po-śhréd-ńee) adj.
m. intermediate; indirect
pośrednik (po-śhred-ńeek) m.
go-between; intermediary
pośredniczyć (po-shred-ńée-
chićh) v. mediate;be a go-between
pośród (po-śh-rood) prep. among
poświadczać (po-śhvyád-chaćh)
v. attest; certify;testify;witness
poświadczenie (po-śhvyad-che-
ńe) n. certificate;attestation
poświęcać (po-shvyáń-tsaćh) v.
sacrifice; sanctify
poświęcenie (po-shvyáń-tse-ńe)
n. devotion; sacrifice
pot (pot) m. sweat;prespiration
potajemny (po-ta-yém-ni) adj.
m. secret; clandestine;underhand
potakiwać (po-ta-keé-vaćh) v.
assent; agree; acquiesce
potas (pó-tas) m. potassium
potaż (pó-tash) m. potash

potąd (po-townt) adv. up to
here ;up to this place
potem (po-tem) adv. after ;
afterwards; then; later on
potencjalny (po-ten-tsyál-ni)
adj. m. potential ;virtual
potęga (po-tán-ga) f. power;
might ;force;impressiveness
potęgowac (po-tán-go-vach) v.
intensify ;raise to a power
potępiac (po-tán-pyach) v.
damn; run down ;condemn
potępienie (po-tán-pye-ne) n.
damnation ;disapproval;blame
potężny (po-tánzh-ni) adj. m.
mighty ;tremendous;powerful
potknąc sie (pot-knownch shán)v.
slip ;trip; stumble;make a slip
potknięcie (pot-knán-che) n.
slip; stumble; trip ; a lapse
potoczny (po-tóch-ni) adj. m.
current; common ;everyday;daily
potok (po-tok) m. stream;brook
potomek (po-tó-mek) m. descendant ; offspring; scion
potomnosc (po-tom-noshch) f.
posterity ;future generations
potomstwo (po-tom-stvo) pl. issue; progeny; offspring;breed
potop (po-top) m. deluge; flood
potrafic (po-tra-feech) v. know
how to do ;manage;be able to do
potrawa (po-tra-ya) f. dish
potrawka (po-trav-ka) f. fric-
assee ;ragout
potrącic (po-trown-cheech) v.
knock; deduct ;poke;push;jostle
po trochu (po-tro-khoo) adv.
little by little ;gradually
potrojny (po-trooy-ni) adj. m.
triple ;triplicate;treble
potrzask (pot-shask) m. trap
potrząsac (po-tzhówn-sach) v.
shake ; brandish; agitate;strew
potrzeba (po-tzhé-ba) f. need;
want;call;emergency;extremity
potrzebny (po-tzhéb-ni) adj. m.
necessary ;needed;wanted
potulny (po-tool-ni) adj. m.
docile ;submissive;humble;meek
poturbowac (po-toor-bó-vach) v.
manhandle; rough up ;beat;maul
batter;knock about;ill-treat;
give a rough handling; hurt

potwarz (po-tvash) f. slander
potwierdzac (po-tvyer-dzach) v.
confirm; attest;corroborate
potwor (po-tvoor) m. monster
potykac się (po-ti-kach shán)
v. stumble; skirmish;joust
potylica (po-ti-lée-tsa) f.
occiput; back part of skull
pouczac (po-oó-chach) v. instruct; teach;give instructions
pouczenie (po-oo-che-ne) n.
instruction;giving instructions
poufalic się(po-oo-fá-lich shán)v
take liberties; familiarize
poufały (po-oo-fá-wi) adj. m.
intimate;unceremonious;free with
too familiar; maty;hob-nobbing
poufny (po-oóf-ni) adj. m. confidential;private;secret
powab (po-vap) m. charm;attrac-
tion;lure;seduction;loveliness
powabny (po-váb-ni) adj. m. attractive; charming;alluring
powaga (po-vá-ga) f. gravity;
seriousness;dignity;prestige
powalac (po-va-lach) v. soil;
dirty; overthrow;kill;slay
powalic (po-va-leech) v. knock
down;overthrow;kill;slay;fell
powała (po-va-wa) f. ceiling
poważac (po-va-zhach) v. respect;esteem;have regard
poważny (po-vazh-ni) adj. m.
earnest; grave;dignified;serious
powątpiewac (po-vównt-pye-vach)
v. doubt;have doubts; be dubious
powetowac (po-ve-to-vach) v.
make up;idemnify oneself;retrieve
powiadac (po-vyá-dach) v. say;
tell; speak ;(the legend)has it
powiadomic (po-vya-dó-meech) v. that
inform; notify; let know
powiastka (po-vyast-ka) f. tale
powiat (po-vyat) m. county;
district; district authorities
powicie (po-vee-che) n. swad-
dling clothes; child delivery
powidła (po-veed-wa) pl. jam;
marmalade; jam
powiedziec (po-vye-dzhech) v.
say; tell; declare
powieka (po-vye-ka) f. eyelid
powielacz (po-vye-lach) m.
mimeograph

powiernica (po-vyer-nee-tsa) f.
confidante;trusted friend
powierzac (po-vye-zhach) v.
confide;charge with a task
powierzchnia (po-vyezhkh-ña) f.
surface;plane; area; acreage
powiesic (po-vye-sheech) v.
hang;supend; hung up;ring off
powiesc (po-vyeshch) f. novel
powiesc sie (po-vyeshch shan)
v. succeed; be successful
powietrze (po-vyet-zhe) n. air
powiew (po-vyev) m. breeze
powiekszac (po-vyank-shach) v.
enlarge;augment;extend; add
powiekszenie (po-vyank-she-ñe)
n. enlargement; magnification
powijaki (po-vee-ja-kee) pl.
swathings;initial stage
powiklac (po-veek-wach) v.
complicate; embroil
powinnosc (po-veen-noshch) f.
duty; obligation
powinowaty (po-vee-no-va-ti)
adj. m. related; akin
powitac (po-vee-tach) v. welcome; salute; bid welcome
powlekac (po-vle-kach) v. cover; drag; coat;smear; spread
powloczka (po-vwoch-ka) f. pillowcase; envelope;covering
powloka (po-vwo-ka) f. (paint)
coat; covering;envelope; shell
powloczysty (po-vwoo-chis-ti)
adj. m. trailing; enticing
powodowac (po-vo-do-vach) v.
cause; bring about; touch off;
effect; induce; give occasion
powodzenie (po-vo-dze-ñe) n.
success; well-being;prosperity
powodzic sie (po-vo-dzhech shan)
v. fare (well; ill);be well off
powojenny (po-vo-yen-ni) adj.
m. post-war; after-war
powoli (po-vo-lee) adv. slow
powolny (po-vol-ni) adj. m.
slow; tardy;leisurely;gradual
powolanie (po-vo-wa-ñe) n. vocation; call;appointment;quot.
powonienie (po-vo-ñe-ñe) n.
sense of smell; smell
powod (po-voot) m. cause; reason;ground; motive;plaintiff

powodz (po-voodzh) f. flood
powoj (po-vooy) m. bindweed
powoz (po-woos) m. carriage
powracac (po-vra-tsach) v. return; come back;resume;recover
powrotny (po-vrot-ni) adj. m.
return; return(ticket)
powrot (po-vroot) m. return
powroz (po-vroos) m. rope
powstanie (po-vsta-ñe) n. rising; uprising; insurrection
powstaniec (po-vsta-ñets) m.
insurgent(against a government)
powstawac (po-vsta-vach) v.
rise up; stand up;revolt;
powstrzymac (po-vstzhi-mach) v.
restrain; refrain; hold back
powszechny (po-vshekh-ni) adj.
m. universal; general; public
powszedni (po-vshed-ñee) adj.
m. everyday; commonplace;daily
powsciagliwosc (povshchowng-
lee-voshch) f. abstinence;
temperance; moderation;restraint
powsciagliwy (povshchowng-lee-
vi) adj. m. reserved; absti-
nent; moderate;temperate
powtarzac (pov-ta-zhach) v. say
again; go over; repeat;reproduce
po wtore (po vtoo-re) adv. secondly; in the second place; then
powtornie (pov-toor-ñe) adv.
anew; again; a second time
powtorny (po-vtoor-ni) adj. m.
repeated; renewed; second-
powyzej (po-vi-zhey) adv. above;
here in before; higher up; over
powziac (pov-zhownch) v. take
up; form ;decide;conceive(a plan)
poza (po-za) f. pose; attitude;
sham
poza (po-za) prep. beyond; besides; except; apart;outside;extra-
pozagrobowy (po-za-gro-bo-vi)
adj. m. beyond the grave;
hereafter, from beyond the grave
pozbawiac (po-zbav-yach) v.
deprive ;dispossess;take away
pozbyc sie (poz-bich shan) v.
rid oneself; get rid;shake off
pozdrawiac (po-zdra-vyach) v.
greet; send one's greetings
pozew (po-zef) m. summons; writ;
citation

poziom (po-żhom) m. level
poziomka (po-żhom-ka) f. wild
strawberry(frujt or plant)
poziomy (po-żho-mi) adj. m.
horizontal;level;uninspired
pozłota (po-zwo-ta) f. gilding
poznać (po-znach) v. get to
know; recognize;taste;acquaint
poznajomić (po-zna-yo-meech) v.
acquaint; introduce
poznanie (po-zna-ńe) n. cogni-
tion; acquaintance; learning
pozornie (po-zor-ńe) adv. ap-
parently; on the surface
pozostać (po-zos-tach) v. remain; stay behind;continue
pozostały (po-zos-ta-wi) adj.
m. remaining; residual;left
pozostawiać (po-zos-tav-yach)
v. leave (behind);bequeath
pozór (po-zoor) m. appearance;
pretext; sham;look;mask;cloak
pozwać (póz-vach) v. summon
pozwalać (po-zva-lach) v. let;
allow; permit; tolerate;suffer
pozwany (po-zva-ni) m. defendant; person sued or accused
pozwolenie (po-zvo-le-ńe) n.
permission;consent; permit
pozycja (po-zyts-ya) f. position; item; status;posture
pozyskać (po-zis-kach) v. gain;
win over ; conciliate
pozytywny (po-zi-tiv-ni) adj.
m. positive; affirmative
pozywać (po-zi-vach) v. sue;
cite; summon; cite(to court)
pożałować (po-zha-wo-vach) v.
repent; regret; take pity
pożar (po-zhar) m. fire (woods,
buildings);conflagration
pożądać (po-zhown-dach) v. desire; covet; lust after
pożądany (po-zhown-da-ni) adj.
m. desirable; welcome;desired
pożądliwy (po-zhownd-lee-vi)
adj. m. greedy; covetus;lewd
pożegnać (po-zheg-nach) v. bid
goodbye; see off; dismiss
pożerać (po-zhe-rach) v. devour
pożoga (po-zho-ga) f. fire; conflagration; ravages (of war)

pożółknąć (po-zhoowk-nownch) v.
grow yellow;turn yellow
pożycie (po-zhi-che) v. intercourse; conjugal life
pożyczka (po-zhich-ka) f. loan
pożyteczny (po-zhi-tech-ni)
adj. m. useful;profitable
pożytek (po-zhi-tek) m. use;
advantage;usefulness; benefit
pożywić (pozhi-veech) v. feed;
nourish; refresh;give food
pożywny (po-zhiv-ni) adj. m.
nutritious; nourishing
pójść (pooyshch) v. go; go away;
go up..;leave;fly;drift;pan out
poki (poo-kee) conj. till; un-
till; as long as;while; when
pół (poow) num. half;semi- ;
demi-;one half; mid(way);hemi-
półbucik (poow-boo-cheek) m.
half boot; low shoe
półgłosem (poow-gwo-sem) adv.
in a low voice;in an undertone
półgłówek (poow-gwoo-vek) m.
half-wit; fool; simpleton; dolt
półka (poow-ka) f. shelf;ledge
półkole (poow-ko-le) n. semicircle; half-circle;hemicycle
półksiężyc (poow-kshań-zhits)m.
half-moon; crescent;the Crescent
półkula (poow-koo-la)f. hemisphere ;half of a sphere
półmisek (poow-mee-sek) m.
charger dish; dish
półnagi (poow-na-gee) adj. m.
half naked ; half dressed
północ (poow-nots) f. midnight;
north; North; the North
północno-wschodni (poow-nots-no
wskhód-ńee)north-east
północno-zachodni (poow-nots-no
zakhód-ńee)north-west
północny (poow-nots-ni) adj.
north ; Northern; Northerly
półroczny(poow-roch-ni) half-
yearly; semi-annual
półświatek (poow-shvya-tek) m.
love industry;demimonde
półtora (poow-tó-ra) num. one
and half; a (day etc.) and half
połurzędowy (poow-oo-zhań-dó-vi)
adj. m. semi-official

połwysep (poow-vi-sep) m. penin-
sula; almost an island
póty (poo-ti) conj. as long
później (poozh-ney) adv. later
on; afterwards ;at a later date
późno (poozh-no) adv. late ;late-
późny (poozh-ni) adj. m. late
prababka (pra-bab-ka) f. great
grandmother
praca (pra-tsa) f. work; job
pracodawca (pra-tso-dav-tsa) m.
employer (employing for wages)
pracowity (pra-tso-vee-ti) adj.
m. industrious; hard-working
pracownik (pra-tsov-neek) m.
worker ;emploee ; clerk;official
praczka (prach-ka) f. wash-
woman ; laundress;washerwoman
prać (prach) v. wash; beat up
pradziad (pra-dzhad) m. great
grandfather; ancestor
pragnąć (prag-nownch) v. be
thirsty; desire; wish;long for
pragnienie (prag-ne-ne) n.wish;
thirst; desire; lust for
praktyczny (prak-tich-ni) adj.
m. practical;sesible;expedient
praktyka (prak-ti-ka) f. practice; usage;apprentiship
praktykować (prak-ti-ko-vach)
v. practice; be in training
pralka (pral-ka) f. washing
machine; washer;wash board
pralnia (pral-na) f. laundry
pranie (pra-ne) n. washing
praojciec (pra-oy-chets) m.
forefather; ancestor
prasa (pra-sa) f. press; print
prasować (pra-so-vach) v. iron
(linen etc.);press; print
prawda (prav-da) f. truth
prawdomówność (prav-do-moov-
noshch) f. truthfulness
prawdopodobny (prav-do-po-dob-
ni) adj. m. probable; likely
prawdziwie (prav-dzheev-ye) adv.
truly; genuinely; indeed
prawdziwy (prav-dzhee-vi) adj.
m. true; real; authentic
prawica (pra-vee-tsa) f. the
Right; right hand; right wing
prawic (pra-veech) v. talk; say

prawidło(pra-veed-wo) n. rule;
boot tree ; law; centering
prawidłowy (pra-veed-wo-vi) adj.
m. regular; correct ;proper
prawie (prav-ye) adv. almost;
nearly ;practically; all but
prawnik (prav-neek) m. lawyer
prawnuczka (prav-nooch-ka) f.
great granddaughter
prawnuk (prav-nook) m. great
grandson
prawny (praw-ni) adj. m. legal;
lawful ;legitimate;rightful
prawo (pra-vo) adv. right;law
prawo (pra-vo) n. law; (driving) license;statute; claim
prawodawca (pra-vo-dav-tsa) m.
legislator;lawmaker;lawgiver
prawodawstwo (pra-vo-dav-stvo)
n. legislation; legislature '
prawomocny (pra-vo-mots-ni)
adj. m. legal; valid
prawosławny (pra-vo-swav-ni)
adj. m. orthodox
prawosc (pra-voshch) f. honesty; integrity; righteousness
prawować się (pra-vo-vach shan)
v. litigate; sue; be engaged
in a lawsuit; be at law with...
prawowity (pra-vo-vee-ti) adj.
m. legal (heir etc.)
prawy (pra-vi) adj. m. honest;
right; rigth hand-;upright;lawful
prażyć (pra-zhich) v. grill;roast
burn; keep heavy gunfire on
prąd (prownd) m. current; flow
stream ;air flow;tendency; trend
prądnica (prownd-nee-tsa) f.
generator ;dynamo
prąd stały (prownd sta-wi) m.
direct current
prąd zmienny (prownd zmyen-ni)
alternating current
prążek (prown-zhek) m. stripe
precyzja (pre-tsiz-ya) f. precision ;accuracy;exactness
precyzować (pre-tsi-zo-vach) v.
define; state precisely ;define
precz ! (prech) adv. go away;
do away with; down with
prefabrykować (pre-fa-bri-ko-
vach)v.prefabricate

prefiks (pre-feeks) m. prefix
prelegent (pre-le-gent) m. lecturer (presenting a lecture)
prelekcja (pre-lek-tsya) f.
lecture (informative talk)
preliminarz (pre-lee-mee-nash)
m. estimate of a budget
premedytacja (pre-me-di-tats-
ya) f. premeditation
premia (prem-ya) f. premium;
bonus;bounty; prize; gift
premier (pre-myer) m. prime
minister ; premier
premiera (pre-mye-ra) f. first
night show;first night
prenumerata (pre-noo-me-ra-ta)
f. subscription(to a paper etc.)
preparat (pre-pa-rat) m. pre —
paration;concoction;specimen
prerogatywa (pre-ro-ga-ti-va)
f. privilege; prerogative
presja (pres-ya) f. pressure
prestiż (pres-teesh) m. prestige; high esteem
pretekst (pre-tekst) m. pretext;
excuse; false reason or motive
pretensja (pre-tens-ya) f. claim;
grudge;debt;pretentiousness
prezerwatywa (pre-zer-va-ti-va)
f. contraceptive sheath
prezent (pre-zent) m. gift
prezes (pre-zes) m. chairman
prezydent (pre-zi-dent) m. president; mayor; Lord Mayor
pręcik (pran-cheek) m. (small)
stick; stamen ;rod; graphite
prędki (prand-kee) adj. m. swift;
quick; rapid; fast; prompt;hasty
prędko (prand-ko) adv. quickly;
fast; 2. soon;at once
prędkość (prand-koshch) f. speed;
swiftness; velocity;impetuosity
prędzej (pran-dzey) adv. quicker
sooner; rather; with all haste
pręga (pran-ga) f. stripe; wale
pręgierz (pran-gesh) m. pillory
pręgowaty (pran-go-va-ti) adj.
m. striped ;with stripes
pręt (prant) m. rod; bar; pole;
switch;stick;wand;twig;perch
prężność (pranzh-noshch) f. resilience; elasticity;energy

prężny (pranzh-ni) adj. m.
elastic; resilient;supple
prężyc (pran-zhich) v. strain
probierczy kamień (pro-byer-
chi kam-yeń) m. touch-stone
problem (prob-lem) m. problem
probostwo (pro-bos-tvo) n.
parsonage; parish; rectory
proboszcz (pro-boshch) m.pas-
tor; parish priest;parson
probówka (pro-boov-ka) f.
test-tube; test glass
proca (pro-tsa) f. sling
proceder (pro-tse-der) m.trade;
(shady)dealings; a plot
procedura (pro-tse-doo-ra) f.
procedure; legal practice
procent (pro-tsent) m. percentage; interest on money
procentować się (pro-tsen-to-
vach shań) v. bring interest
proces (pro-tses) m. lawsuit
procesja (pro-tses-ya) f. procession; moving as in parade
procesować (pro-tse-so-vach)
v. sue; be engaged in a liti-
gation ;litigate a cause
proch (prokh) m. powder; dust
proch strzelniczy (prokh
stzhel-nee-chi) m. gunpowder
producent (pro-doo-tsent) m.
producer; manufacturer; maker
produkcja (pro-dook-tsya) f.
production ;output;performance
produkować (pro-doo-ko-vach)
v. produce; grow;generate;stage
produkt (pro-dookt) m. produkt
profanować (pro-fa-no-vach) v.
profane; desecrate :despoil
professor (pro-fe-sor) m. professor ; teacher
profil (pro-feel) m. profile
profilaktyczny (pro-fee-lak-
tich-ni) adj. m. prophylactic
prognoza (prog-no-za) f. prognosis ; forcast(of weather etc.)
program (prog-ram) m. program
progresja (pro-gres-ya) f.
progression ; sequence
prohibicja (pro-hee-beets-ya)
f. prohibition ;forbiddind
projekcja (pro-yek-tsya) f.
projection (on a screen etc.)

projekt (pró-yekt) m. project
projektować (pro-yek-tó-vach)
v. design ;plan;lay out;draft
proklamować (pro-kla-mó-vach)
v. proclaim ;announce officially
prokurator (pro-koo-rá-tor) m.
public prosecutor
proletariat (pro-le-tár-yat) m.
proletariat ;working class
prolog (pró-lok) m. prologue
prolongować (pro-lon-gó-vach)
v. prolong; extend
prom (prom) m. ferry (boat)
promieniec (pro-mye-ñech) v.
radiate; beam(with joy etc.)
promieniotwórczy (pro-mye-ño-
tvoor-chi) adj. m. radio-
active(matter, isotopes, etc.)
promieniować (pro-mye-ño-vach)
v. radiate;beam;glow;brim over
promienisty (pro-mye-ñees-ti)
adj. m. radial;radiant;rediate
promienny (pro-myen-ni) adj.
m. radiant; beaming;bright
promień (pró-myeń) m. beam;
ray; gleam;radius; fin ray
promocja (pro-móts-ya) f. promotion;conferment of a degree
propaganda (pro-pa-gán-da) f.
propaganda;publicity;boosting
propagować (pro-pa-gó-vach) v.
propagate; publicize;boost
proponować (pro-po-nó-vach) v.
propose;put forwards;suggest
proporcja (pro-pórts-ya) f.
proportion;ratio; relation
proporcjonalny (pro-por-tsyo-
nál-ni) adj. m. proportional
proporzec (pro-pó-zhets) m.
pennon; banner;streamer;jack
propozycja (pro-po-zits-ya) f.
proposal; offer; suggestion
proroctwo (pro-rots-tvo) n.
prophecy; prediction
prorok (pro-rok) m. prophet
prosić (pro-sheech) v. beg;
pray; ask; invite; request
prosię (pró-shañ) n. young pig
proso (pró-so) n. millet
prospekt (prós-pekt) m. prospect;folder;view;panorama
prosperować (pros-pe-ró-vach)
v. prosper;be prosperous;thrive

prostacki (pros-táts-kee) adj.
m. boorish; rude ;vulgar;coarse
prostak (prós-tak) m. boor; gull
prostata (pros-tá-ta) f. prostate (gland, at the of male bladder)
prosto (prós-to) adv. straight;
right; upright;simply;candidly
prostoduszny (pros-to-doósh-ni)
adj. m. simple-hearted ;naive
prostokąt (pros-tó-kownt) m.
rectangle(with four right angles)
prostolinijny (pros-to-lee-ñeey-
ni) adj. m. straightforward
prostopadła (pros-to-pád-wa) f.
perpendicular ;normal; sheer
prostota (pros-tó-ta) f. simplic-
ity ; neatness; boorishness
prostować (pros-tó-vach) v.
straighten; correct;revise
prosty (prós-ti) adj. m. straight;
right; direct simple;vulgar;plain
prostytucja (pros-ti-too-tsya) f.
prostitution; streetwalking
prostytutka (pros-ti-toot-ka) f.
prostitute; streetwalker
proszek (pro-shek) m. powder
(for baking etc.); wafer
proszę (pró-shañ) please
prośba (prósh-ba) f. request;
demand; petition; application
proszkować (prosh-kó-vach) v.
pulverize; grind to powder
protegowany (pro-te-go-vá-ni)
adj. m. protégé,
protekcja (pro-ték-tsya) f. pull;
patronage; backing;influence;push
protest (pro-test) m. protest
protestant (pro-tés- tant) m.
Protestant ; evangelical,
protestantyzm (pro-tes-tan-tizm)
m. Protestantism
proteza (pro-té-za) f. artificial limb or denture
protokół (pro-tó-koow) m. record;
protocol;minutes; official record
prototyp (pro-tó-tip) m. proto-
type; archetype; protoplast
prowadzenie (pro-va-dzé-ñe) n.
management; conduct;leadership
prowadzić (pro-vá-dzheech) v. steer;
lead;conduct; guide; keep; live;
carry on ;show the way;escort;run;
manage (an institution)

prowadzić auto (pro-va-dźheech)
au-to) drive a car
prowiant (pro-vyant) m. provisions;eatables; rations
prowincjonalny (pro-veen-tsyo-
nál-ni) adj. m. provincial
prowizja (pro-veéz-ya) f. co-
mission; percentage; brokerage
prowizoryczny (pro-vee-zo-rich-
ni) adj. m. provisional
prowodyr (pro-vó-dir) m. ringleader; gang leader
prowokacja (pro-vo-káts-ya) f.
provocation; stirring trouble
proza (pró-za) f. prose;dullness
próba (proo-ba) f. trial; test;
proof; ordeal;acid test;try;go
próbka (proob-ka) f. sample
próbny (proob-ni) adj. m.
experimental; tentative ;test-
próbować (proo-bó-vach) v. try;
test; taste;put to test;offer
próchnica (prookh-ńee-tsa) f.
moulder; (tooth) decay;humus
prochno (prookh-no) n. rotten
wood; mould;rot; wood dust
procz (prooch) prep. save;
except;besides;apart from
próg (prook) m. threshold
prószyć (proo-shich) v. sift;
flake; make dust;sprinkle;spray
próżnia (proozh-ńa) f. vacuum
próżniaczy (proozh-ńa-chi) adj.
m. lazy; idle;inactive;leisured
próżniak (proozh-ńak) m. idler
próżno (proozh-no) adv. vainly;
empty-;in vain; to no avail
próżność (proozh-noshch) f.
vanity; false pride;futility
próżny (proozh-ni) adj. m.
1. empty; void; 2. vain
pruć (prooch) v. rip; unsew
pruski (proos-kee) adj. m.
Prussian ; of Prussia
prychać (pri-khach) v. snort
prycza (pri-cha) f. plank-bed
pryk stary (prik sta-ri) adj.
m. old goat; old duffer
prym (prim) m. lead; first
place; superiority;the lead
prymas (pri-mas) m. primate
prymka (prim-ka) f. chewing
tobacco;plug of chewing tobacco

pryskać (pris-kach) v. splash;
spray; fly;clear out;bolt;burst
pryszcz (prishch) m. pimple
prysznic (prish-ńeets) m.
shower bath; shower
prywatny (pri-vat-ni) adj. m.
private; personal;confidential
pryzmat (priz-mat) m. prism
prządka (pzhownd-ka) f. spinner
prząść (pzhownshch) v. spin
przebaczać (pzhe-ba-chach) v.
forgive; pardon; condone
przebaczenie (pzhe-ba-che-ńe)
n. pardon; forgiveness;remittal
przebąkiwać (pzhe-bown-kee-vach)
v. mutter ;hint;allude;mention
przebić (pzhe-beech) v. pierce;
perforate; puncture;stab;recoin
przebieg (pzhe-byeg) m. curse;
run ;progress;process; milage
przebiegać (pzhe-bye-gach) v.
run cross ;take place;proceed
przebiegły (pzhe-byeg-wi) adj.
m. cunning; sly ;wily;crafty
przebierać (pzhe-bye-rach) v.
choose; sort;change clothes;sift
przebijać (pzhe-bee-yach) v.
pierce; puncture;show through
przebłysk (pzhe-bwisk)m.glimpse;
ray; flash; sparkle;glimmer
przebłyskiwać (pzhe-bwis-kee-
vach) v. gleam ;shine;flash
przeboleć (pzhe-bo-lech) v. get
over; put up with ;get over it
przebój (pzhe-booy) m. hit;
success; breakthrough ; clou
przebranie (pzhe-brá-ńe) m.
disguise ;being disguised
przebrnąć (pzhe-brnownch) v.
muddle through; wade thrpugh
przebrzmiały (pzhe-bzhmya-wi)
adj. m. overblown; has-been
przebudowa (pzhe-boo-dó-va) f.
remodeling; rebuilding
przebudzić (pzhe-boo-dźheech)v.
wake up; awake ;rouse;revive
przebyć (pzhe-bich) v. be over
through; surmount; ride out
storm ;travel;cross;pass;dwell
przebywać (pzhe-bi-vach) v.
stay; reside ;dwell;inhabit
przecedzać (pzhe-tse-dzach) v.
filter;strain through a sieve

przeceniac (pzhe-tse-ńach) v.
overrate ;lower the price
przechadzka (pzhe-chádz-ka) f.
walk ;stroll;tour; airing
przechadzac się (pzhe-kha-
dzach śhań) v. take a walk;
stroll ;go for a walk;saunter
przechodzic (pzhe-kho-dzheech)
v. pass (through)
przechodzień (pzhe-kho-dźheń)
m. passerby ; pedestrian
przechowanie (pzhe-kho-va-ńe)
n.safekeeping;storage
przechowywac (pzhe-kho-vi-vach)
v. store;preserve;harbor;keep
przechrzcic (pzhekh-zhcheech)
v. convert; change name
przechwalac (pzhe-khva-lach) v.
talk big;overpraise;extol;puff
przechwycic (pzhe-khvi-cheech)
v. intercept; seize
przechylic (pzhe-khi-leech) v.
tilt; lean; tip; incline
przechytrzyc (pzhe-khit-zhich)
v. outwit; overreach;outsmart
przeciąg (pzhe-chownk) m.
draught; span;spell;time lapse
przeciąc (pzhe-chownch) v. cut;
cross; intersect;slice;cleave
przeciągac (pzhe-chown-gach) v.
draw; drag; delay; stretch
przeciążac (pzhe-chown-zhach)
v. overload;overburden
przecie (pzhe-che) conj. yet;
still; of course but;after all
przeciekac (pzhe-che-kach) v.
leak; ooze; drain; percolate
przecierac (pzhe-che-rach) v.
rub; wipe clear; threadbare;
fret ;polish (shoes);clear up
przecierpiec (pzhe-cher-pyech)
v. endure; bear; suffer
przeciez (pzhe-chezh) conj. yet;
still; after all; now ;though
przeciętny (pzhe-chańt-ni) adj.
m. average ;ordinary;mediocre
przecinac (pzhe-chee-nach) v.
cut; intersect ;slice;cleave
przecinek (pzhe-chee-nek) m.
comma ; point (in mathematics)
przeciskac się (pzhe-chees-kach
shan) v. squeeze through ;push
through;elbow one's way

przeciw (pzhe-cheev) prep.
against; versus ;contrary to
przeciwko (pzhe-cheev-ko) prep.
against; contrary ; versus
przeciwdziałac (pzhe-cheev-
dzha-wach) v. counteract
przeciwległy (pzhe-cheev-leg-wi)
adj, m. opposite; contrary
przeciwlotniczy (pzhe-cheev-
lot-ńee-chi) adj. m. antiair-
craft(artllery, defence etc.)
przeciwnie (pzhe-cheev-ńe) adv.
on the contrary; reverse
przeciwnik (pzhe-cheev-ńeek) m.
opponent ; adversary;enemy;foe
przeciwnosć (pzhe-cheev-noshch)
f. adversity; set-back;reverse
przeciwstawiac (pzhe-cheev-stav-
yach) v. oppose; set against
przeciwwaga (pzhe-cheev-va-ga)
f. counterweight;balance weight
przecudny (pzhe-tsood-ni) adj.
m. most wonderful;just marvellous
przeczący (pzhe-chown-tsi) adj.
m. negative; contradictory
przeczenie (pzhe-che-ńe) n.
negation;negative;denial
przecznica (pzhech-ńee-tsa) f.
side-street ;cross street
przeczucie (pzhe-choo-che) n.
foreboding ;presentiment
przeczulony (pzhe-choo-ló-ni)
adj. m. high-strung; over-
-sensitive;touchy; irritable
przeczyc (pzhe-chich) v. deny;
belie; negate; contradict
przeczyszczac (pzhe-chish-chach)
v. purge; cleanse; scour ;wipe
przeczytac (pzhe-chi-tach) v.
read through ;peruse;read over
przec (pzhech) v. insist on;urge;
press on ;push;exert pressure.
impel;drive;insist;bear down;stri-
przed (pzhet) prep. before; in ve
front of; ahead of; previous
to; from ;since;ago;against
przedajny (pzhe-day-ni) adj. m.
venal ;open to bribery
przedawnienie (pzhe-dav-ńe-ńe)
n. expiration of validity
przedawniony (pzhe-dav-ńó-ni)
adj. m. of expired validity
przeddzień (pzhed-dźheń) m. eve

przede wszystkim (pzhe-de
vshíst-keem) adv. above all;
first; first of all; in the
first place; to begin with
przedhistoryczny (pzhed-hees-
to-rích-ni) adj. m. pre-
historic;before recorded hist.
przedimek (pzhed-ee-mek) m.
article (in grammar)
przedkładać (pzhed-kwa-dach) v.
submit; refer; propose; present; prefer;give priority
przedłużać (pzhed-woo-zhach)
v. lengthen; prolong;extend
przedmieście (pzhed-myesh-che)
n, suburb;outskirts of a city
przedmiot (pzhed-myot) m. object; subject; subject matter
przedmiotowy (pzhed-myo-tó-vi)
adj. m. objective; at issue
przedmowa (pzhed-mó-va) f. preface; foreword;introduction
przedmówca (pzhed-moóv-tsa) m.
previous speaker
przedni (pzhéd-ńee) adj. m.
leading; front; forward;
choice; fine ;foremost;superior
przedostać się (pzhe-dos-tach
shań) v. penetrate;pass through
przedostatni (pzhed-os-tat-ńee)
adj. m. last but one
przedpłata (pzhed-pwa-ta) f.
advance payment;subscription
przedpokój (pzhed-pó-kooy) m.
(waiting-room) lobby; ante-
chamber; anteroom; hall
przedpole (pzhed-pó-le) n. foreground; foreland
przedpołudnie (pzhed-po-woód-ńe)
n. morning; forenoon
przedpotopowy (pzhed-po-to-pó-
vi) adj. m. fossil; antedilu-
vian; fossilized; obsolete
przedramię (pzhed-ram-yań) n.
forearm; antebrachium
przedrostek (pzhed-ros-tek) m.
prefix (in grammar)
przedruk (pzhéd-rook) m. reprint; reimpression;impression
przedrzec (pzhed-zhech) v. tear
up; tear through; rend;
break through;penetrate;burst

przedrzeźniać (pzhed-zhéźh-
ńach) v. ape; mimic; mock;
take off; immitate like an ape
przedsiębiorca (pzhed-shań-byor-
tsa) m. contractor;businessman
przedsiębiorstwo (pzhed-shań-
byor-stvo) n. business; concern; enterprise; firm
przedsiębrać (pzhed-shań-brach)
v. undertake;embark upon
przedsionek (pzhed-shó-nek) m.
lobby; vestibule; porch;auricle
przedsmak (pzhéd-smak) m. foretaste;earnest(of future events)
przedstawić (pzhed-stá-veech)
v. present; represent;recommend
przedstawiciel (pzhed-sta-vee-
chel) m. representative
przedstawicielstwo (pzhed-sta-
vee-chél-stvo) n. agency
przedstawienie (pzhed-sta-vyé-
ńe) n. performance;show;version
przedszkole (pzhed-shko-le) n.
kindergarten; nursery school
przedświt(pzhed-shveet)m. pre-
dawn; daybreak;dawn; harbinger
przedtem (pzhéd-tem) adv. before; formerly;in advance;earlier
przedterminowy (pzhed-ter-mee-
nó-vi) adj. m. advance;
premature; done ahead of time
przedwczesny (pzhed-vches-ni)
adj. m. premature; untimely
przedwczoraj (pzhed-vchó-ray)
adv. the day before yesterday
przedwieczny (pzhed-vyéch-ni)
adj, m. eternal;primeval;ancient
przedwiośnie (pzhed-vyosh-ńe)
n. early spring
przedwojenny (pzhed-vo-yén-ni)
adj. m. prewar; before the war
przedział (pzhe-dźhaw) m. partition; compartment; section
przedzielić (pzhe-dźhé-leech)
v. divide; part;separate
przedzierać (pzhe-dźhe-rach) v.
tear down; tear up; rend
przedziurawić (pzhe-dźhoo-ra-
veech) v. perforate; puncture;
riddle; pierce ;make a hole
przedziwny (pzhe-dźheév-ni) adj.
m. prodigious; admirable; odd

przeforsować (pzhe-for-so-vach)
v. ram through;force through
przegapić (pzhe-ga-peech) v.
let slip; over look;miss
przeginać (pzhe-gee-nach) v.
bend (over); turn up;turn down
przegląd (pzhe-glównt) m. review; inspection; survey
przegłosować (pzhe-gwo-so-vach)
v. outvote; take a vote
przegonić (pzhe-go-neech) v.
overtake; drive out; drive
through; drive away;rush past
przegotować (pzhe-go-to-vach)
v. boil; overcook;overboil
przegrać (pzhe-grach) v.lose
(war; game etc.);gamble away
przegradzać (pzhe-gra-dzach) v.
partition;divide;separate
przegrana (pzhe-gra-na) f. defeat; loss;beating;licking
przegryzać (pzhe-gri-zach) v.
bite through;bite in two
przegroda (pzhe-gro-da) f. partition;division;stall;cell
przegub (pzhe-goop) m. wrist;
ball-and-socket joint
przeholować (pzhe-kho-lo-vach)
v. overshoot; rush into excess
przeistoczyć (pzhe-ees-to-chich)
v. transform; remould;convert
przejaśnienie (pzhe-yash-ne-ne)
n. clearing up;bright interval
przejaw (pzhe-yav) m. symptom;
sign; indication;manifestation
przejawiać (pzhe-ya-veeach) v.
reveal; display; manifest;show
przejazd (pzhe-yazt) m. crossing; passage ;thoroughfare
przejąć (pzhe-yównch) v. take
over; seize;adopt;master;thrill
przejechać (pzhe-ye-khach) v.
pass; ride; cross; run over
przejęty (pzhe-yán-ti) adj. m.
impressed; upset; deeply
stirred ;perturbed;wrapped up
przejmować (pzhey-mo-vach) v.
take over ;seize;penetrate
przejrzeć (pzhey-zhech) v. see
through; recover sight ;revise
przejrzysty (pzhey-zhis-ti) adj.
m. transparent; clear ;sheer

przejście (pzhéy-shche) n. pass;
transition;conversion;roadway
przejściowo (pzhey-shcho-vo)
adv. temporarily;provisionally
przejść (pzheyshch) v. pass;
cross; experience; go across
przekaz (pzhe-kas) m. transfer;
money order;remittance
przekazywać (przhe-ka-zi-vach)
v. transfer; pass on; send on;
transmit;deliver; direct
przekaźnik (pzhe-kazh-neek) m.
relay; repeater; transmitter
przekąsem (pzhe-kówn-sem)adv.iro-
nically; mockingly; spitefully
przekąska (pzhe-kówns-ka) f.
snack; refreshment
przekątna (pzhe-kównt-na) f.
diagonal(line)
przekleństwo (pzhe-kleń-stvo)
n. curse; profanity;damnation
przekład (pzhe-kwat) m. translation; rendering;rearrangement
przekładać (pzhe-kwa-dach) v.
shift; transfer; prefer; move;
translate;reach;put between
przekładnia (przek-wad-ña) f.
gearbox; clutch ;transposition
przekłuć (pzhe-kwooch) v. prick;
pierce; puncture;perforate
przekonać (pzhe-ko-nach) v.
convince; persuade ;bring round
przekonanie (pzhe-ko-na-ñe) n.
conviction ;persuasion;opinion
przekop (pzhe-kop) m. trench;
ditch ; tunnel;cutting;piercing
przekopać (pzhe-ko-pach) v. dig-
through ;turn over; excavate;cut
przekora (pzhe-ko-ra) f. spite
przekraczać (pzhe-kra-chach) v.
overstep; cross ;surpass
przekradać się (pzhe-kra-dach
shań) v. steal through
przekreślić (pzhe-kresh-leech)
v. cross out; delete; annul
przekręcic (pzhe-krán-cheech) v.
twist; distort(a statement)
przekroczenie (pzhe-kro-che-ñe)
n. trespass;offence;transgression
przekroczyć (pzhe-kro-chich) v.
cross; trespass; exceed; offend; violate;transgress(the law)

przekroić (pzhe-kro-eech) v. cut
przekrój (pzhé-krooy) v. cross
section; profile;review,
przekrwienie (pzhe-krvye-ńe) n.
hyperemia;congestion ,
przekształcić (pzhe-kshtaw-
ćheećh) y. transform
przekupić (pzhe-koo-peech) v.
bribe; buy over; corrupt
przekupka (pzhe-koop-ka) f.
huckstress; vendor;wrangler
przekupny (pzhe-koop-ni) adj.
m. venal; bribable ,
przekupstwo (pzhe-koop-stvo) n.
bribery ;graft; corruption
przekwitać (pzhe-kvee-tach) v.
wither; fade; decay;shed blossom
przelatywać (pzhe-la-ti-vach)
v. fly through;cross;run;pass
przelew (pzhé-lef) m. transfusion; transfer;over flow
przelewać (pzhe-le-vach) v.
overfill; transfer; shed
przelękły (pzhe-lań-kwi) adj.
m. frightened ;intimidated
przelęknąć (pzhe-lańk-nownch)v.
frighten ;scare; terrify
przelicytować (pzhe-lee-tsi-
to-vach) v. outbid
przeliczyć (pzhe-lee-chich) v.
miscalculate; count over
przelot (pzhe-lot) m. over-
flight; flight; passage
przelotny (pzhe-lot-ni) adj. m.
fleeting; passing; transient
przeludnienie (pzhe-lood-ńe-ńe)
n. overpopulation; congestion
przeładować (pzhe-wa-do-vach)
v. overload; transship;reload
przeładunek (pzhe-wa-doo-nek)
m. load , transfer,; reloading
przełamać (pzhe-wa-mach) v.
break through;break in two
przełazić (pzhe-wa-zheech) v.
climb over ;creep across
przełącznik (pzhe-wownch-ńeek)
m. switch; shift;commutator
przełęcz (pzhe-wańch) v. (mountain) pass;saddle; col
przełknąć (pzhew-known̆ch) v.
swallow; swollow down
przełom (pzhé-wom) m. breakthrough; turning point;gorge

przełożony (pzhe-wo-zho-ni)
adj. m. principal; superior
przełożyć (pzhe-wo-zhich) v.
transfer; prefer; shift;reach
przełyk (pzhé-wik) m. gullet;
esophagus
przemakać (pzhe-má-kach) v.
ooze; get wet ;be permeable
przemarsz (pzhe-marsh) m.
marching past; march of troops
przemarznąć (pzhe-mar -znownch)
v. be chilled ;freeze stiff
przemawiać (pzhe-ma-vyach) v.
speak; harangue; address
przemądrzały (pzhe-mownd-zha-
wi) adj. m. smart aleck
przemęczać (pzhe-mań-chach) v.
overstrain; overwork ;spend
przemęczenie (pzhe-mań-che-ńe)
n. strain ;overwork; tiredness
przemiał (pzhe-myaw) m. grinding; milling ;meal;grist;shoal
przemiana (pzhe-mya-na) f.change;
transformation; alteration
przemianować (pzhe-mya-no-vach)
v. rename ; change name
przemienić (pzhe-mye-ńeech) v.
change; transform ;alter;turn
przemieścić (pzhe-myesh-cheech)
v. displace ;dislocate; shift
przemijać (pzhe-mee-yach) v.
go by;be over; pass; cease
przemilczeć (pzhe-meel-chech)
v. keep secret;leave unsaid
przemoc (pzhe-mots) f. force;
violence ;constraint;compulsion
przemoczyć (pzhe-mo-chich) v.
soak; drench ;wet;seep; sop
przemoknąć (pzhe-mok-nown̆ch) v.
be soaked ;be permeable;get wet
przemowa (pzhe-mo-va) f. speech;
oration; address :harangue
przemóc (pzhe-moots) v. overcome ;conquer;defeat;master;prevail
przemówić (pzhe-moo-veech) v.
speak up ;make a mistake(speaking)
przemówienie (pzhe-moov-ye-ńe)
n. speech ;address; oration
przemycać (pzhe-mi-tsach) v.
smuggle (into a country,a room etc.)
przemyć (pzhe-mich) v. rinse; scrub;
wash ;give a wash; lavage; flush
przemysł (pzhe-misw) m.industry

przemysłowy (pzhe-mis-wo-vi) adj.
m. industrial;manufacturing
przemyśliwac (pzhe-miśh-lee-
vach) v. ponder; think over
przemyślny (pzhe-miśhl-ni) adj.
m. ingenious;clever;cunning
przemyt (pzhe-mit) m. smuggling
przemytnik (pzhe-mit-ňeek) m.
smuggler; contrabandist
przemywac (pzhe-mi-vach) v.
rinse; wash; scrub;lavage;flush
przeniesc (pzhe-ňeshch) v.
transfer; surpass; carry over;
remove;convey; move; retrace
przenigdy (pzhe-ňeeg-di) adv.
nevermore; never,never
przenikac (pzhe-ňee-kach) v.
penetrate; pierce; permeate
przenikliwy (pzhe-ňeek-lee-vi)
adj. m. penetrating; acute;
sharp; piercing;keen;shrewd
przenocowac (pzhe-no-tso-vach)
v. pass the night;put up
przenosnia (pzhe-nosh-ňa) f.
metaphor; figure of speach
przenosny (pzhe-nosh-ni) adj. m.
portable; mobile;metaphorical
przeobrazac (pzhe-o-bra-zhach)
v. transform; modify;change
przeoczenie (pzhe-o-che-ňe) m.
oversight; omission
przeoczyc (pzhe-o— chich) v.
overlook; leave out;omit
przepadac (pzhe-pa-dach) v. be
lost; be extremely fond;vanish
przepalic (pzhe-pa-leech) v.
burn through;overheat;scorch
przepasac (pzhe-pa-sach) v.
gird ;belt;tie;overfeed
przepaska (pzhe-pas-ka) f. band
przepaść (pzhe-pashch) f. abyss
przepchac (pzhep-khach) v. push
through; pass through;clean out
przepełniac (pzhe-pew-ňach) v.
overfill; cram ; over cram
przepełnienie (pzhe-pew-ňe-ňe) n.
overfill; crowd;excess
przepędzac (pzhe-pan-dzach) v.
drive away; spend ;distil;stay
przepic (pzhe-peech) v. spend
on drinking ; drink away;waste
przepierac (pzhe-pye-rach) v.
launder; wash clothes

przepierzenie (pzhe-pye-zhe-ňe)
n. partition (wall etc.)
przepiękny (pzhe-pyáň -kni)
adj. , very beautiful; gorgeous
przepiłowac (pzhe-pee-wo-wach)
v. saw through; file through
przepiórka (pzhe-pyoor-ka) f.
quail(migratory game bird)
przepis (pzhe-pees) m. 1. regulation; 2. recipe
przepisac (pzhe-pee-sach) v.
1. prescribe; 2. copy
przepłacac (pzhe-pwa-tsach) v.
overpay; pay too much; bribe
przepłukac (pzhe-pwoo-kach) v.
rinse; gargle ;scoup; wash
przepłynąc (pzhe-pwi-nównch) v.
swim across ;row acposs
przepływac (pzhe-pwi-vach) v.
flow; float across; swim
across; row across;sail across
przepocic (pzhe-po-cheech) v.
sweat through ;sweat (a shirt)
przepoic (pzhe-po-eech) v. impregnate ;saturate; fill
przepona (pzhe-po-na) f. diaphragm ;midriff; stiffener
przepowiadac (pzhe-po-vyá-dach)
v. predict ;foretell;repeat
przepracowac się (pzhe-pra-tso-
vach sháň) v. overwork (oneself) ;overstrain oneself
przepraszac (pzhe-pra-shach) v.
apologize ;excuse oneself
przeprawa (pzhe-pra-va) f.
1. passage; crossing ;journey
2. fight ;incident;scene; row
przeprawiac (pzhe-prav-yach) v.
cross over ;carry across
przeproszenie (pzhe-pro-she-ňe)
n. apology ; apologies
przeprowadzac (pzhe-pro-va-dzach)
v. convey; lead; move ;pass
przeprowadzka (pzhe-pro-vadz-ka)
f. moving (form a house etc.)
przepuklina (pzhe-poo-klee-na)
f. hernia ; rupture,
przepustka (pzhe-poost-ka) f.
pass; permit ;liberty; sluice
przepuszczac (pzhe-poosh-chach)
v. let pass ;promote;leak;miss;
let slip;waste;squander away

przepuszczalność (pzhe-poosh-chál-noshćh) f. permeability

przepych (pzhe-pikh) m. luxury; pageantry;splendor;ostentation

przepychać (pzhe-pi-khaćh) v. push through; force through

przepytywać (pzhe-pi-ti-vaćh) v. examine;inquire ;question

przerabiać (pzhe-ra-byaćh) v. do over; revise ;remodel;alter

przerachować (pzhe-ra-kho-vaćh) v. miscalculate; count over

przeradzać się (pzhe-ra-dzaćh shań) v. change (into)

przerastać (pzhe-rás-taćh) v. outgrow; rise above ;surpass

przerazić (pzhe-ra-źheećh) v. terrify; appal; consternation

przerażliwy (pzhe-ražh-lee-vi) adj. m. appalling; terrifying shrill ; awesome; acute;sharp

przerażenie (pzhe-ra-zhe-ńe) n. terror ;horror;dread;dismay

przerażony (pzhe-ra-zho-ni) adj. m. horror stricken

przeróbka (pzhe-roob-ka) f. revision ;reshaping; alteration

przerwa (pzher-va) f. pause; break; recess ; interval

przerys (pzhe-ris) m. tracing

przerysować (pzhe-ri-so-vaćh) v. trace; copy ;retrace

przerwać (pzhér-vaćh) v. interrupt; pause; cut-off

przerzedzić(pzhe-zhe-dźheećh)v. thin out ; decimate(a population)

przerzucać (pzhe-zhoo-tsaćh) v. throw over; shift; move; flip; browse ;transfer; ransack

przerzynać (pzhe-zhi-naćh) v. cut through ;cut in two

przesada (pzhe-sá-da) f. exaggeration ;overstatement

przesadzać (pzhe-sa-dzaćh) v. 1. exaggerate; 2. transplant

przesalać (pzhe-sa-laćh) v. oversalt ;put too much salt

przesąd (pzhe-sownt) m. prejudice; superstition;fallacy

przesądny (pzhe-sownd-ni) adj. m. superstitious ;prejudiced

przesiadać się (pzhe-sha-daćh shań) v. change(places; seats)

przesiedlać (pzhe-shéd-laćh) v. displace; migrate;transplant

przesiewać (pzhe-she-vaćh) v. sift; sieve ;screen out;riddle

przesilać się (pzhe-shee-laćh shań) v. subside ;get over; culminate;overcome;overstrain

przesilenie (pzhe-shee-le-ńe) n. crisis ;turning point

przeskoczyć (pzhe-sko-chićh) v. jump over;vault ;outstrip;skip

przesłać (pzhe-swaćh) v. 1.send ; 2. make bed over ;rearrange a bed

przesłaniać (pzhe-swa-naćh) v. screen off ;veil;cover;hide;shade

przesłanka (pzhe-swan-ka) f. premise ;prerequisite;condition

przesłuchiwać (pzhe-swoo-khee-vaćh) v. interrogate ;question

przesmyk (pzhes-mik) m. strait

przesolony (pzhe-so-lo-ni) adj. m. oversalted;with excess salt

przespać (pzhes-paćh) v. sleep over ;fail to wake up for...

przestać (pzhes-taćh) v. cease

przestanek (pzhes-tá-nek) m. pause; rest ; stop

przestankować (pzhe-stan-ko-vaćh) v. punctuate (written matter)

przestarzały (pzhe-sta-zha-vi) adj. m. obsolete ;time worn

przestawać (pzhe-sta-vaćh) v. 1.cut out; break off; 2. associate; hobnob ;keep company

przestawiać (pzhe-stáv-yaćh) v. displace; transpose ;shift

przestąpić (pzhe-stown-peećh) v. step over;transgress ;cross

przestępca (pzhe-stanp-tsa) m. criminal ;felon; law beaker

przestępny (pzhe-stanp-ni) adj. m. leap (year) ;felonious

przestępstwo (pzhe-stanp-stvo) n. offense; crime ;transgression

przestrach (pzhe-strakh) m. fright; alarm; fear; terror

przestraszyć (pzhe-stra-shićh) v. scare; startle;alarm

przestroga (pzhe-stro-ga) f. warning; admonition;caution

przestronny (pzhe-stron-ni) adj. m. spacious; roomy

przestrzegać (pzhe-stzhe-gach)
v. observe (rules); caution
przestrzelić (pzhe-stzhe-leech)
v. shoot through;shoot down
przestrzenny (pzhe-stzhen-ni)
adj. m. spatial; roomy
przestrzeń (pzhe-stzheń) f.
space ; outer space; room
przestworze (pzhe-stvo-zhe) n.
expanse; infinity ; space,
przesunięcie (pzhe-soo-nan-che)
n. shift; transfer;displacement
przesuwać (pzhe-soo-vach) v.
move; shift ; shove; transfer
przesycać (pzhe-si-tsach) v.
saturate; glut; impregnate
przesyłać (pzhe-si-wach) v.
send ; dispatch; forward
przesyłka (pzhe-siw-ka) f.
shipment ; mail; parcel
przesypiać (pzhe-sip-yach) v.
oversleep; sleep away
przesyt (pzhe-sit) m. glut
przeszczep (pzhe-shchep) m.
transplant; graft; grafting
przeszkadzać (pzhe-shka-dzach)
v. hinder; trouble ;prevent
przeszkoda (pzhesh-ko-da) f.
obstacle ; hitch; obstruction
przeszkolenie (pzhe-shko-le-
ńe) n. training ; course
przeszło (pzhesh-wo) adv.
more than ; over(an amount)
przeszłość (pzhesh-woshch) f.
past ; record;antecedents
przeszukać (pzhe-shoo-kach) v.
search over ; ransack
przeszyć (pzhe-shich) v. sew-
through; pierce; gore;quilt,
prześcieradło (pzhesh-che-rad-
wo) n. bedsheet; sheet
prześcignąć (pzhe-shcheeg-
nownch) v. outdistance; outdo; outstrip;overtake;excel
prześladować (pzhe-shla-do-
vach) v. persecute;harass;haunt
prześladowanie (pzhe-shla-do-
va-ńe) n. persecution;obsession
prześliczny (pzhe-shleech-ni)
adj. m. most beautiful;lovely
prześliznąć (pzhe-shleez-nownch)
v. slip through;glide past
przeświadczenie (pzhe-shvyad-
che-ńe) n. conviction;certitude

prześwietlać (pzhe-shvyet-lach)
v. shine through; fluoroscope
przetak (pzhe-tak) m. riddle
przetaczać (pzhe-ta-chach) v.
1. rollover; 2. transfuse
przetapiać (pzhe-tap-yach) v.
recast; smelt(metals); melt
przetarg (pzhe-tark) m. auction
przetarty (pzhe-tar-ti) adj. m.
threadbare; rubbed through,
przetłumaczyć (pzhe-twoo-ma-
chich) v. translate ; explain
przeto (pzhe-to) conj. therefore;accordingly;consequently
przetrawić (pzhe-tra-veech) v.
digest;ruminate;etch;corrode
przetrwać (pzhe-trvach) v.
survive; outlast;remain;keep
przetrwonić (pzhe-trvo-ńeech)
v. squander,;waste;fritter away
przetrząsnąć (pzhe-tzhowns-
nownch) v. search (shake
through);ransack;comb out
przetrzymać (pzhe-tzhi-mach) v.
endure; outdo; keep waiting
przetwarzać (pzhe-tva-zhach)
v. remake; manufacture
przetwórnia (pzhe-tvoor-ńa) f.
factory; processing plant
przewaga (pzhe-va-ga) f. pre-
dominance ; overbalance ;lead
przeważać (pzhe-va-zhach) v.
outweigh; prevail; overbalance
przeważający (pzhe-va-zha-yown-
tsi) adj. m. prevailing; superior; predominant,
przeważnie (pzhe-vazh-ńe) adv.
mainly; mostly; chiefly;largely
przewiązać (pzhe-vyown-zach) v.
bind up; change dressing
przewidywać (pzhe-vee-di-vach)
v. anticipate; foresee
przewiercić (pzhe-vyer-cheech)
v. drill through (pierce)
przewiesić (pzhe-vye-sheech)v.
sling over;hang over;rehang
przewietrzyć (pzhe-vyet-zhich)
v. ventilate
przewiew (pzhe-vyev) m. draught;
breeze; breath of air;whiff
przewiezienie (pzhe-vye-zhe-ńe)
n. transport ;transportation;
carriage; conveyance

przewijać (pzhe-vee-yach) v.
wrap up; change dressing
przewinienie (pzhe-vee-ńe-ńe)
n. offense; delinquency
przewlekły (pzhe-vlek-wi) adj.
m. protracted; lingering;lasting
przewodni (pzhe-vod-ńee) adj.
m. leading ;guiding(principle)
przewodniczący (pzhe-vod-ńee-
chown-tsi) m. chairman
przewodnik (pzhe-vod-ńeek) m.
guide; conductor; leader
przewodzić (pzhe-vo-dżheech) v.
head; command ;lead;conduct
przewozić (pzhe-vo-żheech) v.
convey; transport;cart across
przewoźnik (pzhe-vozh-ńeek) m.
ferryman;carter; carrier
przewód (pzhe-voot) m. conduit;
channel; wire;procedure
przewóz (pzhe-voos) m. transport ; freight ; cartage
przewracać (pzhe-vra-tsach) v.
overturn; turn over; upset;
toss ; topple; invert;reverse
przewrotność (pzhe-vrót-noshch)
f. perversity; perfidy;deceit
przewrót (pzhe-vroot) m. revolution;upheaval;coup d'état
przewyższać (pzhe-vizh-shach)
v. out do; exceed; surpass
przez (pzhes) prep. : across;
over; through; during; within; in; on;on the other side
przeziębić się (pzhe-zhań-beech
shań) v. catch cold;grow cold
przezimować (pzhe-żhee-mo-vach)
v. winter; hibernate
przeznaczać (pzhe-zna-chach) v.
intend; earmark ; mean; destine; assign; allocate;design
przeznaczenie (pzhe-zna-che-ne)
n. destiny; destination
przezorność (pzhe-zor-noshch) f.
caution; prudence;foresight
przezrocze (pzhe-żhro-che) n.
transparency; slide;open work
przezroczysty (pzhe-żhro-chis-
ti) adj. m. transparent
przezwisko (pzhes-vees-ko) n.
1. nickname; 2. abusive name
przezwyciężać (pzhez-vee-chan-
zhach) v.overcome; conquer

przezywać (pzhe-zi-vach) v. revile; abuse; call names,
przeżegnać się (pzhe-zhég-nach
shań) v. cross oneself
przeżuwać (pzhe-zhoo-vach) v.
chew;masticate; ponder over
przeżycie (pzhe-zhi-che) n.
experience; survival
przeżyć (pzhe-zhich)v.survive;
live through;outlive
przeżytek (pzhe-zhi-tek) m.
relic of the passd;old timer
przędza (pzhań-dza) f. yarn
przędzalnia (pzhań-dzal-ńa) f.
spinning mill;spinning room
przęsło (pzhańs-wo) n. (bridge)
bay; (stair) flight; span
przodek (pzho-dek) m. 1. ancestor; 2. front;heading;end;top
przodować (pzho-do-vach) v.
lead; excel; be the best
przodownictwo (pzho-dov-ńeets-
tvo) n. leadership; hegemony
przodownik (pzho-dov-ńeek) m.
leader;foreman;police inspector
przód (pzhoot) m. front; ahead
przy (pzhi) prep. by; at; near
by; with; on; about; close to
przybić (pzhi-beech)v. nail down
przybiec (pzhi-byets) v. run
up ; hasten;come up running
przybierać (pzhi-bye-rach) v.
dress up; put on; adopt;adorn
przybliżać (pzhi-blee-zhach) v.
bring near;draw near;magnify
przybliżony (pzhi-blee-zho-ni)
adj. m. approximate;very near
przyboczny (pzhi-bóch-ni) adj.
m. side(kick) ; personal (aide);
body (guard);adjutant (officer)
przybory (pzhi-bo-ri) pl. accessories;outfit; tools;tackle
przybór (pzhi-boor) m. rise
(of flood);rise (of a river)
przybrać (pzhi-brach) v. adorn;
put on; assume; adopt;rise;grow
przybrzeżny (pzhi-bzhezh-ni)
adj. m. coastal; riverside
przybudówka (pzhi-boo-doov-ka)
f. annex;addition(to a building)
przybycie (pzhi-bi-che) n. arrival;gain;growth; accession
przybysz (pzhi-bish) m. newcomer

przybytek (pzhi-bi-tek) m. increase; sanctuary;repository przybywać (pzhi-bi-vach) v. 1. arrive 2. increase;rise przychodnia (pzhi-khod-na) f. outpatient clinic;ambulatory przychodzić (pzhi-kho-dźheech) v. come over, around, along, to, again; turn up; arrive przychód (pzhi-khoot) m. income;profit; takings;proceeds przychylać (pzhi-khi-lach) v. incline: comply; bend przychylny (pzhi-khil-ni) adj. m. favorable; kind;friendly przyciągać (pzhi-chown-gach) v. attract; draw near;appeal;lure przyciąganie ziemskie (pzhi-chown-ga-ne zhem-ske ) gravitation; gravitational pull przyciemniać (pzhi-chem-nach) v. dim; darken;shade;black out przycinać (pzhi-chi-nach) v. 1. cut; slip; 2. make fun of przycisk (pzhi-cheesk) m. 1. pressure; 2. accent; 3. paper-weight; weight;emphasis przyciskać (pzhi-chis-kach) v. press; keep down;squeeze przycupnąć (pzhi-tsoop-nownch) v. squat down;crouch;lje in wait przyczaic się (pzhi-cha-eech shań) v. lurk; sulk; ambush;hide przyczepic (pzhi-che-peech) v. attach; fasten;link;fix;pin;hook przyczepic się (pzhi-che-peech shań) v. cling; pick a quarrel; find fault; hold tight; attach przyczepka (pzhi-chep-ka) f. trailer przyczółek (pzhi-choo-wek) m. abutment; bridgehead; beachhead;fronton;frontal;pediment przyczyna (pzhi-chi-na) f.cause; reason; ground; intercession przyczynek (pzhi-chi-nek) m. contribution(to science etc.) przyczyniać (pzhi-chi-nach) v. add; add to; contribute przyczynowość (pzhi-chi-no-voshch) f. causation;causality przyćmiewać (pzhi-chmye-vach) v. dim; tarnish; obscure; outshine; overshadow;darken; eclipse

przydać (pzhi-dach) v. add; apend; lend; add weight przydatny (pzhi-dat-ni) adj. m. useful;helpful;serviceable przydawka (pzhi-dav-ka) f. attribute (gram.);qulifier przydeptać (pzhi-dep-tach) v. thread upon; step on przydługi (pzhi-dwoo-gee) adj. m. lengthy;somewhat too long przydomek (pzhi-do-mek) m. by-name; surname;nickname przydreptać (pzhi-drep-tach) v. trip along; come tripping przydrożny (pzhi-drozh-ni) adj. m. roadside(shrine etc.) przydusić (pzhi-doo-sheech) v. throttle; smother;press down przydybac (pzhi-di-bach) v. overtake; take unawares;nab przydymać (pzhi-dimach) v. foot it along; run up(slang) przydymiony (pzhi-dim-yo-ni) adj. m. smoky; tinted przydział (pzhi-dźhaw) m. allotment; ration;allowance przydzielac (pzhi-dźhe-lach) v. assign; allocate;allot przyganiac (pzhi-ga-nach) v. blame; find fault with; criticize;rebuke;reprimand przygarnąć (pzhi-gar-nownch) v. take up; adopt;hug;grasp;shelter przygasać (pzhi-ga-sach) v. dim; subside; abate;go out;die down przygladać się (pzhi-glown-dach shań) v. observe;look on;scan;see przygnać (pzhi-gnach) v. drive near; bring; run up; hasten przygnębiać (pzhi-gnań-byach) v. depress; deject;dishearten przygnębienie (pzhi-gnań-byene) n. depression; low spirits przygniatać (pzhi-gna-tach) v. crush;overwhelm; oppress; burden; press down;squeeze; pinch przygoda (pzhi-go-da) f. adventure; accident; experience przygodny (pzhi-god-ni) adj. m. occasional; casual; accidental przygotować (pzhi-go-to-vach) v. v. prepare; get ready; worn ; fit; coach; train; make ready; pack up; turn on (the bath)

przygotowanie (pzhi-go-to-va-
ńe) n. preparation;getting ready
przygotowawczy (pzhi-go-to-vav-
chi) adj. m. preparatory;initial
przygrywac (pzhi-gri-vach) v.
1. accompany; 2. play(music)
przygrzewac (pzhi-gzhe-vach) v.
warm up; heat up;swelter
przygwozdzic (pzhi-gvozh-
dzheech) v. nail down;pin down
przyimek (pzhi-ee-mek) m. prep-
osition(relation word)
przyjaciel (pzhi-ya-chel) m.
friend;good friend;close friend
przyjaciołka (pzhi-ya-choow-
ka) f. girl friend;close friend
przyjazd (pzhi-yazt) m. arrival; time of arrival
przyjazny (pzhi-yaz-ni) adj. m.
friendly; amicable; kindly
przyjazń (pzhi-yazhń) f. friendship; friendly relations;amity
przyjaznic się (pzhi-yazh-neech
shań) v. be friends;pal;chum
przyjechac (pzhi-ye-khach) v.
come (over); arrive; come
przyjemnosc (pzhi-yem-noshch) f.
pleasure; enjoyment; gusto;zest
przyjemny (pzhi-yem-ni) adj. m.
pleasant;attractive;nice;cosy
przyjezdny (pzhi-yezd-ni) m.
stranger; sightseer;visitor
przyjeżdżac (pzhi-yezh-dzhach)
v. arrive (by transportation)
przyjęcie (pzhi-yań-che) n.
admission; adoption; reception
przyjęty (pzhi-yań-ti) adj. m.
customary; acceptable
przyjmowac (pzhiy-mo-vach) v.
receive; accept; entertain
przyjscie (pzhiysh-che) n. arrival; coming; advent
przyjsc (pzhiyshch) v. come-
over; come along; come around
przykazac (pzhi-ka-zach) v. order; tell; enjoin to do
przykazanie (pzhi-ka-za-ńe) n.
commandment; injunction
przyklasnąc (pzhi-klas-nownch)
v. applaud;commend;praise
przykleic (pzhi-kle-eech) v.
stick; glue; paste; stick on
(stamp etc.)

przyklękac (pzhi-klań-kach) v.
genuflect; bend the knee
przykład (pzhi-kwat) m. example; instance; pattern; sample
przykładac (pzhi-kwa-dach) v.
1. apply;affix; lend a hand;
2. beat up with;.apply a force
przykładny (pzhi-kwad-ni) adj.
m. exemplary; model(husband)
przykrajac (pzhi-kra-yach) v.
cut off; cut out(garments etc.)
przykrawac (pzhi-kra-vach) v.
cut out(garments etc.);cut off
przykręcac (pzhi-krań-tsach)
v. screw on; 2. turn tight
przykrosc (pzhi-kroshch) f.
annoyance;irritation;vexation
przykry (pzhi-kri) adj. m.
disagreeable;painful;nasty;bad
przykrywac (pzhi-kri-vach) v.
cover; roof over
przykrywka (pzhi-kriv-ka) f.
lid; cover (of friendship etc.)
przykrzyc się (pzhi-kzhich
shań) v. be bored; have nothing to do;pall on;weary;long
przykucnąc (pzhi-koots-nownch)
v. squat down;crouch; squat
przykuc (pzhi-kooch) v.
1. hammer; 2. arrest (attention);chain;grip;rivet;fascinate
przylatywac (pzhi-la-ti-vach)
v. fly in; fly into (a room)
przylądek (pzhi-lown-dek) m.
cape ; tip of land; headland
przyleciec (pzhi-le-chech) v.
fly in; arrive;come running
przylegac (pzhi-le-gach) v.
1. fit; cling; 2. adjoin
przyległy (pzhi-leg-wi) adj.
m. adjacent;adjoining;contiguous
przylepic (pzhi-le-peech) v.
stick; glue on;stick to;post
przylepiec (pzhi-le-pyets) m.
adhesive,tape;court plaster
przylgnąc (pzhil-gnownch) v.
stick; cling; adhere;nestle up
przylot (pzhi-lot) m. plane
arrival(of an airplane)
przylutowac (pzhi-loo-to-vach)
v. solder on; sweat on
przyłączac (pzhi-wown-chach) v.
annex; join; add;connect;attach

przyłączenie (pzhi-wówn-che-
ńe) n. annexation;incorporation
przyłbica (pzhiw-bee-tsa) f.
visor; beaver;welder's helmet
przymawiać (pzhi-máv-yach) v.
criticize;rebuke;pinprick;nettle
przymawiac się (pzhi-máv-yach
śhań) v. hint around for
przymiarka (pzhi-myár-ka) f.
fitting on; trying on clothes
przymierać (pzhi-mye-rach) v.
starve;be half dead;be dying
przymierzac (pzhi-mye-zhach)
v. try on;set to; apply to
przymierze (pzhi-mye-zhe) n.
alliance; covenant; Testament
przymierzyc (pzhi-mye-zhich)
v. try on; set on; apply to
przymieszka (pzhi-myesh-ka) f.
admixture;addition;modicum;dash
przymiot (pzhi-myot) m. (man's)
quality; trait; attribute
przymiotnik (pzhi-myot-ńeek) m.
adjective (grammar)
przymknięty (pzhim-knań-ti)
adj. m. half-closed; shut up
przymocować (pzhi-mo-tso-vach)
v. fasten; fix; secure;attach
przymowka (pzhi-moóv-ka) f.gibe;
hint; allusion;scoff;jeer
przymrozek (pzhi-mró-zek) m.
slight frost;ground frost
przymrużyc oczy (pzhi-mroo-
zhich o-chi) blink; narrow
one's eyes; wink
przymus (pzhi-moos) m. compulsion; constraint; coersion
przymusic (pzhi-moo-śheech) v.
compel;force;oblige;coerce
przymusowy (pzhi-moo-so-vi) adj.
m. obligatory;coercive;forced
przynaglac (pzhi-nág-lach) v.
urge; haste; push on;hustle;spur
przynajmniej (pzhi-náy-mńey)
adv. at least;at any rate;anyway
przynaleźec (pzhi-na-le-zhech)
v. belong; be member(of a party)
przynależnosc (pzhi-na-lezh-
noshch) f.(nationality) membership;affiliation;(national)status
przynależny (pzhi-na-lezh-ni)
adj. m. belonging; appurtenant

przynęta (pzhi-nań-ta) f. bait;
lure; enticement; lure; decoy
przynosic (pzhi-no-śheech) v.
1. bring; fetch; 2. bear;
yield; bring(profit);afford
przyobiecac (pzhi-obye-tsach)
v. promise; give a promise
przyobiecywac (pzhi-ob-ye-tsi-
vach) v. promise;give a promise
przypadac (pzhi-pa-dach) v.
be due; fall; come ; happen
przypadek (pzhi-pá-dek) m.
event; chance; case; incident
przypadkiem (pzhi-pád-kem) adv.
by chance; accidentally
przypadkowo (pzhi-pad-kó-vo)
adv. accidentally;unintentionally
przypadłosc (pzhi-pád-woshch)
f. affliction; ailment; disease
przypalic (pzhi-pa-leech) v.
singe; burn; smoke;scorch;sear
przypasac (pzhi-pá-sach) v.
attach (to belt); grid on
przypatrywac się (pzhi-pa-tri-
vach śhań) v. observe; look at;
contemplate;have a look at
przypatrzyc się (pzhi-pá-tzhich
śhań) v. observe;contemplate
przypędzac (pzhi-pań-dzach) v.
1. come in haste; 2. drive (to)
przypiąc (pzhi-pyównch) v. pin;
fasten;attach;buckle; pin on
przypieczętowac (pzhi-pye-chań-
tó-vach) v. seal up; confirm
przypisek (pzhi-pee-sek) m. note;
postscript; added note
przypisywac (pzhi-pee-si-vach)
v. ascribe; attribute; credit
przypłacac (pzhi-pwa-tsach) v.
pay (with life; health; property etc.); pay (dearly)
przypłynąc (pzhi-pwi-nównch) v.
arrive sailing or swimming;
come to shore; swim up;sail up
przypływ (pzhi-pwif) m. high
tide; inflow;influx; high water
przypodobac się(pshi-po-dó-bach
śhań)v.get into good graces
przypominac (pzhi-po-mee-nach)
v. remind; recollect;resemble
przypomnienie (pzhi-pom-ńe-ńe)
n. reminder; memento;souvenir

przypowieść (pzhi-póv-yeshch) f. tale; parable; allegory
przyprawa (pzhi-prá-va) f. seasoning; spice;relish;sause
przyprawiać (pzhi-práv-yach) v. 1. season; 2. cause a loss
przyprowadzać (pzhi-pro-vadzach) v. bring along; fetch
przypuszczać (pzhi-poósh-chach) v. suppose;let approach;admit
przypuszczalnie (pzhi-pooshchál-ñe) adv. supposedly
przypuszczalny (pzhi-pooshchál-ni) adj. m. supposed
przypuszczenie (pzhi-poosh-cheñe) n. guess; supposition
przyroda (pzhi-ro-da) f. nature
przyrodni brat (pzhi-ród-ñee brát) half brother
przyrodnia siostra (pzhi-ród-ña shós-tra) half sister
przyrodnik (pzhi-ród-ñeek) m. naturalist;natural historian
przyrodzony (pzhi-ro-dzó-ni) adj. m. innate;natural;inborn
przyrost naturalny (pzhi-rost na-too-rál-ni) birthrate
przyrostek (pzhi-roś-tek) m. suffix (grammar)
przyrząd (pzhi-zhównd) m. instrument;tool; appliance;device
przyrządzać (pzhi-zhówn-dzach) v. make ready; prepare;cook
przyrzeczenie (pzhi-zhe-che-ñe) n. promise; plighted word
przyrzekać (pzhi-zhe-kach) v. promise to do(something)
przysadka (pzhi-sád-ka) f. pituitary gland; stipule
przysądzać (pzhi-sówn-dzach) v. award; adjudge; allocate
przysiad (pzhi-shad) m. squat
przysiadać (pzhi-sha-dach) v. sit down; crouch; sit up
przysięga (pzhi-shań-ga) f. oath; sworn attestation
przysięgać (pzhy-shań-gach) v. swear to do; take an oath
przysięgły (pzhy-sháng-wi)adj. m. sworn (jury man)
przysłać (pzhi-swach) v. send in
przysłaniać (pzhi-swa-ñach) v. shade; vail;cover up;screen

przysłona (pzhi-swó-na) f. veil; shade; screen; diaphragm; stop
przysłowie (pzhi-swóv-ye) n. proverb; by word
przysłówek (pzhi-swoó-vek) m. adverb (grammar)
przysłuchiwać się (pzhi-swoo-kheé-vach shañ) v. listen to
przysługa (pzhi-swoó-ga) f. service;good turn;favor;kindness
przysługiwać (pzhi-swoo-geé-vach) v. to have right;be vested
przysłużyć się (pzhi-swoó-shich shañ) v. render service
przysmak (pzhis-mak) m. delicacy
przysmażyć (pzhi-smá-zhich) v. roast; fry a little; brown;devil
przysparzać (pzhi-spá-zhach) v. 1. increase; add to 2. cause (trouble);bring unpleasantness
przyspieszać (pzhish-pyé-shach) v. accelerate; urge;speed up
przyspieszenie (pzhish-pye-sheñe) n. acceleration;speeding up
przysposabiać (pzhis-po-sáb-yach) prepare; adapt; adopt;fit;qualify
przystać (pzhiś-tach) v. join; comply;cohere;fit together;befit
przystanąć (pzhi-stá-nównch) v. stop; pause; halt
przystanek (pzhi-stá-nek) m. stop; station; bus stop etc.
przystań (pzhi-stań) f. small (boat) harbor(inland); port
przystawać (pzhi-sta-vach) v. fit; enlist; coincide; halt
przystawiać (pzhi-stáv-yach) v. place near; set against; put
przystawka (pzhi-stáv-ka) f. side dish; hors-doeuvre
przystęp (pzhi-stánp) m. access
przystępny (pzhi-stánp-ni) adj. m. 1. accessible; 2. moderate
przystojny (pzhi-stóy-ni) adj. m. handsome; decent; suitable
przystosować (pzhi-sto-só-vach) v. adjust; fit;accomodate;adapt
przystrajać (pzhi-strá-yach) v. decorate; adorn; dress; trim
przysunąć (pzhi-soo-nównch) v. move near; push nearer
przyswajać (pzhi-svá-yach) v. acquire; assimilate; adopt(ways)

przysyłać (pzhi-sí-wach) v.
send;send along;send up
przysypac (pzhi-si-pach) v. cover (with earth; snow etc.)
przyszłość (pzhish-woshch) f.
future;days to come;the future
przyszyc (pzhi-shich) v. sew on
przyszykowac (pzhi-shi-ko-vach)
v. prepare; make ready
przysnić się (pzhish-neech shan)
v. appear in a dream
przyśrubowac (pzhi-shroo-bo-vach)
v. screw on; screw down
przyswiadczyc (pzhi-shviad-
chich) v. agree with;attest
przytaczac (pzhi-ta-chach) v.
quote; cite;wheel up;bring up
przytakiwac (pzhi-ta-kee-vach)
v. say yes;assent;acquiesce
przytepic (pzhi-tan-peech) v.
dull; blunt somewhat;dim;befog
przytepienie (pzhi-tan-pye-ne)
n. dullness; bluntness
przytknac (pzhit-known-ch) v.
place touching; set to;apply to
przytłaczac (pzhi-twa-chach) v.
overwhelm;press to earth;crush
przytłumic (pzhi-twoo-meech) v.
damp; deaden;stifle;subdue;dim
przytoczyc (pzhi-to-chich) v.
quote; cite; roll up; bring up
przytomnie (pzhi-tom-ne) adv.
with presence of mind;lucidly
przytomnosc (pzhi-tom-noshch)
f. consciousness;(one's)senses
przytomny (pzhi-tom-ni) adj.m.
conscious;quickwitted
przytrafiac się (pzhi-traf-yach
shan) v. happen; occur;befall
przytrzymac (pzhi-tzhi-mach) v.
hold; detain;keep in place;arrest
przytulic (pzhi-too-leech) v.
snuggle; cuddle ;hug;cuddle;fold
przytułek (pzhi-too-wek) m.
shelter,alms,house;poor house
przytwierdzic (pzhi-tvyerdzheech)
v. fasten; fix;attach;assent
przytyk (pzhi-tik) m. dig; allusion ;tilt;reference;junction
przytykac (pzhi-ti-kach) v.
1. adjoin; 2. set; apply ;border
przy tym (pzhi-tim) adv. besides

przyuczac (pzhi-oo-chach) v.
train; accustom an animal
przywabiac (pzhi-vab-yach) v.
decoy; allure; lure
przywara (pzhi-va-ra) f. vice;
fault;defect;shortcoming
przywiazac (pzhi-vyown-zach) v.
bind;tie;attach;hitch;lash;fasten
przywdziewac (pzhi-vdzhe-vach)
v. put on (clothes)
przywidzenie (pzhi-vee-dze-ne)
n. illusion;delusion;phantasm
przywiezc (pzhi-vyezhch) v.
import; bring; drive up;recall
przywilej (pzhi-vee-ley) m.
privilege; prerogative;charter
przywitac (pzhi-vee-tach) v.
welcome; greet;bid good morning
przywłaszczac (pzhi-vwash-
chach) v. usurp; appropriate
przywodzic (pzhi-vo-dzeech) v.
lead; bring about;remind;drive
przywłaszczenie (pzhi-vwash-
che-ne) n. appropriation;
usurpation (of rights etc.)
przywołac (pzhi-vo-wach) v.
summon; call in;signal;sign
przywozic (pzhi-vo-zheech) v.
bring (by car);import;deliver
przywodca (pzhi-vood-tsa) m.
leader ; ringleader;chietain
przywoz (pzhi-voos) m. import;
delivery ;transport;carriage
przywracac (pzhi-vra-tsach) v.
restore ;bring back;reappoint
przywrocenie (pzhi-vroo-tse-ne)
n. restoration ;reinstatement
przywyknac (pzhi-vik-known-ch)
get accustomed ;get used
przyznac (pzhi-znach) v. award;
admit ;allow;acknowledge;grant
przyzwalac (pzhi-zva-lach) v.
consent; approve ;agree;concede
przyzwoitosc (pzhi-zvo-ee-
toshch) f. decency ;propriety
przyzwoity (pzhi-zvo-ee-ti) adj.
m. decent ;proper;seemly;suitable
przyzwolenie (pzhi-zvo-le-ne)
n. consent ;acquiescence
przyzwyczajac (pzhi-zvi-cha-
yach) v. accustom ;habituate

przyzwyczajenie (pzhi-zvi-cha-
ye-ne) n, habit; custom
przyzywać (pzhi-zi-vach) v.
call in ; call sb;beckon;sign
psalm (psalm) m. psalm
pseudonim (psew-do-neem) m.
pseudonym; pen name
psiarnia (pshar-ña) f. kennel
psie pieniądze (pshe pye-nown-
dze) dirt cheap; dog cheap
psikus (pshee-koos) m. prank
psota (pso-ta) f. prank; mischief; practical joke; trick
psotnik (psot-neek) m. prank-
ster; practical joker;scamp
pstrąg (pstrowng) m. trout; kelt
pstry (pstri) adj. m. 1. mottled;
speckled; 2. uncertain;freaked
psuć (psooch) v. spoil; decay;
waste; corrupt; deprave; damage;put out of order;mess up
psychiatra (psi-khyat-ra) m.
psychiatrist; shrink; alienist
psychiczny (psi-kheech-ni) adj.
m. mental(state,disease etc.)
psycholog (psi-kho-lok) m.
psychologist; behaviorist
pszczelarstwo (pzhche-lar-stvo)
n. beekeeping ; apiculture
pszczelarz (pshche-lash) m. beekeeper; apiarist
pszczoła (pshcho-wa) f. bee
pszenica (pshe-nee-tsa) f. wheat
ptactwo (ptats-tvo) pl. fowl;
birds; the species of birds
ptak (ptak) m. bird;fowl
ptaszek (pta-shek) m. little
bird; small bird; rogue
publicysta (poo-blee-tsis-ta)
m. columnist; journalist
publiczność (poo-bleech-noshch)
pl. public;community; audience
publikacja (poo-blee-kats-ya) f.
publication;something published
puch (pookh) m. down;fluff
puchacz (poo-khach) m. eagle
owl(night bird of prey)
puchar (poo-khar) m. cup; bowl
puchlina wodna (poo-khlee-na
wod-na)f.dropsy ;hydropsy
puchnąć (pookh-nownch) v. swell
puchowy (poo-kho-vi) adj. m.
downy;fluffy;eiderdown

pucołowaty (poo-tso-wo-va-ti)
adj. m. chubby cheeked
pucz (pooch) m. Putsch
pudełko (poo-dew-ko) n. box
(small); tin ; can;hand box
puder (poo-der) m. powder
puderniczka (poo-der-neech-ka)
f. powder box; compact;puff box
pukać (poo-kach)v. knock ;rap
pugilares (poo-gee-la-res) m.
billfold; pocket book;wallet
pukiel (poo-kel) m. curl;lock
pula (poo-la) f. pool;kitty
pularda (poo-lar-da) f. pou-
larde; fowl
pulchny (pool-khni) adj. m.
plump;mellow;loose;spongy
pulower (poo-lo-ver) m. pullover (sweater)
pulpit (pool-peet) m. desk;
lectern; shelf;book rest
puls (pools) m. pulse;vibration
pulsować (pool-so-vach) v.
pulsate;palpitate;throb;vibrate
pułap (poo-wap) m. ceiling
pułapka (poo-wap-ka) f. trap
pułk (poowk) m. regiment;group
pułkownik (poow-kov-neek) m.
colonel; group captain
pumeks (poo-meks) m. pumice
punkt (poonkt) m. point; mark
punktualny (poonk-too-al-ni)
adj. m. punctual;exact;prompt
pupa (poo-pa) f. behind; buttocks; bottom
pupil (poo-peel) m. ward; pupil; favorite
purchawka (poor-khav-ka) f. 1.
puff-ball; 2. grumpy fellow
purpura (poor-poo-ra) f. purple
purytanin (poo-ri-ta-neen) m.
Puritan;man of strict religion
pustelnia (poos-tel-ña) f. her-
mitage;solitary secluded place
pustelnik (poos-tel-neek) m.
hermit; recluse
pustka (poost-ka) f. solitude;
empty (place);emptiness;void
pustkowie (poost-kov-ye) n.
deserted place;desert;solitude
pustoszyć (poos-to-shich) v.
devastate;ravage;lay waste;ruin
pusty (poos-ti) adj.m. empty

pustynia (poos-ti-ña) f. desert
puszcza (poosh-cha) f. primeval
forest; wilderness
puszczać (poosh-chach) v. let
go; let fall; set afloat; free;
fade; drop; let out; emit; start
puszczać się (poosh-chach shän)
v. draw apart; let go; be a
permissive girl; go to bed with
puszek (poo-shek) m. down
puszka blaszana (poosh-ka bla-
sha-na) tin can; tin box
puszysty (poo-shis-ti) adj. m.
downy; fluffy; flossy; flaky; nappy
puścić (poosh-cheech) v. let go;
let free; release; let fall
puzon (poo-zon) m. trombone
(one octave lower than trumpet)
pycha (pi-kha) f. 1. pride;
2. excellent tidbit; fine stuff
pykać (pi-kach) v. puff; pop
pylić (pi-leech) v. dust; be dusty
pył (piw) m. dust; powder
pyskować (pis-ko-vach) v. be
saucy; bark; bawl
pysk (pisk) m. muffle; snout;
mug; muzzle; phiz; rowdyism
pyskaty (pis-ka-ti) adj. m.
foulmouthed; saucy; pert; bawling
pyszałek (pi-sha-wek) m. boaster; braggart; coxcomb
pysznic się (pish-ñeech shän)
v. swagger; prance; swank; strut
pysznie (pish-ñe) adv. proudly;
admirably; in grand fashion
pytać (pi-tach) v. ask; inquire;
question; interrogate
pytanie (pi-ta-ñe) n. question;
inquiry; query; interrogation
pytel (pi-tel) m. bolter
pytlować (pi-tlo-vach) v. sift;
bolt(flour); be a chatterbox
pyton (pi-ton) m. python
pyza (pi-za) f. dumpling
pyzaty (pi-za-ti) adj. m. chubby
rab (rab) m. slave; servant
rabarbar (ra-bar-bar) m. rhubarb
rabat (ra-bat) m. discount; rebate; reduction (in price)
rabin (ra-been) m. rabbi
rabować (ra-bo-vach) v. rob;
maraud; plunder; pirate; take
by force; steal

rabunek (ra-boo-nek) m. robbery; plunder; holdup; spoliation
rabuś (ra-boosh) m. robber;
plunderer; pillager
rachityczny (ra-khee-tich-ni)
adj. m. rickety; rachitic
rachmistrz (rakh-meestsh) m.
accountant; calculator; reckoner
rachować (ra-kho-vach) v. calculate; count; reckon; compute; rely
rachunek (ra-khoo-nek) m. bill;
account; count; calculation; sum
rachunkowość (ra-khoon-ko-
voshch) f. bookkeeping
racica (ra-chee-tsa) f. cloven
hoof; cow hoof
racja (rats-ya) f. reason; right;
ration; propriety; correctness
racjonalizować (ra-tsyo-na-lee-
zo-vach) v. rationalize; improve
racjonalny (ra-tsyo-nal-ni)
adj. m. rational; reasonable
raczej (ra-chey) adv. rather;
sooner; rather than
raczkować (rach-ko-vach) v. go
on all fours; crawl on all four
raczyć (ra-chich) v. deign; be
pleased; treat; condescend; stoop
rad (rad) adj. m. 1. pleased;
glad 2. m. radium
rada (ra-da) f. advice; counsel
radar (ra-dar) m. radar
radca (rad-tsa) m. advisor;
counselor; legal advisor
radcostwo (rad-tsos-tvo) n.
councillorship; post of advisor
radio (rad-yo) n. radio; wireless; broadcasting (system)
radiofonia (ra-dyo-fo-ña) f.
broadcasting; radiotelephony
radioaktywny (rad-yo-ak-tiv-ni)
adj, m. radioactive
radiostacja (rad-yi-stats-ya)
f. radio station
radiodepesza (rad-yo-de-pe-sha)
f. radiotelegram
radioterapia (rad-yo-te-rap-ya)
f. radiotherapy; X-ray therapy
radny (rad-ni) m. alderman
radosny (ra-dos-ni) adj. m. gay;
glad; festive(day etc.)
radość (ra-doshch) f. joy; gladness; delight; merriment; glee

radykalny (ra-di-kál-ni) adj. m. radical;man of radical views

radykał (ra-di-kaw) m. radical

radzić (rá-dżheech) v. deliberate; suggest; advice;counsel

radziecki (ra-dżhéts-kee) adj. m. Soviet;of Soviet Union

rafa (rá-fa) f. reef;rim;ripple

rafineria (ra-fee-nér-ya) f. refinery; refining,works

rafinować (ra-fee-nó-vach) f. refine; purify; distil

raid (rayd) m.sport rally (race)

raj (ray) m. paradise; heaven

rak (rak) m. crayfish; cancer

rakieta (ra—ke-ta) f. 1. rocket; flare; 2. (tennis) racket

rama (rá-ma) f. frame;scheme;case

ramię (ra-myáń) n. shoulder

ramowy (ra-mó-vi) adj. m. frame

rampa (rám-pa) f. ramp; loading platform;bar;barier; float

rana (rá-na) f. wound;injury;sore

randka (ránd-ka) f. date

ranek (ra-nek) m. morning; daybreak; break of day

ranga (ran-ga) f. rank; standing

ranic (ra-neech) v. wound; hurt

ranny (rán-ni) adj. m. 1. wounded; injured; 2. morning; early

rano (rá-no) adv. 1. early; 2. morning; forenoon;too early

rapier (rá-pyer) m. rapier

raport (rá-port) m. report; account; statement; log

raptem (ráp-tem) adv. suddenly; abruptly;no more than;all in all

raptowny (rap-tóv-ni) adj. m. abrupt; sudden;impulsive;heady

rasa (ra-sa) f. race; stock; breed ;(plant)variety; blood

rasizm (ra-sheezm) m. racism

rasowy (ra-só-vi) adj. m. racial; thoroughbred;purebred;racy

raszpla (rásh-pla) f. rasp

rata (rá-ta) f. instalment (payment);part payment(system)

ratować (ra-tó-vach) v. rescue; save; deliver(from danger)

ratownictwo (ra-tov-néets-tvo) n. life saving (system)

ratownik (ra-tov-ńeek) m. lifeguard; rescuer; life saver

ratunek (ra-too-nek) m. rescue; salvation;help;assistance;resort

ratunkowy pas (ra-toon-ko-vi pas) m. life belt; life jacket

ratusz (rá-toosh) m. city hall

ratyfikacja (ra-ti-fee-káts-ya) f. ratification

raut (rawt) m. evening party

raz (ras) m. 1. one time; 2. blow; stroke; buffet

raz (ras) adv. once; at one time; at last; time being

razem (rá-zem) adv. together

razić (rá-żheech) v. 1. strike; 2. offend; 3. dazzle; shock;hit

razowy (ra-zó-vi) adj. m. brown (bread); whole meal (bread)

razowiec (ra-zó-vyets) m. whole meal bread; brown bread

rażący (ra-zhówn-tsy) adj. m. 1. glaring; 2. flagrant; rank

raźnie (ráżh-ńe) adv. cheerfully; briskly; at a lively pace

rąb (równb) m. rim;pane;clearing

rąbać (równ-bach) v. 1. chop;hew; 2. say truth to face ; slash

rączka (równch-ka) f. handle; small hand; handgrip;holder

rączy (równ-chi) adj. m. swift

rdza (rdza) f. rust;mildew;blight

rdzenny (rdzén-ni) adj. m. essential; original;specific

rdzeń (rdzeń) m. core; pith; marrow; gist; essence; log

rdzoodporny (rdzo-od-pór-ni) adj. rust-proof;stainless

reagować (re-a-go-vach) v. react; respond;be suscrptible

rdzewieć (rdze-vyech) v. corrode; rust; get rusty; gather rust

reakcja (re-ak-tsya) f. reaction

reakcjonista (re-ak-tsyo-ńees-ta) m. reactionary

reakcyjny (re-ak-tsiy-ni) adj. m. reactionary;retrograde

reaktywować (re-ak-ti-vo-vach) v. 1. start again; 2. reactivate;bring back to life;recall

realia (re-al-ya) pl. realia; realities

realista (re-a-lees-ta) m. realist; advocate of realism

realizm (re-a-leezm) m. realism

realizować (re-a-lee-zó-vach) v.
actualize; realize;cash(assets)
realność (re-ál-noshch) f. 1.
real estate; 2. reality;the real
realny (re-ál-ni) adj. m. real;
concrete; actual;genuine;true
rebelia (re-bél-ya) f. rebellion;uprising against government
recenzent (re-tsén-zent) m.critic;
reviewer (of books, plays, etc.)
recenzja (re-tsén-zya) f. review (of books, plays, etc.)
recepcja (re-tsep-tzya) f. reception;formal social function
recepis (re-tsé-pees) m. receipt; recipe;written receipt
recepta (re-tsép-ta) f. pre-
scription; doctor's order
rechot (re-khot) m. shrieking
laughter; croak(of frogs)
recydywista (re-tsi-di-vees-ta)
m. recidivist;old offender
recytować (re-tsi-to-vach) v.
recite;give a recitation
redagować (re-da-go-vach) v.
edit;draw up;formulate;draft
redakcja (re-dak-tsya) f. 1.
editing; 2. editor's office
redaktor (re-dák-tor) m. editor
redukcja (re-doók-tsya) f. reduction (in size,price etc.)
redukować (re-doo-kó-vach) v.
reduce; lay off;cut down
referat (re-fé-rat) m. report
referencja (re-fe-rén-tsya) f.
reference; testimonial
referent (re-fé-rent) m. clerk
refleks (re-fleks) m. reflex
refleksja (re-fléks-ya) f. reflection; thought; cogitation
reflektor (re-flek-tor) m. re-
flector; searchlight;headlight
reflektować (re-flek-tó-vach)
v. 1. apply for; want; 2. reflect;bring to reason;moderate
reforma (re-fór-ma) f. reform
reformacja (re-for-máts-ya) f.
reformation; Reformation
reformować (re-for-mo-vach) v.
reform; reorganize
regaty (re-gá-ti) pl. boat race
regencja (re-gén-tsya) f. regency; regency style

regionalny ( re-gyo-nál-ni)
adj. regional; local
regulacja (re-goo-láts-ya) f.
regulation;control;regulator
regularny (re-goo-lar-ni) adj.
m. regular; even;systematic
regulować (re-goo-lo-vach) v.
1. regulate control 2. settle
reguła (re-góo-wa) f. rule
rehabilitować (re-kha-bee-lee-
to-vach) v. rehabilitate
reja (re-ya) f. yardarm
rejent (re-yent) m. notary
public; notary; regent
rejestr (re-yestr) m. register;
file; index;roll;register mark
rejestracja (re-yes-tráts-ya)
f. registration; licensing
rejestrować (re-yes-tro-vach)
v. register; enroll;record
rejon (re-yon) m. region
rejwach (réy-vakh) m. uproar;
hullabaloo;row;hurly-burly
rekin (re-keen) m. shark
reklama (rek-lá-ma) f. advertising; commercial publicity
reklamacja (re-kla-máts-ya) f.
complaint;demand for compensation
reklamować (re-kla-mo-vach) v.
1. complain; 2. advertise
rekolekcje (re-ko-lék-tsye) pl.
retreat;period of contemplation
rekomendacja (re-ko-men-dats-
ya) f. recommendation;reference
rekompensata (re-kom-pen-sá-ta)
f. compensation;recompense
rekonvalescent (re-kon-va-lés-
cent) m. convalescent
rekord (re-kord) m. (sports)
record; (world) record
rekordzista (re-kor-dzhees-ta)
m. record holder;champion
rekreacja (re-kre-áts-ya) f.
recreation;opposing action
rekrut (rék-root) m. recruit;
conscript;recently enlisted man
rekrutować (re-kroo-to-vach)
v. recruit; enlist(new people)
rektor (rék-tor) m. university
president;university head
rektyfikować (rek-ti-fee-ko-
vach)v. rectify;correct; put
right; purify

rekwizycja (rek-vee-zits-ya) f. requisition;seizure

relacja (re-lats-ya) f. 1. report; 2. rate; relation

relatywizm (re-la-ti-veezm) m. relativity; relativism

relegacja (re-le-gats-ya) f. expulsion; relegation

religia (re-leeg-ya), f. religion

religijny (re-lee-geey-ni) adj. m. religious; godly

relikwia (re-leek-vya) f. relic

remanent (re-ma-nent) m. remainder; inventiry;stock

remis (re-mees) m. (sport)draw

remiza (re-mee-za) f. engine - shed ; engine-house; depot;barn

remont (re-mont) m. 1. repair; 2. (horse) remount

remontować (re-mon-to-vach) v. repair; recondition;overhaul

renumeracja (re-noo-me-rats-ya) f. renumeration;recount

ren (ren) m. reindeer; caribou

renegat (re-ne-gat) m. renegade

renifer (re-nee-fer) m. reindeer;(domesticated)arctic deer

renoma (re-no-ma) f. renown

renta (ren-ta) f. rent ; fixed income; annuity; pension

rentowność (ren-tov-noshch) f. profitability;earning capacity

rentgenolog (rent-ge-no-lok) m. radiologist; roentgenologist

rentowny (ren-tov-ni) adj. m. profitable;renumerative

reorganizacja (re-or-ga-nee-zats-ya) f. reorganization

reparacja (re-pa-rats-ya) f. 1. repair; 2. reparation

repatriacja (re-pa-tree-ats-ya) f. repatriation

reperować (re-pe-ro-vach) v. mend; repair;fix; set right

repertuar (re-per-too-ar) m. repertory; repertoire

repetycja (re-pe-tits-ya) f. repetition(of a lesson etc.)

replika (rep-lee-ka) f. 1, replica; 2. rebuttal; 3. (theatre)cue; retort;rejoinder

replikować (re-plee-ko-vach) v. answer back; rejoin; retort

reportaż (re-por-tash) m. 1. account; 2. reporting; commentary;coverage (of event etc.)

represja (re-pres-ya) f. reprisal;repressive measures

reprezentacja (re-pre-zen-tats-ya) f. representation

reprezentant (re-pre-zen-tant) m. representative

reprezentować (re-pre-zen-to-vach) v. represent; display

reprodukcja (re-pro-dook-tsya) f. reproduction;copy;replica

republika (re-poob-lee-ka) f. republic

republikański (re-poob-lee-kań-skee) adj. m. republican

reputacja (re-poo-tats-ya) f. reputation; (character)

resor (re-sor) m. (car) spring

resort (re-sort) m. 1. agency; 2. competence;scope;province

respekt (res-pekt) m. respect

restauracja (res-taw-rats-ya) f. 1. restaurant; 2. restoration (of objects of art etc.)

restrykcja (res-trik-tsya) f. restriction; reservation

restytucja (res-ti-toots-ya) f. restitution; restoration

reszta (resh-ta) f. rest; reminder; change; residue

retoryka (re-to-ri-ka) f. rhetoric;manual of rhetoric

retusz (re-toosh) m. retouch

retuszować (re-too-sho-vach) v. touch up; retouch

reumatyczny (re-oo-ma-tich-ni) adj. m. rheumatic

reumatyzm (re-oo-ma-tizm) m. rheumatism(pain in joint etc.)

rewanż (re-vansh) m. 1. rematch; 2. revenge; get back at

rewelacja (re-ve-lats-ya) f. revelation;striking disclosure

rewers (re-vers) m. 1. receipt; 2. reverse (side etc.)

rewia (rev-ya) f. 1. parade; 2. (theatre) revue

rewidować (re-vee-do-vach) v. 1. revise; 2. search; 3. audit

rewizja (re-veez-ya) f. revision search;audit;inspection;retrial rewizjonizm (re-veez-yó-ńeezm) m. revisionism

rewizyta (re-vee-zi-ta) f. return visit

rewolucja (re-vo-loóts-ya) f. revolution;complete change

rewolucyjny (re-vo-loo-tsiy-ni) adj. m. revolutionary

rewolwer (re-vól-ver) m. revolver; gun (with revolv.cylinder)

rezerwa (re-zer-va) f. reserve

rezerwat (re-zer-vat) m. reservation;game preserve

rezerwować (re-zer-vó-vach) v. reserve; set aside; book

rezerwuar (re-zer-voo-ar) m. reservoir;(storage)tank

rezolutny (re-zo-loot-ni) adj. m. resolute;determined; game

rezonans (re-zo-nans) m. resonance(intesifying vibrations)

rezultat (re-zool-tat) m. result; effect; numerical answer

rezydencja (re-zi-den-tsya) f. residence;dwelling place

rezydent (re-zi-dent) m. resident(not a transient)

rezygnacja (re-zig-nats-ya) f. resignation;patient submission

reżim (re-zheem) m. regime

reżyser (re-zhi-ser) m. stage manager; (film) director

ręcznie (rańch-ńe) adv. by hand

ręcznik (rańch-ńeek) m. towel

ręczny (rańch-ni) adj. m. manual; hand made; wrist(watch)

ręczyć (rań-chich) v. guarantee

ręka (rań-ka) f. hand; arm;touch

rękaw (rań-kav) m. sleeve

rękawica (rań-ka-vee-tsa) f. mitten; gauntlet;mitt;glove

rękawiczka (rań-ka-veech-ka) f. glove(fur lined,velvet, etc.)

rękodzielnik (rań-ko-dzhel-ńeek) m. craftsman;handicraftsman

rękojeść (rań-ko-yeshch) f. hilt; handle; handgrip; helve

rękojmia (rań-koy-mya) f. guaranty; pledge; gage;warranty

rękopis (rań-ko-pees) m. manuscript; script; MS

robactwo (ro-bats-tvo) n.vermin-

robak (ró-bak) m. worm;beetle;grub

rober (ro-ber) m. (bridge) rubber (in card game)

robić (ro-beech) v. make; do;act; work; become; get;feel;turn;knit

robociarz (ro-bo-chash) m. common laborer (slang); mechanic

robocizna (ro-bo-cheez-na) f. wages;cost of labor; labor

roboczogodzina (ro-bo-cho-go-dżhee-na) f. man-hour

robot (ro-bot) m. robot

robota (ro-bó-ta) f. work; job

robotnica (ro-bot-ńee-tsa) f. worker (bee); operative;mechanic

robotnik (ro-bót-ńeek) m. worker; worker;operative;mechanic

robótki (ro-boot-kee) pl. needlework; fancy work

rocznica (roch-ńee-tsa) f. anniversary

rocznie (róch-ńe) adv. yearly

rocznik (róch-ńeek) m. annual; yearbook; annual set; age group

roczny (róch-ni) adj. m. annual; one year's (duration etc.)

rodak (ró-dak) m. compatriot

rodowity (ro-do-vee-ti) adj. m. native; by birth; trueborn

rodowód (ro-dó-voot) m. genealogy; origin;pedigree;descent

rodzaj (ró-dzay) m. kind; sort; gender;type; race; manner;aspect

rodzajnik (ro-dzay-ńeek) m. article (definite or indefinite)

rodzeństwo (ro-dzeń-stvo) n. brothers and sisters

rodzice (ro-dzhee-tse)pl. parents;father and mother

rodzić (ro-dzheech)v. bear; procreate breed; yield (crops)

rodzina (ro-dzhee-na)f. family

rodzinny (ro-dzheen-ni)adj. m. family; native; home(life etc.)

rodzynek (ro-dzi-nek) m. raisin; currant

rogacz (ró-gach) m. 1. stag; 2. cuckold;deceived husband

rogatka (ro-gát-ka) f. tollgate; toll bar; turnpike

rogaty (ro-gá-ti) adj. m.. horned; haughty; deceived (husband)

rogatywka (ro-ga-tív-ka) f.
four-cornered cap(Polish style)
rogowacieć (ro-go-va-chech) v.
grow horny;become corneous
rogowaty (ro-go-va-ti) adj.
corneous ; horny
rogówka (ro-goov-ka) f. cornea
rogóżka (ro-goozh-ka) f. (door)
mat (flat,woven of straw etc.)
roić (ro-yeech) v. 1. dream;
imagine; 2. swarm; teem; run
rojalista (ro-ya-lees-ta) m.
royalist; supporter of the king
rojny (roy-ni) adj. m. teeming;
swarming(crowds etc.)
rojowisko (ro-yo-vees-ko) n.
hive; swarm;gathering place
rok (rok) m. year;a twelvemonth
rok przestępny (rok pzhe-stáñp-
ni) leap year
rokować (ro-kó-vach) v. 1. negotiate 2. expect; promise
rokowania (ro-ko-va-ña) pl. 1.
negotiations; 2. prognosis
rola (ró-la) f. 1. arable land
2. (theatre) part;scroll;weight
rolka (ról-ka) f. roll; spool;
reel;runner;pulley;castor
rolnictwo (rol-ñeets-tvo) v.
agriculture;farming;husbandry
rolnik (ról-ñeek) m. farmer
romans (ró-mans) m. 1. novel;
2. love affair; laison
romantyczny (ro-man-tich-ni) adj.
m. romantic;full of romance
romantyk (ro-man-tik) m. romantic
romantyzm (ro-man-tizm) m. ro-
manticism(literary style etc.)
romański (ro-mań-skee) adj. m.
Romance; Romanesque
romb (romb) m. rhomb;diamond
rondel (ron-del) m. stewpan
rondo (ron-do) n. brim; circular
plaza; traffic circle;circus
ronić (ro-ñeech) v. 1. shed;
2. miscarry;drop;cast;emit;moult
ropa (ró-pa) f. 1. puss; 2. crude
oil;rock oil; naphta;petroleum
ropieć (ró-pyech) v. fester;have
oozing sore; suppurate
ropień (róp-yeñ) m. abscess
ropny (róp-ni) adj. m. purulent;
oil fired; oil-(derrick etc.)

ropucha (ro-poó-kha) f. toad
rosa (ró-sa) f. dew
rosły (rós-wi) adj. m. tall;
big frame; stalwart
rosnąć (rós-nownch) v. grow
rosół (ró-soow) m. broth;
bouillion; clear soup;pickle
rostbef (rost-bef) m. roast-
beef; baked beef
rosyjski (ro-siy-skee) adj. m.
Russian; of Russia
roszczenie (rosh-che-ñe) n.
claim; pretension; pretence
rościć (rosh-cheech)v. claim
roślina (rosh-lee-na) f. plant;
vegetable; living plant
roślinność (rosh-leen-noshch)
f. flora ; vegetation
rowek (ro-vek) m. (small) channel; groove; gutter; rut;furrow
rower (ró-ver) n. bike; cycle
rowerzysta (ro-ve-zhis-ta) m.
cyclist
rozbawiony (roz-ba-vyó-ni) adj.
m. merry; amused;in high spirits
rozbestwić (roz-bést-veech) v.
enrage;turn into a wild beast
rozbicie (roz-bee-che) n. break;
wreck;jumble;defeat;rout; hurt
rozbić (roz-beech) v. smash;
defeat; wreck;shatter;disrupt
rozbiegać się (roz-byé-gach śhań)
v. scatter; run; swarm (through)
rozbierać (roz-byé-rach) v. undress; strip; dismount; analyze
rozbieżny (roz-byézh-ni) adj. m.
divergent;different;discordant
rozbijać (roz-bee-yach) v. break
up; rout; crush;bluster;storm
rozbiór (róz-byoor) m. 1. analysis; 2. dismemberment;partition
rozbiórka (roz-byoor-ka) f. de-
molition;taking to pieces
rozbitek (roz-bee-tek) m. shipwreck person; castaway; wreck
rozbój (roz-booy) m. robbery;
piracy; banditry;highjacking
rozbójnik (roz-booy-neek) m.
bandit;robber;cutthroat;brigand
rozbrajać (roz-bra-yach) v.
disarm(a person etc.);dismantle
(a ship);appease; pacify

rozbrat (róz-brat) m. split;
disunion;break with somebody
rozbrojenie (roz-bro-ye-ñe) n.
disarmament;reduction of arms
rozbrojeniowy (roz-bro-ye-ñó-vi)
adj. m. disarmament
rozbrzmiewać (roz-bzhmyé-vach)
v. resound;ring out; (re)echo
rozbudowa (roz-boo-dó-va) f.
build up; extension;expansion
rozbudować (roz-boo-dó-vach) v.
extend;eplarge;expand;develop
rozbudzić (roz-boo-dźheech)v.
rouse up; wake up ;excite;stir
rozchmurzyć (roz-khmoó-zhich)
v. clear up; brighten up
rozchodzić (roz-khó-dźheech) v.
1. stretch (shoes); 2. spread;
3. come apart
rozchód (róz-khoot) m. expendi-
ture; expenses; outgoings
rozchwytac (roz-khvi-tach) v.
snatch up;scramble for;sweep off
rozchylać (roz-khi-lach) v.
open; force apart spread
rozciągać (roz-chówn-gach) v.
stretch; extend;widen;expand
rozcieńczyć (roz-cheñ-chich) v.
thin; dilute; rarefy;attenuate
rozcierać (roz-che-rach) v. rub;
grind;crush;spread (ointment)
rozcinać (roz-chee-nach) v.
cut up ; dissect; rip open
rozczarować (roz-cha-ró-vach) v.
disappoint;disenchant
rozczesać (roz-che-sach) v. comb
down;brush out(one's hair)
rozczłonkować (roz-chwon-kó-vach)
v. dismember;divide;break up
rozczulić (roz-choo-leech) v.
move; touch;affect;stir(feelings)
rozczyn (róz-chin) m. solution
(chem.); leaven ( yeast )
rozdać (róz-dach) v. distribute
rozdarcie (roz-dár-che) n.
1. tear; 2. disruption
rozdeptać (roz-dep-tach) v.
trample out under foot;tread on
rozdęcie (roz-dañ-che) n. swelling; inflation;expansion
rozdmuchać (roz-dmoo-khach) v.
fan; inflate;blow about;amplify

rozdrapać (roz-dra-pach) v.
1. scratch; 2. snatch up
rozdrażnić (roz-drazh-ñeech)
v. irritate; exasperate; vex
rozdrobnić (roz-drób-ñeech) v.
split up; divide;crumble;morsel
rozdroże (roz-dró-zhe) n.
crossroads; parting of the ways
rozdwoić (roz-dvó-eech) v.
split; cleave; divide in two
rozdymać (roz-di-mach) v. inflate; swell;expand;puff out
rozdział (róz-dźhaw) m. distribution; disunion; parting
(hair);dispensation;chapter
rozdzielać (roz-dźhe-lach) v.
divide; distribute;set at odds
rozdzierać (roz-dźhe-rach) v.
tear up;tear asunder;rend;pierce
rozdźwięk (róz-dźhvyáñk) m.
discord ;dissonance; clash
rozebrać (ro-zéb-rach) v. undress; analyze; take apart
rozedma (ro-zéd-ma) f. emphy-
sema(swelling produced by gas)
rozejm (ro-zeym) m. truce
rozejrzec się (ro-zéy-zhech
śhań) v. look around
rozejsc się (ro-zeyśhch śhań)
v. split; part; separate
rozerwać się (ro-zér-vach śhań)
v. divert oneself;get torn
rozgałęzić (roz-ga-wañ-źheech)
v. branch out; fork off
rozgałęzienie (roz-ga-wañ-źhe-
ñe) n. branching;ramification
rozgardiasz (roz-gárd-yash) m.
bustle; chaos; confusion
rozgarnąć (roz-gar-nównch) v.
rake aside; part;brush apart
rozgarnięty (roz-gar-ñáñ-ti)
adj. m. bright; clever; sharp
rozglądać się (roz-glówn-dach
śhań) v. look around;look for
rozgłaszać (roz-gwá-shach) v.
make known; broadcast
rozgłos (róz-gwos) m. publicity;
fame; renown;repute;notoriety
rozgłosnia (roz-gwóśh-ña) f.
broadcasting station
rozgmatwać (roz-gmát-vach) v.
disentangle; extricate

rozgnieść (roz-gneśhch) v.
flatten; squash (once)
rozgniatać (roz-gna-tach) v.
squash; flatten (often)
rozgniewać (roz-gńe-vach) v.
anger; vex; irritate
rozgoryczenie (roz-go-ri-che-ńe)
n. bitterness; exasperation
rozgoryczyc (roz-go-ri-chich) v.
embitter; exacerbate;disgust
rozgotowac (roz-go-to-vach) v.
cook to a pulp;cook to rags
rozgraniczyc (roz-gra-ńee-chich)
v. delimit; mark boundaries
rozgromic (roz-gro-meech) v.
rout(the enemy);crush(an army)
rozgrywac (roz-gri-vach) v. play
one's game ;put through;carry out
rozgryzc (roz-grizhch) v. bite
through;bite in two;crack(nuts)
rozgrzac (roz-gzhach) v. warm up
rozgrzebac (roz-gzhe-bach) v.
dig up; rake up; scatter
rozgrzeszyc (roz-gzhe-shich) v.
absolve(of sins); forgive
rozgrzewac (roz-gzhe-vach) v.
warm up; rouse; stimulate
rozhukany (roz-khoo-ka-ni) adj.
m. wild; unruly;riotus
rozhustac (roz-khoosh-tach) v.
set swinging; set rocking
roziskrzyc (roz-eesk-zhich) v.
start sparkle; make sparkle
rozjasnic (roz-yash-ńeech) v.
brighten; clear up; clarify
rozjatrzyc (roz-yownt-zhich) v.
exasperate; irritate; chafe
rozjemca (roz-yem-tsa) m. referee; arbiter; umpire
rozjezdzac sie (roz-yezh-dzhach
shań) v. disperse; part
rozjuszyc (roz-yoo-shich) v.
enrage;infuriate; exasperate
rozkapryszony (roz-ka-pri-sho-
ni) adj. m. whimsical; fitful
rozkaz (roz-kas) m. order
rozkiełznac (roz-kéwz-nach) v.
unbridle; unchain; let loose
rozkleic (roz-kle-eech) v. 1.
unglue; weaken; 2. post up
rozkład (róz-kwat) m. dissolution;
decay; disposition; timetable ;
train schedule;breakdown

rozkładac (roz-kwa-dach) v. decompose; spread; display; stagger (hours);lay out; distribute
rozkołysac (roz-ko-wi-sach) v.
set rocking; set swinging;agitate
rozkopywac (roz-ko-pi-vach) v.
dig up; rip up; make excavations
rozkosz (róz-kosh) f. delight
rozkrajac (roz-kra-yach) v.
cut up; carve; slice; divide
rozkręcic (roz-kran-cheech) v.
unscrew; unreel;take to pieces
rozkruszyc (roz-kroo-shich)
v. crush up; grind;disintegrate
rozkrzewic (roz-kzhe-veech) v.
propagate; increase; diffuse
rozkuc (roz-kooch) v. unshackle;
unshoe (horse);unchain;hammer out
rozkulbaczyc (roz-kool-ba-chich)
v. unsaddle; take the saddle off
rozkupic (roz-koo-peech) v. buy
up; buy everything;buy all
rozkwit (roz-kveet) m. bloom
rozkwitac (roz-kvee-tach) v.
flower; burst into flower;beam
rozlatywac sie (roz-la-ti-vach
shań) v. fly away; break up;
scatter;disperse;run away;burst
rozlazły (roz-laz-wi) adj. m.
slack; loose;spread out;sloppy
rozległy (roz-leg-wi) adj. m.
spacious; vast; wide;extensive
rozleniwiac (roz-le-ńeev-yach)
v. make lazy;induce to laziness
rozlepic (roz-le-peech) v. post;
put up;paste up;stick;unstick
rozlew (roz-lev) m. flood
rozlew krwi (roz-lev krvee) m.
bloodshed;killing; slaughter
rozlewac (roz-le-vach) v. spill;
shed; pour(out);ladle out(soup)
rozliczenie (roz-lee-che-ńe) n.
settling; reckoning;settlement
rozliczny (roz-leech-ni) adj.
m. manifold; diverse;numerous
rozliczyc (roz-lee-chich) v.
settle up (accounts);calculate
rozlokowac (roz-lo-ko-vach) v.
put up; make at home; quarter
rozlosowac (roz-lo-so-vach) v.
allot; distribute by lot
rozluźnic (roz-loozh-ńeech) v.
**slacken; relax**;unfasten

rozluźnienie (roz-loozh-ńe-ńe)
n. loosening;laxity;slackness
rozładować (roz-wa-do-vach) v.
unload; discharge(a battery)
rozłam (róz-wam) m. breach;
split;break;division;dissent
rozłamac (roz-wa-mach) v.
break (in two); split
rozłazic się (roz-wa-zheech
shań) v. fall apart; disperse
rozłączenie (roz-wown-che-ńe)
n. separation; disjunction
rozłączyc (roz-wown-chich) v.
disconnect;sever;uncouple
rozłąka (roz-wown-ka) f. separation (of people)
rozłożyc (roz-wó-zhich) v.
spread;lay out;disassemble
rozłupac (roz-woo-pach) v.
split; cleave; rift; slit;
crack(nuts,etc.); rive
rozmach (róz-makh) m. impetus;
dash; grand style ;force;swing
rozmaitosci (roz-ma-ee-tosh-
chee) pl. miscellanea; vaude-
ville theater;variety theater
rozmaity (roz-ma-ee-ti) adj.
m. various; miscellaneous
rozmaryn (roz-má-rin) m. rosemary (Rosmarinus)
rozmarzenie (roz-ma-zhe-ńe) n.
daydream;dreaminess;reverie
rozmawiac (roz-máv-yach) v.
converse; talk; speak with
rozmazac (roz-má-zach) v. blur;
smear;daub; let out (a secret)
rozmiar (róz-myar) m. dimension;
extent;size;proportion;scale
rozmienic (roz-mye-ńeech) v.
change (money);get the change
rozmieszczac (roz-myesh-chach)
v. arrange; dispose;place;put
rozmieszczenie (roz-myesh-che-
ńe) n. distribution; layout
rozmiękczyc (roz-myank-chich) v.
soften; soak;steep;make soft
rozmięknąc (roz-myank-nownch)
v. become soft ;get soaked;sop
rozmijac się (roz-mee-yach shań)
v. miss; swerve from;fail to meet
rozmiłowac się (roz-mee-wo-vach
shań) v. take a liking to

rozminąc się(roz-mee-nownch shań)v.
miss (on road):pass each other
rozmnazac (roz-mna-zhach) v.breed;
multiply; propagate; imcrease
rozmoczyc (roz-mó-chich) v.soak;
steep; wet thoroughly; sodden
rozmoknąc (roz-mók-nownch) v.
become soaked; get soggy
rozmowa (roz-mo-va) f. conversation; talk ;discourse
rozmowny (roz-mov-ni) adj. m.
communicative; talkative
rozmówca (roz-moóv-tsa) m.
interlocutor (in conversation)
rozmówic się (roz-moo-veech
shań) v. talk over;get understood
rozmysł (róz-misw) m. premeditation; consideration; intention
rozmyslac (roz-mish-lach) v.
meditate; ponder how to do
rozmyslanie (roz-mish-la-ńe) n.
meditation; contemplation
rozmyslic się (roz-miśh-leech
shań), v. change one's mind
rozmyslny (roz-miśhl-ni) adj.
m. deliberate;intentional;wilful
roznamiętnic (roz-na-myańt-
ńeech) v. impassion; excite
rozniecic (roz-ńe-cheech) v.
inflame; enkindle a fire;inspire
roznosic (roz-no-sheech) v.
carry around; serve;rout;cut up
rozochocic (roz-o-kho-cheech)
v. make merry;enliven; animate
rozogniac się (roz-og-ńach
shań) n. inflame; excite;flare up
rozpacz (róz-pach) f. despair
rozpad (róz-pat) m. decay;break up
rozpakowac (roz-pa-ko-vach) v.
unpack(one's luggage);unwrap
rozpalic (roz-pa-leech) v.fire up;
ignite; start a fire; set ablaze
rozpamiętywac (roz-pa-myań-ti-
vach) v. contemplate ;reflect upon
rozpaplac (roz-pa-plach) v.
blab out;divulge ; babble out
rozpasany (roz-pa-sá-ni) adj. m.
unbridled; dissolute; licentious
rozpatrywac (roz-pa-tri-vach)
v. consider; act upon ;examine
rozpęd (róz-pańt) m. impetus;
dash ;momentum; taking a run

rozpędzać (roz-pán-dzać) v. pick
up speed; scatter;disperse
rozpętać (roz-pán-tać) v. unshackle; unleash;let loose
rozpiąć (róz-pyówńch) v. unbuckle; undo; stretch; set (sail)
rozpieczętować (roz-pye-chán-
to-vać), v. unseal;open
rozpierać (roz-pyé-rać) v. expand; extend; push aside,
rozpierzchnąc się (roz-pyezh-
khówńch shán) v. scatter
rozpieszczać (roz-pyésh-chać)
v. pamper; spoil;coddle up
rozpiętosc (roz-pyáń-toshch) f.
span; spread; range;strech
rozpinać (roz-peé-nach) v. unbutton; stretch; spread (sails etc.)
rozplątac (roz-plówn-tach) v.
untangle;untie(a knot);unravel
rozplesc (róz-leshch) v. unbraid;
untwine; unplait(hair);unravel
rozpłakać się (roz-pwa-kach shán)
v. burst into tears;start weeping
rozpłaszczyc (roz-pwash-chich) v.
flatten out; flat (metal)
rozpłatać (roz-pwa-tach) v.slit;
split; cleave; split in two
rozpłodowy (roz-pwo-do-vi) adj.
m. (for) breeding; breeding-
rozpłodzić (roz-pwó-dżheech) v.
propagate;cause reproduction
rozpłod (róz-pwoot) m. propagation; reproduction
rozpływać się(roz-pwi-vach shán)v.
melt away;dissolve; flow;spread
rozpoczęcie (roz-po-chán-che) n.
start; outbreak;beginning;start
rozpoczynac (roz-po-chi-nach) v.
begin; start going; open;initiate
rozpogodzić się (roz-po-go-
dżheech shán) v. clear up
brighten up;cheer up;rise spirit
rozporek (roz-po-rek) m. fly; slit
rozporządząc (roz-po-zhówn-dzach)
v. dispose; decree; order;control
rozposcierac (roz-posh-che-rach)
v. unfurl; spread out;expand
rozpowiadac (roz-po-vya-dach) v.
tell tales;divulge; talk about
rozpowszechniac (roz-pov-shekh-
ńach) v. widespread; diffuse
disseminte;propagate; spread

rozpowszechnienie (roz-pov-
shekh-ńe-ńe) n. propagation;
spread;diffusion;prevalence
rozpoznac (roz-póz-nach) v.
recognize; spot; diagnose
rozpoznanie (roz-po-zná-ńe) n.
diagnosis; identification;
reconnaissance;recognition
rozpoznawczy (roz-poz-náv-chi)
adj. m. diagnostic;distinctive
rozpraszać (roz-pra-shach) v.
scatter; dispel; distract;disperse
rozprawa (roz-prá-va) f. trial;
showdown; dissertation; debate
rozprawiac (roz-práv-yach) v.
debate: argue; dispute; reason; talk at length;discuss
rozprawic się (roz-pra-veech
shán) v. settle matters;
fight out;dispose of; floor
rozprężyc (roz-prán-zhich) v.
distend; expand; dilate; re-
sile;deprive of elasticity
rozprostowac (roz-pros-to-vach)
v. straighten;unbend;stretch(legs)
rozproszyc (roz-pró-shich) v.
disperse;scatter;dispel;distract
rozprowadzic (roz-pro-va-
dżheech) v. spread; retail;
distribute; dilute; convey;smear
rozpruc (róz-prooch) v. rip up;
open; unsew;unravel;rip open
rozprzedać (roz-pzhe-dach) v.
sell out;sell(successively)
rozprzedaż (roz-pzhe-dash) f.
sale;complete sale;retailing
rozprzestrzenic (roz-pzhe-
stzhe-ńeech) v. spread;propagate
rozprzegać (roz-pzhán-gach) v.
1. unhitch; 2. disorganize
rozprzężenie (roz-pzhań-zhe-ńe)
n. anarchy; demoralization
rozpusta (roz-poós-ta) f. debauch; riot; libertinism
rozpustnica (roz-poost-ńee-tsa)
f. rake; rip; libertine; debauchee; profligate; libertine
rozpustnik (roz-poost-ńeek) m.
libertine; debauchee; rake;
profligate;rip; reprobate
rozpuszczac (roz-poosh-chach)
v. dissolve; dismiss; let go;
disband;thaw;melt;defrost;unfreeze

rozpuszczalnik (roz-poos'-chál-ñeek) m. solvent;paii iipner
rozpuszczalny (roz-poosu-ch^l-ni) adj. m. soluble;dissolvuble
rozpychać się (roz-pí-khach sháñ) v.shove aside; jostle; elbow one's way;push one's way
rozpylacz (roz-pí-lach) m. sprayer; nozzle; atomizer
rozpylać (roz-pí-lach) v. spray; pulverize; atomize
rozpytywać (roz-pi-ti-vach) v. ask for;inquire for ask questions
rozrachować (roz-ra-kho-vach) v. settle accounts; calculate
rozrachunek (roz-ra-khóo-nek) m. squaring up accounts
rozradzac się (roz-ra-dzach sháñ) v. breed;propagate
rozrastac się (roz-ras-tach shan) v. grow larger; increase; develop; expand
rozrąbać (roz-równ-bach) v. cut asunder; hew apart;chop up
rozrobic (roz-ro-beech) v. stir up; dilute;scheme;intrigue;brawl
rozrodczość (roz-rod-choshch) f. reproduction;reproductiveness
rozróżniać (roz-roozh-ñach) v. distinguish; tell apart;discern
rozruchy (roz-róo-khy) pl. riots; disturbances
rozruszac (roz-roo-shach) v. start up; stir up; put in motion;set in motion;animate
rozrywać (roz-ri-vach) v. burst; disrupt;tear open;entertain
rozrywka (roz-riv-ka) f. amusement; recreation; pastime
rozrządnica (roz-zhównd-ñee-tsa) f. control panel
rozrzedzić (roz-zhe-dzheech) v. dilute; rarefy;thin down;weaken
rozrzewnic (roz-zhev-ñeech) v. move; touch;affect;stir(the soul)
rozrzucac (roz-zhoo-tsach) v. scatter; squander ;distribute
rozrzutność (roz-zhoot-noshch) f. extravagance;lavishness
rozrzutny (roz-zhoot-ni) adj. m. wasteful; extravagant; thriftless;squandering;prodigal; spendthrift; lavish

rozsada (roz-sá-da) f. seedling; seedlings
rozsadzac (roz-sa-dzach) v. space-out;place; seat separately; blow up;explode;split
rozsądek (roz-sówn-dek) m. good sense; discretion;reason
rozsądny (roz-sównd-ni) adj. m. sensible; reasonable; advisable;sound;judicious
rozsiadać się (roz-sha-dach shan)v. sit stretched; sprawl round
rozsiekać (roz-she-kach) v. cut up; slash asunder; hack up
rozsiewac (roz-she-vach) v. saw; disseminate;spread;shed
rozsiodłać (roz-shod-wach) v. unsaddle;take the saddle off
rozsławiac (roz-swav-yach) v. glorify; make famous; extol
rozstac się (roz-stach sháñ) v. part; give up; part with
rozstanie (roz-sta-ñe) n. parting; separation
rozstawać sie (roz-sta-vach sháñ) v. part with; give up
rozstawiac (roz-stav-yach) v. disperse; place apart; space; spread;put at intervals
rozstąpic się(roz-stówn-peech sháñ) v. step aside;come apart;split
rozstęp (róz-stanp) m. gap; space; slit;interval;heave
rozstroic (roz-stro-eech) v. put out of tune; upset; disarray;derange;disorder; untune
rozstroj (róz-strooy) m. upset; disorder;confusion;derangement
rozstrzelać (roz-stzhe-lach) v. 1. scatter; 2. execute by shooting;put before a firing squad
rozstrzygac (roz-stzhi-gach) v. try out; decide; fight out; judge
rozstrzygnięcie (roz-stzhig-nan-che) v. decision; settlement
rozsuwac (roz-soo-vach) v. part; draw aside;separate;expand(a compas)
rozsyłać (roz-si-wach) v. distribute; circulate; send out
rozsypać (roz-sí-pach) v. disperse(a granular substance);spill
rozszarpac (roz-shar-pach) v. tear up; claw; disjoin;mangle

rozszczepiać (roz-shchep-yaćh)
v. split; cleave; fissure
rozszczepienie (roz-shche-pye-
ńe) n. split; diffraction
rozszerzać (roz-she-zhaćh) v.
widen; broaden; enlarge; expand;spread out;extend;open
rozszerzenie (roz-she-zhe-ńe)
n. enlargement; dilation
rozsznurować (roz-shnoo-ro-
vaćh) v. unlace;loosen the lace
rozszyfrować (roz-shif-ro-vaćh)
v. decode; break the code
rozścielać (roz-shćhe-laćh) v.
spread; make the bed
rozśmieszać (roz-shmyé-shaćh) v.
amuse; make laugh;be amusing
rozświecić (roz-shvye-ćheećh) v.
light up;throw light on;shine on
roztaczać (roz-ta-chaćh) v. roll
out; spread;unfold;display;bore
roztajać (roz-ta-yaćh) v. thaw
roztapiać (roz-táp-yaćh) v.
melt; smelt(metal);thaw (ice)
roztargać (roz-tár-gaćh) v.
tear to pieces;ruffle;dishevel
roztargniony (roz-targ-ńo-ni)
adj. m. absentminded ; distracted; scatterbrained ; far-away
rozterka (roz-tér-ka) f. tearing
between; dissension;suspense
roztkliwiać (roz-tkleé-vyaćh) v.
feel for; touch; move;stir
roztłuc (róz-twoots) v. smash up
roztopy (roz-tó-pi) pl. thaw
roztratować (roz-tra-tó-vaćh)
v.run over; trample; tread
under foot;trample to death
roztrąbić (roz-trówn-beećh) v.
broadcast; blaze abroad
roztrącić (roz-trówn-ćheećh) v.
push aside;elbow;part;jostle
roztropność (roz-tróp-noshćh) f.
prudence; thoughtfulness
roztropny (roz-tróp-ni) adj. m.
wise;cautious;circumspect;politic
roztrwonić (roz-trvo-ńeećh) v.
squander(a fortune,money etc.)
roztrzaskać (roz-tzhás-kaćh) v.
smash; shatter; crash to pieces
roztrzepanie (roz-tzhe-pá-ńe) n.
scatterbrain; fickleness

roztrzepany (roz-tzhe-pá-ni)
adj. m. scatterbrain; giddy
roztwór (róz-tvoor) m.(chem.)
solution(colloidal,molal etc.)
roztyć się (róz-tićh shán) v.
grow fat; become fat
rozum (ró-zoom) m. mind; reason; intellect; understanding;
wit;senses; judgment; brains
rozumieć (ro-zoom-yećh) v.
understand; get; perceive
rozumny (ro-zoom-ni) adj. m.
rational; reasonable; wise
rozumować (ro-zoo-mó-vaćh) v.
reason; argue
rozwaga (roz-va-ga) f. thoughtfulness; prudence; reflection;
deliberation; consideration
rozwalać (roz-va-laćh) v. shatter; demolish; smash; sprawl
rozwarty kąt (roz-vár-ti kównt)
m. obtuse angle
rozważać (roz-vá-zhaćh) v.
1. weigh out; 2. consider
rozweselić (roz-ve-sé-leećh) v.
cheer up; put in good humor
rozwiać (róz-vyaćh) v. blow
away; blow to and fro;scatter
rozwiązać (roz-vyówn-zaćh) v.
untie; solve; undo; dissolve;
loosen; unbind; unravel; undo
rozwiązanie (roz-vyówn-zá-ńe)
n. solution; way out; (child)
delivery; realization;execution
rozwiązły (roz-vyównz-wi) adj.
m. fast; dissolute;debauched
rozwidniać (roz-veéd-ńaćh) v.
dawn; be lit up;become lit up
rozwiedziony (roz-vye-dźho-ni)
adj. m. divorced(f .divorcee)
rozwierać (roz-vye-raćh) v.
open wide; fling open
rozwieszać (roz-vyé-shaćh) v.
hang about;stretch; spread out
rozwieść się (róz-vyeshćh shán)
v. divorce; dwell upon
rozwijać (roz-veé-yaćh) v. unwrap; unfold; develop; spread
rozwikłać (roz-veék-waćh) v.
disentangle; unravel; clear up
rozwikłanie (roz-veek-wá-ńe) n.
unraveling; disentanglement

rozwlekać (roz-vle-kach) v.
drag out; protract; spread
rozwlekły (roz-vlek-wi) adj. m.
verbose; lengthy; long-spun
rozwodnić (roz-vod-neech) v.
dilute;water down; weaken
rozwodnik (roz-vod-neek) m. divorced man; divorcee
rozwodowy (roz-vo-do-vi) adj. m.
divorce-(proceedings etc.)
rozwodzic (roz-vo-dzheech) v.
divorce(a married couple)
rozwojowy (roz-vo-yo-vi) adj.
evolutional; developmental
rozwolnienie (roz-vol-ne-ne) n.
diarrhea;lax bowels;open bowels
rozwozic (roz-vo-zheech) v.
transport; deliver (mail etc.)
rozwod (roz-vood) m. divorce
rozwodka (roz-vood-ka) f. divorcee; divorced woman
rozwoj (roz-vooy) m. development; evolution; growth
rozwscieczony (roz-vshche-cho-
ni) adj. m. enraged; furious
rozwydrzony (roz-vid-zho-ni)
adj. m. rampant; wild;lawless
rozzłościć (roz-zwosh-cheech)
v. irritate; make angry;provoke
rozżalenie (roz-zha-le-ne) n.
grudge; resentment;bitterness
rozzarzyc (roz-zha-zhich) v.
inflame; set on fire; fire
rożek (ro-zhek) m. small horn;
croissant;small corner
rozen (ro-zhen) m. roasting spit
rod (rood) m. clan; breed; family; stock;race;origin; line
rog (roog) m. horn; corner; bugle;antler; corner kick(sport)
roj (rooy) m. swarm;hive;cluster
rosc (rooshch) v. grow;age;go up
row (roov) m. ditch;trench;trough
rowiesnik (roo-vyesh-neek) m.
peer of same age;contemporary
rownac (roov-nach) v. equalize;
level; make even; smooth out
rownanie (roov-na-ne) n. equation ;equalization;comparison
rownia (roov-na) f. plane; level
rownie (roov-ne) adv. equally
rowniez (roov-nesh) conj. also;
too; likewise; as well

rownik (roov-neek) m. equator
rownina (roov-nee-na) f.plain;
flat country; level landscape
rowno (roov-no) adv. even;(equi-)
rownoboczny (roov-no-boch-ni)
adj. m. equilateral
rownoczesny (roov-no-ches-ni)
adj. m. simultaneous
rownoległobok (roov-no-leg-wo-
bok) m. parallelogram
rownoległy (roov-no-leg-wi) adj.
m. parallel to;collateral
rownoleznik (roov-no-lezh-neek)
m. parallel(of latitude)
rownomierny (roov-no-myer-ni)
adj. m. even; uniform;steady
rownoramienny (roov-no-ra-myen-
ni) adj. m. isosceles(triangle)
rownorzedny (roov-no-zhand-ni)
adj. m.equal rank;equivalent
rownosc (roov-noshch) f. equality ; parity; identity
rownouprawnienie (roov-no-oo-
prav-ne-ne) n. equality of
rights(of women,men etc.)
rownowaga (roov-no-va-ga) f.
equilibrium; balance ; poise
rownowartosciowy (roov-no-var-
tosh-cho-vi) adj. m. equivalent; equipollent
rownowazny (roov-no-vazh-ni)
adj. m. equivalent;equiponderant
rownowazyc (roov-no-vazhich)
v. balance; equalize; even up
rownoznaczny (roov-no-znach-ni)
adj. m. synonymous;tantamount
rozga (rooz-ga) f. switch; cane
roz (roozh) m. rouge ; pink
roza (roo-zha) f. rose(flower etc.)
rozaniec (roo-zha-nets) m. ro-
sary;beads;telling one's beads
rozdzka (roozhdzh-ka) f. dowsing
rod ; twig;divining rod(or wand)
roznica (roozh-nee-tsa) f. difference ; disparity; dissent
rozniczka (roozh-neech-ka) f.
differential;small difference
roznic sie (roozh-neech shan) v.
differ ; be at variance
roznobarwny (roozh-no-barv-ni)
adj. m.many colored ; motley
roznojęzyczny (roozh-no-yan-
zich-ni) adj. m. many-tongued

różnolity (roozh-no-lee-ti)
adj. m. diverse ; varied
różnorodny (roozh-no-rod-ni)
adj. m. heterogeneous ;varied
różnoznaczny (roozh-no-znach-
ni) adj. m. ambiguous
różny (roozh-ni) adj. m. different miscellaneous;sundry
różowy (roo-zho-vi) adj. m.
pink; rosy ; ruddy ;rose color
rtęciowy (rtań-cho-vi) adj.m.
mercuric(compounds etc.)
rtęc (rtańch) f. mercury
rubaszny (roo-bash-ni) adj. m.
coarse ; ill-mannered
rubin (roo-been) m. ruby (red)
rubryka (roo-bri-ka) f. space;
column;blank space; rubric
ruch (rookh) m. move; movement;
traffic; motion; gesture stir
ruchawka (roo-khav-ka) f. riot
ruchliwy (rookh-lee-vi) adj.m.
busy; mobile; agile;active
ruchomości (roo-kho-mosh-chee)
pl. movables (personal property);belongings;(one's things)
ruchomy (roo-kho-mi) adj. m.
mobile ;moving; shifting flexile
ruczaj (roo-chay) m. brook
ruda (roo-da) f. ore(metallic)
rudera (roo-de-ra) f. run-down
house ; shanty; ruin ;hovel
rudy (roo-di) adj. m. red(haired);russet;ginger;foxy;ruddy
rufa (roo-fa) f. stern ;poop
rugować (roo-go-vach) v. eject;
oust; evict; eliminate ;displace
ruina (roo-ee-na) f. ruin;wreck
ruja (roo-ya) f. heat; rut
rujnować (rooy-no-vach) v.
ruin; undo; destroy ;wreck
ruleta (roo-le-ta) f. roulette
rulon (roo-lon) m. roll;rouleau
rum ( room) m. rum (drink)
rumak (roo-mak) m. charger;
steed; palfrey; courser
rumianek (roo-mya-nek) m. camomile ; chamonile(tea)
rumiany (roo-mya-ni) adj. m.
rosy ; ruddy; browned;florid
rumienić (roo-mye-neech) v.
blush; brown; redden;color
rumieniec (roo-mye-ńets) m.
blush; ruddiness; floridity

rumor (roo-mor) m. racket; uproar; rumble; clatter; din
rumowisko (roo-mo-vees-ko) n.
debris ; rubble; brash
rumuński (roo-moon-skee) adj.
m. Rumanian ;of Rumania
runąc (roo-nownch) v. fall down;
collapse; crash; swoop;resound
runda (roon-da) f. bout; round;
lap; fall (in wrestling)
runo (roo-no) n. fleece; nap
rupiecie (roo-pye-che) n. rubbish; trash; junk; stuff;oddments
ruptura (roop-too-ra) f. hernia
rura (roo-ra) f. tube; pipe
rurka (roor-ka) f. small pipe
rurociąg (roo-ro-chowng) m.
pipeline ;run of pipes;piping
rusałka (roo-saw-ka) f. undine;
naiad;water nymph; vanessa
ruszac (roo-shach) v. move; stir;
touch; start;take away;withdraw
rusznikarz (roosh-nee-kash) m.
gunsmith (man or shop)
rusztowanie (roosh-to-va-ńe) n.
scaffold ; cradle (hanging)
rutyna (roo-ti-na) f. routine
rutynowany (roo-ti-no-va-ni)
adj. m. experienced;conpetent
rwać (rvach) v. pluck; tear;
pull out; pull up; rush ;burst
rwący (rvown-tsy) adj. m. rapid;
racking (pain);swift flowing
rwetes (rve-tes) m. bustle; ado;
racket ; turmoil ;agitation; stir
ryba (ri-ba) f. fish; the Fish
rybak (ri-bak) m. fisherman
rybny staw (rib-ni stav) fish
pond (artficially made)
rybołostwo (ri-bo-woos-tvo) n.
fishery; fishing
rycerski (ri-tser-skee) adj. m.
chivalrous ; courteous
rycerz (ri-tsesh) m. knight
rychło (rikh-wo) adv. soon;
quickly; early; soon after
rychły (rikh-wi) adj. m. speedy;
quick; early; prompt;approaching
rycina (ri-chee-na) f. engraving;
illustration;cartoon;drawing;plate
rycynus (ri-tsi-noos) m. castor
oil; castor oil plant
ryczałt (ri-chawt) m. lump sum;
global sum

ryczec (ri-chech) v. roar; moo;
bellow;low;growl;bray;hoot;yell
ryc (rich) v. dig; root: engrave;
carve;excavate;burrow;plough
rydel (ri-del) m. spade; spud
rydwan (rid-van) m. chariot
rygiel (ri-gel) m. bolt;bar;lock
rygor (ri-gor) m. rigor;severity
ryj (riy) m. snout;phiz;mug(vulg.)
ryk (rik) m. roar;moo;low;yell
rylec (ri-lets) m. burin; graver;
chisel; etching- needle;dry point
rym (rim) m. rhyme;rhyme word
rymarz (ri-mash) m. saddler
rymowac (ri-mo-vach) v. rhyme
rynek (ri-nek) m. market(square)
rynna (rin-na) f. gutter; chute
rynsztok (rin-shtok) m. sewer
rynsztunek (rin-shtoo-nek) m.
armor; armature; outfit ; kit
rys (ris) m. feature; trait
rysa (ri-sa) f.crack; flow; fissure;scratch;rift;crevice;chink
rysopis (ri-so-pees) m. descrip-
tion(of a person for a passport)
rysowac (ri-so-vach) v. draw;
design; sketch;draft;trace;show
rysownica (ri-sov-nee-tsa) f.
drawing board;drafting table
rysownik (ri-sov-neek) m. draftsman; illustrator; designer
rysunek (ri-soo-nek) m. sketch;
drawing ; draft; outline ;cartoon
rysunkowy (ri-soon-ko-vi) adj.m.
tracing; drawing; cartoon;drawn
rys (rish) m . lynx
rytm (ritm) m. rhythm ;cadence
rytmiczny (rit-meech-ni) adj. m.
rhythmic;regular; measured
rytownictwo (ri-tov-neets-tvo)
n. engraving; die sinking
rytownik (ri-tov-neek) m. engraver; die sinker
rytuał (ri-too-aw) m. ritual
rywal (ri-val) m. rival;contestant
rywalizacja (ri-va-lee-zats-ya)
f. rivalry;competition;emulation
ryza (ri-za) f. ream; restraint
ryzyko (ri-zi-ko) n. risk;venture
ryzykowac (ri-zi-ko-vach) v.
risk; venture; gamble; hazard
ryzykowny (ri-zi-kov-ni) adj.m.
risky; hazardous;venturesome

ryż (rizh) m. rice
ryży (ri-zhi) adj. m. red (haired);russet;ginger;foxy;red-brown
rzadki (zhad-kee) adj. m. rare;thin
rzadko (zhad-ko) adv. seldom;thinly
rarely;far apart;exceptionally
rzadkosc (zhad-koshch) f. rarity;sparseness;curiosity; curio
rząd (zhownt) m. row; rank;
file; line up; government
rządca (zhownd-tsa) f. administrator; ruler;land steward
rządowy (zhown-do-vi) adj. m.
governmental;government-;state-
rządzic (zhown-dzheech) v. rule;
govern; control; direct;be in power
rzec (zhets) v. say; utter.
rzecz (zhech) f. thing; matter; act;
stuff; deal ; work; subject;theme
rzeczka (zhech-ka) f. small river;
river; brook; stream
rzecznik (zhech-neek) m. spokesman; attorney ; patent agent
rzeczownik (zhech-ov-neek) m.
noun; substantive (grammar)
rzeczowo (zhe-cho-vo) adv.
factually; terse; business
like ; to the point ;objectively
rzeczoznawca (zhe-cho-znav-tsa)
m. expert;specialist(authority)
rzeczpospolita (zhech-pos-po-
lee-ta) f. republik; commonwealth
rzeczywistosc (zhe-chi-vees-
toshch) f. reality;actuality
rzeczywisty (zhe-chi-vees-ti)
adj. m. real; actual; virtual
rzedniec (zhed-nech) v. grow
thin; become rare;scatter;thin
rzeka (zhe-ka) f. river; stream
rzekomo (zhe-ko-mo) adv. would
be; allegedly ; supposedly ;ostensibly
rzekomy (zhe-ko-mi) adj.m.make
believe; reputed; supposed;
sham; alleged; immaginary;so called
rzemien (zhe-myen) m. leather
strap; leather band; leather belt
rzemieslniczy (zhe-myeshl-nee-
chi) adj. m. trade; craft-
rzemieslnik (zhe-myeshl-neek)
m. artisan; craftsman;tradesman
rzemiosło (zhe-myos-vo) n. (handi)
craft;trade;job;business

rzemyk (zhe-mik) m. small leather
strap ;chin strap; thong
rzepa (zhe-pa) f. turnip
rzepak (zhe-pak) m. rapeseed;cole
rzesza (zhe-sha) f. crowd; Reich
rzeszoto (zhe-sho-to) n. sieve
rzeski (zhesh-kee) adj. m. lively; brisk ; spry; fresh;brisk
rzeskosc (zhesh-koshch) f. vigor
rzetelny (zhe-tel-ni) adj. m.
honest; upright ; fair; real
rzewny (zhev-ni) adj. m. wistful
rzezac (zhe-zach) v. slaughter;
castrate ; circumcise
rzezimieszek (zhe-zhee-mye-shek)
m. cutpurse; thief; pickpocket
rzez (zhezh) f. carnage; massacre;slaughter ; shambles;carnage
rzezba (zhezh-ba) f. sculpture
rzezbiarstwo (zhezh-byar-stvo)
n. sculpture; sculpturing
rzezbiarz (zhezh-byash) m. sculptor;artist creating sculptures
rzezbic (zhezh-beech) v. carve;
cut;sculpture;weather(the earth)
rzeznia (zhezh-na) f. slaughter-
house
rzeznik (zhezh-neek) m. butcher
rzezwic (zhezh-veech) v. refresh
rzezwosc (zhezh-voshch) f. agil-
ity; briskness;sprightliness
rzezwy (zhezh-vi) adj. m. agile;
brisk; smart;spry;lively;bracing
rzezaczka (zhe-zhownch-ka) f.
gonorrhea
rzedem (zhan-dem) adv. in a row
rzedna (zhand-na) f. ordinate
rzepolic (zhan-po-leech) v.
scrape (on fiddle);rasp(the fiddle)
rzesa (zhan-sa) f. eyelash
rzesisty (zhan-shees-ti) adj. m.
profuse; heavy; abundant;copious
rzezic (zhan-zheech) v. death
rattle ; ruckle (in sickness)
rznac (zhnownch) v. cut,carve;
butcher; vulg.:screw;have sex
rzodkiew (zhod-kev) f. radish
rzodkiewka (zhod-kev-ka) f. rad-
ish(the pungent root eaten raw)
rzucac (zhoo-tsach) v. throw;
fling; pitch; dash;hurl; toss
rzucic (zhoo-cheech) v. throw;
cast; plunge; dash; pitch; fling

rzut (zhoot) m. throw; cast;
projection; view; sketch
rzutki (zhoot-kee) adj. m.
brisk; lively; enterprising
rzutkosc (zhoot-koshch) f.
briskness; initiative
rzyc (zhich) f. (vulg.) ass
rzygac (zhi-gach) v. vomit;
belch; spew; eject;emit
rzymski (zhim-skee) adj. m.
Roman; of Rome(church;rite)
rzec (rzhech) v. whinny; neigh
rznac (rzhnownch) v. cut; saw;
engrave; carve; butcher; bang;
play cards; (vulg.): screw
rzniecie (rzhnan-che) n. colic;
bellyache; (slang): beating
rzysko (rzhis-ko) n. stubble-
field; rye field
sabat (sa-bat) m, Sabbath
sabotaz (sa-bo-tash) m. sabotage; act of sabotage
sacharyna (sa-kha-ri-na) f.
saccharine
sad (sad) m. orchard
sadlo (sad-wo) n. leaflard
sadowic (sa-do-veech) v. place;
show to a seat; seat
sadownik (sa-dov-neek) m. fruit-
grower;fruit farmer; orchardist
sadyba (sa-di-ba) f. dwelling ;
house; human habitation; home
sadysta (sa-dis-ta) m. sadist
sadza (sa-dza) f. soot; black
sadzac (sa-dzach) v. show to
a seat; seat;make sit down
sadzawka (sa-dzav-ka) f. pool
sadzic (sa-dzheech) v. plant;
set; run; speed ;stud(decorate)
sadzonka (sa-dzon-ka) f. seedling; quickset; cutting
sadzonejajka (sa-dzo-ne yay-ka)
s. fried eggs sunny side up
safandula (sa-fan-doo-wa) f.
bungler; yes-man; oaf;muff;duffer
safian (sa-fyan) m. morocco
(lather); saffian
sagan (sa-gan) m. kettle ;pot
sak (sak) m. dipnet; sack
sakrament (sa-kra-ment) m. sacrament (of matrimony etc.)
sakwa (sak-va) f. wallet;purse
money-bag; feed-bag ;nose bag

sala (sá-la) f. 1. hall; 2. audience (in a hall)
salaterka (sa-la-tér-ka) f. salad bowl; vegetable dish
salceson (sal-tsé-son) m. headcheese; (mock)brawn
saletra (sa-lét-ra) f. niter; saltpeter;potassium nitrate
salina (sa-leé-na) f. saltworks; saline; salt mine
salmiak (sal-myak) m. ammoniumchloride; sal-ammoniac
salon (sá-lon) m. drawing-room
salonka (sa-lón-ka) f. club car (railroad);parlor car
salutować (sa-loo-tó-vach) v. salute; dip the flag
salwa (sál-va) f. volley;salvo
sałata (sa-wá-ta) f. 1. lettuce; salad; 2. cabman(slang)
sam (sam) adj. m. alone; oneself; myself; yourself; nothing but
samica (sa-meé-tsa) f. female
samiec (sam-yets) m. male
samobójca (sa-mo-boóy-tsa) m. suicide; suicidal man
samobójczy (sa-mo-boóy-chi) adj. m. suicidal;leading to suicide
samobójstwo (sa-mo-boóy-stvo) n. suicide;act of killing oneself
samochód (sa-mó-khood) m. automobile; car;motor car
samochwał (sa-mo-khvaw) m. braggart; boaster; blow hard
samodział (sa-mó-dżhaw) m. homespun (cloth)
samodzielność (sa-mo-dżhél-noshch) f. independence
samodzielny (sa-mo-dżhél-ni) adj. m.self-reliant; independent: self-contained
samogłoska (sa-mo-gwos-ka) f. vowel; vocal
samogon (sa-mó-gon) m. moonshine
samoistny (sa-mo-eést-ni) adj. m. independent;autonomous
samokrytyka (sa-mo-kri-ti-ka) f. self-criticism;self-accusation
samokształcenie (sa-mo-kshtaw-tsé-ńe) n. self-education
samolot (sa-mó-lot) m. airplane
samolub (sa-mó-loob) m. egoist

samolubstwo (sa-mo-loób-stvo) n . selfishness ; egoism
samolubny (sa-mo-loób-ni) adj. m. selfish; self-seeking;egoistic
samoobrona (sa-mo-o-bró-na) f. self-defense
samopas (sa-mó-pas) adv. alone; by oneself; loosely; unheeded
samopoczucie (sa-mo-po-choo-che) n. frame of mind; feeling
samopomoc (sa-mo-pó-mots) f. self-help; mutual aid (society)
samorodek (sa-mo-ró-dek) m. (gold) nugget
samorodny (sa-mo-ród-ni) adj. m. autogenous; natural; virgin
samorząd (sa-mo-zhownt) m. autonomy; self-government
samotnik (sa-mót-ńeek) m. recluse; hermit;solitary;rogue
samostanowienie (sa-mo-sta-no-vyé-ńe) n. self-determination
samotność (sa-mót-noshch) f. solitude; loneliness
samouctwo (sa-mo-oóts-tvo) n. self-education;self instruction
samouczek (sa-moo-oó-tchek) m. handbook (for self-instruction)
samouk (sa-mo--ook) m. self-taught (man);self taught person
samowładczy (sa-mo-vwád-chi) adj. m. autocratic; arbitrary
samowola (sa-mo-vó-la) f. license (arbitrariness);lawlessness
samowystarczalny (sa-mo-vis-tar-chál-ni) adj. m. self-sufficient;self contained;unsubsidized
samozachowawczy instynkt (sa-mo-za-kho-váv-chi eén-stinkt) m. self-preservation instinct
samozapalenie się (sa-mo-za-pa-lé-ńe shäń) n. spontaneous combustion; self ignition
samozwaniec (sa-mo-zva-nets) m. usurper; pretender
sanatorium (sa-na-tór-yoom) m. sanitorium; sanatorium
sandacz (sán-dach) m. perch-pike
sandał (sán-daw) m. sandal
sanie (sá-ńe) pl. sleigh; sledge
sanitariuszka(sa-ńee-tar-yoósh-ka) f. nurse(emergency, military)

sanitarny (sa-ńee-tár-ni) adj.
m. sanitary; health-
sankcja (sánk-tsya) f. sanction
sankcjonować (sank-tsyo-nó-
vach) v. sanction;authorize
sanki (san-kee) pl. sled
sanskryt (sán-skrit) m. San -
skrit; Sanscrit
sapać (sá-pach) v. gasp; pant;
heave; snort;puff and blow;chug
saper (sá-per) m. combat engineer;army engineer; sapper
sardynka (sar-din-ka) f. sardine
sarkać (sár-kach) v. grumble
sarkastyczny (sar-kas-tích-ni)
adj. m. sarcastic(smile etc.)
sarna (sár-na) f. roe deer
sarnia skóra (sár-ńa skoó-ra)
f. buckskin;roe-deer's hide
satelita (sa-te·lée-ta) m. satellite; attendant
satyna (sa-ti-na) f. satin
satyra (sa-ti-ra) f. satire
satysfakcja (sa-tis-fák-tsya)
f. satisfaction; compensation
sączyć się (sówn-chich shán)
v. drip; trickle; distill;
sift ; ooze out; seep;percolate
sąd (sównd) m. judgment ; court
sądownictwo (sówn-dov-ńeets-tvo)
n. judicature ;jurisdiction
sądowy (sówn-do-vi) adj. m. judicial; of court;judiciary
sądzić (sówn-dzheech) v. judge;
think; believe; expect; guess
sąg (sówng) m. cord (of wood)
sąsiad (sówn-shad) m. neighbor
sąsiadka (sówn-shad-ka) f.
neighbor; lady next door
sąsiedni (sówn-shed-ńee) adj.
m. adjacent;neighboring
sąsiedztwo (sówn-shedz-tvo) n.
neighborhood; nearness;proximity
sążeń (sówn-zheń) m. fathom;
cord;approximately six feet
scalić (stsa-leech) v. integrate
scedzić (stse-dzheech) v. strain
off;decant; pour off(a liquid)
scena (stse-na) f. scene; stage
scenariusz (stse-nár-yoosh) m.
scenario; script; screenplay
sceneria (stse-ner-ya) f. scen—
ery;srage decorations;backdrops

sceptyczny (stsep-tích-ni) adj.
m. sceptic; skeptical(smile etc.)
sceptyk (stsép-tik) m. skeptic
schab (skhab) m. pork chop
schadzka (skhádz-ka) f. date
scheda (skhe-da) f. inheritance; inheritance; heirloom
schemat (skhe-mat) m. scheme;
plan;draft;outline; diagram
schematyczny (skhe-ma-tích-ni)
adj. m. schematic (drafting...)
schizma (skheez-ma) f. schism
schlebiać (skhléb-yach) v.
flatter;wheedle;adulate;gratify
schludny (skhloód-ni) adj. m.
neat; clean;trim;slick;tidy
schnąć (skhnównch) v. dry; dry
up; wane; waste;parch;wither
schodki (skhód-kee) pl. steps
(small);small stairs
schodowa klatka (skho-dó-va
klát-ka) staircase
schody (skho-di) pl. stairs
schodzić (skho-dżheech) v. get
down; go down stairs;step down
scholastyka (zkho-las-ti-ka) f.
scholasticism; Scholasticism
schorowany (skho-ro-va-ni) adj.
m. invalid;ailing;ill;sick
schować (skho-vach) v. hide;
pocket;conceal;put away; save
schowek (skho-vek) m. closet;
safe; hiding place; cubby;recess
schód (skhood) m. stair; step
schron (skhron) m. shelter;
pillbox; air raid shelter etc.
schronić się (skhro-ńeech shán)
v. take refuge;take cover
schronisko (skhro-ńees-ko) n.
shelter;hiding place;refuge
schudnięcie (skhood-ńán-che) n.
loss of fat (weight);slimming
schwycić (skhvi-cheech) v.
seize; catch; get hold of
schylać (skhi-lach) v. bend;
bow; incline; stoop down
schyłek (skhi-wek) m. decline
scyzoryk (stsi-zó-rik) m. pocketknife; clasp knife;pen knife
seans (se-ans) m. seance; sitting;showing;performance
secesja (se-tses-ya) f. seces-
sion:Secession style(architecture)

sedes (se-des) m. toilet seat
sedno (sed-no) n. crux; core;
gist; essence(of the matter)
sejm (seym) m. Polish parliament (600 years old)
sekcja (sek-tsya) f. dissection;
section; cross-section ;division
sekret (sek-ret) m. secret
sekretarz (se-kre-tash) m. secretary;reporter; minuter
seksualny (se-ksoo-al-ni) adj.
m. sexual; sex-(appeal,urge etc)
sekta (sek-ta) f. sect
sektor (sek-tor) m. sector
sekunda (se-koon-da) f. second
sekundnik (se-koond-neek) m.
second -hand(of a watch)
sekutnica (se-koot-nee-tsa) f.
shrew; scold; vixen
seledynowy (se-le-di-no-vi) adj.
m. aquamarine;willow green
selekcja (se-lek-tsya) f. selec-
tion(by elimination,natural etc)
seler (se-ler) m. celery
semafor (se-ma-for) m. semaphore
semicki (se-meets-kee) adj. m.
Semitic (character etc.)
seminarium (se-mee-nar-yoom) n.
seminar;seminary;trainning school
sen (sen) m. sleep; dream
senat (se-nat) m. senate (in Poland evolved from royal council
in XV c.);Upper House
senator (se-na-tor) m. senator
senior (sen-yor) m. senior
senny (sen-ni) adj. m. sleepy
sens (sens) m. sense; significance;gist;drift;meaning;point
sensacja (sen-sats-ya) f. sensation; a hit;making a hit
sensacyjny (sen-sa-tsiy-ni) adj.
m. sensational; exciting
sentencja (sen-tents-ya) f.
maxim; dictum; pronouncement
sentyment (sen-ti-ment) m. sentiment;partiality;fondness;feeling
separacja (se-pa-rats-ya) f.
separation(from bed and board)
separatka (se-pa-rat-ka) f. pri-
vate-room; solitary cell
separować (se-pa-ro-vach) v.
separate;isolate

seplenić (se-ple-neech) v.
lisp; have a lisp;speak with lisp
ser (ser) m. cheese
serce (ser-tse) n. heart;kindness
sercowy (ser-tso-vi) adj. m.
cardiac ; love-(affair,secret etc.)
serdak (ser-dak) m. sleeveless
(furred) waistcoat
serdeczność (ser-dech-nośhćh)
f. cordiality;heartiness;caresses
serdeczny (ser-dech-ni) adj.
m. hearty; cordial;sincere
serdelek (ser-de-lek) m. small
sausage (specially smoked)
serenada (se-re-na-da) f. se-
renade (music and song at night)
seria (ser-ya) f. series;
chain; set;train (of events etc.)
serio (ser-yo) adv. seriously
sernik (ser-neek) m. cheese-
cake ; casein
serwatka (ser-vat-ka) f. whey
serweta (ser-ve-ta) f. (small)
table cloth;doily;serviette
serwetka (ser-vet-ka) f. napkin
serwilizm (ser-vee-leezm) m.
servility; humbly submission
serwis (ser-vees) m. dinner set;
service, (tennis),turn of serving
serwować (ser-vo-vach) v.(tennis) serve; do services;aid;help
seryjny (se-riy-ni) adj. m.
serial; consecutive
sesja (ses-ya) f. session
setka (set-ka) f. hundred
setny (set-ni) num. hundredth
sezon (se-zon) m. season
sędzia (san-dzha) m. judge; umpire; referee; magistrate
sędziwy (san-dzhee-vi)adj. m.
aged; old;grey headed;ancient
sęk (sank) m. knot;knag;knar
sękaty (san-ka-ti) adj. m. knotty;knaggy;gnarly;nodose;rugged
sęp (sanp) m. vulture
sfera (sfe-ra) f. sphere;zone
sferyczny (sfe-rich-ni) adj. m.
spherical(geometry,triangle etc.)
sfinks (sfeenks) m. sphinx
sfora (sfo-ra) f. pack of dogs
siać (śhach) v. sow(corn,terror...)
siadać (śha-dach) v. sit down;
take a seat;get stranded;go flat

siano (śhá-no) n. hay

sianokosy (śha-no-kó-si) pl. haymaking; hay cutting

siarczan (śhar-chan) m. sulfate

siarka (śhar-ka) f. sulfur

siarkowy (śhar-kó-vi) adj. m. sulfuric(acid etc.)

siatka (śhat-ka) f. net; screen

siatkówka (śhat-koóv-ka) f. retina; volley-ball

siąść (śhäñśhch) v. sit down

sidło (śhíd-wo) n. snare; trap

siebie (śhé-bye) pron. (for) self; oneself;one;each other

siec (śhets) v. cut; mow; whip

sieczka (śhéch-ka)f.chop straw; chaff; empty head(slang)

sieczna (śhéch-na) f. secant

sieczna broń (śhech-na broń) f. cutting weapons

sieć (śhech) f. net; network; grid;fishing net;trap;snare;web

siedem (śhe-dem) num. seven

siedemdziesiąt (śhe-dem-dźhe-shównt) num. seventy

siedemdziesiąty (śhe-dem-dźhe-shówn-ti) num. seventieth

siedemnasty (śhe-dem-nás-ti) num. seventeenth

siedemnaście (śhe-dem-nash-che) num. seventeen

siedemset (śhe-dém-set) num. seven hundred

siedlisko (śhed-leés-ko) n, seat; abode;habitation;hotbed;nest

siedmiokrotny (śhed-myo-krót-ni) adj. m. sevenfold

siedmioletni (śhed-myo-lét-ñee) adj. m. seven year (old; lasting)

siedzący (śhe-dzówñ-tsi) adj. m. sitting(posture);sedentary

siedzenie (śhe-dzé-ñe) n. seat; bottom; behind

siedziba (śhe-dzhee-ba)f. seat; abode;habitat(of an animal)

siedzieć (śhe-dźhech) v. sit (stay);be perched;be settled

siejba (śhey-ba) f. sowing; sowing time

siekacz (śhe-kach) m. incisor; chopping knife; chopper

siekanina (śhe-ka-ñee-na) f. hash; chopping up;cutting up

siekiera (śhe-ké-ra) f. axe

siekierka (śhe-kér-ka) f. hatchet; small axe

sielanka (śhe-lán-ka) f. idyll

sielankowy (śhe-lan-kó-vi) adj. m. idyllic; pastoral;bucolic

sielski (śhél-skee) adj. m. rural;idyllic; pastoral

siemię (śhe-myáñ) n. bird seed

siennik (śhén-ñeek) m. straw-mattress;pallet;paillasse

sień (śheñ) f. hallway; corridor;vestibule;entrance hall

siepacz (śhe-pach) m. (rough) henchman;hired assassin

sierota (śhe-ró-ta) m. f. orphan;lonsome person;poor fellow

sierp (śherp) m. sickle

sierpień (śher-pyeñ) m. August

siersć (śhérśhch) f. hair (coat)

sierżant (śhér-zhant) m. sergeant (military rank)

siew (śhev) m. sowing; seeds

siewca (śhév-tsa) m. sower

siewnik (śhév-ñeek) m. seeder; sowing-machine

się (śhäñ) pron. self (oneself; myself etc.;of itself);each other

sięgać (śháñ-gach) v. reach

sikać (śhee-kach) v. squirt; spout; gush; piss (vulg.)

sikawka (śhee-káv-ka) f. fire hose; squirt; fire engine

sikora (śhee-kó-ra) f. titmouse

siksa (śheék-sa) f. hussy; small girl piddler

silnik (śhíl-ñeek) m. motor

silnik spalinowy (śhil-ñeek spa-lee-no-vi) combustion engine

silny (śhíl-ni) adj. m. strong; powerful;mighty;hefty;lusty;stiff

silos (śee-los) m. silo;(store)pit

siła (śhee-wa) f. 1. force; might; strength; power; 2. many; much

siłacz (śhee-wach) m. strongman

siłownia (shee-wóv-ña) f. power plant;power station;power house

sinawy (shee-ná-vi) adj. m. bluish; somewhat blue

siniak (shee-ñak) m. bruise

sinus (see-noos) m. sine (of an angle)

siny (shee-ni) adj. m. livid; blue; purple;blue in the face

siodełko (sho-dew-ko) n. bicycle seat;small saddle

siodlarz (shod-lash) m. saddler

siodłać (shod-wach) v. saddle

siodło (shod-wo) n. saddle

sioło (sho-wo) m. hamlet;village

siostra (shos-tra) f. sister

siostrzenica (shos-tshe-nee-tsa) f. niece

siostrzeniec (shos-tshe-nets) m. nephew

siostrzyczka (shos-tzhich-ka) f. little sister

siodemka (shoo-dem-ka) f. seven

siodmy (shood-mi) num. seventh

sito (shee-to) n. sieve;strainer

sitowie (shee-tov-ye) n. bulrush

siusiac (shoo-shach) v. tinkle; urinate ; piss;pee;piddle

siwek (shee-vek) m. grey horse

siwiec (sheev-yech) v. grow gray

siwucha (shee-voo-kha) f. low grade vodka; rot gut

siwy (shee-vi) adj. m. gray; blue; grizzly;grey haired;hoary

skafander (ska-fan-der) m. diving suit ; pressure suit;wind jacket

skakac (ska-kach) v. jump; spring; bounce; leap; pop; skip ; dive

skakanka (ska-kan-ka) f. jumping rope; skipping rope

skala (ska-la) f. scale;extent

skaleczenie (ska-le-che-ne) n. cut; injury; hurt;wound

skaleczyc (ska-le-chich) v. hurt; injure; cut;prick;wound

skalisty (ska-lees-ti) adj. rocky

skalp (skalp) m. scalp

skała (ska-wa) f. rock

skamieniały (ska-mye-na-wi) adj. m. petrified ;fossil-;stone- skamieniec (ska-mye-nech) v. become petrified ;turn into stone

skandal (skan-dal) m. scandal

skarb (skarb) m. treasure; treasury; riches;beloved person;hoard

skarbiec (skar-byets) m. treasury; strong room;safe deposit

skarbnik (skarb-neek) m.treasurer;cashier;paymaster

skarbonka (skar-bon-ka) f. piggy bank;money box;poor box

skarcic (skar-cheech) v. admonish;rebuke;reprimand;scold

skarga (skar-ga) f. complaint; suit; claim; charge;grievance

skarłowaciały (skar-wo-va-cha-wi) adj. m. stunted; dwarfish

skarpa (skar-pa) f. scarp; buttress;slope;escarpment

skarpetka (skar-pet-ka) f. sock;a short stocking

skarżyc (skar-zhich) v. sue; denounce;complain;tell tales

skarżypyta (skar-zhi-pi-ta) m. squealer; informer; telltale

skaza (ska-za) f. tarnish;brab; blot; flaw;defect;spot;speck

skazac (ska-zach) v. condemn; sentence;pass judgement;doom

skazaniec (ska-za-nets) m. condemned man (to death)

skazic (ska-zheech) v. spoil; corrupt; adulterate;pollute

skąd (skownt) adv. from where; since when; where from?

skądinąd (skownd-ee-nownt) adv. otherwise; on the other hand

skąpic (skown-peech) v. skimp; stint; begrudge (food,money...)

skąpiec (skown-yets) m. miser

skapstwo (skownp-stvo) n. parsimony;avarice;stinginess

skąpy (skown-pi) adj. m. stingy; scanty; meager; scant

skiba (skee-ba) f. clod

skinąc (skee-nownch) v. signal; motion;nod; bow (one's head)

skinienie (skee-ne-ne) m. nod; bow; sign ;call;gesture;motion

sklejac (skle-yach) v. glue together;stick;paste; patch

sklejka (skley-ka) f. plywood

sklep (sklep) m. store; shop

sklepienie (skle-pye-ne) n. vault ;vaulting; dome

sklepikarz (skle-pee-kash) m. shopkeeper; tradesman

sklepowa (skle-po-va) f. saleslady; saleswoman

skleroza (skle-ró-za) f. scle-
rosis;hardening of body
skład (skwat) m. composition;
warehouse; store;framework
składać (skwá-dać) v. make up;
compose; piece;fold;set together
składacz (skwá-dach) m. type-
setter; compositor
składany (skwa-dá-ni) adj. m.
compound; folding;miscellaneous
składka(skwád-ka) f. contribution;collection;membership fee
składnia (skwad-ńa) f. syntax
składnica (skwad-ńee-tsa) f.
depository; warehouse;depot
składnik (skwád-ńeek) m. ingredient; component;element
składowe (skwa-dó-ve) n. warehouse fee; storage charges
skłamać (skwa-mać) v. tell
a lie;tell an untruth; lie
skłaniać (skwá-ńach) v. bend;
lean; incline;induce;impel;rest
skłon (skwon) m. slope; bow
skłonność (skwón-noshch) f.
inclination;tendency;disposition
skłonny (skwon-ni) adj. m. disposed; inclined;prone;apt
skłócić (skwoó-čheech) v. stir
up; agitate; cause to disagree
sknera (skné-ra) m.& f. miser
skobel (skó-bel) m. staple
skoczek (skó-chek) m. jumper
skocznia (skóch-ńa) f. ski-
jump (ramp);take off ramp
skoczny (skóch-ni) adj. m. brisk;
lively; vivacious;saltary
skoczyć (skó-chich) v. leap;
jump; spring;make a dash;hurry
skojarzenie (sko-ya-zhé-ńe) n.
association; union;conjunction
skok (skok) m. jump; leap; hop
skok tłoka (skok two-ka) m. piston stroke
skołatany (sko-wa-tá-ni) adj. m.
worn; battered; shattered
skołować (sko-wo-vać) v. confound; muddle; exhaust
skomleć (skom-lech) v. whine
skomplikowany (skom-plee-ko-va-
ni) adj. m. complex; intricate
skonać (skó-nach) v. expire; die

skończyć (skoń-chich) v. finish; end;stop;have done
skoro (sko-ro) conj. after;at;
since; as;quickly;soon;if;once
adv. very soon; by and by
skoroszyt (sko-ró-shit) m.
folder ;letter file
skorowidz (sko-ro-veets) m.
index; indexed note book
skorpion (skór-pyon) m. scor-
pion; Scorpio
skorupa (sko-roo-pa) f. crust;
shell;hull;incrustation;carapace
skory (sko-ri) adj. m. quick;
eager;prompt(to act); swift
skostniały (skost-ńa-wi) adj.
m. ossified;numb;stiff;fossilized
skośny (skóśh-ni) adj. m. slanting; oblique; inclined
skotłować (skot-wo-vać) v. whirl;
bewilder;agitate;swirl; seethe
skowronek (sko-vró-nek) m.
lark; skylark
skowyczec (sko-vi-chech) v.
yelp; whipe;squeal;whimper;whine
skowyt (skó-vit) m. yelp;squeal
skóra (skoó-ra) f. skin; hide;
leather; hide;skin;coat;pelt;derm
skórka (skoór-ka) f. skin; peel;
cryst; cuticle;agnail;pelt;fur
skórny (skoór-ni) adj. m. cuta-
neous; dermal;skin-(disease etc.)
skórzany (skoo-zha-ni) adj. m.
leather made; leathery;leather-
skra (skra) f. spark (poetic)
skracać (skra-tsać) v. short-
en; cut down;lessen;abridge
skradać się (skra-dać śhań) v.
steal; creep up;advance stealthily
skraj (skray) m. border; edge;
brink; margin;fringe;rand;outskirts
skrajać (skra-yać) v. cut off;cut
(cloth);cut up,(to pieces)
skrajność (skray-noshch) f.
extremism; extreme
skrajny (skray-ni) adj. m.
extreme;intense;utmost;ultra;utter
skrapiać (skrap-yać) v.damp;
sprinkle ;moisten; water
skraplać (skrap-lać) v. liquefy; condense;precipitate

skrawek (skra-vek) m. shred;snip;
strip; patch; chip;fragment;patch
skreslić (skresh-leech) v.
sketch; cancel; jot down;delete
skręcać (skrań-tsach) v. twist;
turn off; break (neck);strand
skrępowac (skrań-po-vach) v. tie
up; restrict;embarrass;impede
skręt (skrańt) m. twist; twist-
ing; coil; turn; torsion
skrobaczka (skro-bach-ka) f.rasp;
scraper; foot scraper(for mud)
skrobac (skro-bach) v. scrape;
rasp; scratch; scale (fish)
skromny (skrom-ni) adj. m.coy;
modest;unassuming;simple;lowly
skron (skron) f. temple
skropic (skro-peech) v. liquefy;
sprinkle;water;moisten;damp
skrocic (skroo-cheech) v. abbreviate; shorten ;cut down;curtail
skrot (skroot) m. abbreviation
skrucha (skroo-kha) f. contrition; repentance;compunction
skrupulatny (skroo-poo-lat-ni)
adj. m. scrupulous;precise,exact
skrupuł (skroo-poow) m. scruple
skruszyc (skroo-shich) v. crumble;crush;bring to repentance
skrycie (skri-che) adv. secretly
skryc (skrich) v. hide;obscure
skrypt (skript) m. script; mi-
meographed lecture; I.O.U.
skrytka pocztowa (skrit-ka poch-
to-va) post office box
skrytosc (skri-toshch) f. secrecy; secretiveness
skryty (skri-ti) adj. m. underhanded; secret; reticent
skrzek (skzhek) m. scream; croak
skrzep (skzhep) m. clot; coagu-
lation(of blood);grume;thrombus
skrzepnąc (skzhep-nownch) v. clot;
coagulate;set;freeze;solidify
skrzętnie (skzhańt-ne) adv. sed-
ulously ; diligently;busily
skrzętny (skzhańt-ni) adj. m.
industrious; busy; diligent
skrzydlaty (skzhid-la-ti) adj.
m. winged;wing-shaped;winglike
skrzydło (skzhid-wo) n. wing;
leaf; brim; (fan) arm;extension

skrzynia (skzhi-ña) f. chest;bin;
box;hutch;case;crate;coffer
skrzynka (skzhin-ka) f. box;chest
skrzynka biegow (skzhin-ka
bye-goov) f. gearbox;gear case
skrzypce (skzhip-tse) n. violin; fiddle;person playing fiddle
skrzypek (skzhi-pek) m. violinist; fiddler
skrzypiec (skzhi-pyech) v. crunch;
creak; screech; grind;squeak;gride
skrzywiac (skzhi-vyach) v. bend;
distort; twist;contort;put awry
skrzyżowanie drog (skzhi-zho-
va-ñe droog) pl. f. cross-
roads;crossing;intersection
skrzyżowany (skzhi-zho-va-ni)
adj. m. crossbred; cross-
legged
skubac (skoo-bach) v. nibble;
pluck; pick; fleece:graze;tease
skuc (skooch) v. shackle; chain
skulic (skoo-leech) v. curl up;
cuddle up; squat; lie low;crouch
skup (skoop) m. purchasing center
skupiac (skoop-yach) v. concentrate; bring together; gather
skupienie (skoop-ye-ñe) n. concentration;focussing;compression
skupiony (skoop-yo-ni) adj. m.
collected; concentrated ;dense
skupowac (skoo-po-vach) v. buy;
buy up ;keep buying; buy out
skurcz (skoorch) m. cramp; shrinking;
spasm; twitch; systole;contraction
skurczyc (skoor-chich) v. draw in;
shrink; contract; lessen;diminish
skutecznosc (skoo-tech-noshch)
f. efficiency; efficacy;good trsult
skutecznie(skoo-tech-ñe) adv.
with good result;effectively
skuteczny(skoo-tech-ni) adj. m.
effective;efficient; operative
skutek (skoo-tek) m. effect;
result; outcome; consequence
skuter (skoo-ter) m. motor-
scooter
skutkowac (skoot-ko-vach) v.
have effect; work; operate
skwapliwy (skwap-lee-vi) adj.
m. eager; willing;ready
skwar (skvar) m. scorching heat

skwarek (skva-rek) m. crackling
skwaśniały (skvash-na-wi) adj.
m. sour;turned sour; glum
skwer (skver) m. square
słabiutki (swa-byoot-kee) adj.
m. very weak(in diminutive)
słabnąć (swab-nownch) v. weaken;
grow feeble;decline;diminish
słabość (swa-boshch) f. weakness;
illness;debility;fragility
słabowity (swa-bo-vee-ti) adj.
m. weakly; feeble;fragile;puny
słaby (swa-bi) adj. m. weak;frail
feeble;infirm;faint;flimsy;poor
słać (swach) v. send; make bed;
spread(a table cloth etc.);strew
słaniać się(swa-ńach shań) v.
totter; stagger;lurch; reel
sława (swa-va) f. glory; renown;
fame; celebrity;reputation;repute
sławetny (swa-vet-ni) adj. m.
notorious;famous;ill famous
sławić (swa-veech) v. praise;
celebrate; glorify;laud;blazon
sławny (swav-ni) adj. m. famous;
glorious;celebrated;illustrious
słodkawy (swod-ka-vi) adj. m.
sweetish; slightly sweet
słodki (swod-kee) adj. m. sweet
słodycze (swo-di-che) pl. sweets
słodzić (swo-dżheech) v. sweeten
słoik (swo-eek) m. jar; gallipot;
glass;pot ;small jar;little jar
słojowaty (swo-yo-va-ti) adj. m.
grained;veined ;shownig grain
słoma (swo-ma) f. straw
słomianka (swo-myan-ka) f. straw
mat;doormat;straw plaited basket
słomiany wdowiec (swo-mya-ni
vdo-vyets) m. grass widower
słomka (swom-ka) f. small straw
słonecznik (swo-nech-ńeek) m.
sunflower
słoneczny (swo-nech-ni) adj. m.
sunny;solar(system,year etc.)
słonina (swo-ńee-na) f. lard
słoniowa kość (swo-ńo-va koshch)
f. ivory
słonka (swon-ka) f. wood-cock
słony (swo-ni) adj. m. salty
słoń (swoń) m. elephant
słońce (swoń-tse) n. sun;sunlight

słota (swo-ta) f.foul weather
słotny dzień (swot-ni dżheń) m.
rainy day; bad weather day
słowacki (swo-vats-kee) adj.
m. Slovak; Slovakian
słowianin (swo-vya-ńeen) m.
Slav
słowiański (swo-vyań-skee) adj.
m. Slav; Slavonic
słowik (swo-veek) m. nightingale; good singer
słownictwo (swov-ńeets-tvo) n.
vocabulary; list of words
słownik (swov-ńeek) m. dictionary; vocabulary; language
słowny (swov-ni) adj. m. verbal; reliable; dependable
słowo (swo-vo) n. word; verb
słoworód (swo-vo-rood) m. etymology; origin of words
słowotwórstwo (swo-vo-tvoor-
stvo) n. word formation
słód (swood) m. malt
słój (swooy) m. jar; (tree)
ring;pot;vain;grain
słówko (swoov-ko) n. (little
or sweet) word;nice word
słuch (swookh) m. hearing
słuchacz (swoo-khach) m. listener; student ;hearer;auditor
słuchać (swoo-khach) v. hear;
obey;listen;obey orders
słuchawka (swoo-khav-ka) f.
(tel.) receiver; earphone
słuchowisko (swoo-kho-vees-ko)
m. radio drama;broadcast drama
słuchy (swoo-khy) pl. rumors;
(animal) ears;uncertain news
sługa (swoo-ga) f. servant
słup (swoop) m. pillar; column;
post; pole; pylon; landmark
słupek (swoo-pek) m. pillaret;
small post;stake;stud; rail
słuszność (swoosh-noshch) f.
rightness; equity; rightful-
ness; legitimacy;aptness;justice
słuszny (swoosh-ni) adj. m.
just; fair; right;pertinent;apt
służalczy (swoo-zhal-chi) adj.
m. servile ;cringing;subservient
służąca (swoo-zhown-tsa) f.
maid ;servant; cleaning woman

służący (swoo-zhówn-tsi) m.
servant;manservant;domestic
służba (swoozh-ba) f. service
służbowy (swoozh-bó-vi) adj. m.
official;business(trip etc.)
służyć (swoo-zhich) v. serve
słychać (swi-khach) v. people
say; one hears;be heard
słynąć (swi-nównch) v. be famed
słynny (swin-ni) adj. m. famous
słyszalny (swi-shál-ni) adj. m.
audible;within hearing range
słyszeć (swi-shech) v. hear
smacznego ! (smach-ne-go) exp.
good appetite
smaczny (smach-ni) adj. m. tasty
smagać (sma-gach) v. lash; whip
smagły (smag-wi) adj. m. swarthy
smak (smak) m. taste; relish;
savor;palate;liking;appetite
smakołyk (sma-ko-wik) m. tidbit;
delicacy;dainty;choice morsel
smakować (sma-ko-vach) v. taste
smakowity (sma-ko-vee-ti) adj.
m. savory;appetizing;tasty
smalec (sma-lets) m. lard; fat
smar (smar) m. grease; lubricant
smarkać (smar-kach) v. blow nose
smarkacz (smar-kach) m. squirt;
snot; whippersnapper;raw lad
smarkaty (smar-ká-ti) adj. m.
snotty; callow; raw
smarować (sma-ro-vach) v. smear
smarowidło (sma-ro-vid-wo) n.
grease ; lubricant; ointment
smażyć (sma-zhich) v. fry
smętny (smán-tni) adj. m. melancholy; blue;doleful; dolorous
smoczek (smó-chek) m. nipple;
pacifier;dummy;comforter
smok (smok) m. dragon
smoking (smo-king) m. dinner
jacket; tuxedo;formal jacket
smolny (smól-ni) adj. m. resi-
nous; pitchy;tarry
smoła (smo-wa) f. pitch; tar
smrodliwy (smrod-lee-vi) adj. m.
rank; stinky; smelly; foul
smród (smroot) m. stench; fetor
smucić (smoo-cheech) v. sadden
smukły (smook-wi) adj. m. slender; slim; willowy; gracile
smutek (smoo-tek) m. sorrow;
sadness ; grief; mournfulness

smutny (smoot-ni) adj. m. sad
smycz (smich) f. leash;dog lead
smyczek (smi-chek) m. (violin)
bow; fiddle stick
smyk (smik) m.whippersnapper;
brat; kid; small boy
snop (snop) m. sheaf; bunch
snop światła (snop shvyat-wa)
light beam;light shaft
snuć (snooch) v. spin;reel off
snycerz (sni-tsesh) m. sculptor
sobek (so-bek) m. egoist
sobota (so-bó-ta) f. Saturday
sobowtór (so-bóv-toor) m. double
soból (so-bool) m. sable (fur)
sobor (so-boor) m. synod
socjalista (so-tsya-lees-ta)
m. socialist
socjalizacja (so-tsya-lee-za-
tsya) f. socialization
socjalizm (so-tsya-leezm) m.
socialism
socjologia (so-tsyo-log-ya) f.
sociology ; social science
soczewica (so-che-vee-tsa) f.
lentil; lentils
soczewka (so-chev-ka) f. lens
soczysty (so-chis-ti) adj. m.
juicy ; sappy; mellow; coarse
soda (so-da) f. soda
sodowa woda (so-dó-va vo-da) f.
soda water
sofa (só-fa) f. lounge; sofa
sofistyczny (so-fees-tich-ni)
adj. m. sophistical; captious
sojusz (só-yoosh) m. alliance
sojusznik (so-yoosh-neek) m.
ally;associate joined for a
   common purpose
sok (sok) m. sap; juice
sokół (so-koow) m. falcon
solanka (so-lan-ka) f. salt
spring; solted bread roll:brine
solić (so-leech)v.salt;add salt
Solidarność (so-lee-dar-noshch)s.
Solidarity Labor Union;solidarity
solidarny (so-lee-dar-ni) adj.
m. solidary; sympathetic
solidny (so-leed-ni) adj. m.
solid; firm;sound:reliable;safe
solista (so-lees-ta) m. soloist
soliter (so-lee-ter) m. tapeworm; solitary tree; solitaire
(gem stone)

solniczka (sol-neech-ka) f.
saltshaker; saltcellar
solo (so-lo) adv. solo
solny (sol-ni) adj. m. saline
solony (so-lo-ni) adj. m. salt-
ed ; corned(beef);salt cured
sołtys (sow-tis) m. village
head(officer below wójt)
sonata (so-na-ta) f. sonata
sonda (son-da) f. probe; feeler;
lead;plummet;sounding ballon
sonet (so-net) m. sonnet
sopel (so-pel) m. icicle
sopran (sop-ran) m. soprano
sortować (sor-to-vach) v. sort
sos (sos) m. gravy; sauce
sosna (sos-na) f. pine
sosnina (sosh-nee-na) f. pine-
wood;pine tree;pine branches
sowa (so-va) f. owl
sowity (so-vee-ti) adj. m. lav
ish;ample;abundant;rich
sód (sood) m. sodium
sól (sool) f. salt
spacerować (spa-tse-ro-vach) v.
walk; stroll; walk about
spacja (spa-tsya) f. (print)
space
spaczać (spa-chach) v. warp;
pervert; twist;distort
spaczenie (spa-che-ne) n. dis-
tortion; perversion; warp
spać (spach) v. sleep;slumber
spad (spat) m. slope; drop
spadać (spa-dach) v. fall; drop
spadek (spa-dek) m. fall; inheritance; downfall;slope;dip
spadkobierca (spad-ko-byer-tsa)
m. heir;inheritor;successor
spadochron (spa-do-khron) m.
parachute
spadzisty (spa-dzhees-ti) adj.
m. steep;sloping;precipitous
spajać (spa-yach) v. weld; solder; link;join;unite;bond
spalenizna (spa-le-neez-na) f.
(smell of) burning (smoke)
spalić (spa-leech) v. burn out
spalony (spa-lo-ni) adj. m.
adust; (sport) offside
sparzyć (spa-- zhich) v. burn;
sting ; scald;blister;scorch

spasły (spas-wi) adj. m. fat
spaść (spashch) v. fall; fatten
spawacz (spa-vach) m. welder
spawać (spa-vach) v. weld; solder; weld metal
spawanie (spa-va-ne) n. weld-
ing(of metals etc.)
spazm (spazm) m. spasm;convulsion
spec (spets) m. specialist;expert;
craftsman; dab hand; dab
specjalizacja (spe-tsya-lee-
zats-ya) f. specialization
specjalność (spe-tsyal-noshch)
f. specialty;peculiarity
specjalny (spe-tsyal-ni) adj.
m. special;express;particular
specyficzny (spe-tsi-feech-ni)
adj. m. specific;peculiar
spedytor (spe-di-tor) m. shipping agent; forwarding agent
spekulacja (spe-koo-lats-ya) f.
speculation; venture
spekulant (spe-koo-lant) m.
profiteer; speculator;gambler
spekulować (spe-koo-lo-vach) v.
speculate; profiteer; gamble
spelunka (spe-loon-ka) f, joint
spełniać (spew-nach) v. perform;
fulfill;comply with;accomplish
spędzać (span-dzach) v. round
up (cattle); spend (time);
abort;drive away;gather;pass time
spichlerz (spee-khlesh) m. gran-
ary
spiczasty (spee-chas-ti) adj. m.
pointed;peaked;tapering;sharp
spiec (spyets) v. burn;scorch;
sunblister;blush; parch;sinter
spieniężyć (spye-nan-zhich) v.
cash(checks);sell property)
spieniony (spye-no-ni) adj. m.
foamy;foaming;covered with foam
spierać się (spye-rach shan) v.
argue;contend;quarrel;dispute
spieszny (spyesh-ni) adj. m.
hasty; quick; hurried
spieszyć się (spye-shich shan)
v. hurry; dismount;be eager
spięcie (spyan-che) n. buckle;
short circuit;collision; clash
spiętrzyć (spyan-tzhich) v.
pile up; heap up;bank up;dam up

spiker (spee-ker) m. (radio) announcer; disc jokey;Speaker
spinacz (spee-nach) m. fastener
spinac (spee-nach) v. fasten; pin up; clasp; spur (horse)
spinka (speen-ka) f. clasp
spirala (spee-ra-la) f. spiral; coil;volute;helix;spiral glide
spiralny (spee-ral-ni) adj. m. spiral;helical;involuted
spirytus (spee-ri-toos) m. spirit; alcohol; spirits
spis (spees) m. list; register; inventory;record;roll;census
spis rzeczy (spees zhe-chi) table of contents
spisac (spee-sach) v. record; write down;acquit oneself(well...)
spisek (spee-sek) f. plot; conspiracy; hatching a plot
spiskowiec (spees-ko-vyets) m. conspirator; plotter
spiz (speezh) m. brass; bronze
spizarnia (spee-zhar-na) f. pantry; buttery; cupboard
spizowy (spee-zho-vi) adj. m. brass ; bronze; booming(voice)
splatac (spla-tach) v. braid; interlace;interlock;plait
splatac (splown-tach) v. snarl up; mat;ravel;confuse;muddle up
splesnialy (splesh-na-wi) adj. m. moldy: musty ;mildewy
splot (splot) m. twine; twist; coil;tangle;plaitcoincidence
splunac (sploo-nownch) v. spit
spluwaczka (sploo-vach-ka) f. spittoon ;cuspidor
splacic (spwa-cheech) v. pay off
splaszczyc (spwash-chich) v. flatten out; humble (another)
splata (spwa-ta) f. refund; instalment payment; repayment
splatac figla (spwa-tach feeg-la) v. play a trick;play a joke
splaw (spwav) m. rafting;floating
splawiac (spwav-yach) v. float; get rid;shunt; raft (timber etc.)
splawik (spwa-veek) m. (fishing) float(dipping when fish bites)
splawny (spwav-ni) adj. m. navigable (river, waterway etc.)

splodzic (spwo-dzheech)v. beget; generate;put out;produce
splonac (spwo-nownch) v. burn down;go up in flames; redden
splonka (spwon-ka) f. percussion cap; primer;detonator
sploszyc (spwo-shich) v. scare away; frighten;startle; flush
splowialy (spwo-vya-wi) adj. m. faded (appearance)
splukac (spwoo-kach) v. rinse; flush;swill out;wash away
splywac (spwi-vach) v. flow (down);drift;float(down stream)
spochmurniec (spo-khmoor-nech) v. grow cloudy; gloomy
spocic sie (spo-cheech shan) v. sweat; become sweaty;prespire
spoczynek (spo-chi-nek) m. rest
spoczywac (spo-chi-vach) v. sit; rest; lie down;be at rest;rest on
spod (spot) prep. form under
spodek (spo-dek) m. saucer
spodenki (spo-den-ki) pl. (knee) pants; shorts
spodlic (spod-leech) v. debase; degrade; disgrace; demean
spodnie (spod-ne) n. trousers; pants; slacks; breeches
spodobac sie (spo-do-bach shan) v. take a liking; take a fancy
spodziewac sie (spo-dzhe-vach shan)v.expect; hope for
spogladac (spo-glown-dach) v. look out; look at; contemplate
spoic (spo-eech) v. make drunk; weld; ply with liquor
spoistosc (spo-ees-toshch) f. cohesion; compactness ; density
spoisty (spo-ees-ti) adj. m. compact;cohesive;dense;tenacious
spojenie (spo-ye-ne) n. weld; joint; pubic symphysis
spojowka (spo-yoov-ka) f. conjunctiva
spojrzec (spoy-zhech) v. look; glance at; gaze at;view
spojrzenie (spoy-zhe-ne) n. glance; look; gaze;peep
spokojny (spo-koy-ni) adj. m. quiet; calm; peaceful;still

spokój (spo-kooy) m. peace; calm ;quiet;serenity;placidity
spokrewniony (spo-krev-no-ni) adj. m. related to; related
spoliczkować (spo-leech-ko-vaćh) v. slap face
społeczeństwo (spo-we-cheń-stvo) n. society; public;community
społeczny (spo-wećh-ni) adj. m. social (evil etc.);public;welfare
społem (spo-wem) adv, together in common ;jointly; unitedly
spomiędzy (spo-myań-dzi) prep. from among;from the midst
sponad (spó-nat) prep. from above ; from over(the top of...)
sponiewierać (spo-ńe-vye-rać) v. abuse; ill-treat ; maltreat
spontaniczny (spon-ta-ńeech-ni) adj. m. spontaneous ; voluntary
sporadyczny (spo-ra-dich-ni) adj. m. sporadic ; occasional
sporny (spor-ni) adj. m. controversial ;debatable;questionable
sporo (spó-ro) adv. good deal; a lot of; briskly;quite a few
sport (sport) m. sport;athletics
sportowiec (spor-tó-vyets) m. sportsman;athlete;sporting man
spory (spó-ri) adj. m. pretty big; fast; useful; lasting
sporządzać (spo-zhówn-dzać) v. make up;draw up; make out
sposobić (spo-só-beećh) v. prepare; make ready(colloquial exp.)
sposobność (spo-sób-noshćh) v. opportunity;occasion;chance
sposobny (spo-sób-ni) adj. m. convenient; capable; able
sposób (spó-soop) m. means; way
spostrzegać (spo-stzhé-gać) v. notice ; perceive;observe;spot
spostrzegawczy (spo-stzhe-gáv-chi) adj. m. quick to notice; keen;observant;perceptive
spostrzeżenie (spo-stzhe-zhé-ńe) n. observation ;awareness;notice
sposród (spó-shrood) prep. from amongst;from the midst
spotęgować (spo-tań-gó-vać) v. intensify; increase ;strengthen
spotkać (spot-kać) v. come across; meet ;run across;befall

spotkanie (spot-ka-ńe) n. meeting; date; encounter
spotwarzać (spo-tva-zhaćh) v. calumniate ;defame; slander
spoufalać się (spo-oo-fa-lećh śhań) v. become intimate
spowiadać (spo-vyá-dać) v. confess; listen to confession
spowiednik (spo-vyéd-ńeek) m. confessor (priest)
spowiedź (spo-vyedźh) f. confession; confided secrets
spowijać (spo-vee-yać) v. swathe; wrap ;shroud; cover
spowodować (spo-vo-dó-vać) v. cause ; induce; set off
spoza (spó-za) prep. from behind;from beyond;from outside
spozierać (spo-żhe-rać) v. glance at;look;gaze at
spożycie (spo-zhi-ćhe) n. consumption;intake (food,calories)
spożywać (spo-zhi-vać) v. consume; eat; drink; have a meal
spożywca (spo-zhiv-tsa) m. consumer
spożywcze artykuły (spo-zhiv-che ar-ti-koo-wi) pl, n. groceries;food products
spód (spoot) m. botton; foot
spódnica (spood-ńee-tsa) f. skirt ; petticoat;apron strings
spójnia (spóoy-ńa) f. bond; union; tie; bond; link
spójnik (spóoy-ńeek) m. conjunction
spółdzielczość (spoow-dżhel-choshćh) f. cooperation
spółdzielnia (spoow-dżhel-ńa) f. coop; cooperative
spółgłoska (spoow-gwós-ka) f. consonant (grammar)
spółka (spoow-ka) f. partnership; company ;society
spór (spoor) m. strife; dispute
spóźniać się (spoóżh-ńać śhań) v. be late; be slow;come late
spóźnienie (spoożh-ńe-ńe) n. delay; late coming;late arrival
spóźniony (spoożh-ńó-ni) adj. m. late ;delayed;belated;tardy
spracować się (spra-tso-vać śhań) v. be tired; be exhausted ; have worked hard

spracowany (spra-tso-va-ni) adj.
m. overworked;exhausted; tired
spragniony (sprag-no-ni) adj.
m. thirsty;thirsting for
sprawa (spra-va) f. affair; matter; cause; case;question;job
sprawca (správ-tsa) m. doer;
author; culprit;originator
sprawdzic (správ-dźheech) v.
verify;examine; test; check
sprawdzian (správ-dźhan) m.
test; gauge; criterion;template
sprawiac (správ-yach) v. cause;
bring to pass;occasion;afford
sprawiedliwość (spra-vyed-leé-
voshch) f. justice; equity
sprawiedliwy (spra-vyed-leé-vi)
adj. m. just;righteous;fair
sprawka (správ-ka) f. doing;
trick; small offense; prank
sprawność (správ-noshch) f. efficiency; dispatch; skill
sprawny (správ-ni) adj. m. able;
efficient; deft; dexterous
sprawowac (spra-vó-vach) v. perform;discharge; hold; exercise
sprawowanie (spra-vo-vá-ne) n.
conduct; behavior;performance
sprawozdanie (s.pra-voz-da-ne) n.
report; account;statement
sprawozdawca (spra-voz-dav-tsa)
m. reviewer; reporter
sprawunek (spra-voó-nek) m.
purchase(made while shopping)
sprężać (spran-zhach) v. compress; tense;prestress
sprężarka (sprań-zhár-ka) f.
compressor; air compressor
sprężenie (sprań-zhe-ne) n.
compression;prestress;pretension
sprężyna (sprań-zhi-na) f.
spring; mainspring; impulse
sprężystość (sprań-zhis-toshch)
f. elasticity; energy;resilience
sprężysty (spran-zhis-ti) adj.
m. elastic; springy; energetic
sprostowac (spros-to-vach) v.
rectify; correct; right
sprostowanie (spros-to-vá-ne)
v. rectification;correction
sproszkowac (sprosh-kó-vach) v.
pulverize; levigate;triturate

sprosny (sprosh-ni) adj. m.
obscene; lewd ;foul(language)
sprowadzać (spro-va-dzach) v.
bring; import; fetch; call in
spróchniały (sprookh-ná-wi)
adj. m. rotten;decayed
spróchnieć (sprookh-nech) v.
rot; decay; moulder;grow carious
spryciarz (spri-chash) m. dodger; trickster; slyboots
spryskac (spriś-kach) v. splash
spryt (sprit) m. shrewdness;
cunning; gumption; knack
sprytny (sprit-ni) adj. m.
tricky; clever;cunning; cute
sprzączka (spzhównch-ka) f.
buckle ;clasp
sprzątaczka (spzhówn-tách-ka)
f. cleaning woman;charwoman
sprzątac (spzhówn-tach) v.
tidy up; clean up; clear up;
pich up; take away;snatch away
sprzątanie (spzhówn-tá-ne) n.
clearing; tidying up;housework
sprzeciw (spzhe-cheev) m. objection; opposition; resistance
sprzeciwiac się (spzhe-cheev-
yach shań) v. object; oppose
sprzeczac się (spzhe-chach
shań) v. fight; argue; dispute;
squabble; quarrel;contend about
sprzeczka (spzhéch-ka) f. quarrel; squable;altercation; tiff
sprzeczność (spzhéch-noshch) f.
contradiction; discrepancy
sprzeczny (spzhéch-ni) adj. m.
contradictory; incompatible
sprzedac (spzhe-dach) v. dispose of; sell; trade away
sprzedajny(spzhe-day-ni) adj.
m. venal;corrupt; corruptible
sprzedawca (spzhe-dav-tsa) m.
salesman; shop keeper;dealer
sprzedawczyni (spzhe-dav-chi-
nee) f. saleslady;saleswoman
sprzedaż (spzhe-dash) f. sale
sprzedaż detaliczna (spzhe-
dash de-ta-leéch-na) f. retail;sale at retail prices
sprzedaż hurtowa (spzhe-dash
khoor-tó-va) f. wholesale
sprzeniewierzenie (spzhe-ne-
vye-zhe-ne) n. embezzlement

sprzęgać (spzhán-gach) v. couple; tie; link; team up; connect

sprzęgło (spzhán-gwo) n. clutch; coupling ; coupler;attachment

sprzęt (spzhánt) m. implement; furniture; accessories; utensils; tackle; outfit; chattels

sprzyjać (spzhi-yach) v. favor

sprzykrzyc (spzhik-zhich) v. get sick of; get fed up with

sprzymierzeniec(spzhi-mye-zheńets) m. ally; confederate

sprzymierzony (spzhi-mye-zhó-ni) adj. m. allied;confederated

sprzysięgac się (spzhi-shán-gach shán) v. conspire; plot

sprzysiężenie (spzhi-shán-zhe-ńe) n. plot; conspiracy

spuchnąć (spookh-nównch) v. swell

spulchniac (spoolkh-nach) v. fluff up;loosen;cultivate(soil)

spust (spoost) m. release; catch; slip; trigger; appetite; drain

spustoszenie (spoos-to-she-ńe) n. devastation; ravage ;ruin

spustoszyc (spoos-to-shich) v. devastate; ravage; make havoc

spuszczac (spoosh-chach) v. let down; drop; droop; lower; drain

spuscizna (spoosh-cheez-na) f. inheritance; legacy;heritage

spychacz (spi-khach) m. bulldozer; stripper

spychać (spi-khach) v. push down; relegate; drive away

spytac się (spi-tach shán) v. ask; ask a question

srac (srach) v. shit (vulg.)

srebrnik (srébr-ńeek) m. silver-coin; silversmith

srebrny (srébr-ni) adj. m. silver; of silver

srebro (sréb-ro) n. silver

srebrzyc (sréb-zhich) v. silver-plate;silver;wash with silver

srebrzysty (sreb-zhis-ti) adj. m. silvery(glow,color etc.)

srogi (sró-gee) adj. m. fierce; cruel; severe; srict; grim

sroka (sró-ka) f. magpie

srokaty (sro-ká-ti) adj. m. piebald (horse);with patches

srom (srom) m. disgrace; vulva

sromota(sro-mo-ta)f.shame;ignomity; disgrace

sromotny (sro-mót-ni) adj. m. shameful; disgraceful;infamous

srożyc (sró-zhich) v. rage; torment; storm;oppress;be severe

ssać (ssach) v. suck; exploit

ssak (ssak) m. mammal;mammalian

ssawka (ssav-ka) f. sucker

ssąca pompa (ssówn-tsa póm-pa) f. suction pump

stabilizowac (sta-bee-lee-zó-vach) v. stabilize; fix

stacja (státs-ya) f. station

stacja benzynowa (státs-ya ben-zi-nó-va) f. filling or service station

stacjonowac (sta-tsyo-nó-vach) v. be stationed;be in garrison

staczac (sta-chach) v. roll down; fight (battle)

staczac sie (sta-chach shán) v. roll down; go from bad to worse;be on the down grade

stać (stach) v. stand; be stopped; farewell; ill-afford;rise

stac sie (stach shán) v.become; grow; occur; happen

stadion (stá-dyon) m. stadium

stadło (stá-dwo) n. couple

stadnina (stad-ńee-na) f. stud

stado (stá-do) n. flock; herd

stagnacja (stag-náts-ya) f. stagnation;recession;stagnancy

stajnia (stáy-ña) f. stable

stal (stal) f. steel

stale (stá-le) adv. constantly; always; for ever;incessantly

stalownia (sta-lov-ña) f. steel-mill; steel plant; steel works

stalowy (sta-ló-vi) adj. m. steel; steely; steel gray

stała (sta-wá) f. constant

stałosc (stá-woshch) f. stability; firmness; steadiness

stały (stá-wi) adj. m. stable; permanent; solid; fixed;firm

stamtąd (stam-tównd) adv. from there; from over there;out of it

stan (stan) m. state; status; condition;order; estate; class

stanąć (stá-nównch) v. stand up; stop at; put up; rise; set foot

standaryzować (stan-da-ri-zo-vach) v. standardize
stanik (sta-ñeek) m. bodice; bra; brassiere;waste; corsage
staniol (stañ-yol) m. tin foil
stanowczość (sta-nóv-choshch) f. determination; finality
stanowczy (sta-nóv-chi) adj. m. final; positive; decided ;firm
stanowić (sta-no-veech) v. establish; determine; constitute;; decide; proclaim
stanowisko (sta-no-vees-ko) n. position; post; status; stand
starać się (sta-rach shañ) v. take care; try one's best
staranie (sta-ra-ñe) n.care; endeavor; exertion; pains
staranny (sta-rán-ni) adj. m. careful; accurate; nice;exact
starcie (star-che) n. clash; collision; friction ; squabble
starczy (star-chi) adj. m. senile; v.:it is enough (exp.)
starczyć (star-chich) v. suffice
starodawny (sta-ro-dav-ni) adj. m. old time; ancient;antique
staromodny (sta-ro-mod-ni) adj. m. old fashioned;outmoded
starosta (sta-rós-ta) m. countyhead; wedding host; foreman
starość (sta-roshch) f. old age
staroświecki (sta-rosh-vyétskee) adj. m. old fashioned
starożytność (sta-ro-shit-noshch) f. antiquity; ancient times
starożytny (sta-ro-zhit-ni) adj. m. ancient; antique ;old world
starszeństwo (star-sheñ-stvo) n. seniority ; superiority
starszy (star-shi) adj. m. older; elder; superior(officer)
starszyzna (star-shiz-na) f. the elders; the seniors;the chiefs
start (start) m. take-off; start
startować (star-to-vach) v. start; take off; make a start
staruszek (sta-roo-shek) m. old fellow;old man;old gentleman
stary (sta-ri) adj. m. old
starzec (sta-zhets) m. old man
starzeć się (sta-zhech shañ) v. grow old ;age;grow stale;go bad

stateczny (sta-tech-ni) adj. m. stable; bouyant; staid
statek (sta-tek) m. ship; craft; vessel;boat;steamship
statki (stat-kee) pl. kitchen pots & pans
statua (sta-too-a) f. statue
statut (sta-toot) m. statute
statyka (sta-ti-ka) f. statics
statysta (sta-tis-ta) m. supernumerary (actor);dummy;mute
statystyczny (sta-tis-tich-ni) adj. m. statistical; statistic
statystyka (sta-tis-ti-ka) f. statistics ;returns
statyw (sta-tiv) m. stand; support; tripod
staw (stav) m. pond; joint
stawać się (sta-vach shañ) v. become; grow (scarce,big etc.)
stawiać (sta-vyach) v. place; erect; put; stand; offer; lay down ;post; station;put upright
stawka (stav-ka) f. stake
stąd (stównd) adv. from here; away;therefore;that is why
stągiew (stówń-gyev) f. vat
stąpać (stówn-pach) v. pace; tramp;tread;plod along;lumber
stchórzyć (stkhoo-zhich) v. show fear; shrink with fright
stearyna (ste-a-ri-na)f. stearin (glyceryl tristearate)
stek (stek) m. steak; pile of... (lies; insults etc.); pack of...
stelmach (stel-makh) m. cartwright;wheelwright
stempel (stem-pel) m. stamp; prop; ramrod; punch; die
stemplowany (stem-plo-vá-ni) adj. m. cancelled; used
stenograf (ste-no-graph) m. stenographer;sorthand writer
stenografia (ste-no-graph-ya) f. shorthand ;stenography
stenotypistka (ste-no-ti-peestka) f. stenotypist ; steno
step (step) m. steppe
ster (ster) m. helm; rudder
sterczeć (ster-chech) v. stand out; stick out; tower; bulge
stereoskop (ste-re-os-kop) m. stereoscope

stereotypowy (ste-re-o-ti-po-vi) adj. m. stereotyped
sternik (ster-neek) m. pilot
sterować (ste-ro-vach) v. steer
sterta (ster-ta) f. stack
stebnować (stań-bno-vach) v. stitch; quilt
stęchlizna (stań-khleez-na) f.
fusty smell; musty smell
stęchły (stańkh-wi) adj. m. musty; stale; foul; fusty; frowsty
stękać (stań-kach) v. moan; groan; utter a groan; complain
stępić (stań-peech) v. blunt; dull; take the edge off
stępienie (stań-pye-ne) n. dullness (of knife; mind etc.)
stęskniony (stań-skño-ni) adj. m. sick for; yearning for; hankering for; nostalgic
stężały (stań-zha-vi) adj. m. hardened; stiff; concentrated; solidified; coagulated
stężec (stań-zhech) v. harden; stiffen; coagulate; concentrate
stężenie (stań-zhe-ne) n. concentration; strength(solutions)
stłoczyć (stwo-chich) v. cram; compress; jam; squize; pack; pile up
stłuc (stwoots) v. smash; break; bruise; shatter; injure; beat up
stłuczenie (stwoo-che-ne) n. bruise; break; contusion; injury
stłumiać (stwoom-yach) v. dampen; muffle; deaden; suppress; stifle
sto (sto) num. hundred
stocznia (stoch-ña) f. shipyard
stodoła (sto-do-wa) f. barn
stoik (sto-eek) m. Stoic
stoisko (sto-ees-ko) n. stand
stojak (sto-yak) m. stand
stojący (sto-yown-tsi) adj. m. standing; stagnant; erect; upright
stok (stok) m. slope; hillside
stokroć (sto-kroch)adv.hundred times; a hundred times; hundredfold
stokrotka (sto-krot-ka) f. daisy
stokrotny (sto-krot-ni) adj. m. hundredfold repeated
stolarnia (sto-lar-ña) f. joiner's shop; carpinter's shop
stolarz (sto-lash) m. cabinet-maker; joiner; carpenter

stolec (sto-lets) m. stool (large); bowel movement
stolica (sto-lee-tsa) f. capital( of a country )
stolik (sto-leek) m. small table; nice little table
stolnica (stol-nee-tsa) f. molding board ; paste board
stołeczny (sto-wech-ni) adj. m. metropolitan (taxes); capital(city)
stołek (sto-wek) m. stool
stołować (sto-wo-vach) v. board
stołownik (sto-wov-ñeek) m. boarder
stołówka (sto-woov-ka) f. mess hall; mess; cantine
stonka (ston-ka) f. potato beetle ;potato bug; Colorado beetle
stonoga (sto-no-ga) f. centipede ; wood louse
stop (stop) m. (metal) alloy; melt; traffic sign :stop; halt
stopa (sto-pa) f. foot; standard
stopa procentowa (sto-pa pro-tsen-to-va) f. interest rate
stopa życiowa (sto-pa zhi-cho-va) f. living standard
stoper (sto-per) m. stopwatch
stopić (sto-peech) v. melt
stopień (sto-pyeń) m. (stair) step; degree; grade; extent
stopniały (stop-ña-wi) adj.m. molten away; dwindled; shrunk
stopniec (stop-ñech) v. melt down; melt away; sfrink; dwindle
stopniowo (sto-ño-vo) adv. gradually; little by little
stopniowy (stop-ño-vi) adj. m. gradual; progressive
stora (sto-ra) f. shade; blind
storczyk (stor-chik) m. orchid
stos (stos) m. (wood) pile
stos atomowy (stos a-to-mo-vi) m. atomic pile
stosować (sto-so-vach) v. use
stosownie (sto-sov-ñe) adv. accordingly; properly
stosowny (sto-sov-ni) adj. m. proper; convenient; opportune
stosunek (sto-soo-nek) m. rate; relation; proportion; attitude
stosunek płciowy (sto-soo-nek pwcho-vi) m. sexual intercourse

stosunki handlowe (sto-soon-kee khand-lo-ve) pl. trade relations ;commercial relations
stosunkowy (sto-soon-ko-vi) adj. m. relative; proportional
stowarzyszenie (sto-va-zhi-she-ne) n. association; club
stożek (sto-zhek) m . cone
stożkowaty (stozh-ko-va-ti) adj. m., conical; cone shaped
stóg (stoog) m. stack (rick)
stół (stoow) m. table
stracenie (stra-tse-ne) n. execution; loss ; doom
straceniec (stra-tse-nets) m. desperado; madcap
strach (strakh) m. fear; fright
stracić (stra-cheech) v. lose; execute(a man);shed(teeth etc.)
stragan (stra-gan) m. booth; stand; (market) stall
straganiarz (stra-ga-nash) m. stand owner; stall holder
strajkować (stray-ko-vach) v. go on strike; strike
strapienie (stra-pye-ne) n. worry; distress; heartbreak
strapiony (stra-pyo-ni) adj. m. worried; dejected; distressed
straszak (stra-shak) m. noisy toy pistol; scarecrow; bugaboo
straszliwy (strash-lee-vi) adj. m. horrible; fearsome;awful
straszny (strash-ni) adj. m. awful; terrible;awesome;frightful
straszyc (stra-shich) v. frighten; haunt; threaten; bluff
straszydło (stra-shid-wo) n. scarecrow; fright
strata (stra-ta) f. loss
strategia (stra-teg-ya) f. strategy ;generalship
strategiczny (stra-te-geech-ni) adj. m. strategic
stratny (strat-ni) adj. m. one that lost;being the looser
strawa (stra-ya) f. food ; meal
strawic (stra-veech) v. digest; consume; bear;stomach; stand
strawne (strav-ne) n. food ration (in the army etc.)
straż (strash) f. guard; watch ; safe custody;strict guard;escort

straż pożarna (strash po-zhar-na) f. fire brigade
straż przednia (strash pzhed-na) f. vanguard ;advance guard
straż tylna (strash til-na) f. rearguard ; rear guard
strażak (stra-zhak) m. fireman
strażnica (strazh-nee-tsa) f. guardhouse; watchtower
strażnik (strazh-neek) m. guard; watchman ;sentry
strącic (strown-cheech) v. knock off (apples); throw down
strączek (strown-chek) m . (small) pod ;hull;husk;legume
strąk (strownk) m. pod;hull;husk
strefa (stre-fa) f. zone ;area
streszczac (stresh-chach) v. sum up; summarize;abbreviate
streszczenie (stresh-che-ne) n. resume; summary ;digest
stręczyciel (stran-chi-chel) m. pimp; procurer ; broker
stręczyc (stran-chich) v. procure (women) ; recommend
strofa (stro-fa) f. strophe
strofować (stro-fo-vach) v. reprimand ;admonish;scold;chide
stroic (stro-eech) v. dress up; tune up; make fun ;add beauty
strojny (stroy-ni) adj. m. dressed up; elegant; smart
stromy (stro-mi) adj. m. steep
strona (stro-na) f. side; page; region ; aspect; part; party
stronnictwo (stron-neets-tvo) n. party (political)
stronniczy (stron-nee-chi) adj. m. partial; biased;unfair
stronnik (stron-neek) m. partisan; supporter;follower;henchman
strop (strop) m. ceiling ;roof
stropic (stro-peech) v. discourage ; confound; abash;disconcert
stroskany (stros-ka-ni) adj.m. worried; sorrowful; dejected
strój (strooy) m. attire ;dress
stróż (stroosh) m. watchman
strudzony (stroo-dzo-ni) adj. m. weary ; tired;exhausted
strug (stroog) m. plane (tool)
struga (stroo-ga) f. stream; creek ; trickle;flow in streams

strugać (stroo-gach) v. whittle
struktura (strook-too-ra) f.
structure flow; flux;jet;torrents
strumień (stroo-myen) m. stream;
struna (stroo-na) f. string;
chord; wire; (metal)wire
struna głosowa (stroo-na gwo-
so-va) vocal cord
strup (stroop) m. scab; crust
struś (stroosh) m. ostrich
strych (strikh) m. attic
strychnina (strikh-nee-na) f.
strychnine
stryczek (stri-chek) m. (hanging) rope ;noose;the halter
stryj (striy) m. uncle
stryjeczny brat (stri-yech-ni
brat) m. cousin
strzał (stzhaw) m. shot
strzała (stzha-wa) f. arrow
strzaskać (stzhas-kach) v.
smash to pieces; shatter
strząsać (stzhown-sach) v.shake
off; shake down; flick off
strzec (stzhets) v. guard; protect; watch; keep an eye on
strzelać (stzhe-lach) v. shoot;
fire; slap; score; blunder
strzelanie (stzhe-la-ne) n. shooting (practice); gunfire
strzelanina (stzhe-la-nee-na) f.
gunfire ; shots; gunplay
strzelba (stzhel-ba) f. shotgun
strzelec (stzhe-lets) m. shooter;
rifleman; sniper; gunner; scorer
strzelnica (stzhel-nee-tsa) f.
shooting range;rifle range
strzelniczy proch (stzhel-nee-chi
prokh) m. gunpowder
strzemienne (stzhe-myen-ne) n.
parting drink;stirrup cup
strzemię (stzhe-myan) n. stirrup
strzepać (stzhe-pach) v. brush
off; flick off;shake off(away)
strzęp (stzhanp) m. shred; tatter
strzępić (stzhan-peech) v. shred
strzępić język (stzhan-peech
yan-zik) v. wag one's tongue;
talk breath;talk nonsense
waste
strzyc (stzhits) v. cut; clip;
shear; cut (hair);mow;trim;graze
strzyc uszami (stzhits oo-sha-
mee) v. prick up ears

strzykać (stzhi-kach) v.squirt;
spray;inject; ache
strzykawka (stzhi-kav-ka) f.
syringe; hypodermic syringe
strzyżenie (stzhi-zhe-ne) n.
(hair) cut ; sheep shearing
strzyżony (stzhi-zho-ni) adj.
m. cropped; cut; clipped
student (stoo-dent) m. student
studenteria (stoo-den-ter-ya)
pl. students ;student folks
studiować (stoo-dyo-vach) v.
study ;investigate;peer
studnia (stood-na) f. well
studzić (stoo-dzheech) v.
cool down (one's tea etc.)
studzienny (stoo-dzhen-ni)
adj. m. well-(shaft;water etc.)
stuk (stook) m. knock ;clutter
stukać (stoo-kach) v. knock;
tap; hit;rap;patter;rattle;drum
stulecie (stoo-le-che) n. century ;an age;hundred years
stuletni (stoo-let-nee) adj.
m. hundred years old ;age old
stulić (stoo-leech) v. press
tight; close up; coil up
stwardnieć (stvard-nech) v.
harden; stiffen ;grow callous
stwardniały (stvard-na-wi) adj.
m. hardened; hard ;sclerotic
stwardnienie(stvard-ne-ne) n.
hardening; callosity
stwierdzać (stvyer-dzach) v.
state; find out; confirm
stwierdzenie (stvyer-dze-ne)
n. statement; ascertainment
stworzenie (stvo-zhe-ne) n.
creature; formation;creation
stworzyciel (stvo-zhi-chel) m.
creator ; maker(of the world)
stworzyć (stvo-zhich) v. create :produce;set up;compose
Stwórca (Stvoor-tsa) m. Creator; Maker
styczeń (sti-chen) m. January
styczna (stich-na) f. tangent
styczność (stich-noshch) f.
contact; tangency ;adjacency
stygmat (stig-mat) m. stigma
stygnąć (stig-nownch) v. cool
down; cool off; cool
styk (stik) m. contact; butt

stykać się (sti-kach shán) v.
contact; touch;adjoin;meet
styl (stil) m. style; fashion
stylista (sti-lees-ta) m. styl-
ist
stylistyka (sti-lees-ti-ka) f.
art of composition ;syntax
stylowy (sti-lo-vi) adj. m. stylish; of style;in a given style
stypa (sti-pa) f. wake; funny
confusion; funeral banquet
stypendium (sti-pend-yoom) n.
scholarship; stipend; grant
subiektywny (soo-byek-tiv-ni)
adj. m. subjective
sublokator (soob-lo-ka-tor) m.
lodger ;subtenant
subordynacja (soob-or-di-nats-
ya) f. subordination
subskrypcja (soob-skrip-tsya) f.
subscription
substancja (soob-stan-tsya) f.
substance; matter
subsydiować (soob-sid-yo-vach)
v. subsidize
subtelność (sub-tel-noshch) f.
subtlety; niceness; delicacy
subtelny (soob-tel-ni) adj. m.
subtle;nice;fine;refined
subwencja (soob-ven-tsya) f.
subsidy; grant in aid
suchar (soo-khar) m. dry-bread
ration; cracker; biscuit
sucharek (soo-kha-rek) m. cracker ; biscuit
suchość (soo-khoshch) f. dryness
suchotnik (soo-khot-neek) m. con-
sumptive
suchoty (soo-kho-ti) pl. consumption; phthisis
suchy (soo-khi) adj. m. dry
sufit (soo-feet) m. ceiling
sugerować (soo-ge-ro-vach) v.
suggest;allude;hint
sugestia (soo-ges-tya) f. suggestion; motion; proposal
sugestywny (soo-ges-tiv-ni) adj.
m. suggestive(speech etc.)
suka (soo-ka) f. bitch
sukces (sook-tses) m. success
sukcesja (sook-tses-ya) f. succession; inheritance; devolution

sukienka (soo-ken-ka) f. dress
sukiennice (soo-ken-nee-tse)
n. weaver's or draper's market
hall ; cloth hall
sukiennik (soo-ken-neek) m.
draper; clothier
suknia (sook-na) f. gown
sukno (sook-no) n. cloth
sułtan (soow-tan) m. sultan
sum (soom) m. sheatfish
suma (soo-ma) f. sum; total;
high mass ;entirety;whole
sumaryczny (soo-ma-rich-ni)
adj. m. summary;total;global
sumienie (soo-mye-ne) n. conscience
sumienny (soo-myen-ni) adj. m.
conscientious;scrupulous
sumować (soo-mo-vach) v. sum up
sunąć (soo-nownch) v. glide;
slide; push; move; skim along
supeł (soo-pew) m. knot
surdut (soor-doot) m. frock
coat; overcoat
surogat (soo-ro-gat) m. surro-
gate ; substitute for
surowica (soo-ro-vee-tsa) f.
serum
surowiec (soo-ro-vyets) m.
raw material;staple; rawhide
surowość (soo-ro-voshch) f.
severity; crudeness ;rigor
surowy (soo-ro-vi) adj. m.
severe; raw; coarse; harsh
surówka (soo-roov-ka) f. pig
iron;fruit salad;raw hide
susza (soo-sha) f. drought;
dryness ;dry weather
suszarka (soo-shar-ka) f. (hair)
dryer ; desciccator
suszarnia (soo-shar-na) f. dry-
ing shed ;drying plant;kiln
suszka (soosh-ka) f. blotter
suszyć (soo-shich) v. dry
sutanna (soo-tan-na) f. cassock
sutener (soo-te-ner) m. cadet;
souteneur ; bully ;ponce
suterena (soo-te-re-na) f. basement
sutka (soot-ka) f. nipple
suty (soo-ti) adj. m. copious;
abundant ; lavish;plentiful;rich

suwać (soo-vach) v. shove
suwak (soo-vak) m. slide rule
swada (sva-da) f. eloquence
swar (svar) m. squabble; quarrel;rife;dissensjon
swarliwy (svar-lee-vi) adj. m.
quarrelsome;cantankerous
swastyka (svas-ti-ka) f. swas-
tica; swastika.
swat(svat) m. matchmaker
swatać (sva-tach) v. matchmake
swaty (sva-ti) n. matchmaking
swawola (sva-vo-la) f. anarchy
swawolny (sva-vol-ni) adj. m.
unruly;playful;frolicsome;wilful
swąd (svownd) m. reek; stench
sweter (sve-ter) m. sweater
swędzenie (svan-dzhe-ne) n.
itch; an itch; tingle
swędzic (svan-dzheech) v. itch
swoboda (svo-bo-da) f. freedom;
ease; latitude;liberty
swoboda działania (svo-bo-da
dzha-wa-na) v. freedom to act
swobodny (svo-bod-ni) adj. m.
free; easy;at liberty;loose;lax
swoisty (svo-ees-ti) adj. m.
specific;characteristic
swojski (svoy-skee) adj. m.
homely;familiar;friendly;tame
sworzen (svo-zhen) m. carriage
bolt; lug bolt;cotter;pin
swój (svooy) pron. his; hers;my;
its;our;your;their;one's, own
swój człowiek (svooy chwo-vyek)
m. trustworthy man
sybaryta (si-ba-ri-ta) m. Sy-
barite;sybarite; voluptuary
syberyjski (si-be-riy-skee) adj.
m. Siberian; of Siberia
sycić (si-cheech)v. satiate
syczec (si-chech) v. hiss
syfon (si-fon) m. siphon
sygnalizować (sig-na-lee-zo-
vach) v. signalize; signal
sygnał (sig-naw) m. signal
sygnatura (sig-na-too-ra) f.
(official) signature
sygnet (sig-net) m. signet;
seal ring; imprint;colophon
syk (sik) m. hiss;sizzle;fizzle
sylaba (si-la-ba) f. syllable

sylogizm (si-lo-geezm)m. syllo-
gism;rozumowanje dedukcyjne
sylweta (sil-ve-ta) f. silhou-
ette; outline;profile;figure
symbioza (sim-byo-za) f. symbio-
sis:living together
symbol (sim-bol) m. symbol
symboliczny (sim-bo-leech-ni)
adj. m. symbolic ;symbolical
symbolizować (sim-bo-lee-zo-
vach) v. symbolize
symetria (si-metr-ya) f. symmetry
symetryczny (si-me-trich-ni)
adj, m. symmetrical
symfonia (sim-fon-ya) f. symphony
symfoniczny (sim-fo-neech-ni)
adj. m. symphonic
sympatia (sim-pat-ya) f. liking
sympatyczny (sim-pa-tich-ni)
adj. m. congenial;attractive
sympatyk (sim-pa-tik) m. well-
wisher; sympathizer
sympatyzować (sim-pa-ti-zo-vach)
v. like; go along; feel with
symptom (simp-tom) m. symptom
symulacja (si-moo-lats-ya) f.
simulation;make believe;sham
symulować (si-moo-lo-vach) v.
simulate ;feign;pretend;affect
syn (sin) m. son
synagoga (si-na-go-ga) f. synagogue
syndykat (sin-di-kat) m. syndi-
cate;syndicat;labor union
synek (si-nek) m. sonny
synekura (si-ne-koo-ra) f.
sinecure; cosy job;fat job
synod (si-nod) m. synod
synonim (si-no-neem) m. synonym
synowa (si-no-va) f. daughter
in law
synowiec (si-no-vyets) m. nephew
syntetyczny (sin-te-tich-ni)
adj. m. synthetic
synteza (sin-te-za) f. synthesis
sypać (si-pach) v. strew; pour;
scatter (dry matter);betray secrets
sypialnia (si-pyal-na) f. bedroom ;bedroom furniture suite
sypki (sip-kee) adj. m. loose
(dry);granular(substance);friable

sypki towar (syp-kee to-var) m. granular goods; dry goods

syrena (si-re-na) f. siren; mermaid;hooter;Warsaw's emblem

syrop (si-rop) m. syrup

syryjski (si-riy-skee) adj. m. Syrian; of Syria

system (sis-tem) m. system/ systematyczny (sys-te-ma-tich-ni) adj. m. systematic; neat

syt (sit) adj. m. satiate; full

sytny (sit-ni) adj. m. filling up; nourishing; satiating

sytuacja (si-too-ats-ya) f. situation;circumstances;things

sytuować (si-too-o-vach) v. situate ; locate; position

sytuowany (si-too-o-va-ni) adj. m. situated ; placed;located

syty (si-ti) adj. m. satiate; dilled up; well-fed;nourishing

szabla (shab-la) f. sabre

szablon (shab-lon) m. stencil; pattern; model; stereotype

szablonowy (sha-blo-no-vi) adj. m. routine; stereotype

szach-mat (shakh-mat) m. checkmate (in a chess game etc.)

szachista (sha-khees-ta) m. chess player

szachować (sha-kho-vach) v. check (in chess); check

szachownica (sha-khov-nee-tsa) f. chessboard ;checker board

szachraj (shakh-ray) m. cheat

szachrować (zhakh-ro-vach) v. cheat; swindle; jockey

szachy (sha-khi) pl. chess

szacować (sha-tso-vach) v. evaluate; estimate ;size up

szacunek (sha-tsoo-nek) m. 1. valuation; 2. respect

szafa (sha-fa) f. chest; wardrobe; bookcase ; cupboard

szafir (sha-feer) m. sapphire

szafka nocna (shaf-ka nots-na) f. night table;bedside table

szafot (sha-fot) m. (execution) scaffold

szafować (sha-fo-vach) v. lavish ; squander;be liberal

szafran (shaf-ran) m. saffron

szajka (shay-ka) f. gang

szakal (sha-kal) m. jackal

szal (shal) m. shawl ;scarf

szala (sha-la) f. scale

szalbierstwo (shal-byer-stvo) n. swindle ; fraud;imposition

szalbierz (shal-byesh) m. fraud; swindler ; quack ;impostor

szaleć (sha-lech) v. rage ;rave

szalenie (sha-le-ne) adv. madly; terribly;awfully;like mad

szaleniec (sha-le-nets) m. madman; daredevil ; desperado

szaleńczy (sha-len-chi) adj. m. frantic;mad;insane;reckless

szaleństwo (sha-len-stvo) n. fury; madness ; craze;frenzy

szalik (sha-leek) m. scarf

szalony (sha-lo-ni) adj. m. mad

szał (shaw) m. rage;fury;frenzy

szałas (sha-was) m. tent; shanty ; shed; shelter; chalet;hut

szamotać się (sha-mo-tach shań) v. scuffle; struggle; tussle

szampan (sham-pan) m. champagne

szaniec (sha-nets) m. bastion

szanować (sha-no-vach) v. respect; honor; have regard;esteem

szanowny (sha-nov-ni) adj. m. honorable;worthy; dear(sir)

szansa (shan-sa) f. chance

szantaż (shan-tazh) m. blackmail ; extortion

szantażować (shan-ta-zho-vach) v. blackmail ;make squeal

szantażysta (shan-ta-zhis-ta) m. blackmailer ;extortioner

szarak (sha-rak) m. hare; average man of the street ;yeoman

szarańcza (sha-ran-cha) v. locust ;swarm of locust;swarm

szarfa (shar-fa) f. scarf; sash

szargać (shar-gach) v. besmear; foul up; slander; tarnish;slur

szarlatan (shar-la-tan) m. confidence man; charlatan

szarotka (shar-ot-ka) f. edelweiss

szarość (sha-roshch ) f. greyness; drabness ;dullness; duskiness

szarpać (shar-pach) v. jerk; pull; tear; tousle ; knock about;assail

szaruga (sha-roo-ga) f. gray,
foul weather; gray skies
szary (sha-ri) adj. m. gray;drab
szarzec (sha-zhech) v. loom;
gray ; grow dusky;,show grey
szarzyzna (sha-zhiz-na) f.
grayness; drabness; duskiness
szarża (shar-zha) f. (cavalry)
charge;(military)rank; officer
szarżować (shar-zho-vach) v.
charge, (recklessly);overact
szastac (shas-tach) v. squander
szata (sha-ta) f. garment;gown
szatan (sha-tan) m. satan; devil ; very strong coffee
szatański (sha-tan-skee) adj.
m. devilish; infernal;satanic
szatkowac (shat-ko-vach) v.
cut; chop ; shred;slice
szatnia (shat-na) f. locker
room; coat room,
szatynka (sha-tin-ka) f. dark-
blond, girl;auburn haired woman
szczac (shchach) v. piss (vulg.)
szczapa (shcha-pa) f. split log;
splint; chip ; sliver;thin man
szczaw (shchav), m. sorrel
szczątek (shchown-tek) m. remnant ; vestige ;fragment
szczebel (shche-bel) m.(ladder)
rung; spoke; grade ;round
szczebiot (shche-byot) m. chatter; chirp;babble;prattle;warble
szczebiotac (shche-byo-tach) v.
chirrup ; chirp; chatter;bable
szczebiotanie (shche-byo-ta-ne)
n. chatter; prattle;chirp;warble
szczecina (shche-chee-na) f.
bristle (of hogs);stubble beard
szczególnosc (shche-gool-noshch)
f. peculiarity;singularity
szczególny (shche-gool-ni) adj.
m. peculiar; special; specific
szczegół (shche-goow) m. detail
szczegółowy (shche-goo-wo-vi)
adj. m., detailed ; minute
szczekac (shche-kach) v. bark
szczekanie (shche-ka-ne) n. bark
szczelina (shche-lee-na) f. slot;
crevice; cleft ;slit; rift crack
szczelny (shchel-ni) adj. m.
(water) tight; (air) tight etc.

szczeniak (shche-nak) m. puppy ; kid ; pup
szczep (shchep) m. graft; tribe;
seedling
szczepic (shche-peech) v. graft;
vaccinate; inoculate,
szczepienie (shche-pye-ne) n.
grafting; vaccination,
szczepionka (shche-pyon-ka) f.
vaccine
szczerba (shcher-ba) f. jag;
notch; gap ;nick; chip; dent
szczerbaty (shcher-ba-ti) adj.
m.gap-toothed; jagged
szczerbic (shcher-beech) v. jag
szczerosc (shche-roshch) f.
sincerity ; open-heartedness
szczerozłoty (shche-ro-zwo-ti)
adj. m. pure golden
szczery (shche-ri) adj. m.
sincere ;frank; candid
szczędzic (shchan-dzheech) v.
spare; economize ;grudge;stint
szczęk (shchank) m. clink;clash;
clang ;jangle; rattle
szczęka (shchan-ka) f. jaw
szczękac (shchan-kach) v.
clink; clang ;jangle;rattle
szczęscic się (shchansh-cheech
shan), v. have good luck
szczęscie (shchansh-che) n.
happiness; good luck success
szczęsliwy (shchan-shlee-vi)
adj. m. happy; lucky;successful
szczodrosc (shchod-roshch) f.
generosity ;open-handedness
szczodry (shchod-ri) adj. m.
generous ;abundant; ample
szczoteczka (shcho-tech-ka) f.
small brush; toothbrush
szczotka (shchot-ka) f. brush
szczotkarski (shchot-kar-skee)
adj. m. brush ;brush maker's
szczotkowac (shchot-ko-vach) v.
brush down; bursh;polish(a floor)
szczuc (shchooch) v. hiss; bait;
embitter against ;set dogs on
szczudło (shchood-wo) n. stilt ;
crutch
szczupak (shchoo-pak) m. pike
szczuplec (shchoop-lech) v.
slim down; reduce; diminish

szczupłość (shchoop-woshch) f.
slimness; scarcity ;scantiness
szczupły (shchoop-wi) adj. m.
slim; slender; thin; lean
szczur (shchoor) m. rat
szczycić się (shchi-cheech shan)
v. boast ; take pride; be proud
szczypać (shchi-pach) v. pinch
szczypce (shchip-tse) pl. tongs;
pliers; pincers; clippers
szczypczyki (shchip-chi-kee) pl.
tweezers; forceps
szczypiorek (shchi-pyo-rek) m.
chive
szczypta (shchip-ta) f. pinch
szczyt (shchit) m. top; summit
szczytny (shchit-ni) adj. m.
lofty; sublime ;commendable
szczytowy (shchi-to-vi) adj.m.
pick; culminant ; uppermost;top
szef (shef) m. boss; chief
szelest (she-lest) m. rustle
szeleścić (she-lesh-cheech) v.
rustle; whisper(in the wind)
szelki (shel-kee) pl. suspenders; straps; belts; braces
szelma (shel-ma) f. rogue;
scoundrel; wretch; knave
szelmostwo (shel-most-vo) n.
roguery;rascally trick
szemrać (shem-rach) v. murmur;
grumble;prattle;repine against
szept (shept) m. whisper
szeptać (shep-tach) v. whisper
szepnąć (shep-nownch) v. whisper; murmur; conspire; scheme
szereg (she-reg) m. row; file;
series;range;chain(of events)
szeregować (she-re-go-vach) v.
rank; classify; arrange
szeregowy (she-re-go-vi) adj.m.
series; soldier in the ranks
szermierka (sher-myer-ka) f.
fencing
szermierz (sher-myesh) m. fencer
szeroki (she-ro-kee) adj. m.
wide;broad; ample; extensive
szerokość (she-ro-koshch) f.
width; latitude; breath
szerokotorowa kolej (she-ro-ko-
to-ro-va ko-ley) f. wide gauge
railroad (Russian)

szerszeń (sher-shen) m. hornet;
wasp
szerzenie (she-zhe-ne) n. spread
szerzyć (she-zhich) v. spread
szesnasty (shes-nas-ti) num.
sixteenth
szesnaście (shes-nash-che) num.
sixteen
sześcian (shesh-chan) m. cube
sześcienny (shesh-chen-ni) adj.
m. cubic
sześciokrotny (shesh-cho-krot-
ni) adj. m. sixfold
sześcioro (shesh-cho-ro) num.
six
sześć (sheshch) num. six
sześćdziesiąt (sheshch-dzhe-
shownt) num. sixty
sześćdziesiąty (sheshch-dzhe-
shown-ti) adj. m. sixtieth
sześćset (sheshch-set) num.
six hundred
szew (shev) m. seam ;stitch
szewc (shevts) m. shoemaker
szewstwo (shev-stvo) n. shoe-
making;shoemaking;trade
szkalować (shka-lo-vach) v.
slander;defame; calumniate
szkapa (shka-pa) f. jade
szkaradny (shka-rad-ni) adj.m.
hideous; ugly; abominable;nasty
szklarlatyna (shkar-la-ti-na) f.
scarlet fever;scarlatina
szkarłat (shkar-wat) m. scarlet
szkarłatny (shkar-wat-ni) adj.
m. scarlet;crimson; purple
szkatuła (shka-too-wa) f. casket
szkic (shkeets) m. outline;
sketch; essay; study;draught
szkicować (shkee-tso-vach) v.
sketch; outline; draw up;design
szkicownik (shkee-tsov-neek) m.
sketch pad; sketchbook
szkielet (shke-let) m. skeleton;
framework; shell; carcass
szkiełko (shkew-ko) n. small
glass; pane;slide
szklanka (shklan-ka) f. (drinking)
glass; glassful (of water etc.)
szklany (shkla-ni) adj. m. glass;
glassy(eyes); vitreous
szklarz (shklash) m. glazier

szklić (shkleech) v. glaze;brag
szklisty (shklees-ti) adj. m.
glassy ;glazy;vitreous;hyaline
szkliwo (shklee-vo) n. enamel;
glaze ;(desert)varnish
szkło (shkwo) n. glass;pane
szkocki (shkots-kee) adj.m.
Scottish ; of Scottland
szkoda (shko-da) f. damage;
harm;detriment;mischief
szkodliwy (shkod-lee-vi) adj.m.
harmful ;detrimental;damaging
szkodnik (shkod-neek) m. wrong-
doerpest;nuisance
szkodzic (shko-dźheech) v. harm;
injure;be harmful;cause damage
szkolenie (shko-le-ne) n. training;instruction; schooling
szkolic (shko-leech) v. school;
train;give instruction;instruct
szkolnictwo (shkol-neets-tvo) n.
school system; education
szkolny (shkol-ni) adj. m.
school; scholastic; school-
szkoła (shko-wa) f. school
szkop (shkop) m. Kraut; Hun(vulg.)
szkopuł (shko-poow) m. obstacle
szkorbut (shkor-boot) m. scurvy
szkuner (shkoo-ner) m. schooner
szkwał (shkvaw) m. squall;flaw
szlaban (shla-ban) m. tollgate ;
barrier;train crossing barrier
szlachcic (shlakh-cheets) m.
squire ; nobleman; gentleman
szlachecki (shla-khets-kee) adj.
m. noble ; gentle; gentleman's
szlachetny (shla-khet-ni) adj.
m. noble ; noble-minded ;elegant
szlachta (shlakh-ta) f. gentry
szlafrok (shlaf-rok) m. house-
robe ; wrapper; dressing gown
szlak (shlak) m. trail; track;
border;route;band;selvage;scent
szlam (shlam) m. slime;ooze;slit
szlem (shlem) m. big slam
(bridge)(card game)
szlemik (shle-meek) m. little
slam (card game,bridge)
szlifa (shlee-fa) f. epaulette
szlifierka (shlee-fyer-ka) f.
grinding machine;grinder
szlifierz (shlee-fyesh) m. pol-
isher; cutter;grinder

szlifowac (shlee-fo-vach) v.
polish; burnish;cut(diamonds)
szlochac (shlo-khach) v. sob
szmaciany (shma-cha-ni) adj.
m. rag; made out of rags
szmaragd (shma-ragd) m. emerald; emerald green
szmat (shmat) m. large piece;
long way;a good bit;expanse
szmata (shma-ta) f. clout; rag
szmatławiec (shma-twa-vyets)
m. shabby newspaper; smear
sheet;rag
szmelc (shmelts) m. scrap
szmer (shmer) m. murmur;rustle
szmergiel(shmer-gel)m. emery
szminka (shmeen-ka) f. lipstick; paint;rouge;make up
szmugiel (shmoo-gel) m. smuggle;smuggling;contraband
szmuglowac (shmoo-glo-vach) v.
smuggle(goods)
szmonces (shmon-tses) m. Jewish
quip or joke; nonsense(slang)
szmuklerstwo (shmook-ler-stvo)
n. haberdashery
szmuklerz (shmook-lesh) m.
haberdasher
sznur (shnoor) m. rope; cord
sznurek (shnoo-rek) m. string
sznurowac (shnoo-ro-vach) v.
lace up; lace; tie
sznurowadło (shnoo-ro-vad-wo)
n. shoe lace;lace;shoe string
sznurowany (shnoo-ro-va-ni) adj.
m. laced
sznycel po wiedeńsku (shni-tsel
po vye-den-skoo) m. Wiener
cutlet
szofer (sho-fer) m. chauffeur;
driver;(bus)driver;truck driver
szopa (sho-pa) f. shed;lark;fun
szopka (shop-ka) f. puppet show
szorowac (sho-ro-vach) v. rub;
scour; scrub; wash;grate;run
szorstki(shorst-kee) adj. m.
coarse; rough; crude; harsh
szorstkosc (shorst-koshch) f.
roughness; harshness;bluntness
szosa (sho-sa) f. highway;road
szowinizm (sho-vee-neezm) m.
chauvinism
szósty (shoos-ti) adj.m. num.
sixth

szpada (shpa-da) f. sword
szpagat (shpa-gat) m. string;
(ballet) split;cord;twine;twist
szpaler (shpa-ler) m. double
(tree) row; lane; hedge
szpalta (shpal-ta) f. (newspaper) column;(printer's)slip
szpara (shpa-ra) f. gap; slot;
rift;chink;crack;slit;crevice
szparag (shpa-rak) m. asparagus
szpargał (shpar-gaw) m. scrap-
paper;scrap of paper
szpecić (shpe-cheech) v. disfigure; make ugly;mar beauty
szperacz (shpe-rach) v. ferret-
er; scout;sniper;searcher
szperać (shpe-rach) v. forage;
burrow;poke about;search books
szpetny (shpet-ni) adj. m. ugly
szpic (shpeets) m. spike;peak;
(sharp) point;Pomeranian dog
szpicel (shpee-tsel) m. stool
pigeon; informer;plainclotheman
szpiczasty (shpee-chas-ti) adj.
m. pointed; tapering
szpieg (shpyeg) m. spy; sleuth
szpiegostwo (shpye-gos-tvo) n.
espionage ; spying
szpiegować (shpye-go-vach) v.
spy upon;shadow;watch;eavesdrop
szpik (shpeek) m. marrow
szpikować (shpee-ko-vach) v.
stuff (meat);lard(meat etc.)
szpilka (speel-ka) f. pin(small)
szpilkowy (shpeel-ko-vi) adj.m.
conifer; pegged (soles)
szpinak (shpee-nak) m. spinach
szpital (shpee-tal) m. hospital
szpon (shpon) m. claw; talon
szponder (shpon-der) m. flank
(meat); sirloin
szprotka (shprot-ka) f. sprat
szpryca (shpri-tsa)f. syringe
szprycha (shpri-kha) f. spoke
szprycować (shpri-tso-vach) v.
sprinkle ; syringe
szpulka (shpool-ka) f. bobbin
szpunt (shpoont) m. plug; stopper; bung;peg; tongue;feather
szpuntować (shpoon-to-vach) v.
bung (barrel) ; plug;peg
szrama (shra-ma) f. scar

szranki (shran-kee) pl. lists;
bounds; reins;tilt yard;barriers
szreń (shreń) f. neve; frost
szron (shron) m. hoar-frost;
rime; coat of rime
sztab (shtab) m. staff;headquarters
sztaba (shta-ba) f. bar;(gold)
ingot ;ingot(of silver)
sztabowy (shta-bo-vi) adj. m.
staff (officer)
sztachety (shta-khe-ti) pl.(picket) fence; railing
sztafeta (shta-fe-ta) f. relay
(race); relay race
sztaluga (shta-loo-ga) f. easel
sztanca (shtan-tsa) f. die;
stamp ; punch
sztandar (shtan-dar) m. banner
sztokfisz (shtok-fish) m. stock-
fish; cod; codfish
sztolnia (shtol-ña) f. gallery
sztucer (shtoo-tser) m. rifle
(gun); sporting rifle
sztuciec (shtoo-chets) m. fork
sztuczka (shtooch-ka) f. trick;
small piece; dodge;manoeuvre
sztuczne tworzywo (shtooch-ne
tvo-zhi-vo) n. plastic
sztuczny (shtooch-ni) adj. m.
artificial;sham;false;immitation-
sztućce (shtooch-tse) pl. (table)
silver;knife,fork and spoons
sztuka (shtoo-ka) f. art; piece;
cattlehead; (stage) play;stunt
sztukateria (shtoo-ka-ter-ya) f.
stucco work; stucco
sztukować (shtoo-ko-vach) v.piece;
patch up; eke out; lengthen
szturchać (shtoor-khach) v. poke;
dig; prod; jab; push; jostle
szturm (shtoorm) m. attack;
storm; assault ;onslaught
szturmować (shtoor-mo-vach) v.
storm; attack; assault; harass
sztych (shtikh) m. stab; engraving ;etching;woodcut; spade
sztyft (shtift) m. tag; pin; peg
sztylet (shti-let) m. stiletto;
dagger; poniard; bodkin; spike
sztywnieć (shtiv-ñech) v. stiff-
en ;grow stiff;become stiff
sztywny (shtiv-ni) adj. m. stiff

szubienica (shoo-bye-nee-tsa)
f. gallows; hanging matter
szubrawiec (shoo-bra-vyets) m.
scoundrel; rascal;rogue
szubrawstwo (shoob-rav-stvo) n.
villainy;rascally trick;rabble
szufla (shoof-la) f. shovel
szuflada (shoof-la-da) f. drawer; shunting;shelving
szuja (shoo-ya) f. scoundrel
szukać (shoo-kach) v. look for;
seek;search;cast about for
szukanie (shoo-ka-ne) n. search
szuler (shoo-ler) m. gambler
szum (shoom) m. (wind) noise;hum;
roar;uproar; scum; frost
szumieć (shoom-yech) v. buzz;
roar; froth;hum;rustle;fizz
szumny (shoom-ni) adj. m. roar-
ing; boistrous;noisy;frothy
szumowiny (shoo-mo-vee-ni) pl.
scum; scum of the society
szurgać (shoor-gach) v. shuffle
noisily;scrape foot on the floor
szuter (shoo-ter) m. gravel
szwaczka (shvach-ka) f. seamstress; needlewoman
szwadron (shvad-ron) m. squad-
ron;(cavalry)squadron; troop
szwagier (shva-ger) m. brother-
-in-law
szwagierka (shva-ger-ka) f.
sister-in-law
szwajcar (shvay-tsar) m. doorman; (Szwajcar = Swiss)
szwajcarski (shvay-tsar-skee)
adj. m. Swiss ;of Switserland
szwalnia (shval-ña) f. underwear
factory;tailoring shop
szwargot (shvar-got) m. gibberish; jabber; lingo
szwedzki (shvedz-kee) adj. m.
Swedish; of Sweden
szyb (shib) m.shaft; (oil)well
szyba (shi-ba) f. (glass) pane
szybki (shib-kee) adj. m. quick;
fast; prompt;rapid; sharp;smart
szybko (shib-ko) adv. quickly;
fast; promptly;swiftly; apace
szybkość (shib-koshch) f. speed;
velocity; rate; fastness
szybować (shi-bo-vach) v..glide;
soar;tower;sail;plane

szybowiec (shi-bo-vyets) m.
glider (motorless)
szychta nocna (shikh-ta nots-
na) v. night shift
szycie (shi-che) n. sewing
szyć (shich) v. sew; sew up
szydełko (shi-dew-ko) n.croch-
et needle; crochet hook
szydełkować (shi-dew-ko-vach)
v. crochet
szyderca (shi-der-tsa) m.
scoffer; giber; jailer
szyderczy (shi-der-chi) adj.
m. scoffing; sarcastic
szyderstwo (shi-der-stvo) n.
scoff;jeer;sneer;gibe;derision
szydło (shid-wo) n. awl;pricker
szydzić (shi-dzheech) v. scoff
szyfr (shifr) m. code;cipher
szyja (shi-ya) f. neck;bottleneck
szyk (shik) m. order; elegance;
(battle) array; order;formation
szykana (shi-ka-na) f. chica-
nery;vexation;difficulties;style
szykanować (shi-ka-no-vach) v.
vex; chicane; annoy; nag;pick at
szykować (shi-ko-vach) v. make
ready; prepare;get ready
szykować się (shi-ko-vach shäñ)
v. get ready;be in prospect
szykowność (shi-kov-noshch) f.
elegance;smartness; style;chic
szykowny (shi-kov-ni) adj. m.
smart; elegant;fashionable;chic
szyld (shild) m. sign-board
szyldwach (shild-vakh) m. sentry; military guard
szyling (shi-ling) m. shilling
szympans (shim-pans) m. chim-
panzee
szyna (shi-na) f. rail
szynk (shink) m. bar;saloon;pub
szynka (shin-ka) f. ham
szynkarz (shin-kash) m. barman
szyszak (shi-shak) m. helmet
szyszka (shish-ka) f. (tree)
cone;trobile; bigwig;topdog
ściana (shcha-na) f. wall
ścianka (shchan-ka) f. partition; bulkhead; small wall
ściągać (shchown-gach) v. draw
down or together;cheat in class;
assemble; collect (taxes)

ściągaczka (śhchǒwn-gach-ka)
f. cheat note; crib
ścieg (śhcheg) m. stitch
ściec (śhchets) v. drain off;
run off;trickle down; drip
ściek (śhchek) m. sewer; gutter;
sink; sewage;drain;sewer;gully
ściekać (śhche-kach) v. drain
off; flow down;trickle down
ściemniać (śhchem-nach) v. dark-
en; dim; obscure;dim the lights
ścienny (śhchen-ni) adj. m. mu-
ral(painting);wall (map etc.)
ścierać (śhche-rach) v. rub off;
dust off;grind down;wear off
ścierka (śhcher-ka) f. duster;
rug; kitchen towel;clout
ściernisko (śhcher-nees-ko) n.
stubble field; stubble
ścierń (śhcherń) m. stubble
ścierpły (śhcherp-wi) adj. m.
numb; gone to sleep
ścierwo (śhcher-vo) n. carrion
ścieśniać (śhchesh-nach) v.cramp;
tighten;narrow;restrict;close
ścieżka (śhchezh-ka) f. trail;
pass ;(foot) pass; alley
ścięcie (śhchań-che) n. behead-
ing; cutting off;truncation
ścięgno (śhcháng-no) n. tendon
ścięty (śhchań-ti) adj. m.
truncated;cut off; beheaded
ścigacz (śhchee-gach) m. torpedo boat;motor gun boat
ścigać (śhchee-gach) v. chase;
pursue;run after;hunt;procecute
ścinać (śhchee-nach) v. cut off;
cut down; fell (tree);clip;clot
ścinać się (śhchee-nach śhań) v.
coagulate; congeal;fix;clot;fail
ściółka (śhchóow-ka) f. litter
bed; litter bedding;barn litter
ścisk (śhcheesk) m. throng;press;
crowd; squeeze ;crush;clamp
ściskać (śhchees-kach) v. compress; shake (hand); squeeze;
embrace;clasp;harass;hamper;hug
ścisłość (śhchees-wośhch) f.
exactness; accuracy; compactness; density; reliability
ścisły (śhchees-wi) adj. m.
exact; precise; compact;dense

ścisłe (śhcheesh-le) adv. exactly;tightly; compactly
ślad (śhlat) m. trace; track;
(foot) print; footstep
ślamazara (śhla-ma-za-ra) f.
sluggard; slowheaded person
ślamazarny (śhla-ma-zár-ni)
adj. m. sluggish
śląski (śhlǒwns-kee) adj. m.
Silesian ;of Silesia
śledczy (śhled-chi) adj. m.
inquisitional ; of inquiry
śledzić (śhle-dźheech) v. spy;
watch; investigate; observe
śledziona (śhle-dźho-na) f.
spleen ; milt
śledziowy (śhle-dźho-vi) adj.
m. herring (oil,salad etc.)
śledztwo (śhledz-tvo) n.
investigation ;inquest;inquiry
śledź (śhledźh) m. herring
ślepie (śhlép-ye) n. (animal's)
eye ; eye; lights
ślepnąć (śhlep-nównch) v. go
blind ;loose one's eyesight
ślepa ulica (śhlé-pa oo-lee-
tsa) s. dead end street
ślepota (śhle-pó-ta) f. blindness ;cecity;lack of foresight
ślepy (śhle-pi) adj. m. blind
ślęczeć (śhlań-chech) v. drag
study or reading; drudge;
pore; plod; slog away; boggle
śliczny (śhleech-ni) adj. m.
pretty; lovely; dandy
ślimacznica (śhlee-mach-nee-
tsa) s. road access ramp;helix
ślimak (śhlee-mak) m. snail
ślina (śhlee-na) f. saliva
śliniak (śhlee-nak) m. bib
śliski (śhlees-kee) adj. m.
slippery ; slimy;scabrous
śliwa (śhlee-va) f. plum tree
śliwka (śhleev-ka) f. plum
śliwowica (śhlee-vo-vee-tsa)
f. plum brandy;plum vodka
ślizgacz (śhleez-gach) m.speed-
boat; gliding boat
ślizgać się (śhleez-gach śhań)
v. slide; glide; slip; skate
ślizgawka (śhleez-gáv-ka) f.
skating rink ;kid's slide

slizgowiec (shleez-gó-vyets)
m. hydrofoil; gliding boat;
speed boat
slub (shloob) m. wedding; vow
slubna obrączka (shloób-na ob-
równch-ka) f. wedding ring
slubny (shloob-ni) adj. m. nup-
tial; wedding-(ring);legitimate
slubowac (shloo-bo-vach) v. vow
slusarz (shloó-sash) m. locksmith; ironworker;metal worker
sluz (shloos) m. slime; phlegm
sluza (shloo-za) f. sluice
smiac się (shmyách shań) v.
laugh;chuckle;scoff;make sport
smiałek (shmyá-wek) m. daredevil; mad cap
smiałosc (shmya-woshch) f. bold-
ness;courage;bravery;daring;guts
smiały (shmya-wi) adj. m. bold
smiech (shmyekh) m. laughter
smieci (shmye-chee) pl. rubbish;
garbage;rag;shred;scrap;refuse
smiecic (shmye-cheech) v. litter; throw litter about
smiecie (shmye-che) pl. rubbish;
garbage;refuse;litter;scrap
smiec (shmyech) m. litter; rag
smiercionosny (shmyer-cho-nosh-
ni) adj. m. lethal; deadly
smierc (shmyerch) f. death
smierdziec (shmyér-dzhech) v.
stink; smell; reek(of nicotine)
smiertelnik (shmyer-tel-neek)
m. mortal man
smiertelnosc (shmyer-tél-noshch)
f. mortality; deadliness
smiertelny (shmyer-tel-ni) adj.
m. mortal;deadly;death(throes)
smiesznosc (shmyesh-noshch) f.
comic trait; the ridiculous
smieszny (shmyesh-ni) adj. m.
funny; ridiculous;comic;absurd
smieszyc (shmye-shich) v. make
laugh; cause laughter;amuse
smietana (shmye-tá-na) f. sour-
cream; clotted cream
smietanka (shmye-tan-ka) f.
cream; flower(of society etc.)
smietnik (shmyét-neek) m. garbage can; garbage dump
smiga (shmee-ga) f. (wind mill)
sail

smigło (shmeeg-wo) n. propeller
smigłowiec (shmeeg-wóv-yets)
m. helicopter
sniadanie (shna-da-ne) n. breakfast ; luncheon
sniady (shna-di) adj. swarthy;
sun-tanned;dusky;tawny
snic (shneech) v. dream (about
something);have a dream
sniedz (shnedzh) f. verdigris
snieg (shneg) m. snow;snowscape
sniegowce (shne-góv-tse) pl.
snowboots;overshoes; galishes
snieg pada (shneg pa-da) exp.:
it snows
sniezka (shnezh-ka)f. snowball
snieznobiały (shnezh-no-bya-
wi) adj. m. snow-white
sniezny (shnezh-ni) adh. m.
snowy;snow white; snow-
sniezyca (shne-zhi-tsa) f.
snow-storm; blizzard
spiący (shpyówn-tsi) adj. m.
sleepy;drowsy;slumberous
spiączka (shpyównch-ka) f.
sleeping sickness
spieszyc się (shpye-shich shań)
v. hurry;hasten;be in a hurry
spiew (shpyev) m. song;singing
spiewaczka (shpye-vach-ka) f.
singer (girl or woman)
spiewac (shpye-vach) v. sing
spiewak (shpye-vak) m. singer
spiewnik (shpyev-neek) m.
songbook; hymn-book
spiewny (shpyev-ni) adj. m.
melodious; singsong-(accent)
spioch (shpyokh) m. sleepy
head; lie-abed; slug-abed
spiwor (shpee-voor) m. sleeping
bag
sredni(shréd-nee) adj. m. average; medium; mean(temperature)
srednica (shred-nee-tsa) f. diameter; bore; middle register
srednik (shréd-neek) m. semicolon
srednio (shréd-no) adv. average ; medium- ;fairly well
sredniowiecze (shred-no-vye-
che) n. Middle Ages
sredniowieczny (shred-no-vyech-
ni) adj. m. medieval

środa (śhró-da) f. Wednesday
środek (śhró-dek) m. center;
middle; measures; means; remedy;midst;inside;agent;medium
środkowy (śhrod-ko-vi) adj. m.
central; center-(line);middle
środowisko (śhro-do-vees-ko) n.
surroundings; environment;circle
śródmieście (śhrood-myesh-che)
n.city center; center of town
Śródziemne morze (śhrood-żhem-
ne mó-zhe) n. Mediterranean
sea; Mediterranean
śruba(śhroo-ba) f. screw
śrubokręt (śhroo-bo-kránt) m.
screwdriver; turn-screw
śrut (śhroot) m. (lead) shot
świadczenie (śhvyad-che-ńe) n.
benefit; charge; testimony
świadczyć (śhvyad-chich) v.
witness;attest;bear witness
świadectwo (śhvya-dets-tvo) n.
certificate; bill of health
świadek naoczny (śhvya-dek na-
óch-ni) exp.: eyewitness
świadomość (śhvya-do-moshch) f.
consciousness; awareness
świadomy (śhvya-do-mi) adj.m.
conscious; aware; wilful
świat (śhvyat) m. world
światło (śhvyat-wo) n. light
światłomierz (śhvyat-wó-myezh)
m. lightmeter ; photometer
światopogląd (śhvya-to-pog-lównd)
m. ideology ;outlook on life
światowy (śhvya-to-vi) adj. m.
world; worldly;global;society-
świąteczny (śhvyówn-tech-ni)
adj. m. festive;holiday(mood...)
świątynia (śhvyown-ti-ńa) f.
temple;place of worship
świder (śhvee-der) m. drill;
auger; bore; borer;perforator
świdrować (śhvid-ro-vach) v.
drill;bore;perforate;pierce
świeca (śhvye-tsa) f. candle
świecić (śhvye-cheech) v. light
up; shine; glitter; sparkle
świecki (śhvyets-kee) adj. m.
secular;mundane;laic;lay
świecki ksiadz (śhvyets-kee
kshownts) m. secular priest

świeczka (śhvyech-ka) f. (small)
candle
świecznik (śhvyech-ńeek) m.
chandelier; candlestick
świergot (śhvyer-got) m. twitter;
chirp; warble; chirrup; tweet
świergotać (śhvyer-go-tach) v.
chirp;chirrup;warble; tweet
świerk (śhvyerk) m. fir tree
świerkowy (śhvyer-ko-vi) adj.
m. fir;spruce; of spruce
świerszcz (śhvyershch) m. cricket; grasshopper
świerzb (śhvyezhb) m. scabies
świerzbiec (śhvyezh-byech) v.
itch; be itching
świetlica(śhvyet-lee-tsa) f.
reading hall;community center
świetlik (śhvyet-leek) m. firebug ;glow worm; skylight;fire fly
świetlny(śhvyetl-ni)adj.m.
lighting (gas etc.)
świetność (śhvyet-noshch) f.
splendor; magnificence;glamor
świetny (śhvyet-ni) adj. m.
splendid ;excellent;first rate
świeżo (śhvye-zho) adv. fresh
świeży (śhvye-zhi) adj. m. fresh;
new; recent; fresh;raw;ruddy
święcenie (śhvyan-tse-ńe) n. celebration; blessing ;observance
święcić (śhvyań-cheech) v. celebrate ;keep a holiday; bless
święcone (śhvyań-tso-ne) n. Easter blessed food (Polish style)
święta (śhvyań-ta) pl. holidays
święto (śhvyań-to) n. holiday
świętokradztwo (śhvyań-to-krads-
tvo) n. sacrilege
świętoszek (śhvyan-tó-shek) m.
bigot;sanctimonious hypocrite
świętość (śhvyań-toshch) f. sanc-
tity; holiness; sainthood
święty (śhvyań-ti) adj. m. saint;
holy; saintly; pious;sacred
świnia (śhvee-ńa) f. swine;hog;pig
świnić (śhvee-ńeech) v. make
a mess; litter up; play dirty
świnka morska (śhveen-ka mor-ska)
f. guinea-pig ;cavy
świństwo (śhveeń-stvo) n. dirty
deed ;meanness;nasty stuff;dross

świsnąć (śhvees-nównch) v.
whistle; pilfer; bolt
świst (śhveest) m. whistle
sound; bullet sound
świstak (śhvees-tak) m. marmot
świstawka (śhvees-táv-ka) f.
whistle
świstek (śhvees-tek) m. scrap
of paper; slip of paper
świt (śhveet) m. daybreak; dawn
świtać (śhvee-tach) v. dawn
(upon) ; rise (of sun or moon)
switezianka (śhvee-te-żhán-ka)
f. water-nymph
tabaka (ta-bá-ka) f. snuff
tabakierka (ta-ba-kér-ka) f.
snuffbox
tabela (ta-bé-la) f. table;
index; list
tabletka (tab-lét-ka) f. tablet;
pill blackboard;switchboard;slab;
tablica (tab-lee-tsa) f. board ;
tablica rozdzielcza (tab-lee-
tsa roz-dżhél-cha) switchboard
tabliczka mnożenia (tab-leéch-ka
mno-zhé-ña) f. multiplication
table
tabor kolejowy (tá-bor ko-le-
yó-vi) m. rolling stock (r.r.)
taboret (ta-bo-ret) m. taboret
tabu (tá-boo) n. taboo
tabun (tá-boon) m. horse herd
taca (tá-tsa) f. tray; salver
taczki (tách-kee) m. wheelbarrow
tafla (táf-la) f. plate; slab
taic (tá-eech) v. hide; conceal
tajac (tá-yach) v. thaw; melt
tajemnica (ta-yem-neé-tsa) f.
secret; mystery;secrecy
tajemniczy (ta-yem-neé-chi) adj.
m. mysterious;inscrutable'weird
tajny (táy-ni) adj. m. secret
tak (tak) part. yes; adv. thus;
as;indecl.:like this;so
tak czy tak (tak chi tak) exp.
anyhow; either way;in any case
taki (tá-kee) adj. m. such
taki sam (tá-kee sam) adj. m.
identical ; similar
takielunek (ta-ke-lóo-nek) m.
rig; rigging; tackle

taksa (ták-sa) f. tariff; rate
taksacja (tak-sáts-ya) f. tax-
appraisal
taksowac (tak-so-vach) v. estimate; rate; appraise;value
taksówka (tak-sóov-ka) f. taxi
takt (takt) m. tact
taktowny (tak-tóv-ni) adj. m.
tactful;cosiderate
taktyczny (tak-tich-ni) adj.m.
tactical; political
taktyka (tak-ti-ka) f. tactics
także (ták-zhe) adv. also; too;
as well; likewise; alike
talent (tá-lent) m. talent
talerz (tá-lesh) m. (food)plate;
plateful; disk;planting scalp
talerzyk (ta-lé-zhik) m. small
plate ; ski-stick disk; scale
talia (tál-ya) f. waist; card
deck; tackle; middle
talk (tá-lk) m. talcum ;talc
talon (tá-lon) m. coupon
tam (tam) adv. there; yonder
tama (tá-ma) f. dam; dike
tamowac (ta-mó-vach) v. dam up;
block ; check; stem; clog
tamtejszy (tam-téy-shi) adj. m.
from there; living there
tamten (tám-ten) pron. that
tamtędy (tam-tán-di) adv. that
way; the other way
tamże (tam-zhe) adv. there in;
in the same place;ay which place
tancerka (tan-tsér-ka) f. dancer ; ballet-dancer; partner
tancerz (tán-tsesh) m. dancer
tandeta (tan-dé-ta) f. trashy
products; shoddy goods
taneczny (ta-néch-ni) adj. m.
dancing ;dance-(step;music etc.)
tangens (tán-gens) m. tangent
tani (tá-ñee) adj. m. cheap
taniec (tá-ñets) m. dance
taniec (tá-ñech) v. get cheaper; cheapen grow cheaper
taniość (tá-ñoshch) f. cheap-
ness; low prices
tańczyc (tań-chich) v. dance
tankowiec (tan-kó-vyets) m.
tanker
tapczan (táp-chan) m. couch;
convertible bed

tapeta (ta-pé-ta) f. wallpaper
tapicer (ta-pée-tser) m. upholsterer ;upholsterer's shop
taran (ta-ran) m. battering ram
tarapaty (ta-ra-pá-ti) pl.
trouble; predicament;sad fix
taras (tá-ras) m. terrace
tarasować (ta-ra-so-vach) v.
block;stand in the way ⌐plank
tarcica (tar-chee-tsa) f. deal;
tarcie (tár-che) n. friction;
frictional resistance
tarcza (tár-cha) f. shield;disk
tarczowa piła (tar-chó-va pee-
wa) circular saw
tarczyca (tar-chi-tsa) f. thy-
roid gland
targ (targ) m. country market
targać (tár-gach) v. tear;jerk
targować (tar-gó-vach) v. sell;
bargain; trade; haggle;deal
tarka (tár-ka) f. rasp; grater
tartak (tár-tak) m. sawmill
taryfa (ta-rí-fa) f. tariff
tarzac się (tá-zhach shán) v.
wallow; welter; roll(in mud)
tasak (ta-sak) m. chopper;
cleaver
tasiemiec (ta-she-myets) m.
tapeworm; cestoid; taenia
tasiemka (ta-shem-ka) f. ribbon;
tape
tasować (ta-so-vach) v. shuffle
taśma (tash-ma) f. band; tape
taśma ruchoma (tash-ma roo-kho-
ma) f. belt conveyor
tatarka (ta-tár-ka) f. buckwheat
taternik (ta-tér-neek) m. mountain climber;alpinist
tatuować (ta-too-o-vach) v. tattoo; make a tattoo mark
tatuś (ta-toosh) m. daddy;dad
tchawica (tkha-vee-tsa) f. tra-
chea; windpipe
tchnąć (tkhnównch) v. inspire
tchnienie (tkhne-ne) n. breath
tchórz (tkhoosh) m. skunk; coward;craven;poltroon; funk
tchórzliwy (tkhoo-zhlee-vi)
adj. m. cowardly;chicken-hearted
tchórzostwo (tkhoo-zhoost-vo)
n. cowardice

teatr (te-atr) m. theatre;the stage
teatralny (te-a-tral-ni) adj.
m. theatrical; scenic; stage-
techniczny (tekh-neech-ni) adj.
m. technical(terms,school,staff...)
technik (tekh-neek) m. technician; engineer; mechanic
technika (tekh-nee-ka) f. technique; engineering;technology
technologia (tekh-no-log-ya) f.
technology;production engineering
teczka (tech-ka) f. briefcase;
folder;portfolio;jacket;binder
tegoroczny (te-go-roch-ni)adj.m.
this year's
teka (te-ka) f. (large) briefcase; portfolio;file;folder
tekst (te-kst) m. text;wording
tekstylny (teks-til-ni) adj.m.
textile;textile-;draper-;clothier-
tektura (tek-too-ra) f. cardboard; pasteboard(corrugated)
telefon (te-le-fon) m. telephone;phone;phone receiver
telefonistka (te-le-fo-neest-
ka) f. telephone operator
telefonować (te-le-fo-no-vach)
v. ring up; telephone;call up
telegraf (te-le-graph) m. telegraph;telegraph office
telegraficzny (te-le-gra-feech-
ni) adj. m. telegraphic
telegrafować (te-le-gra-fo-
vach) v. cable; wire; telegraph
telegram (te-le-gram) m. telegram; cable; wire;cablegram
telepatia (te-le-pát-ya) f. te-
lepathy;thought transference
teleskop (te-les-kop)m. telescope; telescopic spring
teleskopowy (te-les-ko-po-vi)
adj. m. telescopic
telewizja (te-le-veez-ya) f.
television; TV
telewizor (te-le-vee-zor) m.
television set;TV set
temat (te-mat) m. subject
temblak (tem-blak) m. sling
temperament (tem-pe-rá-ment)
m. temper;nature;mettle
temperatura (tem-pe-ra-too-ra)
f. temperature; fever

temperować (tem-pe-ro-vach) v.
temper; sharpen; mitigate
temperówka (tem-pe-roov-ka) f.
pencil sharpener
tempo (tém-po) n. rate; tempo
temu (te-mu) adv. ago
ten;ta, to (ten, ta, to) m.f.n.
pron. this
ten sam (ten sam) pron. the
same (man, pencil, etc.)
tendencja (ten-den-tsya) f. tendency;inclination;proclivity
tendencyjny (ten-den-tsiy-ni)
adj. m. biased;tedentious
tenis (te-nees) m. tennis
tenor (te-nor) m. tenor(voice)
tenuta (te-noo-ta) f. land holding; rent;tenure; lease
tenże (tén-zhe) m. pron. the
same (individual etc.)
teolog (te-o-lok) m. theologian
teologia (the-o-log-ya) f. theology; Faculty of Theology
teoretyczny (te-o-re-tich-ni)
adj. m. theoretical;speculative
teoretyk (te-o-re-tik) m. theo-
retician; theorist
teoria (te-or-ya) f. theory
terapia (te-rap-ya) f. therapeu-
ics; therapy
teraz (te-ras) adv. now;nowadays
teraźniejszosć (te-razh-ney-
shoshch) f. present (time)
teraźniejszy kurs (te-razh-ney-
shi koors) m. present rate
teren (te-ren) m. terrain
terenowy samochód (te-re-no-vi
sa-mo-khood) m. cross-country
car (four wheel drive)
terkotać (ter-ko-tach) v. rattle; clatter;chatter(away)
termin (ter-meen) m. term; apprenticeship;time limit(fixed)
termin ostateczny (ter-meen os-
ta-tech-ni) m. deadline
terminator (ter-mee-na-tor) m.
apprentice;terminator
terminarz (ter-mee-nash) m. appointment calendar; agenda
terminologia (ter-mee-no-log-
ya) f. terminology;nomenclature
terminowo (ter-mee-no-vo) adv.
on time;in due time;punctually

termit (ter-meet) m. termite
termometr (ter-mo-metr) m.
thermometer
termos (ter-mos) m. thermos-
bottle;vacuum bottle(flask)
terpentyna (ter-penti-na) f.
turpentine(oil)
terror (ter-ror) m. terror
terroryzować (ter-ro-ri-zo-
vach) v. terrorize; bully
terytorialny (te-ri-tor-yal-
ni) adj. m. territorial
terytorium (te-ri-tor-yoom) n.
territory
testament (tes-ta-ment) m.
testament;(last)will
teściowa (tesh-cho-va) f.
mother-in-law
teść (téshch) m. father-in-law
teza (te-za) f. thesis;argument
też (tesh) adv. also; too;likewise
tęchnąć (tankh-nownch) v. get
musty; grow mouldy;reduce swelling
tęcza (tañ-cha) f. rainbow
tęczowka (tañ-choov-ka) f. iris
tędy (tañ-di) adv. this way
tęgi (tañ-gee) adj. m. stout;
strong; solid; fat;big;portly
tego (tañ-go) adv. stoutly;ably;
amply; mightly ;powerfully
tepak (tañ-pak) m. dullard
tepić (tañ-peech) v. dull;
blunt; destroy; combat; exterminate;oppose ;persecute
tępota (tan-po-ta) f. dullness;
stupidity;obtuseness; stolidity
tępy (tan-pi) adj. m. dull;
point less; slow-witted
tęsknić (tansk-neech) v. long
(for); yearn ; be nostalgic
tęsknota (tansk-no-ta) f. longing ; hankering; nostalgia
tęskny (tansk-ni) adj. m. melancholy;wietful;longing;yearning
tętent (tañ-tent) m. hoof beat
tętnica (tañ-tnee-tsa) f. artery
tętnic (tañt-neech) v. pulsate
tętno (tañt-no) n. pulse;vibrations
tężec (tañ-zhets) m. tetanus
tężeć (tañ-zhech) v. stiffen;
solidify;set;clot;curdle;coagulate;
grow stronger;acquire vigor

tężyzna (tán-zhiz-na) f. vigor
tkacki (tkáts-kee) adj. m. textile ; weaver's;of textiles
tkactwo (tkáts-tvo) n. weaving
tkacz (tkách) m. weaver (man)
tkać (tkáć) v. weave ; poke
tkanina (tka-née-na) f. fabric
tkanka (tkán-ka) f. tissue
tkliwość (tklee-voshch) f. tenderness ;love;affection
tkliwy (tklee-vi) adj. m. tender ;loving;affectionate;sensitive
tknąc (tknównch) v. touch;size
tkwić (tkveech) v. stick;stay
tlec (tlech) v. smoulder
tlen (tlen) m. oxygen
tlenek (tle-nek) m. oxide
tlic się (tleech shán) v.
smoulder; glow ; burn lightly
tło (two) n. background
tłocznia (twóch-ña) f. press
tłoczyc (twó-chich) v. press;
crowd; print; stamp; crush
tłok (twok) m. piston; crowd
tłuc (twoots) v. pound; hammer;
batter; smash; shatter
tłuczek (twoó-chek) m. pestle
tłuczeń (twoó-cheń) m. macadam;
broken stone; road gravel
tłum (twoóm) m. crowd;mob;host
tłumacz (twoó-mach)m. interpreter ; translator
tłumaczenie (twoo-ma-che-ñe) n.
translation;explanation;excuse
tłumaczyc (twoo-má-chich) v.
translate; interpret;justify
tłumic (twoó-meech) v. muffle;
put down; dampen;suppress;stifle
tłumik (twoó-meek) m. muffler
tłumny (twoóm-ni) adj. m. crowded ; numerous ;populous
tłumok (twoó-mok) m. bundle
tłusty (twoós-ti) adj. m. obese;
fat(meat,pig etc.);podgy; oily
tłuszcz (twoóshch) m. fat ;
grease
tłuszcza (twoósh-cha) f. mob
tłuscic (twoósh-cheech) v.
grease ; smear with grease
to (to) pron. it; this; that;so
toaleta (to-a-le-ta) f. toilet
toaletowe przybory (to-a-le-tó-
ve pzhi-bó-ri) pl. toilet-
articles; cosmetics

toast (to-ast) m. toast
tobół (to-boow) m. pack; bundle
toczony (to-chó-ni) adj. m.
turned; shaped;rounded
toczyc (tó-chich) v. roll; machine; wage (war) ;wheel;carry on
toga (tó-ga) f. gown;Roman toga
tok (tok) m. course; progress
tokarka (to-kár-ka) f. lathe
tokarnia (to-kár-ña) f. lathe
tokarz (tó-kash) m. machinist;
turner; lathe operator
tokowac (to-kó-vach) v. toot
tolerancja (to-le-ran-tsya) f.
tolerance;broad-mindedness
tolerowac (to-le-ro-vach) v.
tolerate;suffer;stand for
tom (tom) m. volume
ton (ton) m. sound; tone;note
tona (tó-na) f. ton(metric etc.)
tonacja (to-náts-ya) f. pitch ;
key ; mode; tone
tonaż (tó-nash) m. tonnage
tonąc (tó-nównch) v. drown
toń (toń) f. deep (water);
flood;deep sea;depth of water
topaz (tó-pas) m. topaz
topic (tó-peech) v. drown;thaw;
melt down; smelt (metals);sink
topiel (to-pyel) f. abyss;gulf
topliwy (top-lee-vi) adj. m.
meltable;fusible;liquescent
topniec (top-ñech) v. melt
topografia (to-po-gráf-ya) f.
topography;lay of the land
topola (to-pó-la) f. poplar
toporek (to-pó-rek) m. hatchet
topór (tó-poor) m. (big) hatchet; axe; battle axe
tor (tor) m. track;lane;path
tor kolejowy (tor ko-le-yó-vi)
m. rail -track;railroad track
torba (tó-ba) f. bag; bagful
torcik (tór-cheek) m. small
layer cake
torebka (to-réb-ka) f. (hand)
bag; purse; small bag(or pouch)
torf (tórf) m. peat
torfowisko (tor-fo-vees-ko) n.
peat bog; turbary
torowac (to-ro-vach) v. clear;
pave; clear a path;show the way
torpeda (tor-pé-da) f. torpedo;motor driven rail car

torpedować (tor-pe-do-vaćh) v.
torpedo; scuttle;obstruct
torpedowiec (tor-pe-do-vyets)
m. torpedo boat
tors (tors) m. torso
tort (tort) m. tort (multi-layer) fancy cake
tortura (tor-too-ra) f. torture
torturować (tor-too-ro-vaćh) v.
torture ;torment;put to torture
totalny (to-tal-ni) adj. m. totalitarian; total;entire
towar (to-var) m. merchandise
towarowy dom (to-va-ro-vi dom)
m. department store
towarzystki (to-va-zhis-kee)
adj- m. sociable; social
towarzystwo (to-va-zhist-vo) n.
company ;society;companionship
towarzysz (to-va-zhish) m. companion ;pal;associate;camerade
towarzyszka (to-va-zhish-ka) f.
companion (female);associate
towarzyszyć (to-va-zhi-shićh) v.
accompany ;escort;keep company
tożsamość (tozh-sa-moshćh) f.
identity ; sameness
tracić (tra-ćheećh) v. lose;
waste;shed(leaves); execute
tradycja (tra-dits-ya) f. tradition ;handing down customs etc
tradycyjny (tra-di-tsiy-ni) adj.
m. traditional
traf (traf) m. happenstance;
chance.luck; coincidence
trafem (tra-fem) adv. by chance
trafiac (traf-yach) v. hit
(target) ;guess right; home
trafność (traf-noshćh) f. accuracy ; rightness; soundness
trafny (traf-ni) adj. m. exact;
correct ; right; fit; apt
tragarz (tra-gash) m. porter
tragedia (tra-géd-ya) f. tragedy :very sad or tragic event
tragiczny (tra-geech-ni) adj. m.
tragic ; disastrous;very sad
tragikomedia (tra-gee-ko-méd-ya) f. tragicomedy
trajkotać (tray-ko-tach) v.
chatter; jabber ;rattle;gabble
trak (trak) m. square saw ;frame
saw

trakcja (trak-tsya) f. traction
trakt (trakt) m. highway; course
traktat (trak-tat) m. treaty
traktor (trak-tor) m. tractor
traktować (trak-to-vach) v.deal;
treat; negotiate ; discuss
trampolina (tram-po-leé-na) f.
spring board; diving board
tramwaj (tram-vay) m. tramway
tramwajarz (tram-va-yash) m.
tramway worker
tran (trán) m. (cod or whale)
oil; cod liver oil
trans (trans) m. trance ;ectasy
transakcja (trans-ákts-ya) f.
transaction; deal
transatlantycki (trans-at-lantits-kee) adj. m. transatlantic
transformator (trans-for-ma-tor)
m. transformer;converter
transfuzja (trans-fooz-ya) f.
transfusion(of blood etc.)
transmisja (trans-meés-ya) f.
transmission; broadcast
transmitować (trans-mee-to-vaćh)
v. transmit; broadcast
transparent (trans-pa-rent) m.
(marching) slogans; banner
transport (trans-port) m. transport; haulage; consignment
tranzyt (trán-zit) m. transit
tranzytowy (tran-zi-to-vi) adj.
m. transit-;through(traffic etc.)
trapez (tra-pes) m. trapeze
trapic (tra-peech) v. molest;
pester; worry; annoy; bother
trasa (tra-sa) f. route;(bus)line
trasa podróży (tra-sa pod-roo-zhi) f. itinerary
tratować (tra-to-vach) v. trample; tred down
tratwa (trat-va) f. raft;float
trawa (tra-va) f. grass
trawic (tra-veech) v. digest
trawienie (tra-vye-ne) n. digestion;consumption
trawnik (trav-neek) m. lawn
trąba (trown-ba) f. trumpet;
trunk (elephant); tornado;
twister ;horn;whiflwind; ninny
trąba wodna (trown-ba vod-na) f.
waterspout; wind spout

trąbić (trown-beech) v. bugle;
toot ;hoot; roar; proclaim
trąbka (trownb-ka) f. horn;bugle
trącać (trown-tsach) v. jostle;
elbow; tip; knock; nudge;strike
trącić (trown-cheech) v. jostle;
smell;be fusty;be out of date
trąd (trownd) m. leprosy
trel (trel) m. trill
trelować (tre-lo-vach) v. trill
trema (tre-ma) f. stage fright
trener (tre-ner) m. coach;trainer
trening (tre-neeng) m. training
trenować (tre-no-vach) v. train;
coach; practise(shooting)
trepanacja (tre-pa-nats-ya) f.
trepanation
trepki (trep-kee) pl. sandals
tresować (tre-so-vach) v. train;
tame; drill; break in (horses)
tresura (tre-soo-ra) f. taming;
training(of animals)
treściwy (tresh-chee-vi) adj.m.
concise ; substantial;meaty;pithy
treść (treshch) f. content;jist;
substance; essence;pith;marrow
trębacz (tran-bach) m. trumpeter
trędowaty (tran-do-va-ti) adj.m.
leprous; leper
triumfować (tree-oom-fo-vach) v.
triumph;achieve triumphs;prevail
trochę (tro-khan) adv. a little
bit; a few ;some;awhile;a spell
trociny (tro-chee-ni) pl. sawdust; scraps (of writings etc.)
trofea (tro-fe-a) pl. trophies
trojaki (tro-ya-kee) adj. m.
threefold; triple;treble;triplex
troje (tro-ye) num. three
troki (tro-kee) pl. straps
trolejbus (tro-ley-boos) m.
trolleybus
tron (tron) m. throne;the throne
trop (trop) m. track; trace
tropić (tro-peech) v. track
tropikalny (tro-pee-kal-ni) adj.
m. tropical;of the tropics
troska (tros-ka) f. care; anxiety; worry; concern;solicitude
troskać się (tros-kach shan) v.
care and worry about;be cocerned
troskliwość (tros-klee-voshch)
f. thoughtfulness; care; heed

troskliwy (tros-klee-vi) adj.m.
careful; attentive;thoughtful
troszczyć się (trosh-chich
shan) v. care; be anxious
about ; take care;look after
trotuar (tro-too-ar) m. sidewalk; pavement(for pedestrians)
trójbarwny (trooy-barv-ni) adj.
m. tricolor ;three-colored
trójca (trooy-tsa) f. trinity
trójka (trooy-ka) f. three
trójkąt (trooy-kownt) m.
triangle; set square
trójnasób (trooy-na-soob)
three times as much
trójnik (trooy-neek) m. three-
way (pipe) connection;"T"(-tee)
joint; "Y" joint ; wye ; tee
truchtem (trookh-tem) adv. by
jogging ; by trot;at a trot
trucizna (troo-cheez-na) f.
poison; venom
truć (trooch) v. poison; bother
(slang); molest; worry
trud (troot) m. pains; toil
trudnić się (trood-neech shan)
v. occupy oneself;be engaged
trudno (trood-no) adv.with
difficulty; too bad;hard
trudność (trood-noshch) f.
difficulty; hardshiphandicap
trudny (trood-ni) adj. m.
difficult;hard;tough;laborious
trudzić (troo-dzheech)v. trouble; disturb; cause trouble
trujący (troo-yown-tsi) adj. m.
poisonous; toxic; poison-
trumna (troom-na) f. coffin
trunek (troo-nek) m. drink
trup (troop) m. corpse;cadaver
trupiarnia (troop-yar-na) f.
mortuary; morgue
truskawka (troos-kav-ka) f.
strawberry
truteń (troo-ten) m. drone
trwać (trvach) v. last; persist; stay; remain;linger on
trwały (trva-wi) adj. m. durable
trwanie (trva-ne) n. duration
trwoga (trvo-ga) f. awe; fright
trwonić (trvo-neech) v. waste;
squander; trifle away; fritter
away (money,time, energy etc.)

trwoźliwy (trvozh-leé-vi) adj.
m. timid; fearful; shy
trwożny (trvóżh-ni) adj. m.
anxious; fearful; timid ;shy
trwożyć (trvó-zhich) v. startle;
frighten; scare ;be frightening
tryb (trib) m. manner; mode;
mood; gear; procedure ;course
trybuna (tri-boó-na) f. tribune;
stand; speaker's platform
trybunał(tri-boo-naw) m.tribunal
trychina (tri-kheé-na) f. trichina; trichinosis
trygonometria (tri-go-no-métr-ya)
f. trigonometry(spherical etc.)
tryk (trik) m. 1.ram(ing);2.trik
trykot (tri-kot) m. tricot
trykotowy (tri-ko-tó-vi) adj.m.
tricot; made of tricot
trykotaże (tri-ko-tá-zhe) pl.
hosiery; knittings
trykotowy (tri-ko-tó-vi) adj.m.
knitted(goods,fabric,wear etc.)
trylion (tril-yon) num. trillion
tryskać (tris-kach) v. spurt;
spout; gush ;jet;squirt;flow
trywialny (tri-vyál-ni) adj.m.
trivial; vulgar; coarse; trite
trzask (tzhask) m. crack ; bang
trzaska (tzhás-ka) f. chip(wood)
trzaskać (tzhás-kach) v. crack;
bang ; smash; shatter;knock;hit
trząść (tzhównshch) v. shake
trzcina (tzhcheé-na) f. cane;
reed( of bamboo etc.)
trzcina cukrowa (tzhcheé-na
coo-króva) f. sugar cane
trzcinowy (tzhchee-nó-vi) adj.
m. cane(chair);made out of cane
trzeba (tzhe-ba) v. imp. ought
to;one should ﬔgut;geld
trzebić (tzhé-beech) v. clear;
trzeci (tzhe-chee) num. third
trzec (tzhech) v. rub; grate
trzepaczka (tzhe-pách-ka) f.
whisk; beater;carpet beater
trzepać (tzhe-pach) v. hit
dust out ; beat(carpet); slap
trzepnąć (tzhép-nownch) v. hit;
crump; strike;spank;slap;wag
trzepotać (tzhe-pó-tach) v.
flap; flutter;flicker; toss

trzeszczeć (tzhésh-chech) v.crack;
crackle;creak;crunch;rustle
trzewia (tzhey-ya) pl. bowels;guts
trzewik (tzhe-veek) m. shoe;slipper
trzeźwić (tzhéżh-veech) v. sober up;bring back to consciousness
trzeźwość (tzhéżh-voshch) f.
sobriety;level-headedness
trzeźwy (tzhéżh-vi) adj. m.
sober;clear headed;wide awake
trzęsawisko (tzhǎñ-sa-veés-ko)
n. bog;swamp;quagmire;slough
trzęsienie ziemi (tzhǎñ-she-ñe
żhé-mee) n. earthquake
trzmiel (tzhmyel) m. bumblebee
trznadel (tzhná-del) m. yellow
bunting;yellow hammer;bunting
trzoda (tzhó-da) f. herd;
flock; heard(of swine,pigs etc.)
trzon (tzhon) m. handle; hilt;core
trzonek (tzhó-nek) m. shaft;shank;
handle(of a hammer, axe etc.)
trzonowy ząb (tzho-no-vi zówñb)
m. molar; grinder
trzpień (tzhpyeñ) m. pin
trzpiot (tzhpyot) m. giddy; gay
trzustka (tzhoóst-ka) f. pan-
creas; sweetbread
trzy (tzhi) num. three
trzydziestokrotny (tzhi-dżhes-
to-krót-ni) adj. m. thirtyfold
trzydziestoletni (tzhi-dżhes-to-
lét-ñee) adj. m. thirty year
old(man,oak,house,horse etc.)
trzydziesty (tzhi-dżhes-ti) num.
thirtieth
trzydzieści (tzhi-dżhésh-chee)
num. thirty
trzykrotny (tzhi-krót-ni) adj.
m. threefold
trzylampowy (tzhi-lam-pó-vi)
adj. m. three-lamp
trzyletni (tzhi-lét-ñee) adj.
m. three year old(boy,car etc.)
trzymać (tzhi-mach) v. hold;
keep;cling;clutch;hold on to
trzynasty (tzhi-nás-ti) num.
thirteenth
trzynaście (tzhi-náshche) num.
thirteen
trzypiętrowy (tzhi-pyǎñ-tro-vi)
adj. m. three-story high(house)

trzysta (tzhís-ta) num.
three hundred
tu (too) adv. here;in here
tuba (too-ba) f. tube;horn
tubka (toob-ka) f. small tube
tuberkuliczny (too-ber-koo-
leech-ni) adj. m. tuberculous
tubylczy (too-bíl-chi) adj. m.
native;indigenous; local
tubylec (too-bí-lets) m. native;
aboriginal; local inhabitant
tucznik (tooch-ñeek) m. porker
tuczyc (too-chich) v. fatten
tulejka (too-léy-ka) f. socket
tulic (too-leech) v. hug; fondle
tulipan (too-leé-pan) m. tulip
tułacz (too-wach) m. wanderer;
vagrant ;exile ;homeless wander-
tułaczka (too-wach-ka) f. homeless wandering;wandering life
tułac się (too-wach shañ) v.
wander;be homeless;be in exile
tułów (too-woov) m. torso
tum (toom) m. cathedral;minster
tuman (too-man) m. 1. dust-cloud;
2. dummie;nitwit;duffer
tunel (too-nel) m. tunnel
tupac (too-pach) v. stamp;tramp
tupet (too-pet) m. nerve;chutz-
pah; self-assurance;impudence
tur (toor) m. bison; aurochs
turbina (toor-beé-na) f. turbine
turecki (too-réts-kee) adj. m.
Turkish(saddle,fashion etc.)
turkawka (toor-káv-ka) f. turtledove;wild dove
turkot (toor-kot) m. rumble;rattle
turkotac (toor-ko-tach) v.
rumble ;bump along; rattle
turkus (toor-koos) m. turquoise
turniej (toor-ñey) m. tournament
turysta (too-rís-ta) m. tourist
turystyczny (too-ris-tích-ni)
adj. m. tourist; touring-
tusz (toosh) m. 1. shower; hit;
2. India ink;mascara
tusza (too-sha) f. corpulence
tuszowac (too-shó-vach) v.
1. draw with ink; 2. cover up;
hush up; stifle (a scandal etc.)
tutaj (too-tay) adv. here
tutejszy (too-téy-shi) adj. m.
local;of this place;of our place

tuzin (too-zheen) m. dozen
tuż (toosh) adv. near by;
close by; just before;just after
tuż obok (toosh o-bok) adv.
next too; near by: close by
twardniec (tvárd-ñech) v. hard-
en; stiffen; fix; bind
twardosc (tvar-doshch) f. hardness ; stiffness; severity
twardy (tvar-di) adj. m. hard
twarożek (tva-ró-zhek) m. cottage cheese;small cottage cheese
twarog (tvá-roog) m. cottage
cheese curds; cottage cheese
twarz (tvash) f. face;physionomy
twarzowy (tva-zhó-vi) adj. m.
becoming; facial(bone etc.)
twierdza (tvyér-dza) f. fortress ; stronghold;citadel
twierdzący (tvyer-dzown-tsi)
adj. m. affirmative(answer etc.)
twierdzenie (tvyer-dze-ñe) n.
affirmation; theorem;assertion
twierdzic (tvyér-dzheech) v.
assert; maintain;affirm; say
twornik (tvór-ñeek) m. armature
tworzyc (tvo-zhich) v. create;
form ; compose; produce; make
tworzywo sztuczne (tvo-zhi-vo
shtooch-ne) n. plastic
twoj (tvooy) pron. yours; your
twor (tvoor) m. creation; piece
of work ; origination;outgrowth
tworca (tvoor-tsa) m. creator;
author; maker ;originator
tworczosc (tvoor-choshch) f.
creation;output ;production
tworczy (tvoor-chi) adj. m.
creative ; originative:formative
ty (ti) pron. you(familiar form)
tyczka (tich-ka) f. pole; perch
tyczyc się (ti-chich shañ) v.
concern; regard;refer to
tyc (tich) v. grow fat
tydzień (ti-dzheñ) m. week
tyfus (ti-foos) typhus
tygiel (ti-gel) m. crucible
tygodnik (ti-god-ñeek) m.
weekly (magazine etc.)
tygodniowy (ti-god-ño-vi) adj.
m. weekly (pay etc.)
tygrys (tíg-ris) m. tiger ;type
of German tank in World War II

tygrysica (tig-ri-sheé-tsa) f.
tigeress
tyka (tí-ka) f. perch; pole
tyka miernicza (tí-ka myer-neé-cha) f. surveyor's rod; affect;
tykać (ti-kaćh) v. touch; tick;
tykwa (ti̯k-va) f. pumpkin; strike
tyle (tí-le) adv. so much; as
many; as much; so many; that much
tylekroc (ti-le-kroch) adv. so
many times: that many times
tylko (tíl-ko) adv. only; but; just
tylko co (tíl-ko tso) adv. just
now; a moment ago; this instant
tylna straż (tíl-na strash) f.
rear guard
tylny (tíl-ni) adj. m. back;
hind(leg etc.); rear (light etc.)
tył (tiw) m. back; rear; stern
tym lepiej (tim le-pyey) adv.
so much better
tymczasem (tim-chá-sem) adv.
meantime; during ; at the time
tymczasowo (tim-cha-só-vo) adv.
provisionally; temporarily
tymczasowy (tim-cha-só-vi) adj.
m. temporary; provisional
tynk (tink) m. plaster(work)
tynkować (tin -kó-vach) v.
plaster; rough cast (a wall)
tynktura (tink-too-ra) f. tincture; tinge; light color
typ (tip) m. type; model; guy
typowy (ti-pó-vi) adj. m. typical; standard (article etc.)
tyrada (ti-rá-da) f. tirade
tyran (ti-ran) m. tyrant; bully
tyrania (ti-rań-ya) f. tyranny
tyrański (ti-rań-skee) adj. m.
tyrannical; tyrannous; bullying
tysiąc (ti-shównts) num. thousand
tysiąclecie (ti-shównts-le-che)
n. millennium
tysiącletni (ti-shównts-lét-ńi)
adj. m. millenary
tysięczny (ti-shanch-ni) num.
thousandth
tytan (ti-tan) m. titan; titanium; demon(of work etc.)
tytaniczny (ti-ta-ńeech-ni) adj.
m. titanic ; huge

tytoniowy (ti-to-ńo-vi) adj. m.
tobacco ; of tobacco leaves
tytoń (ti-toń) m. tobacco
tytularny (ti-too-lár-ni) adj.
m. titular; nominal
tytuł (ti-toow) m. title
tytułowa strona (ti-too-wó-va
stro-na) f. title page
tytułować (ti-too-wó-vach) v.
entitle; address; style as a...
u (oo) prep. beside; at; with;
by; on; from; in; (idiomatic)
u boku (oo bo-koo) exp.: at one's
side (to have a helper, a sabre...)
ubarwić (oo-bár-veech) v. color
ubawić się (oo-bá-veech shań)
v. have fun; have a good laugh
ubezpieczać (oo-bez-pye-chach)
v. insure; secure; protect
ubezpieczalnia (oo-bez-pye-chál-
ńa) f. health insurance center; insurence company
ubezpieczenie (oo-bez-pye-che-
ńe) n. insurance; protection
ubezpieczenie życia (oo-bez-pye-
che-ńe zhi-cha) n. life insurance; life assurance
ubezpieczenie społeczne (oo-bez-
pye-che-ńe spo-wéch-ne) n.
social security insurance
ubiec (oo-byets) v. run; pass
ubiegać się (oo-byé-gach shań)
v. solicit; compete for
ubiegły (oo-byég-wi) adj. m.
past; last (year, week etc.)
ubierać (oo-bye-rach) v. dress
ubijaczka (oo-bee-yach-ka) f.
stamper; compactor; kitchen whisk
ubijać (oo-bee-yach) v. stamp;
churn; chip; kill; pack; ram
ubijac interes (oo-bee-yach
een-te-res) v. strike a bargain; strike a deal
ubikacja (oo-bee-káts-ya) f.
toilet; rest room; powder room; W.C.
ubiór (oob-yoor) m. attire; grab
ubliżać (oo-blee-zhach) v. insult ; offend; affront
ubliżający (oo-blee-zha-yówn-
tsi) adj. m. offensive; insulting; disparaging
uboczny produkt (oo-bóch-ni
pró-dookt) m. byproduct

ubogi (oo-bó-gee) adj. m. poor
ubolewać (oo-bo-lé-vach) v,
deplore; feel sympathy, for...
ubolewanie (oo-bo-le-va-ñe) n,
regret; lamentation;sympathy
ubożeć (oo-bó-zhech) v. become
poor; become impoverished
ubój (oo-booy)m. slaughter
ubóstwiać (oo-boost-vyach) v.
idolize; love;be crazy about
ubóstwo (oo-boost-vo) n. poverty;;destitution;meagerness
ubosc (oo-booshch) v. gore
ubrać (oob-rach) v. dress
ubranie (oob-rá-ñe) n. clothes;
decoration:putting in a fix
ubytek (oo-bi-tek) m. decrease
ubytek krwi (oo-bi-tek krvee)
blood loss
ubywać (oo-bi-vach) v. retire;
go; lessen; reduce; decrease
ucałować (oo-tsa-wo-vach) v.
kiss (good night,good bye etc.)
ucho (oo-kho) n. ear; handle;
(needle) eye;ring(of anchors)
uchodzić (oo-kho-dzheech)v. go
away; flee; pass (for)
uchodźca (oo-khódzh-tsa) m.
refugee;displaced person
uchowac (oo-khó-vach) v. save;
preserve;save;retain;keep;rear
uchronic (oo-khro-ñeech) v.
guard; preserve;protect;keep
uchwalac (oo-khva-lach) v.
pass a law ; resolve; decide
uchwała (oo-khvá-wa) f. resolution; vote; law
uchwycic (oo-khvi-chich) v.
grasp; catch; seize; see ;get
uchwyt (ookh-vit), m. handle
uchwytny (oo-khvit-ni) adj.m.
graspable; palpable;audible
uchybiac (oo-khib-yach) v.
fail; offend ; transgress
uchybienie (oo-khi-byé-ñe) n.
offense ; transgression ;insult
uchylac (oo-khi-lach) v. put
aside ; half-open; set ajar
uciążliwy (oo-chown-zhlee-vi)
adj. m. burdensome ; heavy
ucichać (oo-chee-khach) v.
calm down ; be hushed;abate
uciecha (oo-che-kha) f. joy

ucieczka (oo-chech-ka) f. escape ; flight; desertion;recourse
ucielesnić (oo-che-lésh-ñeech)
v. embody ; personify
uciekac (oo-che-kach) v. flee
uciemiężać (oo-che-myañ-zhach)
v. oppress ; burden;tread down
ucierac (oo-che-rach) v. wipe
off; grind ; grate; level;pound
ucierpiec (oo-chér-pyech) v.
suffer ; be hard hit;sustain a loss
ucieszny (oo-chesh-ni) adj. m.
funny ; comical; droll ;amusing
ucieszyc (oo-che-shich) v. gladden ; please; gratify ; delight
ucinac (oo-chee-nach) v. cut off
ucisk (oo-cheesk) m. oppression
uciskac (oo-chees-kach) v. press;
pinch; opress ; hurt ;compress
uciszyc (oo-chee-shich) v. silence ; quiet; still; soothe;lull
uciułac (oo-choo-wach) v. scrape
together ; save ;put aside
uczcic (oóch-cheech) v. honor;
dignify ; celebrate ;commemorate
uczciwy (ooch-chée-vi) adj. m.
honest ; upright; straight
uczelnia (oo-chel-ña) f. school;
college ; academy ;university
uczenie (oo-che-ñe) adv. learned-
ly ; n. learning ; teaching
uczennica (oo-chen-ñee-tsa) f.
schoolgirl;(girl) pupil
uczen (oó-cheñ) m. schoolboy
uczepic (oo-che-peech) v. hang
on ; hitch; hook; attach;fasten
uczesac (oo-che-sach) v. comb
(hair);brush hair;dress hair
uczesanie (oo-che-sa-ñe) n.
hairdo ; hairstyle; coiffure
uczestniczyc (oo-chest-ñee-chich)
- v. take part ; share in;participate
uczestnik (oo-chest-ñeek) m.
participant ;(sport)competitor
uczęszczać (oo-chañsh-chach) v.
frequent; attend(concerts,school...)
uczony (oo-cho-ni) m. scientist;
learned; erudite; scholarly man
uczta (oóch-ta) f. feast;banquet
uczucie (oo-choo-che) n. feeling
uczuciowy (oo-choo-cho-vi)adj.
m. sensitive ; emotional;sentimental
uczuć (oó-chooch) v. feel ;realize

uczyc (oo-chich) v. teach; train
uczyc się (oo-chich shań) v.
learn; study; take lessons
uczynek (oo-chi-nek) m. deed
uczynic (oo-chi-ńeech) v. make
uczynność (oo-chih-noshch) f.
kindness ; helpfulness
uczynny (oo-chih-ni) adj. m.
obliging ; helpful ;cooperative
udany (oo-da-ni) adj. m. successful; put on; sham
udar słoneczny (oo-dar swo-
nech-ni) m. sunstroke
udaremnic (oo-da-rem-ńeech) v.
frustrate; foil; upset; defeat
udawać (oo-da-vach) v. pretend
udawać się(oo-dá-vach shań)v.go;
succeed;manage;pan out;make for
udeptac (oo-dep-tach) v. tread
down; beat a path ;tread on
uderzac (oo-de-zhach) v. hit
uderzenie (oo-de-zhe-ńe) n.
blow; stroke; hit; bump ;impact
udo (oo-do) n. thigh
udobruchac (oo-do-broo-khach)
v. appease; win over; coax
udogodnic (oo-do-gód-ńeech) v.
facilitate; improve
udoskonalenie (oo-dos-ko-na-le-
ńe) n. perfection;improvement
udoskonalic (oo-dos-ko-na-leech)
v. perfect; improve
udostępnic (oo-dos-tánp-ńeech)
v. give access;put within reach
udowodnic (oo-do-vod-ńeech) v.
prove; demonstrate;substantiate
udowodnienie (oo-do-vod-ńe-ńe)
n. evidence; proof;demonstration
udręka (ood-rań-ka) f. anguish;
torment; distress; worry
udusic (oo-doo-sheech) v. strangle; smother; stifle; throttle
udział (oo-dżhaw) m. share;
part; quota;participation
udziałowiec (oo-dżha-wo-vyets)
m. shareholder; partner
udzielac (oo-dżhe-lach) v.
give; grant; furnish; apply
udzielenie (oo-dżhe-le-ńe) n.
giving; granting;dispensing
ufać (oo-fach) v. trust;confide
ufność (oof-noshch) f. confidence; trust; reliance

ufny (oof-ni) adj. confident;
trustful;hopeful;reliant;sanguine
ufundowac (oo-foon-do-vach) v.
found; set up ;endow;establish
uganiac się (oo-ga-ńach shań)
v. chase after;seek(graces,job...)
ugaszczac (oo-gash-chach) v.
entertain ; treat; feast;treat to
uginac (oo-gee-nach) v. bend-
down; deflect; inflect;bow before
ugłaskac(oog-was-kach) v. tame
ugniatac (oog-ńa-tach) v. press-
down ; exert pressure; pinch
ugoda (oo-gó-da) f. agreement
ugodowiec (oo-go-do-vyets) m.
compromiser;advocate of conciliation
ugodowy (oo-go-do-vi) adj.m.
conciliatory ; amicable
ugodzic (oo-gó-dżheech)v.hit;hire
ugór (oo-goor) m. fallow
ugryzc (oog-rishch) v. bite off
ugrzęznac (oo-gzhańz-nownch)
v. stick; be stuck; get bogged
uiszczenie (oo-eesh-che-ńe) n.
payment(of a bill,rent etc.)
uiścic (oo-eésh-cheech) v. pay
up ; remit(a sum); acquit(a debt)
ujadac (oo-ya-dach) v. yelp;quarrel
ujarzmic (oo-yazh-meech) v.
subdue ; enslave ; enthrall;
subjugate
ujawniac (oo-yav-ńach) v. reveal ; disclose;expose;unmask;show
ująć (oo-yownch) v. conceive;
deduct ; seize; grasp; lessen;win
ujednolicic (oo-yed-no-lee-
cheech) v. standardize ;unify
ujemny (oo-yem-ni) adj. m.
negative(value,etc.);unfavorable
ujeżdżac (oo-yezh-dzhach) v.
break in (a horse);smooth(a road)
ujeżdżalnia (oo-yezh-dzhal-ńa)
f. riding school ;manege
ujęcie (oo-yań-che) n. grasp
ujma (ooy-ma) f. detraction
ujmowac (ooy-mo-vach) v. seize
restrain;embrace;apprehend;express
ujmujący (ooy-moo-yówn-tsi) adj.
m. winsome;egaging;prepossessing
ujrzec (ooy-zhech) v. see;glimpse
ujście (ooysh-che) n. escape;
(river) mouth;withdrawal;retreat;
outlet;issue;vent (to indignation)

ukamienowaa (oo-ka-mye-no-vach)
v. stone to death; lapidate
ukazać (oo-ka-zach) v. show
(appear) ; exhibit; reveal
ukasic (oo-kown-sheech) v. bite
ukąszenie (oo-kown-she-ne) n.
bite ; sting
uklęknąc (oo-klank-nownch) v.
genuflect; kneel down
układ (ook-wat) m. scheme; agreement; disposition;system
układać się (ook-wa-dach shan)
v. lay down; negotiate;pan out
układanka (oo-kwa-dan-ka) f.
jigsaw puzzle;building blocks
układny (ook-wad-ni) adj. m. polite ; urbane; affable;mannerly
ukłon (ook-won) m. bow (greeting)
ukłonic się (oo-kwo-neech shan)
v. bow; tip one's hat ; greet
ukłucie (oo-kwoo-che) n. prick;
sting; sharp pain; prod;twinge
ukochać (oo-ko-khach) v. take
a fancy ; grow fond; hug
ukochana (oo-ko-kha-na) adj. f.
beloved ; darling; pet (female)
ukochany (oo-ko-kha-ni) adj. m.
beloved ; darling; pet (male)
ukoic (oo-ko-eech) v. soothe
ukojenie (oo-ko-ye-ne) n. relief ; consolation;allevivtion
ukonczyc (oo-kon-chich) v. complete; finish ; end (school etc.)
ukos (oo-kos) m. slant ; incline
ukosny (oo-kosh-ni) adj. m. oblique ; sloping; skew; diagonal
ukracać (oo-kra-tsach) v. curb;
subdue ; reform; check;put an end
ukradkiem (oo-krad-kem) adv.
stealthily ; by stealth;furtively
ukraiński (ook-ra-een-skee) adj.
m. Ukrainian; of Ukraine
ukrajac (oo-kra-yach) v. cut off
ukręcic (ook-ran-cheech) v.
twist off ; roll up; wrench off
ukrop (ook-rop) m. boiling water ; feverish bustle
ukrocic (ook-roo-cheech) v. repress; curb; reform;put an end to
ukrycie (ook-ri-che) n. hiding
place ; hideaway; hideout;cover
ukrywać (oo-kri-vach) v. hide;
cover up ; conceal; hold back

ukryty (ook-ri-ti) adj. m. hidden; concealed;put out of sight
ukrywac (ook-ri-vach) v. hide
ukształtowac (ook-shtaw-to-
vach) v. shape ; fashion; cast
ukształtowanie (oo-kshtaw-to-
va-ne) n. configuration; for-
mulation ; form; shape
ukuc (oo-kooch) v. hammer out
ul (ool) m. beehive ; hive
ulac (oo-lach) v. pour off;
cast(metal);pour off water
ulatac (oo-la-tach) v. fly off
ulatniac się (oo-lat-nach shan)
v. evaporate; volatize; vanish ; melt away; leak; escape
ulatywac (oo-la-ti-vach) v.
fly away; leak (vapors; odors,
smells) ; rise in the air
uleczalny (oo-le-chal-ni) adj.
m. curable; remediable; medicable
uleczenie (oo-le-che-ne) n.
cure; successful recovery
uleczyc (oo-le-chich) v. heal
ulegac (oo-le-gach) v. yield
ulegly (oo-leg wi) adj. m.
submissive; docile; compliant
ulepszac (oo-lep-shach) v.
improve; better; ameliorate
ulepszenie (oo-lep-she-ne) n.
improvement ; amelioration
ulewa (oo-le-va) f. rainstorm
ulewac (oo-le-vach) v. pour
off; cast (metals);pour(water)
ulga (ool-ga) f. relief;solace
ulezec się (oo-le-zhech shan)
v. mellow; settle;lie quiet
ulica (oo-lee-tsa) f. street
uliczka (oo-lech-ka) f. lane
ulicznica (oo-leech-nee-tsa)
f. prostitute; streetwalker
ulicznik (oo-leech-neek) m.
gamin; guttersnipe ;nipper
ulitowac się (oo-lee-to-vach
shan) v. have pity;take pity
ulotka (oo-lot-ka) f. hand -
bill ; leaflet;throwaway
ultimatum (ool-tee-ma-toom) n.
ultimatum;final offer(demand)
ultrafioletowy (ool-tra-fyo-le-
to-vi) adj. m. ultraviolet
ulubieniec (oo-loo-bye-nets) n.
favorite ; darling; pet

ulubiony (oo-loo-byo-ni) adj.
m. beloved;favorite; pet
ulżyć (ool-zhich) v. relieve
ułamać (oo-wa-mach) v. break
off ; be broken off;come off
ułamek (oo-wa-mek) m. fraction;
fragment;mathematical fraction
ułamkowy (oo-wam-ko-vi) adj.m.
fractional(number,report etc.)
ułan (oo-wan) m. uhlan (Polish
light cavalryman (lancer)
ułaskawić (oo-was-ka-veech) v.
pardon(a condemned person),
ułaskawienie (oo-was-ka-vye-ne)
n. pardon; reprieve
ułatwić (oo-wat-veech) v. facilitate; simplify;make easier
ułatwienie (oo-wat-vye-ne) n.
facilitation; simplification
ułomność (oo-wom-noshch) f. de-
formity; defect ; frailty
ułomny (oo-wom-ni) adj. m. disabled; defective; lame;faulty
ułożony (oo-wo-zho-ni) adj.m.
arranged; well-mannered; set
umacniać (oo-mats-nach) v.
strengthen; fortify; secure
umaczać (oo-ma-chach) v. dip;
wet; soak; sop;have hand in;
umarły (oo-mar-wi) adj. m. deceased; dead
umartwiać (oo-mart-vyach) v.
mortify(a person)
umarzać (oo-ma-zhach) v. amortize; discontinue ; remit
umawiać się (oo-mav-yach shan)
v. make a date (or plan)
umeblować (oo-meb-lo-vach) v.
furnish; fit out; fit up
umeblowanie (oo-meb-lo-va-ne)
n. furniture ;furnishings
umiar (oom-yar) m. moderation
umiarkowany (oo-myar-ko-va-ni)
adj. m. moderate; temperate
umiec (oo-myech) v. know how
umiejętność (oo-mye-yant-noshch)
f. science; skill; know how
umiejscowić (oo-myey-stso-veech)
v. locate; assign a place;place
umierać (oo-mye-rach) v. die
umieszczać (oo-myesh-chach) v.
place; put; set;insert;seat

umilać (oo-mee-lach) v. make
pleasant; add charm:give charm
umilknąć (oo-meelk-nownch) v.
fall silent ; cease talking
umiłowany (oo-mee-wo-va-ni) adj.
m. beloved ; favorite; dear
umizgać się (oo-meez-gach shan)
v. flirt; woo; court; ogle
umizgi (oo-meez-gee) pl. flirt-
ing ; courtship; love making
umniejszać (oo-mney-shach) v.
diminish; lessen belittle;abate
umocnić (oo-mots-neech) v.
strengthen; fortify; beef up
umocnienie (oo-mots-ne-ne) n .
consolidation; fortification
umocować (oo-mo-tso-vach) v.
fasten; hitch; fix; secure
umorzyć (oo-mo-zhich) v. absolve;
amortize; extinguish
umowa (oo-mo-va) f. contract
umowny (oo-mov-ni) adj. m.
contractual; conventional
umożliwić (oo-mozh-lee-veech) v.
v. make possible; enable
umówić ≈ umawiać
umundurowanie (oo-moon-doo-ro-
va-ne) n. uniforms; uniform
umyc (oo-mich) v. wash up
umykać (oo-mi-kach) v. run away
umysł (oo-misw) m. mind; intellect
umysłowy (oo-mis-wo-vi) adj.m.
mental; intellectual; brain-
umyslnie (oo-mishl-ne) adv. on
purpose ; specially; purposely
umyslny (oo-mishl-ni) adj. m.
intentional; deliberate;special
umywać się (oo-mi-vach shan) v.
wash up; be fit for comparison
umywalnia (oo-mi-wal-na) f.
washbasin ; washroom;washstand
unaocznić (oo-na-och-neech) v.
make evident; visualize
unarodowić (oo-na-ro-do-veech)
v. nationalize;put to state control
unarodowienie (oo-na-ro-do-vye-
ne) nationalization
uncja (oon-tsya) f. ounce
unia (oon-ya) f. union
unicestwić (oo-nee-tses-tveech)
v. annihilate ; frustrate

unicestwienie (oo-ńee-tses-tvye-
ńe) n. annihilation;frustration
uniemożliwić (oo-ńe-mozh-leé-
veech) v. make impossible
unieruchomić (oo-ńe-roo-khó-
meech) v. immobilize ; tie up
unieszkodliwić (oo-ńe-shkod-
leé-veech) v. render harmless
unieść (oó-ńeśhch) v. lift up
uniewaźnić (oo-ńe-vaźh-ńeech)
v. annul ; void; cancel; repeal
uniewaźnienie (oo-ńe-vazh-ńe-
ńe) n. annulment; invalidation
uniewinnić (oo-ńe-veén-ńeech)
v. acquit;exculpate; excuse
uniewinnienie (oo-ńe-veen-ńe-ńe)
n. acquittal
uniezaleźnić (oo-ńe-za-leźh-
ńeech) v. make independent
uniform (oo-ńeé-form) m. uniform
unikać (oo-ńeé-kach) v. avoid;
shun; steer clear;abstain from
unikat (oo-ńeé-kat) m. unique
item ; rare specimen;curiosity
uniwersalny (oo-ńee-ver-sal-
ni) adj. m. universal ;versatile
uniwersytet (oo-ńee-ver-si-tet)
m. university
uniźać się (oo-ńeé-zhach śháń)
v. humble oneself;be servile
uniźony (oo-ńee-zho-ni) adj.m.
humble ; servile; cringing
unormowac (oo-nor-mó-vach) v.
normalize; regulate:regularize
unosić (oo-nó-śheech) v. carry
up; lift off;bear (a weight)
unowocześnić (oo-no-vo-chesh-
ńeech) v. modernize
uodpornić (oo-od-pór-ńeech) v.
immunize; harden; inure
uogólnić (oo-o-goól-ńeech) v.
generalize (rules,observations)
uogólnienie (oo-o-gool-ńe-ńe)
n. generalization
uosabiac (oo-o-sá-byach) v.
personify;embody:typify
uosobienie (oo-o-so-bye-ńe) n.
personification;embodiment
upadac (oo-pa-dach) v. fall
down; collapse; topple over
upadek (oo-pa-dek) m. fall;drop
upadłosc (oo-pád-woshch) f.
bankruptcy ; insolvency

upadły (oo-pad-wi) adj. m. fall-
en; bankrupt; insolvent
upajac (oo-pá-yach) v. intoxicate; elate; fuddle ; make drunk
upalny dzień (oo-pál-ni dźhéń)
m. hot day :very hot day
upał (oó-paw) m. (intense) heat
upanstwowić (oo-pań-stvó-veech)
v. nationalize: socialize
upaństwowienie (oo-pań-stvo-vye-
ńe) n. nationalization
uparty (oo-pár-ti) adj. m.
stubborn; obstinate;pigheaded
upatrywać (oo-pa-trí-vach) v.
look for; suspect; perceive
upełnomocnić (oo-pew-no-mots-
ńeech) v. give powers (of attorney); empower; commission
upewnic (oo-pév-ńeech) v. assure ; reassure ; make sure
upic się, (oó-peech śháń) v.
get drunk; be intoxicated
upierać się, (oo-pye-rach śháń)
v. persist; insist; stick to
upinac (oo-peé-nach) v. fasten
on; pin up; tie(one's hair)
upiór (oóp-yoor) m. ghost
upiorny (oo-pyór-ni) adj. m.
ghostly;weird:nightmarish;ghastly
upłynnienie (oo-pwin-ńe-ńe) n.
make fluid;flux; liquefaction
upływ (oóp-wiv) m. run off;
(blood) loss; lapse; expiration
upływać (oo-pwí-vach) v. flow
away; pass; lapse; go by;flow
upłynąć (oo-pwí-nownch) v.
elapse; pass; expire ;sail away
upodobac (oo-po-dó-bach) v.
take a liking ; take to; fancy
upodobanie (oo-po-do-ba-ńe) n.
liking; fancy; predilection for
upodobnić się (oo-po-dób-ńeech
śháń) v. assimilate; conform to
upoic (oo-pó-eech) v. intoxicate; make drunk; elate
upojenie (oo-po-ye-ńe) n. ine-
briation; rapture ;intoxication
upokorzenie (oo-po-kozhe-ńe)
n. humiliation; abasement
upokorzyć (oo-po-kó-zhich) v.
humiliate ;make eat crow;abase
upominac (oo-po-meé-nach) v.
admonish; warn; scold;rebuke

upominek (oo-po-mee-nek) m.
gift; souvenir; present; token
uporać się (oo-po-rach shañ)
v. get over; cope with; negotiate
uporczywy (oo-por-chi-vi) adj.
m. stubborn; obstinate; severe
uporządkować (oo-po-zhownd-ko-
vach) v. put in order; tidy up
uposażenie (oo-po-sa-zhe-ñe)
n. pay; allowance; salary; wages
uposażyć (oo-po-sa-zhich) v.
endow; give allowance
uposledzenie (oo-poshle-dze-ñe)
n. handicap(mental, physical etc.)
uposledzony (oo-po-shle-dzo-ni)
adj. m. feebleminded; deprived
upoważnić (oo-po-vazh-ñeech) v.
authorize; commission; entitle
upoważnienie (oo-po-vazh-ñe-ñe)
n. authorization; full powers
upowszechniac (oo-pov-shekh-
ñach) v. put into general use
upor (oo-poor) m. obstinacy
upragniony (oo-prag-ño-ni) adj.
m. desired; longed for
upraszac (oo-pra-shach) v. request; beg; beseech
uprawa (oo-pra-va) f. culture;
cultivation; agriculture; tillage
uprawiac (oo-prav-yach) v.
cultivate; till(the soil)
uprawnic (oo-prav-ñeech) v. entitle; qualify; legalize
uprawniony (oo-prav-ño-ni)
adj. m. entitled
uprosic (oo-pro-sheech) v. get
by begging; persuade; ask to do
uproscic (oo-prosh-cheech) v.
simplify; reduce; cancel
uprowadzic (oo-pro-va-dzheech)
v. abduct; kidnap; lead away
uprzątać (oo-pzhown-tach) v.
clean up; tidy up; put away; kill
uprząż (oop-zhownsh) f. harness;
(horse); gear of draught animals
uprzedni (oo-pzhed-ñee) adj.
m. previous; prior; foregoing
uprzedzac (oo-pzhe-dzach) v.
anticipate; warn; have bias
uprzedzenie (oo-pzhe-dze-ñe) n.
anticipation; prejudice; notice
uprzedzony (oo-pzhe-dzo-ni) adj.
m. prejudiced; forewarned

uprzejmosc (oo-pzhey-moshch) f.
polite kindness; courtesy
uprzejmy (oo-pzhey-mi) adj.m.
kind; polite; nice; suave; affable
uprzemysłowic (oo-pzhe-mi-swo-
veech) v. industrialize
uprzemysłowienie (oo-pzhe-mi-
swo-vye-ñe) n. industrializa-
tion; development of industry
uprzykrzyc się (oo-pzhik-zhich
shañ) v. get fed up with
uprzystepnic (oo-pzhis—tañp-
ñeech) v. facilitate; make
available; make accessible
uprzytomnic (oo-pzhi-tom-ñeech)
v. realize; impress upon (sb)
uprzywilejowany (oo-pzhi-vee-le-
yo-va-ñi) adj. m. privileged
upuscic (oo-poosh-cheech) v.
let fall; let drop; bleed
upychac (oo-pi-khach) v. staff;
pack tight; cram; ram; fill
urabiac (oo-rab-yach) v. fashion
uraczyc (oo-ra-chich) v. treat
uradowac (oo-ra-do-vach) v.
gladden; delight; rejoice
uradzic (oo-ra-dzheech) v. agree
decide; resolve; contrive
uran (oo-ran) m. uranium
urastac (oo-ras-tach) v. grow
uratowac (oo-ra-to-vach) v.
save; salvage; rescue
uraz (oo-ras) m. injury; complex; resentment; grudge
uraza (oo-ra-za) f. grudge;
rancor; soreness; ill feeling
urazic (oo-ra-zheech) v. hurt;
offend; wound sb's feelings
urągac (oo-rown-gach) v. insult
uregulowac (oo-re-goo-lo-vach)
v. stettle; put in order; pay
urlop (oor-lop) m. leave; fur-
lough; vacation; holiday
urna (oor-na) f. urn; ballot box
uroczy (oo-ro-chi) adj. m.
charming; enchanting; delightful
uroczystosc (oo-ro-chis-toshch)
f. celebration; festivity
uroczysty (oo-ro-chis-ti) adj.
m. solemn; ceremonial; festive
uroda (oo-ro-da) f. beauty;
loveliness; attraction; charm

urodzaj (oo-ró-dzay) m. good
harvest;abundance; harvest;crop
urodzajny (oo-ro-dzáy-ni) adj.
m. fertile; fecund
urodzenie (oo-ro-dze-ńe) n.
birth
urodzić (oo-ró-dźheech) v. give
birth; breed; bear; yield
urodziny (oo-ro-dźheé-ni) n.
birthday; birth
urodzony (oo-ro-dzó-ni) adj.
m. born; born and bred
uroić (oo-ro-eech) v. imagine
urojenie (oo-ro-ye-ńe) n.
fiction; fancy; illusion
urojony (oo-ro-yó-ni) adj.m.
imaginary; abstract; fictitious
urok (oó-rok) m. charm; spell
uronić (oo-ró-ńeech) v. shed;
drop; let fall; lose;shed;miss
urozmaicenie (oo-roz-ma-ee-tse-
ńe) n. variety; diversity;change
urozmaicić (oo-roz-ma-eé-čheech)
v. diversify; vary ;while away
uruchomić (oo-roo-khó-meech) v.
start; put in motion;set going
urwać (oor-vach) v. tear off;
pull off; wrench away; deduct
urwis (oor-vees) m. urchin
urwisko (oor-veés-ko) n. precipice; crag; cliff ; steep rock
urwisty (oor-veés-ti) adj. m.
steep; precipitous; abrupt
urywek (oo-ri-vek) m. fragment
urząd (oózh-ownt) m. office
urządzać (oozh-ówn-dzach) v.
arrange; settle; set up
urządzenie (oo-zhówn-dze-ńe) n.
furniture; installation;gear
urzec (oó-zhets) v. enchant;
bewitch; fascinate;cast a spell
urzeczywistnić (oo-zhe-chi-
veést-ńeech) v. make real;fulfil
urzeczywistnienie (oo-zhe-chi-
veest-ńé-ńe) n. realization
urzędnik (oo-zhánd-ńeek) m.
official; white-collar worker
urzędowanie (oo-zhán-do-vá-ńe)
n. office hours;clerical duties
urzędowy (oo-zhán-do-vi) adj.
m. official(document,capacity...)
urzynać (oo-zhi-nach) v. cut off

usadowić się (oo-sa-dó-veech
śhań) v. sit or settle down
uschły (oós-khwi) adj. m.
dried up; withered;wasted away
usiąść (oó-śhówńshch) v. sit
down; take a seat;perch;alight
usidłać (oo-śheéd-wach) v.
entrap; ensnare ;enmesh;inveigle
usilny (oo-śheél-ni) adj.m.
strenuous; intense; pressing
usiłować (oo-śhee-wó-vach) v.
strive; try hard; attempt
usiłowanie (oo-śhee-wo-vá-ńe)
n. attempt; efford; endeavor
uskarżać się(oos-kár-zhach śhań)
v.complain; grumble (about...)
uskutecznic (oo-skoo-tech-
ńeech) v. bring about;effect
usłuchać (oo-swoó-khach) v.
follow order (advice);obey
usługa (oo-swoó-ga) f. service;
favor; good turn; help
usługiwać (oo-swoo-geé-vach)
v. wait on; serve;attend
usłużyć (oo-swoó-zhich) v.
do a service; do a good turn
usnąć (oó-snównch) v. fall
asleep; go to sleep
uspokoić(oo-spo-kó-eech) v.
calm down; soothe; set at ease
uspołecznic (oos-po-wéch-ńeech)
v. socialize; civilize;collectivize
usposobić (oos-po-só-beech) v.
dispose; predispose; incline
usposobienie (oos-po-so-bye-
ńe) n. disposition;temper;mood
usprawiedliwić (oos-pra-vyed-
leé-veech) v. justify;explain
usprawiedliwienie (oos-pra-
vyed-lee-vye-ńe) n. excuse;
apology; plea; reason;justification
usprawnic (oos-práv-ńeech) v.
rationalize; make efficient
usta (oós-ta) n. mouth; lips
ustalenie (oo-sta-lé-ńe) n.
determination; settlement
ustalić (oo-stá-leech) v. determine; settle; fix; set
ustały (oo-stá-wi) adj. m.
settled (fluid)
ustanawiać (oo-sta-ná-vyach)
v. constitute; enact; set up

ustanowienie (oo-sta-no-vye-ńe)
n. instituting; establishing
ustatkować się (oo-stat-ko-
vach shań) v. settle down
ustawa (oo-sta-ya) f. law; rule
ustawać (oo-sta-vach) v. cease;
be weary ; hardly stand
ustawiać (oo-stav-yach) v. arrange ; place; put; set up
ustawiczny (oo-sta-veech-ni)
adj. m. constant; continual
ustawienie (oo-sta-vye-ńe) n.
dispositon; installation,
ustawodawca (oo-sta-vo-dav-tsa)
m. legislator
ustawodawstwo (oo-sta-vo-dav-
stvo) n. legislation
usterka (oo-ster-ka) f. defect
ustęp (oos-tańp) m. restroom;
paragraph ; passage
ustępliwy (oos-tań-plee-vi) adj.
m. yielding ; compliant
ustępować (oos-tań-po-vach) v.
yield ;withdraw; recede;cease
ustępstwo (oos-tańp-stvo) n.
concession;meeting half way
ustnik (oost-neek) m. mouthpiece
ustny (oost-ni) adj. m. oral;
verbal; spoken
ustosunkowany (oo-sto-soon-ko-
va-ni) adj. m. influential
ustrój (oos-trooy) m. structure;
government system; organism
ustrzec (oos-tzhets) v. guard;
avoid; safeguard ;protect from
usunięcie (oo-soo-nań-che) n.
removal ; withdrawal
usuwać (oo-soo-vach) v. remove
usychać (oo-si-khach) v. wither
usypać (oo-si-pach) v. pile up;
pour out; pour off (sand etc.)
usypiać (oo-sip-yach) v. put to
sleep ;lull to sleep;send to sleep
uszanować (oo-sha-no-vach) v.
respect; spare(life etc)
uszanowanie (oo-sha-no-va-ńe)
n. respect; respects
uszczelka (oosh-chel-ka) f.
gasket ;seal; packing
uszczelniać (oosh-chel-ńach) v.
pack; caulk; stop(a leak etc.)
uszczęśliwić (oosh-chań-shlee-
veech) v. make happy ;delight

uszczerbek (oosh-cher-bek) m.
harm ; damage; loss
uszczuplić(oosh-choop-leech)
v. curtail; reduce ;lessen
uszczypliwy (oosh-chip-lee-vi)
adj. m. sarcastic; biting
uszko (oosh-ko) m. (small) ear;
(needle) eye ; ravioli
uszkodzenie (oosh-ko-dze-ńe)
n. damage; injury ;imperment
uszkodzić (oosh-ko-dzheech) v.
damage ;injure; impair; spoil
uszny (oosh-ni) adj. m. ear
uścisk dłoni (oosh-cheesk dwo-
ńe)m.handshake
uścisnąć (oosh-chees-nownch) v.
embrace; grasp;hug;squeeze(hand)
uśmiać się (oosh-myach shań) v.
laugh heartily;have a good lough
uśmiech (oosh-myekh) m. smile
uśmiechać się (oosh-mye-khach
shań) v. smile; give a smile
uśmiercić (oosh-myer-cheech)
v. kill ; put to death
uśmierzyć (oosh-mye- zhich)
v. calm down;mitigate;alleviate
uśpić (oosh-peech) v. put to
sleep ; anesthetize ;etherize
uświadomić (oosh-vya-do-meech)
v. instruct; initiate;realize
uświadomienie (oosh-vya-do-mye-
ńe) n. consciousness;information
uświetnić (oosh-vyet-ńeech) v.
give prestige; add splendor
utaić (oo-ta-eech) v. conceal
utajony (oo-ta-yo-ni) adj.m.
secret ; latent; potential
utalentowany (oo-ta-len-to-va-
ni) adj. m. talented ; gifted
utarczka (oo-tarch-ka) f. skirmish; encounter; squabble
utarg (oo-tark) m. receipts ;
take ; takings
utargować (oo-tar-go-vach) v.
make a bargain; realize
utarty (oo-tar-ti) adj. m.
usual; well-worn;wide spread
utęsknienie (oo-tańs-khe-ńe-ńe) n.
longing; earnest desire
utknąć (oot-knownch) v. get stuck
stall; stick fast; get to a stop
utlenić (oo-tle-ńeech) v. oxi-
dize(metals);peroxidize(hair)

utłuc (oót-woots) v. pound;
bruise;crush; pestle;mash;grind
utonąć (oo-to-nównch) v. be
drowned ; sink;be lost
utopia (oo-top-ya) f. Utopia
utopic (oo-to-peech) v. sink;
drown(an animal etc.)
utorować (oo-to-ro-vach) v.
clear a path; show the way
utożsamić (oo-tozh-sa-meech) v.
identify with
utracić (oo-tra-cheech) v.loose;
waste ; forfeit a right(etc)
utracjusz (oo-tráts-yoosh) m.
spendthrift; squanderer
utrapienie (oo-trap-ye-ne) n.
worry; torment ; nuisance
utrata (oo-trá-ta) f. loss
utrącać (oo-trówn-tsach) v.
chip; knock of; blackball
utrudniać (oo-trobd-ñach) v.
make difficult; hinder
utrudnienie (oo-trood-ñe-ñe) n.
difficulty ; hindrance
utrwalić (oo-trva-leech) v.
make permanent; fix; record
utrzymanie (oo-tzhi-ma-ñe) n.
living; upkeep; board;support
utuczyć (oo-too-chich) v.
fatten; grow fat;fatten up
utulić (oo-too-leech) v. comfort; console;nestle (face...)
utwierdzić (oo-tvyer-dżheech)v.
confirm; fix; set; consolidate
utworzenie (oo-tvo-zhe-ñe) n.
formation ; initiation;creation
utworzyć (oo-tvo-zhich) v.
create;form ; compose;initiate
utwór (oot-voor)m. work; composition; production;creation
utyć (oo-tich) v. become fat
utykać (oo-ti-kach) v. limp
utylitarny (oo-ti-lee-tár-ni)
adj. m. utilitarian; useful
utyskiwać (oo-tis-kee-vach) v.
complain ; grumble (at,about)
uwaga (oo-vá-ga) f. attention;
remark ; notice;exp.: Caution!
uwalniać (oo-vál-ñach) v. set
free ; rid; let off; dismiss
uważać (oo-va-zhach) v. pay
attention ; be careful; mind;
take care; look after ;
watch out;consider;reckon

uważny (oo-vázh-ni) adj. m.
careful; attentive; watchful
uwiąd (oov-yównt) m. atrophy
uwiązać (oo-vyown-zach) v.
attach; bind; tie; fasten
uwidocznić (oo-vee-doch-ñeech)
v. make evident; show; expose
uwiecznić (oo-vyech-ñeech) v.
perpetuate; immortalize
uwielbiać (oo-vyel-byach) v.
adore; worship; admire
uwielbienie (oo-vyel-bye-ñe) n.
adoration;admiration;worship
uwierać (oo-vye-rach) v. (shoe)
pinch; rub; hurt
uwierzytelnić (oo-vye-zhi-tel-
ñeech) v. legalize;certify;attest
uwierzytelnienie (oo-vye-zhi-
tel-ñe-ñe) n. certification;
accreditation; authentication
uwięzić (oo-vyáń-żheech) v.
imprison;throw into prison
uwijac się (oo-vee-yach śháñ)
v. be busy; bustle about
uwikłać (oo-veek-wach) v. entangle;involve;get entangled
uwłaczać (oov-wa-chach) v. belittle ; insult; outrage;affront
uwłosiony (oo-vwo-śho-ni) adj.
m. hairy; hirsute; pilose
uwodziciel (oo-vo-dżhee-chel)
m. seducer (of women);inveigler
uwodzić (oo-vó-dżheech) v. seduce (men or women)
uwolnic (oo-vol-ñeech) v. free
uwolnienie (oo-vol-ñe-ñe) n.
liberation;rescue; acquittal
uwydatnic (oo-vi-dát-ñeech) v.
accentuate; set off; bring out
uwypuklić (oo-vi-pook-leech) v.
accentuate; set off;protrude
uwzglednic (oovz-gláńd-ñeech)
v. consider; comply; acquiesce
uwzględnienie (oovz-gláńd-ñe-ñe)
n. allowance for;compliance
uzależnić (oo-za-lézh-ñeech) v.
make dependent; subordinate
uzasadnić (oo-za-sád-ñeech) v.
substantiate; justify;motivate
uzasadnienie (oo-za-sad-ñe-ñe)
n. justification; motive
uzbrajać się (ooz-bra-yach śháñ)
v. arm oneself; equip oneself

uzbrojenie (ooz-bro-yé-ñe) n.
arming; armament ; weapons
uzda (óoz-da) f. bridle
uzdolnić (ooz-dol-ñeech) v.
enable ; qualify;capacitate
uzdolnienie (ooz-dol-ñe-ñe) n.
talent ; gift; aptitude
uzdolniony (ooz-dol-no-ni) adj.
m. gifted; talented;capable;apt
uzdrawiać (ooz-dra-vyach) v.
heal; cure;bring back, to health
uzdrowisko (ooz-dro-vees-ko)
n. health resort
uzębienie (oo-zañ-bye-ñe) n.
dentition;toothing(of gears...)
uzgadniać (ooz-gad-ñach) v.
reconcile;coordinate;adjust
uziemienie (oo-źhe-myé-ñe) n.
grounding ; earth
uzmysłowić (ooz-mi-swó-veech)
v. visualize; convey (meaning)
uznawać (ooz-na-vach) v. acknowledge; do justice;confess
uznanie (ooz-ná-ñe) n. recognition ; admission; approval
uzupełniać (oo-zoo-péw-ñach) v.
complete ; fill up;make up
uzurpator (oo-zoor-pa-tor) m.
usurper(who takes without right)
uzyskać (oo-zis-kach) v. obtain;
gain; win ;get; acquire;secure
użerać się (oo-zhe-rach shañ)
v. fight over; quarrel ;wrangle
użyczać (oo-zhi-chach) v.
grant; give; lend; spare;impart
użyć (oo-zhich) v. use; exert;
take (medicine); profit;employ
użyteczny (oo-zhi-téch-ni) adj.
m. useful ; serviceable;helpful
użytek (oo-zhí-tek) m. use
użytkownik (oo-zhit-kóv-ñeek)
m. user (of appartment etc.)
używać (oo-zhi-vach) v. use;
enjoy; exercise right;make use
używalność (oo-zhi-vál-noshch)
f. use;enjoyment;utilization
używalny (oo-zhi-vál-ni) adj.m.
usable; in working order
używany (oo-zhi-vá-ni) adj.m.
used; second-hand ;worn
użyzniać (oo-zhiźh-nach) v.
fertilize; enrich(the soil)

w (v) prep. in ; into; at
we (ve) prep. in; into; at
wabić (va-beech) v. lure
wabik (va-beek) m. decoy; lure
wachlarz (vákh-lash) m. fan;
range( of questions, subjects..)
wada (va-da) f. fault; defect;flaw
wadliwy (wad-leé-vi) adj. m.
faulty;defective;;imperfect
wafel (va-fel) m. wafer; cornet
waga (vá-ga) f. weight; balance;
pair of scales; importance
wagary (va-gá-ri) pl. skipping
school; playing truant; the wag
wagon (va-gon) m. car; wagon
wagon restauracyjny (vá-gon res-
taw-ra-tsíy-ni) dining car
wahać się (va-khach shañ) v.
hesitate ;sway; rock; swing
wahadło (va-khá-dwo) n. pendu-
lum(swinging backwards and forwards)
wahadłowy (va-khad-wó-vi) adj.
m. rocking; swinging; oscilatory
wakacje (va-káts-ye) pl. vacation; holidays;taking a holiday
walać (va-lach) v. soil; stain;dirty
walc (válts) m. waltz
walcować (val-tsó-vach) v. roll;
flatten; mill; laminate
walczyć (val-chich) v. fight; vie;
straggle;be in conflict;contend
walec (vá-lets) m. cylinder; roller
waleczność (va-léch-noshch) f.
bravery ; valor;gallantry;courage
waleczny (va-léch-ni) adj. m.
valiant; brave; gallant;courageous
walić (vá-leech) v. demolish;hit;pile
walijski (va-leéy-skee) adj.m.
Welsh; of Wales
walizka (va-leéz-ka) f. suitcase; valise; portmanteau
walka (vál-ka) f. struggle;
fight; war; battle; wrestling
walny (vál-ni) adj. m. general;
complete; decisive;outstanding
walor (vá-lor) m. value;quality
waluta (va-lóo-ta) f. currency
wał (vaw) m. 1. rampart; dike;bank;
2. shaft; arbor; billow
wałach (va-wakh) m. gelding
wałek (vá-wek) m. roller; shaft;
cylinder ; rolling pin ;wad; roll

wałęsać się (va-wáń-sach śháń)
v. rove; loaf; idle about
wałkoń (váw-koń) m. loafer;
do-nothing; idler
wałkować (vaw-kó-vach) v. roll;
mangle; debate; thresh out
wampir (vám-peer) m. vampire
wandal (ván-dal) m. vandal
wanienka (va-ńén-ka) f. little
tub ; bałhtub; laboratory dish
wanna (van-na) f. bath tub
wapienny (va-pyén-ni) adj.m.
limy; limestone;calcareus
wapień (vá-pyeń) m. limestone
wapno (váp-no) n. lime
wapn (vápń) m. calcium
warcaby (var-tsá-bi) pl. check-
ers; draughts (game)
warchlak (várkh-lak) m. boar-
cub;young wilde boar; piglet
warchoł (vár-khow) m.brawler ;
discord sower; squabbler
warczeć (yar-chéch) v. growl
warga (var-ga) f. lip; labium
wariant (vár-yant) m. variant
wariactwo (var-yáts-tvo) n.
madness;piece of folly; folly
wariat (var-yat) m. lunatic;
insane ; madman; fool;crazy man
wariować (var-yó-vach) v. go
insane ; rave ;go mad; be mad
warkocz (var-koch) m. braid
warkot (vár-kot) m. growl;
whirr; throb; rattle; drone
warowny (va-róv-ni) adj. m.
fortified;made into fortress
warować (va-ró-vach) v. fortify
warstwa (várs-tva) f. layer;
stratum; coat;coating; class
warstwowy (var-stvo-vi) adj.
m. laminar; stratal;foliated
warsztat (vársh-tat) m. workshop; workbench;(weaver's)loom
warsztatowy (var-shta-tó-vi)
adj. m. workshop-(equipment etc.)
warta (vár-ta) f. watch; guard
wartki (várt-kee) adj. m. rapid ; fast(current);animated
wartko(várt-ko) adv. fast; rap-
idly ; impetuously
warto (vár-to) adv. it's
worth (while); it's proper; it's
worth one's while; it pays

wartościowy (var-tosh-chó-vi)
adj. m. valuable; precious
wartość (var-toshch) f. value;
worth ;quality;power;magnitude
wartownik (var-tóv-ńeek) m.
guard; sentry;sentinel
warunek (va-roo-nek) m. condition; requirement; term;stipulation
warunkowy (va-roon-kó-vi) adj.
m. conditional;contingent;provisory
warząchew (va-zhówń-khev) v.
ladle
warzyć (vá-zhich) v. cook; brew
warzywa (va-zhí-va) pl. vegetables: pot herbs;truk garden produce
warzywny (va-zhiv-ni) adj. m.
vegetable ; vegetable-
wasz (yash) pron. your; yours
waśnić (vash-ńeéch) v. saw
discord (among men or women)
wasń ( vaśhń ) f. quarrel
wata (vá-ta) f. cotton wool
watować (va-tó-vach) v. pad;
quilt ;wad (a jacket etc.)
wawrzyn (váv-zhin) m. laurel
waza (vá-za) f. vase;soup tureen
wazelina (va-ze-leé-na) f.
vaseline
wazon (vá-zon) m. flower pot
ważki (vázh-kee) adj. m. grave;
weighty ; ponderable
ważny (vazh-ni) adj. m. important;valid ; significant
ważyć (vá-zhich) v. weigh
ważyć się (va-zhich śháń) v.
dare; weigh oneself;poise;venture
wąchać (vówń-khach) v. smell
wągr (vowńgr) m. blackhead;
scolex; comedo;tapeworm larva
wąs (vowńs) m. moustache;whisker
wąski (vówń-skee) adj. m. narrow; tight(fitting);narrow-(gage)
wąskotorowa kolej (vówns-ko-to-
ró-va kó-ley) f. narrow gauge
railroad
wątek (vowń-tek) m. weft; plot
wątły (vowńt-wi) adj. m. frail
wątpić (vowńt-peech) v. doubt
wątpliwy (vowńt-pleé-vi) adj.
m. doubtful;open to doubt;toss-up
wątroba (vown-tro-ba) f. liver
wątróbka (vown-troob-ka) f.
liver (dish);(calf's) liver

wąwóz (vówn-voos) m. ravine;
gorge; gully ; canyon ; defile
wąż (vównsh) m. snake; hose
wbiec (vbyets) v. run in;run up
wbijać (vbeé-yach)v.hammer in
wbrew (vbrev) prep. in spite
of ; in defiance; against
wbudować (vboo-do-vach) v.
build in; incorporate
w bród (v broot) adv. 1. in
abundance; 2. fording (river)
wcale (vtsá-le) adv. quite
wcale nie (vtsa-le ńe) not at
all (exp,);not in the least
wchłaniać (vkhwa-ńach) v. absorb ; soak up; take in;soak in
wchodzić (wkhó-dźheech) v. enter; get in; set in; climb
w ciągu (v chown-goo) adv.
during ;while; in time of
wciągać (vchówn-gach) v. pull
in ; drag in; inhale;implicate
wciąż (vchównsh) adv. continual-
ly ; constantly;persistently
wcielać (vche-lach) v. incorporate; embody ; merge; realize
wcielenie (vche-le-ńe) n. in-
carnation ; embodiment;merger
wcierać (vche-rach) v. rub in
wcięcie (vchán-che) n. incision
notch.narrow waist;low cut neck
wciskać (vchees-kach) v. press
in; squeeze in;wedge; cram
w czas (v chas) on time
wczasy (vcha-śi) pl. vacations
wczesny (vches-ni) adj. m.
early;in the small hours
wcześnie (vchesh-ńe) adv. early
wczoraj (vcho-ray) adv. yesterday; during yesterday
wczoraj wieczorem (vcho-ray vye-
cho-rem) adv. last night
wczuwać się (vchoo-vach śhań)
v. sympathize; get in spirit
wdarcie (vdár-che) n. invasion
wdawać się (vda-vach śhań) v.
1. intervene; 2. associate
wdech (vdekh) m. aspiration
wdowa (vdó-va) f. widow
wdowiec (vdó-vyets) m. widower
w dół (v doow) adv. down; downwards ; downstairs; (go)lower

wdrapać się (vdra-pach śhań) v.
climb up ; shin up( a tree)
wdrażać (vdra-zhach) v. train;
implant ; accustom to;enter upon
wdychać (vdi-khach) v. breathe;
inhale ; breathe in; imbibe
wdzierać się (vdźhe-rach śhań)
v. break in; struggle up hill
wdziewać (vdźhe-vach) v. put
on (clothes); slip on;take(the veil)
wdzięczność (vdźhańch-nośhch)
f. gratitude ; thankfulness
wdzięczny (vdźhańch-ni) adj.
m. grateful; thankful;graceful;cute
wdzięk (vdźhańk) m. grace;charm
według (ved-wook) prep. according to; after; along;near;next
wegetacja (ve-ge-táts-ya) f.
vegetation; bare existence
wegetarianin (ve-ge-tar-ya-ńeen)
m. vegetarian(on meatless diet)
wegetować (ve-ge-tó-vach) v.
exist barely; vegetate
wejrzeć (véy-zhech) v. glance
in;look in;get an insight;inspect
wejrzenie (vey-zhe-ńe) n.glance
in; (eye)expression; insight
wejście (véysh-che) n . entrance; way in; admission;entry
wejściowy (veysh-cho-vi) adj.
m. entrance-(door;gate,etc.)
wejść (veyshch) v. enter;get in
weksel (vék-sel) m. loan note
welon (vé-lon) m. veil
wełna (vew-na) f. wool
wełniany (vew-ńa-ni) adj. m.
woolen; worsted, wool-(fabric...)
wełnisty (vew-ńees-ti) adj.m.
wooly; fleecy;wool bearing
weneryczna choroba (ve-ne-rich-
na kho-ro-ba) f. venereal
disease
wenezuelski (ve-ne-zoo-él-skee)
adj. m. Venezuelan;of Venezuela
wentyl (ven-til) m. vent;valve
wentylacja (ven-ti-láts-ya) f.
ventilation;ventilation system
wentylator (ven-ti-la-tor) m.
ventilator; ventilating-fan
weranda (ve-rán-da) f. porch
werbel (vér-bel) m. ruffle;
drum-call; drumbeat ;drum

werbować (ver-bo-vach) v. enlist; recruit; canvas
werbunek (ver-boo-nek) m. draft;
recruitment;enlisting;recruiting
wersja (vee-sya) f. version
werwa (ver-ya) f. verve;zip;pep
weryfikować (ve-ri-fee-ko-vach)
v. verify;confirm
wesele (ve-se-le) n. wedding
wesołość (ve-so-wośhćh) f.joy
gaiety; glee; hilarity
wesoły (ve-so-wi) adj. merry;
gay; jolly; gleeful; funny
wespoł (ves-poow) adv. together;
jointly; all together
westchnienie (vest-khne-ne) n.
sigh(of relief etc.)
wesz (vesh) f. louse
wet za wet (vet za vet) exp.:
tit for tat; retaliate
weteran (ve-te-ran) m. veteran
weterynarz (ve-te-ri-nash) m.
vet; veterinary; farrier
wetknąć (vet-knownch) v. stick
in;slip in;tuck away; stuff
wewnątrz (vev-nowntsh) prep.,
adv. inside; within; intra-
wewnętrzny (vev-nantzh-ni) adj.
m. inner;internal; inward
wezbrać (vez-brach) v. swell
wezbrany (vez-bra-ni) adj. m.
flush; overflowing; swollen
wezwać (vez-vach) v. call in
wezwanie (vez-va-ne) n. call
węch (vankh) m. smell; nose
wędka (vand-ka) f. fishing rod
wędkarz (vand-kash) m. angler
wędlina (vand-lee-na) f. meat
products; pork products
wędliniarnia (vand-lee-nar-na)
f. pork-butcher's shop
wędrować (van-dro-vach) v.
wander; roam; rove; hike
wędrowiec (van-dro-vyets) m.
wanderer; tramp; rover
wędrówka (van-droov-ka) f. mi-
gration; roam; tramp;wandering
wędzić (van-dżeech) v. smoke;
cure; meat; bloat fish
wędzidło (van-dżheed-wo) n.
(horse) bit;bridle;curb
wędzonka (van-dzon-ka) f. bacon

węgiel (van-gel)m. coal;crayon
węgielny kamien (van-gel-ni ka-
myen) m. corner stone;corner stone
węgieł (van-gew)m. corner; quoin
węgierski (van-ger-skee) adj.
m. Hungarian; of Hungary
węglan (van-glan) m. carbonate
węglowodan (van-glo-vo-dan) m.
carbohydrate (chemical compound)
węglowodor (van-glo-vo-door) m.
hydrocarbon ;rock oil etc.
węglowy (van-glo-vi) adj. m.
carbonic; coal; carboniferous;
carbon-
węgorz (van-gosh) m. eel
węzeł (van-zew) m. knot; junction; noose; loop; snarl;hitch
węższy (vanzh-shi) adj. m. nar-
rower(than)
wgląd (vglownt) m. insight; view
wglądać (vglown-dach) v. look
into; get an insight;inquire
wgłębić się (vgwan-beech shan)
v. sink; study;go into (matter)
wgryzć się (vgrizhch shan) v.
penetrate; get teeth into...
wiać (vyach) v. blow; beat it
wiadomo (vya-do-mo) v. (imp.)
it is known;everybody knows
wiadomość (vya-do-mośhćh) f.
news; information; message
wiadomy (vya-do-mi) adj. m.
known; a certain;well known
wiadro (vya-dro) n. bucket;pail
wiadukt (vya-dookt) m. viaduct
wianek (vya-nek) m. flower
crown; wreath; maidenhead
wiara (vya-ra) f. faith;belief
wiarogodny (vya-ro-god-ni) adj.
m. reliable; credible;veracious
wiarołomny (vya-ro-wom-ni) adj.
m. unfaithful; treacherous
wiarus (vya-roos) m. veteran
(old guard) breeze
wiatr (vyatr) m. wind;gale;
wiatrak (vyat-rak) m. windmill
wiatrówka (vya-troov-ka) f.
air gun; wind breaker(jacket)
wiąz (vyowns) m. elm (Ulmus)
wiązać (vyown-zach) v. tie; bind
wiązanie (vyown-za-ne) n. tie;
truss; bond; link;fixation;weave

wiązanka (vyown-zan-ka) f. garland; bunch; banquet;cluster

wiązka (vyownz-ka) f. bundle; bunch; cluster;beam(of rays)

wibracja (vee-bra-tsya) f. vibration; jarring ; jar

wichrowac się (vee-khro-vach shan) v. warp; curl

wicher (vee-kher) m. windstorm; gale;strong wind

wichrzyciel (veekh-zhi-chel) m. warmonger; firebrand;instigator

wichrzyc (veekh-zhich) v. make trouble; create discord;tousle

wichura (vee-khoo-ra) f. windstorm; gale; strong wind

wichura sniezna (vi-khoo-ra-shnezh-na) snowstorm;blizzard

wic (veech) v. wind; meander; build nest; curl;m.twig;osier

widelec (vee-de-lets) m. fork

widelki (vee-dew-kee) pl. fork (small);forked branch

widelkowaty (vee-dew-ko-va-ti) adj. m. forked;fork shaped

widly (veed-wi) pl. pitch fork

widmo (veed-mo) n . ghost; phantom ;spectrum;specter

widno (ved-no) adv. 1. evidently; 2. in daylight;in light

widnokrąg (veed-no-krownk) m. horizon ; sea-line ;true horizon

widocznie (vee-doch-ne) adv. evidently;apparently; clearly

widocznosc (vee-doch-noshch) f. visibility ;field of vision

widoczny (vee-doch-ni) adj. m. visible; evident; noticeable

widok (vee-dok) m. view; sight

widokowka (vee-do-kocv-ka) f. picture postcard

widowisko (vee-do-vees-ko) n. show; spectacle; pageant

widownia (vee-dov-na) f. audience; theatre house ;scene

widz (veets) m. spectator

widzenie (vee-dze-ne) n. sight; vision ; visit; hallucination

widzialny (vee-dzhal-ni) adj. m. visible (to the naked eye...)

widziec (vee-dzhech) v. see

wiec (vyets) m. meeting ;rally

wieczerza (vye-zhe-zha) f. supper ;Lord's Supper

wiecznosc (vyech-noshch) f. eternity; ages ;eternal life

wieczny (vyech-ni) adj. m. eternal; perpetual; endless

wieczorek (vye-cho-rek) m. evening (party); nice evening

wieczorem (vye-cho-rem) exp.: in the evening ;during the evening

wieczorny (vye-chor-ni) adj. m. evening -(dress,newspaper,etc.)

wieczorowy (vye-cho-ro-vi) adj. m. nightly; evening (performance)

wieczor(vye-choor),m. evening

wieczysty (vye-chis-ti) adj. m. eternal; perpetual;imperishable

wiedza (vye-dza) f. knowledge; learning;erudition; science

wiedziec (vye-dzhech) v. know

wiedzma (vyedzh-ma) f. witch

wiejska droga (vyey-ska dro-ga) f. village road; country road

wiejski (vyey-skee) adj. m. village; rural; rustic;country

wiek (vyek) m. age; century

wiekowy (vye-ko-vi) adj. m. secular; ancient; aged;very old

wiekuistosc (vye-koo-ees-toshch) f. eternity ; all time

wiekuisty (vye-koo-ees-ti) adj. m. eternal; everlasting

wielbiciel (vyel-bee-chel) m. devotee; admirer; idolator (man)

wielbicielka (vyel-bee-chel-ka) f. devotee; idolatress (woman)

wielbład (vyel-bwownd) m. camel

wielce (vyel-tse) adv. very; greatly; extremely ;very much

wiele (vye-le) adj. m. many; a lot;much; far out;a great deal

wielebny (vye-leb-ni) adj. m. reverend (Father etc.)

Wielkanoc (vyel-ka-nots) f. Easter

wielkanocny (vyel-ka-nots-ni) adj. m. Easter; of Easter

wielki (vyel-kee) adj. m. big; large; great; vast; keen;mighty

wielkoduszny (vyel-ko-doosh-ni) adj. m. magnanimous ;generous

wielkolud (vyel-ko-lood) m.giant

wielkomiejski (vyel-ko-myey-skee) adj. m. metropolitan; urban ; of a large city
wielkość (vyel-koshch) f. greatness; size; dimension
wielobarwny (vye-lo-barv-ni) adj. m. multicolor (ed)
wieloboczny (vye-lo-bóch-ni) adj. m. multilateral ;polygonal
wielokrążek (vye-lo-krown-zhek) m. set of pulleys ; pulley-block
wielokrotny (vye-lo-krót-ni) adj. m. repeated ; multiple
wieloletni (vye-lo-lét-ñi) adj. m. long; years long;many years' wielopiętrowy (vye-lo-pyan-tró-vi) adj. m. multistory
wieloraki (vye-lo-ra-kee) adj. m. manifold ; varied ;multiple
wieloryb (vye-lo-rib) m. whale
wielorybnik (vye-lo-rib-ñeek) m. whaler;whaleman;whaling ship
wielostronny (vye-lo-stron-ni) adj. m. multilateral; many-sided ; versatile; various
wielozgłoskowy (vye-lo-zgwos-ko-vi) adj. m. polysyllabic
wieloznaczny (vye-lo-znach-ni) adj. m. multivocal; ambiguous
wielożeństwo (vye-lo-zheń-stvo) n. polygamy
wieniec (vye-ñets) m. wreath; garland; crown ; chaplet
wieńczyc (vyeń-chich) v. crown
wieprz (vyepsh) m. hog; pig
wieprzownina (vyep-zho-vée-na) f. pork (meat)
wieprzowy (vyep-zhó-vi) adj.m. pork ;pork's;pig's;hog's;porcine
wiercenie (vyer-tse-ñe) n. drilling ; perforation;boring
wiercić (vyer-chich) v. bore; drill ; pester; bother
wiernosc (vyer-noshch) f. fidelity; loyalty ; faith; truth
wierny (vyér-ni) adj. m. faithful ; true;loyal;exact
wiersz (vyersh) m. verse; poem
wiertarka (vyer-tár-ka) f. drill
wiertnictwo (vyert-ñeets-tvo) n. drilling(activity)
wierutny (vye-root-ni) adj.m. stark(liar); notorious; through-and-through ; rank; arrant;born

wierzący (vye-zhown-tsi) adj. m. believer; believing Christian
wierzba (vyezh-ba) f. willow
wierzch (vyezhkh) m. top; brim head; surface; cover; lid
wierzchni (vyezh-khñee) adj. m. upper ; top; outer;outside
wierzchołek (vyezh-khó-wek) m. top; peak; summit; apex;vertex
wierzyciel (vye-zhi-chel) m. creditor; mortgagee; obligee
wierzycielka (vye-zhi-chel-ka) f. creditor (woman)
wierzyc (vyé-zhich) v. believe; trust;rely; believe in God
wierzytelnosc (vye-shi-tel-noshch) f. debt; claim
wieszac (vye-shach) v. hang
wieszadło (vye-shád-wo) v. hanger; peg; ;coat-stand
wieszak (vye-shak) v. rack
wieszcz (vyeshch) m. bard; seer; poet (leading,national)
wieszczy (vyesh-chi) adj. m. prophetic ;visionary
wieś (vyesh) f. village; countryside; hamlet;the villagers
wieśc (vyeshch) 1. f. news 2. v. lead; conduct; draw; succeed ;stand at the head
wiesniaczka (vyesh-ñach-ka) f. countrywoman ;peasant woman
wiesniak (vyesh-ñak) m. countryman; villager; yokel ;rustic
wietrzec (vyet-zhech) v. decay
wietrzyc (vyet-zhich) v. ventilate; smell; nose;aerate
wietrzenie (vyet-zhe-ñe) n. ventilation; decay (of rocks)
wiewiórka (vye-vyoor-ka) f. squirrel ; squirrel fur
wieść (vyezhch) v. carry (on wheels) ;transport ;convey;drive
wieża (vye-zha) f. tower; rook
wieżowiec (vye-zhó-vyets) m. skyscraper ;high-rise(building)
wieżyczka (vye-zhich-ka) f. turret; pinnacle;small tower
więc (vyańts) conj. now; well; therefore ; so;consequently
więcej (vyań-tsey) adv. more
więdnąc (vyánd-nównch) v. wither; fade ; wilt

więcierz (vyań-chezh) m. fishing net;(set taut on hoops)
większosc (vyańk-shoshch) f. majority; the bulk; most
większy (vyańk-shi) adj. m. bigger; larger; greater
więzic (vyań-zheech) v. imprison ;confine; detain;restrain
więzienie (vyań-zhe-ńe) n. prison; confinement; jail;restraint
więzień (vyań-zhen) m. prisoner
więzy (vyań-zi) pl. fetters; restrains; chains; bonds
wigilia (vee-geel-ya) f. Xmas Eve; eve
wiklina (vee-klee-na) f. osier
wikłać (veek-wach) v. entangle
wikt (veekt) m. board; keep
wilczur (veel-choor) m.wolf dog
wilgoc (veel-goch) f. humidity
wilgotny (veel-got-ni) adj. m. moist; humid ; damp; wet
wilia (veel-ya) f. eve
wilk (veelk) m. wolf;wolfskin
wilzyc (veel-zhich) v. moisten
wina (vee-na) f. guilt; fault
winda (veen-da) f. elevator
winiarnia (vee-ńar-ńa) f. wineshop ;vine vault; winery
winic (vee-ńeech) v. accuse; blame for ;fix the blame on
winien (vee-ńen) adj. m. indebted; owing; guilty; at fault
winnica (veen-ńee-tsa) f. vine yard; vine growing plantation
winny (veen-ni) adj. m. guilty
winny (veen-ni) adj. m. of wine; vineous ; vine-; winy
wino (vee-no) n. wine ;grapevine
winogrono (vee-no-gro-no) n. grape
winorosl (vee-no-roshl) f. vine
winowajca (vee-no-vay-tsa) m. culprit; evildoer;the guilty one
winszować (veen-sho-vach) v. congratulate (on having success)
wiosenny (vyo-sen-ni) adj. m. spring -(flowers,month etc.)
wioska (vyos-ka) f. hamlet
wiosło (vyos-wo) n. oar;paddle
wiosłować (vyos-wo-vach) v. row
wiosna (vyos-na) f. Spring (time)

wioslarz (vyosh-lash) m. oarsman ; rower
wiotki (vyot-kee) adj. m. limp
wior (vyoor) m. shaving ; chip
wir (veer) m. whirl; eddy ;vortex
wiraz (yee-rash) m. curve; bend
wirowac (vee-ro-vach) v. whirl
wirówka (vee-roov-ka) f. centrifuge ;hydro-extractor
wirtuoz (veer-too-os) m. virtuoso ;maestro; great musician etc.
wirus (vee-roos) m. virus
wisiec (vee-shech) v.hang; sag
wisiorek (vee-sho-rek) m. pendant
wisnia (veesh-ńa) f. cherry (tree)
wisniak (veesh-ńak) m. cherrybrandy; cherry liqueur
witac (vee-tach) v. greet; welcome; meet to welcome;bid welcome
witamina (vee-ta-mee-na) f. vitamin (A,B,C,D,E etc.)
witryna (vee-tri-na) f. shopwindow ; glass case
wiza (vee-za) f. visa
wizerunek (vee-ze-roo-nek) m. likeness; image;picture; effigy
wizja (veez-ya) f. vision ;view
wizyta (vee-zi-ta) f. call; visit; be on a visit
wizytówka (vee-zi-toov-ka) f. calling card; visiting card
wjazd (vyazt) m. (car) entrance
wjeżdżać (vyezh-dzhach) v. drive in ;ride to the top
wkleic (vkle-eech) v. stick in
wklęsłodruk (vklań-swo-drook) m. copper plate print
wklęsły (vklańs-wi) adj. m. concave; hollow; sunken
wkład (vkwat) m. input; deposit; investment; outlay; inset
wkładać (vkwa-dach) v. put in
w koło(vko-wo) adv. round;in circles; over and over again
wkoło (vko-wo)prep. round; about; in circles [appear;
wkraczać (vkra-chach) v. step in; invade; intervene; enter; stalk
wkradać się (vkra-dach shań) v. steal in; slip in; creep in
wkrapiać (vkrap-yach) v. put drops in; beat up

wkręcać (vkráń-tsach) v. screw
in ; drive in; push into a job
wkroczyc (vkro-chich)v. enter
(formally) ; appear ; invade
wkrótce (vkroot-tse) adv. soon
wkupic się (vkoó-peech śhań) v.
buy way in;pay one's footing
wlac (vlach) v. pour in
wlatywac (vla-ti-vach) v. fly
in ; rush in; dart in; run in
wlec (vlets) v, drag ; tow
wlepic (vle-peech) v. 1. paste
in; 2. glare at; stare at
wlewac (vlé-vach) v. pour in
wlezc (vlezhch) v. crawl in ;
climb up; barge in; step in
wliczenie (vlee-che-ne) n. inclusion; counting in
wliczyc (vlee-chich) v. count
in ; reckon in ;include
w lot (v lot) adv. in a flash;
quickly; in a hurry
wlot (vlot) m. inlet ; intake
wlot kuli (vlot koo-lee) m.
bullet entry
władac (vwá-dach) v. rule ;wield
władca (vwád-tsa) m. ruler
wladny (vwád-ni) adj. m. sovereign ; having the authority
władza (vwa-dza) f. authority
włamac sie (vwá-mach śhań) v.
break in; burglarize
włamanie (vwa-má-ne) n. burglary ; house breaking
włamywacz (vwa-mi-vach) m. burglar; housebreaker; picklock
własnorecznie (vwa-sno-rańch-ne)
adv. personally; with one's
hand ; with one's own hand
własnosc (vwas-noshch) f. property ; characteristic feature
własnowolny (vwas-no-vól-ni)
adj. m. spontaneous;voluntary
własny (vwas-ni) adj. m. own;very
właściciel (vwash-chee-chel) m.
proprietor ; holder ;owner
właściwy (vwash-chee-vi) adj.m.
proper ; right; suitable; due
właściwosc (vwash-chee-voshch) f.
propriety; characteristic
właśnie (vwásh-ne) adv. exactly;
just so; precisely; very; just
as;just now;just then;only just

wraz (vwas) m. manhole ;hatch
włazic (vwá-źheech) v. crawl
in ; barge in; step in;go deep
włączac (vwowń-chach) v. include; switch on; plug in
włącznie (vwówńch-ne) adv. in-
clusively; inclusive;including
włączenie (vwówń-che-ne) n.
inclusion ; merger ;incorporation
włochaty (vwo-khá-ti) adj. m.
hairy ; shaggy; hirsute;nappy
włos (vwos) m. hair ; fur
włosien (vwó-sheń) m. trichina
włoski (vwós-kee) adj.m. Italian; of Italy
włoskowaty (vwos-ko-vá-ti) adj.
m. capillary ; hairlike (tubes)
włoszczyzna (vwozh-chíz-na) pl.
vegetables ; Italian studies
włościanin (vwosh-chá-neen) m.
farmer ; peasant; country man
włożyc (vwó-zhich) v. put in
włóczęga (vwoo-chań-ga) m.
tramp ;rover; vagrant;roam
włóczka (vwóoch-ka) f. yarn
włócznia (vwooch-ńa) f. spear
włóczyc (vwoó-chich) v. drag
włókienniczy (vwo-kyen-ńee-chi)
adj. m. textile(trade,fiber etc.)
włókniarz (vwoók-nash) m.
weaver; textile worker
włóknisty (vwook-ńees-ti) adj.
m. fibrous; stringy;thready
włókno (vwoók-no) n. fibre
wmawiac (vmáv-yach) v. talk
into; persuade ; make believe
wmieszac sie (vmye-shach śhań)
v. interfere; join; mix;mingle
wmuszac (vmoó-shach) v. force
(upon) ; press upon [directly
wnet (vnet) adv. soon; shortly;
wnęka (vmáń-ka) f. niche ;recess
wnętrze (vnáń-tzhe) n. interior
wnętrznosci (vnantzh-nósh-chee)
pl. bowels ; intestines ;entrails
Wniebowzięcie (vńe-bo-vzhań-che)
n. Assumption [put in; infer;
wniesc (vńeshch) v. carry in ;
[ gather;conclude
wnikac (vńee-kach) v. penetrate
wnikliwy (vńee-klee-vi) adj. m.
penetrating;discerning;piercing
wniosek (vnó-sek) m. conclusion;
proposition; suggestion;motion

wnioskodawca (vnos-ko-dáv-tsa)
m. mover; giver of a motion
wnioskować (vnos-ko-vach) v.
conclude; deduct;infer; gather
wnioskowanie (vnos-ko-vá-ñe)
n. conclusion; inference
wnosić (vnó-sheech) v. carry in;
conclude; infer; gather
wnuczka (vnoóch-ka) f. granddaughter
wnuk (vnook) m. grandson
wnyk (vnik) m. snare
woalka (vo-ál-ka) f. veil(hat)
wobec (vó-bets) prep. in the
face of; before; towards
woda (vó-da) f. water;froth; bull
wodnisty (vod-nées-ti) adj. m.
watery; wishy-washy;aqueous
wodno-płatowiec (vod-no-pwa-tó-
vyets) m. hydroplane;water plane
wodny (vód-ni) adj. m. water-
wodociąg (vo-dó-chownk) m. waterworks ; water tap
wodolecznictwo (vo-do-lech-ñeéts-
tvo); n. hydrotherapy;water cure
wodopój (vo-dó-pooy) m. watering spot ; cow-pond;water hole
wodorost (vo-dó-rost) m. seaweed; alga
wodorowa bomba (vo-do-ró-va
bóm-ba) f. H-bomb
wodospad (vo-dó-spat) m. waterfall; cascade
wodotrysk (vo-dó-trisk) m. fountain; waterspout
wodować (vo-dó-vach) v. launch
on water ; splash down(on water)
wodowstręt (vo-dó-vstrańt) m.
hydrophobia; rabies
wodór (vó-door)m. hydrogen
wodza (vo-dza) f. rein;hold;sway
wodzić (vo-dżheech) v. lead;run
wodzirej (vo-dżhee-rey) m. dance
leader; ringleader;bell wether
w ogóle (vo-goó-le) adv. generally; on the whole; in the main
wojak (vó-yak) m. warrior;soldier
wojenny (vo-yén-ni) adj. m. military; war;wartime; of war
województwo (vo-ye-voódz-tvo) n.
province; voivodeship
wojłok (vóy-wok) m. felt (thick)

wojna (vóy-na) f. war ;warfare
wojna domowa (vóy-na do-mó-va)
f. civil war
wojować (vo-yo-vach) v. wage
war ; combat; contend
wojowniczy (vo-yov-ñee-chi)
adj. m. warlike; aggresive
wojownik (vo-yóv-ñeek) m.
(tribal) warrior
wojsko (vóy-sko) n. army;troops
wojskowość (voy-skó-voshch) f.
military science;the army
wojskowy (voy-sko-vi) adj.m.
military ; army(post etc.)
wokalny (vo-kál-ni) adj. m.
vocal ; all around
wokoło (vo-ko-wo) adv. round;
wola (vo-la) f. will;volition
wolec (vo-lech) v. prefer
wolno (vól-no) adv. slowly
wolnomyśliciel (vol-no-mi-
shleé-chel) m.freethinker
wolność (vól-noshch) f. liberty; freedom ; independence
wolnościowy (vol-nosh-chó-vi)
adj. m. for liberation
wolny (vól-ni) adj. m. free
wolt (volt) m. volt
woltomierz (vol-tó-myesh) m.
voltmeter
wołać (vo-wach) v. call;cry
wołanie (vo-wa-ñe) n. call;cry
wołowina (vo-wo-veé-na) f.
beef
wonny (von-ni) adj. m. fragrant; aromatic; sweet-smelling
woniec (vo-ñech) v. scent;
smell ; be fragrant
woń (voń) f. fragrance
woreczek (vo-ré-chek) m. small
bag ; pouch; cyst
worek(vó-rek) m. bag ; sack
wosk (vosk) m. wax
woskować (vos-kó-vach) v. wax
wozic (vo-żheech) v. carry (on
wheels); transport;drive;cart
wozownia (vo-zóv-ña) f. coach
house
woźnica (vożh-ñee-tsa) m. coach-
man ;driver; waggoner
wożenie (vo-zhe-ñe) n. transport; transportation;carriage

wódka (voód-ka) f. vodka
wódz (voots) m. commander;chief
wójt (vooyt) m. village mayor
wół (voow) m. ox ;steer;bullock
wór (voor) m. (big) sack(ful)
wówczas (voóv-chas) adv. then;
that time; at the time
wóz (voos) m. car; cart;wagon
wózek (vóo-zek) m. (small) car
wpadać (vpa-daćh) v. fall in;
rush in; drop in;run into
wpajać (vpá-yaćh) v. put in
(head); implant; instill
wpatrywać się (vpa-trí-vaćh
shań) v. stare;look intently
wpełzać (vpéw-zaćh) v.crawl in;
creep in(into a cave etc.)
wpędzać (vpáń-dzaćh) v. drive
sb in;bring on sb...(death etc)
wpić się (vpeećh shań) v. sink
into; penetrate; bury(teeth)
wpierw (vpyerv) adv. first
wpis (vpees) m. enrollment
wpisać (vpeé-saćh) v. write in
wpisowe (vpee-só-ve) n. registration fee;inscription fee
wplatać (vplá-taćh) v. twine
in; weave ; braid ;intersperse
wplątać (vplǿwn-taćh) v. entangle;implicate;involve
wpłacać (vpwá-tsaćh) v. pay in
wpłata (vpwá-ta) f. payment
wpław (vpwaf) adv. (swim)across
wpływ (vpwif) m. influence; income ; effect; impact of
wpływać (vpwi-vaćh) v. flow in;
influence ; have effect
wpływowy (vpwi-vó-vi) adj. m.
influential
w pobliżu (v po-blee-zhoo) adv.
near ;in the vicinity;close by
w poprzek (v pó-pzhek) prep.
adv. across; crosswise
wpół (vpoow) adv. in half; halfway ; half past;half-;semi-
w pośród (v pósh-rood) adv.
among ;in the midst of
wprawa (vprá-va) f. skill;
practice ; proficiency
wprawdzie (vpráv-dżhe) adv. in
truth ; to be sure; indeed
wprawić (vprá-veećh) v. set in;
train in ; insert; put in

wprawny (vpráv-ni) adj. m.
skillful ;trained; experienced
wprost (vprost) adv. directly;
straight ahead; outright;simply
wprowadzenie (vpro-va-dzé-ńe) n.
introduction; initiation
wprowadzać (vpro-va-dzaćh) v.
usher; introduce; lead in;put in
wprzęgać (vpzháń-gaćh) v. harness, (horse, river etc)
wprzód (vpshoot) adv. ahead; before; first; in the first place
wpuszczać (vpoósh-chaćh) v. let
in; admit; insert;allow to enter
wpychać (vpí-khaćh) v. push in
wracać (vrá-tsaćh) v. return
wrastać (vrás-taćh) v grow in
wraz (vras) prep. together
wrażenie (vra-zhé-ńe) n. impression;sensation;feeling;thrill
wrażliwosć (vrazh-leé-voshćh) f.
sensitivity ; susceptibility
wrażliwy (vrazh-leé-vi) adj. m.
sensitive ; thin-skinned;tender
wreszcie (vrésh-ćhe) adv. at
last ;finally; after all;eventually
wręcz (yráńćh) adv. down right
wręczać (vrań-chaćh) v. hand in
wrodzony (vro-dzó-ni) adj. m.
innate ; inborn; inbred;congenital
wrogi (vro-gee) adj. m. hostile
wrogosć (vró-goshćh) f. hostility ; ill-will; enmity;malevolence
wrona (vró-na) f. crow
wrota (vró-ta) n. gate
wrotki (vrót-kee) pl. roller
skates
wróbel (vró-bel) m. sparrow
wrócić (vróo-ćheećh) v. return
wróg (vrook) m. foe; enemy
wróżba (vroózh-ba) f. omen
wróżbiarz (vroózh-byash) m.
fortune-teller ; soothsayer
wróżka (vroózh-ka) f. fortune-
teller ;palmist; fairy
wróżyć (vroó-zhićh) v. tell
fortunes; foretell ;predict
wryć się (vrićh shań) v. dig in;
sink in ; imbed
wrzask (vzhask) m. scream;yell
wrzaskliwy (vzhas-kleé-vi) adj.
m. shrill;piercing; clamorous

wrzawa (vzha-va) f. noise

wrzący (vzhówn-tsi) adj. m. boiling ; scalding (hot)

wrzątek (vzhówn-tek) m. boiling water

wrzeciono (vzhe-chó-no) n. spindle ; verge

wrzeć (vzhech) v. boil ; rage

wrzesień (vzhe-sheń) m. September

wrzeszczec (vzhesh-chech) v. shriek ; yell; scream; cry

wrzos (vzhos) m. heather

wrzosowisko (vzho-so-vees-ko) n. heath; moor

wrzód (vzhoot) m. abscess

wrzucać (vzhóo-tsach) v. throw in; drop in; put in; cast

wsadzać (vsa-dzach) v. put in; plant ; stick; lock sb up

wschodni (vskhod-ńee) adj. m. east; easterly; eastern

wschodzic (vskho-dźheech) v. shoot up; rise; sprout

wschód słońca (vskhóod swoń-tsa) m. sunrise

wsiadać (vsha-dach) v. get in; mount; get on board; take seat

wsiąkać (vshówn-kach) v. sink in; infiltrate ;percolate

wskazany (vska-za-ni) adj. m. advisable;indicated;desirable

wskazówka (vska-zoóv-ka) f. hint; direction; (clock) hand

wskazujący palec (vska-zoo-yówn-tsi pá-lets) m. forefinger

wskazywać (vska-zí-vach) v. point out;show; indicate

wskaźnik (vskaźh-ńeek) m. index; pointer; indicator;signal

w skos (v skós) adv. slant

wskros (vskrosh) prep. through

wskutek (vskoó-tek) prep. as a result; due to; thanks to

wskrzesic (vskzhe-sheech) v. resuscitate; revive;wake;recall

wspaniałomyślny (vspa-ńa-wo-míshl-ni) adj. m. magnanimous

wspaniałość (vspa-ńa-woshch) f. splendor; grandeur;lordliness

wspaniały (vspa-ńa-wi) adj. m. superb; glorious; grand;great; smashing; magnificient;splendid

wsparcie (vspar-che) n. support

wspierać (vspye-rach) v. support ; prop up; assist; help

wspinac się (vspee-nach shań) v. climb up;toil up hill;rear

wspomagac (vspo-má-gach) v. help

wspominac (vspo-meé-nach) v. remember ; recall; mention

wspornik (vspór-ńeek) m. cantilever (beam);bracket; support

wspólnik (vspól-ńeek) m. partner; accomplice ; associate

wspólny (vspoól-ni) adj. m. common ; joint; combined ;collective

współczesność (vspoow-ches-noshch) f. the present time (day,age)

współczesny (vspoow-ches-ni) adj. m. contemporary ; modern ;present

współczucie (vspoow-choó-che) n. sympathy ; compassion ;pity

współczynnik (vspoow-chin-ńeek) m. coefficient ; factor

współdziałać (vspoow-dźha-wach) v. cooperate ; act jointly

współistniec (vspoow-eést-ńech) v. coexist

współistnienie (vspoow-eest-ńe-ńe) n. coexistence

współpraca (vspoow-pra-tsa) f. cooperation ; team-work

współrzędna (vspoow-zhánd-na) f. coordinate axis

współudział (vspoow-oó-dżhaw) m. participation; share

współwłasciciel (vspoow-vwash-chee-chel) m. joint owner

współzawodnictwo (vspoow-za-vod-ńeéts-tvo) m. competition

współzawodnik (vspoow-za-vod-ńeek) m. competitor; rival

współżyc (vspoów-zhich) v. get along; live together; coexist

wstawac (vsta-yach) v. get up

wstawiac (vsta-vyach) v. set in

wstawiac się (vsta-vyach shań) v. get tipsy; plead for sb

wstąpić (vstówn-peech) v. step in; drop in; step up; enter

wstążka (vstównzh-ka) f. ribbon

wstecz (vstech) adv. backwards

wsteczny (vstech-ni) adj. m. reactionary; reverse;backward

wstęga (vstán-ga) f. (large)
ribbon ; band;sash;wreath;wisp
wstęp (vstánp) m. entrance;
admission ; preface; opening
wstępny (vstánp-ni) adj. m.in-
troductory ; initial;preliminary
wstręt (vstránt) m. aversion
wstrętny (vstránt-ni) adj. m.
hideous ; foul;vile; nasty
wstrząs (vstzhówns) m. shock
wstrząsający (vstzhówn-sa-yówn-
tsi) adj. m. shocking; thrilling
wstrzemięźliwość (vstzhe-myán-
źhleé-vośhćh) f. moderation
wstrzemięźliwy (vstzhe-myan-
żhleé-vi) adj. m. moderate
wstrzykiwać (vstzhi-keé-vaćh)
v. inject; give a shot
wstrzymać (vstzhi-maćh) v. stop;
abstain; put off; hold back
wstyd (vstíd) m. shame; dis -
grace;dishonor;indecency
wstydliwy (vstid-leé-vi) adj.m.
shy; bashful; timid;embarassing
wstydzić się (vsti-dżheećh śhán)
v. be ashamed; blush for sb
wsunąć (vsoo-nównćh) v. slip in;
put in; insert into;tuck in
wsypa (vsí-pa) f.a bad break;
gaffe; give-away of a plot
wsypać (vsi-paćh) v. pour in;
tell on somebody; pour (grain)
wszakże (vshák-zhe) conj. adv.
yet; however; nevertheless
wszcząć (vshównćh) v. start; begin; institute; enter (talks)
wszechmocny (vshekh-móts-ni) adj.
m. omnipotent; almighty
wszechnica (vshekh-ńee-tsa) f.
university
wszechstronny (vshekh-stron-ni)
adj. m. universal; versatile
wszechświat (vshekh-śhvyat) m.
universe; cosmos ; macrocosm
wszelki (vshél-kee) adj. m.
every; all; any; whatever
wszerz (vshesh) adv. broadside
wszędzie (vshán-dźhe) adv. everywhere; on all sides ;all over
wszystek (vshís-tek) adj. m.
whole; all; ever; the whole
wszywać (vshí-vaćh) v. sew in

wścibski (vśhćheéb-skee) m.
busybody; meddler; snooper
wściekać się (vśhćheé-kaćh śhán)
v. rage; rave; be furious
wścieklizna (vśhćhe-kleéz-na) f.
rabies ; madness;hydrophobia
wściekłość (vśhćhek-wośhćh) f.
fury; rage; tantrums;madness
wślad (vśhlad) adv. following
in tracks; following closely
wśliznać się (vśhleéz-nównćh
śhán) v. sneak in; slip in
wśrod (yśhroot) prep. among
wtaczać (vtá-chaćh) v. roll in
wtajemniczyć (vta-yem-ńeé-chićh)
v. initiate; acquaint;instruct
wtargnać (vtárg-nównćh) v. invade; break into; interrupt
wtedy (vte-di) adv. then
wtem (vtem) adv. suddenly
wtenczas (vtén-chas) adv. then;
at that time; at this junction
wtoczyć (vtó-chićh) v. roll in
wtorek (vto-rek) m. Tuesday
wtórny (vtoór-ni) adj. m. secondary ; incidental;repeated
wtrącać się (vtrówn-tsaćh śhán)
v. meddle; cut into; butt in
wtyczka (vtíćh-ka) f. plug
wtykać (vti-kaćh) v. insert
w tył (vtiw) adv. back
wuj (vooy) m. uncle
wujenka (voo-yén-ka) f. aunt
wulgarny (vool-gár-ni) adj. m.
vulgar, coarse; low
wulkan (vóol-kan) m. volcano
wulkanizować (vool-ka-ńee-zó-
vaćh) v. vulcanize ;cure(rubber)
wwozić (v-vó-żheećh) v. import
wwóz (v-voos) m. import;importation
wy (vi) pron. you; you people
wybaczać (vi-bá-chaćh) v. forgive; pardon; buckle out of line
wybawca (vi-báv-tsa) m. savior;
rescuer; liberator ;redeemer
wybawić (vi-bá-veećh) v. save;
deliver ; free;rescue; rid
wybebeszyć (vi-be-bé-shićh) v.
gut (chicken etc.)
wybić (vi-beéćh) v. knock out
(something); strike; cover;kill
wybiec (vi-byets) v. run out

wybieg (vi-byek) m. evasion;
runway; playground;fowl run
wybielic (vi-bye-leech) v. whitewash; bleach;coat with tin
wybierac (vi-bye-rach) v. choose
elect; select; pick out ;mine
wybierak (vi-bye-rak) m. selec-
tor (technical term),
wybieralny (vi-bye-rál-ni) adj.
m. elective; eligible ;electable
wybitny (vi-beet-ni) adj. m.
prominent; eminent ; marked
wybladły (vi-blad-wi) adj. m.
pale; dim; faded; colorless
wybłagac (vi-bwa-gach) v. get by
entreaty; impetrate
wyblakły (vi-blák-wi) adj. m.
faded; dim; dilute;weathered
wyboisty (vi-bo-ees-ti) adj.m.
rough; full of holes; bumpy
wyborca (vi-bór-tsa) m. voter
wyborczy (vi-bor-chi) adj. m.
electoral;election-(precinct...)
wyborny (vi-bor-ni) adj. m. excellent; prime; choice;splendid
wyborowy (vi-bo-ro-vi) adj. m.
choice; select; first rate
wybory (vi-bo-ri) pl. election
wybór (vi-boor) m. choice;option
wybrany (vi-bra-ni) adj. m.
elected; chosen; selected
wybredny (vi-bréd-ni) adj. m.
fastidious; particular;exacting
wybrnąć (vibr-nownch) v. get out;
pull through; wade;clear out of
wybrukowac (vi-broo-kó-vach) v.
pave (the road, the street etc.)
wybryk (vi-brik) m. prank; freak;
antic; whim; frolic;caprice
wybrzeże (vi-bzhe-zhe) n. coast;
beach; sea-shore; sea-coast
wybrzuszenie (vi-bzhoo-she-ñe)
n. bulge; swelling; knob; belly
wybuch (vi-bookh) m. explosion;
eruption; outbreak; outburst
wybudowac (vi-boo-do-vach) v.
build; erect; raise;construct
wycelowac (vi-tse-lo-vach) v.
take aim; level a gun at
wychodek (vi-khó-dek) m. privy
wychodzic (vi-kho-dzheech) v.
get out; walk out; climb out

wychodzca (vi-khódzh-tsa) m.
emigrant; émigré
wychowac (vi-khó-vach) v. bring
up; rear; rise; train; educate
wychowanek (vi-kho-vá-nek) m.
pupil;alumnus; ward ;foster child
wychowanie (vi-kho-vá-ñe) n.
upbringing; manners ; education
wychowawca (vi-kho-vav-tsa) m.
tutor; educator;foster father
wychudły (vi-khoód-wi) adj. m.
gaunt; skinny; haggard ;emaciated
wychwalac (vi-khvá-lach) v.
praise ; exalt; extol;speak highly
wychylac (vi-khí-lach) v. stick
out;empty (glass);bend;incline
wychylac się (vi-khí-lach sháñ)
v. lean out; stick one's neck
out; hang out; appear ;be visible
wyciąg (vi-chównk) m. extract;
elevator; hoist; winch ;excerpt
wyciągac (vi-chówn-gach) v.
pull out; stretch out; derive;
wycie (vi-che) n. howl ;scream
wycieczka (vi-chéch-ka) f. trip;
excursion; outing ;ramble;hike
wyciekac (vi-ché-kach) v. leak
out; flow out; ooze out ;scamper
wycieńczac (vi-cheñ-chach) exhaust
wycieńczenie (vi-cheñ-che-ñe) n.
exhaustion; weakness; debility
wycieraczka (vi-che-rach-ka) f.
wiper; doormat
erase; efface;dust;wear out
wycierac (vi-che-rach) v. wipe;
wycięcie (vi-cháñ-che) n. opening; cut; décolleté ;notch;jag
wycinac (vi-chee-nach) v. cut
out ; carve out; fell;cut down
wycisk (vi-cheesk) m. press;
squeeze; beating (slang)
wyciskac (vi-chees-kach) v.
squeeze out; impress; wring
wycofac (vi-tsó-fach) v. withdraw; remove;retract;call off
wycofanie (vi-tso-fá-ñe) n .
withdrawal; recall;retirement
wyczerpac (vi-cher-pach) v.
exhaust; drain; deplete;scoop
wyczerpanie (vi-cher-pa-ñe) n.
exhaustion; depletion;prostration
wyczesywac (vi-che-sí-vach) v.
comb out; dress hair (beard etc.)

wyczuwać (vi-choo-vach) v. sense;
feel; scent; ascertain;perceive
wyczyn (vi-chin) m. feat; stunt
wyczyszczać (vi-chish-chach) v.
clean; brush ; clean out; polish
wyc (vich) v. howl; roar;shriek
wycwiczony (vich-vee-cho-ni)
adj. m. trained; skilled
wydajnosć (vi-day-noshch) f.
yield; productivity; output
wydajny (vi-day-ni) adj. m.
productive ; effective
wydalac (vi-da-lach) v. dismiss;
sack ; expel; eliminate;excrete
wydalenie (vi-da-le-ne) n. expulsion ; dismissal; excretion
wydanie (vi-da-ne) n. edition
wydarty (vi-dar-ti) adj. m.
torn out;plucked out;snached out
wydarzac się (vi-da-zhach shan)
v. happen; turn out well;occur
wydarzenie (vi-da-zhe-ne) n.
event ; happening;circumstance
wydatek (vi-da-tek) m. expense
wydatkowac (vi-dat-ko-vach) v.
spend ; lay out funds;expend
wydatny (vi-dat-ni) adj. m.
prominent; salient; distinct
wydawac (vi-da-vach) v. spend;
give the change; publish
wydawca (vi-dav-tsa) m. publisher; editor;publishing house
wydawnictwo (vi-dav-neets-tvo)
n. publication; publishing
house;publishing firm
wydąc (vi-downch) v. expand;
puff up; inflate ; blow up
wydech (yi-dekh) m. exhalation
wydeptac scieżkę (vi-dep-tach
shchezh-kan) beat a path (exp.)
wydłubywac (vi-dwoo-bi-vach) v.
scrape out; poke;hollow out
wydłużac (vi-dwoo-zhach) v. prolong; lengthen; elongate
wydma (vid-ma) f. dune;snowdrift
wydobrzec (vi-dob-zhech) v. recover; get better ; improve
wydobycie (vi-do-bi-che) n, output; yield; production
wydobywac (vi-do-bi-vach) v. extract; mine; wring; get;obtain
wydostac (vi-dos-tach) v. bring
out; extricate; obtain;pull out

wydra (vi-dra) f. otter; vulg.:
bitch ; hussy; minx;vixen
wydrapac (vi-dra-pach) v.
scratch out; erase a stain
wydrapac się (vi-dra-pach shan)
v. climp up; scramble up (out)
wydrążac (vi-drown-zhach) v.
hollow out ; drill; excavate
wydrwic (vi-drveech) v. jeer;
mock; cheat; gibe; deride
wydrwigrosz (vi-drvee-grosh)
m. swindler; fraud; take-in
wydusic (vi-doo-sheech) v.
squeeze out; extort; strangle
wydychac (vi-di-khach) v.
breathe out; exhale; emit
wydymac (vi-di-mach) v. puff out;
inflate ; belly out;blow up;bulge
wydział (vi-dzhaw) m. department
wydziedziczac (vi-dzhe-dzhee-
chach) v. disinherit
wydzielac (vi-dzhe-lach) v.emit;
detach; distribute; secrete
wydzielenie (vi-dzhe-le-ne) n.
secretion; assignment; elimination; emanation ;issue
wydzieliny (vi-dzhe-lee-ni) pl.
sercreta; excretions ; discharge
wydzielony (vi-dzhe-lo-ni) adj.
m. emited; segregated; alloted
wydzierac (vi-dzhe-rach) v. tear
out; roar out ; blare out;scramble
wydzierżawic (vi-dzher-zha-veech)
v. lease; farm out ; rent; let out
wydzierżawienie (vi-dzher-zha-
vye-ne) n. leasing;renting
wyegzekwowac (vi-eg-zek-vo-vach)
v. exact; enforce ; carry out
wyekwipowanie (vi-ek-vee-po-va-
ne) n. outfit; equipment
wyeleganciec (vi-e-le-gan-chech)
v. acquire elegance;become elegant
wyeliminowanie (vi-e-lee-mee-no-
va-ne) n. elimination;exclusion
wyga (vi-ga) m. old experienced
hand; sly fox; old stager
wygadac (vi-ga-dach) v. blab out
wygadany (vi-ga-da-ni) adj. m.
glib; eloquent; wordy ;talkative
wyganiac (vi-ga-nach) v. expel;
chase out ; turn out(cattle)
wygarniac (vi-gar-nach) v. rake
out; tell off ; say openly ;shoot

wygasać (vi-ga-sach) v. extinguish; expire; go out; die out
wyginać (vi-gee-nach) v. bend
wygląd (vig-lownd) m. appearance;aspect; air; looks;semblance
wyglądać (vig-lown-dach) v. look out; appear;appear;look
wygładzać (vi-gwa-dzach) v. smooth;level;even; sleek
wygłodzić (vi-gwo-dzheech) v. starve out; underfeed; famish
wygłosić (vi-gwo-sheech) v. pronounce; utter;deliver(speech)
wygnać (vig-nach) v.expel;banish
wygnanie (vig-ña-ñe) n. exile
wygniatać (vi-gña-tach) v. press out; squeeze out; extort; kill
wygoda (vi-go-da) f. comfort
wygodny (vi-god-ni) adj. m. comfortable; cozy; handy
wygolony (vi-go-lo-ni) adj. m. clean-shaven; well shaven
wygotować (vi-go-to-vach) v. boil away; distill; prepare
wygórowany (vi-goo-ro-va-ni) adj. m. excessive; stiff(price)
wygrać (vi-grach) v. win; score
wygramolic się (vi-gra-mo-leech śhań) v. scramble up (out)
wygrana (vi-gra-na) f. winning; victory; prize; a win
wygryzać (vi-gri-zach) v. 1.bite out; corrode; 2. drive out by harassment;oust;bore a hole
wygrzebywać (vi-gzhe-bi-vach) v. dig out; unearth; rake out
wygrzewać się (vi-gzhe-vach śhań) v. bask; warm oneself
wygwizdać (vi-gveez-dach) v. hiss off (stage); whistle away
wyjałowic (vi-ya-wo-veech) v. sterilize; exhaust(brain,soil...)
wyjasnić (vi-yash-ñeech) v. explain; clear up; elucidate
wyjasnienie (vi-yash-ñe-ñe) n. explanation; interpretation
wyjawić (vi-ya-veech) v. disclose;reveal; bring to light
wyjazd (vi-yazt) m. departure
wyjąkać (vi-yown-kach) v. stammer out;stutter out; falter out
wyjątek (vi-yown-tek) m. exception; excerpt; extract

wyjątkowy (vi-yown-ko-vi) adj. m. exceptional;unusual;unique
wyjechać (vi-ye-khach) v. drive away; leave ;come out with
wyjeżdżać (vi-yezh-dzhach) v. leave; drive away ; set out
wyjmować (viy-mo-vach) v. take out; remove; extract; excerpt
wyjście (viysh-che) n. exit; way out; departure;egress
wyka (vi-ka) f. vetch ; tare
wykadzić (vi-ka-dzheech) v. smoke out; fumigate; perfume
wykałaczka (vi-ka-wach-ka) f. toothpick
wykarczować (vi-kar-cho-vach) v. grub out; clear;dig up(trees)
wykaz (vi-kas) m. list; register; roll; schedule;docket
wykąpac (vi-kown-pach) v. bathe
wykipiec (vi-keep-yech) v. boil over (milk,water,soup etc.)
wyklęty (vi-klań-ti) adj. m. cursed; excommunicated
wykluczyc (vi-kloo-chich) v. exclude; expel; shut out ;except
wykład (vik-wat) m. lecture
wykładać (vi-kwa-dach) v. lecture; lay out ; display; cover
wykładnik (vi-kwad-ñeek) m. exponent; expression ; ratio
wykładowca (vi-kwa-dov-tsa) m. lecturer ; instructor
wykłuwać (vi-kwoo-vach) v. stab out; put out; tattoo;prick out
wykoleic (vi-ko-le-eech) v. derail; lead astray;ditch(a train)
wykombinować (vi-kom-bee-no-vach) v. contrive; think out
wykonać (vi-ko-nach) v. execute; do; fulfil ; carry out; perform
wykonalny (vi-ko-nal-ni) adj.m. feasible ; workable;realizable
wykonanie (vi-ko-na-ñe) n. execution;realization;fulfilment
wykonawczy (vi-ko-nav-chi) adj. m. executive ;executory (details...)
wykończenie (vi-koń-che-ñe) n. finish ; trimming ;last touch
wykończyc (vi-koń-chich) v. finish off ; dress; do sb in
wykop (vi-kop) m. excavation ; potato lifting; flying kick

wykopać (vi-ko-pach) v. dig out
wykopalisko (vi-ko-pa-lees-ko)
n. find (archaeological)
wykorzenić (vi-ko-zhe-neech) v.
root out ; uproot; eradicate
wykorzystać (vi-ko-zhis-tach) v.
take advantage ; exploit:use up
wykpić (vik-peech) v. deride
wykraczać (vi-kra-chach) v. step
over; break law,; transgress
wykradać (vi-kra-dach) v. steal;
kidnap ;purloin;pilfer;abduct
wykrajać (vi-kra-yach) v. cut
out ; carve out;make a low cut
wykres (vi-kres) m. graph; chart
wykreslić (vi-kresh-leech) v.
trace; cross out ; draw ;erase
wykręcać (vi-kran-tsach) v. screw
out; distort; elude ; twist
wykręt (vi-krant) m. shift;
excuse ; dodge ;guibble
wykrętny (vi-krant-ni) adj. m.
shifty ;evasive; sophistical
wykroczenie (vi-kro-che-ne) n.of-
fense ; misdemeanor;delinquency
wykroic (yi-kro-eech) v. cut out
wykruszyć (vi-kroo-shich) v.
crumble out ; shell(corn etc.)
wykryć (vi-krich) v. discover;
detect ; reveal(the truth etc.)
wykrztusić (vi-kzhtoo-sheech) v.
cough up; choke out ;hawk up
wykrzyknąć (vi-kzhik-nownch) v.
call out ; shout; cry out
wyksztalcic (vi-kzhtaw-cheech) v.
educate ; train; shape; form
wykup (yi-koop) m. ransom
wykupic (vi-koo-peech) v. buy up
wykurzac (vi-koo-zhach) v. smoke
out (foxes,bees, etc.)
wykwintny (vi-kveent-ni) adj.m.
elegant; exquisite ; urbane
wyleczalny (vi-le-chal-ni) adj.
m. curable;possible to cure
wyleczyć (vi-le-chich) v. cure
wylew krwi (vi-lev krvee)
hemorrhage; blood effusion
wylewac (vi-le-vach) v. pour out;
overflow;spill;bail out water
wylęgać (vi-lan-gach) v. hatch
wylękły (vi-lank-wi) adj. m.
frightened ; scared ;terrified

wyliczac (vi-lee-chach) v.
count up; count out; recite
wylosowac (vi-lo-so-vach) adj.
m. draw out by lots ;toss for
wylot (vi-lot) m.flight departure; nozzle; exhaust; exit
wyludniac (vi-lood-nach) v.
depopulate;desolate;devastate
wyładowac (vi-wa-do-vach) v.
unload; discharge; cram;pack
wyładowanie (vi-wa-do-va-ne)
n. unloading; discharge
wyłamac (vi-wa-mach) v. break
out ;break loose;break away
wyławiac (vi-wav-yach) v. fish
out; spot out; catch (a sound)
wyłaniac (vi-wa-nach) v. evolve;
emerge ; show; appoint;form
wyłączac (vi-wown-chach) v.
exclude; switch off;disconnect
wyłącznik (vi-wownch-neek) m.
switch; circuit-breaker;cut off
wyłączny (vi-wownch-ni) adj.
m. exclusive; sole; only;entire
wyłudzic (vi-woo-dzheech) v.
coax; beguile; trick; fool
wyłom (vi-wom) m. breach; gap
wyłuskac (vi-woos-kach) v. husk;
scale; fleece; shell; hull; pod
wymaczac (vi-ma-chach) v. soak
wymagac (vi-ma-gach) v. require;
expect; demand; need; exact
wymaganie (vi-ma-ga-ne) n. requirement; demand;requisite;need;
wymawiac (vi-mav-yach) v. pronounce; reproach ; cancel;express
wymazac (vi-ma-zach) v. erase;
efface; blot out; smear;use up
wymiana (vi-mya-na) f. exchange
wymiar (vi-myar) m. dimension
wymiatac (vi-mya-tach) v.
sweep out; clean out; sweep
wymieniac (vi-mye-nach) v.
exchange; convert; replace
wymierac (vi-mye-rach) v. die
out; become extinct(gradually)
wymierzac (vi-mye-zhach) v. aim;
measure; assess; survey;mete out
wymię (vi-myan) n. udder ;evade
wymijac (vi-mee-yach) v. pass by;
wymiotowac (vi-myo-to-vach) v.
vomit; be sick;spew up(one's food)

wymogi (vi-mó-gee) pl. require-
ments; exigencies;needs
wymowa (vi-mó-va) f. pronunciation; significance(of facts...)
wymowny (vi-móv-ni) adj. m.
eloquent; telltale; telling
wymóc (vi-moots) v. extort;
compel; wring; force;prevail
wymówienie (vi-moov-ye-ñe) n.
notice (to quit or dismiss)
wymówka (vi-moóv-ka) f. reproach;
pretext; excuse; put-off;evasion
wymusić (vi-moo-shich) v. extort
wymuszenie (vi-moo-she-ñe) n.
extortion;blackmail;shakedown
wymykać się (vi-mi-kač shãn)
v. escape;slip away;sneak out
wymysł (vi-misw) m. fiction;
invention ;fiction; abuse
wymyślać (vi-miśh-lach) v. think
up; call names; invent; abuse
wymyślny (vi-miśhl-ni) adj. m.
clever; ingenious;sophisticated
wymywać (vi-mi-vach) v. wash out
wynagradzać (vi-na-grá-dzach) v.
reward; pay; indemnify;make up
wynagrodzenie (vi-na-gro-dze-ñe)
n. reward; pay; fee; reparation
wynajdywać (vi-nay-dí-vach) v.
find (out); invent; devise
wynajmować (vi-nay-mo-vach) v.
hire ; rent      rent; hire
wynajem (vi-na-yem) m. lease ;
wynalazca (vi-na-láz-tsa) m.
inventor; contriver
wynalazek (vi-na-lá-zek) m. invention ; device;contrivance
wynaleźć (vi-ná-leżhch) v. invent
wynaradawiać (vi-na-ra-dav-yach)
v. denationalize ; divest
wynik (vi-ñeek) m. result; score
wyniosłość (vi-ñós-woshch) f.
eminence; haughtiness ; prance
wyniosły (vi-ñós-wi) adj. m.
lofty; high-handed ;insolent
wyniszczać (vi-ñeesh-chach) v.
ruin ; exhaust; weaken;devastate
wynosić (vi-nó-sheech) v. carry
out; elevate; amount ;wear out
wynudzać (vi-noó-dzach) v. get
by bothering; bore stiff
wynurzenie (vi-noo-zhe-ñe) n.
emergence; (personal) outpouring

wyobraźnia (vi-o-bráźh-ña) f.
imagination ; fancy;empty fancy
wyobrażać (vi-o-brá-zhach) v.
imagine; picture; fancy;suppose
wyobrażenie(vi-o-bra-zhé-ñe) n.
notion; idea ; image;representation
wyodrębniać (vi-od-ranb-ñach)
v. single out; separate; isolate
wyodrębnienie (vi-od-ranb-ñe-
ñe) n. separation; isolation
wyolbrzymiać (vi-ol-bzhí-myach)
v. magnify; exaggerate(very much)
wypaczyć (vi-pa-chich) v. warp
wypad (vi-pat) m. sally; attack
wypadać (vi-pá-dach) v. fall
out; rash out; become; turn
out; happen; occur; work out
wypadek (vi-pa-dek) m. accident;
case ;event; chance;instance
wypadkowa (vi-pad-kó-va) f. resultant (force, effect etc.)
wypakować (vi-pa-kó-vach) v.
unpack; cram ; pack tight
wypalać (vi-pa-lach) v. burn out
wypaplać (vi-páp-lach) v. babble
out ; blurt out(the truth,secret)
wyparcie się (vi-par-che shãn)
n. disclaimer ; repudiation
wyparować (vi-pa-ro-vach) v.
evaporate; vanish into thin air
wypatrywać (vi-pa-tri-vach) v.
watch (for) ; look out;espy;descry
wypełniać (vi-pew-ñach) v. fulfil; fill up ; while away;fill in
wypełnienie (vi-pew-ñe-ñe) n.
fulfilment ; order execution;filler
wypędzać (vi-pán-dzach) v. drive
out; expel ; discharge;dislodge
wypiekać (vi-pyé-kach) v. bake;
wypierać (vipyé-rach) v. oust;
push out;force out;supplant
wypierać się (vi-pye-rach shãn)
v. deny ; repudiate;disown;abjure
wypijać (vi-pee-yach) v. drink
(empty); drink to; drink off
wypinać (vi-pee-nach) v. extend;
strech out ; show one's back side
wypis (vi-pees) m. extract;passage
wypisywać (vi-pee-sí-vach) v.
(write) extract;make out(a check)
wyplątać (vi-plown-tach) v.
extricate ; disentangle;disengage;
free from tangles

wyplątany (vi-plown-tá-ni) adj.
m. disembroiled;extricated
wyplenić (vi-ple-neech) v. weed
out; root out; eradicate
wypluć (vi-plooch) v. spit out
wypłacać (vi-pwa-tsach) v. pay
out; pay up; pay off; repay
wypłacalny (vi-pwa-tsal-ni) adj.
m. solvent; sound (financially)
wypłata (vi-pwa-ta) f. pay (day)
wypłoszyc (vi-pwo-shich) v.
scare away; drive away (cats...)
wypłowiec (vi-pwo-vyech) v. fade
wypłukac (vi-pwoo-kach) v. rinse;
wash out; swill out ;give a rinse
wypływ (vi-pwiv) m. outflow;
discharge; efflux; leakage
wypływac (vi-pwi-vach) v. flow
out; sail out; swim out; rise
wypocic (vi-po-cheech) v. sweat
out; perspire ;be soaked in sweat
wypoczynek (vi-po-chi-nek) m.
rest; repose
wypoczywac (vi-po-chi-vach) v.
rest;have a rest;take a rest
wypogadzac sie (vi-po-ga-dzach
shan) v. clear up; cheer up
wypomniec (vi-pom-nech) v. reproach; remind ;keep reminding
wypornosc (vi-por-noshch) f.
displacement; draught ;buoyancy
wyposażac (vi-po-sa-zhach) v.
equip; endow; fit out; stock
wyposażenie (vi-po-sa-zhe-ne) n.
equipment; outfit; wages ;dowry
wyposazyc (vi-po-sa-zhich) v.
endow; equip; fit out;stock
wypowiadac (vi-po-vya-dach) v.
pronounce; declare ; express
wypowiedzenie (vi-po-vye-dze-ne)
n.(discharge) notice; (war) declaration; renunciation;utterance
wypożyczac (vi-po-zhi-chach) v.
lend out ;borrow from;hire to
wypożyczalnia (vi-po-zhi-chal-na)
f. rental business ;rental agency
wypracowanie (vi-pra-tso-va-ne)
n. (school) composition; elaboration ;/ essay; exercice
wyprac (vi-prach) v. wash out
wypraszac (vi-pra-shach) v.
1. plead; 2. show (the door) ;
give somebody the gate;turn out

wyprawa (vi-pra-va) f. expedition; outfit; tanning;dowry
wyprawiac (vi-pra-vyach) v.
send; tan;plaster;give(a party)
wyprężac (vi-pran-zhach) v.
stretch out; tense(a muscle etc.)
wyprostowac (vi-pros-to-vach)
v. straighten;set streight
wyprowadzac (vi-pro-va-dzach)
v. lead out; move out; trace
wypróbowac (vi-proo-bo-vach)
v. test; try out;put to test
wyprozniac (vi-proozh-nach) v.
empty; clear out; evacuate
wyprzedawac (vi-pzhe-da-vach)
v. sell out; clear out(stock)
wyprzedaż (vi-pzhe-dash) v.
(clearance) sale
wyprzedzac (vi-pzhe-dzach) v.
pull ahead;outpace;overtake
wyprzęgac (vi-pzhan-gach) v.
unharness; unhitch (a horse)
wypukły (vi-pook-wi) adj. m.
convex; bulging; cambered
wypuscic (vi-poosh-cheech) v.
let out; set free; let go;
omit;release;launch;lease out
wypychac (vi-pi-khach) v. oust;
push out; stuff;pack; fill;cram
wypytywac (vi-pi-ti-vach) v.
question;ask questions;inquire
wyrabiac (vi-ra-byach) v.
1. make; form; 2. play pranks
wyrachowany (vi-ra-kho-va-ni)
adj. m. scheming; thrifty
wyratowac (vi-ra-to-vach) v.
rescue; save (a life etc.)
wyraz (vi-ras) m. word; expression; look; term (in vocabulary)
wyrazny (vi-razh-ni) adj. m.
explicit; clear; distinct
wyrażac (vi-ra-zhach) v. express
wyrażenie (vi-ra-zhe-ne) n.
expression; utterance; phrase ;
statement
wyrąb (vi-rownp) m. clearing;
felling; cutting ; slash;fell
wyrąbac (vi-rown-bach) v. cut
out (with axe); clear; hack out
wyręczac (vi-ran-chach) v. help
out; replace; relieve of tasks
wyrobnik (vi-rob-neek) m. laborer; day-laborer ; navvy

wyrocznia (vi-róch-ña) f. oracle
wyrodny (vi-ród-ni) adj. m. degenerate;unnatural(son);base
wyrodzic się (vi-ró-dźheećh śhäñ)
v. degenerate;deteriorate
wyrok (vi-rok) m. sentence; verdict; judgment; pronouncement
wyrostek (vi-rós-tek) m. out-
growth; stripling; teenager
wyrosnięty (vi-rosh-nän-ti)adj.
m. grown up ; overgrown
wyrozumiały (vi-ro-zoo-myá-wi)
adj. m. indulgent; lenient
wyrozumienie (vi-ro-zoo-mye-ñe)
n. sympathetic understanding
wyrób (vi-roob) m. manufacture
wyrównac (vi-róov-naćh) v.
equalize; pay up; smooth
wyrownanie (vi-roov-ná-ñe) m.
leveling;balancing(accounts)offset
wyróżniac (vi-roózh-ñaćh) v.
distinguish ; favor; single out
wyruszyc (vi-roo-shićh) v. start
out;set out;march out;sail away
wyrwac (vir-vaćh) v. extract;
tear out; pull out; run away
wyrywki (yi-riv-kee) pl. random
wyryc (vi-rićh) v. engrave; root
up; dig out;gully;furrow;incise
wyrzec się (vi-zhets śhäñ) v.
renounce;give up; forgo;repudiate
wyrzucac (vi-zhóo-tsaćh) v. expel; throw out; dump; reproach
wyrzut (vi-zhoot) m. reproach
wyrzutnia (vi-zhoot-ña) f. launch
(ing)pad; chute; launcher
wyrzutek (vi-zhóo-tek) m. outcast
wyrzynac (vi-zhi-naćh) v. cut out;
carve; slaughter; bang; slap
wysadzic (vi-sá-dżheećh) v. set
out;land; blow up ; eject;plant
wyschnąc (vis-khnówñćh) v. dry up
wysepka (vi-sép-ka) f. islet
wysiadac (vi-śha-daćh) v. get out
(from car etc.); go bust;get off
wysiadywac (vi-śha-di-vaćh) v.
sit out; hatch out; sit late
wysiedlac (vi-śhed-laćh) v. expel (from home); resettle;eject
wysilac (vi-śhee-laćh) v. exert
wysiłek (yi-śhee-wek) m. effort
wyskoczyc (vi-sko-chićh) v. jump
out; pop up;run out;bale out

wyskok (vis-kok) m. 1. fling;
freak; 2. cam ;ledge;run out
wyskokowy (vis-ko-kó-vi) adj.
m. alcoholic; intoxicating
wyskrobac (vi-skro-baćh) v.
scratch out; erase ;scratch
wyskubac (vi-skoo-baćh) v.
pluck out; pull out(hair etc.)
wysłac (vi-swaćh) v. send off;
dispatch ;emit; let fly
wysłaniec (vi-swa-ñets) m.
messenger; envoy ; deputy
wysłowic (vi-swó-veećh) v. express ;say; utter; speak
wysłuchac (vi-swoo-khaćh) v.
hear out ;give a hearing
wysługiwac się (vi-swoo-gee-
vaćh śhäñ) v. lackey; use s.o.
wysmarowac (vi-sma-ro-vaćh) v.
smear ;lubricate; soil;stain
wysmażony (vi-sma-zhó-ni) adj.
m. well done (meat);cooked
wysmukły (vi-smoók-wi) adj.m.
slender ; slim and tall
wysoce (vi-só-tse) adv. highly
wysoki (vi-só-kee) m. tall;
high ; soaring; lofty;towering
wysokosc (vi-só-koshćh) f.
height; altitude;level;extent
wysokosciomierz (vi-so-kośh-chó-
myesh) m. altimeter
wyspa (vis-pa) f. island; isle
wyspac się (vis-paćh śhäñ) v.
sleep enough; sleep off
wyspowiadac się (vis-po-vya-
daćh śhäñ) v. confess
wyssac (vis-saćh) v. suck out ;
suck dry
wystarac się (vi-sta-raćh śhäñ)
v. procure ;obtain; secure
wystarczyc (vi-stár-chićh) v.
suffice ; do enough;be enough
wystawa (vi-stá-va) f. exhibi-
tion; display (window dressing)
wystawac (vi-stá-vaćh) v. stand
out; stand long time ;stick out
wystawca (vi-stáv-tsa) m. ex-
hibitor; signer (of check)
wystawiac (vi-stáv-yaćh) v.
put out; stick out; sign
(check) ; exhibit ;expose
wystawienie (vi-sta-vyé-ñe) n.
exposition; exposure ;display

wystąpić (vi-stown-peech) v.
step forward;perform;resign
wystąpienie (vi-stown-pye-ne)
n. withdrawal; appearance
występ (vi-stanp) m. protrusion;
(stage) appearance; utteramce
występek (vi-stan-pek) m. felony; crime; vice; offense
występny (vi-stanp-ni) adj. m.
criminal; immoral ; illicit
wystraszyc (vi-stra-shich) v.
frighten away; terrify; scare
wystroic (vi-stro-eech) v. dress
up ; trig out; deck out; adorn
wystrzał (vi-stzhaw) m. shot
wystrzegac się (vi-stzhe-gach
shan) v. avoid ; beware; shun
wystrzelic (vi-stzhe-leech) v.
fire a gun ;shoot out; go off
wystrzępic (vi-stzhan-peech) v.
ravel out ; fray; unravel
wystygac (vi-sti-gach) v. cool
off ; grow cold ;get cold
wysuszyc (vi-soo-shich) v. dry
up ; wither ;parch; shrivel
wysuwac (vi-soo-vach) v. shove
forward ; protrude; put out
wyswobodzic (vi-svo-bo-dzheech)
v. liberate; deliver; free
wysychać (vi-si-khach) v. dry out
wysypac (vi-si-pach) v. pour out
wysypka (vi-sip-ka) f. (skin)
rash ; eruption ;exanthema
wysysac (vi-si-sach) v. suck
wyszczególnić (vi-shche-gool-
neech) v. specify;detail out
wyszeptac (vi-sheptach) v. whis-
per(not vibrating the vocalrchords)
wyszkolic (vi-shko-leech) v.
train ;school; educate ;instruct
wyszpiegowac (vi-shpye-go-vach)
v. spy out; spy out that...
wyszukac (vi-shoo-kach) v. find
out ; hunt up; search out
wyszukany (vi-shoo-ka-ni) adj.m.
choice; unusual ; elaborate
wyszydzac (vi-shi-dzach) v.
scoff at ; jeer; deride
wyszynk (vi-shink) m. liquor
store; liquor retail on licence
wyszywac (vi-shi-vach) v. embroider;desing with needlework

wyscielac (vi-shche-lach) v.
pad; line; strew;cushion
wyscig (vish-cheek) m. race;
contest ; rivalry ;(horse)race
wysledzic (vi-shle-dzheech) v.
spy out; track out;detect
wyśliznąć się (vi-shleez-nownch
shan) y. slip out;slide out
wyśmiac (vish-myach) v. laugh
at; deride ;mock;ridicule
wyśmienity (vish-mye-nee-ti)
adj. m. choice; excellent
wyspiewac (vi-shpye-vach) v.
squeal; sing ; say ;sound praises
wyswiadczyc (vish-vyad-chich)
v. do (favor); do (good);do (wrong)
wyswiechtany (vi-shvyekh-ta-ni)
adj. m. well worn; beat up
wyswietlac (vish-vyet-lach) v.
clear up; project (film)
wytaczac (vi-ta-chach) v. roll
out ; set forth; draw ;turn
wytargowac (vi-tar-go-vach) v.
buy by haggling; haggle a lot
wytarty (vi-tar-ti) adj.m.
worn out; thread bare;shabby
wytchnąć (vi-tkhnownch) v. rest
up ; relax ;take a rest;breathe
wytchnienie (vi-tkhne-ne) n.
rest; break; relax; truce
wytępic (vi-tan-peech) v.extermi-
nate; eradicate; wipe out
wytężac (vi-tan-zhach) v. strain
wytknąć (vit-knownch) v. put out;
point out; reproach; trace
wytłuc (vi-twoots) v. kill off;
break up ; ruin; beat up
wytłumaczenie (vi-two-ma-che-
ne) n. explanation; excuse
wytłumaczyc (vi-twoo-ma-chich)
v. explain; excuse; justify
wytrawny (vi-trav-ni) adj. m.
experienced; dry (wine) ;seasoned
wytrącac (vi-trown-tsach) v.
knock of; deduct; snatch
wytrwały (vi-trva-wi) adj. m.
enduring; persevering; dogged
wytrwanie (vi-trva-ne) n. endurance; persistence ;lasting
wytrwac (vi-trvach) v. persevere
wytrych (vi-trikh) m. pick-a-
-lock; pass-key; skeleton-key

wytrząsć (vi-tzhownshch) v.
shake out ; empty ; jolt
wytrzebic (vi-tzhe-beech) v.
devastate; exterminate ; clear
wytrzeźwieć (vi-tzhezh-vyech) v.
sober up,;get sober; sober down
wytrzymac (vi-tzhi-mach) v. endure; stand;hold out; keep
wytrzymałosc (vi-tzhi-ma-woshch)
f. endurance ; stamina;strength
wytrzymały (vi-tzhi-ma-wi) adj.
m. enduring ; tough; durable
wytworny (vi-tvor-ni) adj. m.
exquisite ;elegant; stylish
wytwórca (vi-tvoor-tsa) m. producer; manufacturer,; maker
wytwórczosc (vi-tvoor-choshch)
v. productivity ; output ;product
wytwornia (vi-tvoor-ña) f. manufacture; factory; plant ;works
wytyczna (vi-tich-na) f. direc-
tive; guideline: guiding rule
wyuzdanie (vi-ooz-da-ñe) n. unbridled license ;adv.dissolutely
wywiad (vi-vyat) m. interview;
reconnaissance ; espionage
wywiazać się (vi-wyown-zach shañ)
v. develop; arise; discharge
(duty); result; set in; evolve
wywierac (vi-vye-rach) v. exert
wywiercac (vi-vyer-tsach) v. bore
out; sink a well;drill a hole
wywlekac(vi-vle-kach) v. drag
out ; tug; bring out ;pull out
wywietrzac (vi-vyet-zhach) v.
ventilate ; air; nose out
wywłaszczac (vi-vwash-chach) v.
expropriate ;dispossess
wywłaszczenie (vi-vwash-che-ñe)
n. expropriation;dispossession
wywnioskowac (vi-vños-ko-vach)
v. infer; draw a conclusion
wywodzic (vi-vo-dzheech) v. lead
out; derive ; deduce ;lead nowhere
wywojowac (vi-vo-yo-vach) v.
fight out ; gain by force
wywołac (vi-vo-wach) v. call;
cause; develop (film); recall
wywozic (vi-vo-zheech) v. export
wywód (vi-voot) m. deduction
wywoz (vi-voos) m. export ;removal
wywracac (vi-vra-tsach) v. overturn; overthrow; reverse ;upset

wywyższac (vi-vizh-shach) v.
exalt; elevate;extol;rise
wyzbyc się (viz-bich shañ) v.
get rid;sell out;get over
wyzdrowiec (vi-zdro-vyech) v.
recover; get well;recuperate
wyziębic (vi-zhañ-beech) v.
chill ;let get cold ;cool
wyzionąc (vi-żho-nownch) v.
expire; give up(the ghost)
wyznaczac (vi-zna-chach) v.
mark out; appoint; point out
wyznanie (vi-zna-ñe) n. denomination; declaration;creed
wyznawac (vi-zna-vach) v. profess;
declare ; hold a belief;confess
wyznawca (vi-znav-tsa) m. believer; follower; advocate
wyzuc (vi-zooch) v. deprive;
take off (shoe) ; strip;divest;
bereave
wyzywac (vi-zi-vach) v. challenge ; call names;abuse;revile
wyzwalac (vi-zva-lach) v. liberate; free;let loose; exempt
wyzwolenie (vi-zvo-le-ñe) n .
liberation; release;exemtion
wyzwolic (vi-zvo-leech) v. liberate; free; release; set free
wyzysk (vi-zisk) m. exploita-
tion; sweating(of labor)
wyzyskiwacz (vi-zis-kee-vach) m.
exploiter; slave driver
wyż (vizh) m. hight; highland;
high pressure; peak; atm.high
wyżarty (vi-zhar-ti) adj. m.
over-fed; corroded; bloated
wyżej (vi-zhey) adv. higher;
above ; mentioned above;higher up
wyżeł (vi-zhew) m. pointer
wyżerac (vi-zhe-rach) v. eat
away; corrode; erode; eat up
wyżłobic (vi-zhwo-beech) v.
hollow out;gully; erode;groove
wyżłobienie (vi-zhwo-bye-ñe) n.
groove; gully; erosion;channel
wyższosc (vizh-shoshch) f. superiority; excellence;predominance
wyższy (vizh-shi) adj. m. higher
(up),; taller; superior;top(floor)
wyżyc (vi-zhich) v. use up;
hardly live ; make ends meet;
pull through;survive;pull through;
find an outlet for...

wyżyć się (vi-zhićh shán) v.
live up; fulfill oneself
wyżymaczka (vi-zhi-mách-ka) f.
wringer (also machine)
wyżymać (vi-zhi-mach) v. wring
wyżyna (vi-zhi-na) f. high
ground; upland;summit(of glory)
wyżywić (vi-zhi-veech) v. feed
wyżywienie (vi-zhi-vye-ñe) m.
food; board; subsistance;diet
wzajemny (vza-yem-ni) adj. m.
mutual; reciprocal; inter-
w zamian (vza-myan) adv. in
exchange; instead; in return
wzbić się (vzbeech shán) v.
soar (up); shoot up; rise
wzbogacić (vzbo-ga-cheech) v.
enrich; add to; dress;make rich
wzbraniac (vzbra-nach) v. forbid; prohibit
wzbroniony (vzbro-ño-ni) adj.m.
forbidden; prohibited
wzbudzać ( vzboo-dzach) v. excite; inspire;arouse; stir
wzburzenie (vzboo-zhé-ñe) n.
agitation; unrest; tumult
wzburzyć (vzboo-zhich) v. stir
up; agitate;dishevel;covulse
wzdąc (vzdównch) v. puff up;fan
wzdłuż (vzdwoosh) prep. along
wzdrygać się (vzdri-gach shán)
v. flinch; object; shudder
wzdychać (vzdi-khach) v. sigh
wzgarda (vzgár-da) f. contempt
wzgardliwy (vzgard-lee-vi) adj.
m. disdainful; scornful
względność (vzgland-noshch) f.
relativity (of understanding...)
względny (vzgland-ni) adj. m.
relative; indulgent; kind of
względy (vzglán-di) pl. favors
wzgórze (vzgoo-zhe) n. hill
wziąć (vżhównch) v. take;possess
wziernik (vżhér-ñeek) m. peep-
hole; scope;view-finder;spy-hole
wzięty (vżhán-ti) adj. m. popular;in demand; in vogue
wzlot (vzlot) m. ascend; rise
wzmacniac (vzmáts-ñach) v. reinforce; brace up; fortify
wzmagać (vzma-gach) v. intensify
wzmianka (vzmyán-ka) v. mention

wzniesienie (vzñe-shé-ñe) n.
elevation; height;erection
wznieść (vzñeshch) v. raise;
elevate; erect; lift; rear
wzniosły (vzñós-wi) adj. m.
lofty; noble; elevated;sublime
wznowić (vznó-veech) v. renew
wznowienie (vzno-vye-ñe) n.
resumption; come back;reissue
wzorowy (vzo-ro-vi) adj. m.
exemplary ;model; perfect
wzór (vzoor) m. pattern; model;
formula; fashion; standard
wzrok (vzrok) m. sight; vision
wzrost (vzrost) m. growth;size;
height; increase; rise;stature
wzruszac (vzroo-shach) v. move;
touch; affect; thrill; stir
wzruszający (vzroo-sha-yown-tsi)
adj. m. touching; moving;pathetic
wzuć (vzooch) v. put on (shoe)
wzuwacz (vzoo-vach) m. shoe
horn(for pulling boots,shoes on)
wzwyż (vzvizh) adv. up; upwards
skok wzwyż (skok vzvizh) m.
high jump
wzywać (vzi-vach) v. call; call
in; summon; cite; ask in
z (z) prep. with; off; together
ze (ze) prep. with; off; together;from(the ceiling etc.)
za (za) prep. behind; for; at;
by; beyond; over(a wall)
zabarwic (za-bár-veech) v. stain;
dye ; tint; color;tinge;tincture
zabarwienie (za-bar-vyé-ñe) n.
color(ing); pigmentation; tinge
zabawa (za-bá-va) f. play; fun;
party; game; recreation;amusement
zabawiac (za-báv-yach) v. entertain ;amuse;dwell;stay; last
zabawka (za-báv-ka) f. toy;trife
zabawny (za-báv-ni) adj. m.
funny; comical; ridiculous
zabezpieczenie (za-bez-pye-ché-
ñe) n. protection ; safety
zabezpieczyc (za-bez-pyé-chich)
v. safeguard; secure ;protect
zabić (za-beech) v. kill; slay;
plug up; nail down;beat(a card)
zabieg (zá-byek) m. measure;
procedure; exertions; fuss

zabiegać (za-bye-gach) v. strive;
try hard ; court; woo; fuss over
zabierać (za-bye-rach) v. take
away ; take along;take on (up)
zabierać się (za-bye-rach śhän)
v. clear out; get ready for
zabijać (za-bee-yach) v. kill;
deaden ; wear out; exhaust
zabijaka (za-bee-ya-ka) m. bully;
blusterer ; swaggerer; hector
zabity (za-bee-ti) adj. m. killed; dead ; out-and-out;thorough
zabliźniać (za-bleezh-nach) v.
form cicatrize ; scar up
zabłądzić (za-bwown-dzheech) v.
go astray; get lost ; stray
zabłąkany (za-bwown-ka-ni) adj.
m. stray (bullet, man,steer,etc)
zabłocić (za-bwo-cheech) v. get
muddy ; muddy (shoes etc)
zabobon (za-bo-bon) m. superstition;belief in omens,stars etc.
zaboleć (za-bo-lech) v. ache
zaborca (za-bór-tsa) m. invader
zabójca (za-booy-tsa) m. killer
zabójczy (za-booy-chi) adj. m.
murderous ; seductive ;lethal
zabójstwo (za-booy-stvo) n. killing; murder ; homicide
zabór (za-boor) m. annexed territory ; annexation;rape(of Peru..)
zabraniać (za-bra-nach) v. forbid
zabrudzać (za-broo-dzach) v.dirty;
soil; make a mess (of something)
zabudować (za-boo-do-vach) v.
build over; build upon; close
zabudowania (za-boo-do-va-na) pl.
buildings (on farm,factory etc.)
zaburzenie (za-boo-zhe-ne) n.
disorder; rout; agitation
zabytek (za-bi-tek) m. relic;
monument(of art,nature etc.)
zachcianka (zakh-chan-ka) f. fad;
fancy; caprice ; whim ;megrim
zachęta (za-khan-ta) f. encouragement; stimulus ;incentive;spur
zachłanność (za-khwan-noshch) f.
greed ; rapacity ;cupidity
zachłysnąć się (za-khwis-nównch
śhän) v. choke;swallow a bad way
zachmurzyć (za-khmoo-zhich) v.
cloud; become gloomy,overcloud

zachmurzenie (za-khmoo-zhe-ne)
n. cloudiness; gloom;gloominess
zachodzić (za-kho-dzheech) v.
call on; occur; arise; become;
set; creep from behind;drop in
zachodni (za-khód-nee) adj. m.
western; westerly
zachorować (za-kho-ró-vach) v.
get sick; fall ill;be taken ill
zachowanie (za-kho-va-ne) n.
behavior; maintainance;manners
zachowawczy (za-kho-vav-chi)
adj. m. conservative
zachowywać (za-kho-vi-vach) v.
preserve; maintain;keep(calm)
zachowywać się (za-kho-vi-vach
śhän) v. behave; survive;go on
zachód (za-khoot) m. west;sunset;
pains; trouble; endeavor
zachód słońca (za-khoot swon-
tsa) m. sunset
zachrypnięty (za-khrip-nan-ti)
adj. m. hoarse;of a hoarse voice
zachwalać (za-khva-lach) v.
praise; crack up;boost;cry up
zachwiać (zakh-vyach) v. rock;
shake; unsettle (balance etc.)
zachwycać (za-khvi-tsach) v.
fascinate; charm ;delight;enchant
zachwyt (zakh-vit) m. fascination; rapture ;enchantment
zaciąg (za-chówng) m. recruitment; levy; draft ;conscription
zaciągać (za-chówn-gach) v.
recruit; drag to; run in debt
zaciekać (za-ché-kach) v. leak;
stain; run down ; fill(up)
zaciekawić (za-che-ka-veech) v.
interest; puzzle; intrigue
zaciekawienie (za-che-ka-vye-ne)
n. interest; curiosity
zaciekły (za-chek-wi) adj. m.
stubborn; bitter; rabid;stiff
zaciemnić (za-chem-neech) v.
obscure; dim; darken ;black out
zacieniać (za-che-nach) v.
shade; darken ;throw shade
zacierać (za-che-rach) v. efface; erase; hush up ;cover up
zaciesniać (za-chesh-nach) v.
tighten up; narrow; limit
zacięty (za-chan-ti) adj. m.
obstinate; stubborn ;dogged

zacinać (za-chee-nach) v. notch;
cut; lash; hack; taper;set(teeth)
zaciskać (za-chees-kach) v.
tighten; clench; squeeze;clasp
zacisze (za-chee-she) n. retreat
zacny (zats-ni) adj. m. worthy;
good; upright;respectable
zacofany (za-tso-fa-ni) adj.m.
backward;old fashioned
zaczaić się (za-cha-eech shan)
v. lie in ambush; lurk; hide
zaczarować (za-cha-ro-vach) v.
enchant; bewitch; cast a spell
zacząć (za-chownch) v. start;
begin; fire away; go ahead
zaczepiac (za-chep-yach) v.
hook on; accost; touch upon
zaczepny (za-chep-ni) adj. m.
aggressive; offensive;provocative
zaczerpać (za-cher-pach) v.
scoop up; dip up; draw; lade
zaczerwienic (za-cher-vye-neech)
v. redden; blush; flush;paint red
zaczynać (za-chi-nach) v. start;
begin; cut (into a new loaf)
zaćmienie (zach-mye-ne) n. e-
clipse ; obfuscation
zad (zad) m. posterior; rump
zadać (za-dach) v. give; put;
deal; associate; treat with
zadanie (za-da-ne) n. task; charge; assignment; problem;job;stint
zadatek (za-da-tek) m. earnest
money ; down payment;installment
zadławić (za-dwa-veech) v. choke
zadłużyc się (za-dwoo-zhich shan)v.
get in debt;debit; take mortgage
zadłużenie (za-dwoo-zhe-ne) n.
debts; indebtedness; liabilities
zadowalający (za-do-va-la-yown-
tsi) adj. m. satisfactory; fair
zadowolic (za-do-vo-leech) v.
satisfy; gratify; please;suffice
zadowolony (za-do-vo-lo-ni) adj.
m. satisfied ; content;pleased
zadra (za-dra) f. sliver; splinter (in one's finger etc.)
zadrapać (za-dra-pach) v. scratch
open; make a scratch; scratch
zadrasnąć (za-dras-nownch) v.
scratch ; wound (pride etc)
zadrażnic (za-drazh-neech) v.
irritate; embitter; inflame

zadrgac (zadr-gach) v. twitch;
vibrate ; tremble; flicker
zadrwic (za-drveech) v. sneer
zaduch (za-dookh) m. bad air;
stuffy air; stink;fustiness;fug
zaduma (za-doo-ma) f. meditation; reverie;musing;wistfulness
zadusic(za-doo-sheech) v.throttle;
smother; choke ;strangle;suffocate
Zaduszki (za-doosh-kee) n.
All Souls Day
zadymka (za-dim-ka) f. snow-
storm; blizzard
zadyszany (za-di-sha-ni) adj.
m. breathless; panting
zadzierać (za-dzhe-rach) v.
tear open; turn up; quarrel
zadzierżysty (za-dzher-zhis-
ti) adj. m. defiant; perky
zadziwiac (za-dzheev-yach) v.
astonish; amaze; astound
zadzwonic (za-dzvo-neech) v.
ring; ring up ; ring for
zagadka (za-gad-ka) f. puzzle;
riddle ;crux; problem;quizz
zagadnienie (za-gad-ne-ne) n.
problem ; question; issue
zagajnik (za-gay-neek) m. grove
shubbery ; scrub ;coppice;copse
zagiąc (za-gyownch) v. bend
zaginiony (za-gee-no-ni) adj.
m. lost ; missing (person)
zaglądac (za-glown-dach) v.
peep; look up; look into
zagłada (za-gwa-da) f. extinc-
tion ; extermination;annihilation
zagłębic (za-gwan-beech) v.
plunge; sink; dip;immerse
zagłodzic (za-gwo-dzheech) v.
starve to death; starve out
zagłuszac (za-gwoo-shach) v.
silence; jam; drown out; stifle
zagmatwac (za-gmat-vach) v.
entangle; confuse; embroil
zagniewany (za-gne-va-ni) adj.
m. angry; cross; sore;in a huff
zagospodarowywac (za-gos-po-da-
ro-vi-vach) v. make property
productive ; manage (an estate)
zagotowac (za-go-to-vach) v.
boil; start boiling; flare up
zagrabic (za-gra-beech) v. rake
over; grab; seize;carve out

zagradzac (za-gra-dzach) v. bar;
fence; obstruct; intercept
zagranica (za-gra-ñeé-tsa) f.
foreign countries;ouside world
zagraniczny (za-gra-ñeech-ni)
adj. m. foreign;external(trde...)
zagrażac (za-gra-zhach) v.
threaten; impend;be imminent
zagroda (za-gro-da) f. farm
house with yard; enclosure
zagrodzic (za-gro-dżeech) v.
fence in; bar; enclose;obstruct
zagrozony (za-gro-żho-ni) adj.
m. threatened; endangered
zagrzebac (za-gzhe-bach) v.
bury (in the grave,in the past...)
zagrzewac (za-gzhe-vach) v.heat;
warm up; animate;inspire;spur
zahaczac (za-kha-chach) v. hook;
question; accost;find fault
zahamowac (za-kha-mó-vach) v.
restrain; put brakes on; stop
zaimek (za-eé-mek) m. pronoun
zainteresowanie (za-een-te-re-
so-va-ñe) n. interest;concern
zaiste (za-eés-te) adv. truly;
indeed; very true; verily; yea
zajadac (za-ya-dach) v. enjoy
eating ; gorge;eat heartily
zajadły (za-yád-wi) adj. m.
fierce; rabid;bitter∫driveway
zajazd (za-yazt) m. motel; inn;
zając (za-yownts) m. hare
zając (za-yownch) v. occupy
zajechac (za-ye-khach) v. drive
up; block; stump ; pull in ;stink
zajęcie (za-yán-che) n. occupation ; work;trade; interest
zajmowac(zay-mo-vach) v. occupy
zajmujący (zay-moo-yown-tsi) adj.
m. interesting; absorbing
zajscie (záysh-che) n. incident
zakalec (za-ka-lets) m. slack
baked bread (or cake)
zakatarzony (za-ka-ta-zho-ni)
adj. m. having a cold
zakatowac (za-ka-to-vach) v.
flog to death;torture to death
zakaz (za-kas) m. prohibition
zakazic (za-ka-zheech) v. infect
zakazywac (za-ka-zí-vach) v.
forbid ; ban; suppress;prohibit;
forbid to do;suppress(activity..)

zakazny (za-kazh-ni) adj. m.
infectious ; contagious
zakąska (za-kowns-ka) f. snack
zaklęcie (za-klań-che) n. spell;
curse;incantation;charm;entreaty
zakład pogrzebowy (za-kwat po-
gzhe-bo-vi) m. funeral parlor
zakład (za-kwat) m. plant;shop;
institute; bet; wager; fold
zakładac (za-kwa-dach) v.
found; initiate; put on; lay
zakładka (za-kwad-ka) f. fold;
book- mark;tuck;pleat;splice
zakładnik (za-kwad-ñeek) m.
hostage (for ransom etc.)
zakłamanie (za-kwa-má-ñe) n.
hypocrisy ;mendacity;distortion
zakłopotanie (za-kwo-po-ta-ñe)
n. embarrassment;confusion
zakłocac (za-kwoo-tsach) v.
disturb; unsettle;ruffle
zakłuwac (za-kwoo-vach) v. stab
to death ; prick ;stick (a pig)
zakochac się (za-ko-khach shań)
v.fall in love ;become infatuated
zakochany (za-ko-kha-ni) adj.m.
in love ; infatuated;enamorated
zakomunikowac (za-ko-moo-ñee-ko-
vach) v. communicate; let
know; convey a message; notify
zakon (za-kon) m. monastic
order ;convent; sisterhood
zakonnica (za-kon-ñee-tsa) f.
nun ;religious (woman)
zakonnik (za-kon-ñeek) m. monk
zakonczenie (za-koñ-ché-ñe) n.
end; ending; termination;tip
zakopac (za-ko-pach) v. bury
zakorkowac (za-kor-ko-vach) v.
plug up;cork up;jam(the traffic)
zakorzenic się (za-ko-zhe-ñeech
shań) v. get roots in;take roots
zakorzeniony (za-ko-zhe-ño-ni)
adj. m. rooted; deep rooted
zakradac się (za-kra-dach shań)
v. creep; steal; sneak(into)
zakrapiac (za-krap-yach) v.
put drops in; sprinkle; have
a drink;ipstil(in one's eyes)
zakres (za-kres) m. range;field;
scope; domain; sphere;realm
zakreslic (za-kresh-leech) v.
outline; mark off; encircle

zakręcić (za-kráń-cheećh) v.
turn; twist; turn off; curl
zakręt (zá-krant) m. curve;bend
turn ∫ turnbuckle ; cap; nut;
zakrętka (za-krant-ka) f. latch;
zakrwawić (za-krvá-veećh) v.
stain with blood;draw blood
zakryć (zá-krićh) v. cover; hide
zakrzatnąć sie (za-kzhównt-
nównćh śhąń) v.get busy;bustle
zakrztusić (za-kzhtoó-śheećh)v.
choke (on food,fish bone etc.)
zakrzywić (za-kzhi-veećh) v.
bend; bend down; bend back
zaksięgować (za-kżháń-gó-vaćh)
v. post; enter in the books
zakup (za-koop) m. purchase
zakurzony (za-koo-zhó-ni) adj.
m. dusty;covered with dust
zakuty (za-koó-ti) adj. m.
shackled; chained; dull (witted)
zakwitnąć (za-kveét-nównćh) v.
blossom out; go moldy
zalążek (za-lówn-zhek) m. germ;
ovule;seed; origin;embryo
zalecać (za-leśtsaćh) v. recommend; advise; enjoin; court; woo
zaledwie (za-léd-vye) adv. barely;
scarcely; merely; but; only just
zalegać (za-le-gaćh) v. be behind (in paying);lie useless;fill
zaległy (za-lég-wi) adj. m. unpaid; overdue;unaccomplished
zalepić (za-le-peećh) v. glue (up)
over; gum up; paste over;seal up
zalesienie (za-le-śhe-ńe) n.
forestation ; afforestation
zaleta (za-le-ta) f. virtue;
advantage; quality; good point
zalew (zá-lev) m. flood; bay;
invasion; deluge;lagoon
zalewać (za-le-vaćh) v. pour
over; flood;submerge;swarm;spill
zależeć (za-le-zhećh) v. depend
zależny (za-lézh-ni) adj.m.
dependent; contingent;subordinate
zaliczać (za-leé-chaćh) v. include; count in; credit;rate;accept
zaliczka (za-leéch-ka) f. earnest
money; down payment;installment
zalotnica (za-lot-neé-tsa) f.
flirt; coquette; kitten(slang)

zalotnik (za-lót-ńeek) m. suit-
or ; wooer; wheedler
zaloty (za-ló-ti) adj. m.
courtship;wooing;love making
zaludniać (za-loód-ńaćh) v.
populate ;bring in population
zaludnienie (za-lood-ńe-ńe) n.
population;population density
załadować (za-wa-dó-vaćh) v.
load up; embark;ship(goods)
załagodzić (za-wa-gó-dźheećh)
v. mitigate; alleviate; soothe
załamać (za-wá-maćh) v. break
down; collapse; crash; slump
załamanie (za-wa-má-ńe) n.
break down; (light) refraction
załatwiać (za-wát-vyaćh) v.
settle; transact; deal;dispose
załączać (za-wówń-chaćh) v.
enclose ; connect;annex;plug in
załącznik (za-wównch-ńeek) m.
enclosure; attachment; annex
załoga (za-wó-ga) f. crew;
garrison; staff; personnel
założenie (za-wo-zhé-ńe) n.
layout; foundation; assumption
założyciel (za-wo-zhi-ćhel) m.
founder; initiator;promotor
zamach (zá-makh) m. attempt;
swing; sweep; coupd'état;spar
zamaczać (za-má-chaćh) v. steep;
dip; wet; soak; drench
zamarzły (za-már-zwi) adj.m.
frozen; frezen over;frozen stiff
zamarznąć (za-már-znównćh) v.
freeze up;freeze over;congeal
zamaskować (za-mas-kó-vaćh) v.
mask; conceal; hide; disguise
zamaszysty (za-ma-shis-ti) adj.
m. brisk; vigorous;dashing;heavy
zamawiać (za-má-vyaćh) v. reserve; order ;book; engage(workers)
zamazać (za-má-zaćh) v. smear
over; soil up; daub;blur(a picture)
zamącić (za-mówn-ćheećh) v.ruffle;
disturb; make turbid; stir a liquid
zamążpójście (za-mównzh-poóy-
śhćhe) n. marriage
zamek (zá-mek) m. lock; castle
zamek błyskawiczny (zá-mek
bwis-ka-veéch-ni) m. zipper
zamęt (zá-mańt) m. confusion;welter

zamężna (za-mánzh-na) adj. f.
married(woman in married state)
zamiana (za-mya-na) f. exchange
zamianować (za-mya-no-vach) v.
nominate ; appoint;design
zamiar (za-myar) m. purpose ;
zamiast (za-myast) prep. instead of;in place;in lieu
zamiatać (za-mya-tach) v. sweep
zamieć (za-myech) f. snowstorm;
blizzard;snow in a windstorm
zamiejscowy (za-myeys-tso-vi)
adj. m. out of town;long distance
zamienić (za-mye-neech)v. change;
convert; replace;swap;turn into
zamienny (za-myen-ni) adj. m.
exchangeable;interchangeable
zamierać (za-mye-rach) v. die
out; fade out ; wither;die away
zamierzać (za-mye-zhach) v. intend; mean;propose;plan;think
zamierzenie (za-mye-zhe-ne) n.
aim; purpose ; plan; project
zamieszać (za-mye-shach) v. stir
up; blend; mix up ; involve
zamieszanie (za-mye-sha-ne) n.
confusion ; disarray;turmoil;stir
zamieszkać (za-myesh-kach) v.
take up residence ;put up;live
zamieszkiwać (za-myesh-kee-vach)
v. inhabit ; reside ;occupy;live
zamilknąć (za-meel-kownch) v.
became silent ; be hushed
zamiłowanie (za-mee-wo-va-ne) n.
predilection ; fondness ;liking
zamknąć (zám-knownch) v. close;
shut; lock ;wind up; fence in
zamoczyć (za-mo-chich) v. wet;
soak; steep; drench ;submerge
zamorski (za-mor-skee) adj. m.
overseas; from overseas
zamożny (za-mozh-ni) adj. m.rich;
wealthy ; affluent ;well to do
zamówić (za-moo-veech) v. order;
reserve ; commission ;book;engage
zamówienie (za-moo-vye-ne) n.
order ; commission ;custom order
zamrażać (za-mrá-zhach) v. freeze
zamroczyć (za-mro-chich) v. dim;
gloom; confuse; darken ;bewilder
zamsz (zamsh) m. chamois; suede
zamulić (za-moo-leech) v. fill
with slime ; silt up (a harbor)

zamurować (za-moo-ro-vach) v.
brick over ; brick up ;wall up
zamydlić (za-mid-leech) v.
soap over ;pull wool over eyes
zamykać (za-mi-kach) v. shut;
conclude ; close (the view etc.)
zamysł (za-misw) m. design
zamyślać się (za-mish-lach shań)
v. contemplate; muse; ponder
zamyślenie (za-mi-shle-ne) n.
reverie; pondering; meditation
zanadto (za-nad-to) adv. too
much ; excess ;beyond measure
zaniechać (za-ne-khach) v.
give up ; wave; desist from
zanieczyścić (za-ne-chish-cheech)
v. soil ; dirty; litter;grime
zaniedbanie (za-ned-bá-ne) n.
neglect; negligence ;sloppiness
zaniemóc (za-ne-moots) v. become ill ; fall ill ;get sick
zaniemówić (za-ne-moo-veech)
v. become speechless (dumb)
zaniepokoić (za-ne-po-ko-eech)
v. alarm ; up set; disturb
zaniepokojenie (za-ne-po-ko-ye-
ne) n. anxiety ; alarm; concern
zaniesć (za-neshch) v. carry
zanik (za-neek) m. disappearance
zanikać (za-nee-kach) v. disappear ;vanish; decay; wither
zanim (za-neem) conj. before ;
zanocować (za-no-tso-vach) v.
stay over night ; put up at
zanotować (za-no-to-vach) v.
note; write down ;take down
zanurzyć (za-noo-zhich) v. dip
zaoczny (za-och-ne) adv. in
absence;(judgement)by default
zaognic (za-og-neech) v. inflame ; irritate ;excite;kindle
zaokrąglić (za-o-krowng-leech)
v. round off ; make even
zaopatrzenie (za-o-pa-tzhe-ne)
n. supplies;equipment;provision
zaopatrzyć (za-o-pa-tzhich) v.
provide ; equip; supply ;fit out;
furnish;stock
zaorać (za-o-rach) v. plough
over (a field etc.);plough up
zaostrzyć (za-os-tzhich) v. sharp-
en; whet; tighten (restrictions);
stimulate(the appetite);intensify

zaoszczędzić (za-osh-chán-dżheech) v. save ; spare(trouble)
zapach (zá-pakh) m. smell;aroma
zapadać (za-pá-dach) v. fall in; sink ; set in; drop; settle
zapakować (za-pa-kó-vach) v. pack up ; stow away; pack off
zapalczywy (za-pal-chí-vi) adj. m. hotheaded; impetuous
zapalenie (za-pa-lé-ne) n. ignition ; inflammation(of the skin...)
zapaleniec (za-pa-le-ńets) m. fanatic ; enthusiastic;hot head
zapalić (za-pá-leech) v. switch on light; set fire ; animate
zapalniczka (za-pal-ñeech-ka) f. (cigarette) lighter
zapalnik (za-pál-ñeek) m. fuse
zapalny (za-pál-ni) adj. m. inflammable ; ardent;impetuous
zapał (za-paw) m. enthusiasm
zapałka (za-paw-ka) f. match
zapamiętać (za-pa-myán-tach) v. remember ; memorize;keep in mind
zaparcie (za-pár-che) n. constipation; denial
zaparzać (za-pá-zhach) v. draw (tea);brew; gall;make(tea);heat
zapas (zá-pas) m. stock; store; reserve ; supply ;fund;refill
zapasowy (za-pa-só-vi) adj. m. spare ; emergency(door,part,etc)
zapaść (zá-pashch) v. collapse
zapaśnik (za-páśh-ńeek) m. wrestler
zapatrywać się (za-pa-tri-vach śhán) v. have opinion; consider; stare ; take example
zapatrywanie (za-pa-tri-va-ñe) n. opinion; view ;slant
zapełnić (za-péw-ńeech) v. fill up ; stop a gap ;fill(a space etc.)
zaperzyć się (za-pé-zhich śhán) v. flare up ; be testy ;get mad
zapewne (za-pév-ne) adv. certainly ; surely; doubtless ;I daresay
zapewnić (za-pév-ńeech) v. assure
zapewnienie (za-pev-ńé-ñe) n. assurance ; protestation ;assertion
zapieczętować (za-pye-chán-to-vach) v. seal up;seal with wax
zapierać sie (za-pye-rach śhán) deny; disavow ;resist;repudiate

zapinać (za-pée-nach) v. button up; fasten;buckle up
zapis (za-pees) m. registration; bequest; record; notation
zapisać (za-pée-sach) v. note down; prescribe; enroll; bequeath; record; write down
zapisek (za-pée-sek) m. note
zaplątać (za-plówn-tach) v. entangle ;snarl;involve
zaplecze (za-plé-che) n. hinterland; base(of supplies etc.)
zapłacić (za-pwá-cheech) v. pay
zapłakany (za-pwa-ká-ni) adj. m. in tears ; tearful;tear stained
zapłata (za-pwa-ta) f. payment
zapłodnić (za-pwód-ńeech) v. fertilize ; inseminate;fecundate
zapłon (za-pwon) m. ignition
zapobiegać (za-po-byé-gach) v. prevent;avert; ward off;stave off
zapobiegliwy (za-po-bye-glée-vi) adj. m. anticipating;thrifty industrious ;thrifty;provident
zapodziać (za-pó-dźhach) v. misplace;mislay; get lost
zapominać (za-po-mée-nach) v. forget;neglect; unlearn
zapomnienie (za-pom-ńé-ńe) n. oblivion; forgetfulness
za pomocą (za-po-mó-tsówn) adv. by means; with help(of a tool...)
zapomoga (za-po-mó-ga) f. hand out; relief; benefit; grant
zapora (za-pó-ra) f. dam; obstacle ; barrier;check;barrage
zapotrzebowanie (za-po-tzhe-bo-vá-ńe)n. (demand) requisition
zapowiadać (za-po-vyá-dach) v. announce ; forecast; pretend
zapoznać (za-póz-nach) v. acquaint ;introduce;instruct
zapożyczać (za-po-zhí-chach) v. borrow ; adopt from ;take from
zapracować (za-pra-tsó-vach) v. earn; get by hard work
zapracowany (za-pra-tso-vá-ni) adj. m. earned; overworked
zapraszać (za-prá-shach) v. invite(to dinner etc.);offer
zaprawa (za-prá-va) f. mortar;v. seasoning; training ;work out

zaprawdę (za-práw-dán) adv. in
deed ; to tell you the truth...
zaprawic (za-pra-veech) v. season ;train; learn;dress;spice
zaproszenie (za-pro-she-ne) n.
invitation (to dinner etc.)
zaprowadzic (za-pro-vá-dżheech)
v. lead in; establish ;initiate
zaprzag (za-zhówng) m. team
zaprzeczac (za-pzhe-chach) v.
deny ; contest ; dispute
zaprzeczenie (za-pzhe-che-ne) n.
denial ; negation;contradiction
zaprzepascic (za-pzhe-pásh-
cheech) v. loose; waste ; miss
zaprzestac (za-pzhes-tach) v.
discontinue; stop ; cease;quit
zaprzęg (za-pzhäng) m. team; cart;
harness ; yoke; carriage;turn out
zaprzyjaznic sie (za-pzhi-yázh-
neech shán) v. make friends
zaprzysiąc (za-pzhi-shownts) v.
swear by oath ;vow; pledge
zaprzysiężony (za-pzhi-shán-zho-
ni) adj. m. sworn in ;pledged
zapusty (za-poós-ti) pl.carni-
val; Shroyetide
zapuszczac (za-poósh-chach) v.
let in (dye); grow (hair);
neglect ; let down;sink into
zapychac (za-pi-khach) v. stuff;
cram ;fill;block ;choke;crowd
zapytanie (za-pi-ta-ne) n. question; inquiry ; query; asking
zapytywac (za-pi-ti-vach) v. ask
zarabiac (za-ráb-yach) v. earn
zaradczy (za-rád-chi) adj. m.
preventive ; remedial(measure)
zaradny (za-rád-ni) adj. m. resourceful (man, boy etc.)
zaranie (za-ra-ne) n. downing
zarastac (za-rás-tach) v. overgrow; cicatrize (a wound)
zaraz (zá-ras) adv. at once;
directly;right away; soon
zaraza (za-rá-za) f. infection;
plague ; epidemic ;pestilence
zarazek (za-rá-zek) m. virus;
germ ; microbe ;(disease)bacteria
zarazem (za-rá-zem) adv. at the
same time ; as well; also
zarazic (za-ra-zheech) v. infect

zarażenie (za-ra-żhe-ne) n.
infection (with a disease etc.)
zardzewiec (zar-dze-vyech) v.
rust ; get rusty;corrode
zaręczyny (za-rán-chi-ni) n.
betrothal; engagement;engagement-
zarobek (za-ró-bek) m. gain;bread;
earnings; wages;livelihood;living
zarobkowac (za-rob-kó-vach) v.
earn working ; earn a living
zarodek (za-ró-dek) m. embryo
zarosły (za-rós-wi) adj. m.
overgrown (with vegetation etc.)
zarost (zá-rost) m. beard; hair
zarosla (za-rósh-la) n. thicket
zarozumiały (za-ro-zoo-myá-wi)
adj. m. conceited ; uppish
zarówno (za-roóv-no) adv. equally; as well ; alike ; both
zarumienic sie (za-roo-mye-neech
shán) v. blush ;flush; brown
zaryglowac (za-rig-lo-vach) v.
bolt a door; bar an entrance
zarys (zá-ris) m. sketch; outline ; broad lines;design;draft
zarząd (zá-zhównd) m. management ; administration; board
zarzadca (za-zhównd-tsa) m.
administrator; manager
zarządzenie (za-zhówn-dze-ne)
n. administrative order
zarzucac (za-zhoó-tsach) v. fill;
give up; reproach ; fling ;cast
zarzut (zá-zhoot) m. reproach;
objection ; accusation; blame
zasada (za-sá-da) f. principle;
alkali; base ; law ;rule;tenet
zasadniczy (za-sad-nee-chi) adj.
m. fundamental;essential; basic
zasadzka (za-sádz-ka) f. ambush
zasądzic (za-sówn-dżheech) v.
sentence ; adjudge to(somebody)
zasępiony (za-sán-pyo-ni) adj.
m. gloomy; despondent;dejected
zasiadac (za-shá-dach) v. take
a seat ; sit down; settle down
zasięg (zá-shánk) m. reach ;scope
zasięgac rady (za-shán-gach rá-
di) v. consult; seek advice
zasiłek (za-shee-wek) m. hand-
out; grant ;relief;subvention
zaskarżyć (za-skár-zhich) v. sue

zasklepić się (za-skle-peech shñ) v. scab; shut oneself up (in); seal up; vault;wall up
zaskoczyć (za-sko-chich) v. surprise; attack unawares;click;lock
zaskórny(za-skoor-ni) adj. m. subcutaneous;underground(water)
zasłabnąć (za-swab-nownch) v. faint; get sick;grow faint;swoon
zasłać (za-swach) v. cover (bed)
zasłona (za-swo-na) f. blind; veil; screen; curtain;shield
zasłonić (za-swo-neech) v. curtain; shade ; shield;cover up
zasługa (za-swoo-ga) f. merit
zasługiwać (za-swoo-gee-vach) v. deserve ; be worthy;merit
zasłużony (za-swoo-zho-ni) adj. m. man of merit ;just; fair
zasmucić (za-smoo-cheech) v. sadden ; pain; distress;grieve
zasmucony(za-smoo-tso-ni) adj. m. sad; grieved;distressed
zasnąć (za-snownch) v. fall asleep; sleep;drop off to sleep
zasobnik(za-sob-neek) m. container; tank;storage tank
zasób (za-soop) m. store; resource ; stock; supply
zaspa (zas-pa) f. snowdrift; dune; drifted sand;drifted snow
zaspać (zas-pach) v. oversleep
zaspokoić (za-spo-ko-eech) v. satisfy; quench; appease;provide
zastanowić się (za-sta-no-veech shñ) v. reflect; puzzle;ponder
zastaw (za-stav) m. pawn; deposit; security;pledge;forfeit;lien
zastawić (za-sta-veech) v. 1. bar; 2. pledge; 3. set a table ; cram a room; lay(snares)
zastąpić (za-stown-peech) v. replace; bar passage;do duty for
zastępca (za-stanp-tsa) adj.m. proxy; substitute ; deputy
zastępczo (za-stanp-cho) adv. replacing; temporary; in lieu
zastępstwo (za-stanp-stvo) n. replacement ;proxy; agency
zastosować (za-sto-so-vach) v. adopt; apply ; employ;make use
zastosować się (za-sto-so-vach shñ) v. comply ; toe the line

zastosowanie (za-sto-so-vá-ñe) n. application; use compliance
zastój (za-stooy) m. stagnation
zastraszyć (za-strá-shich) v. intimidate ;cow;bully;bulldoze
zastrzał (za-stzhaw) m. (knee) brace; strut; boom; cramp
zastrzec (za-stzhets) v. reserve ; stipulate;condition
zastrzeżenie (za-stzhe-zhe-ñe) n. reservation; proviso
zastrzyk (za-stzhik) m. injection ; shot(in the arm)
zastygnąc (za-stig-nownch) v. congeal ; set; harden;petrify
zasuszyć (za-soo-shich) v. dry up ; wither ; shrivel(the skin)
zasuwa (za-soo-va) f. bar; (door) bolt;valve ;shutter
zasuwka (za-soov-ka) f. small bolt ;damper; valve
zasypać (za-si-pach) v. bury; cover; add (to soup);fill up
zasypiać (za-sip-yach) v. cat nap; doze off; fall asleep
zaszczepiać (za-shche-pyach) v. inoculate; graft;instill
zaszczycać (za-shchi-tsach) v. honor; dignify; favor; grace
zaszczyt (zash-chit) m. honor; distinction; privilege;dignity
zaszkodzić (za-shko-dzheech) v. harm; hurt; damage; injure
zasznurować (za-shnoo-ro-vach) v. tie up; lace(shoes);tighten
zaszyć (za-shich) v. sew up
zaszyć się (za-shich shñ) v. hide; burrow ; conceal oneself
zaś (zash) conj. but; whereas; and ; while; specially
zaślepić (za-shle-peech) v. blind; infatuate;blind to facts
zaślepiony (za-shle-pyo-ni) adj. m. infatuated; fanatic ;blind
zaślubić (za-shloo-beech)v. marry ; get married
zaślubiny (za-shloo-bee-ni) pl. wedding ; marriage ;nuptials
zaśmiecić (za-shmye-cheech) v. litter ; clutter up (a room etc.)
zaśniedziały (za-shñe-dzhá-wi) adj. m. rusty; stagnant

zaśrubować (za-shroo-bó-vach)
v. screw tight ; screw on (a lid)
zaświadczenie (za-shvyad-ché-
ne) n. certificate ;affidavit
zaświadczyć (za-shvyád-chich)v.
certify; attest; witness
zaświecić (za-zhvye-cheech) v.
put light on ; light up ;turn on
zataczać (za-tá-chach) v. roll in;
describe(acircle); stagger;wheel
zataić (za-tá-eech) v. conceal;
suppress; keep secret ;hold back
zatamować (za-ta-mó-vach) v.
dam up; stop ; block ;impede
zatańczyc (za-tań-chich) v.
dance; perform a dance
zatapiac (sa-táp-yach) v.flood;
sink ; penetrate ;inundate;scuttle
zatarasowac (za-ta-ra-só-vach)
v. obstruct; block up; bolt
zatarg (zá-tark) m. conflict
zatem (zá-tem) adv. then; consequently; therefore ; and so
zatemperowac (za-tem-pe-ró-vach)
v. sharpen a pencil etc.
zatkac (za-tkach) v. stop up
zatlic sie (za-tleech shań) v.
catch fire ; smoulder
zatłoczony (za-two-chó-ni) adj.
m. crowded ; crammed; cluttered
zatoka (za-tó-ka) f. bay; gulf
zatonąć (za-tó-nownch) v. sink
zator (zá-tor) m. (traffic) jam
zatracic (za-tra-cheech) v. lose;
waste ; lose all sense of
zatroskac(za-tros-kach) v. grieve
zatrucie (za-troo-che) n. poisoning ; intoxication; toxaemia
zatruc (za-trooch) v. poison
zatrudniac (za-trood-nach) v.
employ ; engage ;take on(workers)
zatrzask (zá-tzhask) m. (door)
latch; (snap) fastener lock
zatrzymac (za-tzhi-mach) v. stop;
retain; detain ;arrest; hold
zatwardzenie (za-tvar-dzé-ne) n.
constipation; costiveness
zatwierdzać (za-tvyer-dzach) v.
approve ;confirm; ratify ;affirm
zatwierdzenie (za-tvyer-dzé-ne)
n. ratification; approval;assent
zatwierdzic (za-tvyér-dzheech) v.
ratify; approve ;confirm ;validate

zatyczka (za-tích-ka) f. plug
zatykac (za-tí-kach) v. stop
up ; plug up; insert a plug
zaufac (za-oo-fach) v. confide
zaufanie (za-oo-fá-ne) n. confidence ; trust ;faith; reliance
zaufany (za-oo-fá-ni) adj. m.
reliable; confidential;trusted
zaułek (za-oó-wek) m. alley;
back street ; lane ;recess; nook
zauważyc (za-oo-vá-zhich) v.
notice ; catch sight;remark
zawada (za-vá-da) f. obstruction; nuisance; hindrance
zawadiaka (za-vad-yá-ka) m.
bully; blusterer;swashbuckler
zawadzac (za-vá-dzach) v. hinder; scrape; touch ;be a drag
zawalac (za-vá-lach) v. soil
zawalic (za-vá-leech) v. collapse; obstruct; bury;bungle
zawartosc (za-vár-toshch) f.
contents ; subject (of a book)
zawczasu (za-vchá-soo) adv.
in good time ;in advance
zawczoraj (za-vchó-ray) adv.
the day before yesterday
zawdzięczac (za-vdzhań-chach)
v. owe (gratitude) ; be indebted
zawezwac (za-véz-vach) v. call;
summon ; call in (a doctor etc)
zawiadomic (za-vya-do-meech)
v. inform; give notice ;let know
zawiadomienie (za-vya-do-mye-
ne) n. notification ;information
zawiadowca stacji (za-vya-dóv-
tsa státs-yee) m. stationmaster ;superintendent
zawiasa (za-vyá-sa) f. hinge
zawiązac (za-vyown-zach) v.
tie up ; bind; set up (a club)
zawieja (za-vyé-ya) f. blizzard
za wiele (za vye-le) adv. too
much ; too many (expenses etc.)
za widna (za veéd-na) adv. in
day light; in light;before dark
zawierac (za-vyé-rach) v. contain; conclude; shut ;strike up
zawierucha (za-vye-roo-kha) f.
wind storm ; gale ;(war)clouds
zawieszenie broni (za-vye-shé-
ne bro-ńee) n. armistice ;truce ;
cessation of hostilities

zawietrzna (za-vyétzh-na) f.
lee side(sheltered from the wind)
zawijać (za-vee-yach) v. wrap
up; tuck in; put in at a port
zawikłać (za-veek-wach) v. complicate; entangle;embroil;tangle
zawiły (za-veé-wi) adj. m. intricate; baffling;knotty(problem)
zawinąć (za-vee-nownch) v. wrap
zawinić (za-vee-neech) v. be
guilty;commit an offense
zawisły (za-vees-wi) adj. m.
dependent(on somebody etc.)
zawistny (za-veest-ni) adj. m.
envious;jealous (of something...)
zawiść (za-veeshch) f. envy
zawitać (za-vee-tach) v. call
on; come and see ⌐wrap
zawlec (za-vlets) v. drag;tug;
zawodnik (za-vod-neek) m. competitor (in sport);contestant
zawodowiec (za-vo-do-vyets) m.
professional; specialist
zawody (za-vo-di) pl. (sport)
competition;match;race;game;event
zawodzić (za-vo-dźheech) v.
1. lead; 2. disillusion;lament
zawołać (za-vo-wach) v. call out;
exclaim; shout; cry out; summon
zawołany (za-vo-wa-ni) adj. m.
excellent; perfect;born(poet etc.)
zawozić (za-vo-źheech) v. convey;
take to; cart; deliver;give rides
zawód (za-vood) m. 1. profession;
2. disappointment; deception
zawór (za-voor) m. valve; vent
zawrót głowy (za-vroot gwo-vi) m.
dizziness; vertigo;giddiness
zawstydzic (za-vsti-dźheech) v.
shame; embarrass ;overwhelm
zawsze (zav-she) adv. always;
evermore;(for)ever;at all times
zawszyc (zav-shich) v. louse up
zawziąć się (zav-źhownch śhań) v.
be obstinate; persist ; set on
zawziętosc (zav-źhań-toshch) f.
persistence; obstinacy; keenness
zazdrosny (zaz-dros-ni) adj. m.
jealous; envious;resentful
zazdrosc (záz-droshch) f. envy
zaziębic się (za-źhań-beech śhan)
v. catch a cold

zaznaczyć (za-zna-chich) v.
mark ; make a note; state;
zaznac (záz-nach) v. experience;
taste ; enjoy; undergo
zaznajomic (za-zna-yó-meech)
v. acquaint ; introduce to
zazwyczaj (za-zvi-chay) adv.
usually ; generally; ordinarily
zażalenie (za-zha-le-ńe) n.
complaint; grievance
zażarty (za-zhár-ti) adj. m.
fierce; bitter ;vehement
zażądac (za-zhown-dach) v.
demand ; require; order
zażenowac (za-zhe-nó-vach) v.
shame ;embarrass;confuse;abash
zażyły (za-zhi-wi) adj. m. familiar; intimate ;close;chummy
zażywac pigułki (za-zhi-vach
pee-goow-kee) v. take pills
ząb (zownp) m. tooth; fang;
prong; cog;otch;indentation
ząb mleczny (zownp mlech-ni)
m. milk tooth (of a child etc.)
ząb trzonowy (zownp tzho-nó-vi)
adj. m. molar
ząbkowac (zownb-ko-vach) v.
teethe ; jag;cut one's teeth
zbaczać (zba-chach) v. deviate
zbankrutowany (zban-kroo-to-va-
ni) adj. m. bankrupt; insolvent
zbawca (zbáv-tsa) m. savior
zbawiciel (zba-vee-chel) m.
savior; redeemer; Saviour
zbawicielka (zba-vee-chel-ka)
f. savior ; redeemer
zbawic (zba-veech) v. save;
redeem ; rescue;take(time)
zbawienie (zba-vye-ńe) n. salvation;deliverance;rescue;redemption
zbesztac (zbesh-tach) v. scold
zbezcześcic (zbez-chesh-cheech)
v. desecrate; defile;profane
zbędny (zband-ni) m. superfluous ; redundant; needless;useless
zbieg(zbyek) m. fugitive ;runaway
zbieg okoliczności (zbyek o-ko-
leech-nósh-chee) m. coincidence ;occurrence at the same time
zbiegac (zbye-gach) v. run down
zbiegowisko (zbye-go-vees-ko)
n. concourse; throng; crowd

zbieracz (zbye-rach) m. collector; gatherer ; picker
zbierać (zbye-rach) v. gather; pick; summon; clear; take in
zbieżny (zbyezh-ni) adj. m. convergent; tapering;concurrent
zbijać (zbee-yach) v. knock together; refute;beat down
zbiornik (zbyor-neek) m. tank; reservoir; container;receptacle
zbiór (zbyoor) m. harvest; collection; set; crop;class;series
zbiórka (zbyoor-ka) f. rally; assembly ;meeting;gathering
zbir (zbeer) m. thug; ruffian
zbity (zbee-ti) adj. m.close; 1 beaten up; 2. compact;dense
zblednąć (zbled-nownch) v.pale; grow pale; fade;turn pale
z bliska (zblees-ka) adv. from near ; close up ;from near
zbliżać (zblee-zhach) v. nearby
zbliżyć się (zblee-zhich shan) v. become close; approach;be near
zbliżenie (zblee-zhe-ne) n. rapprochement; close-up
zbliżony (zblee-zho-ni) adj. m. approximate; nearing;congenial
zbłądzic (zbwown-dzheech) v. go astray; make mistake; lose trail ;err; wander off;err;blunder
zbocze (zbo-che) n. (hill) slope
zboczenie (zbo-che-ne) n. deviation; aberration;drift;sag
zbolały (zbo-la-wi) adj. m. aching ; sore; woeful; wretched
zboże (zbo-zhe) n. corn; grain
zbój (zbooy) m. bandit; robber
zbór ewangielicki (zboor e-van-ge-leets-kee)m. Protestant Church; Evangelical Church
zbratać się (zbra-tach shan) v. fraternize; chum up (with)
zbroczony krwią (zbro-cho-ni krvyown) adj. m. blood-stained
zbrodnia (zbrod-na) f. crime
zbrodniarz (zbrod-nash) m. criminal; felon; malefactor
zbroic (zbro-eech) v. arm
zbroja (zbro-ya) f. armor
zbrojony beton (zbro-yo-ni beton) m. reinforced concrete

zbrojownia (zbro-yov-na) f. arsenal; armory ; gunroom
zbryzgac (zbriz-gach) v. spatter ; bespatter; splash
zbrzydnąc (zbzhid-nownch) v. grow ugly; lose good looks
zbudować (zboo-do-vach) v. build
zbudzic się (zboo-dzheech shan) v. wake up ; awake; be roused
zbujać (zboo-yach) v. fool; hoax : pull one's leg
zburzyc (zboo-zhich) v. demolish
zbutwiec (zboo-tvyech) v. molder. ; rot;decompose;decay;spoil
zbydlęcic (zbi-dlan-cheech) v. imbrute;turn into a brute
zbyt (zbit) adv. too, (much)
zbyt wiele (zbit vye-le) adv. too much ; excessively;overzbyt (zbit) m. sale; market
zbyteczny (zbi-tech-ni) adj. m. superfluous ;needless;redundant
zbytek (zbi-tek) m. frills; luxury ;pl.:pranks;follies
zbytni (zbit-nee) adj. m. excessive; undue;more than needed
zbytnik (zbit-neek) m. rogue
zbywać (zbi-vach) v. dispose; dismiss ; put off;sell;lack;want
z czasem ( z cha-sem) adv. with time ;eventually;later
z dala (z da-la) adv. from far
z daleka (z da-le-ka) adv. from far; from afar; away from
zdalnie (zdal-ne) adv. remote; from afar; by remote control
zdanie (zda-ne) n. opinion; judgment; sentence; proposition
zdanie sprawy (zda-ne spra-vi) n. report; account;giving account
zdarzac się (zda-zhach shan) v. happen; take place;occur
zdarzenie (zda-zhe-ne) n. happening; event; incident
zdatnosc (zdat-noshch) f. fitness; capability;suitability
zdatny (zdat-ni) adj. m. able; fit; apt;suitable (for the purpose)
zdawac (zda-vach) v. entrust; submit;turn over;give up;pass(tests)
zdawac się (zda-vach shan) 1. seem; 2. surrender; 3.rely

z dawien dawna (zda-vyen dáv-na) adv. from way back

z dawna (zdáv-na) adv. since a long time; from way back

zdążyć (zhówn-zhich) v. come on time; keep pace; tend

zdechlak (zdékh-lak) m. weakling

zdechły (zdékh-wi) adj. m. peaky; dead (animal); weakly; sickly

zdecydować się (zde-tsi-dó-vach shán) v. decide ; determine

zdejmować (zdey-mó-vach) v. take off ; strip(clothes); snap(photo)

zdenerwowany (zde-ner-vo-va-ni) adj. m. nervous ; excited

zderzak (zdé-zhak) m. bumper

zderzenie (zde-zhe-ñe) n. collision; clash; crash; smash-up

zderzyc się (zdé-zhich shán) v. collide ; clash; run into

zdjęcie (zdyań-che) n. snapshot

zdjęcie rentgenowskie (zdyań-che rent-ge-nóv-skye) n. X-ray picture;X-ray phtograph

zdmuchiwać (zdmoo-khée-vach) v. blow off ; blow out; blow away

zdobić (zdo-beech) v. decorate

zdobycz (zdo-bich) f. booty; spoils;prey; prize;trophy

zdobyc (zdo-bich) v. conquer

zdolność (zdól-noshch) f. ability; capacity ; talent;aptitude

zdolny (zdól-ni) adj. m. clever; able ; capable; fit ;competent

zdołać (zdo-wach) v. be able

zdrada (zdra-da) f. treason

zdradliwy (zdrad-lee-vi) adj.m. treacherous; tricky; unsafe

zdradzac (zdra-dzach) v. betray

zdrajca (zdráy-tsa) adj. m. traitor ; informer; turncoat

zdrapać (zdra-pach) v. scratch off ; scrape off; loosen up

zdrętwieć (zdrant-vyech) v. grow numb ; stiffen ;grow torpid

zdrętwienie (zdrant-vyé-ñe) n. numbness;stiffnes; torpidity

zdrobniały (zdrob-ña-wi) adj.m. diminutive; grown smaller

zdrojowisko (zdro-yo-vees-ko) n. spa ; health resort ;baths

zdrowie (zdrov-ye) n. health ; good constitution;being well

zdrowotne jedzenie (zdro-vót-ne ye-dzé-ñe) n. health food

zdrowy (zdro-vi) adj. m. healthy; sound ; mighty ;in good health

zdrożny (zdrózh-ni) adj. m. vicious ; wicked; wrong ;fatigued

zdrój (zdróoy) m. spring ; spa

zdrów i cały (zdroóv ee tsa-wi) m. safe and sound

zdrzemnąc się (zdzhém-nównch shán) v. doze off; sleep light; catnap; take a nap

zdumienie (zdoo-myé-ñe) n. astonishment ; amazement

zdumiony (zdoo-myó-ni) adj.m. astonished; flabbergasted

zdun (zdoon) m. stove fitter

zdwajac (zdvá-yach) v. double

zdychac (zdi-khach) v. die

zdyszany (zdi-shá-ni) adj.m. breathless ; panting;out of breath

zdziałać (zdżhá-wach) v. accomplish ; achieve ;manage to do

zdziczec (zdżhee-chech) v. grow wild; become savage; turn wild

zdziecinniec (zdżhe-cheen-ñech) v. grow childish(in the old age)

zdzierac (zdżhé-rach) v. strip off; fleece; tear down; peel

zdzierstwo (zdżher-stvo) n. extortion; exorbitance

zdziwaczec (zdżhee-vá-chech) v. become odd; grow whimsical

zdziwic (zdżhee-veech) v. surprise; astonish;make wonder

zdziewienie (zdżhee-vyé-ñe) n. surprise; wonderment;astonishment

zebra (zé-bra) f. zebra

zebrać(zé-brach) v. gather;clear

zebranie (ze-bra-ñe) n. meeting

zecer (zé-tser) m. type setter

zechciec (zékh-chech) v. be willing; feel inclined; choose

zegar (zé-gar) m. clock ;meter

zegar słoneczny (zé-gar swo-néch-ni) sundial

zegarek (ze-gá-rek) m. watch

zegarmistrz (ze-gár-mees tsh) m. watchmaker; watchmaker's shop

zejscie (zéysh-che) n. descent

zejśc (zeyshch) v. descend

zejśc się (zeyshch shán) v. meet; rendez vous;have a date

zelówka (ze-loóv-ka) f.(shoe)sole
zelżeć (zél-zhech) v. lighten
up ;ease; let up ;diminish;abate
zemdlec (zém-dlech) v. faint;
pan out ; swoon ;feel weak
zemsta (zém-sta) f. revenge
zepchnąć (zép-khnównch) v. push
down; drive out ;shove down
zepsuć (zép-sooch) v. damage;
spoil; worsen; pervert;harm;injure
zepsuty (zep-soó-ti) adj. m.
damaged; spoiled ; corrupt ;bad
zerkać (zér-kach) v. squint;peep
zero (zé-ro) n. zero; nought; nil
zerwać (zér-vach) v. pick off;
snap loose; break off; sprain
zerwanie (zer-vá-ńe) n. rupture
zeskakiwać (ze-ska-keé-vach) v.
jump down ; dismount ;jump off
zeskrobywać (se-skro-bi-vach) v.
scrape off ; erase ;srcape clean
zesłać (ze-swach) v. deport;
send down ; send into exile
zesłanie (ze-swa-ńe) n. deportation ; exile; penal colony
zespolić (ze-spo-leech) v. unite
zespół (ze-spoow) m. team; group;
gang ; crew; set; troupe ;complex
zestarzeć się (ze-sta-zhech śhań)
v. grow old ; age; stale;get old
zestawienie (ze-sta-vye-ńe) n.
comparison; balance sheet; list
zestrzelenie (ze-stzhe-le-ńe) n.
shotting down; downing(a plane)
zeszłoroczny (ze-shwo-rócz-ni)
adj. m. last year's (crop etc.)
zeszpecic (ze-shpe-cheech) v.
disfigure ; make look ugly ;deface
zeszyt (ze-shit) m. notebook
zeslizgiwać się (ze-śhleez-gee-
vach śhań) v. glide down; slip
zetknąć się (zet-knównch śhań)
v. meet face-to-face; get in
touch; contact; meet;put in touch
zew (zef) n. call ; appeal;slogan
zewnątrz (zév-nowntsh) adv.& prep.
out; outside; outwards;outdoors
zewnętrzny (zev-náńtzh-ni) adj.
m. exterior;external; outward
zewsząd (ze-vshównt) adv. from
everywhere; from all points
zez (zez) m. squint; crosseye

zeznawać (zez-na-vach) v. declare; testify ;give evidence
zezowac (ze-zó-vach) v. squint
zezwalac (zez-va-lach) v. allow ; give permission ;permit
zezwolenie (zez-vo-le-ńe) n.
permission ; leave;license
zębaty (zán-bá-ti) adj. m.
toothed ; cogged; indented
zębate koło (zán-bá-te ko-wo)
n. cog wheel; gear (wheel)
zęby (zan-bi) pl. teeth; cogs
zgadywać (zga-di-vach) v.
guess ; anticipate ;give a guess
zgadzać się (zgá-dzach śhań)
v. agree ;fit in;see eye-to-eye
zgaga (zgá-ga) f. heartburn
zganic (zga-ńeech) v. blame
zgarnąć (zgár-nównch) v. rake
together ;gather; brush aside
zgasic (zga-śheech) v. put out;
extinguish; switch off; dim
zgęszczenie (zgań-shche-ńe) n.
condensation ; compression
zgiełk (zgyewk) m. uproar;
clamor ; turmoil; tumult
zgięcie (zgyan-che) n. bend;
fold ; inflection ;inflexion
zginać (zgee-nach) v. bend
(over); fold; stoop ; bow
zgliszcza (zgleésh-cha) pl.
cinders ; ashes ;site of fire
zgłaszac (zgwa-shach) v. notify; call for ; tender ;submit
zgłębic (zgwań-beech) v. probe;
sound out ; deepen ;go deeply
zgłodniały (zgwod-ná-wi) adj.
m. hungry ; starving ;hungering
zgłosic (zgwó-śheech) v. notify
zgłoska (zgwos-ka) f. syllable
zgłupiec (zgwoó-pyech) v. grow
silly ; grow stupid ;be astounded
zgnebic (zgnáń-beech) v. depress ; deject; oppress ;dishearten
zgnic (zgńeech) v. rot ;decay ;ret
zgniesc (zgńeshch) v. crush;stub;
squash ; suppress; quell ;squeeze
zgnilizna (zgńee-leez-na) f.
rot; corruption; foul smell
zgniły (zgńee-wi) adj. rotten;foul
zgoda ,zgó-da) f. concord; assent;
consent ;unity; approval ;harmony

zgodnie (zgód-ńe) adv. according;
in concert ; peaceably ;in unison
zgodność (zgód-nośhćh) f. accord
agreement ; unanimity ;consistence;
zgodny (zgód-ni) adj. m. compatible ; good-natured ;unanimous
zgoic się (zgó-eećh śhâń) v.
heal up; heal over ;heal a wound
zgon (zgon) m. death; decease
zgorszyc (zgór-shićh) v. horrify;
scandalize ; shock; arouse
zgorzkniały (zgozh-knâ-wi) adj.
m. sour; embittered;acrimonious
zgotowac (zgo-tó-vach) v. prepare;cook; give (an ovation)
z góry (zgoó-ri) adv. in advance
zgrabny (zgráb-ni) adj. m.skill-
ful; clever; deft; smart;neat;
shapely ; slick; deft;well-built
zgraja (zgra-ya) f. gang; mob
zgromadzenie (zgro-ma-dzé-ńe) n.
assembly ; congress; meeting
zgromadzać się (zgro-má-dzach
śhâń) v. assemble ; gather
zgroza (zgró-za) f. horror
z grubsza (zgroób-sha) adv.
roughly; approximatively
zgryzota (zgri-zó-ta) f. grief
zgryźliwy (zgrizh-leé-vi) adj.
m. sarcastic; peevish; harsh
zgrzac się (zgzhach śhâń) v.
get hot; sweat; become hot
zgrzebło (zgzhéb-wo) n. horse-
comb ; harrow ;curry comb;comb
zgrzyt (zgzhit) m. screech;jar
zguba (zgoó-ba) f. loss; doom;
undoing ; ruin; destruction
zgubic (zgoó-beećh) v. lose;
undo;drop;bring to ruin;destroy
zgubic się (zgoo-beećh śhâń) v.
get lost; get mixed up ;be mislaid
zgubny (zgoób-ni) adj. m. disastrous; fatal; ruinous ;calamitous
zgwałcic (zgvaw-ćheećh) v. rape
ziarnisty (żhar-ńeés-ti) adj.m.
granular ; grainy ;whole grain-
ziarno (żhár-no) n. grain; corn
ziele (żhé-le) n. weed; herb
zieleń (żhé-leń) f. greenery
zielonawy (żhe-lo-ná-vi) adj. m.
greenish;of greenish color
zielony (żhe-ló-ni) adj. m.green;
young and inexperienced (man)

ziemia (żhém-ya) f. earth; land
ground; soil ;native land;district
ziemianin (żhe-myá-ńeen) m.
squire; landowner ; mortal
ziemianka (żhe-myâń-ka) f.
1. dugout; 2. landowner's wife
ziemniak (żhém-ńak) m. potato
ziemski (żhem-skee) adj. m.
earthly ; worldly; landed ;land-
ziewac (żhé-vach) v. yawn; gape
zięba (żhań-ba) f. finch;chaffinch
ziębic (żhań-beećh) v. cool;
chill ;expose to the cold
zięc (żhâńch) m. son-in-law
zima (żheé-ma) f. winter
zimno (żheém-no) n. cold ;chill
zimno (żheém-no) adv. coldly
zimny (żheém-ni) adj. m. cold
zimowac (żhee-mo-vach) v.
hibernate; winter;pass the winter
zioło (żhó-wo) n. herb(mint,sage...)
ziszczac (zeésh-chach) v. realize; fulfill ; carry out (a plan)
zjadac (zyá-dach) v. eat; eat
up ; have food; ruin ; drain
zjadliwy (zya-dleé-vi) adj.m.
biting; caustic ; spiteful ;vicious
zjawa (zyá-va) f. apparition;
ghost ; vision ;specter; phantom
zjawisko (zya-veés-ko) n. fact;
event; phenomenon ;vision ;occurence
zjazd (zyazt) m. meeting; coming; descent ; downhill drive ;slide
zjednoczenie (zyed-no-ché-ńe) n.
union ; unification ;association
zjeść (zjéshćh) v. eat up ;outdo
zjeżdżac (zyézh-dzhać) v. ride
down; slide down ;make way;slate
zlecac (zle-tsach) v. commission;
order ;entrust; instruct;charge with
zlecenie (zle-tse-ńe) n. commission; order; errand; message
z ledwością (zled-vóśh-chôŵ)
adv. hardly; with difficulty
z lekka (zlék-ka) adv. lightly;
softly ; slightly; gently
zlepek (zle-pek) m. agglomerate
zlew (zlef) m. sink;kitchen sink
zlewac (zle-vach) v. pour off;
pour together ; mix ;flunk;whip
zliczyc (zleé-chich) v. count
up; total; add up ; reckon ;tot up

zlikwidować (zlee-kvee-do-vać)
v. liquidate; wind up;destroy
zlodowacenie (zlo-do-va-tse-ne)
n. freezing; glaciation
zlot (zlot) m. rally;flocking in
złagodzenie (zwa-go-dze-ne) n.
mitigation; softening
złagodzić (zwa-go-dźheećh) v.
mitigate ;soothe;lessen;soften
złamać (zwa-mach) v. break;smash
złamanie (zwa-ma-ne) n. fracture
złazić (zwa-żheećh) v. climb
down ; get off; come off;peel off
złączenie (zwown-che-ne) n. connection;junction ;weld link;fuse
złączyc (zwown-chich) v. join;
złe (zwe) n. evil; wrong; ill
zło (zwo) n. evil; devil;harm
złocenie (zyo-tse-ne) n. gilding
złocic (zwo-ćheećh) v. gild
złoczynca (zwo-chin-tsa) m.
evildoer ; criminal;malefactor
złodziej (zwo-dżhey) m. thief
złodziejka (zwo-dżhey-ka) f.
thief ; electrical adapter
złom (zwom) m. scrap; waste
złość (zwośhćh) f. anger; malice;
spite; soreness; resentment
złośliwy (zwosh-lee-vi) adj.m.
malignant; spiteful;malicious
złotnik (zwót-neek) m. goldsmith
złoto (zwó-to) n . gold;gold work
złoty (zwó-ti) adj. m. 1, golden
m. 2. Polish money unit
złowic (zwó-veećh) v. catch;net;
hook (a fish,a husband etc)
złowrogi (zwo-vró-gee) adj.m.
ominous ; sinister;protentous
złoże (zwo-zhe) n. stratum; bed
złożony (zwo-zho-ni) adj. m.
complex; multiple; intricate
złuda (zwoo-da) f. illusion
złudny (zwood-ni) adj. m. illusory; deceptive; illusive
zły (zwi) adj. m. bad; evil;ill;
vicious ; cross; poor;rotten
zmagać sie (zma-gach shán) v.
struggle with; grapple with
zmaganie (zma-gá-ne) n. struggle
zmarły (zmár-wi) adj. m. deceased; dead; defunct; the late
zmarszczka (zmarshch-ka) f.
wrinkle; crease; fold; pucker

zmartwienie (zmar-tvye-ne) n.
worry; sorrow; grief;trouble
zmartwychwstać (zmar-tvikh-
vstać) v. rise form the dead
zmartwychwstanie (zmar-tvikh-
vsta-ne) n. resurrection
zmarznąć (zmar-znownch) v.
freeze ; freeze over; be cold
zmawiac się (zma-vyach shán) v.
conspire ; plot; arrange;collude
zmaza (zmá-za) f. stain; blemish; blot; wet dream; slur
zmazywać (zma-zi-vach) v. wipe
out; efface ; erase; expiate
zmęczenie (zmán-che-ne) n. fatigue ; weariness;lassitude
zmiana (zmyá-na) f. change ;
variation; shift; relay;exchange
zmiatac (zmyá-tach) v. sweep up
zmiażdżyc (zmyázh-dzhich) v.
crush ; overwhelm(the enemy etc.)
zmienic (zmye-ñeech) v. change
zmierzac (zmye-zhach) v. aim;
tend; make one's way;drive at
zmierzch (zmyezhkh) m. dusk;
twilight; decline; fall; dark;
zmierzyć (zmye-zhich) v. measure; gauge ; take aim;make for
zmieszanie (zmye-shá-ne) n.
mix up; confusion, embarrassment
zmiłowanie (zmee-wo-vá-ne) n.
mercy; pity;disposition to forgive
zmniejszenie (zmñey-she-ne) n.
reduction; decrease; relief
zmniejszyc (zmñey-shich) v.
diminish; lessen; abate; reduce
zmoczyc (zmo-chich) v. wet; soak
zmora (zmó-ra) f. nightmare;bane
zmorzyc (zmo-zhich) v. overpower
zmordowac (zmor-do-vach) v.tire
wear; do in; tire out; exhaust
zmowa (zmó-va) f. conspiracy;
collusion; plot;secret deal
zmrok (zmrok) m. dusk; twilight
zmurszały (zmoor-sha-wi) adj.m.
mouldy, decaying; rotten;musty
zmuszac (zmoo-shach) v. coerce;
compel; force; oblige;constrain
zmykac (zmi-kach) v. cut and run;
bolt; scoot off; scurry away
zmylić(zmi-leech) v. fool; mislead; deceive; lose way;outwit

zmysł (zmisw) m. sense; instinct;knack;aptitude;reason
zmysłowy (zmis-wo-wi) adj. m.
sensual;sensory;sense-; lewd
zmyślać (zmish-lach) v. invent;
trump up ; fake up; bluff;cook up
zmyślony (zmish-lo-ni) adj.m.
fictitious; invented; unreal
znaczący (zna-chown-tsi) adj.
m. significant; emphatic;telling
znaczek (zna-chek) m. sign;stamp
znaczny (znach-ni)adj.m. notable;
znać (znach) v. know;know how
znajdować (znay-do-vach) v.
find ; see; meet; experience
znajomość (zna-yo-moshch) f.
acquaintance ; knowledge
znajomy (zna-yo-mi) adj. m.well
acquainted·well known;familiar
znak (znak) m. mark; sign; stamp
znakomity (zna-ko-mee-ti) adj.
m. excellent ; illustrious
znalazca (zna-laz-tsa) m. finder
znaleźne (zna-lezh-ne) n.find-
er's reward;finder's share
znamienny (zna-myen-ni) adj.m.
significant ; characteristic
znamię (zna-myan) n. stigma;
mole ; trait; birthmark
znany (zna-ni) adj. m. noted;
known ; famed; familiar;well known
znawca (znav-tsa) m. expert
znęcać się (znan-tsach shan) v.
torment; harass; ill-treat
znękany (znan-ka-ni) adj. m.
dejected; harassed ; wasted
znicz (zneech) m. (holy) fire;
fireside ; pilot-light
zniechęcać (zne-khan-tsach) v.
discourage ; sicken; indispose
zniecierpliwić się (zne-cher-
plee-veech shan) v. grow impatient ; get vexed;lose patience
znieczulić (zne-choo-leech) v.
anesthetize ; deaden; harden
zniedołężniały (zne-do-wan-zhna-
wi) adj. m. impotent; decrepit;
infirm ; disable; feeble(old man)
zniekształcać (zne-ksztaw-tsach)
v. deform; disfigure ;distort
zniemczać (znem-chach) v.German-
ize; make into a German;force
to accept German identity

znienacka (zne-nats-ka) adv.
all of a sudden;unawares
znienawidzieć (zne-na-vee-
dzheech) v. grow to hate;loathe
znieprawić (zne-pra-veech) v.
deprave; demoralize; debauch
zniesienie (zne-she-ne) n.
abrogation; abolition;repeal
zniesławienie (zne-swa-vye-ne)
n. defamation; slander
zniewaga (zne-va-ga) f. insult
zniewalać (zne-va-lach) v.
coerce; rape; captivate; win
znikać (znee-kach) v. vanish
zniewieściały (zne-vyesh-cha-
wi) adj. m. effeminate;sissy
znikąd (znee-kownt) adv. from
nowhere; out of nowhere
znikomy (znee-ko-mi) adj. m.
perishable;negligible;minute
zniszczeć (zneesh-chech) v. decay; go to ruin; be worn out
zniszczenie (zneesh-che-ne) n.
destruction; ravage;ruin;havoc
zniszczyć (zneesh-chich) v. destroy; ruin; ware out;ravage
zniweczyć (znee-ve-chich) v.
annihilate; wreck; lay waste
zniżać (znee-zhach) v. lower
zniżka (zneezh-ka) f. reduction
decline; slump; drop; fall
znosić (zno-sheech) v. annul;
endure; carry down;ware out
znośny (znosh-ni) adj. m. tolerable; bearable; so-so; fair
znowu (zno-voo) adv. again;anew
znój (znooy) m. toil; sweat
znów (znoof) adv. again; anew
znudzenie (znoo-dze-ne) n.bore-
dom; till one is sick and tired
znużenie (znoo-zhe-ne) n. weariness; fatigue (people,metals etc.)
zobaczyć (zo-ba-chich) v. see
zobojętnić (zo-bo-yant-neech)
v. neutralize;make indifferent
zobojętnieć (zo-bo-yant-nech)
v. grow indifferent;grow listless
zobowiązać (zo-bo-vyown-zach)
v. oblige ;obligate to do
zobowiązanie (zo-bov-yown-za-
ne) n. obligation;commitment
zobrazować (zob-ra-zo-vach) v.
illustrate; describe ;depict

zogniskować (zog-ńees-ko-vach) v. focus; concentrate

zohydzać (zo-khi-dzach) v. defame; make loathsome;sicken of

zoolog(zo-o-log) m. zoologist

zorza północna (zo-zha poownóts-na) f. aurora borealis

zostać (zos-tach) v. remain;stay; become; get to be; be left

zostawiać (zos-táv-yach) v. leave;abandon; put aside

z powodu (zpo-vo-doo) prep. because of; owing to;due to

z powrotem (zpov-ro-tem) adv. back; backwards;on the way back

zrabować (zra-bo-vach) v. rob

z rana (zra-na) adv. in the morning;during the morning

zranić (zra-ńeech) v. wound; injure; hurt(feelings);mangle

zrastać (zras-tach) v. grow into one; fuse; heal up;blend

zrazu (zra-zu) adv. at first

zrażać (zra-zhach) v. discourage; set against; alienate

zrąb (zrownp) m. frame (work); clearing ; trunk; shell

zrąbać (zrown-bach) v. hew; cut down; hack; chop; pick to pieces

zrealizować (zre-a-lee-zo-vach) v. realize; actualize; execute

zredagować (zre-da-go-vach) v. draw up; compose; edit; draft

zresztą (zresh-town) adv. 1. moreover; besides; 2.after all; though; any way;in the end

zręczność (zrańch-noshch) f. cleverness; dexterity; skill

zrobić (zro-beech) v. make; do; turn; execute; perform

zrodzić (zro-dźheech) v. give birth; beget; originate

zrosnąć się (zros-nownch shan) v. grow into one; fuse;blend

zrozpaczony (zros-pa-cho-ni) adj. m. desperate; brokenhearted

zrozumiały (zro-zoo-mya-wi) adj. m. intelligible; understandable

zrozumieć (zro-zoo-myech) v. understand;grasp;see;make out

zrozumienie (zro-zoo-mye-ńe) n. understanding;sympathy; sense; grasp; comprehension; spirit

zrównać (zroov-nach) v. level; make even; align;equalize

zrównoważyć (zroov-no-va-zhich) v. balance; equalize;equilibrate

zróżniczkować (zroozh-ńeech-ko-vach) v. differentiate

zryć (zrich) v. dig up; furrow

zrywać (zri-vach) v. rip; tear off; tear down; pick; quarrel

z rzadka (zzhad-ka) adv. rarely

zrządzenie losu (zzhown-dze-ńe lo-soo) n. fate ;decree of fate

zrzeczenie się (zzhe-che-ńe shań) n. resignation; renunciation ; renouncement;abdication

zrzeszenie (zzhe-she-ńe) n. association; union

zrzęda (zzhań-da) m. grumbler

zrzucac (zzhoo-tsach) v. throw (down); buck off; drop; shed

zrzut lotniczy (zzhoot lot-ńee-chi) m. drop (from plane)

zsiadac (zsha-dach) v. dismount

zstąpic (zstown-peech) v. descend;step down( one time)

zstępować (zstań-po-vach) v. descent; step down

zsyłac (zsi-wach) v. deport;exile

zsyłka (zsiw-ka) f. deportation

zsypywać (zsi-pi-vach) v. heap up; pour off;shoot into

zszyc (zshich) v. sew together

zubożec (zoo-bo-zhech) v. impoverish; grow poor;pauperize

zuch (zookh) m. brave fellow

zuchwalstwo (zookh-val-stvo) n. insolence; audacity; impudence

zuchwały (zookh-va-wi) adj. m. insolent; impudent; bold

zupa (zoo-pa) f. soup

zupełny (zoo-pew-ni) adj. m. entire;whole;total;out and out

zużycie (zoo-zhi-che) n. consumption; wear and tear; waste

zużytkować (zoo-zhit-ko-vach) v. utilize ; use up; exploit

zużyty (zoo-zhi-ti) adj.m. worn out; used up; wasted; trite

zwać (zvach) v. call; name

zwalczyc (zval-chich) v. overpower; overcome; cope; strive

zwalić (zva-leech) v. demolish; fell; collapse; pile up;knock down

zwalniac (zval-nach) v. release; loosen; let go; slow dawn;vacate
zwal (zvaw) m. heap; bank ; pile
zwapnienie (zvap-ńe-ńe) n. calcification adv.densely;closely
zwarcie (zvár-che) n. short (cirquit); contraction;infighting
zwariowac (zvar-yó-vach) v. go mad ; go crazy; alter (a score...)
zwarzyc (zva-zhich) v. boil; nip; frost damage ; turn sour ;blight
zważac (zvá-zhach) v. pay attention ; weigh ( words);consider
zważyc (zvá-zhich) v. weigh; consider ; give heed ;regard
zwąchac (zvówn-khach) v. smell out; get wind; sniff ;scent
zwątpic (zvównt-peech) v. despair of ; lose hope ;give up
zwędzic (zván-dżheech) v. swipe
zweglic (zvang-ieech) v. carbonize ; char; get charred
zwęzic (zvan-żheech) v. narrow down ; contract; restrict ;confine
zwiady (zvya-di) pl. reconnaissance ; scouting ;reconnoitring
zwiastowac (zvyas-tó-vach) v. announce ; herald ;foreshadow
zwiastowanie (zvyas-to-vá-ńe) n. Annunciation
zwiastun (zvyás-toon) m. harbinger ; herald; omen ;forerunner
związac (zvyówn-zach) v. bind; fasten; join; tie up;strap;frame
związek (zvyówn-zek) m. alliance; connection; bond· compound ;tie
zwichnąc (zveékh-nównch) v. strain; dislocate; disjoin; luxate ;warp
zwichnięcie (zveekh-nán-che) n. dislocation ; luxation; sprain
zwiedzac (zvyę-dzach) v. visit; see the sights ; tour; see ;inspect
zwiedzanie (zvye-dzá-ńe) n. sightseeing ;touring
zwierciadło (zvyer-chád-wo) n. mirror ; reflection ;looking glass
zwierz (zvyesh) n. beast of prey
zwierzac się (zvyc-zhach śhán) v. disclose a secret; confide in...
zwierzchnik (zvyézh-khneek) m. boss; superior ; chief; lord ; master; suzerain;feudal lord

zwierzchnictwo (svyezh-khneetstvo) n. sovereignty; superior authority; supremacy; control
zwierzę (zvye-zhąń) n. animal
zwierzyna (zvye-zhí-na) f. game (animals); game
zwierzyniec (zvye-zhi-ńets) m. zoo; zoological garden ;zodiac
zwieszac (zvyé-shach) v. hang low ;droop; dangle ; hang down
zwietrzec (zvye-tzhech) v. decompose ; go stale; spoil
zwiewac (zvyé-vach) v. cut and run; blow away ; run away
zwiędły (zvyańd-wi) adj. m. withered; wilted ;faded
zwiędnąc (zvyańd-nównch) v. wither; wilt; fade
zwiększyc (zvyańk-zhich) v. increase; magnify ; heighten
zwięzły (zvyańz-wi) adj. m. concise; brief ; terse;compact
zwijac (zvee-yach) v. roll up; wind up;coil; twist up ;furl
zwilzac (zveél-zhach) v. moisten; wet; dampen(often)
zwilzyc (zveél-zhich) v. moisten; wet; dampen(one time )
zwinąc (zvee-nównch) v. roll up; wind up; coil up; twist up
zwinny (zveén-ni) adj. m. agile; nimble; deft; dexterous ;lissome
zwisac (zvee-sach) v. hang down; droop; dangle ;sag;beetle
zwlekac (zvle-kach) v. delay
zwłaszcza (zvwash-cha) adv. particularly; chiefly; especially; most of all;specially
zwłoka (zvwó-ka) f. delay;respite
zwłoki (zvwó-kee) n. corpse
zwodzic (zvó-dżheech) v. delude; deceive; let down; lower
zwolenniczka (zvo-len-ńeech-ka) f. adherent; follower;advocate
zwolennik (zvo-len-ńeek) m. adherent; follower; advocate
zwolna (zvól-na) adv. slowly
zwolniec (zvól-ńech) v. slow down; slack off; relax ;slacken
zwolnienie (zvol-ńe-ńe) n. 1. dismissal; release; acquittal ;sack;exemption;2.slowing

zwoływać (zvo-wi-vach) v. call
together: assemble; convene
zwoj (zvooy) m. roll;reel;coil
zwracać (zvra-tsach) v. return;
give back; pay(attention)
zwrot (zvrot) m. 1; turn; 2. restitution 3.revulsion;4.phrase
zwrotka (zvrot-ka) f. stanza
zwrotnica (zvrot-nee-tsa) f.
switch (large); steering
zwrotnik (zvrot-neek) m. tropic
zwrotny (zvrot-ni) adj. m. flexible; returnable;repayable
zwrócić się (zvrob-cheech shan)
v. turn (to); give back
zwycięski (zvi-chans-kee) adj.
m. victorious;triumphant;winning
zwycięstwo (zvi-chans-tvo) n.
victory; triumph; win
zwyciężać (zvi-chan-zhach) v.
conquer ; win; prevail;overcome
zwyczaj (zvi-chay) m. custom;
habit; fashion; usage;practice
zwyczajny (zvi-chay-ni) adj. m.
usual; ordinary; common;simple
zwyczajowy (zvi-cha-yo-vi) adj.
m. customary; regular; usual
zwykły (zvik-wi) adj. m. common
zwyrodniały (zvi-rod-na-wi) adj.
m. degenerate; degenerated
zwyrodnienie (zvi-rod-ne-ne) n.
degeneration ; degradation
zwyżka (zvizh-ka) f. rise;advance
zwyżka cen (zvizh-ka tsen) f.
price rise ;price increase
zygzak (zig-zak) m. zigzag
zysk (zisk) m. gain; profit
zyskać (zis-kach) v. gain ;earn
zyskowność (zis-kov-noshch) f.
profitability;remunerativeness
zyskowny (zis-kow-ni) adj. m.
profitable; lucrative
zza (z-za) prep. from behind
zziajać się (zzha-yach shan) v.
get out of breath;tire oneself out
zzieleniec (zzhe-le-nech) v.
turn green ; become green
zziębnąć (zzhanb-nownch) v. feel
cold;be chilled to the bone
zziębnięty (zzhanb-nan-ti) adj.
m. chilled( to the bone)
zżyć się(zzhich shan) v. grow
familiar ;grow accustomed

żymać (zzhi-mach) v. wring
żżynać (zzhi-nach) v. cut
down; reap; mow (the grass etc.)
żżywać się (zzhi-vach shan) v.
grow familiar ; reconcile
zdźbło (zhdzhbwo) n. stalk;
blade ;trifle; a bit; a little
zle (zhle) adj. n,& adv. ill;
wrong; badly; falsely;mistakenly
zrebak (zhre-bak) m. colt
zrebię (zhre-byan) n. foal;colt
zrenica (zhre-nee-tsa) f. pupil
zrodlany (zhrood-la-ni) adj.m:
spring (water); of spring
zrodło (zhrood-wo) n. spring;
source ; well;fountain head
zrodłosłów (zhrood-wo-swoof) m.
root word; etymology; radical
zrodłowy (zhrood-wo-vi) adj.m.
original; spring (water)
żaba (zha-ba) f. frog
żaden (zha-den) pron. none;
neither; not any; no one ; no-
żagiel (zha-gel) m. sail
żakiet (zha-ket) m. jacket
żal (zhal) m. regret; grief;
sorrow, remorse;grudge; rancor
żalić się (zha-leech shan) v.
complain ; lament;find fault
żaluzja (zha-loo-zya) f. blind
żałoba (zha-wo-ba) f. mourning
żałobny marsz (zha-wob-ni marsh)
m. funeral march
żałosny (zha-wos-ni) adj. m.
lamentable; wretched;plaintive
żałość (zha-woshch) f. grief;
desolation; sorrow ;deep sorrow
żałować (zha-wo-vach) v. regret
żar (zhar) m. heat; glow; ardor
żarcie (zhar-che) n. swill;dub
żargon (zhar-gon) m. jargon
żarliwość (zhar-lee-voshch) f.
ardor; zeal; earnestness
żarliwy (zhar-lee-vi) adj. m.
ardent; zealous;fervent
żarłoczny (zhar-woch-ni) adj.m.
greedy;voracious; gluttonous
żarłok (zhar-wok) m. glutton
żarówka (zha-roov-ka) f. light
bulb; electric bulb ; bulb
żart (zhart) m. joke; jest;quip;
żartować (zhar-to-vach) v. joke
make fun; poke fun; trifle ;jest

żarzyc (zha-zhich) v. glow;anneal
żąć (zhownch) v. mow; cut; reap
żądac (zhown-dach) v. demand;
 require; exact; stipulate
żądanie (zhown-da-ne) n. demand;
 claim;requirement;stipulation
żądło (zhownd-wo) n . sting;fang
żądny (zhownd-ni) adj. m. eager;
 anxious; greedy;avid (of fame etc.)
żądny przygód (zhownd-ni pzhi-
 goot) adventurous (man)
że (zhe) conj. that; then; as
żebrac (zhe-brach) v. beg
żebraczka (zhe-brach-ka) f. beggar; pauper (girl, woman)
żebrak (zhe-brak) m. beggar (man)
żebranina (zhe-bra-nee-na) f.
 beggary; begging; alms
żebro (zhe-bro) n. rib;fin
żeby (zhe-bi) conj. so as; in
 order that;if;may;if only
żeglarski (zhe-glar-skee) adj.m.
 nautical; seaman's (life etc.)
żeglarstwo (zhe-glar-stvo) n.
 sailing;navigation;seamanship
żeglarz (zhe-glash) m. seaman;
 sailor; mariner; seafarer
żeglowac (zhe-glo-vach) v. sail;
 navigate ( the seas,the ocean)
żeglowny (zhe-glow-ni) adj. m.
 navigable (river, canal etc.)
żegluga (zhe-gloo-ga) f. navigation ; shipping; sailing
żegnac (zheg-nach) v. bid farewell; bless;bid good-bye;see off
żelatyna (zhe-la-ti-na) f.jelly
żelazko (zhe-laz-ko) n. press-
 iron ; cutting iron; edger
żelazny (zhe-laz-ni) adj. m. iron
żelazo (zhe-la-zo) n. iron ;armor
żelazobeton (zhe-la-zo-be-ton)
 m. reinforced concrete
żelaztwo (zhe-laz-tvo) n. scrap
 iron; hardware;iron junk
żelbet (zhel-bet) m. reinforced
 concrete
żeliwo (zhe-lee-vo) n. cast iron
żenic (zhe-neech) v. marry
żenowac (zhe-no-vach) v. embarrass
żenski (zhen-skee) adj. m. female
żer (zher) m. food; prey; feeding
żerdka (zherd-ka) f. (small)perch

żerdz (zherdzh) f. perch
żłobek (zhwo-bek) m. crib
żłobic (zhwo-beech) v. channel; erode; furrow; groove
żłob (zhwoop) m. trough; crib
żmija (zhmee-ya) f. viper;
 adder; poisonous snake
żmudny (zhmood-ni) adj. m.
 uphill; toilsome; strenuous
żniwiarka (zhnee-vyar-ka) f.
 harvester; reaper
żniwo (zhnee-vo) n. harvest
żołądek (zho-wown-dek) m.
 stomach
żołądz (zho-wowndzh) f. acorn
żołd (zhowd) m. (soldier's)
 pay
żołdactwo (zhow-dats-tvo) n.
 soldiery ;the soldiery
żołnierz (zhow-nesh) m. soldier
żona (zho-na) f. wife
żonaty (zho-na-ti) adj. m.
 married; family man
żołc (zhoowch) f. bile
żołciowy (zhoow-cho-vi) adj.m.
 gall; peevish; harsh; biting
żołknąc (zhoow-knownch) v. turn
 yellow; become yellow
żołtaczka (zhow-tach-ka) f.
 jaundice; the yellows
żołtawy (zhow-ta-vi) adj. m.
 yellowish;nankeen; sallow
żołtko (zhoowt-ko) n. yolk
żołty (zhoow-ti) adj. m. yellow
żołto-blady (zhoow-to-bla-di)
 adj. yellow-pale; sallow
żołw (zhoowf) m. turtle;tortoise
żołwi krok (zhoow-vee krok) m.
 snail's pace; turtle's gait
żrący (zhrown-tsi) adj. m.
 corrosive; caustic; biting
żubr (zhoobr) m. (European-Po-
 lish) bison; aurochs
żuchwa (zhookh-va) f. jawbone
żuc (zhooch) v. chew;masticate
żucie (zhoo-che) n. chewing;
 mastication; chew;munducation
żuk (zhook) m. beetle;dung beetle
żulik (zhoo-leek) m. swindler;
 rogue; cheat; street urchin
żuławy (zhoo-wa-vi) pl. marsh-
 land ; lowlands;fertile lowlands

żupa (zhoó-pa) f. saltworks
żupan (zhoó-pan) m. old Polish costume; (hist.) district chief
żur (zhoór) m. soup of fermented meal; sour soup
żuraw (zhoó-rav) m. crane;gantry
żurawina (zhoo-ra-vée-na) f. cranberry
żurnal (zhoór-nal) m. fashion magazine
żużel (zhoó-zhel) m. slag; cinder; scoria;clinker;cinder track
żużlobeton (zhoo-zhlo-be-ton) m. slag concrete
żwawo (zhvá-vo) adj. m. briskly; alertly; apace ; jauntily
żwawy (zhvá-vi) adj. m. brisk; quick; lively; spry ;sprightly
żwir (zhveér) m. gravel upkeep
życie (zhi-che) n. life ;pep; życiodajny (zhi-cho-dáy-ni) adj. m. life-giving ; vivifying
życiorys (zhi-chó-ris) m. biography; life history
życzenie (zhi-che-ńe) n. wish; desire ; request ; greeting
życzliwy (zhich-lée-vi) adj.m. favorable; friendly; kindly
życ (zhich) v. be alive; live; exist; subsist; get along
Żyd (zhid) m. Jew
żydowski (zhi-dóv-skee) adj.m. Jewish; Judaic; Yiddish
żydostwo (zhi-dós-tvo) n. Jewry
żydówka (zhi-dóv-ka) f. Jewess
żyjący (zhi-yówn-tsi) adj.m. living ; pl. the living
żyjatko (zhi-yównt-ko) n. animalcule ; tiny animal
żylak (zhi-lak) m. varix
żylakowy (zhi-la-kó-vi) adj.m. varicose; of varicose vein
żylasty (zhi-las-ti) adj. m. venous; stringy; sinewy
żyletka (zhi-lét-ka) f. (razor) blade; safety razor blade
żyla (zhi-wa) f. vein; seam; core; strand; streak; string
żyłka (zhiw-ka) f. veinlet; thread
żyrafa (zhi-rá-fa) f. giraffe
żyrant (zhi-rant) m. endorser
żyrować (zhi-ro-vach) v. endorse

żytni (zhit-ńee) adj. m. rye
żytniówka (zhit-ńoóv-ka) f. corn vodka ; gin; rye vodka
żyto (zhi-to) n. rye
żywcem (zhiv-tsem) adv. alive
żywe srebro (zhi-ve sréb-ro) n. mercury; restless person
żywica (zhi-vée-tsa) f. resin
żywiec (zhi-vyets) m. cattle for slaughter; live bait
żywic (zhi-veéch) v. feed; nourish; cherish ; feel
żywioł (zhi-vyow) m. element
żywiołowy (zhi-vyo-wó-vi) adj. m. elemental; spontaneous; impulsive; impetuous
żywność (zhiv-noshch) f. food; provisions; eatables; fodder
żywo (zhi-vo) adv. quickly; briskly ;exp.; make it snappy!
żywopłot (zhi-vó-pwot) m. hedge
żywość (zhi-voshch) f. animation; liveliness; vivacity; vitality; vigor; esprit
żywot (zhi-vot) m. life; womb; belly ;life (of a saint)
żywotnie (zhi-vot-ńe) adv. vitally; exuberantly;luxuriantly
żywotność (zhi-vót-noshch) f. vitality ; liveliness ;vivacity
żywotny (zhi-vot-ni) m. vital
żywy (zhi-vi) adj. m. alive; lively; vivid; intense; gay; brisk; live;acute; keen; bright
żyzność (zhiz-noshch) f. fertility ; fruitfulness ;richness
żyzny (zhiz-ni) adj. m. fertile; generous (soil): fruitful; fat; fecund; rich

# ENGLISH-POLISH

a (ej) art.jeden; pewien;
pierwsza litera angielskiego
alfabetu; pierwszej kategorii
A-O'k (ej okej) zupełnie gotów
aback (e'baek) adv. wstecz;
w tył: do tylu; nazad
abandon (e'baendon) v. opuszczać ; porzucić ; zarzucić
abandonment (e'baendonment) s.
opuszczenie;brak pohamowania
abashed (e'baeszt) adj. speszony; zmieszany (czymś)
abate ('ebejt) v. osłabiać;
zmniejszać; mitygować;uciszyć
abbey ('aebi) s. opactwo
abbreviate (e'bry:wjejt) v.
skrócić; skracać
abbreviation (e'bry:wjejszyn)
s. skrót: skrócenie; skracanie
ABC ('ej'bi:'si) alfabet
abdicate ('aebdykejt) v. zrzekać się ; abdykować
abdomen ('aebdemen) s. brzuch
abduct (aeb'dakt) v. uprowa-
dzić: porwać; porywać
abhor (eb'ho:r) v. mieć odrazę
abide, abode, abode (e'bajd,
e'boud, e'boud)
abide (e'bajd) v. znosić; obstawać; dotrzymywać; trwać
ability (e'bylyty) s. zdolność
abject ('aebdżekt) adj. podły;
nędzny; nikczemny: skrajny
abjure (eb'dżuer) v. poprzysiąc
able ('ejbl) adj. zdolny; zdatny; utalentowany; poczytalny
abnormal (aeb'no:rmel) adj.
anormalny; nieprawidłowy
aboard (e'bo:rd) adv. na pokła-
dzie; na statku: w pociągu
abode (e'boud) v. był posłuszny
abode (e'boud) s. mieszkanie;
v. zob. abide
abolish (e'bolysz) v. obalić;
znieść: znosić; obalać
abolition (aebe'lyszyn) n. obalenie; zniesienie(zwyczaju etc)
A-bomb ('ejbom) s. bomba atomowa: bomba jądrowa
abominable (e'bomynebl) adj.
ohydny; wstrętny; obrzydliwy

abortion (e'bo:rszyn) s.przerwa-
nie ciąży; poronienie
abound (e'baund) v. obfitować
about (e'baut) adv. naokoło;
około;dookoła; po: o; wobec;przy
about (e'baut) prep. o; przy;
odnośnie; naokoło; wokoło
about to (e'baut tu) gotów do
above (e'baw) adv. powyżej;
w górze; wyżej; na górze
above (e'baw) prep. nad; ponad
above (e'baw) adj. powyższy
abreast(e'brest) adv. obok;
rzędem: ramię przy ramieniu
abridge (e'brydż) v. skrócić
abroad (e'bro:d) adv. zewnątrz;
za granicą: za granicę; w dal
abrogate ('aebrogejt) v. obalić:
unicestwić; odwoływać; znosić
abrupt (e'brapt) adj. nagły;
szorstki; urwany; ostry; oschły
abscess ('aebses) s. wrzód:ropień
absence ('aebsens) s. brak;
nieobecność; niestawiennictwo
absent ('aebsent) adj. nieobecny;v. być nieobecnym
absent-minded ('aebsent'majndyd)
adj. roztargniony
absolute ('aebselu:t) adj. abso-
lutny; zupełny: nieodwołalny
absolutely ('aebselu:tly) adv.
absolutnie; oczywiście
absolve (eb'zolw) v. rozgrzeszyć;
darować: uwolnić; oczyścić
absorb (eb'zo:rb) v. chłonąc;
tłumić; absorbować; łagodzić
abstain (eb'stejn) v. powstrzymywać się; być abstynentem
abstention (eb'stenszyn) s.
wstrzymanie się(od jedzenia...)
abstinence ('aebstynens) s.
wstrzemięźliwość: abstynencja
abstract ('aebstraekt) adj.
oderwany; abstrakcyjny;
s. abstrakcja; streszczenie;
v. streszczać; abstrahować;
odrywać: ukrasc: sprzątnąć
absurd (eb'se:rd) adj. absurdalny; bezsensowny: niedorzeczny
abundance (e'bandens) s. obfitość: znaczna ilość; dostatek

abundant (e'bandent) adj. obfity;liczny;bogaty; zasobny;płodny
abuse (e'bju:s) s. nadużycie; obelga; (e'bju:z) v. obrażać; nadużywać;lżyć;obrzucać obelgami
abyss (e'bys) n. otchłań; przepaść; głębia;pierwotny chaos
acacia (e'kejsze) s. akacja
academic (,aeke'demyk) adj. akademicki;jałowy; s.uczony
academy (e'kaedemy) s. akademia
accelerate (aek'selerejt) v. przyśpieszać; przyśpieszyć
accelerator (aek'selerejter) s. przyśpieszacz; gaźnik; akcelerator; katalizator
accent ('aeksent) s. wymowa; akcent; (aek'sent) v. akcentować; uwydatniać; znakować
accept (ek'sept) v. akceptować; zgadzać się na;zechcieć wziąść
acceptable (ek'septebl) adj. do przyjęcia; znośny; zadawalający; mile widziany
access ('aekses) s. dostęp
accessible (aek'sesybl) adj. dostępny; przystępny
accession (aek'seszyn) s., wstąpienie; dostęp; dojście; przystąpienie;objęcie(urzędu)
accessory (aek'sesery) s. dodatek; adj. dodatkowy; pomocniczy
access road ('aekses roud) droga dojazdowa
accident ('aeksydent) s. traf; wypadek; katastrofa;awaria
accidental (,aeksy'dentl) adj. przypadkowy; nieważny;uboczny
acclimatize (e'klajmetajz) v. aklimatyzować
accommodate (e'komedejt) v. przystosować; zakwaterować; wyświadczyć; załagodzić(spór)
accommodation (e,kome'dejszyn) s. wygoda; dostosowanie; kwatera; pogodzenie się; ugoda
accompaniment (e'kampenyment) s. towarzyszenie; akompaniament
accompany (e'kampeny) v. towarzyszyć;odprowadzać;akompaniować
accomplice (e'komplys) s. współsprawca; współwinny

accomplish (e'kamplysz) v. dokonać; spełnić; zrealizować
accomplished (e'kamplyszt) adj. utalentowany; znakomity; wykończony; z ogłada;skończony
accomplishment (e'kamplyszment) s. osiągnięcie; realizacja; dokonanie;wykonanie: ogłada
accord (e'ko:rd) s. zgoda; v. uzgadniać; dać; licować
according (e'ko:rdyng) prep. według; zależnie od
accordingly (e'ko:rdyngly) adv. odpowiednio; więc; zatem
accost (e'kost) v. zaczepić (kogoś);zagadnąć;przystąpić do
account (e'kaunt) s. rachunek; sprawozdanie; v. wyliczać; wytłumaczyć; uważać; oceniać
account for (e'kaunt fo:r) v. dać powód; wytłumaczyć
accountant (e'kauntent) s. księgowy
accounting (e'kauntyng)s. księgowość
accumulate (e'kju:mju,lejt) v. gromadzić;zbierać;piętrzyć
accuracy ('aekjuresy) s. scisłość; dokładność; celność
accusation (aekju:zejszyn) s. oskarżenie;winienie;oskądzenie
accuse (e'kju:z) v. oskarżać
accused (e'kju:zd) adj. oskarżony; oskarżona
accustom (e'kastem) v. przyzwyczajać; przzyzwyczaić
accustomed (e'kastemd) adj. przyzwyczajony; zwykły;zwyczajny
ace (ejs) s. as; oczko(in cards)
ache (ejk) s. ból; v.boleć
achieve (e'czi:w) v. dokonać; osiągnąć(cel);zdobywać(sławę)
achievement(e'czi:wment) s. osiągnięcie; wyczyn;zdobycz
aching ('ejkyng) adj. bolący
acid ('aesyd) adj. kwaśny; s. kwas; kwaśna substancja
acid trip ('aesyd tryp) halucynacje po narkotyku
acknowledge (ek'nolydż) v. uznać; potwierdzić; przyznać

acknowledgement (ek'noɫlydżment)
s. przyznanie; potwierdzenie;
uznanie; dowód uznania
acoustics (e'ku:styks) pl. akus-
tyka
acquaint (e'kɫejnt) v. zaznajo-
mić; zapoznać; zapoznawac(kogoś)
acquaintance (e'kɫejntens) s.
znajomość; znajomy
acquiesce (,aekɫy'es), v. zgadzać się; przyzwalać (bez oporu); przychylić się(do prośby)
acquire (e'kɫajer) v. nabywać
acquisition (,aekɫy'zyszyn) s.
nabytek; nabycie; zdobycz
acquit (e'kɫyt) v. zwolnić; wy-
wiązac się;spłacić;uniewinnić
acquittal (e'kɫytl) s. zwolnienie;uiszczenie;wywiązanie się
acre (ejker) s. akr; morga;
4047 m²
acrid ('aekryd) adj. żrący;
ostry; cierpki;kwaskowaty
acrimonious (,aekry'mounjes)
adj. szorstki; zjadliwy;
cierpki; zgorzkniały
acrobat ('aekrebaet) s. akrobata
across (e'kros) adv. w poprzek;
na krzyż; prep. przez; na prze-
ɫaj; po drugiej stronie (czegoś)
act (aekt) v. czynić; działac;
postępować; s. czyn; akt; uczynek;akt sztuki;uchwɫa;ustawa
action ('aekszyn) s. działanie;
czyn; akcja; ruch;poces
active ('aektyw) adj. czynny;
obrotny; rzutki; ożywiony;żywy
activity (aek'tywyty) s..dzia-
łalność; czynność;ożywienie;ruch
actor ('aekter) s. aktor
actress ('aektrys) s. aktorka
actual ('aekczuel) adj. istotny;
faktyczny; bieżący; obecny
actually ('aekczuely) adv. rzeczywiście; obecnie;istotnie;nawet
acute (e'kju:t) adj. ostry;
przenikliwy; bystry;przenikliwy
ad (aed) s. ogɫoszenie (reklama)
(slang)
adapt (e'daept) v. dostosować;
przerobić;przystosować;dostrajać

adaptation (,aedaep'tejszyn)
s. przystosowanie;dostrojenie
add (aed) v. dodać; doliczyc
addict ( aedyktʹ) s. naɫogowiec;
v. oddawać; poświęcać się
addicted (e'dyktyd) adj. naɫo-
gowy; naɫogowo poswięcający się
addition (e'dyszyn) s. dodawanie; dodatek; (ponadto)
additional (e'dyszynl) adj.
dodatkowy; dalszy
address (e'dres) s. adres; mowa; odezwa; v. zwracać się;
adresować; skierować(prośbę)
addressee (,aedre'si:) s. ad-
resat; adresatka
adequate ('aedykɫyt) s. stosowny; dostateczny;właściwy
adhere (ed'hjer) v. lgnąć; należeć; trzymać; przylegać
adhesion (ed'hi:żyn) s. lep-
kość; zrost;przynależność
adhesive (ed'hi:syw) adj. lepki; przylegający; s. plaster
adjacent (e' dżejsent) adj.
przyległy; sąsiedni
adjective ('aeddżyktyw) s.
przymiotnik;adj.dodatkowy
adjoin (e'ddżoyn) v. stykać się;
sąsiadować; doɫączać
adjourn (e'ddże:rn) v. odraczać;
przerywać; zakończyć (obrady)
adjust (e'ddżast) v. dostosowywać; uregulować ; nastawić
administer (ed'mynyster) v. dawać; sprawować; administrować
administration (ed,myny'strejszyn) s. zarząd; rząd; administracja; ministerstwo; wymiar
administrative (ed'mynystrej-
tyw) adj. administracyjny
administrator (ed'mynystrejtor)
s. zarządca; administrator
admirable ('aedmerebl) adj.
godny podziwu;zachwycający
admiral ('aedmyrel) s. admiraɫ
admiration (aedmy'rejszyn) s.
podziw;zachwyt;przedmiot podziwu
admire (ed'majer) v. podziwiać
admirer (ed'majrer) s. wielbiciel; wielbicielka

admissible (ed'mysybl) adj. do-
puszczalny; do przyjęcia
admission (ed'myszyn) s. wstęp:
dostęp; przyznanie; uznanie;
(dopływ); bilet wstępu
admission ticket (ed'myszyn'tykyt) bilet wstępu
admit (ed'myt) v. wpuszczac;
uznac; przyjmowac; przyznac
admittance (ed'mytens) s. dostęp; przyjęcie;przyznanie się
admonish (ed'monysz) v. upominac; ostrzegac; pouczac
ado (e'du) s. wrzawa; kłopot;
trudnosci; grymasy; narzekania
adolescence (,aede'lesns) s.
młodosc(pokwitanie-dojrzałosc)
adolescent (,aede'lesnt) adj.
młodociany; dorastający
adopt (e'dopt) adoptowac; przyjmowac; akceptowac; wybierac
adoption (e'dopszyn) s. adopcja;
adaptacja; przyjęcie; przyspo-
sobienie;akceptacja; wybór
adorable (e'do:rebl) adj. godny
uwielbienia; bardzo miły
adoration (,aede:rejszyn) s.
uwielbienie; wielka miłość
adore (e'do:r) v. czcic; uwielbiac; bardzo lubiec; kochac
adorn (e'do:rn) v. zdobic;
upiększac; byc ozdobą
adrift (e'dryft) adv. na fali;
na wodzie bez steru zdany na los
adult ('aedalt) adj. dorosły;
dojrzały; s. osoba dorosła
adulterate (e'dalterejt) v.
fałszowac; podrabiac;zatruwac
adultery (e'daltery) s. cudzo-
łóstwo
advance (ed'waens) v. isc naprzód; pospieszac; awansowac;
przedkładac; popierac; pozy-
czac; adj. wysunięty; wczes-
niejszy; w przodzie
advanced (ed'waenst) adj. postępowy; swiatły; wysunięty
naprzód; stary; przedwczesny
advanced reservation (ed'waenst,
rezerwejszyn) rezerwacja
z góry zamówiona

advantage (ed'waentydż) s. korzysc; pożytek; przewaga
advantageous (,aedwa:n'tejdżes)
adj. korzystny; zyskowny
adverb ('aedwe:rb) s. przy-
słówek(oznaczający czas,sposób...)
adversary ('aedwersery) s.
przeciwnik; wróg; oponent
adverse ('aedwe:rs) adj. wrogi;
przeciwny; szkodliwy;niekorzystny
advertise ('aedwertajz) v.
ogłaszac; reklamowac
advertisement ('edwertysment)
s. ogłoszenie; reklama
advertising ('aedwertajzyng)s.
reklama; ogłoszenia handlowe
advice (ed'wajs) s. rada; in-
formacje;porada;pouczenie
advisable (ed'wajzebl) adj.
wskazany; rozsądny;ostrożny
advise (ed'wajz) v. radzic; po-
wiadamiac; pouczac
adviser (ed'wajzer) s. doradca;
radca(prawny etc.)
advocate ('aedwekejt) v. zalecac; bronic;s.rzecznik;orędownik
aerial ('eerjel) adj. powietrzny; s. antena (radiowa etc.)
aeronautics (eere'no:tyks) s.
aeronautyka; lotnictwo
aeroplane ('eereplejn) s. samolot
aesthetic (i:stetyk) adj.
estetyczny;wrażliwy na piękno
afar (e'fa:r) adv. daleko;z daleka
affair (e'feer) s. sprawa; interes; romans; przedsięwzięcie
affect (e'fekt) v. wpływac; oddziaływac;wzruszac;dotyczyc;udawac
affected (e'fektyd) adj. dotknięty;przejęty; sztuczny
affection (e'fekszyn) s. uczucie;
przywiązanie; choroba; miłość
affectionate (e'fekszynyt) adj.
czuły; kochający;tkliwy;przwiązany
affidavit (aef'ydejwyt) s. poręczenie pod przysięgą
affinity (e'fynyty) s. pokre-
wienstwo;przyciąganie;powinowactwo
affirm (e'fe:rm) v. potwierdzac; zapewniac;zaręczac

affirmation (,aefe:r'mejszyn) s. twierdzenie; oświadczenie; zapewnienie; zatwierdzenie(wyroku)
affirmative (e'fe:rmetyw) adj. pozytywny; twierdzący
afflict (e'flykt) v. gnębić
affliction (e'flykszyn) s. przygnębienie; choroba;ból;cierpienie
affluence ('aefluens) s. dostatek; bogactwo;obfitosc;natłok
affluent ('aefluent) adj. zamożny; s. dopływ (rzeki)
afford (e'fo:rd) v. zdobyć się; dostarczyć ; stać na coś
affront (e'frant) v. znieważać
afficionado (efisienado) s. entuzjasta (walki byków etc.)
aflame (e'flejm) adv. w ogniu; w podnieceniu
afraid (e'frejd) adj. przestraszony;wyrażający rezerwę
African ('aefryken) adj. afrykański
Afro ('aefro) s. (niby) styl afrykański (uczesania,ubioru)
after ('a:fte:r) prep. po; za; odnośnie; według;poniekąd
after all ('a:fte: o:l) prep. jednak; przecież;mimo wszystko
after that ('a:fte: ḍaet) następnie ; potem
afternoon ('a:fte:rnu:n) s. popopołudnie; adj. popołudniowy
afterwards ('aftełerdz) adv. później; potem; następnie
again (e'gen) adv. ponownie; znowu;na nowo;więcej;ponadto
again and again (e'gen end e'gen) wciąż; ciągle
against (e'genst) prep. przeciw; wbrew; na; pod;na wypadek
age (ejdż) s. wiek;stulecie;czas;
aged ('ejdżyd) adj. stary; sędziwy;wiekowy;w podeszłym wieku
age ten (ejdż ten) w wieku lat dziesięciu
agency ('ejdżensy) s. ajencja; działanie;pośrednictwo
agenda (e'dżende) s. agenda; lista ;porządek dzienny
agent ('ejdżent) s. pośrednik; ajent; czynnik ;przedstawiciel

aggravate ('aegrewejt) v. pogarszać; rozjątrzać ;denerwować
aggression (e'greszyn) s. napaść; agresja;napastliwość
aggressive (e'gresyw) adj. napastliwy; zaczepny;napastniczy
aggressor (e'grese:r) s. napastnik; agresor
aghast (e'gaest) adj. przerażony; osłupiały;skonsternowany
agile ('aedżyl) adj. zwinny; obrotny;zręczny;ruchliwy
agitate ('aedżytejt) v. poruszać; miotać; agitować
agitation (,aedżytejszyn) s. poruszenie; agitacja;podniecenie
agitator ('aedżytejter) s. agitator; mieszadło; trzęsarka
agnostic (aegnostyk) s. agnostyk; adj. agnostyczny
ago (e'gou) adv. przed; ...temu
agonize ('aegenajz) v. męczyć się; dręczyć się
agony ('aegeny) s. śmiertelna męka; agonia;katusze; spazm
agree (e'gri:) v. godzić się; zgadzać się; uzgadniać
agree about (e'gri: e'baut) v. zgadzać się co do...
agree to (e'gri: tu) v. zgadzać się na...
agreeable (e'gri:ebl) adj. zgodny; miły; chętny;sympatyczny
agreement (e'gri:ment) s. zgoda; umowa;porozumienie;układ
agricultural(,aegry'kalczerel) adj. rolniczy; rolny
agriculture (,aegry'kalczer) s, rolnictwo; uprawa ziemi
agriculturist (,aegry'kalczeryst) s. rolnik
ague ('ejgju:) s. febra; dreszcze;malaria; zimnica
ahead (e'hed) adv. naprzód; dalej; na przedzie;z przodu
aid (ejd) s. pomoc; pomocnik; v. pomagać; subwencjonować
aide (ejd) s. asystent;pomocnik
ailing ('ejlyŋg)s. choroba
aim (ejm) s. zamiar; cel; v. celować; mierzyć; zamierzać ;skierować;dążyć

aimless (ejmlys) adj. bezcelowy
air (eer) s. 1. powietrze;
2. mina; postawa;wygląd;nastrój
air ('eer) v. 1. wietrzyc;
2. obnosic się; nadawac
air base ('eerbejs) s. baza lotnicza (wojskowa)
air brake ('eer,brejk) s. hamulec na sprężone powietrze
air-conditioning (,eer-ken'dy-
szynyn) s. klimatyzacja
air compressor (,eer-kem'presor)
s. sprężarka
aircraft ('eer-kra:ft) s. samolot;lotnictwo(wiedza,flota etc.)
aircraft carrier ('eer-kra:ft'
kaerje:ṙ) s. lotniskowiec
airfield ('eer-fi:ld) s. lotnisko (do startowania i lądowania)
air force ('eer fo:rs) s. lotnictwo (wojskowe)
airline ('eerlajn) s. linia lotnicza (system transportu)
airmail ('eermejl) s. poczta
lotnicza
airplane ('eerplejn) s. samolot
airport ('eerpo:rt) s. lotnisko
air raid ('eerejd) atak lotniczy
air show ('eerszou) pokaz lotniczy
airsickness ('eersyknys) s.cho-
roba powietrzna
airtight ('eertajt) adj. hermetyczny
air traffic ('eer-traefyk) ruch
lotniczy(samolotów, pasażerów)
airway ('eerƚej) linia lotnicza
airy ('eery) adj. przewiewny
aisle (ajl) s. przejście; nawa
boczna(kościoła)
ajar (e'dża:r) adv. uchylony;
póƚ otwarty;nieco otwarty
akin (e'kyn) adj. pokrewny
alacrity (e'laekryty) s. ochota;
gotowosc; żwawość; skwapliwość
alarm (e'la:rm) s. popƚoch;
strach; sygnaƚ alarmowy;trwoga;
v. alarmowac; trwożyc;płoszyc
alarm clock (e'la:rm,klok) s.
budzik
alas ! (e'laes) excl. niestety
alcohol ('aelkehol) s. alkohol;
spirytus

alcoholic (,aelke'holyk) s.
alkoholik; adj.alkoholowy
alcove ('aelkouw) s. altanka;
alkowa; nisza
alder ('o:lder) s. olcha; ol-
sza
ale (ejl) s, piwo (gorzkie,
angielskie)
alert (e'le:t) adj. czujny;
raźny; żwawy; s.alarm
algae ('aeldżi:) pl. glony;
algi
alias ('ejliaes) adv. inaczej;
alias; vel; s. pseudonim
alibi ('aelybaj) s. alibi; wymówka; v.usprawiedliwiac się
alien ('ejljen) adj. obcy
alienate ('ejljenejt) v. od-
stręczac; odrywac; zrażac
alike (e'lajk) adj. jednakowy;
podobny; adv. tak samo; jedna-
ko; podobnie; zarówno; także
alimony ('aelimeny) s. alimenty
alive (e'lajw) adj. żywy; żyjący; ożywiony;peƚen życia
all (o:l) adj.& pron. caƚy;
wszystek; każdy; adv. caƚkowi-
cie; w peƚni; s. wszystko
all of us (o:l ow as) my
wszyscy; my wszyscy razem
all at once (o:l et Ɫans)wszys-
cy na raz; wszyscy jednocześnie
all the better (o:l dy betetṙ)
tym lepiej
all told (o:l told) wszystkiego
razem ; razem wziąwszy
alleged(e'ledżd) adj. rzekomy
alleviate (e'li:wjejt) v. ƚa-
godzić; zmniejszac
alley ('aely)s. aleja; przejscie; zauƚek; boczna ulica;tor
alliance (e'lajens) s. związek;
sojusz; powinowactwo;skoligacenie
allot (e'lot) v. przydzielac;
losowac; wyznaczac;wyasygnowac
allotment (e'lotment) s. przy-
dziaƚ; dziaƚka; asygnata
allow (e'lau) v. pozwalac; uży-
czac; uznawac; uwzględniac
allow for (e'lau fo:r) v.
uwzględniac; dawać (czas)
allowance (e'lauens) s. przy-
dziaƚ; pozwolenie; kieszonkowe

alloy ('aeloj) s. stop; próba;
domieszka;stop kilku metali
all—round (o:1-raund) adj.
wszechstronny; universalny
allude (e'lu:d) v. robić aluzje
allure (e'lju:) v. wabić; kusić;
oczarować;nęcić;znęcić;zwabić
allusion (e'lu:żyn) s. aluzja;
przymówka;przytyk;napomknienie
ally (e'laj) v. sprzymierzać
się; łączyć;połączyc;skoligacić
ally ('aelaj) s. sprzymierze-
niec; sojusznik
almighty (o:1'majty) adj.
wszechmogący;ogromny;straszliwy
almond ( am 'end) s. migdał
almost ('o:1moust) adv. prawie;
niemal;jak gdyby;o mało;ledwo
almost never ('o:1moust'newer)
prawie nigdy; rzadko kiedy
alms (a:mz) s, jałmużna
aloft (e'loft) adv. wysoko;hen;
w górze; w górę; do góry
alone (e'loun) adj. sam; samotny;w pojedynkę;sam jeden;jedyny
along (e'lo:ng) adv. naprzód;
wzdłuż; z sobą
alongside (e'lo:ngsajd) adv.
obok; wzdłuż ;przy(molu,burcie...)
aloof (e'lu:f) adv. z dala; na
uboczu; z daleka
aloud (e'laud) adv. głosno
alphabet ('aelfebyt) s. alfabet
already (o:1'redy) adv. już;
wcześniej;poprzednio;uprzednio
also (o:1sou) adv. także;również
altar ('o:1ter) s, ołtarz
alter ('o:1ter) v. zmieniać;
poprawiać;odmienić;przemienić
alteration (o:1te'rejszyn) s.
zmiana; poprawka;przemiana
alternate ('o:1ternejt) v. zmieniać się (kolejno);brać kolejno
alternate ('o:1ternyt) adj. co
drugi; na zmianę;kolejny
alternating current (o:1ternej-
tyngkarent) prąd zmienny
alternative (ol-ter'netyw) s.
alternatywa; adj.alternatywny
although (o:1zou) conj. chociaż
altitude ('aeltytju:d) s. wy-
sokość(nad poziomem morza)

altogether (o:1te'gedze:r) adv.
zupełnie; całkowicie
aluminum (e'lumynem) s.
aluminium
alumnus (e'lamnes) s. były
student uczelni
always ('o:1łejz) adv. stale;
zawsze;ciągle;wciąż
am (aem) v. jestem
amass (e'maes) v. gromadzić
amateur ('aemecze:r)s, miłośnik; amator;dyletant
amaze (e'mejz) v. zdumiewać;
zadziwiać;wprawić w zdumienie
amazement (e'mejzment) s. zdumienie; osłupienie
amazing (e'mejzyng)adj. zdumiewający; zadziwiający
ambassador (aem'baesede:r)s.
ambasador; poseł
amber ('aembe:r)s. bursztyn
ambient ('aembient) adj. ota-
czający
ambiguous (aem'bygjues) adj.
dwuznaczny;mętny;zagadkowy
ambition (aem'byszyn) s. ambicja;chęć wybicia się
ambitious (aem'byszes) adj.
ambulance ('aembjulens) s.
ambulans
ambush ('aembusz) s. zasadzka
amen (ej'men) amen
amend (e'mend) v. poprawiać
amendment (e'mendment) s. poprawa; ulepszenie; uzupełnienie
amends (e'mendz) s. odszkodowanie; zadosćuczynienie
American (e'meryken) s. Amerykanin; adj. amervkański
amiable ('ejmjebel) adj. miły;
uprzejmy; sympatyczny
amicable ('aemykebl) adj. po-
lubowny; przyjacielski
amid (e'myd) prep. wśrod; pośród; między; pomiędzy
amidst (e'mydst) prep. wśrod;
pośród; między; pomiędzy
amiss (e'mys) adv. na opak;
błędnie ; źle;niefortunnie
ammo ('aemou) s. amunicja
ammunition (,aemju'nyszyn) s.
amunicja

amnesty (aemnysty) s. ułaskawienie; amnestia
among (e'maŋg) prep. wśród; pomiędzy; między; pośród
amongst (e'maŋgst) prep. wsród;
pomiędzy; między; pośród
amount (e'maunt) v. wynosić;
s. suma; kwota; wynik
amount to (e'maunt tu) v. wy-
nosić(w sumie)
ample ('aempl) adj. rozległy;
dostatni;hojny;suty;obfity
amplifier ('aemplyfajer) v.
wzmacniacz; amplifikator
amplify ('aemplyfy) v. rozszerzać; wzmacniac; przesadzać
amplitude ('aemplytju:d) s.
amplituda; wielkość; obfitość
amply ('aemply) adv. obszernie;
szeroko;zupełnie wystarczajaco
amulet ('aemjulyt) s. amulet
amuse (e'mju:z) v. bawić;ubawić;
śmieszyć: zabawić;rozśmieszać
amusement (e'mju:zment) s. rozrywka; zabawa
amusing (e'mju:zyŋg)adj. zabawny: śmieszny
an (aen; en) art. jeden ;jakiś
anemia (e'ni:mja) s. anemia
anesthetic (e'nystetyk) s.
środek znieczulający
analogous (e'naeleges) adj.
analogiczny; zbieżny
analogy (e'naeledży) s. podobieństwo; analogia
analysis (e'naelysys) s. analiza
analyze (e'naelajz) v. analizo-
wać; rozpatrywać; zanalizować
anathema (e'naetyma) s, klątwa
anatomize (e'naetemajz) v. rozbierać; anatomizować
anatomy (e'naetemy) s. anatomia
ancestor ('aensester) s. przodek
ancestry ('aensestry) s. przod-
kowie; starożytność rodu
anchor ('aeŋker) s. kotwica
anchovy ('aenchewy) s. sardela
ancient ('ejnszent) adj. starodawny; stary;sędziwy;wiekowy
and (aend; end) conj. i; coraz
anecdote ('aenyk,dout)s. dykte-
ryjka ; anegdota

anew (e'nju:) adv. na nowo
angel ('ejndżl) s. anioł
anger ('eaŋger) s. gniew;
złość;v.gniewac;irytować
angina (aendżajna) s. angina
angle ('aeŋgl) s. kąt; narożnik; kątówka v. kluczyć
Anglican ('aeŋglyken) adj.
anglikański
Anglo-Saxon (aeŋglou'saeksen)
adj. anglo-saski
angry (aeŋgry) adj. zagniewany
anguish (aeŋgłysz) s. udręka;
męka;udręczenie;boleść;ból
angular ('aeŋgjuler) adj. kanciasty; narożny; kątowy; gra-
niasty
animal ('aenyml ) s. zwierzę;
stworzenie;adj.zwierzęcy
animate ('aenymejt) v. ożywiać;
adj. ożywiony; żywy
animated cartoon ('aenymejtyd
'ka:rtu:n) film rysunkowy;kres-
kówka
animation (,aeny'mejszyn) s.
ożywianie; ożywienie; żywość
animosity (,aeny'mosyty) s.
uraza; niechęć; animozja
ankle ('aeŋkl) s. kostka u stopy;staw między stopą i łydką
annex ('aeneks) v. przyłączać;
wcielać;s.przybudówka;załącznik
annihilate ('najelejt) v. unicestwić; niszczyć;niweczyć
anniversary (,aeny've:rsery) s.
rocznica adj. doroczny(obchód)
annotation (,aene'tejszyn) s.
uwaga; komentarz;przypis
announce (e'nauns) v. zapowiadać; ogłaszać;oznajmiać
announcement (e'naunsment) s.
zapowiedź; zawiadomienie
announcer (e'naunser) s.
1. zapowiadacz; 2. (radio)
speaker; konferansjer
annoy (e'noj) v. dokuczać;
drażnić; nękać;trapić;martwić
annoyance (e'nojens) s. udręka;
przykrość;irytacja ; kłopot
annoyed (e'nojd) adj. rozgnie-
wany; rozdrażniony;strapiony
annual ('aenjuel) adj. coroczy-
ny; s. rocznik;jednorocznik

annuity (e'njuyty) s. renta
roczna; renta dożywotnia
annul (e'nal) v. unieważniac;
anulowac; skasowac; kasować
anodyne ('aenedajn) s. anodyna;
środek od bólu ,łagodzący
anomalous (e'nomeles) adj. nienormalny; nietypowy
anonym ('aenenym) s. anonim
anonymous (e'nonymes) adj. bez-
imienny; anonimowy
another (e'nadzer) adj.& pron.
drugi;inny; jeszcze jeden
another time (e'nadzer,tajm)
kiedy indziej;innym razem
answer ('aenser) s. odpowiedź;
v. odpowiadac; spełnic(prosbę)
answer for ('aenser fo:r) v.
odpowiadać za(przed kimś)
ant (aent) s. mrówka
antagonist (aen'taegenyst) s.
przeciwnik; przeciwniczka
antagonize (aen'taege'najz) v.
zrażać; narażać; zwalczać
antelope ('aentyloup) s. anty-
lopa
anterior (aen'tierjer) adj. poprzedni;uprzedni;wcześniejszy
anthem ('aentem) s. hymn narodowy
anti ('aenty) pre . przeciw-
anti-aircraft ('aentaj'e:r-
kra:ft) adj. przeciwlotniczy
antibiotic ('aentybajotyk) s.
antybiotyk
antic ('aentyk) adj. dziwaczny;
groteskowy; s. figiel; dzi-
wactwa; błazeństwo
anticipate (aen'tysypejt) v.
przewidywać; uprzedzać
anticipation (aen'tysypejszyn)
s. uprzedzenie; przewidywanie;
przyspieszenie;oczekiwanie
anticlimax ('aenty'klajmaeks)
s. rozczarowanie; zawód
anticyclone (,aenty'sajkloun)
s. antycyklon; wyż(atmosf.)
antidote ('aentydout) s. odtrutka ; antidotum
antifreeze('aentyfri:z) s. mieszanka niemarznąca
antiknock ('aentynok) s. mieszanka przeciwstukowa

antipathy (aen'typety) s. odraza; niechęc (do kogoś)
antiquated ('aentykłejtyd) adj.
przestarzały; staroświecki
antique (aen'ti:k)adj.stary;
starożytny; staromodny
antiquity (aen'tykłyty) s. starożytność; zabytki
antiseptic (aenty'septyk) adj.
antyseptyk; przeciwgnilny
antlers ('aentlerz) pl. rogi
(np. jelenia)
anvil ('aenvyl) s. kowadło
anxiety (aeng'zajety) s. niepokój; troska; pożądanie
anxious ('aeŋkszes) adj. zaniepokojony; zabiegający;pragnący
anxious about ('aeŋkszes e'baut)
troskliwy o...;niepokojący się o...
anxious for ('aeŋkszes fo:r)
pragnący bardzo czegoś
anxious to ('aeŋkszes tu) pragnący żeby;mający ochotę na
any ('eny) pron. jakikolwiek;
któryś; jakiś;żaden;lada;byle
any farther ('eny fa:rdzer) trochę dalej;nieco dalej
any more ('eny mo:r) trochę
więcej; teraz; obecnie
anybody ('eny'body) pron. ktoś;
ktokolwiek; każdy; nikt
anyhow ('enyhau) adv. jakkolwiek
anyone ('enyłan) pron. ktokolwiek; każdy; ktoś; nikt
anything ('enytyng)pron. coś;
cokolwiek; wszystko(oprócz);nic
anything else ('enytyng els)
jeszcze coś; coś więcej
anyway ('enyłej) adv. w każdym
razie; jakkolwiek;byle jak
anywhere ('enyhłeer) adv.gdzie-
kolwiek;byle gdzie; nigdzie
apart (e'pa:rt) adv. osobno;
niezależnie;na boku;od siebie
apart from (e'pa:rt, from) niezależnie od...;poza;oprócz;prócz
apartment (e'pa:rtment) s.
mieszkanie; izba; pokój
apartment house (e'pa:rtment,
haus)blok mieszkalny;kamienica
apathetic (aepe'tetyk) adj.
apatyczny;obojętny;bez uczuć

ape (ejp) s. małpa (bezogonowa)
v. małpować;naśladować;błaznować
apex ('ejpeks) s. szczyt; czubek; wierzchołek
apiary ('ejpjery) s. pasieka
apiece (e'pi:s) adv. na osobę; od sztuki;za sztukę; każdy
aplomb (e'plom) s. pewność siebie; opanowanie; zimna krew
apologize (e'poledżajz) v. usprawiedliwiać; przepraszać
apology (e'poledży) s. usprawiedliwienie; obrona;przeprosiny
apoplexy ('aepepleksy) s. apopleksja ; udar
apostle (e'posl) s. apostoł
apostolic (,aepe'stolyk) adj. apostolski
apostrophe (e'postrefy) s. apostrof; apostrofa
appal (e'po:l) v. przerażać
apparatus (aepe'rejtes) s. aparat; urządzenie;przyrząd;organ
apparent (e'paerent) adj. jawny; pozorny; oczywisty;widoczny
appeal (e'pi:l) v. apelować; odwoływać się;uciekać się do
appeal to (e'pi:l tu) v. zwracać się do...;zwracać się z apelem
appear (e'pier) v. ukazywać się; zjawiać się;pokazywać się
appearance (e'pierens) s. wygląd; pozór; wystąpienie;zjawienie się
appease (e'pi:z) v. łagodzić; uśmierzać; zaspakajać;ugłaskać
append (e'pend) v. dołączać; doczepiać;dodawać;zawieszać
appendicitis (ependy'sajtys) s. zapalenie wyrostka robaczkowego
appendix (e'pendyks) s. dodatek; uzupełnienie;ślepa kiszka
appetite ('aepitajt) s. apetyt
appetizing ('aepitajzing) adj. apetyczny; smakowity
applaud (e'plo:d) v. oklaskiwać; klaskać;bic brawo;przyklasnąć
applause (e'plo:z) s. aplauz; oklaski;poklask;pochwała;aprobata
apple ('aepl) s. jabłko
apple-pie('aeplpaj) s. placek jabłkowy ; szarlotka

applesauce ('aepl so:s) s. purée z jabłek
apple tree ('aepltri:) s. jabłoń
appliance (e'plajens) s. przyrząd; urządzenie;akcesoria
applicant ('aeplykent) s. petent; zgłaszający się;kandydat
application (,aeply'kejszyn) s. podanie; użycie; zastosowanie;przykładanie;pilność
apply (e'plaj) v. używać; stosować; odnosić się;naciskać
apply for (e'plaj fo:r) v. starać się o..;wnosić podanie o
apply to (e'plaj tu) v. zwracać się do..;zgłaszać się do(o coś)
appoint (e'point) v. mianować; wyznaczać; ustanawiać;ustalić
appointment (e'pointment) s. nominacja; oznaczenie czasu i miejsca; umówione spotkanie
apportion (e'po:rszyn) v. wyznaczać; wydzielać;przydzielać
appreciate (e'pri:szjejt) v. cenić wysoko; zyskiwać na wartości;ocenić; oszacować;docenić
appreciation (e'pri:szjejszyn) s. ocena; uznanie; wzrost wartości;zrozumienie czegoś
apprehend (,aepry'hend) v. ująć; pojmać; rozumieć
apprehension (,aepry'henszyn) s. obawa; pojęcie; aresztowanie;lęk
apprehensive (,aepry'hensyw) adj.obawiający się; pojętny
apprentice (e'prentys) s. czeladnik; uczeń; terminator
apprenticeship (e'prentysszyp) s. termin;nauka rzemiosła
approach (e'proucz) v. zbliżać się; podchodzić;s. dostęp
approach road (e'proucz,roud) droga dojazdowa
appropriate (e'prouprjejt) adj. właściwy; odpowiedni;stosowny
appropriation (e'prouprejszyn) s. asygnowanie; przywłaszczenie;przeznaczenie; kredyty
approval (e'pru:wel) s. aprobata; uznanie; zatwierdzenie

approximate (e'proksymyt) adj.
zbliżony; przybliżony; mniej
więcej;v.zbliżać(się);być około
apricot ('ejprykot) s. morela
April ('ejprel) s. kwiecień
apron ('ejpren) s. fartuch;
płyta przednia;przedpole
apropos (aepre'pou) adv. do tego celu; w związku z tym ,,
apt (aept) v. mieć skłonność
apt to (aept tu) v. być skłon-
nym do...;często coś robić
aquarium (e'kłerjem) s. akwarium
aquatic (e'kłaetyk) adj. wodny
aquatic sports (e'kłaetyk
spo:rts) sport wodny
aqueduct ('aekłydakt) s. wodociąg; akwedukty rzymskie
aquiline ('aekłylajn) adj. orli
Arabic (ae'rebyk) adj. arabski
arable ('aerebl) adj. orny
arbitrary ('a:rbytrery) adj. dowolny; samowolny
arbor ('a:rber) s. altanka; wał
napędowy; oś maszyny; drzewo
arc (a:rk) s. łuk
arc lamp (a:rk lemp) lampa łu-
kowa
arcade (a:r'kejd) s. arkada;
podcienie
arch (a:rcz) s. łuk; sklepienie;
podbicie;v. tworzyć łuk
arch (a:rcz) adj.chytry; wierutny;
arcy...;figlarny
archaeologist (a:rky'oledżyst)
s. archeolog
archeology (a:rky'oledży) s.
archeologia
archaic (a:rkejyk) adj. archai-
czny; przestarzały; staroświecki
archangel ('a:rkejndżel) s.
archanioł
archbishop ('a:rczbyszep) s.
arcybiskup
archer ('a:rczer) s. łucznik
archery ('a:rczery) s. łucznic-
two; łuki i strzały
architect ('a:rkytekt) s. architekt;twórca;budowniczy
architecture ('a:rkytekczer) s.
architektura;styl budowy

archives ('a:rkajwz) pl. archi-
wa; archiwum
archway ('a:rczłej) s. skle-
pione przejście: brama
arctic ('a:rktyk) adj. arktycz-
ny; polarny
ardent ('a:rdent) adj. rozpalo-
ny; prażący;płonący;gorliwy
ardor ('a:rder) s. żar; żarliwość; gorliwość; zapał
arduous ('a:rdżues) adj. mozolny; wytrwały; stromy;żmudny
are (a:r) v. są ;jesteś;jesteście
area ('e:rje) s. obszar; zakres;
powierzchnia;teren;okolica;strefa
Argentine ('a:rdżentajn) adj.
argentyński
argot ('a:rgou) s. żargon
(złodziejski)
argue ('a:rgju:) v. wykazywać;
rozumować; spierać się; rozpatrywać; dowodzić;udowadniać
argument ('a:rgjument) s. argument; dowód; sprzeczka;spór
argumentation (,a:rgjumen'tejszyn) s. roztrząsanie; argu-
mentacja; rozumowanie
arid ('aeryd) adj. suchy; jałowy; oschły;wypalony;spieczony
arise, arose, arisen (e'rajz;
e'rouz; e'r:zn)
arise (e'rajz) v. powstawać;
wstawać; wynikać;nadarzyć się
arithmetic (,aeryt'metyk) s.
rachunki; adj. arytmetyczny;
rachunkowy
ark (a:rk) s. arka; skrzynia
arm (a:rm) s. ramię; odnoga;
konar; rękaw; poręcz
arm (a:rm) s. broń (rodzaj);
uzbrojenie; v. uzbroić; opan-
cerzyć; nastawiać (zapłon)
armament ('a:rmement) s. uzbrojenie; zbrojenia; siły zbrojne
armament race ('a:rmement, rejs)
wyścig zbrojeń
armchair (,a:rm'cze:r) s. fotel
armistice ('a:rmystys) s. zawieszenie broni;rozejm
armor ('a:rmer) s. zbroja;
opancerzenie;v.zbroić w płyty
pancerne;opancerzać

armored car ('a:rmerd,ca:r) samochód pancerny
arm-twisting ('a:rm,tłystyŋ) napór na (kogoś); (wykręcanie ręki);nagabywanie kogoś
arms ('a:rmz) pl. broń; uzbrojenie; herby; herb
army ('a:rmy) s. wojsko; armia
aroma (e'roume) s. aromat
arose (e'rouz) v. powstał; wstał; wynikł; zob. arise
around (e'raund) prep. dokoła; naokoło; wokoło; adv. wokół; tu i tam; około; wszędzie
arousal (e'rauzel) s. pobudzenie do czynu (działania)
arouse (e'rauz) v. pobudzić; budzić; wzniecać(uczucia)
arraign(e'rejn) v. pozwać; oskarżyć;atakować pogląd
arrange (e'rejndż) v. układać; szykować; porządkować;ustalać
arrangement (e'rejndżment) s. układ; ułożenie się; urządzenie; zaaranżowanie;porządek;szyk
array (e'rej) v. szykować; przybrać; rozmieszczać; s. szyk; szereg; uszeregowanie;wystawa
arrears (e'rierz) pl. zaległości; długi;zaległe prace(płatności)
arrest (e'rest) s. areszt; aresztowanie; zatrzymanie; v. aresztować; zatrzymywać; wstrzymywać;przyciągać(uwagę)
arrival (e'rajwel) s. przyjazd; przybysz; rzecz nadeszła
arrive (e'rajw) v. przybyć; dojść; osiągnąć;wspólnie ustalać
arrive at (e'rajw,aet) v. dojść do...;wspólnie ustalać
arrogance ('aeregens) s. zarozumiałość; buta; arogancja
arrogant ('aeregent) adj. butny; arogancki; wyniosły
arrow ('aerou) s. strzała; strzałka (kierunkowa)
arrow head ('aerou hed) s. grot
arse (a:rs) s. vulg. rzyć; zadek; dupa ; dupsko
arsenal ('a:rsynl) s. arsenał
arsenic ('a:rsnyk) s. arszenik; arsen; ('a:rsenyk) adj. arsenowy

arson ('a:rsen)s. podpalenie (zbrodnia); podpalanie
art (a:rt) s. sztuka; chytrość; zręczność; rzemiosło;fortel
arterial (a:r'tyerjal) adj. tętniczy; magistralny
arterial road(a:r'tyerjal,roud) magistrala;główna szosa
artery (a:rtery) s. arteria; tętnica; arteria ruchu
artful ('a:rtful) adj. chytry; zręczny; pomysłowy;dowcipny
article ('a:rtykl) s. rodzajnik; artykuł; warunek;paragraf;temat
articulate (a:rtykjulejt) v. wyrażać jasno; adj. artykułowany; wyraźny;stawowy
artifact (,a:rty'faekt) s. wytwór ludzkiej ręki
artificial(,a:rty'fyszel) adj. sztuczny;udany;symulowany
artillery (a:r'tylery) s. artyleria
artisan ('a:rtyzaen) s. rzemieślnik
artist ('a:rtist) s. artysta; artystka
artiste (a:r'ty:st) s. artysta; odtwórca; artysta estradowy
artless ('artlys) adj. niewinny; niedołężny;szczery;otwarty
as (aez; ez) adv. pron. conj; jak; tak; co; jako; jaki; skoro; żeby; choć; z (dniem)
as... as (ez...ez) tak jak
as far as (ez fa:r ez) co do
as many (ez meny) tak wiele
as well (ez łel) również
as well as (ez łel ez) jak także ; tak jak; jak również
as for (ez fo:r) co się tyczy
asbestos (aez'bestes) s. azbest
ascend (e'send) v. piąć się; iść w górę; wznosić się; wracać w przeszłość; wstępować
ascension (e'senszyn) s. wznoszenie się; Wniebowstąpienie
ascent (e'sent) s. wzlot; wzrost;stok; postęp;wchodzenie
ascertain (aeser'tejn) v. stwierdzać; ustalać;konstatować
ascetic (e'setyk) s. asceta; adj. ascetyczny;odmawiający sobie

ascribe (e'skrajb) v. przypisywać; przypisać(coś komuś)
aseptic ('eseptyk) adj. jałowy;
wyjałowiony; aseptyczny
ash (aesz) s. popiół ;jesion
ashamed (e'szejmd) adj. zawstydzony ;zażenowany
ashamed of (e'szejmd ow)adj.
wstydzący się czegoś
ash can (aesz kaen) wiadro na
śmieci; wiadro na popiół
ashen ('aeszen) adj. popielaty
ashes ('aeszyz) s. popioły
ashore (e'szo:r) adv. na brzeg;
na brzegu ; na ląd; na lądzie
ashtray ('aesztrej) s. popielniczka
Ash Wednesday (,aesz'łenzdy) -
Środa Popielcowa
Asiatic (,ej ży'atyk) adj. azja-
tycki
aside (e'sajd) adv. na stronę;
na stronie; na boku;na uboczu
aside from (e'sajd,from) adv.
oprócz; z wyjątkiem; poza;prócz
asinine ('aesynajn) adj. ośli;
głupi; idiotyczny
ask (ae:sk) v. pytać ;zapytywać
ask a question ('ae:sk ej'kłesz-
czyn) stawiać pytanie; pytać
ask to dinner ('ae:sk tu'dyner)
zapraszać na obiad
ask for ('ae:sk fo:r) prosić o...
askance (es'kaens) adv. z ukosa;
zezem ; niepewnie; podejrzliwie
askew (es'kju:) adv. krzywo;
skośnie ; z ukosa
aslant (e'sla:nt) adv. ukośnie;
skośnie ; na ukos; w poprzek
asleep (e'sli:p) adv. we śnie;
adj. śpiący;zdrętwiały;ścierpły
asparagus (es'paereges) s. szparag
aspect ('aespekt) s. aspekt; wygląd; wyraz; faza; postać;
strona;mina;przejaw;wystawa domu
aspen ('aespen) s. osika; osina
asphalt ('aesfo lt) s. asfalt
aspire (es'pajer) v. dążyć; marzyć; wzdychać do...
aspire after (es'pajer'a:fter)
aspirować; dążyć do (czegoś);
mieć aspiracje żeby...

ass (aes) s. osioł;wulg.: dupa
assail (e'sejl) v. napadać;
przystępować;atakować;uderzać
assailant (e'sejlent) s. napastnik
assassin (e'saesyn) s. morderca (najęty); zamachowiec
assassinate (e'saesynejt) v.
zamordować; dokonać zamachu
assassination (e,saesy'nejszyn)
s. morderstwo;zabójstwo;zamach
assault (e'sa:lt) s. napad;
atak; zgwałcenie;v.atakować;bić
assemblage (e'semblydż) s. zebranie; zbiór; zmontowanie
assemble (e'sembl) v. zbierać;
montować;nagromadzać;złożyć
assembly (e'sembly) s. zebranie; zbiórka; montaż
assembly line (e'sembly,lajn)
taśma montażowa;linia montażowa
assent (e'sent) s. zgoda; pogodzenie się;v.zgadzać się;uznawać
assent to (e'sent tu) v. zgadzać się na coś;zatwierdzać coś
assert (e'se:rt) v. twierdzić;
upominać się;dowieść;stawiać się
assess (e'ses) v. szacować;
oceniać; wymierzać; opodatkować;nałożyć podatek
assets ('aesets) pl. własność;
aktywa; wartościowi pracownicy
assign (e'sajn) v. przydzielać;
ustalać; odnosić; przekazywać
assignment (e'sajnment) s. przy-
dzielenie; przypisanie; przekazanie;przydział;podział
assimilate (e'symylejt) v. upodabniać;wcielać; wchłaniać;
asymilować;przyswajać sobie
assist (e'syst) v. pomagać;
brać udział; być przy
assistance (e'systens) s. pomoc;
asysta; wsparcie
assistant (e'systent) s. asystent; pomocnik;adj.pomocniczy
assizes (e'sajzyz) pl. okresowe
sesje sądu (wyjazdowe)w Anglii
associate (e'souszjejt) s. towarzysz; wspólnik-sprzymierze-
niec; rzecz związana z czyms
v. łączyć;obcować ; kojarzyć;
brać do spółki;adj.towarzyszący

association (e,sous,zy'ejszyn) s.
łączenie; współpraca; kojarzenie; przyłączanie się ;związek
assort (e'so:rt) v. sortować;
dobierać; obcować; klasyfikować
assorted (e'so:rtyd) adj. dobrany; posortowany; mieszany
assortment (e'so:rtment) s.
asortyment; wybór; sortowanie
assume (e'sju:m) v. zakładać;
obejmować; przybierać; przypuszczać ;wdziewać;udawać
assurance (e'szu:rens) s. zapewnienie; pewność; ubezpieczenie
assure (e'szu:r) v. zapewniać;
ubezpieczać; zabezpieczać
assured (e'szu:rd) adj. pewny
(siebie); s. ubezpieczony
asthma (aesma) s. dusznica;
astma ; dychawica
astigmatic (,aestyg'maetyk) adj.
astygmatyczny
astir (e'ste:r) adv. poruszony;
w ruchu; na nogach ;ożywiony
astonish (es'tonysz) v. zadziwiać; zdumiewać ;zdziwić
astonished (es'tonyszt) adj.
zdumiony ; bardzo zdziwiony
astonishment (es'tonyszment) s.
zdumienie ; zdziwienie
astray (es'trej) adv. na błędną
drogę; na bezdrożu ;na manowce
astride (es'trajd) adv. okrakiem;
rozstawionymi nogami
astringent (es'tr,ndżent) adj.
ścigający; surowy ;wstrzymujący
astrodome('aestre,doum)s. astro-
kopuła (nad stadionem sportowym)
astrologer (es'troledżer) s.
astrolog
astronaut ('aestreno:t) s. astro-
nauta
astute (es'tu:t) adj. bystry;
przebiegły ;wnikliwy
asunder (e'sander) adv. oddziel-
nie; na boki; na strony
asylum (e'sajlem) s. azyl; schronisko ; przytułek; schronienie
at (aet; et) prep. w; na; u;
przy; pod; z ;za; do; o; po
ate (ejt) v. jadłem; jadłeś; jadł
etc; zob. eat

athlete ('aetli:t) s. atleta;
siłacz; sportowiec
athletic ('aet'letyk) adj.
atletyczny; sportowy
athletics (aet'letyks) pl.atle-
tyka; sport;wychowanie fizyczne
Atlantic (et'laentyk) adj.
atlantycki
atlas ('aetles) s. atlas
atmosphere('aetmesfier) s.
atmosfera ;otoczenie;nastrój
atoll ('aetol) s, atol
atom ('aetem) s. atom
atom bomb ('aetem bom) s. bomba atomowa
atomic (e'tomyk) adj. atomowy
atomic age (e'tomyk ejdż)
epoka atomowa
atomic pile (e'tomyk pajl)
stos atomowy
atomic weight (e'tomyk łejt)
ciężar atomowy
atomize ('aetemajz) v. rozbijać
na atomy ; rozpylać
atomizer ('aetemajzer) s. rozpylacz (cieczy)
atone (e'toun) v. odpokutować;
okupić; załagodzić
atrocious (e'trouszes) adj.
potworny; okropny ;skandaliczny
atrocity (e'trosyty) s. okrucieństwo ;okrutny czyn;ohyda
attach (e'taecz) v. przywiązywać; przyczepiać; przydzielać;
łączyć ;przymocowywać;nalepiać
attachment (e'taeczment) s. załącznik; przymocowanie ;więź
attack (e'taek) v. napadać;
atakować; s. atak; uderzenie
attempt (e'tempt) v. usiłować;
czynić zamach; próbować
s. próba; usiłowanie; zamach
attend (e'tend) v. uczęszczać;
leczyć; obsługiwać ;towarzyszyć
attendance (e'tendens) s. obsługa; opieka; uczęszczanie
attendant (e'tendent) s. obecny; służący ;adj.towarzyszący
attention (e'tenszyn) s. uwaga;
uprzejmość ;troska;opieka
attentive (e'tentyw) adj. uważny; gorliwy; uprzejmy ;pilny

attest (e'test) v. poświadczyć;
stwierdzać;zalegalizować
attic ('aetyk) s. poddasze;
attyka; strych
attitude ('aetitu:d) s. postawa; ustosunkowanie się;poza
attorney (e'te:rny) s. pełnomocnik; adwokat;prawnik
attract (e'traekt) v. przyciągać;zwabić; być pociągającym
attraction (e'traekszyn) s.
przyciąganie;powab;urok;atrakcja
attractive (e'traektyw) adj. pociągający;przyciagajacy; miły
attribute ('aetrybju:t) s, przymiot; cecha;właściwość
attribute (e'trybju:t) v. przypisywać komuś; odnosić do czegoś
attrition (e'tryszyn) s. wy-
niszczenie; ścieranie; skrucha
auburn ('o:bern) adj. (barwa)
kasztanowa; złotobrązowa
auction ('o:kszyn) s. licytacja;
aukcja
auction off ('o:kszyn of) v.
licytować; sprzedawać na licytacji;wystawiać na licytację
audacious (o:'dejszes) adj. odważny; śmiały; zuchwały
audacity (o:'daesyty) s. śmiałość; odwaga; zuchwałość
audible ('o:dybel) adj. słyszalny;odbierany słuchem
audience ('o:djens) s. publiczność; audiencja
audit ('o:dyt) s. sprawdzenie
rachunków; rozliczenie;
v. kontrolować rachunki
aught (a:t) s. coś; nic; zero
August ('o:gest) s, sierpień
august ('o:gast) adj. wyniosły;
dostojny;majestatyczny
aunt (aent) s. ciotka; wujenka;
stryjenka
aurora (o:'ro:re) s. brzask;
jutrznia; jutrzenka; zorza po-
larna
austere (o:s'tier) adj. surowy;
poważny; prosty;czysto użytkowy
austerity (o:s'teryty) s. surowość; powaga; prostota;srogość;
charakter czysto użytkowy

Australian (o:s'trejljen) adj.
australijski
Austrian ('o:strjen) adj.
austriacki;s. Austryjak
authentic (o:'tentyk) adj.
autentyczny; prawdziwy
author ('o:ter) s. autor; pisarz; sprawca
authoritative (o:'torytejtyw)
adj. stanowczy; miarodajny
authority (o:'toryty) s. władza; autorytet; znaczenie;
powaga;moc rozkazywania
authorize ('o:terajz),v. upoważniać; zatwierdzać;aprobować
authorship ('o:terszyp) s.
autorstwo;zawod pisarza
autobiography ('o:tebaj'ogrefy)
s. autobiografia
autograph ('o:tegraef) s. podpis; autograf
automat ('o:temaet) n . restauracja z automatem na monety
automatic (,o:te'maetyk) adj.
automatyczny; machinalny
automation (,o:te'mejszyn) s.
automatyzacja
automobile ('o:temeby:l) s. samochód; auto
autumn ('o:tem) s. jesień
auxiliary (o:g'zyljery) adj.
pomocniczy
avail (e'wejl) v. pomagać;
znaczyć; być przydatny
available (e'wejlebl) adj.
dostępny; osiągalny
avalanche ('aewelaencz) s. lawina; v. spadać lawiną
avarice ('aewerys) s. chciwość;
skąpstwo
avaricious (,aewe'ryszes) adj.
chciwy; skąpy
avenue ('aewynju:)s. bulwar;
aleja;ulica;dojazd;dojście
average ('aewerydż) adj. przeciętny; średni; s. średnia;
przeciętna; v. osiągać średnio; obliczać średnią; wy-
pośrodkowywać;pracować średnio..
averse (e'we:rs) adj. niechętny; czujący odrazę;przeciwny
aversion (e'werżyn) s. odraza;
niechęć

avert (e'we:rt) v. odwracać
(np. myśli; oczy); oddalić(cios)
aviation (,ejwy'ejszyn) s. lotnictwo
aviator ('ejwyejter) s.lotnik
avid ('ewyd) adj. chciwy; zachłanny
avoid (e'woyd) v. unikać; uchylać się; stronić
avow (e'wau) v. wyznawać
avowal (e'wauel) s. wyznanie;
przyznanie się; zeznanie
await (e'łejt) v. czekać; oczekiwać;być a oczekiwaniu
awake; awoke; awoke (e'łejk;
e'łouk; e'łouk)
awake (e'łejk) v. budzić się;
otwierać oczy na...; adj. czujny; przebudzony; na jawie
awaken (e'łejkn) v. budzić;
uświadamiać komus (kogoś)
award (e'ło:rd) v. przysądzać;
wyznaczać; s. nagroda; zapłata; grzywna sądowa
aware (e'łeer) adj. świadomy
away (e'łej) adv. precz; z dala
awe (o:) s. lęk; nabożna część
awful ('o:ful) adj. straszny;
budzący lęk i szacunek
awhile ('ehłajl) adv. na krótko;
przez chwilę;chwilę; króciutko
awkward ('o:kłerd) adj. niezgrabny; niezdarny; kłopotliwy;
nieporęczny;zaklopotany;trudny
awning ('o:nyŋg)s. dach z płot-
na; markiza; zasłona; stora
awoke (e'łouk) v. zbudzony;
zob. awake
awry (e'raj) adv. skośnie; krzywo; na opak; adj. krzywy; błędny; opaczny; wypaczony
ax (aeks) s. siekiera; topor;
v. obcinać siekierą;redukować
axe (aeks) = ax
axes (aeksyz) pl. osie;siekiery
axis ('aeksys) s. oś ;oska
axle ('aeksel) s. oś (koła);
oska(łącząca tylnie koła wozu)
azimuth ('aezymet) s. azymut
azure ('aeżer) s. błękit; lazur;
adj. błękitny; lazurowy

b (bi) b; druga litera alfabetu angielskiego
babble ('baebl) v. paplać; gadać; s. paplanina; gadanina
babe (bejb) s. niemowlę
baboon (be'bu:n) s. pawian
baby ('bejby) s. niemowlę
baby carriage ('bejby kaerydż)
s. wozek dziecinny
babyhood ('bejbyhud) s. nie-
mowlęctwo
bachelor ('baecheler) s. niezamężna; nieżonaty; stopien
uniwersytecki (najniższy)
back (baek) s. tył; grzbiet;
v. cofać się; wycofać się
backbone ('baekboun) s. kręgosłup; stos pacierzowy
back.door ('baek'do:r) s. tylne
drzwi;adj.zakulisowy;potajemny
backfire ('baek'fajer) s. wybuch odwrotny; zawisc; v.
spalić na panewce
background ('baekgraund) s. tło;
dalszy plan; przeszłość czyjaś
back. number('baeknamber)s. zaległy numer;stare wydanie pisma
backseat ('baek'si:t) s. tylne
siedzenie;wycofanie się z akcji
backstairs ('baeksteerz) s.
tylne schody;adj.zakulisowy
backstroke ('baek'strouk) s.
pływanie na plecach; rzut
odbity od lewa w tenisie
back tire ('baek'tajer) s. tylna
opona samochodowa (slang)
backward ('baekłerd) adj. tylny; zacofany;zapóźniony
backwards ('baekłerds) adv.
w tyle; odwrotnie; do tyłu
back wheel('baekhłil) s. tylne
koło (samochodu,ciężarówki)
bacon ('bejkn) s. słonina; bo-
czek; bekon
bacon and eggs ('bejkn end egz)
jajka z boczkiem
bacterium (baek'tierjem) s.
bakteria
bacteria (baek'tierje) pl.
bakterie
bad (baed) adj. zły; niedobry;
przykry;sfałszowany;słaby;zdrożny

bade (baed) v. proponował; oferował cenę; kazał; zob.: bid
badge (baedź) s. odznaka; oznaka (członkostwa, rangi etc.)
badger ('baedżer) s. borsuk; v. zadręczać (narzekaniem)
badly ('baedly) adv. źle; bardzo badly wounded ('baedl 'Żu:ndyd) ciężko ranny ;ciężko zraniony
badminton ('baedmynten) s. rodzaj tenisa (piłka z piórkiem)
bad mouth('baedmaus) v. oczerniać; obgadywać; obmawiać
baffle ('baefl) v. udaremniać; łudzić ;niveczyć;s.przegroda
bag (baeg) s. torba; worek; babsztyl; v. pakować; zwędzić
baggage ('baegydź) s. bagaż
baggage check ('baegydż,czek) kwit bagażowy
baggy ('baegy) adj. workowaty
bag-pipe ('baegpajp) s. kobza
bail (bejl) s. kaucja; poręka
bail out (bejl'ałt) v. zwolnić za kaucją ;wywinąć się z opresji
bailiff ('bejlyf) s. woźny sądowy; komornik ;rządca majątku
bait (bejt) s. przynęta; pokusa
bake (bejk) v. piec; wypalać
baker ('bejker) s. piekarz
bakery (bejkery) s. piekarnia
baking powder ('bejkyŋ,pałder) proszek do pieczenia
balance ('baelens) s. waga; bilans; równowaga; v. równoważyć; bilansować ; wahać się
bald (bo:ld) adj. łysy ;jawny
bale (bejl) s. zwój płótna; bela; v. zob. bail
balk (bo:k) v. opierać się; przeszkadzać; zniechęcać; s. belka ;miedza; zawada .
ball (bo:l) s. 1. piłka; pocisk; kłębek; 2. bal;zabawa taneczna
ballad ('baeled) s. ballada; pieśń (sentymentalna opisowa)
ballast ('baelest) s. balast; v. obciążać balastem
ball bearing ('bo:l'bearyŋ) łożysko kulkowe
ballet ('baelej) s. balet ; zespół baletowy(tancerzy)

ball game('bo:lgejm) s. rozgrywka; gra w piłkę
ballistic (be'lystyk)adj. balistyczny
balloon (be'lu:n) s. balon
ballot ('bealet) s. (tajne) głosowanie; kartka; v. tajnie głosować
ballot box ('baeletboks) s. urna wyborcza
ball-point pen ('bo:l-pointpen) s. kulkowy pisak;długopis
balm (ba:m) s. balsam
balmy ('ba:my) adj. błogi; balsamiczny
balustrade (,baeles'trejd) s. poręcz; balustrada
bamboo (baem'bu:) s. bambus
ban (baen) s. zakaz; klątwa; v. zabraniać;wyjąć spod prawa
banana (be'na:ne) s. banan
band (baend) s. szajka; kapela; taśma; v. wiązać się; przepasywać opaską ;zrzeszać
bandage ('baendydź) s. bandaż; v. bandażować ; obandażować
bandmaster ('baend,ma:ster) s. kapelmistrz
bandstand ('baendstaend) s. estrada
bang (baeŋ) s. huk; zryw; uciecha; bęc; v. trzaskać ;walnąć
banish ('baenysz) v. wygnać; usunąć; wykluczać ;wypędzać
banishment ('baenyszment) s. wygnanie ; banicja
banisters ('baenystez) pl. banistry (schodów); poręcze
banjo ('baendżou) s. rodzaj gitary okrągłej pokrytej skórą
bank ('baeŋk) s.1.brzeg;łacha;nasyp; szkarpa; 2. bank; 3. stoł roboczy; 4. rząd 5.nachylenie toru v. 1. prowadzić bank; 2. składać w banku; 3. piętrzyć; pochylać; 4. polegać 5.obwałować
bank bill ('baeŋk,byl) s. banknot
banker ('baeŋker) s. bankier
banking ('baeŋkyŋg)s. bankowość
bank note('baeŋknout) s. banknot ; papierowy pieniądz

bankrate ('baeŋkrejt) s. stopa dyskontowa; stopa procentowa
bankrupt ('baeŋkrept) s. bankrut
banner ('baener) s. chorągiew; transparent; tytuł (czołowy)
banns (baenz) pl. zapowiedzi
banquet ('baenkłyt) s. bankiet
baptism ('baeptyzem) s. chrzest
baptize ('baeptajz) s. chrzcić
bar (ba:r) s. belka; drąg; rogatka; krata; v. zagradzać; hamować; prep.: oprócz
bar (ba:r) s. 1. izba adwokacka, sądowa; 2. bar; bufet z wyszynkiem ;szynkwas
barb (ba:rb) s. haczyk; docinek; kolec; skaza (na odlewie);szew
barbarian (ba:r'bearjen) s. barbarzyńca; adj. barbarzyński
barbed wire ('ba:rbd,łajer) drut kolczasty
barber ('ba:rber) s. fryzjer (męski); golibroda
barbiturate (ba:r'byczeret) s. lek uspakajający ;nasenny lek
bare (beer) adj. nagi; goły; łysy; v. obnażać ;odkrywać
barefoot ('beerfut) adj.& adv. boso; bosy
bareheaded ('beerhedyd) adj. z gołą głową
barely ('beerly) adv. ledwie; otwarcie; ubogo; zaledwie
bargain ('ba:rgyn) s. ubicie targu; dobre kupno;,v. targować się; spodziewać się
barge (ba:rdż) s. barka; v. pakować się; trynić się
bark (ba:rk) s. 1. kora; 2. szczeknięcie; v. zdzierać korę; garbować korę; szczekać; pyskować; kaszleć;warkliwie mówić; wyszczekać; zakaszleć
barley ('ba:rly) s. jęczmień
barmaid ('ba:rmejd) f. bufetowa; kelnerka; szynkarka
barn (ba:rn) s. stodoła; stajnia; obora; wozownia ;remiza
barometer(be'romyter) s. barometr
barracks ('baereks) pl. koszary; baraki; budyn'-i koszarowe etc.;
wygwizdywanie (zawodników,graczy)

barrel ('baerel) s. beczka; lufa; rura;cylinder;walec;bęben
barren ('baeren) adj. jałowy; wyczerpany;nieurodzajny
barricade (,baery'kejd) s. barykada; v. barykadować się
barrier ('baerjer) s. zapora; zastawa; rogatka;ogrodzenie
barrister ('baeryster) s. adwokat;adwokatka;obrońca;obrończyni
barrow ('baerou) s. taczki
bartender ('ba:rtender) s. barman; bufetowy;bufetowa;barmanka
barter ('ba:rter) v. wymieniać; handlować; s. handel wymienny
base (bejs) n. podstawa; nasada; adj. podły; nędzny; niski
baseball ('bejsbo:l) s. palant amerykański(grany piłką i maczugą)
baseless ('bejslys) adj. bezpodstawny;nieuzasadniony
basement ('bejsment) s. suterena; piwnica ;podziemie
bashful ('baeszful) a. wstydliwy;nieśmiały;trwożliwy;lękliwy
basic ('bejsyk) a. podstawowy; zasadniczy ;zasadowy
basin ('bejsn) s. miednica; zbiornik; dorzecze; zagłębie
basis ('bejsys) pl. fundamenty; podstawy;podłoże;grunt;zasada
bask (baesk) v. wygrzewać się na słońcu;wylegiwać się;pławić się
basket ('ba:skyt) s. kosz; koszyk;v. wrzucać do kosza
basketball ('ba:skytbo:l) s. koszykówka; piłka do koszykówki
bass (bejs) s. bas (głos,śpiewak)
bass (baes) s. okoń; łyko lipowe ; okoń morski lub rzeczny
bastard ('baesterd) s. bękart; bastard;adj. nieślubny;nędzny
baste (bejst) v. fastrygować; polewać tłuszczem pieczeń
bat (baet) s. nietoperz; maczuga; kij;v. mrugać; hulać(slang)
bath (ba:s) s. kąpiel; łazienka
bathe (bejz) v. kąpać; moczyć;
bathing (bejzyŋg)s. kąpanie
bathing cap ('bejzyŋgkaep) czapka kąpielowa

bathing suit ('bejzyŋ sju:t)
strój kąpielowy;kostjum kąpielowy
bathing trunks ('bejzyŋ traŋks)
spodenki kąpielowe
bathrobe ('ba:zroub) s. płaszcz
kąpielowy
bathroom ('ba:zru:m) s. łazienka;ubikacja;ustęp;klozet
bath towel ('ba:z tałel) ręcznik kąpielowy
bathtub ('ba:ztab) s. wanna
baton ('baeton) s. buława; pałka;batuta;pałeczka dyrygenta
battalion (be'taeljen) s. batalion ;pododdział pułku
batter ('baeter) v. tłuc; walić
battered ('baeterd) adj. pobity
battery ('baetery) s. bateria;
komplet; pobicie;zestaw armat
battle ('baetl) s. bitwa ;walka
battleship ('baetlszyp) s. okręt
wojenny
baulk (bo:k) s. przeszkoda;
rozczarowanie;v.przeszkadzać
bawl (bo:l) v. wrzeszczeć; drzeć
się; krzyczeć; zwymyślać
bay (bej) adj. czerwono-brązowy;
gniady (koń); wawrzyn;laur
bay (bej) s. zatoka; wnęka;
przęsło; v. ujadać ; wyć
bay window ('bej'łyndoł) okno
we wnęce
bazaar(be'za:r) s. bazar
be; was; been (bi:; łoz; bi:n)
be (bi:) v. być; żyć; trwać;
dziać się ;istnieć;stawać się
beatnik (bi:tnyk) s. nonkonfor-
mista; (-tka)
be reading (bi:'ry:dyŋ) czytać
właśnie;być w trakcie czytania
beach (bi:cz) s. brzeg; plaża
beachhead ('bi:czhed) s. przyczółek (nad wodą)
beachwear ('bi:człe:r) s.odzież
plażowa ;kostiumy,plaszcze etc.
beacon ('bi:ken) s. sygnał (og-
niowy); latarnia morska
bead (bi:d) s. paciorek; kora-
lik; v. nawlekać korale; per-
lić się ;ozdabiać paciorkami
beak (bi:k) s. dziób ; belfer

beam (bi:m) s. belka; dźwigar;
promień; radosny uśmiech
v.promieniować; nadawać sygnał; rozpromieniać się
bean (bi:n) s. fasola; bób;
ziarnko; łeb; animusz
bear; bore; borne (beer; bo:r;
bo:rn)
bear (beer) s. niedźwiedź;
v. dźwigać; ponosić; znosić;
trzymać się ; rodzić;miec(podpis)
beard (bierd) s. broda (zarost)
bearer ('beerer) s. nosiciel;
okaziciel; zwiastun;karawaniarz
bearing ('beeryŋg)s. zachowanie;
wzgląd; wspornik; rodzenie;łożysko
beast (bi:st) s. bestia; bydle
beastly ('bistly) adj. bydlęcy;
potworny;adv.straszliwie;okrutnie
beast of prey ('bi:st ow prej)
s. drapieżnik
beat; beat; beaten (bi:t; bi:t;
bi:tn)
beat (bi:t) v. bić; bić się;
ubijac ;tłuc;trzepotać;zbić;kuć
beat it ! ('bi:t,yt) excl.:
precz !wynoś się! wynoście się !
beaten ('bi:tn) adj. ubity; wy-
deptany; wyczerpany; znany
beautiful ('bju:teful) adj.
piękny;cudny;wspaniały;swietny
beautify ('bju:tyfaj) v.upięk-
szać; upiększyć
beauty ('bju:ty) s. piękność;
piękno ;uroda;piekna kobieta
beauty parlor ('bju;ty'pa:rler)
salon kosmetyczny
beaver ('bi:wer) s. bóbr;
przedsiębiorczy człowiek
because (bi'ko:z) conj. dlatego; że; gdyż; adv. z powodu
beckon('beken) v. skinąć; nęcić; s. skinienie
become; became; become (bi'kam;
bi'kejm; bi'kam)
become (bi'kam) v. stawać się;
nadawać się ;zostawać kims(czyms)
becoming ('bikamyŋg)adj. stosowny; odpowiedni;twarzowy
bed (bed) s. łoże; łożysko;klomb;
grządka; ławica ;podkład;nocleg

bedclothes ('bedklouz) s. pos´-
ciel; przescieradła,kołdry etc.
bedding ('bedyng)s. pościel
bed linen ('bed,lynyn) s. pościel ;bielizna pościelowa
bedridden ('bed,rydn) adj. obłożnie chory ;złożony chorobą
bedroom ('bedrum) s. sypialnia
bedside ('bedsajd) przy łożu
bedsore ('bedso:r) s. odleżyna
bedtime ('bedtajm) s. pora do
spania ;pora snu
bee (bi:) s. pszczoła
beech (bi:cz) s. buk ;adj.bukowy
beef (bi:f) s. wołowina; siła;
narzekanie ;wyrzekanie(slang)
beefsteak ('be:f'stejk) s. befsztyk (do smażenia lub pieczenia)
beefy ('bi:fy) adj. krzepki;
flegmatyczny ;muskulary
beehive ('bi:hajw) s. ul
beekeeper ('bi:kiper) s. pszczelarz
beeline ('bi:lajn) s. najkrótsza
droga ;linia powietrzna
been (bi:n) v. były, zob. be
beer (bier) s. piwo
beet (bi:t) s. burak
beetle ('bi:tl) s. tłuczek; ubijak;v.ubijać;wystawać;zwisać
beetroot ('bi:tru:t) s. burak
befall (by'fo:l) v. zdarzać się;
przydarzać się; przytrafiać się
before (by'fo:r) adv. przedtem;
dawniej; z przodu;na przedzie
beforehand (by'fo:rhend) adv.
uprzednio; przedtem; z góry
befriend (by'frend) v. zaprzy-
jaźniać się; wspomagać
beg (beg) v. prosić; żebrać
began (b 'gaen) v. zaczęty;
zob. begin
beget; begot; begotten (by'get;
by'got; by'gotn)
beget (by'get) v. płodzić; rodzić; powodować ;wywoływać
beggar ('beger) s. żebrak
begin; began; begun (by'gyn;
by'gaen; by'gan)
begin (by'gyn) v. zaczynać
beginner (by'gyner) s. początkujący ;nowy(człowiek)

beginning (by'gynyng)s. początek ;rozpoczęcie
begun (by'gan) v. p.p. zob.
begin
behalf (by'hae:f) s. w imie-
niu kogos ; poparcie
behave (by'hejw) v. zachowywać się; prowadzić się
behavior (by'hejwjer) v. postępowanie; zachowanie się
behind (by'hajnd) adv. w tyle;
z tyłu; do tyłu; prep. za; poza;
being ('by:yng)s. byt; |s.tyłek
istnienie; istota
belated (by'lejtyd) adj. spózniony ;zapóźniony;późny
belch (belcz) v. zionąć; odbijać się; s. bekanie; bucha-
nie; huk ;odbijanie się
belfry ('belfry) s. dzwonnica
Belgian ('beldżen) adj. bel-
gijski
belief (by'li:f) s. wiara;
wierzenie; zaufanie;przekonanie
believe (by'li:w) v. wierzyć;
sądzić;mieć przekonanie;zakładać
believer (by'li:wer) s. wyznawca; wierzący ;zwolennik
bell (bel) s. dzwon; dzwonek
belligerent (by'lydżerent) adj.
wojujący; wojowniczy;wojenny
bellow ('belou) v. ryczeć;
s. ryk ;ryczenie;porykiwanie
bellows ('belouz) s. miech;
płuca;przedmiot podobny do miecha
belly ('bely) s. brzuch;żołądek
belong (bylong) v. należeć
belongings (bylongynz) pl.
rzeczy; bagaż; przynależności
beloved (by'lawd) adj. ukochany; drogi;s.kochana osoba
below (by'lou) adv. niżej; w
dole; na dół; pod spodem;
prep. poniżej; pod ;w piekle
belt (belt) s. pas; pasek;
strefa; v. bić pasem ;opasywać
bench (bencz) s. ława; ławka;
stół; terasa;miejsce sędziego
bend; bent; bent (bend; bent;
bent)
bend (bend) s. zgięcie; krzywa;
v. giąc;wyginać;przeginać;zginać

beneath (by'ni:s) prep. pod; poniżej; pod spodem; na dół
benediction (,beny'dykszyn) s.
błogosławieństwo
benefactor (,beny'faekter) s.
dobroczyńca; dobrodziej
beneficient(bi'nefyszent)adj.
dobroczynny
beneficial (,beny'fyszel) adj.
pożywny;korzystny;dobroczynny
benefit ('benyfyt) s. korzyść;
dobrodziejstwo;pożytek;zasiłek
benevolent (by'newelent) adj.
dobroczynny;życzliwy;łaskawy
bent (bent) s. sitowie; skłonność; zgięcie; adj. skłonny;
zgięty; zdecydowany;uparty
benzene ('benzi:n) s. benzen
benzine ('benzi:n) s. (lekka)
benzyna (do czyszczenia)
bequeath (by'kłys) v. zostawiać
w spadku;przekazać potomności
bequest (by'kłest) s. zapis;
spadek;spuścizna; legat
bereave; bereft; bereaved
(by'ri:w, by'reft; by'ri:wd)
bereave (by'ri:w) v. pozbawiać;
odzierać;wyzuwać; osierocić
bereft (by'reft) adj. osierocony; pozbawiony;wyzuty
beret ('berej) s. beret
berry ('bery) s. jagoda;ikra
berth (be:rs) s. koja; łóżko;
stoisko;miejsce postoju statku
beseech; besought; besought
(by'si:cz; by'so:t; by'so:t)
beseech (by'si:cz) v. błagać;
upraszać; zaklinać
beside (by'sajd) adv. poza tym;
ponadto; inaczej; prep. obok;
przy; w pobliżu; w porównaniu
besides (by'sajdz) adv. prócz
tego; poza tym; prep.: oprócz;
poza;ponadto w dodatku
besiege (by'si:dż) v. oblegać
best (best) adj.& adv. najlepszy; najlepiej;v.okpiwać
best wishes (best'łyszys) naj-
lepsze życzenia
best of all (best,ow o:l) najlepszy: najlepiej ;a najlepiej...

bestow (by'stou) v. podarować;
składać ;nadawać;użyczać;darzyć
bet (bet) s. zakład; v. zakładać się ;iść o zakład
betray (by'trej) v. zdradzić;
mylić; zawodzić dawać dowód
betrayal (by'trejel) s. zdrada
betrayer (by'trejer) s. zdrajca
better ('beter) adv. lepiej;
lepszy; v. poprawić; przewyż-
szyć ;prześcignąć;prześcigać
better than ('beter dzaen) exp.
więcej (slang); ponad ; lepiej
between (by'tłi:n) prep. między
adv. w pośrodku; tymczasem
beverage ('bewerydż) s. napój
beware (by'łe:r) v. strzec się
beware of the dog (by'łe:r ow
dy dog) strzec się psa; zły
pies
bewilder (by'łylder) v. zmieszać (kogoś);oszołamiać
bewilderment (by'łylderment) s.
zaczarowanie ;oszołomienie;chaos
bewitch (by'łycz) v. zaczarować;oczarować;ujać(kogoś czymś)
beyond (by'jond) adv.& prep.
za; poza; dalej niż; nad; ponad ;dalej(położony etc.)
bias ('bajes) s. uprzedzenie;
fałsz; kierunek; v. skłonić;
nachylić; uprzedzić ;usposabiać
biased ('bajest) adj. stronniczy; uprzedzony ;nastawiony
bib (byb) s. śliniak ;v.popijać
Bible ('bajbl) s. Biblia
bicycle ('bajsykl) s. rower
bid (byd) v. oferować cenę; licytować; kazać; s. oferta na
licytacji ;stawka; zaproszenie
bid farewell (byd fa:rłel)
żegnać się ;pożegnać kogoś
bier (bjer) s. mary(pod trumną)
big (byg) adj. & adv. duży;
wielki; ważny ;głośny;godny
big business (byg'byznys) wielkie interesy ;wielkie korporacje
big wig (byg łyg) s. wielka
szyszka ; ważniak;gruba ryba
bike (bajk) s. rower
bilateral (baj'laeterel) adj.
dwustronny; obustronny

bile (bajl) s. żółć;zgorzkniałość  
bilious ('byljes) adj. żółcio-  
wy;zrzedny;popędliwy;tetryczny  
bill (byl) s. dziób;pika;cypel  
bill (byl) s. rachunek; kwit;  
afisz; plakat; v. ogłaszać;  
afiszować;oblepiać afiszami  
billboard ('byl,bo:rd) s. ta-  
blica ogłoszeniowa  
billfold ('byl,fould) s. port-  
fel( na dokumenty i pieniądze)  
billiards ('byljerdz) s. bilard  
billion ('byljen) s. tysiąc  
milionów (USA); miliard  
bill of exchange ('byl,ow'  
eksczendż) weksel  
billow ('bylou) s. bałwan; kłąb;  
v. piętrzyć; falować;bałwanić się  
bin (byn) s. skrzynia; paka;  
v. pakować; chować do skrzyni  
bind (bajnd) v. wiązać; zobo-  
wiązywać; opatrywać; oprawiać  
binding ('bajndyng)adj. wiążący;  
s. połączenie; oprawa;wiązanie  
binoculars (bajnokjulez) pl.  
lornetka(polowa,teatralna etc.)  
biography (baj'ogrefy) s. bio-  
grafia;opis życia i działalności  
biology (baj'oledży) s. biologia  
birch (be:rcz) s. brzoza  
bird (be:rd) s. ptak ;dziwak  
bird of passage ('be:rd ow  
paesydż) przelotny ptak  
bird of prey ('de:rd ow prej)  
drapieżny ptak  
bird's eye view ('be:rds aj,wju)  
widok z lotu ptaka  
birth (be:rt) s. urodzenie  
birth control ('be:rt kon,troul)  
kontrola urodzin  
birthday ('be:rtdej) s. urodzi-  
ny; początek czegoś  
birthday party ('be:rtdej'  
pa:rty) przyjęcie urodzinowe  
birthplace ('be:rt-plejs)  
miejsce urodzenia  
biscuit ('byskyt) s. bułka;  
sucharek lekko strawny  
bishop ('byszep) s. biskup  
bison ('bajsn) s. bizon  
bit (byt) s. wędzidło; ostrze;  
wiertło; ząb; szczypta;odrobina;  
12½centów;moment;krótki czas

bitch (bycz) s. suka;wulg.kurwa  
bite; bit; bitten (bajt; byt;  
bitn)  
bite (bajt) v. gryźć; kąsać;  
docinać; s. pokarm; przynęta;  
ukąszenie;ciętość;lekki posiłek  
bitter ('byter) adj. gorzki;  
ostry; zły;zgorzkniały;przykry  
blab (blaeb) v. paplać; gadać;  
s. plotkarz; gaduła;plotkarka  
black (blaek) adj. czarny; po-  
nury; s, murzyn;v.czernić  
blackberry ('blaekbery) s. je-  
żyna  
blackbird ('blackbe:rd) s. kos  
blackboard ('blackbo:d) s. ta-  
blica  
blacken ('blaekn) v. czernić  
black eye ('blaekaj) s. pod-  
bite oko  
blackhead ('blaekhed) s. wągier  
blackmail ('blaemejl) s. szan-  
taż; wymuszenie  
black-market ('black ma:rkyt)  
s. czarny rynek  
blackout ('blaekaut) s. za-  
ciemnienie (miasta, okien)  
black pudding ('blaek'pudyng)  
s. kaszanka; kiszka  
blacksmith ('blaeksmys) s. ko-  
wal(wiejski)  
bladder ('blaeder) s. pęcherz  
blade (blejd) s. zdźbło; liść;  
ostrze;płetwa;klinga;wesołek  
blame (blejm) s. wina; nagana;  
v. tajać; ganić ;winić  
blame for ('blejm fo:r) v. wi-  
nić za (coś)  
blameless ('blejmlys) adj. bez  
winy; niewinny  
blank (blaenk) adj. biały;  
pusty; s. puste miejsce; nie-  
wypełniony formularz;ślepak  
blanket ('blaenkyt) s. koc weł-  
niany ;ciepły koc  
blasphemy ('blaesfymy) s. bluź-  
nierstwo;pogarda dla Boga  
blast (bla:st) s. wybuch; pod-  
much; odgłos eksplozji;  
v. wysadzić w powietrze; de-  
tonować; niszczyć  
blast furnace ('bla:st,fe:rnys)  
s. wielki piec hutniczy

blatant ('blejtent) adj. krzykliwy; ryczący; przesądny
blaze (blejz) s. błysk; płomień; wybuch; v. płonąc
bleach (bli:cz) v. wybielac
bleak (bli:k) adj. ponury;
smutny ;wystawiony do wiatru
blear (blier) adj. mętny; zamglony ; niewyraźny
bleat (bli:t) v. beczec
bleed; bled; bled (bli:d; bled;
bled)
bleed (bli:d) v. krwawic
blemish ('blemysz) s. plama;
wada; v. zniekształcic; splamic;poplamić;pobrudzić
blend; blent; blent (blend;
blent; blent)
blend (blend) v. mieszac się;
łączyc się; s, mieszanina
bless (bles) v. błogosławic
bless my soul ('bles,maj'so:l)
excl.: o Boże !
blessed ('blesyd) adj. błogosła-
wiony ;święty; kojący
blessing ('blesyŋg)s. błogosławieństwo ;aprobata;dobra rzecz
blew (blu:) v. zob.: blow
blight (blajt) s. zniszczenie;
zaraza ;v.niszczyć
blind (blajnd) adj. ślepy;
v. oslepic; s. zasłona
blind alley ('blajnd,alej)
ślepa ulica
blindfold ('blajnd,fould)
adj.& adv. na ślepo; z zawiąza-
nymi oczami; v. zawiązywać
oczy ;s. zasłona oczu
blink (blyŋk) v. mrugac;
s. błysk oka ;mignięcie
bliss (blys) s. radosc; błogosc
blithe ('blajz) adj. wesoły
blizzard ('blyzerd) s. snieżyca;
zawieja ;zadymka;zamiec
bloat (blout) v. nadymac; nabrzmiewac;uwędzic;wędzic
bloater ('blouter) s. sledz wędzony ; pikling
block (blok) s. blok; kloc; zeszyt; przeszkoda; v. tamowac;
wstrzymywac;tarasować;zatykać;
zablokować;blokować;zatamować

block up ('blokap) v. zablokować ;zablokowywac;zamurowac
blockade (blo'kejd) s. blokada;
v. blokowac ;robic zator
blonde (blond) s. blondynka
blood (blad) s. krew ;pokrewieństwo
bloodshed ('bladszed) s. krwi
rozlew ; rozlew krwi
bloodshot ('bladszot) adj. nabrzmiały krwią ;zaszły krwią
blood vessel ('bląd,wesl) s.
naczynie krwionosne
bloody ('blady) adj. krwawy
bloom (blu:m) s. kwiecie;
v. kwitnąc ;rozkwitać
blooming (blu:myŋg) adj. kwitnący; przeklęty (slang)
blossom ('blosem) v. kwitnąc;
s. kwiecie ; kwiat
blot (blot) s. plama; v. plamic
blot out ('blot aut).wymazac;
usunąc ;wykreslać;zamazywac
blotter (bloter) s. bibularz;
rejestr aresztowań;suszka
blotting paper ('blotyŋg,pejper)
bibuła ;suszka
blouse (blauz) s. bluza
blow; blew; blown (blou; blu;
bloźn)
blow (blou) s. cios; rzut; rozkwit; v. zakwitac; rozkwitac
blue (blu:) adj. niebieski;
smutny; v. farbowac na niebiesko ;pomalować na niebiesko
bluebell ('blu:bell) s. dzwonek
(kwiat)
blues (blu:s) pl. smutek; przygnębienie ;smutne piosenki
bluff (blaf) s. oszustwo; nabieranie; adj. szorstki; stromy; v. wprowadzac w błąd
bluish ('blu:ysh) adj. niebieskawy
blunder ('blander) s. cięźki
błąd ;v.popełniac błąd (gafę)
blunt (blant) adj. tępy; nieczuły; v. stępic ;przytępić
blur (ble:r) s. plama v. za-
trzec; splamic; zamazac
boar (bo:r) s. dzik; odyniec
board (bo:rd) s. deska; władza
naczelna ;tablica;rada;pokład

boarder ('bo:rder) s. pensjo-
nariusz; pasażer;stołownik
boardinghouse ('bo:rdynghaus)
s. pensjonat
boarding school ('bo:rdyng,sku:l)
s. szkoła z internatem
boardwalk ('bo:rd łok) chodnik z desek
boast (boust) v. chwalić się;
s. samochwalstwo;przechwałki
boat (bout) s. łódź; statek
boat race('bout,rejs) s. regaty; wyścigi łodzi
bob (bob) v. kiwać się; krótko
strzyc; szturchnąć; s. wisiorek; kłąb włosów; szturchnięcie
bobby ('boby) s. angielski policjant
bobsled ('bob sled) s. bob-
slej; sanki z kierownicą etc.
bodice ('bodys) s. stanik
bodily ('bodyly) adj.& adv.
osobiście; fizycznie; całkowicie;gremialnie; cieleśnie
body ('body) s. ciało; karoser-
ja; korpus;grupa;gromada;ogół
bodyguard ('bodyga:rd) s. straż
przyboczna;ochrona osobista
bog (bog) s. bagno
boil (bojl) v. wrzeć; kipieć;
gotować; s. wrzenie; czyrak
boil over ('bojl,ouwer) v. wygotować; wygotowac się
boiled eggs ('bojld egs) gotowane jajka
boiler ('bojler) s. kocioł
boisterous ('bojsteres) adj.
hałaśliwy;niesforny;burzliwy
bold (bould) adj. śmiały; zuchwały; zauważalny;wyrazny
bolster ('boulster) s. miękka
podkładka; v. miękko podeprzeć
bolt (boult) s. zasuwa; bolec;
piorun; wypad; v. zasuwać;
rzucić się; wypaść;czmychać
bomb (bom) s. bomba; v. bombar-
dować;atakować bombami
bombard (bom'ba:rd) v. bombardo-
wać(artylerią lub bombami)
bond (bond) s. więź; obligacja
bone (boun) s. kość;osc
bonfire ('bonfajer) s. płonący
stos ;ognisko (obozowe etc.)

bonnet ('bonyt) s. czapka
(damska) ; czepek
bonny ('bony) adj. piękny; ładny
bonus ('bounes) s. premia
bony ('bouny) adj. kościsty
book (buk) s. książka; v. księgować; rezerwować; aresztować
booked up ('bukt ap) adj. wy-
przedany; pełny
bookcase ('bukkejs) s. półka
na książki
booking clerk ('bukyn,klerk)
s. kasjer kolejowy
booking office ('bukyn,ofys)
biuro biletowe-rezerwacyjne
bookkeeper ('buk,ki:per) s.
księgowy; ksiegowa
bookkeeping ('buk,ki:pyng)s.
księgowość
booklet ('buklyt) s. książeczka
bookseller ('buk,seler) s. księgarz
book shop('bukszop) s. księgarnia
bookstore ('buksto:r) s. księgarnia
boom (bu:m) s. huk; nagła zwyżka; v. zwyżkować; podbijać ceny
boomerang ('bu:meraeng) s. bumerang;v.działać jak bumerang
boor (bu:r) s. prostak; gbur;
chłop; prostaczka
boost (bu:st) v. forsować; podnosić znaczenie; zachwalać;
wzmacniać;rozreklamować
boot (bu:t) s. but; cholewa
booth (bu:s) s. budka; stragan
booty('bu:ty)s.łup. zdobycz
booze('bu:z)s. alkohol pitny
border ('bo:rder) s. granica;
brzeg; rąbek; v. obrębiać;
graniczyć;oblamować;obszyć
bore (bo:r) v. wiercić; drążyć;
nudzić; s. otwór; nudy; nudziarz;natret;rzecz nieznośna
bore (bo:r) v. zob. bear
born (bo:rn) adj. urodzony
borough ('be:rou) s. miasteczko
borrow ('borou) v.(za)pożyczać
bosom ('busem) s.(łono) piers
boss (bo:s) s. szef; v. rządzić
botany ('botenv) s. botanika
botch (bocz) s. fuszerka; lata-
nina; v. partaczyć; fuszerować

both (bous) pron.& adj. obaj;
obydwaj ;obie;obydwie;oboje
bother (bodzer) s. kłopot;
v. niepokoić; dokuczać;dręczyć
bother about (,bodzer e'baut)
v. kłopotać się czyms
bottle ('botl) s. butelka
bottom ('botem) s. dno; spód;
dolina; głąb; adj. dolny;
spodni; podstawowy; v. sięgac
dna; wstawiać dno ;osiągać dno
bough (bau) s. konar ;gałąż
bought (bo:t) v. kupiony; zob.:
buy (zakupiony,przekupiony...)
boulder ('boulder) s. głaz
bounce (bauns) v. odbijać się;
podskakiwać; s. gwałtowne odbicie ;odskok;samochwalstwo
bound (baund) s. granica; adj.
będący w drodze; v. graniczyc
boundary (baundry) s. linia
graniczna ;adj. graniczny
boundless (baundlys) adj. bezgraniczny ; niezmierzony
bouquet (bu:'kej) s. bukiet
kwiatów; zapach (wina)
bout (baut) s. okres; runda;
próba sił ;atak(choroby)
bow (bau) s. łuk; kabłąk; smyczek; ukłon; v. zginać się;
kłaniać się ;wygiąc w kabłąk
bowels ('bauelz) pl. trzewia;
wnętrznosci
bower ('bauer) s. altana; chatka; kotwica przednia
bowl (boul) s. miska; czerpak;
stadion; szala; v. grać kulami (w kręgle); toczyc koło
box (boks) s. skrzynka; pudełko;
loża; boks; v. pakować; oddzielać; uderzac pięścią
boxer ('bokser) s. pieściarz;
bokser
boxing ('boksyng)s. pięściarst-
wo; boks
box office('boks,ofys) s. kasa
w teatrze ;kasa biletów wstepu
boy (boj) s. chłopak; służący
boycott ('bojkot) s. bojkot;
v. bojkotowac
boyfriend ('boy-frend) przyjaciel (dziewczyny);kochanek

boyhood('bojhud) s. wiek chłopięcy ;dzieciństwo chlopca
boyish ('bojysz) adj. chłopięcy
boy-scout ('boj-skaut) harcerz
bra (bra:) s. biustnik; stanik;
biustonosz
brace (brejs) s. klamra; korba;
podpora; v. wzmacniac; krzepic;
podpierac ;spiac klamrą;związac
brace up (brejs ap) v. wytężyc
się; zebrać siły; orzeźwić
bracelet ('brejslyt) s. bransoletka; kajdanek
bracket ('braekyt) s. wspornik;
ramię; nawias; grupa; klamra;
v. brać w nawiasy; grupowac
brag (braeg) v. chełpic się
braggart('braegert) s. samochwał; pyszałek ;bufon;fanfaron
braid (brejd) s. warkocz; plecionka; v. plesć; opasywac
brain (brejn) s. mózg; rozum
brain wave(brejn'ejw) s. swiet-
ny pomysł ;swietna myśl
brake (brejk) s. hamulec
bramble ('braembel) s. krzak ja-
gody ;krzak jeżyny; jeżyna
branch (bra:ncz) s. gałąż; odnoga; filja; v. odgałęziać się;
zbaczac ;rozwidlac się
brand-new (,braen'nju) adj. nowiutki;nowiusieńki;jak z igły
brass (braes) s. mosiądz; spiż;
ranga; starszyzna; instrumenty
dęte ;forsa;pieniądze;czelnosc;
śmiałosc;przedmioty z mosiądzu
brass band(,braes'baend) s. kapela dęta ;orkiestra dęta
brassiere (bre'zier) s. biustnik;
stanik; biustonosz
brat (braet) s. brzdąc; bachor
brave (brejw) adj. dzielny zuch;
v. stawiać czoło ;odważyć się
Brazilian (Bre'zyljen) a. bra-
zylijski ;s.Brazylijczyk
breach (bry:cz) s.naruszenie;
wyłom; zerwanie; v. przełamac
(się); zrobić wyłom ;przerwać się
bread (bred) s. chleb; forsa
(slang);środki utrzymania
bread and butter (bred-en-bater)
chleb z masłem ;środki utrzymania

breadth (breds) s. szerokość;
rozmach; szerokość pogladów
break; broke; broken (brejk;
brouk; brouken)
break (brejk) v. łamać; rujnować; przerywać; s. załamanie;
wyłom; nagła zmiana; wada
break away ('brejk ełej) v.
oderwać (się);uciekać
break down ('brejk dałn) v. za-
łamać(się); s. zepsucie się;
upadek; rozbiór;awaria
break in ('brejkyn) v. włamać
(się);wtargnąć;wtrącić się.
break off ('brejkof) v. urwać;
odłamać;zerwać stosunki
break out ('brejkaut) v. wyrwać
(się);pokryć się pryszczami
break up ('brejkap) v. połamać
(się);rozpadać się;rozejść się.
breakable('brejkebel) adj. kruchy; łamliwy;łatwy do zbicia
breakfast ('brekfest) s. sniadanie; v. jeść śniadanie
breast (brest) s. piers
breaststroke ('brest,strouk)
pływanie żabką
breath (bres) s. oddech; tchnienie ;dech;oddychanie;powiew
breathe (bri:z) v. oddychać;
tchnąć; żyć; dać wytchnać; powiewać;natchnąć;wionąć;szepnąć
breathing ('bri:zyng) s. oddech; wytchnienie ;adj.żywy
breathless (breslys) adj. bez
tchu ;zasapany;zadyszany;zziajany
bred (bred) zob.: breed;wychowany
breeches ('bry:czyz) pl. spodnie do konnej jazdy; bryczesy
breed; bred; bred; (bri:d; bred;
bred)
breed (bri:d) v. rodzić; rozmna-
żać; hodować; s. chów; rasa;
ród ;plemię; ród ludzki
breeder ('bri:der) s. hodowca;
rozsadnik (choroby);rozpłodnik
breeding (bri:dyng) s. hodowla;
obejście; dobre wychowanie
breeze (bri:z) s. wietrzyk;zwada;
v. wiać; śmigać;odejść;oszukać
brevity ('brewyty) s. zwięzłość;
krótkość ; krótkotrwałość

brew (bru:) v. warzyć (piwo);
knuć; s. napój uwarzony; preparat;warzenie;parzenie;odwar
brewery (bru:ery) s. browar
bribe (brajb) v. dawać łapówkę;
przekupywać; s. łapówka
bribery ('brajbery) s. przekupstwo; łapownictwo;korupcja
brick (bryk) s. cegła; kostka;
adj. ceglany; v. obmurować;
zamurować(okno;drzwi,etc.)
bricklayer ('bryk,lejer) s.
murarz
brickwork ('brykłork) s. muro-
wanie;wykonana robota murarska
brickyard ('brykja:rd) s. cegielnia
bridal ('brajdel) adj. ślubny;
weselny;s.ślub;wesele
bride (brajd) s. panna młoda
bridegroom ('brajdgru:m) s, pan
młody; nowożeniec
bridesmaid ('brajdzmejd) s.
druhna ;drużka
bridge (brydż) s. most; mostek;
v. łączyć mostem;zapełnić lukę
bridgehead ('brydżhed) s. przyczółek mostowy;przyczółek
bridle ('brajdl) s. uździenica;
uzda; cuma; v. kiełzać; pow-
ściągać ;opanowywać;okiełzać
bridle path ('brajdl,pas) s.
ścieżka do konnej jazdy
brief (bri:f) s. streszczenie;
odprawa; krótkie majtki;
v. zwięzle streścić; pouczyć;
informować; adj. krótkotrwały;
treściwy; zwięzły;krótki
briefcase ('bri:f,kejs) s.
teczka
brigade (bry'gejd) s. brygada
bright (brajt) adj. jasny;
świetny; bystry; adv. jasno
brighten ('brajtn) v. rozjasnić; błyszczeć; promieniować
brightness (brajtnys) s. jas-
nosć;światło;blask;żywosć
brilliance ('bryljens) s.blask;
wielkie zdolności ;świetność
brilliancy ('bryljensy) s.
świetność ; blichtr; połysk
jasne światło;blask;jasność

brilliant (,bryljent) adj. błyszczący; świetny; wybitny
brim (brym) s. brzeg (naczynia); rondo (kapelusza);v.napełniać
brimful ('brym'ful) adj. pełen
po brzegi;przepełniony
bring; brought; brought (bryng; bro:t; bro:t)
bring (bryng)v. przynosić; przyprowadzać;powodować;zmusić (się)
bring an action ('bryngen'aekszyn) v. wszczynać działanie, akcje
bring about ('brynge'baut) v. uskutecznić;wywoływać;dokonać
bring forth ('bryng,fo:rs) v. ujawniać; wywoływać;urodzić
bring in ( bryngyn)v. wprowadzać; przynosić;wydawać(wyrok etc.)
bring up (bryngap) v. poruszyć; przynieść na górę; przysunąć
brink (brynk) s. skraj; brzeg
brisk (brysk) adj. żywy; raźny; rześki;trzaskający;wesoły
bristle ('brysl) s. szczecina
British ('brytysz) adj. brytyjski; Anglik
brittle ('brytl) a. kruchy
broach (broucz) v. żłobić; zaczynać; poruszać;s.szydło;rożen
broad (bro:d) adj. szeroki; z rozmachem; wyraźny; obszerny s. szeroka płaszczyzna; wulg.: kobieta; adv. szeroko;z akcentem
broadcast ('bro:dka:st) v. transmitować; rozsiewać; szerzyc
broadminded ('bro:d'majndyt) adj. pobłażliwy; z otwartą głową
brochure ('brouszjuer) s. broszura
broke (brouk) adj. złamany; bez grosza; zob. break
broken (brouken) adj. połamany; zepsuty; zob. break
broker (brouker) s. pośrednik; ajent;makler;handlarz narkotyków
bronchia ('bronkje) pl. oskrzela
bronze (bronz) s. brąz; adj.brązowy; v. brązować; brązowiec
brooch (broucz) s. brosza; spinka
brood (bru:d) s. wyląg; potomstwo; v. wysiadywać; tkwić; rozmyślać ponuro;być pogrążonym w myślach

brook (bruk) s. potok;v.ścierpieć
broom (bru:m) s. miotła; v. zamiatać;wymiatać;obmiatać
broth (bros) s. rosół;bulion
brothel ('brodzel) s. burdel
brother ('bradzer)s. brat
brothers and sisters ('bradzers, en'systers) rodzeństwo
brotherly ('bradzerly) adj. braterski
brought (bro:t) adj. przyniesiony; zob. bring
brow (brau) s. brew; czoło; nawias;szczyt;pomost;kładka
brown (braun) adj. brunatny; brązowy; opalony; v. brązowieć; opalać się;przyrumieniać (mięso)
brown paper ('braun,pejpe:r)s. papier pakunkowy
bruise (bru:z) s. siniak; stłuczenie; v. tłuc; otłuc; połamać kości; ranić;zgnieść;wyklepać
brush (brasz) s. szczotka; pędzel; draśnięcie; v. szczotkować; otrzepać; pędzlować
brush up ('brasz ap) v. wygładzić; odświeżyć;zgarnąć szczotką
brutal ('bru:tl) a. brutalny; zmysłowy;zwierzęcy
brutality (bru:'taelyty) s.
brutalstwo ; brutalność
brute (bru:t) s. bydlę; zwierzę ludzkie; adj. tępy; brutalny; bezduszny; bydlęcy;nieokrzesany
bubble ('babl) s. bąbel; bańka; kipienie; v. kipieć; burzyć się; wydzielać bańki;musować
buck (bak) s. kozioł; fircyk; dolar adj. rogowy; męski; zwykły (szeregowy); v. skakać
narowiście; opierać się;ługować
bucket ('bakyt) s. wiadro; czerpak (koparki);tłok;miska
buckle ('bakl) v. spinać; łączyć; wichrować; s. spinka; sprzączka
buckle on ('bakl on) v. pozapinać się ; zapiąć pas ;przypiąć
buckskin ('bakskyn) s. wyprawiona koźla skóra ( też sarnia)
bud (bad) s. pączek; v. pączkować; wyrastać;być w zarodku;rozwijać się;dobrze zapowiadać się

buddy ('bady) s. bliski kolega
budget ('badżyt) s. budżet;
v. budżetowac ;asygnowac
buffalo ('bafelou) s. bawół
buffer ('bafer) s. bufor;
zderzak ;odbój
buffet ('bafyt) s. bufet; kułak; cios ;raz;uderzenie
buffet ('befej) s. niski kredens ;dania barowe
bug (bag) s. owad; pluskwa;
defekt; amator ;insekt;robak
bugle ('bju:gl) s. róg (do
trąbienia) ;v.trąbić;zatrąbić
build; built; built (byld;bylt;
bylt)
build (byld) v. budowac; rozbu-
dowywac ;stworzyć;wznosić
builder ('bylder) s. budowniczy
building ('byldyng)s. budowla
built (bylt) adj. zbudowany;
zob. build
bulb (balb) s. cebula; żarówka
bulge (baldż) v. wzdymac; wybrzu-
szac; wydymac; wytrzeszczac;
s. wypukłość; wzdęcie; wzdyma-
nie się;wybrzuszenie;przewaga
bulk (balk) s. masa; kolos;
większosć ;v.gromadzić;komasować
bulky ('balky) adj. wielki;otyły;
ciężki; masywny ;nieporęczny
bull (bul) s. byk; duży samiec;
głupstwo;nonsens=bull-shit(bul-
szyt)
bullet ('bulyt) s. kula (nabój)
bulletin ('buletyn) s. komunikat; biuletyn
bulletin board ('buletyn,bo:rd)
s. tablica na ogłoszenia
bullion ('buljen) s. złoto i
srebro w sztabach
bully ('buly) v. dręczyć; tyra-
nizowac; s. awanturnik; kłot-
nik; najęty drab; adj. byczy;
żywy; wesoły;świetny;kapitalny
bum (bam) s. włóczęga; nierób;
popijawa; zadek; v. włóczyć
się; cyganic; pic; adj. marny
bumblebee ('bambl-bi:) s.
trzmiel
bump (bamp) v. zderzyc się; łup-
nąc; odbic się z łomotem; nabic guza: s. zderzenie; grzmotnięcie; guz;wybój;wstrząs; uderzenie; wypukłość; zdolności

bumper ('bamper) s. zderzak;
pełny kielich .rekord
bun (ban) s. ciastko drożdżowe;
kok(włósów)
bunch (bancz) s. pęk; banda;
zgraja; guz; v. składac w pęki; skupiac się; kulic się
bunch of grapes ('bancz,ow
grejps) kisć (gałązka) winogron ; pęk winogron
bundle ('bandl) s. tłumok;
wiązka ;v.pakowac(w tobół)
bundle up ('bandl,ap) v. za-
winąc się ;zebrać;zbierać
bungalow ('bangelou) s. domek
letni parterowy
bungle ('bangl) s. partactwo;
v. partaczyc; bałaganic
bunion ('banjen) s. zapalenie
stawu w stopie(bolesny guz)
bunk ('bank) s. koja ;baniąluki
bunk bed ('bank,bed) s. łóżko
piętrowe ; łóżko do podnoszenia
bunny ('bani) s. królik; trus
buoy (boj) s. boja; znak pływający ;pława;v.znaczyć bojami
burden ('be:rdn) s. brzemię;
ciężar; obowiązek; v. obciążac;
przygniatać; obładowywac
bureau ('bjurou) s. komoda;
biuro ;sekretarzyk; urząd
bureaucracy (bju'rokresy) s.
biurokacja
burglar (be:rgler) s. włamywacz
burglary ('be:rlery) s. włama-
nie(zwłaszcza w nocy)
burial ('berjel) s. pogrzeb
burly ('be:rly) adj. krzepki;
tęgi;duży i silny
burn; burnt; burnt (be:rn;
be:rnt; be:rnt)
burn (be:rn) v. palic; płonąc;
zapalic; s, oparzelizna;
dziura wypalona;oparzenie
burner ('be:rner) s. palnik
burning ('be:rnyng) s. palenie
burnt (be:rnt) v. spalony;
zob. burn(przypalony,opalony...)
burst; burst; burst (be:rst;
be:rst; be:rst)
burst (be:rst) v. rozsądzac;
rozrywac; s. wybuch;pęknięcie;
salwa; zryw;szał;grzmot;hulanka

burst of laughter ('be:rst,ow
'lafter) wybuch śmiechu
burst into flames ('be:rst,
yntu'flejms) buchać ogniem
burst into tears ('be:rst,
yntu'tiers) wybuchnąć płaczem ;zalać się łzami
bury ('bery) v. pochowac; zagrzebac; chowac ;zakopywać
bus (bas) s. autobus
bush (busz) s. krzak; gąszcz
bushel ('buszel) s. korzec
(8 galonów);v.przerabiać
bushy ('buszy) adj. nastroszony;
krzaczasty ;gęsty
business ('byznys) s. interes;
zajęcie ;sprawa;przedsiębiorstwo
business hours ('byznys,aurs)
godziny urzędowe
business letter ('byznys,leter)
oficjalny list
businesslike ('byznys,lajk)
adj. rzeczowy ;solidny;powazny
businessman ('byznysman) s.
przedsiębiorca; człowiek inte-
resów ;handlowiec
business trip ('byznys,tryp)
podroż służbowa
bus stop ('bas-stop)s.przysta-
nek autobusowy
bust (bast) s. popiersie; biust;
v. rujnowac; psuc; rozwalic;
niszczyc ;bankrutowac;wybuchnąć
bustle ('basl) v. krzątać się;
zapędzac do pracy; s. rozgardiasz; krzątanina ;bieganina
busy ('byzy) adj. zajęty;
skrzętny; wścibski;ruchliwy
busybody ('byzy,body) wścibski;
złośliwy ;plotkarz;intrygant
but (bat) adv. conj.prep. lecz;
ale; jednak; natomiast; tylko;
inaczej niż; z wyjątkiem
but for ('bat fo:r) exp. oprócz;
bez ; gdyby nie
but now ('bat nau) exp. dopiero
teraz ;dopiero w tej chwili
but once ('bat łans) exp. tylko
raz ;chociaż tylko raz
butcher ('buczer) s. rzeźnik ;kat;
v.zarzynac; mordować; masakrować;brutalnie zabijac;partaczyć

butt (bat) 1. s. drzewce; kolba; nasada; niedopałek papierosa; posladki; cel; przedmiot
kpin; ofiara; tarcza; v. bósc;
trącac; przytykac; 2. s. styk;
zetknięcie; uderzenie głowa
butt in ('bat yn) v. wtrącac
się;przerywać rozmowę
butter ('bater) s. masło; v.
smarowac masłem ;przychlebiać
buttercup ('baterkap) s. jas-
kier
butterfly ('baterflaj) s. motyl;
adj. motyli
buttocks ('bateks) pl. posladki
button ('batn) s. guzik;v.zapinąc
button up ('batn ap) v. zapinac
się ; zapinać na guziki
buttonhole ('batnhoul) s. dziurka od guzika;v.zmuszać do słuchania
buttress ('batrus) s. podpora
buxom ('baksem) adj. dorodny;
okazały;pełny(biust);ładna(babka)
buy; bought; bought (baj; bo:t;
bo:t)
buy (baj) v. kupowac ;przekupić
buyer (bajer) s. nabywca
buzz (baz) s. brzęczenie;
v. brzęczec ;przelotywać nisko
buzzard ('bazed) s. myszołów
by (baj) prep. przy; koło; co(dzień);
przez; z; po;w(nocy);o;według
by myself ('baj majself) ja sam
by and large ('baj end'la:rdż)adv.
ogólnie mowiąc; ogólnie biorąc
by twos ('baj,tuz) dwójkami
by the dozen('baj dy 'dazn) tu-
zinami
by the end ('baj dy,end) przy
końcu ;ku końcowi;z końcem
by land ('baj,laend) lądem
by bus ('baj,bas) autobusem
by day ('baj,dej) za dnia
by-and-by ('baj-end-baj) s.
przyszłosc; adv. wnet ;po chwili
bye-bye ! ('baj'baj) excl.: pa !
by-election (,baj-e'lekszyn) s.
wybory uzupełniające
bygone ('bajgon) adj. miniony;
przestarzały ;s.zdarzenia minione
bygones ('bajgonz) pl. przeszłosc; dawne urazy ;dawne zatargi

bylaw ('bajlo:) s. przepis; zarządzenie(miejscowe etc.)
byname ('bajnejm) s. przydomek
bypass ('baj-pas) s. droga dojazdowa; objazd;v.objeżdżać
by-product (,baj-'prodakt) s. produkt uboczny
byroad (,baj-'roud) s. boczna droga;droga drugorzędna
bystander (,baj-'stander) s. przygodny widz
bystreet (,baj-'stri:t) s. boczna ulica(drugorzędna)
byway ('baj-łej) s. boczna droga;boczne przejście
byword ('baj-,łe:rd) s. przysłowie; przydomek(pogardliwy)
by work ('baj,-łe:rk) s. praca uboczna poza zajęciem głównym
c (si:) litera "c"; trzecia litera alfabetu angielskiego
cab (kaeb) s. taksówka; dorożkaszoferka;budka maszynisty
cabaret (,kaebe'rej) s. lokal taneczny; kabaret;serwis na tacy
cabbage ('kaebydż) s. kapusta
cabin ('kaebyn) s. kabina; chatka;prymitywnie zbudowany domek
cabinet ('kaebynyt) s. szafka; rada ministrów adj.tajny
cabinetmaker ('kaebynyt,mejke:r) s. stolarz meblowy
cable ('kejbl) s. przewód; lina; depesza; v. depeszować; umocowywać liną;przesyłać kablem
cable-car ('kejbl,ka:r) s. wóz linowy; kolejka; linowa
cabman ('kaebmen) s. taksówkarz
cabstand ('kaeb staend) s. postój taksówek
cackle ('kaekl) v. gdakać; gęgać; chichotać; s. gdakanie; gęganie; chichot
cacti ('kaektaj) pl. kaktusy
cactus ('kaektes) s. kaktus
cad (kaed) s. ordynus; cham
café ('kaefej) s. kawiarnia; kawa;restauracja; bar
cafeteria (,kaefy'tierja) s. restauracja samoobsługowa
cage (kejdż) s. klatka; kosz; v. zamykać w klatce

cake (kejk) s. ciastko; kostka (mydła);smażony placek(z ryby)
cake tin ('kejk,tyn) s. forma na ciastko
calamity (ke'laemyty) s. nieszczęście; klęska;niedola
calculate ('kaelkjulejt) v. rachować; sądzić; oceniać
calculation (,kaelju'lejszyn) s. liczenie;ostrozność
calendar ('kaelynder) s, kalendarz;terminarz
calf (kaef) s. cielak; łydka
caliber ('kaelyber) s. średnica wewnętrzna; kaliber; wzorzec; sprawdzian
call (ko:l) v. wołać; wzywać; telefonować; odwiedzać; zawijać do portu; wyzywać; s. krzyk; wezwanie; apel; powołanie; wizyta;nazwanie;rządanie
call for help ('ko:l,fo:r help) wołanie o pomoc;wzywanie pomocy
call names ('ko:l,nejmz) przezywać; wyzywać;ubliżać
call back ('ko:l,baek) odtelefonować; odwołać z powrotem
call at ('ko:l,aet) odwiedzać
call for ('ko:l,fo:r) żądać; chodzić po coś(żeby otrzymać)
call on ('ko:l,on) odwiedzać (kogoś);prosić o wypowiedz
call up ('ko:l,ap) telefonować
caller ('ko:ler) s. gość; odwiedzający;adj.rześki;świerzy
calling ('ko:lyng) s. zawód; powołanie;zatrudnienie;fach
callous ('kaeles) adj. stwardniały; nieczuły;zrogowaciały
calm (ka:m) adj. spokojny; cichy; s. spokój; cisza;opanowanie; v. uspokajać; uciszać;uciszyć się
calm down ('ka:m,dałn) v. uciszyć się;uspokoić się
calorie ('kaelery) s. kaloria
calves (ka:wz) pl. cielaki; łydki
camber ('kaember) v. wyginać; s. wygięcie;wypukłość (jezdni)
came (kejm) v. przyszedł; zob. come

camel ('kaemel) s. wielbłąd
camera ('kaemere) s. aparat
fotograficzny; prywatna izba
camomile ('kaemoumajl) s. rumianek
camouflage ('kaemufla:ż) s. ma-
skowanie; v. maskować (wojsk.)
camp (kaemp) s. obóz; v. obozować; rozlokowywać w namiotach
camp out (kaemp aut) v. obozować w namiocie
campaign (kaem'pejn) s, kampania; akcja; v. odbywać kam-
panię; agitować
camp bed ('kaemp,bed) s. łóżko
polowe;łóżko składane
camper ('kaemper) adj.obozujący;s.
wóz lub przyczepa do obozowania; mieszkalny wóz (turystyczny)
camping ('kaempyng) s. obozowa-
nie; życie obozowe
camping ground ('kaempyng,graund)
obozowisko; miejsce do obozowania
campus ('kaempes) s. teren uniwersytecki lub szkolny
can (kaen) s. puszka blaszana;
ustęp; v. móc; konserwować;
wyrzucać;umieć;zdołać;potrafić
Canadian (ke'nejdjen) adj. kanadyjski
canal (ke'nael) s. kanał ;kanalik
canard (kae'na:rd) s. kaczka
dziennikarska; plotka
canary (ke'nery) s. kanarek
cancel ('kaensel) v. znosić;
kasować;odwoływać;skreślać
cancer ('kaenser) s. rak (choroba); nowotwór
candid ('kaendyd) adj. szczery;
bezstronny;otwarty
candidate ('kaendydyt) s. kandydat;kandydatka
candied ('kaendyd) adj. pocu-
krzony; lukrowany
candle ('kaendl) s. świeca
candlestick ('kaendlstyk) s.
świecznik; lichtarz
candy ('kaendy) s. cukierki;
lukier;cukier lodowaty
cane (kejn) s. trzcina; laska;
pałka; v. chłostać ;wyplatać
trzciną; ukarać trzciną

canned (kaend) adj. zakonserwo-
wany w puszce
cannery (kaenery) s. fabryka
konserw
cannibal ('kaenybel) s. ludożerca; adj. ludożerczy
cannon ('kaenen) s. działo
cannot ('kaenot) v. nie móc
(od cannot);nie potrafić
canoe (ke'nu:) s. czółno; kajak; v. jeździć kajakiem;
wiosłować
canopy ('kaenepy) s. baldachim;
okap;firmament; sklepienie
cant ('kaent) s. żargon; frazes
can't (ka:nt) v. nie móc( od
can);nie potrafić
canteen (kaen'ti:n) s. manierka; menażka; kantyna
canvas ('kaenves) s. płótno
impregnowane
canvass ('kaenves) s. badanie;
zabieganie; v.zabiegać; badać;
starać się o głosy
cap (kaep) s. czapka; pokrywa;
wieko; kapiszon;beret
cap (kaep) v. wkładać czapkę
lub nakrywkę; wieńczyć; zakładać spłonkę; zakasować
capability (,kaepe'bylyty) s.
zdolność;zdatność; możliwość
capable (,kejpebl) adj. zdolny
capacity (ke'paesyty) s. zdolność; kompetencja; pojemność;
właściwość;nośność;objętość
cape (kejp) s. 1. peleryna;
2. przylądek
caper (kejper) v. wywijać kozły;
s. hołubiec; sus; skok
capital ('kaepytl) s. stolica;
kapitał; adj. główny; zasadniczy; stołeczny; fatalny
capital crime ('kaepytlkrajm)
s. morderstwo
capitalism ('kaepytlyzem)s.
kapitalizm
capital letter ('kaepytl,leter)
duża litera
capital punishment ('kaepytl
'panyszment) kara śmierci
capricious (ke'pryszes) adj.
kapryśny

capsize (kaep'sajz) v. wywracac (statek) dnem do góry

capsule ('kaepsju:l) s. kapsuł-ka;torebka;pochewka;kabinka

captain ('kaeptyn) s. kapitan; naczelnik;v.dowodzić

caption ('kaepszyn) s. nagłówek; napis ;poświadczenie;aresztowanie

captivate ('kaeptywejt) v. ujać; czarować; urzekać;zniewalać

captive ('kaeptyw) adj. jeniec

captivity ('kaeptyvyty) s. nie-wola

capture ('kaepczer) s. owładnię-cie; łup; v. pojmać; owładnąc

car (ka:r) s, samochód; wóz

caravan('kaerevaen) s. karawana; wóz kryty;przyczepka mieszkalna

carbohydrate ('ka:rbe'hajdrejt) s. węglowodan

carbon ('ka:rben) s. węgiel; kopia (kalka)

carbon dioxide ('ka:rben daj'oksajd) s. $CO_2$ dwutlenek węgla

carbon paper ('ka:rben,pejper) s. kalka

carburetor ('ka:rbjureter) s. gaźnik

car carrier (ka:r-'kaerjer) s. wóz do przewozu aut

carcass ('ka:r-kes) s. ścierwo; padlina; szkielet

card ('ka:rd) s. karta; bilet; pocztówka;legitymacja; atut

cardboard ('ka:rdbo:rd) s. tek-tura;adj.tekturowy

card box('ka:rdboks) s. karton

cardigan ('ka:rdygen) s. wełnia-na kurta (kamizelka)

cardinal ('ka:rdynl) adj. głów-ny; kardynał

card index ('ka:rd yndeks) s. kartoteka

car papers (ka:r pejpers) s. do-kumenty samochodowe

care (keer) s. opieka; troska; ostrożność;zgryzota;dozór;uwaga

care of (keer ow) c/o: adres (u kogoś)

care for (keer fo:r) v. dbać o kogoś;lubić;kochać;mieć ochotę

career (ke'rier) s. kariera; zawód;tok;pęd;bieg;v. cwałować

carefree (keerfri:) adj. bez-troski

careful (keerful) adj. ostrożny; troskliwy;dbały;pieczołowity

careless (keerles) adj. niedba-ły; nieuważny;nieostrożny

caress (ke'res) s. pieszczota; v. pieścić; popieścić

caretaker ('keertejker) s. dozorca; stróż

careworn ('keerło:rn) s.zgnę-biony kłopotami

carfare ('ka:rfeer) s. opłata za jazdę

cargo ('ka:rgou) s. ładunek

caricature (,kaeryke'czjuer) s. karykatura;v.karykaturować

car mechanic (ka:r-my'kaenyk) s. mechanik samochodowy

carnation ('ka:r'nejszyn) l. s.& adj. ciemno-czerwony;cielis-ty;2. goździk ogrodowy

carnival ('ka:rnywel) s. karna-wał;zapusty

carnivorous (ka:r'nyweres) adj. mięsożerny

carol ('kaerel) s. kolenda; v. kolendować

carp (ka:rp) s. karp; v. cze-piać się;ganić;przycinać

car parking ('ka:r-pa:rkyng) s. parking samochodowy

carpenter ('ka:rpynter) s. cieśla; stolarz

carpet ('ka:rpyt) s. dywan; v. wyścielac dywanem

carriage ('kaerydż) s. wagon; powóz; postawa;kareta;chód

carrier ('kaerjer) s. firma przewozowa; nosnik; tragarz; rozsadnik (zakażenia); lotni-skowiec;okaziciel

carrion ('kaerjen) s. padlina

carrot ('kaeret) s. marchewka

carry ('kaery) v. nosic; wo-zic; zanieść; unosic

carry off ('kaery,of) v. upro-wadzic; zabrać;zdobywać(nagrodę)

carry on ('kaery,on) v. konty-nuować;wytrwać;awanturować się

carry out ('kaery,aut) v. wykonać; przeprowadzić;spełnić
cart ('ka:rt) s. wóz
cartel ('ka:rtel) s. kartel
carter ('ka:rter) s. woźnica
cart horse ('ka:rthors) s.
koń pociągowy
carton ('ka:rten) s. karton
cartoon (ka:r'tun) s. karykatura;v. rysować karykatury
cartoonist (ka:r'tunyst) s.
karykaturzysta
cartridge ('ka:rtrydż) s. nabój
cartwheel ('ka:rt-hłi:l) s.
kołodziej
carve ('ka:rw) v. rzeźbić; krajać;cyzelować;pociać an części
carver ('ka:rwer) s. snycerz
carving ('ka:rwyng) s. rzeźba
cascade (kaes'kejd) s. wodospad;v.spadać jak wodospad
case (kejs) s. l. wypadek; sprawa; dowód; 2. skrzynia; pochwa;
torba; 3. sprawa sądowa;
v. zamykać w pochwie; otaczać
czymś ;oszalować; oprawić
casement ('kejsment) s. rama
okienna; okno z kwaterami
cash (kaesz) s. gotówka; pieniądze; v. spieniężać; inkasować; płacić (gotówka)
cash on delivery (kaesz on
dy'lywery) zapłata przy od-
biorze; C.O.D.
cashier (kae'szjer) s. kasjer
cash register(kaesz'redżyster)
s. kasa (zmechanizowana)
casing ('kejsyng)s. l. powłoka;
pochwa; 2. obudowa; oprawa;
3. łuska; 4. opancerzenie
cask (kaesk) s. beczułka
casket (kaeskyt) s. trumna; urna; szkatuła
cassock ('kaesek) s. sutanna
cast; cast; cast (ka:st; ka:st;
ka:st)
cast (ka:st) s. rzut; odlew;
gips; odcień: v, rzucać; łowić; odlewać; powalić; dzielić
role teatralne
castaway ('ka:st,e'łej) s. wyrzutek ;rozbitek

cast down (ka:st dałn) adj.
przygnębiony.v.deprymować
caste (ka:st) s. kasta
cast iron(ka:stajren) s. żeliwo
castle ('ka:sl) s. zamek
castor oil ('ka:ster,ojl) s.
olej rycynowy
cast steel ('ka:st,sti:l) s.
lana stal
casual ('kaeżuel) adj. przypadkowy; niedbały;dorywczy
casualty ('kaeżuelty) s. wypadek; ofiara wypadku; lista
strat;nieszczęście
cat (kaet) s. kot;jędza
catalog ('kaetelog) s. katalog
catamaran (,kaeteme'raen) s.
dwu-czółnowa łódź
cataract ('kaeteraekt) s. katarakta; ulewa;wodospad
catarrh (ke'ta:r) s. katar
catastrophe (ke'taestrefy) s.
katastrofa
catch; caught; caught (kaecz;
ko:t; ko:t)
catch (kaecz) v. łapać; łowić;
ujmować; słyszeć; wybuchać;
nabawić się; s. łup; połów
catch cold (kaecz kold) v. za-
ziębiać się
catch fire (kaecz fajer) v. zapalać się
catch up (kaecz ap) v. dogonić
catching (kaeczyng)adj. zaraźliwy;s.tryby;uchwyt;zazębienie
category ('kaetygery) s. kategoria
cater ('kejter) v. dostarczać
żywności; obsługiwać
caterpillar ('kaetepyler) s.
gąsie nica (traktora.czołgu etc.)
cathedral (ke'ti:drel) s. katedra
Catholic ('kaetelyk) adj. katolicki; s. katolik
cattle (kaetl) s. bydło rogate
caucus ('ko:kes) s. tajne na-
rady partyjne; klika
caught (ko:t) złapany; zob.
catch
cauldron ('ko:ldren) s,kocioł

cauliflower ('kalyflauer) s. kalafior

cause (ko:z) s. przyczyna; sprawa;racja;motywacja;proces

causeless(ko:zles) adj. przypadkowy ; bezpodstawny

caution ('ko:szyn) s. ostrożnosć; uwaga;v.ostrzegać

cautious ('ko:szes) adj. ostrożny;rozważny;roztropny;uważny

cavalry ('kaevelry) s. kawaleria

cave (kejw) s. pieczara; jaskinia; v. zapadać się; drążyć

cavern ('kaewen) s. jama; jaskinia; grota; pieczara

cavity ('kaewyty) s. wklęsłosć; dziura(w zębie);dół;wydrążenie

cease (sy:s) v. ustawać; przestawać; położyć kres

ceaseless (sy:slys) adj. bezustanny;ciągły; nieprzerwany

cede (si:d) v. ustąpić; cedować

ceiling ('sy:lyng)s. sufit; pułap; górna granica

celebrate ('selybrejt) v. świecić ;uczcić;sławićobchodzić

celebrated ('selybrejtyd) adj. sławny; słynny; głośny

celebration ('selybrejszyn) s. obchód; odprawianie; święcenie

celebrity ('sylebryty) s. sławna osoba;sława;znakomita osobowość

celery ('selery) s. seler (jarzyna)

celibacy ('selybesy) s. bezżeństwo; celibat

cell (sel) s. cela; komórka

cellar ('seler) s. piwnica

Celtic (keltyk) adj. celtycki

cement (sy'ment) s. cement; v. cementować; kleić; utwierdzać ;spoić; złączyć

cemetery ('semytry) s. cmentarz

censor ('sensor) s. cenzor

censorship ('senserszyp) s. cenzura

censure ('senszer) s. nagana; krytyka; v. krytykować

cent (sent) s. cent

centenary (sentynery) adj. stuletni; s. stulecie; setna rocznica

centennial ('sen'tenjel) s. stulecie; adj. stuletni

center ('senter) s. ośrodek; v. ześrodkowywać

centigrade ('sentygrejd) adj. stustopniowy(termometr)

centimeter ('sentymi:ter) s. centymetr

central ('sentral) adj. środkowy; czołowy ; s. centrala

Central Europe ('sentral juerop) Europa Srodkowa

central heating ('sentrel hi:tyng)centralne ogrzewanie

centralize ('sentrelajz) v. centralizować;ześrodkowywać

center ('senter) s. ośrodek

centrum; v. ześrodkowywać; centrować ;skupiać się

century ('senczury) s.stulecie

cereals ('syerjelz) pl, zboża

cerebral ('serybrel) adj. mózgowy

ceremonial (,sery'mounjel) adj. ceremonialny; s. rytuał; ceremonial; ceremonialnosć

ceremonious (,sery'mounjes) adj. drobiazgowy; ceremonialny

ceremony ('serymeny) s. ceremonia;v.sztywno się zachowywać

certain ('se:rtyn) adj. niejaki; pewien;pewny;ustalony;jakiś

certainly ('se:rtnly) adv. napewno; oczywiscie;bezwzględnie

certainty ('se:rtynty) s. pewnosć; pewnik; rzecz pewna

certificate (se'rtyfykyt) s. świadectwo; poświadczenie; v. zaświadczać ;dyplomować

certify ('se:rtyfaj) v. zaświadczać; zapewniać; uznawać za

certitude ('se:rtytju:d) s. pewnosć; przeświadczenie

chafe (czejf) v. trzeć; otrzeć; irytować; s. tarcie; otarcie; irytacja; rozdrażnienie; złość

chaff(cza:f) s. 1. sieczka; 2. żart; naciąganie; wyśmiewać żartobliwie; naciągać

chagrin ('szaegryn) s. smutek; rozczarowanie; v.upokarzać;rozczarowywać boleśnie

chain (czejn) s. łańcuch; syndykat; trust; v, wiązać na łańcuchu; mierzyc;uwiązać; zakuć
chair (czeer) s. krzesło; stołek; fotel; katedra; v. przewodniczyc; sadzać na krześle
chair lift ('czeerlyft)s. wyciąg linowy
chairman ('czeermen) s. przewodniczący; prezes _fkredą
chalk (czo:k) s. kreda;v.pisać
challenge ('czaelyndż) s., wyzwanie; zadanie; v. wyzywać; zarzucać; wzywać;korcić;prowokować
chamber ('czejmber) s. izba; komora;sala;pokój;v.wydrążyć
chambermaid ('czejmbermejd) s. pokojowa
chamois ('szaemła:) s. giemza; ircha; zamsz
champagne ('szaem'pejn) s. szampan
champion ('czaempjen) s. mistrz; obrońca; v. bronic; walczyć o...
championship ('czaempjenszyp) s. mistrzostwo
chance (cza:ns) s. okazja; przypadek; szczęście; szansa;ryzyko; adj. przypadkowy; przygodny; v. zdarzać się; ryzykować; próbować;przytrafić się;natknąc się
chancellor (cza:seler) s. kanclerz; pierwszy sekretarz (ambasady);najwyższy sędzia
chandelier (szaendy'lyer) s. żyrandol; świecznik
change (czejndż) s, zmiana; wymiana; drobne; v. zmienić; przebierać (się); wymieniać
change one's mind ('czejndż, lans'majnd) zmienic czyjeś zdanie (przekonania etc.)
change trains ('czejndż,trejns) v. przesiąsć się (na kolei)
changeable('czejndżebl) adj. zmienny;podlegający zmianom
channel ('czaenl) s. kanał; koryto; łożysko; v, żłobić; przesyłać drogą (urzędową)
chaos ('kejos) s. chaos
chap (czaep) s., chłop; chłopiec; człek; v.pękać; powodować pęknięcia (warg);zarysowywać

chapel ('czaepel) s. kaplica
chaplain ('czaeplyn) s. kapelan
chaps (cza:ps)pl.. skórzane nogawice (kowboja);ochraniacze
chapter ('czaepter) s. rozdział; oddział; v. dzielić na rozdziały
character ('kaerykter) s. charakter; typ; cecha; reputacja; moralność; facet; znak
characteristic ('kaerykterystyk) adj. charakterystyczny; typowy; s. cecha; własność; właściwość
characterize ('kaerykterajz) v. charakteryzować (opisywać)
charge (cza:rdż) s. ciężar; ładunek; obowiązek; piecza; podopieczny; zarzut; opłata; należność; szarża; godło; v. ładować; nasycać; obciążać; zadać; liczyć sobie; oskarżać; atakować; szarżować
charge account (cza:rdż e'kaunt) s. otwarty kredyt (w banku)
charge card (cza:rdż'ka:rd) s. karta kredytowa do zakupów
chariot ('czaerjet) s. wóz; rydwan
charitable ('czaerytebl) adj. litościwy; dobroczynny
charity ('czaeryty), s. miłosierdzie; dobroczynność
charm (cza:rm) s, czar; urok; amulet; v. czarować; oczarować
charming (cza:rmyng)adj. czarujący
chart (cza:rt) s. wykres; mapa morska; v. robić wykres; wytyczać; pokazywać (jak)
charmless (cza:rmlys) adj. bez wdzięku
charter (cza:rter)s. statut; przywilej; dyplom; akt nadania prawa do... v. nadawać; zakładać na statutach; wynajmować statek lub samolot
charter plane (cza:rter plejn) s. wynajęty grupowo samolot
charwoman ('cza:rłumen) s. sprzątaczka; dochodząca sprzataczka;posługaczka

chase 1. (czejs) s. pościg; pogoń; polowanie; v. gonić; ścigać; polować; wyganiac
chase 2. (czejs) s. łożysko; wgłębienie; wykop; v. żłobic
chasm ('kaezem) s. otchłan
chaste (czejst) adj. czysty; niewinny;nieskażony;cnotliwy
chastity ('czaestyty) s. niewinnosć; prostota;dziewictwo
chat (czaet) s. pogawędka; v. gawędzić; gadać;rozmawiać
chatter (czaeter) v. szczebiotać; klapać; s.szczebiot; klapanie; klekot;paplanie;terkot
chatterbox (czaeterboks) s. trajkotka;gaduła;pleciuga
chauffer ('szoufer) s. zawodowy kierowca; przenośny piecyk
cheap (czi:p) adj. tani; marny
cheapen (czi:pen) v. taniec; obniżać wartosć;spadać w cenie
cheat (czi:t) s. oszust; oszustwo; v. oszukiwać; zdradzać (w małżeństwie);okpiwać
check (czek) s. wstrzymanie ; przerwa; sprawdzenie; czek; kwit; szach; a. szachownicowy; kontrolny; pokreślony; v. hamowac; sprawdzac; zakreslac; nadawac; zgadzac się; szachowac;ganić;krytykować;opanowywać
check in (czek yn) v. wmeldowywać się (w pracy,w wojsku etc.)
check out (czek aut) v. wymeldowywać się;zapłacić za hotel
checked (czekt) adj, w kratkę
checkroom (czekrum) s. przechowalnia (bagażu);szatnia
cheek (czi:k) s. policzek; bezczelne gadanie; v. mowic bezczelnie do kogos; stawiać się
cheeky ('czi:ky) adj. bezczelny; zuchwały;pełen tupetu;z tupetem
cheer (czier) s. brawo; hurra; radosć; jadło; v. krzyczec; rozweselac;dodawać otuchy
cheer on ('czier on) v. zachęcać ;zagrzewać;dodawać otuchy
cheer up ('czier ap) v. pocieszac; nabrać otuchy;rozpogodzić
cheerful ('czierful) adj. pogodny; wesoły; ochoczy;rozweselający

cheerless ('czierlys) adj. ponury; smutny; przybity
cheery ('cziery) adj. wesoły; radosny; pogodny
cheese ('czi:z) s. ser
chef (czef) s. kuchmistrz
chemical ('kemykel) adj. chemiczny;s.substancja chemiczna
chemicals ('kemykels) pl. chemikalia;leki:lekarstwa
chemise (sze'mi:z) s. damska koszula luźna i długa
chemist ('kemyst) s. chemik; aptekarz
chemistry ('kemystry) s. chemia
cheque (czek) s. czek (poza USA)
chequered ('czekerd) adj. kratkowany; urozmaicony; burzliwy
cherish ('czerysz) v. lubic; tulic; żywic (uczucie);miłować
cherry ('czery) s. czeresnia; wisniowy kolor; vulg.:prawiczka; adj. wisniowy; vulg.: prawiczy; czerwony
chess (czes) s. szachy
chess-board (czes-bo:rd) s. szachownica
chess man(czesmen) s. figurka szachowa
chest (czest) s. skrzynia; komoda; piers ;płuca;kufer;skrzynka
chestnut ('czesnat) s. kasztan
chest of drawers (czest ow dro:ers) komoda
chew (czu:) v. żuć; przeżuwać; besztac; gderać; s. żucie; tyton do żucia; prymka
chewing gum('czu:yng.gam) s. guma do żucia
chicken ('czykyn) s. kurcze; adj.tchórzliwy; bojący się
chicken out ('czykyn aut) v. stchórzyć;ustąpić ze strachu
chide; chid; chidden (czajd; czyd; czydn)
chide (czajd) v. łajać; droczyć się; skarżyć;besztać; łajać
chicken pox('czykyn poks) s. ospa wietrzna
chief (czy:f) s. wódz; szef; adj. główny; naczelny
chilblain ('czylblejn) s, odmrożenie

child (czajld) s. dziecko
childish ('czajldysz) adj. dziecinny
childless ('czajldlys) adj. bezdzietny
childlike ('czajldlajk) adj. dziecięcy; jak dziecko
children( 'czyldren) pl. dzieci
chill (czyl) s. chłód; dreszcz; v. studzić; mrozić ;oziębiać
chilly (czyly) adj. chłodny; adv. chłodno; zimno
chime ('czajm) s. dzwony grające; rytm; kurant; v. bić w dzwony; wydzwaniać; rymować;zabrzmieć
chimney ('czymny) s. komin; wylot; szkło lampy naftowej
chimney sweeper ('czymny,słi:per) s. kominiarz;adj. kominiarski
chin (czyn) s. broda; v. podciągać brodę do drążka;s.podbródek
china ('czajna) s. porcelana
chinese ('czaj'ni:z) adj. chiński;Chinese s. chińczyk
chink('czyŋk) 1. s. brzęk; v.pobrzękiwać; brzęczec; 2. szpara; szczelina; v. zapychać szpary
chip (czyp) s. drzazga; odłamek; skrawek; v. otłuc; obijać; dokuczać; nabierać; ciosać; ćwierkać; piszczec; nogę podstawiać; złuszczać się;odłupać
chirp (czy:rp) s. świergot; v. ćwierkać; szczebiotać
chisel ('czyzl) s. dłuto; przecinek; v. ciąć; rzeźbić;oszukać
chivalrous ('czywelres) adj. rycerski
chivalry ('czywelry) s. rycerstwo; rycerskość
chive (czajw) s. szczypiorek
chlorine ('klo:ry:n) s. chlor
chloroform ('klo:refo:rm) s. chloroform; v. maczać w chloroformie;usypiać chloroformem
chock (czok) s. klin; v. osadzać na klinach; adv. szczelnie; ciasno; mocno ; w pełni
chocolate ('czoklyt) s. czekolada;adj. czokoladowy(kolor etc.)
choice (czoys) s. wybor; wybranka; adj.wyborowy;doborowy

choir ('kłajer) s. chór
choke (czouk) v. dusić; zadusić; tłumić; dławić; s. durzenie; dławik; gardziel; przewężenie;odgłosy duszenia;zawór
choke down (czouk dałn) v. dławić;zmniejszać gardziel
choke up (czouk ap) v. zatykać
(rurę); zadławić(motor etc.)
choose; chose; chosen (czu:z; czouz; czouzn)
choose (czu:z) v. wybierać; woleć; postanowić;zadecydować
chop (czop) v. rąbać; obcinać; s. rąbnięcie; kotlet;krótka fala
chop down (czop dałn) v. powalić (drzewo etc.); ściać;zrąbać
chord (ko:rd) s. struna; cięciwa;struna głosowa
chorus ('ko:res) s. chór; v. mówić chórem;śpiewać chórem
chose (czouz) v. wybrał; zob. choose
chow (czau) s. jadło (slang)
Christ (krajst) Chrystus
christen ('krisn) v. ochrzcić
Christian ('krystjen) adj. chrześcijański; s. chrześcijanin(slang:cywilizowany)
Christianity (krys'czaenyty) v. chrześcijaństwo
Christian name ('krystjen,nejm) s. imię(inne niż nazwisko)
Christmas ('krysmas) s. Boże Narodzenie
Christmas Day ('krysmas dej) Dzień Bożego Narodzenia
Christmas Eve ('krysmas i:w) wilia, wigilia Bożego Narodzenia
chromium ('kroumjem) s. chrom
chronic ('kronyk) adj. chroniczny;strawszliwy (ból)
chronicle ('kronykl) s. kronika
chronological ( krone'lodżykel) adj. chronologiczny
chubby ('czaby) adj. pucołowaty; pyzaty;mały i gruby
chuck (czak) v. rzucać; gdakać; cmokać; s. kurczątko; dziecina; kochanie;gdakanie;cmokanie

chuckle (czakl) v. chichotac;
s. chichot; zduszony śmiech
chum (czam) v. przyjaźnic się
blisko; s. serdeczny kolega;
współlokator;v.przyjaźnić sie
church (cze:rcz) s. kościół
churchyard (tze:rczja:rd) s.
cmentarz; dziedziniec kościelny; adj. cmentarny
churn (cze:rn) v. robic masło;
kłocić się; burzyc sie; kotłować się; pienic się; s. maślni-
ca; maślniczka;bańka na mleko
chute (szu:t) s. koryto zrzuto-
we; spadek; wodospad; spadochron; tor zjażdżalni dla dzięci
chutzpah (hucpa) s. nachalnosc;
śmiałość;tupet(po nowohebrajsku)
cider ('sajder) s. wino z jabłek
cigar (sy'ga:r) s. cygaro
cigaret(te) (sige'ret) s. papieros
cinder ('synder) s. popiół; żużel; v. spalac na żużel
cinderella (,synde'rele) s. kopciuszek; Kopciuszek
cinder track ('synder-traek) s.
bieżnia żużlowa;tor łużlowy
cine camera ('syni-'kaemere) s.
aparat filmowy
cinema ('syneme) s. kino
cinema projector ('syneme-
prodżekter) s. rzutnik filmowy
cipher ('sajfer) s. cyfra; szyfr;
zero; v. szyfrowac; rachowac
circle ('se:rkl) s. koło; krąg;
obwód; v. otaczac; kręcić się
w koło; opasywc; krążyć;okrążać
circuit ('se:rkyt) s. obwód;
okrężna; okólna (podróż)
circular ('se:rkjuler) s. okólnik; adj. okrągły; kolisty
circulate ('se:rkjulejt) v.
krążyć; cyrkulowac; puszczac
w obieg; być w obiegu
circulation ('se:rkjulejszyn)
s. krążenie; obrót; nakład
circumference (se'rkamfyrens)
s. obwód (koła etc.)
circumcision (se:rkem'syżyn)s.
obrzezanie;obcięcie napletka

circumscribe (,se:rkem'skrajb)
v. opisywac; zakreslac
circumstance ('se:rkemstaens)
s. okoliczności; szczegóły
circus ('se:rkes) s. cyrk;
okrągły plac;rondo; desant(sl.)
cistern ('systern) s. zbiornik
na wodę; cysterna
cite (sajt) v. cytowac; przytaczac; pozywac; wymieniac
w komunikacie;wzywac do sądu
citizen ('sytyzn) s. obywatel
citizenship ('sytyzenszyp) s.
obywatelstwo;cnoty obywatelskie
city ('syty) s. (wielkie) miasto; centrum finansowe;ośrodek
city center ('syty,senter) s.
centrum miasta
city guide ('syty'gajd) s. plan
miasta;przewodnik po mieście
city hall('syty,ho:l) s. zarząd
miasta; magistrat
civics ('sywyks) s. nauka praw
i obowiazkow obywatela[uprzejmy;
civil ('sywl) adj. społeczny;
obywatelski;cywilny(kodeks);
civilian (sy'wyljen) adj. cywilny; s. cywil; obywatel
civility (sy'wylyty) s. uprzej-
mosć; grzeczność
civilization (,sywylaj'sejszyn)
s. cywilizacja;całość kultury
civilize ('sywylajz) v. cywili-
zowac; ucywilizowac
civil marriage ('sywl'maerydż)
s. slub cywilny
civil rights ('sywl,rajts) s.
prawa obywatelskie
civil service ('sywl'se:rwys)
s. służba państwowa
civil war ('sywl,ło:r) s. wojna domowa
clack (klaek) v. klekotac; gdakać; s. klekot; wieko
clad (klaed) adj. odziany; zob.
clothe
claim (klejm) v. żądac; twierdzić; s. żądanie; twierdzenie;
działka;skarga;zażalenie;dług
claimant (klejment) s. rosci-
ciel; pretendent;adj.pilny;rażący

clammy ('klaemy) adj. mokro-
lepki;wilgotny i zimny
clamor ('klaemer) s. zgiełk;
krzyk; v. krzyczeć; robić
wrzawę; wymuszać krzykiem
clamorous ('klaemeres) adj.
zgiełkliwy; krzykliwy
clamp (klaemp) s. klamra; zacisk;v.zaciskać (jak)klamrą
clan (klaen) s. klan; szczep
szkocki;v.tworzyć klikę
clandestine (klaen'destyn) adj.
potajemny; skryty; tajny
clang (klaeng) s.dźwięk: szczęk;
klekot; v. dzwięczeć; szczękać;
klekotać;rozbrzmiewać;dzwonić
clank (klaenk) s. chrzęst;
brzęk; v. brzękać; chrzęścić
clap (klaep) s. huk; klaskanie;
v. łopotać; oklaskiwać; klepać
claret ('klaeret) s. czerwone
wino; bordo; slang:krew
clarify ('klaeryfaj) v. wyjas-
niać; rozjaśniać; oczyszczać
clarity ('klaeryty) s. czystość;
jasność; przejżystość;klarowność
clash (klaesz) s. brzęk; starcie;
v. brzęczeć; ścierać się; kolidować; uderzać w coś
clasp (klaesp) s. klamra; uchwyt; okucie; v. spinać; ściskać
clasp knife ('klaesp-najf) s.
scyzoryk;kozik; nóż składany
class (klaes) s. klasa; lekcja;
rocznik; grupa; v. klasyfikować ;segregować; sortować
classmate ('kla:s,mejt) s. kolega szkolny
classroom ('kla:s,rum) s. klasa
(w szkole); sala szkolna
class struggle (,kla:s's'stragl)
s. walka klas w społeczeństwie
classic ('klaesyk) s. klasyk;
studia klasyczne; adj. klasyczny; uznany autotytet;klasyk
classical ('klaesykel) adj. typowy; klasyczny;humanistyczny
classification (klaesyfy'kejszyn)
s. klasyfikacja;klasyfikowanie
classify ('klaesyfaj) v. klasyfikować; sortować; zaklasyfikować
clatter ('klaeter) v. brzęczeć;
klapać; s. brzęk;łoskot;gwar

clause (klo:z) s. klauzula;
zdanie; punkt umowy
claw (klo:) s. pazur; szpon;
łapa; kleszcze; v. drapać; wydrapać; łapać w szpony
clay (klej) s. glina; sl.trup
clean (kli:n) adj. czysty; wyraźny; zgrabny; adv. całkiem;
zupełnie; poprostu; v, oczys-
cić; opróżniać; ogołocić; wygrać; uprzątnąć;dużo zyskać(sl,)
clean out ('kli:n aut) v. oczys-
cić; opróżniać;wyczyścić
clean up ('kli:n ap) v. po-
sprzątać; wygrać; zrobić na
czysto;robić porządek
cleaner ('kli:ner) s. czyści-
ciel; oczyszczalnik; właściciel pralni;pralnia chemiczna
cleaning ('kli:nyng) s. czyszczenie; sprzątanie;porządki
cleanliness ('klenlynys) s.
czystość;zamiłowanie do czystości
cleanly ('klenly) adj. czysty;
adv. czysto; schludnie
cleanness ('kli:nnys) s. czystość;zamiłowanie do czystości
cleanse (klenz) v. oczyścić;
zmywać (grzechy);oczyszczać
clear (klier) adj. jasny; czysty; bystry; adv. jasno; wyraźnie; z dala; zupełnie; dokładnie; s. wolna przestrzeń
clear away('klier,ełej) v. usunąć (przeszkodę etc.)
clear up ('klier,ap) v. wyjaśnić
clear-cut ('klier,kat) adj. wyraźny; czysty ; poprawny
clearing ('klieryng) s. karczo-
wisko; rozrachunek;obrachunek
clearly ('klierly) adv. wyraźnie; jasno; oczywiście
cleave; cleft; cleft (kli:w;
kleft; kleft)
cleave (kli:w) v. 1. łupać; pękać; rozdwajać; 2. trzymać się
wiernie ; nie odstępować
clef (klef) s. klucz (muzyczny)
cleft (kleft) s. szczelina;
pęknięcie; zob. cleave
clemency ('klemensy) s. miłosierdzie;łagodność (klimatu etc.)

clench (klencz) v. ściskać; zaciskać; zewrzeć się; s. uścisk;
zaciśnięcie; zagięcie;ubić(targ-
clergy ('kle:rdży) s. duchowieństwo ;kler
clergyman ('kle:rdżymen) s.
duchowny; ksiądz; pastor
clerical ('klerykel) adj. urzęd-
niczy; duchowny; biurowy
clerk (kla:rk) s. subjekt;
urzędnik; pisarz; ekspedient
clever ('klewer) adj. zdolny;
sprytny; zręczny;pomysłowy;uprze-
click (klyk) v. szczękać; cmokać; trzaskać; dopiąć swego;
wygrać; s. trzask; zatrzask;
klamka;mlaśnięcie;klekot;brzęk
client ('klajent) s. klient
cliff (klyf) s. urwisko; stroma
ściana; ściana skalna
climate ('klajmyt) s. klimat
climax ('klajmaeks) s. szczyt;
zakończenie; v. stopniowac;
szczytować; kuliminować
climb (klajm) s.wspinaczka;
miejsce wspinania; v. piąc się;
wspinać; wzbijać się;wdrapać się
climb up (klajm ap) v. wspinać
się w górę; wdrapywać się
climber (klajmer) s.taternik;
karierowicz; pnącz (roślina)
clinch (klyncz) v. zaciskać;
zaginać; zanitować;zakończyć
cling: clung; clung (klyng;klang;
klang)
cling (klyng)v. trzymać się;
chwytać się; czepiać się;trwać
clinic ('klynyk) s. klinika; poradnia; adj. kliniczny
clink (klynk) s. dzwonienie;
ciupa ; v. dzwonić (kluczami etc.)
clip 1. (klyp) s. sprzączka
v. spinać; 2. s. strzyżenie;
nożyce; v. strzyc; orznąc
clippings ('klypyns) pl. wycinki (z gazet);okrawki;obrzynki
cloak (klouk) s. płaszcz;maska;
v. okryć płaszczem;wdziewać
clock (klok) s. zegar ścienny
clockwise ('klokłajz) adj. (obrót) w prawo wg. zegarka

clod (klod) s. gruda; ziemia;
gamoń.v.obrzucać grudkami ziemi
clog (klog) s. kłoda; chodak;
v. zatykać; zapychac;zawadzać
cloister ('klojster) s. krużganek; klasztor
close (klouz) v. zamykać; zatykać; zakończyć; zwierać; zgodzić się; s. zakończenie; koniec; miejsce ogrodzone;
adv. szczelnie; blisko; prawie
adj. zamknięty; skąpy; gęsty;
bliski; ścisły;ekskluzywny;skąpy
close to ('klous tu) przy;tuż o-
close by ('klous baj) obok   bok
close down ('klouz dałn) v. zamykać;kończyć (działalność etc.)
close in (klouz yn) v. nadchodzić; ogarniać; okrążyć;otoczyć
closet ('klozyt) s. pokoik;
klozet; kredens
close-up ('klousap) s. zdjęcie
zbliżone; zbliżenie
closing time ('klouzyng,tajm)
s. koniec pracy; zamknięcie
(sklepu);koniec urzędowania
clot (klot) s. skrzep; v. ścinać się; skrzepnąć;zsiadać się
cloth (kloth) s. materiał; szmata; szafa; obrus;sukno;żagiel
cloth-bound (kloth baumd) s.
oprawny w płótno
clothe (klouz) s. materiał; sukno;v.przywdziewać; zamaskować
clothes (klouz) pl. ubranie;
pościel; pranie; odzierz;ubiór
clothes brush ('klouz,brasz) s.
szczotka do ubrań
clothes hanger ('klouz,hanger)
s. wieszak do ubrań
clothesline ('klouz,lajn) s.
sznur na bieliznę do suszenia
clothespin ('klouz,pyn) s.
spinacz do bielizny
clothing (klouzyng) s. odzież;
osłona; bielizna;odzienie
cloud (klaud) s. chmura; obłok;
zasępienie; v. chmurzyć; sę-
pić; rzucać cień ;ufarbować
cloudy ('klaudy) adj. chmurny;
posępny; zamglony; mętny

clove (klouw) s. goździk; ząbek
czosnku: zob. cleave
clover (klouwer) s. koniczyna
clown (klaun) s. błazen; prostak; v. błaznować; wygłupiać się
club (klab) s. klub; pałka;
kij; v, bić pałką; zbijać; łączyć; zrzeszać;stowarzyszać się
clue (klu:)· s. klucz; ślad;
wątek; v. informować(o wątku)
clumsy ('klamzy) adj. niezgrabny; nietaktowny;niekształtny
clung (klang)vprzywarty; zob.
cling
cluster ('klaster) s. grono;
kiść; pęk; kupka; v. tworzyć
pęki; skupiać się; zbierać się
clutch (klacz) s. chwyt; szpon;
sprzęgło;v.trzymać się kurczowo
clutch pedal ('klacz,pedl) s.
pedał sprzęgła
coach (koucz) s. wóz pasażerski;
trener; v. jechać wozem; trenować; uświadamiać;pouczać
coagulate (kou'aegjulejt) v.
stężać; skrzepnąć;koagulować
coal (koul) s. węgiel
coalfield ('koul'fi:ld) s. zagłębie węglowe
coalition (,koue'lyszyn) s.
związek; koalicja;przymierze
coal mine(koul-majn) s. kopalnia
węgla
coal pit ('koul-pyt) s. kopalnia
węgla ;szyb kopalniany
coarse (ko:rs) adj. pospolity;
gruboziarnisty ; szorstki
coast (koust) s. brzeg; v. jechać bez napędu;płynąc brzegiem
coastguard ('koustga:rd) s.
straż przybrzeżna
coat (kout) s. marynarka; surdut; powłoka; v. okrywać; pokrywać warstwą ;powlekać(farbą)
coat hanger('kouthaenger) s.
wieszak (do ubrania)
coating (koutyng) s. powłoka;
warstwa ;pokrycie
coat of arms('kout ow,a:rms) s.
herb; godło
coax (kouks) v. namówić pochleb-
stwem; udobruchać;przymilać się;
wycyganiać; wyczrowywać(z butelki)

cob (kob) s. głąb; kucyk; ła-
będz samiec;kaczan;kutwa;bochenek
cobra ('koubre) s. kobra
cobweb ('kobłeb) s. pajęczyna
cock (kok) s. kogut; kurek;
kran; kutas (vulg.) v. postawić; nastroszyć; napiąć; odwodzić; podnieść; zadzierać;wznieść
cock-and-bull ('koken'bul) exp.:
o żelaznym wilku
cockchafer ('kok,chejfer) s.
chrząszcz
cockle ('kokl) s. kąkol;piecyk
cockpit ('kokpyt) s. kokpit;
kabina;arena do walki kogutów
cockroach('kokroucz) s. karaluch
cocksure ('kokszuer) adj. pewny siebie; zarozumiały
cocktail ('koktejl) s. cocktail
coco ('koukou) s. palma kokoso-
wa; kokos
cocoa ('koukou) s. kakao
coconut ('koukenat) s. orzech
kokosowy
cocoon (ke'ku:n) s. kokon;
oprzęd
cod(kod)s.dorsz;sztokfisz;wąt-
łusz;v.wystrychnąć na dudka
coddle ('kodl) v. podgotować;
pieścić; tuczyć; zepsuć
code (koud) s. kodeks; szyfr;
v. szyfrować ;pisać szyfrem
cod-liver oil ('kod,lywer ojl)
s. tran (lekarski)
coexist ('kouyg'zyst) v. współistniec;koegzystować
coexistence ('kouyg'zystens)
s. współistnienie;współżycie
coffee('kofy) s. kawa
coffee bean ('kofy-bi·:n) s.
ziarno kawy
coffee mill ('kofy-myl) s. młynek do kawy
coffeepot ('kofy-pot) s. maszynka do kawy
coffin ('kofyn) s. trumna
cogwheel ('kog-hłil) s. koło
zębate; tryb
coherence (kou'hierens) s. sens;
spoistość ;związek logiczny
coherency (kou'hierensy) s.
sens; zwartość ;spójność

coherent (kou'hierent) adj. logiczny; zwarty; spoisty
cohesive (kou'hi:syw) adj. spoisty; zwarty ; kleisty
coiffure (kła:'fjuer) s. fryzura; styl uczesania
coil (kojl) s. zwój; cewka; lok; v. zwijać; skręcać; wić się
coin (koyn) s. moneta; v. bić monety; spieniężać; ukuc (nowe pojęcie) ;tłoczyć
coinage (koynydź) s. bicie monety; monety; system monetarny; wymysł;nowe słowo
coincide (kouyn'sajd) v. zbiegać się; pokrywać się; przystawać do siebie; pasować
coincidence (kou'ynsydens) s. zbieg okoliczności; zgodność; przystawanie; zgodność faktów
coke (kouk) s. koks; kokaina; Coca-Cola; v. koksować
cold (kould) s. zimno; przeziębienie; adj.zimny;chłodny;mroźny
cold storage room(kouldstoredżru:m) chłodnia
colic ('kolyk) s. kolka (w brzuchu);ostry ból w brzuchu
collaborate (ke'laeberejt) v. współpracować;kolaborować
collaboration (ke'laeberejszyn) s. współpraca; kolaboracja
collapse (ke'laeps) s. załamanie się; v. załamać się; upaść; opaść; zawalić się;zalamywać
collapsible (ke'laepsebl) adj. składany (mebel,,stół,łóżko etc.)
collar ('koler) s. kołnierz; szyjka; pierścień; obroża; chomąto; piana (na piwie) v.wkładać obrożę; pojmac; ujać
collarbone ('koler-boun) s. obojczyk
colleague ('koli:g) s. kolega (po fachu);współpracownik
collect ('ke'lekt) v. zbierać; odbierać; inkasować
collected (ke'lektyd) adj. skupiony; opanowany ;spokojny
collection (ke'lekszyn) s. zbiór; kolekcja; inkaso ;zainkasowane pieniadze

collective ('ke'lektyw) adj. zbiorowy; wspólny;s. kolektyw
collector ('ke'lektor) s. inkasent; poborca; zbieracz
college ('kolydż) s. uczelnia; kolegium;zrzeszenie;akademia
collide (ke'lajd) v. zderzyć się; kolidować;wejść w kolizję
colliery ('koljery) s. kopalnia węgla
collision (ke'lyżen) s. zderzenie; kolizja
colloquial (ke'loukłjel) adj. potoczny (język);familiarny
colon ('koulen) s. grube jelito; dwukropek
colonel('ke:nl) s. pułkownik
colonial (ke'lounjel) a. kolonialny;s. mieszkaniec kolonii
colonialism (ke'lounjelyzem)s. kolonializm
colonist ('kolenyst) s. osadnik ;mieszkaniec kolonii
colonize ('kolenajz) v. osiedlać; kolonizować
colony ('koleny) s. kolonia
color ('kaler) s. barwa; farba; koloryt; v. barwic; farbować; koloryzować; rumienić się
color bar ('kaler ba:r) s. oddzielenie ras
colored ('kaleret) s. murzyn; kolorowy;adj.przekręcony
colored man ('kaleret men) s. murzyn
colored people ('kaleret'pi:pl) s. murzyni
colorful ('kalerful) adj. pstry; barwny ;żywy;kolorowy
coloring ('kaleryng) s. koloryt; kolorowanie; rumience
colorless ('kalerlys) adj. bezbarwny; nudny;monotonny
colorline ('kalerlajn) s. przedział rasowy
color print ('kaler,prynt) s. chromodruk
colt (koult) s. źrebak
column ('kolem) s. kolumna; stos; trzon; szpalta;formacja
coma ('koume) s. omdlenie; koma; śpiączka;ogon(komety)

comb (koum) s. grzębień; grzbiet
(fali); v. czesać; kłębić sie
combat ('kombet) s. walka;
v. zwalczać; walczyć
combatant ('kombetent) adj.
walczący; s. kombatant;bojownik
combination (komby'nejszyn)s.
kombinacja; zespół;związek
combine-harvester (kembajn-
ha:rwyster) s. kombajn
combustible (kem'bastebl) adj.
palny; s. paliwo; materiały
palne;opał;adj.popędliwy
combustion (kem'bastszyn) s.
spalanie; zapłon
come; came; come (kam; kejm;
kam)
come (kam) v. przybyc; pochodzic; wynosic;dziać się;być
come about ('kam,e'baut) v. zdarzyć się;stać się;odwracać się
come across ('kam,e'cros) v.
natknąc się;dać się przekonać
come along ('kam,e'long) v.
pospieszyc się; nadejść
come around ('kam,e'raund) v.
zmienic zdanie; odwiedzic
come at ('kam,et) v. podejsc;
dotrzec; przyjść o (czwartej...)
come by ('kam,baj) v. dojść do
czegos; minąc; nabyc
come for ('kam,for) v. przyjsc
po cos
come loose ('kam,luz) v. obluzniac się
come off ('kam,of) v. odpasc;
odleciec;puszczać;miec miejsce
come on ('kam,on) v. chodz-że;
przestan; daj spokoj!
come round ('kam,raund) v. zmienic zdanie;przechytrzyc;obejść
come to see ('kam tu si:) v. odwiedzic;przyjść z wizytą
come up to ('kam ap tu) v. podejsc do..;wejść na sam(szczyt)
come-and-go ('kam-en'-go) s.
bieganina;ruch tam i z powrotem
comeback ('kam-'baek) s. powrót : bystra odpowiedz;poprawa
comedian (ke'mi:djen) s. komik;

comedy('komydy) s.komedia

comer ('kamer) s. przybysz
comet ('komyt) s. kometa
comfort ('kamfert) s. wygoda;
pociecha; v. pocieszać; czynic wygodnym;dodawać otuchy
comfortable ('kamfertebl) adj.
wygodny; zadowolony;spokojny
comforter ('kamferter) s. po-
cieszyciel; kołdra;smoczek
comical ('komykel) adj. zabawny; śmieszny;komiczny
comic strips ('komyk,stryps) s.
seryjne obrazkowki;kreskowki
comma ('kome) s. przecinek
command (ke'maend) v. rozkazy-
wać; kazać; rozporządzać; panować nad; dowodzić; s. rozkaz;
nakaz; komenda;dowództwo
commander (ke'maender) s. dowodca; komendant;kapitan(fregaty)
commander-in-chief (ke'maender
yn'czi:f) głownodowodzący
commandment (ke'maendment) s.
przykazanie (boskie)
commend (ke'mend) v. chwalic;
zalecac; polecac opiece
comment ('koment) s. objasnie-
nie; v. robic uwagi krytyczne
lub złosliwe;wypowiadac zdanie
comment on('koment on) v. ko-
mentowac; oceniac (utwor etc.)
commentary('komentery) s. komentarz;uwaga; notatka
commentator('komentejter) s.
komentator; sprawozdawca
commerce ('kome:rs) s. handel
commercial (ke'ke:rszel) adj.
handlowy;s.ogołoszenie(w radiu...)
commissar ('komy'sa:r) s. komisarz w ZSRR
commission (ke'myszyn) s. zlecenie; misja; urząd; v. dele-
gowac; powierzac; objąc; zlecac;zamianowac;upoważniac
commissioner (ke'myszener) s.
delegat; pełnomocnik; komisarz
rządowy;członek komisji rządowej
commit (ke'myt) v. powierzac;
przekazywac; odsyłac; popełniac; wciągac; zobowiazywac
się;oddawac w opiekę;zamykć w
(domu wariatów);obiecywac

commitment (ke'mytment) s. zobowiązanie; dopuszczenie się;
przekazanie;zaangażowanie się
committee (ke'myti:) s. komitet;
komisja;opiekuń(umysłowo chrego)
commodity (ke'modyty) s. towar;
rzecz przydatna;artykuł handlu
common ('komen) adj. wspólny;
publiczny; ogólny; pospolity;
zwyczajny;prosty;publiczny
commoner ('komener) s. człowiek
z gminu; nie szlachcic
common law marriage ('komen,lo:
'maerydż) pożycie na wiarę
common market ('komen'ma:rkyt)
wspólny rynek (Zach.Eur.)
commonplace ('komen-plejs) s.
banał; adj. banalny;oklepany
common sense ('komen,sens)
zdrowy rozsądek
commonwealth ('komen,łels) s.
wspólnota; rzeczpospolita
commotion (ke'mouszyn) s. zamieszki; tumult; poruszenie
commune ('komju:n) s. gmina;
komuna; v. obcować; rozmawiać
communicate (ke'mju:ny,kejt) v.
dzielić się; komunikować; łączyć się;przenosic (ciepło etc.)
communication (ke,mju:ny'kejszyn)
s. łączność; komunikacja; po-
rozumiewanie się;zakomunikowanie
communicative (ke'mju:nykejtyw)
adj. otwarty; rozmowny; towarzyski; przystępny
communion (ke'mju:njen) s. obcowanie; uczestnictwo; wspólnota; komunia;wyznanie wiary
communism ('komju,nyzem) s. komunizm;ruch komunistyczny
communist ('komjunyst) s. komunista;adj. komunistyczny
community (ke'mju:nyty) s. środowisko; społeczność; gmina;
kolektyw; wspólnota;koło;zakon
commute (ke'mju:t) v. zamieniać;
zastępować; łagodzić; dojeżdżać
do pracy;brać bilet okresowy
comose ('koumous) adj. włochaty;
puszysty;włóknisty
compact (kem'paekt) adj. gęsty;
zbity; zwarty; v. ubijać; zbijać; zagęszczać;s.puderniczka

compact ('kempaekt) s. 1. ugoda;
porozumienie; 2. puderniczka
samochód średniej wielkości(USA)
companion (kem'paenjen) s. towarzysz; (coś) do pary
companionship (kem'paenjenszyp)
s. koleżeństwo; towarzystwo
company ('kampeny) s. towarzystwo; załoga; goście; partnerzy;
spółka; kompania;trupa teatralna
comparable ('komperebl) adj.
porównywalny;wytrzymujący porównanie
comparative (kem'paeretyw) adj.
porównawczy; względny; stosunkowy;s, stopień wyższy(przymiot-
nika
compare (kem'peer) v. porówny-
wać; dawać się porównać; stopniować (gram)
comparison (kem'paeryson) s. porównanie;zestawienie
compartment (kem'pa:rtment) s.
przedział; przegroda; komora
wodoszczelna
compass ('kampes) s. kompas;
busola; obwód; obręb;cyrkiel
zasięg v. obchodzić; otaczać;
ogarniać;osiągać;dopiąć
compassion (kem'paeszyn) s;
litość; współczucie
compassionate (kem'paeszynyt)
adj. litościwy;v.litować się
compatible (kem'paetebl) adj.
zgodny;licujący; do pogodzenia
compatriot (kem'paetryet) s.
rodak; ziomek;rodaczka
compel (kem'pel) v. zmuszać;
wymuszać (coś);wzbudzać
compensate ('kompen,sejt) v.
wyrównywać; nagradzać; wypłacić
odszkodowanie; kompensować
compensation (,kompen'sejszyn)
s. rekompensata; wynagrodzenie;
odszkodowanie;wyrównanie
compete (kem'pi:t) v. konkuro-
wać; rywalizować; ubiegać się
compete for (kem'pi:t,fo:r) v.
(o coś) współzawodniczyć;
współubiegać się;prześcigać się
competence ('kompytens) s. fa-
chowość; kwalifikacja; uzdolnienie; zasobność; dobrobyt
competent ('kompytent) adj. własciwy;kwalifikowany;odpowiedni;
kompetentny

competition (,kompy'tyszyn) s.
konkurencja; konkurs; zawody;
współzawodnictwo;tuniej
competitor (kem'petyter) s.
rywal; konkurent; współzawodnik;współzawodniczka;rywalka,
compile (kem'pajl) v. zbierac;
zestawiac; kompilowac
complacent (kem'plejsnt) adj.
zadowolony (z siebie; ze świata);błogi
complain (kem'plejn) v. żalic
się; narzekac; skarżyc; wnosic
zażalenie;wnosić skargę
complaint (kem'plejnt) s. skarga; zażalenie; dolegliwość
complete (kem'pli:t) adj. całkowity; zupełny; kompletny;
v. uzupełniac; udoskonalic;
ukończyc;wypełniać (formularz)
completion (kem'pli:szyn) s.
ukończenie; uzupełnienie;
udoskonalenie;spełnienie(woli)
complexion (kem'plekszyn) s.ce-
ra; płeć; postać; aspekt (charakter);wygląd
complicate ('komply,kejt) v.
wikłac; splątac; komplikowac
compliment ('komplyment) s.
komplement; gratulacje; ukło-
ny; uszanowanie; v. mówic
komplementy; gratulowac
comply (kem'plaj) v. zastosowac
się; spełnic; podporządkowac
się;uczynić zadość;przestrzegać
comply with (kem'plaj,łys) v.
spełniac;przestrzegać czegoś
component (kem'pounent) s.
składnik; część składowa; siła
składowa;adj.składowy
compose (kem'pouz) v. składać;
układać; tworzyc; komponowac;
skupiac (myśli); uspokoic; załagodzić;uspokajać się
composed (kem'pouzd) adj. opanowany; spokojny;stateczny
composer (kem'pouzer) s. kompozytor;kompozytorka
composition (,kempe'zyszyn) s.
skład; układ; ugoda; wypracowanie; budowa;usposobienie
composure (kem'poużer) s. spokój; opanowanie;zimna krew

compote ('kompout) s. kompot
(z puszki);kompotiera
compound (kom'paund) adj. złożony; sprężony; s. związek(chem.)
mieszanka; złożenie; v. mieszac; składac; powiększac;
łączyc;zawrzeć;załatwić
comprehend (,kompry'hend) v.
pojmowac; rozumieć; zawierać
comprehensible (,kompry'hensebl)
adj. zrozumiały;pojętny
comprehensive (,kompry'hensyw)
adj. obszerny; szeroki;rozumo-
wy; wyczerpujący;ogólny;wszech-
stronny
compress (kem'pres) v. ściskać;
s. kompres; okład;v.streszczać
comprise (kem'prajz) v. włączać; obejmowac;składać się
compromise ('kompre,majz) s.
kompromis; ugoda; kompromitacja; narażenie; v. załatwiac
ugodowo; kompromitowac
compulsion (kem'palszyn) s.
przymus; siła przymusu
compulsory (kem'palsery) adj.
przymusowy;przymuszający
compunction (kem'pankszyn) s.
skrucha;żal za grzechy
computation (,kompju'tejszyn) s,
obliczenie; kalkulcja
computer (kem'pju:ter) s. kalku-
lator; komputer; przelicznik
comrade ('komread) s. kolega;
druh; współpracownik
comradeship ('komraedszyp) s.
koleżeństwo; braterstwo
conceal (ken'si:l) v. taic,
ukrywac;przemilczać;zataić
concede (ken'si:d) v. przyznawać; ustępowac; poddawać się
conceit (ken'si:t) s. próżnośc;
zarozumiałosc;mniemanie;koncept
conceited (ken'si:tyd) adj.
próżny; zarozumiały
conceivable (ken'si:webl) adj.
wyobrażalny; zrozumiały
conceive (ken'si:w) v. wymyślic;
wyobrażac; rozumieć; ujmowac;
zajść w ciążę;pojąc;redagować
concentrate ('konsentrejt) v.
skupiac się; stężac;s.roztwór
conception (ken'sepszyn) s. pomysł; poczęcie (dziecka);początek

concern (ken'se:rn) s. interes;
troska; związek; v. tyczyć się;
dotyczyć; obchodzić; niepokoić
się o...;wchodzić w grę
concerned (ken'se:rnd) adj. zainteresowany; zaaferowany;
strapiony; niespokojny
concert ('konsert) s. koncert;
porozumienie; v. ułożyć; ukar-
tować;porozumieć się
concession (ken'se szyn) s.
koncesja; ustępstwo;przyzwolenie
conciliate (ken'syly,ejt) v.
zjednywać; jednać; godzić; łagodzić; pogodzić;udobruchać
conciliatory (ken'syljeto:ry)
adj. pojednawczy
concise (ken'sajs) adj. zwięzły;
treściwy ;krotki i węzłowaty
conclude (ken'klu:d) v. zakończyć; zawierać; wnioskować;
postanawiać ;kończyć się
conclusion (ken'klu:żyn) s. zakończenie; wynik; postanowienie; wniosek; konkluzja; zawar-
cie układu ;wynik ostateczny
conclusive (ken'klu:syw) adj.
rozstrzygający; dowodny
concord ('konko:rd) s. zgoda;
jedność; harmonia;v. zgadzać się
concrete ('konkri:t) s. beton;
konkret; adj. rzeczywisty;
realny; zwarty; stały; konkretny; specyficzny; betonowy
concur (ken'ke:r) v. zgadzać
się; schodzić się;współdziałać
concurrence (ken'ke:rens) s.
zgodność; zbieżność ; zgoda
concussion (ken'kaszyn) s.
wstrząs (mózgu); uderzenie
condemn (ken'dem) v. potępiać;
skazywać ;krytykować;wybrakować
condemnation (,kendem'nejszyn)
s. potępienie; skazanie
condense (ken'dens) v. kondenso-
wać; zgęszczać;streszczać
condenser (ken'denser) s. kondensator; skraplacz
condescend (,kondy'send) v.
zniżać się; raczyć; zezwalać;
zachowywać się z wyższością

condition (ken'dyszyn) s. stan;
warunek; zastrzeżenie; poprawka; v.uwarunkowywać; zastrzegać; naprawiać; przygotowywać; przyzwyczajać;klimatyzować
conditional (ken'dyszynl) adj.
warunkowy;uzależniony;zależny
condole (ken'doul) v. składać
kondolencje;współczuć;ubolewać
condolence (ken'doulens) s.
wyrazy współczucia;kondolencje
conduct (kon'dakt) s. prowadzenie; sprawowanie; prowadzenie
się; sprawowanie się; kierownictwo; v. prowadzić; wieść;
przewodzić;dyrygować;dowodzić
conduction (kon'dakszyn) s.
przewodzenie (fiz.)
conductor (kon'dakter) s. kierownik; przewodnik; dyrygent;
przewód;odgromnik;piorunochron
cone (koun) s. stożek; szyszka;
v. nadawać kształt stożka
confection (ken'fekszyn) s.
sporządzanie; konfitura; słodycze; konfekcja (damska)
confectioner (ken'fekszyner) s.
cukiernik;właściciel cukierni
confectionery (ken'feksznery)
s. cukiernia; wyroby cukier-
nicze
confederacy (ken'federesy) s.
konfederacja; sojusz; związek; spisek; sprzysiężenie
confederate (ken'federyt) adj.
sprzysiężony; v. jednoczyć;
spiskować; knuć;sprzymierzać
confederation (ken,fede'rejszyn)
s. sprzymierzenie; skonfedero-
wanie; konfederacja
confer (ken'fe:r) v. naradzać
się; nadawać ;przyznawać
conferee (,konfe'ri:) s. uczestnik konferencji; nagrodzony
conference ('konferens) s. narada; liga;zebranie;zjazd
confess (ken'fes) v. wyznać;
przyznać się; spowiadać się
confession (ken'feszen) s. wyznanie; spowiedź; przyznanie
się ; religia

confessor (ken'feser) s. spowiednik; ksiądz spowiednik
confide (ken'fajd) s. ufać (komuś); zwierzać sie; powierzać
confidence ('konfydens) s. zaufanie; bezczelność; pewność;
ufność; zwierzenie;śmiałość
confident ('konfydent) adj.
dufny; bezczelny ;przekonany
confidential (,konfy'denczel)
adj. tajny; poufny; zaufany;
poufały;intymny
confine ('konfajn) v. ograniczać; odosabniać;s,kres;granica
confinement (kon'fajnment) s.
uwięzienie; ograniczenie; odosobnienie; połóg; poród
confirm (ken'fe:rm) v. potwierdzać; zatwierdzać; umacniać;
bierzmować;utwierdzać;pokrzepić
confirmation (,konfer'mejszyn)
s. potwierdzenie; zatwierdzenie; bierzmowanie;pokrzepienie
confiscate ('konfyskejt) v. kon-
fiskować; skonfiskować
conflagration (,konfle'grejszyn)
s. pożar; pożoga
conflict ('konflykt) s. zatarg;
starcie; konflikt; kolizja
conform (kon'fo:rm) v. dostosować; upodabniać;dostrajać
conformity (kon'fo:rmyty) s.
zgodność; dostosowanie się
confound (kon'faund) v. mieszać;
zawieść; pokrzyżować;poplątać
confound it ! (kon'faund,yt) exp.;
do licha ! niech to diabli wezmą!
confront (ken'frant) v. stawiać
czoło; konfrontować;unaocznić
confuse (ken'fju:z) v. zmieszać
(kogoś; siebie);wikłać;gmatwać
confusion (ken'fju:żyn) s. nieład; zamieszanie;bałagan;chaos
congeal (ken'dżi:l) v. mrozić;
ścinać; marznąc;zakrzepnąć
congestion (ken'dżestczyn)s.
przeludnienie; przeciążenie
(ruchu); przekrwienie
conglomerate (ken'glomerejt) v.
skupiać; zlewać w jedną masę
congratulate (ken'graetju,lejt)
v. gratulować;składać(komuś)
gratulacje;pogratulować

congratulation (ken,graetju'-
lejszyn) s. gratulacje; gra-
tulowanie; gratulacja
congregate ('kongry,gejt) adj.
zbiorowy; v. skupiać; zbierać
(się); gromadzić (się)
congregation (,kongry'gejszyn)
s. zbieranie; zgromadzenie
congress ('kongres) s. zjazd;
zebranie; parlament USA
conjecture (ken'dżekczer) s.
domysł; przypuszczenie;
v. przypuszczać; mniemać
conjugal ('kondżugel) adj.
małżeński
conjugate ('kondżu,gejt) v.
odmieniać się; kopulować;
parzyc się;adj.połączony
conjugation (,kondżu'gejszyn)
s. koniugacja; zespalanie się;
kopulacja;odmiana czasownika
conjunction (ken'dżankszyn) s.
zbieg; związek; skojarzenie;
spójnik; połączenie
conjunctive mood (ken'dżanktyw,
mu:d) s. tryb łączący
conjure (kan'dżuer) v. zaklinać; błagać;robić sztuczki
conjure ('kandżer) v. czarować
conjurer ('kandżerer) s. czarownik; magik;kuglarz
connect (ke'nekt) v. łączyć;
wiązać;mieć połączenie
connected (ke'nektyd) a. zwarty (logiczny); ustosunkowany
connection(xion) (ke'nekszyn)
s. połączenie; pokrewieństwo
conquer ('konker) v. zdobyć;
zwyciężyć; pokonać
conqueror ('konkerer) s. zdobywca; zwyciezca
conquest ('konkłest) s. podbój; zdobycie;zawojowanie
conscience ('konszyns) s. sumienie;świadomość zła i dobra
conscientious (,konszy'enszes)
adj. sumienny;skrupulatny
conscious ('konszes) adj. przytomny; świadomy;naumyślny
consciousness ('konszesnys) s.
świadomość;całość myśli i uczuć
conscript ('konskrypt) s.& adj.
poborowy ;s.rekrut;v.rekwirować;
brać do wojska

consecrate ('konsy,krejt) v.
poświęcać;adj.poświęcony
consecutive (ken'sekjutyw)
adj. kolejny;nieprzerwany;skut-
consent (ken'sent) s. zgoda;kowy
v. zgadzać się;przyzwalać
consequence ('konsykłens) s.wy-
nik; znaczenie; konsekwencja
consequently ('konsykłently)
adv. a zatem; przeto; tym samym;w skutek tego; więc
conservative (ken'se:rwatyw)
adj. ostrożny; zachowawczy;
konserwatywny; s. konserwatys-
ta; środek konserwujący
conserve (ken'se:rw) v. konserwować; zachowywać; zabezpieczać; s. konserwa owocowa
consider (ken'syder) v. rozważać; rozpatrywać; uważać; szanować; mieć wzgląd;sądzić
considerable (ken'syderebl)
adj. znaczny;adv.znacznie
considerate (ken'syderyt) adj.
myślacy; uważający; troskliwy
consideration (ken,syde'rejszyn)
s. wzgląd; rozważanie; warunek;
uprzejmość; rekompensata
consign (ken'sajn) v. przekazać;
powierzać;złożyć do(banku,grobu..)
consignment(ken'sajnment) s.
przesyłka ; powierzenie
consist (ken'syst) v. składać
się; polegać;zgadzać się
consistency (ken'systensy) s.
konsystencja; solidność; sta-
łość; zgodność;logiczność
consistent (ken'systent) adj.
zgodny; stały; konsekwentny
consolation (,konse'lejszyn) s.
pocieszenie; pociecha;ukojenie
console (ken'soul) v. pocieszać;
s. konsola; wspornik;podpora
consolidate (ken'solydejt) v.
utwierdzać; scalać; jednoczyć
consonant ('konsenent) s. spółgłoska; adj. spółgłoskowy;
zgodny; harmonijny
conspicuous ('ken'spykjues) adj.
widoczny; zwracający uwagę
conspiracy (ken'spyresy) s. spisek; konspiracja; zmowa; umowa

conspirator (ken'spyreter) s.
spiskowiec; konspirator
conspire (ken'spajer) v. konspirować;spiskować;uknuć
constable ('kanstebl) s. policjant; posterunkowy
constant ('konstent) adj. stały; trwały;s. liczba stała
consternation (,konste:rnejszyn)
s. przerażenie;osłupienie
constipation (,konsty'pejszyn)
s. zatwardzenie; zaparcie
constituency (ken'stytjuensy)
s. okręg wyborczy; wyborcy
constituent (ken'stytjuent)
adj. składowy; s. wyborca;
część składowa; element
constitute ('konsty,tju:t) v.
stanowić; ustanawiać; wyznaczać
constitution (,konsty'tju:szyn)
s. statut; konstytucja; struktura; założenie;układ psychiczny
constitutional (,konsty'tu:szenl)
adj. zasadniczy; istotny; zdrowotny;s.przechadzka dla zdrowia
constrain (ken'strejn) v. wymuszać; zmuszać; ograniczać;
więzić; zniewalać;przymuszać
constraint (ken'strejnt) s.
przymus; skrępowanie; ograniczenie swobody(ruchów etc.)
construct (ken'strakt) v. budo-
wać; tworzyć; rysować(figury geom.)
construction (ken'strakszyn)
s. budowa; konstrukcja;układ;
konstruowanie;ujęcie;interpretacja
constructive (ken'straktyw)
adj. twórczy; konstruktywny
consul ('konsel) s. konsul
consular ('konsjuler) adj.
konsularny
consulate ('konsjulyt) s. konsulat;uprawnienia konsula
consulate general ('konsjulyt'
'dżenerel) s. konsulat generalny
consult (ken'salt) v. radzić
się; informować się
consultation (,konsel'tejszyn)
s. porada; konsultacja
consultative (ken'saltetyw) a.
doradczy; konsultatywny

consume (ken'sju:m) v. spożywać; zużywać; trawić; niszczeć; marnieć;uschnąć
consumer (ken'sju:mer) s. kon-
sumer; spożywca;odbiorca
consummate(ken'samyt) a. doskonały;wielkiej miary;skończony
consummate('kensemejt) v. spełniać małżeństwo
consumption (ken'sampszyn) s.
zużycie; suchoty; pylica
contact ('kontaekt) s. styczność; stosunki; znajomości
v. kontaktować; porozumiewać
się;stykać się;zetknąć się
contact lenses ('kontaekt,lenzys)
pl. szkła kontaktowe
contagious (ken'tejdżes) a. zaraźliwy ; zakaźny;udzielający się
contain (ken'tejn) v. zawierac;
opanowywać się; wiązać;hamować
container (ken'tejner) s. zasob-
nik; zbiornik; naczynie
contaminate (ken'taemynejt) v.
zakazić;skalać;deprawować
contamination (ken'taemynejszyn)
s. kontaminacja; zakażenie; ska-
żenie; ujemny wpływ
contemplate ('kontemplejt) v.
oglądać; rozważać; liczyć się
z (czyms); medytować;planować
contemplation ('kontemplejszyn)
s. oglądanie; kontemplacja;
rozważanie;planowanie;medytacja
contemplative ('kontemplejtyw)
adj. kontemplacyjny; zamyślony
contemporary (ken'temperery)
adj.& s. wspołczesny (rówiesnik)
contempt (ken'temt) s. pogarda;
lekceważenie;obraza (sądu· etc.)
contemptible (ken'temtebl) adj.
godny pogardy, lekceważenia
contemptuous (ken'temtjues) adj.
pogardliwy;nadęty;lekceważący
contend (ken'tend) v. spierać
się; walczyć;rywalizowac;upierać
się
content 1. (ken'tent) adj. zadowolony; s. zadowolenie; v. zadowalać
content 2. ('kontent) s. zawar-
tość; tresc; objętość; pojemność;powierzchnia;kubatura;istota

contented (ken'tentyd) adj. zadowolony; zaspokojony
contents ('kontents) s. zawar-
tość(pojemnika,treści
contest ('kontest) s. rywalizacja; spór; v. walczyć; spierać się; ubiegać; kwestionować
context ('kontekst) s. kontekst
continent ('kontynent) s. kontynent; część świata
continental ('kontynentl) adj.
kontynentalny; s. mieszkaniec
kontynentu
continual (ken'tynjuel) adj.
ciągły; powtarzający się;stały
continuance (ken'tynjuens) s.
ciągłosć; trwanie; przebieg;
ciąg dalszy;odroczenie;pobyt
continuation (ken,tynju'ejszyn)
s. kontynuacja; ciąg dalszy
continue (ken'tynju:) v. kontynuować; ciągnąc dalej; trwać;
ciągnąc się ;odroczyć;upierać
continuous (ken'tynjues) adj. się
nieprzerwany ;stały;ciągły
contort (ken'to:rt) v. skręcać;
wykrzywiać ;zwichnąć;przekrzywić
contour ('kontuer) s. zarys;
kontur,warstwica;v.konturować
contraceptive (,kontre'septyw)
s. środek zapobiegający za-
płodnieniu ;adj.antykoncepcyjny
contract ('kontraekt) s. umowa;
układ; kontract ;obietnicą
contract (ken'traekt) v. sciągać; kurczyć; zobowiązywać
contractor (ken'traekter) s.
przedsiębiorca (budowlany etc.)
contradict (,kontre'dykt) v.
zaprzeczać ;posprzeczać się
contradiction (,kontre'dykszyn)
s. sprzeczność ;zaprzeczenie
contradictory (,kontre'dyktery)
adj. sprzeczny,przekorny;kłótliwy
contrary ('kontrery) adj. przeciwny; s. przeciwieństwo;
adv. w przeciwieństwie
contrariwise ('kontrery,łajz)
adv. odwrotnie; natomiast
contrast (ken'traest) v.prze-
ciwstawiać; kontrastować;
s.kontrast; przeciwieństwo

contribute (ken'trybjut) v.,
przyczynić się; dostarczyć;
współdziałać;zasłużyć się
contribution (,kontry'bju:szyn)
s. przyczynek; wkład; ofiara;
kontrybucja;datek;wsparcie
contributor (ken'trybjuter) s.
ofiarodawca; współpracownik
(pisarz);współpracowniczka
contrite (ken'trajt) adj. skruszony ;pełen skruchy
contrivance (ken'trajwens) s.
pomysł; sztuczka; fortel; wynalazek;wynalazczość;pomysłowość
contrive (ken'trajw) v. wymyślić; wynaleźć; doprowadzić do
czegoś; zaplanować;wykombinować
control (ken'troul) v. sprawdzać; rządzić; kontrolować;
opanować; s. kontrola; sterowanie; regulowanie; ster;władza
controller (ken'trouler) s.
kontroler;regulator;zarządca
controversial (,kentre'we:rżel)
adj. sporny; sprzeczający się
controversy ('kontre,we:rsy)
s. spór;kłótnia;polemika;dysputa
contuse (ken'tju:z) v. stłuc;
kontuzjować
convalesce (,konwe'les) v. wyzdrowieć i odzyskać siły
convalescence (,konwe'lesens)
s. wyzdrowienie
convalescent (,konwe'lesnt) s.
rekonwalescent; ozdrowieniec
convenience (ken'wi:njens) s.
wygoda; korzyść;dogoność
convenient (ken'wi:njent) adj.
wygodny;łatwy do osiągnięcia
convent ('konwent) s. zakon
convention (ken'wenszyn) s.·
zjazd; zgromadzenie; układ;
umowa; konwent;zebranie
conventional (ken'wenszynl)
adj. zwyczajowy; konwencjonal-
ny; umowny;powszechnie stosowany
conversation (,konwer'sejszyn)
s. rozmowa; konwersacja
converse (ken'we:rs) v. rozmawiać;obcować;prowadzić rozmowę
converse ('konwe:rs) s. rozmowa;
adj. odwrotny; s.rzecz odwrotna

conversion (ken'we:rżyn) s.od-
wrócenie; przemiana; nawrócenie;przeistoczenie
convert (ken'we:rt) v. zmieniać; nawracać; przekształcać;
odwracać;przemieniać;przystosować
convert ('konwert) s. neofita
convertible (ken'we:rtybl) adj.
wymienialny; s. otwarty samochód z podnoszonym dachem
convey (ken'wej) v. przewozić;
przenosić; przesyłać; przekazywać; komunikować;zapisywać
conveyance (ken'wejens) s. przewóz; przenoszenie; uzmysławia-
nie; pojazd; przekazanie
conveyor belt (ken'wejer,belt)
s. przenośnik taśmowy
convict ('konwykt) s. skazaniec;
więzień; v. udowadniać; przekonywać; uznać winnym
conviction (ken'wykszyn) s.
przeświadczenie; przekonanie;
zasądzenie;skazanie
convince (ken'wyns) v. przekonać;przekonywać
convoy ('konwoj) s. konwój;
eskorta; straż
convoy (kon'woj) v. konwojować
convulsion (ken'valszyn) s.
drgawki; wstrząs; konwulsje
convulsive (ken'walsyw) adj.
konwulsyjny;niepohamowany
cook (kuk) s. kucharz; kucharka; v. gotować; preparować
cooking (kukyng) s. gotowanie
cool (ku:l) adj. chłodny;
oziębły; spokojny; v. chłodzić;
studzić; ochłonąć; s. chłód
cooler ('ku:ler) s. chłodnica;
element chłodzący;więzienie
coolness ('ku:lnys) s. chłód;
zimna krew;opanowanie;spokój
co-op (kou'op) s. spółdzielnia
cooperate (kou'operejt) v.
współpracować; współdziałać
cooperation (kou,ope'rejszyn)
s. współpraca; współdziałanie
kooperacja; spółdzielczość
cooperative (kou,ope'rejtyw)
adj. spółdzielczy; uspołecznio-
ny; uczynny; współpracujący

cooperator

coope̦rator (kou'ope,rejter) s.
współpracownik; współdzielca
coordinate (kou'o:rdynejt) adj.
współrzędny; współrzędna
cop (kop) s. policjant (slang)
v. złapać; wygrać; buchnąć;
nakryć ;porwać; ukraść(slang)
coPartner (kou'pa:rtner) s.
uczestnik; wspólnik; udziało-
wiec(we wspólnym interesie)
cope ('koup) v. uporać; dawać
sobie radę; pokrywać; zwień-
czać; s. kapa;peleryna(duża)
copilot ('kou'pajlot) s. ko-
pilot;zastępca pilota
copious ('koupjes) adj. obfity;
suty; bogaty;płodny;obfitujący
copper ('koper) s. miedź; v.mie-
dziowac; slang: glina; policjant;miedziak;kocioł,z miedzi
copy ('kopv) v. kopiować; przepisywać; naśladować; s. kopia;
odpis; odbitka; egzemplarz;
wzór; model;rękopis do druku
copybook ('kopy,buk) s. zeszyt
copyright ('kopy,rajt) s. prawo
autorskie.v.chronić prawem autor-
coral ('korel) s. koral ┐skim
cord (ko:rd) s. sznur; lina;
v. wiązać; ustawiać w sągi
cordial ('ko:rdżel) adj. serdeczny; nasercowy;s.lek nasercowy
cordiality (,ko:rdy'aelyty) s.
serdeczność; kordialność
corduroys ('ko:rde,rojz) pl.
sztruksowe spodnie
core (ko:r) s. rdzeń v. usuwać
rdzeń; wycinać rdzeń
cork (ko:rk) s, korek;v.korkować
corkscrew ('ko:rk,skru:) s. korkociąg;adj.w kształcie korkociąga
corn (ko:rn) s. 1. ziarno; zboże; kukurydza; 2. nagniotek
corner ('ko:rner) s. róg; narożnik; kąt; zakręt; zapędzać do
kąta; zmuszać; monopolizować
cornered ('ko:rnerd) adj. rogaty;
schwytany;zapędzony w ślepą ulicę
cornet ('ko:rnyt) s. kornet;
trąbka (mosiężna)
cornflakes ('ko:rn,flejks) pl.
płatki z kukurydzy

coronary disease('korenery dy
'zi:z)s.choroba wieńcowa┐nacja
coronation(,kore'nejszyn)s.koro-
coroner('korener)s. sędzia śledczy, lekarz sądowy(oględziny zwłok)
corporal ('ko:rperel) adj. cielesny; osobisty; s. kapral
corporation (,ko:rpe'rejszyn)
s. korporacja; zrzeszenie;
osoba prawna zbiorowa
corpse (ko:rps) s. trup;zwłoki
corpulent ('ko:rpjulent) adj.
tęgi; otyły; gruby;tłusty
corral (ke'rael) s. ogrodzenie
dla bydła; tabór; v. zamykać
w ogrodzeniu; łapać; ustawiać
tabor;wpędzać do ogrodzenia
correct (ke'rekt) adj, poprawny;
v. korygować; karcić; prostować;leczyć;naprawiać
correction (ke'rekszyn) s. poprawka; korektura ;kara
correspond (,korys'pond) v.
odpowiadać; korespondować
correspondence (,korys'pondens)
s. zgodność; korespondencja
correspondent (,korys'pondent)
s. korespondent; adj. odpowiedni; zgodny z; odpowiadający
corridor ('korydo:r) s. korytarz
corrigible ('korydżybl) adj.
dający się poprawić;uległy
corroborate (ke'robe,rejt) v.
potwierdzić ;potwierdzać
corrode (ke'roud) v. zżerać;
rdzewieć; niszczec; niszczyć
corrosion (ke'roużyn) s. koroz-
ja; zżeranie; niszczenie
corrugate ('korugejt) v.
marszczyć; fałdować;karbować
corrugated iron('korugejtyd'
'ajron) s. pofałdowana blacha
corrupt (ke'rapt) adj. zepsuty;
sprzedajny;v.korumpować;psuć się
corruption (ke'rapszyn) s. zepsucie; korupcja;rozkład;fałszowanie
corset ('ko:rsyt) s. gorset;
sznurówka;v.wkładać gorset
cosmetic (koz'metyk) s. kosmetyk; adj. kosmetyczny
cosmetician (koz'metyszyn) s.
kosmetyczka

cosmonaut ('kozme,no:t) s. kosmonauta ;astronauta (w USA)
cost; cost; cost (kost; kost; kost)
cost (kost) v. kosztowac; s. koszt; strata; cena
costly ('kostly) adj. kosztowny; wspaniały;drogi;cenny
costume ('kostju:m) s. kostium; strój; v. przystroic w kostium
cosy ('kouzy) adj. przytulny; v. przytulic się
cot (kot) s. łóżko składane; szałas; schronienie
cottage ('kotydż) s. chata; dworek;domek letniskowy
cottage cheese ('kotydż, czi:z) s. biały ser krowi z kwaśnego mleka
cotton ('kotn) s. bawełna; v.polubic; kapowac;adj.bawełniany
cotton wool ('kotn,łul) s. wata
couch (kaucz) s. tapczan; posłanie; łóżko;v.rozsiadac się;wlcmówic
cougar ('ku:ger) s. puma; kuguar
cough (kof) s. kaszel; v. kaszlec ; wykaszlec ,zakaszlec,mógł
could (kud) v. mógłby; zob.:can;
council ('kaunsyl) s. rada; konsylium; sobór;zarząd (miejski etc.)
councilor ('kaunsyler) s. radny; radca; członek zarządu)
counsel ('kaunsel) s. rada; zamysł; radca prawny; v. radzic; doradzac; przyjmowac radę
count (kaunt) v. liczyc; sądzic; liczyc się; znaczyc; s. rachuba; liczenie; suma; zarzut; hrabia
countdown (kaunt-dałn) s. liczenie do startu (rakiety)
count in (kaunt yn) v. brac w rachubę; wliczac; włączyc
count out (kaunt aut) v. wyliczyc; nie brac w rachubę
countenance ('kauntynens) s. mina; wyraz twarzy; śmiałość; pewność siebie; animusz; fantazja; v. zachęcac; popierac; zatwierdzac;usankcjonowac
counter ('kaunter) s. 1. kantor; lada; licznik; żeton; 2. przeciwieństwo; cios odbijający; napiętek; adj. przeciwny; prze-

ciwlegly; podwójny; v. sprzeciwiac się; reagowac; uderzac;
adv. przeciwnie; na przekór; wbrew (instrukcjom,poleceniom..)
counteract (,kaunter'aekt) v. przeciwdziałac;neutralizowac
counterbalance ('kaunter,-,baelens) s. przeciwwaga
counterespionage ('kaunter'-'espje,na:ż) s. kontrwywiad
counterfeit ('kaunterfyt) adj. fałszywy; podrobiony:v.udawac;
counterintelligence \fałszowac ('kaunteryn'tylydżens) s. kontrwywiad
counterpart ('kaunter,pa:rt) s. odpowiednik; duplikat
countess ('kauntys) s. hrabina; hrabianka
countless ('kauntlys) adj. niezliczony; nie do zliczenia
country ('kantry) s. kraj; ojczyzna; wieś; prowincja
country house ('kantry-'haus) s. dom wiejski;dom na wsi
countryman ('kantrymen) s. rodak; wiesniak;człowiek ze wsi
countryside ('kantry,sajd) s. okolica; krajobraz;ludzie ze wsi
country town ('kantry,tałn) s, miasteczko; duża wieś
county ('kaunty) s. powiat; hrabstwo ;adj.powiatowy
couple ('kapl) s. para; v. łączyc; parzyc się; żenic
coupling ('kaplyng) s. złącze; skojarzenie; sprzęgło
coupon ('ku:pon) s. odcinek; kupon wymienny(w sklepie,banku...)
courage ('karydż) s. odwaga
courageous (ke'rejdżes) adj. odważny; śmiały;dzielny;waleczny
courier ('kurjer) s, posłaniec; goniec;kurier; agent turystyczny
course (ko:rs) s. bieg; kierunek; ruch naprzód; droga; danie; kolejność; bieżnia; warstwa; kurs; ciąg; v. gnac; pędzic; ścigac; uganiac się
court (ko:rt) s. podwórze; hala; dwór; hotel; sąd; v.zalecac się; wabic; zabiegac;

courteous ('ke:rcjes) adj. grzeczny; uprzejmy i miły

courtesy ('ke:rtysy) s. grzeczność; uprzejmość; kurtuazja; (darmowa) usługa; gest przez grzeczność; adj.grzecznościowy

courtly ('ko:rtly) adj. układny;wytworny; dworski;dostojny

courtmartial ('ko:rt'ma:rszel) s. sąd wojenny;v.sądzić sadem wojskowym

court of justice ('ko:rt,ow 'dżastys) s. sad

courtroom ('ko:rt.ru:m) s. sala sądowa (rozpraw)

courtship ('ko:rtszyp) s. zaloty; umizgi do kobiety

courtyard ('ko:rt,ja:rd) s. podwórze; dziedziniec

cousin ('kazyn) s. kuzyn; kuzynka; krewny;cioteczny brat(siostra)

cover ('kawer) s. koc; wieko; oprawa; osłona; koperta; nakrycie (stołu); pokrycie; v. kryć; pokryć (klacz);ubezpieczać; dać opis;nakrywać;rozlać;chować;przejechać

coverage ('kawerydż) s. pokrycie ubezpieczeniem; zasięg radiowy; omówienie w prasie

covering ('kaweryng) s. osłona; pokrycie (dachu);przykrycie

covert ('kawert) s. schronienie; adj. ukryty; potajemny;przebrany

covet ('kawyt) v. pożądac (cudzego);patrzyć z zawiścią

covetous (kawytes) adj. chciwy; pożądliwy; łapczywy;zawistny

cow (każ) s. krowa; v. zastraszyc się; przestraszyć się

coward ('kauerd) s. tchorz; adj. tchórzliwy; bojaźliwy

cowardice ('kauerdys) s. tchórzostwo ;tchorzliwość

cowardly ('kauerdly) adj. tchórzliwy; adv. tchórzliwie

cowboy ('każboj) s. konny pastuch;pastuch bydła;krowiarz

cower ('kauer) v. skulic się; kucnąć; przykucać do ziemi

cowherd ('każ,he:rd) s. pasterz bydła; pastuszka

cowhide ('każ,hajd) s. krowia skóra; skóra wołowa

cowshed ('każ,szed) s. krowia szopa; obora

cowslip ('każ,slyp) s. pierwiosnek(kwiat bagienny)

coxcomb ('koks,koum) s. błazen; fircyk; pajac;głupi zarozumialec

coxswain ('kok,słejn) s. sternik na regatach

coy (koj) adj. skromny; nieśmiały; ostrożny; cichy;udający

cozy (kouzy) adj. wygodny; przytulny;s.okrycie czajnika

crab (kraeb) s. krab; rak; (wulg.) menda; v. łowić kraby; krytykować; rujnować;narzekać

crab louse ('kraeb,laus) s. wesz łonowa

crack (kraek) s. trzask; rysa; szpara; próba; dowcip; v. trząskać; żartować; łupać; uderzyć; rujnować; adj. wysokiej jakości; doskonały

crack a joke (kraek e dżok) v. palnąć żart;palnąć kawał

crack a smile('kraek,e'smajl) v. (slang) uśmiechnąć się

cracker ('kraeker) s. sucharek; petarda; łupacz;kłamstwo

crackpot ('kraekpot) s. wariat; bez piątej klepki (slang)

crackle ('kraekl) v. trzeszczeć; s. trzeszczenie; pajęczyna; porcelana zdobiona

cradle ('krejdl) s. kołyska; kolebka; wywrotka; v. kraść w kołysce; kołysać; kosić (kosa z ramą);płukać złoto

craft (kraeft) s. rzemiosło; branża; sztuka; cech; podstęp; chytrość; biegłość; pojazd

craftsman ('kraftsmen) s. rzemieślnik;mistrz w swoim zawodzie

crafty ('kra-fty) adj. sprytny; zręczny; podstępny;przebiegły

crag (kraeg) s. skała (stroma); turnia;nawis skalny

cram (kraem) v. tłoczyć; napychać; opychać; wytłaczać; wkuwać (się); s. tłok; ciżba; wkuwanie się do egzaminu;ścisk; kłamstwo; uczenie się do egzaminu intensywnie i w pośpiechu

cramp (kraemp) s. skurcz; klamra; zwornik; v. ściskać; krępować; ograniczać; adj. scisnięty; stłoczony; nieczytelny; sztuczny ;uchwycony w imadło
cranberry ('kraenbery) s. żurawina; brusznica błotna
crane (krejn) s. żuraw; dźwig; v. podnosić; wyciągać szyję
crank (kraenk) s. korba; dziwak; bzik; v. puszczać w ruch (korba); kręcić; wydębić
crank up ('kraenk,ap) v. zapuszczać (motor);uruchomić(motor)
crape (kraep) s. gra w kości; brednie; bzdury;nonsens
crape (krejp) s. krepa
crash (kraesz) s. huk; łomot; upadek; katastrofa; ruina; krach; samodział; v. trzaskać; huczeć; roztrzaskiwać; wpaść na...; adv. z hukiem;z trzaskiem ;z łomotem;z hałasem
crash helmet ('kraesz,helmyt) s. kask ochronny (motocyklisty)
crash landing ('kraesz;laendyng) s. rozbicie się przy lądowaniu
crate (krejt) s. stare pudło; skrzynia; paka; v. pakować w skrzynie;wkładać do pak
crater ('krejter) s. krater
crave (krejw) v. pożądać; pragnąc; prosić usilnie; błagać
crawfish ('kro:fysz) s. rak; v. wycofywać się(rakiem)
crawl (kro:l) v. pełzać; czołgać się; wlec; roić się; s. czołganie; pływanie kraulem; ciarki;basen do hodowli raków
crayfish ('krejfysz) s. rak (rzeczny);rak morski bez kleszczy
crayon ('krejen) s. kredka; rysunek kredką; v. rysować kredką; szkicować;narysować węglem
crazy ('krejzy) adj. zwariowany; pomylony; walący się (np.dom)
crazy about ('krejzy,e'baut) zwariowany na punkcie czegoś
creak (kri:k) v. skrzypieć; trzeszczeć; s. skrzypienie; pisk; zgrzyt; trzask; trzeszczenie;pisknięcie; zgrzytnięcie

cream (kri:m) s. śmietana; śmietanka; krem; v. ustać się; zbierać śmietankę; zabielać
cream cheese (kri:m,czi:z) s. ser śmietankowy (biały i miękki)
creamy ('kri:my) adj. śmietankowy ; jak śmietana
crease ('kri:s) s. fałda; kant (spodni); v. fałdować; plisować; prasować; zmiąć ;pomiąc
create (kry:'ejt) v. tworzyć; wywoływać ;zapoczątkować;powodować
creation (kry'ejszyn) s. stworzenie; kreacja; świat ;wszechświat
creative (kry'ejtyw) adj. twórczy ;wynalazczy;tworzący
creator (kry'ejter) s. twórca
creature ('kry:czer) s. stwór; istota; kreatura (dominowana)
credentials (kry'denszelz) pl. dokumenty; listy uwierzytelniające (tożsamość posła etc.)
credibility gap (,kredy'bylyty gaep) s. niedowierzanie; luka w zaufaniu ;brak zaufania
credible ('kredybl) adj. wiarogodny ; wiarygodny
credit ('kredyt) s. kredyt; wiara; autorytet; powaga; uznanie; chluba; v. dawać wiarę; zapisywać na rachunek; zaliczac ;przypisywać(coś komuś)
creditable ('kreditebl) adj. zaszczytny; chlubny;godny pochwały
credit card ('kredyt ka:rd) karta kredytowa do zakupów
creditor ('kredyter) s. wierzyciel(handlowy,prywatny etc.)
credulous ('kredjules) adj. łatwowierny;zbyt łatwowierny
creed (kri:d) s. wiara; wierzenia; głębokie przekonania
creek (kri:k) s. potok; zatoka
creep; crept; crept (kri:p; krept; krept)
creep (kri:p) v. pełzać; wkradać się; mieć ciarki; s. pełzanie; ciarki; obsuwanie; poślizg; nędzny typ;pełzanie się
creeper ('kri:per) s. pnącz
cremate (krymejt) v. spalać zwłoki na popiół

crept (krept)v.podpełzał; zob.:
creep
crescent ('kresnt) s. półksiężyc; adj. półksiężycowy; rosnący; przybywający;s.rogalik
cress (kres) s. rzeżucha
crest (krest) s. czub; grzebień; grzywa; pióropusz; kita;
hełm; klejnot; grzbiet; v.for-
mować grzbiet; osiągnąć szczyt
crestfallen (krest-folen) adj.
z opadnietym czubem; speszony;
zawstydzony; przygnębiony
crevasse (kry'waes) s. szczelina; pęknięcie (w lodowcu etc.)
crevice ('krewys) s. szczelina; rysa; pęknięcie; szpara
crew (kru:)s. załoga; drużyna;
zgraja; zob. crow
crib (kryb) s. żłób z pętami;
stajnia; obora; ciupka; pokoik;
domek; kojec; plagiat; v. stła-
czać; wyposażac w żłoby; ocemb-
rować; zwędzic;używać ściągaczki
cricket ('krykyt) s. swierszcz;
krykiet; v. grać w krykieta
crime (krajm) s. zbrodnia
criminal ('krymynl) s. zbrodniarz; kryminalista; adj. :
zbrodniczy; kryminalny
crimson ('krymzn) s. & adj. kar-
mazyn(owy); v. zabarwiać na
karmazynowo; zaczerwieniać się
cringe (kryndż) s. uniżonosc;
v. kulic; kurczyć się; kłaniać
się; płaszczyć sie (usłużnie)
cripple ('krypl) kulawy; kaleka
v. okulawic; osłabiać; kuleć;
utykać; okaleczyc;przeszkadzać
crisis ('krajsys) s. przesilenie; kryzys:krytyczna sytuacja
crises ('krajsi:z) pl. prze-
silenia; kryzysy; opały
crisp (krysp) adj. rzeski;
chrupki; energiczny; v.robic
kruchym;marszczyć; kędzierza-
wic;fryzowac; ufryzować
critic ('krytyk) s. krytyk
critical ('krytykel) adj. kryty-
kujący; krytyczny; trudny do
nabycia; ważny(moment etc.)

criticism ('krytysyzem) s. krytyka; krytycyzm;znajdowanie błędów
criticize ('krytysajz) s. krytykować; ganic; znajdywać błędy
croak (krouk) v. rechotac; kra-
kac;s. rechot;rechotanie;krakanie
crochet ('krouszej) v. robic
na szydełku ; szydełkować
crockery ('krokery) s. naczynia gliniane(dzbany, słoje etc.)
crocodile ('krokedajl) s. krokodyl; adj.krokodylowy
crocus ('kroukes) s. krokus;
szafran(z rodziny irysów)
crook (kruk) s. hak; zagięcie;
krzywizna; kanciarz; krzywic;
wyginac; krasć; kantowac
crooked (krukyd) adj. zakrzy-
wiony; krzywy; wypaczony;
zgarbiony; cygański; szachraj-
ski; oszukańczy;zgięty;wygięty
crop (krop) s. plon; biczysko:
bacik; całość; przycinanie;
krótko strzyżone włosy; ucinek;
v. strzyc; skubać; zbierać;
zasiewać; obrodzic; wyłaniac
się; uprawiać ziemię: obradzać
crop up (krop ap) v. nagle
zjawiać się; wyskoczyć nagle
cross (kros) s. krzyż; skrzyżowanie; mieszaniec; kant;
cygaństwo; v. żegnać się;
krzyżować; przecinać coś; isc
w poprzek; przekreslać;
udaremnic; adj. poprzeczny;
skosny; krzyżujący; przeciwny; gniewny; opryskliwy
cross out ('kros,aut) v. wykreślać;skreslać;przekreslać
cross-examination ('kros -
ig'zaemynejszyn) s. przesłuchanie; badanie (w sledztwie)
crossing ('krosyng) s. skrzyżowanie; przejście lub przejazd na druga stronę (rzeki...)
crossroads ('krosroudz) pl.
rozstaje; skrzyżowanie dróg
crossword puzzle ('krosłord-
'pazl) s. krzyżówka
crouch (kraucz) v. kulić się;
kurczyć; przysiąsc;gotować się
                              do skoku

crow (krou) s. kruk; wrona;
pianie; wesoły pisk; v. piać;
piszczec wesoło;krzyczeć z rados-
crowbar ('krouba:r) s. drąg;
lewar; łom(do podważania etc.)
crowd (kraud) s. tłum; tłok;
banda; mnóstwo; v. tłoczyć;
natłoczyć; napierać; wpychać;
śpieszyć; przepełniać
crowded ('kraudyd) adj. zatłoczony; zapchany;przeludniony
crown (kraun) s. korona; wieniec; v. wieńczyć; koronować
crucial ('kru:szel) adj. decydujący; przełomowy; krytyczny
crucifixion (,kru:sy'fykszyn)
s. ukrzyżowanie; krucyfiks
crucify (kru:syfaj) v. ukrzyżo-
wać;torturować;znęcać się
crude (kru:d) adj. surowy;
szorstki; niepożyty;obskórny
cruel (kruel) adj. okrutny
cruelty ('kuelty) s. okrucieństwo; znęcanie się(nad kimś)
cruet ('kru:yt) v. flaszeczka;
ampułka;buteleczka(na ocet etc.)
cruise (kru:z) v. krążyć; lecieć; podróżować; s. wycieczka
morska; przejażdżka; rejs
crumb (kram) s. okruch; (slang)
drań; v. kruszyć; drobić; dodawać okruszyn;obtoczyć(w bułce)
crumble ('kramb) v. kruszyć (się)
crumple ('krampl) v. zmiąć;
zmarszczyć;załamywać się
crumple up ('krampl,ap) v. po-
miąć; zawalic się;załamać się
crunch (krancz) v. miażdżyc;
chrupać; s, chrupanie; chrzęst
crusade (kru:'sejd) s. wyprawa
krzyżowa;v.iść z krucjata
crusader (kru:'sejder) s. krzy-
żowiec;aktywny działacz,
crush (krasz)v. kruszyc; miażdżyć; miąć; s, miażdżenie;
tłok; ciżba; zadurzenie się
crusher (kraszer) s. łamacz;
miażdżarka;druzgocący cios
crust (krast) s. skorupa; skóra;
v. zaskorupiać (się)
crutch (kracz) s. kula; podpórka ;laska;v.podpierać się

cry (kraj) s. krzyk; płacz;
wrzask; okrzyk; hasło; v.krzy-
czec; płakac; urągać; ujadać
cry-baby ('kraj,bejby) s. mazgaj; beksa; płaksa(dziecinna)
crying ('krajyng) s. wołanie;
płacz adj. płaczący;skandalicz-
ny cry of rage ('kraj,ow'rejdż)
s. krzyk szału (wściekłości)
crypt (krypt) s. krypta
crystal ('krystl) s. kryształ;
szkiełko od zegarka;adj.kryszta-
łowy crystalline ('krystelajn) adj.
krystaliczny;kryształowy
crystallize ('krystelajz) v.
krystalizować się
cub (kab) s. szczenie (dzikie-
go zwierza); zuch;młodzik
cube (kju:b) s. sześcian; kostka; (slang) facet; v. podnosić do sześcianu; obliczać
kubaturę;formować w sześciany
cube root ('kju:b,ru:t) s.
pierwiastek sześcienny
cubicle ('kju:bykl) s. pokoik;
mała sypialnia;małe mieszkanie
cuckoo ('kuku) s. kukułka;
głuptas;kukanie;dureń
cucumber ('kju:kamber) s. ogórek
cuddle ('kadl) s. tulić;
pieścić; kulić się;gnieździć
cudgel ('kadżel) s. pałka; się
v. bić pałką
cue (kju:) s. wskazówka; nastrój; ogonek (do sklepu); kij
bilardowy; warkocz;v.dać wska-
zówkę cuff (kaf) s. mankiet; kajdan-
ki; v. bić pięścią; uderzać;
kułakować;potarmosić;szturchać
cuff links ('kaf,lynks) pl.
spinki do mankietów
culminate ('kalmynejt) y.
szczytować; kulminować
culmination (,kalmy'nejszyn) s.
kulminacja; punkt szczytowy
culprit ('kalpryt) s. oskarżony; winowajca;winowajczyni
cultivate ('kaltywejt) v. uprawiać; rozwijać; kultywować;
pielęgnować; spulchniać

cultivation (‚kaltu'wejszyn)
s. uprawa; kultura; kultywo-
wanie;kultura duchowa
cultivator ('kaltyvejter) s.
plantator; kultywator;rolnik
cultural ('kalczerel) adj.
kulturalny;kulturowy
culture ('kalczer) s. kultura;
uprawa; v. uprawiać; hodować;
kształcić;hodować bakterie
cultured ('kalczerd) adj.
kulturalny;oczytany;wykształcony
cumulative ('kju:mjulejtyw)
adj. łączny; kumulacyjny;
skumulowany; kumulujący się
cunning('kanyng) s. chytrość;
przebiegłość; adj. chytry;
przebiegły; miły; ładny
cup (kap) s. kubek; kielich;
czasza; filiżanka; v. wgłę-
biać; stawiać bańki
cupboard ('kaberd) s. kredens;
szafka;półka na kubki
cupola ('kju:pele) s. kopuła;
piec kopułowy; żeliwiak
cur (ke:r) s. kundel; szelma
curable ('kjuerebl) adj. uleczalny; wyleczalny
curate ('kjueryt) s. wikary
curb (ke:rb) s. krawężnik;
łańcuszek; wędzidło; oszczep;
twarda spuchlizna; v. okiełzać; hamować; ograniczać
curd (ke:rd) s. twaróg; tłuszcz
curdle (ke:rdl) v. ścinać;
zsiadać się;formować w gródki
cure (kjuer) s. kuracja; lek;
lekarstwo; v. uleczyć; wyleczyć; zaradzić; wykurować
cure-all ('kjuero:l) s. pana-
ceum;lek na wszystkie dolegliwoś-
ci
curfew ('ke:rfju:) s. godzina
policyjna: capstrzyk
curio ('kjuerjou) s. okaz;
osobliwość;unikat; rzadkość
curiosity (‚kjurj'osyty) n.
ciekawość; osobliwość
curl (ke:rl) s. kędzior; lok;
pukiel; skręt; spirala; wir
v. kręcić; skręcać; zwijać;
marszczyć; złościć;skulić się
curl up ('ke:rl ap) v.zwinąć (się)

curly ('ke:rly) adj. kędzierzawy; kręty ;falujący;kręcony
currant ('karent) s. porzeczka;
rodzynek bez pestki
currency ('karensy) s. waluta;
obieg; potoczność; popularność
current ('karent) adj. bieżący; obiegowy; obiegający; powszechnie znany; panujący (pogląd);.s. prąd; bieg; nurt;
tok ;strumień;natężenie pradu
curriculum (ke'rykjulem) s.
plan studiów ;program nauki
curriculum vitae (ke'rykjulem,
wajti:) s. życiorys
curse (ke:rs) s. przekleństwo;
klątwa; v. przeklinać; wykli-
nać; kląć; bluźnić;złorzeczyć
cursed (ke:rsyd) adj. przeklęty; cholerny; adv. paskudnie;
cholernie ;po diable
curt (ke:rt) adj. krótki; zwięzły,lakoniczny;szorstki;suchy
curtail (ke:r'tejl) v. obcinać;
skracać; zmniejszać ;uczszuplać
curtain ('ke:rtn) s. zasłona;
firanka; kurtuna; v. zasłaniać
curtsy ('ke:rtsy) s. dyg; v. dy-
gać;złożyć głęboki ukłon
curve (ke:rw) s. krzywa; krzywizna; krzywka; v. wyginać
(się); wykrzywiać (się);zakręcać
cushion ('kuszyn) s. poduszka
custody ('kastedy) s. opieka;
nadzór; areszt ;przetrzymanie
custom ('kastem) s. zwyczaj;
klientela; zrobiony na zamówienie ;nawyk;stałe zaopatrywanie się
customary ('kastemery) adj. zwyczajny; zwyczajowy;s.zbiór praw
customer ('kastemer) s. klient
customhouse ('kastem-haus) s.
komora celna ;urząd celny
custom-made ('kastem-mejd) adj.
zrobiony na zamówienie
customs ('kastemz) pl. cło
customs clearance ('kastemz;
klierens) s. odprawa celna
customs declaration('kastemz,
decle'rejszyn) s. deklaracja
celna (przy przekraczaniu gra-
nicy etc.)

customs examination ('kastemz
ig,zamy'nejszyn) s. rewizja
celna (bagażu,towarów etc.)
cut; cut; cut; (kat; kat; kat)
cut (kat) s. cięcie; przecięcie; wycięcie; ścięcie; odrzy-
nek; krój; styl (krawiecki);
wykop; drzeworyt; v. ciąc;
zaciąć; skaleczyć; ranić; krajać; kroić; przycinać; kosić;
rznąc; rzeźbić; szlifować; wycinać; obcinac; uciąc; ścinać
cut down ('kat,dałn) v. obniżać;
redukować;wyciąc w pień(wroga)
cut in ('kat,yn) v. wtrącać się
cut off ('kat,of) v. odcinać;
przerwać(dopływ);wydziedziczać
cut out ('kat,aut) v. wykroić;
przestać;zaprzestać (palić etc.)
cut up ('kat,ap) v. posiekać;
skrytykować;wypatroszyć;siec
cute (kju:t) adj. miły; ładny;
chytry; sprytny;ciekawy;bystry
cuticle ('kju:tykl) s. naskórek
cuticle scissors ('kju:tykl'-
'syzez) s. nożyczki od naskórka
cutlery ('katlery) s. wyroby
nożownicze; sztuce
cutlet ('katlyt) s. kotlet (bity);kotlet mielony(mięsny,rybi )
cut-off ('katof) s. odcięcie;
skrót; wyłącznik; wycinek; za-
wor(wodny,parowy,gazowy etc.)
cutout ('kat aut) = cut-off
cutpurse ('kat pe:rs) s. rzezimieszek; kieszonkowiec;opryszek
cutter ('kater) s. kuter; przecinek; przykrawacz; odcinacz
cutting ('katyŋg) adj. bolesny;
przenikliwy; cięty;s.sadzonka
cycle (sajkl) s. cykl; rower;
v. jechać na rowerze; obiegać
cyklicznie(tam i nazad,w koło...)
cyclist ('sajklyst) s. rowerzysta;
rowerzystka ; cyklista;cykilstka
cyclone ('sajkloun) s. cyklon
cylinder ('sylynder) s. walec;
cylinder;bęben(rewolweru etc.)
cynic ('synyk) s. cynik
cynical ('synykel) adj. cynicz-
ny (pomysł,programçzłowiek etc.)
cynicism('syny,syzem)s.cynizm

cypress ('sajprys) s. cyprys
cyst (syst) s. cysta; torbiel
czar (za:r) s. car; (od nafty;
sportu;komisarz generalny USA)
Czech (czek) adj. czeski
Czechoslovak ('czekou,slouwaek)
adj. czechosłowacki
d (di) czwarta litera alfabetu
angielskiego; oznaczenie centa
dab (daeb) v. musnąc; klepać;
dotknąc; dziobnąc; s. muśnie-
cie; klaps; stuknięcie; dziobnięcie;plama;bryzg;odrobina
dachshund ('daekshund) s. jamnik ;a.jamniczy;jamnika
dad (daed) s. tato; tatuś
daddy ('daedy) s. tatuś
daffodil ('daefedyl) s. żółty
narcyz ;żonkil;adj.bladożółty
daffy ('daefy) adj. zwariowany
daft ('daeft) adj. pomylony;
głupkowaty; zwariowany
dagger ('daeger) s. sztylet;
v. sztyletować ;s. odsyłacz
daily ('dejly) adj. codzienny;
adv. codziennie; s. dziennik
dainty ('dejnty) adj. wyszukany; wyborowy; delikatny;
gustowny; miły; wybredny
daiquiri ('daikery) s. rum z
sokiem cytrynowym, cukrem
i lodem (po amerykańsku)
dairy ('deery) s, mleczarnia
dairyman ('deerymen) s. mleczarz;właściciel mleczarni
daisy (dejzy) s. stokrotka;
ładny okaz(człowieka)
dale (dejl) s. dolina
dally ('daely) v. marudzic;
igrać; flirtować;tracić czas
dam (daem) s. tama; zapora
damage ('daemydż) s. szkoda;
uszkodzenie; odszkodowanie;
(slang) koszt; v. uszkodzic;
poniesc szkody; uwłaczać
dame (dejm) s. dziewczyna;
kobieta; pani(starsza)
damn (daem) v. potępiać; prze-
klinac; adj. przeklęty
damnation (daem'nejszyn) s. potępienie; excl.: psiakrew; cholera;a niech to piorun trzaśnie!

damp (daemp) v. zwilżyc; skropic; tłumic; ostudzic; amortyzowac; butwiec; s. wilgoc; przygnębienie; zwątpienie dampen ('daempen) v. wilgotniec ; zwilgotniec;zwilżyć dance (da:ns) s. taniec; zabawa taneczna; v. tańczyc; skakac; kazac tańczyc; huśtac dancer ('da:nser) s. tancerz; tancerka; baletnica dancing ('da:nsyŋg) s. taniec; adj. tańczący;do tańca dandelion ('daendylajon) s. mniszek lekarski; mlecz dandruff ('daendref) s. łupież danger ('dejndżer) s. niebezpieczeństwo; groźba dangerous ('dejndżeres) adj. niebezpieczny;niepewny(grunt...) dangle ('daeŋgl) v. dyndac; bujac; kręcic się;nadskakiwać Danish (dejnysz) adj. duński dapper ('daeper) adj. wytworny; elegancki;dobrze ubrany;zwinny dare (deer) v. śmiec; ważyc się; wyzywac; s. wyzwanie daring ('deeryng) adj. śmiały; s. śmiałośc; odwaga dark (da:rk) adj. ciemny; ponury; s. ciemnośc; mrok; cień; murzyn;tajemniczośc;niewiedza dark-brown ('da:rk brałn) adj. ciemno-brazowy darken (da:rkn) v. zaciemniac darkness ('da:rknys) s. ciemnośc; ciemnota; śniadosc darling ('da:rlyŋg) s. kochanie; ulubieniec; adj. kochany; ulubiony; ukochany darn (da:rn) v. cerowac; s.cera; adj. (slang) przeklęty dart (da:rt) s. żądło; szybki ruch; oszczep; zryw; v. pędzic; rzucac; wybuchac;strzelac dash (daesz) v. roztrzaskac; rzucac się; pędzic; popisywać się; zakropic; opryskąc; nieweczyc; mieszac; oniesmielac; odbic; naszkicowac; s. uderzenie; zderzenie; plusk; barwna plama; szczypta; przy-

mieszka;myślnik; kreska; pęd; skok; rozmach; rozpęd; popis dash-board ('daeszbo:rd) tablica rozdzielcza; zestaw zegarów (lotniczych, samochodowych, etc,) ; błotnik dashing (daeszyŋg) adj. dziarski; z werwą; z rozmachem data ('dejte) pl. dane; podstawa odniesienia ;dane liczbowe data processing ('dejte'prousesyŋg) s. przetwarzanie danych date (dejt) v. datowac; nosic datę; chodzic z kims; s. data; spotkanie; randka; umówienie się; palma daktylowa; daktyl date from ('dejt,from) data z... (dnia, miejsce) dative case('dejtyw,kejs) trzeci przypadek ;celownik datum ('dejtem) s, dana (fakt; szczegół);punkt wyjściowy daub (do:b) v. babrac; mazac; oblepiac; s. tynk; polepa; plama; kicz sknocony ;gips daughter ('do:ter) s. córka daughter-in-law ('do:ter,yn lo:) s. synowa dawdle ('do:dl) v. próżniaczyc; mitrężyc ;wałkonić się dawdle away ('do:dl,a'łej)v. marnowac czas;trcić czas dawn (do:n) v. świtac; zaświtac; dniec; jasniec; s. świt; brzask; zaranie;zdanie sobie sprawy day (dej) s. dzien; doba daybreak('dejbrejk)s.świt;brzask day by day('dej,baj dej)exp.: dzień w dzień ;dzień po dniu daydream('dejdri:m)s. marzenie;v. marzyc;budować zamki na lodzie day in day out(dej,yn'dej aut)exp. codziennie; dzień w dzień daylight('dejlajt)s.swiatło dzienne: biały dzień ⌡(dzienny) day nursery('dej,ne:rsery)s.żłobek day off('dej of)s.dzień wolny days to come('dejs,tu kam) exp.: przyszłość day's work(dejz,łe:rk)s. dniówka daytime ('dejtajm)s. dzień od świtu do zmroku

daze (dejz) v. oszałamiać;
otumaniać; oślepiać; s. oszołomienie; otumanienie
dazzle (daezl) v. oślepiać;
olśniewać; zamaskować;
s. oślepiający blask
dead (ded) adj.& s. zmarły;
martwy; wymarły; matowy
dead body (ded'body) s. zwłoki
dead center ('ded'senter) s.
punkt martwy, zwrotny
deaden ('deden) v. zabijać siły, uczucia etc.: tłumić;
osłabiać; stępiać; zmartwieć;
obumrzeć; pozbawiać blasku,
połysku, zapachu;znieczulać
dead end('dedend)s.ślepa(ulica)
deadline('dedlajn)s.nieprzekra-
czalny termin;ostateczna granica
deadlock ('dedlok) s. impas;
martwy punkt;v. powodować impas
deadly (dedly) adj. śmiertelny;
adv. śmiertelnie;nieludzko
deadweight ('dedłejt) s. ciężar własny (urządzenia); kula
u nogi;kamień u szyi
deaf (def) adj. głuchy
deafen (defn) v. ogłuszać
deafening (defnyŋg) adj. ogłu-
szający
deal; dealt; dealt (di:l; delt;
delt)
deal (di:l) v. zajmować się;
traktować o: załatwiać; przestawać z; postępować; handlować; rozdzielać (karty)
s. ilość; sprawa;sporo;wiele
deal with ('di:l łyt) v. postępować z ···;mieć do czynienia
dealer ('di:ler) s. kupiec;
handlarz;rozdający karty
dealing ('di:lyŋg)s. postępowanie z; stosunki; transakcje
dealt (delt) zob. deal
dean (di:n) s. dziekan
dear (kier) adj. kochany; drogi
dear Sir ('dier,se:r) exp.: szanowny panie;Drogi Panie
dear me ! (kier mi) exp.: ojej !
mój Boże ! czyżby! ależ nie!
death (deß) s. śmierć; zgon
deathly (deßly) adj. śmiertelny;
adv. śmiertelnie;grobowo;trupio

debar ('dyba:r) v. wykluczać;
zabraniać (komuś);zakazywać
debase (dy'bejs) v. obniżać;
poniżać; fałszować;upadlać
debate (dy'bejt) v. roztrząsać;
rozważać; debatować;s.debata
debauchery ('dy'bo:czery) s.
rozpusta;wyuzdanie;rozwiązłość
debit ('debyt) s. debet; obciążenie rachunku
debrief (dy'bri:f) s. przesłu-
chania po (akcji); v. przesłuchiwać po (akcji)
debris ('dejbri:) pl. gruzy
debt (det) s. dług
debtor ('deter) s. dłużnik;
dłużniczka
decade ('dekejd) s. dziesięcio-
letni okres
decadence ('dekejdens) s. de-
kadencja; chylenie się ku
upadkowi; schyłek; upadek
decapitate (dy'kaepytejt) v.
ścinać głowę;pozbawić wodza
decay (dy'kej) v. gnić; rozpa-
dać się; psuć się; s. upadek;
ruina; zanik; rozkład; gnicie
decease (dy'si:s) v. umierać;
s. zgon ; śmierć
deceased (dy'si:st) adj. zmarły; s. nieboszczyk
deceit (dy'si:t) s. oszukańst-
wo; podstęp; złuda ; fałsz
deceitful (dy'si:tfel) adj.
kłamliwy; zwodniczy;podstępny
deceive (dy'si:w) v. okłamywać;
zwodzić; łudzić; zawodzić
deceiver (dy'si:wer) s. oszu-
kaniec; zwodziciel; kłamca
decelerate (dy:'selerejt) v.
zwalniać;zmniejszać szybkość
December (dy'sember) s. grudzień
decency ('di:snsy) s. przyzwoitość; obyczajność;dobre obyczaje
decent ('di:sent) adj. przyzwoity; porządny; znośny
deception (dy'sepszyn) s. łu-
dzenie; okłamywanie; podstęp;
zawód; szachrajstwo;oszukanie
decide (dy'sajd) v. rozstrzygać;
postanawiać; decydować sie;
zadecydować; skłaniać się

decided (dy'sajdyd) adj. zdecydowany; stanowczy;definitywny
decimal ('desymel) adj. dziesiętny;s. ułamek dzisiętny
decipher (dy'sajfer) v. odcyfrować; rozszyfrować;rozwiazać
decision (dy'syżyn) s. rozstrzygnięcie; postanowienie; decyzja; zdecydowanie; stanowczosc; wygrana na punkty (sport);ustalenie;rezolutność
decisive (dy'sajsyw) adj. decydujący; rozstrzygający; zdecydowany; stanowczy
deck (dek) s. pokład; pomost; podłoga; talia; v. pokrywac pokładem; przystrajac
deck chair (dek,czeer) s. leżak (do opalania się na statku)
declaration (dekle'rejszyn) s. deklaracja; zapowiedź; oświadczenie (oficjalne)
declare, (dy'kle:r) v. deklarowac; oswiadczac; zeznawac; ogłaszac; uznawac za; stwierdzac;wykazac;dawac do oclenia
declension (dy'klenszyn) s. deklinacja (gram.); przypadkowanie; odchylenie; upadek
decline (dy'klajn) v. uchylac (się); pochylac (się);skłaniac (się); isc ku schyłkowi; opadac; obnizac; podupadac; marniec; słabnąc; zanikac; przypadkowac;s.schyłek;utrata;spadek
declivity (dy'klywyty) s. pochyłosc; spadzistosc;stok;skłon
decode (, dy'koud)v.rozszyfrowac
decorate('dekerejt)v.ozdabiac;odznaczac; udekorowac; upiększac
decompose (,dy:kem'pouz)v.rozkładac się; rozłożyc się;gnic
decoration (,deke'rejszyn) s. ozdoba; odznaczenie;medal etc.
decorative (,deke'rejtyw) adj. ozdobny; dekoracyjny
decorator ('dekerejter) s. dekorator; architekt wnętrz
decoy ('dy:koj) s. wabik; przynęta; v. wabic; usidlac; zwabiac; wciągac w pułapkę;zaciągac sidła;wabic w pułapkę

decrease ('dy:kri:s) v. zmniejszac; słabnąc; obnizac; s. zmniejszenie; spadek(cen)
decree (dy'kri:) s. dekret; rozporządzenie; wyrok rozwodowy; postanowienie o seperacji; v. zarządzac; dekretowac; rozporządzac;nakazywac dekretem
decrepit (dy'krepyt) adj. zgrzybiały; wyniszczony
decry (dy'kraj) v. potępic; okrzyczec;zohydzic;obgadac
dedicate ('dedykejt) v. dedykowac; poswięcac; inaugurowac
dedication ('dedykejszyn) s. dedykacja; poswięcenie;otwarcie
deduce (dy'du:s) v. wnioskowac; dedukowac; wywodzic (rodowód)
deduct (dy'dakt) v. potrącac; odciągac;odejmowac;odtrącac
deduction (dy'dakszyn) s. potrącenie; odciągnięcie; wnioskowanie; wniosek;wywód
deed (di:d) s. czyn; wyczyn; akt; v. przekazywac aktem (własnosc);przelewac pieniądze
deep (di:p) adj. głęboki; s. głębia; adv. głęboko
deepen('di:pn) v. pogłębiac
deep-freeze ('di:p,fri:z) s. (głębokie) zamrożenie
deeply ('di:ply) adv. głęboko
deep-rooted ('di:p'ru:tyd) adj. głęboko zakorzeniony
deer, (dier) s. jelen; sarna; łos; łania ;daniel;renifer
deface (dy'fejs) v. szpecic - zniekształcac; zacierac
defame (dy'fejm) v. zniesławic
defeat, (dy'fi:t) v. pokonac; pobic; unicestwic; udaremnic; uniemozliwic; uniewaznic prawnie;s.klęska;udaremnienie
defect (dy'fekt) s. brak; wada; błąd; defekt; v. odpasc; skłonic do odstępstwa;odstąpic
defective (dy'fektyw) adj. wadliwy; wybrakowany; niepełny
defence (dy'fens) = defense
defend (dy'fend) v. bronic
defendant (dy'fendent) s. pozwany;oskarżony; obrońca

defender (dy'fender) s. obrońca (prawo i sport)
defensive (dy'fensyw) adj. obronny; defensywny; s. defensywa; byc'w defensywie
defense (dy'fens) s. obrona
defenseless (dy'fenslys) adj. bezbronny
defer (dy'fe:r) v., odraczać; ustępować; ulegać;mieć wzgląd
defiant (dy'fajent) adj. zbuntowany; nieufny;buntowniczy
deficiency (dy'fyszynsy) s. brak; niedobór; należność niezapłacona ; niedostatek;słabość
deficit ('defysyt) s. deficyt; niedobór ; nadwyżka rozchodu
defile ('dy:fail) v. kalać; plugawić; brukać; bezcześcić; iść szeregami;defilować
define (dy'fajn) v., określać; definiować; zakreślać (granice); zarysować;określać
definite ('defynyt) adj. określony; wyraźny; pewny; prostolinijny;określający(rodzajnik)
definition (,drfy'nyszyn) s. określenie; definicja; ostrość; czystość;oznaczenie
definitive (dy'fynytyw) adj. ostateczny; definitywny; stanowczy;konkluzywny;definiujący
deflate (dy'flejt) v. wypuszczać powietrze (z dętki); zmniejszać obieg,znaczenie etc.)
deform (dy'fo,rm) v. szpecić; znieksztaźcać;oszpecać
deformed (dy'fo:rmd) adj. ułomny; szpetny;zniekształcony
defrost ('dy:frost) v. odmrozić
defunct ('dy'fankt) adj. zmarły; zlikwidowany;już nie istniejący
defy (dy'faj) v. stawiać czoło; rzucać wyzwania (by zrobić,wykazać)
degenerate (dy'dżeneryt) adj. zwyrodniały; s. degenerat
degrade (dy'grejd) y. poniżać; obniżać; wyrodnieć;znieważać
degree (dy'gri:) s. stopien (np. naukowy, ciepła etc.)
dejected (dy'dżektyd) adj. przygnębiony ;zgaszony(człowiek) zdeprymowany;strapiony

dejectedly (dy'dżektydly) adv. z przygnębieniem;z niechęcią
delay (dy'lej) v. odraczać; opóźniać; zwlekać; s. odroczenie; zwłoka; opóźnienie
delegate ('delegejt) s. zastępca; wysłannik; v. delegować; udzielać delegacji; zlecać (władzę);udzielać(władzy)
delegation (,dely'gejszyn) s. delegacja;grupa delegatów
deliberate (dy'lyberejt) adj. rozmyślny; spokojny; v. rozmyślać; rozważać; obradować; naradzać się (dy,ly'berejt)v.
delicacy ('delykesy) s. delikatność; smakołyk;takt
delicate ('delykyt) adj. delikatny; wyśmienity;taktowny
delicatessen (,delyka'tesn) s. sklep z delikatesami
delicious (dy'lyszes) adj. rozkoszny;bardzo smaczny etc.
delight (dy'lajt) s. rozkosz; v. zachwycać się; rozkoszować się; lubować się
delightful (dy'lajtful) adj. zachwycający; czarujący
delinquency (dy'lynkłensy) s. zaniedbanie; wina; przestępstwo;nie płacenie należności
delinquent (dy'lynkłent) a. winny; zaniedbany; zalegający z zapłatą (podatkiem); s. winowajca; przestępca (nieletni)osoba zalegająca etc.
deliver (dy'lywer) v. doręczać; zdawać; wydawać; wygłaszać; zadawać; uwalniac;podawac
deliverance (dy'lywerens) s. uwolnienie ;wygłoszenie(opinii)
deliverer (dy'lywerer) s. zbawca ;oswobodziciel;wybawca
delivery (dy'lywery) s. dostawa; wydawanie; wygłaszanie; podanie; poród; przekazanie
deluge ('delju:dż) s. potop
delusion (dy'lu:żyn) s. urojenie; zwodzenie ;ułuda;iluzja
delusive (dy'lu:syw) adj. złudny;oszukańczy;bałamutny;zwodniczy
demand (dy'ma:nd)s. zadanie;popyt; v.zadać; dopytywać się

demeanor (dy'mi:ner) s. zachowanie się;postępowanie: postawa
demented (dy'mentyd) adj. obłąkany;oszalały;umysłowo chory
demi-('demy) pref. pół-
demilitarized ('dy:mylyterajzd)
adj. zdemilitaryzowany
demise (dy'majz) s. zgon; przekazanie spadku; v. przekazywać
testamentem lub zgonem
demobilize (dy:,moubylajz) v.
demobilizować;zdemobilizować
democracy (dy'mokresy) s. demokracja
democrat ('demokreat) s. demo-
krata; demokratka
democratic (,deme'kraetyk) adj.
demokratyczny
demolish (dy'molysz) v. burzyć;
niszczyć; obalać; demolować
demon ('di:men) s. diabeł; demon;doskonały zawodnik sportowy
demonstrate ('demenstrejt) v.
wykazywać; udowadniać; demon-
strować;urządzać manifestację
demonstration (,demen'strejszyn)
s. wykazywanie; okazywanie;
demonstracja;adj.wzorcowy;pogla-
demonstrative (dy'menstrejtyw)
adj. wylewny; dowodowy; wskazujący;dowodzący;ekspansywny
demurrage (dy'me:rydż) s. prze-
stój; opłata za postojowe
den (den) s. nora; jaskinia;
ustronie; cicha pracownia
denial (dy'najel) s. zaprzeczenie; odmowa;wyparcie się
denomination (dynomy'nejszyn)
s. nazwa; miano; określenie;
wyznanie (rel.);kategoria
denounce (dy'nauns) v. oskarżać;
donosić; wypowiadać;denuncjować
dense (dens) adj. gęsty; zwarty;
tępy (człowiek);niepojętny
density ('densyty) s. gęstość;
zwartość; grupota;spoistość
dent (dent) s. wgłębienie; wrąb;
znaczenie;v.szczerbić;wyginać
dental ('dentl) adj. zębowy;
dentystyczny;stomatologiczny
dentist ('dentyst) s. dentysta;
dentystka; stomatolog

denture (denczer) s. (sztuczne) uzębienie; szczęka
deny (dy'naj) v. zaprzeczyć;
odrzucić; odmawiać; wypierać
się;zdementować; przeczyć
depart (dy'pa:rt) v. odjeżdżać;
odbiegać;robić dygresje;odejść
department (dy'pa:rtment) s.
wydział; ministerstwo; dział
department store (dy'pa:rtment,
sto:r) s. dom towarowy
departure (dy'pa:rczer) s. odjazd; rozstanie; odchylenie
depend on (dy'pend on) v. polegać na...;zależeć od
depend upon (dy'pend,apon) v.
być zależnym od..;być na utrzy-
depends (dy'pends)v. zależy
deplorable (dy'plo:rebl) adj.
godny pożałowania;opłakany
deplore (dy'plo:r) v. ubolewać;
boleć nad...;wyrażać ubolewanie
depolarize (dy'poulerajz) v.
depolaryzować;rozwiać złudzenia
depopulate (dy'popjulejt) v.
wyludniać;pustoszyć;opustoszyć
deport (dy'po:rt) v. zsyłać;
deportować; zachowywać się
depose (dy'pouz) s. składać;
zeznawać;usunąć(z tronu etc.)
deposit (dy'pozyt) s. osad;
warstwa; kaucja; depozyt;
v. składać; osadzać; depono-
wać; nawarstwiać;złożyć (jaja...)
depositor (dy'pozyter) s. de-
ponent; osadnik
depot (depou) s. stacja kole-
jowa; skład;remiza; kadra
depraved (dy'prejwd) adj. zde-
prawowany;zepsuty moralnie
depress (dy'pres) v. przygnębiać; deprymować; spychać
w dół(ceny);deprymować;martwić
depression (dy'preszyn) s.
przygnębienie; depresja
deprive (dy'prajw) v. odzierać;
wykluczać; umartwiać się; pozbawiać;odwołać (z urzędu etc.)
depth (deps) s. głębokość;
głębia; głębina;dno(nędzy etc.)
deputy ('depjuty) s. zastępca;
deputowany; poseł; wice-

derail (dy'rejl) v. wykoleic
(się)(czyjś plan,zamiar etc.)
derange (dy'rejndż) v. pomieszac; rozstrajać; psuć; zakłócać; powodować obłęd
deride (dy'rajd) v. wysmiewac
derision (dy'ryżyn) s. szyderstwo; posmiewisko; drwina
derisive (dy'rajsyw) adj.kpią-
cy; ironiczny;wart smiechu
derive (dy'rajw) v. uzyskiwac;
czerpać; wywodzic; pochodzic
derogatory (dy'rogeto:ry) v.
pomniejszający; uszczuplający;
uwłaczający ; szkodliwy,
descend (dy'send) v. zejsc;spasc
zniżać się;pochodzic; opadac
descendant (dy'sendent) s. po-
tomek(przedka;rodziny;grupy etc.)
descent (dy'sent) s. zejscie;
spadek; pochodzenie;nagły atak
describe (dys'krajb) v. opisywać; okreslac;przerysowywac
description (dy'skrypszyn)
s. opis;sposób opisywania
desegregate (dy'segrygejt) v.
(Am.) zniesc podział rasowy
desert ('desert) adj. pustynny;
pusty; s. pustynia;pustkowie
desert (dy'ze:rt) v. porzucac;
opuszczac; dezerterować; s.za-
służenie; zasługa;nagroda;kara
deserted (dy'ze:rted) adj.
opuszczony;bezludny
deserter (dy'ze;rter) s. dezer-
ter;dezerterka;zbieg;zbiegła
desertion (dy'ze:rszyn) s.
opuszczenie; dezercja;porzucenie
deserve (dy'ze:rw) v. zasługiwać na...;miec zasługi wobec...
design (dy'zajn) s. zamiar;
plan; szkic; v. pomyslec; zamierzac; przeznaczac; projekto-
wac;zamyslac;uplanować;kreslic
designate ('dezygnejt) v. wyznaczac; okreslac; desygnowac
designer (dy'zajner) s. projek-
tant; konstruktor; rysownik;
intrygant;projektodawca;autor
desirable (dy'zajerebl) adj. pożądany;pociągający;atrakcyjny
celowy;mile widziany;wskazany

desire (dy'zajer) v. pożądac;
pragnąc; życzyc sobie
desirous (dy'zajeres) adj. żądny;pragnący;spragniony
desk (desk) s. biuro; referat;
pulpit; ambona ;ławka szkolna
desk set ('desk set) s. zestaw
przyborów do pisania
desolate ('deselyt) adj.
opuszczony; posępny;wyludniony
desolate (deselejt) v. pusto-
szyc; wyludniac; opuszczac
desolation (,dese'lejszyn) s.
wyludnienie; spustoszenie;
pustka; żałosc; strapienie
despair (dys'peer) s. rozpacz
despairingly (dys'peeryngly)
adv. rozpaczliwie;beznadziejnie
desperate ('desperyt) adj.
rozpaczliwy;beznadziejny;zacie-
desperation (,despe'rejszyn)
s. rozpacz; desperacja
despise (dys'pajz) v. pogar-
dzac;gardzic;lekceważyć
despite (dys'pajt) s. przekora; złość; prep. pomimo;
wbrew;na przekór(komuś,czemuś)
despond (dys'pond) v. przygnę-
biac się;s.przygnębienie
despondent (dys'pondent) adj.
przygnębiony; zniechęcony
dessert (dy'ze:rt) s. deser;
legumina; ciastka
destination (desty'nejszyn) s.
miejsce przeznaczenia
destine ('destyn) v. przezna-
czac(z góry);przeznaczyć
destiny ('destyny) s. przezna-
czenie(wypadków,ludzi...);los
destitute ('destytju:t) adj.
bez srodków;pozbawiony;w nędzy
destroy (dy'stroj) v. burzyć;
niweczyc;zabijać;zagładzać
destroyer (dy'strojer) s.kontr-
torpedowiec; niszczyciel
destruction (dys'trakszyn) s.
zniszczenie;ruina;zguba;zagłada
destructive (dy'straktyw) adj.
niszczycielski;s.niszczyciel
detach (dy'taecz) v. odczepic;
odłączyc; odpiąc; odwiazac;
odkomenderowac;odlepiac;urwac

detached (dy'taeczt) adj. odosobniony; obojętny;niezależny
detail ('di:tejl) s. szczegół;
wyszczególnienie; v. wyłuszczać; przydzielać do zadań
detain (dy'tejn) v. wstrzymywać; więzić; przeszkadzać
detect (dy'tekt) v. wykrywać;
wyśledzić;wypatrzyć;przychwycić
detection (dy'tekszyn) s. wy-
krywanie; wyśledzenie
detective (dy'tektyw) s. detek-
tyw; adj. detektywistyczny
detention (dy'tenszyn) s. więzienie; zatrzymanie;przetrzymanie
deter (dy'te:r) v. odstraszać
od...;pohamować;oniesmielać
detergent (dy'te:rdżent) s.&
adj. czyszczący (środek)
deteriorate (dy'tierjerejt) s.
psuć; marnieć;tracić na wartości
determination (dyte:rmy'nejszyn)
s. określenie; postanowienie;
ustalenie; orzeczenie;wygaśnięcie
determine (dy'te:rmyn) v. rozstrzygać; określać; postanawiać; ustalać;zdefiniować
deterrent (dy'terent) adj. od-
straszający; s.(czynnik) od-
straszający;środek zaradczy
detest (dy'test) v. nienawidzić;
czuć wstręt;nie cierpieć
detestable (dy'testebl) adj.
wstrętny; nienawistny;obmierzły
detonate ('detounejt) v. wybuchać; powodować wybuch
detour ('dy:tuer) s. objazd
devaluation (,dy:vaelju'ejszyn)
s. dewaluacja;zdewaluowanie
devaluate('dy:waelju:ejt)v.dewalu-
ować;obniżać wartość;zdewaluować
devastate ('devestejt) v. pustoszyć;niweczyć;dewastować
develop (dy'velop) v. rozwijać
(się); wywoływać (zdjęcia)
development (dy'velepment) s.
rozwój; rozbudowa; osiedle;
wywołanie(filmu);ewolucja
deviate ('di:wyejt) v. zbaczać;
odchylać;schodzić z drogi
device (dy'wajs) s. plan; pomysł;
urządzenie; dewiza; hasło;środek

devil ('dewl) s. chart; diabeł
devilish ('dewlysh) adj. szatański; diabelski;adv.diabelsko
devise (dy'wajz) v. zapisać
(komuś); wymyślać; obmyślać
devoid (dy'woyd) adj. pozbawiony;próżny;czczy;wolny od.,.
devote (dy'wout) v. poświęcać;
ofiarować;oddawać się
devoted (dy'vouted) adj. oddany;przywiązany (do kogoś)
dew (dju:) s. rosa; świeżość;
powiew; v. rosić; zraszać
dew point ('dju:point)
temperatura powstawania rosy
dexter ('dekster) a. prawy
dexterity (deks'teryty) s.
zręczność; bystrość;sprawność
diabetes (,daje'by:ty:z) s.
cukrzyca;choroba cukrowa
diagram ('dajegraem) s. wykres;
schemat; diagram
dial ('dajel) s. tarcza nume-
rowa (zw. zegarowa);
v. mierzyć; nakręcać (numer)
dial tone ('dajel,toun) s.
sygnał połączenia (tel.)
dialect ('dajelekt) s. gwara;
narzecze; dialekt
dialog(ue) ('dajelog) s. rozmowa; dialog(na scenie etc.)
diameter (dai'aemyter) s. średnica; długość średnicy
diamond('dajemend) s. diament;
romb; a. diamentowy; romboidalny;s.boisko do gry w palanta
diaper ('dajeper) s. pielusz-
ka; wzór romboidalny;
v. przewijać; ozdabiać w romby
diaphragm ('dajefraem) s. przepona; membrana;przesłona
diarrhea (daje'rye) s. biegunka
diary ('daiery) s. dziennik
dice (dajs) v. grać w kości;
kratkować; pl. od die=kostka do
dictate (dyktejt) s. nakaz; gry
v. dyktować;narzucać(wolę etc.)
dictation (dyk'tejszyn) s.
dyktat; dyktowanie ;nakaz
dictator (dyk'tejter) s. dyktator;dyktujący dyktando;dyk-
tujący na głos (tekst;list etc.)

dictatorship (dyk'tejterszyp)
s. dyktatura;władza nieograniczo-
na;
dictionary ('dykszeneerys.słow-
nik;mała encyklopedia
did (dyd) v. zrobić; zob.: do
die (daj) v. umierać; zdech-
nąć; zginąć; s. matryca;
sztanca; pl. zob,: dice
die-hard ('daj-ha:rd) adj.
twardy; nieustępliwy; s. zagorzały bojownik(szermierz etc.)
diet ('dajet) s. dieta; zjazd;
sejm; v. trzymać na diecie
differ ('dyfer) v. różnic się;
nie zgadzać się(z opinią etc.)
difference ('dyferens) s. różnica; sprzeczka; nieporozumienie
different ('dyferent) adj. różny; odmienny; niezwykły
difficult ('dyfykelt) adj.
trudny;cieżki; niełatwy
difficulty ('dyfykelty) s.
trudność; przeszkoda
diffident ('dyfydent) adj. nieśmiały; bez wiary we własne
siły;bez zaufania do siebie
diffuse (dy'fju:z) adj. rozwlekły; rozproszony; v. rozle-
wać; szerzyć; rozpraszać
dig; dug; dug (dyg; dag; dag)
dig (dyg) v. kopać; ryć; rozumieć; ocenić; bawic się; kuć
się; s. szarpnięcie; przytyk;
kujon;szturchnięcie;docinek
digest (dy'dżest) v. trawić;
przetrawiac; s. streszczenie;
skrót; przegląd;zbiór praw
digestible (dy'dżestebl) adj.
strawny;łatwy do przyswojenia
digestion (dy'dżestszyn) s.
trawienie; wygotowanie
diggings ('dygynz) s. kopalnia
(złota); mieszkanie
dignified ('dygnyfajd) adj. dostojny;godny;pełen godności
dignity ('dygnyty) s. godność;
dostojenstwo;powaga;zaszczyt
digress ('daj'gres) v. zbaczać;
odbiegać od rzeczy (tematu etc.)
digs (dygz) s, mieszkanie; pokój; buda; melina
dihedral (daj'hi:drel)adj.(kąt)
między dwoma ścianami

dike (dajk) s. tama; grobla;
v. osuszać rowem; otamować
dilapidated (dy'laepydejtyd)
adj. zniszczony;walący się
dilate (daj'lejt) v. rozszerzać; rozwodzic się;rozciągać
diligence ('dylydżens) n. pilność;przykładanie się do pracy
diligent ('dylydżent) adj. pilny;przykładający się do pracy
dill (dyl) s. koper ogrodowy
dill-pickle ('dyl,pykl) s. kiszony ogorek
dilute (daj'lju:t) v. rozpusz-
czać; rozcieńczać; rozrzedzać;
adj. rozpuszczony; rozcieńczo-
ny; rozrzedzony; rozwodniony;
wypłukany; wybladły;spłowiały
dim (dym) v. przyćmić; zaciem-
nic; zamglić; adj. przyćmiony;
blady zamazany; niewyrazny
dime (dajm) s. dziesięcio-
centowa moneta U.SA.
dimension (dy'menszyn) s. wymiar; rozmiar; wielkość
diminish (dy'mynysz) v. zmniejszać; zwęzać;uszczuplać;niknąć
diminutive (dy'mynjutyw) adj.&
s. drobniutki; zdrobniały;
zdrobnienie:malutka kobieta
dimple ('dympl) s. dołek (w
twarzy) ; v. robić dołki; miec
dołki (w twarzy etc.)
dine (dajn) v. jeść obiad;
jesć; mieć na obiedzie
diner (dajner) s. stołówka
wagon restauracyjny; osoba
jedząca;restauracja
dining car ('dajnyng,ka:r) s.
wagon restauracyjny
dining room ('dajnyng,ru:m)
s. jadalnia;pokój jadalny
dinner ('dyner) s. obiad
dinner-jacket ('dyner,dżaekyt)
s. smoking
dinner-party ('dyner,pa:rty)
s. przyjęcie; obiad proszony
dip (dyp) v. zanurzać; czerpać;
farbować; pograżać; płukać;
nachylać sie; opadać; s. zanurzenie; zamoczenie; rozczyn;
nachylenie; obniżenie; łojówka;
sos do macznia;skok do wody

diphtheria (dyfteria) s. dyfteryt; błonica
diploma (dy'plouma) s. dyplom
diplomacy (dy'ploumesy) s. dyplomacja;takt
diplomat ('dyplemaet) s. dyplomata;człowiek taktowny
diplomatic(,dyple'maetyk) adj. dyplomatyczny; taktowny
direct (dy'rekt) v. kierować; kazać; zarządzić; dowodzić; zaadresować;nakierowywać; wymierzać polecić; dyrygować;adj. prosty; bezpośredni; otwarty; szczery; wyraźny; adv. wprost; prosto; bezpośrednio
direct current (dy'rekt'karent) s. prąd stały
direction (dy'rekszyn) s. kierunek; kierowanie; kierownictwo; zarząd; wskazówka; adres
directions (dy'rekszyns) pl. instrukcje; przepisy; przepis
directly (dy'rektly) adv. bezpośrednio; wprost; od razu; zaraz;natychmiast;dokładnie
director (dy'rektor) s. dyrektor; reżyser; celownik; kierownik;zarządzający
directory (dy'rektery) s. książka adresowa; telefoniczna(lub przepisów);skorowidz
dirigible ('dyrydżebl) adj.& s. sterowy; sterowiec
dirt (de:rt) s. brud; błoto; świństwo; ziemia; język plugawy; mówienie oszczrstw;plotki
dirt-cheap (de:rt'czi:p) adv. za bezcen; adj, bardzo tani; tani jak barszcz;śmiesznie tani
dirty (de:rty) adj. brudny; sprosny; podły; wstrętny
disability (,dyse'dylyty) s. inwalidztwo; niemoc;niemożność
disabled (dysejbld) s. kaleka; inwalida wojenny
disadvantage (dysed'wa:ntydż) s. niekorzyść; wada; strata; szkoda; niekorzystne położenie;v.szkodzić;zaszkodzić(komu)
disadvantageous (dysaedwa:ntejdżes) adj. niekorzystny; szkodliwy;ujemny

disagree (dyse'gri:) v. nie zgadzać się; różnić się; nie służyć (jedzenie; klimat)
disagreeable (,dyse'gri:ebl) adj. nieprzyjemny; niemiły
disagreement (,dyse'gri:ment) s. niezgoda; różnica
disallow (,dyse'lau) v. niepozwalać; nie dopuszczać
disappear (,dyse'pier) v. znikać;zapodziewać się; przepaść
disappearance (,dyse'pierens) s. zniknięcie;zanik;zginięcie
disappoint (dyse'point) v. zawieść;rozczarować;nie spełnić
disappointment (dyse'pointment) s. zawód; rozczarowanie
disapproval (dyse'pru:wel) s. potępienie; niechęć;desaprobata
disapprove (dyse'pru:w) v. potępiać; ganić;źle widzieć(kogoś)
disarm (dys'a:rm) v. rozbroić; unieszkodliwić;odebrać broń
disarmament (dys'a:rmement) s. rozbrojenie;a.rozbrojeniowy
disarrange ('dyse'rejndż) v. rozstrajać; dezorganizować
disarray (,dyse'rej) v. wprowadzać nieład; rozstrajać; s. nieład; zamieszanie; bałagan;niekompletny strój
disaster (dy'za:ster) s. nieszczęście; klęska(żywiołowa etc.)
disastrous (dy'za:stres) adj. katastrofalny; zgubny;fatalny
disbelief ('dysby'li:f) s. niewiara; niedowierzanie;nieufność
disbelieve ('dysby'li:w) v. niewierzyć; niedowierzać
disc (dysk) s. krążek; tarcza; płyta; dysk;płyta gramofonowa
discard (dys'ka:rd) v. wyrzucać; odrzucać;zarzucać;zaniechać
discard ('dyska:rd) s. odrzucenie; odrzucona (rzecz lub osoba);odpadek;rzecz wybrakowana
discern (dy'se:rn) v. rozróżniać;odrożniać;rozpoznawać
discharge (dys'cza:rdż) v. rozładować; odciążać; zwalniać; wypuścić; wystrzelić; s. rozładowaniewystrzał; zwolnienie; wydzielina;odpływ;odchody;ropa

disciple (dy'sajpl) s. uczeń;
wyznawca;jeden z apostołów
discipline ('dyscyplyn) s.
dyscyplina; karność; v. karać; ćwiczyć; musztrować
disc-jockey (dysk'dżoki) s.
nadający muzykę z płyt ;
(disk jockey)
disclaim (dys'klejm) v. wypierać się;rezygnować;zrzekać się
disclcse (dys'k-ouz) v. odsłaniać; ujawniać;wyjawiać;odkryć
discolor (dys'kaler) v.
discomfort (dys'kamfert) s. niewygoda; niepokój; v. sprawiać
niewygody lub złe samopoczucie;krępować;żenować;dolegać
discompose (,dyskem'pouz) v.
niepokoić; mieszać;zmieszać
disconcert (,dysken'ser:t) v.
żenować; krzyżować plany
disconnect ('dyske'nekt) v. od-
łączyć; oderwać; odhaczyć
disconnected ('dyske'nektyd)
adj. bez związku; bezładny;
rozłączony; chaotyczny
disconsolate (dys'konselyt) adj.
niepocieszony; posępny
dicontent ('dysken'tent) s. niezadowolenie; adj. niezadowolony; v. wywoływać niezadowolenie ;wywoływać rozgoryczenie
discontented ('dysken'tentyd)
adj. niezadowolony; rozgory-
czony; zniecierpliwiony
discontinue ('dysken'tynju:) v.
zaprzestawać; przerywać; ustawać ;zakończyć; zaniechać
discord ('dysko:rd) s. niezgoda; różnica; dysonans;niesnaski
discordance ('dysko:rdens) s.
niezgodność ;dysonans
discotheque ('dyskoutek) s.
dyskoteka; nocny lokal z muzy-
ką z płyt do tańca
discount ('dyskaunt) s. dyskont;
rabat; odjęcie; v. potrącać;
odliczać; nie dawać wiary
discourage (dys'karydż) v. zniechęcać; odstraszać;być przeciwnym
discover (dys'kawer) v. wynaleźć; odkryć; odsłaniać;zobaczyć

discoverer (dys'kawerer) s.
odkrywca; wynalazca
discredit (dys'kredyt) v. dys-
kredytować; przynosić ujmę;
pozbawiać zaufania; s. utrata zaufania i dobrego imienia;
niewiara;zła opinia(kogo ,czego)
discreet (dys'kri:t) a. rozsądny; dyskretny; z rezerwą
discrepancy (dys'krepensy) s.
sprzeczność ;rozbieżność
discretion (dys'kreszyn) s.
swoboda decyzji; rozwaga;
powściągliwość; dyskrecja
discriminate (dys'krymynejt),
v. odróżniać; dyskryminować;
robić różnicę;wyróżniać
discriminate against (dys'krymynejt e'genst) wprowadzać
dyskryminację w stosunku do..
discuss (dys'kas) v. dyskuto-
wać; roztrząsać ;debatować
discussion (dys'kaszyn) s.
dyskusja; debata ;debaty
disdain (dy'dejn) s. pogarda;
wzgarda;v.gardzić;lekceważyć
disease (dy'zi:z) s. choroba
diseased (dy'zi:zd) adj. chory; schorzały;cierpiący na...
disembark ('dysym'ba:rk) v.wy-
ładować; wysiadać; lądować
disengage ('dysen'gejdż) v.
odczepiać; wyłączać;odwikłać
disengaged ('dysyn'gejdżd) adj.
wolny; nie zajęty;zwolniony
disentangle ('dysyntaengl) v.
wyplątać; rozplątać;wywikłać
disfavor ('dys'fejwer) s. niełaska; dezaprobata; v. odnosić się nieprzychylnie; z niechęcią traktować;dezaprobować
disfigure (dys'fyger) v. zniekształcić ;zeszpecić
disgrace (dys'grejs), s. hańba;
niełaska; v. hańbić; znieśła-
wić; pozbawiać łaski;narobić wsty-
disgraceful (dys'grejsfel) adj.
haniebny; hańbiący;sromotny;niecny
disguise (dys'gajz) v. przebierać; ukrywać; maskować; z..taić;
s. charakteryzacja; udawanie;
pozory ;zamaskowanie; maska

disgust (dys'gast) s. odraza;
wstręt; obrzydzenie; v. budzić odrazę, wstręt, obrzydzenie, rozgoryczenie,oburzenie
disgusting (dvs'gastyng)adj.
wstrętny; obrzydliwy;oburzający
dish (dysz) s. półmisek; naczynie;potrawa; danie; v. nakładac; podawac; drążyc;okpiwać
dishes ('dyszyz) pl. statki;
naczynia;smaczne potrawy
dish-cloth ('dysz,klos) s.
ścierka do wycierania talerzy
disheveled (dy'szeweld) adj.
rozczochrany; zaniedbany
dishonest (dys'onyst) adj. nieuczciwy; nie godny zaufania
dishonesty (dys'onysty) s. nie-
uczciwość;nieuczciwy postępek
dishonor (dys'oner) s. hańba;
dyshonor; niehonorowanie;v.lżyc
dishonorable (dys'onerebl) adj.
haniebny; podły;bez czci i wiary
dishwasher ('dysh,łoszer) s.
pomywacz(ka)
dish-water (dysz,ło:ter) s. pomyje
disillusion (,dysy'lu:żyn) s.
rozczarowanie;otrzeźwienie
disincline (,dysyn'klajn) v.
zniechęcac; miec niechęc
disinclined (,dysyn'klajnd) adj.
zniechęcony;źle usposobiony
disinfect (,dysyn'fekt) v. od-
każac ;zdyzenfekować
disinfectant (,dysyn'fektent)
s. środek odkażający
disinherit ('dysyn'heryt) v.
wydziedziczyc; wydziedziczac
disintegrate (dys'yntegrejt) v.
rozpadac (się); rozkładac (się)
disinterested (dys'yntrystyd)
adj. bezinteresowny; nie zainteresowany;obiektywny
disjoint(dys'dżoint)v. rozłączac;
rozdzielac;zwichnac;rozerwać
disk (dysk) s. krążek; tarcza;
płyta gramofonowa; dysk
dislike (dys'lajk) v. nie lubic;
miec odrazę; s. odraza; niechęc;awersja; wstręt

dislocate ('dyslekejt) v.
zwichnąc; przesunąc;zatrącic
disloyal (,dys'lojel) adj. niewierny; nielojalny; zdradziecki
dismal ('dyzmel) adj. nieszczęsny; ponury; posępny
dismantle (dys'maentl) v. roz-
montowywac; ogołacac; odzie-
rac;rozbroic;pozbawiać
dismay (dys'mej) s. trwoga;
przestrach; v. przerażac;
konsternowac;skonsternować
dismember (dys'member) v. roz-
członowac; rozebrac na części
dismiss (dys'mys) v. odprawiac;
zwalniac; odsuwac od siebie
dismissal (dys'mysel) s. zwolnienie; dymisja;rozejście się
dismount ('dys'maunt) v. zsiadac z konia; wyjmowac z opra-
wy; wysadzac z siodła
disobedience (dyse'bi:djens)
s. nieposłuszeństwo; opór
disobedient (dyse'bi:djent)
adj. nieposłuszny; oporny
disobey (,dyse'bej) v. nie-
słuchac; byc nieposłusznym
disoblige (,dyse'blajdż) v.
lekceważyc; bagatelizowac
disorder (dys'o:rder) s. nieporządek; zamieszki;zaburzenie
disorderly (dys'o:rderly )adj.
nieporządny; niesforny; gorszący; burzliwy;bezładny
disown (dys'oun) v. wypierac
się; zaprzeczac; nie uznawac
disparage (dys'paerydż) v.
poniżac; ubliżac; dyskredyto-
wac;uwłaszczac;lekceważyć
dispassion (dys'paeszyn) s.
beznamiętnosc; odiektywizm
dispassionate (dys'paeszynat)
adj. beznamiętny;obiektywny
dispatch (dys'paecz) s. wysył-
ka; wysłanie; sprawnosc; szyb-
kosc; szybkie załatwienie;
v. wysyłac; załatwiac
dispel (dys'pel) v. rozwiewac
(obawy);rozpędzac(chmury)
dispensable (dys'pensebl) adj.
zbędny; niekonieczny;do uchyle-
nia

dispense (dys'pens) v. wydzielac; wymierzac; wydawac;
udzielac;sporządzac(lekarstwo)
dispense with (dys pens łys)
v. pomijac; obyc się
disperse (dys'pe:rs) v. roz-
praszac; rozpędzac; rozjeż-
dżac się; rozsiewac;płoszyc
displace (dys'plejs) v. prze-
mieszczac; wypierac; usuwac
display (dys'plej) v. wystawiac; popisywac się; s. wystawa; popis; pokaz;parada
displease (dys'pli:z) v. ura-
żac; drażnic; gniewac; dotykac; oburzac; irytowac
displeased (dys'pli:zd) adj.
urażony; zirytowany; niezadowolony;obrażony;poirytowany
displeasure (dys'pleżer) s.
niezadowolenie; gniew;irytacja
disposal (dys'pouzel) s. rozkład; zbyt; sprzedaż; przekazanie; rozporządzenie;niszczeni
dispose (dys'pouz) v. rozmieszczac; rozporządzic; pozbyc
się; sprzedac;usunąc;niszczyc
disposed (dys'pouzd) adj. skłonny; usposobiony(dobrze,źle etc.)
disposition (dys'pouzyszyn) s.
skłonnosc; pociąg; zarządzenie; dyspozycje;rozporządzanie
disproportionate (,dyspre'po:r-
sznyt) adj. nieproporcjonalny
dispute (dys'pju:t) s. spór;
kłótnia; v. sprzeczac się;
kłócic się; kwestionowac
disqualify (dys'kłolyfaj) v.
dyskwalifikowac
disquiet (dys'kłajet) v. niepokoic; s. niepokój; adj. niespokojny;zaniepokojony
disregard (,dysry'ga:rd) v. pomijac; lekceważyc;s.lekceważe-
disrepute (,dysry'pju:t) s. nie
niesława;hańba; zła reputacja
disrespectful (,dysry'spektfel)
adj. niegrzeczny; niedelikatny
disrupt (dys'rapt) v. rozrywac;
rozdzierac;przerwac; obalic
dissatisfaction ('dysseatys'-
faeksyn) s. niezadowolenie

dissatisfied (dys,satys'fajd)
adj. niezadowolony
dissension (dy'senszyn) s. wasn;
niezgoda; swary
dissent (dy'sent) s. róznica;
rozbieżnosc zdań; v. różnic
się w zapatrywaniach;odstępstwo
dissimilar ('dy'symyler) adj.
niepodobny; różny
dissipate (dy'sypejt) v. roz-
praszac; marnowac; trwonic;
marnotrawic;rozgonic;hulac
dissociate (dy'souszjejt) v.
rozłączac; zrywac(z kims,czyms)
dissolute ('dyselu:t) adj. rozwiązły; rozpustny
dissolution (,dys'elu:szyn) s.
rozkład; zanik; rozpuszczenie;
rozwiązanie;smierc;zgon;rozpad
dissolve (dy'zolw) v. rozpuszczac; rozkładac; niszczyc;
rozwiązywac; zanikac;skasowac
dissuade (dy'słejd) v. odradzac;
odwodzic (kogos);wyperswadowac
distance ('dystens) s. odległosc;
odstęp; oddalenie;v.zdystansowac
distant ('dystent) adj. daleki;
odległy; powsciągliwy;z rezerwą
distaste (,dys'tejst) s. niesmak;
niechęc; odraza; awersja
distasteful (,dys'tejstful) adj.
odstręczający;wstrętny;przykry
distend (dys'tend) v. rozdymac;
rozszerzac;nabrzmiewac;nadąc
distill (dy'styl) v. przekrap-
lac; destylowac;przesączac;kapac
distinct (dys'tynkt) adj. odmienny; odrębny; wyrazny; dobitny
distinction (dys'tynkszyn) s.
rozróznienie; wyróżnienie;
wytwornosc; podział;wyrazistosc
distinctive (dys'tynktyw) adj.
odrózniający sie;charakterystyczny
distinguish (dys'tyngłysz) v.
rozrózniac; klasyfikowac;odznaczyc
distinguished (dystyngłyszt)
adj. wybitny; znakomity;
dystyngowany;odznaczający się
distort (dys'to:rt) v. wykrzywiac; wykręcac; przekręcac
distract (dys'traekt) v. odrywac; rozproszyc; oszołomic

distracted (dys'traektyd) adj.
oszalały; w rozterce; skłopo-
tany;roztargniony;rozproszony
distraction (dys'traekszyn) s.
dystrakcja; roztargnienie;
rozrywka; rozterka; szalenst-
wo;zamieszanie;odwrócenie uwagi
distress (dys'tres) s. męka;
strapienie; niedostatek; potrzeba; niebezpieczeństwo
distressed (dys'trest) adj.
umęczony; udręczony;w niedoli
distribute (dys'trybju:t) v.
udzielac; rozmieszczac;rozdać
distribution (dys'tryju;szyn)
s. rozdział; podział; dystry-
bucja;roznoszenie;a.rozdzielczy
district ('dystrykt) s. okręg;
powiat; dystrykt;dzielnica;rejon
distrust (dys'trast) s. nie-
ufność; niedowierzanie; v.nie-
ufac; niedowierzac;podejrzewac
disturb (dys'te:rb) v. prze-
szkadzac; niepokoic; zakłócac;
mącic; zaburzyc;denerwować
disturbance (dys'te:rbens) s.
zakłócenie; zaburzenie; naruszenie;burda;awantura;rozruchy
disuse (dys'ju:z) v. zarzucenie; nieużywanie;s.nieużywanie
ditch (dycz),s. rów; v. kopac;
drenowac; utknąc w rowie; rzucac do rowu(samolot w morze)
dive (dajw) v. nurkowac; zanurzac się; skakac z trampoliny;
s. nurkowanie; zanurzenie; melina;lot nurkowy;pikowanie;knajpa
diver ('dajwer) s. nurek;skoczek
z trampoliny;ptak nurkujący
diverge (daj'we:rdż) v. rozcho-
dzic się; odchylac się; zbaczac;
odbiegac;rozbiegac się
diverse (daj'we:rs) adj. odmienny; rozmaity;inny;zmienny
diversion (daj'we:rżyn) s.odchy-
lenie;objazd;rozrywka;dywersja
diversion (dy'we:rżyn) s. zboczenie; dywersja; rozrywka;odwróce-
nie uwagi;oderwanie uwagi
diversity (daj'we:rsyty) s. roz-
maitosc;różnorodność;urozmaicenie

diversity (dy'we:rsyty) s. od-
mienność;roznorodność;rozmaitość
divert (daj'we:rt) v. odwracac (uwagę); odrywać; rozer-
wac; rozbawic;bawic(kogoś)
divide (dy'wajd) v. dzielic;
rozdzielac; oddzielać; różnic
divide by (dy'wajd,baj) v.
dzielic przez...(liczbę)
divine (dy'wajn) adj. boski;
boży; v. wróżyc; przepowiadac
diving ('dajwyŋg) s. skakanie
z trampoliny;pikowac samolotem
divinity (dy'wynyty) s. bóstwo;
boskosc; teologia
divisible (dy'wyzebl) adj. podzielny (przez,na etc.)
division (dy'wyżyn) s. podział;
rozdział; dzielenie; dział;
wydział; oddział; dywizja
divorce (dy'wo:rs) s. rozwód;
rozdzielenie; v. rozwodzic
się; oddzielac;a.rozwodowy
dizzy ('dyzy) adj. wirujący;
oszołomiony;v.oszałamiac
do (du:) v. czynic; robic; wykonac; zwiedzac;przyrządzać
do away ('du,ełej) v. zniesc;
pozbyc się; zabic;skasowac
do not ('du not) = don't (dont)
nie(rób);nie(idź);nie(stój,etc.)
do in ('du,yn) v.uwięzic; zlikwi-
dowac; zabic;wsadzić do paki
do up ('du,ap) v. przerobic;
odnowic; zmęczyc;upudrowac etc.
do well (,du'łel) v. miec się
dobrze; powodzic się
do without (,du'łyşout) v.oby-
wac się bez (kogoś,czegos)
do you know? (du: ju nou) expr.
czy pan wie (zna) ? czy pan słyszał?
docile ('dousajl) adj. uległy;
posłuszny;pojętny;giętki;łagodny
dock (dok) s. dok; basen; molo;
miejsce oskarżonego; v. umies-
cic w doku; cumowac przy molu
dockyard (dokja:rd) s. stocznia
doctor ('dakter) s. lekarz;
doktor (medycyny;filozofii etc.)
doctrine ('daktryn) s. doktryna

document ('dokjument) s. dokument;v. udokumentować
documentary (,dokju'mentery)s.
adj. dokumentarny (film etc.)
dodge (dodż) v. uchylić; uniknąć; zwodzić; s, unik; kruczek; sztuczka;odskok;kiwanie
doe (dou) s. łania ;pl.:does (douz)
does (daz) v. on czyni; robi;
zob.: do
dog (dog) s. pies;uchwyt;klamra
dog-catcher (dog'kaeczer) s.
rakarz; oprawca; hycel
dogged ('dogyd) adj. uparty;
zawzięty;wytrwały
doggie ('dogi) s. psina
dogma ('dogme) s. dogmat
dog-tired ('dog'tajerd) adj.
skonany; ledwo żywy;zmęczony
doings ('du:yngs) pl. sprawki;
uczynki; wyprawiania;psoty
dole ( doul) s. zasiłek; zapomoga; smutek;v.mało dawać
doll (dol) s. lalka; (slang)
dziewczyna;v.wystroić się
dollar ('doler) s. dolar
dollish ('dolysz) adj. lalko-
waty(a);lalusiowaty
dolorous ('douleres) adj.
smętny; żałosny; zbolały
dolphin ('dolfyn) s. delfin
dome (doum) s. kopuła; sklepienie;v.nakrywać kopułą
domestic (de'mestyk) adj. domowy; krajowy; domatorski;
s. służący; służąca
domesticate (de'mestykejt) v.
oswajać; zadomowić
domicile ('domysajl) s, miejsce zamieszkania; v. osiedlać;
zamieszkać na stałe
dominate ('domynejt) v. domi-
nować; gorować; przeważać;
panować;mieć zwierzchnictwo
domination ('domynejszyn) s.
władza; panowanie; przewaga
domineer (,domy'nier) v. domi-
nować; rządzić się; rozkazy-
wać;tyranizować;panoszyć się
domineering (,domy'nieryng)
adj. tyranizujący; apodyktyczny; despotyczny; władczy

donate (dou'nejt) v. podarować
donation (dou'nejszyn) s. daro-
wizna, donacja; dar
done (dan) adj. zrobiony; uczy-
niony; zob.: do
donkey ('donky) s. osioł
donor ('douner) s. donator;
dawca (krwi etc.);darujący
doom (du:m) s. zguba; zły los;
śmierć; potępienie; v. potępiać; skazać na zgubę;przesądzać
Doomsday ('du:mzdej) s. dzień
sądu ostatecznego
door (do:r) s. drzwi;brama
door handle ('do:r,haendl) s.
klamka
doorkeeper ('do:r,ki:per) s.
dozorca;portier; oddźwierny
doorknob ('do:r,nob) s. klamka
doormat ('do:r,maet) s, wycieraczka (przy drzwiach)
doorway ('do:r,łej) s. wejście
dope (doup) s. maź; lakier; narkotyk; informacja (poufna);
głupiec (slang). v. narkotyzo-
wać; zaprawiać;fałszować
dormitory ('do:rmytry) s. dom
studencki; sypialnia
dose (dous) s. dawka; dodatek;
dawkowanie; v. dawkować (lekarstwo); mieszać; fałszować
(wino);leczyć;dozować
dot (dot) s. kropka; punkt;
v. kropkować; rozsiewać
dote (dout) v. wariować; kochać
przesadnie; dziecinnieć
double ('dabl) adj. podwojny;
dwukrotny; fałszywy; v. pod-
wajać; adv. podwójnie;w dwójnasób
double up ('dabl,ap) v. składać
się we dwoje; zsuwać się (razem);przybiegać;dzielić pokój
double bed ('dabl,bed) podwójne
łóżko
double-breasted ('dabl,brestyd)
adj. dwurzędowy(płaszcz,marynarka)
double-decker ('dabl-'deker) s.
dwupokładowiec; dwupiętrowiec
double-park ('dabl²pa:rk) v.
parkować podwójnie (na jezdni)
double-room ('dabl,ru:m) s.
pokój dwuosobowy(w hotelu etc.)

doubt (daut) s. wątpliwość; niedowierzanie; v. wątpić; powąt-
piewać; niedowierzać
doubtful ('dautful) adj. wątpliwy; niepewny;niezdecydowany
doubtless ('dautlys) adv. nie-
wątpliwie; bez wątpienia
douche (du'sz) s. natrysk
dough (dou) s. ciasto; (slang)
forsa; pieniądze
doughnut ('dounat) s. pączek
(z dziurą)
dove (daw) s. gołąb(ica)
down (daŕn) s. wydma; puch;
meszek ;puszek;piórka
down (daŕn) adv. na dół; niżej;
nisko; v. obniżać; poniżać;
przewrócić; strącić; przełknąć
downcast ('daŕnka:st) adj.
przybity; przygnębiony; ze
spuszczonymi oczyma
downfall ('daŕnfo:l) s. upadek;
klęska; ruina ; zguba
downhill ('daŕn'hyl) adj. opa-
dający; s. spadek ;adv.na dół
downpour ('daŕnpo:r) s. ulewa
downright ('daŕhrajt) adv. zupełnie; wprost; adj. zupełny;
szczery; otwarty; uczciwy
downstairs ('daŕn'steerz) adv.
na dół; w dole ;na dole;pod nami
downtown ('daŕntaŕn) s. centrum
miasta; adv. w śródmieściu;
adj. śródmiejski
downwards ('daŕnŕódz) adv.
w dół; ku dołowi ;na dół;z góry
downy ('daŕhy) adj. puszysty;
(slang):chytry ;falisty;puchaty
dowry ('daŕry) s. posag; wiano;
dar wrodzony ; talent
doze (douz) s. drzemka; v. drzemać; zdrzemnąć się; zasnąć
dozen ('dazn) s. tuzin
drab (draeb) s.& adj. brudno-
brunatny; nudny; szary; brudas;
prostytutka; v. puszczać się
draft (dra:ft) s. szkic; brulion
zarys; przekaz; pobór; rysunek;
v. szkicować; projektować; rysować; odkomenderować;wyżłobić
draftsman ('dra:ftsmen) s. kreślarz; rysownik; projektodawca

drag (draeg) v. wlec; ciągnąć;
s. pogłębiarka; pojazd; wleczenie; opór czołowy
dragon ('draegen) s. smok
dragonfly ('draegenflaj) s.
ważka
drain (drejn) v. odwadniać;
wysączać; ociekać; s. dreń;
spust; ściek;rów odwadniający
drainage ('drejnydż) s. odwad-
nianie; wody ściekowe; obszar odpływowy (rzeki)
drainpipe ('drejnpajp) s.dren
drake (drejk) s. kaczor
drama ('dra:ma) s. dramat
dramatic (dre'maetyk) adj.
dramatyczny;jak w sztuce;żywy
drank (draenk) s. pijak; pijany; zob.: drink
drape (drejp) v. upinać; spadać fałdami; drapować;s.kotara
drastic ('draestyk) adj. drastyczny ;gwałtowny; surowy
draught (draeft) s. przeciąg;
ciąg; łyk; dawka; zanurzenie
statku ;wyporność;a.pociągowy
draw; drew; drawn (dro:; dru:;
dro:n)
draw (dro:) v. ciągnąć; wyciągać; przyciągać; czerpać; wdychać; ściągać (wodze); spuszczać (wodę); napinać (łuk);
wlec ;rysować; kreślić
draw near(dro:nier) v. zbliżać
się;przybliżać się
drawback (dro:baek) s. strona
ujemna; v. cofać się(draw back)
draw up (dro:,sp) v. podciągać
(się); redagować; zbliżać się;
zrównać się; ustawiać(wojsko)
drawer ('dro:er) s. szuflada;
kreślarz; rysownik;bufetowy
drawers ('dro:ers) pl. kalesony; majtki (damskie,dziecięce...)
drawing ('dro:yng) s. rysunek
drawing pen ('dro:yng,pen) s.
grafion ;piórko kreślarskie
drawing room ('dro:yng,ru:m)
s. salon ;wagon salonowy
drawn (dro:n) adj. nierozstrzygnięty; ciągniony; wychudzony;
zob.: draw(wyciągnięta:szabla)

drawn-out (dro:n aut) adj.
przewlekły ;wyciągniety(z pochwy)
dread (dred) s. strach; postrach; lęk; v. bać się bardzo; lękać się; adj. straszny
dreadful (dredful) adj. przeraźliwy; okropny ;straszny
dream; dreamt; dreamt (dri:m;
dremt; dremt)
dream (dri:m) v. śnić; marzyć;
s. sen; marzenie;mrzonka;uroje-
nie
dreamt (dremt) v. miec sen,
marzenie; zob.: dream
dreamy ('dri:my) adj. marzycielski; mglisty;niewyraźny
dreary ('dryery) adj. posępny;
ponury;smętny;melancholijny
dregs (dregz) pl. osady; męty
drench (drencz) v. zmoczyć;
przemoczyć ;s. ulewa
dress (dres) s. ubiór; strój;
szata; suknia; v. ubierac;
stroic; opatrywac; czyscic;
czesać; przyrządzać; wykańczać; wyprawiac ;wygarbowac
dress down ('dres dałn) v.
besztac ; czyścic (konia)
dress up ('dres,ap) v. stroic
dressing ('dresyng) s. przyprawa; opatrunek; nawóz ;ubiór
dressing-case ('dresyng,kejs)
s. neseser
dressing-gown('dresyn,gołn) s.
podomka; szlafrok
dressing-room (?dresyng,ru:m) s.
garderoba ;ubieralnia;umywalnia
dressing-table ('dresyng,tejbl)
s. toaleta (mebel)
dressmaker ('dresmejker) s.
krawiec damski; krawcowa
drew (dru:) zob.: draw
drift (dryft) s. dryf; znoszenie; biernosc; prąd; dążnosc;
tresc; zamleć; zaspa; nanos
v. dryfowac; znosić; plątac
się; nanosic;płynąc z prądem
drill 1. (dryl) s. świder; wiertarka; dryl; musztra; v. wiercic; swidrowac; cwiczyć; muszt-
rowac;drążyć;sortowac(wagony)
drill 2. (dryl) s. rowek do sia-
nia; siewnik rzędowy; v. siać;
obsadzac w rowkach

drink; drank; drunk ('drynk;
draenk; drank)
drink ('drynk) v. pic; przepi-
jac; s, napój; woda (morze)
drip (dryp) v. kapac; ociekac;
ciec; s. kapanie; okap; piła(sl);
nudziara ;kapka;kropla(wody etc.)
drip-dry ('dryp,draj) s. bielizna niewymagająca prasowa-
nia (schnąca na wieszaku etc.)
dripping ('drypyng) s. tłuszcz
spod pieczeni; adj. kapiący;
ociekający ; przemoczony
drive; drove; driven (drajw;
drouw; drywn)
drive (drajw) v. pędzic; gnac;
wiezc; powozic; prowadzic; napędzac; jechac; wbijac ;drążyć
s. przejażdżka; obława; napęd;
droga; dojazd ;energia;pościg
drive at (drajw et) v. kierowac (rozmowę ku...)
drive out (drajw,aut) v. wy-
jeżdzac (z garażu;wypędzać
drive-in (drajw,yn) s. obsługa
w samochodzie :bank; jadłodajnia; kino; sklep;poczta
drive-in movies (drajw,yn
mu:wiz) kino do oglądania
z samochodu
driven (drywn) v. napędzany;
zob.: drive
driver (drajwer) s. kierowca
driving license ('drajwyng-
lajsens) s. prawo jazdy
drizzle ('dryzl) s. mżący
deszcz; v. mżyc; adj. mżący;
drobny (deszcz)
drone (droun) s. truten; bucze-
nie; dudniący mowca; v. zbijac
bąki; buczec; dudnic(monotonnie)
droop (dru:p) v. opadac; zwisac;
zwieszac (głowę); s. zwis;
spadek (tonu); utrata (otuchy)
drop (drop) v. kapac; ciec;
upuszczac; spadac; opadac;
s. kropla; cukierek; spadek
(temperatury);łyk;kieliszek;zniż-
ka;kotara;upadek;obniżenia
drop in ('drop,yn) v. wpasc (do
kogos);wejść na chwilę
dropout (dropaut) s. osoba prze-
rywająca (studia lub szkołę)

drove (drouw) zob.: drive

drown (draun) v. tonąc; topic;
tłumic; głuszyc; zagłuszac

drowsy ('drauzy) adj. senny;
śpiący; ospały;na pół spiący

drudge (dradż) s. niewolnik;
popychadło; v. harowac

drug (drag) s. lek; lekarstwo;
v. narkotyzowac; przesycac

drug-addict ('drag,aedykt) s.
narkoman

drugstore ('drag,stor) s. apteka; drogeria

drum (dram) s. bęben; v. bębnic;zwoływac bębnieniem;zjedny-
drummer ('dramer) s. dobosz <sup>wac</sup>

drunk (drank) adj. pijany;
zob.: drink

drunken driving (dranken
drajwyng) s. kierowanie po
pijanemu (samochodem etc.)

dry (draj) adj. suchy;wytrawny
(wino) v. osuszac; suszyc; (łzy)
zeschnąc;wyjaławiac;wycieracʹ

dry up (draj,ap) v. wycierac;
wysychac;zapomniec;zaniemówic

dry-clean ('draj kli:n) v.
oczyścic chemicznie (sucho)

dry goods('drajgudz) pl. materiały do szycia;konfekcja

dual ('dju:el) adj. podwójny;
dwoisty;dwudzielny;wspólny

duchess ('daczys) s. księżna

duck (dak) s. kaczka; unik; v.
zanurzyc; zrobic unik;nurkowac

duct (dakt) s. przewód; kanał

dud (dad) s. poroniony pomysł;
safanduła; nieuk; niewypał;
strach na wróble;adj.niezdolny

dude (d(j)u:d) s. elegancik;
laluś; turysta;goguś;wycieczko-
dude ranch ('du:d,ra:nch) ran-<sup>wicz</sup>
czo wakacyjne(dla mieszczuchów)

due (dju:) adj. należny; płatny;
należyty; adv. w kierunku na
(wschód); s. to co się należy;
należności; opłata;składka

due to ('dju:,tu) exp. z powodu

duel ('dju(;)el) s. pojedynek

dug (dag) s. cycek; wymię; zob.:
dig

dug2.(dag)s. dójka

dugout ('dagaut) s. ziemianka;
łódź drążona; okop; schron

duke (dju:k) s. książe

dull (dal) adj. tępy; głuchy;
ospały; niemrawy; nudny; ponury; ciemny;v.tępic;tłumic

duly ('dju:ly) adv. właściwie;
należycie; punktualnie;słusznie

dumb (dam) adj. niemy; milczący; głupi;v.odbierac mowę

dumbfounded (dam'faundyd) adj.
osłupiony;osłupiały;oniemiały

dummy ('damy) s, imitacja; bałwan; manekin; (wulg.) niemowa;
adj. udany; podstawiony; imitowany ; na niby; niby to

dump (damp) s. śmietnisko; hałda;
magazyn; v. zwalac; rzucac; zarzucac (towarem obcym)

dun (dan) s. wierzyciel; inkasent długów; v. napastowac
o zapłatę długu;a.ciemnobrązowy

dune (dju:n) s. wydma ;diuna

dung (dang)s. nawóz; gnój; bagno moralne; v. nawozic; użyzniac
ziemię ; gnoic

dungeon ('dandżen) s. loch;baszta
v. więzic w lochu lub baszcie

dupe (du:p) s. ofiara; wystrychnięty na dudka ;v. okpic;nabrac

duplicate ('dju:plykyt) adj.
podwójny; s. duplikat; w dwu
egzemplarzach; v. podwajac;
duplikowac (niepotrzebnie)

duplicity (dju:'plysyty) s. dwulicowosc; podstęp ;fałsz;obłuda

durable ('djuerebl) adj. trwały

duration (dju'rejszyn) s. trwanie; czas trwania

duress (dju'res) s. przymus

during ('djueryng) prep. podczas; w czasie ;w ciągu;przez;za

dusk (dask) s. zmierzch; mrok;
cien; adj. ciemny; mroczny;
v. zacmic; zamroczyc

dust (dast) s. pył; kurz; prochy; pyłek; v. odkurzac; trzepac; kurzyc się; posypywac

dust bowl ( dast,boul) s. kraj
suszy i burz(zamieci)piaskowych

dustcover ('dast, kawer) s.
obwoluta; pokrowiec od kurzu

duster ('daster) s. odkurzacz;
wiatr z kurzem;zmoitka
dust-pan ('dast,paen) s. śmiet-
niczka;łopatka na śmieci
dust-storm ('dast,sto:rm) s.
wicher z tumanami kurzu
dusty ('dasty) adj. zakurzony;
pokryty kurzem; suchy; nudny
Dutch (dacz) adj. holenderski;
w niełasce; lichy
duty ('dju:ty) s. powinność;
obowiązek; szacunek; służba;
uległość; cło; podatek od
sprzedaży;funkcja;obowiązki
dwarf (dło:rf) s. karzeł;
krasnoludek; adj. karłowaty;
v. pomniejszać; karlec; skar-
lec;skarłowacieć;zmniejszać
wzrost
dwell; dwelt; dwelt (dłel;
dłelt; dłelt)
dwell (dłel) v. mieszkać; zatrzymywać się; rozwodzić się
(o czyms); zwlekać;przystanąć
dwelling (dłelyng) s. mieszkanie;pomieszczenie mieszkalne
dwelt (dłelt) v. mieszkał...
zob,: dwell
dwindle (dłyndl) v. maleć; top-
nieć; marnieć; kurczyc się;
tracić znaczenie;zwyrodnieć
dye (daj) v. barwić; farbować;
s. barwa; barwik;farba
dying (dajyng) v. umierający;
zanikający; zob.: die
dyke (dajk) s. grobla; rów;
tama;v.ogroblić;ochronić tamą
dynamic (daj'naemyk) adj. dyna-
miczny;energiczny;z wigorem
dynamics (daj'naemyks) s. dyna-
mika (sił działających razem)
dynamite ('dajne,majt) s. dynamit;v.wysadzać dynamitem
dynamo ('dajne,mou) s. dynamo
dynasty ('dajnesty) s. dynastia
dysentery ('dysnetry) s. czer-
wonka; dyzenteria(krwawa)
e (i:) piąta litera angielskiego
alfabetu
each (i:cz) pron. każdy;za(sztukę)
each other ('i:cz, odzer)siebie;
nawzajem (dwie osoby);sobie

eager ('i:ger) adj. gorliwy;ostry;
żądny;ożywiony pragnieniem;żywy
eagerness('i:gernyss) s. gorliwość;skwapliwość;pochopność
eagle ('i:gl) s. orzeł;a.orli
ear (ier) s. ucho; słuch; kłos
(zboża);a.uszny;dotyczący uszu
eardrum ('ierdram) s. bębenek
ucha; błona bębenkowa(ucha)
early ('e:rly) adj. wczesny;
adv. wcześnie;przedwcześnie
earn (e:rn) v. zarabiać; zasługiwać;zapracowć;zdobywać(sławę)
earnest ('e:rnyst) adj. poważny;
gorliwy; s. powaga;zadatek;dowód
earnings ('e:rnynz) pl. zarobki
earphone ('ierfoun) s. słuchawka;loki ułożone na uszach
**earring** ('ieryng) s. kolczyk
earshot ('ier,szot) w zasięgu głosu ;w zasięgu słuchu
earth (e:rs) s. ziemia;świat;glę-
ba
earthen ('e:rsen) adj. ziemisty; gliniany;wypiekany z gliny
earthenware ('e:rsen,łe:r) s.
wyroby garncarskie(wypiekane)
earthly ('e:rsly) adj. ziemski
earthquake('e:rs,kłejk) s.
trzęsienie ziemi
earthworm ('e:rs,łe:rm) s.
(glista) ;dżdżownica
ease (i:z) v. łagodzić; uspokoić;
odciążyć; s. spokój; wygoda;
beztroska;ulga;łatwość;bezczynność
easel ('i:zl) s. sztaluga
easily ('i:zyly) adv. łatwo;
lekko; swobodnie;bez trudności
east (i:st) s. wschód; adj.
wschodni; adv. na wschód
Easter ('i:ster) s. Wielkanoc
eastern ('i:stern) adj. wschodni;człowiek wschodu;prawosławny
eastwards ('i:stłerdz) adv. ku
wschodowi;na wschód;adj.wschodni
easy (i:zy) adj. łatwy; beztroski; wygodny; adv. łatwo;
swobodnie; lekko;s.odpoczynek
easy chair ('i:zy,czeer) s.
fotel (klubowy) miękki
eat; ate; eaten (i:t; ejt: i:tn)
eat (i:t) v. jeść (posiłek)

eat up ('i:t,ap) v. wyjeść
eaten (i:tn) adj. zjedzony;
zob. eat
eaves (i:wz) pl. okap(dachu)
eavesdropping ('i:wzdropyng)
s. podsłuchiwanie(rozmowy)
ebbtide ('ebtajd) s. odpływ
w morze;v.odpływać(jak morze)
ebony ('ebeny) s. heban
eccentric (ik:sentryk) adj.
dziwaczny; s. ekscentryk;
dziwak; mimośród;dziwaczka
ecclesiastic (ik,ly:zi'eastyk)
adj. kościelny; s. duchowny
echo ('ekou) s. echo; v. odbijać się echem; powtarzać za
kims; odbijać głos
eclipse (i'klyps) s. zaćmienie;
v. zaciemniac;zaćmiewać
ecology (i'koledży) s. ekologia;
związek między środowiskiem
a organizmem(część biologii)
economic (,i:ke'nomyk) adj;
ekonomiczny;gospodarczy
economical (,i:ke:nomykel) adj.
oszczędny; ekonomiczny
economics (,i:ke'nomyks) pl.
nauka o ekonomii (gospodarce)
economist (i'konemyst) s. ekono-
mista;specjalista od gospodarki
economize (i:kone,majz) v.
oszczędzac;zmniejszać wydatki
economy (i,konemy) s. ekonomia;
gospodarka;oszczędnosć
economy class (i'konemy,kla:s)
s. druga klasa (w pociągu;
samolocie);klasa turystyczna
ecstasy ('ekstesy) s. zachwyt;
ekstaza; uniesienie;siódme niebo
eddy ('edy) s. wir; v. wirować
edelweiss ('ejdl,wajs) s. szarotka (kwiat górski)
edge (edż) s. ostrze; krawędź;
kraj; v. ostrzyć; obszywać;
wyślizgać się;przysuwać po trochu
edging ('edżyng) s. brzeg; ob-
szywka; lamówka;skraj
edgy ('edży) adj. nerwowy;
podniecony;o ostrych kantach
edible('edybl) adj. jadalny
edict ('i:dykt) s. edykt; dekret

edifice ('dyfys) s. budowla;
gmach (duży i imponujący)
edifying ('edyfajyng) adj. po-
uczający(zwłaszcza moralnie)
edit ('edyt) v. redagować; wydawac;zarządzać gazetą etc.
edition (i'dyszyn) s. wydanie;
nakład (ksiązki,gazety etc.)
editor (e'dyter) s. redaktor;
wydawca;pisarz"od redakcji"
editorial (,edy'to:rjel) s.
artykuł od redakcji; adj.
redakcyjny; redaktorski
educate ('edju:kejt) v. kształcić; wychowywać;płacić za szko-
education (,edju'kejszyn) s. łę
wykształcenie; nauka; oświata;
wychowanie; tresura;wiedza
educational (,edju'kejszenl)
adj. kształcący; wychowawczy
educator ('edju,kejter) s.
wychowawca; wychowawczyni
eel (i:l) s. węgorz
effect (i'fekt) s. skutek; wrażenie; v. wykonywać; dokonywać
effects (i'fekts) pl. ruchomości; dobytek;manatki
effective (i'fektyw) adj. skuteczny; wydajny; rzeczywisty;
efektowny;wchodzący w życie
effeminate (i'femynyt) adj.
zniewieściały;nie męski;słaby
effervescent (,efer'wesnt) adj.
musujący; kipiący;tryskający ży-
efficacy ('efykesy) s. skutecznosć;dawanie porzadanych wyników
efficiency (i'fyszensy) s. wydajnosć; skuteczność; spraw-
nosć(przy minimum nakładów)
efficient(i'fyszent) adj. skuteczny; wydajny; sprawny
effigy ('efydży) s. wizerunek;
podobizna; czyjas kukła
effort ('efert) s. wysiłek;
usiłowanie;wyczyn;próba;popis
effusive (i'fju:syw) adj. wylewny;wylany;ekspansywny;wulka-
egg (eg) s. jajko; v. namawiać;
namawiac;podbechtać;podniecać
eggcup ('eg,kap) s. kieliszek
na jajko;kieliszek do jaj

**egghead** ('eg,hed) s. intelektualista (nieżyciowy)

**egoism** ('egou,zyem) s. egoizm

**egress** ('i:gres) s. wyjście; wyjazd; uchodzenie;wypływ

**Egyptian** (i'dżypszen) adj. egipski

**eiderdown** ('ajder,dałn) s. kaczy puch; kołdra;pierzyna

**eight** (ejt)num.osiem; s. ósemka; ośmioro;ośmiu wioślarzy

**eighteen**('ejt'i:n) num. osiemnaście; osiemnaścioro;osiemnaątka

**eightfold** ('ejt,fould) num. ośmiokrotny; adv. ośmiokrotnie ;osiem razy

**eighty** ('ejty) num. osiemdziesiąt; s. osiemdziesiątka

**either** ('ajdzer) pron. każdy (z dwu); obaj; obie; oboje; jeden lub drugi;adv.także;też

**either... or** ('ajdzer..o:r) albo... albo

**ejaculate** (i'dżaekju,lejt) v. zawołać; krzyknąć;wytrysnąć

**eject** (i'dżekt) v.wyrzucać (się); eksmitować;usuwać

**elaborate** (i'laebe,rejt) v. opracować; adj. wypracowany; staranny;skomplikowany

**elapse** (i'laeps) v. minąć; przeminąć ;przemijać

**elastic** (i'laestyk) adj. sprężysty; rozciągliwy; elastyczny; s. guma; gumka(do majtek...)

**elated** (i'lejtyd) adj. podniecony; uniesiony; dumny

**elbow** ('elboł) s. łokiec; zakręt; kolanko; v. szturchać; przepychać się; zakręcać

**elbow grease** ('elboł,gri:s) s. ciężka praca; wysiłek

**elder** ('elder) s. człowiek starszy; adj. starszy (z dwoch);należący do starszyzny

**elderly** ('elderly) adj. podstarzały; starszy;starszawy

**eldest** ('eldyst) adj. najstarszy (syn)(w rodzinie)

**elect** (i'lekt) v. wybrać; postanawiać; decydować; adj.wybrany; wyborny; wyborowy

**election** (i'lekszyn) s. wybór; wybory (głosowaniem)

**elector** (i'lekter) s. wyborca;

**electric** (i'lektryk) adj. elektryczny;bursztynowy;electryzujący

**electrical engineer** (e'lektrykel,endży'nier) s. inżynier elektryk

**electric chair** (i'lektryk,cze:r) s. krzesło elektryczne (do egzekucji) (w USA)

**electrician** (ilek'tryszen) s. elektryk (monter) (instalator)

**electricity** (ilek'trysyty) s. elektryczność;prąd elektryczny

**electrify** (i'lektryfaj) v. elektryfikować; elektryzować

**electrocute** (i'lektrekju:t) v. uśmiercić prądem elektrycznym

**electron** (i'lektron) s. elektron

**elegance** ('elygens) s. elegancja

**elegant** ('elygent) adj. elegancki;dostojny;doskonały

**element**('elyment) s. żywioł; pierwiastek; część składowa; ogniwo; część podstawowa

**elemental** (,ely'mentl) adj. żywiołowy; zasadniczy; elementarny; podstawowy;konieczny

**elementary** (,ely'mentery) adj. elementarny; zasadniczy; niepodzielny; pierwiastkowy

**elementary school** (,ely'mentery sku:l) s. szkoła powszechna

**elephant** ('elyfent) s. słoń

**elevate** ('ely,wejt) v. podnosić; unosić; wynosić (wzwyż)

**elevation** (ely'wejszyn) s. wysokość; godność; fasada; podwyższenie

**elevator** ('ely,wejter) s. winda; dźwig; wyciąg; spichlerz

**eleven** (i'lewn) num. jedenaście; s. jedenastka; jedenaścioro

**eleventh** (i'lewnt) num. jedenasty; jedenastka

**eligible** ('elydżebl) adj. nadający się; odpowiedni na wybór

**eliminate** (i'lymy,nejt) v. usuwać; wydzielać;pozbywać się;nie brać pod uwagę;opuszczać

elimination (i,lymy'nejszyn)
s. eliminacja ;pozbycie się
elk (elk) s. łoś
ell (ell) s. łokieć (miara)
ellipse (i'lyps) s. elipsa
elm (elm) s. wiąz
elongate (i'longejt) v. wydłużać się;adj.wydłużony
elope (i'loup) v. uciekać
z ukochanym (potajemnie)
eloquence ('eloukłens) s. elo-
kwencja; krasomówstwo
eloquent ('elokłent) adj. elo-
kwentny; wymowny(też w piśmie)
else (els) adv.inaczej; bo
inaczej; w przeciwnym razie;
poza tym; jeszcze;adj.różny in-
elsewhere (els'hłer) adv. gdzie
indziej;w innym miejscu
elude (i'lu:d) v. ujść; wymknąć
się;obejść prawo;uchylić się
elusive (ilu:syw) adj. nieuchwytny; wymykający się
emanate ('eme,nejt) v. wydobywać; pochodzić;wydzielać się
emancipate (i'maens,ypejt) v.
wyzwolić; wyemancypować
embalm (im'ba:lm) v. zabalsamo-
wać; napełnić aromatem
embankment (im'baeŋkment) s.
nasyp; grobla; nabrzeże
embargo (em'ba:rgou) s. zakaz
handlowania, wjazdu, wyjazdu
embark (im'ba:rk) v. ładować
(się); wsiadać (na statek);
rozpoczynać (przedsięwzięcie)
embark upon (im'ba:rk e'pon) v.
rozpoczynać ;przedsięwziąć
embarrass (im'baeres) v. zakłopotanie; wikłać; przeszkadzać;powodować zadłużenie
embarrassing (im'baeresyŋg)
adj. żenujący; kłopotliwy;
krępujący;zawstydzający
embarrassment (im'baeresment)s.
zakłopotanie; powikłanie;
skrępowanie;zaaferowanie
embassy ('embesy) s. ambasada
embed (im'bed) v. osadzić; sa-
dzić;wmurować;wryć;wkopać
embedded (im'bedyd) adj. osadzo-
ny; wsadzony;wryty;wmurowany
embellish (im'belysz) v. upiększać;ozdabiać;podkolorowywać

embers ('emberz) pl. niewygas-
łe węgle; żar;palące się polana
embezzle (ym'bezl) v. sprzeniewierzać (pieniądze,własność etc.)
embitter (im'byter) v. rozgory-
czać; zatruwać; pogarszać
emblem ('emblem) s. godło; wzór
embody (im'body) v. wcielać;
uosabiać; zawierać;włączać
embolden (im'boulden) v. ośmielać; rozzuchwalać;dodać śmiałości
embolism (embelyzem) s. zator
embrace (im'brejs) v. uścisnąć
się; obejmować; przystępować!
imać się; korzystać; s. uścisk;
objęcie ;włączenie(do kategorii)
embroider (im'brojder) v. hafto-
wać;wyszywać;upiększać opowiadanie
embroidery (im'brojdery) s. haft;
hafciarstwo;upiększanie opowiadania
emerald ('emereld) s. szmaragd
emerge (y'me:rdż) v. wynurzać
się; wyłaniać;wyniknąć;nasunąć się
emergency (y'me:rdżensy) s.
nagła potrzeba; stan wyjątkowy
emergency brake (y'me:rdżensy,
,brejk) s. ręczny hamulec
w samochodzie;hamulec zapasowy
emergency call (y'me:rdżensy,kol)
s. wzywanie pogotowia (nagłe)
emergency exit (y'me:rdżensy,
,eksyt) s. wyjście zapasowe
emergency landing (y'merdżensy,
, laendyŋg)s. przymusowe lądowanie (samolotu)
emigrant ('emygrent) s. wychodzca; emigrant;adj.wychodzczy
emigrate ('emygrejt) v. emigro-
wać; wywędrować;przeprowadzać się
emigration (,emy'grejszyn) s.
emigracja; wychodzstwo
emigré ('emygrej) s. emigrant
(polityczny);a.emigracyjny(rząd)
eminent ('emynent) adj. dostojny; wybitny; wyniosły; wysoki
eminently ('emynently) adv.
szczególnie; wybitnie;wysoce
emit (y'myt) v. wydawać; wysyłać (światło); fale radiowe;
ciepło; opinie); wypuszczać
(banknoty);nadawać(audycje)
emotion (y'mouszyn) s. wzruszenie; emocja; uczucie(miłości,stra-
chu,gniewu,oburzenia,współczucia)

emotional (y'mouszynel) adj.
emocjonalny;poruszający uczucia
emperor ('emperer) s. cesarz
emphasis ('emfesys) s. nacisk;
emfaza;uwypuklenie;uwydatnienie
emphasize ('emfesajz) v. podkreślać; kłaść nacisk;uwypuklać
emphatic (ym'faetyk) adj. dobitny; wyraźny; stanowczy;
emfatyczny;mówiący z naciskiem
empire ('empajer) s. cesarstwo;
imperium ;adj.empirowy
emplacement (yn'plejsment) s.
umiejscowienie; stanowisko
employ (ym'ploj) v. zatrudniać;
używać; zajmować się; poświęcać (czas);posługiwać się
employee (,emploj'i:) s. pracownik;siła (robocza,biurowa...)
employer (em'plojer) s. pracodawca;pracodawczyni;szef
employment (ym'plojment) s. za-
trudnienie; używanie; zajęcie
employment agency (ym'plojment
'ejdżensy) agencja pośrednict-
wa pracy;biuro zatrudnienia
empower (ym'pałer) v. upełnomocnić; upoważniac;umożliwiać
empress ('emprys) s. cesarzowa
emptiness ('emptynys) s. pustka
empty ('empty) adj. pusty; próżny; v. wypróżniać; wysypywać;
wylewać;wpływać(do morza)
emulate ('emjulejt) v. rywalizować; współzawodniczyć
enable (y'nejbl) v. umożliwiać;
upoważniać;dawać możność
enact (y'naekt) v. postanawiać;
uchwalać; grać (rolę); odgrywać (sztukę); uprawomocnić
enamel (y'naemel) s. emalia;
szkliwo(na zębach etc.)
encase (yn'kejs) v. wsadzać do
pochwy; oprawiać;wpakowywać
enchant (yn'czaent) v. zaczarować; oczarować; zachwycać
encircle (yn'se:rkl) v. otaczać;
okalać;okrążać;okrążyć;otoczyć
enclose (yn'klouz) v. ogradzać;
zamykać; dołączać; załączać;
zawierać;okrążyć(wroga)

enclosure (yn'kloużer) s. ogrodzenie; załącznik;ogradzanie
encounter (yn'kaunter) s. spotkanie; potyczka; pojedynek;
v. natknąć się; spotykać się;
potykac się; mieć utarczkę
encourage (yn'ka:rydż) v. zachęcać; ośmielać; popierać;
dodawać odwagi;pomagać
encouragement (yn'ka:rydżment)
s. zachęta; ośmielenie; po-
pieranie;dodanie odwagi
encroach (yn'kroucz) v. wdzierać się; naruszać; wkraczać
na cudze;targnąć się na cudze
encumber (yn'kamber) v. krępować; tarasować; obarczać; za-
wadzać;obciążać(długami etc.)
end (end) s. koniec; cel;
skrzydłowy w nożnej piłce;
v. kończyć (się); skończyć;
dokończyć;położyć kres
endanger (yn'dejndżer) v. narażać na niebezpieczeństwo
endear (yn'dier) v. czynić
drogim; lubianym;przymilać się
endeavor (yn'dewer) v. starać
się; usiłować; s. usiłowanie;
wysiłek; dążenie;zabiegi;próba
ending ('endyng) s. zakończenie; końcówka (wyrazu etc.)
endless ('endlys) adj. niekończący się; nieskończony;
ustawiczny;wieczny;ciągły
endorse (yn'do:rs) v. potwierdzać; popierać; podżyrować;
notować na odwrocie
endow (yn'dał) v. uposażyć;
wyposażyć;ufundować;zapisywać
endurance (yn'djuerens) s. wytrzymałość; cierpliwość
endure (yn'djuer) v. znosić
(ból); cierpieć; wytrzymać;
przetrwać; ostać się
enema ('enyme) s. lewatywa
enemy ('enymy) s. wróg; przeciwnik; adj. wrogi; nieprzyjacielski;przeciwny
energetic (,ene:r'dżetyk) adj.
energiczny; z wigorem
energy ('enerdży) s. energia

enervate ('ene:rwejt) v. osłabiać (nerwowo,na zdrowiu)wyczerpywać

enervate (y'ne:rwyt) adj. słaby; bez energii;wyczerpany

enfold (yn'fould) v. zawijać; obejmować;zapakowywać

enfranchise (un'fraenczajz) v. wyzwalać; nadawać prawo wyborcze; uwalniać;uwłaszczać

engage (yn'gejdż) v. zajmować; angażować; skłaniać; ścierać się;zaręczyć;zobowiązywać się

engaged (yn'gejdżd) adj. zajęty; zaręczony; włączony

engagement (yn'gejdżment) s. zobowiazanie; zaręczyny

engine ('endżyn) s. silnik; parowóz; maszyna; motor

engine-driver ('endżyn,drajwer) s. maszynista (kolejowy)

engineer (,endży'nier) s. inżynier;v.planować;zręcznie prowadzić

engineering (,endży'nieryng)'s. technika; mechanika; inżynieria;zarząd dróg,maszyn etc.

engine trouble ('endżyn'trabl) s. zepsucie silnika (samochodowego);kłopot z silnikiem

English ('yŋglysz) adj. angielski (język)

english ('yŋglysz) v. uderzyć piłkę fałszem; s. fałsz; podkręcona piłka; v. zangielszczyć

engorge (yn'go:rdż) v. pożerać

engrave (yn'grejw) v. rytować; ryć; grawerować;wyryć;wyrytować

engraving (yn'grejwyŋg) s. sztych;rytownictwo;grawiura

engross (yn'grous) v. pochłaniać; monopolizować (rozmowę)

enigma (y'nygme) s. zagadka

enjoin (yn'dżoyn) v. nakazywać; zarządzać; zakazywać;zalecać

enjoy (yn'dżoj) v. cieszyć się; rozkoszować;mieć;posiadać

enjoyment (yn'dżojment) s. uciecha; korzystanie z uprawnienia; rozkosz; przyjemność

enlarge (yn'la:rdż) v. powiększać; poszerzać;zwalniać z ciupy

enlargement (yn'la: rdżment) s. powiększenie; poszerzenie

enlighten (yn'lajtn) v. oświebiać; oswietlać;objasniać

enlist (yn'lyst) v. zaciągać (się); werbować;wsptępować

enliven (yn'lajwn) v. ożywiać

enmesh (yn'mesz) v. wplatać (w sieć); usidlać;usidlić

enmity ('enmyty) s. wrogosc; nieprzyjazn;nienawiść

enormous (y'no:rmes) adj. olbrzymi; ogromny; kolosalny

enough (y'naf) adj.,s.& adv. dosyć; dość;na tyle;nie więcej

enounce (y'nauns) v. ogłaszać; wymawiać;wypowiadać;wymówić

enquire (yn'kłajer) v. pytać; dowiadywać się;rozpytywać się

enquiry (yn'kłajry) s, pytanie; śledztwo;badania;pytanie

enrage (yn'rejdż) v. rozwścieczać;doprowadzać do wściekłości

enraged (yn'rejdżd) adj. rozwścieczony; rozwścieczona

enrapt (yn'raept) adj. zachwycony;pogrążony w zachwycie

enrapture (yn'reapczer) v. zachwycać;oczarowywać;porywać

enrich (yn'rycz) v. wzbogacać; użyźniać;ozdobić;ozdabiać

enrol(1) (yn'roul) v. zaciągać (się); zapisywać (się)

ensue (yn'su:) v. wynikać; następować;wypływać (z czegos)

ensure (yn'szuer) v. zabezpieczać; zapewniać;asekurować

entangle (yn'taeŋgel) v. gmatwać; wplątać;zmieszać;komplikować

enter ('enter) v. wchodzić; wpisywać;penetrować;wkładać;wpisywać

enter into ('enter,yntu) v. wdawać się; brać udział;zawierać

enter upon ('enter,apon) v. wchodzić w posiadanie; przystępować do tematu; zaczynać

enterprise ('enterprajz) s. przedsięwzięcie; przedsiębiorstwo; przedsiębiorczość

enterprising ('enterprajzyŋg) adj. przedsiębiorczy;ryzykujący

entertain (,enter'tejn) v. zabawiać; przyjmować; żywić; nosić się;brać pod uwagę

entertainer (,enter'tejner) s. artysta (kabaretowy)
entertainment (,enter'tejnment) s. rozrywka; zabawa; uciecha
enthusiasm (yn'tju:zjaezem) s. zapał; entuzjazm
enthusiast (yn'tju:zaest) s. entuzjasta;zapaleniec
enthusiastic (yn'tu:zy'aestyk) adj. entuzjastyczny;zapalony
entice (yn'tajs) v. znęcić; zwabić(nagrodą,przyjemnością)
entire (yn'tajer) adj. cały; całkowity;nietknięty
entirely (yn'tajerly) adv. całkowicie; jedynie; wyłącznie;kompletnie;niepodzielnie
entitle (yn'tajtl) v. uprawniać; tytułować; zatytułować;nadawać
entity ('entyty) s. byt; istnienie; jednostka;istota
entrails ('entrejlz) pl. jelita wnętrzności;wnętrze ziemi
entrance ('entrens) s. wejście; wstęp(za opłatą);dostęp;wjazd
entrance (,en'traens) v. przejmować; wprawiać w trans
entrance fee ('entrens,fi:) opłata za wstęp;bilet wstępu
entreat (yn'tri:t) v. błagać
entreaty (yn'tri:ty) s. błaganie; usilna prośba
entrust(yn'trast) v. powierzać
entry ('entry) s. wejście; wpis; hasło (słownika);uczestnik wyścigu
entry permit ('entry,per'myt) pozwolenie wejścia; wjazdu
enumerate (y'nju:merejt) v. wliczać; sporządzać wykaz
envelop (yn'welep) v. owijać; otaczać; ogarniać;okryć(całkiem)
envelope ('enweloup) s. koperta; otoczka ;teczka(papierowa)
envenom (yn'wenem) v. zatruwać
enviable ('enwjebl) adj. godzien zazdrości;godny pażądania
envious (enwjes) adj. zazdrosny; zawistny;pełen zazdrości
environment (yn'wajerenment) s. otoczenie; środowisko
environmental pollution (yn'wajerenmentel pel'u:szyn) zanieczyszczanie środowiska

environs (yn'wajerenz) s. okolice podmiejskie ;przedmieścia
envoy ('enwoj) s. wysłannik
envy ('enwy) s. zawiść; zazdrość; przedmiot zazdrości
epic ('epyk) adj. epicki; s. epos (o bohaterstwie)
epidemic (,epy'demyk) s. epidemia; adj. epidemiczny
epidermis (,epy'de:rmys) s. naskórek; skóra (powierzchnia)
epilepsy ('epylepsy) s. epilepsja ; padaczka
epilog(ue) ('epylog) s. epilog
episode ('epysoud) s. epizod
epitaph ('epytaef) s. napis na grobie(ku pamięci zmarłego)
epoch (i:'pok) s. epoka
equal ('i:kłel) adj. równy; jednaki; jednakowy; jednostajny; zrównoważony; s. równy (stanem); v. równać się; dorównywać; wyrównywać;wyrównywać
equality (i'kłolyty) s. równość
equalize (i'kłelajz) v. wyrównywać; równać;zrownywać(się)
equanimity (,i:kłe'nymyty) s. opanowanie; spokój; równowaga
equate (i'kłejt) v. równać;
equation (i'kłejżyn) s. równanie; równoważenie ;bilansowanie
equator (i'kłejter) s. równik
equilibrium (,i:kłý'lybrjem) s. równowaga
equip (i'kłyp) v. wyposażać; zaopatrywać ;uzbrajać;ekwipować
equipment (i'kłypment) s. wyposażenie; ekwipunek;sprzęt
equitable ('ekłytebl) adj. słuszny; sprawiedliwy
equivalent (i'kływelent) adj. równowartościowy; równoznaczny; równej wielkości;s.równowa-
era ('yere) s. era ważnik
erase (y'rejz) v. wycierać; wymazywać ;zatrzeć;zacierać
erect (y'rekt) adj. prosty; wyprężony; najeżony ;v.budować;stawiać
erection (y'rekszyn) s. podniesienie; wyprostowanie; najeżenie; erekcja; budowla; montaż

erosion (y'rouźyn) s. wyżera-
nie; żłobienie; erozja
ermine ('e:rmyn) s. gronostaj
erotic (y'rotyk) adj. erotyczny; miłosny; s. erotyk; ero-
toman; wiersz erotyczny
err (e:r) v. błądzić; być
w błędzie;grzeszyć; zgrzeszyć
errand ('erand) s. posyłka;
zlecenie; cel;sprawunek
erratic (y'raetyk) adj. błędny;
nieobliczalny;dziwny;s.dziwak
erroneous (y'rounjes) adj.
błędny;mylny;fałszywy
error ('erer) s. błąd
erudite ('erudajt) adj. uczony; s. erudyta (b.oczytany etc.)
erupt (y'rapt) v. wybuchać;
wyrzucać; przerzynać (się);
wysypywać się;wybuchać lawa,
eruption (y'rapszyn) s. wybuch;
przerzynanie się; wysypka
escalation (,eske'lejszyn) s.
wzmożenie;rozszerzenie się
escalator ('eskelejter) s. ru-
chome schody; ruchoma skala
płac(wg. kosztów utrzymania etc.)
escape (ys'kejp) s. ucieczka;
wyciekanie; wchodzenie;ocalenie;
v. wymknąć się; zbiec; wyjść
cało; uchodzić;ratować się ucieczką
escort ('esko:rt) s. eskorta;
konwój; mężczyzna towarzyszą-
cy kobiecie; kawaler;v.eskorto-
escort (i'sko:rt) v. eskortować
especial (ys'peszel) adj.
szczególny; wyjątkowy; specjalny; szczególny; główny
especially (ys'peszely) adv.
szczególnie; zwłaszcza
espionage (,espje'na:dż) s. wywiad; szpiegostwo;szpiegowanie
esprit (es'pri:) s. żywość; życie; dowcip;silne poczucie humo-
espy (ys'paj) v. spostrzegać;
wyśledzić;wykombinować
essay ('esej) s. esej; szkic
literacki; próba; v. próbować;
wypróbować;poddać próbie
essence ('esens) s. esencja;
istota czegoś; wyciąg; treść
istotna treść;sedno sprawy;olej

essential (y'senszel) adj. niezbędny; istotny; zasadniczy;
zupełny; eteryczny; s. cecha
istotna, nieodzowna, zasadni-
cza;rzecz podstawowa,konieczna
establish (ys'taeblysz) v. zakładać; osądzać; ustalać;
wprowadzać;udowodnić;ufundować
establishment (yz'taeblyszment)
s. założenie; osadzenie; ustalenie; ustanowienie; zakład;
gospodarstwo;koła rządzące;
organizacja państwowa lub wojskowa;firma;przedsiębiorstwo
estate (ys'tejt) s. majątek;
stan majątkowy;położenie w ży-
estate tax (ys'tejt,taeks) s.ciu
podatek spadkowy (majątkowy)
esteem (ys'ti:m) v. cenić;
szanować; poważać; s. poważanie; szacunek;dobra opinia
estimate ('estymejt) v. oceniać;
szacować; s. szacunek; kosztorys; ocena;opinia;oszacowanie
estimation (,esty'mejszyn) s.
szacowanie; poważanie; szacunek;zdanie;mniemanie;sąd
estrange (ys'trejndż) v. od-
stręczać; zrażać;zniechęcać
estray (ys'trej) s. stworzenie
bezpańskie, zgubione
estuary ('estjuery) s. ujście
(rzeki) do morza (oceanu)
eternal (y'ternl) adj. wieczny;
odwieczny;bez początku i końca
eternity (y'ternyty) s. wiecz-
ność;trwnie bez końca i odpoczyn-
ether ('i:ter) s. eter ku
ethics ('etyks) pl. etyka
ethnic ('etnyk) adj. etniczny;
pogański;odrębny zwyczajami i je-
etymology (,ety'moledży) s. ety-zykiem
mologia;pochodzenie i rozwój słów
eulogy ('ju:ledży) s, mowa
pochwała (pogrzebowa)
eunuch ('ju:nek) n. eunuch;
rzezaniec;człowiek wykastrowany
European (,ju:re'pi:en) adj.
europejski; s. Europejczyk
evacuate (y'waekjuejt) v. ewa-
kuować; opróżniać; wypróżniać;
wydalać;usuwać; wycofywać się

evacuation (y,waekju'ejszyn) s.
ewakuacja; wypróznienie (się)
evade (y'wejd) y. ujsc; unik-
nąc; obchodzic; wymykac się;
wykręcac się; pomijac
evaluate (y'waeljuejt) v. obliczac; oceniac; analizowac
evaporate (y'waeperejt) v. paro-
wac; ulatniac się; poddawac
parowaniu;wyparowywac;umrzec
evasion (y'wejzyn) v. uniknię-
cie; wymknięcie się; obejscie;
wykręt;oszustwo(podatkowe);wykręt
evasive (y'wejsyw) adj. wykrętny; wymijający; nieuchwytny
eve (i:w) s. wilia; wigilia
even ('i:wen) adj. rowny;
jednolity; parzysty; adv. nawet; v. rownac; wyrownac;
zemscic się;wygladzac;ujednosta
even-handed ('i:wen,haendyd) adj.
sprawiedliwy; bezstronny
evening ('i:wnyng) s. wieczor
evening dress ('i:wnyn, dres)s.
stroj wieczorowy
evening paper ('i:wnyn'pejper)
gazeta wieczorna
evensong ('i:wensong) s. nieszpory; piesn wieczorna
event (y'went) s. wydarzenie;
możliwosc; wynik; rezultat; zawody (sportowe);konkurencja
eventful(y'wentful) adj. burzliwy; pamiętny; pełen wydarzeń
eventual (y'wenczuel) adj.
w końcu pewny
eventually (y'wenczuely) adv.
w końcu napewno
ever ('ewer) adv. w ogóle; niegdys;kiedys; jak tylko; ile tylko; kiedykolwiek;jeszcze wciąż
ever after (,ewer'after) do tego czasu;już od tego czasu
ever since (,ewer'syns) od tego
czasu ; od kiedy (był etc.)
everlasting (,ewer'lastyng)adj.
wieczny; ciągły; nieustanny
evermore ('ewer'mi:re) adv.
zawsze; na zawsze; na wieki
every ('ewry) adj. każdy; wszelki; co(dzien, noc, rano etc.)
every other day ('ewry,odzer'dej)
co drugi dzień

everybody ('ewrybody) pron.
każdy; wszyscy(ludzie)
everyday ('ewrydej) adj. codzienny; powszedni; zwykły
everyone ('ewryłan) pron.
każdy; wszyscy;każda rzecz
everything ('ewrytyng) pron.
wszystko (co jest, etc.)
everywhere ('ewryhłer) adv.
wszędzie; gdziekolwiek
evidence ('ewydens) s. znak;
dowód; swiadectwo; oczywistosc;
jasnosc; v. swiadczyc; dowodzic (czegos);manifestowac
evident ('ewydent) adj. oczywisty; widoczny;jawny;jasny
evil ('i:wl) adj. zły;fatalny
evildoer ('i:wl-duer) s.
złoczyńca
evince (y'wyns) v, wykazywac;
okazywac (życzenie);przejawiac
evoke (y'wouk) v. wywoływac;
wydobywac; zdobywac (odpowiedz)
evolution (,ewe'lu:szyn) s.
rozwój; ewolucja; rozwinięcie
(się); pierwiastkowanie
evolve (y'wolw) v. rozwijac;
wypracowywac; wytwarzac (ciepło etc.);rozwijac się stopniowo
ewe (ju:) s. owca
ex-(eks) pref. były; była;
prep. bez; ze; s. (litera)"x"
exacerbate (eks'aeserbejt) v.
draznic; pogorszyc; irytowac
exact (yg'zaekt) adj. dokładny;
scisły; v. wymagac; sciągac;
egzekwowac ;wymuszac
exactitude (yg'zaektytju:d)s.
scisłosc; dokładnosc;punktual-
exactly (yg'zaektly) adv. dokładnie; scisle; własnie;
zgadza się ;punktualnie; ostro
exactness (yg'zaektnys) s. dokładnosc; precyzja
exaggerate (yg'zaedżerejt) v.
przesadzac; wyolbrzymiac
exaggeration (yg'zaedże'rejszyn)
s. przesada; wyolbrzymienie
exalt (yg'zo:lt) v. wywyższac;
podnosic;wychwalac;chwalic
exam (yg'zaem) s. egzamin
(slang); klasówka; egzamin w
szkole lub na uniwersytecie

examination (yg, zaemy'nejszyn)
s. egzamin; badanie;rewizja
examine (yg'zaemyn) v. badac;
sprawdzac; egzaminowac; rozpatrywac; rewidowac; przesłu-
chiwac;przeprowadzac sledztwo
example (yg'za:mpl) s. przykład; wzor; precedens
exasperate (yg'za:sperejt) v.
rozjątrzac; rozgoryczac; pogarszac; powodowac rozpacz
excavate ('ekskewejt) v. kopac; odkopac; wykopac; drą-
zyc;pogłębiac;wybierac(ziemię)
exceed (yk'si:d) v. przewyższac; celowac; przekraczac
exceedingly (ek'si:dynly) adv.
niezmiernie; nadzwyczajnie
excel (yk'sel) v. przewyzszac;
wybijac się; celowac(w czyms)
excellence (yk'selens) s. wyższosc; doskonałosc; zaleta
excellent (yk'selent) adj. doskonały; wyborny;swietny;celuja-
except (yk'sept) conj. chyba
że...; żeby;oprucz;poza;wyjąwszy
except (yk'sept) v. wykluczac;
wyłączac; prep. z wyjątkiem;
pominąwszy; wyjąwszy;chyba że
exception (yk'sepszyn) s. wyjątek; wyłączenie; zarzut;obiekcja
exceptional(yk'sepszenl) adj.
nadzwyczajny; wyjątkowy
excess (yk'ses) s. nadmiar;
nadwyżka;a.nadmierny;nad-
excess fare(yk'ses,fe:r) s. dopłata do biletu
excessive (yk'sesyw) adj. nadmierny;zbytni;nieumiarkowany
excess luggage (yk'ses,lagydż)
nadwyżka bagażu
exchange (yks'czendż) s. wymiana; zamiana; giełda; centrala
telefoniczna; v. wymienic;_towy
zamienic (się);a.wymienny;walu-
excitable (yk'sajtebl) adj. pobudliwy;pobudzajacy;podniecaja-
excite (yk'sajt) v. pobudzac; -
podniecac;prowokowac
excited (yk'sajtyd) adj. podniecony; zdenerwowany

excitement (yk'sajtment)
podniecenie; zdenerwowanie
exciting (yk'sajtyng) adj.
emocjonujący; pasjonujący
exclaim (yks'klejm) v. zawołac;
wykrzyknąc; zaprotestowac
exclamation (,ekskla'mejszyn)
s. okrzyk; krzyk; wykrzyknik
exclamation mark (,ekskla'mejszyn,ma:rk) wykrzyknik
exclude (yks'klu:d) v. wykluczac; wydalac; usuwac
exclusion (yks'klu:żyn) n.
wykluczenie; wydalenie; usunięcie; wyłączenie
exclusive (yks'klu:syw) adj.
modny; wykluczający; wyłączny;
jedyny ; ekskluzywny
excursion (yks'ker:żyn) s. wycieczka;dygresje;a.wycieczkowy
excuse (yks'kju:z) v. usprawiedliwiac; przepraszac; darowac; zwalniac; s. usprawiedliwienie; wymowka ;pretekst
excuse me (yks'kju:z,mi)
przepraszam; przepraszam pana
excusable (iks'kju:zebl) adj.
usprawiedliwiony;wybaczalny
execute ('eksykju:t) v. wykonac (wyrok, plan); stracic
(skazanca);nadawac ważnosc
execution (,eksy'kju:szyn) s.
wykonanie; egzekucja;stracenie
executive (yg'zekjutyw) adj.
wykonawczy; s. władza wykonaw-
cza; stanowisko kierownicze
exemplary (yg'zemplery) adj.
wzorowy; przykładny; przykła-
dowy;wymierzony dla odstraszenia
exempt (yg'zempt) v. zwalniac;
adj. wolny; zwolniony; s. osoba zwolniona;człowiek zwolniony
exercise ('eksersajz) s. cwiczenie; wykonywanie (zawodu);
korzystanie; v, cwiczyc; używac;
wykonywac;spełniac;pełnic
exercise book ('eksersajs,buk)
s. zeszyt (szkolny)
exert (yg'ze:rt) v. wytężac
(się); wysilac (się); wywierac
(nacisk, wpływ, etc);zabiegac

exertion (yg'ze:rszyn) s. wy-
tężenie; wysiłek; wywieranie
exhale (eks'hejl) v. wyziewać;
wydychać; zionąć; parować
exhaust (yg'zo:st) v. wydychać;
wyczerpywać; wyciągac; wypróżniać; odgazować; s. wydech; wydmuch; rura wydechowa; opróżnianie (z powietrza);
aspirator;rura wydechowa(auta)
exhaust fumes (yg'zo:st,fjums)
gazy wydechowe(z motoru)
exhaustion (yg'zo:stszyn) s.
wyczerpanie; opróżnienie; zużycie; pochłonięcie;zmęczenie
exhaust-pipe (yg'zo:st,pajp)
s. rura wydechowa (w aucie)
exhibit(yg'zybyt) s. wystawa;
pokaz; eksponaty; v. wystawiać; okazywać; pokazywać;
wykazywać; popisywać się
czyms;przedkładać;mieć wystawę
exhibition(,eksy'byszyn) s.
wystawa; wystawianie; pokazy-
wanie;pokaz; widowisko;popis
exhibitor(yg'zybyter) s. wystawca; wystawczyni
exile ('eksajl) s. wygnanie;
tułaczka; emigracja; wygnaniec; v. wygnać na banicję
exist (yg'zyst) v. istnieć;być;
żyć; egzystować ;zdarzać się
existence (yg'zystens) s. istnienie; byt; egzystencja
existent (yg'zystent) a. istniejący;będacy;znajdyjący się
exit ('eksyt) s. wyjście; odejście; ujście; wylot; swobodne
wyjście; v, wychodzić; kończyć
(slang);schodzić ze sceny
exit visa ('eksyt,wyza) s. wiza wyjazdowa
expand (yks'paend) v. rozszerzać; powiększać; wzrastać;
rozprężać; rozwijać; rozru-
szać;rozpościerać;powiększać
expanse (yks'paens) s. bezmiar;
rozległa przestrzeń; ekspansja
expansion (yks'paenszyn) s.
rozszerzanie; rozprężanie się;
ekspansja; rozposcieranie;
rozwijanie (się);ilość ekspansji

expansive (yks'paensyw) adj.
rozszerzalny; rozległy; roz-
prężalny; obszerny; wylewny
expect (yks'pekt) v. spodziewać się; przypuszczać;zgadywać
expectation (,ekspek'tejszyn)
s. oczekiwanie; nadzieja;
widoki;prospekt;przewidywanie
expedient (yks'pi:djent) adj.
celowy; wygodny; oportunistycz-
ny; korzystny; s. środek; zabieg; sposób;wybieg;fortel
expedition (,ekspy'dyszyn) s.
wyprawa; ekspedycja; sprawnosc;
szybkosć;pospiech;marsz do akcji
expel (yks'pel) v. wypędzać;
wydalać; usuwać; wyrzucać
expend (yks'pend) v. wydawać;
zużywać;poświęcać czas etc.
expense (yks'pens) s. koszt;
wydatek;rachunek;strata;ofiara
expensive (yks'pensyw) adj.
drogi; kosztowny;wysoko wycenio-
experience (yks'pierjens) s.  ny
doswiadczenie; przeżycie;
v. doswiadczać; doznawać;
poznać (coś);przeżywać;przechó-
experienced (yks'pierjenst)  dzić
adj. doswiadczony;doznany
experiment (yks'peryment) s.
próba; eksperyment; doswiadczenie; v. eksperymentować;
robić doswiadczenia
expert ('ekspe:rt) s. biegły;
ekspert; znawca; adj. biegły;
swiatły;mistrzowski;wykonany
        przez eksperta
expiration (,ekspi'rejszyn) s.
wygasnięcie: upłynięcie; wydech; wyzionięcie ducha;smierc
expire (yks'pajer) v. wygasać;
upływać; wydychać; wyzionąc
ducha;umierać;kończyć sie
explain (yks'plejn) v. wyjaśnić; objasnic; wytłumaczyć
explanation (,eks'plaenejszyn)
s. wyjasnienie; wytłumaczenie
explicable ('eksplykebl) adj.
dający się wyjasnic
explicit (yks'plysyt) adj. jasny; wyrazny; szczery; otwarty;definitywny;wygadany

explode (yks'ploud) v. wybuchać; explodować; demaskować (fałsz) ;obalić(teorię etc.)
exploit (yks'ploit) v. użytkować; exploatować; wyzyskiwać
exploit ('eksploit) s. wyczyn
exploration (,eksplo:'rejszyn) s. poszukiwanie; badanie
explore (yks'plo:r) v. badać; sondować;wybadać;przebadać
explorer (yks'plo:rer) s. badacz; sonda ;odkrywca;odkrywczyni
explosion (yks'ploużyn) s. explozja; wybuch (kłótni etc.)
explosive (yks'plousyw) s, materiał wybuchowy; adj. wybuchowy;mogący wybuchnąć
exponent (yks'pounent) adj. interpretujący; s. eksponent; wyraziciel; interpretator; wykładnik (potęgi);przedstawiciel
export (yks'po:rt) v. wywozić; eksportować; s. wywóz; eksport; towar wywozowy;wywożenie
expose (yks'pouz) v. wystawiać (na wpływ); poddawać (czemuś); odsłaniać; demaskować; eksponować; naświetlać; porzucać (dziecko);zrobić zdjęcie
exposé (,ekspou'zej) s.. zdemaskowanie; odsłonięcie skandalu
exposition (,ekspe'zyszyn) s. wystawa; wykład; przedstawienie; wyjaśnienie; opis; naświetlenie; ekspozycja; porzucenie (dziecka)
exposure (yks'poużer) s. wystawienie (na zimę. etc); ujawnienie; zdemaskowanie; naświetlenie;jedno zdjęcie na filmie
exposuremeter (yks'poużer'mi:ter) s. swiatłomierz
expound (yks'paund) v. wykładać; wyjaśnić szczegółowo;przedstawić
express (yks'pres) s. ekspres ; przesyłka pośpieszna; adj. wyraźny; umyślny; dokładny; adv. pośpiesznie;expresem
expression (yks'preszyn) s. wyrażenie; wyraz; ekspresja; ton; wydawanie; wytłoczenie;zwrot wyciśnięcie;wyżymanie

expressive (yks'presyw) adj. wyrażający; wyrazisty: ekspresyjny;pełen wyrazu
expressly (yks'presly) adv.wyraźnie; kategorycznie; naumyślnie;specjalnie;formalnie
express way (yks'pres,łej) s. drogą przelotcwa (bez skrzyżowań jednopoziomowych)
expulsion (yks'palszyn) s. wydalenie; wyrzucenie; wypędzenie;wygnanie;wyparcie
exquisite ('ekskłyzyt) adj. wyborowy; wyborny; wyśmienity; nadzwyczajny; ostry; przeszywający;s.lalus';goguś;pięknis
extent ('ekstent) adj. pozostały; jeszcze istniejący
extemporaneous (eks,tempe'rejnjes) adj. zaimprowizowany
extend (yks'tend) v wyciągac (się); rozciągać (się);przeciągać (się); rozszerzać (się); dawać i udzielać; przedłużać; powiększać;rozpościerać się
extendible (yks'tendybl) adj. rozszerzalny; rozciągalny
extension (yks'tenszyn) s. rozciąganie; wyciąganie; rozwinięcie; przedłużenie; zasięg; rozmiar; zakres ;skrzydło(domu)
extensive (yks'tensyw) adj. obszerny; rozległy ;ekstensywny
extent (yks'tent) s. obszar; rozmiar; zasięg; miara; stopień; wysokość ;oszacowanie
extenuate (yks'tenjnejt) v. zmniejszać; łagodzić
exterior (eks'tierjer) s. powierzchowność; wygląd zewnętrzny; strona zewnętrzna ;fasada
exterminate (yks'te:rmynejt) v. tępić (np; pogląd);wyniszczyć
external (eks'te:rnal) adj. zewnętrzny; zagraniczny
extinct (yks'tynkt) adj. wygasły; zgasły ;zanikły;wymarły
extinguish (yks'tyngłysz) v. zgasić; zagasić; niszczyć; unicestwić; umierać ;tępić
extirpate ('ekster,pejt) v. wykorzeniać;plewić; tępić

extol (yks'tol) v. wysławiać;
wynosić pod niebiosa
extort (yks'tort) v. wymuszać;
zdzierać(pieniadze);wydrzeć
extra ('ekstre) adj. specjalny; dodatkowy; luksusowy;
nadzwyczajny; ponad normę;
adv. nadzwyczajnie; dodatkowo;
s. dodatek; dopłata; rzecz
szczególnie dobra;statysta
extra charge ('ekstre,cha:rdź)
s. dopłata;nadpłata
extract ('ekstraekt) s. wyciąg;
ekstrat;wyjątek;wypis
extract (yks'traekt) v. wyciągać; wydobywać; wypisywać
extraction (eks'traekszyn) s.
wyciągnięcie; wydobycie; wyr-
wanie (zęba); pochodzenie;ród
extradite ('ekstredajt) v.
wydawać (przestępcę przez granicę)do miejsca zbrodni
extraordinary (yks'tro:rdnery)
adj. niezwykły; nadzwyczajny
extravagance (yks'traewygens)
s. przesada; rozrzutność;
nieumiarkowanie; głupstwo;
niedorzeczność; ekstrawagancja
extravagant (yks'traewegent)
adj. rozrzutny; przesądny;
zwariowany;wygórowany;szalony
extravaganza (yks,traeve'gaenze)
s. ekstrawagancja;fantazja
extreme (yks'tri:m) adj. skrajny; krańcowy; najdalszy; ostatni; s. kraniec; ostateczna
granica; ostateczność;skrajność
extremity (yks'tremyty) s. koniec; kraniec; skrajność; kran-
cowość; kończyna; krytyczne
położenie;potrzeba;ostateczność
extrude (yks'tru:d) v. wypierać; wyrzucać; przeciągać lub
ciągnąć odlew;wytłoczyć
exuberant (yg'zju:berent) adj.
wybujały; pełen życia; kwitnący; wylewny; płodny; obfity
exult (yg'zalt) v. triumfować;
unosić się radością
eye (aj) s. oko;wzrok;v.patrzeć
eyeball ('ajbo:l) s. gałka oczna
w oczodołach za powiekami

eyeball to eyeball ('ajbo:l,tu
'ajbo:l) oko w oko
eyebrow ('ajbrau) s. brew
eyeglasses ('ajgla:sys) pl.
okulary;lupy;monokle
eyelash ('ajlaesz) s. rzęsa
eyelid ('ajlyd) s. powieka
eyesight ('aj-sajt) s. wzrok
eyewash ('ajłosz) s. woda do
oczu; mydlenie oczu (slang)
eyewitness ('aj'łytnes) s.
świadek naoczny
f (ef) szósta litera angielskiego alfabetu; stopień "f"
failure = niedostatecznie
fable (fejbl) s. bajka
fabric ('faebryk) s. tkanina;
materiał; osnowa; szkielet;
budowa; wytwór;a.sukienny
fabricate ('faebrykejt) v. tworzyć; wymyślać; zmyślać; mon-
towac;wyssać z palca;sfałszować
fabulous ('faebjules) adj. ba-
jeczny;legendarny;fantastyczny
facade (fe'sa:d) s. fasada
face (fejs) s. twarz; oblicze;
mina; grymas; czelność; śmiałość; powierzchnia lica; prawa strona; obuch; v. stawiać
czoła; stanąć wobec; napoty-
kać; stać frontem do..; wykładać powierzchnię;oblicować
face-lifting ('fejs-lyftyng) v.
operacyjnie usuwać zmarszczki
facetious (fe'si:szes) adj.
żartobliwy;krotochwilny
facilitate (fe'sylytejt) v.
ułatwiać; udogadniać;uprzy-
stępniać
facility (fe'sylyty) s. łatwość;
zręczność; udogodnienia; układ-
ność; swada;zgodność
fact (faekt) s. fakt; stan
rzeczywisty;podstawa twierdzenia
factor ('faekter) s. czynnik;
współczynnik; część;okoliczność
faculty ('faekelty) s. zdolność;
władza; wydział; fakultet; gro-
no profesorskie;dar; zmysł
fad (faed) s. moda; kaprys;konik;
bzik;chwilowa moda;dziwactwo
fade (fejd) v. więdnąć; bled-
nąć; zanikać;płowieć;pełznąć

fail (feil) v. chybić; zawodzić;
nie udać się; brakować; bankru-
tować; omieszkać; słabnąć;
załamać się; zamierać;zepsuć się
failure ('fejljer) s. niepowodzenie; brak; upadek; zawał
(serca); niezdara; stopień
niedostateczny; pechowiec
faint (fejnt) adj. słaby; omdlały; bojaźliwy; s. omdlenie;
v. mdleć; słabnąć;zasłabnąć
fair (feer) adj. piękny; jasny;
uczciwy; honorowy; czysty;
pomyślny; niezły; adv. prosto;
honorowo; pomyślnie; pięknie;
v. wypogadzać się; wygładzać;
przepisywać na czysto; s. targ;
targi; jarmark;targowisko
fairly ('feerly) adv. słusznie;
uczciwie; całkowicie; zupełnie;
dość;rzetelnie;wręcz;poprostu
fairplay ('feer'plej) szlachetne
postępowanie;czysta gra
fairness ('feernys) s. piękność;
jasność; sprawiedliwość; bezstronność; uczciwość;uroda
fairy ('feery) s. czarodziejka;
adj. zaczarowany;czarodziejski
fairy-tale ('ferrytejl) s. bajka
faith (fejs) s. wiara; zaufanie;
wierność; wyznanie;słowność
faithful ('fejsful) adj. wierny;
uczciwy;sumienny;skrupulatny
faithless ('fejslys) adj. niewierny; wiarołomny;zdradziecki
fake (fejk) v. fałszować; oszukiwać; podrabiać; s. fałszerstwo;
oszustwo;kant;lipa;szwindel
falcon ('fo:lken) s. sokół
fall; fell; fallen (fo:l; fel:
fo:len)
fall (fo:l) v. padać; opadać;
wpadać; marnieć; zdarzać się;
przypadać; s. upadek; spadek;
jesień;opad;schyłek;obniżka
fall back ('fo:l, baek) v. cofać się
fall ill ('fo:l,yl) v. zachorować;rozchorować się
fall in love ('fo:l,yn'law) v.
zakochać się

fallout ('fo:laut) s. skutek
uboczny; pył radioaktywny;
wrażenie na publiczności i
prasie(z wypowiedzi,planów)
fall out ('fo:l,aut) v. poróżnić się; rozejść się! (komenda)
fall short ('fo:l,szo:rt) v.
nieosiagnąć; niewywiązać się
fallen ('fo:len) upadły; zob.
fall
false (fo:ls) adj. fałszywy;
kłamliwy;adv.zdradliwie;fałszy-
falsehood ('fo:lshud) s. fałsz;
kłamstwo;nieprawda;kłamliwość
falsify ('fo:lsyfaj) v. fałszować; przekręcać; kłamać; zawodzić;podrabiać;oszukać
falter ('fo:lter) v. chwiać się;
wahać się; potykać się; jąkać
się; s. chwiejność; jąkanie
fame (fejm) s. sława; wieść;fa-
famed (fejmd) adj. sławny; znany; głośny; słynący z
familiar (fe'myljer) adj. zażyły; poufały; znany; obeznany
familiarity (fe,myly'aeryty)
s. zażyłość; poufałość; obez-
nanie;znajomość;zażyłość
familiarize (fe'myljerajz) v.
obeznać; obznajomić; oswoić;
spoufalić;spopularyzować
family ('faemyly) s. rodzina;
adj. rodzinny
family name ('faemyly,nejm) s.
nazwisko
family tree ('faemyly,tri:) s.
drzewo genealogiczne
famine ('faemyn) s. głód; klęska głodu; ogólne braki wszystkie-
famish ('faemysz) v. głodzić;
wygłodnieć; głodować;morzyć gło-
famous ('fejmes) adj. znany;
sławny;znakomity;świetny;nie byle
fan (faen) v. wachlować; roz-
dmuchiwać; wiać; rozpościerać;
wywiewać; s. wachlarz; wentylator; wialnia; żagiel i
śmigło (wiatraka); entuzjasta;
miłośnik;kibic;a.wachlarzowaty
fanatic (fe'naetyk) adj. zagorzały; fanatyczny; s, fanatyk

fanciful ('faensyful) adj. dziwaczny; kaprysny; fantastyczny;zmyslony;wyszukany;fantazyjny
fancy ('faensy) s. urojenie; zludzenie; fantazja; kaprys; humor; pomysł; chetka;a.pstry...
fancy dress ball('faensy'fres, ,bo:l) s. bal kostiumowy
fancy-free ('faensy,fri:) adj. wolny od trosk; niezakochany
fancywork ('faensy,łe:rk) s. robótki reczne
fang (faeng) s. ząb jadowity; kieł;sztyft;korzen;v.dławic pom-
fantastic (faen'taestyk) adj.
fantastyczny;s.fantastyk
far (fa:r) adv. daleko
far away ('fa:r,ełej) adv. hen; daleko;adj.daleki;odległy
far from ('fa:r,from) adv. bynajmniej; daleko od
fare (feer) s. pasażer; bilet pasażerski; pożywienie; potrawa; v, być w położeniu. miec sie; wiesc sie; czuc się; odżywiac się; jadac; podróżowac
farewell (,feer'lel) s. pożegnanie; adj. pożegnalny; v. żegnaj; do widzenia
farfetched (,fa:r'feczt) adj. przesadny; naciągany; wyszukany;nierozsadny
far-flung (,fa:r'flang) adj. szeroko rozrzucony; rozgałęziony;zakrojony na szeroka skale
farm (fa:rm) s. ferma; gospodarstwo rolne; kolonia hodowlana; v. uprawiac; dzierżawic; wydzierżawiac; wynajmowac; podzstwo dzierżawiac;prowadzic gospodar-
farmer ('fa:rmer) s. rolnik; farmer; dzierżawca;hodowca
farmhand ('fa:rm,haend) s. parobek;robotnik rolny
farmhouse ('fa:rm,haus) s. dworek; gospodarski dom mieszkalny
farming ('fa:rmyng)s. rolnictwo; gospodarka rolna; dzierżawa
farm worker (,fa:rm'łe:rker) s. robotnik rolny; parobek
farmyard ('fa:rm,ja:rd) s. podworze fermy;podworze gospodarskie na fermie

farsighted ('fa:r'sajtyd) adj. przewidujacy; dalekowidz; dalekowzroczny;dalekowidz
farther('fa:rdzer) adj. dalszy; adv. dalej;ponadto;poza tym; prócz-tego
farthest ('fa:rdzest) adj. najdalszy; adv. najdalej;najpóźniej
fascinate ('faesynejt) v. urzekac; czarowac; fascynowac; hipnotyzowac;zachwycic
fascination (,faesy'nejszyn) s. urok; czar;oczarowanie;olśnienie
fascist ('faeszyst) s. faszysta; adj. faszystowski;faszystowska
fashion ('faeszyn) s. moda; fason; kształt; wzór; sposób; v. kształtowac; fasonowac; modelowac; urabiac
fashionable ('faesznebl) adj. modny; s. człowiek wytworny
fast (faest) adj. szybki; przytwierdzony; mocny; twardy; zwodniczy; adv. mocno; pewnie; trwale; v. poscic; s. post
fasten ('faesn) v. umocowac; zamykac;przymocowac
fastener ('faesner) s. przymocowanie (np. gwoźdź); spinacz zatrzask; zasuwka
fastidious (fes'tydjes) adj. wybredny; grymasny; wymagający
fat (faet) s. tłuszcz ; tusza; adj. tłusty; tuczny; głupi; tepy;urodzajny;zyskowny
fatal ('fejtl) adj. fatalny; śmiertelny; nieuchronny
fate ('fejt) s. los; przeznacznie; zguba;fatum;v.los rzadzi...
father ('fa:dzer) s. ojciec
fatherhood ('fa:dzerhud) s. ojcostwo;starszenstwo(w slużbie)
father-in-law ('fa:dzerynlo:) s. teść;ojciec meza lub żony
fatherland ('fa:dzerlaend) s. ojczyzna; ojczysty kraj
fatherly ('fa:dzerly) adj. ojcowski;jak ojciec;dobrotliwy
fathom ('faedzem) s. sążeń
fathomless ('faedzemlys) adj. bezdenny; niezgłebiony
fatigue (fe'ti:g) s. zmeczenie (człowieka lub materiału);służba porzadkowa;v.trudzić;meczyć

fatten ('faetn) v. tuczyć; tyć; urzyźniać ziemie: utyć;utuczyć

faucet ('fo:syt) s. kurek (od wody); czop; tuleja

fault ('fo:lt) s. błąd; wada; wina; uskok; usterka;brak;defekt

faultless ('fo:ltlys) adj. bez-błędny; nienaganny;doskonały

faulty ('fo:lty) adj. wadliwy; nieprawidłowy;niescisły;błędny

favor ('fejwer) s. łuska;uprzej-mość; upominek; v. sprzyjać; zaszczycać; faworyzować

favorable ('fejwerebl) adj. życzliwy; łaskawy; sprzyjający; korzystny(dla kagoś,czegoś)

favorite ('fejweryt) s. ulubie-niec; faworyt; adj. ulubiony

fawn (fo:n) v. ocielić; łasić się; przymilać (się); s. je-lonek; sarenka; adj. brunatny; płowy;płaszczyć się(przed kimś)

fear (fier) s. strach; obawa; v. bać się; obawiać się

fearful ('fierful) adj. okropny; straszny; wystraszony; bojaź-liwy; bojący się;pełen strachu

fearless ('fierlys) adj. nie-ustraszony;bardzo odważny

feast (fi:st) s. święto; odpust; biesiada; v. ucztować; sycić się; ugaszczać pragnienie

feat (fi:t) s. wyczyn; czyn (bohaterski);(dokazana)sztuka

feather ('fedzer) s. pioro; v. zdobić piórami

featherbed ('fedzerbed) s. pier-nat;pierzyna;lekka praca

feathered ('fedzerd) adj. upie-rzony; pokryty piórami

feathery ('fedzery) adj. pucho-waty; miękki jak puch:leciutki

feature ('fi:czer) s. cecha; rys; atrakcja; film długo-metrażowy;v.cechować;odgrywać

February ('februery) s. luty

fed (fed) adj. karmiony; zob. feed

federal ('federel) adj. związko-wy; federalny

federation (,fede'rejszyn) s. federacja; konferencja

fee (fi:) s. opłata; wpisowe; należność; honorarium; v. płacić honorarium;płacić wpisowe

feeble ('fi:bl) adj. słaby

feed: fed; fed (fi:d; fed; fed)

feed (fi:d) v. karmić; paść; zasilać; s. pasza; obrok; za-silacz; posuw

feeder (fi:der) s. boczna (dro-ga); dopływ; przewód zasila-jący

feel; felt; felt (fi:l; felt; felt)

feel (fi:l) v. czuć (się); od-czuwać; macać; dotykać

feel well ('fi:l,łel) v. czuć się dobrze; być zdrowym

feel bed('fi:l,baed) v. czuć się źle

feeler ('fi:ler) s. macka; son-da; próbny balon; szperacz

feeling ('fi:lyng) s. dotyk; uczucie; odczucie; poczucie; takt; wrażliwość; adj. wrażli-wy; czuły; współczujący; szcze-ry; wzruszony; szczery

feet (fi:t) pl. stopy; nogi

fell (fel) v. ścinać (drzewo); zob. fall

felloe ('felou) s. dzwono(koła)

fellow ('felou) s. towarzysz; człowiek; chłop; gość; facet; odpowiednik;wykładowca;adjunkt

fellow being ('felou bi:yng) s. bliżni

fellow citizen ('felou'sytyzen) s. współobywatel

fellowship ('felouszyp) s. udział; wspólnota; związek; towarzystwo; przyjaźń; cech

felon ('felen) s. przestępca; adj. okrutny; zły;zbrodniczy

felony ('feleny) s. przestępstwo; zbrodnia

felt (felt) czuły; zob.; feel

felt (felt) s. wojłok; filc

female ('fi:mejl) s. kobieta; niewiasta; samica; adj. żeński; kobiecy; wewnętrzny (gwint)

feminine ('femynyn) adj. żeński; kobiecy; zniewieściały; s. ro-dzaj żeński;a,rodzaju żeńskiego

fen (fen) s. bagno; trzęsawisko;nizina bagienna
fence (fens) s. płot; ogrodzenie; szermierka; v. ogrodzic;
fechtowac się;odpowiadac wykrętnie
fencing ('fencyng) s. szermierka;płot;ogrodzenie;paserstwo
fend for ('fend,fo:r) v. zaspokajac potrzeby;utrzymywac
fend off ('fend,of) v. odbijac;
odparowywac;chronic;ochraniac
fender ('fender) s. błotnik;
(zderzak);zasłona;zderzak
fennel ('fenel) s. koper
ferment ('fe:rment) s. ferment;
fermentacja; v. wywoływac ferment; podniecac; fermentowac
fermentation (,fe:rmen'tejszyn)
s. fermentacja; ferment
fern (fe:rn) s. paproc
ferocity (fe'rosyty) s. dzikosc;
okrucienstwo; srogosc
ferry ('fery) v. przeprawiac
promem; kursowac; s. prom
ferryboat ('ferybout) s. prom
fertile ('fe:rtajl) adj. żyzny;
płodny;zapłodniony;obfitujący
fertility (fer'tylyty) z. żyz-
nosc; płodnosc;urodzjnosc
fertilize ('fe:rtylajz) v. użyzniac;nawozic;zapładniac;zapylac
fertilizer ('fe:rtylajzer) s.
nawoz sztuczny
fervent ('fe:rwent) adj. żarliwy; gorący;płomienny;gorliwy
fester ('fester) v. jątrzyc (się)
ropiec; gnic; s. ropiejąca rana; mały wrzod;ropniak;zajad
festival ('festewel) adj. świąteczny;odswiętny;s.swięto
festive ('festyw) adj. uroczysty;
wesoły; radosny;biesiadny
festivity (fes'tywyty) s. wesołosc; zabawa; uroczystosc
fetch (fecz) v. isc po cos;
przyniesc; przywiezc;s.odległosc
fetter ('feter) v. skuc; spętac
feud (fju:d) s. lenno; wasn ro-
dowa;wojna między klanami
feudal ('fju:dl) adj. feudalny
fever ('fy:wer) s. gorączka
feverish ('fy:werysz) adj. go-
rączkowy;rozgoraczkowany

few (fju:) adj.& pron. mało;kilka;
niewielu ; nieliczni;kilku;kilko-
ro
fiance (fi'a:nsej) s. narzeczo-
ny(a)
fib (fyb) s. kłamstwo; v. cyganic;okładac;s. cios;uderzenie
fiber ('fajber) s. włokno; siła ducha;charakter;łyko;budowa
fibrous ('fajberes) adj.
włoknisty; łykowaty
fickle ('fykl) adj. zmienny;
niestały;płochy; wietrzny
fiction ('fykszyn) s. fikcja;
urojenie; beltrystyka;wymysł
fictitious (fyk'tyszes) a.
fikcyjny; urojony; fałszywy
fiddle ('fydl) v. grac na
skrzypcach; baraszkowac;
s. skrzypce
fiddler ('fydler) s. skrzypek;
skrzypaczka
fidelity (fy'delyty) s. wiernosc; dokładnosc; scislosc
fidget ('fydżyt) v. wiercic
się; niepokoic się; s. niepokoj; człowiek niespokojny
fidgety ('fydżyty) adj. wiercą-
cy sie; niespokojny;niecirpliwy
field (fi:ld) s. pole; boisko;
drużyna; dziedzina; v. ustawiac na boisku; zatrzymac
(piłkę);poprowadzic do akcji
field-events('fi:ld,y wents) pl.
lekkoatletyka
field-glasses('fi:ld,glasys) pl.
lornetka polowa
field-gun('fi:ld,gan) s. działo
polowe
fiend ('fy:nd) s. zły duch;
szatan; demon; nałogowiec;
zagorzalec
fierce (fiers) adj. dziki; srogi; zażarty; wsciekły; zaw-
ziety;nieopanowany;gwałtowny
fiery ('fajery) adj. ognisty;
płomienny; palący; zapalny;
burzliwy;popędliwy;choleryczny
fife (fajf) s. piszczałka; v.
grac na piszczałce (na fujarce)
fifteen ('fyf'ti:n) num. piet-
nascie;piętnascioro;piętnastka
fifteenth ('fyf'ti:nt) num.
piętnasty;jedna piętnasta czesc

fiftieth ('fyftjet) num. pięć-
dziesiąty;jedna piędziesiąta
fifty ('fyfty) num. pięcdziesiat
fig (fyg) s. figa; strój
fight; fought; fought (fajt;
fo:t; fo:t)
fight (fajt) s. walka; bitwa;
zapasy; bój; duch do walki;
mecz bokserski; v. walczyć
(przeciw lub o coś);bić się
fighter ('fajter) s. bojownik;
zapaśnik; samolot myśliwski
figurative ('fygjurejtyw) adj.
obrazowy; przenośny;symboliczny
figure ('fyg'er) s. kształt;
postać; wizerunek; cyfra;
wzór; v. figurować; liczyc;
rachować; oznaczać cenami;
wyobrażać; przedstawiać
figure out ('fyger,aut) v.obli-
czać; wynosić;składać się na
figure skating ('fyger, skejtyŋg)
s, jazda figurowa na łyżwach
file (fajl) s. rejestr; archiwum; seria; pilnik; v. archi-
wować; defilować; piłować pil-
nikiem; wnosić (podanie; skargę);iść rzędem(rzedami);maszero-
wać
fill (fyl) v. napełniac; plom-
bować ząb; obsadzac; s. wypełnienie; napicie i najedzenie do
syta; nasyp;ładunek;porcja
fill in ('ful,yn) v. zapełniać;
wypełniać (formularze,blankiety)
fill up ('fyl,ap) v. wypełniać;
zapełniać;nabierać benzyny
fillet ('fylyt) s. wstążki;
zraz zawijany; dzwonko; v.prze-
pasywać;wycinać filety
fillet ('fylej) v. dzielic na
dzwonka ;wycinać dzwonka
filling ('fylyŋg) s. nadziewka;
plomba; wątek ;zapas benzyny
filling station ('fylyŋg,st'ejszyn) s. stacja benzynowa
filly ('fyly) s. żrebica; koza;
młoda dziewczyna ;dzierlatka
film (fylm) s. powłoka; błona;
warstwa; film; mgiełka; bielmo;
v. pokrywać błoną; filmować
filter ('fylter) s. filter; sączek; v. filtrować; przeciekać

filth (fyls) s. brud; plugastwo
filthy (fylsy) adj. brudny; plugawy;niegodziwy;sprośny
fin (fyn) s. płetwa; v. obcinać płetwy; ruszać płetwami
finagle ('fy'nejgl) v. oszukiwać; wyłudzac;nabierać
final ('fajnl) adj. końcowy;
ostateczny; s. finał (sport;
egzamin etc)coś ostatecznego
finally ('fajnly) adv. w końcu;
wreszcie; na końcu;ostatecznie
finance (faj'naens) s. finanse;
skarbowość; v. finansować;
udzielać pożyczki
financial (faj'naenszel) adj.
pieniężny; finansowy
financier (,fynaen'sjer) s. fi-
nansista; v. spekulować;
sprzeniewierzać pieniądze
finch (fynch) s. łuszczak;ptak
z krótkim dziobem
find; found; found (fajnd;
faund; faund)
find (fajnd) v. znajdować;
konstatować;dowiedzieć się
find out (fajnd, aut) v. wykryć;
wynaleźć; dowiedzieć się
finder ('fajnder) s. znalazca;
odkrywca;wizier;dalekomierz
finding ('fajndyŋg) s. odkrycie; stwierdzenie;dane;wniosek
fine (fajn) adj. piękny; misterny; czysty; przedni; wyszukany;
świetny; dokładny; adv. świet-
nie; wspaniale; s. grzywna;
kara; v. ukarać grzywną
finery ('fajnry) s. szyk; elegancja; strojny ubiór
finger ('fyŋger) s. palec;
kciuk; v. przebierać w palcach;
wskazywać palcem;brać palcami
finger nail ('fyŋger,nejl) s.
paznokieć
finger print ('fyŋger,prynt)
odcisk palca
finish ('fynysz) s. koniec; wykończenie; v. kończyć; skończyć; wykończyć;dokończyć
finite ('fajnajt) adj. skończony; ograniczony;końcowy
Finnish ('fynusz) adj. fiński

fir (fe:r) s. jodła ;jedlina
fire ('fajer) s. ogień; pożar
fire alarm ('fajer,e'la:rm) s.
sygnał pożarowy ;alarm pożarowy
firearm ('fajera:rm) s. broń
palna (armaty.strzelby etc.)
firebug ('fajer,bag) s. świetlik ;robaczek swietojanski
fire brigade ('fajerbry,gejd)
s. straż pożarna
fire department ('fajer,dy'-
pa:rtment) s. miejska straż
pożarna;straż ogniowa
fire engine ('fajer'endżyn) s.
wóz straży ogniowej(pompa)
fire escape ('fajerys,kejp) s,
we
wyjscie zapasowe;schody zapaso-
fire extinguisher ('fajeryks,-
,tyngłyszer) s. gaśnica
fireman ('fajermen) s. strażak
fireplace ('fajer-plejs) s.
kominek; palenisko
fireproof ('fajerpru:f) adj.
ogniotrwały; ognioodporny
fireside ('fajersajd) s. przy
kominku;kominek;ognisko domowe
firewood ('fajerʌud) s. drzewo
opałowe; drewno opalowe
fireworks ('fajerłe:rks) pl.
ognie sztucznie;hałasliwe sceny
firm (fe:rm) s. firma; adv. mocno; adj. pewny; stanowczy;
trwały; v. ubijać; osadzać
(mocno);umacniac sie
firmness ('fe:rmnys) s. sta-
łość; trwałość; stanowczosc;
jędrnosc;moc;energia
first ('fe:rst) adj. pierwszy;
adv. najpierw; po raz pierwszy;
początkowo; na poczatku
first of all ('fe:rst,ow'o:l)
przede wszystkim;najpierw
first aid ('fe:rst,ejd) pierw-
nek
sza pomoc;dorazna pomoc;opatru-
first aid kit ('fe:rst,ejd kyt)
podreczna apteczka; zestaw
pierwszej pomocy(opatrunkow etc)
firstborn ('fe:rstbo:rn) adj.
pierworodny(syn, dziecko etc.)
first class ('fe:rst'klas) s.
kosci
pierwsza klasa;a.najlepszej ja-
first-class ('fe:rst'klas) adj.
pierwszorzedny; wspanialy

first floor ('fe:rst flo:r) s.
parter(w Anglii pierwsze piętro)
first hand ('fe:rst,haend) adj.
bezposredni; z pierwszej ręki
firstly ('fe:rstly) adv. po
pierwsze; najpierw
first name ('fe:rst,nejm) s.
imię (chrzestne)
first-rate ('fe:rst,rejt) adj.
pierwszorzędny; adv. pierwszo-
rzędnie ;bardzo dobrze
firth (fe:rs) n. odnoga morska;
zatoka (zwłaszcza w Szkocji)
fish (fysz) s. ryba;v.łowić ryby
fishbone ('fyszboun) s. osć
fisherman ('fyszemen) s. rybak
fishery ('fyszery) s. rybołóstwo; teren połowu lub hodowli
fishing ('fyszyng) s. wędkarst-
wo; rybołóstwo; połów
fishing line ('fyszyng,lajn) s.
linka; żyłka (od wedki)
fishing rod ('fyszyng,rod) s.
wędka
fishing tackle ('fyszyng,taekl)
s. sprzęt rybacki
fishmonger ('fyszmanger) s.
handlarz ryb;sklep z rybami
fission ('fyszyn) s. dzielenie;
rozbicie (atomu);rozszczepienie;
rozerwanie
fissure ('fyszer) s. szczelina;
pęknięcie; v. rozszczepiac;
pękac; łupac (się)
fist (fyst) s. pięsc ;v.uderzac
fit (fyt) s. atak (choroby;
gniewu etc.); krój; dopasowa-
nie; adj. dostosowany; odpowiedni; nadajacy się; gotow;
zdatny; dobrze leżący; v. spros-
tac; dobrze leżec;przygotowac sie
fit on (fyt on) v. przymierzac
fit out (fyt aut) v. zaopatrywac; s. wyposażenie; umeblowanie
fitness ('fytnys) s. stosownosc;
kondycja;trafnosc(uwagi);przyzwo-
itosc
fitter ('fyter) s,. monter; krawiec dokonywujacy przymiarek;slu-
sarz
fitting ('fytyng) s. okucie;
oprawa; przymiarka; adj. odpowiedni; wlasciwy;trafny;stosowny
five (fajw) num. pieć ;piecioro;
piata(godzina);piatka (numer opu-
wia)

fix (fyks) v. umocować; przyczepiać; ustalać; utkwić; ustalać; zgęszczać; tężec; krzepnąć; urządzic kogoś(źle); usytuować; zaaranżować wynik (zapasów); s. kłopot; dylemat; położenie nawigacyjne (statku,samolotu etc.) fix up (fyks,ap) v. naprawić; uporządkować;ulokować(kogoś) fixed (fykst) adj. trwały; stały;nieruchomy;niezmienny fixedly ('fyksydly) adv. stale; trwale; uporczywie fixture ('fyksczer) s. urządzenie przymocowane fizz (fyz) s. syk; napój musujący; v. syczec; musowac flabbergast ('flaebergaest) v. zdumiec; odebrać mowę (ze zdumienia);oszołamiać flabby ('flaeby) adj. zwiotczały; obwisły; miękki; słaby; niedbały;bez charakteru flag (flaeg) s. flaga; chorągiew; lotka; v. wywieszać flagę; sygnalizować flagstone ('flaeg,stoun) s. płyta brukowa; płyta chodnikowa flak (flaek) s. artyleria przeciwlotnicza (niemiecka) flake (flejk) s. płatek; łuska; iskra; v. prószyć; odpryskiwać; łuszczyć;padać płatkami flake oft ('flejk;of) v. złuszczać (się);odpadac płatkami flame (flejm) s. płomień;miłość; v. zionąc; błyszczec; płonąc; opalać; migotac;byc podnieconym flank (flaenk) s. bok; flanka; v. flankowac; strzec flanki flannel ('flaenl) s. flanela; v. wycierać flanelą; ubierać we flanelę (lekka wełnę) flap (flaep) s. trzepot; klapnięcie; klapa; poła; płat; pokrywa; v. trzepotac; zwisac; klapnąc;uderzyc czyms płaskim flare (fleer) v. błyszczec; sygnalizować; popisywać się; rozszerzac się;s.jasny płomień flare up (fleer ap) s. wybuch; błysk; v.wybuchnąć (gniewem; płomieniem)reagować gwałtownie

flash (flaesz) s. błysk; blask; adj. błyskotliwy; fałszywy; gwarowy; v. zabłysnąć; sygnalizować; pędzic; mknąć; wysyłać (natychmiastowo wiadomości etc.) flashbulb ('flaeszbalb) s. żarówka (do zdjęć);flesz flashlight ('flaeszlajt) s. latarka (elektryczna) flashy ('flaeszy) adj. błyskotliwy(chwilowo);jaskrawy;krzykliwy flask (flaesk) s. flaszka; flakon; kolba;opleciona flaszka wina flat (flaet) adj. płaski; płytki; nudny; równy; stanowczy; oczywisty; matowy; bezbarwny; adv. płasko; stanowczo; dokładnie; s. płaszczyzna; równina; mieszkanie; przedziurawiona dętka ;v.rozpłaszczyc;matować flatten ('flaetn) v. spłaszczyc (się);matowiec;wietrzec;równać flatter ('flaeter) v. pochlebiac flattery ('flaetery) s. pochlebstwo; schlebianie komus flavor ('flejwer) s. smak; zapach; v. dawac smak;miec posmak flaw (flo:) s. skaza; rysa; pęknięcie; v. psuc; pękać flawless ('flo:les) adj. bez skazy;(przedstawienie)bez usterek flax (flaeks) s. len flaxen(fkak'sn)adj.płowy;lniany flea (fli:) s. pchła fled (fled) zob. flee fledgling ('fledźlyng) s. świeżo opierzony ptak;żółtodziób flee; fled; fled (fli:; fled; fled) flee (fli:) v. uciekać;pierzchać fleece (fli:s) s. runo; wełna; czupryna; puch; v. strzyc; skubac; pokrywac puchem fleet (fli:t) s. flota; park pojazdów; v, mknąc; przemknąc; mijac; adv. płytko; adj. płytki flesh (flesz) s. ciało; miąższ fleshy ('fleszy) adj. mięsisty; tłusty;cielesny;zmysłowy flew (flu:) zob. fly flexible (fl'eksybl) adj. giętki; gibki; układny; obrotny; elastyczny;łatwo przystosowywujący się; ustępliwy;poddajacy się flick (flyk) s. przytyk; śmignięcie; smuga; v. śmignąć; trzepnąć; rzucać się; trzepotać się;zapalać zapalniczkę flicker ('flyker) s. mig; miganie; drganie; trzepot; v. migać; drgać; trzepotać; machać;lekko się poruszać flier ('flajer) s. lotnik; ulotka;pośpieszny pociąg etc. flight (flajt) s. lot; przelot; ucieczka;kondygnacja schodów flight engineer ('flajt,endży'- nier) s. mechanik pokładowy flimsy ('flymzy) adj. cienki; wątły; słaby (papier,wymówka...) flinch (flyncz) v. uchylać się; cofać się; drgać;s.unik fling; flung; flung (flyng; flang; flang) fling (flyng) v. rzucać (się); powalić; wypaść; wierzgać fling open('flyn,oupen) v. rozewrzec (gwałtownie) flint (flynt) s. krzemień; krzesiwo ;kamyk do zapalniczki flip (flyp) v. prztykać ; rzucać;wyprztykiwać;s.prztyk flippant ('flypent) adj. niepoważny; impertynencki flipper ('flyper) s. płetwa nożna; graba ;łapa;błona pławna flirt (fle:rt) v. flirtować; machać; s. flirciarz; flirciarka; machnięcie(raptowne) flirtation (,fle:r'tejszyn) s. flirt ;powierzchowny romans flit (flyt) v. biegać; fruwać; wyjechać;poruszać się zwinnie float (flout) v. unosić się; pływać na powierzchni; spławiać; puszczać w obieg; lansować; s. pływak; tratwa; platforma na kołach; gładzik do tynku ;niezdecydowany ruch flock (flok) s. trzoda; stado; tłum; v. tłoczyć się; iść tłumem; gromadzić się floe (flou) s. kra (lodowa) flog (flog) v. chłostać; smagać; bić ;biczować się flood (flad) s. powódź; wylew; potok; v. zalewać; nawadniać

floodlights ('flad,lajts) pl. reflektory (szeroko-stożkowe) flood tide ('fladtajd) s. przypływ (morza) ;fala powodziowa floor (flo:r) s. podłoga;dno floor cloth ('flo:rklo:s) s. szmata do podłogi ;linoleum floor lamp ('flo:r,laemp) s. lampa stojąca na podłodze floor show ('flo:r,szou) s. przedstawienie kabaretowe flop (flop) s. klapanie; klapa; fiasco; v. klapnąć; załamać się; zrobić klapę;a.dziadowski florist ('floryst) s. kwiaciarz; kwiaciarka ;hodowca kwiatów flounder ('flaunder) s. flądra; brnięcie; v. brnąć; brodzić; błądzić; występać (mowę) flour (flauer) s. mąka; v. mleć na mąkę;dodawać mąki(posypywać) flourish ('flarysz) s. fanfara; wymachiwanie; v. kwitnąć; zdobić kwiatami; wymachiwać flow (flou) s. strumień; prąd; przepływ; dopływ; v. płynąć; lać się; zalewać;ruszać się płynnie flower (flauer) s. kwiat; v. kwitnąć;być w rozkwicie flown (floun) zob. fly fluctuate ('flaktjuejt) v. falować; wahać się;być niezdecydowanym flu (flu:) s. grypa;influenca fluent ('fluent) adj. płynny; biegły i wymowny(mówca;pisarz...) fluff (flaf) s. puch;v.trzepać;knocić fluffy (flafy) adj. puszysty ;lekki fluid ('flu:yd) s. płyn; adj. płynny ;płynnie poruszający się flung (flang) zob. fling flunk (flank) v. oblać (egzamin) spalić (ucznia); nie zdać;zawalić flurry ('fle:ry) s. wichura; ulewa; śnieżyca; podniecenie; rozgardiasz; v. oszałamiać; denerwować;wprowadzać zamieszanie flush (flasz) v. rumienić się; napełniać; spłukiwać; s. rumieniec; rozkwit; blask; adj. wylewający się; krzepki; rumiany; równy; etc.; adv. równo; prosto ;gładko;pełno;poziomo;sowicie(wyposażać w pieniądze)

fluster ('flaster) s. podniecenie; niepokój; v. podniecać; oszałamiać; kręcić się
flute (flu:t) s. flet;rowkowa<sup>nie</sup>
flutter ('flater) s. trzepotanie; dygotanie; niepokój; v. trzepotać; drzeć; dygotać; płoszyc;powodowac'trzepotanie
flux (flaks) s. prąd; przepływ; potok; płynność; krwotok; przypływ;pasta do lutowania
fly (flaj) s, mucha;klapka
fly; flew; flown( flaj; flu; floun), v. latać; lecieć; powiewać; uciekać; przewozić samolotem; puszczać (latawca)
fly across (,flaj e'kros) v. przelatywać (przez)
flyblown ('flaj-bloun) adj. popstrzony przez muchy
fly into a rage ('flaj,yntu ej'rejdź) v. wpaść w pasję
flyer ('flajer) s. lotnik
flying ('flajyng)adj. latający; lotny; lotniczy; krótkotrwały;samolotowy;pośpieszny
flying boat ('flajynbout) s. hydroplan (do wodowania)
flying buttress ('flajyn,batrys) s. łuk przyporowy
flying machine ('flajyng ,meszi:n) s. samolot
flying time ('flajyng,tajm) s. czas przelotu;czas lotu
fly weight ('flaj,łejt) s. waga musza (112 funtów lub mniej)
flywheel ('flajhłi:l) s. koło zamachowe (do regulowania szyb<sup>kości</sup>
foal (foul) s. źrebię
foam (foum) s, piana; v. pienić się ;a.pianowy;piankowy
foamy ('foumy) adj. pieniący się ;pienisty;spieniony
focus ('foukes) s. ognisko; ogniskowa; v. skupiac; ogniskowac; koncentrowac;zesrodkowy-<sup>wać</sup>
fodder ('foder) s. pasza
foe (fou) s. wróg ;przeciwnik
fog (fog) s. mgła;v.otumaniać
foggy ('fogy) adj. mglisty
foible ('fojbl) s. słabostka;lek-ka słabość charakteru; słabość; watłość

foil (fojl) s. folia; tło; floret; trop; ślad; v. udaremnic; zacierać (ślad) ;niweczyć
fold (fould) s. fałda; zagięcie; zagroda (owiec) v. składać; zaginać (się); splatać; zamykać owce (w owczarni);faldować
folder ('foulder) s. składana teczka; broszura;falcownik
folding ('fouldyng) adj. składany; rozsuwany;s.fałd;fałda
folding boat ('fouldyng bout) składana łódź(turystyczna etc.)
folding chair ('fouldyng, czeer) składane krzesło(kampingowe etc.)
foliage ('fouljydź) s. listowie; liście (rosnące);ulistnienie
folk (fouk) s. ludzie; krewni; lud; rasa; adj. ludowy;folklorys-<sup>tyczny</sup>
folklore ('fouklo:r) s. folklor
folksy ('fouksy) adj. towarzyski; prosty;ludzki
folk song ('fouksong) s. pieśń ludowa (regionalna etc.)
follow ('folou) v. isć za; następować za; śledzić; rozumieć (kogoś) wnikać;gonić;wynikać
follower ('folouer) s. stronnik; zwolennik; uczeń; pomocnik
following ('folouyng) s. zwolennicy; adj. następujący; następny;s.orszak;świta;posłuch;autory-<sup>tet</sup>
folly ('foly) s. szaleństwo
foment (fou'ment) s. podżegać; podsycać;nagrzewać;pobudzać
fond (fond) adj. kochający; czuły; łatwowierny;głupio ,czuły
fondle ('fondl) v. pieścić
fondness ('fondnys) s. czułosc; miłosc; zamiłowanie;pociag
food (fu:d) s. żywnosc; strawa; pokarm; jedzenie;a.żywnościowy;
fool (fu:l) s. głupiec; głuptas; błazen; v. błaznowac; wyśmiewać; oszukiwać ;okpiwać;partaczyć
foolhardy ('fu:l,ha:rdy) adj. szaleńczy; wariacki; lekkomyślny ;nieroztropny;gwałtowny
foolish ('fu:lysz) adj. głupi
foolishness ('fu-lysznys) s. głupota ; głupstwo;bzdura;nonsens
foolproof ('fu:l,pru:f) adj. niezawodny ;nie do zepsucia

foot (fut) s. stopa; dół; spód; miara (30,5 cm);piechota;v.płaścić
foot the bill ('fut,ty'byl) v. zapłacić rachunek
football ('fut,bo:l) s. piłka nożna; futbol;piłka do nożnej
foot brake ('fut,brejk) s. hamulec nożny(w samochodzie)
foothills ('futhylz) pl. podgórze(przy łancuchu górskim)
foothold ('futhould) s. oparcie (dla nóg); miejsce gdzie można stanąć;pewna pozycja
footing ('futyng) s. fundament; ostoja; podstawa; położenie
footpath ('futpas) s. ścieżka dla pieszych; chodnik
footprint ('futprynt) s. ślad stopy
footstep ('fut,step) s. odgłos kroku; ślad;długość kroku
for (fo:r) prep. dla; zamiast; z; do; na; żeby; że; za; po; co do; co się tyczy; jak na; mimo; wbrew; po coś; z powodu; conj. ponieważ; bowiem; gdyż; albowiem; dlatego że
for two vears ('fo:-tu-je:rs) przez dwa lata
forbade (fe:r'bejd) zob. forbid
forbear ; forbore; forborne (fo:'beer; fe'bo:r; fe'bo:rn) forbear ('fo:r'beer) v. znosić cierpliwie; powstrzymywac(się) s. wyrozumiałość; przodek
forbid; forbade; forbidden (fer'byd; fe:r'bejd; fer'bydn) forbid (fe'rbyd) s. zakazywac; zabraniac; niedopuszczac; uniemożliwiac;nie pozwalać
forbidding (fe'rbydyng) adj. odpychający; posępny; ponury
forbore (fer'bo:r) zob. forbear
forborne (fer'bo:rn) zob. forbear
force (fo:rs) s. siła; moc; potęga; sens; v, zmuszać; pędzic; wpychać; forsowac
forced landing ('fo:rst,laendyng) przymusowe lądowanie
forceps ('fo:rsyps) pl. kleszcze; szczypce;szczypczyki

forcible ('fo:rsybl) adj. gwałtowny; przymusowy; przekonywujący ;mocny;dosadny;bezprawny
ford (fo:rd) v.przeprawiac się brodem; s. bród (płytkie miejsce)
fore (fo:r) adj. przedni; adv. na przedzie; s, przednia część
foreboding (fo:r'boudyng) s. przeczucie (złego) ;złe przeczucie
forecast ('fo:r-ka:st) v. przewidywac; s. przewidywanie
forefather ('fo:r,fa:dzer) s. przodek ; antenat
forefinger ('fo:rfynger) s. palec wskazujący
forefoot ('fo:r-fut) s. przednia noga (zwierzęcia)
foregone (fo:r'gon) adj. przesądzony ;miniony
foreground ('fo:rgraund) s. pierwszy plan (obrazu)
forehead ('fo:ryd) s. czoło
foreign('foryn) adj. obcy; obcokrajowy ;cudzozieski
foreign currency (,foryn'karensy) s. obca waluta
foreigner ('foryner) s. cudzoziemiec; cudzoziemka,obcokrajowiec
foreign policy ('foryn,polysy) polityka zagraniczna
foreign trade ('foryn,trejd) handel zagraniczny
foreleg ('fo:rleg) s. przednia noga (zwierzęcia)
foreman ('fo:rmen) s. majster; sztygar; starszy przysięgły
foremost ('fo:r,maust) adj. głowny; przedni; adv. przede wszystkim ;w pierwszym rzędzie
forenoon ('fo:rnu:n) s. przedpołudnie ;s.przedpołudniowy
foresee ('fo:rsi:) v. przewidywać ;przewidziec;wiedziec z góry
foresight ('fo:rsajt) s. przezorność; przewidywanie; muszka celownika (przy strzelbie etc.)
forest ('foryst) s. las; v. zalesiac ;a. lesny; w lesie
forester ('foryster) s. leśniczy; lesnik;ptak leśny;ćma leśna
forestry ('forystry) s. lesnictwo; lasy ;wiedza o lesie

foretaste ('fo:rtejst) s. przedsmak;zapowiedź tego co ma nasta-
pic
foretell; foretold; foretold
(fo:rtel; fo:'rtould; fo:'r-
tould)
foretell (fo:r'tel) v. przepo-
wiadać; zapowiadać;wróżyć
forever (fe'rewer) adv. wiecz-
nie; na zawsze; ustawicznie
foreword ('fo:rde-rd) v. przedmowa; przedsłowie;słowo wstępne
forfeit ('fo:rfyt) s. grzywna;
fant; zastaw; utrata; v. stra-
cić(w skutek konfiskaty);utracić
forge ('fo:rdż) s. kuźnia; huta:
v. kuć; fałszować; posuwać się
z trudem;wykuwać sobie przyszłość
forgery ('fo:rdżery) s. fałszerstwo;podrobiony dokument
forget; forgot; forgotten
(fer'get; fer'got; fer'gotn)
forget (fer'get) v. zapominać;
pomijać; przeoczyć;zaniedbać
forgetful (fer'getful) adj. za-
pominający;zapominalski;niepomny
forget-me-not (fer'getmyna:t) s.
niezapominajka
forgive; forgave; forgiven
(fer'gyw; fer'gejw; fer'gywn)
forgive (fer'gyw) v. przebaczać; darować ;odpuszczać
forgiveness (fer'gywnys) s. przebaczenie; darowanie; wybaczenie
forgiving (fer'gywyŋg)adj. wyrozumiały; pobłażliwy
forgo (fo:r'gou) v. powstrzymywać się; obchodzić się bez
czegoś ;zrzekać się czegoś
forgot (fer'got) zob. forget
fork (fo:rk) s. widły; widelec;
widełki; v. rozwidlać (się);
brać na widły;spulchniać(ziemię)
forlorn (fer'lo:rn) adj. zapuszczony; opuszczony; beznadziejny; rozpaczliwy;niepocięszony
form (fo:rm) v. formować (się);
kształtować (się); utworzyć
(się); organizować (się); wy-
tworzyć; s, forma; kształt;
postać; formuła; formułka; formularz;.blankiet;styl;układ
formal ('fo:rmel) adj. formalny;
urzędowy; oficjalny;s.strój wieczorowy

formation ('fo:rmejszyn) s. for-
macja; szyk; układ; tworzenie
(się); kształtowanie; formowa-
nie (się); powstawanie;budowa
formative ('fo:rmetyw) adj. for-
mujący; kształtujący; tworzą-
cy (się);słowotwórczy
former ('fo:rmer) adj. & pron.
poprzedni; były; miniony; dawny;s. formierz;giser;wzornik
formerly ('fo:rmerly) adv. dawniej; przedtem; poprzednio
formidable ('fo:rmydebl) adj.
straszny;strszny;potężny;ogrom-
ny
formulate ('fo:rmjulejt) v.
formułować;wyrażać;redagować
fornicate ('fo:rnykejt) v.
cudzołożyć ;spółkować bez ślubu
forsake; forsook; forsaken
(fer'sejk; fer'suk; fer'sejken)
forsake (fer'sejk) v. opuszczać;
porzucać;poniechać;zaprzeć się
fort (fo:rt) s. fort
forth (fo:rs) adv. naprzód; dalej;wobec;na zewnątrz etc.
forthcoming (fo:rs'kamyŋg) adj.
zbliżający się;nadchodzący
forthwith ('fo:rs'łys) adv.
bezzwłocznie;natychmiast
fortieth ('fo:rtyjes) num.
czterdziesty;czterdziesta(część)
fortify ('fo:rtyfaj) s. wzmacniać; fortyfikować;umacniać
fortnight ('fo:rtnajt) s. dwa
tygodnie (czternaście nocy)
fortran ('fo:rtraen) = formula
translation, język dla progra-
mów na komputery
fortress ('fo:rtrys) s. twierdza; forteca ;warownia
fortunate ('fo:rcznyt) adj.
szczęśliwy;pomyślny;udany
fortunately ('fo:rcznytly) adv.
na szczęście; szczęśliwie
fortune ('fo:rczen) s. szczęście; los; majątek;traf;ślepy los
forty ('fo:rty) num. czterdzies-
ci;czterdziestka;czterdziešcioro
forward ('fo:rłerd) adj. przedni; naprzód; postępowy; wczesny; chętny; gotowy; v. przyśpieszać; ekspediować; s. napastnik (w sporcie);gracz w ataku

forwards ('fo:rłerds) adv. naprzód; dalej;adj.frontowy;śmiały
foster-child ('foster.czajld)
s. wychowanek; wychowanka
fought (fo:t) zob, fight
foul (faul) adj. zgniły;plugawy;
wstrętny; adv. nieuczciwie;
wbrew regułom; s, nieuczci-
wosc; v, zawalać (się); za-
brudzić (się);plugawić się;kalać
found (faund) v. 1. uzasadniać;
zakładać; odlewać; 2. zob.
find
foundation (faun'dejszyn) s.
podstawa; założenie; fundament; fundacja;podwalina
founder ('faunder) s. odlew-
nik; założyciel; v. zatonąc;
przepaść;okulawic;zatopic'
foundling ('faundlyng) s.
podrzutek ; znajda
fountain ('fauntyn) s. fontanna; źródło;wodotrysk;poijalnia
fountainpen ('fauntyn,pen) s.
wieczne pióro
four (fo:r) num; cztery;czworo;
fourscore ('fo:rskor) num.
osiemdziesiąt
four-stroke engine ('fo:r,strok-
'endżyn) motor cztero-taktowy
fourteen ('fo:rti:n) num. czter-
nascie;czternaścioro;czternastka
fourth ('fo:rą) num. czwarty
fourthly (fo:rsly) adv. po
czwarte;na czwartym miejscu
fowl (faul) s. drób; ptaki
fox (foks) s. lis; v.przechytrzyć
fraction ('fraekszyn) s. ułamek;część;odłam;frakcja
fracture ('fraekczer) s. złamanie; v. złamac;łamac się
fragile ('fraedżajl) adj. kruchy; łamliwy;słabowity;wątły
fragment ('fraegment) s. fragment;urywek;odłamek;okruch
fragrance ('frejgrens) s. zapach; woń; aromat
fragrant ('frejgrent) adj. pachnący;aromatyczny;wonny
frail (frejl) adj. kruchy; wątły;lekkomyslny;s.kosz;plecionka
frailty ('frejlty) s. słabosć;
wątłosć ;chwila słabosci

frame ('frejm) s. oprawa; rama;
struktura; szkielet; v. opra-
wiac; kształtować; wrabiać
frame of mind ('frejm,ow'majnd)
s. nastrój; nastawienie psychiczne;usposobienie do czegos'
frame-house ('frejm,haus) s.
drewniany dom (typowy w USA)
framework ('frejm,łe:rk) s.
struktura; zrąb;szkielet;wiąza-nie
franchise ('fraenczajz) s.
przywilej; prawo do prowadzenia filii lub firmy,do głosowa-nia
frank (fraenk) adj. szczery;
otwarty;v.wysyłać bez opłaty
frankness ('fraenknys) s.
szczerosć; otwartosć
frantic ('fraentyk) adj.
wariacki; szalony;zapamiętały
fraternal (fre'te:rnl) adj.
braterski;bratni;bracki
fraternity (fre'te:rnyty) s.
braterstwo;korporacja studencka
fraud (fro:d) s. oszustwo;oszust
fray (frej) v. strzępic; wycierac; s. bójka; burda
freak (fri:k) s. kaprys; wybryk; potwor;a.fantazyjny
freckle ('frekl) s. pieg; v.po-
krywać piegami;powodowac piegi
free (fri:) adj. wolny; bezpłatny; nie zajęty; v. uwolnic;
wyzwolic; oswobodzic; adv.wol-
no; swobodnie; bezpłatnie
free and easy ('fri:,end'i:zy)
adj. beztroski;bez ceremonii
freedom ('fri:dem) s. wolnosć;
swoboda;nieskrępowanie;prawo do
freemason ('fri:,mejsn) s.
mason; wolnomularz
free port ('fri:, port) s.
wolnocłowy port
freethinker ('fri:tynker) s.
wolnomysliciel;wolnomyslicielka
freeway ('fri:łej) s. szosa
przelotowa wieloliniowa
freewheel ('fri:hłi:l) s. wolne koło (np, od roweru)
freeze (fri:z; froze; frozen (fri:z;
frouz; frouzn)
freeze (fri:z) v. marznąc; za-
marzac;krzepnąc;przymarznąc;
mrozić;wyrugować(konkurenta)

freezing point ('fri:zyn,point)
s. punkt zamarzania
freight (frejt) s. przewóz;
fracht; v. przewozić; frachto-
wać statek;a.towarowy(pociag etc.)
freighter ('frejter) s. frach-
towiec; statek towarowy
French (frencz) adj. francuski
frenzy ('frenzy) s. szał; szaleństwo;v.doprowadzać do szału
frequency ('fri:kłensy) s.
częstość; częstotliwość
frequent ('fri:kłent) adj. częsty; rozpowszechniony; v.
uczęszczać; odwiedzać; bywać
fresh (fresz) adj. świeży; nowy;
zuchwały; niedoświadczony; adv.
świeżo; niedawno;dopiero co
freshman ('freszmen) s. student
pierwszego roku
freshness ('fresznys) s. świeżość; zuchwałość;zuchwalstwo
freshwater ('fresz;ło:ter) adj.
słodkowodny; s. woda słodka
fret (fret) v. gryźć się: niepokoić się; s. rozdrażnienie;
niepokój;zdenerwowanie;irytacja
fretful ('fretful) adj. rozdrażniony; drażliwy;nerwowy;wzburzo-
ny;
friar ('frajer) s. mnich; zakonnik ; biała plamka
friction ('frykszyn) s. tarcie;
ścieranie się; ucieranie
Friday ('frajdy) s. piątek
fridge (frydż) s. lodówka
(slang)
fried (frajd) adj. smażony
friend (frend) s. znajomy; zna-
joma; przyjaciel;kolega;klient
friendly ('frendly) adj. przyjazny; przychylny ;życzliwy
friendship ('frendszyp) s. przyjaźń osobista; dobra znajomość;
znajomość powierzchowna; stosunki koleżeńskie lub handlowe
fright (frajt) s. strach;prze-
rażenie;strach na wróble
frighten ('frajtn) v. straszyć
frightened ('frajtnd) adj.prze-
straszony ;zastraszony;wylękniony
frightful ('frajtful) adj.
straszny; przerażający;strszliwy;
alarmujący;nieprzyjemny;wstrętny

frigid ('frydżyd) adj. zimny;
lodowaty; oziębły;zimna(kobieta)
frill (fryl) v. plisować;
s. falbanka; pl. fochy; fanaberie;niepotrzebne ozdóbki
fringe (fryndż) s. frędzla; ob-
rębek; v. obrębiać; obramowywać; ograniczać;wystrzępić
frisk (frysk) v. brykać; s.sus;
podskok; skok;v.rewidować
frisky ('frysky) adj. rozbrykany; ożywiony; swawolny
fro (frou) exp.: to and fro;
tu i tam; tam i z powrotem
frock (frok) s. sukienka; habit;mundur;surdut;anglez
frog (frog) s. żaba; strzałka
(w kopycie konia);vulg.Francuz
frolic ('frolyk) s. wybryk;figiel
swawola; v. dokazywać; swawolić; figlować; adj. rozbawiony; swawolny; figlarny
frolicsome ('frolyksem) adj.
figlarny; swawolny;rozbawiony
from (from) prep. od; z; przed
(zimnem); ze;(ponieważ; żeby)
from under (from ander) prep;
spod (czegos)
from... to (from... tu) exp.
stąd... dotąd ;od ..,do
front (frant) s. przód; front;
czoło; adj, przedni; frontowy;
czołowy; v. stawiać czoło;
stać frontem; konfrontować
front-door ('frant,do:r) s.
główne drzwi wejściowe
frontier ('frantjer) s. granica ; a. pograniczny
front-page ('frant,pejdż) s.
strona tytułowa;a.sensacyjny
front tire ('frant,tajer) s.
przednia opona (samochodu)
front-wheel ('frant,hłi:l) s.
przednie koło (wozu)
front wheel drive ('frant,
hłi:l'drajw) s. napęd na
przednie koła (auta,etc.)
frost (frost) s. mróz; przymrozek; oziębłość;v.zmrozić;oszro-
frostbite ('frost,bajt) s. uníc
odmrożenie(nosa,reki,stopy etc.)
frosted ('frostyd) adj. matowy;
oszronionya matowy odcien

frosty ('frosty) adj. mroźny; oszroniony; lodowaty

froth (froþ) s. piana; szumowiny; v. pienić się;ubijać białko

frothy (froþy) adj. spieniony

frown (fraun) v. marszczyć brwi; s. zachmurzone czoło; wyraz dezaprobaty;niezadowolona mina

froze (frouz) zob. freeze

frozen food ('frouzn, fu:d) s. mrożonki;mrożona żywność

frugal ('fru:gel) adj. oszczędny;tani; skromny(posiłek etc.)

fruit (fru:t) s. owoc; v. owocować;a. owocowy

fruitcake ('fru:t,kejk) s. świąteczne ciasto z kandyzowanymi owocami i orzechami

fruitful ('fru:tful) adj. owocny;owocujący;zyskowny;wydajny

fruitless ('fru:tlys) adj. bezowocny; bezpłodny;nieudany

frustrate (fra'strejt) v. udaremnic; zniechęcić; zawieść

fry (fraj) v. smażyć;s.narybek

frying pan (frajyn,paen) s. patelnia

fuel (fjuel) s. paliwo; opał

fugitive ('fju:dżytyw) s. zbieg; adj. zbiegły; przelotny

fulfill (ful'fyl) v. spełnic; wykonac; dokonac; skonczyc

fulfilment (ful'fylment) s. spełnienie; wykonanie; dokonanie;wypełnienie;wysłuchanie

full(ful) adj. pełny; pełen; zapełniony; całkowity; kompletny; cały; adv. w pełni; całkowicie

full board ('ful'bo:rd) s. pełne utrzymanie;wikt i opierunek

full moon ('ful'mu:n) s. pełnia księżyca

fullness (ful'nys) s. pełność; dokładność;drobiazgowość

full-time ('ful'tajm) adj. pełnoetatowy; całkowicie zajęty

fumble ('fambl) v. szperac; partaczyc; s. gmeranie; partactwo; niezdarność;niezdarnę zagranię

fume (fju:m) v. dymic; kopcic; s. dym (ostry); wyziew(przykry) gazy spalinowe;zapach;won;napad gniewu;wybuch gniewu

fun (fan) s. uciecha; zabawa; wesołość; śmiech;powód do wesołości

in fun (yn,fan) adv. żartem; make fun (mejk fan) v. dokuczac; kpic;wyśmiewac się

function ('fankszyn) v. działac; funkcjonowac; s. działanie; funkcja; praca; obowiązek; impreza; uroczystość;czynność

functionary ('fanksznery) s. urzędnik; funkcjonariusz

fund (fand) s. fundusz

fundamental (,fande'mentel) adj. podstawowy; s. zasada; podstawa zasada;nakaz;podstawa

funeral ('fju:nerel) s. pogrzeb; adj. pogrzebowy;żałosny

funereal (fju'njerjel) adj. żałobny;pogrzegowy

funicular railway (fju'nykjuler'rejlłej) kolejka linowa

funnel ('fanl) s. lej; lejek; komin (maszyny parowej etc.)

funny ('fany) adj. zabawny; śmieszny; dziwny;humorystyczny

fur (fe:r) s. futro;v.okładać

furious ('fjuerjes) adj. wściekły; rozjuszony;gwałtowny;zaciekły

furl (fe:r) v. składac (się); złożyc (się);s.zwitek;zawinięcie

furnace ('fe:rnys) s. piec (centralny);palenisko;piekło

furnish ('fe:rnysz) v. zaopatrzyc; dostarczyc; umeblowac; wyposażyc;uzbrajac;meblowac

furniture ('fe:rnyczer) s. umeblowanie; urządzenie

furrier ('farjer) s. kuśnierz

furrow ('farou) s. bruzda; zmarszczka; koleina; v. orac; przeorac; zryc;ryc;pruc;żłobic

further ('fe:rdżer) adv. dalej; dodatkowo; adj. dalszy; dodatkowy; v. pomagac; ułatwiac; posuwac naprzód;sprzyjac;popierac

further more ('fe:rdżermo:r) adv. ponadto; oprócz tego; w dodatky

furtive ('fe:rtyw) adj. skryty; potajemny;ukradkowy;skradający się

furuncle ('fjuerankl) s. czyrak

fury ('fjuery) s. szał; furja; pasja; gwałtowna siła; jędza; megiera;siła burzy;siła wiatru

fuse (fju:z) v. stopić; s. za- gallon ('gaelen) s. miara płynu
palnik; bezpiecznik; korek (ok. 4,5 litra)(am.gal.=3,78 l.)
fuselage ('fju:zyla:ż) s. kad- gallop ('gaelep) v. galopować;
łub (samolotu)bez skrzydeł i o- s. galop; cwał;galopada
fusion ('fju:żen) s. stopienie; gallows ('gaelouz) s. szubieni-
spawanie; zlewanie się ca;kobylica;szelki;a.szbieniczny
fuss (fas) v. niepokoić; dener- galore (gr'lo:r) s. mnóstwo;
wować; krzątac się; s. wrzawa; adv. w bród;bardzo wiele
zamieszanie; krzątanina gamble ('gaembl) s. hazard; ry-
fussy ('fasy) adj. grymasny; zyko; v. uprawiać hazard; ry-
hałaśliwy; nieznośny;zrzędny zykować;igrać;spekulować
futile ('fju:tajl) adj. darem- gambler ('gaembler) s. gracz-
ny; bezskuteczny; próżny hazardzista; ryzykant
future ('fju:tczer) s. przy- gambol (gaembel) v. podskaki-
szłość; adj. przyszły(czas...) wać; s. podskok; skok
fuzzy ('fazy) adj. kędzierzawy; game (gejm) s. gra; zabawa; za-
kręty; puszysty; niewyraźny; wody; sztuczki; machinacje;
zamazany(obraz,pojęcie etc.) adj. dzielny; odważny; kulawy;
g (dżi:) siódma litera angiel- v. uprawiać hazard
skiego alfabetu gamekeeper ('gejm,ki:per) s.
gab (gaeb) s. gadanie (slang) gajowy; leśnik
gable ('gejbl) s. szczyt (da- gander ('gaender) s. gąsior
chu)trójkąt płaszczyzn dachu gang (gaeng) s. banda; szajka;
gad-fly ('gaedflaj) s. giez; grupa;v.łaczyc się w bandę
bąk;osoba zaczepna jak giez gangster ('gaengster) s. gans-
gag (gaeg) s. knebel; v. kneb- ster; bandyta
lować; nałożyć kaganiec; gangway ('gangłej) s. przejście;
zamknąć debatę;oszukiwać kładka;chodnik w kopalni
gage (gejdż) s. wskaźnik; mia- gaol= jail (dżejl) s. więzienie;
ra; rękojmia; v, mierzyć; ciupa;v.uwięzić;wsadzać do więzie-
oceniać; zastawiać;sadzic gaoler= jailer ('dżejler) s. do-
gaiety ('gejety) s. wesołość zorca więzienny;strażnik więzienny
gaily ('gejly) adv. wesoło gap (gaep) s. szpara; luka;otwór;
gain (gejn) s. zysk; zarobek; przerwa;odstęp;wyrwa;przełęcz;wyłom
korzyść; v. zyskiwać; zdo- gape (gejp) v. gapić się; zie-
bywać; pozyskiwać; wygrywać; wać; s. ziewanie; gapienie się
osiągać;mieć korzyść;wyprzedzać garage (gaera:dż) s. garaż;
gait (gejt) s. chód;bieg(konia) v. garażować; zagarażować
gaiter ('gejter) s. kamasz; garbage ('ga:rbydż) s. odpadki;
getr śmieci;bezwartościowe publikacje
gale (gejl) s. poryw wiatru; garden ('ga:rdn) s. ogród;uprawiać o-
sztorm;wybuch śmiechu;zefir gardener ('ga:rdner) s. ogrodnik
gall (go:l) s. żółć; złość; go- gardening ('ga:rdenyng) s. og-
rycz;tupet;otarcie;v.urazić... rodnictwo(warzywne,kwiatowe etc.)
gallant ('gaelent) s. bawida- gargle ('ga:rgl) v. płukać
mek; galant; adj. piękny; gardło;v.płyn do płukania gardła
dzielny; waleczny; szarmancki garland ('ga:rlend) s. girlanda
gallery ('gaelery) s. arkady; garlic ('ga:rlik) s. czosnek
galeria; krużganek;balkon;chór garment ('ga:rment) s. część
galley ('gaely) s. galera; ubrania;szaty;v.odziewać
kuchnia na statku;szufelka garnish ('ga:rnusz) v. ozdabiać;
galley proof ('gaely,pru:f) s. s. ozdoba; przybranie (potraw)
odbitka na korektę(szczotkowa) upiększenia literackie

garret ('gaeret) s. poddasze; strych; mansarda;sl.:łeb

garrison ('gaerysn) s. załoga; garnizon; v. garnizonować

garter ('ga:rter) s. podwiązka

gas (gaes) s. gaz; benzyna

gaseous ('gejzjes) adj. gazowy

gash (gaesz) s. skaleczyć się; s. szrama; skaleczenie;blizna

gasket ('gaeskyt) s. uszczelka

gas-meter ('gaes,mi:ter) s. gazomierz;zegar gazowy

gasoline ('gaesely:n) s. gazolina; benzyna

gasp (ga:sp) v. ciężko dyszeć; sapać; s. ciężki oddech

gas station ('gaes,stejszyn) s. stacja benzynowa

gas-stove ('gaes'stouw) s. kuchenka gazowa;kuchnia gazowa

gate (gejt) s. brama; furtka; wrota; szlaban; ilość publiczności;wpływy kasowe ze wstępu

gateway ('gejtłej) s. przejscie; wjazd; brama wjazdowa

gather ('gaedzer) v. zbierać; wnioskować;wzbierać;narastać

gather speed ('gaedzer spi:d) nabierać szybkości;rozpędzać się

gathering ('gaedzeryng) s. zebranie;nagromadzenie; ropień

gaudy (go:dy) adj. jaskrawy; krzykliwy; s. obchód(uroczysty)

gauge (gejdż) s. wskaźnik; miara; skala; v. kalibrować; oceniać;szacować; oszacować

gaunt (go:nt) adj. chudy; nędzny;wycienczony;ponury;posępny

gauze ('go:z) s. gaza; siateczka;mgiełka;gaza metalowa

gave (gejw) zob. give

gay (gej) adj. wesoły; jaskrawy; pstry; rozpustny; s. pederasta;pedzio;pedał

gaze (gejz) s. spojrzenie; v. przyglądać się;przypatrywać się

gaze at (gejz aet) v. wpatrywać (się)w kogoś, w coś

gear (gier) v. włączyć (napęd) s. przybory; bieg; układ

gear change ('gier,czeindż) zmiana biegów

gearbox ('gier,boks) s. skrzynka biegów;skrzynia biegów

gearing ('geryng) s. przekładnia;mechanizm napędowy

gear wheel ('gier-hłi:l) s. tryb; koło zębate

geese (gi:s) pl. gęsi

gem (dżem) s. klejnot;perła

gender ('dżender) s. rodzaj; płeć; wytwór; potomstwo

general ('dżenerel) adj. ogólny; powszechny; generalny; naczelny; główny; nieścisły; ogólnikowy; s. generał; wódz

generalize ('dżenerelajz) v. uogólniać; mówić ogólnikami

generally ('dżenerely) adv. ogólnie; zazwyczaj; powszechnie; najczęściej; w ogóle

generate ('dżenerejt) v. rodzić; wytwarzać;płodzić; wywoływać

generation ('dżenerejszyn) s. powstawanie; pokolenie

generator ('dżenerejter) s. prądnica; sprawca;generator

generosity (,dżene'rosyty) s. szczodrość; wspaniałomyślność

generous ('dżeneres) adj. hojny; wielkoduszny; suty; obfity; bogaty; żyzny;mocny; krzepiący

genial ('dżi:njel) adj. wesoły; łagodny; miły;jowialny;ożywczy

genitive (dżenytyw) s. (gram.) dopełniacz;adj.wesoły;łagodny

genius (dżi:njes) s. geniusz; duch; talent;duch epoki etc.

genocide ('dżenousajd) s. ludobójstwo(stematyczne mordowanie)

gentle ('dżentl) adj. łagodny; delikatny; subtelny.stopniowy

gentleman ('dżentlmen) s. pan; człowiek honorowy; dżentelmen

gentlemanly ('dżentlmenly) adj. dżentelmeński; honorowy

gentleness ('dżentlnys) s. łagodność; delikatność

gentlewomen ('dżentl,łumen) s. szlachcianka; dama;dama dworu

gentry ('dżentry) s. ziemiaństwo; szlachta; światek

genuine ('dżenjuyn) adj. prawdziwy; autentyczny; szczery

geography (dży'ogrefy) s. geografia; fizyczne cechy rejonu
geologist (dży'oledżyst) s. geolog
geology (dży'oledży) s. geologia
geometry (dży'omytry) s. geometria
germ (dże:rm) s. zarodek; zarazek; nasienie; pączek
German ('dże:rmen) adj. niemiecki(jezyk,człowiek)s.Niemiec
germinate ('dże:rmynejt) v. kiełkować; rozwijac się
gerund (dżerend) s. rzeczownik odsłowny(z końcówką:"ing")
gestation ('dżes'tejszyn) s. ciąża
gesticulate ('dżes'tykjulejt) v. gestykylować; mówic na migi
gesture ('dżesczer) s. gest
get; got; got (get; got; got) get (get) v. dostac; otrzymac; nabyć; zawołać; łupać; przyniesć; zmusic; musić; miec; dostac się; wpływac;wsiadać
get about (,get e'baut) v. poruszac się;rozchodzić się
get along (,get e'long) v. dawac sobie radę; współpracować
get away (,get e'łej) v. uciec; odejsc;wyjeżdżać;oderwac się
get in (,get'yn) v. wejsc; wsiąsc
get off (,get'of) v. wysiasć,
get on (,get'on) v. wdziewac; posuwac się; robic dalej
get out (,get'aut) v. wysiąsć; wyjmowac; wyciągać;wynosić się
get to (,get'tu) v. dotrzec; przyjsć; musiec;byc zamuszonym
get together (,get te'gedżer) v. zebrac się; s. zebranie
get up (,get'ap) v. wstac;zbudzić się
get-up ('getap) s.wygląd;ubior
get ready (,get'redy) v. przygotowac(się);przygotowywać się
get to know ('get,tu'nou) v. zapoznac się (bliżej)
geyser ('gajzer) s. gejzer
ghastly ('ga:stly) adj. ohydny; upiorny; blady;adv.okropnie
gherkin ('ge:rkyn) s, korniszon
ghost (goust) s. duch; cień;widmo

ghostly ('goustly) adj. upiorny
giant ('dżajent) s. olbrzym
gibbet ('dżybyt) s. szubienica
gibe ('dżajb) s. kpina; drwina; v. kpić; szydzic; wysmiewac
giblets ('dżyblyts) pl. podróbki (np. kurze);podroby
giddy ('gydy) adj. zawrotny; mający zawrót głowy; roztrzepany; v. przyprawiac o zawrót głowy
gift (gyft) s. dar; upominek; talent; uzdolnienie;a.darowany
gifted ('gyftyd) adj. utalentowany;mający naturalne zdolności
gigantic (dżaj'gantyk) adj. olbrzymi; gigantyczny;kolosalny
giggle ('gygl) s. chichot; v. chichotac;głupio śmiac się
gild (gyld) v. złocic; pozłocic;nadać lepszego wyglądu
gill (gyl) s. skrzela; wąwoz; potok;jedna czwarta galona
gilt (gylt) adj. pozłacany; s. złocenie; pozłocenie
gin (dżyn) s. jałowcówka
ginger ('dżyndżer) s. imbir
ginger bread ('dżyndżer,bred) s. piernik;przesadne dekoracje
gingerly ('dżyndżerly) adj. ostrożny; delikatny; adv. ostrożnie; delikatnie; niesmiało
gipsy ('dżypsy)s. cygan
giraffe (dży'ra:f) s. żyrafa
gird; girt; girt (ge:rd; ge:rt; ge:rt)
gird (ge:rd) v. opasac;kpić.s.kpina
girder ('ge:rder) s. dzwigar; belka; wzdłużnik
girdle ('ge:rdl) s. pas; v. opasac; okrążyć;opasywać lekkim gorsetem
girl (ge:rl) s. dziewczyna;ukochana
girlhood ('ge:rlhud) s. wiek dziewczęcy; dziewczeta (kraju etc.)
girl scout ('ge:rl skaut) s. harcerka
girl's name ('ge:rls,nejm) s. panieńskie nazwisko
girt (ge:rt) zob. gird
girth (ge:rt) s. popręg; obwód
gist (dżyst) s. tresc; istota; sedno; esencja; osnowa;sens; główna tresc

give; gave; given (gyw; gejw;
gywn)
give (gyw) v. dac; dawac; byc
elastycznym; zawalic' się;
ustąpic; s. elastycznosc;
ustępstwo pod naciskiem
give away (,gyw e'łej) v. wydawac; zdradzac;wydawac córkę,
give in (,gyw'yn) v. ustępowac;
podawac(nazwisko);uznawac w koncu
give up (,gyw'ap) v. poddac się;
ustąpic; zaniechac;dac za wygraną
give way (,gyw'łej) v. zrobic
miejsce; ustąpic;obsunąc się
glacier ('glaesjer) s. lodowiec
glad (glaed) adj. rad; wesoły;
radosny;dający radosc;ochoczy
gladly ('glaedly) adv. z przy-
jemnoscią; chętnie;wlasciwie
gladness ('glaednys) s. wesołosc; pogoda ducha; przyjemnosc
glamorous ('glaemeres) adj. czarujący; wspaniały; fascynujący
glance (gla:ns) v. spojrzec;
zesliznąc się; błyszczec; połyskiwac; s. rzut oka; błysk;
połysk;rekoszet;odbicie się
glance at ('gla:ns et) v. spojrzec na (cos);rzucic spojrzenie
gland (glaend) s. gruczoł
glare (gleer) v. błyskac; razic;
wlepiac wzrok; s.błysk; blask
glass (gla:s) s. szkło; szklanka;lampka;kieliszek;szyba etc.
glasses ('gla:sys) pl. okulary;
szkła
glassy ('gla:sy) adj. szklisty;
szklany;przezroczysty;bez wyrazu
glaze (glejz) v. szklic; oszklic
glazier ('glejzjer) s. szklarz
gleam (gli:m) s. połysk; v. połyskiwac;zjawic się nagle
glee (gli:) s. wesele; radosc
glen (glen) s. dolina(zaciszna)
glib (glyb) adj. gładki; żwawy;
płynny; wygadany(zanadto)
glide ('glajd) s. poslizg; szy-
bowanie; v. slizgac się; szybowac; powodowac poslizg
glider ('glajder) s. szybowiec
glimmer ('glymer) v. migotac;
słabo swiecic; s. słabe swiatło;
migotanie;słabe postrzeganie

glimpse (glymps) s. mignięcie;
przelotne spojrzenie; v. ujrzec w przelocie;zerknąc
glint (glynt) s. błysk; odblask; v. błysnąc; zamigotac
glisten ('glysn) s. połysk;
v. połyskiwac;lsnic;iskrzyc się
glitter ('glyter) v. swiecic
się; błyszczec; s. połysk;
blask; pretensjonalnosc
gloat ('glout) v. napawac się;
gloat over patrzec;pożerac oczami
gloat over ('glout,ower) v.
napawac się (cudzym nie-
szczęściem);unosic się
globe (gloub) s. globus; kula
ziemska;jabłko krolewskie;gałka
gloom (glu:m) s. smutek; mrok;
przygnębienie; v. zasmucac
(się); zaciemniac (się);posęp-
nieć
gloomy ('glu:my) adj. ponury;
mroczny;posępny;przygnębiony
glorify ('glo:ryfaj) v. chwalic; wychwalac; gloryfikowac
glorious ('glo:rjes) adj. sławny; wspaniały;przepiękny;chlubny
glory ('glo:ry) s. chwała; sława; v. szczycic się; chlubic
się;chwalic się;chełpic się
gloss (glos) s. połysk; v. po-
lerowac;interpretowac(błędnie)
glossary ('glosery) s. słownik
(przy tekscie);glosarjusz
glossy ('glosy) adj. lsniący
glove (glaw) s. rękawiczka
glow (glou) v. żarzyc się; pałac; s. jarzenie; zapał; żar-
liwosc;łuna;rumieniec;jasnosc
glowworm ('glou,łe:rm) s. ro-
baczek swiętojański
glue (glu:) s. klej; v. kleic;
zalepiac;wlepiac(oczy);zlepic
glutton ('glatn) s. żarłok
gluttonous ('glatnes) adj.
żarłoczny;jedzący zbyt dużo
gluttony ('glatny) s. żarłocz-
nosc;zwyczaj jedzenia za dużo
glycerine (,glyse'ry:n) s.
gliceryna
gnarled ('na:rld) adj. sękaty;
wykrzywiony; węzłowaty
gnash (naesz) v. zgrzytac zębami
jak w złości

gnat (naet) s. komar;owad
gnaw (no:) v. gryźć; wgryzać;
ogryzać; nękać(stałym bólem)
go; went; gone (gou; lent; gon)
go (gou) v. iść; chodzić; jechać; stać się;być na chodzie
go about (,gou e'baut) v. za-
jąć się (czymś);afiszować się
go along (,gou e'long) v. towarzyszyć; zgadzać się;iść sobie
go away (,go e'łej) v. iść
precz; odchodzić;wyjeżdżać
go back (,gou'bek) v. wracać;
cofać się;sięgać wstecz
go by (,gou'baj) v. mijać
go on (,gou'on) v. iść naprzód;
ciagnąć dalej; kontynuować
go out (,gou'aut) v. wychodzić
(z kims); gasnąć;bywać(u ludzi)
go through (,gou'tru) v. przechodzić; brnąć przez ;przebrnąć
go under (,gou'ander) v. to-
nąć; ulegać; zniknąć;umrzeć
goad (goud) s. kolec; bodziec;
v. popędzać; drażnić; prowokować;doprowadzać do zrobienia
goal (goul) s. cel; meta; bramka
goalie (gouli) s. bramkarz
go-between (,gouby'tły:n) s.
pośrednik; stręczyciel
goblet ('goblyt) s. kieliszek;
czara;puchar;kielich na nóżce
goblin ('goblyn) s. chochlik
god (god) s. Bóg; bożek;bóstwo
godchild ('godczajld) s. chrześ-
niak; chrześniaczka
goddess ('godys) s. bogini
godfather ('god,fa:dzer) s.chrztu
ojciec chrzestny;v.trzymać do
godless ('godlys) adj. bezboż-
ny;grzeszny;niegodziwy;nikczemny
godmother ('god,madzer) s.
matka chrzestna
goggles ('goglz) pl. okulary
ochronne; gogle;okrągłe okulary
going ('gouyng)s. chodzenie;
jazda ;tempo;adj.ruchliwy;istnie-
going rate ('gouyn,rejt) bieżący kurs (dolara,oprocentowania)
gold (gould) s. złoto,adj.złoty
gold digger ('gould,dyger)
poszukiwacz złota ; naciagaczka

golden ('gouldn) adj. złoty
gold-plated ('gould,plejtyd)
s. plater złoty ;platerowany
goldsmith ('gould,smys) s.
złotnik golfa
golf (golf) s. golf ;v.grać w
golf course ('golf,ko:rs) s.
pole golfowe
gondola ('gondele) s. gondola
(np. balonu);otwarty,niski wagon
towarowy
gone (gon) v. zob. go
good (gud) adj. dobry; s. dobro; pożytek; zaleta;wartość
better ('beter) lepszy;
best (best) najlepszy
good at it ('gud,et'yt) dobry
w tym; dobrze to robi
good-bye (,gud'baj) s. do widzenia; pożegnanie
good-for-nothing ('gudfe:r,na-
syng) s. nicpoń ;hultaj;łobuziak
good-looking ('gud'lukyng)adj.
przystojny; ładny
good-natured ('gud'nejczerd)
adj. dobroduszny;poczciwy
goodness ('gudnys) s. dobroć
good will ('gud'łyl) s. dobra
wola;wartość reputacji firmy
goose(gu:s) s. gęś; pl. geese
(gi:s) gęsi;gęsie mięso;dureń
gooseberry ('gusbery) s. agrest
gooseflesh ('gu:sflesz) s. gę-
sia skórka (z zimna,strachu etc.)
gopher ('goufer) s. suseł;
v. grzebać;ryć;plądrować gospo-
gore (go:r) v. bość; klinować; darkę
s, klin w krawiectwie;posoka
gorge ('go:rdz) s. wąwoz; żar-
łoczność; treść żołądka; prze-
jedzenie; gardziel; v, obżerać
się; pożerać; połykać;opychać się
gorgeous ('go:rdżes) adj. wspaniały; okazały; suty; ozdobny;
wystawny;wspaniały;cudowny
gospel ('gospel) s. ewangielia
gossip ('gosyp) s. plotka;
plotkarz; plotkarka; v. plotkować;pisać popularne artykuły
got (got) zob. get
Gothic ('gotyk) adj. gotycki
gotten ('gotn) = got; zob. get
gourd (go:rd) s. bania; tykwa

gourmet ('guermej) n. smakosz

gout (gaut) s. gościec;podagra

govern ('gawern) v. rządzić; rządzać w ry-
kierować; dowodzić;trzymać w ry-

governess ('gawernys) s. guwer-
nantka;nauczycielka;instruktor-
ka

government ('gawernment) s.

rząd; ustrój;okręg;a.rządowy

governor ('gawerner) s. gubernator; zarządca;naczelnik;szef

gown (gaun) s. suknia; toga;
v. układać togę;ubierać suknię

grab (graeb) v. łapać; zagar-
niać; grabić; s. łapanie;
chwyt; zagarnięcie;porwanie

grace (grejs) s. łaska; wdzięk;
przyzwoitość; v. czcić; ozdabiać; dodawać wdzięku;zaszczy-
cić

graceful ('grejsful) adj. pełen
wdzięku; wdzięczny;łaskawy

gracious ('grejszes) adj. łaskawy; miłosierny;exp. goodness gracious!('gudnys'grejszes) Boze miłosierny!

grade (grejd) s. stopień; klasa; nachylenie; v. stopniować;
dzielić na stopnie; cieniować;
równać teren;niwelować;profilo-
wać

grade crossing ('grejd'krosyng)
s. skrzyzowanie dróg; przejazd
przez tory(jedno poziomowe)

grade school('grejd'sku:l) s.
szkoła podstawowa

gradient ('grejdjent) s. nachylenie; stopień nachylenia

gradual ('graedżuel) adj. stopniowy;po trochu

graduate ('graedżuejt) s. absol-
went; v. stopniować; ukończyć
studia;adj. podyplomowy(kurs)

graduation (,graedżu'ejszyn) s.
ukończenie wyższych studiów;
ka
stopniowanie;cechowanie;podział

graft (gra:ft) v. szczepić; dawać łapówkę; przeszczepiać;
s. szczepienie; łapówka; przeszczep ;szufla(pełna ziemi)

grain (grejn) s. ziarno; zboże;
odrobina; grań; włókno; słój;
v. granulować; ziarnować

gram (graem) s. gram;1/28uncji

grammar ('graemer) s. gramatyka

grammar school ('graemer-sku:1)
s. szkoła podstawowa

grammatical (gre'maetykel) adj.
gramatyczny (poprawny)

gramme (graem) s. gram (ang.)

gramophone ('graemefoun) s.
patefon; gramofon

grand (graend) adj. wielki; główny; wspaniały; świetny; okazały;
(slang):1000 dolarów;całkowity

grandchild ('graen,chajld) s.
wnuk

granddaughter ('graen,do:ter) s.
wnuczka

grandeur ('graendżer) s. wielkość; dostojność; okazałość;
wspaniałość;majestat;blask;pompa

grandfather ('graend,fa:dzer)s.
dziadek

grandma ('graenma:) s. babcia

grandmother ('graen,madzer) s.
babka

grandpa ('graenpa:) s. dziadzio

grandparents ('graen,pearents)
pl. dziadkowie

grandson ('graensan) s. wnuk

grandstand ('graenstaend) s.
wać
główna trybuna;Xpopisywać się

granny ('graeny) s. babunia

grant (gra:nt) v. nadawać; udzielać; uznawać; zgadzać się na;
przekazywać; s,pomoc; przekazanie tytułu własności;darowizna

granulated ('graenjulejtyd) adj.
ny
ziarnisty;rozdrobniony;granulowa-

grape (grejp) s. winogrona

grapefruit ('grejp-fru:t) s.
greipfrut(owoc lub drzewo)

grape-sugar ('grejp,szuger) s.
cukier gronowy

grapevine ('grejp-wajn) s. wino-
ka
rośl; poczta pantoflowa; szep-
tanka;źródło kaczek prasowych

graph (fraef) s. wykres; krzywa

graphic ('graefyk) adj. graficz-
ny; plastyczny; obrazowy(dosadny)

grasp (gra:sp) v. łapać; chwytać; pojmać; pojmować; dzierżyć; s. chwyt; uchwyt; pojęcie;
panowanie;zrozumienie;kontrola

grass (gra:s) s. trawa; (slang):
marijuana; "pot";haszysz

grasshopper ('gra:s,hoper) s.
konik polny (z czterema skrzydłami) ży; świetny; znakomity; wspa-
grass widower ('gra:s,łydouer)
s. słomiany wdowiec
grate (grejt) s. krata; ruszt;
v. trzeć, ucierać; zgrzytać;
skrzypieć;irytować;być irytują-
cym
grateful ('grejtful) adj.
wdzięczny;dobrze widziany
grater ('grejter) s. tarko;
tarło;raszpla;tarnik do drzewa
gratification (,graetyfy'kejszyn)
s. zaspokojenie; wynagrodzenie; gratyfikacja;łapówka
gratify ('graetyfaj) v. dogadzać; uprzyjemniać; zadawalać;
przekupywać·wynagradzać
grating ('grejtyŋg) s. krata;
adj. zgrzytliwy; ochrypły
gratis ('grejtys) adv. gratis;
bezpłatnie; adj. bezpłatny;
gratisowy ;darmowy
gratitude ('graetytju:d) s.
wdzięczność(za pomoc etc.)
gratuitous (gre'tjuites) adj.
bezpłatny; niepotrzebny
gratuity (gre'tjuity) s. napiwek; zasiłek przy zwolnieniu
grave ('grejw) s. grób; adj.
poważny; v. wyryć; wryć;wykopać
gravel ('grawel) s. żwir; piasek;v.psypywać żwirem; kłopotać
graveyard ('grejwja:rd) s. cmentarz; nocna zmiana w pracy
gravitation (,graewy'tejszyn)
s. ciążenie(ciał);grawitacja
gravity ('graewyty) s. siła
ciężkości; ciężkość; powaga
(np. sytuacji);ciężar(gatunkowy)
gravy ('grejwy) s. sos mięsny;
sok;dodatkowy zysk;osobista korzyść
gray (grej) adj. szary; zob.
grey ;v.szarzeć;s.szary kolor
graze (grejz) v. paść; drasnąć;
s. draśnięcie; muśnięcie;odarcie
grazing land ('grejzyŋg,laend)
s. pastwisko; pastwiska
grease (gri:s) s. tłuszcz; smar;
v. brudzić; smarować; nasmarować smarem(samochod etc.)
grease gun ('gri:s,gan) s. sma-
rownica wyciskowa ;towotnica
greasy('gri:sy)adj.tłusty;śliski

great (grjet) adj. wielki; du-
żły; świetny; znakomity; wspaniały ;zamiłowany;doniosły;pra-
greatcoat ('grejt'kout) s.
palto; płaszcz;opończa
great grandchild ('grejt'graend-
czajld) s. prawnuk
great grandfather ('grejt'-
graendfa:dzer) s. pradziadek
great grandmother ('grejt'-
grand,madzer) s. prababka
greatness ('grejtnys) s. wielkość; ogrom;wielkoduszność;powa-
ga
greed (gri:d) s. chciwość; zachłanność;żądza(władzy etc)
greedy (gri:dy) adj. chciwy;
zachłanny; łakomy; łapczywy;
żądny;zarłoczny;spragniony
Greek adj. grecki; (niezrozumiały);s.język grecki;Grek
green (gri:n) adj. zielony;
naiwny; młody; niedoświadczony; świeży; s. zieleń; zieleni-
na; trawnik;v.zielenić;naciągać
greenback ('gri:nbaek) s.
(slang) dolar(banknot)
greenhorn ('gri:nhorn) s. nowicjusz ;żółtodziub
greenhouse ('gri:nhaus) s.
cieplarnia
greenish ('gri:nysh) adj. zie-
lonkawy
greet ('gri:t) v. kłaniać się;
pozdrawiać; ukazać się; dojść
do (uszu);zaprezentować się
greeting ('gri:tyŋg)s. pozdrowienie; powitanie;pozdrowienia
grew (gru:) zob. grow
grey (grej) adj. szary; siwy;
s. szarość; v. szarzeć; si-
wiec(ortografia brytyjska)
greyhound ('grejhaund) s.
chart(wysoki;chudy,szybki ,pies)
grid (gryd) s. krata; sieć;
siatka ;sieć wysokiego napięcia
grief (gri:f) s. zmartwienie;
zgryzota ;smutek;żal
grievance ('gri:wens) s. uraza;
krzywda; skarga; zażalenie
grieve (gri:w) v. martwić;
krzywdzić; smucić ;zasmucić
grievious ('gri:wes) adj. dre-
czący; przykry ;ciężki;smutny

grill (gryl) s. rożen; krata;
potrawa z rusztu; v. smażyć
na różnie; przesłuchiwać
grim (grym) adj. srogi; ponury;
okrutny;groźny;odrażający
grimace (gri'mejs) s. grymas;
v. grymasić
grime,(grajm) s. brud; v. bru-
dzić(sadzą, smarem etc.)
grimy ('grajmy) adj. brudny;
wysmarowany; zatłuszczopy
grin (gryn) v. szczerzyć zęby;
uśmiechać się; s. uśmiech
grind; ground; ground (grajnd;
graund; graund)
grind,(grajnd) v. ostrzyc; toczyć; mleć; zgrzytać; trzeć;
harować; s. mlenie; harówka;
kujon;ciężka rutyna;kucie się
grindstone ('grajnd,stoun) s.
kamień szlifierski:harówka
grip (gryp) s, uchwyt; trzonek;
rękojeść; uścisk dłoni;walizka;
v. chwycić; złapać; trzymać
gripes (grajps) pl. kolka
gristle ('grysl) s. chrząstka
grit (gryt) s. żwir; piasek;
odwaga; wytrzymałość;charakter;
v. zgrzytać; skrzypieć;posypy-
groan (groun) s. jęk; v. jeczec
grocer ('grouser) s. właściciel
sklepu spożywczego
groceries ('grouserys) pl. towary spożywcze
grocery ('grousery) s. sklep
spożywczy;artykuł spożywczy
groin (grain) s. pachwina
groom (grum) s, parobek; pan
młody; v. obrzadzac; przygotowywać do objęcia stanowiska
groove (gru:w) s. bruzda; rowek; rutyna; v. żłobić; rowkować;nacinac zwojnik;gwintować
grope (group) v. szukać po omacku; iść po omacku;iść na slepo
gross (grous) adj. gruby; ordynarny; prostacki; całkowity;
hurtowy; tłusty; niesmaczny;
spasły; wybujały; s. 12 tuzi-
nów; v. uzyskac brutto...
ground (graund) s. grunt;zie-
mia; podstawa; podłoże; teren;
dno(morza);osad;powod;przyczyna

dno; v. l. osiąść na mieliźnie;
uziemiać; gruntować; zagrunto-
wać; v. 2. zob. grind
ground control ('graund,ken'troul)
kontrolna stacja (lotów)
ground crew ('graund.kru:) s.
załoga, ekipa na ziemi
ground floor ('graund,flo:r) s.
parter(bliski poziomu gruntu)
ground glass ('graund,glas) s.
tłuczone szkło
groundhog ('graundhog) s. świstak (amerykański)
groundless ('graundlys) adj.
bezpodstawny;gołosłowny
groundnut ('graundnat) s. orzeszek ziemny
ground staff ('graund,staf) s.
personel naziemny(lotnictwa etc.)
groundwork ('graundłerk) s. podstawa; podłoże; zasada; fundament;tło;osnowa;kanwa(utworu)
group (gru:p) s. grupa; v. gru-
pować;rozsegregowywać na grupy
grove (grouw) s. gaj
grow; grew; grown( grou; gru:
groun)
grow (grou) v. rosnąć; stawać
się; dojrzewać; hodować; sadzic
growl (graul) s. ryk; pomruk;
warczenie; v. mruknąć; warknąć;
burczeć; warczeć; odburknąć;
gderac;mrukliwie odpowiadać
grown (groun) v. zob. grow
grown-up ('groun,ap) adj. dorosły; s. dorosły człowiek
growth (groug) s. rozwój; wzrost;
uprawa; narosl;porost;przyrost
grub, (grab) .v karczować; dłubac: harować; wcinać (jedzenie)
grubby (graby) adj. brudny;
niechlujny;robaczywy
grudge (gradż) v. żałować; ską-
pić; zazdroscic; miec niechęc;
s. żal; uraza; niechęc
gruel (gruel) s. kaszka; kleik;
v. wymęczyc;zadawać bobu(komuś)
gruesome ('gru:sem) adj. okropny
gruff (graf) adj. burkliwy;
gburowaty; ochrypły;gruby(głos)
grumble ('grambl) v. narzekać;
utyskiwać;gderac;skarżyć się;
s.narzekanie; pomruk;szemranie

grumbler (grambler) s. zrzęda
grunt (grant) s. kwik; v. kwiczeć;chrząkać;wymruczeć
guarantee (,gaeren'ti:) v.
gwarantować; poręczać; s. poręczyciel;poręka;rękojmia
guarantor (,gaeren'to:r) s.
poręczyciel; poręczycielka
guaranty (,gaerenty) s. gwarancja; poręka;rękojmia;poręczenie
guard (ga:rd) v. pilnować;chronić; s. strażnik; opiekun;
obrońca; bezpiecznik
guard against ('ga:rd.e'genst)
v. zabezpieczać się przed...
guardhouse ('ga:rdhaus) s.
wartownia;tymczasowy areszt
guardian ('ga:rdjen) s. opiekun; kustosz;adj.opiekuńczy
guardianship ('ga:rdjenshyp)s.
opieka; opiekuństwo; kuratela
guess (ges) v. zgadywać; przypuszczać; myśleć; s. zgadywanie; przypuszczenie;zgadnięcie
guest (gest) s. gość
guest house ('gesthaus) s. pensjonat; osobny domek dla gości
guest room ('gestru:m) s. pokój gościnny;gościnna sypialnia
guidance ('gajdens) s. kierownictwo; poradnictwo;kierowanie
guide (gajd) s. przewodnik; doradca;v.wskazywać drogę;prowadzić
guidebook ('gajdbuk) s. przewodnik (książka)dla turystów
guild (gyld) s. cech; związek
guildhall('gyld'ho:l) s. dom
cechowy; ratusz;dom związkowy
guile (gajl) s. oszustwo
guileless ('gajllys) adj.
szczery; otwarty(w postępowaniu)
guilt (gylt) s. wina;przestępstwo
guiltless ('gyltlys) adj. niewinny;wolny od zarzutu
guilty ('gylty) adj. winny
guinea pig ('gynypyg) s. świnka morska;przedmiot experymentów
guitar (gy'ta:r) s. gitara
gulf (galf) s. zatoka; przepaść; wir; v. pochłaniać
gull (gal) s. mewa;v.oszukiwać
gullet (galyt) s. przełyk; gardło; gardziel

gully ('galy) s. wąwoz; ściek; kanał; v. żłobić;wyżłobić;poryć
gulp (galp) s. łyk; duży kęs
gulp down (galpdałn) v. łykać; dławić się; hamować łzy
gum (gam) s. dziąsło; guma; v. kleić;wydzielać żywicę
gun (gan) s. strzelba; armata; pistolet;działo;wystrzał armatni
gunpowder ('gan,pałder) s. proch strzelniczy;proch armatni
gurgle ('ge:rgle) v. bulgotać; bełkotać;s.bulgotanie;szemranie
gush (gasz) s. ulewa; wylew; v. tryskać; lać się;wytrysnać
gust (gast) s. podmuch; wybuch
gut (gat) s. kiszka; v. patroszyć;wypalić wnętrze (domu)
guts (gats) pl. wnętrzności
gutter ('gater) v. wyżłobić; okapywać; s. rynna; rynsztok; rów; wyżłobienie; adj. rynsztokowy; brukowy(dziennik)
guy (gaj) s. facet; człek; cuma; v. cumować; uwiązać
gym (dżym) s. sala gimnastyczna; gimnastyka(przedmiot w szkole)
gymnasium (dżym'nejzjem) s. sala gimnastyczna;hala sportowa
gymnastics (dżym'naestyks) s. gimnastyka;ćwiczenia fizyczne
gynecologist (,gajny'koledżyst) s. ginekolog
gypsy ('dżypsy) s. cygan; cyganka;cyganeria;język cygański
gyrate (,dżaje'rejt) v. wirować; kręcić się(wg.koła lub spirali)
h (ejcz) ósma litera angielskiego alfabetu (prawie niema)
haberdasher ('haeberdaeszer) s. kupiec galanteryjny;szmuklerz
habit ('haebyt) s. zwyczaj; nałog; usposobienie; przyzwyczajenie; habit; v. odziewać się
habitation (,haeby'tejszyn) s. miejsce zamieszkania;zamieszkiwanie
habitual (he'bytjual) adj. zwykły; nałogowy; zwyczajny
hack (haek) v. siekać; rąbać; kopać; kaszleć; s. szrama; motyka; szkapa; najemnik; taksówka; adj. wynajęty; spowszedniały; banalny;oklepany;szablonowy

hacksaw ('haekso:) s. piła do
metalu (z drobnymi zębami)
had (haed) zob. have
haddock ('haedek) s. łupacz
h(a)emorrhage ('hemerydż) s.
krwotok;v. mieć krwotok
hag (haeg) s. wiedźma; czarownica;brzydka zła kobieta
haggard ('haegerd) adj. wynędz-
niały; strapiony; wychudły
hail (hejl) s. grad; powitanie;
v. grad pada; witać; pozdrawiać; zawołać;walić jak gradem
hair (heer) s. włos; włosy
hairbrush ('heerbrasz) s.
szczotka do włosów
haircut ('heerkat) s. ostrzyże-
nie;styl strzyżenia włosów
hairdo ('heerdu:) s. uczesanie;
fryzura;styl uczesania
hairdresser ('heer,dreser) s.
fryzjer damski
hairdryer ('heer,drajer) s. suszarka do włosów(elektryczna)
hairless ('h-erlys) adj. bez-
włosy; łysy;wyłysiały
hairpin ('heerpyn) s. szpilka
do włosów
hairy (heery) adj. włochaty
half (ha:f) s. połowa; adj.pół;
adv. na pół; po połowie
half an hour ('ha:f,en'aur) s.
pół godziny
half brother ('ha:f,bradzer)
s. przyrodni brat
half-breed ('ha:f,bri:d) s.
mieszaniec
halftime ('ha:f'tajm) s. przerwa; pół etatu;a.pół-etatowy
halfway ('ha:f'łej) adv. w pół
drogi; w połowie drogi
hall (ho:l) s. sień; sala; hala;
dwór; gmach publiczny;westybul
hallo ! (he'lou) excl.;czesć !
halo ! czolem! dzień dobry!
halo ('hejlou) s. nimb; aureola
halt (ho:lt) v. zatrzymać; utykać; kulec; wahać się; s.po-
stój; przystanek;utykanie
halter ('ho:lter) s. kantar pa-
stewny; stryczek;v.nakładać kan-
halve (ha:w) v. przepołowic ;po
dzielic się po połowie

ham (haem) s. szynka
hamburger ('haembe:rger) s. sie-
kany kotlet wołowy; bułka z
siekanym kotletem wołowym
hamlet ('haemlyt) s. wioska;
sioło; malutka wieś
hammer ('haemer) s. młotek;
v. bić młotkiem; walić
hammock ('haemok) s. hamak
hamper ('haemper) v. zawadzac;
krępowac; s. kosz z wiekiem
hamster ('haemster) s. chomik
hand (haend) s. ręka; dłoń;
pismo; v. podac; zwijac; pomagac;a.podręczny;przenosny
hand back ('haend,baek) v. od-
dac; podac do tyłu
hand down ('haend,dałn) v. przekazac; dac w spadku;podac w dół
hand in ('haend,yn) v. wręczyc
hand over ('haend,ouwer) v.,
wręczvc; podac; dostarczyc
handbag ('haendbaeg) s. damska
torebka
handbill ('haendbyl) s. ulotka
handbook ('haend-buk) s. podręcznik; poradnik
hand brake ('haend,brejk) s.
hamulec ręczny
handcuff ('haendka:f) s. kajdany; v. zakuwac w kajdany
handful ('haendful) s. garsc;
garstka; kłopotliwa osoba
handicap ('haendykaep) s. przeszkoda; uposledzenie; trudnosc
handicraft ('haendykra:ft) s.
rzemiosło; rękodzieło (tkactwo
etc.)
handkerchief ('henkerczy:f) s.
apaszka; chustka do nosa
handle ('haendl) s. trzonek;
rękojesc; uchwyt; sposób;
v. dotykac; manipulowac; traktowac; załatwiac; dac radę;
handlowac;zarzadzac;kontrolowac
handlebar ('haendlba:r) s. kie-
rownica( od roveru)
hand luggage ('haend,lagydż) s.
bagaż ręczny
handmade ('haend'mejd) adj.
ręcznie zrobiony
handrail ('haend,rejl) s. poręcz; bariera;balustrada

handshake ('haend,shejk) s. uścisk dłoni(w pozdrowieniu,targu)

handsome ('haensem) s. przystojny; szczodry;znaczny(datek)

handwork ('haend,łe:rk) s. robota ręczna;praca fizyczna

handwriting ('haend,rajtyŋg) s. pismo; charakter pisma

handy ('haendy) adj. zręczny; wygodny; bliski;pod ręką

hang; hung; hung (haeŋg; haŋg; haŋg)

hang (haeŋg) s. wieszać; powiesić; rozwiesić; wywiesić; zwisać; s. nachylenie; pochyłość;powiązanie;orientacja

hang around ('haeŋg e'raund) v. wałęsać się;obijać się

hang out ('haeŋg'aut) v. wywieszać; wychylać się

hang up ('haeŋg,ap) v. zaczepić się; powiesić słuchawkę; opóźniać (pracę);wstrzymywać

hangar ('haeŋger) s. hangar

hang-glider ('haeŋg'glajder) s. lotnia; skrzydło Rogali

hangings ('haeŋyŋz) s. kotary; portiery;draperie;obicia;firanki

hang loose ('haeŋ,lu:z) v. być rozluźniony w akcji (sportowej); zwisać swobodnie

hangover ('haeŋg,ouwer) s. (slang) kac; przeżytek

hanky-panky ('haeŋky-paenky) s. hokus-pokus;też rozwiązłość

haphazard ('haep'haezerd) s. los szczęścia; przypadek; adj. przypadkowy; dorywczy; adv. przypadkowo;na chybił trafił

happen ('haepen) v. zdarzać się; trafić się; przypadkowo być (gdzieś);mieć(nie)szczęście

happen on ('haepen,on) v. przypadkiem spotkać;natknąć się na

happening ('haepenyŋg) s. wydarzenie; wypadek;zdarzenie

happily ('haepyly) adv. szczęśliwie;na szczęście;trafnie

happiness ('haepynys) s. szczęście; zadowolenie; radość

happy ('haepy) adj. szczęśliwy; zadowolony;właściwy (wybór); mądra (rada); radosny

happy-go-lucky ('haepy,gou'laky) adj. beztroski

harass ('haeres) v. niepokoić; trapić; dręczyć; nękać

harbor ('ha:rber) s. przystań; port; v. gościć; dawać schronienie; zawijać do portu

hard (ha:rd) adj. twardy; surowy; trudny; ciężki; ostry; adv. usilnie; wytrwale; ciężko; z trudem; siarczyście

hard by ('ha:rd,baj) adv. blisko;tuż obok; w pobliżu

hard up ('ha:rd,ap) być w kłopotach pieniężnych

hard of hearing (ha:rd,ow'hieryŋg) adj. głuchawy

harden ('ha:rdn) v. twardnieć; uodpornić; stabilizować

hardheaded ('ha:rd'hedyd) adj. trzeźwy; praktyczny;twardy człowiek

hardhearted ('ha:rd'ha:rtyd) adj. nieczuły; niemiłosierny

hardly ('ha:rdly) adv. ledwie; zaledwie; prawie; z trudem; surowo;chyba nie; rzadko

hardness ('ha:rdnys) s. twardość; wytrzymałość;odporność

hardship ('ha:rdszyp) s. trudność; trudy; męka; znój

hardware ('ha:rdłeer) s. wyroby żelazne;towary żelazne

hare (heer) s. zając;królik

harebell ('heer-bel) s. dzwonek okrągłolistny

hark (ha:rk) v. słuchaj; uważaj; odejdź;słuchaj uważnie

harm (ha:rm) s. szkoda; krzywda; v. szkodzić; krzywdzić

harmful ('ha:rmful) adj. szkodliwy;szkodzący;zadający ból

harmless ('ha:rmlys) adj. nieszkodliwy; niewinny

harmonious (ha:rmounjes) adj. harmonijny;melodyjny;zgodny

harmonize ('ha:rmenajz) s. uzgadniać; harmonizować

harmony ('ha:rmeny) s. harmonia (dzwięków,ludzi);zgoda

harness ('ha:rnys) s. uprząż; v. zaprzęgać;zużytkować(wiatr...)

harp (ha:rp) s. harfa; v. gadać w kółko; grać na harfie

harpoon (ha:'rpu:n) s. harpun;
v. ugodzić harpunem
harrow ('haerou) s. brona; v.
bronować; dręczyć; szarpać;
ranić; pustoszyć; niszczyć
harsh (ha:rsz) adj. szorstki;
żrący; ostry; cierpki; przykry; surowy;nieprzyjemny
hart (ha:rt) s. rogacz (dorosły)(powyżej pięcioletni)
harvest('ha:rwyst) s. żniwa;
zbiory; zbiór; urodzaj; plony; v. zbierać (zboże); zbierać (plony);sprzątać z pól
harvester ('ha:rwyter) s. żniwiarz; żniwiarka (mechaniczna)
has (haez) (on,ona.ono) ma;
zob. have
hash (haesz) s. siekane mięso;
v. siekać;knocić;przemieszać
haste (hejst) s. pospiech
hasten (hejstn) v.przyśpieszać;
spieszyć;być szybkim
hasty ('hejsty) adj. pospieszny; prędki; porywczy;niecier-
hat (haet) s. kapelusz ᵖˡⁱʷʸ
hatch (haecz) v. wysiadywać;
wylęgać; wykłuwać; knuć; za-
kreskować; s. wyląg; łuk;
drzwiczki; śluza; kreska
hatchet ('haeczyt) s. toporek
hatchet man('haeczyt,men) s.
człowiek przeprowadzający ʲᵇᵒᵗᵉ
czystkę(odrabiający brudną ro-
hate (hejt) s. nienawiść;
v. nienawidzieć;nieznosić
hateful ('hejtful) adj. nienawistny;zasługujący na nienawiść
hatred ('hejtryd) s. nienawiść
haughtiness ('ho:tynys) s.pysz-
ność; hardość;zarozumialstwo
haughty ('ho:ty) adj. hardy;
pyszny;zarozumiały;wzgardliwy
haul (ho:l) s. wleczenie; holowanie; ładunek; połów; zysk;
v. wlec; ciągnąć; holować;
wozić; transportować;taszczyć
haunch (ho:ncz) s. biodro z udem
haunt (ho:nt) v. nawiedzać;
s, miejsce często odwiedzane;
melina; spelunka;legowisko
have; had; had (haew; haed;
haed)

have (haew) v. mieć; otrzymać;
zawierać; nabyć; musieć
have-not ('haev,nat) adj. nieposiadający; biedny
have on ('haew on) v. mieć na
sobie;być ubranym w
have to do ('haew,tu'du) v. musieć (coś) robić
haven ('hejwn) s. przystań; port;
v. dawać schronienie; wprowadzać do portu
havoc ('haewek) s. spustoszenie
hawk (ho:k) s. jastrząb; packa;
chrząknięcie; v. polować
z jastrzębiem; sprzedawać na
ulicy; chrząkać głośno
hawthorn ('ho:torn) s. głóg
hay (hej) s. siano
haycock ('hejkok) s. stóg siana
hayfever ('hej'fi:ver) s. uczu-
lenie; katar sienny
hayloft ('hej-loft) s. strych
na siano (w stodole etc.)
hayrick ('hejryk) s. stóg siana
haystack ('hejsta:k) s. stóg
siana (w polu, na łące etc.)
hazard ('haezerd) s. przypadek;
traf; ryzyko; v. ryzykować
hazardous ('haezerdes) adj. ryzykowny; hazardowny; niebezpieczny
haze (hejz) s. lekka mgła
hazel ('hejzl) s. leszczyna;
kolor orzechowy
hazel-nut ('hejzl-nat) s. orzech
laskowy
hazy ('hejzy) adj. mglisty;
zamglony; nieco podchmielony
H-bomb ('ejcz bom) s. bomba wodorowa
he (hi:) pron. on
head (hed) s. głowa: łeb; szef;
naczelnik; nagłówek; szczyt;
v. prowadzić; kierować (się)
head over heels ('hed,ouwer'-
hi:ls) do góry nogami; na łeb
na szyję; panicznie;w panice
head or tail ('hed,o:r'tejl)
orzeł czy reszka
headache ('hedejk) s. ból głowy
headgear ('hedgi:r) s. nakrycie głowy;ubiór głowy

heading ('hedyŋ g)s. nagłówek
headland ('hedlend) s. przylądek (daleko wysunięty w morze)
headlights ('hedlajts) pl.
główne światła samochodu
headline ('hedlajn) s. nagłówek (w gazecie);wiadomość w skró-cie
headlong ('hedloŋg) adv. na
łeb na szyję; na złamanie karku; na oślep;głową na przód
headmaster ('hedma:ster) s.
dyrektor (szkoły)
headphones ('hedfouns) pl.
słuchawki(radiowe,gramofonowe)
headquarters ('hed'kło:terz)
pl. kwatera główna;główne biuro
headstrong ('hedstroŋg) adj.
zawzięty; uparty;bezwzgledny
headway ('hedłej) s. postęp
heal (hi:l) v. leczyć; łagodzić; uspakajać;wyleczać się
heal up ('hi:l,ap) v. zagoic
health (hels) s. zdrowie
health resort (hels ry'zo:rt)
s. uzdrowisko
healthy (helsy) adj. zdrowy;
potężny;spowodowany zdrowiem
heap (hi:p) s. kupa; gromada;
v. gromadzic; ładować na stos;
obsypywać dużą ilością
hear; heard; heard (hier; he:rd;
he:rd)
hear (hier) v. słyszec; usły-
szec; sluchac; dowiedzieć się
heard (he:rd) zob. hear
hearing ('hieryŋg)s. słuch;
posłuch; przesłuchanie; rozprawa;zasięg głosu;słyszenie
hearsay ('hiersej) s. pogłoska
hearse (he:rs) s. karawan
heart (ha:rt) s. serce; odwaga; otucha; sedno;symbol serca
heartbreaking ('ha:rtbrejkyŋg)
adj. rozdzierający serce
heartburn ('ha:rtbe:rn) s.
zgaga; pieczenie w żołądku
hearth (ha:rs) s. palenisko
heartless ('ha:rtlys) adj. nieczuły; bez serca
heart transplant ('ha:rt,traens-
pla:nt) przeszczepienie serca
hearty ('ha:rty) adj. serdeczny;
szczery; otwarty;pożywny;obfity;
solidny;dobry;krzepki;rześki

heat (hi:t) s. gorąco; upał;
żar; ciepło; uniesienie; pasja; popęd płciowy (zwierząt)
heater ('hi:ter) s. grzejnik;
piec
heath (hi:s) s. wrzos; wrzo-
siec; wrzosowisko
heathen (hi:zen) adj. pogański;
s. poganin. ciemniak
heather ('hedzer) s. wrzos
heating ('hi:tyŋg)s. ogrzewanie
heave; hove; hove (hi:w; houw;
houw)
heave (hi:w) v. unosic; dźwigać; podwazać; nabrzmiewac;
wyciągac; sapac; s. dźwignię-
cie; przesunięcie
heaven ('hewn) s. niebo; raj;
niebiosa
heavenly ('hewnly) adj. niebieski; niebiański; boski
heaviness ('hewynys) s. cięż-
kosć; ociężałość
heavy ('hewy) adj. ciężki; duży; ponury; zrozpaczony
heavy-handed ('hewy'haendyd)
adj. niezgrabny; nietaktowny;
bezwzględny
heavy traffic ('hewy'traefyk)
ciężki ruch (np. kołowy)
heavyweight ('hewyłejt) s.
waga ciężka
hectic ('hektyk) adj. gorący;
dziki; niszczący; rozgorącz-
kowany
hedge (hedż) s. płot; żywopłot;
ogrodzenie; zapora; ubezpieczenie; v. ogradzać; wykręcać się;
ubezpieczać się w spekulacji
hedgehog ('hedżhog) s. jeż;
świnka morska
heed (hi:d) s. troska; dbałosć;
uwaga; wzgląd; ostrożność;
v. uważać; baczyć
heedful ('hi:dful) adj. uważny;
ostrożny
heedless ('hi:dlys) adj. niedbały; nieostrożny; nieuważny
heel (hi:l) s. pięta; obcas;
przechył; łajdak; v.dotykać
piętą; podbijać obcas;zaopatry-
wać; przechylac się;tupać obca-sem

he goat ('hi:gout) s. kozioł
heifer ('hefer) s. jałówka
height (hajt) s. wysokość;
wzniesienie; wyniosłość;
szczyt;najwyższa granica
heighten (hajtn) v. podnosic,
podwyższac;powiększać etc.
heinous ('hejnes) adj. potworny; ohydny;nienawistny;haniebny
heir (eer) s. spadkobierca;
dziedzic; następca
heiress ('eerys) s. spadkobier-
czyni; następczyni; dziedzicz-
ka (majątku, tytułu etc.)
held (held) zob. hold
helicopter ('helykopter) s.
śmigłowiec; helikopter
hell (hel) s. piekło; psiakrew ! miejsce nędzy i okrucień-stwa
hello ('he'lou) excl.: hallo !
helm (helm) s. ster;v.sterować
helmet ('helmyt) s. hełm; kask
help (help) v. pomagać; usługiwac; nakładać (jedzenie)
s. pomoc; pomocnik; robotnik
helper ('helper) s. pomocnik
helpful ('helpful) adj. pomocny; przydatny; użyteczny
helping ('helpyng) s. porcja
(jedzenia);udzielanie pomocy
helpless ('helplys) adj. bezradny; bez pomocy ;słaby
helplessness ('helplysnys) s.
bezradność ;słabość
helter-skelter ('helter'skelter)
adv. na łapu-capu; na łeb na
szyję; s. popłoch; bezładny
pospiech(w bałaganie)
hem (hem) s. brzeg; obrąbek;
chrząkanie; v. obrębiać; otoczyc; pochrząkiwać; wahać się
hem in ('hem,yn) v. okrążyć;
zamknąć; obrębić
hemisphere ('hemysfier) s. półkula (zachodnia,wschodnia etc.)
hemline ('hemlajn) s. obrąbek
(spódnicy)
hemlock ('hemlek) s. szalej;
cykuta jadowita; drzewo tsuga
hemp (hemp) s. konopie; adj.
konopny (sznur etc.)
hemstitch ('hemstycz) s. mereż-
ka; v. mereżkować(ozdobnie)

hen (hen) s. kura; kwoka; baba
hence (hens) adv. stąd; odtąd;
a więc; przeto; dlatego
henceforth (hens'fo:rs) adv.
odtąd; na przyszłość;od teraz
hen coop ('henku:p) s. kurnik
hen house ('henhaus) s, kurnik
henpecked ('henpekt) s. pantoflarz;adj.będący pod pantoflen
her (he:r) pron. ją; jej; adj.
jej (należący)do niej
herald ('hereld) s. zwiastun;
v. zwiastować; wprowadzac
heraldry ('hereldry) s. heral-
dyka;pompa; ceremonia
herb (he:rb) s. zioło (jednoroczne)
herd (he:rd) s. trzoda; stado;
pastuch; v. iść stadem;zganiac
w stado; pasć;popędzać stadem
herdsman ('he:rdzmen) s. pasterz; pastuch
here (hier) adv. tu; tutaj; oto
here you are (,hier'ju:,a:r)
exp.;tu pan ma !proszę bardzo !
hereafter ('hier'a:fter) adv.
odtąd; poniżej; potem; w życiu pozagrobowym; s, przyszłość; przyszłe życie
hereby ('hier'bay) adv. przez
to; w ten sposób; skutkiem
tego; w pobliżu
hereditary (hy'redytery) adj.
dziedziczny; odziedziczony;
tradycyjny;przekazany dziedzicz-nie
herein ('hie'ryn) adv. tutaj;
tam że; wobec tego; w tych
warunkach;w tym(rozdziale etc.)
hereof ('hier'ow) adv. tego;
o tym ;w odniesieniu do tego
heresy ('herysy) s. herezja
hereupon ('hiere'pon) adv.
potem; skutkiem tego; o tym
herewith ('hier'łys) adv. ni-
niejszym ;w ten sposób
heritage ('herytydż) s. spuści-
na; spadek; dziedzictwo
hermit ('he:rmyt) s. pustelnik;
odludek;eremita;pustelnica
hero ('hierou) s. bohater
heroic ('hierouyk) adj. bohaterski ;heroiczny;epiczny; bardzo wymowny; podniosły

heroine ('hierouyn) s.bohaterka
heroism ('hierouyzem) s.
bohaterstwo (w czynach i ce- ʃchach)
heron ('heren) s. czapla
herring ('heryŋg)s. śledz
hers (he:rz) pron. jej
herself (he:r'self) pron. ona
sama; ona sobie; ja sama
hesitate ('hezytejt) v. wahać
się ;byc niepewnym;zatrzymać ʃsię
hesitation (,hezytejszyn) s.
wahanie;być niezdecydowanym
hew; hewed; hewn (hju:; hju:d;
hju:n)
hew (hju:) v. rąbać; ciosac;
kuc; wyrąbywać(ścieżkę etc.)
hewn (hju:n) zob: hew
hey (hej) excl.; hej ! ej że!
heyday ('hejdej) s. pełnia;
rozkwit; świetny nastrój
hi (haj) excl.; hej ! (pozdrowienie) ; cześć! czołem!
hiccup; hiccough ('hykap) s.
czkawka; v. miec czkawkę
hid (hyd) zob, hide
hidden (hydn) zob. hide
hide; hid; hidden (hajd; hyd;
hydn)
hide (hajd) v. chować; ukrywać;
s. kryjówka; skóra (zwierzęca)
hide-and-seek ('hajd,en si:k)
exp.: zabawa w chowanego
hideous ('hydjes) adj. ochydny;
wstrętny ;paskudny;odrażający
hiding ('hajdyŋg)s. kryjówka;
skórobicie ; lanie;manto
hiding place ('hajdyŋg'plejs)
s. kryjówka; melina
hi-fi ('haj'faj) = high-fideli-
ty ('haj fy'delyty) wiernie
odtwarzający dźwięk (aparat)
high (haj) adj. wysoki; wyniosły; silny;cienki(głos)
highbrow ('hajbrau) s. intelektualista;a. intelektualny
high diving('hajdajwyŋg) s.
skakanie z wieży do wody
high jump('hajdżamp) s. skok
wzwyż (w sporcie)
highlands ('hajlend) s. pod-
górze; góry;górzysty kraj
highlights ('hajlajts) pl. główne punkty (np. programu)

highly ('hajly) adv. wysoko; wysoce; wielce; zaszczytnie
highness ('hajnys) s. wysokość
(tytuł); wyniosłość
high-pitched ('haj'pyczt) adj.
wysoki; ostry; cienki (głos)
spadzisty; stromy (dach)
high-powered ('haj'pałerd) adj.
potężny
high-pressure ('haj'preszer)
adj. wysokiego ciśnienia; na-
chalny
highroad ('haj'roud) s. szosa;
główna droga
high-school ('haj'sku:l) s.
gimnazjum; szkoła srednia
high-strung ('haj'straŋg)adj.
nerwowy; napięty; wrażliwy
high-tide ('haj'tajd) s. przypływ
highway ('haj'łej) s. szosa
highwayman ('haj,łejmen) s.
rozbójnik
hijack ('hajdżaek) v. rabować;
grabić
hike (hajk) v. włóczyć się;
wędrować; wyciągać do góry;
s. wycieczka; podwyżka
hilarious (hy'leerjes)adj.wesoły;
hałaśliwie wesoły
hill (hyl) s. górka; pagórek;
kopiec; v. sypać kopiec
hillbilly ('hylbyly) s. pro-
wincjał
hillside ('hyl'sajd) s. stok
hilly ('hyly) adj. pagórkowaty;
górzysty
hilt (hylt) s. rękojeść; garda
him (hym) pron. jego; go; jemu;
mu
himself (hym'self) pron. się;
siebie; sobie; sam; osobiście;
we własnej osobie
hind (hajnd) s. parobek; łania;
adj. tylny; zadni
hinder ('hynder) v. przeszkadzać; powstrzymywać
hind leg ('hajnd,leg) s. tylna
noga
hindrance ('hyndrens) s. przeszkoda ; zawada;zawadzanie
hindsight('hajnd,sajt)s.zrozu-
mienie co trzeba było zrobić

hinge (hyndż) s. zawiasa; v.ob-
racać; zależeć; zawiesić na
zawiasach;wisieć na zawiasach
hinny (hyny) s. muł (z oślicy
i ogiera)
hint (hynt) s. aluzja; przytyk;
wskazówka; v. napomknąć; dać
do zrozumienia;zrobić aluzję
hinterland ('hynter,laend) s.
zaplecze; daleki teren
hip (hyp) s. biodro; naroże
dachu; chandra;adj.biodrowy
hippie (hypi:) s. niekonformista; adj. zbuntowany przeciw
tradycji (wyobcowany)
hippopotamus (hype'potemes) s.
hipopotam
hire (hajer) s. najem; opłata
za najem; v. najmować; wynajmować; dzierżawić;odnajmować
hire out ('hajer aut) v. wynaj-
mować(się do pracy,na służbę...)
hire purchase ('hajer'pe:rczys)
wynajem - zakup na raty
his (hyz) pron. jego
hiss (hys) v. syczeć; gwizdać;
s. syk; gwizd;głoska sycząca
historian (hys'to:rjen) s.
historyk;historyczka
historic (hys'toryk) adj. histo-
ryczny;sławny w historii
history ('hystory) s. historia;
dzieje; przeszłość (znana)
hit (hyt) s. uderzenie; przytyk; sukces; sensacja; v. uderzyć; utrafić; natrafić; zabić
hit and run ('hyt,en'ran) adj.
uciekający od wypadku (drogowego); walczący podjazdowo;
dorywczy i niepewny
hitman ('hytmen) s. najemny
zabójca;najemny morderca
hit or miss (hyt o:r mys) adv.
na chybił trafił;przypadkiem
hit upon ('hyte'pon) v. natrafić (na coś,na kogoś)
hitch (hycz) s. zacisnięcie;
węzeł; przeszkoda; szarpnięcie;
uchwyt; służba (wojskowa)
v. doczepić; uczepić; pociągnąć; szarpnąć; przywiązać; za
czepić się;ciągnąć szarpiąc

hitchhike ('hycz,hajk) v. jechać autostopem
hitchhiker ('hycz,hajker) s.
jadący autostopem
hither ('hydzer) adv. dotąd;
tutaj;adj. bliżej
hitherto ('hydzer'tu:) adv.
dotychczas; do tej pory
hive (hajw) s. ul; rojowisko;
v. umieszczać w ulu; wchodzić
do ula;zbierać do ula
hoard (ho:rd),v. gromadzić;
zbierać; s. zapas. zbiór; skarb
hoarfrost ('ho: r'frost) s.
szron(na trawie,włosach etc.)
hoarse (ho:rs) adj. zachrypnięty; v. zachrypnąć;mieć chrapliwy
hoax (houks) v. bujać; nabie-głos
rać; s. bujda; kaczka;kawał
hobble ('hobl) s. pętą; utyka-
nie; v. utykać; kuleć; pętać
hobby ('hoby) s. hobby; pasja
(np. filatelistyka)
hobbyhorse ('hobyho:rs) s.
konik na kiju do zabawy(na biegu-nach)
hobgoblin ('hob,goblyn) s.
skrzat; chochlik
hobnob ('hobnob) v. być za pan
brat;blisko się zadawać
hobo('haubou) s. włóczęga
hock (hok) s. pęcina; v. zastawić (się) w lombardzie
hockey ('hoky) s. hokej
hoe (hou) s. motyka; graca;
v. gracować;okopywać motyką
hog (hog) s. wieprz; człowiek
zachłanny; v. łapać dla siebie; jechać środkiem; wyginąć
łukowato w środku;zagarniać so-bie
hoist (hojst) s. dźwig; wyciąg;
v. wyciagać ładunek w górę;
wywieszać(flagę);podciągać do góry
hold; held; held (hould; held;
held)
hold (hould) v. trzymać; posiadać; zawierać; powstrzymywać;
uważać; obchodzić; wytrzymywać; trwać; s. chwyt; pauza;
pomieszczenie; więzienie;
twierdza;silny wpływ;uchwyt
hold back ('hould,baek) v.
powstrzymać; zataić;wahać się

hold on ('hould,on) v. trzymać
się; wytrzymywać;powstrzymać
holdup ('hould'ap) s. zatrzymanie; zator; napad rabunkowy
holder ('houlder) s. właściciel; posiadacz; uchwyt
holding ('houldyng) s. posiadłość; portfel akcji; dzierżawa;uchwyt;ujęcie;trzymanie
hole (houl) s. dziura; nora;
dołek; v. dziurawić; przedziurawić;przekopywać(tunel)
holiday ('holedy) s. święto;
wakacje; urlop;adj.wesoły;ra-/
holidaymaker   ('holedy,mejker)
s. wczasowicz; letnik; turysta;wycieczkowicz;letniczka
holler ('holer) v. wrzeszczeć;
krzyczeć(po prostacku)
hollow ('holou) s. dziupla;
dziura; kotlina; dolina;
adj. wklęsły; dziurawy; fałszywy; głuchy; pusty; czczy;
głodny;nieszczery;adv.pusto
hollow out ('holou,aut) v.
drążyć;wydrążyć;żłobić
holly ('holy) s. ostrokrzew
holy ('holy) adj. święty
homage ('homydż) s. hołd
home (houm) s. dom; ojczyzna;
kraj; schronisko; bramka;
adj. domowy; rodzinny; krajowy; wewnętrzny; ojczysty
homeless ('houmlys) adj. bezdomny;bez dachu nad głowa
homely ('houmly) adj, swojski;
pospolity; nieładny; prosty;
skromny;niewybredny;niewyszu-/
homemade   ('houm'mejd) adj.
domowego wyrobu; krajowy
homesick   ('houm-syk) adj.
stęskniony za domem rodzinnym;
stęskniony za (czyms swoim)
homesickness   ('houm,syknys)
s. nostalgia;tęsknota za domem
home team ('houm-ti:m) s. drużyna miejscowa (sportowa)
home trade ('houm-trejd) s.
handel wewnętrzny
homewards ('houm ledz) adv. ku
domowi (ojczyźnie);do domu

homework ('houmłerk) s. zadanie
domowe;odrabianie lekcji
homicide ('homy,sajd) s. zabójca; zabójstwo
honest ('onyst) adj. uczciwy;
prawy; przyzwoity; szczery;
adv. naprawdę
honesty,('onesty) s. zacnosć;
prawosć; rzetelnosć; uczciwosć
honey ('hany) s. miód;słodycz
honeycomb ('hany,koum) s. (woskowy) plaster pszczeli;
v. dziurawić; przenikać
honeymoon ('hany,mu:n) s. miodowy miesiąc;v.spędzić miodowy miesiąc
honk (honk) s. krzyk gęsi; głos
trąbki, klaksonu; v. trąbić;
(slang; wymyślać)
honorary ('onerery) adj. honorowy (np. urząd);bezpłatny
honor ('oner) s. cześć; uczciwosć; cnota; tytuł sędziego;
v. czcić; zaszczycać; honorować
honorable ('onerebl) adj. czcigodny; uczciwy; szanowny; honorowy; zaszczytny;poważany
hood (hud) s. kaptur; kapturek;
maska; buda; v. zaopatrywać
w kaptur; przykrywać
hoodlum ('hu:dlem) s. opryszek;
chuligan;łobuz
hoodwink ('hudłynk) v. oczy mydlic; zmylic;zawiązywać oczy
hoof ('hu:f) s. kopyto; v. kopać; iść; tańczyć;iść pieszo
hook (huk) s. hak; v. zahaczyć;
zakrzywić (sie);złapać (męża)
hoop (hu:p) s. obręcz; v. otaczać obręczą;wykrzyknąć
hooping cough ('hu:pyng-kof) s.
koklusz; krztusiec,zob.whooping-
cough
hoot (hu:t) s. hukanie; odgłosy
niezadowolenia; v. hukać; gwizdać; wyć; trabić;wygwizdać
hooves (hu:wz) pl. kopyta
hop (hop) s. chmiel; skok; po-
tancówka; v. podskakiwać; po-
derwać (sie); przeskakiwać
hope (houp) s. nadzieja; v.
mieć nadzieję;spodziewać sie;ufać;
żywić nadzieję

hopeful ('houpful) adj, pełen
nadziei; ufny; obiecujący;
rokujący nadzieje
hopeless ('houplys) adj. beznadziejny; rozpaczliwy; zrozpaczony; zdesperowany
horde (ho:rd) s. horda; gromada
horizon (he'rajzen) s. horyzont
widnokrąg; warstwa oznaczona
horizontal (,hory'zontel) adj.
poziomy; horyzontalny; widno-
kręgowy; s. płaszczyzna po-
zioma;poziom równy i płaski
horn (ho:rn) s. róg; trąbka;
syrena; kula (siodła)
v. bóść; przebóść;wmieszać się
hornet ('ho:rnyt) s. szerszeń
horny ('ho:rny) adj. rogowy;
zrogowaciały;rogaty;jak róg
horrible ('horebl) adj. straszny; okropny;szokujący;paskudny
horrid ('horyd) adj. straszny;
ohydny; odrażajacy;paskudny
horrify ('horyfaj) v. przerażać;
oburzać;ciężko szokować
horror ('horer) s. groza; wstręt;
odraza; przerażenie;dreszcz
horse ('ho:rs) s. koń; konnica;
jazda; kozioł z drzewa
horseback ('ho:rs,baek) s.
grzbiet koński;adv. konno
horsefly ('ho:rs,flaj) s.giez
horsehair ('ho:rs,heer) s.
włosie końskie;sztywna tkanina
horseman ('ho:rsmen) s. jeździec
horse opera ('ho:rs'opere) s.
film kowbojski (nie-realistyczny)
horseplay ('ho:rs,plej) s. ordy-
narna zabawa (brutalna)
horsepower ('ho:rs,pałer) s.
koń mechaniczny= 746 watów
horse race ('ho:rs,rejs) s.
wyścigi konne
horseradish ('ho:rs,raedysh)
s. chrzan; a. chrzanowy
horseshoe ('ho:rs,szu) s. podkowa;a.w kształcie podkowy
horticulture('ho:rty,kaltczer)
s. ogrodnictwo
hose (houz) s. pończochy; wąż do
podlewania(wiedza i praktyka)
hosiery ('haouzery) s. trykotaże;
pończochy

hospitable ('hospytebl) adj.
gościnny; szczodry dla gości
hospital ('hospytl) s. szpital;
lecznica;a. szpitalny
hospitality (, hospy'taelyty)
s. gościnność
host (houst) s. gospodarz; ży-
wiciel; chmara;czereda;tłum
hostage ('hostydż) s. zakładnik; zastaw;zakładniczka
hostel ('hostel) s. dom studencki; bursa ;zajazd
hostess ('houstys) s. gospodyni; stewardesa; fordanserka
hostile ('hostajl) adj. wrogi;
nieprzyjemny; antagonistyczny
hostility (hos'tylyty) s. wro-
gość; stan wojny;ostra opozycja
hot (hot) adj. gorący; palący;
pieprzny; ostry; nielegalny;
świeży; pobudliwy; adv. gorąco
hotbed ('hot,bed) s. inspecty;
wylęgarnia;siedlisko;rozsadnik
hot dog ('hot,dog) s. kiełbas-
ka w bułce;kiełbaska smażona
hotel (hou'tel) s. hotel
hothead ('hot,hed) s. człowiek
zapalczywy; raptus;a.porywczy
hothouse ('hot,haus) s. cieplarnia; oranżeria
hot-pants (,hot'paents) exp.
obcisłe damskie szorty;
vulg.:panna puszczalska
hot water bottle (hot'ło:ter'
botl) s. gorąca butelka
hound (haund) s. ogar; łajdak;
v. tropić; szczuć; podjudzać
hour ('auer) s. godzina; pora
hourly ('auerly) adj. cogo-
dzinny; adv. co godzinę;
ustawicznie;z godziny na godzinę
house (haus) s. dom; zajazd;
teatr; widzowie; v. gościć;
dawać pomieszczenie; mieszkać
housekeeper ('haus,ki:per) s.
najęta gosposia ;pomoc domowa
housekeeping ('haus,ki:pyng) s.
gospodarka domowa
housemaid ('haus,mejd) s. pokojówka; pomoc domowa
housewife ('haus,łajf) s.
gospodyni (niepracująca poza
domem)

housework ('haus,ƚe:rk) s. prace domowe;sprzątanie i gotowanie

housing ('hauzyŋg) s. pomieszczenie; kolonia; osƚona; pokrywa; czaprak;obudowa

hove (houw) zob. heave

hover ('hower) v. unosic się; kręcic się; byc w niepewności; s. stan niepewności; unoszenie się;wahanie się;przywieranie

how (hau) adv. jak; jak ?sposób

how do you do ('hau,du'ju:du) exp.:dzień dobry !; dobry wieczór ! (jak się pan(i) ma ?)

how are you ('hau,a:r'ju) exp.: jak się pan(i) ma ?

how about ('hau,e'baut) exp.: może ?; pozwolisz ? etc.

how much ('hau,macz) exp.: ile ?

how many ('hau,meny) exp.: ile? ilu ? jak wielu?

how much is it ? ('hau,macz'yz, yt) ile to kosztuje ?

however (hau'ewer) adv. jakkolwiek; jednak; niemniej

howl (haul) s. wycie; ryk; ſkiem v. wyc; wyganiac (gonic)wrzas-

howler ('hauler) s. gruby błąd

hub (hab) s. piasta; ośrodek; slang: maż;środek(rozgrywki)

hubbub ('habbab) s. gieƚk;gwar; awantura; wrzawa;tumult

hubby ('haby) s. mężulek (slang)

huckleberry ('hakelbery) s. ſda) borówka amerykańska(krzak i jago-

huddle together ('hadl,tu'gedzer) v. przytulac się; tulic się

huddle up ('hadl,ap) v.skulic się zwinać się w kƚębek

hue (hju:) s. barwa; odcień

hug ,(hag) s. uścisk; chwyt zapaśniczy; v. ściskac; przyciskac; tulic (sie);uściskać

huge (hju:dż) adj. ogromny

hull (hal) s. ƚuska; kadƚub; v. ƚuszczyc; godzic w kadƚub

hullabaloo ('halebelu:) s. harmider;zgieƚk;wrzawa;gwar

hullo (he'lou) excl.: hola! halo!

hum (ham) v. nucic; buczec; mruczec; chrząkac; s. pomruk; chrząkanie; wahanie się; blaga

human ('hju:men) adj. ludzki; s. istota ludzka

humane ('hju:mejn) adj. ludzki; humanitarny ;litościwy

humanitarian (hju,maeny'teerjen) adj. humanitarystyczny; s. humanitarysta;filantrop

humanity (hju'maenyty) s. ludzkosc; rasa ludzka; cechy ludzkie; dobre uczynki

humble ('hambl) adj. pokorny; uniżony; skromny; v. upokażac; poniżac; poniżyć

humbleness ('hamblnys) s. pokora; bezpretensjonalność

humbug ('hambag) s. oszustwo; blaga; bujda; oszust; blagier; v. blagowac; oszukiwac; nabie-ſhi rac;wyƚudzac opowiadaniem bred-

humdrum ('hamdram) adj. nudny; banalny; monotonny; s. szarzyzna; banalnosc; nudziarz

humidity (hju'mydyty) s. wilgoc; wilgotnosc(powietrza etc.)

humiliate (hju'myly,ejt) v. upokarzac; poniżac;martwic

humiliation (hju,:myly'ejszyn) s. upokorzenie; poniżenie

humility (hju'mylyty) s. skromnosc; pokora ducha etc.

humming-bird ('hamyŋg,byrd) s. koliber

humor ('hju:mer) s.humor; nastroj; kaprys; wesołość; v. dogadzac; zaspakajac; zadowalac; ustępowac; dostosowac się do zachcianek etc.

humorous ('hju:meres) adj. śmieszny; pocieszny; peƚen humoru; zabawny;komiczny

hump ,(hamp) s. garb; v. garbic się; wyginac w ƚuk

humpback ('hampbaek) s. garbus

hunchback ('hancz,baek) s. garbus;garb na plecach

hundred ('handred) num. sto; s. setka;niezliczona ilość

hundredth ('handredt) num. setny; jedna setna

hundredweight ('handred,ƚejt) s. cetnar angielski

hung (haŋg) zob. hang

Hungarian (han'geerjen) adj.
węgierski ;s. Węgier
hunger ('hanger) s. głód;
v. głodować; łaknąć; głodzić
hunger strike ('hanger-strajk)
s. strajk głodowy
hungry ('hangry) adj. głodny;
zgłodniały; pożądliwy; ubogi;
jałowy ; nieurodzajny;łaknący
hunt (hant) s. polowanie;
teren łowiecki; v. polowác;
gonić; przeszukiwać; szukać
hunter ('hanter) s. myśliwy
hunting ('hantyng) s. polowanie; adj. myśliwski
hunting ground ('huntyng,graund)
s. teren myśliwski
huntsman ('hantsmen) s. myśliwy; łowca
hurdle ('he:rdl) s. opłotki;
v. poraç się; skakac przez
płotki; grodzic;przebijac się
hurdler ('he:rdler) s. zawodnik
wyścigów (z płotkami)
hurdle race ('he:rdl,rejs) s.
wyścigi (z płotkami) przez płotki
hurl (he:rl) s. rzut; v. rzucać
hurrah (he'ra:) excl.; hura !
hurray (he'rej) excl.; hura !;
v. krzyczeć hura (z radości etc.)
hurricane ('haryken) n. huragan; orkan tropikalny
hurried ('haryd) adj. pospieszny
hurry ('hary) s. pospiech
hurry up ! ('hary,ap) v. spiesz
się ! ruszaj się!
hurt; hurt; hurt; (he:rt;
he:rt; he:rt)
hurt (he:rt) v. ranic; kaleczyc;
urazić; uszkodzić; boleć; dokuczać; s. skaleczenie; rana;
szkoda; krzywda; uraz; uszkodzenie ;ból;ujma;ranka
husband ('hazbend) s. mąż;
v. gospodarować oszczędnie;
wydawać za mąż
husbandry ('hazbendry) s. rolnictwo; uprawa; hodowla
hush (hasz) s. cisza; spokój;
milczenie; v. cicho ! sza !;
uciszyć się; milczec; tuszować (coś);ululać; załagodzić

hush up ('hasz,ap) v. siedzieć
cicho; zatuszować (coś)
husk (hask) s. łuska; v. łuszczyć; wyłuszczać;złuszczać
husky ('hasky) adj. krzepki;
suchy; zachrypniety; łuszczas-
ty; s. pies eskimoski; język
eskimoski
hustle ('hasl) s. pospiech;
krzątanina; bieganina; popy-
chanie; v. spieszyc się; krzątać się; popychac; pchac się;
szturchac; popędzac; wypchnąć
hut (hat) s. chata; barak; chałupa; v. mieszkać w chałupie
hutch (hacz) s. skrzynia; klatka; domek; v. wkładac cos do
skrzyni;s.kurnik;chlewik;chatka
hybrid ('hajbryd) s. mieszaniec;
adj. mieszany;mieszanego pochodze-
hydrant ('hajdrent) s. hydrant
hydraulic ('haj'dro:lyk) adj.
hydrauliczny
hydro ('hajdrou) adj. wodo- ;
wodoro-; wodny
hydrocarbon ('hajdrou'ka:rben)
s. węglowodór
hydrochloric acid (,hajdrou'-
klo:ryk,asyd) s. kwas solny
hydrogen ('hajdrydżen) s. wodór
hydrogen bomb ('hajdydżen,bom)
s. bomba wodorowa
hydroplane ('hajdrou,plejn) s.
wodnopłatowiec; slizgacz
hyena (haj'y:ne) s. hiena
hygiene ('hajdżi:n) s. higiena
hymn (hym) s. hymn; v. śpiewać
hymn ;chwalić hymnem
hyphen ('hajfen) s. łącznik;
v. używać łącznika
hypnotize ('hypne,tajz) v.
hipnotyzować
hypocrisy (hy'pokresy) s. hipo-
kryzja ;udawanie cnoty etc.
hypocrite ('hypekryt) s. hipokryta ;obłudnik;obłudnica
hypocritical (,hypou'krytykel)
adj. obłudny; hipokryzyjny;
dwulicowy ;udający cnotę etc.
hypodermic (,hajpe'de:rmyk)
adj. podskórny (zastrzyk)

hypothesis (haj'potysys) s.
hipoteza;niesprawdzona teoria
hysterectomy (,histe'rektemy)
s. wycięcie macicy
hysteria (hys'tyerje) s. histeria;wybuch podniecenia
hysterical (hys'terykel) adj.
histeryczny;podlegający histerii
hysterics (hys'teryks) pl.
atak histerii
hysterotomy (,histe'rotemy)
s. operacja macicy
I (aj) pron. ja; dziewiąta litera angielskiego alfabetu
I-beam ('aj,bi:m) s. belka
dwuteówka (stalowa)
ice (ajs) s. lód; lody; v. zamrażać; mrozić; lukrować
Ice Age('ajsejdż) s. epoka lodowa;epoka lodowcowa
iceberg ('ajsbe:rg) s. góra lodowa (na morzu)
ice-cream ('ajskri:m) s. lody
icicle ('ajsykl) s. sopel
ice floe ('ajs-flou) s. kra
icing ('ajsyŋ) s. lukier
icy ('ajsy) adj. lodowaty
idea (aj'die) s. idea; pojęcie;
pomysł;wyobrażenie; myśl;plan
ideal (aj'diel) adj. idealny;
s. ideał; model doskonały
idealize (aj'dielajz) v. ideali-
zować;wyidealizować
identical (aj'dentykel) adj.
taki sam; identyczny; tożsamos-
ciowy;zupełnie podobny
identification (ajdentyfy'kejszyn) s. utożsamienie; identy-
fikacja ;stwierdzenie tożsamości
identification papers (aj,denty-
fy'kejszyn'pejpers) s. dowód
tożsamości; dowód osobisty
identify (aj'dentyfaj) v. utożsamić; identifikować
identity (aj'dentyty) s. tożsamość; identyczność
identity card (aj'dentyty ka:rd)
s. dowód osobisty
ideological (,ajdye'lodżykel)
adj. ideologiczny
idiom ('ydjem) s. wyrażenie
zwyczajowe; wyrażenie idioma-
tyczne; dialekt ;typowy styl

idiot ('ydjet) s. idiota ;dureń
idiotic (,ydy'otyk) adj. idiotyczny ;bardzo głupi
idle ('ajdl) adj. niezajęty;
bezczynny; leniwy; pusty;
czczy; jałowy; zbyteczny;
v. próżnować; być na wolnym
biegu;być bez pracy;obijać się
idle away ('ajdle'łej) v. marnować (czas) ;roztrwonić czas
idleness ('ajdlnys) s. bezczynność; lenistwo; próżniactwo;
daremność;bezpodstawność
idol ('ajdl) s. bożyszcze; bałwan;posąg bożka
idolize ('ajdelajz) v. ubóstwiać; uwielbiać; bałwochwalić
idyl ('ydyl) s. sielanka; idyl-
la;opis raju na wsi(w poezji)
if (yf) conj. jeżeli; jeśli;
gdyby; o ile; czy; żeby(tylko)
iffy (yffy) adj. wątpliwy
(slang) gdybowany
igloo ('iglu:) s. eskimoska
chata kopulasta ze śniegu
ignite (yg'najt) v. zapalić
ignition (yg'nyszyn) s. zapłon;
zapalenie; elektryczny zapłon
ignition key (yg'nyszyn,ki:)
s. klucz do zapłonu (w aucie)
ignoble (yg'noubl) adj. nędzny;
podły; haniebny; niecny; marny;
niegodziwy;niskiego pochodzenia
ignorance ('ygnerens) s. nie-
świadomość; ignorancja; nieuctwo; ciemnota;obskurantyzm
ignorant ('ygnerent) adj. nieświadomy; ciemny; bez wykształcenia ;zdradzający ignorancję
ignore (yg'no:r) v. pomijać;
lekceważyć; odrzucać;nie zważać
ill (yl) adj. zły; chory; słaby; lichy; s. zło; adv. źle;
nie bardzo ;kiepsko;niepomyślnie
ill-advised ('yled'wajzd) adj.
nierozsądny; nierozważny
ill-affected ('yle'fektyd) adj.
źle usposobiony ;nieżyczliwy
ill-bred ('yl'bred) adj. źle
wychowany ;grubiański
illegal (y'li:gel) adj. bezprawny; nielegalny ;samowolny;
przeciw prawu i ustawom

illegible (y'ledżybl) adj. nieczytelny;źle napisany(wydrukowany)
illegitimate (,yly'dżytymejt)
adj. bezprawny; nieprawny;
nieprawowity; nieślubny
ill-fated ('yl-fejdyd) adj.
fatalny; nieszczęśliwy;nieszczęś-
ill-humored ('yl'hju:merd)
adj. w złym humorze
illicit (y'lysyt) adj. bezprawny; niedozwolony;niewłaściwy
illiterate (y'lyteryt) s. analfabeta; adj. niepiśmienny
ill-judged ('yl'dżadżd) adj.
nierozważny; nierozsądny
ill-mannered ('yl'maenerd) adj.
źle wychowany;grubiański
ill-natured ('yl'nejczerd) adj.
zły; złośliwy; opryskliwy
illness ('ylnys) s. choroba
illogical (y'lodżykel) adj.
nielogiczny;nierozsądny
ill-tempered ('yl'temperd) adj.
w złym humorze;zły;kłótliwy
ill-timed ('yl'tajmd) adj. nie
na czasie;niefortunny
ill-treat ('yl'tri:t) v. maltretować; znęcac się(nad kims)
illuminate (y'lju:mynejt) v.
oświetlać; oswiecać; uświetniac
illumination (y,lju:my'nejszyn)
s. oświecenie; oświecenie;
uswietnianie;rozjaśnienie
illusion (y'lu:żyn) s. złudze-
nie; iluzja; złuda
illusive (y'lu:syw) adj. złudny; iluzyjny;iluzoryczny;zwodni-
illusory (y'lu:sery) adj. złudny; iluzoryczny;zwodniczy
illustrate ('yles,trejt) v.
wyjasniac; ilustrować
illustration (,yles'trejszyn)
s. ilustracja; ilustrowanie
illustrative ('yles,trejtyw)
adj. objaśniający; ilustru-
jący(przykład,zdarzenie etc.)
illustrious (y'lastrjes) adj.
znakomity; wybitny; sławny
ill will ('yl'łyl) s. niechęc
image ('ymydż) s. wizerunek;
obraz; wcielenie; v. wyobrażac; odzwierciadlac; ucieles-
niac; dawać obraz(wyobrażenie)

imagery ('ymydżery) s. wizerun-
ki; podobizny; gra wyobrazni;
porownanie przez przykłady
imaginable (y'maedżynebl) adj.
wyobrażalny; możliwy;do pomyśle-
imaginary (y'maedżynery) a.
urojony; zmyslony;nierzeczywisty
imagination (y,maedży'nejszyn)
s. wyobraznia; fantazja; urojenie;tworzenie nowych pomysłów
imagine (y'maedżyn) v. wyobrażac sobie;przypuszczać;myśleć
imbecile ('ymby,syl) adj. uposledzony; głupi; niedorozwinięty; cherlawy; s. człowiek
uposledzony; imbecyl(niedorozwi-
imitate ('ymytejt) v. nasladowac; małpowac;imitowac;wzorowac
imitation (,ymy'tejszyn) s. na-
sladowanie; nasladownictwo;
imitacja;falsyfikat;podróbka
immaterial (,yme'tierjel) adj.
nieistotny; bezcielesny;błachy
immature (,yme'tjuer) adj. niedojrzały;niewyrobiony;niedorosły
immeasurable (y,meżerebl) adj.
niezmierzony; ogromny;bezmierny
immediate (y'mi:djet) adj.
bezpośredni; natychmiastowy;pil-
ny;nagły
immediately (y'mi:djetly) adv.
natychmiast; bezpośrednio
immense (y'mens) adj. olbrzymi;ogromny;świetny;kpitalny
immerse (y'me:rs) v. zanurzać;
pogrążać;ochrzcić przez zanużenie
immigrant ('ymygrent) s. imigrant; adj. imigrujący;osadniczy
immigrate ('ymygrejt) v. imigro-
wac;przywędrowac;sprowadzac osad-
immigration (,ymy'grejszyn) s.
imigracja;urząd imigracyjny
imminent ('ymynent) adj. nad-
chodzący; grozny;nadciagający;blis
immobile (y'moubajl) adj. nieruchomy;przytwierdzony na stałe
immoderate (y'moderyt) adj.
nieumiarkowany;niepohamowany;nad-
immodest (y'modyst) adj. nieskromny; bezczelny; zuchwały
immoral (y'morel) adj. niemoralny;nieetyczny;rozpustny
immorality (ym'e-ral'ety)s.rozpus-
ta; niemoralnosc

immorality (,yme'raelyty) s.
niemoralność;rozpusta
immortal (y'mo:rtl) adj. nie-
śmiertelny; wiekopomny
immortality (,ymo:r'taelyty) s.
nieśmiertelność
immovable (y'mu:webl) adj.nie-
ruchomy; niezmienny; nieczuły; nieugięty;niewzruszony
immune (y'mju:n) adj. odporny;
uodporniony;wolny(od przepisów)
imp (ymp) s. skrzat; diablik
impact ('ympaekt) v. wgnia-
tać; s. zderzenie; uderzenie;
wpływ;wstrząs;kolizja;działanie
impair (ym'peer) v. uszkadzać;
osłabiać; nadwyrężać;umniejszać
impart (ym'pa:rt) v. dawać;
udzielać;zakomunikować
impartial (ym'pa:rszel) adj.
bezstronny; sprawiedliwy
impartiality ('ym,pa:rszy'aelyty) s. bezstronność;sprawiedli-
impassable (ym'pa:sebl) adj.
nieprzebyty; nie do przebycia
impassive (ym'paesyw) adj.
niewzruszony; obojętny;nieczuły
impatience (ym'pejszens) s.
zniecierpliwienie; niecierpli-
wość;irytacja(z powodu czegoś)
impatient (ym'pejszent) adj.
niecierpliwy; zniecierpliwiony;palący się do;podrażniony
impediment (ym'pedyment) s.
przeszkoda; utrudnienie
impend (ym'pend) v. grozić;
zbliżać się;zagrażać(z bliska)
impenetrable (ym'penytrebl)
adj. nieprzenikniony; niedostępny;niezglebiony;nie do prze-
imperative (ym'peretyw) adj.bicia
stanowczy; rozkazujący; konieczny;naglący;niezbędny
imperceptible (,ym-pe'rseptebl)
adj. niedostrzegalny;nieuchwyt-
imperfect (ym'pe:rfykt) adj.
niedoskonały; niedokończony;
wadliwy; niezupełny;niedokonany
imperial (ym'pierjel) adj.
cesarski; imperialny; do-
stojny;rozkazujący;majestatycz-
imperialism (ym'pierjelyzem)s.
imperializm(budowanie imperium)

imperil (ym'peryl) v. zagrażać;
narazić na niebezpieczeństwo
imperious (ym'pierjes) adj.
władczy; naglący;nakazujący
imperishable (ym'peryszebl) adj.
niezniszczalny; nieprzemijają-
cy;trwały;wieczysty
impermeable (ym'pe:rmiebl) adj.
nieprzemakalny; nieprzenikniony;nieprzepuszczający
impersonal (ym'pe:rsenl) adj.
nieosobowy; nieosobisty
impersonate(ym'pe:rsenejt) v.
wcielać; uosabiać; odgrywać
kogoś;personifikować
impertinence (ym'pe:rtynens) s.
niestosowność; impertynencja;
niewłasciwość; natręctwo ;nietakt
impertinent (ym'pe:rtynnent) adj.
niestosowny; impertynencki;
bezczelny; natrętny;bez związku
imperturbable (,ympe:r'te:rbebl)
adj. niewzruszony; spokojny
impervious (ym'pe:rwjes) adj.
nieprzepuszczalny; niedostępny
impetuous (ym'petjues) adj.
popędliwy; porywczy; gwałtowny
implacable (ym'plekebl) adj.
nieubłagalny; nieprzejednany
implement ('ymplyment) s. narzędzie; środek; sprzęt;
v. uzupełniać; urzeczywistniać;
wykonać;uprawomocniać;spełniać
implicate ('ymplykejt) v. uwikłać; owijać; włączać;wplątać;wmie-
implication (,ymply'kejszyn) s.
uwikłanie; włączenie; sugestia
implicit (ym'plysyt) adj. rozu-
miejący się sam przez się;
niezaprzeczalny;domniemany;ślepy
implore (ym'plo:r) v. błagać
imply (ym'plaj) v. zawierać
w sobie; mieścić; sugerować;
zakładać ;nasuwać wniosek
impolite (,ympo'lajt) adj. nieuprzejmy; niegrzeczny
import (ym'po:rt) s. import;tresć
v. oznaczać; importować; przywozić z zagranicy;a.importowy
import ('ympo:rt) s. treść;
znaczenie;ważność;doniosłość
importance (ym'po:rtens) s.
znaczenie; ważność;doniosłość

important (ym'po:rtent) adj.
ważny; znaczący; doniosły
importation (,ympo:r'tejszyn)
s. przywóz; importowanie
importune (ym'po:rtju:n) v.
dokuczać; żądać natarczywie;
narzucać się;naprzykrzać się
impose (ym'pouz) v. nadawać;
narzucać; oszukiwać; imponować;narzucać;nakładać obowiązek
impose upon (,ym'pouz e'pon)
v. narzucać się komuś;okpiwać
imposing (ym'pouzyng) adj.
imponujący;wspaniały;okazały
impossibility (ym,posy'bylyty)
s. niemożliwość
impossible (ym'posybl) adj.
niemożliwy(do zrobienia,zniesienia
impostor (ym'poster) s. oszust
(podszywający się);szarlatan
impotence ('ympotens) s. niemoc; zniedołężnienie (płciowe);nieudolność;niesprawność
impotent ('ympotent) s. bezsilny; impotent; nieudolny
impracticable (ym'praektykebl)
adj. niewykonalny;krnąbrny
impregnate ('ympregnejt) v. za-
płodniać; impregnować; nasycać;wpoić;zaszczepić;nasiąkać
impress (ym'pres) v. odcisnąć;
wycisnąć; robić wrażenie;
s. odcisk; odbicie; piętno
impression (ym'preszyn) s. wrażenie; druk; odbicie; nakład
impressive (ym'presyw) adj. robiący wrażenie; uderzający;
podniosły;wstrząsający;frapujący
imprint (ym'prynt) v. odbijać;
wpajać; wydrukować; wbijać
w pamięć;wyryć w pamięci
imprint ('ymprynt) s. odbicie;
nadruk; odcisk;piętnc;znak fir-
imprison (ym'pryzn) v. uwięzić
imprisonment (ym'pryznment) s.
uwięzienie(kara więzienia)
improbable (ym'probebl) adj.
nieprawdopodobny
improper (ym'proper) adj. niewłaściwy; nieprzyzwoity;zdrożny
improve (ym'pru:w) v. poprawić;
udoskonalić; ulepszać(jakość)

improvement (ym'pru;wment) s.
poprawa; udoskonalenie; wy-
korzystanie(sposobności);poprawa
improvise ('ymprowajz) v. improwizować;sklecić na poczekaniu
imprudent (ym'pru:dent) adj. nierozsądny; nieopatrzny; nierozważny;nieoględny;niebaczny
impudence ('ympjudens) s. bez-
wstyd; bezczelność; tupet
impudent ('ympjudent) adj. bezwstydny; bezczelny;zuchwały;z tu-
impulse ('ympals) s. impuls;poryw;
popęd;pęd;siła napędowa;bodziec
impulsive ('ympalsyw) adj. im-
pulsywny; porywczy; pobudliwy
impunity (ym'pju:nyty) s. bez-
karność;swoboda od skutków(kary)
impure (ym'pjur) adj. nieczysty; zanieczyszczony
impute (ym'pju:t) v. oskarżać;
przypisywać(zbrodnię;błąd etc.)
in (yn) prep. w; we; na; za; po;
do; u; nie-
in and out ('yn,end'aut) exp.:
na wylot; wchodzić i wychodzić
in a week ('yn,ej'łi:k) exp.: za
tydzień;w ciągu tygodnia
in my opinion ('yn,maj e'pynjen)
exp.: według mnie;moim zdaniem
in order that ('yn.o:rder'daet)
exp.: ażeby;w celu;poto żeby
in pairs ('yn,peers) exp.: parami
in Shakespeare ('yn,Szekspir)
u Szekspira;w sztukach Szekspira
inability (,yne'bylyty) s. niezdolność;niemożność
inaccessible (ynaek'sesybl) adj.
niedostępny; nieprzystępny
inaccurate (yn'aekjuryt) adj.
nieścisły; niedokładny
inactive (yn'aektyw) adj. bezczynny;bierny;obojetny;inertny
inadequate (yn'aedykłyt) adj.
nieodpowiedni; niewystarczalny
inadmissible (,yned'mysebl)
adj. niedopuszczalny;nie do przy-jęcia
inadvertent (,yned'we:rtent)
adj. nieuważny; niedbały; nie-
rozmyślny;mimowolny;nieumyślny
inalterable (yn'o:lterebl) adj.
niezmienny

inanimate (yn'aenymyt) adj.
martwy; nieożywiony; bezduszny; nieorganiczny
inappropriate (,yne'prouprjyt)
adj. niewłaściwy;niestosowny
inapt (yn'aept) adj. niezdatny
inarticulate (,yna:r'tykjulyt)
adj. nieartykułowany; niewyraźny; niemy;słabo mówiący
inasmuch (,ynez'macz) adv.
o tyle; ponieważ; wobec tego;
że; skoro;zważywszy;jako że
inasmuch as (,ynez'macz,aez)
adv. gdyż ;o tyle że;o tyle o
inattentive (,yne'tentyw) adj.
nieuważny; nie uważający
inaudible (yn'o:debl) adj. nie-
słyszalny;nie uchwytny dla ucha
inaugural (y'no:gjurel) adj.
inauguracyjny
inaugurate (y'no:gjurejt) v.
otwierać uroczyście; inaugurować;uroczyście zapoczątkowy-
inborn ('yn'bo:rn) adj. wrodzony ;przyrodzony;z natury
incalculable (yn'kaelkjulebl)
adj. nieobliczalny;nieprzewi-
incapable (yn'kejpebl) adj.
niezdolny; nie będący w stanie
incapacitate ('ynke'paesytejt)
v. czynić niezdatnym; dyskwa-
lifikować;uznać za niezdatnego
incapacity (,ynke'paesyty) s.
niezdolność; nieudolność
incarnate (yn,ka:rnejt) adj.
wcielony; v. wcielać; ucieles-
niać (się);być wcieleniem
incautious (yn'ko:szes) adj.
nierozważny; niebaczny
incendiary (yn'sendjery) adj.
zapalający; podżegający;
s. podpalacz; podżegacz
incense ('ynsens) s. kadzidło
incense (yn'sens) v. rozwscie-
czać; doprowadzać do szału
incertitude (un'se:rtytju:d) s.
niepewność; niepokój
incessant (yn'sesnt) adj. ustawiczny; bezustanny; stały
incest ('ynsest) s.kazirodztwo
a.kazirodczy
inch (yncz) s. cal (2.54 cm)
v. posuwać cal po calu

incident ('ynsydent) s. zajście;
wydarzenie; incydent; adj. pa-
dający; związany;prawdopodobny
incidental (,ynsy'dentl) adj.
przypadkowy; uboczny;drugorzędny
incidentally (,ynsy'dently) adv.
przypadkowo; ubocznie; nawiasem mówiąc;mimochodem;przy spobnoś-
ci
incinerate (yn'synerejt) v.
spalić; spopielić;palić na popiół
incise (yn'sajz) v. naciąć; wyryć;wyrzeźbic;wygrawerować
incision (yn'syżyn) s. nacięcie;
cięcie; cietość; bystrość;ostrość
incisive (yn'sajsyw) adj. przenikliwy; ostry; tnący; bystry;
sieczny; zjadliwy;wcinający się
incisor (yn'sajzer) s. siekacz
(ząb)każdy z przednich zębów między
zębami
incite (yn'sajt) v. zachęcać;
podburzać;podżegać;namawiać
inclement (yn'klement) adj.
surowy;ostry (klimat etc.)
inclination (ynkly'nejszyn) s.
skłonność; nachylenie;pociąg
incline (yn'klajn) v. miec
skłonność; pochylać się
inclose (yn'klous) v. ogrodzic;
załączyć; włączyć;zamknąć
include (yn'klu:d) v. zawierać;
włączać; wliczać(w cenę);obejmować
inclusive (yn'klu:syw) adj.
włączony;obejmujący;adv.włącznie
incoherent (,ynkou'hierent) adj.
bez związku; nieskoordynowany
income ('ynkam) s. dochód
income tax ('ynkam,taeks) s.
podatek dochodowy
incoming ('yn,kamyng) adj. nad-
chodzący;następujący; przyra-
stający; s. przybycie; dochód
incomparable (yn'komperebl)
adj. niezrównany; nie do porów-
nania; nieporównywalny
incompatible (,ynkem'paetebl)
adj. niezgodny; sprzeczny
incompetent (yn'kompytent) adj.
niekompetentny; nieudolny
incomplete (,ynkem'pli:t) adj.
niezupełny; nieukończony
incomprehensible (yn,kompry'-
hensebl) adj. niepojęty; niezrozumiały

inconceivable (,ynken'si:webl) adj. niepojęty; nieprawdopodobny; nieprawdopodobny

inconclusive (,ynken'klu;syw) adj. nieprzekonywujący; nierozstrzygający;nie decydujący

inconsequent (yn'konsykŁent) adj. bez związku; niekonsekwentny; nielogiczny

inconsiderable (,ynken'sydęrebl) adj. nieznaczny; niepokaźny

inconsiderate (,ynken'syderyt) adj. bezwzględny; nierozważny

inconsistent (,ynken'systent) adj. niejednolity; niekonsekwentny; niezgodny;bez związku

inconsolable (,ynken'soulebl) adj. niepocieszony;nieutulony

inconstant (yn'konstent) adj. zmienny; niestały; nieregularny

inconvenience (,ynken'wi:n jens) s. niewygoda; kłopot; v. niepokoić; przeszkadzać; sprawiać kłopot;deranżować

inconvenient (,ynken'wi:njent) adj. niewygodny; niedogodny; kłopotliwy; uciążliwy

incorporate (yn'ko:rperejt) v. jednoczyć; wcielać; zrzeszać (yn'ko:rperyt) adj. zrzeszony

incorporated (yn'ko:rperejtyd) adj. zarejestrowany; zalegalizowany;wcielony; złączony

incorrect (,ynke'rekt) adj. niepoprawny; nieścisły: błędny

incorrigible (yn'korydżybl) adj. niepoprawny;nie do poprawienia

increase (yn'kri:s) v. wzrastać; zwiększać się; pomnażać się; wzmagać się;rozmnażać się ; s. ('ynkri:s) wzrost; przyrost; podwyżka;rozrost;mnożenie się

increasingly (yn'kri:syngly) adv. coraz więcej; coraz bardziej; coraz to; wciąż

incredible (yn'kredebl) adj. nie do wiary; niewiarygodny; nieprawdopodobny;nie do pomyśle-nia

incredulous (yn'kredjules) adj. nie

incriminate (yn'krymynejt) v. obwiniać; oskarżać;pomawiać; objąć (kogoś) oskarżeniem

incubator ('ynkjubejter) s. wylęgarka; inkubator

incur (yn'ke:r) v. narażać się; ponieść; zaciągać;natknąć się na

incurable (yn'kjuerebl) adj. nieuleczalny;s.człowiek nieuleczal-ny

indebted (yn'detyd) adj. dłużny; zobowiązany; wdzięczny;zawdzięcza-jący

indecency (yn'di:sensy) s. nieskromność; nieprzyzwoitość

indecent (yn'di:sent) adj. nieprzyzwoity;obrażający moralność

indecision (,yndy'syżyn) s. chwiejność; niezdecydowanie

indecisiveness (,yndy'sajsywnys)s. chwiejność; niezdecydowanie

indecisive (,yndy'sajsyw) adj. nie rozstrzygnięty; niezdecydowany;chwiejny;nie rozstrzygający

indeed (yn'di:d) adv. naprawdę; istotnie; rzeczywiście; faktycznie;wprawdzie; co prawda;właściwie

indefatigable (,yndy'faetygebl) adj. niestrudzony; niezmordowany

indefinite (yn'defynyt) adj. nieokreślony;niewyraźny;nie sprecy-zowany

indelible (yn'delybl) adj. niezatarty; trwały;nie do zmazania

indelicate (yn'delykyt) adj. niedelikatny; nietaktowny;niestosowny

indemnify (yn'demnyfaj) v. dawać odszkodowanie; zabezpieczać przed(np. szkodą);powetować

indemnity (yn'demnyty) s. odszkodowanie; zabezpieczenie przed...;wynagrodzenie

indent (yn'dent) v. naciąć; wyciąć; wyrznać; zamówić; zawierać umowę; tłoczyć; s. wgłębienie;nacięcie;karbowanie

indent ('yndent) s. wcięcie; nacięcie; karbowanie; zamówienie

independence (,yndy'pendens) s. niezależność; niepodległość; niezależność materialna

independent (,yndy'pendent) adj. niepodległy; niezależny (materialnie);osobny;oddzielny

indescribable (,yndys'krajbebl) adj. nieopisany; nie do opisania (poza możliwościami opisania)

indeterminate (,yndy'te:rmynyt) adj.nieokreślony;niewyraźny

index ('yndeks) s. wskaźnik;
indeks; v. umieszczać spi-
sie (indeksie);robić indeks
Indian ('yndjen) adj. indiański;
hinduski ⌐babie lato
Indian Summer ('yndjen'samer)
exp.: słoneczne dni w jesieni;
India-rubber ('yndje'raber) s.
guma (naturalna,elastyczna)
indicate ('yndykejt) v. wskazywać; stwierdzać; wymagać
indication (,yndy'kejszyn) s.
wskazówka; wskazanie; znak
indicative (yn'dyketyw) adj.
oznajmiający; dowodzący
indicator ('yndykejter) s.
wskaźnik; indykator; licznik
indict (yn'dajt) v. oskarżyć
indictment (yn'dajtment) s.
oskarżenie; akt oskarżenia
indifference (yn'dyferens) s.
obojętność ;nieistotność;błacho ść)
indifferent (yn'dyfrent) adj.
obojętny;mierny;błachy;neutralny
indigent ('yndydżent) adj.
ubogi; biedny;s.biedak;biedaczka
indigestible (,yndy'dżestebl)
adj. niestrawny ;źle strawny
indigestion (,yndy'dżestczyn) s.
niestrawność
indignant (yn'dygnent) adj.
oburzony (na niesprawiedliwość..)
indignation (,yndyg'nejszyn) s.
oburzenie
indirect (,yndy'rekt) adj; pośredni; okrężny; nieuczciwy
indiscreet (,yndys'kri:t) adj.
nierozważny; niedyskretny
indiscretion (,yndys'kreszyn)
s. nierozwaga; niedyskrecja;
uchybienie(słowem,czynem etc.)
indiscriminate (,yndys'krymynyt)
adj. bezkrytyczny; pomieszany
indispensable (,yndys'pensebl)
adj. nieodzowny; niezbędny;
konieczny;niezastąpiony
indisposed (,yndys'pouzd) adj.
niezdrów; niedysponowany; niechętny;bez zapału;niedomagający
indisposition (,yndyspe'zyszyn)
s. niedyspozycja; niechęć; odraza;dolegliwość;niedomaganie

indisputable (,yndys'pju:tebl)
adj. bezsporny;niezaprzeczalny
indistinct (,yndys'tynkt) adj;
niewyrazny;niejasny;mętny
individual (,yndy'wydjuel) adj.
pojedyńczy; odrębny; s. jednostka; osobnik;okaz;chłowiek
individualist (,yndy'wydjuelyst)
s. indiwidualista;individualistka
indivisible (,yndy'wyzebl) adj.
niepodzielny;nieskończenie mały
indolence ('yndelens) s. lenistwo; opieszałość;próżniactwo
indolent ('yndelent) adj. leniwy;opieszały;obojętny;niebolesny
indomitable (yn'domytebl) adj.
nieposkromiony; nieugięty
indoor ('yndo:r) adj. domowy;
wewnętrzny; pokojowy;zakładowy
indoors ('yndo:rz) adv. w domu;
pod dachem ;do domu;do mieszkania
indorse(yn'do:rs) v. potwierdzić (podpisem)
induce (yn'dju:s) v. skłonić;
namówić; powodować; wnioskować;pobudzić;nakłonić;powodować
induct (yn'dakt) v. wprowadzać;
tworzyć; brać do wojska
indulge (yn'daldż) v. pobłażać;
znosić; ulegać; dogadzać; używać sobie ;dawać upust;zaspokajać
indulgence (yn'daldżens) s. do-
gadzanie; nałog; oddawanie się;
pobłażanie; odpust;uleganie
indulgent (yn'daldżent) adj. pobłażliwy ;ulegający;folgujący
industrial (yn'dastrjel) adj.
przemysłowy (towar,robotnik etc.)
industrial area (yn'dastrjel'
eerje) s. teren przemysłowy
industrial city (yn'dastrjel'
syty) s. miasto przemysłowe
industrialist (yn'dastrjelyst)
s. przemysłowiec
industrialize (yn'dastrjelajz)
v. uprzemysławiać
industrious (yn'dastrjes) adj.
skrzętny; pilny; pracownity
industry ('yndastry) s. przemysł; pilność; pracowitość;
skrzętność;gałaź przemysłu;właś-
ciciele i zarządcy przemysłu

ineffective (,yny'fektyw) adj.
bezskuteczny; niesprawny
inefficient (,yny'fyszent)
adj. niewydajny; niesprawny
inequality (,yny'kľolyty) s.
nierówność; niewystarczalność;
zmienność(krajobrazu);niestałość
inert (y'ne:rt) adj. bezwľadny;
ociężaľy; obojętny; opieszaľy
inertia (y'ne:rszja) s. inercja; bezwľad; ociężalość
inestimable (yn'estymebl) adj.
nieoceniony;bezcenny
inevitable (yn'ewytebl) adj.
nieunikniony; nieuchronny
inexact (,ynyg'zaekt) adj. nieścisły; niedokľadny
inexcusable (,ynyks'kju:zebl)
adj. niewybaczalny; nie-
usprawiedliwiony;nie do darowa-
inexhaustible (,ynyg'zo:stebl)
adj. niewyczerpany; nieprzebrany; niestrudzony;bez dna
inexpensive (,ynyks'pensyw) adj.
niedrogi; niekosztowny; tani
inexperience (,ynyks'pierjens)
s. niedoświadczenie;brak wprawy
inexplicable (yn'eksplykebl)
adj. niewytľumaczalny; nie-
wyjasniony;zagadkowy
inexpressible (,yneks'presebl)
adj. niewysľawiony; niewyra-
żalny;niewymowny
inexpressive (,ynyks'presyw)
adj. bez wyrazu
infallible (yn'faelebl) adj.
nieomylny; niezawodny; niechybny;bezbľędny;zawsze słuszny
infamous ('ynfemes) adj. haniebny; niesľawny; hanbiący;podľy
infamy ('ynfemy) s. hanba; nie-
sľawa; podľość;utrata praw obywa-
infancy ('ynfensy) s. nie-
mowlectwo; dziecinstwo
infant ('ynfent) s. niemowlę;
dziecko;noworodek;a.dziecinny
infantile ('ynfentajl) adj.
dziecięcy;infantylny;niemowlęcy
infantry ('ynfentry) s. piechota (wojsko)
infatuated with (yn'faetjuejtyd
łyą) adj. szalejący za...;rozko-
chany w;nierozsądnie zakochany

infect (yn'fekt) v. zakazic;
zarazic; zatruwać
infection (yn'fekszyn) s. zakażenie; zarażenie; zaraza
infectious (yn'fekszes) adj. zakaźny; zaraźliwy;infekcyjny
infer (yn'fe:r) v. wnioskować;
zawierac w sobie pojęcie
inference ('ynferens) s. wniosek; konkluzja;domniemanie
inferior (yn'fierjer) adj.
niższy; podrzędny; posledni
inferior to (yn'fierjer,tu)
adj. ustępujący; gorszy
inferiority (yn,fiery'oryty) s.
niższość;poczucie niższości
infernal (yn'fe:rnel) adj. piekielny; diabelski; szatański
infest (yn'fest) v. nawiedzac;
trapic;byc utrapieniem
infidelity (,ynfy'delyty) s.
niewiara; niewierność
infiltrate ('ynfyltrejt) v.
wsiąkac; przesiąkać; przenikać
infinite ('ynfynyt) adj. nieskończony; bezgraniczny; niezliczony; ogromny;bezkresny
infinitive (yn'fynytyw) s. bezokolicznik;adj.nieokreślony
infinity (yn'fynyty) s. nie-
skończoność
infirm (yn'fe:rm) adj. sľaby;
niedoľężny;dotknięty niemocą
infirmary (yn'fe:rmery) s.
szpital; lecznica; izba chorych
infirmity (yn'fe:rmyty) s. niemoc; słabość; zniedoľężnienie
inflame (yn'flejm) v. zapalić;
rozognic; pobudzac;zagrzewać
inflammable (yn'flaemebl) adj.
zapalny; pobudliwy; palny
inflammation (,ynfle'mejszyn)
s. zapalenie; zaognienie
inflammatory(yn'flaemeto:ry)
adj. podżegający; zapalny
inflate (yn'flejt) v. nadąc;
rozdąc; powodować inflacje
inflation (yn'flejszyn) s.
inflacja; nadymanie; nadmu-
chanie;zwyżka cen
inflect (yn'flekt) v. zginąc;
skrzywic; odmieniac;naginać

inflexible (yn'fleksebl) adj.
sztywny; nieugięty;nieelastycz-
inflection(yn'flekszyn) s.
fleksja; modulacja; końcówka;
wygięcie ;nadgięcie;odchylenie
inflict (yn'flykt) v. zadać;
narzucać; zsyłać(na kogoś)
infliction (yn'flykszyn) s.
zadanie (ciosu) narzucanie;
przykrość;nieszczęście;strapie-
influence ('ynfluens) s. wpływ
v. wywierać wpływ;oddziaływać
influential (,ynflu'enszel)
adj. wpływowy(polityk etc.)
influenza (,ynflu'enza) s.
grypa; influenca
inform (yn'fo:rm) v. powiado-
mić; nadawać; donosić;ożywić
inform against(yn'fo:rme'genst)
v. donosić na (kogoś)
information (,ynfer'mejszyn)
s. wiadomość; wiedza; objas-
nienie;informacja;doniesienie
information desk (,ynfer'mejszyn,desk) punkt informacyjny (w banku,hotelu,na wystawie)
information officer (,ynfer'-
mejszyn 'ofyser) oficer in-
formacyjny(w banku etc.)
informative (yn'fo:rmetyw)
adj. objaśniający; pouczający
informer (yn'fo:rmer) s. donosiciel; konfident;konfidentka
infuriate (,yn'fjuerjejt) v.
rozwścieczać; rozjuszać
infuse (yn'fju:z) v. wlewać;
zalewać; zaparzać;dodać(odwagi)
ingenious (yn'dżi:njes) adj.
pomysłowy; dowcipny(pomysł)
ingenuity (,yndży'njuyty) s.
pomysłowość;oryginalność;dowcip
ingot ('yŋgot) s. sztaba
ingratiate (yn'grejszjejt) v.
wkradać się w łaski czyjeś
ingratitude(yn'graetytju:d) s.
niewdzięczność
ingredient (yn'gri:djent) s.
składnik (mieszanki etc.)
ingress ('yngres) s. wejście
inhabit (yn'haebyt) v. zamieszkiwać; mieszkać
inhabitable (yn'haebytebl)adj.
mieszkalny(godny zamieszkania)

inhabitant (yn'haebytent) s.
mieszkaniec; mieszkanka
inhale (yn'hejl) v. wdychać; zaciągać się (dymem);wziewać
inherent (yn'hierent) adj. nieodłączny; własciwy;wrodzony
inherit (yn'heryt) v. dziedziczyć; być spadkobiercą
inheritance (yn'herytens) s.
spadek; spuścizna; dziedzictwo
inhibit (yn'hybyt) v. wstrzymywać; wzbraniać; zakazywać
inhibition (,ynhy'byszyn) s.
zakaz; zahamowanie; wstrzymanie
inhospitable (yn'hospytebl) adj.
niegościnny
inhuman (yn'hju:men) adj. nieludzki; okrutny;brutalny etc.
initial (y'nyszel) adj. początkowy;v.znaczyć własnymi inicjała-mi
initiate (y'nyszjejt) v. zapoczątkować; wprowadzać; zainicjo-
wać; wtajemniczać;s.nowicjusz
initiation (y,nyszy'ejszyn) s.
wprowadzenie;zapoczątkowanie
initiative (y'nyszjetyw) s.
inicjatywa; adj. początkowy
inject (yn'dżekt) v. wstrzyknąć
injection (yn'dżekszyn) s.
zastrzyk;wstrzyknięcie;a.wytrysko-wy
injudicious -(,yndżu'dyszes) adj.
nierozważny; nieroztropny
injure ('yndżer) v. zranić;
uszkodzić; krzywdzic; zepsuć
injurious (yn'dżuerjes) adj.
szkodliwy; krzywdzący; obelżywy;przynoszący ujmę;obraźliwy
injury ('yndżery) s. szkoda;
krzywda; rana; uszkodzenie
injustice (yn'dżastys) s. niesprawiedliwość; krzywda
ink (yŋk) s. atrament; tusz
inkling ('yŋklyŋg)s. wzmianka;
podejrzenie; przypuszczenie
ink-pot ('yŋk,pot) s. kałamarz
inland ('ynlend) s. wnętrze
kraju; adj. z głębi kraju;
wewnętrzny; adv. w głębi
w głąb kraju;w głębi kraju
inlet ('ynlet) s. wstawka; zatoka; wlot; wejście;a.wlotowy
inmate ('ynmejt) s. mieszkaniec;
lokator; współ-(więzień etc.)

inmost ('ynmoust) adj. głęboko
utajony; skryty;najtajniejszy
inn (yn) s. gospoda; oberża
innate ('y'nejt) adj. wrodzony
inner ('yner) adj. wewnętrzny
innermost ('ynermoust) adj.
głęboko ukryty; najskrytszy
inner tube ('yner,tju:b) s.
dętka(samochodowa,rowerowa)
innkeeper ('yn,ki:per) s.
oberżysta;właściciel zajazdu
innocence ('ynesns) s. niewinność; naiwność;prostoduszność
innocent ('ynesynt) adj. niewinny; naiwny; nieszkodliwy;
niemądry; s. prostaczek;
niewiniątko; głuptas
innovation (,ynou'wejszyn) s.
innowacja;wprowadzanie zmian
innumerable (y'nju:merebl) adj.
niezliczony; bez liku
inoculate (y'nokjulejt) s.
szczepić;wpajać;oczkować roślin
inoffensive (,yne'fensyw) adj.
nieszkodliwy; spokojny;obojętny
inpatient ('ynpejszent) s.
pacjent leżący w szpitalu
inquest ('ynkłest) s. śledztwo
inquire (yn'kłajer) s. pytać
się; dowiadywać się; dociekać
inquiry (yn'kłajry) s. badanie;
zasięganie informacji; śledztwo; poszukiwanie;ankieta;wywiad
inquisitive (yn'kłyzytyw) adj.
badawczy; ciekawy;wścipski
insane (yn'sejn) adj. chory
umysłowo;zwarjowany;bez sensu
insanity (yn'saenyty) s. obłęd
insatiable (yn'sejszjebl) adj.
nienasycony;niezaspokojony;chciwy
insatiate (yn'sej'szjyt) adj.
nienasycony;niezaspokojony
inscribe (yn'skrajb) v, wpisać;
napisać;umieszczać na liście
inscription (yn'skrypszyn) s.
napis; dedykacja
insect ('ynsekt) s. owad
insecure (,ynsy'kjuer) adj. niepewny; niezabezpieczony
insensible (yn'sensybl) adj.
nieświadomy; bez zmysłów;w stanie omdlenia;niedostrzegalny

insensitive (yn'sensytyw) adj.
nieczuły; niewrażliwy
inseparable (yn'seperebl) adj.
nierozłączny;nieodstępny
insert (yn'se:rt) v. wstawiać;
wkładać; s. wkładka; wstawka
insertion (yn'se:rszyn) s. wkładka; wstawka; włożenie; wsta-
wienie;przyczep;przyczepienie
inshore (yn'szo:r) adv. blisko
brzegu; przy brzegu; adj. przybrzeżny; bliski brzegu
inside 'ynsajd) s. wnętrze;
adj. wewnętrzny;adv.wewnatrz
inside (yn'sajd) adv. wewnątrz
inside out ('ynsajd'aut) exp.:
na lewą stronę (np. marynarki)
insight ('ynsajt) s. wgląd;
intuicja;wnikliwość
insignificant (,ynsyg'nyfykent)
adj. mało znaczący;błachy
insincere (,ynsyn'sier) adj.
nieszczery;zwodny;dwulicowy
insinuate (yn'synjuejt) v. in-
synuować; podsuwać;sugierować
insipid (yn'sypyd) adj. mdły;
tępy; bez sensu;głupi;ckliwy
insist (yn'syst) v. nalegać;
nastawać;utrzymywać;obstawać
insist on (yn'syst,on) v. domagać się;upierać się;nastawać
insolent ('ynselent) adj. bezczelny;zuchwały;butny;wyniosły
insoluble (yn'soljubl) adj. nierozpuszczalny;nie do rozwiązania
insolvent (yn'solwent) adj. niewypłacalny; s. bankrut;bankrutka
insomnia (yn'somnja) s. bezsen-
ność (nie normalna)
insomuch (,ynsou'macz) adv.
o tyle; do tego stopnia;tak dalece
inspect (yn'spekt) v. oglądać;
doglądać; mieć nadzór;badać
inspection (yn'spekszyn) s.
przegląd; oglądanie; inspekcja;
doglądanie;sprawdzanie;kontrola
inspector (yn'spekter) s. inspektor;nadzorca;kontroler
inspiration (,ynspe'rejszyn) s.
natchnienie ;wdech;wdychanie
inspire (yn'spajer) v. natchnąć;
podsunąć; zainspirować;wdychać

install(yn'sto:1) v. instalować;
wprowadzać na stanowisko
installation (,ynsto:'lejszyn)
s. instalacja; wprowadzenie
na stanowisko;zamontowanie
instal(l)ment (yn'sto:lment)
s. część całości; rata
instance ('ynstens) s. wypadek;
przykład ;v.przytaczać przykład
instant ('ynstent) adj. nagły;
natychmiastowy; bieżący;
s. moment; chwila (szczególna)
instantaneous (,ynsten'tejnjes)
adj. natychmiastowy; momentalny ;zdarzający się w momencie
instantly (yn'stently) adv.
natychmiast; momentalnie
instead (yn'sted) adv. zamiast
tego; natomiast; w miejsce
instead of (yn'sted,ow) adv.
zamiast (kogoś, czegoś)
instigate ('ynstygejt) v. podżegać;podjudzać;prowokować
instigator ('ynstygejter) s.
podżegacz;prowokator;poduszczy-
ciel
instil(l) (yn'styl) v. wsączać;
wpajać (uczucia etc.);wkraplać
instinct ('ynstynkt) s. instynkt;adj.tchnący(czymś);pełen
instinctive (yn'stynktyw) adj.
instynktowny; odruchowy
institute ('ynstytju:t) s. instytut; v. zakładać; ustanawiać; zarządzać(śledztwo etc.)
institution (,ynty'tju:szyn) s.
instytucja; ustanowienie
instruct (yn'strakt) v. uczyć
instruction (yn'strakszyn) s.
pouczenie; nauka; instrukcja
instructive (yn'straktyw) adj.
pouczający; kształcący
instructor (yn'strakter) s.
nauczyciel;wykładowca;instruktor
instructress (yn'straktrys) s.
nauczycielka ;instruktorka
instrument ('ynstrument) s.
instrument; przyrząd;dokument
insubordinate (,ynseb'o:rdnyt)
adj. niesforny; nieposłuszny
insufferable (yn'saferebl) adj.
nieznośny; nie do zniesienia
insufficient (,ynse'fyszent)
adj. niedostateczny;nieodpowiedni

insulate ('ynsjulejt) v. izolować;oddzielać;odosabniać
insult ('ynsalt) s. zniewaga;
insult, (yn'salt) v. lżyć; znieważać;uchybiać;zelżyć
insupportable (,ynse'po:rtebl)
adj. nie do zniesienia; nieznośny;nieuzasadniony
insurance (yn'szuerens) s.
ubezpieczenie;a.ubezpieczeniowy
insurance policy (yn'szuerens'-
polysy) s. polisa ubezpieczeniowa;polisa asekuracyjna
insure (yn'szuer) v. ubezpieczać
(się);asekurować;zabezpieczać
insurmountable (,ynse:r'maun-
tebl) adj. niepokonany
insurrection (,ynse'rekszyn) s.
powstanie; insurekcja
intact (yn'taekt) adj. nietknięty ;nie uszkodzony
integrate ('yntygrejt) v. scalić; uzupełnić; całkować
integrity (yn'tegryty) s. uczciwość; rzetelność; czystość;
prawość ;niepodzielność
intellect ('yntylekt) s. rozum;
umysł;rozsądek;wybitne umysły
intellectual (,ynty'lekczuel)
adj. intelektualny; umysłowy;
s. intelektualista;inteligent
intelligence (yn'telydżens) s.
inteligencja; informacja; wywiad;wiadomości;nowiny;informac-
ja
intelligent (yn'telydżent) adj.
inteligentny;łatwo uczący się
intelligentsia (yn'tely'dżencja)
s. inteligencja (warstwa kraju)
intelligible (yn'telydżybl) adj.
zrozumiały; jasny;wyraźny
intemperate (yn'temperyt) adj.
nieumiarkowany; bez umiaru
intend (yn'tend) v. zamierzać;
przeznaczać; mieć na myśli
intense (yn'tens) adj. napięty;
usilny; gorliwy;wytężony;uczucio-
wy
intensify (yn'tensyfaj) v.
wzmóc; wzmocnić; napiąć;wzmagać
intensity (yn'tensyty) s. inten-
sywność; wzmożenie;natężenie
intensive (yn'tensyw) adj. intensywny; wzmożony ;silny; wzmacniający

intent (yn'tent) s. plan; zamiar; adj. ważny; zamierzający; zajęty;pochłonięty;zdecydowany
intent on (yn'tent on) adj. pochłónięty; zajęty czyms
intention (yn'tenszyn) s. zamiar; cel;zamierzenie(czynu)
intentional (yn'tenszenel) adj. umyślny; celowy;zamierzony
inter (yn'te:r) v. grzebać
intercede (,ynte:r'si:d) v. wstawiać się; orędować
intercept ('ynte:rsept) v. przechwycić; przejąć; przerwać; udaremnić; podsłuchać
intercession (,ynter'seszyn) s. wstawiennictwo;orędownictwo
interchange (,ynte:r'czejndż) s. wzajemna wymiana; v. wymieniać się; zmieniać się
intercourse ('ynterko:rs) s. stosunek; obcowanie;spółkowanie
interdict (,ynter'dykt) s. zakaz; v. zakazywać;zabraniać
interest('yntryst) s. zainteresowanie; ciekawość; odsetki; interes;procent;v.zainteresować
interested ('yntrystyd) adj. zaciekawiony; zainteresowany
interesting ('yntrystyng) adj. ciekawy; interesujący
interfere (,ynter'fier) v. wtrącać się; wdawać się; kolidować; zakłócać;dokuczać
interfere with (,ynter'fier,łys) v. mieszać się do kogos
interference (,ynter'fierens) s. wtrącanie się; zakłocenie
interior (yn'tierjer) adj. wewnętrzny; środkowy; s. wnętrze głąb kraju;głąb duszy(serca)
interior decorator (yn'tierjer 'dekerejter) s. architekt wnętrz; sprzedawca mebli
interjection (,ynter'dżekszyn) s. okrzyk; wykrzyknik
interlude (ynter'lu:d) s. przerwa; antrakt
intermediary (,ynter'mi:diery) adj. pośredni; pośredniczący; s. pośrednik;piśredniczka;pośrednie stadium;pośrednia forma;pośredni produkt; agent

intermediate (,ynter'mi:djet) adj. pośredni; środkowy; średni;s.pośrednik;v.pośredniczyć
intermingle (,ynter'myngl) v. mieszać (się); pomieszać (się)
intermission (,ynter'myszyn) s. przerwa;pauza; antrakt
intermittent (,ynter'mytent) adj. przerywany; niemiarowy
intern (yn'te:rn) v. internować; odbywać praktykę lekarską; intern ('ynte:rn) s. praktykant lekarski w szpitalu
internal ('ynte:rnl) adj. wewnętrzny; krajowy; domowy
international (,ynter'naeszenl) adj. międzynarodowy; s. międzynarodówka; zawody międzynarodowe;zawodnik międzynarodowy
interpose (,ynter'pouz) v. wstawać; wtrącać (się); przerywać
interpret (yn'ter:pryt) v. tłumaczyć i objaśniać; interpretować;rozumieć(opatrznie etc.)
interpretation (yn,te:rpry'tejszyn) s. interpretacja; tłumaczenie;sposób zrozumienia
interpreter (yn'te:rpryter) s. tłumacz (ustny)
interrogate (yn'teregejt) v. wypytywać; przesłuchiwać
interrogation (yn,tere'gejszyn) s. przesłuchanie; pytanie
interrogative (,ynte'rogetyw) adj. pytający (np. ton)
interrupt (,ynte'rapt) v. przerywać; zasłaniać (widok)
interruption (,ynte'rapszyn) s. przerwa (w czynności etc.)
intersect (,ynte:r'skt) v. przecinać (się);pokrzyżować)się)
intersection (,ynter'sekszyn) s. przecinanie się; skrzyżowanie
interval ('ynterwel) s. odstęp; przerwa;antrakt;okres(pogody)
intervene (,ynter'wi:n) s. wdawać się; interweniować; zdarzyć sie; zajść;być między(dwoma etc.)
intervention (,ynter'wenszyn) s. interwencja; wdanie się
interview ('ynterwju:) s. wywiad; rozmowa; v. mieć wywiad; widzieć się z kimś (dla wywiadu)

interviewer ('ynterwju:er) s.
przeprowadzający wywiad
intestines, (yn'testynz) pl.
wnętrzności ; jelita
intimacy ('yntymesy) s. zażyłość; intymność; poufałe sto-
sunki(płciowe);poufałość
intimate ('yntymyt),adj. zażyły; wewnętrzny; intymny;
v. zawiadamiać; dawać do zrozumienia;s.serdeczny przyjaciel
intimation (,ynty'mejszyn) s.
zawiadomienie; danie do zrozumienia;napomknięcie;znak(czegoś)
intimidate (yn'tymydejt) v.
zastraszyć; onieśmielić
into ('yntu:) prep. do; w; na
intolerable· (yn'tolerebl) adj.
nieznośny;nie do zniesienia
intolerant (yn'telerent) adj.
nietolerancyjny; nie znoszący
czegoś (cudzych przekonań etc.)
intoxicate (yn'toksykejt) v.
upić; upajać; odurzać się
intransitive (yn'traensytyw)
adj. & s. nieprzechodni
intrepid (yn'trepyd) adj. nie-
ustraszony ;śmiały;odważny
intricate ('yntrykyt) adj. zawiły ;trudny do zrozumienia
intrigue (yn'tri:g) s. intryga;
potajemna miłość; v. intrygo-
wać; potajemnie utrzymywać
stosunek miłosny; zaciekawiać
introduce (,yntre'dju:s) v.
wprowadzać (coś lub kogoś);
przedstawiać; rozpoczynać; wsu-
wać; wysuwać; wkładać;zapoznawać
introduction (,yntre'dakszyn) s.
wstęp; wprowadzenie; włożenie;
wsunięcie; przedstawienie
(kogoś);przedmowa;innowacja etc.
introductory (,yntre'daktery)
adj. wstępny; wprowadzający
intrude (,yn'tru:d) v. wpychać
(sie); wciskać (sie); wedrzec
(sie); narzucać (sie) (komuś)
intruder (yn'tru:der) s. natręt;
intruz; nieproszony gość
intrusion (yn'tr:żyn) s. wcis-
nięcie (sie); wepchnięcie (sie);
narzucanie (sie); wdarcie (sie)
w cudze prawa

intuition (,yntju'yszyn) s.
intuicja;przeczucie;wyczucie
inutile (yn'ju:tyl) adj. niepotrzebny; bezcelowy;bezużyteczny
invade (yn'wejd) v. najeżdżać;
wdzierać się; zalewać; owła-
dać; ogarniać; wtargnąć
invader (yn'wejder) s. najeżdż-
ca ;okupant
invalid (yn'weli:d) s. chory;
inwalida ;kaleka;człowiek słaby
invalid (yn'waelyd) adj. nieważny ;nieprawomocny
invalidate (yn'daelydejt) v.
unieważniać (prawnie etc.)
invaluable (yn'waeljuebl) adj.
bezcenny; nieoceniony
invariable (yn'weeryebl) adj.
niezmienny;stały;równomierny
invariably (yn'v-eryebly) adv.
niezmiennie;stale;równomiernie
invasion (yn'wejżyn ) s. inwazja; najazd; wdarcie (się)
invective (yn'wektyw) s. in-
wektywa; obelga; napaść (słow-
na);obelżywe słowa
invent, (yn'went) v. wynaleźć;
wymyślić;zmyślić(coś na kogoś)
invention (yn'wenszyn) s. wynalazek; wymysł; zmyślenie
inventive (yn'wentyw) adj. pomysłowy; wynalazczy
inventor (yn'wentor) s. wynalazca (w nauce,mechanice etc.)
inverse (yn'we:rs) adj. odwrotny; s. odwrotność (czegoś)
inversion (yn'we:rżyn) s. od-
wrócenie; inwersja; homo-
seksualizm ;wynicowanie
invert (yn'we:rt) v. odwrócić;
przestawić; s. homoseksualista
inverted commas (yn'we:rtyd -
'komes) cudzysłów
invest (yn'west) v. inwestować;
wyposażać; oblegać; obdarzać
investigate (yn'westygejt) v.
badać; prowadzić dochodzenie
investigation (yn,westy'gejszyn) s. badanie; dochodzenie; śledztwo;rozpatrzenie;do-
ciekanie
investigator (yn'westygejtor)
s. badacz ;agent(prokuratury)

investment (yn'westment) s.
inwestycja; lokata; oblężenie;osaczenie;obleczenie
invincible (yn'wynsebl) adj.
niepokonany; niezwyciężony
inviolable (yn'wajelebl) adj.
nienaruszalny; nietykalny;
niepogwałcony ;niezniszczalny
invisible (yn'wyzybl) adj.
niewidoczny; niewidzialny
invitation (,ynwy'tejszyn) s.
zaproszenie (pisemne,słowne)
invite (yn'wajt) v. zapraszać;
wywoływać; ściągać; nęcić;
zachęcać; prosic o (radę)
invoice ('ynwojs) s. faktura;
v. fakturować
invoke (yn'wouk) v. wzywać;
odwoływać się; wywoływać
involuntary (yn'wolentery) adj.
mimowolny; nieumyślny; bez-
wiedny (czyn,ruch etc.)
involve (yn'wolw) v. gmatwać;
wikłać; wmieszać; komplikco-
wać; obejmować; wymagać
invulnerable (yn'walnerebl)
adj. nie do zranienia; nienaruszalny; nie do zdobycia
inward ('ynłerd) adj. wewnętrzny; adv. wewnątrz;w sercu etc.
inwards ('ynłerds) adv. wewnątrz ;w duchu ; w myśli
iodine ('ajoudi:n) s. jod
I.O.U. =I owe you ('ajou'ju:) s.
kwit; skrypt dłużny
irascible (y'raesybl) adj.
gniewliwy; popędliwy; wybuchowy;skory do gniewu
iridescent (,yry'desnt) adj.
mieniący się; tęczowy
iris ('ajerys) s. tęczówka
Irish ('ajerysz) adj. irlandz-
ki;s. Irlandczyk
iron ('ajern) s. żelazo; żelazko;(pistolet; rewolwer;)adj.
żelazny; v. zakuwać; prasować
ironic(al) (aj'ronyk(el)) adj.
ironiczny; drwiący;uczczypliwy.
ironing ('ajernyng) s. prasowa-
nie (bielizna etc.)
ironmonger ('ajern,manger) s.
handlarz wyrobów żelaznych;wła-
ciciel sklepu żelaznego

iron mold ('ajernmould) s.
plama od rdzy
ironworks ('ajernłe:rks) s. huta żelaza ;przetwórnia żelaza
irony ('ajereny) s. ironia
irradiate (y'rejdjejt) v. oswietlać; naświetlać; oświecać;
rozjaśniać; rozpromienić
irrational (y'raesznel) adj.
nieracjonalny; nierozumny;
niewymierny;s.liczba niewymierna
irreconcilable (y'rekesajlebl)
adj. nieprzejednany; nie dający się pogodzic(z wiarą etc.)
irrecoverable (,yry'kawerebl)
adj. niepowetowany; nie do
odzyskania;stracony bezpowrotnie
irredeemable (,yry'di:mebl)
adj. niewymienny; beznadziejny;nieodwracalny;nieodkupny
irregular (y'regjuler) adj. nieregularny; nierówny; nieporządny; nielegalny;nieprawidłowy
irrelevant (y'relywent) adj.
nieistotny; niestosowny; oderwany; od rzeczy;nie do rzeczy
irremovable (,yry'mu:webl) adj.
nieusuwalny;nie do pokonania
irreparable (y'reperebl) adj.
niepowetowany;nie do naprawie-
irreplaceble (,yry'plejsebl) adj.
niezastąpiony;nie do zastąpienia
irrepressible (,yry'presybl)
adj. niepohamowany;nieodparty
irreproachable (,yry'prouczebl)
adj. nienaganny; bez zarzutu
irresistible (,yry'zystybl) adj.
nieodparty;porywający;gwałtowny
irresolute (y'rezelu:t) adj.
niezdecydowany; chwiejny
irrespective (t.yrys'pektyw) adj.
niezależny; adv. niezależnie;
bez względu na...;bez szacunku
irresponsible (,yrys'ponsybl)
adj. nieodpowiedzialny;nieobli-
irretrievable (,yry'tri:webl)
adj. bezpowrotnie stracony
irreverent (y'rewerent) adj.
lekceważący; uchybiający
irrevocable (y'rewekebl) adj.
nieodwołalny; nie do odwołania
irrigate ('yrygejt) v. nawadniać; przepłukiwać; oświeżać

irritable ('yrytebl) adj.
draźliwy; wraźliwy; nerwowy;
przewraźliwiony;skory do gniewu
irritate ('yrytejt) v. denerwować; irytować; draźnić;
rozdraźniac;uniewaźnić prawnie
irritation (,yry'tejszyn) s.
irytacja; rozdraźnienie
is (yz) v. jest; zob. be
island ('ajlend) s. wyspa;
wysepka (na bruku)
isle (ajl) s. wyspa; v. źyć
na wyspie ;zrobić (jak)wyspę
isn't ('yznt) = is not; exp.:
nie jest (w domu etc.)
isn't it ? ('yznt yt) nieprawda ? czy nie prawda?
isolate ('ajselejt) v. odosab-
niac; izolować;osamotnić
isolated ('ajselejtyd) adj.
odosobniony;osamotniony
isolation (,ajse'lejszyn) s.
odosobnienie; izolacja; wyodrębnienie;osamotnienie
issue ('yszu:) s. wydanie;
przydział; zeszyt; spor; problem; argument; wynik; koniec;
ujście; wyjście; wypływ; potomstwo; upuszczenie; dochod;
v. wysyłać; wypuszczać; wydawać; dawać w wyniku; wychodzic; pochodzić;emitować
isthmus ('ysmes) s. przesmyk;
międzymorze ;ciesn; węzina
it (yt) pron. to; ono
Italian (y'taeljen) adj. włoski
itch ('ycz) s. swędzenie;
świerzb;chętka; v. czuc swędzenie; swędzic;miec ochotę
item ('ajtem) s. pozycja; punkt
programu; artykuł; wiadomość;
adv. podobnie; takźe;teź dotyczy
itemize ('ajte,majz) v. wy-
szczegolniac(rachunek,spis)
itinerary (aj'tynerery) s. marszruta; szlak; przewodnik;
adj. podroźny; drogowy
its (yts) pron. jego; jej; swoj
itself (yt'self) pron. się; siebie; sobie; sam; sama; samo
ivory ('ajwery) s. kość słoniowa;klawisz fortepianu;biel kre-
mowa;adj.z kości słoniowej;biały

ivy ('ajwy) s. bluszcz
j (dźej) dziewiąta litera
angielskiego alfabetu
jab (dźaeb) s. szturchaniec;
dźgnięcie; v. szturchać; dźgac
jack (dźaek) s. lewarek; dźwignia; przyrząd; walet; flaga;
gniazdko elektr.; złącze
jack up ('dźaek,ap) v. podnieść
lewarkiem;wyśrubowanie(cen)
jackal ('dźaeko:1) s. szakal;
sługus;harować za kogoś
jackass ('dźaekaes) s. osioł;
dureń; bałwan;menda;niedojda
jackdaw ('dźaekdo:) s. kawka
jacket ('dźaekyt) s. marynarka;
źakiet; kurtka; okładzina; obwoluta; osłona; v. okrywac; nakładac okładzinę;wkładać do teki
jack-in-the-box ('dźaek-yn-dy-
boks) s. figurka wyskakująca
z pudełka;typ ognia sztucznego
jackknife ('dźaeknajf) s.
scyzoryk; nóż składany
jack-of-all-trades ('dźaek,ow-
'o:1,trejds) majster do
wszystkiego;majster klepka
jackpot ('dźaek,pot) s. główna
wygrana; pula
jackscrew ('dźaekskru:) s. lewar śrubowy (podnośnik)
jag (dźaeg) s. ostry występ;
zadarcie; nacięcie; podniecenie; popijawa; zabawa; v. po-
szarpac; postrzepic; ząbkowac
jagged ('dźaegyd) adj. po-
strzępiony;wyszczerbiony;szczerbaty
jaguar ('dźaegjuer) s. jaguar
jail (dźejl) s. ciupa; więzienie;v. więzic; uwięzic(kogoś)
jam (dźaem) s. tłok; zator; korek; zła sytuacja; v. stłoczyc;
zablokowac; zaciąc; zagłuszyc
janitor ('dźaenitor) s. portier;
dozorca;sprzątacz biurowy etc.
January ('dźaenjuery) s. styczeń ; a.styczniowy (dzień etc.)
Japanese (,dźaepe'ni:z) adj.
japoński; s.Japończyk
jar (dźa:r) s. słoj; słoik;
zgrzyt; kłotnia; drganie;
v. zgrzytac; draźnić; wstrząsac; kłocić się ;trząsc;razic

138

jaundice ('dżo:ndys) s. żół-
taczka ;v.powodować żółtaczkę
javelin ('dżaewlyn) s. oszczep
jaw (dżo:) s. szczęka; v. ględzic; gadać;wstawiać mowę
jaw-bone ('dżo:boun) s. kość
szczękowa; v. nakłaniać słowami (pod presją)
jazz (dżaz) s. muzyka jazzowa;
v. kłamać;adj.zgrzytliwy;krzyk-
liwy
jazz it up ('dżaz,yt'ap) v.
ożywiać; ulepszać (coś)
jay (dżej) s. sójka; dudek;
pleciuga; gaduła (arogancki)
jay-walker ('dżej,ło:ker) s.
nieprawidłowo przechodzący
jezdnię ;roztrzepaniec
jealous ('dżeles) adj. zazdrosny; baczny (nadzór);zawistny
jealousy ('dżelesy) s. zazdrość;
zawiść ;wybuch zazdrości
jeep (dżi:p) s. łazik; samochód
terenowy (silnie zbudowany)
jeer (dżier) s. kpina; szyderstwo; drwina; v. drwić; kpić;
wykpiwać (ordynarnie i złośliwie)
jelly ('dżely) s. galareta;
kisiel;v.zgalarecieć;robić gala-
jellyfish ('dżelyfysz) s. meduza;człowiek słabej woli
jeopardize ('dżepe,dajz) v. narazić na niebezpieczeństwo
jerk (dże:rk) s. szarpnięcie;
skręt; skurcz; pchnięcie; bzik;
frajer; v. szarpać; targać;
pchnąć; rzucać się;wzdrygać się
jerky ('dże:rky) adj. urwany;
trzesący; bzikowaty;spazmatyczny
jersey ('dże:rzy) s. sweter
jest (dżest) s. żart; dowcip;
zabawa; pośmiewisko; v. żartować; dowcipkować;przekomarzać się
jester ('dżester) s. błazen;
trefniś; błazen nadworny
jet (dżet) s. strumień; wytrysk;
płomień; dysza; rozpylacz; odrzutowiec; v. tryskać;a.czarny
jak smoła
jet engine (,dżet'endżyn) s.
motor odrzutowy
jet lag('dżet,laeg) s.ujemny
efekt zmiany sfer czasu na
pasażera samolotu odrzutowego

jet plane ('dżet,plejn) s. samolot odrzutowy;odrzutowiec
jet-propelled ('dżet-pre,peld)
adj. odrzutowy
jet set ('dżet,set) s. złota
młodzież; prominenci
jetty (dżety) s. grobla; molo;
adj. czarny jak smoła
jewel ('dżu:el) s. klejnot;
drogi kamień; v. ozdabiać
klejnotami; osadzać na kamie-
niach(zamontować)
jeweler ('dżu:eler) s. jubiler;własciciel sklepu jubiler-
skiego
jewelry ('dżu:elry) s, klejno-
ty; biżuteria;kosztowności
Jewish ('dżu:ysz) adj. żydowski
jibe (dżajb) v. zgadzać się;
pasować (do czegoś);harmonizo-
wać
jiffy ('dżyfy) s. mig; chwi-
leczka;momencik;skundka
jiggle ('dżygl) v. kołysac;
lekko hustać;wstrząsąc zrywnie
jingle ('dżyngl) v. brzękac;
szczękac; dzwonić; s. brzęk;
szczęk; wierszyk(rymy);dzwonek
job (dżob) s. robota; zajęcie;
zadanie; posada; v. pracować;
robić; handlowac; wynajmować
job (dżob) v. ukłuć; dźgnąc;
dziobnąc; s. dźgnięcie;praca;
dziobnięcie;zadanie;robota;fach
jobless ('dżoblys) adj. bezrobotny ;bez pracy
job-work ('dżobłerk) s. praca
na akord (zob. piece-work)
jockey ('dżoky) s. dżokej;
v. oszukać; nabrać;pchać się na
pozycje
jocular ('dżokjuler) adj. wesoły; żartobliwy;krotochwilny
jocularity (,dżokju'laeryty)
s. wesołość; żartobliwość;
żarty;ktotochwilność;figlarność
jocund ('dżoukend) adj. wesoły
jog (dżog) s. potrącenie; poruszenie; trucht; rógwystęp;
v. potrącać; poruszać; przebiedować; biec truchtem;telepać
jog-trot ('dżog'trot) s.
trucht;a.monotonny;jednostajny

join (džoyn) v. łączyć; przyłączac (się); przytykac do;
spotykac się;brac udział
joiner ('džojner) s. stolarz
joint (džoynt) v. spajac;łą-
czyc; cwiartowac; kantowac;
s. spojenie; fuga; złącze;
zestawienie; zawiasa francuska;
część; lokal; melina; a. wspólny; połączony;dzielący się z kims
joint stock ('džoynt,stok) adj.
akcyjny (bank);udziałowy
joke (džouk) s. żart; dowcip;
figiel; v. żartowac z kogos;
dowcipkowac;wysmiac;zadrwic
joker ('džouker) s. żartownis;
dowcipnis; gosc; facet; džo-
ker; pułapka; trudnosc
jolly ('džoly) adj. wesoły; miły; podochocony; adv. szalenie;
bardzo; v. przychlebiac; nabierac; zachęcac;mitygowac;ugłas-
jolt (džoult) v. wstrząsac;
podrzucac; s. wstrząs; podrzu-
cenie; szarpnięcie;podskok
jostle ('džosl) v. rozpychac
(się); roztrącac; szarpac się;
walczyc (z kims); s. pchniecie;
starcie;szturchnięcie;tłok;scisk
jot down ('džot,dałn) v. zapi-
sac napredce;zanotowac pospiesz-
journal ('džе:rnl) s. dziennik;
czasopismo; czop;os w łożysku
journalism ('dže:rnlyzem) s.
dziennikarstwo
journey ('dže:rny) v. podrożowac;
s. podroż;jazda;wycieczka
journeyman ('dže:rnymen) s. cze-
ladnik(nauczony rzemiosła)
jovial ('džouwjel) adj. wesoły;
jowialny;pełen dobrego humoru
joy (džoj) s. radosc; uciecha
joyful ('džoyful) adj. radosny;
wesoły;zadowolony(bardzo)
joyous ('džojes) adj.=joyful
jubilant ('džu:bylent) adj.
triumfujący; rozradowany
jubilee ('džu:byli:) s. jubileusz; wielka radosc;a.jubileuszowy
judge (džadž) v. sądzic; osądzac;
rozsadzac; s. sędzia; znawca;
znawczyni;człowiek biegły w oce-

judgment ('džadžment) s.
sąd; sądzenie; wyrok; rozsądek;opinia; ocena; decyzja
judicial (džu'dyszel) adj. sądowy; sędziowski; bezstronny;
krytyczny;sądownie zastrzeżony
judicious (džu'dyszes) a. rozsądny;rozumny;wykazujący rozum
jug (džag) s. dzbanek; koza;
ciupa; v. gotowac; wsadzac do
kozy, ciupy;dusic (potrawkę)
juggle ('džagl) v. żonglowac;
cyganic; robic sztuczki;
s. kuglarstwo;żonglerka
juggler ('džagler) s. kuglarz;
żongler;oszust;kanciarz
jugglery ('džaglery) s. kuglarstwo;podstęp;oszukaństwo;żon-
Jugoslav ('ju:gou'sla:v) adj.
jugosłowianski;Jugosłowianin
juice (džu:s) s. sok; tresc;
benzyna; elektrycznosc;
v. wyciskac sok; doic
juicy ('džu:sy) adj. soczysty;
jędrny;barwny;deszczowy etc.
juke box ('džuk,boks) s. auto-
mat-gramofon(na monety)
July (džu:laj) s. lipiec
jumble ('džambl) s. pomieszac;
kotłowac; mieszanina; galimatias; bigos;trzęsąca jazda
jumble-sale ('džambl,sejl) s.
wyprzedaż wysortowanych to-
warow(często dobroczynna)
jump (džamp) s. skok; sus; podskok; wyskok; v. skakac; pod-
skoczyc; wskoczyc; wyskoczyc;
wyprzedzac; podnosic cenę;
wykoleic;poderwac się;rzucac
jumper ('džamper) s. skoczek;
typ sukni (bez rękawow)
jumpy ('džampy) adj. nerwowy;
zmienny;nierówny;kapryśny
junction ('džankszyn) s. połączenie; złącze; stacja węzło-
wa; węzeł;skrzyżowanie(drog)
juncture('džankczer) s. połączenie; stan rzeczy; krytycz-
na chwila; chwila;przesilenie
June (džu:n) s. czerwiec
jungle ('džangl) s. dżungla;
gaszcz zarosli,lian etc.

junior ('dżu:njer) s. junior;
młodszy; student trzeciego
roku (USA);a.młodszy;z młodszych
junk ('dżąnk) s.złom; szmelc;
narkotyki; v. wyrzucać
junkie ('dżanki) s. narkoman
jurisdiction (,dżurys'dykszyn)
s. wymiar sprawiedliwości;
sądownictwo;zasięg władzy
jurisprudence (,dżurys'pru:-
dens) s. prawoznawstwo
juror ('dżuerer) s. sędzia
przysięgły; ławnik; zaprzysiężony;juror
jury ('dżuery) s. sąd przysięgłych; sąd konkursowy
just (dżast) s. sprawiedliwy;
słuszny; dokładny; adv. własnie; poprostu; zaledwie; przecież; dokładnie; moment wczes-
niej;ściśle;równie;tak samo
just now ('dżast,nał) exp.:
właśnie teraz;przed chwilą
justice ('dżastys) s. sprawiedliwość; słuszność; sę-
dzia(pokoju,sądu najwyższego)
justification (,dżastyfy'kejszyn) s. uzasadnienie;
usprawiedliwienie;wykazanie
justify ('dżastyfaj) v. usprawiedliwić; wytłumaczyć; umoty-
wować; uzasadnić;dać dowody
justly ('dżastly) adv. słusznie;
poprawnie;właściwie;sprawiedli-
jut (dżat) s. występ;v.wystawać
jut out ('dżat,aut) v. wystawać;
sterczeć(na zewnątrz);występować
juvenile ('dżu:wynajl) adj.
małoletni; nieletni; s. wyrostek; młodzik;podrostek
juvenile court ('dżu:wynajl,-
,ko:rt) s. sąd dla nieletnich
juvenile delinquent ('dżu:wy-
najl,dy'lynkłent) s. młodociany przestępca
juxtaposition (,dżakstepe'zyszyn) s. zestawienie; bezpos-
rednie sąsiedztwo(tuż obok)
k (kej)jedenasta litera angielskiego alfabetu
kangaroo (,kaenge'ru:) s. kangur;a.samosądny;nielegalny
kayak ('kajaek)s.kajak;s.kajakowy

keel (ki:l) s. stępka; kil;
v. wywracać do góry stępką
keen (ki:n) adj. ostry; dotkliwy; żywy; cięty; serdeczny;
gorliwy; zapalony; bystry;
przenikliwy; wrażliwy; czuły
keen on ('ki:n.on) adj. palący się do..;czujący miętę
keep; kept; kept (ki:p; kept;
kept)
keep (ki:p) v. dotrzymywać;
przestrzegać; dochować; obchodzić; strzec; pilnować; utrzymywać; prowadzić; trzymać(się)
powstrzymywać się; mieszkać;
kontynuować; s. utrzymanie;
jedzenie; wikt;umocnienie
keep away ('ki:p,ełej) v. trzymać się z daleka;odstraszać
keep back ('ki:p,baek) v. powstrzymać; nie zbliżać się
keep down ('ki:p,dałn) v. trzymać w ryzach; tłumić; kulić
się;utrzymywać na niskim pozio-mie
keep in('ki:p,yn) v. zatrzymywać; nie wychodzić; pozostawać;nie pokazywć się
keep off ('ki:p,of) v. nie dopuszczać; trzymać się z dala
keep on ('ki:p,on) v. kontynuować; iść dalej;nudzić;męczyć
keep on doing ('ki:p,on'du:yŋg)
v. robić dalej; nie przestawać;nie dawać spokoju;nudzić
keep out ('ki:p, ałt) v. nie
wchodzić; trzymać się na uboczu;nie pozwolić wejść;odpędzać
keep talking ('ki:p'to:kyŋg)v.
mówić dalej;kontynuować rozmowę
keep time ('ki:p'tajm) v. być
punktualnym;zapisywać czas pracy
keep to oneself ('ki:p,tu'łan-
self) v. trzymać się na uboczu; żyć w odosobnieniu
keep up ('ki:p,ap) v. dotrzymywać; utrzymywać w porządku;
nie dawać iść spać; trzymać
się w dobrym stanie;czuwać
keep up with ('ki:p,ap'łys) v.
śledzić; dotrzymywać (kroku)
keeper ('ki:per) s. opiekun;
dozorca; strażnik; konserwator;
klamra; kotwica magnesu;skobel

keeping ('ki:pyŋg) s. opieka; zgoda; harmonia;a.do przechowywania
keepsake ('ki:psejk) s. upominek; pamiątka od kogoś
keg (keg) s. beczułka;100 funtów
kennel ('kenl) s. psiarnia; psia buda; ściek; v. trzymac w budzie; mieszkać w norze
kept (kept) v. zob. keep
kerb stone ('ke:rb,stoun) s. krawężnik (ang.) zob. curb
kerchief ('ke:rczyf) s. chustka (na głowę);chustka do nosa
kernel ('ke:rnl) s. jądro; ziarno;sedno sprawy;istotna rzecz
ketchup ('keczap) s. sos pomidorowy (gotowy) do mięsa
kettle ('ketl) s. kocioł; czajnik; imbryk na herbatę
kettledrum ('ketl,dram) s.bębenkocioł(półkulisty)miedziany
key (ki:) s. klucz; klawisz; klin; ton; rafa; wysepka; v. stroić; zamykać kluczem lub zwornikiem;adj.ważny;kontrolujacy
keyboard ('ki:bo:rd) s. klawiatura (maszyny do pisania etc.)
keyhole ('ki:houl) s. dziurka od klucza (w drzwiach etc.)
keynote ('ki:nout) s. nuta kluczowa ;myśl przewodnia
keystone ('ki:stoun) s. zwornik;zasada;główna część
kick (kᴧk) s. kopniak; kopnięcie; wierzgnięcie; wykop; strzał; odrzut; skarga; narzekanie; przyjemność; uciecha; krzepa; miłe podniecenie; opór; v. kopać; wierzgać; skrzywić się; protestować; opierać się
kickback ('kᴧkbaek) s. łapówka za kontrakt;dawanie łapówki
kick downstairs ('kᴧkdaⁱn'steerz) v. degradować; zrzucać ze schodów (kopniakiem)
kick-off ('kᴧkof) s. rozpoczęcie meczu; pierwszy strzał
kick out ('kᴧk aut) v. wyrzucić; wykopać ; pozbyć się
kick the bucket ('kᴧk,dy'bakyt) v. umrzeć; odwalić kitę; wyciagnać nogi;wykitować

kid (kyd) s. koźlę; dzieciak; smyk; młodzik; blaga; bujda; v. urodzić koźlę; bujać; nabierać; żartować;dowcipkować
kid glove ('kydglaw) s. rękawiczka;adj.galowy;delikatny
kidnap ('kydnaep) v. porywać; uprowadzać;ukraść dziecko etc.
kidnapper ('kydnaeper) s. porywacz (dziecka;zakładnika etc.)
kidney ('kydny) s. nerka; rodzaj;a.w kształcie nerki
kidney bean ('kydny,bi:n) s. fasola szparagowa; piesza
kill (kyl) v. zabijać; uśmiercać; wybić; zatrzymać (piłkę, motor) ścinać (piłkę); s.upolowane zwierzę; zabicie; mord
kill time (,kyⁱl'tajm) v. zabijać czas; marnować czas
killer ('kyler) s. zabójca; morderca; narzędzie śmierci
kiln (kyln) s. piec do wypalania lub wysuszania cegieł etc.
kilogram(me) ('kylougraem) s. kilogram;a. kilogramowy
kilometer ('kyle,mi:ter) s. kilometr; a. kilometrowy
kilt (kylt) s. spódniczka męska (szkocka); v. podkasać; plisować pionowo;s.spódnica szkocka
kin (kyn) s. rodzina; krewni; ród; adj. spokrewniony;pokrewny
kind (kajnd) s. rodzaj; jakość; gatunek; charakter; natura; adj. grzeczny; uprzejmy; życzliwy;łagodny;wyrozumiały
kindergarten ('kynder,ga:rtn) s. przedszkole (do szesciu lat wieku)
kindhearted ('kajnd'ha:rtyd) adj. dobrotliwy;współczujacy
kindle ('kyndle) v. rozpalić; rozżarzyc; rozniecać; podniecać;zapalać się
kindly ('kajndly) adj. uprzejmie; życzliwie; adj. dobry; dobrotliwy; życzliwy;adv.uprzejmie
kindness ('kajndnys) s. dobroc; uprzejmość; łaskawość; życzliwość ;życzliwy postępek
kindred ('kyndryd) s. krewni; pokrewieństwo; adj.pokrewny

king (kyŋg) s. król
kingdom ('kyŋgdom) s. królestwo;monarchia;świat(roslin etc.)
kingsize ('kyŋgsajz) adj. wielki; duży;krolewskich wymiarów
kingly ('kyŋgly) adj. królewski
kinsman ('kynzmen) s. krewny;
powinowaty (męszczyzna)
kipper ('kyper) s. śledź wędzony; ryba suszona; v. suszyć;
wędzić i solić; zasuszać(ryby)
kiss (kys) s. całus; v. całować; pocałowac;lekko dotknąc
kit (kyt) s. przybory; narzę-
dzia; wyposażenie; zestaw;
komplet; torba; bagaż; ceb-
rzyk; kubeł;komplet(narzędzi)
kitchen ('kyczn) s. kuchnia
kitchenette ('kyczynet) s.
kuchenka(mała w kawalerce etc.)
kite (kajt) s. latawiec;v.szybo-
wać;
kitten ('kytn) s. kotek
knack (naek) s. spryt; sztuczka; chwyt; dryg; talent
knapsack ('naepsaek) s. plecak
knave (nejw) s. łajdak; łotr;
szelma; walet;naciągacz;kanalia
knavery ('nejwery) s. łajdactwo; szelmostwo;niegodziwość
knead ('ni:d) v. miesić; gniesć;
masowac;kształcić(charakter)
knee ('ni:) s. kolano;v.klękac
knee breeches ('ni:bryczyz) pl.
spodnie do kolan
kneel; knelt; knelt (ni:l; nelt;
nelt)
kneel ('ni:l) v. klękac
knelt(nelt) zob. kneel
knew (nju:) zob . know
knickerbockers ('nikerbockers)
s. pumpy; krótkie spodnie
spięte pod kolanami
knickknack ('niknaek) s. cacko;
fatałaszek; przysmaczek
knife (najf) s. nóż; v. krajac;
kłuć nożem; zakłuc;zadzgać nożem
knight (najt) s. rycerz; v. nadawać szlachectwo;nobilitować
knit; knit; knit (nyt; nyt; nyt)
knit (nyt) v. robić na drutach;
dziac; marszczyc (brwi); łączyc; ściągac;powodować zrośnię-
cie(kości);spajac(cementem)

knitting (nytyŋg) s. dzianie;
trykotarstwo ;dziewiarstwo
knives (najwz) pl. noże; pl.od
knife
knob (nob) s. guzik; guz; gałka; sęk;uchwyt;pokrętło;rączka
knock (nok) s. stuk; uderzenie;
pukanie; stukac; pukać; zapu-
kac; uderzyc; zderzyc; szturchac;zderzyc się
knock down ('nok,dałn) v. powalic; obniżac cenę;rozkręcac
knock out ('nok,aut) v. nokau-
towac; wybijac; wymęczyc
knock over ('nok,ower) v. przewracac; przewrócić
knocker ('noker) s. kołatka na
drzwiach;malkontent;opukiwacz
knot (not) s. węzeł; kokarda;
sęk; zgrubienie; dystans morski 1853 m; v. wiązac; zawiązywac; komplikowac; motac
knotty ('noty) adj. węzłowaty;
sękaty; zawiły; zagadkowy
know; knew; known (nou; nju:;
noun)
know (nou) v. wiedziec; umiec;
znac; móc odróżniac; poznac
know-how ('nouhau) s. umiejęt-
nosc; znajomość rzeczy
knowingly ('nouyŋgly) adj. świadomie; naumyslnie; chytrze
knowledge ('noulydż) s. wiedza;
nauka; znajomość;zasięg wiedzy
knowledgeable ('nolydżebl) adj.
dobrze poinformowany; mądry
knuckle ('nakl) s. staw palca;
kastet; uderzac kośćmi palców
kotow ('kou,tał) = kowtow
kowtow ('koł,tał) v. bic czołem; płaszczyc się; s. ukłon
starochiński czołem do ziemi
Kraut (kraut) adj. szkopski
(niemiecki); kapuściany
kudos ('kju:dos) s. nagroda
lub uznanie za znaczne osiągnięcie; sława (slang)
Ku Klux Klan ('kju:,kluks'klaen)
s. rasistowska tajna organizacja w USA przeciw murzynom,
żydom i katolikom
kulak (ku:'la:k) s. zamożny
chłop; kułak

1                        143                    landing-stage

1 (el) dwunasta litera alfabetu
angielskiego; klauzura; kolanko (rury); kątownik
lab (laeb) s. (slang):labora-
torium; a. laboratoryjny
label ('lejbl) s. nalepka; etykieta; naklejka; przezwisko;
v. przylepiać etykiety (na
coś; komuś);przezywać
labor ('lejber) s. praca; robota; trud; mozół; wysiłek;
klasa robotnicza; poród;
v. ciężko pracować; mozolić
się; borykać się; łudzić się;
brnąć; opracować; rozwodzić
się; rodzić;szczegółowo opracowywać
laboratory (lae'boretery) s.
laboratorium; pracownia
laborious (le'bo:rjes) adj.
pracowity; mozolny; wypracowany;ciężko pracujący
labor union('lejber'ju:njen)
s. związek zawodowy
laborer ('lejberer) s. robotnik płatny na godzinę(fizyczny)
laborite ('lejberajt) s. członek partii pracy (w Anglji)
lace (lejs) s. sznurówka; sznurowadło; koronka; v. sznuro-
wać; przetykać; koronkować;
urozmaicać; chłostać; zakra-
piać (wódkę);młócić;bić;walić
lack (laek) s. brak; niedostatek; v. brakować; nie mieć
czegoś;być bez czegoś
laconic (le'konyk) adj. lakoniczny; zwięzły; treściwy
lacquer ('laeker) s. lakier;
v. lakierować;emaliować
lad (laed) s. chłopak; chłopiec
ladder ('laeder) s. drabina;
v. pruć; rozpruć;puszczać oczka
ladder proof ('laeder,pru:f)
adj. nie prujące się (np. pończochy);nie puszczający oczek
laden ('lejdn) adj. obciążony;
obarczony;pogrążony(w smutku)
lading ('lejdyng)s. fracht; za-
ładowanie; ładunek (statku etc.)
ladle ('lejdl) s. warząchew;
czerpak; chochla; v. czerpać;
nalewać warząchwią (czerpakiem)

lady ('lejdy) s. pani; dama
lady killer ('lejdy,kyler) s.
pożeracz serc niewieścich
ladylike ('lejdylajk) adj. wytworny; zniewieściały
lag (laeg) s. zaleganie; opóź-
nianie; zwłoka;v. zalegać;
wlec się z tyłu; nie nadążać
lag behind ('laeg,by'hajnd) v.
pozostawać w tyle;zalegać
lager ('la:ger) s. wystałe piwo
lagoon (le'gu:n) s. laguna
laid (lejd) zob. lay
lain (lejn) zob. lie
lair (leer) s. barłóg; legowisko; szałas; v.iść na legowisko
lake (lejk) s. jezioro;a.jeziorny
lamb (laem) s. jagnię; baranina
lame (lejm) adj. kulawy; ułomny; v. okulawić; okaleczyć
lament (le'ment) s. lament;
biadanie; v. lamentować; biadać; opłakiwać; narzekać; ubolewać;zawodzić;być w żałobie
lamentable ('laementebl) adj.
opłakany; godny ubolewania;
żałosny;wyrażający ubolewanie
lamentation (,laemen'tejszyn) s.
lament; biadanie;lamentacja
lamp (laemp) s. lampa; latarka;
kaganek; v. świecić; oświetlać;
gapić się;zobaczyć;widzieć
lamppost ('laemppoust) s. słup
latarniany ;latarnia uliczna
lamp shade ('laempszejd) s.
abażur
lance (la:ns) s. lanca; lansjer;
lancet; v.kłuć; przebijać lan-
cą lub lancetem; rozcinać
land (laend) s. ląd; ziemia;
grunt; kraj; v. wyciągać na ląd;
wyładować; zdobyć (np. nagrodę)
landholder ('laend,houlder) s.
właściciel ziemski; dzierżawca
landing ('laendyng) s. lądowanie;
pomost; przystań; półpiętrze
landing field ('laendyng,fi:ld)
s. lotnisko polowe ;lądowisko
landing gear ('laendyng,gier)
s. podwozie (z kołami-samolotu)
landing stage ('laendyng,stejdż)
s. pomost pływający ; wyładunek

landlady ('laend,lejdy) s.
właścicielka domu, hotelu
etc.;gospodyni (pensjonatu)
landlord ('laend,lo:rd) s.
właściciel domu czynszowego;
gospodarz odnajmujący pokój
landmark ('laendma:rk) s. punkt
orientacyjny; słup graniczny
landowner ('laend,otner) s.
właściciel ziemski
landscape ('laendskejp) s.
krajobraz; v. kształtować
teren i ogród (upiększać)
landslide ('laendslajd) s.
osuwisko; lawina głosów
landslip ('laendslyp) s. osuwisko; obsunięcie się ziemi
lane (lejn) s. tor; uliczka;
szlak; przejście; linia ruchu kołowego ;trasa(samolotu)
language ('laengłydż) s. mowa;
język mowiony i pisany
languid ('laengłyd) s. ospały;
omdlały; słaby; ociężały; powolny; rozmarzony; tęskny
languish ('laengłysz) v. omdle-
wać; marnieć; ginąć z tęsknoty ;mieć wyraz zadumy
languor ('laenger) s. omdlenie;
osłabienie;ociężałość; ospa-
łość; tęsknota; rozmarzenie;
powolność;brak wigoru;słabość
lank (laenk) adj. mizerny; wysoki; chudy; wychudzony;
prosty; gładki ;długi i płaski
lanky ('laenky) adj. wychudzony; wysoki i chudy
lanolin ('laenolyn) s. lanolina
lantern ('laentern) s. latarnia
lap (laep) s. łono; podołek;
poła; okrążenie; zanadrze;
dolinka; chlupotanie; lura;
v. spowijać; otulać; zakładać
(jak dachówki); wystawać;
chłeptać; chlupotać;chlupać
lapel (le'pel) s. klapa
(płaszcza)dochodząca kołnierza
lapse (laeps) s. lapsus; upływ;
okres; omyłka; v. potknąć się;
odstąpić; omylić się; upłynąć;
stracić ważność; minąć; przechodzić;pogrążyc się w stan...

larceny ('la:rseny) s. kradzież
larch (la:rcz) s. modrzew
lard (la:rd) s. smalec; v. szpikować; naszpikowywać;ozdabiać :scytatami
larder ('la:rder) s. spiżarnia
large (la:rdż) adj. wielki;
rozległy; obfity; hojny
largely ('la:rdżly)adv. znacz-
nie; hojnie; suto; w dużym
stopniu; w dużej ilości;głównie
lark (la:rk) s. skowronek; zabawa; uciecha; v. figlować;
żartować; przeskakiwać
larva ('la:rwa) s. larwa
larynx ('laerynks) s. krtań
lascivious (le'syvjes) adj.
lubieżny;wzbudzający lubieżność
lash (laesz) s. bicz; uderzenie;
nagana; rzęsa; v. chłostać; machać; walić; pędzić; uwiązać
lass (laes) s. dziewczyna;
dziewczę; młoda kobieta
lasso (lae'su:) s. lasso;
v. chwytać na lasso
last (laest) adj. ostatni; ubiegły; ostateczny; adv. po raz
ostatni; ostatnio; wreszcie;
w końcu; v. trwać; wytrzymac;
wystarczyc; długo służyc;
s. koniec; kres; wytrzymałość;
kopyto szewskie ;ostatnie dziecko
last but one ('laest,bat'łan)
exp.: przedostatni
lasting ('la:styng) adj. stały;
trwały ;długo trwały
lastly ('la:stly) adv. w końcu;
na końcu ;w konkluzji;ostatecznie
last night ('laest,najt) exp.
wczoraj wieczór
last name ('laest,nejm) s. nazwisko
latch (laecz) s. zasuwka; rygiel; zatrzask; v. zamykać na
zasuwkę, rygiel lub zatrzask
latch onto ('laecz,ontu) v.
uczepić się kogoś
late (lejt) adj. & s. późny;
spózniony; były; zmarły; adv.
późno; poniewczasie; niegdyś
lately ('lejtly) adv. ostatnio
later on ('lejter,on) adv.
później; potem; dalej

lath (laeŋ) s. łata; deseczka;
v. pokrywać łatami(do tynkowa-
nia)
lathe (lejz) s. tokarnia; koło
garncarskie; v. toczyć (na
tokarni); obrabiać(na obrabiarce)
lather ('laedzer) s. piana;
mydliny; v. mydlić (brodę);
zapienić (się); prać; łoić
Latin ('laetyn) adj. łaciński;
s. łacina; łacinnik
latitude ('laetytju:d) s. szerokość (geograficzna); szerokość poglądów; zakres; roz-
miary; wolność; swoboda (np.
działania); tolerancja
latter ('laeter) adj, drugi;
końcowy; schyłkowy;ostatni
latterly ('laeterly) adv. ostatnio; niedawno; później
lattice ('laetys) s. kratownica; v. kratować;ułożyć w kratę
laudable ('lo:debl) adj. chwalebny ;godny pochwały
laugh (laef) v. śmiać się; za-
śmiać się;roześmiać się
laugh at ('laef,et) v. wyśmiewać ;uśmiać sie(z czegoś)
laugh away ('laef,e'łej) v. zbyć
śmiechem
laugh off ('laef,of) v. obrócić
w żart;pokryć zmieszanie śmiechem
laughter ('laefter) s. śmiech
launch (lo:ncz) v. puszczać
w ruch; spuszczać na wodę;
miotać; rzucać; zadawać; wydawać; s. szalupa; spuszczenie
na wodę (statku,okrętu,etc.)
launching pad ('lo:nczyŋg,paed)
s. wyrzutnia (rakiet)
launderette (lo:n'dret) s. pralnia samoobsługowa
laundry ('lo:ndry) s. pralnia;
bielizna do prania
laurel ('lorel) s. wawrzyn;
laur; v. wieńczyć wawrzynem
lavatory ('laewetery) s. umywalnia; ustęp; umywalka
lavender ('laewynder) s. lawenda; v. wkładać lawendę w bieliznę ;a. lawendowy
lavish ('laewysz) adj. hojny;su-
ty; rozrzutny; v. nie szczędzić
pieniędzy, miłości etc.)

law (lo:) s. prawo; ustawa; reguła; sądy;posłuszeństwo prawu
lawful ('lo:ful) adj, legalny;
słuszny; prawowity; z prawego
łoża; prawnie uznany
lawless ('lo:lys) adj. bezprawny; łamiący prawo; rozpustny
lawn (lo:n) s. trawnik; murawa
lawsuit ('lo:sju:t) s. proces
(sądowy) ;sprawa sądowa
lawyer ('lo:jer) s. prawnik;
adwokat ;radca prawny
lax (laeks) adj. luźny; nieszczelny; niedbały; nieścisły;
mający rozwolnienie;wolny
laxative ('laeksetyw) adj.& s.
przeczyszczający (środek)
laxity ('laeksyty) s. luźność;
nieścisłość; niedokładność;
niedbalstwo;rozwiązłość
lay; laid; laid( lej; lejd;
lejd)
lay (lej) v. kłaść; uspokajać;
układać; skręcać (się); zaczaić
się; spać z kims; s. położenie; układ; spanie (z kims);
adj. świecki; laicki; niefachowy; lay- zob. lie
layout ('lejout) s. rozkład;
plan ;założenie; układ
lay out ('lej.aut) v. układać;
projektować; powalić (slang):
zabić; wydatkować; wyłożyć
lay up ('lejap) v. zbierać;
gromadzić; przechowywać
layer ('lejer) s. warstwa; od-
kład; kura niosąca; zakładają-
cy się;pokład
layman ('lejmen) s. człowiek
świecki; laik
lazy ('lejzy) adj. leniwy;
próżniaczy;ociężały
lead (led) s. ołow; v. pokrywać
ołowiem; obciążać ołowiem
lead; led; led (li:d; led;led)
lead (li:d) v. prowadzić; kierować; dowodzić; naprowadzać;
nasunąć; namówić; dyrygować;
przewodzić; s. kierownictwo;
przewodnictwo; przewaga; prym;
wskazówka ;przykład;powodzenie
leaden ('ledn) adj. ołowiany;
ciężki;ociężały;ponury;szary

leader ('li:der) s. przywódca; lider; przewodnik; prowadzący leading ('li:dyng) adj. kierowniczy; naczelny; główny; s. kierownictwo; prowadzenie; przewodnictwo;przywództwo leaf (li:f) s. liść; kartka; pl. leaves (li:wz) leaflet (li:flyt) s. listek; ulotka (często złożona) league (li:g) s. liga; związek; mila; v. łączyć (się) w ligę leak (li:k) s. dziura; otwór; przeciekanie; v. ciekąć; przeciekać; wyciekać (sekrety);wysączać; zaciekać leakage (li:kydż) s. przeciekanie (sekretów); wyciekanie (pieniędzy); rozproszenie leaky ('li:ky) adj. dziurawy; nieszczelny; cieknący; niedyskretny;nie dochowujący sekretu lean; leant; leant (li:n; lent; lent) lean (li:n) v. nachylać (się); pochylać (się); opierać(się) (o coś); adj. chudy; s. chude mięso;nachylenie;skłonność leant (lent) v. zob. lean leap; leapt; leapt (li:p; lept; lept) leap (li:p) v. skakać; przeskoczyć; s. skok; podskok leapt (lept) zob . leap leap-year ('li:pye:r) s. rok przestępny learn; learnt; learnt (le:rn; le:rnt; le:rnt) learn (le:rn) v. uczyć się; dowiadywać się;zapamiętać learned ('le:rnyd) adj. uczony learner ('le:rner) s. uczący się; uczeń; uczennica learning ('le:rnyng) s. nauka; wiedza; erudycja;umijętności learnt (le:rnt) v. zob. learn lease (li:s) s. dzierżawa; v. dzierżawić;wydzierżawić leash (li:sh) s. smycz least (li:st) adj. najmniejszy adv. najmniej; w najmniejszym stopniu; s. najmniejsza rzecz; drobnostka najmniej ważna

leather ('ledzer)s. skóra; adj. skórzany; v. pokrywać skórą; oprawiać w skórę ;sprać(rzemieniem) leave; left; left (li:w; left; left) leave (li:w) v. zostawiać; opuszczać; odchodzić; odjeżdżać; pozostawiać; s. pożegnanie; urlop; pozwolenie leaven (lewn) s. drożdże leaves (li:wz) pl. liście; zob. leaf lecture ('lekczer) s. wykład; nagana; v. wykładać; udzielać nagany;przemawiać do sumienia lecturer ('lekczerer) s. wykładowca(w uczelni,klasie etc.) led (led) zob. lead ledge (ledż) s. występ; stopień; półka; gzyms; listwa; rafa lee (li:) s. strona zawietrzna; osłona;adj.zawietrzny;osłonięty leech (li:cz) s. pijawka leek (li:k) s. por leer (lier) s. spojrzenie z ukosa; v. łypać okiem znacząco (chytrze,złośliwie,pożądliwie) left (left) adj. lewy; adv. na lewo; s. lewa strona; zob. leave left-hand ('left,haend) s. lewa ręka;adj.lewoskrętny;lewostronny left-handed ('left'haendyd) s. mańkut; adj. leworęki; niezgrabny;wątpliwy;nieszczery left side ('left,sajd) s. lewa strona (drogi,samochodu etc.) leg (leg) s. noga; nóżka; podpórka; odcinek;kończyna;udziec legacy (legesy) s. spadek; spuścizna;dziedzictwo;zapis legal ('li:gel) adj. prawny; prawniczy ;ustawowy;legalny legation (li'gejszyn) s. poselstwo (wlacznie z posłem) legend ('ledżend) s. legenda legendary ('ledżendery) adj. legendarny ;tradycyjny legible ('ledżebl) adj. czytelny ;łatwo czytelny legion ('li:dżen) s. legion; legia ;wojsko;wielka ilość; mnóstwo;tłumy;mnogość

legislation (,ledžys'lejszyn)
s. prawodawstwo; ustawodawstwo
legislative ('ledžysletyw) adj.
prawodawczy; ustawodawczy
legislator ('ledžyslator) s.
prawodawca; poseł do parlamen-
tu (sejmu,senatu etc.)
legitimate (ly'džytymyt) adj.
ślubny; prawowity; słuszny;
uzasadniony;logiczny;rozsadny
leg-pull ('legpu:l) s. kawał;
żart; sztuczka;naciąganie
leisure ('li:żer) s. wolny czas;
swoboda od zajęć;wolne chwile
leisurely ('li:żerly) adv. swobodnie; bez pośpiechu; adj.
mający czas; spokójny; robiony
w wolnym czasie
lemon ('lemen) s. cytryna;
tandeta;adj.cytrynowy;z cytryn
lemonade ('lemenejd) s. lemo-
niada(z soku cytrynowego etc.)
lend; lent; lent (lend; lent;
lent)
lend (lend) v. pożyczać; użyczać; udzielac
length (lenks) s. długość
lengthen ('lenksen) v. przedłużać; wydłużać(sie);podłużać
lengthwise ('lensłajz) adv. adj.
wzdłuż; na długość
lenient ('li:njent) adj. wyrozumiały; łagodny
lens (lenz) s. soczewka; objektyw ;lupa
lent (lent) s. post; zob. lend
leopard ('leperd) s. lampart
leper ('leper) s. trędowaty;
trędowata
leprosy ('lepresy) s. trąd
less (les) adj. mniejszy; adv.
mniej; s. coś mniejszego;
prep. bez;nie tak dużo(wiele)
lessen (lesn) v, zmniejszac(się);
maleć; pomniejszać
lesser ('leser) adj. mniejszy
lesson (lesn) s. lekcja; nauczka;urywek z Biblji;wykład
lest (lest) conj. ażeby nie; że
let; let; let (let;let;let)
let (let) v. zostawić; wynajmować; dawać; puszczać ; pozwalać

let alone ('let,e'loun) s. zostawić w spokoju; dać spokoj
let down ('let,dałn) v. robić
zawód; spuszczać; opuszczać;
upokorzyć;odmawiać pomocy
let go ('let,gou) v. wypuszczać;
zwalniać; pozwolić odejść
let know ('let,nou) v. zawiadomić; doniesć;powiadomić
let up ('let,ap) v. zelżec;
złagodnieć; się zelżenie
lethal ('li:sel) adj. śmiertelny; zgubny;śmiercionośny
letter ('leter) s. litera; list;
czcionka; v. drukować; oznaczać literami:kaligrafować
letter-box ('leter,boks) s.
skrzynka pocztowa
letter-carrier ('leter'kaerjer)
s. listonosz
lettuce ('letys) s. sałata (gło-
wiasta);liście sałaty
leukemia (lju'ki:mje) s. białaczka;leukemia
level ('lewl) s. poziom; płaszczyzna; równina; poziomnica;
adj. poziomy; adv. poziomo;
równo; v. zrównywać; celować
level crossing('lewl'krosyng)
s. skrzyżowanie dróg (koli-
zyjne)w jednej płaszczyźnie
lever ('li:wer) s. dźwignia;
lewar; v. podważać; podnosić
dźwigiem(lewarem)
levity ('lewyty) s. lekkomyśl-
nosć
levy ('lewy) v. pobierać; nakładać (podatek); s. pobór
lewd (lu:d) adj. zmysłowy; lubieżny;pożądliwy;sprośny
liability (,laje'bylyty) s.
odpowiedzialność; obowiązek;
obciążenie; zadłużenie;ryzyko
liable ('lajebl) adj. odpowiedzialny; podlegający; podatny;
skłonny;narażony;mający widoki
liable to ('lajebl,tu) adj.
skłonny do…;adv. łatwo(zgnije)
liaison (ly'ejzo:n) s. łącznosć;
związek; romans (nielegalny)
liar ('lajer) s. kłamca; łgarz
libation(laj-bej'szyn)s.libacja

libel ('lajbel) s. paszkwil;
oszczerstwo; zniesławienie
(publiczne w piśmie; filmie
etc.);v.zniesławiac´
liberal ('lyberel) s. liberał;a.
liberalny; hojny;tolerancyjny
liberate ('lyberejt) v. uwalniac; zwalniac;wyzwalać
liberation ('lyberejszyn) s.
uwolnienie; oswobodzenie
liberator ('lyberejter) s.
oswobodziciel;wyzwoliciel
liberty ('lyberty) s. wolnosć;
swoboda;nadużywanie wolnosci
librarian (laj'breerjen) s.
bibliotekarz
library ('lajbrery) s. biblioteka; księgozbiór
lice (lajs) pl. wszy; zob.
louse
license(ce) ('lajsens) s. licencja; pozwolenie; upoważnienie; swoboda; rozpusta;
v. upoważniac; udzielac´ poz-
wolenia; nadużywać wolności
licensee (,lajsen'si:) s. posiadacz zezwolenia; koncesjo-
nariusz;własciciel licencji
lichen ('lajken) s. liszaj
lick (lyk) s. liznięcie; odrobina; cios; raz; wybuch;
energia; v. lizać; polizac´;
wylizać; bic; smarowac´
licking ('lykyŋg)s. (slang);
bicie; pobicie; młocka
lid (lyd) s. wieko; powieka;
pokrywa ;nakrywka;przykrywka
lie !. lay ; lain (laj; lej;
lejn)
lie (laj) v. leżec; s. układ;
położenie;konfiguracja;legowisko
lie 2. lied; lied (laj; lajd;
lajd)
lie (laj) v. kłamac; s. kłamstwo;łgarstwo;fałsz
lie down('laj,dałn) v. kłasc´
się;położyć się;nie reagować
lie in ('laj,yn) v. byc w poło-
gu; leżeć w (łóżku)
lie over ('laj,ouwer) v. byc´
odroczonym; zostac´ przez noc
lieutenant (lef'tenant; lu:te-
nant) s. porucznik

life (lajf) s. życie; życiorys;
zob. pl. lives
life assurance ('lajfe'szuerens)
s. ubezpieczenie na życie
life belt ('lajfbelt) s. pas
ratunkowy
lifeboat ('lajfbout) s. łódz´
ratunkowa
lifeguard ('lajfga:rd) s. ratownik
life insurance ('lajf,yn'szuerens) s. ubezpieczenie na życie
life jacket ('lajfdżaekyt) s.
kurta ratownicza;kamizelka ratun-
lifeless ('lajflys) adj. bez
życia; martwy;zamarły;wymarły
lifelike ('lajflajk) adj. jak
żywy(człowiek,osoba,stworzenie)
life sentence ('lajf,sentens)
s. kara dożywocia(wyrok)
life-style ('lajfstajl) s. styl
życia; modła życia;sposób życia
lifetime ('lajf,tajm) s. życie; całe życie
lift (lyft) s. dźwig; winda;
przewóz; podniesienie; wzniesienie; v. podnieśc; dźwignąc;
podnosic´ się; kraśc; spłacić
(np. dom); kopnąc;buchnąd;awanso-
lift-off ('lyft,of) s. start
lotu (np. rakiety)
ligament ('lygement) s. ścięgno
ligature ('lygeczuer) s. przywiązanie; ligatura; podwiąza-
nie;bandaż;nić chirurgiczna
light; lit; lit (lajt; lyt;lyt)
light (lajt) s. światło; oswietlenie; ogien; adj. swiet-
ny; jasny; łatwy; lekki; błahy; słaby; beztroski; niefrasobliwy; lekkomyślny; v.świe-
cić; oświecac; zapalać; ujaw-
nic; poświęcic; rozjasnic;
przyswiecic; zsiadac; wsiadac;
wpaśc; wyjechac; adv. lekko
light up ('lajtap) v. zaświe-
cic; rozjasnic; oświecić
lighten ('lajtn) v. ulżyc; zel-
życ; oswiecac; rozjasnić się;
błysnąc; błyskac´ się
lighter ('lajter) s. zapalniczka; latarnik ;lampiarz

lighthouse ('lajthaus) s. latarnia morska

lighting ('lajtyng) s. oświetlenie; oświetlanie

light-minded ('lajt'majndyd) adj. lekkomyślny;roztargniony

lightness ('lajtnys) s. jasnosc; lekkosc; łagodnosc; łatwosc; lekkomyslnosc

lightning ('lajtnyng)s. błyskawica; piorun;a.błyskawiczny

lightning rod ('lajtnyng,rod) s. piorunochron;odgromnik

lightweight ('lajt-łejt) s. waga lekka; adj. lekkiej wagi; błachy(127 do 135 funtowy boks)

light-year ('lajt,je:r) s. rok świetlny(ok.6x10¹²mil=10x10¹²km.)

lignite ('lygnajt) s. węgiel brunatny; lignit

like (lajk) v. lubiec; upodobac sobie; (chciec); miec zamiłowanie, ochotę; adj. podobny; analogiczny; typowy; adv. podobnie; w ten sam sposób; s. drugi taki sam; rzecz podobna; conj. jak; tak jak;po; w ten sposób; niby to;niczym

like that ('lajk'dzaet) adv. tak; w ten sposób;właśnie tak

likelihood ('lajklyhud) s. prawdopodobieństwo

likely ('lajkly) adj. możliwy; prawdopodobny; odpowiedni; nadający się; obiecujący; adv. pewnie; prawdopodobnie

likeness ('lajknys) s. podobieństwo; podobizna; pozory

likewise ('lajkłajz) adv. także; również; podobno; podobnie;w ten sam sposób;też

liking ('lajkyng) s. sympatia; upodobanie; zamiłowanie

lilac ('lajlek) s. bez; adj. lila; liljowy;blado siny

lily ('lyly) s. lilja;a.jak lilja

lily of the valley ('lyly,ow' 'dy,waely) s. konwalia

limb (lym) s. kończyna; konar; brzeg; krawędz;ramie;noga;skrzydło

lime 1. (lajm) s. wapno; v. wapnic; adj. wapienny

lime 2. (lajm) s. lipa; cytrus (dzika cytryna);a.cytrusowy

limelight ('lajmlajt) s. swiatło wapienne; światło reflektorow; widok publiczny

limestone ('lajmstoun) s. wapien; a. z wapienia

limey ('lajmy) s. (slang):Brytyjczyk (wulg.) zwłaszcza marynarz

limit ('lymyt) s. granica; kres; v. ograniczac; ustalac granic

limitation (,lymy'tejszyn) s. ograniczenie; zastrzeżenie; prekluzja;przedawnienie

limited liability ('lymytyd,laje'bylyty)s. ograniczona odpowiedzialnosc

limp (lymp) adj. wiotki; bez sił; osłabiony; v. kulec; chromac

line (lajn) s. linia; kreska; bruzda; lina; sznur; przewód; granica; zajęcie; zainteresowania; szereg; rząd; linka; v. liniowac; wyscielac; podbic podszewką;służyc za podszewkę

lineup ('lajnap) s. uszeregowanie; rząd; ustawianie w rząd

line up ('lajnap) v. ustawic w rząd; uszeregowac

lineaments ('lynjements) pl. rysy twarzy;cechy szczególne

linear ('lynjer) adj. liniowy; linijny; wąski i długi

linen ('lynyn) s. płotno; bielizna; adj. lniany; płocienny

linen closet('lynen'klozyt) s. schowek na bieliznę

liner ('lajner) s. samolot pasażerski; statek pasażerski

linger ('lynger) v. ociągac się; zwlekac; pozostawac w tyle; marudzic; tkwic; wlec życie

lingerie ('le:nżeri) s. damska bielizna ;damskie artykuły bielizniane

lining ('lajnyng) s. podszewka; podkład; okładzina; zawartosc

link (lynk) s. ogniwo; więz; spinka; 20,1 cm; v. połączyc; zczepiac; związac; sprzęgac

links (lynks) pl. wydmy; boisko golfowe ;wydmy piaszczyste

lion (lajon) s. lew ;a.lwi;lwie

lioness (lajonys) s. lwica
lip (lyp) s. warga; brzeg;
ostrze; bezczelne gadanie;
v. dotykać wargami; mruczec
lipstick ('lypstyk) s. kredka
do warg; pomadka do ust
liquid ('lykłyd) s. płyn;
adj. płynny;niestały;nie ustalony
liquor ('lyker) s. napój alko-
holowy; sok; odwar;bulion
liquorice ('lykorys) s. lu-
krecja
lisp (lysp) v. seplenic; seplenic jak niemowle;s.seplenienie
list (lyst) s. lista; spis;
listwa; krawędz; v. wciągaćna
listę; obramowywać; przechylac (się); pochylać (się);
s. pochylenie; przechył
listen ('lysen) v. słuchac;
usłuchac;przysłuchiwac się
listen in ('lysen,yn) v. pod-
słuchiwac;posłuchac(radia etc)
listen to ('lysen,tu) v. usłuchac kogos (czyjejs rady)
listener ('lysener) s. słuchacz
listless ('lystlys) adj. apatyczny; obojętny; zobojętnia-
ły;bierny(z powodu choroby)
lit (lyt) zob. light
liter ('li:ter) s. litr
literal ('lyterel) adj. literal-
ny; dosłowny; prozaiczny; li-
terowy;rzeczowy(umysl etc.)
literary ('lyterery) adj. literacki;obeznany w literaturze
literature ('lytereczer) s. literatura; pismiennictwo
lithe (lajs) adj, giętki; gibki; łatwo gnący się
litter ('lyter) s. smieci; pod-
sciołka ; barłog; v. smiecic;
podscielac; urodzic szczenia-
ki;porozrzucac niechlujnie
litter bin ('lyter,byn) s.
smietnik ;kosz na smiecie
little ('lytl) adj. mały; niski;
nieduzy; adv. mało; niewiele
little bit ('lytl,byt) adv.
trochę ;bardzo mało;troszeczkę
little one ('lytl,łan) s.
dziecko ;dziecina;dzieciatko

little by little ('lytl,bay'
'lytl) exp. po trochu; stopniowo;po mału;po malutku
live (lyw) v. życ; mieszkac;
przeżywać; przetrwac; ocalic
live (lajw) adj. żywy; żyjący;
ruchliwy;energiczny;niewyeksplo-
live on ('lyw,on) v. życ    ˙dowany
z czegos; życ czyms
live wire ('lajw'łajer) s.
przewód pod napięciem
livelihood ('lajwly,hud) s.
utrzymanie;srodki do życia
lively ('lajwly) adj. żywy;
wesoły; ożywiony; żwawy; gorący;rześki;pełen życia;jaskrawy
liver ('lywer) s. wątroba;
wątróbka ;a.wątroby
livery ('lywery) adj. wątrobia-
ny; chory na wątrobę; opryskliwy; s. liberia; utrzymanie
konia; wynajem (wozów)
lives (lajws) pl. żywotny;
zob. life
livestock ('lajwstok) s. żywy
inwentarz ;zwierzęta domowe
livid ('lywyd) adj. siny;
wsciekły ;posiniaczony
living ('lywyng) s. życie;
utrzymanie; tryb życia
living room('lywyn,ru:m) s.
salon; bawialnia; pokój
lizard ('lyzerd) s. jaszczurka
load (loud) s. ładunek; waga;
ciężar; obciążenie; v. łado-
wac; załadowac; naładowac;
obciążać; nasycac; fałszowac
load up ('loud,ap) v. brac ładunek; opychac się
loader ('louder) s. ładowniczy;
maszyna do ładowania
loading ('loudyng) s. ładunek;
ładowanie ;a.ładunkowy(pomost)
loaded words ('loudyd,łe:rds)
s. słowa tendencyjne (nie-
sprawiedliwe)(uwłaszczajace)
loaf (louf) s. bochenek; głowa
(cukru); pl. loaves (louvz)
v. wałęsac się;marnować czas
loafer ('loufer) s. włóczęga;
łazik; próżniak ;nieród;wałkoń;
wygodny bucik sportowy

loam (loum) s. gleba ilasta;
ił ;zaprawa gliniana(murarska)
loan (loun) s. pożyczka;
v. pożyczać ; pożyczać
loath (lous) adj. niechętny
loathe (lous) v. nienawidzieć;
czuć wstręt
loathsome ('loussem) adj.
wstrętny; obrzydliwy; ohydny
loaves (louwz) zob. loaf
lobby ('loby) s. przedpokój;
kuluar; v. urabiać senatora
lub posła na czyjąś korzyść
(przekupywać)
lobbyist('lobyst) s. inter-
wencjonalista kuluarowy (często oficjalnie rejestrowany
w USA); lobbyista
lobe (loub) s. płat (np. płucny)
lobster ('lobster) s. homar
local ('loukel) adj. lokalny;
miejscowy;s.oddział związku zawodowego
locality (lou'kaelyty) s.okolica;
miejscowość; strefa;rejon
localize ('loukelajz) v. umiejscowić; lokalizować
locate ('loukejt) v. umieścić;
znaleźć; osiedlić się
located ('loukejtyd) adj. zamieszkały; umieszczony;znaleziony
location ('loukejszyn) s. położenie; ulokowanie; miejsce
zamieszkania;miejsce zaznaczone
loch (lok) s. jezioro; wąska
zatoka (zwłaszcza w Szkocji)
lock (lok) s. zamek; zamknięcie;
śluza; lok; v. zamykać (na
klucz);przechodzić śluzę
lock in ('lokyn) v. zamykać
(wewnątrz); otaczać (górami etc.)
locker ('loker) s. szafka; kabina; skrzynia; schowek
lock out ('lokaut) v. wykluczać;
s. lokaut ( lockout )
locksmith ('loksmys) s. ślusarz
locomotive ('louke,moutyw) s.
lokomotywa; adj. ruchomy
locust ('loukest) s. szarańcza;
akacja
lodge ('lodż) s. chata; loża;
kryjówka; domek myśliwski; nora
v. przenocować; zdeponować;
umieszczać; wnosić (skargę)etc.

lodger ('lodżer) s. lokator
lodging ('lodżyng) s. mieszkanie (tymczasowe,wynajęte etc.)
loft (loft) s. strych; poddasze;chór;v.podbić pilkę golfową
lofty ('lofty) adj. wzniosły;
wyniosły; wysoki;dumny;hardy
log (log) s. kłoda; kloc; log;
dziennik operacyjny (statku;
szybu) v. wycinać drzewa;
ciąć na kłody; wciągać do
dziennika okrętowego etc.
logbook ('logbuk) s. dziennik
pokładowy;książka raportowa
log cabin ('log,kaebyn) s. chata (z belek) (z okrąglaków)
logic ('lodżyk) s. logika
logical ('lodżykel) adj. logiczny;rozumujący poprawnie
loin (loin) s. lędźwie; polędwica; comber;krzyże;biodra
loiter (lojter) v. marudzić;
wałęsać się; guzdrać; mitrę-
żyć;kręcić się podejrzanie
lol (lol) v. rozwalać się;
opierać się niedbale; wywieszać
(język psa); zwisać
loneliness ('lounlynys) s. samotność;osamotnienie;odludność
lonely ('lounly) adj. samotny
lonesome ('lounsom) adj.
osamotniony; odludny
long (long) adj. długi; długo-
trwały; v. tęsknić; pragnąć
(czegoś); adv. długo; dawno
long ago (,long'egou) adv.
dawno temu;adj.dawno miniony
long before ('long,befor) adv.
dużo wcześniej;znacznie wcześniej
long since ('long,syns) adv.
dawno temu ; od dawna
long distance call ('long'dystans,kol) s. telefon między-
miastowy;rozmowa międzymiastowa
longing ('longyng) s. pragnienie;
tęsknota;ochota;adj.tęskny
long jump ('long,dżamp) s.
skok w dal
longshoreman ('long,szo:rmen)
s. doker; robotnik portowy
long-sighted ('lon'sajtyd) adj.
dalekowzroczny; przewidujący
long spun ('lon'span)a.rozwlekły

long-term ('lon'term) adj.
długoterminowy;długofalowy
long-winded ('lon'łyndyd)
adj. gadatliwy; długo mówiący;(koń) ze zdrowymi płucami
look (luk) s. spojrzenie; wygląd; v. patrzec; wyglądac
look after ('luk,a:fter) v. doglądac; opiekowac się(kimś)
look at ('luk,et) v. patrzec
na (kogoś, na coś)
look for ('luk,fo:r)v. szukac
look forwards ('luk fo:rłerds)
v. oczekiwać; cieszyc się
look into ('luk,yntu) v. badac; wglądac
look on ('luk,on) v. przypatrywac się;przyglądac się;kibicowac
look out ('luk,aut) v. byc
na baczności;wyjrzec;wyszukac
look over ('luk,ouwer) v.
przeglądac;przejrzec
look around ('luk,e'raund) v.
rozglądac się;poszukiwać wzrokiem
look up ('luk,ap) v. szukac;
odwiedzac; patrzec w górę
looker-on('luker'on) s. widz;
przygladający się ;kibic
looking-glass ('lukynglass) s.
lustro; zwierciadło
lookout ('luk,aut) s. widok;
uwaga; czaty;czujnosc
look out ('luk,aut) v. wyjrzec;
uważac; wyszukac;byc w pogotowiu
loom (lu:m) s. krosna; warsztat
tkacki; v. wynurzac się; zagrażac;grozic;zamajaczyc
loop (lu:p) s. pętla; węzeł;
supeł; v. robic pętlę, kokardę;
podwiązywac;splatac (się)
loophole ('lu:p,houl) s. strzelnica; droga ucieczki (od podatków);wykręt; luka;furtka
loose (lu:s) adj. luzny; rozluzniony; obluzniony; wolny;
na wolności; rzadki; sypki;
rozwiązły; s. upust; v. luzowac; obluzniac; zwalniac
loosen ('lu:sn) v. rozluzniac
(się); obluzniac (się); rozwalniac;leczyc zatwardzenie
loot (lu:t) s. łupy; (nadużycia
urzędnika);v.plądrowac;szabrowac

lop (lop) v. obcinac; ciąc; zwisac; plątac się; waręsac się;
s. scięcie; obcięte (gałęzie)
lop off ('lop,of) v. obciąc
lope (loup) v. biec susami;
pędzic krotkim galopem; s.
krótki galop; sus
lord (lo:rd) s. pan; władca;
magnat; Bog; v. grac pana;
nadawac tytuł lorda
lorry ('lory) s. ciężarówka;
platforma; lora;przyczepa
lose; lost; lost (lu:z; lost;
lost)
lose (lu:z) y. stracic; schudnąc; zgubic; zabłądzic; niedosłyszec; spoznic się; przegrac; byc pokonanym,pozbawionym
loss (los) s. strata; utrata;
zguba; ubytek;szkoda;kłopot
lost (lost) adj. stracony; zgubiony; zob. lose
lot (lot) s. doba; las; losowanie; udział; działka; parcela; grupa; zespół; partia;
sporo; wiele; v. parcelowac;
dzielic; losowac;adv.bardzo dużo
loth (lous) adj. niechętny;
wstrętny;z ciężkim sercem
lotion ('louszyn) s. płyn
(leczniczy)
lottery ('lotery) s. loteria
lotto ('lotou) s. loteryjka
loud (laud) adj. głosny; smrodliwy; krzykliwy; adv. na cały
głos; głosno;w głosny sposób
loudspeaker ('laud'spi:ker) s.
głosnik; megafon
lounge (laundż) y. próznowac;
wylegiwac; łazic; s. lokal;
salonik; hall; włoczęga;
wolny krok;wygodna kanapa
louse (laus) s. wesz; pl. lice
lousy ('lauzy) adj. zawszony;
wstrętny;dobrze zaopatrzony (sl.)
lout ('laut) s. gbur; prostak
love (law) s. kochanie; miłosc;
lubienie; ukochana; ukochanie;
gra na zero; v. kochac; lubic;
byc przywiązanym ;piescic;umizgac się
love-affair ('lawefeer) s. romans; przygoda miłosna;osobiste
troski w sprawach miłosnych

loveless ('lawlys) adj. nieko-
chany; nie kochający; bez
miłości;nie kochany przez nikogo
lovely ('lawly) adj. śliczny;
uroczy; rozkoszny;przyjemny(bar-
lovemaking ('law,mejkyng) s.
zaloty; umizgi; spoŁkowanie
lover ('lawer) s. kochanek;
miłośnik; amator czegoś
loving ('lavyng) adj. kochający;
s. kochanie; miłość
low (lou) s. ryk (bydŁa); ryczeć; adj. niski; niewysoki;
słaby; przygnębiony; cichy;
podŁy; mały; adv. nisko; nie-
wysoko; słabo; skromnie; cicho; szeptem; marnie; podle
lower ('louer) adj. niższy;
dolny; młodszy; adv. niżej;
v. obniżac; zniżać; spuszczac; poniżyć; sciszyć;
zmniejszyć; osłabiać; opadać;
spadać;ryczeć(jak bydło)
low-grade ('lougrejd) adj.
niskoprocentowy; niskiej
jakości;kiepski;tandetny
lowland ('loulend) pl. nizina;
adj. nizinny
lowly ('louly) adj. skromny;
adv. skromnie;bez pretensji
low-necked('lou'nekyd) adj.
dekoltowany (głęboko)
low-pressure ('lou'preszer) s.
niskie cisnienie; adj. nisko-
prężny;pod niskim ciśnieniem
low tide ('lou'tajd) s. odpŁyw
(morza)
loyal(lojel) adj. lojalny;
wierny(krajowi,ideaŁom etc.)
loyalty ('lojelty) s. lojalność;
wierność
lozenge ('lozyndż) s. romb;
tabletka; pastylka
lubber ('laber) s. niezdara;
niedoŁęga;niezdarny marynarz
lubricant ('lu:brykent) s. smar;
adj. smarujący; smarowniczy
lubricate ('lu:brykejt) v. smarowac; oliwic;robic śliskim
lubrication ('lu:brykejszyn) s.
smarowanie; oliwienie
ubricity(lu:'brysyty)s.smarowność;

lucid ('lu:syd) adj. świecacy;
jasny; błyszczacy; klarowny;
przezroczysty; czysty;oczywisty
luck (lak) s. los; traf; szczęscie; szczęśliwy traf;powodzenie
luckily ('lakyly) adv. na
szczęście; szczęśliwie
luckless ('laklys) adj. niefortunny; nieszczęśliwy
lucky ('laky) adj. szczęśliwy
lucky fellow ('laky'felou) s.
szczęściarz
ludicrous ('lu:dykres) adj.
śmieszny; nonsensowny; absurdalny;komicznie głupi
lug (lag) v. wlec; pociągać;
przytŁaczac; s. wleczenie;
szarpanie; ucho; uchwyt
luggage ('lagydż) s. bagaż; walizki
luggage carrier ('lagydż'kaerjer)
s. bagażowy
luggage rack ('lagydż'raek) s.
półka na walizki
luggage slip ('lagydż'slyp) s.
kwit bagażowy
luggage van ('lagydż'waen) s.
wóz bagażowy
lukewarm ('lu:kŁo:rm) adj. cie-
pł
awy; letni; obojętny; ozięb-
Ły.; niezainteresowany
lull(lal) v. ukołysać; uciszyć;
uśmierzyć; s. cisza; zastój
lullaby ('lalebaj) s. kołysanka
lumbago (lam'bejgou) s. lumbago;
ischias
lumbar ('lamber) adj. lędźwiowy
lumber ('lamber) s. budulec
(drewniany); rupiecie; graty;
v. zwalać; wycinać; ciężko
stąpac; poruszac się ociężale
lumberjack ('lamber'dżaek) s.
drwal(przygotowujący do tartaku)
lumber mill ('lambermyl) s.
tartak
luminous ('lu:mynes) adj.
świetlny; jasny; adj. świecą-
cy; wyjasniający;zrozumiały
lump (lamp) s. bryŁa; gruda; masa; hurt; guz; niezdara; niedo-
Łęga; v. zwalać; gromadzić;
dojsc do Ładu;zcierpiec;znosić

lump of('lamp,ow) s. kawałek
lump sugar ('lamp,szu:ger) s.
gruda cukru
lump sum ('lamp,sam) s. suma
całościowa
lunar ('lu:nar) adj. księżyco-
wy;mierzony ruchem księżyca
lunar module ('lu:nar,modjul)
s. kapsula do lądowania na
Księżycu
lunatic ('lu:netyk) s. wariat
(chory umysłowo); adj. obłąkany; zwariowany; lunatyk
lunch (lancz) s. obiad (popołudniowy); v. jeść obiad;
goscic obiadem
lunch-hour ('lancz'auer) s.
przerwa obiadowa (w południe)
lung (lang) s. płuco
lunge (landż) s. wypad;
pchnięcie; v. pchnąć; zrobic
wypad;spowodować wypad
lurch (le:rcz) v. opuszczac
w potrzebie; słaniac się na
nogach; przechylac się; s.
nagłe przechylenie się (na
bok);trudna sytuacja
lure (ljuer) s. przynęta; wabik; urok; powab; v. kusic;
nęcic; wabic;przywabiac
lurk (le:rk) v. czaic się;
s. czaty ; ukrycie
luscious ('laszes) adj. sło-
dziutki; ckliwy ;soczysty
lush (lasz) adj. bujny; soczysty;miękki i pełen soku
lust (last) s. żądza; lubiez-
nosc; namiętnosc; pożądli-
wosc; v. pożądac(namiętnie)
luster ('laster) s. blask; połysk; swiecznik; swietnosc;
v. glansowac; wyswiecac
lusty ('lasty) adj. krzepki;
pełen wigoru (młodzieńczego)
lute (lu:t) s. lutnia; glina;
v. lepic gliną;kitowac
luxate ('laksejt) v. zwichnąc
(np. nogę)(staw)
luxation (lak'sejszyn) s.
zwichnięcie (nogi w kostce;
stawu biodrowego etc.)

luxurious (lag'żjuerjes) adj.
zbytkowny; luksusowy;zmysłowy
luxury ('lakszery) s. zbytek;
luksus;rozkosz;a.od zbytku
lying ('lajyng) adj. kłamliwy;
zob. lie; s. kłamstwo; adj.le-
żący; zob. lie; s. leżenie;
posłanie;pozycja leżąca
lying-in (,lajyng'yn) adj. po-
łozniczy; połogowy; s. połog
lymph (lymf) s, limfa; szczepionka; wysięk; serum, (czy-
sta woda)
lynch (lyncz) v. zlinczowac;s.
linczowanie;zabijanie bez wyro-ku
lynx (lynks) s. rys
lyre ('lajer) s. lira
lyric ('lirik) adj. liryczny;
s. słowa piesni; poemat liryczny;tekst piosenki
lysol ('lajsol) s. lizol
m (em) trzynasta litera alfabetu
angielskiego;cyfra rzymska:1000
ma'am (maem) s. pani (madam)
mac (maek) s.nieprzemakalny materiał (płaszcz) mackintosh
machine (me'szi:n) s. maszyna;
machina (polityczna) v. obrabiac maszynowo;adj.maszynowy
machine-made (me'szi:nmejd) adj.
maszynowy; maszynowo robiony
machine-gun (me'szi:ngan) s.
karabin maszynowy
machinery (me'szi:nery) s, maszyneria;maszyneria;aparat
machinist (me'szi:nyst) s, maszynista (np. tokarz)(szwaczka)
macho (ma:czou) s. bardzo męski
mężczyzna (slang)
mack (maek) s. zob. mac
mackintosh ('maekyntosz) s.
zob. mac
mad (maed) adj. obłąkany; szalony; zły; wsciekły; v. doprowadzac do obłędu; byc obłąkanym
madam ('maedem) s. pani; (panienka)(w zwrocie:proszę pani)
madcap ('maedkaep) s. narwaniec
madden ('maedn) v. rozwscieczac;
szalec; wsciekac sie;wariowac
made (mejd) v. zrobiony; zob.
make (wykombinowany;fabryczny...)

madman ('maedmen) s. wariat;
szaleniec;furiat;obłąkaniec
madness ('maednys) s. obłęd;
obłąkanie; furia; wściekłość;
wścieklizna;szał;szaleństwo
magazine (maege'zi:n) s. czasopismo; magazynek (na kule);
skład broni dla wojska
maggot ('maeget) s. dziwactwo;
chimera; larwa
magic ('maedżyk) s. magia; adj.
magiczny; działający jak magia
magician (me'dżyszyn) s. czarodziej; magik
magistrate ('maedżystrejt) s.
sądownik; stróż prawa
magnanimous (maeg'neanymes)
adj. wielkoduszny
magnet ('maegnyt) s. magnes
magnetic (maeg'netyk) adj.
magnetyczny; przyciągający
magnificence (maeg'nyfysns) s.
wspaniałość; świetność;
okazałość
magnificent (maeg'nyfysnt)adj.
wspaniały; okazały
magnify ('maegnyfaj) v. powiększać; potęgować; wyolbrzymiać
magpie ('maegpaj) s. sroka;
gaduła
maid (mejd) s. dziewczyna;
dziewka; panna ;służąca
maiden ('mejden) s. dziewczyna;
panna; adj. panieński; dzie-
wiczy; świeży; nowy
maidenly ('mejdenly) adj.
dziewczecy; panieński
maiden name ('mejden,nejm) s.
nazwisko panieńskie
mail (mejl) s. poczta; kolczu-
ga; v. wysyłać pocztą
mailbag ('mejl,baeg) s. worek
pocztowy
mailbox ('mejl,boks) s, skrzynka pocztowa
mailman (mejlmen) s. listonosz
mail-order house ('mejlorder,
,haus) s. firma sprzedająca
przez pocztę (z katalogu)
maim (mejm) v. okaleczyć
main (mejn) s. główny (przewód)
adj. główny; najważniejszy

mainland ('mejnlaend) s. konty-
nent(w odróżnieniu od bliskich
wysp)
mainly('mejnly) adv. głównie;
przeważnie;po większej części
main road('mejnroud) s. główna
droga;główna szosa
main street ('mejn.stri:t) s.
główna ulica
maintain (men'tejn) v. utrzymywać (w dobrym stanie); trzymać (pozycję); podtrzymywać;
zachowywać; twierdzić; mieć
na utrzymaniu;bronić;pomagać
maintenance ('mejntenens) s.
utrzymanie; utrzymywanie; poparcie; wyżywienie
maize (mejz) s. kukurydza
majestic (medżestyk) adj. majestatyczny
majesty ('maedżysty) s. majestat;godność;wielkość
major ('mejdżer) s. major; pełnoletni; przedmiot kierunkowy
specjalizacji; adj. większy;
główny; ważniejszy; pełnoletni;
starszy;v.specjalizować się w stu-
diach
majorette ('mejdżeret) s. tancerka na defiladach i w przer-
wach meczów w USA
majority (me'dżoryty) s.
większość;a. wiekszościowy
major road ('mejdżer,roud) s.
droga główna;ważniejsza droga
make; made; made (mejk; mejd;
mejd)
make (mejk) v. robić; tworzyć;
sporządzać;powodować; wynosić;
doprowadzać; ustanawiać; stać
się; postanowić etc.
make-believe ('mejk,by'li:w) s.
udawanie; pozory
make off ('mejkof) v. uciec;
uciekać .gwiznąć coś komuś
make up ('mejkap) v. uzupełnić;
wynagrodzić; sporządzić; zmonto-
wać; ucharakteryzować
makeup ('mejkap) s. makijaż;
charakteryzacja; układ (gra-
ficzny); stan (kogoś,czegoś)
make up your mind ('mejk,ap'-
'jo:r,majnd) exp.: zdecyduj się
(czego chcesz,co wolisz, na co
masz ochotę,gdzie jedziesz etc.)

maker ('mejker) s. wytwórca;
sprawca; producent; fabrykant;
konstruktor( Maker= Bóg)
makeshift ('mejkszyft) s. namiastka; urządzenie prowizo-
ryczne;adj.prowizoryczny
malady ('maeledy) s. choroba
male (mejl) s. mężczyzna; samiec; adj. męski; samczy;
wewnętrzny; obejmowany
malediction (,maely'dikszyn) s.
przekleństwo; złorzeczenie
malefactor ('maelyfaekter) s.
złoczyńca; zbrodniarz
malevolent (me'lewelent) adj.
niechętny; wrogi
malice ('maelys) s. złośliwość;
zła wola; zły zamiar
malicious (me'lyszys) adj.
złośliwy; zły;powodowany złością
malignant (me'lygnent) adj.
złośliwy; zjadliwy
malnutrition ('maelnju'tryszyn)
s. niedożywienie
malt (mo:lt) s. słód; v. słodo-
wać ;adj. słodowy;zcukrzony
maltreat (mael'tri:t) v. ponie-
wierać; maltretować
mamma (me'ma:) s. mama;gruczoł mlekowy
mammal (me'ma:l) s. ssak;a.ssakowy
man (maen) s. człowiek; mężczyzna; mąż; v. obsadzać (np. zało-
gą); pl. men (men)
manacle('maenekl) s. kajdany;
v. zakuwać w kajdany
manage ('maenydż) v. kierować;
zarządzać; posługiwać się; obchodzić się; opanowywać; poskramiać; radzić sobie
manageable ('maenydżebl) adj.do
pokierowania (możliwy,łatwy)
management ('maenydżment) s.
zarząd; kierownictwo; dyrekcja;
posługiwanie się; obchodzenie
się ;sprawne zarządzanie
manager('maenydżer) s. kierownik
zarządzający; gospodarz
manageress ('maenydżeres) s.
kierowniczka
mane (mejn) s. grzywa
maneuver (me'nu:wer) s. manewr;
v. manewrować;manipulować

manger ('mejndżer) s. żłob; koryto
mangle ('maengl) s. magiel;
v. maglować; poszarpać; pokale-
czyc; poprzekręcać
manhood ('maenhud) s. męskość;
ludność męska ;wiek męski
mania ('mejnje) s. bzik; obłęd;
mania;zbytni entuzjazm;szał
maniac ('mejnjaek) s. maniak;
szaleniec;adj.umysłowo chory
manifest ('maenyfest) adj. jawny; oczywisty; v. manifestować;
ujawniać; s. manifest okrętowy (szczegółowa lista ładunku)
manifold ('maenyfould) adj.
różnorodny; wieloraki; wielokrotny; v. powielać (tekst)
manipulate (me'nypjulejt) v.
manipulować; umiejętnie; zręcz-
nie pokierować (niesprawiedliwie)
mankind (,maen'kajnd) s. ludzkość; rodzaj ludzki
mankind ('maenkajnd) pl. mężczyź-
ni ;cały rodzaj męski
manly('maenly) adj. dzielny;
mężny; męski;adv.po męsku
manner ('maener) s. sposób; zwyczaj; zachowanie (się); wychowanie; maniera;procedura;rodzaj
manoeuvre (me'nu:wer) s. manewr;
v. namewrować(pisownia brytyjska)
man-of-war ('maenew'ło:r) s.
okręt wojenny;uzbrojony statek
manor ('maener) s. dwór; rezydencja (w Anglii:duży majatek)
man power('maen,pałer) s. siła
robocza; rezerwy ludzkie
mansion ('maenszyn) s. rezydencja; pałac;duży dwor
manslaughter ('maen,slo:ter) s.
zabójstwo (bez premedytacji)
mantelpiece ('maentlpi:s) s.
gzyms kominka (obramowanie)
manual ('maenjuel) s. podręcznik;
manuał; adj. ręczny;ręcznie zrobio-ny
manufacture (,maenju'faekczer)
v. wyrabiać; s. wyrób; produkcja; produkt (zwłaszcza masowy)
manufacturer (,maenju'faeccze-
rer) s. wytwórca; producent;
fabrykant;przedsiębiorstwo wytwór-cze

manure (me'njuer) s. nawóz;
v. nawozić (gnój)
manuscript ('maenjuskrypt) s.
rękopis; adj. ręcznie pisany
many ('meny) adj. dużo; wiele
many-sided ('meny'sajdyd) adj.
wielostronny; wieloboczny;
wszechstronny
map (maep) s. mapa; plan;
v. planować; robic mapę
maple ('mejpl) s. klon
marble ('ma:rbl) s. marmur; kul-
ka do zabawy; adj, marmurowy;
v. marmurkować (np. papier)
March (ma:rcz) s. marzec
march (ma:rcz) s. marsz; v.ma-
szerować
mare (meer) s. klacz; kobyła
margarine ('ma:rdże,ri:n) s.
margaryna
margin ('ma:rdżyn) s. margines;
brzeg; krawędź; nadwyżka;
rezerwa
marine (me'ri:n) adj. morski;
s. marynarka; żołnierz piecho-
ty desantowej (USA)
mariner ('maeryner) s. marynarz;
żeglarz
maritime ('maerytajm) adj. morski
mark (ma:rk) s. marka (pieniądz)
slad; znak; oznaczenie; nota;
cenzura; cel; uwaga; v. oznaczać; określać; notować; zwracać uwagę
marked (ma:rkt) adj. wybitny;
wyrazny; znaczny
mark out ('ma:rk,aut) v. wyznaczać; wytyczać (np. granicę)
market ('ma:rkyt) s. rynek;
zbyt; targ; v. robić zakupy;
sprzedawać na targu
marketing ('ma:rkytyŋg) s. orga-
nizowanie rynku;handlowanie
market-place ('ma:rkytplejs) s.
rynek; plac targowy
marksman ('ma:rksmen) s. strzelec (doborowy)
marmalade ('ma:rmelejd) s.
marmolada (pomarańczowa)
marmot ('ma:rmet) s. świstak
marriage ('maerydż) s. małżen-
stwo (skojarzenie);a.slubny

marriageable ('maerydżebl) adj.
na wydaniu;odpowiedni do małżeństwa
marriage certificate ('maerydż,
ser'tyfykyt) s. świadectwo
slubu
married ('maeryd) adj. żonaty;
zamężna; małżeński; ślubny
married couple ('maeryd,kapl)s.&
adj. para małżeńska
marrow ('mearou) s. szpik
(kostny); dynia
marry ('maery) v. poslubić;
udzielać ślubu; ożenić (się)
brać ślub; pobierać się;
wychodzić za mąż
marsh (ma:rsz) s. moczary; bagno;błota;a.bagienny
marshal ('ma:rszel) s. marszałek; mistrz ceremonii; komisarz policji; v. uszykować
(uroczyscie); przetaczać wagony;uporządkować;uszykować
marshy ('ma:rszy) adj. bagnisty; bagienny;błotnisty
marten ('ma:rtyn) s.kuna
martial ('ma:rszel) adj. wojenny; wojowniczy; wojskowy
martyr ('ma:rter) s. męczennik; v. zamęczac;zadręczać
marvel ('ma:rwel) s. cudo; cud;
v. podziwiać; dziwić się
marvelous ('ma:rwyles) adj.
cudowny; zdumiewający
mascot ('maesket) s. maskotka
masculine ('maeskjulyn) adj.
męski;płci męskiej
mash (maesz) s. zacier; papka;
mieszanka; v. warzyć; tłuc na
papkę; umizgać się
mashed potatoes ('maeszt,pe'tej-
tous) s. gniecione ziemniaki
mask (ma:sk) s. maska; v. zamaskować; maskować
mason ('mejsn) s. murarz; ka-
mieniarz;v.wymurować;murować
masonry ('mejsnry) s. murarstwo;
obmurowanie;kamieniarstwo
masque (ma:sk) s. maskarada;
pantomima (amatorska)
mass (maes) s. mszą; masa; rzesza; v. gromadzić; zrzeszać
massacre ('maeseker) s. masakra; v. masakrować;urządzić rzez

massage ('maesa:ż) s. masaż;
v. masować ;zrobić masaż
massif ('maesyw) s, masyw
gorski
massive ('maesyw) adj. masywny;
ciężki;zwarty;bryłowaty;ciężki
mast (ma:st) s. maszt
master ('ma:ster) s. mistrz;
nauczyciel; pan; gospodarz;
szef; kapitan statku; panicz;
v. panować; kierować; nabywać (np.wprawy);owładnąć
master key ('ma:sterki:) s.
wytrych
masterly ('ma:sterly) adj.
mistrzowski
master of ceremony ('ma:ster,ow-
sere'mouny) s. mistrz ceremonii
masterpiece ('ma:sterpi:s) s.
arcydzieło
mastership ('ma:sterszyp) s.
mistrzostwo; władza; panowanie; zwierzchnictwo
mastery ('ma:stery) s. władza;
panowanie; mistrzostwo
mat (maet) s. mata; v. plątać;
adj. matowy(bez połysku)
match (maecz) s. zapałka; lont;
mecz; dobór; małżeństwo;
v. swatać; współzawodniczyc;
dobierać;dorównywac
matchless ('maeczlys) adj. niezrównany;nie mający równego
matchmaker ('maecz,mejker) s.
swat; swatka;aranżujący mecze
mate (mejt) s. kolega; małżonek;
samiec; pomocnik; łączyc ślu-
bem; parzyc (się); pobierać
się;zadawać mata(w szachach)
material (me'tierjal) s. materiał; tworzywo; tkanka; adj.
materialny; cielesny
maternal (me'te:rnl) adj. macierzyński; matczyny
maternity (me'te:rnyty) s. ma-
cierzynstwo;adj.położniczy
maternity hospital (me'te:rnyty'
'hospytl) s. szpital położniczy
mathematician (,maetyme'tyszyn)
s. matematyk
mathematics (,maety'maetyks) s.
matematyka

math (maes) s. matematyka
(slang)
matriculate (me'trykjulejt) v.
immatrykulować; zdawać wstepny
egzamin (uniw.);zapisać się na.,.
matrimony ('maetrymeny) s. małżeństwo;akt ślubu
matron ('mejtren) s. matrona;
kobieta zamężna; (gospodyni)
matter ('maeter) s. rzecz;
tresć; materiał; substancja;
sprawa; kwestia; v. znaczyc;
mieć znaczenie;odgrywać role
matter-of-fact ('maeter,ow'faekt)
adj. rzeczowy; praktyczny
mattress ('maetrys) s. materac
mature (me'tjuer) adj. dojrzały;
płatny; v. dojrzewać; stawać
się płatnym(np.pożyczka)
maturity (me'tjueryty) s. dojrzałość; termin płatności
mauve (mouw) s. kolor różowo-
liliowy ;adj.różowo-liliowy
maw (mo:) s. żołądek; wole
maxim ('maeksym) s. maksyma
maximum ('maeksymem) s. maksi-
mum
May (mej) s. maj
may (mej) v. byc może; might
(majt) mógłby
maybe ('mejbi:) adv. byc może;
może byc;możliwe że
may I ? ('mej aj) czy mogę ?
may-bug ('mejbag) s. chrabąszcz
mayor (meer) s. burmistrz
maypole ('mejpoul) s. słup do
tańca "gaik", 1-go maja
maze (mejz) s. labirynt; gmatwanina; v. w błąd wprowadzic;
oszołomic;dezorientować;mieszac
mazurka (me'ze:rke) s. mazur;
mazurek
me (mi:) pron. mi; mnie; mną;
(slang): ja
meadow ('medou) s. łąka
meager ('mi:ger) adj. chudy;
cienki; skromny;nie obradzający
meal (mi:l) s. posiłek; grubo
mielona maka;czas posiłku
mealtime ('mi:1-tajm) s. pora
posiłku(ustalona zwyczajem)
mealy('mi:ly)adj.mączysty;nie-
szczery;słodziutki; oblesny

mean; meant; meant (mi:n;
ment; ment)
mean (mi:n) v. myśleć; przypuszczać; znaczyć; s. przeciętna; średnia; środek;
adj. ubogi; nędzny; podły;
marny; skąpy;tandetny;skąpy
meaning ('mi:nyŋg) s. znaczenie; sens; treść; adj. znaczący;mający zamiar
meaningless ('mi:nyŋglys) adj.
bez sensu; bez znaczenia
meant (ment) przeznaczony;
zob. mean
meantime ('mi:n'tajm) adv.
tymczasem;w tym samym czasie
meanwhile ('mi:n,hłajl) adv.
tymczasem
measles ('mi:zlz) s. odra
measure ('mežer) s. miara;
miarka; środek; zabieg; sposób; v. mierzyć; mieć rozmiar; oszacować;być...wzrostu
measureless ('mežerlys) adj.
bezmierny; nieskończony
measurement ('mežerment) s.
wymiar; miara; mierzenie
meat (mi:t) s. mięso; danie
mięsne;treść (książki etc.)
mechanic (my'kaemyk) s. mechanik ;rzemieślnik;technik
mechanical (my'kaenykel) adj.
mechaniczny
mechanics (my'kaenyks) s. mechanika
mechanism ('mekenyzem) s. mechanizm;maszyneria
mechanize ('mekenajz) v. zme-
chanizować
medal ('medl) s. medal
meddle ('medl) v. wmieszać się;
wtrącać się w cudze sprawy
mediaeval (,medy'i:wel) adj.
średniowieczny
mediate ('my:djejt) adj. pośredni; v. pośredniczyć
mediator ('my:djejt) s. rozjemca; mediator
medical ('medykel) adj. lekarski; medyczny
medical certificate ('medykel,
,sertyfykyt) s. świadectwo lekarskie

medicated ('medykejtyd) adj.
leczony; zaprawiony substancją
leczniczą
medicinal (me'dysynl) adj. leczniczy; lekarski; medyczny
medicine ('medysyn) s. medycyna;
lek; lekarstwo; v. leczyć lekarstwami
medieval (,medy'i:wel) adj.
średniowieczny
mediocre ('my:djouker) adj. mierny; średni; przeciętny
meditate ('medytejt) v. obmyślać;
rozmyślać; medytować
meditation (,medy'tejszyn) s.
rozmyślanie ;planowanie
meditative ('medytejtyw) adj.
zadumany; zamyślony; medyta-
cyjny ;kontemplacyjny
Mediterranean (,medyter'rejnjen)
adj. śródziemnomorski
medium ('mi:djem) s. środek;
średnia; przewodnik; środek
obiegowy; środowisko; rozpuszczalnik; sposób; środkowa droga; adj. średni;adv.średnio
medley ('medly) s. mieszanina;
pstrokacizna; rozmaitości
meek (mi:k) s. potulny; łagodny; skromny ;bez wigoru
meet; met; met (mi:t; met;met)
meet (mi:t) v. spotykać; zbierać
się; gromadzić; iść na kompromis; zgadzać się; zaspokajać;
s. spotkanie; zbiórka; miejsce
spotkania; spotkanie sportowe;
zawody(na bieżni etc.)
meet with ('mi:t,łys) v. spot-
kać się z (kims);doświadczyć
meeting ('mi:tyŋg) s. spotkanie;
połączenie się; posiedzenie;
zgromadzenie; wiec; zawody;
konferencja; pojedynek
melancholy ('melenkely) s. melancholia; adj. smutny; melan-
cholijny;zasmucający;ponury
mellow ('melou) adj. słodki;
miękki; soczysty; uleżały; zła-
godzony (wiekiem); łagodny; wesoły; pogodny; podchmielony;
dojrzały; miły; świetny; przyjemny; v. dojrzewać; zmiękczać;
uleżeć się;łagodnieć; łagodzić

melodious (my'loudjes) adj.
melodyjny ;harmonijny
melody ('meledy) s. melodia;
piosenka
melon ('melen) s. melon
melt (melt) s. stop; stopienie;
topnienie; wytop; v. topic;
topniec; roztapiac (się);
rozpuszczac; przetapiac; od-
lewac; wzruszyc;roztkliwiac
melting point ('meltyng'point)
s. temperatura topnienia
member ('member) s. członek;
człon(odrożniajacy się)
membership ('memberszyp) s.
członkowstwo; przynaleznosc;
skład członkowski
membrane ('membrejn) s. błona;
przepona; membrana
memoir ('memła:r) s. pamiętnik;
życiorys;autobiogrfia
memorable ('memerebl) adj. pamiętny;znaczny
memorial (my'no:riel) s. pomnik; memorial; petycja; posąg (na pamiatkę)
memorize ('memerajz) v. za-
pamiętywac; uczyc się na pamięc
memory ('memery) s. pamięc;
wspomnienie
men (men) pl. mężczyzni; robot-
nicy; zob.: man
menace ('menes) s. grozba; za-
grożenie; v. grozic; zagrażac
mend (mend) s. naprawa; na-
prawka; reperowac; zaszyc
menial ('mi:njel) s. sługa;
służalec; adj. czarno-robo-
czy; służalczy; służebny
mental ('mentl) adj. umysłowy;
pamięciowy; psychiatryczny;
s. (slang) umysłowo chory
mental hospital ('mentl'hospytl)
s. szpital psychiatryczny
mentality (men'taelyty) s.
umyslowosc; mentalnosc
mention ('menszyn) v. wspominac; wymieniac; nadmieniac;
wzmiankowac; s. wzmianka
menu ('menju:) s. jadłospis
meow (mi:'au) v. miauczec jak kot

mercantile ('me:rkentajl) adj.
handlowy; kupiecki
mercenary ('me:rsynery) adj.
najemny; wyrachowany; s. najemnik; żołnierz najemny
merchandise('me:rczendajz) s.
towar(y); v. handlowac
merchant('me:rczent) s. kupiec;
handlowiec; adj. handlowy;
kupiecki
merciful ('me:rsyfúl) adj. miłosierny; litosciwy
merciless ('me:rsylys) adj. bezlitosny; niemiłosierny
mercurial (me:r'kjuerjel) adj.
rtęciowy; żywy; bystry; rozgarnięty; zmienny
mercy ('me:rsy) s. miłosierdzie;
litosc; łaska;rzecz pomyslna
mercy killing ('me:rsy'kylyng)
s. eutanazja; zabojstwo z li-
tosci
mere (mjer) adj. zwykły; zwyczajny;nie więcej niż
merely ('mjerly) adv. tylko; jedynie; zaledwie; po prostu
merge (me:rdż) v. roztapiac
(się); zlewac; łączyc (się)
merger ('me:rdżer) s. połączenie; zlanie się; fuzja
meridian (me'rydjen) s. południk; zenit; szczyt; adj. południowy; szczytowy
merit ('meryt) s. zasługa; zaleta; odznaczenie; v. zasługiwac
meritorious (,mery'to:rjes) adj.
chwalebny; zasłużony
mermaid ('me:rmejd) s. rusałka;
syrena
merriment ('meryment) s. uciecha; radosc; wesołosc
merry ('mery) adj. wesoły; radosny; podochocony;odswiętny;
podchmielony
merryandrew ('mery'aendru:) s.
błazen; trefnis;wesołek
merry-go-round ('merygou,raund)
s, karuzela
merry-making ('mery,mejkyn) s.
zabawa;uciecha;weselenie się
mesh (mesz) s. siatka; siec;
układ siatkowy; v. łapac w
siec; zazebiac;wplatac

mess (mes) s. nieporządek; bałagan; bród; świństwo; paskudztwo; paćka; papka; zupa;
bigos; posiłek wspólny; stołówka; wspólny stół; v. za-
babrać; zapaskudzić; zabru-
dzić; zabałaganić; pokpić;
sfuszerować; obijać się; bawić; dawać jeść (posiłek);
stołować się (wspólnie)
mess up (,mes'ap) v. zepsuć;
zaprzepaścić; sknocić;zagmat-
wać;pobrudzić;zabałaganić
message ('mesydż) s. wiadomość;
orędzie; morał; wypowiedź;
v. komunikować;podawać;posłać
messenger ('mesyndżer) s. posłaniec; zwiastun
messy ('mesy) adj. kłopotliwy;
zapaskudzony; sfuszerowany;
brudny etc. upaćkany;niechlujny
met (met) v. zob. meet
metal ('metl) s. metal; v. pokrywać metalem;a.metalowy
metallic (my'taelyk) adj. meta-
liczny; metalowy;metalurgiczny
meteor ('mi:tjer) s. meteor
meteorology (,mi:tjero'ledży)
s. meteorologia
meter ('mi:ter) s. metr; licznik; v. mierzyć;a.metrowy
method ('meted) s. metoda; me-
todyka; metodyczność; sposób
methodical (me'todykel) adj.
metodyczny;systematyczny
meticulous (my'tykjules) adj.
drobiazgowy; szczegółowy;
drobnostkowy; pedantyczny
metric system ('metryk'system)
s. system metryczny
metropolitan (,metre'polyten)
adj. wielkomiejski; metropoli-
talny; s. mieszkaniec metro-
polii; metropolita (duchowny)
mew (mju:) v. miauczeć;pierzyć się
Mexican ('meksyken) adj. meksy-
kański;Meksykanin;Meksykanka
miaow (mi:'au) v. miauczeć
mica ('maike) s. mika; łuszczyk
mice (majs) pl. myszy; zob.:
mouse
micron('majkron)s. mikron

microphone ('majkrefoun) s. mikrofon
microscope ('majkreskoup) s. mikroskop;podczas;pośród;między-
mid (myd) adj. środkowy;prep. w;
midday ('myddej) adj. południowy;
s. południe
mid summer (,myd'samer) exp.
w środku lata
middle ('mydl) s. środek; kibić;
stan; adj. środkowy; v. składać w środku; kopać na środek
middle aged ('mydl'ejdżd) adj.
w średnim wieku
Middle Ages ('mydle'ejdżys) s.
średniowiecze
middle class ('mydl,kla:s) s.
klasa średnia; klasa średnioza-
można;a.ze średniozamożnej klasy
middle name ('mydl,nejm) s. drugie imię
middle sized ('mydl,sajzd) adj.
średniej wielkości; średni
middleweight ('mydl,łejt) s.
waga średnia; adj. średniej
wagi (148 do 160 funtów)
middling ('mydlyng) adj. średni;
przeciętny; adv. średnio
midge ('mydż) s. muszka
midget ('mydżyt) s. karzełek;
maleństwo; adj. miniaturowy
midland ('mydlend) s. środek
kraju; adj. leżący w środku
kraju; w głębi kraju
midmost ('mydmoust) adj. leżący
w samym środku;prep.pośród
midnight ('mydnajt) s. północ;
adj. północny; o północy
midway ('myd'łej) s. połowa drogi; adv. w połowie drogi
midwife ('mydłájf) s. położna;
okuszerka
might (majt) s. moc; potęga;
v. mógłby; zob.: may
mighty ('majty) adj. potężny;
adv. bardzo; wielce
migrate ('maj,grejt)v. wędrować;
przesiedlać się
migratory ('maj,gretery) adj.
wędrowny(ptak etc.)
mild (majld) adj. łagodny; powolny; potulny; słaby;delikatny

mildew ('myldju:) s. plesn;
v. plesniec;rdzewiec (o zbozu)
mildly ('majldly) adv. łagod-
nie; umiarkowanie;oglednie
mildness ('majldnys) s. łagodnosc; nieostrosc
mile (majl) s. mila; 1,609 km
mil(e)age ('majlydż) s. milaż;
odległosc w milach
milestone ('majlstoun) s. kamien milowy
military ('mylytery) adj. wojskowy; pl. wojskowy; wojsko
milk (mylk) s. mleko; v. doic
(krowy); wykorzystac; exploatowac;podsłuchiwac (telefon)
milking machine ('mylkyng,ma'-
'szi:n) s. maszyna do dojenia
milkman ('mylkmen) s. mleczarz
milk shake ('mylkszejk) s. mieszany napoj mleczny
milksop ('mylksop) s. mamin-
synek;fajtlapa;oferma;niedołęga
milky ('mylky) adj. mleczny;
zniewiesciały; koloru mleka
mill (myl) s. młyn; huta; fabryka; (1/1000); walcownia;
krawędz ząbkowana; v. mlec;
frezowac; pilsnic; kręcic się
miller ('myler) s. młynarz
millet ('mylyt) s. proso
milliner ('mylyner) s, modniarka; modystka
million ('myljen) num. milion
millionaire('myljeneer) s. milioner
millionth ('myljent) num.
milionowy; jedna milionowa
(częsc)
milt (mylt) s. mlecz rybi. ;
v. zapładniac ikrą
mimic ('mymyk) s, nasladowca;
imitator; v. nasladowac; małpowac; adj. nasladowniczy;udany,
mimiczny;zmyslony;fikcyjny
mince (myns) v. siekac; mowic
bez ogrodek; cedzic (słowa);
drobic nogami; s. siekane
mięso; nadzienie mięsne
mincing (mynsyng) adj. mizdrzą-
cy się; afektowany;sztucznie
zachowujący się(wykwintny)

mind (majnd) s. umysł; pamięc;
zdanie; opinia; postanowienie;
zamierzenie; v. pamietac; zważac; przejmowac się; baczyc;
miec cos przeciwko;byc posłusznym
mind your own business ('majnd;-
jo:'ołn'byznys) pilnuj swego
nosa; nie wtrącaj się
minded ('majndyd) adj. nastawio-
ny na; skłonny do; gotow; gotowy
mindful ('majndful) adj. pomny;
dbały; uważający; troskliwy
mindless ('majndlys) adj. nierozumny; niedbały; nieuważający
mine (majn) pron. moj; moje; mo-
ja; s. kopalnia; podkop; mina;
bomba; v. kopac;.podkopywac;
exploatowac; minowac
miner ('majner) s. gornik
mineral ('mynerel) s. minerał;
adj. mineralny;zawierający mine-
 rały
mingle ('myngl) v. mieszac się;
przyłączac się (do innych)
miniature ('mynjeczer) s. miniatura; adj. miniaturowy
minimum ('mynymem) s. minimum;
adj. minimalny;najmniejszy
mining ('majnyng) s. gornictwo;
adj. gorniczy; kopalniany
miniskirt ('myny,ske:rt) s. spod-
nica (mini) (b. krotka)
minister ('mynyster) s. duchowny;
minister; v. stosowac; przyczy-
niac się; udzielac; pomagac
ministry ('mynystry) s. dusz-
pasterstwo; kler; duchowienstwo;
ministerstwo; gabinet ministrow;
służba; pomoc;posługa
mink (mynk) s. norka; adj. z norek; z futer norek
minor ('majner) adj. mniejszy;
mało ważny; młodszy; nieletni;
s. człowiek niepełnoletni
minority (maj'noryty) s. mniejszosc; niepełnoletnosc
minster ('mynster) s. katedra;
koscioł klasztorny
minstrel ('mynstrel) s. bard;
spiewak przebrany za murzyna
mint (mynt) s. mięta; mennica;
majątek; żrodło; v. bic pieniądze; wymyslac; twonzyc; kuc

minute ('mynyt) s. minuta; chwilką; notatka; v. szkicować; protokołować; (maj'nju:t) adj.
szczegółowy;bardzo mały;znikomy
miracle ('myrekl) s. cud;a.cudowny
miraculous (my'raekjules) adj. cudowny ;nadprzyrodzony
mirage ('myra:dż) s. miraż; fata morgana ;złudzenie wzrokomire ('majer) s. muł; błoto; bagno; v. grzęznąć (w trudnościach); zabłocić się
mirror ('myrer) s. zwierciadło; v. odzwierciedlać
mirth (me:rs) s. wesołość; radość ;uciecha(pełna śmiechu)
miry ('majry) adj. błotnisty; mulisty ; bagnisty
mis-(mys) przedrostek: nie; źle; (błędnie) nie-;źle-
misadventure ('mesed'wenczer) s. niepowodzenie;zła przygoda
misanthrope ('myzentroup) s. mizantrop ;wróg ludzkości
misapply ('myse'plaj) v. nadużyć; źle zastosować
misapprehend ('mys,aepry'hend) v. nie pojąć; źle zrozumieć
misbehave ('mysby'hejw) v. nieodpowiednio zachowywać się
miscalculate ('mys'kaelkjulejt) v. przeliczyć się;przerachować się
miscarriage (mys'kaerydż) s. poronienie; omyłka;niepowodzenie
mischief ('myszyf) s. szkoda; krzywda; psota; utrapienie; złośliwość; figiel; figlarność; licho; szkodnik;bieda;niezgoda
mischievous ('myszczywes) adj. szkodliwy; niegodziwy; niesforny; niegrzeczny;psotny
misdeed ('mys'di:d) s. przestępstwo; zły czyn(karygodny)
misdemeano(u)r ('mysdy'mi:ner) s. wykroczenie;złe sprawowanie
miser ('majzer) s. sknera; chciwiec; skąpiec; kutwa
miserable ('myzerebl) adj. nędzny; chory; marny; żałosny
miserably ('myzerebly) adv. nędznie; marnie; żałośnie
misfortune ('mys'fo:rczen) s. nieszczęście; pech; zły los

misgiving (mysgywyŋg) s. złe przeczucie; obawa;powątpiewanie
misguide (,mys'gajd) v. wprowadzać w błąd;sprowadzać na manowce
mishap ('myshaep) s. (mały; nieważny) wypadek(niepowodzenie)
misinform ('mysyn'form) v. źle informować;zwieść z drogi
mislay (mys'lej) v. zatracić; zob. lay; zagubić;zapodziać
mislead (mys'li:d) v. wprowadzić w błąd; zob. lead;zbałamucić
mismanage (,mys'maenydż) v. źle prowadzić;źle pokierować
misplace (,mys'plejs) v. zatracić; położyć; nie na miejscu
misprint (,mys'prynt) v. błędnie wydrukować; s. omyłka druku; błąd drukarski
mispronounce ('myspre'nauns) v. błędnie wymawiać;źle wymawiać
misrepresent (,mysrepry'zent) v. przekręcić; błędnie przedstawić;fałszywie przedstawić
Miss (mys) s. panna; panienka
miss (mys) v. chybić; nie trafić; nie znaleźć; nie dostać; brakować; tęsknić; zacinać się; s. pudło; niepowodzenie; opuszczenie; chybienie
miss out ('mys,aut) v. wypuścić (słowo); chybić;nie dostać
missile ('mysajl) s. pocisk; rakieta; adj. nadający się do rzucania (oszczep;rakieta etc.)
missing ('mysyŋg) adj. nieobecny; brakujący; zaginiony
mission ('myszyn) s. misja; delegacja; v. wysyłać z misją; zakładać misje ;a.misyjny
missionary ('mysznery) s. misjonarz ;adj.misjonarski
misspelling ('mys'spelyŋg) s. błąd ortograficzny
mist (myst) s. lekka mgła; v. zachodzić parą (mgiełką)
mistake (mys'tejk) s. omyłka; nieporozumienie; v. pomylić (się) (co do faktu lub człowieka); źle zrozumieć; mylić się
mistaken (mys'tejken) adj. mylny; błędny;pomylony;nie mający zrozumienia sytuacji etc.

mistakenly (mys'tejknly) adv.
błędnie;pomyłkowo;nierozsądnie
Mister ('myster) s. pan (używane z nazwiskiem); skrót Mr.
(bez nazwiska niegrzecznie !)
mistletoe (mysltou) s. jemiołka, jemioła;liście jemioły
mistress ('mystrys) s. kochanka; nauczycielka; (myzys) s.
pani; (skrót Mrs); zob.Mister
mistrust (mys'trast) v. podejrzewac; nie ufac; s. niedowierzanie; nieufnosc
misty ('mysty) adj. mglisty;
zamglony;niejasny;nieokreslony
misunderstanding ('mysande r-staendyng) s. nieporozumienie
misuse ('mys'ju:z) v. nadużywac; zle uzywac; ('mys'ju:s)
s. nadużycie; złe użycie
mite (majt) s. molik; kruszyna;
drobiazg; grosz (wdowi); berbec;mała sumka pieniędzy
mitigate ('mytygejt) v. koic;
usmierzac; łagodzic; łagodniec; ukoic;złagodzic
mitten ('mytn) s. rękawiczka
bez palcow; (slang):rękawica
bokserska(zimowa etc.)
mix (myks) v. mieszac; obcowac;
wspołżyc; s. mieszanka; mieszanina; zamieszanie
mix-up ('myks'ap) s. gmatwanina; platanina;zamieszanie;bójka)
mixed up with ('mykst'ap,łys)
adj. zamieszany (w cos)
mixture ('myksczer) s. mieszanka; mieszanina;mikstura
moan (moun) s. jęk; v. jęczec;
lamentowac;mowic jęczac
moat (mout) s. fosa; row;
v. opasywac fosą
mob (mob) s. tłum; motłoch;
banda; v. napastowac; atakowac tłumnie;stłoczyc się
mobile ('moubajl) adj. ruchomy;
ruchliwy; zmienne; s. rzeźba-kompozycja wiszaca(abstrakcyj-na)
mock (mok) v. wykpic; przedrzezniac; zmylic; stawiac czoło;
żartowac z kogos; s. kpiny;
przedrzezanianie;nasladownictwo;
adj.fałszywy; udany; pozorny

mockery ('mokery) s. kpiny;
smiech; posmiewisko;pokrzywianie się
mode (moud) s. sposob; tryb; moda;rzecz modna(lub zwyczajowa)
model ('modl) s. model; wzor; modelka; manekin; v. modelowac
moderate ('moderyt) adj. umiarkowany; sredni; s. człowiek umiarkowany (w poglądach etc.)
moderate ('moderejt) v.powsciągac; uspokoic (się);prowadzic(zebranie)
moderation (,mode'rejszyn) s.
umiarkowanie; umiar;spokój
modern ('modern) adj. wspołczesny;
nowoczesny; nowozytny
modernize ('modernajz) v. unowoczesnic (się);modernizowac
modest ('modyst) adj. skromny
modesty ('modysty) s. skromnosc
modification (,modyfy'kejszyn) s.
modyfikacja; łagodzenie z lekka
modify ('modyfaj) v. modyfikowac;
zmieniac częsciowo; łagodzic
modulate ('modjulejt) v. modulowac; regulowac; dostosowywac
module ('modju:l) s. moduł; kabina (astronauty)
moist (mojst) adj. wilgotny
moisten(mojsen) v. wilgnąc; zwilżac (sobie usta etc.);wilgotnjec
moisture ('mojsczer) s. wilgoc;
wilgotnosc;lekkie zamoczenie
molar (mouler) s. trzonowy (ząb);
adj. trzonowy
mole (moul) s. kret; grobla; molo; znamię;brodawka etc.
molecule ('molykju:l) s. molekuła; cząsteczka
molest (mou'lest) v. napastowac;
dokuczac; molestowac;naprzykrzac się
mollify ('molyfaj) v. łagodzic;
miękczyc; mięknąc;usmierzac
moment ('moument) s. chwila; moment; waga; znaczenie; motyw;
powod;doniosłosc;ważnosc
momentary ('moumentery) adj.
chwilowy; mijajacy;lada chwila
monarch ('monerk) s. monarcha;
krol;duży motyl tropikalny
monarchy ('monerky) s. monarchia
monastery ('monestery) s. klasztor (głownie męski);miejsce za
mieszkania mnichow (zakonnic)

Monday ('mandy) s. poniedziałek; a. poniedziałkowy

monetary ('manytry) adj. monetarny;pieniężny;walutowy

money ('many) s. pieniądze

money-order ('many,o:rder) s.
przekaz pieniężny

monger ('manger) s. handlarz;
przekupień;kupiec

monk (mank) s. mnich

monkey (manky) s, małpą; v. dokazywać; małpowac;wygłupiać sie

monkey business ('manky'byznys)
s. małpie figle (dokuczliwe)

monkey wrench ('manky'rencz) s.
francuski klucz (dostosowywalny)

monolog(ue) ('monelog) s. monolog ;a.monologowy

monopolize (me'nopelajz) v.
monopolizować; skupiac na sobie uwagę wszystkich etc.

monopoly (me'nopely) s. monopol

monotonous (me'notnes) adj.
monotonny; jednolity

monotony (me'notny) s. monotonia

monster ('monster) s. potwór;
adj. olbrzymi;potworny;okrutny

monstrous ('monstres) adj. potworny; ogromny;okrutnie zły

month (mant) s. miesiąc

monthly ('mantly) adj. miesięcz-
ny; adv. miesięcznie; s. mie-
siecznik;adv.co miesiac;na miesiąc

monument ('monjument) s. pomnik

moo (mu:) v. ryczeć; s. ryk
(krowy)

mood (mu:d) s. humor; nastrój;
(gram.) tryb;usposobienie

moody (mu:dy) adj. ponury; maja-
cy humory;markotny

moon (mu:n) s. księżyc;a.księżyco-wy

moonlight ('mu:nlajt) s. światło
księżyca; v. miec kilka posad
równocześnie

moonlit ('mu:nlyt) adj. oświe-
cony księżycem

moonshine ('mu:nszajn) s. światło księżyca; alkohol pędzony
nielegalnie lub przemycony

Moor (muer) adj. mauretański;
s. Maur

moor (muer) s. otwarty teren łowiecki; wrzosowisko; bagno;
trzęsawisko; v. cumowac; umocowac;przybijac do brzegu

moorings ('mueryns) pl. kotwica
martwa; miejsca przycumowania

moose (mu:s) s. łoś amerykański

mop (mop) s. szmata do podłóg;
grymas; v. wycierac; zgarniac;
robic miny;spuścić manto

moral ('morel) s. morał; pl.
moralnosc;adj.moralny;obyczajny

morale (me'rael) s. nastroj;
duch (w wojsku,w narodzie)

morality (me'raelyty) s. moralność; moralizowanie; etyka

moralize ('morelajz) v. umoral-
niac; moralizowac

morass (me'raes) s. moczar; bagno;mokradła;grzęzawiska

morbid ('mo:rbyd) adj. chorobliwy; chorobowy;niezdrowy;schorzały

more (mo:r) adv. bardziej; więcej; adj. liczniejszy;dalszy

morel (mo'rel) s. (grzyb)
smardz;psianka;a.psiankowaty

more or less ('mo:r,or'les) adv.
mniej więcej;w przybliżeniu

moreover (mo:'rouwer) adv. co
więcej; prócz tego;nadto;poza tym

morgue (mo:rg) s. morga (na
zwłoki) ; kostnica;a.kostnicy

morning ('mo:rnyng) s. rano;
poranek; przedpołudnie

morose (mo'rous) adj. ponury;
zasępiony;przygnębiony;markotny

morphine ('mo:rfi:n) s. morfina ;a.morfinowy

morsel ('mo:rsel) s. kęs; kąsek;
kawałek; smakołyk; v. dzielic
na kawałki;rozdrabniac;rozparce-lowywac

mortal ('mo:rtl) s. smiertelnik;
adj. smiertelny; straszny

mortality (mo:'rtaelyty) s.
smiertelnosc;liczba ofiar

mortar ('mo:ter) s. moździerz;
zaprawa murarska; v. tynkowac;
kłasc zaprawę; strzelac z
moździerza;związac zaprawą

mortgage ('mo:rgydż) s. hipoteka; v. hipotekowac

mortician (mo:r'tyszen) s.
przedsiębiorca pogrzebowy
mortification (mo:rtyfy'kejszyn) s. upokorzenie; umartwia-
nie się;wstyd;gangrena
mortify ('mo:rtyfaj) v. zamie-
rac; ranic (uczucia); upokarzac; umartwiac (się);
powsciągac;zgangrenowac
mortuary ('mo:rtjuery) s. trupiarnia; kostnica;a.pogrzebowy
mosaic (mou'zejyk) s. mozaika;
adj. mozaikowy;mojżeszowy
mosque (mosk) n. meczet
mosquito (mes'ki:tou) s. komar;
moskit;a.moskitowy
moss (mos) s, mech; v. pokrywac
mchem (torfowiskiem)
most (moust) adj. największy;
najliczniejszy; adv. najbardziej; najwięcej; s. najwięk-
sza ilosc;maksimum
mostly ('moustly) adv. przeważnie; głównie;po największej częs-
moth (mos) s. cma; mol
moth-eaten ('mos,i:tn)adj.zje-
dzony przez mole;przestarzały
mother ('madzer) s. matka;v.mat-
mother country ('madzer'kantry)
s. ojczyzna;kraj rodzinny
motherhood ('madzer,hud) s. macierzyństwo
mother-in-law ('madzer,yn'lo:)
s. tesciowa
motherly, ('madzerly) adj. ma-
cierzynski
mother tongue ('madzer,tang) s.
język ojczysty
motif (mou'ti:f) s. motyw
(artystyczny);główny temat
motion ('mouszyn) s. ruch; wniosek; stolec; v. kierowac skinieniem, znakiem; skinąc na
kogos znaczącym gestem
motionless ('mouszenlys) adj.
bez ruchu; unieruchomiony
motion picture ('mouszyn'pykczer) s. film ruchomy
motivate ('moutywejt),v. uzasad-
niac; pobudzac kogos;zachęcac
motive ('moutyw) s. motyw; podnieta; adj. napędowy;poruszający

motor ('mouter) s. motor; adj.
ruchowy; mechaniczny; samochodowy; v. jezdzic; przewozic
samochodem;prowadzic wóz
motorbike ('mouter,bajk) s.
motocykl;rower z motorkiem
motorboat ('mouter,bout) s.
motorowka;łódź motorowa
motorcycle ('mouter,sajkl) s.
motocykl
motorcyclist ('mouter,sajklyst)
s. motocyklista
motoring ('mouteryng) s. jazda
samochodem;automobilizm
motorist ('mouteryst) s. auto-
mobilista; kierowca
motorize ('mouterajz) s. motory-
zowac;zmotoryzowac
mottle ('motl) s. cętka; plamka;
v. cętkowac;nakrapiac;upstrzyc
motto (motou) s. motto;dewiza
mo(u)ld (mould) s. plesń; ziemia;
modła; forma; v. plesniec; od-
lewac; kształtowac;urabiac
moulder ('moulder) v. gnic;
pruchniec; niszczyc się; kruszyc się;zgłupiec;s.odlewacz
mouldy ('mouldy) adj. splesniały
zgniły;stęchły;przeżyty;nudny
moult (moult) v. liniec;s.linienie
mound (maund) s. hałda; kopiec
mount (maunt) s. oprawa; podstawa; wierzchowiec; v. stanąc (na);
wsiąsc (na konia); podniesc;
wchodzic; oprawic; osadzic; wyposazyc;zmontowac;wyrezyserowac
mountain ('mauntyn) s. góra; sterta; adj. gorski; gorzysty
mountaineer (,maunty'nier) s.
goral; alpinista
mountainous ('mauntynes) adj.
gorzysty;olbrzymi;zawrotny
mourn (mo:rn) v. byc w żałobie;
opłakiwac;pogrążac się w smutku
mournful ('mo:rnful) adj. żałobny;ponury;przygnębiony
mourning ('mo:rnyng) s. żałoba
mouse (maus) s. mysz; pl. mice
(majs);podbite oko;v.myszkowac
moustache (mos'ta:sz) s. wąsy
mouth (maus) s. usta; ujscie; wylot;v.mowic przesadnie (patosem)

**mouth** (mou<u>s</u>) v. deklamować;
brać w usta; robić złą minę
**mouthful** ('mausful) s. pełne
usta; kęs; dźwięk trudny do
wymówienia; powiedzieć do
rzeczy;ważne słowa;dużo czegoś
**mouthpiece** ('mauspi:s) s. ustnik; rzecznik;kiełzno
**mouthwash** ('mausłosz) s. woda
do ust;płukanka do ust
**move** (mu:w) s. ruch; pociągnięcie; krok; zmiana mieszkania;
przeprowadzka; v. ruszać się;
posuwać; przesuwać; postępować; przeprowadzać się; wzruszać; nakłonić; zwracać się;
wnosić;zrobić ruch;działać
**move in** ('mu:wyn) v. wprowadzać się;wtargnąć ;wejść;
**move on** ('mu:w,on) v. jechać
dalej; iść dalej;ruszyć(w drogę)
**move out** ('mu:w,aut) v. wyprowadzać się;wynieść się
**movement** (mu:wment) s. ruch;
poruszenie; przemieszczenie;
mechanizm; wypróżnienie
**movies** ('mu:wyz) s. (slang)
kino ;film niemy;film
**moving** ('mu:wyng) adj. ruchomy;
wzruszający; s. przeprowadzka
**moving violation** ('mu:wyn,wa-
je'lejszyn) przestępstwo drogowe w czasie jazdy (autem)
**mow; mowed; mown** (moł; mołd;
mołn)
**mow** (moł) v. kosić(trawę)
**mower** ('młer) s. kosiarz
**mown** (mołn) v. zob. mow
**Mr.** (myster) s. pan (używane
z nazwiskiem)
**Mrs.** (mysyz) s. zamężna pani
(używane z nazwiskiem)
**much** (macz) adj.& adv. wiele;
bardzo; dużo;sporo;niemało
**much too much** (,macz'tu,macz)
exp. dużo za dużo ; zbyt dużo
**mucus** ('mju:kes) s. śluz
**mud** (mad) s. błoto; brud
**muddle** ('madl) v. nurzać się;
mącić; bełtać; mieszać; brnąć;
wikłać się; s. powikłanie;
trudne położenie ;nieład;zamęt

**muddle through** ('madl,tru:) v.
przebrnąć;wybrnąć z kłopotów
**muddy** ('mady) adj. zabłocony;
błotnisty; mętny ;v.błocić;mącić
**muff** (maf) s. zarękawek; fuszerka; fuszer; v. fuszerować
**muffle** (mafl) v. tłumić; owinąć;
otulić;s.pysk(przeżuwaczy,gryzoni)
**muffler** ('mafler) s. tłumik;
szal; rękawica bokserska;szalik
**mug** (mag) s. dzban; kubek; gęba
**mulberry** ('malbery) s. morwa
**mule** (mju:l) s. muł (zwierzę)
**mull** (mal) v. rozmyślać; pokpić;
sfuszerować; zagrzać i zapra-
wić (np. piwo); s. bałagan;
muslin; przylądek; tabakiera
**mullion** ('malion) s. pret; drążek okienny;słupek okienny
**multiple** ('małtypl) s. wielokrot-
na; adj. wielokrotny;złożony
**multiplication** (,maltyply'kejszyn) s. mnożenie;rozmnażanie się
**multiplication table** (,malty-
ply'kejszyn tejbl) s. tabliczka mnożenia
**multiply** ('małyplaj) v. mnożyć
(się);rozmnażać się;pomnożyć
**multitude** ('maltytju:d) s. mnóstwo; tłum;pospólstwo;mnogość
**mumble** ('mambl) s.mruknięcie;
bąknięcie; v. mruknąć; bąknąć;
żuć bezzębnymi dziąsłami;mamrotać
**mummy** ('mamy) s. mumia; miazga;
brunatny barwik; mamusia
**mumps** ('mamps) s. (choroba);
świnka ; zapalenie ślinianki
**munch** (mancz) v. chrupać;schrupać
**municipal** (mju:'nysypel) adj.
miejski; samorządowy; komunalny
**municipality** (mju:,nysy'paelyty)
s. zarząd miasta;miasteczko
**mural** ('mjuerel) s. malowidło
ścienne; fresk;adj.ścienny
**murder** ('me:rder) s. mord; mor-
destwo ;v.mordować;paskudzić(rolę)
**murderer** ('me:rderer) s. morderca
**murderess** ('me:rderys) s. morder-
czyni
**murderous** ('me:rderes) adj. morderczy; śmiercionośny

murmur ('me:rmer) s. mrucze-
nie; pomruk; pomrukiwanie;
szmer; szmeranie; sarkanie;
v. mruczec; szmerac
muscle ('masl) s. mięsień;
muskuł ;v. pchac się na siłę
muscle bound ('masl,baund) adj.
z zerwanymi mięśniami
muscular ('maskjuler) adj.
mięśniowy; krzepki; muskularny;wykonany muskułami etc.
muse (mju:z) v. dumac ;s.zaduma
museum (mju:'ziem) s. muzeum
mush (masz) s. papka; kulesza
(z kukurydzy);v.isc po śniegu
mushroom ('maszrum) s. grzyb;
pieczarka polna; dorobkiewicz;
v. zbierac grzyby; rozszerzac
się (jak grzyby po deszczu)
music ('mju:zyk) s. muzyka;
nuty ;konsekwencje postępku(sl)
musical ('mju:zykel) adj. muzyczny; muzykalny; s. komedia
lub film muzyczny
music hall ('mju: zykho:l) s.
teatr rewiowy
musician ('mju:zyszen) s. muzyk (zawodowy)
music stand('mju:zyk,staend) s.
pulpit (na nuty)
musk (mask) s. piżmo
musket ('maskyt) s.muszkiet
muskrat ('mask,raet) s.
piżmoszczur; futro piżmoszczura
Muslim ('muslym) adj. muzułman-
ski; s. muzułmanin
muslin ('mazlyn) s. muslin
musquash ('maskłosz) s. piżmo-
wiec;piżmoszczyr
mussel('masl) s. małz
must (mast) s. moszcz winny;
stęchlizna; szał; v. musiec;
adj. konieczny;nieodzowny
mustache ('mastasz) s. wąsy
mustard ('masterd) s. musztarda
muster ('master) v. musztrować;
zbierac (się); s. przegląd;
zebranie; zbior; apel;zebrani
muster in ('master,yn) v. za-
ciągac do wojska (powołac)
muster out ('master,aut) v. zwalniac z wojska

musty ('masty) adj. stęchły; za-
plesniały;zbutwiały;przestarzały
mute (mju:t) adj. niemy;v.tłumic
mutilate ('mju:tylejt) v. okaleczyc; psuc;okroic(tekst książki)
mutineer (,mju:ty'nier) s.
buntownik; winny buntu
mutinous ('mju:tynes) s. buntowniczy ; zbuntowany
mutiny ('mju:tyny) s. bunt;v.bun-
tować
mutter ('mater) v. mamrotac; mruczec; szemrac (przeciw); szeptac; pomrukiwac; s. mamrot; pomruk; szemranie; narzekanie
mutton ('matn) s. baranina;a.bara-
ni
mutton chop ('matn,czop) s.
kotlet barani
mutual ('mju:tjuel) adj. wzajemny; wspólny; obustronny;wspólny
muzzle ('mazl) s. wylot lufy;
pysk; kaganiec; v. nakładac
kaganiec (psu;dziennikarzowi etc.)
my (maj) pron. moj;moja;moje;moi
myelitis (,maje'lajtys) s. zapalenie rdzenia pacierzowego
myriad ('myryed) s. krocie; ro-
je; 10.000; miriada; adj. niezliczony; wielostronny
myrrh (me:r) s. mirra
myrtle ('me:rtl) s. mirt
myself (maj'self) pron. ja sam;
sam osobiscie; siebie; sobie
mysterious (mys'tierjes) adj.
tajemniczy;niezgłębiony
mystery ('mystery) s. tajemnica;
tajemniczośc ;misterium
mystify ('mystyfaj) v. wprowadzac w błąd; okrywac tajemnicą
myth (mys) s. mit; postac mi-
tyczna; bajka;mistyfikacja
mystic ('mystyk) s. mistyk;
adj. mistyczny; tajemniczy
n (en) czternasta litera
angielskiego alfabetu
nab (naeb) v. capnąc; złapac;
przydybac;aresztowac;przyłapac
nag (naeg).v. gderac; dokuczac;
dręczyc; s. szkapa;kucyk;konik
nail (nejl) s. gwóźdz; pazno-
kiec; pazur; v. przybijac;
utkwic(wzrok); ujawnic(kłam-
przygwoździc; chwytac stwo)

naive (na:'i:w) adj. naiwny
naked ('nejkyd) adj. nagi; goły; goła(prawda etc.);obnażony
name (nejm) s. imię; nazwa;
nazwisko; v. nazywać; mianować; wymieniać;naznaczyć(datę)
nameless ('nejmlys) adj. bez-
imienny; nieznany; niesłychany; nieopisany;anonimowy
namely ('nejmly) adv. mianowicie; właśnie;żeby(wyjaśnić)
nanny ('naeny) s. niańka; koza
nanny -goat ('naeny,gout) s.
koza (żywicielka,mlekodajna)
nap (naep) v. drzemać; zdrzemnąć się;s.drzemka; meszek;puch;
włos;stroszenie meszku
nape(nejp) s. kark
nappy ('naepy) adj. mocny;
podchmielony; puszysty; v. napój; piwo; półmisek; serwetka
narcosis (na:r'kousys) s. narkoza;uśpienie narkotykami
narcotic(na:r'kotyk) adj.narko-
tyczny; s. narkotyk; narkoman
narrate (nae'rejt) v. opowiadać (coś);opowiedzieć
narration (nae'rejszyn) s. opowiadanie ;opowieść
narrative ('naeretyw) adj. nar-
racyjny; s. opowiadanie
narrator (nae'rejter) n, narrator;opowiadający;opowiadacz
narrow ('naerou) adj. wąski;
ciasny; ograniczony; s. przesmyk; cieśnina; v. zwężać;
ścieśniać; kurczyć się; zmniejszać się; redukować do...
narrow -minded ('naerou'majndyd)
s. ciasny; ograniczony
nasty ('na:sty) adj. obrzydliwy; wstrętny; nieznośny; grozny: brudny; nieprzyzwoity
nation ('nejszyn) s. naród;
kraj; państwo
national ('naeszenl) adj. narodowy; państwowy; s. członek
narodu; obywatel; ziomek
nationality (,naesze'naelyty)
s. narodowość; obywatelstwo
nationalize ('naesznelajz) v.
upaństwowić; nadawać obywatelstwo (imigrantom etc.)

native ('nejtyw) adj. rodzinny;
krajowy; miejscowy; wrodzony;
naturalny; prosty; s. tubylec;
autochton; człowiek miejscowy
native language ('nejtyw'laengłydż) s. ojczysty język
nativity (ne'tywyty) s. narodzenie
natural ('naeczrel) adj. naturalny; przyrodniczy; przyrodzony; doczesny; fizyczny; przyrodni; pierwotny; nieślubny;
dziki; s. biały klawisz (pia-
nina); kasownik (muzyczny)
naturalize ('naeczerelajz) v.
naturalizować (się); aklimatyzować (się); robić naturalnym;
przyswajać sobie; pozbawiać
cech nadprzyrodzonych
naturally ('naeczrely) adv. na-
turalnie ;z przyrodzenia;oczywiś-
cie
natural-science ('naeczerel'sajens) s. przyroda; nauka przy-
rody; przyrodoznawstwo
nature ('nejczer) s. natura;
przyroda; usposobienie; rodzaj
naught (no:t) s. nic; zero
naughty ('no:ty) adj. niegrzeczny; nieposłuszny; nieprzyzwoity
nausea ('no:sje) s. nudność;
mdłość; choroba morska; obrzydzenie; wstręt;chęć wymiotowania
nauseating ('no:sjejtyng)adj.
obrzydliwy; przyprawiający
o mdłości ,wymioty etc.
nautical ('no:tykel) adj. ma-
rynarski; morski
nautical mile ('no:tykel,majl)
s. mila morska; 1853 m.
naval (nejwel) adj. morski
naval base ('nejwel,bejz) s.
baza morska (wojskowa)
nave (nejw) s. 1. nawa; 2. piasta (u koła)
navel ('nejwel) s. pępek (ośrodek)
navigable ('naewygebl) adj.
spławny; żeglowny; sterowny;
podatny do żeglugi
navigate ('naewygejt) v. żeglo-
wać; kierować; (np.balonem)
navigation (,naewy'gejszyn) s.
żegluga;podróż morska;nawigacja

navigator ('naewygejter) s.
żeglarz; nawigator

navy (nejwy) s. marynarka
wojenna;granatowy kolor

nay (nej) adv. nie; nawet; co
więcej; s. sprzeciw

near (nier) adj. bliski; dokładny; v. zbliżac się; adv. blisko; prawie; oszczędnie

nearby ('nier'baj) adj. pobliski; sąsiedni; adv. w pobliżu

nearly ('nierly) adv. prawie;
blisko; oszczędnie;nie całkiem

nearness ('niernys) s. bliskość

nearsighted ('nier-sajtyd) s.
krótkowzroczny

neat (ni:t) adj. schludny;
zgrabny;proporcjonalny

neatness ('ni:tnys) s. schlud-
nosć;prostota; porządek; gus-
townosć;dobre proporcje

necessary ('nesysery) adj. konieczny; potrzebny;wynikający

necessitate (ny'sesytejt) v.
wymagać; czynić koniecznym

necessity (ny'sesyty) s. potrzeba; koniecznosć; artykuł
pierwszej potrzeby; niedostatek;los;zrządzenie los

neck (nek) s. szyja; kark;
szyjka; przesmyk;v.pieścić się

necklace ('neklys) s. naszyjnik

neck-tie ('nektaj) s. krawat

nee (nej) z domu (nazwisko
panieńskie)

need (ni:d) s. potrzeba; trud-
nosći; bieda; v. potrzebowac;
musiec; cierpiec biedę

needful (ni:dful) adj. potrze-
bujący; potrzebny;konieczny

needle ('ni:dl) s. igła;v.kłuć

needless ('ni:dlys) adj. niepotrzebny; zbyteczny;zbędny

needy ('ni:dy) adj. będący
w potrzebie, w biedzie etc.

negate (ny'gejt) s. zaprzeczac;
negowac ; anulowac

negation (ny'gejszyn) s. zaprzeczenie; odmowa; niebyt

negative ('negetyw) adj. przeczący; negatywny; odmowny;
ujemny; s. zaprzeczenie;odmowa;
forma przecząca;wartość ujemna;

negatyw; v. sprzeciwic się;
odrzucac(np. plan)

neglect (ny'glekt) v. zaniedbywac; nie zrobić; s. zaniedbanie; pominięcie; lekceważenie

negligent ('neglydżent) adj.
niedbały; opieszały;nieuważny

negotiate (ny'gouszjejt) v. pertraktowac; omawiac; załatwiac;
przezwyciezac;przebic się przez

negotiation (ny,gouszy'ejszyn)
s. pertraktacje; omawianie

Negress ('ni:grys) s. murzynka

Negro ('ni:grou) s. murzyn; adj.
murzynski

neigh (nej) s. rżenie; v. rżeć

neighborhood ('nejberhud) s.
sąsiedztwo; sąsiedzi; okolica

neighboring ('nejberyng) adj.
sąsiedni; sąsiadujący

neither ('ni:dzer) pron. & adj.
żaden (z dwoch); ani jeden
ani drugi; ani ten ani tamten;
conj. też nie;jeszcze nie

neither... nor ('ni:dzer...no:r)
exp. ani,.. ani

neon ('ni:en) s. neon;a.neonowy

neon sign('ni:en,sajn) s. reklama neonowa

nephew ('nefju:) s. siostrzeniec; bratanek

nerve (ne:rw) s. nerw; siła;
energia; odwaga; opanowanie;
zuchwalstwo; tupet; czelnosć;
v. dodawac siłȳ, odwagi

nervous ('ne:rwes) adj. nerwowy

nervousness ('ne:rwesnys) s.
nerwowosć; zdenerwowanie

nest (nest) s. gniazdo; wyląg
v. budowac; gnieździć się

nestle ('nesl) v. skulić; stu-
lic się; przytulic się;urządzic
się
nestle down ('nesl,dałn) v.
usadawiac się (wygodnie)

nestle up to ('nesl,ap'tu) v.
przytulic się (do kogos)

net (net) adj. czysty; netto;
s. siatka; sieć; v. łowic sie-
cią; trafic w siatkę; zarobic
na czysto (na sprzedarzy etc.)

nettle ('netl) s. pokrzywa;
v. parzyc pokrzywą; draznic;
irytowac;docinac(komus)dopiekac

network ('net,łe:rk) s. sieć
(np. elektryczna)
neurosis (nju:rousys) s. nerwica;zaburzenia psychiczne
neuter ('nju:ter) adj. nijaki;
neutralny; bezstronny; bezpłciowy; s. człowiek bezstronny; rodzaj nijaki
neutral ('nju:trel) adj. bezstronny; neutralny; obojętny;
pośredni; nieokreślony; bezpłciowy; s. państwo neutralne
neutrality (nu'traelyty) s.
neutralność;obojetność
neutralize ('ny:trelajz)v.neutra-
lizować;unieszkodliwiać;zobo-
jętniać
neutron ('nu:tron).s. neutron
never ('never) adv. nigdy;
chyba nie; wcale; ani nawet
nevermore ('newer'mo:r) adv.
nigdy wiecej(przenigdy)
nevertheless (,newerty'les) adj.
niemniej; jednak; pomimo tego
new (nju:) adj. nowy; świeży;
nowoczesny;adv.znowu;na nowo
newborn ('nju:,bo:rn) adj. nowo urodzony; s. noworodek
newcomer (nju:'kemer) adj. no-
woprzybyły; s. przybysz
news (nju:z) s. nowiny; wiadomości; aktualności;zadrzenia
newscast ('nju:z,ka:st) s. na-
dawanie wiadomości
newspaper ('nju:s,pejper) s.
dziennik (gazeta);tygodnik etc.
newsreel ('nju:sri:l) s. kronika filmowa
newsstand ('nju:staend) s.kiosk
z gazetami
new year ('nju:je:r) s. nowy
rok; pierwszego stycznia
New Year's Eve ('nju:,je:rs'i:w)
s. Sylwester( 31go grudnia)
next (nekst) adj. następny;
najbliższy; sąsiedni; adv. następnie; potem; z kolei; tuż
obok;prep.obok;najbliżej
next but one ('nekst,bat'łan)
adj. przedostatni
next day ('nekst,dej) exp. na-
stępnego dnia
next door ('nekst,do:r) adj.
(dom) obok; sąsiedni(budynek)

next to ('nekst,tu) prep. obok
nibble at ('nybl,et) v. obgry-
zać; nadgryzać; brać (przynętę); s. ogryzanie; dziobanie
nice (najs) adj. miły; sympatyczny; przyjemny; uprzejmy;
ładny; wybredny; dokładny
nicely ('najsly) adv. przyjem-
nie; miło; grzecznie; ściśle;
dokładnie; skrupulatnie
nicety ('najsyty) s. delikatność; subtelność; zawiłość;
drobiazgowość; dokładność;
drobny szczegół; małe rozróż-
nienie;precyzja;akuratność
niche (nycz) s. nisza; v. chować (się)w niszy
nick (nyk) s. karb; otłuczenie;
moment; v. karbować; podcinać;
przecinać; trafić; natrafić;
odgadnąć; oszukać; złapać
nickel ('nykl) s. nikiel; 5 centów USA; v. niklować
nick-nack ('nyk,naek) = knickknack; ozddbka;świecidełko
nickname ('nyknejm) s. zdrobnia-
łe imię; przezwisko; v. nazywać
zdrobniale; przezywać
niece (ni:s) s. siostrzenica;
bratanica
niggard ('nyged) s. sknera; adj.
żałujący (czegoś); skąpiący
night (najt) s. noc; wieczór
night cap ('najtkaep) s. kieliszek przed snem; czepek do spania;szklanka wina przed snem
nightclub ('najtklab) s. nocny
lokal (rozrywkowy)
nightgown ('najtgałn) s. damska
koszula nocna;nocny ubiór
nightingale ('najtyngejl) s.
słówik; a. słowikowy; słowika
nightly ('najtly) adv. co noc;
w nocy;adj. nocny; jak noc
nightmare ('najtmeer) s. koszmar; przerażające doświadczenie
night school ('najtsku:l) s.
szkoła wieczorowa
nightshirt ('najtsze:rt) s.
koszula nocna
nighty ('najty) s. koszulka
nocna (dziecinna,kobieca)

nil (nyl) s. nic; zero

nimble ('nymbl) adj. zwinny;
zgrabny;bystry;żywy;żwawy

nine (najn) num. dziewięć;
s. dziewiątka;dziewięcioro

ninepins ('najnpynz) pl. kręgle

nineteen ('najn'ti:n) num.
dziewiętnaście;dzewiętnastka

nineteenth ('najn't:ns) num.część
dziewiętnasty;dzewiętnasta

ninetieth ('najntyys) num.
dziewiędziesiąty

ninety ('najty) num. dziewięć-
dziesiąt;dzewiędziesiątka

ninth ('najns) num. dziewiąty

ninthly ('najnsly) adv. po
dziewiąty (raz)

nip (nyp) v. uszczypnąć; przy-
chwycić; odszczepić; stłumić;
zmrozić; buchnąć; ukraść; popędzić; polecieć; ucinać;
niszczyć;s.ukąszenie;uszczypnięcie

nipoff ('nypof) v. zemknąć

nipple ('nypl) s. brodawka
sutkowa; smoczek; złącze
gwintowane rury; wzniesienie;
pagórek;bańka;złączka;nasówka

niter ('najter) s. saletra

nitrogen ('najtrydżen) s. azot

no (nou) adj. nie; żaden;
odmowa; adv. nie; bynajmniej;
nic;wcale nie;s.odmowa;sprzeciw

no one ('nou,łan) adj. żaden;
ani jeden; nikt (w ogóle)

nobility (nou'bylyty) s. szla-
chetność; szlachta

noble (noubl) adj. szlachetny;
szlachecki; wspaniały; wielkoduszny; s. szlachcic

nobleman (noublmen) s. szlachcic

nobody ('noubedy) s. nikt;
człowiek bez znaczenia

nod (nod) v. skinąć głową;
ukłonić się; drzemać; przyzwalać skinieniem;być nachylonym

noise ('nojz) s. hałas; zgiełk;
wrzawa; szum; odgłos; szmer;
v. rozgłaszać coś;rozgłosić

noiseless ('nojzlys) adj. cichy;
bezszelestny;nie hałaśliwy

noisy ('nojzy) adj. hałasliwy;
krzykliwy; wrzaskliwy

nomadic ('noumaedyk) adj. wędrowny; koczowniczy ;wędrujący

nominal ('nomynl) adj. nominalny;
imienny; symboliczny;tylko z nazwy

nominate ('nomynejt) v. mianować; wyznaczać; obierać

nomination (,nomy'nejszyn) s.
nominacja

nominative ('nomynetyw) s. mianownik (gram.); ta sprawa(sądowa)

non- (non) prefix nie-; bez-;

nonalcoholic ('non,aelke'holic)
adj. bezalkoholowy

noncommissioned ('nonke'myszend)
adj. bez rangi oficerskiej
(podoficer)

noncommital ('nonke'mytl) adj.
wymijający;nie zobowiazujący(się)

nonconducting ('nonken'daktyng)
adj. nieprzewodzący

nonconformist ('nonken'fo:rmyst)
dyskontent; niekonformista

nondescript ('nondyskrypt) adj.
nieokreślony; s. człowiek nie-
określony(trudny do opisania)

none (non) pron. nikt; żaden;
nic; adv. wcale nie; bynajmniej
nie

nonexistence (,nony'ksystens)
s. niebyt;nie istnienie

nonfiction (,non-'fykszyn) s.
reportaże; opowieść prawdziwa;
opisy faktów (w dziennikach etc.)

nonsense ('nonsens) s. niedorzeczność; nonsens; głupstwo

nonskid ('nonskyd) adj. prze-
ciwślizgowy; nie ślizgający
się (samochód, opona etc.)

nonsmoker ('non'smouker) s.
osoba niepaląca; przedział dla
niepalących(w pociągu etc.)

nonstop ('non'stop) adj. bezpośredni;bez lądowania; bez
postoju; nieprzerwany (lot etc.)

nonunion ('non'ju:njen) adj.
nie należący do związku zawodowego;nie uznający związku zawodowego

nonviolence ('non'wajelens) s.
(polityka) bez gwałtów

noodle ('nu:dl) s. makaron; kluska; cymbał; pała; głupek;łeb

nook (nuk) s. kącik; zakątek

noon (nu:n) s. południe

noose (nu:s) s. pętla; stryczek; sidła; lasso; v. usidlić; zrobic pętlę

nor (no:r) conj. też nie

norm (no:rm) s. norma;wzorzec; standard

normal ('no:rmel) adj. normalny; prostopadły; prawidłowy; s. stan normalny; prostopadła

normalize ('no:rmelajz) v. normalizować; unormować

Norman ('no:rmen) adj. normański ;Normandczyk;Normandka

north (no:rs) adv. na północ; s. północ; adj. północny

northeast (no:rs'i:st) adj. północno-wschodni

northerly ('no:rdzerly) adj. północny; adv. na północ

northerner ('no:rdzerner) s. człowiek z północnych stanów

northward ('no:rsłerd) adj. północny; adv. na północ

northwest ('no:rs'łest) adj. północno-zachodni; adv. na północny-zachód; s. północny-zachód

Norwegian (no:rłi:dżen) adj. norweski ;s.Norweg

nose (nouz) s. nos; węch; wylot; dziób; v. węszyć; pocierać nosem; wtykać nos

nosegay ('nouzgej).s. wiązanka; bukiet

nostril ('noustryl) s. nozdrze; chrapy; dziura w nosie

nosy ('nouzy) adj. wścibski; śmierdzący; aromatyczny; nosacz wielki;stęchły;cuchnący

not (not) adv. nie ;ani(jeden)

not a (not ej) adv. żaden

notable ('noutebl) adj. znakomity; sławny; wybitny; s. dostojnik ;wybitny człowiek

notary public ('noutery'pablyk) s. notariusz

notation (nou'tejszyn) s. znakowanie; notacja; symbol

notch (nocz) s. nacięcie; karb; przełęcz; v. nacinać; karbować; rowkować ;s.krok(dalej)

note (nout) s. nuta; znak; znamie; uwaga; notatka; banknot; v. zapisywać; zauważać

note down ('nout'dałn) v. zanotować;zapisywać

notebook ('noutbuk) s. zeszyt; notatnik ;notes; notesik

noted ('noutyd) adj. znany; znakomity; wybitny

notepaper ('nout,pejper) s. papier listowy ;blok

noteworthy ('nout,łe:rsy) adj. godny uwagi; wybitny ;osobliwy

nothing ('nasyng) s. nic; drobiazg; adv. nic; nie; w żaden sposób ;bynajmniej nie;wcale nie

nothing but ('nasyng'bat) s. nic tylko.. (coś najlepszego)

notice ('noutys) v. zauważyć; spostrzec; traktować grzecznie; powiadamiać; s. zawiadomienie; uwaga; recenzja ;spostrzeżenie

noticeable ('noutysebl) adj. godny uwagi; widoczny

notification (,noutyfy'kejszyn) s. zawiadomienie ;zgłoszenie

notify (noutyfaj) v. zawiadomić

notion ('nouszyn) s. pojęcie; wyobrażenie; zamiar ;wrażenie

notorious ('nou'to:rjes) adj. notoryczny; osławiony ;jawny

notwithstanding (,noutłys'staendyng) adv. jednakże; niemniej; mimo; prep. pomimo(tego);mimo

nought (no:t) s. nic; zero

noun (naun) s. rzeczownik

nourish ('narysz) v. żywić; karmić ;utrzymywać

nourishing ('naryszyng) adj. pożywny ;pokrzepiający

nourishment ('naryszment) s. pokarm; pożywienie; żywienie; karmienie ;żywność; jedzenie

novel ('nowel) s. powieść; opowieść; nowela; adj. nowy; nowatorski; osobliwy ;oryginalny

novelist ('nowelyst) s. powieściopisarz

novelty ('nowelty) s. nowość; innowacja ;oryginalność

November (nou'wember) s. listopad; adj. listopadowy

novice ('nowys) s. nowicjusz;
neofita; początkujący

now (nał) adv. teraz; obecnie;
dopiero co; otóż; a więc;
s. teraźniejszość; chwila
obecna; chwila dzisiejsza

now and again ('nał,ende gejn)
exp. od czasu do czasu

now and then ('nał,end'dzen)
exp.;nieraz; od czasu do czasu; czasem;co jakiś czas

nowadays ('nałe,dejz) adv.
obecnie; dzisiaj; s. obecne
czasy;dzisiejsze czasy

nowhere ('nouhłer) adv. nigdzie; s. niepowodzenie etc.

noways ('noułejz) adv. bynajmniej ; wcale nie

noxious ('nokszes) adj. szkodliwy; niezdrowy (moralnie etc.)

nozzle ('nozl) s. dysza; rozpylacz; dziób; wylot (rury etc.)

nuclear ('nu:kli:er) adj. jądrowy; o napędzie nuklearnym

nuclear fission('nu:kli:er'fyszyn) v. rozszczepienie jądra

nuclear power plant ('nu:kli:-
er'pałer'pla:nt) s. elektrownia atomowa

nuclear reactor ('nu:kli:er,ri:-
'aekter) s. reaktor nuklearny

nucleus ('nu:kljes) s. jądro

nude (nju:d) adj. nagi; goły:
nie ważny (prawnie); s. człowiek nagi; nagość; akt

nudge (nadż) v. trącać lekko;
s. trącenie łokciem

nugget ('nagyt) s. bryłka; złoty samorodek

nuisance ('nju:sns) s. zawada;
naruszenie porządku publiczne-
go; osoba sprawiająca zawade

null and void ('nal,end'woid)
exp. nieważny; bez znaczenia;
unieważniony;nic nie zanczący

numb (nam) adj. ścierpły; zdręt-
wiały; odrętwiały; v. drętwieć;
odurzać;paralizować;zdrętwieć

number ('namber) s. liczba; numer; ilość; v. liczyć; numerować; wyliczać; zaliczać

numberless ('namberlys) adj.
niezliczony; bez numeru

number plate ('namber'plejt) s.
płyta z numerem rejestracji
samochodu;motoru etc.

numeral ('nju:merel) adj. liczbowy; cyfrowy; s. liczebnik;
cyfra(pisana,mówiona etc.)

numerous ('nju:meres) adj. liczny; obfity;liczebny;rytmiczny

nun (nan) s. zakonnica:mniszka

nunnery('nanery) s. zakon żeński

nuptials ('napszels) pl. zaślubiny;gody;wesele;ślub

nurse (ne:rs) s. pielęgniarka;
pielęgniarz; mamka; osłona;
v. pielęgnować; leczyć; opie-
kować się; żywic; podsycać;
szanować; obejmować; karmić;
pić powoli;(piersią) niańczyć

nursery ('ne:rsery) s. pokój
dziecinny; żłobek; przedszkole; ochronka; wylęgarnia;
szkółka (roślin)(drzewek)

nursery school ('ne:rsery'sku:l)
s. przedszkole

nursing bottle ('ne:rsyng'botl)
s. flaszka do karmienia

nursing home ('ne:rsyn'houm)
s. przytułek - lecznica dla
starych i kalekich;dom zdrowia

nut (nat) s. orzech; bzik; dziwak; nakrętka; zakrętka;
v. szukać i zbierać orzechy

nutcracker ('natkraeker) s.
dziadek do orzechów

nutmeg ('natmeg) s. gałka
muszkatołowa

nutria ('nju:trje) s. nutria
(futro);nutrie

nutrient ('nju:trjent) adj.
pożywny; odżywczy ;s.odżywka

nutriment ('nju:tryment) s.
środek odżywczy

nutrition (nju'tryszyn) s. odżywienie; pokarm

nutritious (nju'tryszes) adj.
pożywny; odżywczy

nutshell ('natszel) s. łupka
od orzecha; istota rzeczy;
sama treść(w paru słowach)

nutty ('naty) adj. orzechowy;
pomylony; zbzikowany;dziwaczny;
zwariowany;pikantny;zakochany

nuzzle ('nazl) v. wsadzać nos
(w coś); ryć; węszyć; wtulać
się(twarzą w czyjeś ramię)
nylon ('najlon) s. nylon; pończochy nylonowe
nymph (nymf) s. nimfa
nymphomania (,nymfe'mejnia) s.
nimfomania(kobieca żądza miłos-
o (ou) piętnasta litera
angielskiego alfabetu;zero
oak (ouk) s. dąb;a.dębowy
oar (o;r) s. wiosło; v. wiosłować
oarsman ('o:rzmen) s. wioslarz
oasis (ou'ejsys) s. oaza ;
zielonei żywne miejsce wsród
pustynnej okolicy
oat (out) s. owies
oatmeal ('outmi:l) s. owsianka ʃstwo;świętokradztwo etc.
oath (ous) s. przysięga;przeklen-
obedience (e'bi:djens) s. po-
słuszeństwo
obedient (e'bi:djent) adj. posłuszny
obey (e'bej) v. słuchać; być
posłusznym (rozsądkowi etc.)
obituary ('bytjuery) s. nekrolog; adj. pośmiertny; żałobny
object ('obdżykt) s. przedmiot;
rzecz; cel; śmieszny człowiek;
dopełnienie; v. zarzucać coś;
być przeciwnym ;sprzeciwiać się
objection (eb'dżekszyn) s. zarzut; sprzeciw; przeszkoda;
trudność; wada; niechęc
objective (eb'dżektyw) s. cel;
objektyw; adj. przedmiotowy;
obiektywny;rzeczywisty
obligation (obly'gejszyn) s.
zobowiązanie; obowiązek; obligacja;dług(wdzięczności etc.)
oblige (e'blajdż) v. zobowiązywać; spełniać prosbę
obliging (e'blajdżyng) adj.
uprzejmy; uczynny ;usłużny
oblique (e'bli:k) adj.posredni;
ukosny; skosny; kręty; nieszczery; potajemny;v.iść na ukos
obliterate (e'blyterejt) s. zacierać; zamazywać; wykreślić;
zniszczyć;skasować (zanczek etc.)

oblivion (e'blywjen) s.
zapomnienie; niepamięc
oblivious (o'blywjes) adj. za-
pominający; niepomny; nieswia-
domy; dający zapomnienie
oblong('oblong)adj. podłużny;
s. podłużny przedmiot
obscene (ob'si:n) adj. sprosny;
nieprzyzwoity; niemoralny
obscure (eb'skjuer) adj. ciemny;
skromny; niejasny; ukryty; nieznany; v. zaciemniac; przyciem-
niac; zacmiewać
obsequies ('obsykłyz) pl. pogrzeb
observance (eb'ze:rwens) s. obrzęd; zwyczaj; przestrzeganie;
szacunek;poszanowanie;rytuał
observant (eb'ze:rwent) adj.
uważny; przestrzegający; spostrzegawczy;bystry; czujny
observation (,obzer'wejszyn) s.
obserwacja; spostrzeżenie;
uwaga;spostrzegawczość
observatory (eb'ze:rweto:ry) s.
obserwatorium;punkt obserwacyjny
observe (eb'ze:rw) v. obserwować;
przestrzegac; obchodzić; zauważać;wypowiedzieć uwagę;zbadać
observer (eb'ze:rwer) s. obserwator;człowiek przestrzegający praw
obsess (eb'ses) v. opętać; prze-
sladować;nie dawać spokoju;nawiedzać
obsession (eb'seszyn) s. obsesja;
opętanie ;natręctwo (myślowe)
obsolete ('obseli:t) adj. przestarzały; szczątkowy;zarzucony
obstacle ('obstekl) s. przeszkoda; zawada
obstetrics (ob'stetryks) s. po-
łożnictwo
obstinacy ('obstynesy) s. upior
obstinate ('obstynyt) adj. uparty; uporczywy;zawzięty;wytrwały
obstruct (eb'strakt) v. tamować;
zagradzac; zasłaniac; wstrzymywać;wywoływać zator;zawadzać
obtain (eb'tejn) v. uzyskać;
trwać; panować;obowiązywać
obtainable (eb'tejnebl) adj.
osiągalny (do nabycia etc.);
możliwy do nabycia

obtrusive (eb'tru:syw) adj.
natarczywy; natrętny
obvious ('obwjes) adj. oczywisty; rzucający się w oczy
occasion (e'kejżyn) s. sposobność; okazja; powód
occasional (e'kejżenl) adj.
przypadkowy; okazyjny;
okolicznościowy; rzadki
Occident ('oksydent) s. Zachód (jako kultura, ekonomia
etc.)-całość geogaficzna
occult (o'kalt) adj. tajemny
occupant ('okjupent) s. mieszkaniec; posiadacz (faktyczny)
occupation (,okju'pejszyn) s.
okupacja; zawód; zajęcie;
zajmowanie;zamieszkiwanie
occupy ('okjupaj) v. okupować;
zajmować (się czyms);zatrudniać
occur (e'ke:r) v. zdarzać się;
przychodzic na mysl; poja-
wiac się;dziac sie;trafić sie
occurrence(e'karens) s. wydarzenie; przypadek;występowanie
ocean ('ouszen) s. ocean;a.ocea-
o'clock (e'klok) adv. na zegarze;według zegara
October (ok'touber) s. październik ;a,październikowy
ocular ('okjuler) adj. oczny;na-
oczny;na oko;okiem;s.okular
oculist ('okjulyst) s. okulista
odd (od) adj. nieparzysty;
dziwny; dziwaczny; zbywający;
pozostały; dodatkowy;od pary
odds (ods) pl. szanse; fory;
nadwyżka; różnica; drobne
szczegóły; spór; nierówność
(w grze);sprzeczność;różnica
odds-and-ends ('ods,end'ends)
exp.: resztki; rupiecie
oddity ('odyty) s. osobliwość;
dziwak;dziwactwo;dziwna rzecz
odor ('ouder) s. odor; won;
slad; reputacja;sława;posmak
of (ow) prep. od; z; o; w
of Cracow (ow'Krakau) exp.:
z Krakowa(pochodzeniem etc.)
of charity (ow'chaeryry) exp.
z miłosierdzia
off (of) adv. od; z; na boku;
precz; zdala; przy;prep.z dala

offshore (of'szo:r) adv. przy
wybrzeżu ;adj.od lądu(na morze)
offense (e'fens) s. obraza; za-
czepka; przekroczenie,ofenzywa
offend (e'fend) v. obrażac; razić; występować przeciw (np.
prawu);zawinić;wykroczyc
offender (e'fender) s. winowajca ;przestępca;strona winna
offensive (e'fensyw) adj. obraz-
liwy; drażniący; przykry; cuch-
nący; zaczepny; s. ofensywa;
postawa zaczepna
offer ('ofer) s. oferta; propozycja (np. ślubu); v. ofia-
rowac (się); oswiadczyć (się);
oferowac; nastręczyć się; nada-
rzyc się;występować z propozycją
offering ('oferyng) s. ofiara
office ('ofys) s. biuro; urząd;
obowiązek; służba urzędowania;
posada;funkcja;stanowisko;gabi-net
officer ('ofyser) s. urzędnik;
oficer; policjant; v. obsadzac
kadra; dowodzić; kierować
official (e'fyszel) s. urzędnik;
adj. urzędowy; oficjalny
officious (e'fyszes) adj. narzucający się; natrętny; gorliwy;
nieurzędowy;nieoficjalny
offish ('ofysz) adj. chłodny;
sztywny; z rezerwą;nieprzystępny
offset (o':fset) s. offsetowy
druk; gałąź; odgałęzienie;
odrosl; potomek; wyrównanie;
kompensata;v.wynagradzać;rozras-tać się
offspring ('o:fspryng)s. potomek;
wynik; potomstwo
often ('o:fn) adv. często
oh ! (ou) excl.:och !; ach !
oil (ojl) s. oliwa; olej; ropa;
nafta; farba olejna; v. oliwic;
smarowac; przetapiac;pochlebiac
oilcloth ('ojlklos) s. cerata
oily ('ojly) adj. oleisty;
olejny; tłusty; oblesny;służalczy
ointment ('oyntment) s. masc
O.K., okay ('ou'kej) adv. w porządku; tak; adj. b. dobry;
s. zgoda; v. zaaprobować (coś)
old (ould) adj. stary; staroświecki; doswiadczony; były
s.dawne czasy;dawno temu

old age ('ould,ejdż) s. starosć
old-age ('ould ejdż) adj. dawny; stary; starczy
old-fashioned ('ould'faeszend)
adj. staromodny; staroświecki
old-time ('ould,tajm) adj.
dawny
old town ('ould,tałn) s. starów-
ka; stare miasto
olive ('olyw) s. oliwka; drzewo oliwne; (kolor) oliwkowy;
oliwa stołowa
olive-branch ('olywbra:ncz) s.
gałązka oliwna
Olympic Games (ou'lympyk,gejms)
pl. igrzyska olimpijskie
ombudsman (om'bu:dz,men) s.
rzecznik ludu - załatwia skar-
gi na biurokratów
omelet(te) ('omlyt) s. omlet
omen ('oumen) s. omen; wróżba;
znak ;v. być wróżbą;być znakiem
ominous ('omynes) adj. złowieszczy ; źle wróżący
omission (e'myszyn) s. opuszczenie; zaniedbanie
omit (ou'myt) v. opuszczac;
pomijac; zaniedbywac
omnipotent (om'nypetent) adj.
wszechmocny;wszechmogący
omniscient (om'nysjent) adj.
wszechwiedzący
on (on) prep. na; ku; przy; nad;
u; po; adv. dalej; przed siebie; naprzod ;przy sobie
on and on ('on,end'on) exp.: coraz dalej;bez końca;wciąż
on demand (,on dy'ma:nd) exp.:
na żądanie
on the street ('on,dy'stri:t)
exp.: na ulicy
on to ('ontu) exp. na; do
once (łans) adv. raz; nagle;
naraz; zaraz; kiedys; niegdys;
dawniej; s. raz; conj. raz;
gdy; skoro ;od razy;zarazem etc.
one (łan) num. jeden; adj. pierwszy; pojedynczy; jedyny; pewien;
s. dowcip; kieliszek; pron. ten;
który;ktos; niejaki;s.jedynka
one Adams ('łan,aedems) exp.: pewien Adams ;niejaki Adams

one day ('łan,dej) exp.pewnego
dnia; kiedys;niegdys
one by one ('łan,baj'łan) adv.
pojedynczo;jeden za drugim
one antoher (,łan e'nadzer) adv.
jeden drugiego; wzajemnie
oneself (łan'self) pron. się;
siebie; sobie; sam; osobiscie;
samodzielnie; samotnie
one-sided ('łan'sajdyd) adj.
jednostronny
one-up-manship ('łan,ap'-men-
szyp) s. "wyscig" nerwów
(w zatargu etc)
one-way ('łan,łej) adj. jedno-
kierunkowy(ruch)
onion ('anjen) s. cebula
onlooker ('onluker) s. widz
only ('ounly) adj. jednyny; jedynak; adv. tylko; jedynie;
ledwo; dopiero; conj. tylko
że;coż z tego ,kiedy...
onward ('onłerd) adj. naprzód;
ku przodowi; adv. naprzód;
dalej;dalej naprzod
ooze (u:z) v. sączyc się; wydzielac się; ciec; s. szlam;
muł; wyciek; rzadkie błoto
opaque (ou'pejk) adj. nieprzezroczysty; matowy; mętny;
niejasny; s. rzecz matowa;
nieprzezroczysta
open ('oupen) adj. otwarty; rozwarty; dostępny; wystawiony;
jawny; odsłonięty; wakujący;
otwarty; wolny; v. otworzyc;
zwierzyc się; umożliwic; rozpoczynac; rozchylic;udostępnic
open air ('oupen,eer) s. swieże
powietrze; wolna przestrzeń
opener ('oupener) s. otwieracz
(np. puszek);przyrząd do otwie-
rania
open-handed ('oupn'haendyd) adj.
szczodry; hojny
open-hearted ('oupn,ha:rtyd) adj.
szczery; serdeczny
opening ('oupynyng) s. otwor; wylot; otwarcie; początek; zbyt
adj. początkowy; wstępny
openly ('oupnly) adv. otwarcie;
szczerze; publicznie; bez ogrodek;po prostu; wprost(powiedzieć)

open-minded ('oupn'majndyd)
adj. z otwartą głowa; bez
przesądów; bez stronny
opera ('opere) s. opera
opera glasses ('operegla:sys) s.
lornetka (teatralna)
operate ('operejt) v. działać;
zadziałać; oddziaływać; pracować; operować (kimś; kogoś);
wywoływać; prowadzić; kierować; obsługiwać;spekulować
operation (,ope'rejszyn) s.
działanie; czynności; operacja;
obsługiwanie; akcja
operative ('oprejtyw) adj. skuteczny; działający; praktyczny; operacyjny;s.pracownik;agent
mechanik; robotnik; detek-
tyw; agent wywiadu
operator ('operejter) s. operator; pracownik; obsługujący
maszynę; telefonista; kierownik; przemysłowiec; finansi-
sta; spekulant
opinion (e'pynjen) s. pogląd;
opinia; zdanie;zapatrywnie;sąd
opponent (e'pounent) s. przeciwnik; oponent; adj. przeciwny; przeciwległy
opportunity (,oper'tju:nyty)
s. sposobność; okazja
oppose (e'pouz) v. przeciwstawiać; sprzeciwiać się
opposed (e'pouzd) adj. przeciwny;przeciwdziałający
opposite ('epezyt) adj. przeciwny; przeciwległy; odmienny; adv. na przeciwko;na przeciw
s. przeciwieństwo;odwrotność
opposition (,ope'zyszyn) s.
sprzeciw; opór; opozycja;
przeciwstawienie (się); przeciwieństwo;a.opozycyjny
oppress (e'pres) v. przygniatać; uciskać; ciemiężyć;
gnębic; nużyć; męczyć
oppression (e'preszyn) s. ucisk
oppressive (e'presyw) adj.
uciążliwy; dręczący; gnębiciel-
ski; ciężki; duszny;deprymujący
opt (opt) v. wybierać z dwu
alternatyw;optować na rzecz cze-goś

optical ('optykel) adj. optyczny; wzrokowy;pomocny w widzeniu
optician (op'tyszen) s. optyk
optimism ('optymysem) s. opty-
mizm;pogodny pogląd na życie
optimize ('optymajz) v. używać
najwydajniej,najsprawniej
option ('opszyn) s. możnosć wyboru; opcja; wybór; v. wybrać
alternatywę
or (o:r) conj. lub; albo; czy;
ani; inaczej; czyli; s. złoto;
adj. złoty
or else ('o:rels) exp. bo jak
nie..; w przeciwnym razie
oral ('o:rel) adj. ustny; do-
ustny; s. egzamin ustny
orange ('oryndż) s. pomarańcza;
adj. pomarańczowy
orangeade ('oryn'dżejd) s.
oranżada(z pomarańcz ,cukru)
orator ('oreter) s. mówca
orbit ('o:rbyt) s. orbita;
oczodół; v. latać w orbicie
(ziemi)(słońca etc.)
orchard ('o:rczerd) s. sad
orchestra ('o:rkystra) s.
orkiestra
ordain (o;r'dejn) v. wyświęcać;
mianować; nakazywać; przeznaczać;zarządzać;nakazać
ordeal (o:r'di:l) s. ciężka
próba; ciężkie doświadczenie
order ('o:rder) s. rozkaz; zlecenie; zarządzenie; przekaz;
porządek; szyk; układ; stan;
zakon; order; obrzęd; zamówienie; zadanie; v. rozkazać; zamawiać; komenderować; zarządzać;
wyświecać; porządkować
orderly ('o:rderly) s. posługacz; ordynans; adj. adv.
porządny; czysty; dokładny;
skromny; spokojny; dyżurny
ordinal ('o:rdynl) s. liczebnik
porządkowy; adj. porządkowy
ordinary ('o:rdnry) adj. zwyczajny; zwykły; przeciętny;
pospolity; typowy; s. rzecz
zwykła,codzienna,przęcietna
ore (o:r).s. ruda; kruszec;
a. kruszcowy;rudowy

organ ('o:rgen) s. narząd;
organ; organy;czasopismo
organic ('o:rgaenyk) adj. organiczny;usystematyzowany
organization (,o:rgenaj'zejszyn) s. organizacja; organi-
zowanie;struktura;zrzeszenie
organize ('o:genajz) v. organizować;zrzeszyć;nadawać ustrój
organizer('o:genajzer) s. organizator
orgy ('o:rdży) s. orgia
Orient ('o:rjent) adj. orien-
talny; wschodni;s.Wschód(bliski)
orient ('o:rjent) v. oriento-
wać;ukierunkowywać;ustawiać
origin('orydżyn) s. pochodzenie;
poczatek;źródło;geneza
original (e'rydżynel) adj.
oryginalny; początkowy;
s. oryginał; dziwak
originality (e,rydży'naelyty)
s. oryginalność
originate (e'rydżynejt) v. zapoczątkować; powstawać
ornament ('o:rnament) s. ozdoba; v. ozdabiać,upiększać
ornamental (,o:rne'mentl) adj.
ozdobny; dekoracyjny; zdobni-
czy;upiększający
orphan ('o:rfen) s. sierota;
adj. sierocy; osierocony
orphanage ('o:rfenydż) s. sie-
rociniec; sieroctwo
orthodox ('o:tedoks) adj. pra-
wowierny; prawosławny
oscillate ('osylejt) v. drgać;
wahać się; oscylować
ostrich ('ostrycz) s. strus
other ('adzer) pron. inny; drugi; adv. inaczej;odmiennie
otherwise ('adzerłajz) adv.
inaczej; poza tym; skądinąd
ought (o:t) v, powinien; trzeba;
żeby; należy; zobowiazany etc.
ounce (auns) s. uncja; odrobina; lampart;1/16 funta
our ('aur) adj. nasz
ours ('auerz) pron. nasz
ourselves (auer'selwz) pl.pron.
my; my sami;(dla)nas etc.
oust (aust) v. usuwać; wypierać; wyrzucać;wywłaszczać

out (aut) adv. na zewnątrz;
precz; poza; na dworze; poza
domem;nieobecnym(być) etc.
out-and-out (auten'aut) adj.
całkowity; adv. całkowicie
out of ('autow) adv. z; bez;
poza ;nie (modne,rozsądne)
outbalance (aut'baelens) v.
przeważyć;przewyższać
outbid (aut'byd) v. przelicytować;dać więcej (niż inny)
outbreak ('autbrejk) s. wybuch
(np. wojny)(epidemii etc.)
outburst ('autbe:rst) s. wybuch (np. gniewu)(vulkanu)
outcast ('autka:st) s. wyrzutek; wygnaniec; adj. wygnany
outcome ('autkam) s. wynik;
rezultat;konsekwencje
outcry ('autkraj) s. okrzyk;
wrzawa;silny protest
outdoors ('aut'do:rz) adj. na
wolnym powietrzu; s. wolna
przestrzeń;adv.zewnatrz(domu)
outer ('auter) adj. zewnętrzny
outermost ('auter'moust) adj.
najbardziej zewnętrzny
outfit ('autfyt) s. wyposażenie; drużyna; zespół; towarzystwo; zestaw narzędzi; v. wyposażyć; zaopatrywać;wyekwipować
outgoing ('aut,gouyng)adj. od-
chodzacy; odjeżdżający; przyjazny;komunikatywny;towarzyski
outgrow (aut'grou) v. przerastać; wyrastać z..; wyrosc(z ró-
snli)
outing ('autyng) s. wycieczka(na
otwarte morze,do lasu etc.);wy-jpad
outlast (aut'la:st) v. przetrwać (cos,kogos);wytrwać dłużej
outlaw ('aut-lo:) v. zakazywać;
wyjmować spod prawa; s. przestępca; banita;notoryczny krymi-malista
outlet ('autlet) s. wylot; rynek zbytu; wyjscie; ujscie
outline ('autlajn) s. zarys;
szkic; v. konturować; szkicować; przedstawiać(plany etc,)
outlive (aut'lyw) v. przeżyć;
przetrwać;wytrwać dłużej
outlook ('autluk) s. widok; po-
glad; obserwacja; widoki
(na przyszłość);czaty

outnumber (aut'namber) v. przewyższac liczebnie;byc liczniej-
out-of-date (autew'dejt) adj.
przestarzały; niemodny
outpatient ('aut,pejszent) s.
pacjent dochodzący (z domu)
output ('autput) s. wydajnosc;
wydobycie; moc; produkcja
outrage ('autrejdż) s, gwałt;
zniewaga; v. gwałcic; znie-
ważac;uragac(zdrowemu rozsądko-
outrageous (aut'rejdżes) adj.
wołający o pomstę; bezecny;
gwałtowny;skandaliczny;obrażają-
outright (aut'rajt) adj. całkowity; zupełny; stanowczy; bezpośredni; adv. odrazu; całkowicie; zupełnie; otwarcie
outrun (aut'ran) v. przegonic;
wyscignąc
outside ('aut'sajd) s. okładka;
fasada; strona zewnętrzna; adj.
zewnętrzny; adv. zewnątrz;
oprócz; z wyjątkiem
outside right ('aut'sajd'rajt)
exp. na zewnątrz po prawej
outsider ('aut'sajder) s. człowiek obcy; niewtajemniczony;
laik; obcy zawodnik
outsize ('autsajz) s. wielkosc
nietypowa, za duża
outskirts ('aut,ske:rts) s.
krance; kraj; peryferie
outspoken (aut'spouken) adj.
szczery; otwarcie wypowiedzia-
ny, bez ogródek,prosto w oczy
outspread (aut'spred) adj. rozpostarty; rozpowszechniony
outstanding ('autstaendyng)
adj. wybitny; wyróżniający się;
otwarty; niezałatwiony; zaległy; wystający; sterczący
outstretched (aut'streczt) adj.
rozpostarty; wyciagnięty
outward ('autłerd) adj. zewnetrz-
ny; powierzchowny; pozorny;
cielesny; s. strona zewnętrzna;
wygląd zewnętrzny;adv.na zewnątrz
outweigh (aut'łej) v. przeważyc
outwit (aut'łyt) v. przechytrzyc
oval ('ouwel) s. owal; adj.
owalny;owalnego kształtu

oven ('own) s. piekarnik; piec
over ('ouwer) prep. na; po;
w; przez; ponad; nad; powyżej;
adv. na drugą stronę; po powierzchni; całkowicie; od początku; zbytnio; znowu; raz
jeszcze(odrabiac zadanie etc.)
over again ('ouwer,e'gejn) adv.
na nowo; jeszcze raz
over-and-over ('ouwer,end'ouwer) adv. w kółko
overall ('ouwero:l) adj. ogólny; wszystko obejmujący;
pl. s. kombinezon roboczy
overboard ('ouwerbo:rd) adv.
(zaniechac) za burtę (wyrzucic)
overburden (,ouwe'rbe:rden) v.
przeładowywac; s. ciężar po-
kładow (np. nad kopalnią);
nadmiar ciężaru;ciężar warstw
overcast ('ouwerka:st) adj. za-
chmurzony; mroczny; ponury;
obrębiony; v. mroczyc; chmu-
rzyc (się); obrębiac
overcharge (,ouwer'cza:rdż) v.
przeciążac; zdzierac (pieniądze); stawiac za wysokie ceny
overcoat ('ouwerkout) s. płaszcz
overcome (,ouwer'kam) v. pokonac
overcrowd (,ouwer'kraud) s. za-
tłoczyc;przepełniac
overdo (,ouwerdu:) v. przeciążac; przesadzac; przegotowywac;
niszczyc przesadą;robic za dużo
overdraw (,ouwer'dro:) v. wyczerpac (konto); przesadzac;
pisac czeki bez pokrycia
overdue (,ouwer'dju:) adj. zaległy;zapóźniony(pociąg etc.)
overestimate (,ouwer'esty,mejt)
v. przecenic; s. za wysoka
ocena;zbyt duże oczekiwania
overflow (,ouwer'flou) v. przepełniac; przelewac; s. wylew;
przelew;kanał przelewowy etc.
overgrow (,ouwer'grou) v. obrastac; przerastac; rosnąc
nadmiernie;rośc zbyt szybko
overhang ('ouwer'haeng) v. zwisac; sterczec; zagrażac;
s. występ; zwis; nawis (dachu);
występ(skały);zwis(skalny etc.)

overhaul ('ouwer'ho:l) v.gruntownie naprawić; gruntownie zbadać; s. gruntowny remont
overhead ('ouwer'hed) s. wydatki administracyjne; adv., powyżej; na górze; adj. górny
overhear (,ouwer'hier) v. usłyszeć przypadkiem; podsłuchać
overheat ('ouwerhi:t) v. przegrzać; s. nadmiernie gorąco; przegrzanie
overjoyed (,ouwer'dżojd) adj. nieposiadający się z radości
overlap (,ouwer'laep) v. zachodzić na siebie; s. zachodzenie (na siebie)
overload (,ouwer'loud) v.przeładowac;s.nadmierny ciężar; przeciążenie(dachu etc.)
overlook (,ouwer'luk) v. przeoczyć; puszczać płazem; miec widok z góry; nadzorować; wybaczyć; widok z góry; nadzór
overlord ('ouwerlo:rd) s. suzeren; samodzierżca
over-night ('ouwer'najt) adv. przez noc; poprzedniego wieczoru; adj. nocny; na noc
overpass (,ouwer'oa:s) s.skrzyżowanie wiaduktem; przejazd wiaduktem; v. przecinać; przekraczać; przewyższać; przezwyciężać; pomijac(w kolejce etc.)
overrate ('ouwer'rejt) v. przeceniac;spodziewać się zbyt dużo
overrule (,ouwer'ru:l) v.,opanowac; uchylac; odrzucać; unieważniac;zmieniać czyjeś postanowienie)
overrun (,ouwer'ran) v. najechać; zalewac; przelewać; s. przekraczanie ceny umówionej
overseas ('ouwer'si:z) adv. za morzem; do krajów zamorskich; adj. zamorski
oversee ('ouwer'si:) v. dozorować; doglądać
overseer ('ouwer'si:er) s. nadzorca
overshadow ('ouwer'szaedou) v. przyćmiewac; zaćmiewać
oversight ('ouwersajt) s. przeoczenie

oversleep ('ouwer'sli:p) v. zaspać; przespać
overstrain ('ouwer'strain) v. przemęczać; s. przeciążenie; przemęczenie
overtake ('ouwer'tejk) v. doganiac; przeganiac; zaskoczyć
overthrow ('ouwer'srou) v., przewrócić; obalić; pobić; s. obalenie
overtime ('ouwertajm) s. godziny nadliczbowe; adv. nadprogramowa; adj. nadprogramowy; v. prześwietlic; przeeksponować
overtone ('ouwertoun) s. niedomówienie; sugestia; akcent; główna nuta
overture ('ouwer,tjuer) s. rozpoczęcie rokowan; propozycja; uwertura; v. proponować
overturn (,ouwer'te:rn) v. wywracac; obalac; s. przewracanie; przewrót;podbój
overweight (,ouwer'łejt) s. nadwaga; dodatkowa waga; otyłość; adj. ponad normalną wagę
overwhelm (,ouwer'hłelm) v. przygniatac; przywalac; zalewac; rujnowac; ogarniac
overwork ('ouwer'łe:rk) v. przepracowywać się; przeciążać pracą; zmuszać do za ciężkiej pracy; przemęczać się; s. nadmierna praca
ovulate ('ouwjulejt) v. jajeczkować; wytwarzać jaja
owe (oł) v.byc winnym; zawdzięczać
owing ('ołyng) adj. dłużny; należny; prep. z powodu; skutkiem
owing to ('ołyng,tu) prep. ponieważ
owl (aul) s. sowa
own (ołn) v. miec; posiadać; przyznawać (się); adj. własny; rodzony
owner ('ołner) s. właściciel
ownership ('ołnerszyp) s. własność; posiadanie
ox (oks) s. wół; pl. oxen

oxen ('oksen) pl. woły; zob.ox
oxide ('oksajd) s. tlenek
oxidation (oksy'dejszyn) s.
utlenienie; oksydacja
oxidize (oksydajz) v. utleniac
oxygen (oksydżen) s. tlen
oyster ('ojster) s. ostryga
ozone ('ouzoun) s. ozon
p (pi:) szesnasta litera
angielskiego alfabetu
pa (pa:) s. tato
pace (pejs) s. krok; chod;
v. kroczyc; mierzyc krokami;
ustalac rytm kroku; cwiczyc
krok (np. konia); przebywac
(drogę);chodzic(tam i na zad)
pacer ('pejser) s. regulator
rytmu (serca; kroku etc)
pacific (pe'syfyk) adj. spokojny; pokojowy
pacify ('paesyfaj) v. uspakajac; zaspokajac
pack (paek) s. pakunek; tłumok;
toboł; stek; sfora; okład;
kupa; v. pakowac; opakowac;
owijac; stłoczyc; napychac;
objuczyc; zbierac w stado
pack up ('paek,ap) v. spakowac
package ('paekydż) s. pakunek;
paczka
package deal ('paekydż'di:1)
s. przyjęcie złożonej propo-
zycji bez zmian
packer ('paeker) s. pakier;
przedsiębiorca od pakowania
artykułow żywnosciowych; maszyna do pakowania
packet ('kaekyt) s. pakiet;
v. zawijac
packing ('paekyng) s. pakowa-
nie; opakowanie; uszczelka;
okładzina; tampon
packthread ('paektred) s. szpagat
pact (paekt) s. pakt; układ
pad (paed) s. wysciołka; notes;
blok (papieru); bibularz; Łapa; podkładka; v. wysciełac;
wywoływac; rozdymac
padding ('paedyng) s. obicie;
wysciołka; podbicie; podszy-
cie; rozwadnianie tekstu

paddle ('paedl) s. wiosełko
kajakowe; v. wiosłowac
paddock ('paedek) s. wybieg
(konski)
padlock ('paedlok) s. kłodka
v. zamykac na kłodkę
pagan ('pejgen) s. poganin;
adj. pogański
page (pejdż) s. stronnica;
karta; paz; goniec
pagent ('paedzent) s. widowisko
(np. historyczne)
paid (pejd) adj. zapłacony; płatny; zob. pay
pail (pejl) s. wiadro
pain (pejn) s. bol; cierpienie;
trud; starania; v. zadawac bol;
bolec; dolegac
painful ('pejnful) adj. bolesny;
przykry
painless (pajnlys) adj. bezbolesny
paint (pejnt) s. farba; szminka;
v. malowac
paintbrush ('pejntbrasz) s. pędzel
painter ('pejnter) s. malarz
painting ('pejntyng) s. malarstwo; obraz
pair (peer) s. para; parka; stadło; v. dobierac do pary; stanowic parę
pajamas (pe'dża;mez) pl. piżama
pal (pael) s. kumpel; druh; przyjaciel
palace ('paelys) s. pałac
palate ('paelyt) s. podniebienie
pale (pejl) s. pal; granica; adj.
blady; v. otaczac palami; blednąc; spowodowac bledniecie
pallor ('paeler) s. bladosc
palm (pa:m) s. palma; dłon;
piędz; v. ukrywac w dłoni; dotykac dłonią
palpitation (,paelpy'tejszyn)
s. palpitacja; mocne bicie serca;kołatanie serca;drżenie;dygotá-nie
pamper ('paemper) v. rozpiesz-
czac;przekarmiac;zbyt pobłażác
pamphlet ('paemflyt) s. broszura natury polemicznej na tematy
bieżące, kontrowersyjne etc.

pan (paen) s. patelnia; rondel;
rynka; szalka; panewka; gęba;
kra; v. gotować na patelni;
udawać się; krytykować
pancake ('paen,kejk) s. naleśnik; adj. płaski
pane (paen) s. szyba; krata;
ścianka; płaszczyzna
panel ('paenl) s. tafla; oto-
czyna; płyta; wstawka; tablica (rozdzielcza); komitet;
lista (przysięgłych; lekarzy
etc); czaprak
pang (paeng)s. ostry ból; męka;
wyrzuty (sumienia etc.)
panhandler (,paen'haendler) s.
kwestarz; ksiądz z tacą
panic ('paenyk) s. panika; popłoch; v.wpaść w panikę; wywoływać panikę,;poddać się panice
pan-Slavism ('paen'sla:wyzem)
s. panslawizm
pansy ('paensy) s. bratek
pant (paent) s. zadyszka;
v. sapać; dyszeć
panther ('paenter) s. pantera
panties ('paentyz) pl. majtki
(damskie)
pantry ('paentry) s. spiżarnia
pants (paents) pl. spodnie; kalesony
panty hose ('paenty'houz) s.
rajstopy; pończochy z majtkami
pap (paep) s. papka; bzdury;
sutka; brodawka piersiowa
papa ('pa:pe) s. papa; tata
paper ('pejper) s. papier; gazeta; tapeta; rozprawa nauko-
wa; papierowe pieniądze; adj.
papierowy; rzekomy; v. zawinąć
w papier; tapetować
paper-backed ('pejper.baekt)
adj. w papierowej okładce;
kieszonkowe wydanie książki
paper-bag ('pejper,baeg) s.
torba papierowa
paper-hanger ('pejper,haenger)
s. tapeciarz
paper-hangings ('pejperhaengyngs)
pl. tapety
paper-money ('pejper'many) s.
pieniądze papierowe

paper-weight ('pejper,łejt) s.
przycisk
par (pa:r) s. stan równości;
norma
parable ('paerebl) s. przypowieść
parachute ('paere,szu:t) s.
spadochron
parachutist ('paere,szu:tyst)
s. spadochroniarz
parade (pe'rejd) s. parada; pochód; rewia; defilada; popisywać się; obnosić się (z
czyms)
paradise ('paere,dajs) s. raj;
adj. rajski
paragraph ('paere,gra:f) s.
ustęp; odnośnik; notatka;
v. dzielić na ustępy; pisać
notatkę
parallel ('paere,lel) adj.
równoległy; odpowiedni (czemuś)
s., równoległa; równoleznik; porównanie; v. być równoległym;
kłaść równolegle; zestawiać;
znaleźć odpowiednik
paralyze ('paere,lajz) v. pa-
raliżować; porażać
paralysis (pe'raelysys) s. paraliż
paramount ('paere,maunt) adj.
główny; najważniejszy; kapitalny; najwyższy
parasite ('paere.sajt) s. pasożyt
parcel ('pa:rsl) s. paczka;
działka; v. dzielić; pakować
w paczki
parch ('pa:rcz) v. wysuszać
(się); prażyć; cierpieć z
pragnienia
parchment ('pa:rczment) s. pergamin
pardon('pa:rdn) s. ułaskawienie;
przebaczenie; v. przebaczać;
darować ;ułaskawiać
pardon me ('pa:rdn,mi:) exp.:
przepraszam
pardonable ('pa:rdnebl) adj.
wybaczalny
pare (peer) v. obcinać; obierać; obskrobać

parent ('peerent) s. ojciec;
matka; rodziciel;rodzicielka
parental (pe'rentl) adj. ro-
dzicielski
parenthesis (pe'rentysys) s.
nawias
parentheses (pe'renty,si:z) pl.
nawiasy
parings ('peerynz) pl. łupiny;
obrzynki
parish ('paerysz) s. parafia
parishioner (pe'ryszener) s.
parafianin
park (pa:rk) s. park; postój
samochodów; v. parkować
parking ('pa:rkyng) s. postój
samochodów; parkowanie
parking garage ('pa:rkyng'gae-
ra:ż) s. garaż parkingowy
parking lot ('pa:rkyn,lot) s.
plac parkingowy
parking meter ('pa:rkyn'mi:ter)
s. licznik do płacenia za
parking(na ograniczony czas)
parking ticket ('pa:rkyn'tykyt)
s. mandat karny za złe parkowanie lub za niezapłacenie
parkway ('pa:rkłej) s. cztero-
liniowa szosa, przedzielona
roślinnością
parliament ('pa:rlyment) s.
parlament
parliamentary (,pa:rly'mentery)
adj. parlamentarny
parlo(u)r ('pa:rler) s. salon;
sala; pokój (przyjęć)
parquet ('pa:rkej) s. parkiet;
v. wyłożyć parkietem
parrot ('paeret) s. papuga;
v. powtarzać jak papuga
parsley ('pa:rsly) s. pietruszka; a. pietruszkowy
parry ('paery) v. parować; odpierać; s. odparcie
parson ('pa:rsn) s. proboszcz
parsonage ('pa:rsnydż) s. plebania
part (pa:rt) s. część; ustęp;
udział; rola; strona; przedział (włosów); v; rozchodzić
(się); rozdzielać; dzielić;
pękać; robić (przedział); wyjeżdżać;adj.mniejszy niż całość

partake (pa:r'tejk) v. brak
udział; dzielić coś z kims;
zob. take
partaken (pa:r'tejkn) v. zob.
partake
partial ('pa:rszel) adj. stronniczy; częściowy; mający słabo-
bość do...;nie pełny
partiality (,pa:rszy'aelyty) s.
stronniczość; upodobanie
participant (pa:r'tysypent) s.
uczestnik;adj.uczestniczący
participate (pa:r'tysypejt) v.
brać udział
particle ('pa:rtykl) s. cząstka;
odrobina; partykuła
particular ('per'tykjuler) adj.
szczególny; szczegółowy; specjalny; prywatny; grymaśny
dokładny; uważny; dziwny; nie-
zwyczajny; ostrożny; s. szczegół; fakt
particularity (per,tykju'laeryty)
s. osobliwość; szczegółowość;
drobiazgowość; wybredność
particularly (per,tykju'laerly)
adv. osobliwie; szczególnie
particulars (per'tykjulers) s.
dane osobiste
parting ('pa:rtyng) s. przedzia-
łek (włosów); rozstanie; rozdział; pożegnanie; rozdroże;
zgon
partition (pa:r'tyszyn) s. podział; rozbiór; rozdział; v.
dzielić; przegradzać
partition off (pa:rtyszyn,of)
v. oddzielać
partly ('pa:rtly) adv. częścio-
wo;po części; poniekąd
partner ('pa:rtner) s. wspólnik
partnership ('pa:rtnerszyp) s.
spółka
partook (pa:r'tuk) v. zob. partake
partridge('pa:trydż) s. kuropatwa
part-time ('pa:rt,tajm) adv.
na niepełnym etacie; na niepełnym czasie;adj.niepełnetatowy
party ('pa:rty) s. partia; przyjęcie towarzyskie; towarzystwo;
grupa;strona; uczestnik;osobnik

pass (pa:s) s. przełęcz; odnoga
rzeki; przepustka; wypad; bilet; umizg; sztuczka; v, przechodzic; mijac; pomijac; zdac;
przekazac; wymijac; wyprzedzac;
przeprowadzic; przewyzszac;
spędzac; puszczac w obieg; podawac; odchodzic; umierac;
dziac się; krążyc
pass away ('pa:se,łej) v. odchodzic;umierac
pass by ('pa:s,baj) v. mijac;
pomijac
pass for ('pa:s,fo:r) v. uda-
wac (kogoś)
pass out ('pa:s,aut) v. zemdlec;
umrzec; wyjsc
pass round ('pa:s,raund) v.
podawac wkoło (np. gosciom)
pass through ('pa:s,tru) v.
przechodzic (przez, na wskros)
passable ('paesebl) adj. nadający się do przebycia;
(stopien) dostateczny; znosny
passage ('paesydż) s. przejscie;
przejazd; przeprawa; przelot;
upływ; korytarz; urywek tekstu
passenger ('paesyndżer) s. pasażer; pasażerka
passer-by ('pa:ser'baj) s. prze-
chodzien
passion ('paeszyn) s. namiętnosc;
pasja; Męka Panska; stan bierny
passionate ('paeszenyt) adj. namiętny; porywczy; zapalczywy;
żarliwy ;ognisty
passive ('paesyw) adj. bierny;
s. strona bierna
passport ('pa:s,po:rt) s. paszport
password('pa:s,łoːrd) s. hasło
past (pa:st) adj. przeszły;
miniony; ubiegły; prep. za;
obok; po; przed; adv. obok;
s. przeszłosc; czas przeszły
paste (pejst) s. pasta; ciasto;
klej mączny; klajster; masa;
makaron; uderzenie (slang);
v. przylepiac; oblepiac;
obic (kogoś)
pasteboard ('pejst,bo:rd) s.
karton; tektura; adj.tekturo-
wy; kartonowy; lichy

pastime ('pa:s,tajm) s. rozrywka (po pracy etc.)
pastry('pejstry) s. wyroby cu-
kiernicze; ciastka
past tense ('pa:st tens) s.
czas przeszły (gram.)
pasture ('pa:sczer) s. pastwisko
pat (paet) s. głaskanie; kle-
panie; krążek (np. masła);
v. pogłaskac; poklepac; po-
chwalic (kogos) adv. trafnie;
w sam raz; adj. trafny; biegły ;na czasie;zupełnie własciwy
patch (paecz) s. łata; plama;
skrawek; polko; zagon; grządka; klapka (na oko); przepaska; v. łatac; załatac; szyc
z łat; sztukowac; naprawic;
skleic; załagodzic
patch pocket ('paecz,pokyt) s.
naszywana kieszen
patchwork ('paecz,łe:rk) s.
łatanina; szachownica
pate (pejt) s. slang: głowa;
łeb; pała;szczyt głowy
patent ('paetnt) s. patent;
v. opatentowac; a. patentowa-
ny; opatentowany ;oczywisty
patent ('pejtnt) adj. jasny;
otwarty; oczywisty ;chroniony
patentem
patent-leather ('paetnt'ledzer)
s. skora lakierowana
paternal (pe'te:rnl) adj. ojcowski; po ojcu
paternity (pe'te:rnyty) s.
ojcostwo; pochodzenie po ojcu;
autorstwo(książki,planu etc.)
path (pa:s) s. sciezka; tor;
droga ruchu; zob. paths
pathetic (pe'tetyk) adj. żałosny; smutny; uczuciowy;
wzruszający; rozrzewniający
paths (pa:sz) pl. sciezki; tory;
drogi ruchu
patience ('pejszens) s. cierpli-
wosc; pasjans
patient ('pejszent) adj. cierpliwy; wytrwały; s. pacjent;
pacjentka; chory; chora
patio ('pa:ti:o) s. ogrodek
wewnętrzny ; taras

patriot ('pejtryet) s. patry-
jota
patriotic(,paetry'otyk) adj.
patriotyczny
patriotism ('paetrye,tyzem) s.
patriotyzm
patrol (pe'troul) v. patrolo-
wac; s. patrolowanie; patrol
patrolman (pe'troulmen) s. policjant (drogowy USA)
patron ('pejtren) s. klient;
opiekun; patron
patronage ('paetrenydż) s.
opieka; poparcie; klientela;
US rozdawanie posad etc.;
protekcjonalnosc; przywileje;
posady
patronize ('paetre,najz) v. popierac; protegowac; traktowac
protekcjonalnie
patsy ('paecy) s. oferma przez
wszystkich zawsze nadużywana
patter ('paeta) s. stukot; traj-
kot; trajkotanie; gwara; kle-
panie; szybka recytacja; żargon; v. stukac; bębnic; traj-
kotac; klepac (np. pacierze);
odklepywac; klapac; gadac
pattern ('paetern) s. probka;
wzor; uklad; material na suknię lub ubranie (USA); zespol;
cechy charakterystyczne; sla-
dy kul (na tarczy) v. wzoro-
wac; modelowac; ozdabiac wzo-
rami
paunch ('pa:ncz) s. (duży)
brzuch; żoładek krowy
paunchy ('pa:nczy) adj. brzu-
chaty ;z wydatnym brzuchem
pause (po:z) s. przerwa; pauza;
v. robic przerwę; wahac się
pave (pejw) v. brukowac; torowac drogę
pavement ('pejwment) s. bruk;
posadzka; materiał do bruko-
wania
pavement-café ('pejwment'kaefej)
s. kawiarnia ze stolikami na
chodniku
paw (po:) s. łapa; (slang):
tatuś; v. uderzac łapą lub
kopytem; miętosic w łapach;
macac (poufale)

pawn (po:n) s. zastaw; fant;
pionek; v. zastawiac; dawac
w zastaw
pawnbroker ('po:n,brouker) s.
lichwiarz pożyczający pod zastaw; własciciel lombardu
pawnshop ('po:n-szop) s. lom-
bard; sklep zastawniczy
pay; paid; paid (pej; peid;
peid)
pay (pej) v. płacic; zapłacic;
wynagradzac; udzielac (uwagi);
dawac (dochod); opłacac (się)
s. płaca; zapłata; pobory;
wynagrodzenie; adj. płatny
(np. automat telefoniczny);
opłacalny
pay back ('pej baek) v. zwrocic
dług; odpłacac
payday ('pej dej) s. dzień wy-
płaty
pay down ('pej dałn) v. dawac
zadatek; płacic pierwszą ratę
gotowka
pay for ('pej,fo:r) v. płacic
(za cos)
pay in ('pej,yn) v. wpłacac
pay off ('pej,of) v. spłacac
pay out ('pej,aut) v. wydatkowac; wypuszczac linę (na statku); wypłacac; płacic
pay up ('pej,ap) v. wyrownywac
(dług); zapłacic
payable ('pejebl) adj. płatny;
dochodowy; opłacający się
payee ('pej'i:) s. odbiorca
płatnosci
payer ('pejer) s. płatnik
payment ('pejment) s. płatnosc;
wypłata; zapłata
pea (pi:) s. groch; ziarnko
grochu
peace (pi:s) s. pokoj; pojednanie; spokoj
peaceful ('pi:sful) adj. spokojny; pokojowy
peach (pi:cz) s. brzoskwinia;
wspaniała rzecz, dziewczyna,
człowiek; v. (slang):sypac;
donosic (na kogos)
peacock ('pi:,kok) s. paw;
v. pysznic się jak paw, chodzic
jak paw; paradowac

peak (pi:k) s. (ostry) szczyt; wierzchołek; daszek (u czapki); szpic; garb (krzywej)

peak hour ('pi:k'auer) s. godzina szczytu ruchu

peal (pi:l) s. huk; łoskot; bicie w dzwony; huczny śmiech; zespół dzwonów; v. huczec; bic w dzwony; grac (cos) hucznie

peanut ('pi:nat) s. orzeszek ziemny; drobnostka; a; drobny; prowincjonalny

pear (peer).s. gruszka

pearl (pe:rl) s. perła

peasant ('pezent) s. chłop; wiesniak; adj. chłopski

peat (pi:t) s. torf

peat bog ('pi:t'bog) s. torfowisko

pebble ('pebl) s. kamyk; otoczak; v. granulowac; obrzucac kamykami

peck (pek) v. dziobac; wcinac (jedzenie); dziobnąc; cmoknąc (męza); stukac; wydziobac; dłubac; odziobac; v. dziobniecie; cmok; slad dziobania

peculiar (py'kju:ljer) adj. szczegolny; dziwny; osobliwy; charakterystyczny;dziwaczny

peculiarity (py'kju:li'aeryty) s. własciwosc; cecha; osobliwosc; dziwacznosc

pedal ('pedl) s. pedał; nuta pedałowa; v. pedałowac; naciskac pedał; ('pi:dl) adj. pedałowy; nozny

peddle ('pedl) v. sprzedawac po domach; byc domokrążcą; wydzielac po trochu

peddler ('pedler) s. domokrążca

pedestal ('pedystl) s. piedestał; podstawa;stawiac na piedestał

pedestrian (py'destrjen) adj. pieszy; przyziemny; prozaiczny; s. piechur;pieszy człowiek

pedestrian crossing (pu'destrjen'krosyng) v. przejscie dla pieszych; zebra: pasy

pedigree ('pedygri:) s. rodowód; drzewo genealogiczne

pedlar('peler)s.przekupień;hand-

peek ('pi:k) v. podglądac

peel (pi:l) s. skóra; skórką; łupa; v. obierac; zdzierac; łuszczyc się; (slang):rozbierac (się)

peep (pi:p) v. zerkac; podglądac; wynurzac (się); wychodzic niepostrzezenie

peeping Tom ('pi:pyng,tom) s. podglądający natręt

peer (pier) s. rowny (komus) stanem, pochodzeniem etc.

peerless ('pierlys) adj. niezrownany

peevish ('pi:wysh) adj. drazliwy; zły; gniewny;zirytowany

peg (peg) s. czop; kołek; zatyczka; szpunt; v. zakołkowac; przymocowac kołkami

pelican ('pelyken) s. pelikan

pelt (pelt) s. futro; kanonada; grzmocenie; pospiech; v. ostrzeliwac; obrzucac; obsypywać gradem; rzucac zniewagi; obsypywac zniewagami; walic

pelvis ('pelwys) s. miednica; a. miedniczny

pen (pen) s. pioro; kojec; ogrodzenie; schron; (slang):więzienie; v. pisac; układac list; zamykac w ogrodzeniu

penal ('pi:nl) adj. karny; karalny

penalty ('penlty) s. kara

penalty kick ('penlty,kik) s. karny strzał (do bramki)

penance ('penens) s. pokuta

pence (pens) pl. grosze; zob. penny

pencil ('pensl) s. ołowek; rysowac; pisac

pencil sharpner ('pensl'sza:rpner) s. strugaczka do ołowka

pendant ('pendent) s. wisiorek; proporzec; adj. wiszący; zwisający; nierozstrzygnięty; toczący się; do rozstrzygnięcia

pending ('pendyng) adj. niezałatwiony; będacy w toku; wiszący; prep.: aż do; podczas

penetrate ('peny,trejt) v. przenikac; przepajac; przedostawac się przez ;wtargnąc;zanurzyc

penetration (,peny'trejszyn)
s. penetracja; przenikanie;
przenikliwość

pen friend ('penfrend) s. znajomy z listów

penguin ('pengłyn) s. pingwin

penholder ('pen,houlder) s.
piórnik; obsadka; stojak na
pióro

penicillin (,peny'sylyn) s.
penicylina

peninsula(py'nynsjule) s. pół-
wysep

penitent ('penytent) s. żałujący grzesznik; pokutnik; adj.
żałujący; skruszony

penitentiary (,peny'tenszery)
s. więzienie; adj. karany
więzieniem; poprawczy

penknife ('pen.najf) s. scyzoryk

penniless ('penylys) adj. w nędzy; bez grosza

penny ('peny) s. cent; grosz;
pl. pennies ('penyz); Br.pl.
pence (pens)

pennyworth ('penyłe:rs) s. wartość centa; exp. za centa

pension ('penszyn) s. renta;
emerytura; pensjonat; v. wyznaczać pensje; pensjonować

pension off ('penszyn,of) v.
przenosić na emeryture

pensive ('pensyw) adj. zamyślony

penthouse ('penthaus) s. mieszkanie z ogrodem na szczycie
budynku; przybudówka na dachu

people ('pi:pl) s. ludzie;
ludność; lud; v. zaludniać

pep (pep) s. animusz; werwa;
wigor; adj. ożywiony; wesoły;
dowcipny; dodający animuszu

pep pills ('pep,pyls) pl. pigułki podniecające

pep up ('pep,ap) v. ożywić; dodać animuszu

pepper ('peper) s. pieprz; papryka; v. pieprzyć; kropić;
zasypywać kulami; dać lanie

per (pe:r) prep. przez; za; na;
według; co do;za pośrednictwem

perceive (per'si:w) v. uświadamiać sobie; odczuć; dostrzegać;
spostrzegać

percent (per'sent) s. odsetek;
od sta

percentage (per'sentydż) s. odsetek; procent; od sta

perceptible (per'septebl) adj.
dostrzegalny

perception (per'sepszyn) s.
spostrzeganie;percepcja

perch (pe:rcz) s. okoń; grzęda;
żerdź; pręt; v. siedzieć na
grzędzie; sadzać na grzędzie

percussion (per'kaszyn) s. uderzenie; zderzenie;bicie(bębna)

peremptory (per'emptery) adj.
stanowczy; apodyktyczny; ostateczny; nieodwołalny

perfect ('pe:rfykt) adj. doskonały; zupełny; v. udoskonalić;
wykończyć

perfect tense ('perfykt'tens)
s. gram. czas przeszły dokona-
ny

perfection (per'fekszyn) s.
doskonałość; szczyt; wykończenie; udoskonalenie

perforate ('pe:rferejt) v.
przedziurawiać; dziurkować;
przenikać; przebijać się

perform (per'fo:rm) v. wykonywać; odgrywać; spełniać; występować

performance (per'fo:rmens) s.
przedstawienie; wyczyn; wykonanie; spełnienie

performer (per'former) s. wy-
konawca

perfume ('pe:rfju:m) s. perfuma;
zapach ; (pe'rfju:m) v. perfu-
mować

perhaps (per'haeps, praeps) adv.
może; przypadkiem

peril ('peryl) s. niebezpieczeństwo; ryzyko; v. narazić
na niebezpieczeństwo

perilous ('peryles) adj. niebezpieczny; ryzykowny

period ('pieried) s. okres;
period; menstruacja; kropka;
kres; pauza;miesiączka;a.stylowy

periodic (,piery'odyk) adj.
okresowy; periodyczny
periodical (,piery'odykel) s.
czasopismo; periodyk; adj.
okresowy; periodyczny
perish ('perysz) v. zgiąc;
niszczyc; nękać; trapic; gnębic; ginąc (przedwczesną śmiercią)
perishable ('peryszebl) adj.
zniszczalny; s; łatwo psujący się towar
perjury ('pe:rdżery) s. krzywoprzysięstwo; złamanie
obietnicy
perm (pe:rm) s. trwała ondulacja
permanent ('pe:rmenent) adj.
trwały; permanentny
permanent wave ('pe:rmenent,
,łejw) s. trwała ondulacja
permeable ('pe:rmjebl) adj.
przepuszczalny; przenikalny
permission (per'myszyn) s. pozwolenie; zezwolenie
permit (per'myt) s. pisemne
zezwolenie; pozwolenie; v.pozwalac; zezwalac; dopuszczac
perpendicular (,pe:rpen'dykjuler) adj. prostopadły; s, prostopadła; pion
perpetual (per'petjuel) adj.
wieczny; wieczysty; trwały;
dożywotni
persecute ('pe:rsy,kju:t) v.
prześladowac
persecution (,pe:rsy'kju:szyn)
s. prześladowanie
persecutor ('pe:rsy,kju:ter) s.
prześladowca
persevere (,pe:rsy'wier) v.
wytrwac
persist (pe'rsyst) v. obstawac;
wytrwac; upierac się
persistence (per'systens); persistency (per'systensy) s. wytrwałosc; uporczywosc; trwałosc
persistent (per'systent) adj. wytrwały; uporczywy; trwały
person ('pe:rson) s. osoba;
człowiek
personage ('pe:rsonydż) s.
osobistosc;ważny człowiek

personal ('pe:rsenel) adj. osobisty; robiący osobiste uwagi;
s. wiadomosc osobista
personality (,pe:se'naelyty) s.
osobowosc; powierzchownosc;
postawa; indywidualnosc; pl.
wycieczki (uwagi) osobiste
personify (pe:r'sony,faj), v.
uosabiac; personifikowac
personnel (,pe:rse'n el) s.
personel
personnel manager (,pe:rse'-
'nel'maenydżer) s. kierownik
oddziału personalnego; personalny
perspiration (,pe:rspy'rejszyn)
s. pocenie się; pot
perspire (,pe:r'spajer) v. pocic się; wypacac się
persuade (pe:r'słejd) v. przekonywac; namawiac
persuasion (pe:r'słejżyn) s.
perswazja; przekonywywanie;
namawianie; przekonanie; wyznanie; wierzenie
persuasive (pe:r'słejsyw) adj.
przekonywujący; s. motyw; pobudka (do czegos)
pert (pe:rt) adj. smiały; arogancki; (slang) żwawy
pertain (per'tejn) v. nalezec
do czegos; byc własciwym czemus; odnosic się; wchodzic
w zakres
perusal (pe'ru:zal) s. przestudiowanie; dokładne przeczytanie
peruse (pe'ru:z) v. czytac
uważnie; studiowac (np. twarz)
pervade (per'wejd) v. przenikac;
owładnąc; ogarniac; szerzyc się
perverse (per'we:rs) adj. przewrotny; przekorny; wyuzdany
pesky ('pesky) adj. (slang) dokuczliwy; natrętny;cholerny
pessimism ('pesy,myzem) s. pesymizm ;spodziewanie się najgorszego
pest (pest) s. plaga; zaraza
pet (pet) s. faworyt; ulubieniec (np. pies); adj; ulubiony; v. (slang) piescic; byc
w złym nastroju; gniewac się ;
migdalic się; wypiescic

petal ('petl) s. płatek

petition (py'tyszyn) s. petycja; prosba; podanie; v, prosic; wnosic podanie

petrify ('petry,faj) v. zamieniac (się) w kamien; powodowac kostnienie

petroleum (py'trouljem) s. ropa naftowa; olej skalny

pet shop ('petszop) s. sklep zwierzątek pokojowych

petticoat ('petykout) s. halka; spódniczka; kobieta; adj. kobiecy

petty ('pety) adj. drobny

petty cash (,pety'kaesz) s. gotówka podręczna

pew (pju:) s. ławka (koscielna)

pharmacy ('fa:rmesy) s. apteka; farmacja

phase (fejz) s. faza (np. rozwojowa); aspekt

pheasant ('feznt) s. bażant

philanthropist (fy'laentrepyst) s. filantrop

philologist (fy'loledżyst) s. filolog ;lingwista;językoznawca

philology (fy'loledży) s. filologia; językoznawstwo;ligwistyka

philosopher (fy'losefer) s. filozof

philosophize (fy'lose,fajz) v. filozofowac

philosophy (fy'losefy) s. filozofia

phone (foun) s. telefon (slang)

phonetic (fou'netyk) adj. fonetyczny

phon(e)y (founy) adj. fałszywy; udawany; s. rzecz fałszywa; podrabiana;ktos udający

photo ('foutou) s. fotka; fotografia; v. fotografowac

photograph ('foute,gra:f) s. fotografia; zdjęcie; v. fotografowac

photographer (fe'togrefer) s. fotograf; fotografik

photography (fe'tegrefy) s. fotografia; fotografika

phrase (frejz) s. wyrażenie; zwrot; v. wyrażac; wypowiadac wyrażeniami lub słowami

physical ('fyzykel) adj. fizyczny; cielesny

physician ('fyzyszyn) s. lekarz

physicist ('fyzysyt) s. fizyk

physics ('fyzyks) s. fizyka

physique (fy'zi:k) s. budowa ciała; rozwój; wygląd fizyczny;kondycja;siła muskularna

piano (py'aenou) s. fortepian; pianino

pick (pyk) v. wybierac; dorabiac; kopac; krytykowac; dłubac; obierac; zbierac; usuwac; oskubac; wydziobac; krasc; okrasc; s, kilof; dłuto; wybór; czółenko; nitka wątka

pick-off ('pyk,of) v. zedrzec; wystrzelac pojedyńczo(wrogów)

pick out ('pyk,aut) v. wybrac; dobrac; doszukiwac się

pick over ('pyk,ouwer) v. przebierac;wybierac co lepsze

pick up ('pyk,ap) v. podnosic; brac; nauczyc się; zarabiac; odnaleźc; odzyskac; przyjsc do siebie; poznac się; s. adapter; lekka ciężarówka

picket ('pykyt) s. palik; kół; pikieta; posterunek; v. rozstawiac pikiety strajkowe; służyc jako pikieta; zabezpieczac pikietami

pickle ('pykel) s. kiszony ogórek; marynata; kłopot; łobuz; v. marynowac; kisic; wytrawiac

pickpocket ('pyk,pokyt) s. złodziej kieszonkowy; kieszonkowiec

picnic ('pyknyk) s. piknik; majówka; v. brac udział w pikniku, majówce,posiłku na dworze

pictorial (pyk'to:rjel) adj. obrazowy; ilustrowany; malowniczy; malarski; s.(czaso)pismo ilustrowane; ilustracja (trzywymiarowa)techniczna

picture ('pykczer) s. obraz; film; rysunek; rycina; portret; widok; v. odmalowywac; przedstawiac; opisywac; wyobrazac sobie; dawac obraz czegos

picturesque (,pykcze'resk) adj. malowniczy;żywy i przyjemny

pie (paj) s. placek; szarlotka; pasztet; pasztecik;(ptak) sroka

piece(pi:s) s. kawałek; częsc; sztuka; moneta; utwor; v. łączyc; zeszyc; łatac; naprawiac

piecework ('pi:s,łe:rk) s. robota na akord

pier (pier) s. pomost ładunkowy; molo; falochron; filar (np. mostu)

pierce (piers) v. przewiercac; wnikac; przedziurawiac; przebijac; przedostawac się

piercing (piersyŋg) adj. przeszywający; ostry; rozdzierający ;przenikający

piety ('pajety) s. pobożnosc

pig (pyg) s. wieprz; swinia; prosię; v. prosic się

pigeon ('pydżyn) s. gołąb; v. oszukiwac

pigeon-hole ('pydżyn,houl) s. przegrodka; v. umieszczac w przegrodkach

pigheaded ('pyg'hedyd) adj. uparty ; głupi

pigskin ('pyg,skyn) s. swinska skora; (slang):piłka; siodło

pigtail ('pyg,tejl) s. warkocz

pike(pajk) s. rogatka; dzida; pika; szpic; ostrze; szczupak

pile (pail) s. stos; sterta; kupa; pal; słup; puszek; meszek; włos; v. układac w stos; gromadzic na kupe;stawiac w kozły

pile up ('pail,ap) v. walic na kupę; s. zwalenie na kupę

piles (pailz) pl. hemoroidy

pilfer ('pylfer) v. ukrasc; zwędzic; buchnąc

pilgrim ('pylgrym) s. pielgrzym

pilgrimage ('pylgrymydż) s. pielgrzymka

pill (pyl) s. pigułka; tabletka

pillar ('pyler) s. filar; słup; podpora

pillbox('pylboks)s. bunkier; pudełeczko na pigułki;kapelusz

pillion ('pyljen) s. tylne siodełko (np. na motocyklu)

pillory ('pylery) s. pręgierz; v. stawiac pod pręgierzem

pillow ('pylou) s. zagłowek; jasiek; poduszka; podkładka v. spoczywac; opierac (np. głowę)

pillowcase ('pylou,kejs) s. poszewka

pillow slip ('pylou,slyp) s. poszewka

pilot ('pajlet) s. pilot; sternik; v. pilotowac; sterowac; przeprowadzic

pimp (pymp) s. stręczycielka; alfons; v. stręczyc

pimple ('pympl) s. pryszcz; wągier

pin (pyn) s. szpilka; sztyft; sworzen; kołek; kręgiel v. przyszpilic; przymocowac

pincers ('pynserz) pl. kleszcze; obcęgi

pinch (pyncz) v. szczypac; gniesc; cisnąc; przycisnąc; przyskrzynic; krępowac; dokuczac;doskwierac; podważac łomem; s. uszczypnięcie; szczypta; łom; (slang) aresztowanie; obława; kradziez

pinch bar ('pyncz ba:r) s. łom (ze stopką)

pine (pajn) s. sosna; ananas; v. usychac

pineapple ('pajnaepl) s. ananas

pinion ('pynjen) s. kołko zębate; wrzeciono zębate; wał przekładni; koniec piora; lotka v. podcinac (skrzydła); pętac; przywiazywac

pink (pynk) s. rożowy kolor; radykał (komunizujacy); goździk; v. urazic do żywego; przekłuwac

pinnacle ('pynekl) s. szczyt; wieżyczka; v. zwienczac; postawic na szczycie; stanowic szczyt

pint (pajnt) s. połkwarcie; 0.47 litra ; 1/8 galona

pioneer (,paje'nier) s. pionier; saper; v. torowac drogę

pious (pajes) adj. pobożny

pip (pyp) s. pestka; oczko; gwiazdka; ziarnko; punkcik; pypeć; dzwięk gwizdka; v. piszczec; wykluwac się; pobic; trafic; postrzelic

pipe (pajp) s. rura; rurka; przewod; piszczałka; (slang) łatwizna; drobiazg; v. doprowadzac rurami; włączyc; połączyc; prowadzic dzwiękiem fujarki; grac na fujarce; grac na kobzie; gwizdac; piszczec

pipeline ('pajp,lajn) s. rurociąg;(slang):informator; v. przesyłac rurociągiem

piper (pajper) s. kobziarz

pipes (pajps) s. kobza

pirate (pajeryt) s. korsarz; pirat; statek piracki; maruder; v. grabic; uprawiac korsarstwo; wydawac bezprawnie (książki)

pistol ('pystl) s. pistolet

piston ('pysten) s. tłok

pit(pyt) s. doł; jama; kopalnia; pestka; v. puszczac do walki; robic dołki; wkładac do dołu; wyjmowac pestki

piston-stroke ('pysten,strouk) s. suw tłoka

pitch (pycz) v. rozbijac (oboz); umieszczac; rzucac; ustawiac; chwiac się; upasc ciężko; kołysac (na fali); przechylac; wybierac; ostro pracowac; rzucac się na...; smołowac; s. stopien; najwyzszy punkt; wzniesienie; wzdłuzne kołysanie statku: spadek dachu; odstęp między (falami; zębami koł etc.);skok (uzwojenia, sruby); smoła

pitcher ('pyczer) s. dzban; rzucający piłką

piteous ('pytjes) adj. żałosny; nędzny

pitfall ('pytfo:l) s. pułapka; wilczy doł

pith (pys) s. miękisz; rdzen; tężyzna; moc; v. wyjmowac rdzen; przecinac rdzen w celu zabijania bydła (w rzezni etc.)

pitiable ('pytjebl) s. żałosny; godny pożałowania

pitiful ('pytyful) adj. litosciwy; żałosny; nędzny

pitiless ('pytylys) adj. bezlitosny

pity ('pyty) s. litosc; wspołczucie; szkoda; v. litowac się; wspołczuc; żałowac kogos

pivot ('pywet) s. czop; os; osrodek ;v.obracac jak na osi

pivotal ('pywetel) s. adj. centralny ;kardynalny;kluczowy;decydujący

placard ('plaeka:rd) s. afisz; plakat; (ple'ka:rd) v. rozlepiac plakaty

place (plejs).s. miejsce; miejscowosc; plac; ulica; dom; mieszkanie; zakład; krzesło; posada; v. umieszczac; położyc; ulokowac; dac stanowisko; pokładac; powierzyc; okreslac

placid ('plaesyd) adj. łagodny; spokojny

plague (plejg) s. plaga; dżuma; zaraza; v. dręczyc

plaice (plejs) s. płastuga pospolita

plaid (plaed) s. sukno; pled w kratę ;rysunek w kratę

plain (plejn) adj. wyrazny; prosty; gładki; szczery; płaski; rowny; adv. jasno; szczerze; s. rownina

plain clothesman ('plejn,klozmen) s. tajny policjant

plaintiff ('plejntyf) s. powod (zaskarżający); powodka

plaintive ('plejntyw) adj. żałosny; płaczliwy

plait (plejt) s. plecionka; warkocz; fałda; zakładka; v. plesc; splatac; fałdowac

plan (plaen) s. plan; v. planowac; zamierzac

plane (plejn) s. płaszczyzna; rownina; poziom; samolot; płat (skrzydła); strug; wiornik; gładzik; platan (owoc); v. slizgac; zeslizgiwac się; heblowac

planet ('plaenyt) s. planeta

plank ('plaenk) s. deska; tarcica; punkt programu (politycznego w USA); v.pokrywac deskami

plank down ('plaeņk,daŉn) v.
wybulić gotówkę
plant ('pla:nt) s. roslina;
fabryka; zakład; wtyczka;
(slang) oszustwo; włamanie;
kant; v. zasadzać; zakładać;
umieszczać; pozorować; ukrywać; wtykać; sadzić(rosliny)
plantation (plaen'tejszyn) s.
plantacja
planter ('pla:nter) s. plantator; maszyna do sadzenia;
skrzynka na kwiaty
plaque (plaek) s. tablica (pa-
miątkowa); odznaka
plaster ('pla:ster) s. tynk;
wyprawa wapienna; przylepiec
v. tynkować; wyprawiać; po-
wlekać; zalepiać; oblepiać
plaster cast ('pla;ster,ka:st)
s. odlew gipsowy; opatrunek
gipsowy
plaster of Paris ('pla:ster of
'paerys) s. gips
plastic ('plaestyk) s. plastyk;
sztuczne tworzywo; adj. plastyczny; giętki
plastics ('plaestyks) s. tworzy-
wa sztuczne
plate (plejt) s. talerz; danie;
płyta; taca; tafla; v. platerować; opancerzać
platform ('plaet,fo:rm) s.
platforma; podium; trybuna;
rampa; program polityczny
platinum ('plaetynem) s. platyna
platter ('plaeter) s. półmisek
plausible ('plo:zebl) adj. pozornie słuszny, prawdziwy,
uczciwy; obłudnie przymilny
play (plej) s. gra; zabawa;
sztuka; v. grać; bawić się;
zagrać; udawać
play back('plej,baek) v. repro-
dukować; przegrywać
playboy ('plej,boj) s. lekko-
duch
player ('plejer) s. gracz; muzyk; aktor; zawodnik
playful ('plejful) adj. wesoły;
żartobliwy ;figlarny; filuterny;
swawolny;rozbawiony;zabawny;
rozbrykany;ożywiony

playground ('plej,graund) s.
boisko; park
playhouse ('plej,haus) s. teatr
playmate ('plej,mejt) s. towarzysz zabaw(dziecinnych,intym-
nych)
play-off ('plejof) s. rozgrywka
poremisowa
play off ('plej.of) v. rozgrywać partię poremisową
plaything ('plejţyņg) s. zabawka
playwright ('plej,rajt) s. dra-
maturg
plea (pli:) s. usprawiedliwienie;
wywód; apel; prosba
plead (pli:d) v. bronić; błagać;
powoływać się
plead guilty ('pli:d'gylty) v.
przyznawać się do winy
pleasant ('plesnt) s. przyjemny;
miły; wesoły
please (pli:z) v. podobać się;
zadowalać
please ! (pli:z) v. proszę
pleased (plizd) adj. zadowolony
pleasing ('pli:zyņg) adj. przyjemny; miły
pleasure ('pleżer) s. przyjemność; adj. rozrywkowy
pleat (pli:t) s. fałda; v. plisować
pledge (pledż) v. zobowiązywać
(się); zastawiać; s. zastaw;
gwarancja; przyrzeczenie
plenipotentiary (,plenype'tenszery) s. pełnomocnik; adj.
pełnomocny
plentiful ('plentyful) adj. obfity; liczny
plenty ('plenty) s. obfitość;
mnóstwo; adv. zupełnie;
nadto;adj.obfity;liczny;obszerny
pliable ('plajebl) adj. giętki
pliers ('plajerz) pl. szczypce
plight (plajt) s. trudności;
stan; położenie; przyrzeczenie;
v. ręczyć; dawać słowo
plod (plod) v. mozolić się;
ślęczeć; s. harowanie; kucie
plod along ('plod,e'loņg) v.
wlec się;mozolić się;trudzić się
plot (plot)s. osnowa; fabuła;
spisek;działka; wykres; mapa;
v.knuć; spiskować;nanosić na
mapę; planować; dzielić

plough (plau) s. pług; v. orać
plow (plau) s. pług; v. orać
plowshare ('plau-szeer) s.lemiesz
pluck (plak) v. wyrwać; zerwać;
szarpnąć
pluck up courage ('plak,ap'karydź) exp.: zdobyć się na odwagę
plucky ('plaky) adj. śmiały;
odważny
plug (plag) s. czop; zatyczka;
kurek; reklama; świeca (silnika); v. zatykać
plug up ('plag,ap) v. zatkać
plum (plam) s. śliwka; rodzynka; gratka; adv. pionowo
plumage ('plu:mydż) s. upierzenie
plumb (plam) adj. pionowy; zupełny; adv. pionowo; prosto;
dokładnie; zupełnie; s. pion
murarski; sonda; v. pionować;
sondować
plumber ('plamer) s. hydraulik
plumbing ('plambyng) s.instalacja wodociągowo-ściekowa budynku
plume (plu:m) s. pióro; pióropusz; v. ozdabiać piórami;
czyścić pióra
plummet ('plamyt) s. pion murarski; v. spadać pionowo
plump (plamp) adj. pulchny;
tęgi; stanowczy; otwarty;
v. tuczyć; tyć; wypełniać
(się); ciężko upaść; upuścić;
rzucić; popierać w wyborach
masowym głosowaniem; adv. prosto; nagle; ciężko; s. upadek
plum pudding('plam'pudyng)s.
budyń świąteczny
plunder ('plander) s. grabierz;
rabunek; łup; v. plądrować;
łupić; grabić
plunge (plandż) v. pogrążać
(się) ; zanurzać (się); wpadać;
spadać; s. skok do wody; pływalnia
plunk (plank) v. brząkać; wybulić; s. brzęk; adv. z brzękiem; prościutko;v.ciskać;rzucać;
upaść ciężko;szarpać(struny);
strzelić do kogoś;s.sl.:dolar

pluperfect ('plu:'pe:rfykt)
adj. zaprzeszły; s. czas zaprzeszły; plusquamperfectum
plural ('pluerel) s. liczba
mnoga; adj. pluralny; mnogi
plus (plas) prep. plus; więcej;
adj. dodatni; dodatkowy;
s. znak plus; dodatek
plush (plasz) s. plusz; adj.
pluszowy; okazały
ply (plaj) v. uprawiać gorliwie;
używać czegoś; zasypywać (np.
pytaniami) ; kursować po...;
s. warstwa; grubość; skłonność;
pasmo
plywood ('plaj,łud) s. sklejka;
dykta
pneumatic (nju'maetyk) adj.
pneumatyczny
pneumonia (nju'mounje) s. zapalenie płuc
poach (poucz) v. uprawiać kłusownictwo; grzęznąc; rozrabiać;
udeptywać; rozmiękać; gotować
jajko na miękko bez skorupki
poached egg ('pauczt,eg) s.
jajko gotowane na miękko bez
skorupki
poacher ('pouczer) s. kłusownik
pocket ('pokyt) s. kieszeń;
dziura (powietrzna) v. wkładać do kieszeni
pocketbook ('pokyt,buk) s.
portfel
pocketknife ('pokyt,najf) s.
scyzoryk
pocket money ('pokyt,many) s.
kieszonkowe
pod (pod) s. strączek; kokon;
stadko; obsada; v. rodzić
strączki; łuszczyć; spędzać
razem
poem (pouim) s. wiersz ; poemat
poet (pouyt) s. poeta
poetess ('pouytys) s. poetka
poetic (pou'etyk) adj. poetyczny ; poetycki;poetycznie piękny
poetry ('pouytry) s. poezja
pogrom ('pougrem, pe'grom) s.
pogrom
poignant ('pojnent) adj.przejmujący; uszczypliwy; cięty;
ostry; dotkliwy;wzruszający

point (point) s. punkt; ostry
koniec; szpiczaste narzędzie;
przylądek; kropka; pointa; cecha; sedno; sens; v. zaostrzać;
celować; wskazywać; punktować;
kropkować;dowodzić;dążyć;pokazywać
point at ('point,aet) v. wyce-
lować; wskazać
point of view ('point,ow'wju:)
s. punkt widzenia
point out ('point,aut) v. wskazywać; uwydatnić
point to ('point,tu) v. wskazać
kierunek (kogoś, coś )
pointed ('pointyd) adj. spiczasty; ostry; cięty; zjadliwy
point-blank ('point'blaenk) adj.
(strzelać) na wprost, bezpośredni; bezceremonialny; bez
ogródek; adv. bezpośrednio;
z bliska; wprost; bez ogródek;
w prostej linii; bez zastano-
wienia się
pointer ('pointer) s. wskaźnik;
wskazówka
poise (pojz) s. równowaga; postawa; swoboda; stan zawiesze-
nia; stan niepewności; v. rów-
nowazyć; ważyć w rękach; za-
wisnąć w powietrzu; być przy-
gotowanym do ataku
poison ('pojzn) s. trucizna;
v. truć; zatruć; zakazić
poisonous ('pojznes) adj. trujący; jadowity; szkodliwy
poke (pouk) v. wtykać; wpychać;
szturchać; dłubać; sterczeć;
wtrącać się; plątać
poker ('pouker) s. pogrzebacz;
poker
polar ('pouler) adj. polarny
polar bear ('pouler beer) s.
biały niedźwiedź
Pole (poul) s. Polka; Polak
pole (poul) s. biegun; słup;
żerdź; dyszel; maszt
pole jump ('poul dżamp) s. skok
o tyczce
police (pe'li:s) s. policja;
v. rządzić; pilnować; utrzymywać porządek
policeman (pe'li:smen) s. policjant

police officer (pe'li:s,ofyser)
s. policjant
police station (pe'li:s,stejszyn)
s. komisariat
policewoman (pe'li:s,łumen) s.
policjantka
policy ('polysy) s. polityka
rządzenia; polityka postępowa-
nia; mądrość polityczna; polisa ubezpieczeniowa
polio ('pouljou) s. poliomyeli-
tis (,poliou,maje'lajtis) s.
paraliż dziecięcy; choroba
Haine-Medina
Polish ('poulysz) adj. polski
(język) (obywatel etc.)
polish ('polysz) v. polerować;
gładzić; pochlebiać; nabierać
połysku; s. pasta (do butów);
połysk; politura; polor
polite (pe'lajt) adj. grzeczny;
uprzejmy; kulturalny
politeness (pe'lajtnys) s.
grzeczność; ogłada; kultura;
uprzejmość
political (pe'lytykel) adj.
polityczny
politician (,poly'tyszyn) s.
polityk; politykier
politics ('polytyks) s. polityka
poll (poul) s. głosowanie; reje-
strowanie głosów; wyniki głosowania; lista; wykaz; lokal
wyborczy; urny wyborcze; ankieta; głowa; tył głowy; obuch
v. oddawać głosy; obliczać
głosy; rejestrować; dostawać
głosy; strzyc włosy; obcinać
rogi
pollen ('polyn) s. pył kwiato-
wy
pollute (pe'lju:t) v. zanie-
czyszczać; skazić
pollution (pe'lju:szyn) s. ska-
żenie; zanieczyszczenie
pomp (pomp) s. pompa
pompous ('pompes) adj. napuszony; nadęty; pompatyczny
pond (pond) s. staw
ponder ('ponder) v. rozważać;
rozmyślać;przemyśliwać;dumać;
zastanawiać się;zadumać się

ponderous ('ponderes) adj.
ciężki; niezgrabny
pontoon (pon'tu:n) s. ponton
pony ('pouny) s. kuc; bryk;
v. odpisywać; ściągać;zrzynać
poodle ('pu:dl) s. pudel(pies)
pool (pu:l) s. kałuża; sadzawka; pływalnia; v. składać się
razem; zbierać się w grupę
poor (puer) adj. biedny; ubogi; lichy; marny; słaby;
kiepski; nędzny; skromny
poorhouse ('puer,haus) s.
przytułek
poorly ('puerly) adv. licho;
kiepsko; skąpo; skromnie;
biednie; ubogo; adj. nie-
zdrów
pop (pop) s. trzask; puknię-
cie; strzał; napój musujący;
lombard; tatuś (slang);
v. strzelać; pukać; nagle wyrzucać; nagle wsadzać; skakać;
wściekać się
popcorn ('pop,ke:rn) s. su-
cha prażona kukurydza
pop in ('pop,yn) v. wskoczyć
pop out ('pop,aut) v. wyskoczyć
pope (poup) s. papież
poplar ('popler) s. topola
poppy ('popy) s. mak
popular ('popjuler) adj, ludowy; rozpowszechniony; popularny (tani)
popularity (,popju'laeryty) s.
popularność
populate ('popjulejt) s. zaludniać
population ('popjulejszyn) s.
ludność
populous ('popjules) adj. ludny; gęsto zaludniony
porch (po:rch) s. weranda; ga-
nek; portyk
porcupine ('po:rkjupajn) s.
jeż; jeżozwierz; kolczatka
pore (po:r) v. rozmyslać; ślęczeć; wpatrywać się; s. por
(skóry)
pore over ('po:r,ouwer) v. rozmyslać nad czymś;ślęczeć (nad
książką );zagłebiać się

pork (po:rk) s. wieprzowina
porous ('po:res) adj. porowaty
porpoise ('po:rpes) s. morswin;
ssak morski
porridge ('porydż) s. owsianka
port (po:rt) s. port; przystań;
otwór; otwór ładunkowy; postawa; trzymanie się; prezentowa-
nie (broni); wino porto; lewa
burta; sterowanie w lewo
portable ('po:rtebl) adj. przenosny; polowy
porter ('po:rter) s. tragarz;
kolejarz od sypialnego wagonu
portion ('po:rszyn) s. część;
porcja; udział; posag; los;
v. dzielić; przydzielać
portion out ('po:rszyn,aut) v.
wydzielać; wyposażać
portly ('po:rtly) adj. dostojny; godny; tęgi; postawny;
okazały
portrait ('po:rtryt) s. portret
pose (pouz) v. pozować; upozo-
wać; stawiać (np. problem);
kłopotać (za pytaniem); s. poza
posh (posz) adj. elegancki; szykowny; v. wyelegantować się
position (pe'zyszyn) s. położenie; stanowisko; postawa;
twierdzenie; umieszczenie;
v. umieszczać; ulokować
positive ('pozetyw) ˉadj. pozytywny; stanowczy; ustanowiony;
zupełny; dodatni; pozytywistycz-
ny; s. znak dodatni; wartosc
dodatnia; pozytyw
possess (pe'zes) v. posiadac;
opanować; opętać; przepajać
possessed (pe'zest) adj. opęta-
ny
possession (pe'zeszyn) s. posiadanie; posiadłość; własnoćć;
dobytek;opanowanie
possessor (pe'zeser) s. posiadacz; właściciel
possibility (pose'bylyty) s.
możliwosc; moznosc;ewentualnosc
possible ('posebl) adj. możliwy; ewentualny
possibly ('posebly) adv. może;
wogóle możliwe; możliwie

post (poust) s. słup; posada;
posterunek; poczta; v. ogłaszać; wywieszać; zalepiać
plakatami

postage ('poustydż) s. opłata
pocztowa

postage stamp ('poustydż,staemp)
s. znaczek pocztowy

postal ('poustel) adj. pocztowy

postal order ('poustel'o:rder)
s. przekaz pocztowy

postcard ('poust,ka:rd) s.
pocztówka

post code ('poust,koud) = zip-
code ('zyp,koud) pocztowy
numer kierunkowy

poster ('pouster) s. plakat

poste restante ('poust'resta:-
nt) s. list lub przesyłka do
odebrania na poczcie

posterity (po'teryty) s. potomnosc

post-free ('poust'fri:) adj.
wolny od opłaty pocztowej

posthumous ('postjumes) adj.
pośmiertny

postman ('poustmen) s. listonosz

postmark ('poust,ma:rk) s.
stempel pocztowy

postmaster ('poust,ma:ster) s.
naczelnik poczty

post office ('poust,ofys) s.
poczta

post office box ('poust,ofys'-
'boks) s. skrytka pocztowa

postpaid ('poust,pejd) s.
opłata pocztowa z góry uisz-
czona

postpone (poust'poun) v. odłożyć; odroczyć; odwlekać

postscript ('pous,skrypt) s.
dopisek; postscriptum

posture('posczer) s. postawa;
stan; położenie; v. przybrać
postawę; pozować

postwar ('poust'ło:r) adj.
powojenny

posy ('pouzy) s. bukiet

pot (pot) s. garnek; imbryk;
czajnik; nocnik; doniczka;
wazonik;rondel;dzban;kocioł;
kufel;słój;puchar;więcierz;łuza

szklanka; haszysz; v. wsadzać
do garnka; polować; strzelać

potato (po'tejtou) s. ziemniak

potent ('potent) adj. potężny;
skuteczny; jurny

potion ('pouszyn) s. dawka; napój

potter ('poter) s. garncarz;
v. grzebać się; włóczyc się;
łazic

potter about ('poter,e'baut)
v. włóczyc się

potty ('poty) adj. marny; lichy;
błachy; łatwy; stuknięty; pomylony; zbzikowany

pouch (paucz) s. worek; torba;
brzuszysko; ładownica; sakiewka; v. nadawać formę worka;
łykac

poulterer ('poulterer) s.
handlarz drobiu

poultice ('poultys) s. okład;
v. kłasc okład

poultry ('poultry) s. drob

pounce (pauns) s. szpon; nagły
atak z góry; v. rzucać się na
cos; trybować; pumeksować; posypywać (rysunek) proszkiem
(kolorowym)

pound (paund) s. funt (pieniądz;
waga); stuk; tupot; uderzenie;
tłuczenie; walnięcie; ogrodzenie; magazyn; areszt; v.tłuc;
walić; tupać;biegać; więzić;
zamykać

pour (po:r) v. wysypać; posypać; lać; polać; wylać; rozlać;
nalać

pour out ('po:r,aut) v. wysypać;
wylać

pout (paut) v. dąsać się; wydymać; s. wydęcie warg; kwasna
mina

poverty('powerty) s. bieda;
ubóstwo

powder ('pałder) s. proch; pył;
puder; proszek; v. posypywać;
pudrować; proszkować

powder room ('pałder,ru:m) s.
toaleta damska

power ('pałer) s. potęga; moc;
energia; siła; własnosc; władza; mocarstwo; v. napędzać;
wspomagać;dostarczać energii

power brake ('pałer,brejk) s.
serwohamulec; wspomagany hamulec
powerful ('pałerful) adj, potężny; mocny
powerless ('pałerlys) adj.
bezsilny
power plant ('pałer,plaent)
s. siłownia
power station ('pałer,stejszyn)
s. elektrownia
powwow ('pał,łał) v. naradzac
się co do taktyki; leczyc;
s. sejmik Indian; odprawa ofi-
cerska; czarownik indiański
practicable ('praektykebl) adj.
wykonalny; możliwy do prze-
prowadzenia
practical ('praektykel) adj.
praktyczny
practice ('praektys) s. praktyka; cwiczenie; v. praktykowac;
uprawiac; cwiczyc
practise ('praektys) v. = practice
practitioner(praek'tyszener) s.
zawodowiec; praktykujący lekarz
prairie('preery) s. preria
praise (prejz) s. pochwała;
v. chwalic; sławic
praiseworthy ('prejz,że:rsy)
adj. chwalebny; godny pochwały
pram (praem) s. ręczny wózek
prance (praens) v. stawac dęba;
tańczyc; paradowac; hasac;
kazac koniowi stawac dęba
prank (praenk) s. psota; figiel; v. wystroic; popisywac
się
prattle ('praetl) v. paplac;
s. paplanina
prawn ('pro:n) s. krewetka;
v. łowic krewetki
pray (prej) v. modlic się; prosic; błagac
prayer ('prejer) s. modlitwa;
prośba
prayer book ('prejer,buk) s.
modlitewnik; książka do
nabożeństwa
pre-(pri:-)prefix,przed-;z góry

preach (pri:cz) v. głosic; kazac;
wygłaszac
preacher (pri:czer) s. kaznodzieja; pastor
precarious (pry'keeries) s. niepewny; niebezpieczny; dowolny
precaution (pry'ko:szyn) s. prze-
zornosc; srodek ostrożnosci
precede (pry:'si:d) v. poprzedzac;
miec pierwszeństwo
precedence (pry'si:dens) s. pierwszeństwo;nadrzędnosc
precedent (pry'si:dent) adj.
uprzedni; poprzedzający
precedent ('presydent) s. precedens
precept('pry:sept) s. nakaz;
przykazanie; nauka moralna; reguła
precinct ('pry:synkt) s. okręg
(wyborczy); obręb; granice
precious ('preszes) adj. drogi;
cenny; afektowany; wyszukany;
wspaniały; adv. bardzo; niezwykle
precipice ('presypys) s. prze-
pasc
precipitate (pry'sypytejt) s.
opad; osad; przyspieszac (zdarzenia);skraplac (się); rzucac;
spadac
precipitation (pry,sypy'tejszyn)
s. opady; przyspieszanie; po-
chopnosc; upadek; strącanie
precipitous (pry'sypytes) adj.
przepascisty; spadzisty
precis ('prejsi:) s. skrót; v.
robic skrót
precise (pry'sajs) adj. dokładny; wyrazny; v. precyzowac;
wyszczególniac
precision (pry'syżyn) s. precyzja;
dokładnosc
precocious (pry'kouszes) adj.
przedwczesny; przedwczesnie roz-
winięty; kwitnący
preconceived ('pry:ken'si:wd)
adj. uprzedzony do; powzięty
z góry
predatory ('predetery) adj. łu-
pieżczy; grabieżczy; drapieżny
predecessor ('pry:dyseser) s.
poprzednik; przodek

predetermine ('pry:dy'te:rmyn)
v. z góry ustanowic; z góry
okreslic; z góry zadecydowac
predicament (pry'dykement) s,
kłopot; kłopotliwe położenie
predicate ('predy,kejt) v.
opierac się na czyms; łączyc
się z czyms; przypisywac czemus; orzekac o czyms; miescic
pojęcie czegos; ('predykyt) s.
cecha; orzecznik; adj. orzecze-
niowy; dopełnienie orzeczenia
predict (pry'dykt) v. przepowiadac
prediction (pry'dykszyn) s.
przepowiednia
predisposition ('pri:dyspe'zyszyn) s. skłonnosc; predyspo-
zycja
predominant(pry'domynent) adj.
przeważający; panujący; góru-
jący
predominate (pry'domynejt) v.
górowac; przeważac
preface ('prefys) s. przedmowa;
wstęp
prefect ('pry:fekt) s. prefekt
prefer (pry'fe:r) v. wolec;
przekładac; dawac awans
preferable ('preferebl) adj.
lepszy
preferably ('preferebly) adv.
raczej
preference ('preferens) s.
pierwszenstwo; uprzywilejowa-
nie; możność wyboru; rzecz bardziej ulubiona, upodobana
preferment (pry'fe:rment) s.
wybór; awans
prefix ('pry:fyks) s. przedrostek; prefiks; tytuł przed
nazwiskiem; v. umieszczac
przedrostek; umieszczac na
wstępie
pregnancy ('pregnensy ) s. ciaza
pregnant ('pregnent) adj. brze-
mienny; doniosły; sugestywny;
płodny ;ciężarna (kobieta)
prejudice ('predżudys) s. uprzedzenie; szkoda; v. uprzedzac się
do kogos; szkodzic (komuś);
rozpowszechniac uprzedzenie

prejudiced ('predżudyst) adj.
uprzedzony ;mający uprzedzenie
preliminary (pry'lymynery) adj.
wstępny; przygotowawczy;
s. wstęp
prelude ('prelju:d) s. wstęp;
preludium; v. grac preludium;
dawac wstęp do czegos
premature (,preme'tjuer) adj.
przedwczesny; przedwczesnie
dojrzały
premeditate (pry'medy,tejt) v.
obmyslac; rozważac
premier ('premjer) adj. pierwszy; najważniejszy; premier;
prezes rady ministrow
premises ('premysys) pl. lokal;
obejscie
premium ('pri:mjem) s. nagroda;
premia
preoccupied (pry:'okju,pajd)
adj. pochłonięty; zaabsorbowany
preparation (,prepe'rejszyn) s.
przygotowywanie; przyrządzanie
prepare (pry'peer) v. przygoto-
wywac (się); szykowac (się);
przyrządzac
prepay ('pry'pej) v. opłacac
z góry
preposition (,prepe'zyszyn) s.
przyimek
prepossess (,pry:po'zes) v.
wpoic; usposobic; natchnąc
prepossessing (prype'zesyng)
adj. miły; sympatyczny
preposterous (pry'posteres) adj.
niedorzeczny; absurdalny
prerequisite (pry'rekłyzyt) adj.
& s. (warunek) wstępny; podstawowy
prescribe (prys'krajb) v. przepisac; nakazac; zaordynowac
prescribtion (prys'krypszyn) s.
nakaz; przepis; recepta
presence ('presens) v. obecnosc
presence of mind ('prezens,ow'
'majnd) v. przytomnosc umysłu
present ('preznt) s. upominek;
prezent; teraźniejszosc; adj.
obecny; niniejszy; teraźniejszy;v.stawiac się;nadarzyć się

present tense ('presnt,tens) s.
czas teraźniejszy

presentation (,prezen'tejszyn)
s. przedstawienie; ofiarowa-
nie; podarek; darowanie; przedłożenie

presentiment (pry'zentyment) s.
przeczucie

presently ('prezently) adv.
wkrótce; niebawem; zaraz

preservation (,preze:r'wejszyn)
s. zachowanie; ochrona; zabezpieczenie

preserve (pry'ze:rw) v. zachowywać; chronić; przechowywać;
konserwować; ochraniać;
s. konserwa; rezerwat

preside (pry'zajd) v. przewod-
niczyć

president ('prezydent) s. prezydent

press (pres) s. prasa; dzienni-
ki; tłocznia; druk; drukania;
nacisk; tłok; ścisk; pospiech;
v. cisnąć; ściskać; przyciskać;
ciążyć; pracować; naglić; narzucać; wciskać; tłoczyć

press in ('pres-yn) v. wciskać

pressing ('presyng) adj. naglący; natarczywy

pressure ('preszer) s. ciśnienie; napór; parcie

prestige (pres'ty:dż) s. prestiż (szacunek i uznanie)

presumable(pry'zju:mebl) adj.
przypuszczalny

presume (pry'zju:m) v. przypuszczać; wykorzystywać (kogoś);
ośmielać się

presumedly (pry'zju:mydly) adv.
przypuszczalnie

presuming (pry'zju:myng) adj.
zarozumiały

presumption (pry'zampszen) s.
przypuszczenie; założenie;
zarozumiałość

presumptuous (pry'zamptjues)
adj. zarozumiały

presuppose (pry:se'pouz) v.
przypuszczać; zakładać z góry;
stawiać warunek

pretend (pry'tend) v. udawać;
pretendować

pretender (pry'tender) s. pretendent

pretense (pry'tens) s. udawanie;
pozór; pretensja; pretensjonalnosc

pretension (pry'tenszyn) s.
aspiracje; roszczenie; preten-
sjonalność; pretensja

preterite ('preteryt) adj.
przeszły; s. czas przeszły

pretext ('pry:tekst) s. pretekst;
pozor;

pretext (pry'tekst) v. wymawiać
się; powoływać się

pretty ('pryty) adj. ładny;
adv. dość; dosyć

prevail (pry'wejl) v. przeważać;
brać górę; przekonać; panować
(np. zwyczaj)

prevalent ('prewelent) adj. panujący; przeważający

prevent (pry'went) v. zapobiec;
powstrzymywać

prevention (pry'wenszyn) s. za-
pobieganie; środek zapobiegający

preventive (pry'wentyw) adj.
zapobiegawczy; prewencyjny

previous ('pry:wjes) adj. poprzedni; wcześniejszy od...;
przedwczesny; nagły; pochopny

previous to ('pry:wjes,tu) adv.
przed czyms

previously ('pry:wjesly) adv.
wcześniej

prewar ('pri:'ło:r) adj.
przedwojenny

prey (prej) s. zdobycz; łup;
ofiara; v. grabić; trawić

price (prajs) s. cena; koszt;
v. wyceniać

priceless ('prajslys) adv.
bezcenny; nieoceniony

prick (pryk) s. ukłucie;
(wulg.) penis; v. kłuć; przekłuwać

prick up one's ears ('pryk,ap-
'łans,eerz) s. nadstawiać
uszu; postawić uszy

prickle ('prykl) s. kolec;
ciern; v. ukłuć; jeżyć się

prickly ('prykly) adj. kolczasty

pride (prajd) s. duma; pycha; ambicja; chluba; v. być dumnym z czegoś;chełpić się;pysznić się

priest (pri:st) s. kapłan; duchowny

primarily ('prajmeryly) adv. głównie; przede wszystkim

primary ('prajmery) adj. główny; zasadniczy; pierwotny; s. wybór kandydatów (U.S.A.)

primary school ('prajmery,sku:1) s. szkoła podstawowa

prime ('prajm) adj. pierwszy; najważniejszy; główny;v.przygotować

prime minister ('prajm-'mynyster) s. premier

primer ('prajmer) s. elementarz; podręcznik (elementarny)

primitive ('prymytyw) adj. prymitywny; pierwotny

primrose ('prymrous) s. pierwiosnek

prince ('pryns) s. książę

princess (pryn'ses) s. księżna; księżniczka

principal ('prynsepel) adj. główny; s. kierownik; zleceniodawca; kapitał; sprawca

principality (prynsy'paelyty) s. księstwo

principle ('prynsepl) s. zasada; reguła;podstawa;źródło;składnik

prink (prynk) v. stroić się; muskać się

print (prynt) s. ślad; odcisk; druk; pismo; fotka; v. wycisnąć; wytłoczyć; wydrukować; być w druku;drukować się;odbić

printed matter ('prynted'maeter) v. druki;materiały drukowane

printer ('prynter) s. drukarz

printing ('pryntyng) s. druk; drukowanie; nakład;a.drukarski

printing ink ('pryntyng,ynk) s. farba drukarska

printing office ('pryntyn,ofys) s. drukarnia

prior ('prajer) adj. wcześniejszy; ważniejszy; s. przeor

prior to ('prajer,tu) adv. przed czymś;wcześniej od czegoś

priority ('praj'oryty) s. pierwszeństwo;starszeństwo

prison ('pryzn) s. więzienie

prisoner ('pryzner) s. więzień

privacy ('prajwesy) s. odosobnienie; samotność; utrzymanie w dyskrecji (tajemnicy); życie prywatne, intymne, osobiste

private ('prajwyt) adj. prywatny; tajny; ukryty; s. szeregowiec;(private parts=genitalia)

private hotel ('prajwyt,hou'tel) s. pensjonat

privation (praj'wejszyn) s. prywacja; niedostatek

privilege ('prywylydż) s. przywilej;prawdziwa satysfakcja

privileged ('prywylydżd) adj. uprzywilejowany;zaszczycony

prize (prajz) v. podważyć; zajmować; cenić; nagroda; premia; wygrana; łup;a.kapitalny.v.cenić

prizefighter ('prajz,fajter) s. zawodowy bokser

prizewinner ('prajz,łyner) s. laureat; zdobywca nagrody

pro (prou) s. zawodowiec (slang) adv. za; dla;prep. pro(forma etc.)

probability (proba'bylyty) s. prawdopodobieństwo;widoki;szanse

probable ('probebl) adj. prawdopodobny;wiarogodny;mający szanse

probation (pro'bejszyn) s. okres próbny; próba;zawieszenie kary

probe (proub) s. sonda; v. sondować; zagłębiać się;badać w śledztwie

problem ('problem) s. problem; zadanie; zagadnienie;a.problemowy

procedure (pre'si:dżer) s. postępowanie; procedura(sądowa)

proceed (pre'si:d) v. isc dalej; postępować;kontynuować;zaskarżać

proceed from (pre'si:d,from) v. wychodzić z...;iść dalej z...

proceedings (pre'si:dyngs) pl. sprawozdanie (z sesji etc.)

proceeds ('prousi:dz) pl. zysk; dochody;przychód (ze sprzedaży)

process ('prouses) s. przebieg; proces; postęp; v. obrabiać; przerabiać; załatwiać; procesować;poddawać procesowi;mleć

procession (pre'seszyn) s. pochód; procesja;kontynuowanie; prowadzenie dalej;dalszy rozwój

proclaim (pre'klejm) v. proklamować; ogłaszać; zakazywać; wskazywać;wprowadzać ograniczenia
proclamation (,prokle'mejszyn) s. proklamacja; obwieszczenie
procrastinate (pre'kraesty,nejt) v. zwlekać; odkładać na później
procure (pre'kjuer) v. postarać się; stręczyć do nierządu
prodigal ('prodygel) adj. marnotrawny; s. marnotrawca;utracjusz
prodigious (pre'dydżes) adj. niezwykły; cudowny; olbrzymi
prod (prod) v. szturchać; kłuć; drażnić; popędzać; s. dżgnięcie; bodziec; szpikulec
prodigy ('prodydży) s. dziwo; cud;genialne dziecko etc.
produce ('produ:s) s. produkty; plony; wynik; produkcja; wydajność; wydobycie;produkty rolne
produce (pre'dju:s) v. wytwarzać; produkować; dostarczać; wydobywać; wystawiać; okazywać
producer ('produ:ser) s. wytwórca (filmowy); producent
product ('predakt) s. produkt; wynik; iloczyn;wytwór(natury etc.)
production (pre'dakszyn) s. wytwórczość; wydobycie; produkcja; utwór;produkty;a.produkcyjny
productive (pre'daktyw) adj. wydajny; produktywny; produkcyjny; urodzajny; żyzny
profess (pre'fes) v. twierdzić; zapewniać; udawać; wyznawać; uprawiać (zawód);być profesorem
professed (pre'fest) adj. jawny; rzekomy; zawodowy
profession (pre'feszyn) s. zawód; wyznanie; zapewnienie; oświadczenie;śluby zakonne
professional (pre'feszenl) s. zawodowiec; adj. zawodowy; fachowy;należący do wolnego zawodu
professor (pre'feser) s. profesor; wyznawca;nauczyciel(tańca)
proficiency (pre'fyszensy) s. biegłość; sprawność
proficient (pre'fyszent) adj. biegły; sprawny; s. mistrz;biegły;znający(obcy język);fachowiec

profile ('proufajl) s. profil; szkic biograficzny; v. przedstawiać z profilu; profilować
profit ('profyt) s. zysk; dochód; korzyść; pożytek; v. korzystać; być korzystnym; przydawać się;mieć zyski
profitable ('profytebl) adj. korzystny;intratny;zyskowny
profiteer (,profy'tier) v.paskować; spekulować; s. paskarz; spekulant(na czarnym rynku etc.)
profound (pro'faund) adj. głęboki;gruntowny;s.otchłań
profusion (pro'fju:żyn) s. obfitość; rozrzutność;nadmiar
prognoses (prog'nousi:z) pl. prognozy; rokowania
prognosis (prog'nousys) s. prognoza; rokowanie
program ('prougraem) s. program; plan; audycja; przedstawienie; v. planować
progress ('prougres) s. postęp; bieg; rozwój;kolejne etapy etc.
progress (pro'gres) v. robić postępy; iść naprzód;być w toku
progressive (pro'gresyw) adj. postępowy;stopniowy;s.postępowiec
prohibit (pro'hybyt) v. zakazywać; zabraniać
prohibition (,prouy'byszyn) s. zakaz; prohibicja
project ('prodżekt) s. projekt; plan;przedsięwzięcie;schemat
project (pro'dżekt) v. projektować; miotać; rzutować; sterczeć; wystawać;wyświetlać(na ekranie)
projection (pro'dżekszyn) s. rzut; planowanie; projektowanie; rzutowanie; wystawanie; projekcja; wyświetlanie
projector (pro'dżekter) s. rzutnik;aparat projekcyjny
proletariat (,proule'teerjet) s. proletariat;robotnicy przemysłowi
prolog ('proulog) s.prolog
prolong (prou'long) v. przedłużać; wydłużać;prolongować(spłaty)
promenade (,promy'nejd) s. przechadzka;przejażdżka; deptak; promenada; v.przechadzać się

prominent ('promynent) adj. wydatny; wybitny; sterczący; wystający; wyróżniający się;sławny

promise ('promys) s. obietnica;
przyrzeczenie; v. obiecywać;
przyrzekać; zaręczać; zapewniać;robić obietnice;zapowiadać się

promising('promysyng) adj. obiecujący; rokujący nadzieje

promontory ('promento:ry) s.
przylądek; wyrostek

promote (pre'mout) v. popierać;
promować; awansować; (slang)
oszukiwać; kombinować

promoter (pre'mouter) s. organizator;krzewiciel; inspirator

promotion (pre'mouszyn) s. po-
pieranie; ułatwienie; awans;
promowanie; lansowanie

prompt (prompt) adj. szybki;
natychmiastowy; v. nakłaniać;
pobudzać; podpowiadać; sufle-
rować;adv.punktualnie;co do mi-nuty

prompter ('prompter) s. sufler
(w teatrze);podżegacz

promptly ('promptly) adv. natychmiast; z miejsca; bezzwłocznie; punktualnie

prone (proun) adj. leżący twarzą na dół; stromy; skłonny

prong (prong) s. ząb (wideł);
róg; v. kłuć; przebijać;
zaopatrywać w zęby

pronoun ('prounaun) s. zaimek

pronounce (pre'nauns) v. oświad-
czać; wymawiać; mieć wymowę;
wypowiadać się

pronto ('prontou) adv. (slang):
prędko; już;natychmiast;zaraz

pronunciation (pra,nansy'ejszyn)
s. wymowa;zapis fonetyczny

proof (pru:f) s. dowód; próba
(np. złota); sprawdzian; wy-
próbowanie; korekta; próbna
odbitka; adj. odporny; wypró-
bowany;sprawdzony;nieprzemakalny

prop(up) ('prop,ap) v. podpierać; s. podpórka;ostoja;oparcie

propagate ('prope,gejt) v. roz-
mnażać (się); rozszerzać; propagować; przekazywać

propagation (,prope'gejszyn) s.
rozmnażanie się; propagowanie

propel (pre'pel) v. napędzać;
poruszać; pędzić

propeller (pre'peler) s. śmigło;
śruba (okrętowa)

proper ('proper) adj. właściwy;
własny; przyzwoity

properly ('properly) adv. właściwie; słusznie; przyzwoicie

property ('property) s. własność;właściwość;cecha;nierucho-mość

prophecy ('profysy) s. proroctwo

prophet ('profyt) s. prorok;
apostoł

proportion (pre'po:rszyn) s.
proporcja; stosunek; rozmiar;
część; v. dostosowywać; rozdzielać;dawkować;dozować

proportional (pre'po:rsznl) adj.
proporcjonalny (do czegoś)

proposal (pre'pouzel) s. propozycja; projekt; oświadczyny

propose (pre'pouz) v. proponować; przedkładać; zamierzać

proposition (,prope'zyszyn) s.
propozycja; sąd; zagadnienie;
twierdzenie; v. robić nie-
przyzwoite propozycje

proprietary (pre'prajetery) adj.
należący; będący prywatną
własnością; s. właściciel;
własność

proprietor (pre'prajeter) s.
właściciel;posiadacz;gospodarz

propulsion (pre'palszyn) s. napęd; bodziec; popędzanie

prose (prouz) s. proza;v.nudzić

prosecute ('prosy,kju:t) s. ścigać prawnie; prowadzić (np.
studia);nie zaniedbywać;pilno-wać

prosecution (,prosy'kju:szyn)
s. oskarżenie

prosecutor ('prosy,kju:ter) s.
prokurator; oskarżyciel

prospect ('prospekt) s. widok;
perspektywa; ewentualny klient;
potencjalne złoża; v. przeszukiwać (okolice); próbnie
exploatować kopalnie; szukać
złota etc.;badać(teren etc.)

prospective (pres'pektyw) adj.
przyszły; ewentualny

prospectus (pres'pektes) s.
prospekt (nowego przedsiębiors-twa)

prosper ('prosper) v. prosperować; sprzyjać powodzeniu

prosperity (pros'peryty) s. dobrobyt; powodzenie; konjunktura; pomyślność

prosperous ('prosperes) adj. mający powodzenie; kwitnący; pomyślny; zamożny

prostate (pros'tejt) s. prostata; gruczoł krokowy

prostitute ('prosty,tu:t) s. prostytutka; v. prostytuować (się);adj.wszeteczny;rozpustny

prostrate ('prostrejt) v. powalić (np. ze zmęczenia); adj. leżący twarzą w dół; powalony; wyczerpany; bezsilny; kłaniający się ;leżący plackiem

protect (pre'tekt) v. chronić; bronić; ochraniać;zabezpieczać

protection (pre'tekszyn) s. ochrona; opieka; protekcja; list żelazny; wymuszanie pieniędzy przez grożenie gwałtem

protective (pre'tektyw) adj. ochronny;zapobiegawczy

protector (pre'tekter) s. opiekun; protektor; ochraniacz

protest (pro'test) v. protestować; zapewniać;oponować

protest ('proutest) s. protest

protestant ('protystent) s. ewangielik; protestant

protestation (proutes'tejszyn) s. uroczyste zapewnienie; protest;zaprotestowanie

protract(pre'traekt) v. przeciągać; przedłużać; wystawiać; przedstawiać w skali

protrude (pre'tru:d) v. wystawać; wysuwać ;sterczeć

proud (praud) adj. dumny; napawający dumą;piękny;szczęśliwy

prove (pru:w) v. udowadniać; wykazać (się); uprawomocnić; poddawać próbie; okazywać się

proverb ('prowe:rb) s. przysłowie ;przypowieść

proverbial (pre'we:rbjel) adj. przysłowiowy

provide (pre'wajd) v. zaopatrywać; przygotowywać; postarać się; sprzyjać; postanawiać; zaplanować

provide for (pre'wajd,fo:r) v. zaopatrywać (dla kogoś)

provided that (pre'wajdyd,daet) exp.: pod warunkiem że...; o ile

providence ('prowydens) s. opatrzność; oszczędność; przezorność; skrzętność

province ('prowyns) s. prowincja; zakres; dziedzina

provincial (pre'wynszel) adj. zaściankowy; prowincjonalny; s. człowiek z prowincji

provision (pro'wyżyn) s. klauzula; dostawa; przygotowanie się; (pl.) prowianty; v. prowiantować; zaopatrywać w żywność;zaprowiantować

provisional (pro'wyżenl) adj. prowizoryczny; tymczasowy

provocation (,prowe'kejszyn) s. prowokacja; rozdrażnienie; podniecenie;spowodowanie

provocative (pro'woketyw) adj. prowokujący; zaciekawiający; drażniący;wyzywający

provoke (pre'wouk) v. prowokować; podniecać; pobudzać; wywoływać; podżegać;jątrzyć

prowl (praul) v. grasować; s. grasowanie (po łup)

proxy ('proksy) s. zastępstwo; pełnomocnik

prude (pru:d) s. świętoszka

prudence ('pru:dens) s. rozwaga; roztropność ;ostrożność

prudent ('pru:dent) s. rozważny; roztropny;ostrożny

prudish ('pru:dysz) adj. pruderyjny;przesadnie skromny

prune (pru:n) s. śliwka (suszona) v. obcinać (np. gałązki); oczyszczać (z czegoś)

psalm (sa:m) s. psalm

pseudonym ('sju:de,nym) s. pseudonim;fikcyjne nazwisko

psyche ('sajki:) s. dusza; duch; umysł (zwierciadło odchylone)

psychiatrist (saj'kajetryst) s. psychiatra

psychiatry (saj'kajetry) s. psychiatria

psychological (,sajke'lodżykel) adj. psychologiczny

psychologist (saj'koledżyst) s. psycholog

psychology (saj'koledży) s. psychologia

pub ·(pab) s. Br., knajpa

puberty ('pju:berty) s. dojrzałość płciowa

public ('pablyk) s. publiczność; adj. publiczny; obywatelski

publication (,pably'kejszyn) s. opublikowanie; ogłoszenie; publikacja;wydanie książki

public house ('pablyk,haus) s. szynk; oberża

publicity (pab'lysyty) s. rozgłos; reklama;a.reklamowy

publish ('pablysz) v. publikować; wydawać; ogłaszać; rozgłaszać;wydać drukiem

publisher ('pablyszer) s. wydawca; nakładca

publishing house ('pablyszyng,- haus) s. firma wydawnicza

pudding ('pudyng) s. budyń

puddle ('padl) s. kałuża

puff (paf) v. pykać; sapać; dmuchać; reklamować; pudrować; s. puszek; pyknięcie; dmuchnięcie; blaga reklamowa; pierzyna;kłąb dymu;zwoj włosów

puff paste ('paf,pejst) s. francuskie ciasto

puffy ('pafy) adj. dychawiczny; nadęty; pękaty; napuszony; otyły; porywisty;dychawiczny

pull (pul) v. pociągnąć; szarpnąć; wyrwać; wyciągać; przeciągać; wiosłować;zciągnać

pull down ('pul,dałn) v. spuścić; rozbierać (np. budynek); osłabiac;sciagac(store etc.)

pull for ('pul,fo:r) v. popierać

pull in ('pul,yn) v. wciągać

pull off ('pul,of) v. ściągać; zdobywać;potrafić;zdołac;stapac

pull out ('pul,aut) v. wyrwać; wycofać; s. wycofanie się

pulley ('puli) s. bloczek; blok krążkowy; v. podnosic bloczkiem

pullover ('pul,ouwer) s. pulower

pulp (palp) s, miazga; miąższ; papka; v.rozcierac na miazgę

pulpit ('pulpyt) s. ambona; kazalnica;kaznodzieje; kazanie

pulpy ('palpy) adj. papkowaty; miąższowy

pulsate (pal'sejt) v. tętnic; pulsowac;drgać;trząść się

pulse (pals) s. tętno; puls; v. tętnic; pulsować

pulverize ('palwerajz) v. proszkować (się); rozpylać; ścierać w proch;zemleć na proch

pump (pamp) s. pompa; lakierek; v. pompowac;pytać uporczywie

pump gun ('pamp,gan) s. strzelba (do repetowania)

pumpkin ('pampkyn) s. dynia

pun (pan) s. gra słów (dwuznacznych); v. robić kalambury

punch (pancz) s. uderzenie (pięścią); poncz; przebijak; krzepa; siła; sztanca; kułak; rozmach; v. dziurkować; tłoczyć; walic; szturchać

punctual ('panktjuel) adj. punktualny; punktowy

punctuate ('panktju,ejt) v. przestankować; przerywać

punctuation (,panktju'ejszyn) s. interpunkcja

punctuation mark (,panktju'ejszyn ma:rk) s. kropka; znak przestankowy

puncture ('pankczer) s. przebicie; punkcja; v. przekłuwać; przedziurawiac;przebic

pungent ('pandżent) adj. kłujący; ostry; cierpki; zjadliwy; gryzący;sarkastyczny;pikantny

punish ('panysz) v. karać;dać bobu

punishment ('panyszment) s. kara;sromotna klęzka (na boisku)

pupil ('pju:pl) s. zrenica; uczeń; wychowanek;małoletni;niepełnoletni

puppet ('papyt) s. kukiełka; marionetka;a.kukiełkowy;marionetkowy

puppet ·show ('papyt,szou) s. występy marionetek

puppet state ('papyt,stejt) s. państwo marionetkowe

puppy ('papy) s. szczenie; szczeniak; piesek;zarozumialec

purchase ('pe:rczes) s. zakup;
kupno; dźwignią; v. kupić;
okupić;nabywać; podnosić (np.
kotwicę);sprawiać sobie

purchaser (pe:rczeser) s. nabywca; kupujący

pure (pjuer) adj. czysty; zupełny; szczery; niewinny; nie
zepsuty,zwykły;czystej krwi

purgative ('pe:rgetyw) adj. przeczyszczający; s. środek na
przeczyszczenie

purgatory ('pe:rgetery) s. czyś-
ciec; adj. oczyszczający

purge (pe:rdż) v. przeczyszczać;
oczyścić; usuwać; dawać na
przeczyszczenie; s. oczyszczenie; czystka; środek przeczyszczający;rafinowanie;klarowanie

purify ('pjuery,faj) v. oczyszczać (się);klarować;rafinować

purity ('pjueryty) s. czystość

purloin (pe:rloyn) v. ukraść;
sciągać;porwać

purple ('pe:rpl) s. purpura;
adj. purpurowy; v. robić purpu-
rowym;robić szkarłatnym

purpose ('pe:rpes) s. cel. zamiar; skutek; decyzja; wola;
v. zamierzać;mieć na celu;plano-
wać

purposeful ('pe:rpesful) adj.
celowy; znaczący; rozmyślny;
zdecydowany; stanowczy

purposeless ('pe:rpeslys) adj.
bezcelowy; bezsensowny; daremny; próżny(wysiłek etc.)

purposely ('pe:rpesly) adv. naumyślnie; celowo; rozmyślnie

purr (pe:r) v. mruczeć; mrucze-
nie; pomrukiwać;s.pomruk

purse (pe:rs) s. sakiewka; torebka damska; kiesa; nagroda;
v. ściągać (się);marszczyć(czoło)

pursue (per'sju:) v. ścigać; tropić; isć dalej; uprawiać (np.
zawód); działać wg.planu; prześladować; kontynuować; towarzyszyć;spełniać(obowiazek)

pursuer(per'sju:er) s. ścigający;
prześladowca ;dążący do czegoś

pursuit (per'sju:t) s. pościg; po-
goń; zawód; zajęcie; rozrywka

pursy (pe:rsy) adj. dychawiczny; wydęty; otyły;sciągnięty

purvey (pe:r'wej) v. dostarczyć;
zaopatrywać; być dostawcą

purveyor (pe:rwejer) s. dostawca

pus (pas) s. ropa

push (pusz) s. pchnięcie; suw;
nacisk; wypad; wysiłek; energia; dryg; bieda; kryzys; zdecydowanie; v. pchać; posunąć;
szturchnąć; nakłonić; dopingować; odpychać; spychać; pomiatać; robić karierę;ponaglać

push along ('pusz,e'long) v. isć
dalej; ciagnąć się dalej; jechać dalej; spieszyć się

push around ('pusz,a'round) v.
pomiatać kims

pusher ('puszer) s. popychacz;
(uliczny): sprzedawca narkotyków

puss (pus) s. kociak; dziewczyna; (slang):gęba;kot(tygrys)

pussycat ('pusy,kaet) s. kociak;
pliszka; (wulg.) narząd płciowy
żeński; ('pasy) adj. ropny

put; put; put (put; put; put)

put (put) v. kłasc; stawiać;
umieszczać; wsadzać; pouczać;
przedkładać; ujmować; wystawiać; dodawać; wlewać; szacować; nakładać; opierać; składać;
narażać; wypychać (np. kule);
zanosić (np. prosby); s. rzut;
adj. nieruchomy(pozostający na)

put back ('put,baek) v. przestawić do tyłu;odłożyć z powrotem

put down ('put,dałn) v. położyć;
stłumić;spuscić w dół;zapisywać

put forth ('put,fo:rs) v. wydobyć; wytężyć(siły);wydawać(pismo)

put off ('put,of) v. odłożyć;
odroczyć ;zbywać;odwieść ;pozbyć się

put on ('put,on) v. wdziewać;
przybierać; tyć;udawać;dodawać

put out ('put,aut) v. zwichnąć;
zgasić; wytężyć (się); produkować; wydawać;wysunać(rękę etc.)

put together (,put'tugedzer) v.
łączyć; montować; powiązać;
zbierać(myśli);kojarzyć;zliczyć

put up('put,ap) v. ustawiac;
wywieszac; cierpiec; wetknac;
schowac;dzwigac do góry;ustawic
putrefy ('pju:try,faj) v.gnic;
ropiec;ulegac zepsuciu
putrid ('pju:tryd) adj. zgniły;
zepsuty; cuchnacy; smierdzacy;
wstretny; obrzydliwy
putty ('paty) s. kit; szpachlów-
ka; v. szpachlowac; zakitowac
putty knife ('paty,najf) s.
szpachla
puzzle ('pazl) s. zagadka; łami-
migłówka; zakłopotanie;
v. intrygowac; wprawiac w zakłopotanie; odgadnac; wymyslic
puzzler ('pazler) s. łamigłówka
pyjamas (pe'dza:mez) pl. pizama
pyramid ('pyremyd) s. piramida;
ostrosłup; v. zarabiac na
spekulacji; wznosic (sie)
piramidalnie;budowac jak piramide
python ('pajsen) s. pyton
q (kju:) siedemnasta litera
angielskiego alfabetu (q.=kwarta)
quack (kłaek) s. znachor; szarlatan; kwakanie; v. uprawiac
znachorstwo; gadac jak szarlatan; kwakac
quad (kłod) (skrót): s. kwadrat;
czworokat
quadrangle (kło'draengl) s.
czworokat
quadruped ('kładru,ped) adj.
czworonozny
quadruple (kło'drupl) adj.
czterokrotny; cztery razy
wiekszy;czterokrotnie wiekszy
quadruplets (kło'dru:plets) s.
czworaczki
quail (kłejl) s. przepiórka;
v. drzec przed czyms
quaint (kłejnt) adj, malowniczy; troche dziwaczny
quake (kłejk) s. trzesienie
(ziemi); v. trzasc sie (np.
z zimna)(ze strachu etc.)
quaky (kłejky) adj. trzesacy
sie; grzaski
qualification (,kłolyfy'kejszyn)
s. warunek; okreslenie; kwalifikacja; uzdolnienie(do pracy)

qualified ('kłolyfajd) adj. wy-
kwalifikowany; uwarunkowany;
kwalifikujacy sie
quality ('kłolyty) s. jakosc;
gatunek; własciwosc; zaleta
qualm (kło:m) s. mdłosci; nud-
nosci; obawa; wyrzuty; skrupuły
quandary ('kłondery) s. zakłopotanie; kłopot;dylemat
quantity ('kłontyty) s. ilosc;
wielkosc; hurt; obfitosc
quarantine ('kłorenti:n) s.
kwarantanna; v. izolowac
quarrel ('kło:rel) s. kłotnia;
zerwanie; spor; sprzeczka;
v. kłocic sie; sprzeczac sie;
zerwac z soba;robic wyrzuty
quarrelsome ('kłorelsem) adj.
kłotliwy; swarliwy
quarry ('kłory) s. kamieniołom;
kopalnia odkrywkowa; łup; zdobycz; płytka; szybka; v. łamac;
wygrzebywac; wydobywac; exploatowac;szperac(za wiadomosciami)
quarter ('kło:ter) v. cwiartowac; kwaterowac; rozpłatac;
stacjonowac; s. cwierc; cwiartka; kwadrans; kwatera; 25 cen-
tow (moneta); kwadra; dzielnica;
strona swiata; czynniki wpływo-
we (pl.) sfery(rzadzace);kwartal
quarterly ('kło:terly) adj. kwartalny; adv. kwartalnie; s. kwar-
talnik;pismo kwartalne
quartet(te) (kło:r'tet) s. kwar-
tet; czworka
quarto ('kło:rtou) s. format
cwiartkowy
quaver ('kłejwer) s. drzenie
głosu; tryl; v. drzec; drgac;
wibrowac; trelowac
quay (ki:) s. molo;nadbrzeze
queasy ('kłi:zy) adj. przeczulony; mdlejacy; grymasny;wrazliwy
queen (kłi:n) s. królowa;królówka
queen bee ('kłi:n.bi:) s. krolo-
wa pszczoła
queer (kłir) adj. dziwny; dziwaczny; nieswoj; podejrzany; fałszywy; pederasta; v. zepsuc;
wpakowac w zła sytuacje; mdlic

quench ('kłencz) v. gasić; tłumić; nagle oziębiać (metal)

querulous ('kłerules) adj. narzekający; zrzędny;płaczliwy

query ('kłiery) s. zapytanie; pytajnik; znak zapytania; v. pytać; kwestionować

quest (kłest) s. poszukiwanie; śledztwo; v. szukać

question ('kłesczyn) s. pytanie; zagadnienie; kwestia; wątpliwości; v. wypytywać; przesłuchiwać; badać; kwestionować; pytać się;przeegzaminować

questionable ('kłesczenebl) adj. wątpliwy (moralnie); sporny; niepewny; niejasny

question mark ('kłesczyn,ma:rk) s. znak zapytania

questionnaire (,kłejstje'neer) s. kwestionariusz

queue (kju:) s. warkocz; ogonek; kolejka; v. czekać w kolejce;czekać w ogonku

queue up ('kju:,ap) v. ustawiać się w kolejce

quibble ('kłybl) s. kruczek; v. szukać wykrętów

quick (kłyk) adj. prędki; szybki; bystry; pomysłowy; żywy; lotny; rudonośny; adv. szybko; chyżo; v. przyspieszać; ożywiać (się);zwiększać szybkość

quicken ('kłyken) v. przyspieszać; pobudzać; ożywiać się; wrócić do życia

quickly ('kłykly) adv. szybko; prędko; z pospiechem

quickness ('kłyknys) s. prędkość; ostrość

quicksand ('kłyk,saend) s. grząski piasek

quicksilver ('kłyk,sylwer) s. rtęć; żywe srebro

quick-tempered ('kłyk'temperd) adj. porywczy

quick-witted ('kłyk'żytyd) adj. bystry; rozgarnięty

quid (kłyd) s. funt szterling; prymka;kawałek do żucia

quiet ('kłajet) adj. spokojny; cichy; s. spokój; cisza;

v. uspokoić (się); uciszyć (się);uspokajać;zciszyć;ucichnąć

quiet down ('kłajet dałn) v. uspakajać;przyciszyć;ucichnąć

quietness ('kłajetnys) s. spokój; cisza;łagodność;skromność

quietude (kłajetju:d) s. spokój (ducha)

quill (kłyl) s. lotka; dutka; kolec; szpulka; pióro

quilt (kłylt) s. pikowana kołdra; pikowana narzuta; v. pikować; watować; robić kołdry; zszywać;sprawić lanie

quince (kłyns) s. pigwa

quinine ('kłajnajn) s. chinina

quintal ('kłyntl) s. cetnar; kwintal

quintuple ('kłyntjupl) adj. pięciokrotny

quintuplets ('kłyntjuplyts) pl. pięcioraczki

quit (kłyt) v. przestać; odejść; odjechać; zabrać się; wyprowadzić się; opuszczać; porzucać; rezygnować; adj. wolny;uwolniony

quite (kłajt) adv. całkowicie; zupełnie; raczej; wcale

quiver ('kływer) s. kołczan; drżenie; drganie; v. drzeć; drgać; trzepotać skrzydłami

quixotic ('kłyks,otyk) s. marzyciel w stylu Don Kichota

quiz (kłyz) s. klasówka; egzamin; badanie; przesłuchanie; kawał; v. egzaminować; badać; przesłuchiwać'przeglądać;kpić

quota ('kłouta) s. udział; kontyngent;norma

quotation (kłou'tejszyn) s. cytata: cytowanie; notowanie; przytaczanie(bieżącej ceny)

quotation marks (kłou'tejszyn, ,ma:rks) pl. cudzysłów

quote (kłout) v. cytować; przytaczać; umieszczać w cudzysłowie; notować; podawać kurs; powoływać się na kogoś

quotient ('kłouszent) s. iloraz r (a:r) osiemnasta litera angielskiego alfabetu

rabbi ('raebaj) s. rabin

rabbit ('raebyt) s. królik

rabble ('raebl) s. motłoch

rabid ('raebyd) adj. wściekły; szalony;rozjuszony;rozzłoszczony

rabies ('raebi:z) s. wścieklizna; wodowstręt

raccoon (ra'ku:n) s. pracz pospolity

race (rejs) s. rasa; plemię; szczep; ród; rodzaj; bieg; gonitwa; wyścigi; prąd; kanał; v. ścigać (się); gonić (się); pędzić; iść w zawody

racer ('rejser) s. wyścigowiec

racial ('rejszel) adj. rasowy

racing ('rejsyŋg) adj. wyścigowy; s. wyścigi; biegi

racist ('rejsyst) s. rasista

rack (raek) s. ruina; zagłada; zniszczenie; koło tortur; wieszak; drabina stajenna; półka; stojak; zębatka; szybki kłus; v. niszczeć; łamać kołem; torturować; cedzić; szarpać; męczyć; dręczyć

racket ('raekyt) s. rakieta; rak; zabawa; hulanka; awantura hałas; afera; granda; nieuczciwe interesy; kant; v. hałasować; hulać; bumblować; zabawiać się; awanturować się

racketeer (,raeky'tier) s. szantażysta; opryszek; v. szantażować; robić grandę

racoon (re'ku:n) s. szop

racy ('rejsy) adj. typowy; cięty; żywy; dosadny; aromatyczny; pikantny; nieprzyzwoity

radar ('rejder) s. radar

radiance ('rejdjens) s. promieniowanie; blask; promienność

radiant ('rejdjent) adj. promieniujący; promienny; rozpromieniony;rzucający promienie

radiate ('rejdyejt) v. promieniować (ciepłem, światłem etc.)

radiation (,redy'ejszyn) s. promieniowanie;zrodło promieniowania

radiator ('rejdy'ejter) s. grzejnik; kaloryfer; chłodnica (samochodowa);radiowa antena nadawcza;radioaktywna substancja wydzielająca promienie

radical ('raedykel) s. pierwiastek; radykał; adj. zasadniczy; radykalny; podstawowy; pierwiastkowy; korzeniowy

radio ('rejdjou) s. radio; adj. radiowy; v. nadawać przez radio ;wysyłać drogą radiową

radioactive ('rejdjou'aektyw) adj. radioaktywny; promieniotwórczy

radio set ('rejdjou,set) s. aparat radiowy; odbiornik radiowy

radiotherapy ('rejdjou-'terepy) s. radioterapia

radish ('raedysz) s. rzodkiewka

radius ('rejdjes) s. promień

raffle ('raefl) s. loteria fantowa; rupiecie; v. sprzedawać na loterii; kupować los

raft (raeft) s. tratwa; (slang): mnóstwo; v. spławiać na tratwie; robić tratwę

rafter (raefter) s. krokiew

rag (raeg) s. szmata; łachman; łupek; dachówka; v. (slang): besztać; dokuczać

rage (rejdż) s. szaleć; wściekać się; s. szał; wściekłość; namiętność

ragged (raegyd) adj. szmatławy; obdarty; podarty; poszarpany; kosmaty; zapuszczony; zaniedbany; wadliwy; chropowaty

raid (rejd) s. obława; nalot; najazd; v. urządzać obławę; najeżdżać ;dokonywać napadu

rail (rejl) s. poręcz; szyna; kolej; listwa; erekcja (slang); v. ogradzać poręczami; kłaść szyny; przewozić koleją; drwić; gorzko narzekać ;pomstować

rail in ('rejl,yn) v. przywozić koleją (materiały,towar)

rail off ('rejl,of) v. wywozić koleją (ludzi;towary etc.)

railing ('rejlyŋg) s. sztachety; ogrodzenie; poręcz;balustrada

railroad ('rejlroud) s. kolej; v. przewozić koleją; przepychać pośpiesznie (np.ustawę); (slang) wpakowywać niesłusznie do więzienia

railway ('rejlłej) s. kolej;
tor kolejowy;tor na szynach
railway man('rejlłej,men) s.
kolejarz
rain (rejn) s. deszcz; v. pada
deszcz; spadać deszczem
rainbow ('rejn,boł) s. tęcza
raincoat ('rejnkout) s. płaszcz
nieprzemakalny
rainfall ('rejn,fo:l) s. opad;
ilość opadów
rainproof ('rejn,pru:f) adj.
nieprzemakalny
rainy ('rejny) adj. deszczowy;
dżdżysty; mokry od deszczu
rainy day ('rejny,dej) exp.
czarna godzina
raise (rejz) v. podnosić;
wskrzeszać; wznosić; wynosić;
hodować; wychowywać; wysuwać;
wytaczać; wzniecać; zrywać;
wywoływać; budzić; zbierać
(np. fundusze); wydobywać;
przerywać (np. oblężenie);
znosić (zakaz); s. podwyżka
(płac); podwyższenie
raisin ('rejzyn) s. rodzynek
rake (rejk) v. grabić; przegrze-
bać; grzebać; ostrzeliwać
(wzdłuż); obrzucać wzrokiem;
nachylać do tyłu; uganiać się
za zwierzyną; s. grabie; grab-
ki; rozpustnik
rake-off ('rejk,of) s. niele-
galna prowizja;łapówka
rake out ('rejk,aut) v. wygrzebywać; wygarniać (popiół etc.)
rakish ('rejkisz) adj. zgrabny;
rozpustny; hulaszczy;(pozornie)
szybki (okręt)(z wygladu)
rally ('raely) s. zbierać (się);
skupiać (się); przyjsć do siebie; ochłonąc; okrzepnąć; ulegać poprawie (giełda); żartować
z kogoś; s. zbiórka; wiec;
okrzepnięcie; ożywienie walki
bokserskiej; wymiana ciosów;
poprawa (konjunktury)
ram (raem) s. tryk; baran; ta-
ran; tłok; dźwig hydrauliczny;
bijak; v. uderzyć; zderzyć się;
ubijać; wtłaczać; bic taranem;
upychać;ugniatać;najechać;zanu-

ramble ('raemb) v. włóczyc się;
przechadzać się; pnąc się (np.
o bluszczu); mówić bez związku;
odbiegać od tematu;s.wędrówka
ramify ('raemyfaj) v. rozgałę-
ziać (się); odgałęzienie (się)
ramp (raemp) s. rampa; v. rzucac się; stawac na tylnych
łapach;opadać pochyło;szaleć
rampart (raempa:rt) s. wał;
szaniec; v. umacniać (szańcem)
ran (raen) v. zob. run
ranch (raencz) s. rancho (gospodarstwo hodowlane) v. prowadzic rancho(farmę etc.)
rancher ('raenczer) s. właściciel rancha
rancid ('raensyd) adj. zjełczały (tłuszcz, oliwa etc.)
rancor ('raenker) s. uraza; za-
jadłość; zawziętość; złość
random ('raendem) s. na chybił
trafił; adj. przypadkowy;
pierwszy lepszy;nie planowany
rang (raeng)v. zob. ring
range (rejndż) s. skala; zasięg;
rozpiętość; nosność; strzelnica; pasmo; obszar; wędrówka;
pastwisko; piec kuchenny;
s. ustawiać; układać; klasyfikować; wędrować; nastawiać teleskop; mieć zasięg; wstrzeliwać się; ciągnąc się; zaliczać
się;rozciągać się;sięgać;nieść
range finder ('rejndż,fajnder) s.
dalekomierz ; odległosciomierz
ranger (rejndżer) s. strażnik
lesny; policjant; komandos;
wędrowiec;desantowiec etc.
rank (raenk) s. ranga; stan;
stanowisko; v. ustawiać rzędem;
układać; klasyfikować; zaszere-
gować; przewyższać rangą; mieć
rangę; adj. wybujały; zjełczały;
smierdzący; zupełny; jaskrawy;
obrzydliwy; sprosny;wierutny
ransack ('raensaek) v. przetrząsać; pladrować;grzebać
ransom ('raensem) s. okup; zwolnienie za okupem; v. wykupić;
zwalniać za okupem
rant (raent)v.deklamować z patosem;s.tyrada;bombastyczna mowa

rap (raep) v. dać klapsa; stukać; krytykować; s. klaps; kołatanie; nagana; zarzut; skazanie na więzienie; odrobina
rapacious (re'pejszes) adj. drapieżny;chciwy
rape (rejp) s. zgwałcenie (kobiety); zniewolenie; splądrowanie; uprowadzenie; v. gwałcić (kobietę); uprowadzać; plądrować;pogwałcić neutralność
rapid ('raepyd) adj. prędki; szybki; bystry; stromy
rapidity('raepydyty) s. szybkość; bystrość;rwący nurt(rzeki)
rapids ('raepyds) pl. progi (na rzece); wodospad
rapt (raept) adj. zaabsorbowany; zachwycony;urzeczony;oczarowany
rapture ('raepczer) s. zachwyt; uniesienie;wzięcie żywcem do nieba
rare (reer) adj. rzadki; niedopieczony (np. kotlet); na pół surowy;nie dosmażony;adv.rzadko
rarity ('reeryty) s. rzadkość
rascal ('raeskel) s. hultaj; łobuz; adj. hultajski
rascally ('raeskely) adj. hultajski; łobuzerski
rash (raesz) s. wysypka skórna; ulewa; powódź; adj. pochopny; popędliwy; nieprzemyślany
rasher ('raeszer) s. płatek (np. szynki)
rasp (raesp) s. raszpla; pilnik; zgrzytanie; v. drapać; skrobać; drażnić; chrapliwie mówić
raspberry (ra:zbery) s. malina
rat (raet) s. szczur; łamistrajk; donosiciel; v. polować na szczury; zdradzać; donosić;zaprzedawać
rats (raets) pl. szczury; bzdura
rate (rejt) s. stopa; stosunek; proporcja; wysokość; poziom; szybkość; cena; stawka; opłata; podatek; stopień; klasa; v. szacować; oceniać; ustalać; zaliczać; opodatkować; zasługiwać; besztać; wymyślać
rate of exchange ('rejt of yks'czejndż) s. kurs wymiany
rate of interest (,rejt of 'yntryst) s. stopa procentowa

rather ('raedzer) adv. raczej; chętniej; dość; nieco; do pewnego stopnia;poniekąd;zamiast
ratify ('raetyfaj) v. zatwierdzać; ratyfikować
ration ('raeszyn) s. przydział; porcja; racja; v. racjonować; sprzedawać na kartki
rational ('raeszynl) adj. rozumny; rozsądny; racjonalny; wymierny;sensowny
rationalize ('raeszyne,lajz) v. racjonalizować; usprawiedliwiać
rattle ('raetl) v. grzechotać; szczekać; brzęczeć; stukać; trzaskać; terkotać; paplać wiersze; s. grzechotanie; terkot; stuk; paplanina; gaduła
rattler ('raetler) s. grzechotnik
rattlesnake ('raetl,snejk) s. grzechotnik
ravage ('raewydż) s. spustoszenie; zniszczenie; v. pustoszyć; niszczyć;plądrować
rave (rejw) v. bredzić; majaczyć; szaleć; wściekać się; wyć; zachwycać się; v. wrzask; wycie; zaślepienie; przesadna pochwała (entzjastyczna)
raven (rejwn) s. kruk; adj. kruczy; (raewen) s. grabież; łup; v. pożerać; szukać łupu; mieć szalony apetyt
ravenous ('raewynes) adj. wygłodniały; zgłodniały; żarłoczny; drapieżny
ravine (re'wi:n) s. parów;jar; wąwóz
raving (rejwyng) adj. bredzący; szalony; porywający (np. pięknością); s. atak furii; bredzenie; majaczenie
ravish ('raewysz) v. porywać (kobietę); gwałcić (kobietę)
raw (ro:) adj. surowy; otwarty (np. rana); wrażliwy; nieokrzesany; brutalny; nieprzyzwoity; s. gołe ciało; surówka; v. ocierać (skórę)
ray (rej) s. promień; promyk; (ryba) płaszczka; v. promieniować; naświetlać; prześwietlać wysyłać promienie(światła etc.)

rayon ('rejon) s. sztuczny jedwab

razor ('rejzer) z. brzytwa

razor blade ('rejzer'blejd) s. żyletka; ostrze brzytwy

re (ri:) prep. w sprawie; tyczy; dotyczy; przedrostek : znowu; od nowa

reach (ri:cz) v. osiągać; wyciągnąć, (np. rękę) dosięgnąć; dotrzec; docierać; sięgnąć; s. sięgnięcie; zasięg; połać; przestrzeń ;pobliże;granice

reach out ('ri:cz,aut) v. wyciągnąć (rękę etc.)

react (ri:'aekt) v. reagować; oddziaływać; przeciwdziałac

reactor (ri:'aekter) s. reaktor (np. jądrowy)

read; read; read (ri:d; red; red)

read (ri:d) v. czytać; tłumaczyć; interpretować

read out ('ri:d,aut) v. wydalać kogos ;wyczytywać

readout ('ri:daut) s. odczyt wyników komputera

read to ('ri:d tu) v. czytać komus

reader ('ri:der) s. czytelnik; korektor; lektor; czytanka; wypisy;recenzent(wydawnictwa)

readily ('redyly) adv. łatwo; chętnie;ochoczo;bez tudu

readiness ('redynys) s. gotowość; pogotowie; obrotność; ciętość; przytomność umysłu

reading ('ri:dyng)s. czytanie; oczytanie; interpretacja; lektura; czytelnictwo; adj. czytający

readjust ('ri:e'dżast) v. dopasować na nowo

ready ('redy) adj. gotów; gotowy; przygotowany; adv. w przygotowaniu; gotowy; v. przygotowywać

ready-made ('redy'mejd) s. konfekcja; adj. gotowy

ready-to-wear ('redy,tu'łeer) s. odzież fabrycznej produkcji

real (ryel) adj. prawdziwy; rzeczywisty; realny; istotny; prawdziwy;autentyczny;faktyczny

real estate('ryel,ys'tejt) s. nieruchomość; realność

realism ('ryelyzem) s. realizm

realistic ('ryelyst) s. adj. realistyczny

reality (ty'aelyty) s. rzeczywistość; realizm; prawdziwość

realization (,ryelaj'zejszyn) s. realizacja; spełnienie; wykonanie; spieniężenie; uświadomienie sobie

realize ('ry:e,lajz) v. urzeczywistnić; realizować; uprzytamniać; zdawać sobie sprawę; uzyskiwać; zdobywać (majątek)

really ('ryely) adv. rzeczywiscie; naprawdę; doprawdy; faktycznie; istotnie

realm (relm) s. królestwo; dziedzina; sfera; zakres

realpolitik (rej'a:lpouly'tyk) s. polityka egoistyczna

realtor ('ryelter) s. pośrednik sprzedaży nieruchomości

realty ('ryelty) s. nieruchomość

reap (ry:p) v. żąć; zbierać plony, owoce pracy etc.

reaper ('ry:per) s. żniwiarz: żniwiarka

reappear ('ry:e'pier) v. zjawić się ponownie;znowu ukazac się

rear (rier) s. tył; tyły; ustęp; v. stawać dęba; hodować; wychowywać; wznosić (się); wybudować; wystawiać

rear guard('rier,ga:rd) s. tylna straż

rear-light ('rier,lajt) s. tylne światło samochodu

rearm ('ry:'a:rm) v. ponownie uzbrajać

rearmament ('ry:'a:rmement) s. remilitaryzacja

rearmost (rie:r,moust) adj. końcowy ;ostatni

rearview mirror ('rier,wju:'-'myrer) s. (tylne) lusterko w samochodzie (do sprawdzania ruchu za samochodem)

rearrange ('ry:erejndż) v.
przestawiać; zmieniać (porządek) ;poprawic(fryzurę etc.)
rearwards ('rierłedz) adv.
wstecz;ku tyłowi; na tył
reason ('ri:zn) s. rozum; powód; uzasadnienie; motyw; przesłanka; rozsądek; v. rozumować;
rozważać; wnioskować; rozpra-
wiać; przekonywać; dowodzic
reason out ('ri:zn,aut) v.
przemyślać;wrozumować;dociekać
reason with ('ri:zn,łyз) v.
przekonywac kogoś
reasonable ('ri:znebl) adj.
rozumny; rozsądny; umiarkowany; słuszny; racjonalny
reassure (,ry:a'szuer) v. zapewniać; upewniać; ubezpieczac
na nowo; uspakajac; przywracać
zaufanie;upewniać na nowo
reassuring (,ry:a'szueryng)
adj. uspokajający
rebate (ry'bejt) s. rabat;
zwrot (części kwoty); v. udzielać rabatu; potrącać (z rachunku) ;zamortyzować;przytępiać
rebel ('rebel) s. buntownik;
v. buntować się; adj. zbuntowany; buntowniczy
rebellion (ry'beljen) s. bunt;
powstanie
rebellious (ry'beljes) adj.
zbuntowany; buntowniczy; niesforny;oporny;zbuntowany
rebirth (ry'be:rз) s. odrodzenie;odżywanie
re-book ('ry:buk) v. zamawiać
na nowo (program teatralny;
bilety lotnicze etc.)
rebound (ry'baund) s. odbicie;
odskok; rykoszet; v. odskaki-
wać; odbijać (się) (sobie na
kimś)
rebuff (ry'baf) s. ofuknięcie;
odrzucenie; v. ofuknąć; dać
odprawę;odesłać z kwitkiem
rebuild('ry:byld) v. odbudowy-
wać; przebudowywać
rebuke (ry'bju:k) s. nagana;
v. upominać; łajać
recall (ry'ko:l) v. odwoływać;
przypominać (sobie);wycofywać;
cofać (obietnicę);s.nakaz powrotu

recap ('ry:kaep) s. opona ponownie gumowana; v. ponownie
wulkanizować opony; powtarzac
dla podsumowania
recapture ('ri:'kaepczer) v.
odzyskac; s. odzyskanie
recede (ry'si:d) v. cofać się;
oddalac sie; maleć; słabnąć
receipt (ry'si:t) s. pokwitowanie; odbiór; recepta
receive (ry'si:w) v. otrzymy-
wać; dostawać; odbierać; przyjmować (np. gości)
receiver (ry'si:wer) s. odbiornik (radiowy); słuchawka (telefoniczna); odbiorca; syndyk;
zarządca upadłości
recent ('ri:snt) adj. niedawny;
świeży; nowy
recently ('ri:sntly) adv. niedawno; swieżo; ostatnio;współ-
reception (ry'sepszyn) s. przyjęcie; odbiór; recepcja
reception desk (ry'sepszyn,desk)
s. biuro do przyjmowania inte-
resantów;portiernia;biuro przyjęć
receptionist (ry'sepszynyst) s.
recepcjonistka; sekretarka
przyjmująca klientów;portier
recess (ry'ses) s. przerwa
(między lekcjami); ferie;
wgłębienie; nisza; wnęka;
v. odraczać; wkładać do wnęki;
robic wnękę;rozjeżdżać się na
recession (ry'seszyn) s. cof-
nięcie; recesja (gospodarcza);
wgłębienie; wnęka:kryzys;zastój
recipe ('rysypy) s. przepis;
recepta
recipient (ry'sypjent) adj. od-
biorczy; s. odbiorca; zdobywca
nagrody; osoba obdarowana
reciprocal (ry'syprekel) adj.
wzajemny; odwrotny; s. odwrot-
nosć (w matematyce)
recital (ry'sajtl) s. przedstawienie; opowiadanie; recytacja;
koncert;deklamowanie utworu
recite (ry'sajt) s. recytować
(wiersz); wyliczać
reckless ('reklys) adj. (nie-
bezpiecznie) lekkomyślny;
nieuważający;na oślep;wariacki
brawurowy;szaleńczy;zuchowaty

reckon ('reken) v. liczyc; sądzic; myśleć że;polegać na
reckon up ('reken,ap) v. zli-
czac;zsumować; podsumowywać
reckon with ('reken,łys) v.
liczyc się (z kims)
reckoning ('rekenyŋg) s. oblicza-
nie (położenia); rachuba; obrachunek;kalkulacja;rozliczenie
reclaim (ry'klejm) v. odzyski-
wac (pod uprawę); użyzniać;
przerabiać odpadki; wyprowadzać z (zaniedbania; błędu
etc.);zażądać zwrotu;dochodzić
recline (ry'klajn) v. kłasc się;
wyciągać się; złozyć (np. głowę);spoczywać poł leżąc
recognition (,rekeg'nyszyn) v.
rozpoznanie; uznanie; pozdrowienie; dowod uznania
recognize ('rekeg,najz) v. rozpoznawac; pozdrowić; uznawać;
przyznawac; udzielać (głosu)
recoil (ry'kojl) v. wzdrygać się;
cofac się; kopać (np. kolbą);
odskoczyc; odbijać; s. odskok;
odrzut; odbicie; wzdrygnięcie
się
recollect (reke'lekt) v. wspominac; przypominać sobie; zbierać
na nowo;przypominać sobie z trudem
recollection (,reke'lekszyn) s.
wspomnienie; pamięć
recommend (reke'mend) v. polecać;
zalecać;dobrze świadczyć
recommendation(,rekemen'dejszyn)
s. polecenie; zlecenie
recompense ('rekem,pens) v. odpłacac; dawać odszkodowanie;
s. wynagrodzenie; zadośćuczynie-
nie;odszkodowanie;rekompensata
reconcile ('rekensajl) v. godzić
(sprzeczności); zażegnać (spór);
pojednac;pogodzić się
reconciliation (,reken,syly'ejszyn) s. pojednanie; pogodzenie
reconsider (,ri:ken'syder) v.
ponownie rozważyc; reasumować
reconstruct (,ri:ken'strakt) v.
odbudowywac; odtwarzać
reconstruction ('ri:ken'strakszyn) s. rekonstrukcja; odbudowa

record ('reko:rd) v. zapisywać;
notowac; rejestrować; zazna-
czac; nagrywać; s. zapiska;
archiwum; rejestracja; dokument; przeszłość (czyjaś); pamięć o kims; nagranie; rekord
recorder (ry'ko:rder) s. re-
gistrator; aparat zapisujący;
pisak;pisarz archiwista
record holder ('reko:rd,houlder)
s. rekordzista; mistrz
recording ('reko:rdyŋg) s. nagranie (płyta)
record player ('reko:rd,plejer)
s. adapter
recourse (ry'ko:rs) s. ucieka-
nie się (ratunek)
recover (ry'kawer) v. odzyskac;
nadrabiac; powetować sobie;
uzyskac; przywracać; wyzdrowieć;
ochłonąc; przyjsć do siebie
recovery (ry'kawery) s. odzyskanie (pozycji); wyzdrowienie;
poprawa (gospodarcza)
recreation (,rekry'ejszyn) s.
rozrywka; zabawa; odtworzenie
recruit (ry'kru:t) s. rekrut;
poborowy; v. werbować; uzupełniac (stan zatrudnienia)
rectangle ('rektaengl) s.
prostokąt; a.prostokątny
rectify ('rektyfy) v. prostować
(np. błąd); poprawiać (np.
plan); usuwać (np. nadużycia)
rector ('rekter) s. proboszcz;
rektor
rectory ('rektery) s. probostwo
recur (ry'ke:r) v. powtarzać
się; przypominać się; nawiązy-
wać do czegoś (wielokrotnie)
recurrent (ry'karent) adj. po-
wracający; nawracający
red (red). adj. czerwony;
s. czerwień; lewicowiec; komunista ;radykał(skrajny);forsa(sl.)
red-bait('redbejt) v. oskarżać
o komunizm (USA)
red-blooded('red,bladyd) adj.
męski; krzepki ;jurny
redden ('reden) v. zaczerwie-
nić się ;zarumienić się
reddish ('redysz) adj. czerwo-
nawy

redeem (ry'di:m) v. wykupywać;
okupywać; wybawiać; zbawiać;
odkupić; zamienić;kompensować
redemption (ry'dempszyn) s.
wykup; okupienie; odkupienie;
wybawienie;umorzenie;zbawienie
red-handed ('red'haendyd) adj.
splamiony krwią; exp. na gorącym uczynku
red letter day ('red'leter dej)
s. dzień specjalny; dzień
świąteczny
redouble (ry'dabl) v. podwoić
(się); zwijać się
reduce (ry'dju:s) v. zmniejszać (się); chudnąć; redukować; ograniczać; obniżać; dostosować; sprowadzać; doprowadzać; rozcieńczać; osłabiać;
odtleniać; wytapiać
reduction (ry'dakszyn) s.
zmniejszenie; redukcja; obniżka; sprowadzenie; dostosowanie; odtlenianie; wytapianie
reed (ri:d) s. trzcina; słoma;
fujarka; strzała; płocha
tkacka; stroik (muzyczny)
reeducation ('ry:edju'kejszyn)
s. przeszkolenie ponowne
reef (ri:f) s. rafa; skała podwodna; ref; v. refować
reek (ri:k) s. odor; para; dym;
v. śmierdziec; parować; dymić;
wędzic; ociekać (krwią)
reel (ri:l) s. szpula; cewka;
rolka; chwianie się; kręcenie
się; v. nawijać; odwijać; rozwijać; recytować; chwiać się;
zataczać się; kręcić się; dostawać zawrotu głowy; dawać zawrót
głowy;zachwiać sie na nogach
reel off ('ri:l,of) v. odwijać
reel up ('ri:l,ap) v. nawijać
reelect ('ri:y'lekt) v. ponownie wybierać
reenter ('ri:'enter) v. ponownie wchodzić (w posiadanie etc.)
reentry ('ri:'entry) s. ponowne wejście;rewindykacja
re-establish (,ry:ys'taeblysz)
v. ponownie: zakładać; ustanawiać; ustalać; wprowadzać

refer (ry'fe:r) v. odsyłać; po-
wiązywać; skierować; odwoływać;
cytować; odnosić się; dotyczyć;
powoływać się
referee (refe'ri:) s. sędzia
sportowy; rozjemca; v. sędzio-
wać
reference ('refrens) s. odsyłacz; odnosnik; odwoływanie
się; aluzja; informacja; referencja; stosunek; związek;
wzgląd;przelotna wzmianka
reference book ('referens,bu:k)
s. tekst podręczny;podręcznik
reference library ('referens
laj'brery) s. biblioteka podręczna naukowo-informacyjna
refill (ry:'fyl) s. ponowne;
napełnienie; wypełnienie; nowy
zapas; v. ponownie napełniać,
wkładać,zapełniać etc.
refine (ry'fajn) v. oczyszczać;
rafinować; wysubtelniać; roz-
prawiać subtelnie
refinement (ry'fajnment) s.
rafinowanie; wyrafinowanie;
subtelność; wytworność
refinery (ry'fajnery) s. rafineria
reflect (ry'flekt) v. odbijać;
odzwierciadlać; rozmyślać; zastanawiać się; krytykować;
przynosić (zaszczyt; ujmę)
reflection (ry'flekszyn) s. odbicie; odzwierciedlenie; odbicie światła; zarzut; rozwaga;
namysł;wzmianka;pomysl;wstyd
reflex ('ry:fleks) s. odruch;
refleks; odbicie; odzwierciedlenie; adj. refleksyjny; odbity; wygięty; v. poddawać
refleksom; wyginac wstecz
reflexive (ry'fleksyw) adj.
odbijający; pełen zadumy;
refleksyjny
reform (ry'fo:rm) v. reformować;
poprawić; usuwać; ulegać refor-
mie; s. reforma; poprawa
reformation (,refer'mejszyn) s.
reformacja; poprawa
reformer (ry'fo:rmer) s. refor-
mator(moralności,warunków etc.)

refract (ry'fraekt) v. załamywać
światło;wyginać promień światła
refractory (ry'fraektery) adj.
oporny; uporczywy; krnąbrny;
odporny; ogniotrwały
refrain (ry'frejn) v. powstrzymywać się; s. refren
refresh (ry'fresh) v. odświeżyć;
wzmacniać; pokrzepiać
refreshment (ry'freszment) s.
odpoczynek; wytchnienie; od-
świeżenie; zakąska
refrigerator (ry'frydże,rejter)
s. lodówka; chłodnia
refuel ('ry:'fjuel) v. zaopatrzyć w paliwo; dodać paliwa
refuge ('refju:dż) s. schronienie; azyl;przytułek;v.schronić się
refugee (,refju'dżi:) s. zbieg;
uchodźca; uciekinier
refund (ry'fand) s. zwrot; spła-
ta; v. zwracać pieniądze
refusal (ry'fju:zel) s. odmowa;
prawo opcji; wbijanie do oporu
refuse (ry'fju:z) v. odmawiać;
odrzucać; adj. odpadowy; s. odpadki; rupiecie
refute (ry'fju:t) v. zbijać
(np. twierdzenie)
regain (ry'gejn) v. odzyskać;
wrócić (do zdrowia)
regard (ry'ga:rd) v. spoglądać;
zważać; uważać; dotyczyć;
s. wzgląd; spojrzenie; szacunek; uwaga;pozdrowienia;ukłony
regarding (ry'ga:rdyng) prep.
odnośnie;co się tyczy;w sprawie
regardless (ry'ga:rdlys) adv.
w każdym razie; adj. nie zważa-
jący; bez względu (na kłopoty
etc.);nie liczac się(z wydatka-mi)
regard of (ry'ga:rd,ow) exp. co
się tyczy ; w sprawie etc.
regent ('ri:dżent) s. regent;
opiekun; członek zarządu
regime (ry'żi:m) s. ustrój; re-
żym; tryb życia; system; rządy
regiment ('redżyment) s. pułk;
zastęp; v. organizować; ko-
szarować; wcielać do pułku
region ('ri:dżen) s. okolica;
sfera; rejon; obszar; dzielnica

register ('redżyster) v. rejestrować; zapamiętywać; wysyłać
polecony list; prowadzić rejestr;
wstrzeliwać się; wyrażać minami
registered letter ('redżysterd,
,leter) s. list polecony
registration (,redzys'trejszyn)
s. rejestracja; meldunek;
ilość zarejestrowana
regret (ry'gret) s. ubolewanie;
żal; v. żałować czegoś
regrettable(ry'gretebl) adj.
godny ubolewania
regular ('regjuler) adj. regularny; stały; zawodowy; poprawny;
przepisowy; s. regularny (żołnierz; ksiądz etc.); stały gość;
wierny partyjnik
regularity (,regju'laeryty) s.
regularność; systematyczność
regulate ('regjulejt) v. regulować;przystosowywać do wymogów
regulation (,regju'lejszyn) s.
przepis; regulowanie; adj.
przepisowy; zwykły
rehearsal (ry'he:rsel) s. próba;
powtarzanie
rehearse (ry'he:rs) v. odbywać
próbę; powtarzać
reign (rejn) v. panować; władać;
s. władza; panowanie
rein (rejn) v. kierować wodzami;
trzymać na wodzach
reins (rejns) pl. wodze
reindeer ('rejn.dier) s. renifer
reinforce (,ri:yn'force) v.
wzmocnić;popierać;dodać sił
reject (ry'dżekt) v. odrzucić;
odpalić; zwracać; ('rydżekt)
s. wybrakowany towar; niezdatny
do wojska;coś odrzuconego
rejection (ry'dżekszyn) s. odrzucenie; odmowa; wybrakowany towar;oblanie studenta;odkosz
rejoice (ry'dżojs) v. radować;
cieszyć się; weselić się
rejoicing (ry'dżojsyng) s. radość;uradowanie;adj.uradowany
rejoin ('ri:dżoyn) v. ponownie
łączyć (się); zestawiać połama-
ne części; odpowiadać na zarzut

relapse (ry'laeps) s. nawrót;
pogorszenie; v. ponownie popa-
dać; zapadać z powrotem
relate (ry'lejt) v. opowiadać;
referować; łączyć się
related (ry'lejtyd) adj. bliski;
spokrewniony; spowinowacony;
związany;pokrewny;powinowaty
relation (ry'lejszyn) s. sprawozdanie; opowiadanie; stosunek; związek; pokrewieństwo;
powinowactwo; krewny
relationship (ry'lejszynszyp)
s. stosunek; pokrewieństwo;
powinowactwo;zależność
relative ('reletyw) adj.
względny; stosunkowy; podrzędny; zależny; dotyczący;
adv. odnośnie; w sprawie;
s. krewny; zaimek względny
relax (ry'laeks) v. odprężać
(się); osłabnąć; rozluźniać
się; łagodnieć; odpoczywać
relaxation (,ry:laek'sejszyn)
n. odprężenie; odpoczynek;
rozrywka; złagodzenie
relay(ry'lej) s. bieg rozstawny; wzmacniacz;v.przekazywać;
zmieniać (tor);kłaść na nowo
relay race (re'lej,rejs) s.
bieg rozstawny; bieg sztafe-
towy
release (ry'li:z) v. wypuszczać; uwalniać; zwalniać;
s. zwolnienie; uwolnienie;
puszczenie (do druku); spust;
wyzwalacz;wypuszczenie(filmu)
relent (ry'lent) v. łagodnieć;
mięknąć;dać się wzruszyć
relentless (ry'lentlys) adj.
nieugięty; bezlitosny; nieprzejednany;nieustępliwy;srogi
relevant ('relewent) adj.
istotny; trafny; na miejscu;
należący do rzeczy
reliability (ry,laje'bylyty) s.
rzetelność; solidność; pewność
reliable (ry'lajebl) adj. pewny; solidny; rzetelny
reliance (ry'lajens) s. zaufanie; otucha
reliant (ry'lajent) adj. ufny
w siebie;liczący na kogoś;zależ-
ny od czegoś

relic ('relyk) n. zabytek; relikwia;pozostałość;resztka
relief (ry'li:f) n. odprężenie;
ulga; urozmaicenie; zapomoga;
pomoc; zmiana (np. warty);
płaskorzeźba;uwypuklenie
relieve (ry'li:w) v. nieść pomoc, ulgę; ulżyć (sobie);
oddać mocz; ożywić; zmieniać
wartę; zluzować; uwypuklić
(na tle czegoś);uwydatnić
religion (ry'lydżyn) s. religia;
obrządek; wyznanie; zakon
religious (ry'lydżes) adj. pobożny; religijny; zakonny;
s. zakonnik; zakonnica
relinquish (ry'lynkłysz) v. porzucać; wyrzekać się czegoś;
zaniechać; zrzekać się; rezygnować;wypuścić coś z rąk
relish ('relysz) s. smak; posmak;
przyprawa; przysmak; urok; zamiłowanie; v. smakować w czyms;
czynić smaczniejszym; przyprawiać; mieć dobry smak; być
przyjemnym;dodawać smaku
reluctance (ry'laktens) s. niechęć; opór(magnetyczny);wstręt
reluctant (ry'laktent) adj. niechętny; oporny
rely on (ry'laj,on) v. polegać
na czyms lub kims;liczyc na
remain (ry'mejn) v. pozostawać
remains (ry'mejns) pl. pozosta-
łości; resztki; przeżytki;
zwłoki; szczątki
remainder (ry'mejnder) s. reszta; pozostałość; remanent
remand (ry'maend) v. odsyłać
(do niższej instancji lub więzienia); s. odesłanie do
więzienia; człowiek odesłany
z powrotem
remark (ry'ma:rk) v. zauważyć;
zrobić uwagę; s. uwaga
remarkable (ry'ma:rkebl) adj.
wybitny; godny uwagi
remedy ('remydy) s. lekarstwo;
środek; rada; v. leczyć; za-
radzać;naprawiać
remember (ry'member) v. pamiętać;
przypominać; pozdrawiać; modlić
się za kogoś;mieć w pamięci

remembrance (ry'membrens) s.
wspomnienie; pamiątka; pamięc; pozdrowienie;ukłony
remind (ry'majnd) v. przypominac coś komuś;przypomnieć
reminder (ry'majnder) s. przypomnienie; upomnienie; ponaglenie;ktoś przypominający
reminiscent (,remy'nysnt) adj.
przypominający; wspominający;
pełen wspomnień
remiss (ry'mys) adj. niedbały;
ospały; niechlujny
remit (ry'myt) s. przekazywać
(pieniądze); darować (dług);
odpuszczać (grzechy); odsyłać; przywracać; łagodzić;
łagodnieć; słabnąc
remitance (ry'mytens) s. przesyłka pieniężna; wypłata
remnant ('remnent) s. resztka;
pozostałość; ślad czegoś
remodel (ry'modl) v. przera-
biac; odnowić; przemodelować
remonstrate ('remenstrejt) v.
protestować
remorse (ri'mo:rs) s. wyrzuty
sumienia; skrupuły
remorseless (ri'mo:rslys) adj.
bezlitosny ;nie skruszony
removal (ry'mu:wl) v. usunięcie; przeprowadzka
remove (ry'mu:w) v. usuwać;
przewozic; zdejmować; przeprowadzac się; opuszczać;
s. przeprowadzka; odległość;
stopień;oddalenie
remover (ry'mu:wer) s. usuwacz
(plam); środek do usuwania
renaissance (ry'nesens) s. odrodzenie;renesans;a.renesansowy
rend; rent; rent (rend; rent;
rent)
rend (rend) v. drzeć; targać;
wydzierać; urągać; rozdzierać
render ('render) v. uczynić;
zrobić; oddawać; okazywać;
składac; wydawać; płacić; odpłacać; oczyszczać; wytapiac;
tynkować; s. odpłata (np.
w naturze); pierwsza warstwa
tynku

rendezvous ('ra:ndy,wu:) s.
randka; umówione spotkanie;
miejsce spotkań
renew (ry'nu:) v. odnawiać; po-
nawiac; wznawiać; odświeżać;
prolongować
renewal (ry'nu:el) s. odnowienie (np. kontraktu)
renounce (ry'nauns) v. zrzekać
się; zrezygnować; wyrzekać się;
wypowiadać; odstępować; nie-
uznawać
renovate (ry'nowejt) v. odnowić;
naprawić
renown (ry'naun) s. sława; rozgłos; pogłoska
renowned (ry'naund) adj. sławny
rent 1. (rent) v. zob. rend
rent 2. (rent) s. komorne;
czynsz; renta; najem; rozdarcie; szczelina; rozłam; parów;
v. wynajmować; dzierżawić; pobierać czynsz; być wynajmowanym
rental ('rentl) s. czynsz; komorne; wypożyczanie; adj. czynszowy
rental agency ('rentl'ejdżensy)
s. biuro wynajmu (narzędzi;
mieszkań etc)
rent free ('rent'fri:) adj.
wolny od opłaty czynszowej
repair (ry'peer) v. pójść;
uczęszczać; naprawiać; reperowac; remontować; powetować;
wynagrodzić; s. naprawa; remont; stan
repair shop (ry'peer,shop) s.
warsztat naprawy
reparation (repa'rejszyn) s.
naprawa; remont; odszkodowanie
repartee (repa:r'ti:) s. ripos-
ta; cięta odpowiedź; odcina-
nie się
repay (ry:'pej) v. spłacić;
zwrócić; wynagrodzić; odwza-
jemnic się; oddać
repeat (ry:'pi:t) v. powtarzać
(się); repetować; odbijać się;
robić powtórkę; robić ponownie;
odtwarzać; s. powtórka; powtórzenie; powtórne zamówienie
a.powtórny;wielokrotny

repel (ry'pel) v. odpierać;
odrzucać; odtrącać; budzić
odrazę,niechęć, wstręt etc.
repent (ry'pent) v. żałować
repentance (ry'pentens) s.
skrucha; żal
repentant (ry'pentent) adj.
żałujący; pełen skruchy
repetition (,repy'tyszyn) s.
powtórzenie; powtórka
replace (ry'plejs) v. zastępować; zwracać; oddawać; umieszczać z powrotem; przywrócić;
wymienić
replacement (ry'plejsment) s.
zastępstwo; zastępca; zastąpienie; wymiana (części)
replenish (ry'plenysz) v. ponownie napełniać; wypełniać;
uzupełniać
replay (ry'plej) v. ponownie
rozgrywać; ('ry:plej) s. ponowna rozgrywka
reply (ry'plaj) v. odpowiadać;
s. odpowiedź
report (ry'po:rt) v. opowiadać;
meldować; dawać sprawozdanie;
zdawać sprawę; pisać sprawozdanie; referować; s. raport;
sprawozdanie; komunikat;
opinia; huk; wybuch; pogłoska
reporter (ry'po:rter) s. dzien-
nikarz; sprawozdawca; reporter
repose (ry'pouz) s. odpoczynek;
spokój; v. odpoczywać; spo-
czywać; polegać; opierać; po-
kładać
represent (,repry'zent) v.
przedstawiać; reprezentować;
wyobrażać; grać (kogoś)
representation (,repryzen'tejszyn) s. przedstawicielstwo;
reprezentacja; przedstawienie;
wyobrażenie
representative (,repry'zente-
tyw) adj. przedstawiający;
reprezentujący; wyobrażający;
s. przedstawiciel; reprezentant (poseł na sejm)
repress (ry'pres) v. tłumić;
hamować; powstrzymywać; po-
skromić

reprieve (ry'pri:w) v. zawieszać; odraczać; dawać odroczenie; s. odroczenie; darowanie,
zmiana kary (śmierci)
reprimand ('reprymaend) v. karcić; udzielać nagany; s. nagana
reproach (ry'proucz) v. robić
wyrzuty; wymawiać; s. wyrzut;
zarzut; wymówka
reproachful (ry'prouczful) adj.
pełen wyrzutu
reproduce (,rypre'du:s) v. odtwarzać;reprodukować; rozmna-
żać; wznawiać
reproduction (,ri:pre'dakszyn)
s. reprodukcja; rozmnażanie
się; płodzenie
reproof (ry'pru:f) s. nagana
reprove (ry'pru:w) v. ganić
reptant ('reptent) adj. pełzra-
jący
reptile ('reptajl) s. gad; płaz;
gadzina; adj. pełzający; ga-
dzinowy
republic (ry'pablyk) s. republika; rzeczpospolita
republican (ry'pablyken) adj.
republikański; s. republikanin
repugnance (ry'pagnens) s. odraza; niechęć; niezgodność;
sprzeczność
repugnant (ry'pagnent) adj.
odrażający; oporny; sprzeczny;
niezgodny
repulse (ry'pals) v. odpierać;
odrzucać; odtrącać; s. odparcie; odrzucenie; odmowa
repulsive (ry'palsyw) adj. odrażający; wstrętny; odpychający;budzący odrazę
reputable ('repjutebl) adj.
szanowany; zaszczytny
reputation (,repju'tejszyn) s.
reputacja; sława; dobre imię
repute (ry'pju:t) s. reputacja;
sława; v. uważać za coś
request (ry'kłest) s. prosba;
życzenie; zadanie; zapotrzebowanie; v. prosić o pozwolenie;
upraszać ;poprosić o przysługę
require (ry'kłajer) v. żądać;
nakazywać;wymagać;być wymaganym

required (ry'kłajerd) adj.
obowiązkowy;wymagany;żądany
requirement (ry'kłajerment) s.
wymaganie; zadanie; potrzeba
requisite ('rekłyzyt) adj. wy-
magany; s. rzecz konieczna,
potrzebna; rekwizyt
requisition (,rekłyzyszyn) s.
zadanie; nakaz; zapotrzebowanie; v. wydawać zapotrzebowanie; zapotrzebowywać; rekwiro-
wać;zarzadać dostaw
requite (ry'kłajt) v. odwzajemniać się;wynagradzać;zemścić się
rescue ('reskju:) v. ratować;
wybawiać; odbijać z więzienia;
s. ratunek; odbicie z więzienia; odebranie przemocą
research (ry'se:rcz) s. poszukiwanie; badanie
researcher (ry'se:rczer) s. badacz (naukowy etc.);badaczka
resemblance (ry'zemblens) s.
podobieństwo
resemble (ry'zembl) v. być po-
dobnym (z wyglądu)
resent (ry'zent) v. czuć urazę
resentful (ry'zentful) adj.
urażony;obrażony;zawzięty
resentment (ry'zentment) s.
uraza;złość;oburzenie;obraza
reservation (,rezer'wejszyn) s.
zastrzeżenie; zarezerwowanie;
miejsce zarezerwowane; rezerwat (np. indiański); rezerwa;
zapas;ograniczenie
reserve (ry'ze:rw) v. odkładać;
zastrzegać; zarezerwować;
s. rezerwa; zapas; rezerwat;
zastrzeżenie; warunek
reserved (ry'ze:rwd) adj.zare-
zerwowany; powściągliwy; pełen rezerwy;z rezerwą;zastrzeżony
reservoir ('reserwła:r) s.
zbiornik; zbiór; pokład kopalniany; v. składać w zbiorniku
reside (ry'zajd) v. mieszkać;
tkwić;spoczywać w;osadzać się
residence ('rezydens) s. miejsce zamieszkania; pobyt (stały)
residence permit ('rezydens,-
per'myt) s. prawo pobytu

resident ('rezydent) s. stały
mieszkaniec; adj. zamieszkały;
umiejscowiony;zamieszkujący
residue ('rezydju:) s. reszta;
pozostałość;reszta spadkowa
resign (ry'zajn) v. zrzekać się;
wyrzekać się; godzić się z losem
resignation (,rezyg'nejszyn) s.
dymisja; zrzeczenie się; wyrzeczenie się;pogodzenie się(z losem)
resigned (ry'zajnd) adj. zrezyg-
nowany;w stanie spoczynku
resin ('rezyn) s. żywica; v. zaprawiać żywicą
resist (ry'zyst) v. opierać się;
stawiać opór; być odpornym;
powstrzymywać się
resistance (ry'zystens) s. opór;
sprzeciw; wytrzymałość; odporność; opornica;a.oporowy
resistant (ry'zystent) adj. odporny; opierający się; s. coś
lub ktoś odporny,opierający się
resolute ('rezelu:t)adj. rezolutny; śmiały; zdecydowany
resolution (,rese'lu:szyn) s.
uchwała; postanowienie; rezo-
lucja; śmiałość; rozłożenie;
rozwiązanie;rozkład(sił)
resolve (ry'zolw) s. postanowienie; decyzja; stanowczość;
v. rozkładać; rozwiązywać;
uchwalać; decydować; postanawiać; usuwać;przemieniać;skłaniać
resolved (ry'solwd) adj. zdecydowany; śmiały
resonance ('resnens) s. oddźwięk;
odgłos ; rezonans
resonant ('reznent) adj. rezonu-
jący; rozbrzmiewający
resort (ry'zo:rt) v. uciekać się;
uczęszczać; s. uzdrowisko;
uczęszczanie; ucieczka; ucieka-
nie się; ratunek; wyjście
resort to (ry'zo:rt,tu) v. uciekać się do...
resound (ry'zaund) v. rozbrzmiewać; odbijać; opiewać; obiegać;
wypowiadać się;odbijać się echem
resource (ry'so:rs) s. zasoby;
środki; bogactwa; zaradność;
pomysłowość;zasoby naturalne

resourceful (ry'so:rsful) adj.
zaradny; pomysłowy
respect (rys'pękt) v. szanować; dotyczyc; zważać;
s. wzgląd; szacunek; poważanie;związek;łacznosć;pozdrowienia)
respectable (rys'pektebl) adj.
chwalebny; godny szacunku;
poważny; pokaźny
respectful (rys'pektful) adj.
pełen szacunku
respectfully (rys'pektfuly)
adv. z poważaniem; z uszanowa-
niem
respecting (rys'pektyŋg) prep.
odnośnie do...
respective (rys'pektyw) adj.
odpowiedni;poszczególny
respectively (rys'pektywly)
adv. odpowiednio; każdemu
z osobna;kolejno
respiration (,respy'rejszyn)
s. oddech; oddychanie
respite ('respajt) s. wytchnienie (krótkie); odroczenie;
v. odraczać (stracenie); przynosić (krótką) ulgę
resplendent (rys'plendent) adj.
błyszczący silnie;jasny
respond (rys'pond) v. odpowiadać; reagować; byc czułym
respondent (rys'pondent) adj.
odpowiadający; wrażliwy;
s. pozwany; obrońca
response (rys'pons) s. odpowiedź; odzew; reakcja; oddźwięk;odezwanie się
responsibility (rys,ponse'bylyty) s. odpowiedzialność
responsible (rys'ponsebl) adj.
odpowiedzialny (wobec; przed)
rest (rest) s. odpoczynek;
spokój; przerwa; przestanek;
podpórka; pomieszczenie;
schronienie; reszta; v. spo-
czywać; odpoczywać; dawać odpoczynek; uspokoić; byc spo-
kojnym; podpierać się; polegać
restaurant ('resterent) s. restauracja ;jadłodajnia
restful ('restful) adj. spokojny; uspokajający;wypoczęty

restless ('restlys) adj. niespokojny; bezsenny;niesforny
restlessness ('restlysnys) s.
niepokój;zniecierpliwienie
restoration (,reste'rejszyn) s.
odnowienie; rekonstrukcja; restytucja; odtworzenie
restore (rys'to:r) v. przywracać; uleczyć; odnawiać; restau-
rowac; restytuować; zwracać;
rekonstruować; odtwarzać
restrain (rys'trejn) v. powstrzymywać; powsciągać; krępować;
ograniczać;trzymać w ryzach
restraint (rys'trejnt) s. skre-
powanie; uwięzienie; zamknięcie w szpitalu psychiatrycznym;
wstrzemięźliwosć; umiar
restrict (rys'trykt) v. ograniczać do; zamykać w (granicach)
restriction (rys'trykszyn) s.
ograniczenie
rest room('rest,rum) s. ustęp;
toaleta
result (ry'zalt) s. rezultat;
wynik; v. wynikać; dawać w wyniku;wypływać;pochodzić
result in (ry'zalt,yn) v. kon-
czyć się na
resultant (ry'zaltent) adj. wy-
nikający;(np. siła) wypadkowa
resume (ry'zju:m) v. wznawiać;
ponownie podejmować; obejmować;
zajmować; odzyskiwać; ciągnąć
dalej; streszczać;odzyskać
resumption (ry'zampszyn) s.
wznowienie; odzyskanie; podjęcie
na nowo;powrót do czegos
resurrection (,reze'rekszyn) s.
odżycie; zmartwychwstanie;
wskrzeszenie;wznowienie(zwyczaju)
retail ('ri:tejl) s. detal; adj.
detaliczny; v. sprzedawać de-
talicznie; szczegółowo opowiadać;adv.detalicznie;a.detaliczny
retailer (ri:'tejler) s. sklepikarz; detalista; plotkarz
retain (ry'tejn) v. zatrzymywać;
zapamiętywać; zgodzić (do pracy);zachowywać(tradycje)
retaliate (ry'taeliejt) v. od-
wzajemniac się; brać odwet

retaliation (ry,taely'ejszyn)
s. odwet;zemsta;odpłata

retell ('ri:'tel) v. ponownie
opowiedziec;powtorzyc

retention (ry'tenszyn) s. zatrzymanie (np. moczu); zdol-
nosc zatrzymywania; pamięc

retinue ('retynu:) s. orszak;
swita;czeladz;poczet(dostojnika)

retire (ry'tajer) v. wycofywac
(się); isc na spoczynek;
pensjonowac;s.sygnał odwrotu

retired (ry'tajerd) adj. emery-
towany; ustronny;odosobniony

retirement (ry'tajerment) s.
przejscie w stan spoczynku;
ustronie; odosobnienie; wy-
cofanie(weksla);odwrot

retort (ry'to:rt) v. odpłacac
się; odcinac się; odparowac;
ripostowac; s. retorta; ri-
posta; odwet; odwrocenie
(oskarżenia) ; cięta odpowiedz

retrace (ry'trejs) v. odtwo-
rzyc; przypomniec sobie; badac początek               (1)

retrace (ry:'trejs) v. ponownie liniowac; kopiowac (2)

retract (ry'traekt) v. cofnąc
się; odwołac; chowac się;
wciagac(się)(pazury)

retreat (ry'tri:t) v. cofac
się; s. odwrot; wycofanie się
w zacisze; kryjowka; odosobnienie; przytułek ;ustronie

retribution (,retry'bju:szyn)
s. odpłata; kara; nagroda

retrieve (ry'tri:w) v. odzyskac; powetowac; odszukac; uratowac; uprzytomnic sobie;
aportowac; s. odzyskanie; od-
szukanie; powetowanie; urato-
wanie ;ruch wsteczny(powrotny)

retrospect ('retrespekt) s.
spojrzenie wstecz; rozważanie
przeszłosci; v. rzucac okiem
wstecz; nawiązywac do (przeszłosci);patrzyc w przeszłosc

retrospective('retrespektyw)
adj. retrospektywny; działający wstecz;z mocą retroaktywną

return (ry'te:rn) v. wracac;
przynosic dochod;złożyc(zezna-nie);

obracac w..; oddawac; odwzajem-
nic; odpowiedziec; wybrac;
s. powrot; nawrot; dochod;
zysk; zwrot; rewanż; sprawozdanie (np podatkowe)

return flight (ry'te:rn,flajt)
s. lot powrotny

return ticket (ry'te:rn,tykyt)
s. powrotny bilet

reunification ('ri:ju:nyfy'kejszyn) s. ponowne zjednoczenie

reunion ('ri:'ju:njen) s. zjazd;
ponowne połączenie; zebranie

revaluation (ri:'waelju'ejszyn)
s. ponowna ocena; przewartoscio-
wanie(po ponownej ocenie)

revaluate (ri:'waelju':ejt)v.
ponownie ocenic; przewartoscio-
wac(dom w celach podatkowych)

revamp (ry:'waemp) v. przera-
biac; reorganizowac; rewidowac;
okapowac (buty) ;odnowic

reveal (ry'wi:1) v. ujawniac;
objawiac; odsłaniac; s. rama
okna w karoserii

revel ('rewl) s. zabawa; hulanka; v. hulac; używac sobie

revelation (,rewy'lejszyn) s.
ujawnienie; objawienie; odsłonięcie; rewelacja ;odkrycie

revenge (ry'wendż) s. zemsta;
msciwosc; v. pomscic; zemscic
się(za zniewage,krzywde etc.)

revengeful (ry'wendżful) adj.
msciwy

revenue ('rewy,nu:) s. dochod
(z podatkow)

revenue office ('rewy,nu:'ofys)
s. urząd podatkowy (finansowy)

revere (ry'wier) v. czcic;
odnosic się z czcią

reverence ('rewerens) s. czesc;
szacunek; wielebnosc

reverend ('rewerend) adj. czcigodny; wielebny; s. duchowny

reverse (ry'we:rs) s. odwrot-
nosc; rewers; tył; niepowodzenie; wsteczny bieg; adj. odwrotny; przeciwny; wsteczny;
v. odwracac; zmieniac kierunek; obalac (np. przepis)

reverse gear (ry'we:rs,gier) s.
wsteczny bieg(w samochodzie)

reverse side (ry'we:rs,sajd)
s. odwrotna strona
review (ry'wju:) v. przeglądać; pisać recenzje; przeglądać w myśli; dokonywać przeglądu; s. recenzja; przegląd; rewia;ponowny przegląd
reviewer (ry'wju:er) s. recenzent; krytyk
revile (ry'wajl) v. wyzywać; wymyślać; przezywać
revise (ry'wajz) v. przejrzeć; zrewidować; przerabiać
revision (ry'wyżyn) s. rewizja; przejrzane wydanie; przeróbka
revival (ry'wajwel) s. ożywienie; odżywanie; powrót do życia;powrót do stanu użyteczności
revive (ry'wajw) v. wskrzeszać; przywracać do życia; wznawiać; ożywiać; odżywać; wracać do przytomności
revolt (ry'woult) s. bunt; powstanie; v. buntować się; wzdrygać się; mieć odrazę; budzić odrazę
revolution (,rewe'lu:szyn) s. obrót; rewolucja
revolutionary (,rewe'lu:sznry) adj. rewolucyjny; s. rewolucjonista
revolutionist (,rewe'lu:szynyst) s. rewolucjonista
revolutionize (,rewe'lu:szn,ajz) v. zrewolucjonizować; wywoływać rewolucje
revolve (ry'wolw) v. obracać; krążyć; obracać się; obmyślać
revolving (ry'wolwyng) adj. obrotowy
reward (ry'Xo:rd) s. nagroda; wynagrodzenie; v. wynagradzać
rheumatism ('ru:metyzem) s. reumatyzm; gościec stawowy
rhubarb ('ru:ba:rb) s. rabarbar; (slang):kłótnia
rhyme (rajm) s. rym; rymować się
rhythm ('rytm) s. rytm
rhythmic ('rytmyk) adj. rytmiczny; miarowy
rib (ryb) s. żebro; żeberko; wręga; v. żeberkować; nabierać; wyśmiewać;droczyć się;płytko orać
ribbed(rybd)adj.żebrowany

ribbon ('ryben) s. taśma; pasek; strzęp; wstążka; v. drzeć na strzępy, paski; ozdabiać wstążką;wić się wstęgą
rice (rajs) s. ryż
rich (rycz) adj. bogaty; kosztowny; suty; obfity; tuczący; pożywny; soczysty; mocny (zapach); pełny; tłusty (np. pokarm); pocieszny (zdarzenie)
riches ('ryczyz) pl. bogactwo; bogactwa
richness ('rycznys) s. bogactwo; pełnia
rick (ryk) s. stóg; v. ustawiać w stogi; stawiać stóg
rickets ('rykyts) s. choroba angielska; krzywica; rachityzm
rickety ('rykyty) adj. chwiejny; koślawy; rachityczny
rid (ryd; rid; ridded (ryd; ryd; 'rydyd)
rid (ryd) v. uwalniać się od...; oczyszczać się; pozbywać się
ridden ('rydn) zob. v. ride
riddle ('rydl) s. zagadka; v. zadawać zagadki; mówić zagadkami; rozwiązywać zagadki
ride; rode; ridden (rajd; roud; 'rydn)
ride (rajd) v. pojechać; jechać (też statkiem); jeździć; tyranizować; wozić; nosić; dokuczać; s. przejażdżka; jazda; nabieranie (kogoś); droga
rider ('rajder) s. jeździec; dżokej; dodatek; poprawka; klauzula; ciężarek przesuwany; nasadka;poprawka na dokumencie
ridge (rydż) s. grzbiet (też góry); krawędź; kalenica; pasmo górskie; wał; skiba; grobla; v. pokrywać skibami; robić krawędzie; marszczyć
ridicule ('rydy,kju:l) v. wyśmiewać się; s. kpiny
ridiculous (ry'dykju:les) adj. śmieszny; bezsensowny
riding ('rajdyng) s. konna jazda; adj. jadący;do konnej jazdy
rifle (rajfl) s. karabin; gwintówka; gwint;strzelec; v.gwintować (lufę); strzelać;ograbić; okraść; pokrzyżować

rift (ryft) s. szczelina; różnica zdań; v. rozszczepiać się ;pęknąć;popękać
rig (ryg) v. zaopatrywać; klecić; montować; stroić; robić kanty; manipulować ceny; s. sprzęt (wiertniczy); wóz z koniem; kostium; machlojka
right (rajt) adj. prawa; prawy; poprawny; prawoskrętny; prosty (też kąt); właściwy; słuszny; dobry; odpowiedni; prawidłowy; w porządku; zdrowy; adv. w prawo; na prawo; prosto; bezpośrednio; bezzwłocznie: dokładnie; słusznie; dobrze; s. prawa strona; prawo; dobro; słuszność; sprawiedliwość; pierwszeństwo; v. naprostować; naprawić; sprostować; odpłacać; mścić; usprawiedliwiać
right ahead ('rajt,e'hed) exp. wprost ;na wprost;przed siebie
right away ('rajt,e'łej) exp. zaraz ;natychmiast;już teraz
righteous ('rajtszes) adj. sprawiedliwy; prawy ;słuszny
rightful ('rajtful) adj. słuszny; sprawiedliwy; prawowity; należny z prawa;prawy
right-hand ('rajt,haend) adj. praworęki; położony na prawo
right-handed ('rajt-'haendyd) adj. praworęczny; dostosowany do prawej ręki; idący wg.ruchu zegara; obracający się w prawo (gwint etc.)
right of way ('rajt,ow'łej) exp.; prawo pierwszeństwa na drodze; prawo przejazdu; grunt pod drogą (kolej)(pod szosą etc.)
rightist ('rajtyst) s. prawicowiec; adj. prawicowy
rightly ('rajtly) adv. sprawiedliwie; słusznie; poprawnie; właściwie;na miejscu
rigid ('rydżyd) adj. sztywny; nieugięty; surowy;nieustępliwy
rigor ('ryger) s. rygor; surowość; zesztywnienie
rigorous ('rygeres) adj. surowy; rygorystyczny

rim (rym) s. brzeg; krawędź; obręcz; powierzchnia wody (przy żeglowaniu); v. robić krawędź; posuwać wzdłuż krawędzi;dawać oprawę(do okularów)
rimple ('rympl) v. marszczyć
rind (rajnd) s. kora; łupina; skórka; v. zdzierać korę
ring (ryng) s. pierścień; obrączka; kółko; koło; zmowa; szajka; słój; arena; ring (bokserski); v. otaczać; kołować; krajać w kółko
ring; rang; rung (ryng; raeng; rang)
ring (ryng) v. dzwonić; dźwięczeć; brzmieć; rozbrzmiewać; wydzwaniać; telefonować; wybijać czas na zegarze kontrolnym; sprawdzać monetę dźwiękiem; s. dzwonek; dzwony; dźwięk; brzęk; telefonowanie
ring off ('ryng,of) v. skończyć rozmowę telefoniczną
ring the bell ('ryng,dy'bel) v. dzwonić (do drzwi etc.)
ring up ('ryng,ap) v. wybijać kwotę (na kasie rejestracyjnej);zatelefonować(do kogoś)
ringleader ('ryng,li:der) s. prowodyr; herszt
rink (rynk) s. ślizgawka; tor jazdy na wrotkach; boisko do gry w kule
rinse (ryns) v. płukać; s. wypłukanie
rinse out ('ryns,aut) v. wypłukać ;przepłukiwać
riot ('rajot) s. zgiełk; zamęt; rozruchy; bunty; rozpusta; hulanka; rozprężenie; orgia; v. buntować się; robić rozruchy, zamieszki; hulać; używać sobie;uprawiać rozpustę
riotous ('rajetes) adj. buntowniczy; rozpustny; hulaszczy; hałaśliwy; bujny;oporny;niesforny
rip (ryp) v. odrywać; zrywać; łupać; rozpruwać; piłować wzdłuż; pękać; pędzić; s. rozprucie; rozpustnik; hulaka; szkapa; rzecz nie warta nic; wir;wzburzona powierzchnia wody

ripe (rajp) adj. dojrzały
ripen ('rajpn) v. dojrzewac;
przyspieszac dojrzewanie
ripeness ('rajpnys) s. dojrza-
łosc
ripple ('rypl) s. zmarszczki
(na wodzie); fale (na włosach);
falowanie; grzebien do lnu;
v. marszczyc; falowac; roz-
czesywac; rozwodzic się
rise; rose; risen (rajz; rouz;
'ryzn)
rise (rajz) v. podniesc się;
stanąc; wstawac; powstawac;
buntowac się; wzbierac; wzbijac się; wzmagac się; spros-
tac; s. wschod; wznoszenie
się; podwyżka; wzrost; powodzenie; początek; stopien
risen ('ryzn) v. zob. rise
riser (rajzer) s. osoba wstają-
ca; pionowy przewod (też rura);
podstawka stopnia (na schodach)
rising ('rajzyng) s. wzniesienie; powstanie; zmartwychwstanie; bąbel; pryszcz; zaczyna-
nie ciasta; adj. podnoszący
się; wzrastający; wschodzący
risk (rysk) s. ryzyko ; niebezpieczenstwo; v. narazac się;
ryzykowac; ponosic ryzyko
risky ('rysky) adj. niebezpieczny; ryzykowny; pikantny; drastyczny
rite (rajt) s. obrządek; obrzęd
(slubny); rytuał
rival ('rajwel) s. rywal; wspoł-
zawodnik; v. rywalizowac
rivalry ('rajwelry) s. rywalizacja; wspołzawodnictwo
river ('rywer) s. rzeka
riverboat ('rywer, bout) s. statek rzeczny; łodz rzeczna
riverside ('rywer, sajd) s.
brzeg rzeki
rivet ('rywyt) s. nit; v. nito-
wac; utkwic; przykuc
rivulet ('rywjulyt) s. rzeczuł-
ka; mały strumien; mały potok
road (roud) s. droga; kolej;
reda; v. topic
road hog ('roud, hog) s. pirat
drogowy (lekcewazący przepisy)

road map ('roud, maep) s, mapa
drogowa; mapa samochodowa
roadside ('roud, sajd) s. bok
drogi; adj. przydrozny
roadsign ('roud, sajn) s. znak
drogowy
roam (roum) v. włoczyc się;
s. włoczęga; wędrowka
roar (ro:r) v. ryczec; huczec;
s. ryk; huk(armat); ryk(smiechu)
roars of laughter ('ro:rs, ow-
'lafter) exp. wybuchy smiechu
roast (roust) v. piec; opiekac;
przypiekac; wypalac; osmieszac;
krytykowac ostro; s. pieczen;
pieczenie; kpiny; krytyka
ostra; adj. pieczony
roast beef ('roust, bi:f) s.
pieczen wołowa
roast meat ('roust, mi:t) s.
pieczone mięso
rob (rob) v. grabic; rabowac;
ograbic; pozbawiac (czegos)
robber ('rober) s. rabus
robbery ('robery) s. rabunek
robe (roub) s. podomka; suknia;
szata; płaszcz kąpielowy; toga; v. przyodziewac; przyoblekac
robin ('robyn) s. drozd; rudzik
robot ('roubot) s. robot
robust ('roubast) adj. krzepki;
trzezwy; szorstki; hałasliwy;
ciężki; silny; mocny
rock (rok) s. kamien; skała;
forsa; kołysanie; taniec
(rock and roll); pl. kostki
lodu w napoju; v. kołysac się;
bujac się; hustac się; wstrząsac; wypłukiwac piasek; płuka-
kac (się); a. kamienny; skalisty
rocker ('roker) s. biegun; łyżwa holenderka
rocket ('rokyt) s. rakieta;
v. wznosic się
rocket power ('rokyt'pałer) s.
napęd rakietowy
rocketry ('rokytry) s. bron
rakietowa; technika rakietowa
rocking chair ('rokyng, czeer)
s. krzesło na biegunach
rocky ('roky) adj. skalisty;
chwiejny; kamienisty; skalny

rod (rod) s. pręt; drąg; rózga; wędka; (pręt = 5.029 m)
rode (roud) v. zob. ride
rodent ('roudent) s. gryzoń
roe (rou) s. sarna; łania; ikra we wnętrzu ryby;sperma ryb
rogue (roug) s. łobuz; łajdak; psotnik; słoń samotnik
roguish ('rougysz) adj. psotny; figlarny; łobuzerski
role (roul) s. rola
roll (roul) s. rólka; zwój; zwitek; rulon; bułka; rożek; spis; wykaz; rejestr; lista; wokanda; wałek; walec; wałek; kołysanie (się); werbel; huk; toczyć; wałkować; tarzać; grzmieć; dudnić; rozlegać się; zataczać beczkę; toczyć koło; kręcić; obracać; wymawiać "r"; rozwałkowywać ;wałkować
roll up ('roul,ap) v. zawinąć (rękawy); kłębić się; podjeżdżać; skumulować (się)
roller ('rouler) s. wałek; rolka; kółko; długa tocząca się fala ;narzędzie do wałkowania
roller coaster ('rouler'kouster) s. kolejka wysokogórska; wesołe miasteczko
roller-skate ('rouler'skejt) s. wrotka
rolling mill ('roulyn,myl) s. walcownia
Roman ('roumen) adj. rzymski
romance (rou'maens) s. romans średniowieczny; powieść miłosna; sprawa miłosna; adj. romański; v. romansować; koloryzować; przesadzać;pisać romanse
romantic (rou'maentyk) adj. romantyczny; s. romantyk
romp (romp) s. urwis; zbytki; swawole; figle; igraszki; v. figlować; dokazywać; uganiać; łatwo wygrać (wyścigi)
rompers ('rompers) pl. kombinezon do zabawy dla dziecka
roof (ru:f) s. dach; v. pokrywać dachem
roof over ('ru:f,ouwer) v. pokrywać dachem

rook (ruk) s. gawron; szuler; wieża (w szachach); v. ograć; oszukać; zdzierać skórę
room (rum) s. pokój. miejsce; mieszkanie; izba; wolna przestrzeń; sposobność; powód; v. dzielić pokój lub mieszkanie;mieszkać lub odnajmować pokój
room-mate ('rum,mejt) s. współmieszkaniec; współlokator
roomy ('rumy) adj. przestronny; obszerny
roost (ru:st) s. grzęda; v. siedzieć na grzędzie
rooster (ru:ster) s. kogut
root (ru:t) s. korzeń; nasada; podstawa; istota; źródło; sedno; pierwiastek; v. posadzić; zakorzenić; ryć; szperać; wygrzebywać; popierać; dopingować
root out ('ru:t,aut) v. wykorzeniać; wyrywać z korzeniami
rope (roup) s. sznur; powróz; lina; stryczek; v. związać; przywiązać; łapać na lasso; ogradzać sznurami; ciągnąć na linie; przyciągać; zdobywać; obśliznąć
rope off ('roup,of) v. ogradzać linami
rose (rous) s. róża; kolor różowy; rozetka; v. zarożowić; zob. rise
rosy ('rouzy) adj. różowy
rot (rot) s. zgnilizna; rozkład; zepsucie; głupstwa; brednie; motylica; v. gnić; butwieć; rozkładać się
rotary ('routery) adj. rotacyjny; obrotowy
rotate ('routejt) v. obracać (się); kolejno zmieniać (się); wirować ;adj.kółkowy
rotation (rou'tejszyn) s. rotacja; ruch obrotowy; obracanie (się); płodozmian; ciągła wymiana; kolejne następstwo
rotor ('router) s. wirnik
rotten ('rotn) adj. zgniły; zepsuty; zdemoralizowany; lichy; kiepski; marny;chory na motylicę ;do niczego;do chrzanu

rotund (rou'tand) adj. okrągły; zaokraglony; szumny;
przysadkowaty

rough (raf) adj. szorstki; chropowaty; ostry; nierówny; wyboisty; nieokrzesany; brutalny;
drastyczny; cierpki; nieprzyjemny; nieociosany; surowy;
gruby; burzliwy; gwałtowny;
hałaśliwy; ciężki; pobieżny;
przybliżony; prymitywny;
wstępny; szkicowy; adv. ostro;
szostko; grubiańsko; z grubsza; s. nierówny teren; stan
naturalny - nieobrobiony;
hacel;huligan; v. być szorst-
kim; szorstko postępować;
hartować (się); jeżyć (się);
burzyc (się); szlifować z grubsza; pasować z grubsza; obrabiac z grubsza; szkicować;
przebiedować; ujeżdżać (konia);
robic coś z grubsza; podkuwać
hacelami

roughness ('rafnys) s. szorst-
kosć; grubiaństwo; chamstwo

rough-neck ('rafnek) s. członek
obsługi szybu; łobuz; brutal;
chuligan

round (raund) adj. okragły; za-
okrąglony; kolisty; okrężny;
tam i nazad; kulisty; sferyczny; adv. wkoło; kołem; dookoła; prep. dookoła; s. koło;
obwód; kula; obrót; krąg; bieg
cykl; ciąg; zasięg; seria;
objazd; obchód; runda; za-
okrąglenie; pasmo (np. trudności); przechadzka; v. zaokra-
glac; wygładzać; okrążyć; obchodzic; opływać

round off ('raund,of) v. za-
okraglac

round out ('raund,out) v. za-
okraglac się; tyc

round up ('round,ap) v. spędzac
(bydło)

round-up ('round'ap) s. spędza-
nie bydła

roundabout ('raundebaut) adj.
okrężny; s. rondo; karuzela

round trip ('raund,tryp) s. podroż
roz tam i nazad

rouse (rauz) v. pobudzić;
wzniecac; ruszyc; ożywiac;
podsycac; wyrywać; wypłoszyc;
obudzic się; otrzasnąc się

roustabout ('rauste,baut) s.
robotnik portowy; robotnik
przemysłu naftowego

route (ru:t) s. droga; trasa;
marsz; szlak

routine (ry:'ti:n) s. rutyna;
tok zajęc

rove (rouw) v. wałęsac się;
błądzic wzrokiem; łowic; skręcac włókno; s. niedoprzęd

rover ('rouwer) s. wędrowiec;
włóczęga; korsarz; pirat

row (roł) s. szereg; rząd;
jazda łodzią; v. wiosłować

row (rał) s. zgiełk; hałas;
kłótnia; bójka; burda; nagana;
bura; v. besztać; pokłocic się

row-boat ('roł,bout) s. łódz
wiosłowa

rower ('rołer) s. wioslarz

rowing boat ('rołyngbout) s.
łódz wiosłowa

royal ('rojel) adj. krolewski

royalty ('rojelty) s. krolew-
skosć; honorarium autorskie

rub (rab) v. trzec; potrzec;
wytrzec; wycierać; głaskać;
nacierac; s. tarcie; nacie-
ranie

rub down('rab,daln) v. nacierac;wcierac

rub in ('rab,yn) v. wcierać;
wytykac

rub off ('rab,of) v. zetrzec

rub out ('rab,aut) v. wymazac

rubber('raber) s. guma; masa-
żysta; pl. kalosze; v. pokrywac gumą; odwracac (głowę)

rubberneck ('raber,nek) s.
ciekawski; turysta; gapa

rubber plant ('raber,plaent)
s. kauczukowa roślina

rubbish ('rabysz) s. śmiec;
gruz; tandeta; nonsens; brednie; głupstwa; bzdury

rubble ('rabl) s. gruz; rumowisko skalne; kamień łamany

ruby ('ru:by) s. rubin

rucksack ('ruksaek)s. plecak

rudder ('rader) s. ster
ruddy ('rady) adj. rumiany;
czerstwy; czerwony; v. ru-
mienic się
rude (ru:d) adj. szorstki;
niegrzeczny; ostry; surowy;
prosty; pierwotny; nagły;
gwałtowny; krzepki
ruff (raf) s. kołnierz; kreza; batalion; bojownik; bicie atutem; v. przebic atutem
ruffian ('rafjen) s. zbój;
łotr
ruffle ('rafl) s. kreza; ża-
bot; mankiet koronkowy;
kłopot; zamieszanie; marsz-
czenie; v. marszczyc (po-
wierzchnię); rozwiewac; roz-
czochrac; nastroszyc; wzbu-
rzyc (się)
rug (rag) s. pled; kilim; dywan
rugby ('ragby) s. (sport) rugby
ruin ('ruyn) s. ruina; v. rujnowac (się); zniszczyc (się)
rule (ru:l) s. przepis; prawo;
reguła; zasada; rządy; panowanie; postanowienie; miarka;
linijka; v. rządzic; panowac;
kierowac; orzekac; postana-
wiac; liniowac
rule out ('ru:l,aut) v. wykluczac
ruler ('ru:ler) s. władca;
liniał; linijka
rum (ram) s. rum; adj. dziwny
rumble ('rambl) v. dudnic;
grzmiec; turkotac; s. huk;
grzmot; dudnienie; tylne
miejsce w pojeździe na bagaż
lub służącego
ruminant ('ru:mynent) adj.
przeżuwajacy; s. przeżuwacz
rummage ('ramydż) s. szperanie; przetrząsanie; wyprzedaż
resztek; v. grzebac; prze-
trząsac
rumor ('ru:mer) s. pogłoska;
słuchy; v. puszczac pogłoski
rump (ramp) s. zad; kuper;
comber; kadłub

rumple ('rampl) v. zmiąc; zmięto-
sic; mierzwic; czochrac
run; ran; ran (ran; raen; raen)
run (ran) v. biec; biegac; pędzic; spieszyc się; jechac; płynąc; kursowac; obracac się;
działac; funkcjonowac; pracowac;
uciekac; zbiec; prowadzic; toczyc się; wynosic (sumę); roz-
pływac się; łzawic; głosic;
spotykac; narzucac się; molestowac; zderzyc się; sprzeciwiac
się; wpasc etc.; s. bieg; przebieg; bieganie; rozbieg; rozpęd;
przebieg; passa; sekwens; okres;
seria; ciąg; dostęp; wybieg;
pastwisko; zjazd; tor
run about ('ran,e'baut) v. biegac tu i tam; s. wędrowiec;
adj. wędrowny
run across ('ran,e'kros) v. spot-
kac przypadkowo
run after ('ran,aefter) v. gonic
run away ('ran,e'łej) v. uciekac;
poniesc
run down ('ran,dałn) v. przeje-
chac; wyczerpac; wytropic
run in ('ran,yn) v. wpasc na...;
dotrzec
run off ('ran,of) v. uciekac;
recytowac; drukowac
run out ('ran,aut) v. skończyc
się; wygasnąc; wydrukowac
run over ('ran,ouwer) v. przeje-
chac; przepełniac
run up ('ran,ap) v. dobiec; dojsc
do..; dodac; wysrubowac; s. dochodzenie do celu
rung (rąg) s. poprzeczka; szczebel; szprycha; v. zob. ring
runner ('raner) s. goniec; biegacz; posłaniec; wozny; akwizytor; łopatka; obsługujący maszynę; chodnik; przemytnik; płoza;
za; łożysko slizgowe; wałek
running ('ranyng) adj. bieżący;
biegający; będacy w biegu; cieknący; ropiejący; w ruchu; ruchomy; ciągły; nieustanny; pochyły;
nieprzerwany; s. bieg; wyscig;
kandydowanie; funkcjonowanie;
ropienie; kierownictwo

running board ('ranyng,bo:rd)
s. stopien; pomost
runway ('ran,łej) s. bieżnia
(do łądowania); tor (jezdny)
rupture ('rapczer) s. złamanie;
zerwanie; przepuklina; v.
przerywac; zrywac; poderwac
się (miec przepuklinę)
rural ('ruerel) adj. wiejski
ruse (ru:z) s. podstęp
rush (rasz) v. pędzic; poganiac; ponaglac; rzucac się na
cos; przeskakiwac; wysyłac
pospiesznie; zdobywac szturmem; zdzierac (pieniądze);
słac sitowiem; s. pęd; ruch;
pospiech; napływ; atak; intensywny popyt; sitowie
rush hour ('rasz,auer) s. godzina szczytu; chwila uderze-
nia
Russian ('raszyn) adj. rosyjski ;s.Rosjanin
rust (rast) s. rdza (zbożowa)
v. rdzewiec;niszczyc się
rust-eaten ('rast.i:tn) adj.
zardzewiały
rustic ('rastik) adj. wiejski;
prostacki; s. wiesniak; prostak
rustle ('rasl) v. szelescic;
krasc bydło; krzątac się;
s. szelest
rusty ('rasty) adj. zardzewiały; zaniedbany; wyszły z wprawy ;podniszczony
rut (rat) s. koleina; bruzda;
utarty szlak; rutyna; nawyk;
rowek; wyżłobienie; ruja;
-bekowisko; rykowisko
ruthless ('ru:tlys) adj. bezlitosny; bezwzględny; niemiłosierny
rutted ('ratyd) adj. rozjeżdzo-
ny; wyjeżdżony
rutty ('raty) adj. wyjeżdżony
rye (raj) s. żyto; żytniówka
rye whisky (raj,hisky)
szkocka żytnia wódka
s (es) dziewiętnasta litera
alfabetu angielskiego
's skrót: is, has, us

saber ('seiber) s. szabla; pałasz; v. ciąc; ranic; scinac
sable ('sejbl) s. soból; czern;
adj. czarny;sobolowy(z futer)
sabotage ('saebeta:ż) s. sabo-
taż; v. sabotowac
sabre ('sejber) s. szabla; zob.
saber
saccharin ('saekeryn ) s. sacharyna
sack (saek) s. worek; torebka;
sak; luzny płaszcz; plądrowa-
nie; v. pakowac do workow;
zwalniac z pracy; plądrowac
sacrament ('saekrement) s. sakrament
sacred ('sejkryd) adj. poswięco-
ny; nienaruszalny
sacrifice ('saekryfajs) s. ofiara; wyrzeczenie (się); v. ofia-
rowywac; poswięcac; wyrzekac
się w zamian za cos innego
sacrilegious (,saekry'lydżes)
adj. swiętokradzki
sad (saed) adj. smutny; bolesny;
posępny; ponury; okropny
sadden ('saedn) v. zasmucac (się);
posmutniec
saddle ('saedl) s. siodło;
v. siodłac; obarczac; wkładac
ciężar (komus)(na kogos)
sadness ('saednys) s. smutek
safe (sejf) adj. pewny; bezpieczny; s. schowek bankowy;
kasa pancerna; spiżarnia
wietrzona; (slang):kondon
safeguard ('seifga:rd) v. ochraniac; zabezpieczac; gwarantowac;
s. zabezpieczenie; gwarancja
safety ('sejfty) s. bezpieczenstwo; zabezpieczenie; bezpiecznik ; adj.dajacy bezpieczenstwo
safety belt ('sejfty,belt) s.
pas bezpieczenstwa (np. w samochodzie)
safety lock ('sejfty,lok) s. zamek bezpieczenstwa
safety pin ('sejfty,pyn) s.
agrafka
safety razor ('sejfty,rejzer) s.
maszynka do golenia się żyletka-
mi (które się wymienia po zużyciu)

safety-valve ('sejfty,waelw)
s. klapa bezpieczeństwa; zawór bezpieczeństwa
sag (saeg) v. obwisać; zwisać;
wyginać (się); przechylać się;
spadać w cenie; s. zwis; wygięcie; spadek (ceny)
sagacity (se'gaesyty) s. rozwaga; mądrość; roztropność;
bystrość
said (sed) v. zob. say
sail (sejl) s. żagiel; podróż
morska; żaglować; kroczyć okazale; sterować okrętem; bawić się modelem statku
sail-boat ('sejl,bout) s. żag-
lówka
sailing-ship('sejlyng,szyp) s.
statek żaglowy
sailor ('sejlor) s. żeglarz;
marynarz
saint (sejnt) s. & adj. święty
sake (sejk) s. czyjeś dobro;
wzgląd
salad ('saeled) s. sałata
salary ('saelery) s. pensja;
pobory; wynagrodzenie
sale (sejl) s. sprzedaż; wyprzedaż
saleslady ('sejls'lejdy) s.
sprzedawczyni
salesman ('sejlsmen) s. sprzedawca
salesmanager (,sejls'maenydżer)
s. kierownik działu sprzedaży
saliva (se'lajwa) s. ślina
sallow ('saelou) adj. ziemisty;
blady; żółtawy; v. dawać żółtawy odcień; s. iwa (wierzba)
sally ('saely) s. wypad; wycieczka z oblężenia; docinek
(cięty)
sally out ('saely,aut) v. wy-
ruszać w podróż
salmon ('saemen) s. łosoś; adj.
łososiowy; łososiowego koloru
saloon (se'lu:n) s. bar; szynk;
sala (zabaw); salon (na okrę-
cie)
salt (so:lt) s. sól; adj; słony; v. solić
saltcellar ('so:lt,seler) s.
solniczka

salt-free ('so:lt,fri:) adj.
bezsolny; pozbawiony soli
salty ('so:lty) adj. słony
salutation (,saelju:'tejszyn)
s. pozdrowienie; przywitanie
salute (se'lu:t) s. pozdrowienie; salutowanie; honory wojskowe; salwa (powitalna);
v. pozdrowić; powitać; salutować; odbierać defiladę; przejść
przed kompanią honorową
salvation (sael'wejszyn) s.
zbawienie; ratunek; wybawienie
salve (sa:w) v. natrzeć; złagodzić; uspokoić; s. maść; balsam
same (sejm) adj. ten sam; taki
sam; jednostajny; monotonny;
adv. tak samo; identycznie;
bez zmiany; pron. to samo
sample ('sa:mpl) s. próbka;
wzór; v. próbować; dawać próbki
sanatorium (,saene'to:rjem) s.
sanatorium
sanctify ('saenkty,faj) v.
uświęcać; poświęcać
sanction ('saenkszyn) v.
usankcjonować; s. sankcja
sanctuary ('saenkczuery) s.
przybytek; azyl
sand (saend) s. piasek; v. posypywać piaskiem; obrabiać papie-
rem ściernym
sandal ('saendl) s. sandał; rzemyk; v. wkładać sandały; przywiązywać rzemykiem
sandwich ('saendłycz) s. kanapka;
sandwicz; v. wkładać (między)
sandy ('saendy) adj. piaskowy;
piaskowego koloru
sandy beach ('saendy,bi:ch) s.
plaża
sane (sejn) adj. zdrowy na umysle; rozsądny; normalny
sang (saeng) v. zob. sing
sanitarium (,saeny'teerjem) s.
sanatorium
sanitary ('saenytery) adj. hi-
gieniczny; zdrowy
sanitary napkin ('saenytery
'naepkyn) s. podpaska higie-
niczna

sanitation (,saeny'tejszyn) s.
higiena; kanalizacja; urządzenia sanitarne
sank (saeŋk) v. zob. sink
Santa Claus (,saenta'klo:z)
s. Dziadek Mróz; Święty Miko-
łaj
sap (saep) s. żywica; sok; głupiec; kujon; nudziarstwo; sa-
pa; podkopywanie; v. wyciągać
soki; usuwać biel z drzewa;
podkopywać; podmywać; kopać
sapę
sappy ('saepy) s. soczysty; pełen wigoru; energiczny
sarcasm ('sa:rkaezem) s. sar-
kazm
sardine (sa:r'di:n) s. sardynka
sash (saesz) s. szarfa; rama
okienna do pionowego suwania
okien; v. instalować ramy
okienne
sash window ('saesh'łyndou) s.
suwane okno
sat (saet) v. zob. sit
Satan ('sejtn) s. szatan
satchel ('saeczel) s. torba
z rzemieniami na plecy
satellite ('saete,lajt) s. satelita
satin ('saetyn) s. atlas; adj.
atlasowy; v. satynować (papier)
satire ('saetajer) s. satyra
satirize ('saety,rajz) v. wykpiwać; wyśmiewać; satyryzo-
wać
satisfaction (,saetys'faekszyn)
s. zadowolenie; satysfakcja;
spłacenie długu ;zaspokojenie
satisfactory (,saetys'faektery)
adj. zadawalający; odpowiedni
satisfy ('saetys,faj) v. zaspokoić; uiścić; spełnić; zadowalać; odpowiadać; przekonywać
Saturday ('saeterdy) s. sobota
sauce (so:s) s. sos; kompot;
v. przyprawiać jedzenie; na-
gadać komuś ;stawiać się
saucebox ('so:s,boks) s. impertynent ;zuchwalec
saucepan ('so:spen) s. patelnia; rondel

saucer ('so:ser) s. spodek
saunter ('so: nter) s. przechadzka; przechadzać się; chodzić
powolnym krokiem
sausage ('sosydż) s. kiełbasa
save (sejw) v. ratować; oszczędzać; zachowywać pozory; zbawiać;
uniknąć; zyskiwać (czas); prep.
oprócz; wyjąwszy; poza; pominąwszy; conj. że; poza tym;
chyba że; z wyjątkiem
save for a car ('sejw,fo:r'ej-
,ca:r) exp.; oszczędzać na samochód
saver ('sejwer) s. osoba oszczę-
dzająca; przedmiot oszczędzający
(np, czas)
saving ('sejwyŋg) adj. zbawienny;
oszczędny; prep. wyjąwszy
savings-bank ('sejwyŋz'baeŋk) s.
kasa oszczędności
savior ('sejwjer) s. zbawca;
zbawiciel
savor ('sejwer) s. smak; aromat;
powab; v. mieć smak; pachnieć;
smakować; nadawać smak
savory ('sejwery) adj. smaczny;
apetyczny; smakowity; pikantny;
aromatyczny
saw; sawed; sawn (so:; so:d;
so:n)
saw (so:) v. zob. see; piłować;
s. piła
sawdust ('so:,dast) s. trociny
sawmill ('so:,myl) s. tartak
Saxon ('saeksn) adj. saksoński;
saski ; s. Sas
say; said; said (sej; sed; sed)
v. mówić; powiedzieć; odprawiać; twierdzić
sayso ('sejso) s. rozkaz; powiedzenie; ostatnie słowo
saying ('sejyŋg) s. powiedzonko;
powiedzenie
scab (skaeb) s. strup; parch;
świerzb; łamistrajk
scaffold ('skaefeld) s. rusztowanie; platforma; estrada; szafot; v. stawiać rusztowanie
scaffolding ('skaefeldyŋg) s.
rusztowanie
scald (sko:ld) v. oparzyć; wy-
parzyć; pasteryzować; s. opa-
rzenie

scale (skejl) s. skala; podziałka; układ; drabina;
szalka; łuska; kamień nazębny;
v. wyłazić; wdzierać się;
mierzyć (podziałką); ważyć;
łuszczyć; łuskać; złuszczać
się
scale down ('skejl,dałn) v.
zmniejszać (proporcjonalnie)
scale up ('skejl,ap) v. powiększać (proporcjonalnie)
scales ('skejls) pl. waga
scalp ('skaelp) s. skalp; skóra na głowie; v. oskalpować;
złośliwie krytykować
scan (skaen) v. badawczo przeglądać; skandować; mieć rytm
scandal ('skaendl) s. skandal;
zgorszenie; oszczerstwo;
plotki
scandalous ('skaendeles) adj.
skandaliczny; gorszący;
oszczerczy
Scandinavian (,skaendy'nejw-
jan) adj. skandynawski
scant (skaent) adj. skąpy;
ograniczony; ledwo wystarczający; niedostateczny
scapegoat ('skejp,gout) s. kozioł ofiarny
scar (ska:r) s. blizna; szrama;
wyrwa; urwisko; v. pokieresz-
wać (się); zabliźniać się
scar over ('ska:r,ouwer) v.
zabliźnić
scarce (skeers) adj. rzadki;
niewystarczający
scarcely ('skeersly) adv. zaledwie; ledwo; z trudem;
z trudnością
scarcity ('skeersyty) s. niedostatek; niedobór; brak
scare (skeer) s. popłoch; panika; strach; v. nastraszyć;
przestraszyć; siać popłoch
scare away ('skeere,łej) v.
odstraszać
scarecrow ('skeer,krou)s.
straszydło; strach na wróble
scarf (ska:rf) s. szalik;
chustka na szyję; szarfa
scarfs (ska:rfs) pl. styk;
złącza

scarlet ('ska:rlyt) s. szkarłat;
adj. szkarłatny
scarlet fever ('ska:rlyt,fi:wer)
s. szkarlatyna ; płonica
scarp (ska:rp) s. skarpa; urwisko
scarred (ska:rd) adj. poznaczo-
ny bliznami; poszarpany
scarves (ska:rwz) pl. zob.scarf;
chusty na szyję; szarfy etc.
scathing ('skejzyng) adj. kostyczny; zjadliwy; niszczący
scatter ('skaeter) v. rozpraszać (się); rozsypywać; roz-
rzucać; rozwiewać; posypywać;
rozpierzchnąć (się)
scavenge ('skaewyndż) v. czys-
cić; oczyszczać; wyrzucać spa-
liny; być zamiataczem ulic
scene (si:n) s. scena; miejsce
zdarzeń; widowisko; widok; obraz; awantura publiczna
scenery (si:nery) s. widok;
krajobraz; dekoracje sceniczne
scent (sent) v. węszyc; wiet-
rzyć; wydawać zapach; s. zapach; nos (węch); perfumy
sceptic ('skeptyk) s. sceptyk;
adj. sceptyczny ;powątpiewający
sceptical ('skeptykel) adj.
sceptyczny;powątpiewający we wszystko
schedule ('skedżul) s. rozkład
jazdy; wykaz; zestawienie; tabela; taryfa; harmonogram; lista; plan; v. planować; wciagac
na listę ;naznaczać wg. planu
scheme (ski:m) s. intryga; podstęp; plan
scholar ('skoler) s. uczony;
stypendysta; uczeń ;student
scholarship ('skolerszyp) s.
poziom naukowy; stypendium;
erudycja ;systematyczna wiedza
school (sku:l) s. szkoła; katedra; nauka; ławica; adj. szkolny; v. szkolić; kształcić; nauczać; wyćwiczyć; tworzyć ła-
wicę;karcic; sprawdzać naukę
schoolboy ('sku:l,boj) s.
uczeń
schoolgirl ('sku:l,ge:rl) s.
uczennica

schooling ('sku:lyŋ) s. nauka;
szkolenie; wykształcenie
schoolmaster ('sku:l,ma:ster)
s. kierownik szkoły
schoolmate ('sku:l,mejt) s. kolega szkolny
school of driving ('sku:l,ow-
'drajwyŋg) s. nauka jazdy
(samochodem)
schooner ('sku:ner) s. skuner;
szklanka na piwo
science ('sajens) s. wiedza;
nauka; umiejętność
scientific ('sajentyfyk) adj.
naukowy; umiejętny
scientist ('sajentyst) s. uczony; przyrodnik; naukowiec
scissors ('syzez) s. nożyce;
nożyczki
scoff (skof) v. szydzić; kpić;
drwić; s. pośmiewisko; szyderstwo; kpiny; drwiny
scold (skould) v. besztać;
skrzyczeć; obrugać; łajać;
złorzeczyć; s. jędza; sekutnica; megiera
scone (skon) s. placek trójkątny z jęczmiennej mąki
scoop (sku:p) v. zaczerpnąć;
wygarnąć; wybrać; s. czerpak;
szufelka; chochla; kubeł; sensacyjna wiadomość
scooter ('sku:ter) s. skuter;
hulajnoga
scope (skoup) s. zasięg; zakres;
dziedzina; meta; sposobność;
możliwość
scorch (sko:rcz) v. spalić;
przypiekać; przypalać; dopie-
kać; wypłowieć; pędzić samochodem jak szalony; s. poparzenie
score (sko:r) v. zdobyć (punkt);
podkreślić; zanotować; zapisać;
wygrać; osiągnąć; strzelić
bramkę; s. ilość (zdobytych
punktów lub bramek); zacięcie;
rysa; znak; dwadzieścia
scorn (sko:rn) s. lekceważenie;
wzgarda; v. lekceważyć; gardzić; odrzucać z pogardą
scornful ('sko:rnful) adj. pogardliwy (i zagniewany); odrzuca-
jący z gniewem i pogardą

Scot (skot) adj. szkocki
Scotch (skocz) adj. szkocki
scot-free ('skot'fri:) adj.
cały; nietknięty; niezraniony;
gratis; bezpłatny
scoundrel ('skaundrel) s. kanalia; łotr
scour ('skauer) v. podmyć; szo-
rować; przepłukiwać; poszukiwać; grasować; przetrząsać;
s. podmycie; przemywanie;
przepłukiwanie
scout (skaut) s. harcerz; zwia-
dowca; v. iść na zwiady; robić
rekonesans
scoutmaster ('skaut,ma:ster)
s. harcmistrz
scowl (skaul) v. chmurzyć się;
patrzeć spode łba; groźnie;
patrzeć; s. zła mina; grozne
spojrzenie; krzywa mina
scramble ('skraembl) s. ubija-
nie się; gramolenie się; do-
bijanie się; robienie jajeczni-
cy; v. ubijać się; gramolić się;
dobijać się; robić jajecznicę
scrambled eggs ('skraembld,egs)
s. jajecznica
scrap (skraep) s. szmelc; odpadki; skrawki; wycinki; bójka; v. wyrzucać na szmelc; odrzucać; wycofać; bić się
scrape (skrejp) s. skrobanie;
tarapaty; szurnięcie; ciułanie;
draśnięcie; v. skrobać; drasnąć;
ciułać; szurnąć
scrape off ('skrejp,of) v. ze-
skrobać
scrape out ('skrejp,aut) v. wy-
skrobać
scrape together (skrejp,tu'gedzer) v. uciułać
scrap iron('skraep,ajern) s.
złom żelazny
scrappy ('skraepy) adj. niejednolity; bez związku; frag-
mentaryczny
scratch (skraecz) s. draśnięcie;
zadrapanie; rozdarcie; skrobanie; linia startu; adj. do pisania (np. brulion; brulionowy);
v. drapać (się); zadrasnąć;
gryzmolić; wydrapać; wykreślić

scream (skri:m) s. krzyk; pisk;
gwizd; kawał; v. krzyczec
przenikliwie; śmiac się hałas-
liwie i histerycznie
screech(skri:cz) s. zgrzyt;
pisk; skrzypienie; v. zgrzytac; piszczec; skrzypiec
screen (skri:n) s. zasłona; osłona; siatka na komary; ekran;
sito; siewnik; filtr (swiatła)
v. zasłaniac; osłaniac; zabezpieczac; wyswietlac; przesie-
wac; sortowac; badac; przesłu-
chiwac; filmowac; izolowac
screw (skru:) s. sruba; prope-
ler; smigło; zwitek; wyzyskiwacz; dusigrosz; (slang): stosunek płciowy; v. przysrubo-
wac; wyduszac; naciskac; wykrzywiac; zabałaganic; obracac się; (slang): spółkowac;
wkopac (kogos) ;oszukac
screwdriver ('skru:,drajwer) s.
srubokręt; wodka z sokiem poma-
rańczowym
scribble ('skrybl) s. gryzmoły;
bazgranina; v. gryzmolic;
bazgrac; pisac naprędce
script (skrypt) s. rękopis;
scenariusz
scripture ('skrypczer) s. Pismo Swięte
scroll (skroul) s. zwitek;
krzywa; spirala
scrub (skrab) s. zarosla; zagajnik; karłowate drzewo; pętak; niepozorny człowiek; szo-
rowanie; v. szorowac; oczysz-
czac;adj.lichy;marny;maławy
scruple ('skrupl) s. skrupuł;
v. wahac się; miec skrupuły
scrupulous ('skru;pjules) adj.
sumienny; dokładny; skrupulatny; pedantyczny
scrutinize ('skru:tynajz) v.
badac szczegółowo
scrutiny ('skru:tyny) s. dokładne badanie
scuff (skaf) s. włoczenie nogami; wytarte miejsca; v. powłoczyc nogami; wycierac; rozrzucac; porysowac ;musnąc;ze-
drzec;zdzierac;szurac

scuffle (skafl) s. włoczenie nogami; szamotanie się; utarczka;
bojka; v. szamotac się; bic się;
powłoczyc nogami;szurac;zaszurac
sculptor ('skalpter) s. rzezbiarz
sculpture ('skalpczer) s. rzezba;
v. rzezbic
scum (skam) s. szumowiny; v.
zbierac szumowiny, wytarzac
scurf (ske:rf) s. łupiez;strup;par-
chy
scurvy ('ske:rwy) s. szkorbut;
adj. podły; nędzny
scuttle ('skatl) s. wiaderko;
szybka ucieczka; właz; v. pędzic; uciekac; robic dziury
w dnie; zatapiac
scuttlebutt ('skatelbat) s. kadz;
pogłoska
scythe (sajz) s. kosa; v. kosic
sea (si:) s. morze; fala
sea breeze ('si:'bri:z) s. wiatr
od morza
seafarer ('si:,feerer) s. żeglarz;
podróżnik morski
seafood ('si:fu:d) s. potrawy
morskie (ryby; skorupiaki)
sea gull ('si:gal) s. mewa
seal (si:l) s. foka; futro foki;
uszczelka; zagadka; plomba;
pieczątka; piętno; znak; v.po-
lowac na foki; uszczelniac; plom-
bowac; pieczętowac; zalakowac
seal up ('si:l,ap) v. zaplombo-
wac; uszczelnic; zamknąc; zalakowac; zapieczętowac
sea level('si:,lewl) s. poziom
morza
sealskin ('si:lski:n) s. futro
z fok
seam (si:m) s.szew; rąbek; pokład; blizna; szpara; szczelina; v. łączyc szwami; pękac;
pokiereszowac
seaman ('si:men) s. marynarz;
żeglarz
seamstress ('semstrys) s.
szwaczka
seaplane ('si:,plejn) s. hydroplan
seaport ('si:,po:rt) s. port
morski

sea-power ('si:,paŕer) s. potęga morska
search (se:rcz) s. poszukiwanie; badanie; szperanie; rewizja; v. badać; dociekać;
szukać; przetrząsać; rewidować
searching ('se:rczyŋg) adj.
badawczy; przenikliwy
seashore ('si:,szo:r) s. wybrzeże; brzeg morski
seasick ('si:,syk) adj. chory
na morską chorobę
seaside ('si:'sajd) s. wybrzeże morskie
season ('si:zn) s. pora roku;
pora; sezon; v. zaprawiać;
przyprawiać; okrasić
seasonable (si:znebl) adj. stosowny; odpowiedni; właściwy na
porę roku; w porę
seasonal ('si:zenl) adj. sezo-
nowy
seasoned ('si:znd) adj. zaprawiony; wdrożony; przyprawiony;
pikantny; wystały
seasoning ('si:znyŋg) s. przyprawa
season ticket ('si:sn'tykyt) s.
abonament; karta wstępu; bilet (np. na serię przedstawień)
seat (si:t) s. siedzenie; ławka;
krzesło; miejsce siedzące;
siedlisko; siedziba; gniazdo;
v. posadzić; usadowić; wybierać (do sejmu); siąść; osadzić
seat belt ('si:t,belt) s. pas
ochronny w samolocie lub samochodzie; pas beapieczeństwa
seaward ('si:łerd) adv. ku
(otwartemu) morzu; adj. skiero-
wany ku morzu
seaweed ('si:łi:d) s. wodorost
seaworthy ('si:,łe:rsy) adj.
zdatny do podróży morskiej
(m.in. wodoszczelny)
secession (sy'seszyn) s. secesja; oddzielenie się
seclude (sy'klu:d) v. odosabniać (się)
secluded (sy'klu:dyd) adj. odosobniony

seclusion (sy'klu:żyn ) s. odosobnienie; ustronie; zacisze
second ('sekend) adj. drugi;
wtórny; powtórny; ponowny; za-
stępczy; zapasowy; drugorzędny;
v. poprzeć; sekundować; s. sekunda; moment; chwila; drugi;
sekundant; delegat; zastępca
secondary ('sekendery) adj.
drugorzędny; wtórny; pochodny
secondary school ('sekendery-
,sku:l) s. szkoła średnia
second floor ('sekend,flo:r) s.
pierwsze piętro
secondhand ('sekend,haend)
adj. z drugiej ręki; używany
secondly ('sekendly) adv. po
drugie
second-rate ('sekend'-rejt)
adj. drugorzędny; lichy; kiepski
secrecy ('si;krysy) s. tajemnica; skrytość; dyskrecja
secret ('si:kryt) adj. tajny;
tajemny; sekretny; skryty;
ustronny; dyskretny; s. tajemnica; sekret; pl. wstydliwe
części ciała
secretary ('sekretry) s. sekretarz; sekretarka; sekretarzyk
secretary of state ('sekretry-
,ow'stejt) minister spraw
zagranicznych USA
secrete (sy'kri:t) v. wydzielać;
ukrywać
secretion (sy'kri:szyn) s. wydzielina; wydzielanie; ukrycie
section ('sekszyn) s. część;
wycinek; etap; oddział; grupa;
dział; ustęp; paragraf; sekcja;
przekrój; żelazo profilowe;
przedział; drużyna robocza;
v. dzielić na części; robić
przekrój
sector ('sekrer) s. wycinek;
odcinek
secular ('sekjuler) adj. świecki; wiekowy; stuletni; s.
ksiądz świecki
secularize (,sekjulerajz) s.
sekularyzować

secure (sy'kjuer) v. zabezpieczać (się); umacniać; uzyskiwać; zapewniać sobie; adj;
spokojny; bezpieczny; pewny
security (sy'kjueryty) s. bezpieczeństwo; zabezpieczenie;
pewność; zastaw; papier wartościowy; zbytnia ufność
sedan (sy'daen) s. samochód
4-osobowy
sedate (sy'dejt) v. uspokajać
(lekarstwami); adj. spokojny;
opanowany; zrównoważony
sedative ('sedetyw) adj. & s.
(środek) uspakajający, nasen-
ny
sediment ('sydyment) s. osad;
nanos; (skała osadowa)
seduce (sy'du:s) v. uwodzić
seduction (sy'dakszyn) s. uwo-
dzenie; pokusa; poneta; powab
seductive (sy'daktyw) adj. kuszący; necący
sedulous ('sedjules) adj. pilny; skrzętny; staranny; skwapliwy
see; saw; seen (si:, so:,si:n)
see (si:) v. zobaczyć; widzieć;
ujrzeć; zauważyć; spostrzegać; doprowadzić; odprowadzić;
zwiedzać; zrozumieć; odwiedzać; przeżywać; dożyć; uważać; zastanawiać się; dopil-
nować
see off ('si:,of) v. odprowadzać
see out ('si:,aut) v. odprowadzić do drzwi
see through ('si:,tru:) v.prze-
prowadzić do końca; doczekać
się końca
see to ('si:,tu) v. troszczyć
się o...
seed (si:d) v. obsiewać; obsypywać się; zasiewać; wybierać;
s. nasienie; zarodek; plemię
seek; sought; sought (si:k;
so:t; so:t)
seek (si:k) v. szukać; starać
się; chcieć; zadać; nastawać;
usiłować; próbować; przetrząsać; dążyć

seek out ('si:k,aut) v. odszuki-
wać; wykrywać
seem (si:m) v. zdawać się; robić
wrażenie; okazywać się; mieć
wrażenie
seeming (si:myng) adj. pozorny;
widoczny
seemingly ('si:myngly) adv. na
pozór; widocznie
seemly ('si:mly) adj. właściwy;
przyzwoity
seen (si:n) v. zob. see
seep (si:p) v. sączyć się; wyciekać
seesaw ('si:so:) s. huśtawka
(na desce); adj. wahadłowy;
huśtawkowy; s. huśtać się; wahać się; adv. (poruszać czyms)
do góry i na dół
segment ('segment) s. odcinek;
segment; v. podzielić na części
segregate('segry'gejt) v. oddzielać; segregować
segregation ('segry'gejszyn) s.
oddzielenie; segregacja
seize (si:z) v. uchwycić; złapa-
pać; zrozumieć; owładnąć; sko-
rzystać; zaciąć się; zatrzeć
się; zablokować się
seizure ('si:zer) s. zagarnięcie;
zawładnięcie; zajęcie; napad;
atak apopleksji; zatarcie; za-
blokowanie ;atak drgawek
seldom ('seldem) adv. rzadko;
z rzadka
select (sy'lekt) v. wybierać;
wyselekcjonować; adj. wybrany;
doborowy; ekskluzywny
selection (sy'lekszyn) s. wybór;
dobór; selekcja
self (self) prefix. samo; auto-
matycznie; s. jaźń; osobowość;
własne dobro; pl.selves (selwz)
self-acting ('self'aektyng) adj.
samoczynny
self-command ('self,ke'ma:nd) s.
spokój; panowanie nad sobą;
opanowanie
self-confidence ('self,konfydens)
s. pewność siebie; tupet
self-conscious ('self'konszes)
adj.niesmiały; zażenowany

self-control ('self,ken'troul)
s. zimna krew; opanowanie
self-defense ('self,dy'fens) s.
 samoobrona
self-employment ('self,ym'plojment) samozatrudnienie
self-government ('self'gawen-
 ment) s. samorząd; autonomia
self-interest ('self'yntryst)
 s. interesowność; własne dobro
selfish ('selfysz) adj. samolubny; egoistyczny
self-made ('self'mejd) adj.
 przez samego siebie osiagnięty
self-possessed ('self,pe'zest)
 adj. opanowany; spokojny
self-reliant ('self,ry'lajent)
 adj. na sobie polegający
self-respect ('self,rys'pekt) s.
 poczucie własnej godności
self-righteous ('self'rajczes)
 adj. nadmiernie pewny siebie
self-service ('self'se:rwys) s.
 samo-obsługa
sell; sold; sold (sel; sould;
 sould)
sell (sel) v. sprzedawac; za-
 przedawać; sprzyniewierzyc;
 wykiwac; miec zbyt; byc na
 sprzedaż; wyprzedawać
sell out ('selaut) v. wyprzedawać
seller ('seler) s. sprzedawca
selves (selwz) pl. zob. self
semblance ('semblens) s. pozór;
 podobieństwo
semen ('si:men) s. nasienie
semicolon ('semy'koulen) s.
 średnik
semifinal ('semy'fajnl) s. pół-
 finał
senate ('senyt) s. senat
senator ('seneter) s. senator
send; sent; sent (send; sent;
 sent)
send (send) v. posyłac; wysyłac;
 nadawac; transmitować; wystrze-
 liwac; sprawiac; wywoływać
send away ('send,e'łej) v. odprawiac; wypędzac
send for ('send,fo:r) v. zawołac; zamawiac; kazac przyniesc

send in ('send,yn) v. posłac;
 nadesłac
send off ('send'o:f) v. wysyłac;
 odprowadzac (np. na lotnisko);
 pożegnac kogos (na stacji)
sender ('sender) s. nadawca;
 nadajnik (np. radiowy)
send-off ('send'o:f) s. pożegnanie
senior ('si:njer) adj. starszy
 (np. rangą); s. starszy człowiek; senior; student ostat-
 niego roku
sensation (sen'sejszyn) s. wrażenie; doznanie; uczucie; sensacja
sensational (sen'sejszenl) adj.
 sensacyjny; wrażeniowy
sense (sens) s. zmysł; poczucie; uczucie (np. zimna); świadomość (czegos); rozsądek;
 znaczenie; sens; v. wyczuwac;
 czuc; rozumiec
senseless ('senslys) adj. bez
 sensu; nierozumny; nieprzytomny
sensibility (,sensy'bylyty) s.
 wrażliwosc
sensible ('sensybl) adj. rozsądny; świadomy; przytomny;
 wrażliwy; odczuwalny; pozna-
 walny; sensowny
sensitive ('sensytyw) adj.
 wrażliwy; delikatny
sensual ('senszuel) adj. zmysłowy (też seksualnie)
sensuous ('senszues) adj. zmysłowy (nie seksualnie)
sent (sent) v. zob. send
sentence ('sentens) s. zdanie;
 powiedzenie; wyrok; sentencja;
 v. wydawac wyrok; skazywac
sentiment ('sentyment) s. sentyment; uczucie; opinia; zdanie;
 życzenie; sentymentalnosc
sentimental (,senty'mentl) adj.
 uczuciowy; sentymentalny
sentimentality (,senty'ment'aelyty) s. uczuciowosc; czułost-
 kowosc; sentymentalnosc
sentry ('sentry) s. posterunek;
 wartownik

separable ('seperebl) adj. roz-
łączny

separate ('seperejt) v. rozłączyc; rozdzielic; oddzielic;
oderwac; odseparowac (się);
odgrodzic; rozszczepic;

separate ('sepryt) adj. odrębny;
oddzielny; osobny; indywidualny; poszczególny

separation (,sepe'rejszyn) s.
separacja; rozdzielenie; oddzielenie; rozłączenie

September (sep'tember) s.
wrzesien

septic ('septyk) adj. septyczny;
zakaźny

sepulcher ('sepelker) s. grób;
v. składac do grobu

sequel ('si:kłel) s. ciąg dalszy; wynik; następstwo

sequence ('si:kłens) s. następstwo; kolejnosc; porządek;
progresja

serene (sy'ri:n) adj. pogodny;
spokojny; s. spokojne morze;
pogodne niebo etc. v. rozpogo-
dzic

sergeant ('sa:rdżent) s. sierżant

serial('sierjel) a. seryjny;
periodyczny; kolejny; odcin-
kowy

series ('sieri:z) pl. seria;
szereg; rząd

serious ('sierjes) adj. poważny

sermon ('se:rmen) s. kazanie;
nagana

serpent ('se:rpent) s. wąż

serum ('sierem) s. surowica

servant ('se:rwent) s. służący;
sługa; służąca; urzędnik
(panstwowy)

serve (se:rw) s. służyc; odby-
wac służbę (też kadencję;
praktykę etc.); nadawac się;
obsłużyc; podawac; sprzedawac;
dostarczyc; wręczyc; potrakto-
wac; postępowac; spełniac
fukcje; sprawowac urząd; odby-
wac karę (więzienia); zaserwo-
wac

service ('se:rwys) s. służba;
obsługa; praca; urząd; zaopatrzenie; instalacja;
uprzejmosc; grzecznosc; przysługa; pomoc; użytecznosc;
nabożenstwo; serw; serwis
(stołowy); wręczenie; v. doglądac; naprawic; kryc (sami-
ce)

serviceable ('se:rwysebl) adj.
pożyteczny; użyteczny; praktyczny; wygodny; mocny; trwały

service-station('se:rwys-'stejszyn) s. stacja obsługi
i sprzedaży benzyny

session ('seszyn) s. posiedzenie; siedzenie; półrocze

set; set; set (set; set; set)
set (set) v. stawiac; ustawiac;
wstawic; urządzic; umieszczac;
przykładac; nastawiac; osadzac;
wbijac; wyznaczac; ustalac;
sądzic; nakrywac; składac;
wysadzac (czyms); scinac się;
okrzepnąc; adj. zastygły; nieruchomy; zdecydowany; stały;
ustalony; s. seria; garnitur;
skład; komplet;zespół; grupa;
szczepek; zachod: ustawienie;
układ; twardnienie; gęstosc;
rozstęp; oszalowanie

set at ease ('set,et'i:z) v.
uspokoic

set-back ('setbaek) s. pogorszenie; nawrot; zahamowanie

set free ('set,fri:) v. uwolnic

set off ('set,of) v. uwydatnic;
wyodrębnic; wystrzelic; wysadzic; wywołac; wyruszyc; wy-
jeżdżac

set out ('set,aut) v. wystawiac;
ozdabiac; wykładac; wyruszac;
zacząc się

set to ('set,tu) v. zabierac
się (do czegos)

set up ('set,ap) v. ustawiac;
zakładac; zaczynac; zaopatrywac; roscic; wysuwac; przywracac; podnosic; założyc; podawac
się (za kogos)

settee (se'ti:) s. kanapa; sofa
setting ('setyŋg) s. otoczenie;
oprawa; ułożenie; układ; inscenizacja
settle (setl) v. osiedlić (się);
umieścić (się); uregulować;
osadzic (się); ustalic; roz-
strzygnąc; zapłacic (dług);
zamieszkać; usadowić (się);
uspokoic (się); zawierać (umowę); układać (się)
settle down ('setl,dałn) v.
ustatkować sie; osiedlić się;
zabrac się do czegoś
settlement ('setlment) s. osiedle; osada; kolonia; osiadanie;
sedymentacja; załatwienie; rozstrzygnięcie; ustalenie
settler ('setler) s. osadnik;
kolonista
set-up ('set,ap) s. postawa;
układ; drużyna; dodatki do
alkoholu; (slang):ukartowane
zawody; łatwa sprawa
seven ('sewn) num. siedem;
s. siódemka
seventeen ('sewn'ti:n) num.
siedemnaście; s. siedemnastka
seventh ('sewent) adj. siódmy
seventy ('sewnty) num. siedemdziesiąt; s. siedemdziesiątka
sever ('sever) v. odrywać; odłączyc; zrywac; urywac; roz-
chodzic się
several ('sewrel) adj. kilku;
kilka; kilkoro
severe (sy'wier) adj. surowy;
srogi; ostry; dotkliwy; bolesny; zacięty
severity (sy'weryty) s. surowość; srogość; ostrość; za-
ciętosc; ciężki stan
sew; sewed; sewn (sou; soud;
soun)
sew (sou) v. szyc; uszyc
sewage ('sju:ydż) s. scieki
sewer ('suer) s. kanał sciekó-
wy; v. kanalizować;
sewer ('souer) s. osoba szyjąca
sewerage ('su:erydż) s. kanalizacja; system kanalizacyjny
sewing ('souyŋg) s. szycie

sewing-machine ('souyŋgme,szi:n)
s. maszyna do szycia
sewn (soun) v. zob. sew
sex (seks) s. płec
sex appeal ('sekse'pi:l) s.
atrakcyjnosc płciowa; seksapil
sexton ('seksten) s. grabarz
sexual ('sekszjuel) adj. seksualny; płciowy
Sejm (sejm) s. sejm
shabby ('szaeby) adj. brudny;
skąpy; odrapany; wytarty;
nędzny; podły
shack (szaek) s. buda; szałas;
dom
shack up ('szaek,ap) v. spędzac
noc z kims (slang)
shackle ('szaekl) s. kajdany;
klamra; pęta; v. zakuwać;
szczepiać
shade (szejd) s. cień; odcien;
abażur; stora; pl. ustronie;
piwnica na wino; v. zasłaniac;
zamroczyc; cieniowac
shadow ('szaedou) s. cień
(czyjś); v. pokrywac cieniem;
sledzic kogoś
shady ('szejdy) adj. cienisty;
nieczysty; mętny
shaft (szaeft) s. drzewce; trzon;
strzała; promień; wał; trzonek;
dyszel; szyb
shaggy ('szaegy) a. włochaty;
krzaczasty
shake; shook; shaken (szejk;
szuk; szejken)
shake (szejk) v. potrząsać;
uscisnąc dłoń; grozic (palcem);
wstrząsać; drżec; dygotać;
s. dygotanie; dreszcze; drżenie; potrząsanie
shake-up ('szejkap) s. otrząsnię-
cie (się); czystka (slang)
shaky ('szejky) adj. drżący;
rozklekotany; słaby; zachwiany;
chwiejący się
shale (szejl) s. łupek
shall (szael) v. będę; będziemy;
musisz; musi; muszą (zrobić)
shallow ('szaelou) s. mielizna;
adj. płytki; powierzchniowy;
v. spłycac; płyciec; obniżac
poziom (wody)

sham (szaem) adj. fałszywy;
oszukańczy; sztuczny; udawany; symulowany; upozorowany;
s. poza; symulowanie; symu-
lant; pozór; udawanie; v.uda-
wać, symulować
shambles ('szaemblz) pl. jatki; rzeź
shame (szejm) s. wstyd; v.wsty-
dzić się
shame on you ! ('szejm,on'ju:)
exp.: wstydź się !
shameful ('szejmful) adj. sromotny; haniebny
shameless ('szejmlys) adj. bezwstydny; bezczelny
shampoo (szaem'pu:) s. szampon;
mycie głowy szamponem; v. myć
szamponem
shank (szaenk) s. goleń; trzonek; uchwyt
shape (szejp) v. kształtować;
rzeźbić; modelować; formułować; wyobrazić; s. kształt;
kondycja; postać; zjawa; widmo; model
shaped ('szejpt)adj. ukształto-
wany
shapeless('szejplys) adj. bezkształtny; nieforemny; niezgrabny
shapely ('szejply) adj. kształtny; foremny; zgrabny
share (szeer) s. udział; należ-
na część; lemiesz; v. rozdzie-
lić; dzielić (się); podzielać;
brać udział
share-holder ('szeer,houlder)
s. akcjonarjusz
shark (sza:rk) s. rekin
sharp (sza:rp) adj. ostry; bystry; pilny; wyraźny; chytry; do-
minujacy; inteligentny; adv.
punktualnie; szybko; biegiem
sharpen ('sza:rpen) v. ostrzyć;
temperować; obostrzyć; zaostrzyć
sharpener ('sza:rpner) s. temperówka; narzędzie do ostrze-
nia
sharpness ('sza:rpnys) s. ostrość; bystrość; chytrość; pilność

sharp-witted ('sza:rp'łytyd)
adj. bystry; dowcipny; rozgarnięty
shatter ('szaeter) v. gruchotać; roztrzaskac; niweczyć;
szarpać
shave; shaved; shaven (szejw;
szejwd; szejwn)
shave (szejw) v. golić (się);
oskrobać; strugać; s. golenie;
muśnięcie
shaven (szejwn) v. zob. shave
shaving ('szejwyng) v. golenie;
skrobanie; wiórkowanie; s.
wiór
shawl(szo:l) s. szal
she (szi:) pron. ona
sheaf (szi:f) s. snop; wiązka;
wiązanka; plik; pl. sheaves
(szi:wz)
shear; sheared; shorn (szier;
szierd; szo:rn)
shear (szier) v. ścinać; ucinać; ostrzyc; s. ścinanie; pl.
nożyce (shears)
sheath (szi:s) s. pochwa; futerał; powłoka; prezerwatywa
sheaves (szi:wz) pl. od sheath
shed (shed) s. szopa; buda;
v. zrzucać; strącac; pozbywać
(się); pogubić; ronić; przelewać (krew); wydzielać; promieniować
sheep (szi:p) pl. owce
sheep dog ('szi:p,dog) s. owczarek
sheepish ('szi:pysz) adj. bojaźliwy; nieśmiały; zakłopota-
ny; zbaraniały; ogłupiały
sheer (szier) v. schodzić z kur-
su; skręcać nagle; adj. zwykły;
jawny; czysty; zwyczajny; stromy; prostopadły; pionowy;
przejrzysty; przewiewny; lekki;
adv. zupełnie; pionowo; stromo
sheet (szi:t) s. arkusz; prześcieradło; gazeta; tafla; obszar; warstwa; v. pokrywać
prześcieradłem; okrywać brezen-
tem
sheet iron ('szi:t,ajren) s.
blacha stalowa

shelf (szelf) s. półka; rafa;
mielizna; pl. shelves (szelwz)
shell (szel) s. łupina; skorupa; powłoka; osłona; łupina;
pancerz; muszla; szkielet;
łuska; pocisk; granat; gilza;
v. ostrzeliwać z armat; wyłus-
kiwać
shellfish ('szel,fysz) s. sko-
rupiak; mięczak
shelter ('szelter) s. schronienie; ochrona; osłona; v. chronic; osłaniać; udzielać schro-
nienia; zabezpieczać
shelve (szelv) v. odkładać (na
półkę); wkładac do szuflady;
opadać (wzdłuż stoku)
shelves (szelwz) pl. zob.shelf
shepherd ('szeperd) s. pastuch;
pasterz; v. pasć; (pilotować)
prowadzić
shield (szi:ld) s. tarcza;
osłona; v. osłaniać; ochraniać
shift (szyft) v. zmieniać (np.
biegi); przesuwać; przełączyc;
zwalić; s. przesunięcie; zmiana; szychta; wykręt; wybieg
shiftless ('szyftlys) adj. niezaradny
shifty ('szyfty) adj. zmienny;
fałszywy; chytry
shilling ('szylyng) s. szyling
shin (szyn) s. goleń; v. kopać
w goleń
shine; shone; shone (szajn;
szon; szon)
shine (szajn) v. zabłyszczeć;
zajaśnieć; oczyścić na połysk;
s. jasność; blask; (slang):
granda; awantura; sympatia
shingle ('szyngl) s. gont; szyld;
wywieszka; kamyk; v. pokryć
gontami; krótko ostrzyc
shingles ('szynglz) pl. półpa-
siec
shiny('szajny) adj. błyszczący;
wypolerowany
ship (szyp) s. okręt; statek;
samolot; v. załadować; zaokrę-
tować; posyłać
shipment ('szypment) s. załadunek; przesyłka; fracht

shipowner ('szyp,ołner) s. armator
shipping ('szypyng) s. flota
handlowa; żegluga; załadunek;
usługi żeglugowe; przesyłka;
adj. spedycyjny; okrętowy
shipping company ('szypyng'kampeny) s. firma okrętowa; armator
shipwreck ('szyp,rek) s. rozbicie statku; v. ulec rozbiciu;
spowodować rozbicie statku;
rozbić się
ship-wrecked('szyp,rekt) s. rozbitek
shipyard('szyp,ja:rd) s. stocznia
shire ('szajer) s. hrabstwo
(powiat)
shirk (sze:rk) v. uchylać się;
wymigiwać się; s. nierób; wy-
migiwacz
shirt (sze:rt) s. koszula
shirt sleeves ('sze:rt,sli:wz)
pl. rękawy od koszuli; bez
marynarki; adj. prosty; domowy
shit (szyt) v. wulg.: srać; s.gow-
no
shitty ('szyty) adj. wulg.: za-
srany
shiv (szyw) s. majcher (slang)
shiver ('szywer) v. drżeć;
trząsć się; rozbijać się w kawałki; s. dreszcz; kawałek
shock (szok) s. wstrząs; cios;
uderzenie; starcie; porażenie;
czupryna; kopka; v. wstrząsać;
gorszyć; oburzać; porazić
shock absorber ('szok-eb,so:r-
ber) s. tłumik drgań; amorty-
zator
shocking('szokyng) adj. okropny; wstrętny; skandaliczny;
oburzający; niestosowny
shoddy ('szody) adj. tandetny
shoe; shod; shod (szu:, szod,
szod)
shoe (szu:) s. but; półbucik;
trzewik; okucie; podkowa;
nakładka (hamulca); obręcz;
nasada; v. obuwać; podkuwać

shoehorn ('szu:,ho:rn) s. łyżka do butów; wzuwacz
shoelace ('szu:,lejs) s. sznurowadło
shoemaker ('szu:,mejker) s.
szewc
shoestring ('szu:,stryŋg) s.
sznurowadło; bardzo mały kapitał
shoeshine ('szu:,szajn) s.
czyszczenie butów (na połysk)
shone (szon) v. zob. shine
shook (szuk) v. zob. shake
shoot; shot; shot (szu:t; szot;
szot)
shoot (szu:t) v. strzelić; wystrzelić; zastrzelić; rozstrzelać; zrobić zdjęcie; na-
kręcić film; mknąć; przemknąć;
spłynąć; rwać; kiełkować;
s. pęd; kiełek; polowanie;
progi; plac zwozu śmieci
shooter ('shu:ter) s. strzelec;
rewolwer
shooting ('shu:tyŋg) adj. mkną-
cy; pędzący; strzelający
shooting gallery ('shu:tyŋg,gae-
lery) s. strzelnica
shooting-star ('shu:tyŋg,sta:r)
s. spadająca gwiazda
shooting-party ('shu:tyŋg,pa:r-
ty) s. wyprawa łowiecka; polowanie
shop (szop) s. sklep; pracownia;
warsztat; zakład; v. robić zakupy
shopkeeper ('szop,ki:per) s.
kupiec; sklepikarz
shoplifter ('szop,lyfter) s.
złodziej sklepowy
shopping center ('szopyŋg,sen-
ter) s. skupisko sklepów;
ośrodek zakupów
shopping mall ('szopyŋg,mol) s.
skupisko sklepów wzdłuż krytej
hali ;pasaż handlowy
shop window('szop'łyndoł) s.
wystawa
shore (szo:r) s. brzeg; wybrzeże; podpora; v. podpierać;
podstęplować
shorn (szo:rn) v. zob. shear

short (szo:rt) adj. krótki;
niski; zwięzły; oschły; niecały; niewystarczający; adv.
krótko; nagle; za krótko;
s. skrót; zwarcie; pl. szorty
shortage ('szo:rtydż) s. brak;
niedobór; deficyt
short circuit ('sho:rt'se:rkyt)
s. krótkie spięcie; zwarcie
shortcoming ('sho:rt'kamyŋg)
s. wada; niedociągnięcie; brak;
niedobór
shorten ('szo:rtn) v. skracać
shorthand ('szo:rthaend) s.
stenografia
shortly ('szo:rtly) adv. wkrótce; niebawem
shortness ('szo:rtnys) s. krótkość; niedobór
shorts ('szo:rts) pl. szorty;
kalesony (krótkie)
shortstory ('szo:rt,sto:ry) s.
nowela
short-sighted ('szo:rt'sajtyd)
adj. krótkowzroczny; nieprze-
widujący
short-term ('szo:rt'term) adj..
krótkoterminowy; krótko-
trwały
short-winded ('szo:rt'łyndyd)
adj. zasapany; krótko mówiący
shot (szot) v. zob. shoot; ładować broń; s. strzał; pocisk;
śrut; zastrzyk; docinek; adj.
mieniący się
shotgun ('szotgan) s. dubeltówka; śrutówka; strzelba
should (szud) v. tryb warunkowy
od shall
shoulder ('szoulder) s. ramię;
plecy; łopatka; pobocze; v.
brać na ramię; rozpychać się
shout (szałt) s. krzyk; okrzyk;
wrzask; v. krzyczeć; wykrzy-
kiwać
shove (szaw) v. popychać; posuwać (coś); s. pchnięcie
shovel ('szawl) s. łopata;
szufla; v. przerzucać łopatą
lub szuflą
show; showed; shown (szou;
szoud; szoun)

show (szou) v. pokazywać; wskazywać; s. wystawa; przedstawienie; pokaz

show around ('szou,e'raund) v. oprowadzać

show off ('szou,o:f) v. popisywać się; paradować; starać się imponować

show up ('szou,ap) v. demaskować; zjawiać się; ukazywać się

show business ('szou'byznyz) s. przemysł widowiskowy

shower ('szałer) s. tusz; prysznic; przelotny deszcz; grad; stek; przelotnie kropić; obsypywać; oblewać

shower bath ('szałer,ba:t) s. tusz; prysznic

shown (szołn) v. zob. show

showy ('szoły) adj. ostentacyjny; okazały

shrank (szraenk) s. zob. shrink

shred (szred) s. strzęp; v. ciąć na strzępy

shrew (szru:) s. złośnica; sekutnica; sorek

shrewd (szru:d) a. przenikliwy (np. obserwator)

shriek (szri:k) v. wrzeszczeć; piszczeć; rechotać; s. wrzask; pisk; gwizd (ostry)

shrill (szryl) adj. ostry; przenikliwy; przeraźliwy; v. rozlegać się przenikliwie; adv. przenikliwie

shrimp (szrymp) s. krewetka; karzełek; v. łowić krewetki

shrine (szrajn) s. przybytek; relikwiarz; v. umieszczać w przybytku

shrink; shrank; shrunk (szrynk; szraenk; szrank)

shrink (szrynk) v. kurczyć (się) wzbraniać (się) wzdrygać się; s. kurczenie się; (slang):psychiatra

shrinkage ('szrynkydż) s. kurczenie się; ubytek na wadze

shrivel ('szrywl) v. kurczyć (się)

Shrovetide ('szrouwtajd) s. ostatki; zapusty

Shrovetide Tuesday ('szrouwtajd'tju:zdy) s. tłusty wtorek

shrub (szrab) s. krzew; krzak

shrubbery ('szrabery) s. krzaki

shrubby ('szraby) adj. krzaczasty

shrug (szrag) s. wzruszenie ramion; v. wzruszyć ramionami

shrunken ('szrankn) v. zob. shrink

shudder ('szader) s. dreszcz; (slang):nudziarz; v. zadrzeć; wzdrygać się

shuffle ('szafl) v. wlec się; powłóczyć; kręcić; tasować; mieszać; s. krok suwany; krętactwo; tasowanie (kart); wleczenie się; szuranie

shun (szan) v. unikać; wystrzegać się; s, baczność; uwaga

shut; shut; shut (szat; szat; szat)

shut (szat) v. zamykać (się); przytrzasnąć; adj. zamknięty

shut down ('szat,dałn) s. zamknięcie; wstrzymanie pracy; v. zamykać; kłaść koniec; zasłaniać; (o zakładzie) stanąć

shut up ('szat,ap) v. pozamykać; zamknąć gębę; zamilknąć; bądź cicho; wulg.:stul pysk!

shutter ('szater) s. okiennica; zasłona; migawka; regulator organów; v. zamykać okiennice

shy (szaj) adj. płochliwy; wstydliwy; nieśmiały; nieufny; ostrożny; skąpy; szczupły; v. płoszyć się; stronić; rzucać; s. rzut (w coś)

shyness ('szajnys) s. skromność; nieśmiałość

shyster ('szajster) s. chytry (polityk) bez zasad; adwokat-krętacz

sick (syk) adj. chory; znudzony; chorowity; skażony zarazkami; chorobowy

sickbed ('sykbed) s. łóżko chorego; łoże boleści

sick benefit ('syk'benefyt) s. zasiłek chorobowy

sicken ('sykn) v. zaczynać chorować; wywoływać obrzydzenie; brzydzić (się)

sickle ('sykl) s. sierp

sick leave ('sykli:w) s. zwolnienie lekarskie; urlop chorobowy

sickly ('sykly) adj. chorowity; słabowity; niezdrowy; chorobliwy; ckliwy

sickness ('syknyś) s. choroba; wymioty; nudności

sick room ('syk-ru:m) s. izba chorych; pokój chorego

side (sajd) s. strona; adj. uboczny; v. stać po czyjejś stronie

side by side ('sajd,baj'sajd) exp.: obok siebie; jeden przy drugim

side arms ('sajda:rmz) pl. broń boczna (np. szable)

sideboard ('sajdbo:rd) s. kredens

sidecar ('sajd,ka:r) s. przyczepa do motocykla

sided ('sajdyd) adj. stronny; mający strony

side dish ('sajd,dysz) s. przystawka

side-kick ('sajdkyk) s. (slang): kompan; pomagier

sideroad ('sajd,roud) s. boczna droga

side line ('sajd,lajn) v. odsuwać na bok; zapobiegać

sidewalk ('sajd-ło:k) s. chodnik; trotuar

sidewalk café ('sajdło:kaefej) s. kawiarnia na chodniku

sidewards ('sajdłedz) adv. bokiem; w bok

sideways ('sajdłejz) adv. bokiem; na poprzek; adj. boczny

side with ('sajd,łys) v. brać czyjąś stronę

siege (si:dż) s. oblężenie

sieve (syw) s. sito; rzeszoto; przetak; v. przesiewać

sift (syft) v. przesiewać; przebierać; oddzielać; prószyć; posypywać

sigh (saj) s. westchnienie; v. wzdychać

sight (sajt) s. wzrok; widok; celownik; przeziernik

sighted ('sajtyd) adj. spostrzeżony

sightly ('sajtly) adj. dający dobry widok; miły; przyjemny

sightseeing ('sajtsi:yńg) s. zwiedzanie; adj. turystyczny

sightseeing tour ('sajtsi:yńg-,tu:r) s. zwiedzanie z wycieczką; wycieczka krajoznawcza

sightseer ('sajtsi:er) s. turysta; zwiedzający

sign (sajn) s. znak; omen; godło; napis; wywieszka; szyld; skinienie; oznaka; objaw; ślad; znak drogowy; hasło; odzew; v. znaczyć; naznaczyć; podpisać; skinąć

sign up ('sajn,ap) v. zapisywać się

sign out ('sajn,aut) v. wypisywać się

signal ('sygnl) s. sygnał; znak; v. sygnalizować; zapowiadać; dawać znak

signature ('sygnyczer) s. podpis; sygnatura; klucz

signature-tune ('sygnyczer,tju:n) s. oznaczenie tonacji

signboard ('sajnbo:rd) s. wywieszka; szyld; godło

signet ('sygnyt) s. sygnet; pieczątka; v. pieczętować

significance (syg'nyfykens) s. wyraz; ważność; znaczenie

significant (syg'nyfykent) adj. istotny; znaczący; doniosły; znamienny; ważny

signification (syg'nyfykejszyn) s. znaczenie

signify ('sygnyfaj) v. znaczyć; mieć znaczenie; oznaczać; zaznaczać

signpost ('sajn,poust) s. drogowskaz

silence ('sajlens) s. milczenie; cisza; v. nakazywać milczenie; cicho !

silencer ('sajlenser) s. tłumik
silent ('sajlent) adj. milczący;
cichy; małomówny
silk (sylk) s. jedwab; adj.
jedwabny
silken ('sylkn) adj. jedwabny;
jedwabniczy
silky ('sylky) adj. jedwabisty
sill (syl) s. próg; podkład;
parapet
silly ('syly) s. głupiec; adj.
głupi; ogłupiały
silver ('sylwer) s. srebro;
v. posrebrzać; adj. srebrny;
srebrzysty
silvery ('sylwry) adj. srebrzysty
similar ('symyler) adj. podobny; rzecz podobna
similarity (,symy'laeryty) s.
podobieństwo
simmer ('symer) v. wolno gotować (się); burzyć się wewnątrz;
s. gotowanie na wolnym ogniu
simple ('sympl) adj. prosty;
zwykły; naturalny; szczery; naiwny; głupkowaty; zwyczajny
simplicity(sym'plysyty) s.
prostota
simplification (,symplyfy'kejszyn) s. uproszczenie
simplistic ('symplystyk) adj.
zbyt upraszczający
simplify ('symplyfaj) v.upros-
cić; ułatwić
simply ('symply) adv. po prostu
simulate ('symjulejt) v. udawać; naśladować
simultaneous (symel'tejnjes)
adj. równoczesny; jednoczesny
sin (syn) s. grzech; v. grze-
szyć
since (syns) adv. odtąd; potem;
conj; skoro; ponieważ; od czasu jak
sincere (syn'sier) adj. szczery
sincerely (syn'sierly) adv.
szczerze
sincerity (syn'seryty) s. szcze-
rość
sinew ('synu:) s. ścięgno
sinews ('synu:s) pl. muskulatu-
ra; siła; moc

sinewy ('synuy) adj. muskularny; mocny
sing; sang; sung (syng; saeng;
sang)
sing (syng) v. śpiewać; wyć;
zawodzić; bzykać; świstać;
opiewać; s. śpiew; świst
singe (syndź) v. opalać; osma-
lać
singer (synger) s. śpiewak
single ('syngl) adj. pojedynczy; jeden; samotny; szczery;
uczciwy; s. bilet w jedną
stronę; gra pojedyncza; v. wybierać; wyróżniać
single out ('syngl,aut) v. wybierać
single-handed ('syngl'haendyd)
adj. adv. w pojedynkę; na
własną rękę; samodzielny; samodzielnie
single room ('syngl'ru:m) s.
pojedynczy pokój
single ticket ('syngl'tykyt) s.
bilet w jedną stronę
singles bar ('syngls,ba:r) s.
bar dla samotnych
singular ('syngjuler) adj.
osobliwy; niezwykły; pojedynczy; liczba pojedyncza
singularity (,syngju'laeryty)
s. osobliwość; niezwykłość;
niezwykły człowiek
sinister ('synyster) adj.
zbrodniczy; złowieszczy; lewy
sink; sank; sunk (synk; saenk;
sank)
sink (synk) v. zatonąć; zato-
pić; zagłębić (się); opuścić;
obniżyć; pogrążyć; zanikać;
zmaleć; wykopywać; ukrywać;
wyryć; zainwestować; amortyzo-
wać; s. zlew; ściek; bagno
zepsucia
sinking ('synkyng)s. uczucie
mdłości (np. z przerażenia)
sinner ('syner) s. grzesznik
sip (syp) s; łyk; popijanie;
v. popijać
sir (se:r) s. pan; v. nazywać
panem; exp.: proszę pana !
sirloin (se:rloyn) s. polędwica
sister (syster) s. siostra

sister in law ('syster yn,lo:)
s. szwagierka

sit; sat; sat (syt; saet; saet)

sit (syt) v. siedziec; przesia-
dywac; usiąsc; zasiadac; obra-
dowac; lezec; pozowac

sit down ('syt,dałn) v. usiąsc

sit up ('syt,ap) v. wyprostowac się siedząc; czuwac;
usiąsc prosto

site (sajt) s. miejsce; plac
(np. budowy); położenie;
v. umieszczac

sitting ('sytyng) s. posiedzenie; sesja

sitting-room ('sytyng,ru:m) s.
bawialnia; salon

situated ('sytjuejtyd) adj.
umieszczony; stojący; usytuo-
wany

situation (,sytu'ejszyn) s. położenie; posada; sytuacja

six (syks) num. szesc; s. szost-
ka

sixteen ('syks'ti:n) num. szes-
nascie; s. szesnastka

sixth (sykst) num. adj. szosty;
s. jedna szosta

sixthly ('sykstly) adv. po
szoste

size (sajz) s. wielkosc; numer;
format; klajster; krochmal;
rzadki klej; v. sortowac wg
wielkosci; oceniac wielkosc;
nadawac się; krochmalic; usz-
tywnic klejem

sized-up ('sajzd,ap) adj. oce-
niony (co do wielkosci, siły
lub waznosci)

sizzle ('syzl) v. skwierczec;
s. skwierczenie

skate (skejt) s. łyzwa; wrotka;
płaszczka; szkapa; pętak; pa-
tałach; v. slizgac się; jezdzic na wrotkach

skater ('skejter) s. łyzwiarz;
wrotkarz

skeleton ('skelytn) s.szkielet

skeptic ('skeptyk) adj. sceptyczny; s. sceptyk

sketch ('skecz) s. szkic; skecz;
zarys; v. szkicowac;przedstawic
w ogolnych zarysach(w krotkich
słowach);robic wstępny rysunek

sketch block ('skecz,blok) s.
szkicownik

sketchbook ('skecz,bu:k) s.
szkicownik

ski (ski:) s. narta; wyrzutnik
bomb; v. jezdzic na nartach

skid (skid) s. deska; płoza;
podporka; klin hamowniczy;
poslizg; zarzucenie; v. slizgac się; zarzucac; umieszczac
na płozach; hamowac

skier ('ski:er) s. narciarz

skiing ('skiyng) s. narciarstwo; jazda na nartach

ski lift ('ski lyft) s. wyciąg narciarski

skill ('skyl) s. zręcznosc;
wprawa

skilled ('skyld) adj. wykwali-
fikowany; wykonany fachowo

skillful ('skylful) adj. zręczny; wprawny

skillet (skylyt) s. patelnia;
(slang): draka

skim (skym) v. zbierac (smie-
tankę); szumowac; przebiegac
wzrokiem; puszczac po powierzchni; szybowac; s. zbieranie;
mleko zbierane; adj. zbierany

skimmer ('skymer) s. warzęchwa;
cedzidło

skimp (skymp) v. skąpic

skimpy (skympy) adj. skąpy; za
mały; niewystarczający

skin (skyn) s. skora; skorka;
cera; szawłok; (slang):oszust;
v. zdzierac skorę; pokrywac
naskorkiem; sciągac z siebie

skin-deep('skyn'di:p) adj.
powierzchowny

skindiver ('skyn'dajwer) s.
płetwonurek

skindiving ('skyn'dajwyng) s.
sportowe nurkowanie (z płetwami) skora i kosci

skinny ('skyny) adj. chudy;

skip (skyp) v. skakac; przeskakiwac; odskakiwac; pomijac;
(slang):uciekac; s. skok;
przeskok; kapitan sportowy

skipper ('skyper) s. szyper;
kapitan statku; skoczek; kapitan druzyny

skirt ('ske:rt) s. spódnica;
poła; wulg.:kobietka; przepona; brzeg; v. jechać brzegiem;
obchodzić; leżeć na skraju
skit ('skyt) s. skecz; satyra;
mnóstwo
skoal (skoul) excl.:na zdrowie!
skull (skal) s. czaszka
sky (skaj) s. niebo; klimat
skyjack ('skaj,dźaek) s. porwanie samolotu w locie; v. porwać samolot w locie(uprowadzać)
skyjacker ('skaj,dżaeker) s.
pirat powietrzny
skylark ('skajla:rk) s. skowronek; v. dokazywać; swawolić
skylight ('skajlajt) s. okno
dające górne światło; okno
w suficie
skyscraper ('skaj.skrejper) s.
drapacz chmur
skywards ('skajłerdz) adv.
ku niebu
slab (slaeb) s. płytka; v. krajać na płytki (kromki)
slack (slaek) adj. luźny; wolny; rozlazły; opieszały; ospały; leniwy; niedbały;
v. zluźniac; zwalniac; popusz-
czac; zaniedbywać; gasić (np.
ogień); s. luźna część; lenistwo; zastój; bezczelność;
miał węglowy ;zwis;impertypencja
slacken (slaeken) v. rozluzniac
(się); zwalniac; poluzniac
(się); popuszczać; zaniedbywać; gasić (np. wapno)
slacks (slaeks) pl. (luzne)
spodnie
slain (slejn) zabity; zob.slay
slake (slejk) v. gasic (np.
wapno); wywierac (np.zemstę)
slam (slaem) v. zatrzasnąć (się);
(slang) krytykować ostro; pobić; s. trzaśnięcie; ostra
krytyka; ciupa
slang (slaeng) s. gwara; żargon;
slang; adj. gwarowy; żargonowy;
v. nawymyślać komuś
slangy (slaengy) adj. gwarowy
slant (sla:nt).s. pochyłosc;
skos; tendencja; punkt widze-

nia; spojrzenie; adj. ukosny;
v. isć skosnie; pochylać (się);
odchylać (się); być nachylonym
slap (slaep) s. klaps; plasnię-
cie; v. plasnąć; dać klapsa;
uderzyc; narzucić; adv. nagle;
prosciutko; regularnie
slapstick ('slaep,styk) s. laska
arlekina; błazeńska komedia
slash ('slaesz) v. pokiereszo-
wać; przeciąc; hłostać; smagać;
walic; ciąć; s. cięcie; szrama;
przecięcie; wyrąb; odpadki
drzewne; porosłe (krzakami) moczary
slate(slejt) s. łupek; dachówka
łupkowa; tabliczka do pisania;
lista (kandydatów w USA); v.po-
krywac dachówkami; umieszczać
na liscie kandydatów; łajać;
wymyślać; krytykować
slate pencil ('slejt'pensl) s.
rysik
slattern ('slaete:rn) s. brudas;
flejtuch; kocmołuch
slaughter ('slo:ter) v. rznąc;
zabijac; wymordowac; s. ubój;
rzez; masakra
Slav (sla:w) adj. słowiański
slave (slejw) adj. niewolniczy;
s. niewolnik; v. harować
slavery ('slejwery) s. niewol-
nictwo
slay; slew; slain (slej; slu:,
slejn) v. zabic; usmiercać
sled (sled) s. sanie; v. wozic
saniami
sledge hammer ('sledź-haemer)
s. oburęczny młot
sleek (sli:k) adj. gładki; uli-
zany; v. gładzic; wygładzac
sleep; slept; slept (sli:p;
slept; slept)
sleep (sli:p) v. spac; spoczywac; dawac nocleg; s. sen;
spanie; drzemka
sleep off ('sli:p,of) v. ode-
spac   wtyczka (szpiegowska etc.)
sleeper ('sli:per) s. człowiek
śpiący; dźwigar; potencjalny
przedmiot rozgłosu;truteń;leń
sleeping-bag ('sli:pyng,baeg)
s. śpiwór

sleeping car ('sli:pyng,ca:r)
s. wagon sypialny
sleeping partner ('sli:pyng-
'pa:rtner) s. cichy wspólnik
sleeping pill ('sli:pyng,pyl)
s. pigułka nasenna
sleepless ('sli:plys) adj. bezsenny
sleepwalker ('sli:p,ło:ker) s.
lunatyk
sleepy ('sli:py) adj. śpiący
sleet (sli:t) s. słota; deszcz
ze śniegiem; gołoledź
sleeve (sli:w) s. rękaw; tuleja; łuska; nasadka; tuba;
zanadrze
sleeved ('sli:wd) adj. z ręka-
wami
sleigh (slej) v. saneczkować
(się); jechać saniami
slender ('slender) adj. wysmukły;szczupły; wiotki; nikły;
skromny; niewielki; słaby
slept (slept) v. zob. sleep
slew (slu:) v. zob. slay
slice (slajs) s. kromka; płatek;
plasterek; kawałek; łopatka
kuchenna; v. krajać na kromki;
kawałki etc. przecinać; wiosłować; wyjmować łopatką
slick (slyk) adj. gładki; tłusty; oślizgły; miły; pociągający; pierwszorzędny; adv. gładko; prościutko; s. tłusta plama (na morzu); szerokie dłuto
slicker ('slyker) s. gładki
płaszcz od deszczu; oszust
slid (slyd) v. zob. slide
slide; slid; slid (slajd; slyd;
slyd)
slide (slajd).v. suwać (się);
sunąć (się); ślizgać (się);
s. ślizganie się; suwak; pro-
wadnica ślizgowa; poślizg;
przeźrocze; zrzutnia
slide rule('slajd,ru:l) s. suwak logarytmiczny
slight (slajt) adj. wątły; niewielki; drobny; skromny; nieznaczny; v. lekceważyć;
s. lekceważenie

slim (slym) adj.szczupły; wysmukły; słaby; (slang):chytry;
v. wyszczuplać; odchudzać (się)
slime (slajm) s. szlam; muł;
śluz; płynna smoła ziemna;
v. zamulać; odmulać; zwilżać
(np. śliną)
slimy (slajmy) adj. mulisty;
zamulony; oblesny; oślizgły
sling; slung; slung (slyng;
slang; slang)
sling (slyng) s. proca; rzut;
pętla (np. do ładowania dzwi-
giem); temblak; rzemień do
strzelby itp. v. rzucać;
strzelać z procy; podnosić na
pętli; zawieszać na (np. rze-
mieniu)
slinger ('slynger) s. procarz
slinky ('slynky) adj. ukradko-
wy; (slang):mający ruchy węża
slip; slipped; slipped (slyp;
slypd; slypd)
slip (slyp) v. pośliznąć (się);
wyśliznąć (się); ześliznąć
(się); popełnić nietakt; zrobić błąd; przepuścić (np.okaz-
je); wymknąć się; zerwać się;
zapomnieć; spuszczać (np. ze
smyczy); s. poślizg; potknięcie; pomyłka; błąd; przemówienie się; zsuw; halka; świstek
(papieru); pochylnia
slip off ('slyp,of) v. zdejmować; rozbierać się; ześlizgi-
wać się; spadać
slip on ('slyp,on) v. wdziewać
slip out ('slyp,aut) v. wymknąć się
slip up ('slyp,ap) s. błąd; za-
chwianie się; przemówienie się;
zsuw; ślizg; v. zrobić błąd;
pomylić się; potknąć się
slipper ('slyper) s. pantofel
slippery ('slypery) adj. śliski; niebezpieczny; ryzykowny;
nieuczciwy; nieczysty; drażliwy; delikatny; wykrętny;
chytry
slit; slit; slit (slyt; slyt;
slyt)

slit (slyt) v. rozszczepić;
rozedrzeć wzdłuż; s. szpara;
szczelina; rozcięcie
slobber ('slober) s. ślina; roz-
czulenie; v. oślinic się; roz-
czulic się
slogan ('slougen) s. slogan;
hasło; powiedzonko (np. rekla-
mowe)
sloop (slu:p) s. slup (łódz)
slop (slop) v. rozlewac; przepełniać płynem; rozpryskiwać;
s. kałuża; brudna woda; pomyje; lura
slop over ('slop,ouwer) v.
przelewac się przez wierzch
slope (sloup) s. pochyłosc;
spadek; nachylenie; spadzistosc; stok; skarpa; zbocze;
pochylnia; v. byc pochylonym;
miec nachylenie; nachylac;
pochylac; wałęsac się; łazi-
kowac
sloping (sloupyng) adj. pochyły; skosny
sloppy ('slopy) adj. błotnisty;
pochlapany; zaniedbany; rozlazły; ckliwy
slot (slot) s. szczelina; rozcięcie; trop; slad; v. roz-
ciąc; naciąc; wyżłobic
sloth (slous) s. lenistwo; le-
niwiec
slot-machine ('slotme,szi:n)
s. (grający lub sprzedający)
automat na monety
slouch (slaucz) s. przygarbie-
nie; niedbała postawa; wałkon;
v. garbic się; isc ociężale;
opuszczac rondo kapelusza
slough (slau) s. bagno; trzęsawisko
slaugh (slaw) v. leniec; zrzucac skorę
sloven ('slawn) s. niechlujny;
brudas; flejtuch; fuszer;
partacz
slovenly ('slawnly) adj. niechlujny; partacki
slow (slou) adj. powolny; nie-
gorliwy; nieskory; opieszały;
leniwy; tępy; nudny; adv. wolno; powoli

slow down ('slou,dałn) v. zwalniac; przyhamowac
slow-motion ('slou'mouszyn) s.
zwolnione tempo; w zwolnionym
tempie
slowworm ('slou,łe:rm) s. padalec
sluggish ('slagysz) adj. ospały; leniwy; powolny
sluice ('slu:s) s. śluza; ściek;
rynna; v. puszczac wodę (ze
stawu etc). spłukiwac; zalewac; chlusnąc; spływac ze
sluzy
slums (slamz) s. dzielnica nędzy
slumber ('slamber) v. spac lekko; drzemac; s. sen; drzemka;
spokoj; bezczynnosc
slung (slang) v. zob . sling
slush (slasz) s. chlapa; odpadki tłuszczowe; smar; fundusz
z odpadkow; tajny fundusz na
przekupstwo; v. opryskac; wysmarowac; pokrywac zaprawą
slut (slat) s. flejtuch; kocmołuch; plucha; pinda; szmata;
flądra; suka
sly (slaj) ad. szczwany; chytry;
filuterny
slyboots ('slajbu:ts) s. urwis;
spryciarz; chytrus (udający
głupiego)
smack (smaek) s. posmak; odrobina; trzask; mlasnięcie;
cmoknięcie; klaps; jednomasz-
towiec; v. cmokac; strzelac
z bata; dac w pysk; oblizywac
(wargi)
smacking ('smaekyng) adj.
zgrabny; razny; mocny (wiatr)
small (smo:l) adj. mały; drobny; niewielki; skromny; ciasny;
nieliczny; nieznaczny; małostkowy; adv. drobno; na małą ska-
lę; cicho; s. drobna rzecz;
mała częsc
small change ('smo:l,czejndż)
s. drobne (pieniądze)
small hours ('smo:l,auers) pl.
bardzo wczesne ranne godziny
smallish ('smo:lysz) adj. ma-
ławy

small of the back ('smo:1,ow-
'dy,baek) s. krzyże
smallpox ('smo:1,poks) s. ospa
smart (sma:rt) adj. dotkliwy;
cięty; zreczny; żwawy; dowcipny; szykowny; zgrabny; elegancki; v. piec; palic (np.
w oczy); cierpiec; szczypac;
parzyc; odczuwac bolesnie;
pokutowac
smart aleck('sma:rt,alek) s.
Jedrek-medrek
smash (smaesz) v. rozbic; rozwalic; roztrzaskac; zmiazdzyc;
potluc; palnąc; rozgromic;
upadac; zbankrutowac; scinac
piłkę
smashing('smaeszyng) adj. nadzwyczajny; niezwykły
smattering('smaeteryn) s. znajomosci po łebkach; wiedza
powierzchowna
smear (smier) v. osmarowac;
zasmarowac; wlepic komus sma-
ry; s. plama; smar
smell; smelt; smelled (smel;
smelt; smeld)
smell (smel) s. wech; won; zapach; odor; smrod; v. pach-
niec; tracic; miec zapach;
smierdziec; miec powonienie;
obwachiwac; czuc zapach;
zwietrzyc; zwąchac; poczuc
smelt (smelt) v. sob. smell;
stapiac; wytapiac (metal);
s. stynka (ryba)
smile (smajl) v. usmiechac się;
s. usmiech
smite; smote; smitten (smajt;
smout; 'smytn)
smite (smajt) v. uderzac; po-
razic; powalic; zabic; nękac;
karac; oczarowac; s. cios;
uderzenie;s probo
smith (smys) s. kowal
smithy (smysy) s. kuznia
smitten ('smytn) v. zob.smite
smock (smok) s. chałat; kitel;
v. ubierac chałat; ozdabiac
rysunkiem szachownicy
smog (smog) s. mgła zanieczysz-
czona dymem (Londyn,Los Angeles)

smoke (smouk) s. dym; palenie;
papieros; v. dymic; kopcic; wykurzac; wyjawiac; wykadzac; oka-
dzac; okopcic; uwędzic; przypa-
lac; palic (tyton)
smoke-dried ('smouk,drajd) adj.
wędzony
smoker ('smouker) s. palący; pa-
lacz
smoking ('smoukyng) s. palenie
(tytoniu)
smoking car ('smoukyng,ka:r) s.
wagon dla palących
smoking compartment ('smoukyng-
kaem,pa:rtment) s. przedział
dla palących
smoky ('smouky) adj. dymiący;
przydymiony; zadymiony; okopcony
smolder ('smoulder) v. tlic się;
s. tlenie się; dym
smooch (smu:cz) v. brudzic; walac; całowac się; sciskac się;
migdalic się
smooth (smu:s) adj. gładki; spokojny; łagodny; v. gładzic; łagodzic; adv. gładko; s. wygła-
dzenie
smooth down ('smu:s,dałn) v.
wygładzic; uspakajac (się)
smother ('smadzer) v. stłumic;
stłamsic; obcałowywac; zatuszo-
wac; okrywac
smudge (smadż) v. poplamic; za-
brudzic; s. plama; kleks; brud
smuggle ('smagl) v. przemycac
smuggler ('smagler) s. przemytnik
smut (smat) v. poplamic; s. brud
z sadzy; sprosnosci; tłuste
kawały; sniec
smutty ('smaty) adj. sprosny;
brudny od sadzy
snack (snaek) s. zakąska
snack bar ('snaek,ba:r) s. bufet; bar
snafu (snae'fu:) v. zabałaganic;
s. bałagan (slang)
snail (snejl) s. slimak
snake (snejk) s. wąż; v. wic
się; wlec (za sobą);pełzac jak
wąż;przybierac kształt węża

snap (snaep) v. łapać zębami;
warczeć; błysnąć; urwać; złamać; chwytać; zapalić się do;
przerwać szorstko; poprawić
się; mieć się na baczności;
zatrzasnąć (się); strzelać
z bicza; pstryknąć; sfotografować; spiesznie załatwiać;
machnąć ręką lekceważąco;
s. ugryzienie; warknięcie;
trzask; zatrzask; dociskacz;
zdjęcie; rzecz łatwa; adj.
prosty; łatwy; dorazny; nagły
snap bolt ('snaep,boult) s.
zatrzask u drzwi
snap fastener('snaep,fa:sner)
s. zatrzask
snappish ('snaepysz) adj.
zgryzliwy; kostyczny
snappy ('snaepy) adj. zgryzliwy; kostyczny; zwawy; prędki
snapshot ('snaepszot) s. zdjęcie migawkowe; strzał na chybił trafił
snare (sneer) v. usidłać; łapać w sidła; s. sidła; pułapka
snarl (sna:rl) s. warknięcie;
plątanina; v. warczec; plątać (się); zaplątać; robić
zator
snatch (snaecz) v. złapać;
wyrwać; s. złapanie; urywek;
strzęp; mig
sneak (sni:k) v. chyłkiem zakradać się; przemykać się;
zerkać; zwiać; s. podły
tchórz
sneakers ('sni:kers) pl. trzewiki; trampki
sneer (snier) v. uśmiechać się
szyderczo; kpić; drwić; s.
szyderstwo; szydercze spojrzenie
sneeze (sni:z) v. kichać;
s. kichnięcie
sniff (snyf) v. prychać; pociągać nosem; krzywić się na
coś; powąchać; obwąchać; zwąchać; wyczuc; s. prychnięcie;
pociągnięcie nosem

sniffle ('snyfl) s. katar; pociąganie nosem; v. pociągać
nosem
snipe (snajp) s. bekas; strzał
z ukrycia; v. z ukrycia: strzelać; trafic, zabić
sniper ('snajper) s. strzelec
wyborowy; strzelec z ukrycia
snivel ('snywel) s. śluz z nosa;
biadolenie; udawanie; v. smarkać się; skamleć; biadolić;
płakać; rozczulać się
snob (snob) s. człowiek wywyższający się
snoop (snu:p) v. myszkować;
wścibiać nos; s. szpicel
snoop around ('snu:p,e'raund)
v. przemyszkowywać; szpiegować
snooze (snu:z) s. drzemka;
v. drzemać; zdrzemnąć się
snore (sno:r) v. chrapać; s.
chrapanie
snort (sno:rt) v. parskać;
s. parsknięcie
snout (snaut) s. ryj; pysk; morda; wylot
snow (snou) s. śnieg; (slang):
kokaina; heroina; v. ośnieżyć;
śnieg pada; zasypać śniegiem;
pobić na głowę; omamiać
snowball ('snoubo:l) s. kula
śnieżna; v. bić się śniegiem;
rosnąć jak lawina
snow blindness ('snou'blajndnys)
s. śnieżna ślepota
snowdrift ('snou'dryft) s. zaspa śniezna
snowdrop ('snoudrop) s. śnieżyczka
snow job ('snou,dżob) s. naciąganie pochlebstwami
snow-white ('snou'hłajt) adj.
śnieznobiały
snowy ('snoły) adj. śnieżny;
śniegowy
snub (snab) v. ofuknąć; dać po
nosie; traktować lekceważąco;
nagle zatrzymać; adj. perkaty;
zadarty nos; s. bura; ofuknięcie;ostra odprawa;afront;ucieranie nosa komus;przywodzenie
kogoś do porządku

snuff(snaf) s. tabaka; proszek
do zażywania przez nos; zapach;
opalony koniec knota; v. zażywać tabakę; pociągać nosem;
czyścić koniec knota
snug (snag) adj. przytulny;
wygodny; ukryty; v. tulić się;
zrobić przytulnym
snuggle ('snagl) v. przytulić
się
so(sou) adv. tak; a więc; w ta-
kim razie; a zatem; też; tak
samo; bardzo to; także; excl.:
to tak ! no, no !
so far ('sou fa:r) adv. jak
dotąd ; jak do tej pory
soak (souk) v. moczyć (się);
nasycać (się); przenikać; na-
moknąć; (slang):wyciągać (od
kogoś) pieniądze; mocno uderzyć; s. moczenie (się); woda
do moczenia; popijawa; zastaw
soap (soup) s. mydło; pochlebstwo; wazelinowanie się (komuś); v. mydlić (się); pochlebiać; adj. mydlany; myd-
larski
soap box ('soup,boks) s. skrzynia od mydła; mównica (np.
uliczna). v. przemawiać na
ulicy, w parku etc.
soap opera ('soup'opere) s.
(popołudniowe) przedstawienie
radiowe lub telewizyjne pełne
małżeńskich kryzysów, tragedii,
cierpień, płaskiej czułostko-
wości i melodramatycznych za-
kończeń
soar (so:r) v. wznosić się;
osiągać wyżyny; iść w górę
(np. ceny)
sob (sob) v. łkać; szlochać;
s. łkanie; szloch
sober ('souber) adj. trzeźwy;
wstrzemięźliwy; stateczny;
zrównoważony; rzeczowy; poważny; spokojny; v. trzeźwieć;
wytrzeźwieć; wytrzeźwiać ;
otrzeźwieć; opanować się
sober up ('souber,ap) v. wytrzeźwieć
sober-minded ('souber,majndyd)
adj.stateczny; zrównoważony

so-called ('sou-ko:ld) adj.
tak zwany
soccer ('soker) s. piłka nożna
sociable ('souszebl) adj. towarzyski; przyjacielski; gro-
madny; stadny
social ('souszel) adj. społeczny; socjalny; s. zebranie
towarzyskie
social democrat ('souszel'de-
mekraet) s. socjaldemokrata
socializm ('souszelyzem) s.
socjalizm
social security ('souszel-
sy'kjueryty) s. ubezpiecze-
nia społeczne
socialist ('souszelyst) s.
socjalista; adj. socjalistycz-
ny
social worker ('souszel'łerker) s. pracownik społeczny;
pracownik urzędu opieki spo-
łecznej
socialize ('souszelajz) v.
upaństwowić; uspołecznić
social welfare ('souszel,łel-
feer) s. opieka społeczna
society (so'sajety) s. towarzystwo; społeczeństwo; społeczność; spółka (np. akcyj-
na)
sock (sok) s. skarpetka; cios;
szturchaniec; v. cisnąć w kogoś; uderzyć; walnąć; adv.
prosto (np. w nos)
socket ('sokyt) s. oprawka;
oczodół; zębodół; gniazdko;
wydrążenie
sod (sod) s. darń; darnina;
wulg.;skurwysyn; sodomita
sofa ('soufe) s. kanapa; sofa
soft (soft) adj. miękki; delikatny; przyciszony; łagodny;
słaby; głupi; wygodny
soft drink ('soft,drynk) s.
napój bezalkoholowy
soft goods ('soft,gu:ds) pl.
tekstylia
soften ('softn) v. zmiękczyć;
osłabić; złagodzić; złagodnieć; zmięknąć
soil (sojl) s.gleba; rola; ziemia; brud;plama; v.zabrudzić;
powalać; poplamic;wysmarować

sojourn ('sedże:rn) s. pobyt;
v. przebywać; zatrzymywać (się)
sold (sould) v. sprzedany; zob.
sell
soldier ('souldżer) s. żołnierz
najemnik; adj. żołnierski;
v. służyć w wojsku
sole (soul) s. podeszwa; podwalina; zelówka; stopa; spodek;
sola; adj. jedyny; wyłączny
solemn ('solem) adj. solenny;
uroczysty; poważny
solicit (se'lysyt) v. prosić;
zwracać się (o coś); nagabywać; ubiegać się; zwracać (np.
uwagę)
solicitor (se'lysyter) s. radca prawny; akwizytor; agent
firmowy
solicitous (se'lysytes) adj.
pragnący; troszczący się o...;
niepokojący się
solicitude (se'lysytju:d) s.
troska; pieczołowitość;
troskliwość
solid ('solyd) adj. stały; masywny; lity; trwały; mocny;
rzetelny; solidny; ciało stałe; bryła
solidarity (,soly'daeryty) s.
solidarność
solidity (so'lydyty) s. masywność; trwałość; rzetelność
soliloquy (se'lylekły) s. monolog; mówienie do siebie
solitary ('solytery) adj. samotny; odosobniony; odludny;
pojedyńczy; wyjątkowy; adj.
pustelnik; odludek; samotnik
solitude ('solytju:d) s. samotność; osamotnienie; odludne
miejsce
solo ('soulou) adj. adv. w pojedynkę; adj. jednoosobowy;
s. solo
soloist ('soulyst) s. solista
soluble ('soljubl) adj. rozpuszczalny; możliwy do rozwiązania
solution (so'ljuszyn) s. roz-
czyn; roztwór; rozwiązanie
(problemu)

solve (solw) v. rozwiązywać
(np. problemy)
solvent ('solwent) adj. wypłacalny; rozpuszczający; s.
rozpuszczalnik
somber ('somber) adj. mroczny;
ciemny; posępny; ponury
some (sam) adj. jakiś; pewien;
niejaki; nieco; trochę; kilku;
kilka; kilkoro; niektórzy;
niektóre; sporo; niemało; nie
byle jaki; adv. niemało; mniej
więcej; jakieś; pron.: niektórzy; niektóre; kilku; kilka
some more ('sam,mor) exp.: nieco
więcej
somebody ('sambedy) pron. ktoś;
s. ktoś ważny
someday ('samdej) adv. kiedyś
somehow ('samhał) adv. jakoś;
w jakiś sposób
someone ('samłan) pron. ktoś;
s. ktoś
somersault ('samerso:lt) s.
salto; koziołek
something ('samsyng) s. coś;
coś niecoś; ważna osoba; adv.
trochę; nieco; (slang):co się
zowie
sometime ('samtajm) adj. były;
adv. kiedyś; swego czasu
sometimes ('samtajmz) adv. niekiedy; czasem; czasami
someway ('sam,łej) adv. jakoś
somewhat ('samhłot) adv. nieco;
do pewnego stopnia; niejaki
somewhere ('samhłe:r) adv.
gdzieś
son (san) s. syn
song (song)s. pieśń; śpiew
song-bird ('songbe:rd) s. ptak
śpiewający
song-book ('songbuk) s. śpiewnik
sonic ('sonyk) adj. dźwiękowy
sonic boom ('sonyk,bu:m) s.
grzmot samolotu przekraczającego szybkość dźwięku
son-in-law ('san,ynlo:) s. zięć
sonnet ('sonyt) s. sonet
soon (su:n) adv.wnet; niebawem;
wkrótce; zaraz; niedługo

sooner ('su:ner) adv. wczes-
niej; adj. chętnie
soot (sut) s. sadza; kopeć;
v. brudzić sadzą; użyźniać
sadzą
soothe (su:z) v. uspakajać;
uciszać
sooty ('suty) adj. okopcony;
zakopcony; czarny jak sadza
sophisticated (se'fystykejtyd)
adj. wyszukany; wyrafinowany;
wymyślny; doświadczony
sophomore ('sofemo:r) s. student drugiego roku
sorcerer ('so:rserer) s. czarownik; czarodziej
sorceress ('so:rserys) s. czarodziejka
sorcery ('so:rsery) s. czary
sordid ('so:rdyd) adj. brudny
(np. zysk); nikczemny; podły;
skąpy
sore (so:r) adj. bolesny; drażliwy; wrażliwy; dotkliwy; dotknięty; złoszczący się; zmartwiony; adv. srodze; bardzo;
akrutnie
sore throat ('so:r,trout) s.
zapalenie gardła; angina
sorrow ('sorou) s. zmartwienie;
żal; smutek ; narzekanie;
v. martwić się; boleć za...
sorrowful ('sorouful) adj.
smutny; zmartwiony; przykry
sorry ('so:ry) adj. żałujący;
zmartwiony; przygnębiony;
nędzny; marny
sorority (se'ro:ryty) s. korporacja studentek (w USA)
sort (so:rt) s. rodzaj; gatunek; sorta; v. sortować
sortie ('so:rty) s. wypad wojskowy; lot bojowy
so-so ('sou-sou) adj. taki sobie; adv. tak sobie
sought (so:t) v. zob. seek
soul (soul) s. dusza
soulless (soulys) adj. bezduszny
sound (saund) s. dźwięk; ton;
szmer; cieśnina wodna; pęcherz
pławny; sonda; v. dźwięczeć;

brzmieć; grać (na trąbce); bić
na alarm; głosić; opukiwać;
wymawiać; zabierać głos; chwalić się; sondować; zanurzać
się do dna
soundless ('saundlys) adj. bezdźwięczny
soundproof ('saundpru:f) adj.
dźwiękoszczelny
soundwave ('saundłejw) s. fala
dźwiękowa
soup (su:p) s. zupa
sour ('sauer) adj. kwaśny;
skwaszony; cierpki; v. kisnąć;
kwasić się; zniechęcać się
source (so:rs) z. źródło
south (saus) adj. południowy;
z. południe; adv. na południe
southeast ('saus'i:st) s. południowy wschód; adj. południowo-
wschodni; adv. na południowy
wschód
southern ('sadzern) adj. południowy; s. południowiec
southernmost (,sadzern'moust)
adj. najbardziej na południe
southwards ('sausłerdz) adv.
ku południowi; na południe
southwest ('saus'łest) s. południowy zachód; adj. południowo-zachodni; adv. na południowy zachód
southwesterly ('saus'łesterly)
adj. południowo zachodni
souvenir ('su:venier) s. pamiątka
sovereign ('sawryn ) s. suweren;
władca; adj. suwerenny; wyniosły; najwyższy
sovereignty('sawrenty) s. su-
werenność; zwierzchnictwo;
najwyższa władza
Soviet ('souwjet) adj. sowiecki;
radziecki
sow; sowed; sown( sou; soud;
soun)
sow (sou) v. siać; zasiewać; po-
siać
sow (sau) s. maciora; koryto
odlewnicze
sown (soun) v. zob. sow
spa (spa:) s. zdrojowisko; zdrój
mineralny; (USA) sport zdrowotny za opłatą

space (spejs) s. przestrzeń;
miejsce; obszar; odstęp; okres;
przeciąg (czasu); chwila;
v. robić odstępy; rozstawiać
spacecraft ('spejs,kra:ft) s.
pojazd międzyplanetarny
spaceship ('spejs,szyp) s. statek międzyplanetarny(kosmiczny)
space suit ('spejs;sju:t) s.
kombinezon międzyplanetarny
spacious ('spejszes) adj. przestronny; obszerny
spadę (spejd) s. łopata; v. kopać łopatą
spades (spejdz) pl. piki (w kar-
tach)
spadework ('spejd-łe:rk) s.
praca przygotowawcza
span; spanned; spanned (spaen;
spaend; spaend)
span (spaen) v. zob. spin; sięgać (np. przez rzekę); rozciągać się (np. nad rzeką); obejmować (pamięcią); mierzyc pie-
dzią; posuwać się stopniowo;
łączyc brzegi; s. piędz; rozpiętość; przeswit; przęsło;
przeciąg (czasu) zasięg; roz-
ciągłość; para; zaprzęg
spangle ('spaengl) s. świecidełko; błyskotka; v. pokrywać
swiecidełkami; błyszczeć swiecidełkami
spangled ('spaengld) adj. pokryty (swiecidełkami)
Spanish ('spaenysz) adj. hisz-
pański
spank ('spaenk) s. klaps; v. dawać klapsa; popędzać klapsami;
isć kłusem
spanking (spaenkyng) s. skoro-
bicie; lanie; adj. chyży; zamaszysty; silny; solidny; swiet-
ny; adv. bardzo (slang)
spanner ('spaener) s. sciegno
(mostu); klucz do nakrętek
gasienica miernikowa
spare (speer) v. oszczędzać; za-
oszczedzic; odstępowac; obywać
sie; zachować; przeznaczac;
szanować (uczucia); szczędzić;
a. zapasowy; oszczędny; skromny;

drobny; szczupły; wolny (np.
czas) s. część zapasowa; koło
zapasowe
spare time ('speer,tajm) s.
wolny czas
spare tire ('speer,tajer) s.
koło zapasowe
sparing ('speeryng) adj. oszczędny; wstrzemięzliwy
spark (spa:rk) s. iskra; zapłon;
wesołek; zalotnik; v. iskrzyc
się; sypać iskrami; zapalać się;
dawać początek; zalecać się
grać galanta
spark plug ('spa:rk,plag) s.
swieca samochodowa (zapłonowa)
sparrow ('spaerou) s. wróbel
sparse (spa:rs) adj. rzadki;
z rzadka; rozsiany; szczupły
spasm ('spaezem) s. skurcz;
spazm; napad (kaszlu)
spastic ('spaestyk) adj. skur-
czowy; spazmatyczny; chory na
paraliż kurczowy
spat (spaet) v. zob . spit;
kłocic się; dawać klapsy; składać jaja (przez ostrygi); s.
jaja mięczaków; kłótnia;
klaps; lekki cios
spatial ('spejszel) adj. przestrzenny
spawn (spo:n) s. ikra; skrzek;
nasienie; v. składać (ikrę;
skrzek); wylęgać się; płodzic;
zasiewac grzybnię
spayed (spejd) adj.(samica)
z usuniętymi jajnikami; bez-
płodna: wytrzebiona
speak; spoke; spoken (spi:k;
spo:k;'spoken)
speak (spi:k) v. mówic; przema-
wiac; szczekać na rozkaz; grać;
sygnalizować do statku
speak out ('spi:k,aut) v. wypowiadac (się); mówic otwarcie;
mowic głosno
speak up ('spi:k,ap) v. wypowie-
dziec się bez osłonek
speaker ('spi:ker) s. mówca;
głosnik; marszałek sejmu; przewodniczący

spear (spier) s. dzida; włócznia; oszczep; kopia; oścień; źdźbło; v. przebijać dzidą; kłuć; wystrzelić w górę

spearhead ('spierhed) s. ostrze dzidy; czołówka; v. prowadzić; być na czele

special ('speszel) adj. specjalny; wyjątkowy; osobliwy; dodatkowy; nadzwyczajny; s. dodatkowy autobus; nadzwyczajne wydanie; reklamowa dzienna zniżka ceny w sklepie

specialist ('speszelyst) s. specjalista

speciality (,speszy'aelyty) s. specjalność; specjalna cecha

specialize ('speszelajz) v. wyspecjalizować (się); wyszczególniać; precyzować; różniczkować(się); ograniczać (się)

specially ('speszely) adv. specjalnie; szczególnie

specialty ('speszelty) s.specjalność; specjalizacja

species ('spi:szi:z) s. gatunek; rodzaj; postać czegoś

specific (spy'syfyk) adj. określony; wyraźny; gatunkowy; charakterystyczny; specificzny

specify ('spesyfaj) v. wyszczególniać; precyzować; konkretyzować; sporządzić specyfikację

specimen ('spesymyn) s. okaz; przykład; wzór; typ; próba; numer okazowy

spectacle ('spektekl) s. widowisko

spectacles ('spektekls) pl. okulary

spectacular (spek'taekjuler) adj. widowiskowy; efektowny; sensacyjny; okazały; s. film widowiskowy "wielki"

spectator ('spektejter) s. widz

speculate ('spekjulejt) v. spekulować; rozmyślać nad..; rozważać

speculation (,spekju'lejszyn) s. spekulacja; domysł; rozmyślanie

sped (sped) v. zob. speed

speech (spi:cz) s. mowa; przemówienie; język; wymowa; przemowa

speechless ('spi:czlys) adj. (chwilowo) niemy; oniemiały; (slang): pijany (kompletnie)

speed; sped; sped (spi:d; sped; sped)

speed (spi:d) v. pospieszyć; popędzić; pędzić; odprawić; kierować spiesznie; popierać (np. sprawę); s. szybkość; prędkość; bieg

speedboat ('spi:dbout) s. ślizgacz

speed limit ('spi:d,lymyt) s. ograniczenie szybkości

speedometer (spi'domyter) s. szybkościomierz

speed up ('spi:d,ap) v. przyspieszyć; s. przyspieszenie

speedy ('spi:dy) adj. szybki

spell; spelled; spelt (spel; speld; spelt)

spell (spel) v. przeliterować (poprawnie); napisać ortograficznie; znaczyć; mozolnie odczytywać; sylabizować; zaczarować; urzec; dać (wytchnienie); odpoczywać; zaczarować; pracować na zmiany; s. chwila pracy; chwila; okres; pewien czas; zaklęcie; czar

spellbound ('spel baund) adj. zaczarowany; urzeczony; oczarowany

spelling ('spelyng) s. pisownia

spelt (spelt) v. zob. spell

spend; spent; spent (spend; spent; spent)

spend (spend) v. wydawać (np. pieniądze); spędzać (czas); zużywać (się); wyczerpywać; tracić (np. siły); składać ikrę

spent (spent) v. wyczerpany; wydany; zob. spend

sperm (spe:rm) s. sperma; nasienie męskie

spew (spju:) v. wypluwac; wymiotowac; wyrzucac z siebie

sphere (sfier) s. kula; globus; ciało niebieskie; sfera (np. działalności)

spice (spajs) s. wonne korzenie; pikanteria; v. przyprawiac korzeniami; dodawac pikanterii

spicy ('spajsy) adj. korzenny; zaprawiony korzeniami; aromatyczny; pikantny; nieco nieprzyzwoity; elegancki; żywy; ostry

spider (spajder) s. pająk

spike (spajk) s. cwiek; bretnal; kolec; gwozdz do szyn; szpic; ostrze; fanatyk religijny; kłos; v. przymocowywac gwozdziami; zaostrzac konce; ranic kolcami; zagważdżac armatę; zaprzeczac pogłoskom; odpierac; zakrapiac alkoholem; wspinac się na słup ostrymi okuciami(na butach)

spiky ('spajky) adj. kolczasty; wydłużony; ostro zakończony; fanatyczny religijnie

spill; spilled; spilt (spyl; spyld; spylt)

spill (spyl) v. rozlewac (się): rozsypywac (się); uchylac żagiel z wiatru; wyspiewac; wygadac (się); powiedziec wszystko; popsuc sprawę; s. rozlanie; rozsypanie; ilosc rozlana; ilosc rozsypana; odłamek; zatyczka; upadek; fidybus do zapalania swiec

spilt (spylt) v. zob. spill

spin; spun; span (spyn; span; spaen)

spin (spyn) v. snuc; prząsc; kręcic (się); puszczac bąka; toczyc na tokarni; łowic ryby na błyszczkę; zawirowac; s. kręcenie (się); zawirowanie; ruch wirowy; przejażdżka; korkociąg (w locie)

spinach ('spynycz) s. szpinak

spinal column ('spajnel 'kolem) s. stos pacierzowy ;kręgosłup

spinal cord ('spajnel'ko:rd) s. rdzeń kęgowy

spindle ('spyndl) s. wrzeciono; oś; wał; 14400 jardow lnu; 15120 jardow bawełny; v. miec kształt wrzecionowaty

spine ('spajn) s. kręgosłup; grzbiet; ciern

spinning mill ('spynyŋg,myl) s. przędzarnia

spinster ('spynster) s. stara panna

spiny ('spajny) adj. ciernisty; kolczasty; trudny

spiral ('spajerel) s. spirala; adj. spiralny; v. poruszac się spiralnie; szybko isc w gorę (np. ceny); nadawac kształt spirali

spire ('spajer) s. iglica; hełm wieży; zwoj; spirala; ostry szczyt; szpic; pęd; v. strzelac w gorę; nakładac hełm na wieżę

spirit ('spyryt) s. duch; intelekt; umysł; zjawa; odwaga; nastawienie; nastrój; v. zachęcac; ożywiac; rozweselac; zabierac (potajemnie)

spirits ('spyryts) s. spirytus; alkohol

spirited ('spyrytyd) adj. ożywiony; z werwą; napisany z zacięciem

spiritual ('spyryczuel) adj. duchowy; duchowny; natchniony; s. murzynska piesn religijna

spit; spat; spat (spyt; spaet; spaet)

spit (spyt) v. pluc; zionac; splunąc; wypluc; lekceważyc; fuknąc; parsknąc; mżyc; kropic; pryskac; nadziewac na rożen; s. plucie; slina; parskanie; mżenie; jaja owadow; rożen; językowaty połwysep; głebokosc łopaty

spite (spajt) s. złosc; uraz; złosliwosc; v. zrobic na złosc; in spite of= wbrew; pomimo

spiteful ('spajtful) adj. złosliwy; msciwy

spittle ('spytl) s. plwocina; ślina

splash (splaesz) y. chlapać; pryskać; plusnąć; rozpryskać; upstrzyć; s. rozprysk; plusk; zakropienie; plamka; sensacja

splash down ('splaesz,daźn) v. wodować; s. wodowanie

spleen (spli:n) s. śledziona; przygnębienie; splin; złość

splendid ('splendyd) adj. wspaniały; świetny; doskonały

splendor ('splender) s. wspaniałość; przepych, blask

splint (splynt) s. łupek; szyna; patyk; kość piszczelowa; v. wstawiać w szyny złamaną kość

splinter ('splynter) s. drzazga; odłamek

split; split; split (splyt; splyt; splyt)

split (splyt),v. łupać; pękać; rozszczepiać (się); dzielić; oddzielać (się) odchodzić; s. pęknięcie; rozszczepienie; rozdwojenie; odejście

splitting ('splytyŋg) adj. rozsadzający; ostry; gwałtowny

splutter ('splater) v. pryskać; opryskać; mówić bezładnie; s. pryskanie; szybka gadanina; zgiełk

spoil; spoilt; spoiled (spojl; spojlt; spojld)

spoil (spojl) v. psuć (się); zepsuć (się); (slang): krasć; sprzątnąć; przetrącić

spoils (spojls) pl. łupy (też w polityce)

spoilsport ('spojl'spo:rt) s. psujący zabawę

spoilt ('spojlt) v. zob.spoil

spoke (spouk) v. zob. speak; s. szczebel; szprycha

spoken ('spoukn) v. zob. speak

spokesman (spouksmen) s. rzecznik

sponge (spandż) s. gąbka; wycior; tampon; pieczeniarz; pasożyt; v. myć gąbką; chłonąć; łowić gąbki; wyłudzać; wsysać; pasożytować

sponger ('spandżer) s. pasożyt; pieczeniarz (slang)

sponge cake ('spandż'kejk) s. biszkopt

spongy ('spandży) adj. gąbczasty

sponsor ('sponser) s. patron; organizator; gwarant; ojciec chrzestny; v. wprowadzać; być gwarantem; popierać; opłacać (np. program telewizyjny)

spontaneous (spon'tejnjes) adj. spontaniczny; samorzutny; naturalny; odruchowy

spook (spuk) s. zjawa; duch; upiór

spool (spu:l) s. cewka; rolka; szpulka; nawijać na (rolkę etc).

spoon (spu:n) s. łyżka; v. czerpać (łyżką); durzyć się w kims

spoon out ('spu:n,aut) v. drążyć; nabierać

spoon-fed ('spu:n,fed) adj. rozpieszczony; łyżką karmiony

spoonful ('spu:nful) s. łyżka czegoś

spore (spo:r) s. zarodnik; v. wytwarzać zarodniki

sport (spo:rt) s. sport; zawody; zabawa; rozrywka; sportowiec; (slang): człowiek dobry, elegancki, lubiący zakładać się; v. bawić się; uprawiać sport; obnosić się z czymś; popisywać się; wyśmiewać się

sportive ('spo:rtyw) adj. żartobliwy

sportsman ('spo:rtsmen) s. sportowiec; myśliwy

sporty ('spo:rty) adj. (slang): sportowy; krzykliwy (ubiór); modny

spot (spot) s. plama; skaza; kropka; cętka; plamka; miejsce; lokal; odrobina; punkt; dolar; krótkie ogłoszenie; v. plamić (sie); umiejscowić (np. zepsucie); poznawać; wyróżniać; rozmieszczać; adj. gotowy; gotówkowy; dorywczy

spotless ('spotlys) adj. bez skazy

spotlight ('spotlajt) s. reflektor szczelinowy; v. rzucac swiatło (na cos)
spout (spaut) s. wylot; rynna;
wylew; dziobek; strumien;
pochyłe koryto; v. wyrzucac
z siebie płyn; tryskac;
chlusnąc; recytowac
sprain (sprejn) s. bolesne
wykręcenie (nie zwichnięcie);
v. wykręcic
sprang (spraeng) v. zob.
spring
sprat (spraet) s. szprotka
(sledz); v. łowic szproty
sprawl (spro:l) v. rozwalac
się; gramolic się; rozłazic
się; rozrzucac; byc rozrzu-
conym; s. rozwalenie się;
rozłazenie się; rozkrzewia-
nie się
spray (sprej) s. rozpylony
płyn; krople z rozpylacza;
płyn do rozpryskiwania;
spryskiwacz; grad (kul); gałązka; v. opryskiwac; roz-
pryskiwac (się)
spread; spread; spread (spred;
spred; spred)
spread (spred) v. rozposcierac (się); rozszerzac (się);
posiac; rozsmarowywac; rozkładac; pokrywac; nakrywac;
rozklepywac; s. rozpostar-
cie; rozpiętosc; zasięg;
szerokosc; pasta; narzuta;
(slang): smarowidło na chleb
sprig (spryg) s. gałązka;
latorosl; młokos; szyft;
v. ozdabiac gałązkami
sprightly ('sprajtly) adj. żywy; dziarski; wesoły
spring; sprang; sprung (spryng;
spraeng; sprang)
spring (spryng) v. skakac;
sprężynowac; wypłynąc; puscic
pędy (pąki); zaskoczyc; spowodowac wybuch; paczyc się;
puszczac oczko.; pękac; s.wios-
na; skok; sprężyna; zrodło;
zdroj; prężnosc; adj. wiosenny; sprężynowy; zrodlany

springboard ('spryng,bo:rd)
s. trampolina; odskocznia
springtime ('spryngtajm) s.
wiosna
sprinkle ('sprynkl) v. posypac;
pokropic; s. deszczyk
sprint (sprynt) s. krotki bieg;
krotki zrywny wysiłek; v.bieg
na krotki dystans
sprinter (sprynter) s. sprinter;
biegacz krotkodystansowy
sprout (spraut) s. pęd; odrosl;
v. puszczac pędy; wyrastac
spruce (spru:s) s. swierk;
smrek; adj. elegancki; schludny; v. stroic się
sprung (sprang) v. zob. spring
spun (span) v. zob. spin
spur (spe:r) v. pogardliwie od-
trącac; pospieszyc; popędzac;
s. odtrącenie z pogardą
sputter ('spater) v. pryskac
(slina); bełkotac; s. pryskanie; plwociny; bełkot
spy (spaj) s. szpieg; tajniak;
szpiegowanie; v. szpiegowac;
wybadac; czatowac; wypatrzec
squabble ('skłobl) s. sprzeczka; sprzeczac się
squad (skłod) s. oddział; grup-
ka; (lotny) patrol; woz patro-
lowy; v. formowac grupki
squall (skło:l) s. szkwał; kłopot; wrzask; v. wiac gwałtownie; wrzeszczec
squander ('skłonder) s. marnotrawstwo; v. trwonic; marnotrawic
square ('skłeer) s. kwadrat;
czworobok (budynkow); plac;
kątownik; węgielnica; adj.
kwadratowy; prostokątny; prostopadły; uporządkowany; zupełny;
uczciwy; v. robic kwadratowym
prostym; podnosic do kwadratu;
płacic (dług); adv. w sedno;
rzetelnie; wprost
squash (skłosz) v. ubijac (się);
gniesc (się); miazdzyc;
s. miazga; tłok; rodzaj tenisa;
napoj owocowy; mała dynia
squat; squat; squat (skłot;
skłot; skłot)

squat (skłot) v. kucać; przycupnąć; nielegalnie koczować
na gruncie; adj. przysadzisty;
niski; szeroki; s. osoba przy-
sadzista; kucki
squeak (skłi:k) v. piszczeć;
skrzypieć; mówić piskliwie;
(slang): zdradzać (sekrety);
sypać; przepychać się z trudnością; s. pisk; trudne osiąg-
niecie czegos
squeal (skłi:l) v. piszczeć;
kwiczeć; (slang): awanturować
się; sypać; wydawać (kogoś);
s. pisk; kwik; sypanie (kogoś, czegoś)
squeamish ('skłi:mysz) adj.
wybredny; pruderyjny; przesadny; wrażliwy
squeegee ('skłi:dżi:) s. przyrząd w kształcie litery T do
usuwania wody z mytych szyb
squeeze (skłi:z) v. ściskać;
wyciskać; wygniatać; wciskać;
odciskać; ściesnić; s. ucisk;
nacisk; odcisk; tłok; scis-
niecie
squeezer ('skłi:zer) s. wy-
ciskacz (soku)
squid (skłyd) s. przynęta
z mątwy; kałamarnica (ryba)
squint (skłynt) s. zez; ukosne
spojrzenie; zerknięcie; skłonność; v. mrużyć oczy; wysiłać
wzrok; zezować; skłaniac się;
adj. zezowaty; zerkający
squirm (skłe:rm) v. wić się
(z bólu); płonać (ze wstydu);
kręcić się niespokojnie;
s. skręcanie się
squirrel ('skło:rel) s. wiewiórka
squirt (skłe:rt) v. strzykać;
tryskać; s. strzykawka; struga; pętak
stab (staeb) v. dźgnąc; pchnąc;
ugodzić; ranić; s. pchnięcie;
dzgnięcie; rana kłuta
stability (ste'bylyty) s.sta-
łosć; statecznosć; stabil-
nosć; równowaga
stabilize ('stejbylajz) v.
ustalać; stabilizować

stable ('stejbl) s. stajnia;
stadnina; v. trzymać konie
w stajni; adj. stały; stanowczy; trwały
stack (staek) s. stóg; stos;
sterta; komin; kupa; v. układać w stogi; ustawiać w kozły;
układać podstępnie przeciwko
komus
stadium('stejdjem) s. stadion;
faza; stadium (czegoś)
staff (staef) s. laska; drzewce; sztab; personel; adj.
sztabowy; v. obsadzać persone-
lem
stag (staeg) s. rogacz; jeleń;
samotny mężczyzna
stage (stejdż) s. scena; stadium; etap; rusztowanie; pomost; postój; v. wystawiać;
odegrać (sztukę); urządzać;
inscenizować; adj. teatralny;
sceniczny
stagecoach ('stejdż-koucz) s.
dylizans
stage-manager ('stejdż'maenydżer) s. reżyser
stagflation ('staegflejszyn)
s. stagnacja, rosnące bezrobocie i inflacja jednocześnie
stagger ('staeger) v. zataczać
się; wahać się; chwiać się;
układać w zygzak lub w odstę-
pach; porażać; s. układ skosny; zachodzący na siebie w od-
stępach lub zygzakowaty; zataczanie się; pl. zawroty głowy
staggering ('staegeryng) adj.
przerażający; oszałamiający;
rozbrajający
stagnant ('staegnent) adj. za-
stały; stojący; będący w za-
stoju
stain (stejn) v. plamić (się);
brudzić; szargać; barwić; ko-
lorować; farbować; drukować
tapety; s. plama;barwik; bej-
ca do drzewa
stained ('stejnd) adj. zabar-
wiony (np. szkło)
stainless ('stejnlys) adj. nierdzewny (stal); nieskalany

stair (steer) s. stopień; pl.
schody
stair case ('steer,kejs) s.
klatka schodowa
stair way ('steerłej) s. schody
stake (stejk) s. słup; słupek;
kołek; palik; stawka; kowa-
dełko blacharskie; v. przy-
twierdzać kołkami; wytaczać;
przywiązywać do słupa; stawiać na coś
stake out ('stejk,aut) v.
wziąć pod obserwację; wyznaczać granicę
stake-out ('stejkaut) s. zasadzka (slang)
stale ('stejl) adj. stęchły;
nieświeży; zwietrzały;
czerstwy; przestarzały;
v. czuć nieświeżym
stalk (sto:k) v. kroczyć; pod-
kradać się; podchodzić; s.(majestatyczny) chód; podkrada-
nie się; podchodzenie; wysoki komin; łodyga; nóżka (kie-
liszka)
stall (sto:l) v. działać opóź-
niająco; zwlekać; przewlekać;
kręcić; zwodzić; przetrzymy-
wać; dławić motor; utykać;
grzęznąć; trzymać bydło w obo-
rze; zaopatrywać w przegrody
s. stajnia; obora; stragan;
kiosk; przegroda; komora
(w kopalni); (slang): trik;
kruczek
stallion ('staeljen) s. ogier
stalwart ('sto:lłert) s. bojownik partyjny; adj. dzielny;
krzepki; stanowczy
stammer ('staemer) v. jąkać się;
s. jąkanie się
stamp (staemp) v. stemplować;
wytłaczać; tupać; kruszyć;
wbijać (w pamięć); przylepiać
znaczki pocztowe; s. stempel;
pieczątka; znaczek; piętno;
cecha; pokrój; tupnięcie; ubijak do kruszenia (rudy)
stanch (staencz) v. tamować
krwotok; adj. wierny; stały;
krzepki; szczelny

stand; stood; stood (staend;
stud; stud)
stand (staend) v. stać; stanąć;
wytrzymać; znosić; przetrzymać;
zostać; utrzymywać się; stawiać
opór; znajdować się; być; postawić; (slang): płacić; s. stanie;
stanowisko; stojak; trybuna;
postój; łan; ława dla świadków;
unieruchomienie; umywalka
stand back ('staend,baek) v.
stać w tyle; zachowywać rezerwę
stand by ('staendbaj) v. popierać; być w stanie pogotowia
stand off ('staend,of) v. cofać
się
stand-off ('staend,of) s. nie-
rozegrana (równowaga sił)
stand out ('staend,aut) v. wyróżniać się; kontrastować;
wytrwać
stand up ('staend,ap) v. wstawać; powstawać; stawać w obro-
nie; nie ustępować; stawiać
czoło
standard ('staenderd) s. sztandar; norma; miernik; wzorzec;
wskaźnik; stopa (życiowa);
próba; słup; podpórka; adj.
znormalizowany; normalny; typowy; przeciętny; wzorcowy;
klasyczny; literacki (język)
standardize ('staenderdajz) v.
normalizować; dostosowywać do
normy; mierzyć wzorcem; porów-
nywać z wzorcem
standing ('staendyng) adj. stojący; na pniu; pionowy; stały;
s. stanie; stanowisko; znaczenie; poważanie; reputacja;
czas trwania
standing room ('staendyng,ru:m)
s. miejsce stojące
standoffish ('staend'ofysz) adj.
nieprzystępny; trzymający się
z dala
standpoint ('staend,poynt) s.
punkt widzenia; punkt obserwacyjny
standstill ('staendstyl) s. zastój; przerwa; martwy punkt;
unieruchomienie

stank (staeŋk) v. zob. stink

star (sta:r) s. gwiazda;
gwiazdor; gwiazdka; v. ozdabiać gwiazdkami; być gwiazdo-
rem; adj. gwiezdny; występu-
jący w głównej roli

starboard ('sta:rberd) s. prawa burta; v. sterować na prawo

starch (sta:rcz) s. skrobia;
sztywność; krochmal; v. na-
krochmalić;(slang):siła

starchy ('sta:rczy) adj. na-
krochmalony; skrobiowaty;
sztywny

stare (steer) v. patrzec; gapić się; wpatrywać się; zwracać uwagę; s. nieruchomy
wzrok; wytrzeszczone oczy;
zagapione spojrzenie

stare at ('steer,aet) v. gapić
się na...

stark (sta:rk) adj. sztywny;
zupełny; czysty; wierutny;
ponury; posępny; adv. zupełnie; całkowicie

starling ('starlyŋg) s. szpak

starlit ('sta:rlyt) adj.
gwiaździsty; oświetlony
gwiazdami; wygwieżdżony

starry ('sta:ry) adj. gwiaździsty; usiany gwiazdami; promienny; marzycielski; rozmarzony

stars-spangled ('sta:r-spaeŋgld)
adj. usiany gwiazdami (flaga
USA)

start (sta:rt) v. zacząc; ru-
szyć; startować; zerwać się;
podskoczyć; wyruszyć; zabierać się; uruchamiać; obsuwać;
rozpoczynać; wszczynać; s.po-
czątek; start; wymarsz; poderwanie się; obsunięcie się;
zdobywanie przewagi

starter ('sta:rter) s. starter;
rozrusznik; startujący zawodnik; pierwsze danie; kierownik ruchu

startle ('sta:rtl) v. zaskoczyć; zaniepokoić; podrywać;
wzdrygać się; przestraszać;

s. zaniepokojenie; poderwanie
się

startling ('sta:rtlyŋg) adj.
sensacyjny; zdumiewający; niepokojący

staryation (sta:r'wejszyn) s.
głód; głodowanie; głodzenie;
przymieranie głodem

starve (sta:rw) v. głodowac;
zagłodzić; przymierać z głodu,
zimna; łaknąć; zmuszać (głodem, brakiem)

stash (staesz) v. (slang): chować na potem; s.schowanie;
schowek

state (stejt) s. panstwo; stan;
zajęcie; parada; pompa; cere-
moniał; stan prac; adj. państwowy; stanowy; uroczysty;
paradny; formalny; v. stwierdzać; wyrażać; określać; wyrażać (też symbolami)

state department ('stejt,dy'-
'pa:rtment) w USA ministerstwo spraw zagranicznych

stately ('stejtly) adj. uroczysty; okazały; adv. uroczyscie; okazale

statement ('stejtment) s. wyrażenie; twierdzenie; sprawozdanie; wyciąg; oświadczenie;
deklaracja; zeznanie

state room ('stejt,rum) s. prywatny pokój; kabina; przedział

state side ('stejt,sajd) adj.
amerykanski; w stanach

statesman('stejtsmen) s. mąż
stanu

statesmanship ('stejtsmenszyp)
s. rozum polityczny

static ('staetyk) adj. statycz-
ny; nieruchomy

station ('stejszyn) s. stacja;
stanowisko; stan; pozycja życiowa; godność; punkt; stacja
telewizyjna; radiowa, etc.

stationary ('stejsznery) adj.
niezmienny; stały; nieruchomy;
pozycyjny

stationmaster ('stejszyn,ma:-
ster) s. naczelnik stacji

station wagon ('stejszyn,łaegn)
s. samochód typu kombi
statistics (ste'tystyks) s.
statystyka
statue ('staeczu:) s. posąg
statute ('staetju) s. ustawa;
prawo; statut; nakaz
staunch (sto:ncz) v. tamować
krwotok; tamponować; adj. oddany; wierny; zagorzały
stay; stayed; staid (stej;
stejed; stejd)
stay (stej) s. pobyt; zwłoka;
odroczenie; opóźnienie; zawieszenie; podpora; wanta;
zatrzymanie; przerwa; wytrzymałość; v. zostać; przebywać;
wytrzymać; odraczać; kłaść
kres; zaspakajać (głód)
stay away ('stej,ełej) v.
trzymać się z dala
stay up ('stej,ap) v. nie siadać
stay with ('stej,łys) v. mieszkać u kogoś
stead (sted) s. miejsce; na
miejsce; pożyteczność
steadfast ('sted,fa:st) adj.
stały; nieruchomy; niezachwiany; niewzruszony; mocny;
pewny
steady ('stedy) adj. mocny;
silny; pewny; stały; rzetelny;
równy; stateczny; excl.:powo-
li ! prosto ! naprzód ! stój!
v. dawać równowagę; odzyskiwać
równowagę; s. podpora; (slang):
ukochany
steak (stejk) s. stek; befsztyk; płat (np. mięsa)
steal; stole; stolen (sti:l:
stoul; stoulen)
steal (sti:l) v. kraść; wykraść;
wejść ukradkiem; zakradać się;
skradać się; s. kradzież;
rzecz ukradziona; rzecz ku-
piona prawie że za darmo; dar-
mocha (slang)
stealth (stels) s. tajemni-
czość; ukradkowość
stealthy ('stelsy) adj. ukrad-
kowy; tajemny

steam (sti:m) s. para; v. parować; dymić; płynąć pod parą;
gotować w parze; umieszczać
pod parą
steam up ('sti:m,ap) v. zamglić
(się); zajść mgłą lub parą
steamer ('sti:mer) s. parowiec
steamship ('sti:m,szyp) s. parowiec
steel (sti:l) s. stal; pręt
stalowy; adj. stalowy; ze
stali; v. pokrywać stalą; kar-
tować
steelworks ('sti:l,łe:rks) s.
stalowania
steep (sti:p) v. moczyć się;
rozmiękczać; impregnować; po-
grażyc się; rozpijać się;
adj. stromy; nieprawdopodobny;
wygórowany; przesadny
steepen ('sti:pn) v. nagle
podnosić ceny; robić stromym
steeple ('sti:pl) s. strzelista
wieża; ostra wieżyczka
steer (stier) v. sterować; kierować; prowadzić; s. wskazówka; młody wół na mięso
steering wheel ('stieryng,hłi:l)
s. kierownica; koło sterowe
stem (stem) s. pień; łodyga;
szpulka; trzon; trzonek; nóżka; v. pochodzić; tamować; powstrzymywać; iść pod prąd;
zwalczać
stench (stencz) s. smród; odor;
fetor
stenographer ('stenegraefer) s.
stenograf; stenografistka
step (step) s. krok; stopień;
takt; szczebel; schodek;
v. stąpać; kroczyć; iść; tańczyć; podnosić; wzmagać; przyciskać nogą; mierzyć (krokami)
stepchild ('step,czajld) s.
pasierb
stepfather ('step,fa:dzer) s.
ojczym
stepmother ('step,madzer) s.
macocha
stereo ('steriou) s. stereoskop;
dwugłosnikowe radio-adapter;
adj. stereofoniczny

sterile ('sterajl) adj. wyjałowiony; jałowy; sterylny;
bezpłodny

sterilize ('stery,lajz) v. wy-
jałowić; wysterylizować

sterling (,ste:rlyŋg) s. pieniądz pełnowartościowy; adj.
solidny; niezawodny

stern (ste:rn) adj. surowy;
srogi; s. rufa; zad; zadek;
tył; pośladki

sternness ('ste:rnys) s. surowość; srogość

stew (stu:) v. gotować;dusić
(się); martwić się; wkuwać
się; s. potrawa duszona; kłopot; staw na ryby

steward ('stu:erd) s. zarządca;
ekonom; kelner; v. zarządzać;
być stewardem

stewardess ('stu:erdys) s.
stewardesa

stewpan ('stu:,paen) s. rondel; garnek

stick; stuck;stuck (styk;
stak; stak)

stick (styk) v. wtykać; przekłuwać; kłuć; wbijać; zarzy-
nać; przyklejać; naklejać;
utkwić; utknąć; ugrzęznąć;
przyczepiać (się); trzymać
się (tematu); oszukiwać;
s. pałka; patyk; laska; kij;
tyczka; żerdź

stick out ('styk,aut) v. wystawiać; sterczeć; zadać

stick to ('styk,tu) v. trzymać się (tematu); przylepiać

stick up ('styk,ap) v. terroryzować (bronią); brać w obro-
nę; podnosić; przeciwstawiać
się

sticky ('styky) adj. lepki;
kleisty; grząski; parny;
(slang): marny; nieprzyjemny

stiff (styf) adj. sztywny;
twardy; kategoryczny; zdręt-
wiały; "słony"; wygórowany;
trudny; ciężki; silny;
s. (slang): trup; umrzyk;
niedojda; włóczęga; facet;
pedant

stiffen ('styfn) v. usztywniać;
podnieść (wymagania); zgęszczać;
zesztywnieć

stifle (stajfl) v. dusić (się);
tłumić; przygaszać; tuszować

stile (stajl) s. przełaz; kołowrot; pionowa rama drzwi

still (styl) adj. spokojny; cichy; nieruchomy; martwy (przedmiot); milczący; adv. jeszcze;
jednak; wciąż; dotąd; niemniej;
mimo to; v. uspokoić (się); uciszyć; destylować; s. destylar-
nia (też wódki)

stillness ('stylnys) s. cisza;
spokój; bezruch

stilt (stylt) s. szczudło

stilted ('styltyd) adj. na
szczudłach; nienaturalny;
sztuczny; na wspornikach

stimulant ('stymjulent) s. bodziec; podnieta; alkohol;
środek podniecający; zachęta;
adj. pobudzający

stimulate ('stymjulejt) v. pobudzać; zachęcać

stimulating ('stymjulejtyŋg)
adj. podniecający; pobudzający

stimulation ('stymjulejszyn)
s. podnieta; zachęta; podniecenie

stimulus ('stymjules) s. bodziec;
zachęta; podnieta

sting; stung; stung (styŋg;
staŋg; staŋg)

sting (styŋg) v. kłuć; parzyć;
kąsać; szczypać; palić; rwać;
gryźć; s. żądło; ukłucie; poparzenie; piekący ból; uszczyp-
liwość; zjadliwość

stingy ('styndży) adj. skąpy

stink; stank; stunk (styŋk;
staenk; staŋk)

stink (styŋk) v. cuchnąć; śmier-
dzieć; zasmradzać; wyganiać
smrodem; (slang): poczuć smrod
s. smród

stipulate ('stypjulejt) v. za-
żądać; uwarunkować; zastrzegać
w umowie

stir (ste:r) v. ruszać; poruszać;
grzebać; mieszać; wzniecać; podniecać; s. poruszenie; podniecenie; ruch; (slang): więzienie

stirrup ('styrep) s. strzemię;
pocięgiel; okucie do wspinania się
stitch (stycz) s. szew; ścieg;
oczko; kłucie; v. szyc; zaszyc; zeszywać
stoat (stout) s. gronostaj; v.
zaszywać niewidocznym ście-
giem
stock (stok) s. zapas; zasób;
bydło; pień; strzon; kłoda;
łożysko; ród; rasa; surowiec;
kapitał udziałowy; akcje giełdowe; obligacje; wywar; v. zaopatrywać; zagospodarować; za-
rybiać; mieć na składzie;
adj. typowy; seryjny; w stałym zapasie; repertuarowy
stockade (sto'kejd) s. palisada;
częstokół; obóz
stockbroker ('stok,brouker) s.
makler giełdowy
stock exchange ('stok,eks'-
'czejndż) s. giełda
stockholder ('stok,houlder) s.
akcjonariusz; udziałowiec
stocking ('stokyŋg) s. pończocha
stocky ('stoky) adj. krępy
stock market ('stok-'ma:rkyt)
s. giełda
stole (stoul) v. zob. steal;
s. stuła; etola
stolen ('stouln) v. zob. steal
stolid ('stolyd) adj. obojętny;
flegmatyczny
stomach ('stamek) s. żołądek;
brzuch; apetyt; ochota;
v. jeść; przełykać (obelgę);
znosić
stone (stoun) s. kamień; głaz;
skała; pestka; adj. kamienny;
v. ukamieniować; obkładać
(mur) kamieniem; wyjmować
pestki; upijać (się) na umór
stonewall ('stoun-ło:l) v. od-
mówić zaciekle jakiejkolwiek
kooperacji
stoneware ('stoun-łeer) s. naczynia kamionkowe
stony ('stouny) adj. kamienny;
kamienisty; skamieniały;
pestkowy

stood (stud) v. zob. stand
stool (stu:l) s. stołek; sedes;
taboret; stolec; klęcznik; podnóżek; pniak puszczający pędy;
wabik; v. puszczać pędy
stoop (stu:p) v. schylać się;
ugiąć się; poniżyć się; raczyć;
garbić się; s. pochylenie;
przygarbione plecy; weranda;
taras (przy domu)
stooping ('stu:pyŋg) adj. przy-
garbiony
stop (stop) v. zatrzymywać;
powstrzymywać; wstrzymywać;
zatykać; zaplombować; zagrodzić;
zablokować; zamknąć; zaprzestawać; niedopuścić; stanąć; przestać; exp.:przstan ! stój !
dosyć tego !; s. zatrzymanie
(się); stop; postój; przystanek; zatkanie; zator; zatyczka;
zderzak; ogranicznik
stop by ('stop,baj) v. wstąpić
do kogoś na chwilę
stopover ('stop'ouwer) s. zatrzymanie się w podróży
stoppage ('stopydż) s. wstrzymanie; zatrzymanie (się); zatwardzenie
stopper ('stoper) s.korek; zatyczka; v. zatykać; umocować
liną
stopping ('stopyŋg) s. plomba
(w zębie); zatrzymanie; zatkanie
storage ('sto:rydż) s. skład;
przechowywanie; magazynowanie
store ('sto:r) s. zapas; sklep;
skład; mnóstwo; składnica;
v. magazynować; mieścić w sobie; zaopatrywać; wyposażać
store up ('sto:r,ap) v. zama-
gazynować; zachować
storehouse ('sto:rhaus) s.
skład; magazyn; skarbnica; kopalnia
storekeeper ('sto:r,ki:per) s.
sklepikarz; kupiec
storey ('sto:ry) s. piętro
storeyed ('sto:rjed) adj. pięt-
rowy (angielska pisownia)
storied ('sto:rjed) adj. pięt-
rowy

stork (sto:rk) s. bocian
storm (sto:rm) s. burza; wichura; sztorm; zawierucha;
szturm; v. szalec (burza etc.)
wpasc do pokoju; wypasc z pokoju (jak burzą); rzucac gromy; szturmowac; brac szturmem
stormy ('sto:rmy) adj. burzliwy; zwiastujący burzę
story ('sto:ry) s. opowiadanie; opowiesc; powiastka; historia; bajka; anegdota; gawęda; zmyslanie; nowela;
piętro
story teller ('sto:ry,teler)
s. gawędziarz; kłamczuch
stout (staut) adj. dzielny;
krzepki; gruby; s, mocny np.
porto (wino); mocne piwo;
tęga osoba
stove (stouw) s. piec (też kuchenny); cieplarnia; v. zob.
stave; hodowac w cieplarni
stow (stou) v. wypełniac; układac szczelnie; miescic; wsuwac; chowac; przesłac (slang)
stow away ('stou,e'łej) v.
jechac na gapę
stowaway ('stouełej) s. pasażer na gapę
straggling ('straeglyng) adj.
sporadyczny; rozposcierają-
cy się; rzadki
straight (strejt) adj. prosty;
bezposredni; celny; szczery;
otwarty; rzetelny; zwykły;
s. prosta linia; prosty odcinek (toru); adv. prosto;
wprost; na przełaj; po prostu;
pod rząd; należycie; nieprzer-
wanie; ciągiem
straightaway ('strejt,ełej)
adv. natychmiast ;bez zwłoki
straight ahead ('strejt,ehed)
adv. na wprost
straighten ('strejtn) v. wy-
prostowac(się); poprawic (się)
straightforward (strejt'fo:r-
łerd) adj. łatwy; jasny; prosty; prostolinijny;szczery;
uczciwy
strain (strejn) v. prężyc; na-

prężac; naciągac; wytężac; od-
kształcac; naduzywac; nadwerę-
żac; przeciążac; robic gwałtowne wysiłki; cedzic; przecedzac;
s. napręzenie; napięcie; obciążenie; przemęczenie; zwichnięcie; nadwerężenie; wysiłek; od-
kształcenie; rasa; odmiana;
rys
strainer ('strejner) s. sito;
sączek; cedzidło; rozciągacz;
napinacz
strait (strejt) v. sciesniac;
byc w trudnosciach
straited circumstances ('strej-
tyd,ser'kamstenses) s. kłopoty pienięzne
straiten ('strejtn) v. zbied-
niec; zubożec
strait jacket ('strejt'dżaekyt)
s. kaftan bezpieczenstwa
straits (strejts) pl. ciesnina
morska; kłopoty finansowe;
braki czegos
strand (straend) s.skręt; zwitek; pasmo; nitka; warkocz;
sznur; rys; kosmyk; brzeg; plaża; v. splatac; osadzac na
mieliznie; osiąsc na mieliznie
strange (strejndż) adj. obcy;
dziwny; niezwykły; nieznany;
niewprawny
stranger ('strejndżer) s. obcy;
nieznajomy; człowiek nieobez-
nany; exp.:panie tego !
strangle ('straengl) v. dusic;
trzymac za gardło; zadusic
strap (straep) s. rzemien; pasek; rzemyk; tasma; uchwyt;
rączka; chłosta; bicie;
v. na pasku umocowywac;
ostrzyc; bic paskiem; zalepiac
plastrem
strategic (stre'ti:dżyk) adj.
strategiczny
strategy ('straetydży) s.
strategia; taktyka
straw (stro:) s. słoma
strawberry ('stro:bery) s.
truskawka
stray (strej)v. zabłądzic; za-
błąkac się; schodzic na manowce; s. zbłąkane zwierzę; dziecko bez opieki; adj.zabłąkany

strays (strejs) pl. zaburzenia
atmosferyczne (np. w radiu)
streak (stri:k) s. smuga; pasek; pasmo; prążek; rys;
pierwiastek;passa; v. rysować paski, prążki; błyskawicznie poruszać się; wpadać
nagle dokądś
streaky ('stri:ky) adj. prążko-
wany; w paski; zmienny; nierówny (slang)
stream (stri:m) s. strumień;
potok; rzeka; struga; prąd;
v. płynąć (strumieniami);
ociekać; tryskać; powiewać
street (stri:t) s. ulica
streetcar ('stri:tka:r) s.
tramwaj
strength (strenks) s. moc; siła; stężenie; natężenie;
ilość; skład (ludzi)
strengthen ('strenksn) v.
wzmocnić (się); wzmagać; dać
przewagę
strenuous (strenjues) adj.
męczący; żmudny; mozolny; wy-
tężony; zawzięty; pracowity;
energiczny; silny
stress (stres) s. nacisk; akcent; napór; wysiłek;
v. kłaść nacisk; podkreślać;
naciskać
stretch (strecz) s. naciągać
(się); naprężać; napinać; nadużywać; przeciągać; rozciągać (się); ciągnąć się; sięgać; powiesić (kogoś); s. napięcie; rozciąganie; przeciąganie się; nadużycie; połać;
okres służby; przeciąg czasu;
prosty odcinek toru; (slang):
pobyt w więzieniu
stretcher ('streczer) s. nosze
strew; strewed; strewn (stru:,
stru:d; stru:n)
strew (stru:) s. posypać; roz-
rzucić; porozrzucać
strewn (stru:n) v. zob. strew
stricken (stri:ken) v. zob.
strike; adj. dotknięty; nawie-
dzony; rażony; udręczony
stride; strode; stridden
(strajd; stroud; stridn)

stride (strajd) v. kroczyć;
przekroczyć; stać okrakiem
(nad czymś); s. krok; rozkrok
strife (stajf) s. spór; walka;
współzawodnictwo
strike; struck; stricken (strajk;
strak; strykn)
strike (strajk) v. uderzać; bić
(monetę); walić; kuć; wykrze-
sać; zapalić (zapałkę); natrafić; zastrajkować; porzucać
robotę; chwytać (przynętę);
s. strajk; strychulec; wybicie
monety; natrafienie (żyły, np.
złotodajnej); chwycenie przy-
nęty; nieudane uderzenie palan-
tem; zwalenie wszystkich kręgli
naraz
strike off ('strajk off) v. od-
rapywać; ścinać; wykreślać;
drukować kilka egzemplarzy
strike out ('strajk,aut) v.
uderzać na odlew; zacząć; ukuć;
wymyślić
striker ('strajker) s. strajku-
jący; młotek (w dzwonku)
striking ('strajkyng) adj.
uderzający
string; strung; strung (stryng;
strang; strang)
string (stryng) v.zawiązać;
przywiązać; zaopatrzyć w struny; stroić; napinać; podniecać;
powiesić kogoś; ciągnąć sie
(klej); obwieszać; s. sznurek;
szpagat; powróz; sznurowadło;
tasiemka; cięciwa; struna;
żyła; włókno; rząd; stek
(głupstw)
strip (stryp) v. obdzierać;
ogałacać; obnażać; zdzierać;
rozbierać (się); wydobyć do
końca; ścierać (gwint); ciąć
na paski; s. pasek; skrawek;
seria komiksów
strip-tease ('strypti:z) s.
rozbieranie się na scenie
stripes (strajps) pl. paski;
prążki; naszywki; chłosta;
cięgi
striped ('strajpt) adj. pa-
siasty; w pasy

strive; strove; striven
('strajw; strouw; strywn)
strive (strajw) v. starac´ się;
usiłowac´; dążyc´; borykac´ się;
zwalczac´
striven ('strywn) v. zob.strive
strode (stroud) v. zob. stride
stroke (strouk) s. uderzenie;
cios; cięcie; raz; porażenie;
ciąg; pociagnięcie (pióra);
rys; kreska; ruch (wiosła);
wysiłek; suw; skok (tłoka);
takt; głaskanie; v. znaczyc´;
przekreślac´; nadawac´ tempo;
głaskac´; ugłaskac´
stroke of luck ('strouk,ow'lak)
exp.: los szczęscia
stroll (stroul) v. przechadzac´
się; spacerowac´; wędrowac´;
s. przechadzka
stroller ('strouler) s. space-
rowicz; włóczęga; aktor
wędrowny; wozek (dziecięcy)
strong (strong) adj. mocny;
silny; będacy w liczbie...;
mocarstwowy; potężny; trwały;
solidny; wyskokowy; przekonywujący; ordynarny
strongbox ('strong,boks) s.
sejf; kasa ogniotrwała
strongroom ('strong,rum) s.
skarbiec
strove (strouw) v. zob.strive
struck (strak) v.zob. strike
structure ('strakczer) s. budowa; struktura; budowla; wiązanie; splot; v. nadawac´
kształt
struggle ('stragl) v. szarpac´
się; szamotac´ się; walczyc´;
usiłowac´; s. walka;borykanie
strum (stram) v. rzępolic´;
brzdąkac´; s. brzdęk; brzdąkanie
strung (strang) v. zob. string;
adj. napięty
strut (strat) v. kroczyc´ ma-
jestatycznie; rozpierac´;
s. krok majestatyczny; zastrzał; rozpora
stub (stab) s. pniak; korzen:
resztka; niedopałek; grzbiet

(biletu); v. karczowac´; ga-
sic´ (papierosa)
stubble ('stabl) s. rżysko;
sciernisko; twardy zarost
stubborn ('stabern) adj. uparty
stuck (stak) v. zob. stick
stud (stad ) s. sworzen; gwoźdź;
guz; trzon; słup; rozporka;
ogier; stadnina; v. nabijac´
(np. gwoździami; guzami);
usiewac´ czyms; byc´ rozsianym;
podpierac´ (słupami)
student ('stu:dent) s. student;
badający cos; znawca czegos
studio ('stju:djou) s. studio;
pracownia
studio couch ('stju:djou,kaucz)
s. tapczan
studious ('stu:djes) adj. pilny; staranny; dbały; wyszukany
study ('stady) s. pracownia;
gabinet; nauka; przedmiot nauki, staran´, troski, zadumy,
marzenia; v. badac´; studiowac´;
dociekac´; uczyc´ się
stuff (staf) v. napychac´; opy-
chac´ (się); tuczyc´ (się); fa-
szerowac´; wpychac´; wkuwac´;
s. materia; materiał; glina;
rzecz; rupiecie (brednie)
stuffing ('stafyng) s. nadzienie; farsz; nadziewka; wysciołka
stuffy ('stafy) adj. zatęchły;
duszny; ciężki; nudny; zatka-
ny (nos); (slang): ważny;
tępy; skwaszony; zły; purytan-
ski
stumble ('stambl) v. potykac´
(się); utykac´; natknąc´ się;
zawahac´ (kogos); miec´ skrupuły; czuc´ się dotkniętym;
s. potknięcie się
stumblebum ('stambl,bam) s.
(slang): zawalidroga; prozniak
stump (stamp) s. pniak; głąb;
kikut; ogarek; resztka; niedopałek; kulas; krzykactwo; agitacja (polityczna); kuc´; klocek;
przysądkowaty człowiek; v. kar-
czowac´; obcinac´; zdumiec´ (się);
agitowac´; wyzwac´ kogos; cho-
dzic´ na protezie

stun (stan) v. ogłuszyc; oszołomic; s. oszołomienie (uderzenie hukiem)

stung (stąg) v. zob. sting

stunk (stank) v. zob. stink

stunning ('stanyŋg) adj. nadzwyczajny; szlagierowy; kapitalny

stupefy ('stu:pyfaj) v. ogłupiac; odurzac; wprawiac w osłupienie

stupid ('stu:pyd) adj. głupi; odurzony; nudny; s. głupiec

stupidity ('stu:pydyty) s. głupota; głupstwo

stupor ('stu:per) s. osłupienie; odurzenie; apatia

sturdy ('ste:rdy) adj. krzepki; dzielny; solidny; s. motylica

stutter ('stater) v. jąkac (się) s. jąkanie się

sty (staj) s. chlew; burdel; jęczmień (w oku); v. życ w chlewie; trzymac w chlewie

style (stajl) s. styl; maniera; sposób; fason; wzór; kształt; rylec; szyjka; tytuł; nazwa; format; wskazówka; v. formowac stylowo; okreslac mianem

stylish (śtajlysh) adj. szykowny; stylowy; wytworny

suave (sła:w) adj. gładki; łagodny; uprzejmy

subdivision (,sabdy'wyżyn) s. dzielnica (miasta; osiedla); podział

subdue (seb'du:) s. ujarzmiac; poskramiac; przyciszac; tłumic; łagodzic; podbijac

subject ('sabdżykt) s. podmiot; przedmiot; temat; tresc; tworzywo; (sab'dżekt) motyw; poddany; osobnik; v. podporządkowac; ujarzmic; podbic; narazic; poddac czemus; adj. poddany; uległy; podległy; narażony; podatny; podlegający; ujarzmiony; adv. pod warunkiem; z zastrzeżeniem; z uwzględnieniem czegos

subjective('sabdżektyw) adj. subiektywny; podmiotowy

subjunctive mood (seb'dżanktyw, ,mu:d) s. tryb warunkowy

sublime (se'blajm) adj. wzniosły; wyniosły; podniosły

submachine-gun ('sabme'szi:ngan) s. (automatyczny) pistolet maszynowy

submarine (sabme'ri:n ) s. łódz podwodna

submariners (sabme'ri:ners) pl. załoga łodzi podwodnej

submerge (seb'me:rdż) v. zalewac; zatapiac; zanurzac (się); zakrywac

submission (seb'myszyn) s. uległosc; poddanie się; przedłożenie (opinii)

submissive (seb'mysyw) adj. uległy

submit (seb'myt) v. poddawac (się); przedkładac

subnormal (sab'no:rmel) adj. niżej normy; cofnięty w rozwoju

subordinate(se'bo:rdnyt) adj. zależny; podporządkowany; s. podwładny; (se'bo:rdnejt) v. podporządkowywac

subordinate clause (se'bo:rdnyt,klo:z) s. zdanie podrzędne

subscribe (seb'skrajb) v. zaprenumerowac; podpisywac (np. obraz); pisac się na cos; dawac na cel

subscribe for (seb'skrajb,fo:r) v. zapisywac się na (nową) książkę

subscribe to (seb'skrajb,tu) v. abonowac gazetę

subscriber (seb'skrajber) s. abonent; człowiek popierający

subscription (seb'skrypszyn) s. prenumerata; przedpłata; podpisanie; zgoda pisemna; podpis dołączony

subsequent ('sabsykłent) adj. następny

subsequently ('sabsykłently) adv. następnie

subside (seb'sajd) v. klęsnąc; opadac; osadzac się; osiadac; uspokajac się subsidiary (seb'sydjery) adj. pomocniczy; subsydiowany (zależny); s. pomocnik

subsidiary company (seb'sydjery'kampeny) s. firma zależna od innej firmy

subsidize ('sabsydajz) v. zasiłkować; zasilać; opłacać; przekupywać

subsidy ('sabsydy) s. zasiłek (państwowy); subwencja; danina

subsist (seb'syst) s. istnieć; egzystować; utrzymywać się przy życiu; żyć czyms

subsistence (seb'systens) s. utrzymanie; istnienie

substance ('sabstens) s. istota; treść; sens; sedno; substancja; znaczenie; rzeczywistość; majątek

substandard (sab'staenderd) adj. poniżej poziomu; ordynarny (język)

substantial (sab'staenszel) adj. materialny; rzeczywisty; solidny; zasadniczy; ważny; bogaty; wpływowy; konkretny; treściwy

substantive ('sabstentyw) adj. rzeczywisty; niezależnie istniejący; zasadniczy; poważny; rzeczownikowy; wyrażający istnienie; s. rzeczownik

substitute ('sabstytut) s. namiastka; zastępca

substitution (,sabsty'tuszyn) s. zastepstwo; zastąpienie

subtitle ('sabtajtl) s. podtytuł; napis na filmie

subtle ('sabtl) s. subtelny; delikatny; cienki; rzadki; chytry; bystry

subtract (sab'traekt) v. odejmować

suburb ('sabe:rb) s. przedmieście

suburban ('sabe:rben) adj. podmiejski

subway ('sabłej) s. kolejka podziemna

succeed (sek'si:d) v. mieć pocy

wodzenie; udawać się; następować po kims

success (sek'ses) s. powodzenie; sukces; rzecz udana; człowiek mający sukces

successful (sek'sesful) adj. udały; mający powodzenie

succession (sek'seszyn) s. następstwo; kolej; kolejność; sukcesja; spadkobiercy; szereg

successive (sek'sesyw) adj. kolejny

successor (sek'seser) s. następca; dziedzic; spadkobierca

succumb (se'kam) v. ulegać (pokusie); poddawać się; umierać

such (sacz) adj. taki; tego rodzaju; pron. taki; tym podobny

suck (sak) v. ssać; korzystać; wyzyskiwać; wchłaniać; wciągać; (slang): nabierać; dac się nabrać; podlizywać się komus; s. ssanie; wciąganie; (slang): łyk

suckle ('sakel) v. karmić piersią; dawać piers; ssać piers

suckling ('saklyng) s. osesek; młode w okresie ssania

sudden ('sadn) adj. nagły

sudden death ('sadn,det) s. nagła śmierc; rozstrzygnięcie w następnej rozgrywce

suddenly ('sadnly) adv. nagle; raptowanie; nieoczekiwanie

suds (sadz) pl. mydliny; (slang): piwo

sue (su:) v. skarżyc; zaskarżac; pozywać; upraszać; ubiegać się

suede (slejd) s. zamsz

suet ('su:yt) s. łój; adj. łojowy

suffer ('safer) v. cierpiec; ucierpieć; ścierpieć; doznac (czegos); zostać straconym

suffer from ('safer,from) v. być chorym(na cos)

sufferable ('saferebl) adj. znośny

sufferer ('saferer) s. cierpiący

suffice (se'fajs) v. wystarczyc

sufficiency(se'fyszensy) s. wystarczająca ilość; zapasy

sufficient (se'fyszent) adj. dostateczny; wystarczający

suffix ('safyks) s. przyrostek

suffocate ('safokejt) v. udusic; zadusic

sugar ('szuger) s. cukier; słodkie dziecko; (slang): forsa; v. słodzic

sugar-cane ('szugerkejn) s. trzcina cukrowa

suggest (se'dżest) v. sugerowac; proponowac; nasuwac; podsuwac; poddawac (mysl)

suggestion (se'dżestszyn) s. sugestia; wskazówka; mysl; poddawanie; podsuwanie; slad (czegos)

suggestive (se'dżestyw) adj. przypominający; nasuwający (mysl). dwuznaczny

suicide (,su:y'sajd) s. samobójstwo; samobójca; v. popełnic samobójstwo

suit (su:t) v. dostosowac; odpowiadac; służyc; wybrac; byc odpowiednim; zadowalac; pasowac; s. garnitur; ubranie; komplet; skarga; proces; prosba; zaloty; staranie się; zestaw

suit yourself ('su:tjor,self) exp.:rób co chcesz

suitable ('su:tebl) adj. własciwy; stosowny; odpowiedni

suitcase ('su:tkejs) s. walizka

suite (sli:t) s. swita; orszak; szereg; zestaw (mebli); apartament; garnitur; komplet; suita

suitor ('su:ter) s. zalotnik; petent; pretendent; strona; konkurent

sulfate ('salfejt)s. siarczan; v. zakwaszac; zamieniac na siarczan

sulfur ('salfer) s. siarka; v. siarkowac

sulk (salk) v. byc w złym humorze; s. zły humor; człowiek w złym humorze

sulky ('salky) adj. w złym humorze; ponury; s. jednokonny dwukołowy wózek

sullen ('salen) adj. ponury; posępny; flegmatyczny; powolny

sulphur ('salfer) s. siarka; v. siarkowac

sultry ('saltry) adj. parny; duszny; gwałtowny; gorący; namiętny

sum (sam) s. suma; w sumie; rachunek; v. dodawac; zbierac; podsumowywac

sum up ('sam,ap) v. dodawac; zbierac; podsumowywac

summarize ('samerajz) v. streszczac; zbierac; podsumowywac

summary ('samery) s. streszczenie; skrót; adj. pobieżny; dorazny; krótki

Summer ('samer) s. lato; v. spędzac lato

Summer resort ('samer ry'so:rt) s. letnisko

Summer school ('samer,sku:1) s. szkoła w lecie, w czasie wakacji

summit ('samyt) s. szczyt

summon ('samen) v. wzywac (oficjalnie); zdobywac się(na odwagę)

summons ('samens) pl. wezwanie urzędowe; v. doręczac wezwanie urzędowe

sun (san) s. słońce; v. nasłoneczniac (się)

sunbath ('sanba:s) s. kąpiel słoneczna

sunbathe ('sanbejz) v. opalac się

sunbeam ('sanbi:m) s. promien słonca

sunburn ('sanbe:rn) s. opalenizna

Sunday ('sandy) s. niedziela

sundial ('sandajel) s. zegar słoneczny

sundries ('sandryz) s. różności;
rozmaitości

sundry ('sandry) adj. różny;
rozmaity

sung (sang) v. zob. sing

sunglasses (san,gla:sys) pl.
okulary od słońca

sunk (sank) v. zob. sink

sunken ('sanken) v. zob. sink;
adj. zapadnięty; zatopiony;
podwodny

sunny ('sany) adj. słoneczny

sunny side up ('sany,sajd ap)
exp.:jaja sadzone

sunrise ('san-rajz) s. wschód
słońca

sunshade ('sanshejd) s. parasol
od słońca

sunset ('sanset) s. zachód
słońca

sunshine ('sanszajn) s. blask
słońca; pogoda. wesołość

sunstroke ('sanstrouk) s. porażenie słoneczne

sup (sap) s. łyk; v. częstować
kolacją; zjeść kolacje; pić
małymi łykami

super ('su:per) adj. pierwszorzędny; wspaniały; kwadratowy;
prefix: nad-; prze-; s. statysta; nadzorca; szlagier;
przebój (filmowy); najlepszy
gatunek

superabundant ('su:per,e'bandent) adj. nadmierny; przebo-
gaty

superb (se:'pe:rb) adj. wspaniały

super-duper (,su:per-'du:per)
adj. (slang): b. dobry; luksusowy; bardzo elegancki

superficial (,su:per'fyszel)
adj. powierzchowny; powierzchniowy

superfluous (su'pe:rflues)
adj. zbędny; zbyteczny

super-highway (su'per-hajłej)
s. (m,in. 4-pasmowa) autostrada

superhuman(,su:per'hju:man)
adj. nadludzki

superintend (,su:peryn'tend)
v. nadzorować; doglądać; kierować

superintendent (,su:peryn'tendent) s. nadzorca; dozorca;
nadinspektor

superior (su:'pierjer) adj.
wyższy; nieprzeciętny;
pierwszorzędny; przewyższa-
jący; lepszy; nadęty; wyniosły;
s. zwierzchnik; przełożony;
starszy rangą

superiority,(su:,pie:ry'oryty)
s. wyższość

superlative (su:'pe:rlatyw)
adj. najwyższy; s. szczyt;
superlatyw; stopień najwyższy

superman ('su:permen) s. nadczłowiek

supermarket ('su:per'ma:rkyt)
s. supersam; duży sklep samo-
obsługowy (żywnościowy)

supernatural (,su:per'naeczerel) adj. nadprzyrodzony

supernumerary (,su:per'nju:me-
ryry) adj. nadliczbowy; nie-
etatowy; statysta

superscription (,su:per'skrypszyn) s.napis u góry; nadpis;
adres; napis

supersede (sju:per'si:d) v.
zastąpić; wypierać; zajmować
miejsce

supersonic (,su:per'sonyk)
adj. ultradźwiękowy; ponad-
dźwiękowy

superstition (su:per'styszyn)
s. zabobon; przesądy

supervise ('su:perwajz) v.
nadzorować; doglądać

supervisor ('su:perwajzer)
s. inspektor; nadzorca

supper ('saper) s. wieczerza;
kolacja

supple ('sapl) adj. giętki;
gibki; v. stawać się gibkim

supplement ('saplyment) s.
dodatek; uzupełnienie;
v. uzupełniać

supplementary ('saplymentery)
adj. dodatkowy; uzupełniają-
cy

supplication (,saply'kejszyn)
s. błaganie; prosba
supplier (se'plajer) s. dostawca
supply (se'plaj) s. zapas;
aprowizacja; zaopatrzenie;
dostarczenie; dostawy; kredyty; podaż; dopływ; zasilanie;
v. dostarczac; zaopatrywac;
zaradzic; zastępowac
support (se'po:rt) s. utrzymanie; podtrzymanie; podpora;
poparcie; pomoc; wspornik;
dźwigar; rama; łożysko; podłoże; ostoja; v. podtrzymy-
wac; utrzymywac; podpierac;
popierac; wytrzymywac; znosic; tolerowac
suppose (se'pouz) v. przy-
puszczac; zakładac; sądzic
supposed (se'pouzd) adj. domniemany; przypuszczalny;
rzekomy
supposedly (se'pouzdly) adv.
rzekomo; przypuszczalnie
supposition (sape'zeszyn) s.
przypuszczenie; domniemanie
suppress (se'pres) v. tłumic;
zgniatac; znosic; zatrzymywac (krwawienie); usuwac;
taic
suppression (se'preszyn) s.
stłumienie; zgniecenie;
zniesienie; usunięcie; prze-
milczenie; zatajenie
suppurate ('sapjurejt) v. ropiec
supremacy (se'premesy) s.
zwierzchnictwo; przewaga; najwyższa władza; supremacja
supreme (se'pri:m) adj. najwyższy; doskonały; ostateczny
surcharge (se:r'cza:rdż) s.
nadpłata; nadmierny ciężar;
dodatkowy ciężar; opłata (kar-
na); przeładowanie; v. ściągac opłatę podatkową; nakładac grzywnę; przeładowac;
przedrukowac (znaczek)
sure (szuer) adj. pewny; niezawodny; niemylny; bezpieczny;
exp.: napewno !; zgadza się !

adv. z pewnoscią; pewnie; napewno; niezawodnie; niechybnie
sure enough ('szuer,y'naf) adv.
faktycznie
surely ('szuerly) adv. pewnie;
z pewnoscią
surety ('szuerty) s. ręczyciel;
gwarancja; zabezpieczenie;
kaucja; pewnosc
surf (se:rf) s. (łamiące się)
fale przybrzeżne
surface (se:rfys) s. powierzchnia; v. wypływac na powierzchnię; wykanczac powierzchnię
surfboard ('se:rfbo:rd) s. pojedyncza (deska); narta wodna;
v. jeździc na desce na falach
ku brzegowi
surfriding ('se:rf,rajdyng) v.
zjeżdżac z fal ku brzegowi
surge (se:rdż) s. gwałtowny
impuls; fala uskokowa; falowanie; fala; v. nagle wzbierac;
drgac; popuscic; kołysac;
hustac; zeslizgiwac się
surgeon ('se:rdżen) s. chirurg
surgery ('se:rdżery) s. chi-
rurgia; operacja; sala opera-
cyjna
surgical ('se:rdżykel) adj.
chirurgiczny
surly ('se:rly) adj. grubianski;
zgryźliwy
surmise ('se:rmajz) s. domysł;
v. domyslac się czegos
surmount (ser'maunt) v. pokony-
wac; wychodzic na (górę);
przechodzic przez; pokrywac;
wznosic się
surmounted by (ser'mauntyd baj)
adj. pokonany przez
surname ('se:rnejm) s. nazwisko;
przydomek; (se:r'nejm) v.
przezywac; nadawac przydomek
surpass (se:r'paes) v. przewyższac; przechodzic (oczekiwania)
surpassing (se:r'paesyng) adj.
nieprzescigniony; niezrównany
surplus (se:r'plas) s. nadwyżka; nadmiar; superata; nadwyżka
produkcyjna; wartosc dodatkowa;
adj. stanowiący nadwyżkę; nadwyżko-
wy; zbywający

surprise (ser'prajz) s. niespodzianka; zaskoczenie; zdziwienie; v. zaskoczyć; zdziwić;
zmuszać; złapać na gorącym
uczynku; adj. nieoczekiwany;
niespodziewany

surprised (ser'prajzd) adj. za-
skoczony; złapany na gorącym
uczynku

surrender (se'render) s. poddanie się; wyrzeczenie się;
v. poddawać się; oddawać się;
wyrzekać się czegoś

surround (se'raund) v. otaczać;
okrążać

surroundings (se'raundyngs) pl.
otoczenie

survey (se:r'wej) s. przegląd;
oględziny; inspekcja; pomiary;
plan (topograficzny); opis;
ankieta; statystyka; v. przeglądać; robić pomiary; wymierzać; oglądać

surveying (se:r'wejyng) s.
miernictwo

surveyor (se:r'wejer) s. mierniczy; inspektor celny

survival (ser'wajwel) s. przeżycie; przeżytek

survive (ser,wajw) v. przeżyć;
dalej żyć

survivor (ser'wajwer) s. człowiek pozostały przy życiu

susceptible (se'septybl) adj.
wrażliwy; drażliwy; podatny;
dopuszczający

suspect (sęs'pekt) v. podejrzewać kogoś; ('saspekt) adj.
podejrzany

suspected (ses'pektyd) adj.
podejrzany

suspend (ses'pend) v. zawiesić;
powstrzymać (się chwilowo)

suspended (ses'pendyd) adj.
zawieszony w czynnościach

suspenders (ses'penders) pl.
podwiązki; szelki

suspense (ses'pens) s. niepewność; zawieszenie; nierozstrzyg-
nięcie

suspension (ses'penszyn) s. zawieszenie; zawiesina; wstrzymanie

suspension bridge (ses'penszyn-
,brydż) s. wiszący most

suspicion (ses'pyszyn) s. podejrzenie; v. podejrzewać

suspicious (ses'pyszes) adj.
podejrzany; nieufny

sustain (ses'tejn) v. podtrzymywać; dźwigać; cierpieć; doznawać; ponosić; potwierdzać;
utrzymywać; uznawać (słuszność)

sustenance ('sastynens) s. pożywienie; utrzymanie

swab (słob) s. wycior; wacik
chłonący; ścierka na kiju;
gamoń; epoleta; v. wycierać;
ścierać; wuszorować

swab up ('słob,ap) v. wytrzeć

swagger (słaeger) v. parądować;
dumnie chodzić; chełpić się;
pysznić się;odstraszyć; nakłaniać strachem

swallow ('słolou) v. połykać
(np. zniewagę); przełykać;
dać się nabrać; odwołać (słowa); s. przełykanie; łyk; kęs;
przełyk; jaskółka

swam (słaem) v. zob. swim

swamp (słomp) s. bagno; v. zalewać; pochłaniać; przysłaniać; grzęznąc

swampy (słompy) adj. bagnisty;
błotnisty

swan (słon) s. łabędź

swap (słop) v. zamieniać (się);
wymieniać (się); s. zamiana;
wymiana

swarm (sło:rm) s. mrowie;
mnóstwo; rój; v. roić (się);
wyroić; obfitować (w coś);
wspinać się; wdrapywać się

swarthy ('sło:rty) adj. śniady;
smagły

swathe (słejz) v. spowijać;
s. zawinięcie; bandaż

sway (słej) v. kołysać (się);
chwiać (się); zachwiać (się);
rządzić czymś; władać;
s. chwianie się; władza

swear; sware; sworn (słeer;
sło:r; sło:rn)

swear (słeer) v. przysięgać;
poprzysiąc

sweat (słet) s. poty; pot; harówka; v. pocić się; pracować ciężko; (slang): harować; szwejsować; fermentować; wyświechtywać monety; wydzielać (żywicę)

sweat out (słet,aut) v. wypacać (się); (slang): ciężko pracować; wyduszać z kogoś coś; wyciągać pieniądze szantażem; wyciągać odpowiedzi torturami; odsiadywać więzienie

sweater ('słeter) s. sweter; wyzyskiwacz robotników

sweatshop ('słet,szop) s. zakład wyzyskujący robotników

sweatshirt ('slet,sze:rt) s. koszula trykotowa

Swedish ('słi:dysz) adj. szwedzki

sweep; swept; swept (słi:p; słept; słept)

sweep (słi:p) v. zamiatać; wymiatać; zmiatać; oczyszczać; wygrywać (np. wszystkie medale); porywać (słuchaczy); przewalić się przez coś (burza; wichura; powódź); ogarniać; obejmować; rozciągać się; sunąc uroczyście; ślizgać się; śmigać; zwalać (kogoś z nóg); ostrzeliwać; etc. s. zamiatanie; zdobycie; zagarnięcie; ogołocenie; śmieci; śmignięcie; machnięcie; zasięg; robienie zakrętu; etc.

sweeper ('słi:per) s. zamiatacz; zamiataczka; zmiotka

sweeping ('słi:pyng) adj. szeroki; wspaniały; rozległy; daleko idący

sweepings ('słi:pyngs) pl. śmieci

sweepstake ('słi:pstejk) s. wyścigi; loteria; nagroda (zbiorowa) w wyścigach

sweet (słi:t) adj. słodki; przyjemny; miły; rozkoszny; dobrze osłodzony; deserowy; melodyjny; świeży; łagodny; zakochany

sweeten ('słi:tn) v. słodzić; osładzać; stawać się słodkim; (slang): zwiększać stawkę; zwiększac zastaw

sweetheart ('słi:t-ha:rt) s. ukochana; ukochany

sweetness ('słi:tnys) s. słodycz

sweetpea ('słi:tpi:) s. groszek pachnący

swell; swollen; swelled (słel; słoulen; słeld)

swell (słel) v. puchnąć; wzdymać (się); nadymać (się); wydymać (się); rozdymać; wzbierać; wzrastać; potęgować się; s. wydęcie; zgrubienie; nabrzmienie; wzbieranie; wzburzona fala (morze); (slang): wytworniak; gruba ryba

swelling ('słelyng) s. spuchlizna; wzdęcie; obrzęk; wezbranie (rzeki)

swept (słept) v. zob. sweep

swerve (słe:rw) s. odchylenie; zboczenie; v. zbaczać; odchylać (się)

swift (słyft) adj. prędki; rączy; chyży; żywy; s. nawijak przędzy; traszka; jaszczurka; jerzyk

swiftness ('słyftnys) s. prędkość; chyżość

swim; swam; swum (słym; słaem; słam)

swim (słym) v. płynąć; przepływać; pływać (w wyścigach); pławić; ociekać czymś; unosić się na powierzchni; iść z prądem; kręcić się (w głowie); s. pływanie; nurt (życia); woda (do pływania); głębia; pęcherz pławny

swimmer ('słymer) s. pływak

swimming ('słymyng) s. pływanie

swimming pool ('słymyng,pu:l) s, pływanlnia

swimming suit ('słymyng,sju:t) s. kostium kąpielowy

swindle (słyndl) s. oszustwo; v. oszukiwać

swine (słajn) s. świnia

swing ; swung; swang (słyng;
slang;słaeng)

swing (słyng) v. huśtać (się);
kołysać (się); wahać (się);
bujać (się); machać; wywijać;
przerzucać (się) na coś; porywać (za sobą); pociągać
(za sobą); s. huśtanie (się);
kołysanie (się); ruch wahadłowy; zmiana pracy; objazd (te-
renu); rytm; przerzucanie się;
kołyszący chód; taniec (swing)

swing bridge ('słyng,brydź) s.
most wahadłowy

swing door ('słyng,do:r) s.
drzwi wahadłowe

swing wheel ('słyng,hłi:l) s.
koło rozpędowe (zamachowe)

swirl (słe:rl) s. wir; wirowanie; skręt; lok; v. wirować;
kręcić się; unosić się (wiru-
jąc)

Swiss (słys) adj. szwajcarski

switch (słycz) s. pręt; zwrotnica; przekładnia; wyłącznik;
przełącznik; kontakt; śmignięcie; v. bić prętem; machać;
wyrywać; zmieniać; przełączać;
włączać; rozłączać (się); wyłączać (się); włączać (np.
światło)

switch off ('słycz,of) v. wyłączać

switch on ('słycz,on) v. włączać

switchboard ('słyczbo:rd) s.
tablica rozdzielcza; łącznica
(telefoniczna etc.)

swollen ('słoulen) v. zob.swell
adj. opuchnięty; wzdęty;
wezbrany

swoon (słu:n) v. zemdleć; omdlec; zamierać; s. omdlenie

swoop down on ('słu:p,dałn on)
v. zaatakować z góry; runąć
na cos

swoop up ('słu:p,ap) v. porywać; s. spadnięcie; porwanie

swop (słop) v. zamieniać; wymieniać; s. zamiana; wymiana

sword (so:rd) s. pałasz; szpada;
miecz; szabla; bagnet (slang)

swore (sło:r) v. zob. swear

sworn (sło:rn) v. zob. swear;
adj. zaprzysiężony; przy-
sięgły

swum (słam) v. zob. swim

swung (słang)v. zob. swing

sycamore ('sykemo:r) s. jawor;
klon; figowiec

syllable ('sylebl) s. sylaba;
zgłoska

symbol ('symbel) s. symbol;
v. symbolizować

symbolic (,sym'bolyk) adj.
symboliczny

symbolism ('symbelyzem) s.
symbolizm

symmetric (sy'metryk) adj. symetryczny

symmetry ('symytry) s. symetria

sympathetic (,sympe'tetyk) adj.
współczujący; życzliwy; sympatyczny; współbrzmiący;
s. współczulny; łatwy do za-
hipnotyzowania

sympathize ('sympetajz) v.
współczuć; miec zrozumienie;
sympatyzować z kims

sympathy ('sympety) s. współczucie; solidarność; sympatia

symphony ('symfeny) s. symfonia

symptom (sympten) s. symptom

synagogue ('synegog) s. bożni-
ca; synagoga

synchronize ('synkrenajz) s.
działać równocześnie; synchronizować; pokazywać jednakowo
(czas); uzgadniać (zegary)

synonym ('synenym) s. synonim

synonymous (sy'nonymeş) adj.
równoznaczny z czyms

syntax ('syntaeks) s. składnia

synthesis ('syntysys) s. synteza

syntheses ('syntysi:s) pl. syn-
tezy

synthetic (syn'tetyk) adj.
sztuczny; syntetyczny

syphilis ('syfylys) s. kiła; sy-
filis

syringe ('syryndż) s. strzykawka; v. strzykać (wodą)

syrup ('syrep) s. syrop

system ('systym) s. system

systematic (,systy'maetyk) adj. systematyczny

t (ti:) dwudziesta litera alfabetu angielskiego

tab (taeb) s. patka; wieszak (przyszyty); język (buta); naszywka; języczek; ucho; przywieszka; rachunek; kontrola; pilnowanie; v. prowadzic ewidencję; tabelowac; zaopatrywac w (języczek lub ucho etc.)

table ('tejbl) s. stół; stolik; tablica; tabela; tabliczka (np. mnożenia); płyta; płaskowyż; blat; v. kłasc na stole; odraczac (na długo); wciągac na agendę; adj.stołowy

tablecloth ('tejbl,klos) s. obrus

tableland ('tejbl-laend) s. płaskowyż

tablespoon ('tejbl-spu:n) s. łyżka stołowa (do zupy)

tablespoonful ('tejblspu:nful) s. pełna łyżka (pół uncji)

tablet ('taeblyt) s. tabletka; tabliczka (do pisania)

taboo (te'bu:) s. tabu; v.zakazywac; adj. zakazany

tacit ('taesyt) adj. milczący; cichy; niemy

taciturn ('taesyte:rn) adj. małomówny

tack (taek) s. gwóźdź tapicerski; papiak; pluskiewka; fastryga; kurs (polityki); taktyka; stan lepki; prowiant; żywnosc; jedzenie; v. przyczepiac; przybijac (lekko); fastrygowac; zmieniac kurs; lawirowac; hałasowac

tackle ('taekl) s. zestaw przyborów (do łowienia, golenia); wielokrążek; takielunek; złapanie i trzymanie; v. zewrzec się; borykac (się); złapac i trzymac; zmagac (się); brac się do czegoś (ostro); umocowywac; porac (się)

tacky ('taeky) adj. lepki; niemodny; marny

tact (taekt) s. takt; wyczucie; dotyk

tactful ('taektful) adj. taktowny

tactics ('taektyks) pl. taktyka

tactile ('taektajl) adj. dotykowy; dotykalny

tactless ('taektlys) adj. nietaktowny

tad (taed) s. berbec

tadpole ('taedpoul) s. kijanka

tag (taeg) s. skuwka; etykieta; kartka; strzęp; przywieszka; znaczek tożsamosci; marka; mandat karny (pisany);ucho; igliczka; wieszadło (przyszyte); błyszczka; dodatek; morał; frazes; banał; cytat; refren; ogon; zabawa w gonionego; v. przyczepiac: skuwkę; kartkę; znaczek, markę; ucho; wieszadło, igliczkę; ogon; dawac: mandat karny, morał; bawic się w gonionego; tańczyc odbijanego; wymierzac wyrok; przeznaczac; włóczyc się za kims; dołączyc do czegos

tail (tejl) s. ogon; tył; koniec; tren; poła; posladki; buńczuk; warkocz; swita; cień (chodzący za kims); v. dodawac ogon; obrywac ogonki; sledzic (krok w krok); zamykac pochód

tailcoat (,tejl'kout) s. frak

taillight ('tejl,lajt) s. tylne swiatło (wozu)

tailor ('tejler) s. krawiec; v. szyc odzież

tailor-made ('tejlermejd) adj. uszyty na zamówienie

tail wind ('tejlłynd) s. wiatr w plecy

taint (tejnt) s. skaza; zaraza; plama; v. plamic; kazic; zepsuc; plugawic

taintless ('teintlys)adj. bez skazy

take; took; taken (tejk; tuk; 'tejkn)

take (tejk) s. brać; wziąć; łapać; chwytać; zdobywać (twierdzę); zajmować (miejsce); rezerwować; zażywać; pić; jeść; odczuwać; rozumieć; pojechać; notować; zrobić (zdjęcie); zadać sobie (trud); dostawać (napadu); przyjmować (radę; karę; etc.); mierzyć swoją temperaturę; godzić się(na traktowanie); nabierać (połysku); iść (za przykładem) s. połów; zdjęcie; wpływy (do kasy)
take along (,tejke'long) v. zabrać ze sobą
take down ('tejk,dałn) v.zdejmować; rozmontowywać
take-in ('tejk'yn) s. oszukanie; naciąganie
take off ('tejk,of) v. rozbierać; kasować; małpować; wystartować; odjąć; usunąć
takeoff (tejkof) s. start; skok; skocznia; karykatura; parodia; naśladowanie; odbicie; lista materiałów
take out (tejk aut) v. podejmować (poza domem); wyprowadzać; wynieść;wyrywać; wykupić; odjąć; oddzielić
takeover ('tejkouwer) s. opanowanie firmy przez manipulacje giełdowe lub finansowe
take over ('tejk,ouwer) v. przejmować (firmę); przyjmować (obowiązki);dominować
take up ('tejk,ap) v. ponosić; wchłonąć; wziąć (miejsce); zacząć (uczyć się); zadawać się;brać;zcieśniać; besztać
taken ('tejkn) v. zob. take; adj. zabrany; porwany; zdobyty; nabrany; oszukany
talc(taelk) s. talk; v. posypywać talkiem
tale (tejl) s. opowiadanie; plotka; wymysł
talent ('taelent) s. talent (do czegoś); dar; uzdolnienie
talk (to:k) v. mówić; rozmawiać; plotkować; namawiać;

s. rozmowa; dyskusja; pogadanka; plotka: gadanie; mowa
talkative ('to:ketyw) adj. rozmowny; gadatliwy
talk-to ('to:k,tu) s. bura
tall (to:l) adj. wysoki; (slang): nieprawdopodobny
tall talk ('to:l,to:k) s, przechwałki
tallow ('taelou) s. łój; v. tuczyć; smarować łojem
talon ('taelen) s. szpon; pazur; rygiel; łapa ludzka; palec
tame ('tejm) v. oswajać; poskramiać; ujarzmić; okiełzać; łagodzić; przytłumić; upokorzyć
tamper ('taemper) s. ubijak; v. majstrować; manipulować; zmieniać coś nielegalnie
tan (taen) s. opalenizna; kolor (brązowy) brunatny; kora garbarska; v. garbować; opalać się (na słońcu); brązowiec; wyłoic komus skórę
tangent ('taendżent) adj. styczny; s. styczna; szczegół oderwany; zmiana tematu (od rzeczy); zmiana kierunku rozmowy
tangerine (taendże'ri:n) s. mandarynka
tangle ('taengl) s. plątanina; v. plątać (się); wikłać (się); (slang): pobić się z kims
tank (taenk) s. tank; zbiornik; cysterna; czołg; (slang): więzienie; v. nabierać do zbiornika; (slang): popić sobie
tankard ('taenkerd) s. kufel
tanner ('taener) s. garbarz
tantalize ('tae ntalajz)v. dręczyć (zwodną) nadzieją; łudzić
tantrum ('taentrem) s. napad złości
tap (taep) v. stukać; odszpuntować; napoczynąć; robić punkcje; naciąć; ciągnąc sok; wykorzystywać; gwintować; podsłuchiwać (telefon); s. czop: szpunt; kurek; zawór; gwintownik; zaczep; odczep

tape (tejp) s. taśma; tasiemka; tasiemiec; (slang): wódka; v. wiązać taśmą (przylepcem); mierzyć; (slang):oceniać kogoś

tape measure ('tejp,meżer) s. miara na taśmie (krawiecka)

taper ('tejper) s. stopniowe zwężanie (się); stożek; ubytek; osłabianie; stoczek; świeczka

taper off ('tejper,of) v. zwężać się stopniowo; cichnąć stopniowo; kończyć się spiczasto

tape recorder ('tejp-ry,ko:rder) s. magnetofon

tape recording ('tejp;ry,ko:rdyng) s. nagranie na taśmę

tapestry ('taepystry) s. gobelin; arras; v. zdobić gobelinami

tapeworm ('tejpłor:m) s. soliter; tasiemiec

tar (ta:r) s. smoła; dziegieć; ter; v. smołować; terować

target ('ta:rgyt) s. cel; obiekt; tarcza strzelnicza; v. kierować do celu; celować; ustalać cel

tariff ('taeryf) s. cło; taryfa; cennik; c. clic wg taryfy; układać taryfę celną

tarnish ('ta:rnysz) v. matowieć; przyćmiewać; brudzić (się); brukać (się); tracić połysk; s, matowienie; skaza

tart ('ta:rt) adj. cierpki; zgryźliwy; s. ciastko owocowe; (slang): kurewka

tartan ('ta:rten) s. materiał w kratę szkocką

task ('taesk) s. zadanie (specjalne); lekcja zadana; przedsięwzięcie; v. wyznaczać zadanie; wystawiać na próbę; rugać

taskforce ('taesk,fo:rs) s. oddział (grupa) do specjalnego zadania

taskmaster ('taesk,ma:ster) s. nadzorca (kontrolujący wykonanie zadania)

tassel ('taesel) s. kutas; kitka; v. ozdabiać kutasami; kitkami

taste (tejst) s. smak; gust; posmak; zamiłowanie; v. smakować; kosztować; czuć smak; mieć smak; doznawać (czegoś)

tasteful ('tejstful) adj. gustowny; w dobrym smaku

tasteless ('tejstlys) adj. bez gustu; bez smaku

tasty ('tejsty) adj. smakowity; smaczny

ta-ta (tae'-ta:) exp. do widzenia; pa ! pa !

tattoo (te'tu:) v. bębnić palcami; tatuować; s. capstrzyk; tatuaż

taught(to:t) v. zob. teach

taunt (to:nt) v. urągać; wymyślać komuś; zwymyślać kogoś; s. urąganie; wymyślanie; adj. wysoki (np, maszt)

taut (to:t) adj. napięty; naprężony; w dobrej formie; w dobrym stanie

tax (taeks) s. podatek; wysiłek; ciężar; obciążenie; v. opodatkować; obarczać; obciążać; nadwerężać; sprawdzać; wymagać wysiłku; zarzucać coś

taxation (taek'sejszyn) s. opodatkowanie

tax collector ('taekske,lekter) s. poborca podatkowy

taxi ('taeksy) s. taksówka; v. jechać taksówką;wieźć taksówką

taxidriver ('taeksydrajwer) s. taksówkarz

taximeter ('taeksy,mi:ter) s. licznik (w taksówce); taksometr

taxpayer ('taeks,pejer) s. podatnik

tax return ('taeks,ry'te:rn)s. podatek (zapłata ze sprawozdaniem)

tea (ti:) s. herbata; herbatka; podwieczorek; v. pić i częstować herbatą

teabag ('ti:baeg) s. woreczek papierowy z herbatą

teach; taught; taught (ti:cz;
to:t; to:t)
teach (ti:cz) v. uczyc (się);
nauczac; wykładac
teacher (ti:czer) s. nauczyciel
teacup ('ti:kap) s. filiżanka
na herbatę
teakettle ('ti:,ketl) s. imbryk; czajnik
team (ti:m) s. zespół; drużyna; zaprzęg; v. zaprzęgac;
jezdzic zaprzęgiem
team up ('ti:map) v. łączyc
się razem ( do pracy etc.)
teamwork ('ti:młe:rk) s. praca zespołowa
teapot ('ti:pot) s. mały czajnik
tear; tore; torn (teer; to:r;
to:rn)
tear (teer) v. drzec; targac;
rwac; kaleczyc; wydrzec (rane)
pędzic; s. dziura; rozdarcie;
wybuch pasji; kropla; łza;
(slang) hulanka
tearoom ('ti:ru:m) s. herbaciarnia
tease (ti:z) v. draznic; nudzic; s. dokuczanie; nudziarstwo
teat (tyt) s. cycek (wulg.;ko-
biecy)
technical ('teknykel) adj.
techniczny; formalny; spekula-
cyjny
technician ('teknyszyn) s.
technik
technique (tek'ni:k) s. technika malowania, rzezby etc.
tedious ('ti:dies) adj. nudny
teem (ti:m) v. roic sie; obfi-
towac; oprozniac; wylewac
teen (ti:n) s. szkoda; zgryzota
teens (ti:nz) pl. wiek 12 do
18 lat
teeny ('ti:ny) adj. malenki
teeth (ti:s) pl. zęby; zob.
tooth
teethe (ti:s) v. ząbkowac
teetotaler (ti:'toutler) s.
abstynent
telegram('telygraem)s. telegram

telegraph ('telygra:f) s. telegraf
telephone ('telyfoun) s. telefon; v. telefonowac
telephone booth('telyfoun,bu:s)
s. kabina telefoniczna
telephone call('telyfoun,ko:1)
s. rozmowa telefoniczna
telephone directory ('telyfoun,
dyrektory) s. książka telefoniczna
telephone exchange ('telyfoun-
eksczendż) s. centrala telefoniczna na zagranicę
telephone kiosk ('telyfoun-
kiosk) s. kiosk telefoniczny
teleprinter ('tely,prynter) s.
dalekopis
telescope ('telyskoup) s. teleskop
teletypewriter (,tely'tajpraj-
ter) s. dalekopis
televise ('telywajz) v. nadawac przez telewizję
television ('telywyżyn) v. telewizja
television set('telywyżyn,set)
s. telewizor; odbiornik telewizyjny
televisor ('telywajzer) s.
telewizor
tell;told; told (tel; tould;
tould)
tell (tel) v. (o kims; o czyms):
mowic; opowiadac; powiedziec;
wskazywac; pokazywac; kazac;
poznac; sprawdzic; policzyc;
poznawac; wiedziec; doniesc;
oskarzyc; skarżyc; miec znaczenie; odbijac się na kims;
odrozniac
teller ('teler) s. narrator;
kasjer; liczący głosy
telltale ('teltejl) s. plotkarz; okolicznosc ostrzegaw-
cza; wskaznik odchylenia
(steru); aparat sprawdzający,
ostrzegawczy; adj. ostrzegawczy; wymowny
temper ('temper) s. usposobienie; humor; gniew; złosc; domieszka;mieszanka; stan; har-
townosc; v.łagodzic; hartowac

temperament ('temprement) s.
temperament; usposobienie;
skala temperowana; temperatura skali

temperance ('temperens) s.
umiarkowanie; powściągliwość;
obstynencja; wstrzemięźliwość

temperate ('temperyt) adj.
umiarkowany; powściągliwy;
wstrzemięźliwy

temperature ('tempereczer) s.
temperatura; ciepłota

tempest ('tempyst) s. burza;
v. zaburzać

tempestuous (tem'pestjues) adj.
burzliwy

temple ('templ) s. świątynia;
skroń; ucho od okularów; rozciągacz tkacki

temporal ('temperel) adj. doczesny; czasowy; skroniowy;
s. kość skroniowa

temporary ('temperery) adj.
chwilowy; tymczasowy

tempt (tempt) v. kusić; nęcić

temptation (temp'tejszyn) s.
pokusa; kuszenie

tempting ('temptyng) adj. ponętny; nęcący; kuszący

ten (ten) num. dziesięć; s.
dziesiątka

tenacious (ty'nejszes) adj.
wytrwały; nieustępliwy; trwały; wierny; czepny; ciągliwy;
mocny; spoisty

tenant ('tenent) s. lokator;
dzierżawca; v. zamieszkiwać;
dzierżawić

tend (tend) v. skłaniać się:
zmierzać; służyć; doglądać;
obsługiwać

tendency ('tendensy) s. skłonność; tendencja

tender ('tender) adj. delikatny; miękki; kruchy; wrażliwy;
czuły; niedojrzały; młody;
młodociany; uważający; dbały; łamliwy; drażliwy; wy-
wrotny; v. oferować; przedło-
żyć; założyć; s. oferta; środek płatniczy; dozorca; tender; statek pomocniczy-za-
opatrzeniowy

tenderloin ('tenderloyn) s.
polędwica

tenderness ('tendernyss) s. czułość; dbałość; delikatność

tendon (tenden) s. ścięgno

tendril (tendryl) s. wąs; wic

tenement house (tenymenthaus) s.
dom czynszowy

tennis ('tenys) s. tenis

tennis court ('tenys'ko:rt) s.
kort tenisowy

tense (tens) s. czas (np. przyszły) adj. naprężony; napięty

tension (tenszyn) s. naprężenie;
napięcie; prężność

tent (tent) s. namiot

tentacle (tentekl) s. macka;
czułek

tenth (tens) adj. dziesiąty

tenthly (tensly) adv. po dzie-
siąte

tepee ('ti:pi:) s. namiot indiański (stożkowy)

tepid ('tepyd) adj. letni; ciepławy; bez zapału

term (te:rm) s. okres; czas
trwania; przeciąg; semestr; kadencja; termin; wyrażenie;
określenie; kres; v. określać;
nazywać;

terms (te:rms) pl. warunki
(kontraktu, porozumienia) stosunki wzajemne

terminal ('te:rmynel) adj. końcowy; terminowy; ostateczny;
s. zakończenie; końcówka;
uchwyt; końcowa stacja

terminate ('te:rmynejt) v. skończyć; zakończyć; kończyć (się);
ograniczać; upływać; rozwiązywać (umowę); ustawać; wygasać;
upływać; wymawiać pracę

termination (,te:rmy'n ejszyn)
s. koniec; wypowiedzenie (pracy); wygaśnięcie; zakończenie;
końcówka

terminus (te:rmynes) s. końcowa stacja; kres; koniec; granica

termite ('te:rmajt) s. termit

terrace ('teres) s. taras; terasa; ulica wzdłuż zbocza;
v. robić terasy

terraced ('terest) adj uformo-
wany w terasy
terrible ('terybl) adj. straszliwy; straszny; okropny
terrific ('te'ryfyk) adj. przerażający; (slang): fantastyczny; pierwszej klasy
terrify ('teryfaj) v. przerażać
territorial (,tery'torjel) adj.
terytorialny
territory ('teryto:ry) s. obszar; rejon; (terytorium bez
praw stanu np. w USA)
terror ('terer) s. terror;
przerażenie; postrach
terrorize ('tereraiz) v. siac
strach; przerażać; terroryzować
test (test) s. próba; sprawdzian; test; egzamin; odczynnik; skorupa; v. sprawdzać;
poddawać próbie; oczyszczać
(metal)
testament ('testement) s.
testament
testify ('testyfaj) v. świadczyć; dawać świadectwo; zaświadczać; poswiadczać
testimonial (,testy'mounjel)
s. świadectwo (moralności);
polecenie; nagroda w uznaniu
zasług
testimony ('testymouny) s.
świadectwo
testy ('testy) adj. drażliwy;
popędliwy; pobudliwy
tetanus ('tetenes) s. tężec
text (tekst) s. tekst
textbook (' tekstbuk) s. podręcznik
textile ('tekstail) s. tkanina; adj. tkacki; tekstylny
texture ('teksczer) s. budowa; tkanina; struktura;
tkanie
than (dzaen) con, aniżeli; niż;
od
thank (taenk) v. dziękować;
s. podziękowanie; dzięki
thank you ('taenkju:) exp.:
dziękuję
thank you very much ('taenkju:-
'wery,macz) exp.:bardzo dziękuję

thankful ('taenkful) adj.
wdzięczny; dziękczynny
thankless ('taenklys) adj. niewdzięczny
thanks ('taenks) pl. podziękowanie; dzięki
Thanksgiving Day ('taenksgy-
wyng,dej) s. dzień święta
dziękczynienia (USA)
that (daet) adj. & pron. pl.
thouse (dzous); tamten; tam-
ta; tamto; ten; ta; to; ów;
owa; owo; pl. tamci; tamte;
ci; te; owi; owe; adv. tylu;
tyle; conj. że; żeby; aby;
skoro
thatch (taecz) s. strzecha;
v. pokrywać strzechą
thaw (tso:) s. odwilż; rozkroch-
malenie się; v. tajać; odtajać;
taje; jest odwilż
the (przed samogłoską dy; przed
spółgłoską de; z naciskiem dy:)
przyimek określony rzadko
kiedy tłumaczony; ten; ta; to;
pl. ci; te; ten właśnie , etc.
adv.  tym; im...tym
theater ('tieter) s. teatr;
kino; widownia; amfiteatr
theatrical (ti:aetrykel) adj.
teatralny; sceniczny; aktorski
theatricals (ti:'aetrykels) pl.
przedstawienie (amatorskie)
theatrics (ti:'aetryks) s.
sztuka teatralna
thee (di:) archaiczna forma;
ty używana przez kwakrów
theft (teft) s. kradzież
their (dzeer) zaimek; ich
theirs (dzeers) zaimek dzier-
zawczy: ich
them (dzem) przypadek zależny
od: they , (np.: im; nimi;
nich)
theme (ti:m) s. temat; zadanie;
wypracowanie
themselves (dzem'selwz) pl.oni
sami; one same
then (dzen) adv. wtedy; wówczas;
po czym; potem; następnie; później; zatem; zaraz; poza tym;
ponadto; conj.a więc; no to;wo-
bec tego; ale przecież; adj.ów-
czesny;s.przedtem;uprzednio;
dotąd; odtąd;

theologian (tie'loudźjen) s.
teolog

theology (tie'oledźy) s. teologia

theoretic(al) (tie'retyk-el)
adj. teoretyczny

theory (tiery) s. teoria

therapy (terepy) s. leczenie;
terapia

there (dzeer) adv. tam; w tym;
co do tego; oto; własnie; potem; tędy; dlatego; z tego;
na to; s. ta miejscowość; to
miasto; to miejsce

thereabout ('dzeerebaut), adv.
w tych stronach; gdzieś tam
mniej więcej; coś około tego

thereafter ('dzeera:fter) adv.
poźniej; odtąd

there are (dzeer'a:r) exp.; są

thereby ('dzeer'baj) adv. przez
to; w ten sposób; skutkiem
tego

therefore ('dzeer,fo:r) adv.
dlatego; zatem więc

therein (,dzeer'yn) adv. w tym;
w nim; w niej

there is (,dzeer'ys) exp.; jest

thereupon ('dzeer,e'pon) adv.
skutkiem tego

therewith (,dzeer'łys) adv.
tym; z tym; w następstwie tego

there you are (,dzeer'ju:,a:r)
exp.; proszę; tu jest to !
tu pan to ma ! etc.

thermometer (ter'momyter) s.
termometr

thermos ('termos) s. termos

these (di:z) pl. od this

thesis ('ti:sys) s. teza; praca dyplomowa; pl. theses
('ti:syz)

they (dzej) pl. pron. oni; one
(ci; ktorzy)

they say (dzej sej) exp.;podob-
no (mowią)

thick (tyk) adj. gruby; gęsty;
zbity; rzęsisty; stłumiony;
niewyraźny; mętny; ponury;
tępy; ochrypły; (slang): blat-
ny; spoufalony; s. gruba część;
duren; głuptas; adv. gęsto;
grubo; ochryple; tępo

thicken ('tykn) v. pogrubiać
(sie); zagęszczać (się)

thicket ('tykyt) s. gaszcz;
gęstwina

thickness ('tyknys) s. grubość;
warstwa; gęstość

thief (ti:f) s. złodziej;
pl. thieves ( ti:ws)

thigh (taj) s. udo

thimble ('tymbl) s. naparstek;
końcówka (metalowa liny)

thimbleful ('tymblful) s. odrobina; naparstek

thin (tyn) adj.cienki (sos;
głos etc). rzadki; szczupły;
słaby (kolor.etc.); (slang):
paskudny; v. rozcienczać;
szczuplec;przerzedzać(się)

thine (tajn) sob. thy; stara
forma: twoj; twoje

thing (tyng) s. rzecz; przedmiot;
uczynek; coś; krzyk mody; warunek; urojenia; przywidzenia;
pl. zwierzęta; rzeczy; odzież;
ubrania; ruchomości; sytuacja;
konjunktura;wszystko; nieruchomości; głupstwa

think; thought; thought (tynk;
'to:t;'to:t)

think (tynk) v. myśleć; pomyśleć;
zastanawiac się; rozważać; rozmyślać (się); wymyślić; wyobrażac sobie; uważać za; miec zdanie; miec za; zapomnieć (rozmyślnie); miec na mysli; rozwiązywać; etc.

think over ('tynk'ouwer) v. prze-
myśliwać; zastanawiac się

think up ('tynk,ap) v. wymyślać;
wykombinować; rozwiązać

third (te:rd) adj. trzeci

third degree (,te:rd,dy'gri:)
exp.; trzeci stopień (przesłuchi-
wania na policji—głupi, przykry i męczący)

thirdly ('te:rdly) adv. po trzecie

third party (,te:rd'pa:rty) s.
strona trzecia; osoby trzecie

thirdrate ('te:rd'rejt) adj.
trzeciorzędny

Third World ('te:rd'We:rld) s.
trzeci swiat (poza Europą,
Chinami, Indią oraz Ameryką)
thirst ('te:rst) s. pragnienie;
żądza; v. pragnąc
thirsty ('te:rsty) adj. spragniony; żądny; suchy; wyschnię-
ty; (slang): ciężki
this (tys) adj. & pron. pl.
these (ti:z) ten; ta; to; tak;
w ten sposób; tyle; obecny;
bieżący; adv. tak; tak daleko; tyle; tak dużo
thistle ('tysl) s. oset
thorn ('to:rn) s. kolec; ciern;
krzak cierniowy; v. kłuc;
drażnic
thorny ('to:rny) adj. kolczasty;
ciernisty; drażliwy
thorough (terou) adj. dokładny;
zupełny; całkowity; sumienny;
adv. na wskros; na wylot
thoroughbred ('te:rou,bred)
adj. rasowy; czystej krwi;
s. koń rasowy
thoroughfare ('te:rou,feer)
s. arteria komunikacyjna;
przejazd; ulica
thoroughly (te:rouly) adv. zupełnie; dokładnie; całkowicie;
na wskros; sumiennie; gruntownie
those (douz) pl. od that
thou (dau) biblijne: ty
though (tou) conj. chociaż;
chociażby; gdyby; adv. jednak;
pomimo tego; przecież
thought (to:t) v. zob. think;
s, mysl; namysł; zastanowienie
się; pomysł; oczekiwanie; rozwaga; zamiar; pl. zdanie; pogląd; odrobina;troszkę
thoughtful ('to:tful) adj. za-
myslony; zadumany; rozważny;
uważający; dbały; uprzejmy;
(oryginalnie) myslący
thoughtless ('to:tlys) adj.bez-
myslny; nieuważający; nierozważny
thousand ('tauzend) num.tysiąc
thousandth ('tauzendt) adj.
tysięczny

thrash (traesz) s. młocic; walic; bic; prac; dyskutowac;
s. młocenie; walenie
thrashing (traeszyng) s, młocka;
lanie
thread (tred) s. nic; nitka;
przędza; sznurek; wątek; żyłka;
krok (śruby); zwojnik (nici);
gwint; v. nawlekac (igłę);
przetykac; nacinac gwint (zwojnik); przepychac się
threadbare (tredbeer) adj. wytarty; wyswiechtany; wyszarza-
ły
threat (tret) s. grozba; po-
grozka
threaten ('tretn) v. grozic;
zagrażac; odgrażac się
threatening ('tretnyng) adj.
grożący; zagrażający; grozny
three (tri:) num. trzy; s.trój-
ka
threefold ('tri:fold) adj.
potrójny
threescore ('tri:sko:r) num.
szescdziesiąt
threestage ('tri:stejdż) adj.
trójfazowy; trzystopniowy
thresh (tresz) v. młocic; roz-
trzasac; obgadac szczegółowo;
omowic gruntownie; s. młocka
thresher ('treszer) s. młockarnia
threshing ('treszyng) s. młocenie
threshing machine ('treszyng,me-
'szi:n) s. młockarnia
threshold ('treszould) s. próg
threw (tru:) v. zob. throw
thrice (trajs) adj. trzykrotnie
thriftlees (tryftlys) adj. rozrzutny
thrifty (tryfty) adj. oszczędny; rozrastający się; kwitnący
thrill (tryl) v. przejmowac
(się); drgac; s. dreszcz;
dreszczyk; drganie; powiesc
sencacyjna; szmer (serca)
thriller (tryler) s. dreszczowiec; powiesc sensacyjna (kry-
minalna); sztuka sensacyjna;
opowiesc sensacyjna

thrilling (trylyŋg) adj. podniecający; przejmujący; sensacyjny
thrive; throve; thriven
(trajw; trouw; trywn)
thrive (trajw) v. dobrze : rosnąc, chować się, rozwijać się,
miewać się, kwitnąc, prosperować
thro(tru:) = through
throat (trout) s. gardło; szyja; wlot; gardziel; wąskie
przejscie; v. żłobić; żłobko-
wać; mówic gardłowo
throb (trob) v. pulsowac; drgac;
bic; tetnic; rwac; s. pulsowa-
nie; drganie; bicie serca;
dreszcz; warkot maszyny
thrombosis (trom'bousys) s.
skrzep
throne (troun) s. tron; v. tro-
nować; wprowadzac na tron
throng (tro:ng)s. tłum; tłok;
rzesza; masa; v. tłoczyc się;
zatłaczac; napierać na
throstle (trosl) s. drozd;
przędzarka
throttle ('trotl) s. gardziel;
dławik; przepustnica; zawor
dławiący; v. dusic; regulowac
dławikiem
through (tru:) prep. przez; po-
przez; po; wskros; na wylot;
ze; z; skutkiem; na skutek;za;
dzięki; z powodu; adv. na
wskros; na wylot; adj. przelo-
towy; bezpośredni; skończony
(np. życiowo)
throughout ('tru:,aut) prep. po-
przez; przez cały; od poczatku
do końca; wszędzie; całkowicie;
adv. na wskros
throw (trou) v. zob. thrive
throw; threw; thrown (trou;
tru:, troun)
throw (trou) v. rzucac; ciskać;
zarzucac; zrzucac; skręcac;
powalic; narzucac; modelowac
na kole; odrzucac; marnowac;
s. rzut; ryzyko; szal; narzuta;
uskok

throw up ('trou,ap) v. wymiotować; rzucac w górę; podrzucać
thrown ('troun) v. zob. throw
thru (tru:) = through
thrum (tram) v. rzępolic; bębnić; robic z nitek; odcinac
luzne nitki; s. brzdąkanie;
odcięta nitka; krajka
thrush (trasz) s. drozd; choroba strzałki kopyta końskiego;
pleśniawka
thrust; thrust; thrust (trast;
trast; trast)
thrust (trast) v. wpychać;
wsadzac; wtykac; wrazic; pchac
(się); przepychać się; wysuwać (się); szturchać; przebijac; wepchnąc; narzucac (się);
wtracac (się); zadawac pchnięcie; pchnąc; s. pchnięcie;
dzgnięcie; wypad; wypchnięcie;
nacisk; siła : napędu, ciągu,
pędu; zrzut; parcie; uwaga;
przytyk
thud (tad) s. łomot; łoskot
(głuchy); v. łomotac; upadac
z łoskotem
thug (tag) s. bandyta; zbir
thumb (tam) s. kciuk; duży palec; władza (domowa); talent
ogrodniczy; zasada (praktycz-
na); v. kartkowac; brudzic
palcami; niszczyc; walac; grac
niezgrabnie; prosic o podwiezienie; wyprosic (gestem)
thumb a lift (tam a lyft) v.
prosic o podwiezienie (autostopem)
thumbtack ('tam-taek) s. pi-
neska; pluskiewka
thump ('tamp) s. grzmotnięcie;
v. grzmocic; walic; isc ciężko
thunder ('tander) s. grzmot;
burza; grom; piorun; v.
grzmiec; rzucac gromy; pioru-
nowac; miotac (grozby)
thunderstorm ('tander-sto:rm)
s. burza z piorunami
thunderstruck ('tander-strak)
adj. rażony piorunem; oszołomiony

Thursday ('te:r-zdej) s. czwartek

thus (tas) adv. tak; w ten sposób; tak więc; a zatem

thus far ('tas,fa:r) adv. jak
dotąd

thus much ('tas,mach) adv. tyle

thwart ('tlo:rt) v. udaremnic;
pokrzyżowac; psuc szyki; adj.
poprzeczny; przeciwny; niepo-
mysIny; s. poprzeczna Iawka
wioslarska

thy (taj) pron. twój; twoje;
zob. thine

tick (tyk) s. kleszcz; tykanie;
moment; wsyp; kredyt; sprawne
działanie; v. tykac; kupowac
na kredyt; sprzedawac na kredyt (slang); ustalac sprawne
działanie

tick away ('tyke'Iej) v. znaczyc tykaniem

tick off ('tykof) v. odliczac;
besztac; odfajkowac

ticker ('tyker) s. telegraf; zegarek; serce (slang)

ticket ('tykyt) s. bilet; kwit;
znaczek; wywieszka; lista
kandydatów (USA); v. zaopatrywac w bilet, etykietkę; umieszczac na liscie kandydatów

ticket office ('tykyt'ofys) s.
kasa biletowa

tickle ('tykl) v. laskotac; lech-
tac; swędzic; rozsmieszac; bawic; cieszyc; s. laskotanie;
lechtanie; swędzenie

tidal wave ('tajdellejw) s. ol-
brzymia fala przypIywu skutkiem
trzęsienia ziemi

tide (tajd) n. przypIyw & odpIyw
morza; fala; okres; v. przy-
pIywac falą; płynąc z falą;
wybrnąc

tidy ('tajdy) adj. schludny;
czysty; niemały; spory;
s. zbiornik na odpadki; pokrowiec na mebel; v. oporządzic;
sporządzac; oporządzac (się);
porządkowac

tie (taj) v. wiązac; zawiązac;

przywiązac; łączyc; sznurowac;
remisowac; zawrzec slub; unie-
ruchomic; s. węzeł; krawat;
podkład kolejowy; próg; remis;
sznur; rozgrywka; półbucik

tie up ('taj,ap) v. zawiązywac;
unieruchamiac

tier (tier) s. piętro; rząd;
węzeł; zwój; kondygnacja;
rzecz wiążąca; fartuszek;
v. spiętrzac się (też warstwa-
mi)

tiger ('tajger) s. tygrys; jaguar; kugar; zawadiaka; pracujący zapamiętale

tight (tajt) adj. zaciśnięty;
mocny; zwarty; szczelny; spoisty: obcisły; wąski; nabity;
wstawiony; zalany; skąpy; niewystarczający; silny; mocny;
uparty; adv. zwarcie; ciasno;
szczelnie; obcisle; mocno;
silnie

tighten ('tajtn) v. zaciskac
(się); uszczelniac; napinac
(się)

tightfisted ('tajt-,tystyd)
adj. sknera; kutwa

tight fitting ('tajt-fytyng)
adj. obcisły; opięty

tightrope ('tajt-roup) s. lina akrobatyczna

tights (tajts) pl. trykot ba-
letnicy, akrobaty etc.;
w Anglii rajstopy

tigress ('tajgrys) s. tygrysica

tile (tajl) n. dachówka; kafe-
lek; dren; (slang): cylinder;
v. pokrywac dachówkami; wykładac kaflami (płytami)

till (tyl) prep. aż do; dopiero;
dotychczas; aż; dopóki nie;
dotąd; v. uprawiac (ziemię);
s. szufladka na pieniądze; kasa podręczna

tilt (tylt) s.przechylenie;
przechył; nachylenie; natarcie
kopią; plandeka; daszek;
v. przechylac (się); nachylac
(się); nacierac kopią; (pełnym)
pędem leciec; zaopatrywac w
daszek

timber ('tymber) s. drzewo; budulec; drewno; belka; wręga; las; charakter; v. zaopatrywać w budulec; podpierać belką

timberland ('tymber'laend) s. obszar lasu budulcowego

timberwork ('tymber:že:rk) s. konstrukcja drewniana

timber yard ('tymber,ja:rd) s. skład (drzewa) budulca

time (tajm) s. czas; pora; raz; takt; v. obliczać czas zużyty; ustalać czas; wybierać czas; robić we właściwym czasie; nastawiać (przyrząd); regulować (zegar); synchronizować; harmonizować; trzymać takt; excl.: czas ! (zamykać lokal etc.)

time and again ('tajm end,e'-'gen) exp.: ciągle; ustawicznie

time bomb ('tajm,bom) s. bomba zegarowa

time is up ('tajm'ys,ap) exp.: koniec (zabawy; rozmowy etc)

timely ('tajmly) adv. na czasie; w porę; adj. aktualny; odpowiedni; właściwy; punktualny

timetable ('tajm,tejbl) s. rozkład jazdy, zajęć etc.

timeless ('tajmlys) adj. wieczny; ponadczasowy (niekończący się)

timid ('tymyd) adj. niesmiały; bojaźliwy

timidity (ty'mydyty) s. bojaźliwość

timorous ('tymeres) adj. bojaźliwy

tin (tyn) s. cyna; blacha; puszka blaszana; blaszanka; folia cynowa; pieniądze; adj. cynowany; blaszany; dziadowski (kubek); v. cynować

tinfoil ('tynfojl) s. folia metalowa; cynfolia; staniol

tinge (tyndž) s. odcień; lekkie zabarwienie; v. zabarwiać lekko

tingle ('tyngl) s. mrowienie; swierzbienie; kłucie; v. czuć kłucie; mrowienie; kłuc

tinkle ('tynkl) v. dzwonic; brzęczec; (siusiać) s. dzwonienie

tinned (tynd) adj. cynowany

tinopener ('tyn,oupner) s. otwieracz puszek (narzędzie)

tint (tynt) s. odcień; zabarwienie; v. zabarwiać

tinware ('tynžeer) s. wyroby blaszane

tiny ('tajny) adj. drobny; malusieński; malutki

tip (typ) s. koniec (np. palca); koniuszek; szczyt; zakończenie; skuwka; okucie; napiwek; poufna informacja; wiadomosć; rada; wskazówka; trącenie; przechylenie; skład smieci; v. wykańczać koniec; okuwać; przechylać (się); ważyć; przewracać (się); dać napiwek; informować (poufnie); trącać lekko; dotykać; uderzać ukosem (piłkę); przeważać

tip off ('typ,of) v. ostrzegać

tip-off ('typof) s. poufne ostrzeżenie (informacja)

tipster ('typster) s. człowiek udzielający poufnych informacji (o wyscigach etc.)

tipsy ('typsy) adj. podchmielony; pijany; chwiejny; niepewny

tiptoe ('typtou) s. koniec palca u nogi; v. chodzic na palcach; adv. na palcach (u nóg)

tire ('tajer) v. męczyć (się); nudzic (się); nakładać obręcz, oponę; przystroic; s. obręcz; opona; strój

tired ('tajerd) adj. znęczony; znużony; znudzony

tireless ('tajerlys) adj. niestrudzony

tiresome ('tajersem) adj. męczący; nudny

tissue ('tyszu:) s. tkanka; tkanina; siatka; bibułka

tissue paper (tyszu:,pejper) s. bibułka; papier toaletowy; papier płótnowany

tit (tyt) s. sikora
tit for tat ('tyt,fo:r taet)
exp.: wet za wet
titbit ('tytbyt) s. smakołyk
titilate ('tytylejt) s. łech-
tac
title ('tajtl) s. tytuł; nagło-
wek; napis; tytuł rodowy; tytuł prawny; prawo; czystosc
złota w karatach
titled ('tajtld) adj. utytuło-
wany
titter ('tyter) v. chichotac;
s. chichot
tittle-tattle ('tytl-'taetl)
v. plotkowac; s. plotkowanie
to (tu:; tu) prep. do; aż do;
ku; przy; w stosunku do;
w porównaniu z; w stosunku
jak; stosownie do; dla; wobec;
względem; za (zależnie od
ustaleń zwyczajowych)
toad (toud) s. ropucha
to and fro ('tu:end,rou) exp.:
tam i z powrotem
toast (toust) s. grzanka; toast;
v. robic granki;wznosic toast
tobacco (te'baekou) s. tytoń
tobacconist (te'baekounyst) s.
sprzedawca wyrobów tytoniowych
toboggan (te'bogen) s. saneczki;
v. sankowac się; spadac (ceny)
today (te'dej) adv. dzisiaj;
dzis; s. dzien dzisiejszy
toddle ('todl) v. dreptac; drobic nóżkami; s. drobienie nóz-
kami; dreptanie; pędrak
toddler ('todler) s. pędrak;
berbec
to-do (te'du:) s. zamieszanie;
rwetes
toe (tou) s. palec u nogi; nosek;
szpic; stopa wału (tamy); występ z przodu; przednia częsc
kopyta; hacel; dno odwiertu;
v. kopnąc; cerowac palec u pon-
czochy; podporządkowac się;
stawac na starcie; stosowac się
do linii (też partyjnej); ukośnie wbijac gwoździe; krzywo
chodzic (palcami zbyt do wewnątrz lub na zewnątrz)

toffee ('tofi) s. karmelek
toffy ('tofy) s. karmelek
(smietankowy)
together (te'gedzer) adv. razem; wspólnie; naraz; równo-
czesnie
toil (tojl) s. znój; mozół;
trud; mozolic się; trudzic
się; harowac
toilet ('tojlyt) s. ustęp;
toaleta; ubranie; adj. toaletowy
toilet paper ('tojlyt,pejper)
s. papier toaletowy
toils (tojlz) s. sidła; matnia
token ('toukn) s. znak; dowód
autentycznosci; symbol; pamiątka; żeton; bon; adj. symboliczny; niewiążący
told (tould) v. zob. tell
tolerable ('tolerebl) adj.
znosny; nienajgorszy; dosyc
zdrowy
tolerance ('tolerens) s. tolerancja; luz; wyrozumiałosc
tolerant ('tolerent) adj. to-
lerancyjny; wyrozumiały; tole-
rancki
tolerate ('tolerate) v. znosic;
tolerowac; cierpiec
toleration (,tole'rejszyn) s.
znoszenie; tolerancja; tolero-
wanie
toll (toul) s. opłata (np. telefoniczna); myto: mostowe;
drogowe; miejski podatek; try-
but; danina; dzwonienie;
v. uiszczac opłatę; wydzwaniac;
dzwonic jednostajnie; wabic
(zwierzynę)
toll bar ('toulba:r) s. szlaban
tollgate ('toulgejt) s. rogatka
wjazdowa na płatny most lub
autostradę
tomato (te'mejtou) s. pomidor
tomatoes (te'mejtouz) pl. pomi-
dory
tomb (tu:m) s. grób; grobowiec;
v. pochowanie
tombstone (tu:m-stoun) s. kamien nagrobny; nagrobek

tomcat ('tom'kaet) s. kocur

tomorrow (te'mo:rou) s.& adv. jutro

ton (tan) s. tona (2000 funtow) (slang): mnostwo

tone (toun) s. ton; normalny stan (np. ciała; organizmu); brzmienie; v. stonować się; stroic; harmonizować

tone down ('toun,dałn) v. złagodzic; stonować

tongs (tonz) s. szczypce; kleszcze; obcęgi

tongue (tan) s. język; mowa; ozor; v. dotykać językiem; łajac; mlec jezykiem

tonic ('tonyk) adj. wzmacniający; elastyczny; krzepiący; s. srodek tonizujacy

tonight (te'najt) s. dzis wieczor; dzisiejsza noc; adv. dzis wieczorem; gwara: ubiegłej nocy; wczoraj wieczor

tonnage ('tanydż) n. tonaż; opłata od tony ładunku

tonsil ('tonsel) s. migdałek

tonsillitis (,tonsy'lajtys) s. zapalenie migdałkow

tony (touny) adj.(slang): szykowny

too (tu:) adv. tak; także; ponadto; do tego; zbytnio; zanadto; zbyt; za; na dodatek; też

took (tuk) v. zob. take

tool (tu:l) s. narzędzie; obrabiarka; v. obrabiac; oporządzac

tool up ('tu:l,ap) v. oprzyrzą- dzac

tools (tu:ls) pl. przybory; sprzęt

tooth (tu:s) s. ząb; pl. teeth (ti:s) v. uzębiac; wcinac zęby; ząbkowac; szczepiac zębami trybow

tooth ache ('tu:s ejk) s. bol zęba

tooth brush ('tu:s,brasz) s. szczotka do zębow

toothless('tu:slys) adj. bezzębny

toothpaste ('tu:spejst) s. pasta do zębow

toothpick ('tu:spyk) s. wykałaczka

top (top) s. wierzchołek; czubek; szczyt; wierzch; powierzchnia; gora; bociane gniazdo; przykrywka; bąk; fryga; adj. wierzchni; zewnętrzny; gorny; wyższy; najwyższy; szczytowy; maksymalny; v. nakrywac; wienczyc; uwienczac; przewyższac; stanowic wierzch; osiągnąc szczyt; scinac szczyt; przeskoczyc (przez cos); położyc kres; mierzyc wysokosc; wznosic się

topaz ('toupez) s. topaz

topic ('topyk) s. temat (rozmowy)

topple ('topl) v. przechylac; wywracac

topple down ('topldałn) v. przewrocic

top secret (,topsi:kryt) adj. scisle tajny

topsy-turvy ('topsy'te:rwy) adj. do gory nogami; v. przewracac do gory nogami; s. rozgardiasz; bałagan; galimatias

torch (to:rcz) s. pochodnia; znicz; kaganek; palnik (do lutowania etc.)

tore (to:r) v. zob. tear

torment ('to:rment) s. męka; udręka; (to:r'ment) v. męczyc; dręczyc

torn (to:rn) v. zob. tear

tornado (,to:r'nejdou) s. trąba powietrzna; tornado

torrent ('to:rent) s. potok (rwacy); ulewny deszcz; burza

torsion ('to:rszyn) s. skręt; skręcanie

tortoise ('to:rtes) s. żołw (słodkowodny)

torture ('to:rczer) s. tortura; męka; v. torturowac; męczyc; dręczyc; wykręcac; przekręcac

tosh (tosz) s. bzdury; brednie; banialuki

toss (to:s) v. rzucać się;
podrzucać; zarzucać; podnosić;
niepokoić; kłopotać; przewracać się (w łóżku); podbijać
(piłkę); wypaść z pokoju;
kołysać się na boki; s. rzut;
losowanie; upadek (z konia)
toss about (,to:s e'baut) v.
przewracać się (po czymś)
toss up ('to:s,ap) v. przewracać; grać w orła i reszkę
toss-up ('to:sap) s. 50%
prawdopodobieństwa; orzeł
czy reszka ?;rzecz wątpliwa
total ('total) a. ogólny; zupełny; całkowity; totalny;
kompletny; v. zliczać; wynosić ogółem; (slang): niszczyć
całkowicie (np. samochód
w wypadku)
totalitarian (tou,taely'tear-
jen) adj. totalitarny; tota-
listyczny; s. totalista
totter ('toter) v. chwiać się;
zataczać się; s. chwianie
się; zataczanie się (dziecka)
touch (tacz) v. dotykać; stykać (się); wzruszać (się);
poruszać (coś); brać; wydobywać; zabarwiać;lekko uszkadzać; cechować; mierzyć; retuszować; rabnąć kogoś na
pieniądze (slang); s. dotyk;
dotknięcie; pociągnięcie;
odrobina; kontakt; lekka (choroba); rys; nuta (np.złości);
obmacywanie;cecha; probierz;
naciąganie na pieniądze(slang)
touch down ('tacz,daln) v. lądować;uzyskiwać 6 punktów
touchdown (taczdaln) s. lądowanie;gol w futbolu(6 punktów)
touching ('taczyng) adj. wzruszający; rozrzewniający; adv.
odnośnie (do czegoś)
touchy ('taczy) adj. drażliwy;
obraźliwy; przewrażliwiony
tough (taf) adj. twardy;trudny;
ciężki; łobuzerski; adv. trudno; s. człowiek: trudny, twardy; łobuz; chuligan

tour (tuer) s. objazd; wycieczka; tura; przechadzka; służba
(wojskowa); v. objeżdżać; ob-
wozić
tourist ('tueryst) s. turysta;
klasa turystyczna
tourist-agency ('tueryst'ejdżensy) s. biuro podróży
tournament ('tuernement) s.
turniej
tousle ('tauzl) v. szarpać;
mierzwić; czochrać; targać;
s. rozczochrane włosy;rozczo-
chranie
tow (tou) v. holować; ciągnąć;
s. holowanie; lina holownicza;
przedmiot holowany; włókna
lniane; paździory
towards (to:rdz; 'toterdz) prep.
ku; w kierunku; dla; w celu;
na (coś)
tow-boat ('taubout) s. holownik
towel ('tauel) s. ręcznik;
v. wycierać ręcznikiem
tower ('tauer) s. wieża; wznosić (się); sterczeć; wzbijać
się
town (taln) s. miasto
town councilor (,taln'kaunsyler)
s. radny miejski
town hall ('taln,ho:l) s. ratusz
towrope ('touroup) s. lina
holownicza
toy (toj) s. zabawka; cacko;
v. bawić się; cackać się; robić niedbale; flirtować (też
np. z pomysłem)
toxic ('toksyk) adj. trujący;
jadowity
trace (trejs) s. ślad;postronek;
drążek przekaznikowy; v. iść
śladami; kopiować rysunek;
przypisywać czemuś; wytyczać;
nakreślać; kreślić
track (traek) s.tor; koleina;
ślad; trop; bieżnia; rozstaw
kół; v. śledzić; tropić; zostawiać ślady; zabłocić; zawalać; zakładać tor; mieć
rozstęp kół; ciągnąć liną
z brzegu

track down ('traek,dawn) v.
wytropic; wysledzic; schwytac
track and field events ('traek-
,end-fi:ldy'wents) s. lekkoatletyka
track events (traek y'wents)
s. biegi; zawody na biezni
traction engine (traekszyn-
endzyn) s. lokomotywa; pociągowy motor; traktor
tractor ('traekter) s. ciągnik;
traktor
trade (trejd) s. zawód; zajęcie;
rzemiosło; handel; wymiana;
klientela; branza; kupiectwo;
v. handlowac; wymieniac; frymarczyc; przewozic towary;
kupczyc; przehandlowac
trademark ('trejd,ma:rk) s.
znak ochronny; v. przybijać
znak ochronny; rejestrowac
znak ochronny
trader ('trejder) s. handlowiec;
statek handlowy; spekulator
giełdowy
trade-union ('trejd'ju:njen)
s. związek zawodowy
trade unionist ('trejd'ju:n-
jenyst) s. działacz związku
zawodowego
tradition (tre'dyszyn) s. tradycja
traditional (tre'dyszynel) adj.
tradycyjny
traffic ('traefyk) s. ruch(kołowy, pasazerski,towarowy,
telegraficzny, telefoniczny,
drogowy, etc.); v. handel
czyms; frymarczyc; kupczyc
traffic island ('traefyk-aj-
lend) s. wysepka na jezdni
traffic jam('traefyk-dzaem)
s. zator ruchu
traffic lights ('traefyk-
lajts) pl. semafory uliczne
traffic regulation ('traefyk,re-
gju'lejszyn) s. przepisy ruchu
traffic sign ('traefyk,sajn)
s. znak drogowy
traffic-cop ('traefyk,kop) s.
policjant ruchu (drogowego)

tragedy ('traedzydy) s. tragedia
tragic ('traedzyk) adj. tragiczny
tragical ('traedzykel) = tragic
trail (trejl) v. pociągnąc (się);
powlec (się);holowac; wlec (się)
pozostawac w tyle; isc za tro-
pem; scigac; wydeptywac (sciez-
kę); nosic (karabin poziomo
przy boku); s. szlak; sciezka;
trop; ogon; smuga; struga;
bruzda; koleina
trailer ('trejler) s. przyczepa
(do samochodu); przyczepa to-
warowa, mieszkalna, turystyczna, etc.; maruder; pnąca (się)
roslina
train (trejn) v. szkolic; kształ-
cic; przyuczac; wytresowac;
cwiczyc (się); trenowac (się);
kierowac na kogos (np. wzrok);
wlec; s. pociąg; tren; ogon;
sznur; szereg; następstwo;
orszak; swita; porządek; wątek;
łancuch
trainer ('trejner) s. trener;
instruktor; samolot szkolny
training ('trejnyng) s. zaprawa; trening; cwiczenie; szkolenie
trait (trejt) s. cecha
traitor ('trejtor) s. zdrajca
tram (traem) s. tramwaj
tramp (traemp) v. stąpac; włóczyc się; wędrowac pieszo;
isc pieszo; s. włóczęga;tramp;
wędrowiec; statek (nieregular-
nej zeglugi)
trample ('traempl) v. deptac
trance (tra:ns) s. trans; uniesienie; ekstaza
tranquil ('traenkłyl) adj. spokojny
tranquility ('traen'kłylyty) s.
spokój
tranquilize ('traenkłylajz) v.
uspokajac
tranquilizer ('traenkłylajzer)
s. srodek uspakajający
transact (traen'saekt) v. załatwiac; pertraktowac; przeprowadzac

transaction (traen'saekszyn)
s. transakcja; przeprowadze-
nie sprawy; pl. sprawozdania
naukowe; rozprawy
transalpine (traens'aelpajn)
adj. transalpejski
transatlantic (traenzet'laentyk) adj. transatlantycki
transcend (traen'send) v.
przewyższac; przescignać;
gorowac
transcribe (traens'krajb) v.
nagrywac na tasmie; przepi-
sywac
transcript ('traenskrypt) s.
kopia; transkrypcja
transfer (traens'fe:r) y.
przemiescic; przeniesc (się);
przewozic; przekazac; s.prze-
niesienie; przewoz; przedruk;
przekaz; przelew; odstąpienie
transferable (traens'fe:rebl)
adj. przenosny
transform (traens'fo:rm) v.
przekształcic; zmienic postac
transformation (,traensfer'-
'mejszyn) s. przekształcanie;
przeobrażenie
transfuse (traens'fjuz) v.
przelac; przetoczyc (krew)
transfusion (traens'fjużyn) s.
transfuzja
transgress (traens'gres) v.
naruszyc; zgrzeszyc
transgression (traens'greszyn)
s. naruszenie; grzech; wykroczenie
transgressor (traens'greser)
s, grzesznik
transient ('traenzjent) adj.
przechodni; przejeżdżający;
przelotny
transistor (traen'syster) s.
tranzystor
transit ('traensyt) s.przejazd;
przelot; przewoz; tranzyt;
teodolit
transition (traen'syszyn) s.
przejscie; zmiana
transitive ('traensytyw) adj.
przechodni

translate (traens'lejt) v. prze-
tłumaczyc; przełożyc
translation (traens'lejszyn)
s. tłumaczenie; przekład
translator (traens'lejter) s.
tłumacz
translucent (traenz'lu:sent)
adj. przeswiecający; poł-
przezroczysty
transmission (traenz'myszyn) s.
przekładnia; transmisja
transmit (traenz'myt) v. przekazywac; nadawac; transmitowac
transmitter (traenz'myter) s.
nadajnik; przekaznik
transparent (traens'peerent)
adj. przezroczysty
transpire (traens'pajer) v. pocic się; wyparowac; okazywac
się; zdarzyc się
transplant (traens'pla:nt) v.
przeszczepiac; przesadzac;
s. przesadzanie; przeszczep
transport (traens'po:rt) v.
przewozic; zachwycac; s.prze-
woz; zachwyt; uniesienie
transportation (,traenpo:r'tejszyn) s. przewoz; transport;
deportacja; zesłanie
trap (traep) s. pułapka; potrzask; sidła; zasadzka; podstęp; syfon; skała wylewna;
(slang): jadaczka; pl.:manatki;
v. złapac w pułapkę; zaopatrywac w pułapkę; zatrzymywac
(w czyms); przykrywac czapra-
kiem; puszczac rzutki
trap-door ('traep'do:r) s.
drzwi zapadowe; zapadnia
trapeze (tre'pi:z) s. trapez
trapper ('traeper) s. traper;
mysliwy; zastawiający pułapki;
nadzorca szybow powietrznych
w kopalni
trappings (traepyngz) s.ozdoby;
stroj ozdobny; czaprak
trash (traesz) s. smieci; ru-
pieci; tandeta; odpadki; bzdury; hołota; v. obdzierac (z
lisci, gałązek)

travel ('traewl) v. podróżować
(też za interesem); poruszać
się (części maszyny); przesuwać się; biec (w terenie);
przechodzić (oczami po czymś);
poruszać się żwawo; błądzić;
s. (daleka) podróż; ruch (pojazdów); suw (maszynowy);
przesunięcie

travel agency ('traewl'ejdżensy)
s. biuro podróży

traveler ('traewler) s. podróżnik; wodzik nitkowy; komiwojażer

traveler's check ('traewlers,-
,czek) s. z góry wykupiony
czek do użytku w podróży

traveling bag ('traewlyng,baeg)
s. torba podróżna

traverse (trae'we:rs)v. przecinać; przesuwać na bok; przechodzić; omawiać; pokrzyżować;
zaprzeczyć formalnie; nakiero-
wywać (działo); obracać (się)
jak na osi

travesty ('traewysty) s. trawe-
stia; parodia; v. trawestować;
parodiować

trawl (tro:l) s. włók; włók;
traf; niewód; siec;- worek do
holowania;v.ciągnąć niewód; łowić niewodem, włókiem, wędką
ciągnioną za łodzią

trawler ('tro:ler) s. trawler

tray (trej) s, taca; szufladka
(też wkładowa)

treacherous ('treczeres) adj.
zdradziecki; niebezpieczny;
zdradliwy; zawodny; perfidny

treachery ('treczery) s. zdrada; zdradzieckość; zdradliwość;
perfidia

treacle ('tri:kl) s. syrop; melasa; sok (drzewny)

tread; trod; tro(den), (tred;
trod; 'trodn)

tread (tred) v. deptać; stąpać
(po czyms); nadepnąć; tłoczyć;
wdeptywać; iść (ścieżką); wy-
deptać (ścieżkę) ; gnieść;
s. stąpanie; krok; podnóżek;

guma opony dotykająca jezdni;
szyna; bieżnik; podeszwa (dotykająca ziemi); stopień

treadle ('tredl) s. pedał;
v. pedałować

treadmill ('tredmyl) s. kierat
(cylindryczny ze stopniami)

treason('tri:zn) s. zdrada

treasure ('treżer) s. skarb;
v. zaskarbiać; cenić; strzec
skarbu

treasure up ('treżer,ap) v.
przechowywać jak skarb

treasurer ('treżerer) s. skarbnik

treasury ('treżery) s. urząd
skarbowy; skarbnica

Treasury Department ('treżery,-
,dy'pa:rtment) s. ministerstwo
skarbu (USA)

treat (tri:t) v. traktować; po-
traktować; obchodzić się z
kims; uważać kogoś za; brać
coś (za żart); leczyć coś; poddawać działaniu; pertraktować;
fundować (komuś); s. przyjęcie;
uczta; majówka; poczęstunek;
zabawa; przyjemność; rozkosz

treatise ('tri:tys) s. traktat;
rozprawa

treatment ('tri:tment) s. traktowanie; leczenie

treaty ('tri:ty) s. traktat;
układ; umowa

treble ('trebl) adj. potrójny;
wysoki; ostry; przenikliwy;
sopranowy; s. sopran; wysoki
dźwięk; v. potrajać (się)

tree (tri:) s. drzewo; forma;
kopyto; rama siodła; belka;
nadproże; krokiew; szubienica;
v. zapędzić (na drzewo); wsa-
dzić (na kopyto)

treeless ('tri:lys) adj. bez-
drzewny

tree-trunk ('tri:,trank) s.
pień roślina trójlistna;

trefoil ('trefojl) s. koniczyna trójlistna;adj.trójlistny

trellis ('trely) s. krata; altana; v. kratować winorośl;
nadawać formę kraty

tremble ('trembl) v. trząść
się; drżeć; dygotać; s.drże-
nie; drżączka
tremendous (try'mendes) adj.
straszny; olbrzymi
tremor ('tremer) s. drżenie;
drganie; trzęsienie (ziemi)
tremulous ('tremjules) adj.
drżący
trench (trencz) s.rów; okop;
bruzda; cięcie; rów strzelec-
ki; v. kopać rów; okopywać
się; kłaść do rowu; żłobić;
ciąć; przecinać; podkopywać
się; graniczyć
trench up ('trencz,ap) v.
wdzierać się (bezczelnie)
w cudze (prawa etc.)
trend (trend) s. dążność; ogól-
na tendencja; ogólny kierunek;
v. dążyć; mieć tendencję;
kształtować się; ciągnąć się
trespass ('trespas) v. wdzierać się w cudze; nadużywać;
naruszać; wykraczać; grze-
szyć; v. przekroczenie; wykroczenie; grzech; szkoda wy-
rządzona na cudzym terenie
trespasser ('trespaser) s.
człowiek naruszający przepisy,prawo (czyjeś)
tress (tres) s. warkocz; v.za-
platać warkocz
trestle ('tresl) s. kozioł;
kobylica; most filarowy
trial ('trajel) s. próba; proces sądowy; zmartwienie; zawody eliminacyjne; adj. próbny; doświadczalny
trial and error ('trajel end'-
'erer) exp.: chaotyczne próby
(w nieznane)
triangle ('trajaengl) s. trójkąt
triangular (traj'aengjular) adj.
trójkątny
triangulate (traj'aengjulejt)
v. mierzyć (trójkątami) przy
pomocy triangulacji
tribe (trajb) s. plemię; szczep
tribunal (traj'bju:nl) s. try-
bunał ; sąd

tribune ('trybju:n) s. trybuna;
mównica; gazeta; trybun (ludu)
tributary ('trybjutery) adj.
pomocniczy; płacący daninę;
haracz; s. dopływ; kraj płacący daninę
tribute ('trybju:t) s. haracz;
danina
trick (tryk) s. podstęp; chwyt;
sztuczka; sposób; nawyk; maniera; psota; fortel; (slang):
dziecko; dziewczynka; v. oszukać; okpić; wyłudzić; płatać
figla; zawodzić; zaskakiwać
trick up ('tryk,ap) s. wystroić
trickle ('trykl) v. sączyć (się);
przeciekać; przesączyć; puszczać ciurkiem; kroplami;
s. struga (mała)
tricky ('tryky) adj. podstępny;
chytry; sprytny; trudny; zawiły; zręczny
tricycle ('trajsykl) s. rower
na trzech kołach
trifle ('trajfl) s. drobiazg;
drobnostka; błachostka; bagatela; odrobina; głupstewko; byle
co; stop cyny i ołowiu; biszkopt z kremem; v. nie brać po-
ważnie; poflirtować; baraszkować; paplać; bagatelizować
trifling ('trajflyŋg) adj. płochy;
chy; błachy; znikomy
trigger ('tryger) s. spust;
cyngiel; zapadka; v. pociągać
za spust; wywoływać; dawać początek; zaczynać (akcję)
trill (tryl) s. trel; wibrująca
spółgłoska; v. wymawiać z wi-
bracją; trząść głosem; trelować; wymawiać wibrująco
trillion ('tryljen) = USA billion ('byljen) num. trylion
trim (trym) v. oporządzać;
usuwać niepotrzebne (gałęzie;
tłuszcz etc.); przybierać (li-
stwą; tasmą etc); rozkładać
poprawnie ładunek; poprawiać
(opinię); być oportunistą;
zmyć komuś głowę; dać komuś lanie; wyprowadzić w pole; besztać; rugać; s. stan; forma;

nastrój; gotowość; porządek;
strój; ozdoby; listwy; tasmy;
wstążki do poprawienia wyglądu; dekoracja wystawy; oporzą-
dzenie; obcięcie; równowaga
lotu; wyposażenie wnętrza
(np. samochodu, domu etc,)
adj. schludny; porządny;
uporządkowany; wysprzątany
trimming ('trymyŋg) s. ozdoby;
uporządkowanie; przystrzyżenie;
garnirowanie
trimmings ('trymyŋgs) s. zrzyn-
ki i obrzynki z przybierania;
dodatki do potraw; obcinki
Trinity ('trynyty) s.Trójca Sw.
trinket ('trynkyt) s. ozdóbka
(na suknie); świecidełko;
błahostka
trip (tryp) s. podróż; wycieczka; jazda; trans narkomana;
potknięcie; podstawienie nogi;
zgrabny krok; wyzwalanie za-
padkowe lub wychwytowe; błąd;
pomyłka; v. potknąć się; iść
lekkim krokiem; drobić nóżkami;
tańczyć (lekko); pomylić się;
podstawiać noge; złapać na błędzie; wyzwalać; odczepiać kotwicę; przesuwać wychwytem kot-
wicowym; obracać reje; spuszczać nagle część maszyny
tripe (trajp) s. flaki (też potrawa); byle co; paskudztwo;
lichota
triple (tripl) adj. potrójny;
s. potrójna ilość; trójka;
v. potrajać (się)
triplets ('tryplyts) pl. trojacz-
ki
tripod ('trajpod) s. trójnóg;
statyw
triumph ('trajęmf) s. triumf;
v. triumfowac
triumphal (traj'amfel) adj.
triumfalny
triumphant (traj'amfent) adj.
zwycięski; triumfalny
trivial ('trywiel) adj. trywialny; błahy; płytki; banalny;
znikomy
trod (trod) v. zob. tread

trodden ('trodn) v. zob. tread
trolley car ('troly car) s.
tramwaj; wywrotka (woz)
trombone (trom'boun) s. puzon
troop (tru:p) s. grupa; gromada; trupa teatralna; rota;
pol szwadronu; s. iść gromadą;
gromadzić się; formować w ro-
ty (pułk)
trophy ('troufy) s. trofeum
tropic ('tropyk) adj. podzwrotnikowy; tropikalny; s. zwrotnik
tropical ('tropykel) adj. tropikalny; gorący; namiętny
trot (trot) s. kłus; trucht;
bryk (szkolny); (slang): biegunka
trouble ('trabl) s. kłopot;
zmartwienie; zaburzenie; niepokój; trud; dolegliwość; fatyga; bieda; awaria; uszkodzenie; defekt; v. martwić (się);
dręczyć (się); dokuczać; niepokoić (się); kłopotać (się)
troublesome ('trablsem) adj.
kłopotliwy
trough (trof) s. koryto; rynna;
rów (też między falami); niec-
ka; łęk; synklina
trouser leg ('trauserleg) s.
nogawka
trousers ('trauzez) pl. spodnie
trouseau ('tru:sou) s. wyprawa
(ślubna)
trout (traut) s. pstrąg; v. łowić pstrągi
truant ('tru:ent) s. wagarowicz;
opuszczający pracę; adj. próż-
niacki; wałęsający (się); v.
chodzić na wagary; opuszczać
pracę
truce (tru:s) s. rozejm; zawieszenie broni
truck (trak) s. ciężarówka;
taczki; wózek; podwozie na kołach; lora; drobne towary; warzywa; wymiana; interes; śmieci; brednie; stosunki z kimś;
v. przewozić wozem; ładować na
wóz; wymieniać się z kimś; obnosić towar; utrzymywać stosunki z kimś

truck farm ('trak,fa:rm) s.
gospodarstwo warzywne

trudge (tradż) s. trudny marsz;
v. trudzić się marszem; odby-
wac z trudem drogę

true (tru:) adj. prawdziwy;
wierny; scisły; dokładny; praw-
domowny; czysty; faktyczny;
szczery; lojalny; dobrze do-
pasowany; s. prawda; właściwe
położenie; v. regulować; wyre-
gulowac; adv. prawdziwie; dokładnie; exp.: to jest prawda !

truly ('tru:ly) adv. prawdziwie;
dokładnie

true-blue ('tru:blu:) adj. bez-
kompromisowy; prawdziwie oddany

trump (tramp) s. atut; as; zuch;
złoty człowiek; trąba; v. bic
atutem; roztrąbic

trump up ('tramp,ap) v. wyssac
z palca; zmyslac (zarzuty);
preparowac (zarzuty)

trumpet ('trampyt) s. trąbka;
dzwięk; trębacz; v. grac na
trąbie; trąbic; roztrąbic

truncheon ('tranczen) s. pałka
policjanta; buława marszałka

trunk (trank) s. pien; trzon;
tułow; tors; kadłub; głowny kanał; głowna linia; trąba słoniowa; kufer; bagażnik;
pl. spodnie (krotkie)

trunk line ('trank-lajn) s.
linia międzymiastowa (też telefoniczna w Anglii)

trunk road ('trank-roud) s.
szosa głowna

truss (tras) s. wieżba; wspornik;
kratownica; wiązanie dachowe;
wiązka (siana); pas przepukli-
nowy; v. związac (np. dach);
przywiązac; wieszac (zbrodnia-
rza)

trust (trast) s. pewnosc; zaufanie; wiara; nadzieja; kredyt;
opieka; powiernictwo; trust;
v. zaufac; miec zaufanie; ufac;
wierzyc; polegac (na pamięci
swojej etc.) powierzac; kredy-
towac

trustful ('trastful) adj. ufny

trusting ('trastyng) adj. ufny;
pełen zaufania

trustworthy ('trast,łe:rty) adj.
godny zaufania; pewny

truth (tru:s) s. prawda; praw-
dziwosc; rzetelnosc

truthful ('tru:sful) adj. prawdo-
mowny; prawdziwy (np. opis)

truths (tru:sz) pl. prawdy

try (traj) v. probowac; wyprobo-
wac; sądzic; sprawdzic; kosztowac; doswiadczyc; starac się;
męczyc; s. proba. usiłowanie;
wysiłek

trying (trajyng) adj. przykry;
męczący; nieznosny; irytujący;
ciężki

try on ('traj,on ) s. przymierzac

try out ('traj,aut) v. wyprobo-
wywac

T-square ('ti:,skłeer) s. węgielnica

tub (tab) s. balia; ceber; kadz;
wanna; kąpiel; łodz terningowa
(wiosłowa); oszalowanie;
v. wsadzac do wanny; prac;
szalowac

tube (tju:b) s. rura; wąż; dętka; tubka; tunel (kolei pod-
ziemnej); v. zamykac w rurze;
zaopatrywac w rury; nadawac
kształt rury

tuberculosis (tjube:rkju:lou-
sys) s. gruzlica

tuck (tak) v. wtykac; wsuwac;
podwijac; zawijac (rąbek);
otulac; zbierac w fałdy; obrębiac; schowac; (slang): pa-
łaszowac; wcinac; wieszac
(skazanca); s. fałd; fałda;
obręb; koncha

tuck in ('takyn) v. otulac
(w łóżku)

tuck up ('tak,ap) v. podkasac

Tuesday ('tju:zdy) s. wtorek

tuft (taft) s. pęk; pęczek;
kisc; kępa; kitka; brodka;
pikowanie; v. robic pęki; dawac pęki; rosc pękami; pikowac

tug (tag) v. ciągnąć (z trudem)
holować; wciągać; s. holownik;
gwałtowne pociągnięcie

tug-of-war ('tag,ow łor) s.
przeciąganie liny (próba sił,
zawody); zażarta walka o przewagę

tuition (tju'yszyn) s. czesne;
nauczanie; lekcje (płatne)

tulip ('tju:lyp) s. tulipan

tumble ('tambl) v. upaść; zwalić (się); potknąć się; ząta-
czać się; kołysać się; hustać
się; wywalić się; gramolić się;
rzucać się; biegać na oślep;
cisnąć; zwichrzyc; (slang):
kapować; iść do łóżka; v.zwa-
lenie; pobicie rekordu; upadek;
sztuka akrobatyczna; bałagan

tummy ('tamy) s. żołądek;
brzuch (dziecka)

tumor ('tu:mer) s. tumor;
obrzęk; guz ; nowotwór

tumult ('tu:malt) s. zgiełk;
wrzawa; tumult; podniecenie;
zaburzenie

tumultuous ('tu:altjues) adj.
burzliwy; podniecony; hałaśliwy

tun (tan) s. beczka; kadź (252
galonów); v. wlewać do beczki;
przechowywać w beczce

tuna ('tu:na) s. tunczyk

tune (tu:n) s. melodia; nastrój;
harmonia; v. stroić; dostroić;'
harmonizować; nucić

tune in ('tu:n,yn) v. nastawiać
(radio etc.)

tune up ('tu:n,ap) v. nastrajać
(np. motor)

tunnel ('tanl) s. tune;; nora;
v. przekopywać tunel, korytarz,
norę; przekopywać się

turbine ('te:rbyn) s. turbina

turbot ('te:rbet) s. skarptur-
bot (ryba)

turbulent ('te:rbjulent) adj.
wzburzony; burzliwy; gwałtowny;
buntowniczy

turf (te:rf) s. torf; darn;
v. pokrywać darniną; (slang):
drałować (piechotą)

Turk (te:rk) adj. turecki

turkey ('te:rky) s. indyk;
v.mówić bez ogrodek

Turkish ('te:rkysz) adj. turecki

Turkish bath ('te:rkysz,ba:s)
s. parowka; kąpiel parowa;
łaznia

turmoil (te:rmojl) s. zamieszanie; zgiełk; niepokoj; podniecenie

turn (te:rn) v. odwrócić (się);
odkręcić (się); przekręcać
(się); skręcać (się); zwracać
(się); odwracać (się); odpierać
(atak); napadać; zmieniać się;
nawracać (się); popełniać
(zdradę); stawać się (np. kato-
likiem); wyswiadczać; obracać;
kierować; robić skręt; wyprawiac; odprawiać; toczyć (na
kole); puścić w ruch; okazać
się; zdarzać się; zwolnić; wyganiac; wyrzucać etc.
s. obrot; kolej; z kolei; po
kolei; tura; zakręt; zwrot;
skręt; punkt zwrotny; przełom;
kształt; forma; przechadzka;
transakcja; wstrząs; atak;
przysługa; numer (popisowy);
kolejnosc; postępowanie wobec
kogos

turn away ('te:rn,e'łej) v. odwracać się od ; porzucić

turn back ('te:rn,baek) v. za-
wrócić (z drogi)

turn down ('te:rn,dałn) v. odmówic; przyciszać; odrzucać

turn off ('te:rn,of) v. zakręcić (kurek); skręcić; wyłączać
(swiatło), odprawić

turn on ('te:rn,on) v. puszczać
(wodę); włączać (swiatło); od-
kręcać (kurek)

turn out ('te:rn,aut) v. wyrzucać (za drzwi); wyrabiać; zwalniać (z pracy)

turn over ('te:rn,ouwer) v. odwracać; rozważać; miec obrót;
wydawać (policji); przekazywać

turn round ('te:rn raund) v.
przekręcać; odwracać; zmieniać
przekonania ; przekabacić

turn to ('te:rn,tu) v. zabrac
sie (do czegos)

turn up ('te:rn,ap) v. odwracac;
zawinac (rekawy); podkrecac;
przychodzic; zglosic sie;
przytrafic (sie)

turncoat ('te:rn,kout) s. zdrajca

turning point ('te:rnyng,poynt)
s. punkt zwrotny

turnip ('te:rnyp) s. rzepa

turnout ('te:rnaut) s. stawie-
nie sie; ilosc obecnych;ekwipunek

turnover ('te:rn,ouwer) s. zmiana; kapotaz; przewrocenie; placek; przemieszczanie (ludzi,rzeczy

turnpike ('te:rn,pajk) s. kolo-
wrot; rogatka;autostrada(platna)

turnstile ('te:rnstajl) s. kolo-
wrot(do wchodzenia pojedynczo)

turnup ('te:rnap) s. traf; zamieszanie; czesc wywrocona;
cos podwinietego; podwiniecie

turpentine ('te:rpentajn) s.
terpentyna; v. terpentynowac;
zbierac terpentyne

turret ('te:ryt) s. wiezyczka;
imak wielonozowy

turtle ('te:rtl) s. zolw (morski)

turtledove ('te:rtl,daw) s.
turkawka

tusk (task) s. kiel; zab (u bro-
ny); v. bosc; kluc; rozdzierac
klami

tutor ('tu:ter) s. nauczyciel
prywatny; korepetytor; opiekun
(studentow); v. uczyc kogos;
miec opieke nad kims; powsciagac
(sie); byc korepetytorem; uczyc
sie pod nadzorem nauczyciela

tutorial ('tu:terjel) adj. wychowawczy; opiekunczy

TV (ti:wi:) s. telewizja

tuxedo (tak'si:dou) s. smoking
(USA)

twang (tlaeng) s. brzek (struny);
mowienie przez nos; v. brzeczec;
rzepolic; brzdakac; mowic przez
nos

tweed(tli:d) s. material welnia-
ny lub welniano-bawelniany z
szorska powierzchnia

tweet (tli:t) s. cwierkanie;
v. cwierkac

tweezers (tli-zez) s. szczypczyki (kosmetyczne itp.)

twelfth (tlelfs) adj. dwunasty

twelve (tlelw) num. dwanascie;
s. dwunastka

twentieth ('tlentyjes) adj.
dwudziesty

twenty (tlenty) num. dwadzies-
cia; s. dwudziestka

twice (tlajs) adv. dwa razy;
podwojnie; dwukrotnie

twiddle ('tlydl) s. obracanie;
v. krecic; obracac; przebierac palcami; proznowac

twig (tlyg) v. zrozumiec; po-
lapac sie; spostrzec; zauwa-
zyc; rozpoznawac; s. galazka;
rozdzka czarodziejska

twilight ('tlajlajt) s. zmrok;
polcien; polmrok; zmierzch

twin (tlyn) s. blizniak; adj.
blizniaczy; v. rodzic sie jako blizznieta; laczyc (sie)
scisle ze soba

twin-engined ('tlyn'endzynd)
adj. dwumotorowy

twinkle (tlynkl) v. migotac;
blyszczec; mrugac; s. migotanie; blysk; mrugniecie

twirl (tlre:rl) v. wirowac;
krecic (sie); s. wirowanie;
krecenie sie; zakretas; piruet

twist (tlyst) v. skrecac (sie);
zwijac (sie); zwichnac (sie);
zawirowac; wykrzywiac (twarz);
przekrecac; pokrecic (sie);
wic (sie); powiklac (sie);
tanczyc (twista); wykrecac;
przewijac sie (przez tlum)
s. skret; szpagat; przedza;
lina (skrecona); splot; obrot;
przekrecenie (znaczenia);
zwichniecie; sklonnosc;
strucla

twitch(tlytcz)v. szarpac; wyrwac; wydrzec; wykrzywic (sie);
poruszyc sie gwaltownie;
s. skurcz; szarpniecie;pociag-
niecie(za rekaw);drgawka; tik;
drganie(powieki);spazm;kurcz

twitter ('tłyter) v. ćwierkać;
świergotać; chichotać; drżeć
(ze strachu etc.); s. świergot; chichot; podniecenie;
zdenerwowanie

two (tu:) num. dwa; s. dwójka

two-bit ('tu:byt) adj. tandetny;
marny; (slang): wart 25 centów;
rzecz mała; rzecz bez znaczenia

twofold ('tu:fould) adj. podwójny; adv. podwójnie; dwojako

two-piece ('tu:pi:s) adj. dwu-
częściowy

two-stroke ('tu:,strouk) adj.
dwutaktowy; dwusuwowy

two-way ('tu:,łej) adj. dwukie-
runkowy (np. ruch); dwutorowy;
dwuwartościowy

type (tajp) s. typ; wzór; przykład; symbol; klasa; okaz;
czcionka; kaszta (drukarska);
v. pisać na maszynie; ustalać
typ; symbolizować; wyznaczać
role

typewriter ('tajp,rajter) s. maszyna do pisania

typhoid ('tajfoyd) adj. tyfusowy; s. tyfus; dur brzuszny

typhoon (taj'fu:n) s. tajfun;
burza (morska) w układzie
wielkiego wiru

typhus ('tajfes) adj. tyfusowy

typical ('typykel) adj. typowy;
charakterystyczny

typify ('typyfaj) v. uosabiać;
stanowić typ; zapowiadać

typist ('tajpyst) s. maszynistka

tyrannical (ty'raenykel) adj.
tyrański

tyrannize ('tyrenajz) v. tyranizować

tyranny ('tyreny) s. tyrania

tyrant ('tajerent) s. tyran

tyre ('tajer) s. opona; obręcz;
v. nakładać oponę (obręcz)

u (ju:) dwudziesta pierwsza litera alfabetu angielskiego

ubiquity (ju'bykłyty) s. wszech-
obecność

U-boat ('ju:bout) s. łódź podwodna (niemiecka)

udder ('ader) s. wymię

ugly ('agly) adj. brzydki; paskudny

uhlan ('u:la:n) s. ułan

ulan ('u:la:n s. ułan

ulcer ('alser) s. wrzód

ultimate ('altymyt) adj. ostateczny; ostatni; końcowy; podstawowy; s. ostateczny wynik;
podstawowy fakt

ultimatum (alty'mejtem) s. ultimatum

umbrella (am'brela) s. parasol

umpire ('ampajer) s. sędzia
sportowy; rozjemca; v. sędzio-
wać; rozstrzygać jako arbiter

unabashed ('ane'baeszt) adj.
niespeszony; niezmieszany;
nie zbity z tropu

unabated ('an,e'bejtyd) adj.
niesłabnący; niezmniejszony

unable ('an'ejbl) adj. niezdolny; nieudolny

unacceptable ('ane'kseptebl)
adj. nie do przyjęcia

unaccountable ('ane'kauntebl)
adj. niewytłumaczony; niezrozumiały; dziwny; nie
tłumaczący się nikomu

unaccustomed ('ane'kastemd)
adj. niezwykły; nie przyzwyczajony

unacquainted ('ane'kłejntyd)
adj. nie obznajomiony

unaffected (,ane'fektyd) adj.
niekłamany; naturalny

unanimous (ju'naenymes) adj.
jednogłosny

unapproachable (,ane'prouczebl)
adj. niedostępny; niezrównany

unarmed ('an'a:rmd) adj. bezbronny; nie uzbrojony

unashamed ('an,e'szejmd) adj.
bezwstydny

unassisted ('an,e'systyd) adj.
nie wspomagany

unassuming ('an,e'sju:myng)
adj. skromny; bezpretensjonalny

unauthorized ('an'o:terajzd)
adj. nieupoważniony

unavoidable ('an,e'wojdebl) adj.
nieunikniony; niechybny

unaware ('ane,e'żeer) adj.nie-
świadomy; niepoinformowany
unawares ('ane'żeerz) adv.nie-
świadomie; znienacka; niespo-
dziewanie ;nic nie wiedząc
unbalanced ('an'baelensd) adj.
niezrównoważony
unbar ('an'ba:r) v. odryglować
unbearable (an'beerebl) adj.
nieznośny; nie do wytrzymania
unbecoming ('an,by'kamyng)adj.
niestosowny; niewłaściwy;
nieodpowiedni; nietwarzowy
unbelievable (,anby'li:webl)
adj. niewiarygodny; nieprawdopodobny
unbelieving (.anby'li:wyng)
adj. niewierzący; niedowierza-
jacy
unbending ('an'bendyng) adj.
nieugięty; niezłomny
unbiased ('an'bajest) adj.
bezstronny
unbidden ('an'bydn) adj. nieproszony
unborn baby ('an'bo:rn'bejby)
adj. przyszłe dziecko; nie-
urodzone (jeszcze) dziecko
unbounded (an'naundyd) adj.
bez granic; bezgraniczny
unbroken (an'brouken) adj.
nieprzerwany; niezbity; nie
ujeżdżony (koń)
unbutton ('an'batn) v. odpiać;
rozpiać (się)
uncalled-for (an'ko:ld,fo:r)
adj. niewłaściwy; niezasłużony;
niczym nie usprawiedliwiony
uncanny (an'kaeny) adj. niesamowity
uncared-for ('an'keerd,fo:r)
adj. porzucony; zaniedbany
unceasing (an'si:syng) adj.
bezustanny; nieprzerwany
uncertain (an'se:rtn) adj. niepewny; wątpliwy
unchallenged (an'chaelyndż)
adj. niekwestionowany
unchangeable (an'chejndżebl)
adj. stały; niezmienny
unchanged (an'chejndżd) adj.
niezmieniony

unchecked (an'czekt) adj. niepowstrzymany; niepohamowany;
nieposkromiony
uncivil ('an'sywyl) adj. niegrzeczny; nieuprzejmy; nieokrzesany; grubiański
uncivilized ('an'sywylajzd)
adj. dziki; niecywilizowany;
barbarzyński
uncle ('ankl) s. wujek; stryjek
unclean ('an'kli:n) adj. nieczysty; plugawy; sprośny
uncomparable ('an'komperebl) adj.
nieporownywalny
uncommon ('an'komen) adj. niezwykły; rzadki; adv. niezwykle;
nadzwyczaj
uncommunicative ('an-ke'mju:ny-
ketyw); adj. małomówny; skryty;
niekomunikatywny
uncomplaining ('an-kem'plejnyng)
adj. cierpliwy; nienarzekający
unconcern ('anken'se:rn) s.
beztroska; niefrasobliwosć;
obojętnosć
unconcerned ('anken'se:rnd) adj.
obojętny; niefrasobliwy; beztroski
unconditional ('an-ken'dyszynl)
adj. bezwarunkowy
unconfirmed ('an-ken'fe:rmd) adj.
nie potwierdzony
unconscious (an'kouszes) adj.
nieprzytomny; zemdlony; nieświadomy; s. podswiadomość
unconsciousness (an'konszesnys)
omdlenie; nieprzytomność
unconstitutional ('an,konsty'-
'tju:szynl) adj. niezgodny
z konstytucja
uncontrollable ('an,kon'troulebl)
adj. nieposkromiony; niepohamowany
unconventional ('an-ken'wenszynl)
adj. niekonwencjonalny; oryginalny
unconvinced ('an-ken'wynst) adj.
nieprzekonany
unconvincing ('an-ken'wynsyng)
adj. nieprzekonywujący
uncouth (an'ku:s) adj. nieokrzesany; niezręczny; niezgrabny

uncover (an'kawer) v. odkryć;
demaskować
uncultivated ('an'kaltywejtyd)
adj. nieuprawny; leżący odłogiem; niekulturalny
uncultured ('an'kalczerd) adj.
niewykształcony; niekulturalny
undamaged ('an'daemydżd) adj.
nieuszkodzony
undecided ('an-dy'sajdyd) adj.
niezdecydowany; niepewny;
nieokreslony; nierozstrzygnięty
undefined ('andy'fajnd) adj.
nieokreslony; mglisty
undeniable (,andy'najebl) adj.
niezaprzeczalny
under ('ander) prep. pod; poniżej; w; w trakcie; zgodnie
z; z; adv. poniżej; pod spodem; adj. spodni; niższy;
dolny; podrzędny; podwładny
underbid ('ander'byd) v. zob.
bid; składać niższą ofertę
w przetargu
undercarriage ('ander,kaerydż)
s. podwozie
underclothes ('ander;klousz)
pl. bielizna
underclothing ('ander-klousyng)
s. bielizna
underdeveloped (ander,dy'welept) adj. zacofany; nie wywołany poprawnie; niedorozwinięty
underdone ('ander'dan) adj.
półsurowy; niedogotowany
underestimate ('ander'estymejt)
v. niedoceniać; za nisko
oszacować
underfed ('ander'fed) v. niedożywiony
undergo (,ander'gou) v. zob.go;
doznawać czegos; przechodzić
cos; doswiadczyc; poddawac się
(operacji)
undergraduate (,ander'graedjuit)
s. student bez stopnia bachelor
underground ('ander,graund) adj.
podziemny; zaskórny; tajny;
s. kolej podziemna; ruch oporu;

adv. (,ander'graund)pod ziemią;
skrycie; tajnie
undergrowth ('ander-grous) s.
poszycie (lasu)
underline ('anderlajn) v. podkreslać; s. podkreslenie; podpis pod ilustracją; zawiadomienie (u spodu afisza teatralnego) o następnej sztuce
undermine (,ander'majn) v. podkopywać (zdrowie etc.) podmywać (brzegi etc.)
undermost ('andermoust) adj.
najniższy
underneath (,ander'ni:s) adv.
pod spodem; poniżej; na dole;
pod spod
underpass (,ander'pa:s) s.
przejazd poniżej poziomu (w
skrzyżowaniu bezkolizyjnym)
underpay ('ander'pej) v. za mało płacic
underprivileged ('ander'prywylydżd) adj. upośledzony
undershirt ('andersze:rt) s.
podkoszulek
undersigned ('ander'sajnd) adj.
(niżej) podpisany
undersized ('ander'sajzd) adj.
zbyt mały; małego wzrostu
under soil ('ander,sojl) s.
podglebie
understaffed ('ander'sta:ft)
adj. mający zbyt mały personel
understand; understood; understood (,ander'staend; ander'-stud; ,ander'stud)
understand (,ander'staend) v.
rozumiec; domyslać się; orientowac się; znac; wywnioskowac;
wiedzieć jak; umiec dobrze
understandable (,ander'staendebl) adj. zrozumiały
understanding (,ander'staendyng)
adj. pełen zrozumienia; s. zrozumienie; warunek; (wyższa)
inteligencja; porozumienie;
rozum
understatement (,ander'stejtment) s. zbyt skromne wyrażanie się; niedomówienie

undertake (,ander'tejk) v.zob.
take; przedsiębrać; podejmo-
wac się; ręczyc; zobowiązy-
wac się do czegos; byc przed-
siębiorcą pogrzebowym
undertaker (,ander'tejker) s.
przedsiębiorca pogrzebowy
undertaking (,ander'tejkyŋg) s.
przedsięwzięcie; zobowiązanie;
obietnica; przyrzeczenie;
przedsiębiorstwo pogrzebowe
undervalue (,ander'waelju) v.
niedoceniac; za nisko szacować
underwear ('anderłeer) s. bielizna
underwood ('ander,łu:d) s. poszycie (lasu)
underworld ('ander,łe:rld) s.
podziemie; świat podziemny;
pl. antypody
underwrite ('ander-rajt) v.
zob. write; zakontraktowac
(ubezpieczenie); podpisac(się);
wydawac (polisę ubezpieczenio-
wą); zobowiazywac się
underwriter ('ander-rajter) s.
ajent ubezpieczeniowy
undeserved ('andy'ze:rwd) adj.
niezasłużony; niesłuszny
undesirable (andy'zajerebl)
adj. niepożądany: niedogodny;
s. człowiek niepożądany
undeveloped (andy'welopt) adj.
nierozwinięty; niewywołany
undies (andyz) pl. bielizna
(damska i dziecięca)
undignified (an'dygnyfajd) adj.
niegodny; bez godności
undiminished (an'dymynszt) adj.
niezmniejszony
un-disciplined (an'dysyplind)
adj. niezdyscyplinowany; nie-
karny
undisputed (,andys'pju:tyd)
adj. bezsporny; niezaprzeczony
undisturbed ('andys'te:rbd) adj.
niezakłocony
undo; undid; undone ('an'du;
'an'dyd, an'dan)
undo ('an'du:) v. robic nieby-
łym; uniewazniac; usuwac;
niszczyc; rujnowac; rozpakowac;

rozwiązac; otwierac; rozpinac;
przekreslac
undreamt-of ('an'dremt,ow)
adj. nieprawdopodobny; nie do
pomyslenia; niesłychany
undress (an'dres) v. rozbierac
(się); odbandazowywac; s. negliż; zwykłe ubranie
undressed (an'drest) adj. nie
przyrządzony; chropowaty; nie
opatrzona (rana); rozebrany
undue (an'dju:) adj. przesadny;
nadmierny; postronny; niewłas-
ciwy; jeszcze niepłatny (np.
rachunek)
undutiful (an'djutyful) adj.
nieobowiązkowy
uneasy (an'i:zy) adj. niespokojny; niepokojący; nieswoj;
zażenowany; nieprzyjemny;
krępujacy; budzący niepokoj
uneducated (an'edjukejtyd)
adj. niewykształcony; bez
wykształcenia
unemployed (an'emplojd) adj.
bez pracy; bezrobotny; nie-
wykorzystany; nie zużytkowany
unemployment (an'emplojment)
s. bezrobocie
unendurable ('anyn'djuerebl)
adj. nie do zniesienia
unenviable ('an'enwjebl) adj.
nie do pozazdroszczenia
unequal ('an'i:kłol) adj. nie-
rowny; nie na wysokości (zadania)
unequaled ('an'i:kłold) adj.
niezrównany
unequivocal ('any'kływokel) adj.
niedwuznaczny; wyrazny; jasny
unerring ('an'e:ryŋg) adj.
nieomylny; niezawodny
uneven ('an'i:wen) adj. nieparzysty; niejednolity; nierówny
uneventful ('an,y'wentful)
adj. nieurozmaicony; spokojny;
jednostajny
unexpected ('anyks'pektyd)
adj. niespodziewany; nieoczekiwany
unfailing (an'fejlyŋg) adj.
niezawodny; niewyczerpany

unfair (an'feer) adj. niesprawiedliwy; krzywdzący; nieuczciwy; nieprzepisowy

unfaithful (an'fejsful) adj.
niewierny; wiarołomny; nieścisły

unfamiliar ('anfe'myljer) adj.
nieznany; nieobznajomiony;
obcy

unfashionable ('an'faeszenebl)
adj. niemodny

unfasten ('an'fa:sn) v. odczepić (się); odpiąć (się); od-
wiązywać (się); odryglować
(się); rozluźnić (się)

unfavorable ('an'fejwerebl)
adj. niepomyślny; nieżyczliwy;
niesprzyjający; nieprzychylny

unfeasible (an'fi:sebl) adj.
niewykonalny

unfeeling (an'fi:lyng) adj.
bez uczucia; bez serca; okrutny

unfinished ('an'fynyszt) adj.
niewykończony; niedokończony

unfit ('an'fyt) adj. nie nadający się; niezdatny; niezdolny; nieodpowiedni; v. czynić
niezdolnym do czegoś

unflappable ('an'flaepebl) adj,
nie do wytrącenia z równowagi

unfold ('an'fould) v. ujawniać
(się); rozwijać (się); otwierać; odsłonić

unforseen ('an'fer,si:n) adj.
nieprzewidziany; niespodziewany

unforgettable ('an-fer'getebl)
adj. pamiętny; niezapomniany

unforgiving ('an-fer'gywyng)
adj. niewybaczający; nieprzejednany

unforgotten ('an-fer'gotn)adj.
niezapomniany

unfortunate (an'fo:rcznyt) adj.
niefortunny; pechowy; niepomyślny; nieszczęśliwy

unfortunately (an'fo:rcznytly)
adv. niestety; nieszczęśliwie

unfounded (an'faundyd) adj.
bezpodstawny

unfriendly (an'frendly) adj.
nieprzyjazny; nieprzychylny

unfurnished (an'fe:rnyszt) adj.
nieumeblowany

ungainly (an'gejnly) adj. niezdarny; niezgrabny

ungenerous (an'dżeneres) adj.
małostkowy; nie szczodry

ungentle (an'dżentl) adj. nie-
łagodny

unget-at-able ('anget'aetbl)
adj. niedostępny (slang)

ungovernable (an'gawernebl)adj.
dziki; niesforny; krnąbrny;
nieopanowany

ungraceful (an'grejsful) adj.
niewdzięczny; nieuprzejmy

ungrateful (an'grejful) adj.
niewdzięczny

unguarded ('an'ga:rdyd) adj.
niebaczny;nieopatrzny; nierozważny; niestrzeżony

unhappy (an'haepy) adj. nieszczęśliwy; pechowy; zmartwiony;nieudany

unharmed ('an'ha:rmd) adj. nietknięty

unharness ('an'ha:rnys) v. wy-
przęgać; zdejmować zbroję; etc.

unhealthy (an'helsy) adj. niezdrowy

unheard-of (an'he:rd,ow) adj.
niesłychany; niebywały; nieprawdopodobny

unheeded (an'hi:dyd) adj. niezauważony; niedostrzeżony

unheeding (an'di:dyng) adj. nieuważający; niedostrzegający

unhesitating      (an'hezytejtyng)
adj. nie wahający się

unhoped-for (an'hopt,fo:r) adj.
niespodziewany; nieoczekiwany

unhurt (an'he:rt) adj. nieuszkodzony; bez szwanku

unicorn ('ju:nyko:rn) s. jedno-
rożec; jednoróg

unification (,ju:nyfy'kejszyn)
s. zjednoczenie; zcalenie;
ujednolicenie

uniform ('ju:nyfo:rm) adj.
jednolity; równomierny; jednostajny; s, mundur; uniform

uniformity ('ju:ny'fo:rmyty)
s. jednolitość; jednostajność ;
ujednolicenie;ujednostajnienie

unilateral ('ju:ny'laeterel)
adj. jednostronny
unimaginable (any'maedżynebl)
adj. nie do pomyslenia
unimaginative (any'maedżynejtyw)
adj. bez wyobraźni; bez polotu
unimportant ('anym'po:rtent)
adj. nieważny; błahy; mało
ważny
uninhabitable('anyn'haebytebl)
adj. nie do mieszkania; nie
do życia
uninhabited ('anyn'haebytyd)
adj. niezamieszkały
uninjured ('an'yndżerd) adj.
bez szwanku; nie uszkodzony;
bez obrażeń
uninspired ('anyn'spajerd) adj.
banalny
unintelligible ('anyn'telydżebl)
adj. niezrozumiały
unintentional ('anyn'tenszynl)
adj. mimowolny; nie zamierzony
uninteresting ('anyn'terestyng)
adj. nudny; nieciekawy; nie-
interesujący
uninterrupted ('anyn'teraptyd)
adj. nieprzerwany; ciągły;
bezustanny
uninvited ('anyn'wajtyd) adj.
nieproszony
uninviting ('anyn'wajtyng) adj.
nie zachęcający; odpychający;
nieapetyczny
union ('ju:njen) s. połączenie;
złącze; łączność; związek;
zjednoczenie; małżeństwo; zgoda; łącznik; złączka; godło
unionist ('ju:njenyst) s.
związkowiec; zwolennik związku
union Jack ('ju:njen'dżaek) s.
flaga angielska
unique (ju:'ni:k) adj. wyjątkowy; jedyny; niezrównany
unisex ('ju:ny'seks) adj. styl
(wyrobów) do użytku obu płci;
odzież, przybory toaletowe,
zakład fryzjerski etc.
unison ('ju:nyzn) adj. zgodnie
(razem)
unit ('ju:nyt) s. jednostka;
zespół

unite (ju:'najt) v. łączyć; jed-
noczyc; zjednoczyć
united (ju:'najtyd) adj. połączony; zjednoczony; łączny
unity ('ju:nyty) s. jedność
(czasu, miejsca, działania, etc);
jednostka; jednolitość; harmonia; zgoda
universal (ju:ny've:rsel) adj.
powszechny; ogólny; uniwersalny
universe ('ju:nyvers) s. wszechświat; świat; ludzkość; kosmos
university (,ju:ny'wersyty) s.
uniwersytet; wszechnica; uczelnia
unjust ('an'dżast) adj. niesprawiedliwy
unkempt ('an'kempt) adj. nie-
uczesany; rozczochrany; niechlujny
unkind (an'kajnd) adj. niedobry;
okrutny
unknown ('an'noun) adj. nieznany;
niewiadomy
unlace ('an'lejs) v. rozsznurować
unlawful ('an'lo:ful) adj. bezprawny; nielegalny
unlearn ('an'le:rn) v. oduczać
(się); zob, learn
unless (an'les) conj. jeżeli
nie; chyba że
unlike ('an'lajk) adj. niepodobny; odmienny; prep. odmiennie;
inaczej; w przeciwieństwie
unlikely (an'lajkly) adj. nieprawdopodobny; nieoczekiwany;
nie rokujący
unlimited (an'lymytyd) adj.
nieograniczony; bezgraniczny;
dowolny
unload ('an'loud) v. rozładowy-
wać; zrzucać ciężar
unlock ('an'lok) v. otwierać
zamek; otworzyć
unlocked ('an'lokt) adj. otwarty; niezamknięty
unlooked-for (an'lukt,fo:r)
adj. nieoczekiwany; niespodziewany; nieprzewidziany
unloosen ('an'lu:sn) adj. rozluźniony; rozwiązany; rozsznu-
rowany

unlucky (an'laky) adj. pechowy; niefortunny; niepomyślny; nieszczęśliwy

unmanageable (an'maenydżebl) adj. niesforny; krnąbrny

unmanly (an'maenly)adj. zniechecający; odbierający odwagę; adv. zniechecająco

unmarried (an'maeryd) adj. nieżonaty; niezamężna

unmistakabe ('anmys'tejkbl) adj. niewątpliwy; wyrazny; niedwuznaczny

unmoved (`an'm:wd) adj. niewzruszony

unnatural (an'naeczrel) adj. sztuczny; nienaturalny; wbrew naturze; nienormalny

unnecessary (an'nesysery) adj. zbędny; zbyteczny; niepotrzebny

unnoticed ('an'noutyst) adj. niezauważony; (pominięty)

unobtainable ('anęb'tejnebl) adj. nie do nabycia(otrzymania)

unobtrusive ('aneb'tru:syw) adj. skromny; dyskretny; nie narzucający się

unoccupied ('an'okjupajd) adj. wolny; nie zajęty

unoffending ('ane'fendyng) adj. nieszkodliwy; (niewinny)

unofficial ('ane'fyszel) adj. nie urzędowy; nieoficjalny

unpack ('an'paek) v. rozpakowywac (się)

unpaid ('an'pejd) adj. niezapłacony; (bezinteresowny)

unparalleled (an'paereleld)adj. niezrównany; niespotykany; bezprzykładny; niesłychany

unpardonable (an'pa:rdnebl) adj. niewybaczalny

unperceived (an'per'si:wd)adj. niespostrzeżony

unperturbed ('an-per'te:rbd) adj. spokojny; nie zaniepokojony; nie przejmujący się

unpleasant (an'plezent) adj. nieprzyjemny; przykry; niemiły

_wyciągnąc z kontaktu

unplug (an'plag) v. odczopowac;

unpolished ('an'polyszt) adj. niewyczyszczony; niewygładzony

unpopular (an'popjuler) adj. m. niepopularny; niemile widziany

unpopularity ('an,popju'laeryty) s. niepopularnosc; złe przyjęcie

unpractical ('an'praektykel) adj. niepraktyczny; nierealny

unpracticed (an'praektyst) adj. nie wypraktykowany; niewprawny

unprecedented (an'presydentyd) adj. bezprzykładny; bez precedensu; niesłychany

unprejudiced (an'predżudyst) adj. bezstronny; nie mający przesądów

un-premeditated ('anpry:'medytejtyd) adj. bez premedytacji; nienaumyślny

unprepared ('anpry'peerd) adj. nieprzygotowany; nieprzyrządzony

unprincipled (an'prynsepld) adj. bez skrupułów; niegodziwy

unproductive (an'prodaktyw) adj. niewydajny; nie wytworczy; niepłodny;

unprofitable (an'profytebl) adj. niepopłatny; niekorzystny; nierentowny

unprovided-for ('an-pre'wajdyd-,fo:r) adj. niezabezpieczony; bez srodków do życia

unqualified ('an'kłolyfajd) adj. niewykwalifikowany; bez kwalifikacji; niesprecyzowany; nieograniczony (np. zaufanie)

unquestionable (an'kłesczynebl) adj. bezsporny; niewątpliwy

unquestioned (an'kłesczynd) adj. niezaprzeczony; niepytany

unreasonable (an'ri:znebl) adj. nierozsądny; niedorzeczny; wygórowany (w cenie)

unrefined ('anry'faind) adj. niesubtelny; niewyrafinowany; niewykształcony

unreliable ('anry'lajebl) adj. niepewny; niesolidny

unreserved ('anry'ze:rwd) adj.
otwarty; szczery; bez zastrże-
zeń; całkowity; niezarezerwo-
wany

unresisting ('anry'zystyŋg)
adj. nieodporny; nieopierają-
cy się

unrest ('an'rest) s. niepokój;
zamieszki; niepokoje

unrestrained ('anrys'trejnd)
adj. niepowstrzymany; niepohamowany; nieopanowany

unrestricted ('anrys'tryktyd)
adj. nieograniczony; (niedostępny)

unrip ('an'ryp) v. porozpruwać

unripe ('an'rajp) adj. niedojrzały

unrivaled (an'rajweld) adj.
niezrównany; bezkonkurencyjny

unroll ('an'roul) v. rozwinąć
(zwój; rolkę)

unruffled (an'rafld) adj. niezmącony; niezakłócony; zachowujący równowagę

unruly (an'ru:ly) adj. niesforny

unsafe ('an'sejf) adj. niepewny;
ryzykowny; niebezpieczny

unsanitary ('an'saenytery) adj.
niehigieniczny; szkodliwy;nie-
zdrowy

unsatisfactory ('an,saetys'faektery) adj. niezadawalający;
niedostateczny

unsatisfied (an'saetysfajd) adj.
niezadowolony; niezaspokojony

unsavory ('an'sejwery) adj.
niesmaczny; przykry

unscrew('an'skru:) v. odśrubo-
wać; rozśrubować; odkręcić
(gwint)

unscrupulous ('an'skru:pjules)
adj. bez skrupułów; niegodziwy

unseen (an'si:n) adj. nie widziany; niewidoczny

unselfish (an'selfysz) adj.bez-
interesowny

unsettled ('an'setld) adj. za-
burzony; zakłócony; nieustalo-
ny; niezapłacony; rozstrojony

unshaven (an'szejwn) adj. nie-
ogolony

unshrinkable (an'szrynkebl)
adj. nie kurczący się (w praniu)

unshrinking (an'szrynkiŋg) adj.
nie wahający się; nie wzdry-
gający się

unskilled (an'skyld) adj. niewprawny; niewykwalifikowany

unskilful (an'skylful) adj.
niewprawny; niezręczny

unsociable (an'souszebl) adj.
nietowarzyski

unsocial (an'souszel) adj. nie-
socjalny; niespołeczny

unsolvable (an'salwebl) adj.
nierozwiązalny; nierozpuszczalny

unsolved (an'solwd) adj. nie-
rozwiązany; nierozpuszczony

unsophisticated (,anso'fystykejtyd) adj. prosty; naturalny; prawdziwy

unsound (an'saund) adj. niezdrowy; spróchniały; słaby;
niepewny; ryzykowny; błędny;
niesolidny

unspeakable (an'spi:kebl) adj.
niewypowiedziany;nie do opisania

unspoiled (an'spojld) adj.
niezepsuty; nierozpieszczony
(dziecko)

unspoken ('an'spouken) adj.
nie mówiony (np. prawo)

unspoken-for (an'spoukn;fo:r)
adj. niezamówiony

unspoken-of ('an'spoukn) adj.
nie omawiany

unstable (an'stejbl) adj. niepewny; chwiejny;niezrównowa-
żony

unsteady ('an'stedy) adj.
chwiejny; chwiejący się; niezdecydowany; nieustabilizowany;
zmienny; niepewny

unstressed ('an'strest) adj.
nieakcentowany; niepodkreślony;
nieobciążony

unsuccessful ('an-sek'sesful)
adj. nieudany; bez powodzenia;
nieudały; nie mający powodzenia; bezowocny

unsuitable ('an'sju:tebl) adj.
niewłaściwy; niestosowny;
nieodpowiedni
unsure (an'szuer) adj. niepewny; zawodny
unsurpassed ('an-ser'pa:st)
adj. nieprześcigniony; niezrównany
unsuspected ('an-ses'pekyd)
adj. (zupełnie) niepodejrzany
unsuspecting('an-ses'pektyng)
adj. nieczego nie podejrzewa-
jący
unsuspicious ('an-ses'pyszes)
adj. ufny; niepodejrzliwy
unthinkable ('an'tynkebl) adj.
nie do pomyślenia; nieprawdopodobny
unthinking ('an'tynkyng) adj.
bezmyślny
untidy (an'tajdy) adj. niechlujny;niestaranny; rozczor-
rany; zaniedbany; nie posprzą-
tany
untie(an'taj) v. rozwiązywać
(się); rozsupłać; uwalniać
(się) z więzów; usuwać (trudności)
until (an'tyl) prep. & conj.
do; dotychczas; dopiero; aż
untimely (an'tajmly) adj. nie
w porę; przedwczesny; nie na
czasie; wczesny; adv. przed-
wcześnie; w nieodpowiedniej
chwili
untiring (an'tajeryng) adj.
niezmordowany
unto ('antu:) prep,= to; do;
ku; aż do
untold (an'told) adj. niewypowiedziany; nieprzeliczony
untouchable (an'taczebl) adj.
niedotykalny
untouched (an'taczt) adj. nietknięty; nieskazitelny; nieczuły
untried (an'trajd) adj. niewy-
próbowany
untroubled (an'trabld) adj.
spokojny; beztroski

untrue ('an'tru:) adj. nieprawdziwy; fałszywy; niewierny;
sprzeniewierzający się
untrustworthy ('an'trast,łe:rsy)
adj. niegodny zaufania; niepewny
untruth ('an'tru:s) s. nieprawda;
kłamstwo
unused ('an'ju:zd) adj. nie używany; nie przyzwyczajony; nie
stosowany
unusual (an'ju:żuel) adj. niezwykły; wyjątkowy
unutterable (an'aterebl) adj.
niewysłowiony; niewypowiedziany
unvarying (an'weery-yng) adj.
jednostajny; nieurozmaicony;
nie zmieniający (się)
unvoiced (an'woist) adj. bez-
głosny; bezdźwięczny
unwanted (an'łontyd) adj. niepożądany; niepotrzebny; zbędny; zbyteczny
unwarranted ('an'łorentyd) adj.
nieusprawiedliwiony; bezpodstawny
unwholesome ('an'houlsem) adj.
niezdrowy; szkodliwy
unwilling ('an'łylyng) adj.
niechętny
unwind ('an'łajnd) v. zob.wind;
rozwijać (się); odprężać (się);
(slang): odpoczywać sobie
unwise ('an'łajz) adj. niemądry;
nieostrożny; nieroztropny
unworthy (an'łe:rsy) adj. niegodny; niegodziwy; niewart;
niezasługujący; ujemny
unwrap ('an'raep) v. rozwijać
(się); rozpakować; odsłonić
(się); odwijać (się)
unyielding ('an'ji:ldyng) adj.
nieustępliwy; twardy; nieugięty
up (ap) adv. do góry; w górę;
w zwyż; w górze; wyżej; na;
tam (gdzie); na górze; wysoko;
wyżej; aż (do); aż (po); na
(piętro); pod (górę); v. podnosić; zrywać się; podbijać
(cenę); zaczynać

up-and-about ('apend,ebaut)
exp.:(znowu) na nogach (po
chorobie)
up-and-coming ('ap,end'komyŋg)
exp.:(slang): obiecujący;
rzutki; przedsiębiorczy (człowiek)
up-and-doing ('ap,end'duyŋg)
exp.: (slang): czynny; ruchliwy
up-and-up ('ap,end'ap)być uczciwym
up to('ep,tu )adv.aż do pogodny
upbeat('apbi:t)adj.optymistyczny;
upbringing (' p,bryŋgyŋg) s.
wychowanie ; wychowywanie
uphill ('ap'hyl) adj. wznoszą-
cy (się); stromy; trudny;
uciążliwy; adv. stromo; pod
górę; w górę
upholster (ap'houlster) v.
obijać (meble); wyścielać;
pokrywać; urządzać
upholsterer (ap'houlsterer)
s. tapicer; dekorator
upholstery(ap'houlstry) s.
tapicerstwo; meble wyścielane
upkeep ('apki:p) s. utrzymanie;
koszty utrzymania szanie się
upmanship('apmen,szyp)s.wywyż-
upon (e'pon)prep.=on; na; po
upper ('aper) adj. wyższy; górny; wierzchni; s. przyszwa
uppermost ('aper,moust) adj.
najwyższy; adv. na górze; na
górę
uppish ('apysh) adj. zadziera-
jący nos do góry (slang)
upright ('ap'rajt) adj. wypro-
stowany; prosty; uczciwy; prawy; adv. pionowo; s. pionowy
słup; podpora; pianino; pozycja pionowa
uprising (ap'rajzyŋg) s. powstanie; wstawanie
uproar ('ap,ro:) s. zgiełk;
wrzawa; harmider; tumult
upset ('apset) v. zob. set;
przewracać (się), pokonywać;
wzburzać; rozstrajać; rozku-
wać; pogrubiać; skręcać; roz-
klepywać; s. wywrócenie (się);
porażka; podniecenie; zaburzenie; rozstrój; niepokój;

bałagan; sztanca do kucia
upside-down ('apsajd'dałn)adv.
do góry nogami; do góry dnem;
adj. odwrócony do góry nogami
upstairs ('ap'steerz) adv. na
górę; na górze
upstart ('ap-sta:rt) s. par-
wenjusz
upstream ('ap'stri:m) adv. pod
prąd; w górę rzeki
uptight ('ap'tajt) adj. (slang);
napięty; naprężony (nerwowo)
up-to-date ('ap-tu-'dejt) adj.
bieżący; nowoczesny
upwards (apłerdz) adv. w górę;
ku górze; na wierzch; wyżej;
powyżej (czegoś)
uranium (ju'rejnjem) s. uran
urbane (e:r'bejn) adj. grzeczny; układny; wytworny
urchin ('e:rczyn) s. ulicznik;
urwis; łobuz; smyk; jeżowiec;
jeżak; czesak
urge (e:rdż) v. poganiać; popędzać; ponaglać; przyspieszać; nalegać; pilić; namawiać; s. pragnienie; impuls;
tęsknota; pociąg; bodziec
urge on ('e:rdż,on) v. namawiać
na coś
urgent (e:rdżent) adj. pilny;
naglący; gwałtowny; natarczywy; nalegający
urine ('jueryn) s. mocz; uryna
urn (e:rn) s. urna
usage ('ju:sydż) s. zwyczaj;
praktyka; obchodzenie (się);
używanie (zwrotów, języka po-
prawnego)
use (ju:s) s. użytek; używanie;
użycie; posługiwanie; zastosowanie; pożytek; korzyść; zwyczaj; praktyka; obrządek; przyzwyczajenie; v. używać; korzystać; wykorzystać; zużywać; zużyć; wyczerpać; traktować;
obejść się; mieć zwyczaj
used (ju:zd) adj. przyzwyczajony; używany; stosowany
useful ('ju:zful) adj. użyteczny;
pożyteczny; dogodny; wygodny;
(slang):doskonały; sprawny;
biegły; zdolny

useless ('ju:zlys) adj. niepotrzebny; bezużyteczny; zbyteczny; bezcelowy; nieużyteczny; do niczego
use up ('ju:s,ap) v. zużyć (wszystko); wyczerpać (np. pracą
usher ('aszer) s, odźwierny; woźny; bileter; rozprowadzający na miejsca (w kinie; w kościele etc.) v. wprowadzać; zapoczątkować
usher in ('aszer,yn) v. wprowadzać do
usherette (,asze'ret) s. bileterka (rozprowadzająca)
usual ('ju:zuel) adj. zwykły; zwyczajny; normalny; zwyczajowy; utarty
usually ('ju:żuely) adv. zwykle; zazwyczaj
usurer ('ju:żerer) s. lichwiarz
usury ('ju:żury) s. lichwa
utensil (ju'tensyl) s. sprzęt; naczynie; narzędzie
utility (ju'tylyty) s. pożytek; użyteczność; firma dostarczająca gaz, elektryczność lub wodę ludności w USA
utilize ('ju:tylajz) v. zużytkować; spożytkować; wykorzystać
utmost ('atmoust) adj. najwyższy; ostateczny; skrajny; największy; najdalszy; ostatni
utter ('ater) adj. całkowity; zupełny; kompletny; skończony; skrajny; ostatni; v. wydawać (głos); powiedzieć; wypowiedzieć (hasło itp.); wyrażać; wystawiać (czeki); podrabiać (np. dokumenty); puszczać (w obieg)
utterance ('aterens) s. wypowiedz; wymowa; wyrażenie; zeznanie; oświadczenie
uvula ('ju:wjula) s. języczek miękkiego podniebienia
v (wi:) dwudziesta druga litera alfabetu angielskiego
vacancy ('wejkensy) s. wolne mieszkanie; wolne pokoje motelowe; wakans; próżnia; pustka; bezczynność

vacant ('wejkent) adj. pusty; próżny; wolny; wakujący;bezczynny; bezmyślny; obojętny
vacate (we'kejt) v. opróżniać; opuszczać; unieważniać
vacation (we'kejszyn) s. wakacje ferie; opróżnienie; zwolnienie (mieszkania); ewakuacja
vaccinate ('waeksynejt) v. szczepić
vaccination ('waeksynejszyn) s. szczepienie
vaccine ('waeksi:n) s. szczepionka
vacuum ('waekjuem) s. próżnia
vacuum bottle ('waekjuem'botl) s. termos
vacuum cleaner ('waekjuem'kli:-ner)s. odkurzacz
vacuum flask ('waekjuem,fla:sk) s. termos
vagabond ('waegebond) adj. włóczęgowski; wędrowny; s. włóczęga; nierób; próżniak
vagary ('wejgery) s. kaprys; chimera
vague (wejg) adj. niejasny; niewyraźny; nieokreślony; nieuchwytny; niewyraźny; wymijający; niezdecydowany
vain (wejn) adj. próżny; zarozumiały; czczy; pusty; gołosłowny; daremny; bezcelowy
valance ('waelens) s. krótka podłużna zasłona (światła); rodzaj adamaszku
vale ('wejl) s. dolina; pożegnanie; excl.;żegnajcie !
valerian (we'lerjen) s. waleriana
valet ('waelyt) s. służący; v. usługiwać
valiant ('waeljent) adj. dzielny; s. zuch
valid ('waelyd) adj. słuszny; ważny; uzasadniony
valley ('waely) s. dolina; koryto fali; wewnętrzny kąt płaszczyzn dachu
valor ('waeler) s. dzielność
valuable ('waeljuebl) adj. wartościowy; cenny; kosztowny; s.(pl)kosztowności;biżuteria

valuables ('waljuebls) pl.
kosztowności

valuation (,walju'ejszyn) s.
oszacowanie; cena

value ('waelju:) s. wartość;
cena; stopień jasności barwy
(w obrazie); v. szacować; cenić; oceniać

valueless ('waelju:lys) adj.
bezwartościowy

valuer ('waelju:er) s. taksa-
tor

valve (waelw) s. zawór; wentyl;
klapa; zastawka

van (waen) s. kryty wóz (cię-
żarowy); czoło armii; v. przewozić krytym wozem; badać rudę pukaniem

vane (wejn) s. chorągiewka (od
wiatru); łopatka śmigła;
brzechwa bomby; skrzydło wiatraka

vanilla (we'nyle) s. wanilia

vanish ('waenysz) v. znikać;
zanikać

vanity ('waenyty) s. próżność;
pycha; marność; czczość; toaleta; źródło próżności; rzecz
bez wartości

vanitycase ('waenyty,kejs) s.
kosmetyczka

vantage ('waentydż) s. korzyst-
na pozycja; przewaga (w tenisie)

vaporize ('wejporajz) v. wyparować; zamieniać się w parę

vapor (wejpor) s. para; mgła;
v. parować; gledzić

vaporous ('wejperes) adj.
mglisty; zamglony

variable ('weerjebl) adj. zmienny; niestały; s, zmienny wiatr

variance ('weerjens) s. rozbież-
ność; niezgodność

variant ('weerent) s. odmiana;
wariant; adj. odmienny; różny

variation (,weery'ejszyn) s,
zmiana; odmiana; wariant;
wariacja

varicose vein ('waerykous,wejn)
s. żylak

varied ('waeryd) adj. różnorodny;
różny; urozmaicony

variety (we'rajety) s. rozmai-
tość; urozmaicenie; różnorod-
ność; wielostronność; teatr
rozmaitości; kabaret; szereg;
odmiana

various ('weerjes) adj. różny;
rozmaity; urozmaicony; wiele;
kilka; kilkakrotnie

varnish ('wa:rnysz) s. pokost;
politura; werniks; polewa;
v. pokostować; werniksować

Varsovian (wa:r'souwjen) adj.
warszawski; s. warszawiak

vary ('weery) v. zmieniać (się);
urozmaicać; różnić się; nie podzielać zdania

vase (wejz) s. waza; wazon

vat (waet) s. zbiornik; kadź;
cysterna

vault (wo:lt) s. sklepienie;
podziemie; piwnica; grobowiec;
skok o tyczce; v. przesklepiać;
osklepić; przeskoczyć; skoczyć
o tyczce

vaulting horse ('wo:ltyng,ho:rs)
s. kozioł (przyrząd gimnastyczny)

veal(wi:l) s. cielęcina

vegetable ('wedżytebl) s. jarzyna

vegetarian (,wedży'teerjen) adj.
jarski; s. jarosz; wegetarianin

vegetate ('wedżytejt) v. wegetować; rosnąć

vehemence ('wi:ymens) s. gwał-
towność; porywczość; wybucho-
wość

vehement ('wi:yment) adj. gwałtowny; porywczy; wybuchowy

vehicle ('wi:ykl) s. pojazd;
środek; narzędzie; przymieszka
do farby

veil (wejl) s. welon; woalka;
wstąpienie do klasztoru; zasłona (maska); chrypka; v. zasłaniać; ukrywać

vein (wejn) s. żyła (też złota);
usposobienie; natura; nastrój;
wena; v. żyłkować

velocity (wy'losyty) s. szybkość

velvet ('welwyt) s. aksamit;
delikatna skórka; (slang);
zarobek; forsa; adj. aksamit-
ny

venal ('wi:nl) adj. sprzedajny

vend (wend) v. sprzedawać

vender ('wender) s. (uliczny)
sprzedawca; automat do sprzedaży

vending machine ('wendyŋg,me'-
'szi:n) s. automat do sprzedaży

venerable ('wenerebl) adj.
czcigodny; wielebny

venerate ('wenerejt) v. czcić

venereal (wy'njerjel) adj.
weneryczny; chory wenerycznie;
przeciwwenervczny; płciowy

Venetian blind (wy'ni:szyn,-
,blajnd)s. żaluzja (wenecka)

vengeance ('wendżens) s. zemsta; pomsta

venison ('wenzn) s. dziczyzna

venom ('wenem) s. jad

venomous('wenemes) adj. jadowity

vent (went) s. odwietrznik;
wentyl; otwór wentylacyjny;
rozcięcie w tyle marynarki;
ujście; upust; v. dawać upust
czemuś; wyładowywać (złosć);
rozgłaszać; wietrzyc; wiercić
otwór wentylacyjny

ventilate ('wentylejt) v.
wentylowac; wietrzyc; prze-
dyskutowac

ventilator ('wentylejtor) s.
wentylator; wietrznik

ventriloquist (wen'trylokłyst)
s. brzuchomówca

venture ('wenczer) s. ryzyko;
stawka; spekulacja; impreza;
interes; próba; v. odważać
się; osmielac się; ryzykować;
smiec; narazic się

veranda (we'raende) s. weranda

verb (we:rb) s. czasownik;
słowo

verbal ('we:rbel) adj. ustny;
słowny; werbalny; czasownikowy

verdict ('we:rdykt) s. wyrok;
werdykt; osąd; orzeczenie

verdure ('we:rdżer) s. zieleń

verge ('we:rdż) s. skrąj; brzeg;
krawędź; v. graniczyc; zbliżać
się; chylic się; skłaniac się;

verge on ('we:rdż,on) v. graniczyc

verification (,weryfy'kejszyn)
s. uwierzytelnienie; sprawdzenie

verify ('weryfaj) v. sprawdzać;
potwierdzac; udowadniac

vermicelli (we:rmy'sely) s. cienki makaron

vermiform appendix (we:rmy'fo:rm-
e'pendyks) s. slepa kiszka;
wyrostek robaczkowy

vermin ('we:rmyn) s. robactwo;
świat przestępczy

vernacular (we:r'naekjuler) adj.
rodzimy; miejscowy; krajowy;
s. gwara; język rodzinny; do-
sadne powiedzenie

versatile ('we:rsetail) adj.
wszechstronny

verse (we:rs) s. wiersz; strofa

versed ('we:rst) adj. doswiadczony; wprawiony (w czymś)

version ('we:rżyn) s. wersja;
przekład; przekręcenie macicy

vertebra ('we:rtybre) s. krąg

vertebrae ('we:rtybri:) pl.
kręgi

vertical ('we:rtykel) adj. pionowy; szczytowy; s. pionowa
płaszczyzna; linia

very ('wery) adv. bardzo; absolutnie; zaraz; własnie; adj.
prawdziwy; sam; skończony(drań)

vessel ('wesl) s. naczynie; pojemnik; statek; okręt

vest (west) s. kamizelka; v. nadawać; przekazac; przysługiwac
komuś; przypadac komuś; odzie-
wac w szaty; przykrywac ołtarz

vestry ('westry) s. zakrystia

vet ('wet) s. weterynarz

veteran ('weteran) s. weteran

veterinary ('weterynery) s.
weterynarz

veto ('wi:tou) s. weto; v. zakładać weto

vex (weks) v. złościć; dręczyc; dokuczać

vexation (wek'sejszyn) s. dokuczanie; drażnienie; zniecierpliwienie; irytacja; udręka; przykrosc; zaniepokojenie

vexatious (wek'sejszes) adj. dokuczliwy; irytujący; przykry; nieznosny

via ('waje) prep. przez; wia

vibrate (waj'brejt) v. zadrgać; zadrzeć; oscylować; wprawiac w drganie lub ruch wahadłowy

vibration (waj'brejszyn) s. drganie; drżenie; wibracja; oscylacja; ruch wahadłowy

vibrator (waj'brejter) s. wibrator; oscylator

vicar ('wyker) s. wikary; wikariusz; zastępca

vice (wajs) imadło; zacisk; rozpusta; występek; nałog; narów; wada; v. zaciskać w imadle

vice versa ('wajsy'we:rsa) adv. odwrotnie

vicinity (wy'synyty) s. sąsiedztwo; pobliże

vicious ('wy'szes) adj. błędny; występny; złosliwy; wadliwy; zepsuty; dokuczliwy; narowisty; rozpustny

victim ('wyktym) s. ofiara

victor ('wykter) s. zwycięzca

victorian (wyk'to:rjan) adj. wiktorjanski

victorious (wyk'to:rjes) adj. zwycięski

victory ('wyktery) s. zwycięstwo

victuals ('wytlz) s. prowianty; wiktuały

video ('wydjou) s. telewizja; adj. telewizyjny

view (wju:) v. oglądać; rozpatrywac; zbadać; zapatrywać się; s. obejrzenie; spojrzenie; wizja; zasięg wzroku; widok; przegląd umysłowy; pogląd; zapatrywanie; intencja; zamiar; cel; ocena

viewer ('wju:er) s. widz (telewizyjny etc.)

viewpoint ('wju:,pojnt) s. punkt widzenia; zapatywanie

vigil ('wydżyl) s. czuwanie; wigilia

vigilance ('wydżylens) s. czujnosc; bezsennosc

vigilant ('wydżylent) adj. czujny

vigor ('wyger) s. krzepkosc; tężyzna; rzeskosc; energia; siła; moc

vigorous ('wygeres) adj. krzepki; mocny; jędrny; energiczny

vile (wajl) adj. podły; nędzny; marny

village ('wylydż) s. wies

villager ('wylydżer) s. wiesniak (raczej nieokrzesany)

villain ('wylen) s. łajdak; łotr; nikczemnik; łobuziak

villainous ('wylenes) adj. łajdacki; niegodziwy

villainy ('wyleny) s. łajdactwo

vim (wym) s. tężyzna

vincible ('wynsybl) adj. przezwyciężalny

vindicate ('wyndykejt) v. oczyszczać z zarzutu, oskarżenia, podejrzenia; rehabilitowac; usprawiedliwiac; bronic; dochodzic; dowodzic

vindication (,wyndy'kejszyn) s. obrona; windykacja; usprawiedliwienie: oczyszczenie się (z zarzutu); rehabilitacja

vindictive (wyn'dyktyw) adj. msciwy; karzący

vine (wajn) s. winna latorosl; winorosl

vinegar ('wynyger) s. ocet; v. kwasic

vineyard ('wynjerd) s. winnica

vintage ('wyntydż) s. rocznik wina; winobranie; robienie wina; model (roczny)

violate ('wajelejt) v. gwałcic; zgwalcic (kobietę)

violation (,waje'lejszyn) s. pogwałcenie; zgwałcenie; gwałt; zbeszczeszczenie; naruszenie (też praw ruchu)

violence ('wajelens) s. gwałtownosc; gwałt; przemoc
violent ('wajelent) adj. gwałtowny; niepohamowany; wściekły
violet ('wajelyt) s. fiołek; adj. fioletowy (np. promień)
violin (,waje'lyn) s. skrzypce
violinist (,waje'lynyst) s. skrzypek
viper ('wajper) s. żmija
virgin ('we:rdżyn) s. dziewica
virginity (we:r'dżynyty) s. dziewictwo
virile ('wyrajl) adj. męski
virility (wy'rylyty) s. męskosć; wiek męski; cechy męskie
virtual ('we:rczuel) adj. zasadniczy; właściwy; faktyczny; prawdziwy; rzeczywisty
virtually ('we:rczuely) adv. rzeczywiscie; faktycznie; praktycznie biorąc
virtue ('we:rczju:) s. cnota; prawosć; czystosć; skutecznosć; siła; moc
virtuoso (,we:rczju'ouzou) s. wirtuoz; miłosnik- znawca sztuki
virtuous (,we:rczjues) adj. cnotliwy; prawy
virulent ('wyrulent) adj. jadowity; złosliwy; zjadliwy
virus ('wajeres) s. wirus; jad (chorobowy)
visa ('wi:za) s. wiza; v. wiza; v. wizowac
viscosity(wys'kosyty)s.lepkosć;
visibility ('wyzy'bylyty) s. widocznosć
visible (wyzybl) adj. widoczny; wyrazny; widzialny
vision ('wyżyn) s. widzenie; wzrok; wizja; dar przewidywania; v. okazywac wizję; miec wizję
visit('wyzyt) v. odwiedzac; wizytowac zwiedzac; nawiedzac; karac; udzielac się; gawędzic; s. wizyta; odwiedziny; pobyt
visitor ('wyzyter) s. gosc; przyjezdny; zwiedzający; inspektor

vista ('wysta) s. perspektywa; wizja; widok
visual ('wyżjuel) adj. wzrokowy; optyczny
visualize ('wyżjuelajz) v. wyobrażac sobie; uwidaczniac; uzmysławiac
vital ('wajtl) adj. witalny; życiowy; żywotny; zasadniczy; smiertelny
vitality (waj'taelyty) s. żywotnosć; żywosć
vitamin ('wajtemyn) s. witamina
vivacious (wy'wejszes) adj. żywy
vivacity (wy'waesyty) s. żywosć
vivid ('wywyd) adj. żywy
vivify ('wywyfaj) v. ożywiac
vivisection ('wywyseks zyn) s. wiwisekcja
vixen ('wyksen) s. liszka; lisica; jędza
vixenish ('wyksenysz) adj. jędzowaty
vocabulary (wou'kaebjulery) s. słownik (specjalny); słownictwo
vocal ('woukel) s. samogłoska; adj. głosowy; wokalny; głosny; natarczywy
vocalist ('woukelyst) s. spiewak; wokalista
vocation (wou'kejszyn) s. zawód; zamiłowanie; powołanie; skłonnosć
vogue (woug) s. moda; popularnosć
voice (wois) s. głos; dzwięk samogłoskowy; strona (czasownika); v. wymawiac; wyrażac; dawac wyraz czemus; wymawiac dzwięcznie; udzwięczniac; pisac partie głosowe do muzyki; stroic
void (woid) s. próżnia; pustka; adj, próżny; pusty; pozbawiony czegos; wolny od czegos; wakujący; nieważny; v. uniewaźniac; wydalac; wyprózniac (się); oddawac (mocz)
void of ('woid,ow) exp.:bez

volatile ('woletyl) adj. lotny;
ulatniający się; zmienny
volcano (wol'kejnou) s. wulkan
volley ('woly) s. salwa; potok;
odbicie (piłki); wolej;
v. dać salwę; wypuszczać salwę; podawać wolejem; miotać
potokiem (przekleństw);leciec
salwą; odbijać w locie
volleyball ('woly,bo:l) s.
siatkówka
volt (woult) s. wolt (elektr.)
wolta; v. robić woltę
voltage ('woultydż) s. napięcie
prądu; woltaż
voluble ('woljubl) adj. gładki;
potoczysty; ze swadą
volume ('wolju:m) s. tom; objętość; masa; ilość; pojemność;
rozmiar; siła
voluntary ('wolentery) adj.
ochotniczy; dobrowolny; wolą
kontrolowany; spontaniczny;
samorzutny; s. specjalny wyczyn z wyboru sportowca; gra
solo na organie
volunteer ('wolentier) s. ochotnik (bezpłatnie pracujący);
v. robić z własnej ochoty;
zgłaszać się na ochotnika;
podejmować coś dobrowolnie;
być ochotnikiem
voluptuous (we'lapczues) adj.
zmysłowy; lubieżny
vomit ('womyt) v. wymiotować;
wyrzucać; pobudzać do wymio-
tów; s. wymioty; środek wy-
miotny
voodoo ('wu:du:) s. wiara w
czary; czarownik;v.zaczarować
voracious (we'rejszes) adj.
żarłoczny
voracity (we'raesyty) s. żar-
łoczność
vote (wout) s. głos; głosy;
głosowanie; prawo głosowania;
uchwała; wotum (zaufania);
v. głosować; uchwalać; orze-
kać; uznawać powszechnie za
cos
vote down ('wout,dałn) v. odrzucać w głosowaniu

voting paper ('woutyŋg'pejper)
s. kartka wyborcza
vouch (waucz) v. ręczyć; gwarantować; potwierdzać; zapewnić
voucher ('wauczer) s. dowód
kasowy
vouch for ('waucz,fo:r) v. ręczyć za kogoś
vouch safe (waucz'sejf) v. (łas-
kawie) raczyć
vow (wau) s. ślub (też zakonny);
przymierze; v. przysięgać;
ślubować; składać śluby
vowel ('wałel) s. samogłoska
voyage ('wojydż) s. podróż
(statkiem)
voyager ('wojedżer) s. podróżnik
vulcanize ('walkenajz) s. wulkanizować
vulgar ('walger) adj. ordynarny;
wulgarny; prostacki; gminny;
pospolity; powszechny
vulgarity ('wal'gaeryty) s.
wulgarność; wyrażenie wulgarne
vulnerable ('walnerebl) adj.
czuły; wrażliwy; mający słabe
miejsce; narażony na cios; pod-
datny na zranienie; niezabe z-
pieczony
vulpine ('walpajn) adj. lisi;
przebiegły; chytry
vulture ('walczer) s. sęp;(slang)
vulturine (walczeryn) adj. sępi
w ('dablju:) dwudziesta trzecia
litera alfabetu angielskiego
wabble ('łobl) v. (slang); roz-
klekotać; roztrząsnąć; rozchwiać;
s. rozchwianie; rozklekotanie
wack (łaek) s. (slang); oryginał;
dziwak
wacky ('łaeky) adj.(slang):
zwariowany;zdziwaczały; nieobliczalny
wad (łod) s. tampon; wałek (zwi-
nięty); wata (w uszach); przybitka naboju w strzelbie;
(slang): forsa; plik (banknotów);
v. zatykać (tamponem); watować;
przybijać (nabój); wypychać;
zwijać w wałek
wadding ('łodyŋg) s. watowanie;
watolina; wata; wełna (do utyka-
nia); podkład; przybitka

[jszakal
[slang]

waddle ('łodl) v. chodzic kołysząc się w biodrze jak
kaczka; s. kaczy krok
wade (łejd) y. brodzic; brnąc;
przechodzic w bród; brodze-
nie
wafer ('łejfer) s. wafel;
opłatek; naklejka urzędowa
(pieczątkowa); v. zapieczę-
towywac naklejką
waffle ('łofl) s. wafel z ciasta naleśnikowego
waft ('łaeft) v. popychac (lekko); posuwac; posyłac (cału-
sa); przepędzac; unosic (w
powietrzu). s. śmignięcie
skrzydła; powiew; podmuch;
tchnienie; przelotne uczucie;
smuga (swiatła)
wag (łaeg) v. kiwac (ogonem);
poruszac się; wahac się; chodzic tam i spowrotem; merdac
wage (łejdż) s. płaca; zarobek;
zapłata; v. prowadzic (np.
wojnę)
wage earner ('łejdż,e:rner) s.
człowiek zarobkujący
wages ('łejdżyz) s. zapłata
wager ('łejdżer) s. zakład;
v. zakładac się o coś
wagon ('łaegen) s. ciężki wóz
(kryty); lora; wóz policyjny;
furgon
wail (łejl) v. zawodzic; lamentowac; opłakiwac; v. zawodze-
nie; lament; płacz
wainscot ('łejnsket) s. boazeria;
ozdobne obicie scian drzewem
waist (łejst) s. talia; stan;
pas; kibic; stanik; sródokrę-
cie; zwężenie
waistcoat ('łeiskout) s. kamizelka
wait (łejt) v. czekac; oczekiwac;
czyhac; czatowac; czaic się;
obsłużyc; obsługiwac kogos;
s. czekanie; oczekiwanie; zasadzka; czaty
wait at table('łejtettejbl) v.
usługiwac przy stole
waiter ('łejter) s. kelner
wait on('łejton) v.obsługiwac

waiting (łejtyŋg) s. czekanie;
oczekiwanie; wyczekiwanie; zasadzka
waiting list (łejtyŋg,lyst) s.
lista kolejnosci (kandydatów,
klientów)
waiting room(łejtynrum) s.po-
czekalnia
waitings (łejtyns) pl. kolędni-
cy
waitress (łejtryss) s. kelnerka
wake; woke; woken (łejk; łouk;
łoukn)
wake (łejk) v. obudzic (się);
nie spac; pobudzic; rozbudzic;
wzbudzic; wskrzesic; czuwac
przy (zwłokach); s. niespanie;
czuwanie przy zwłokach; kilwater; fala w ślad za statkiem
(motorówką); slad (po kims, po
czyms)
wake up ('łejk,ap) v. obudzic
(się); ocknąc się; oprzytom-
niec; zdawac sobie sprawę;
zbudzic
wakeful ('łejkful) adj. czuwa-
jący; bezsenny; czujny
waken ('łejkn) = woken (łouken)
v. zob. wake
waken ('łejkn) v. zbudzic;
obudzic; ożywiac; wzbudzic;
wskrzesic (np. zmarłego)
walk (ło:k) v. isc; przechadzac się; chodzic; kroczyc;
isc stępa; jechac stępa;
wejsc; zejsc; s. chód; krok;
przechadzka; spacer; marsz;
deptak; aleja; odległosc prze-
byta
walk about ('ło:ke,baut) v.
włóczyc się; łazic
walk along ('ło:ke,loŋg) v.
chodzic sobie
walk away ('ło:ke,łej) v. odchodzic; (w zawodach): łatwo
wygrywac
walk back ('ło:k,baek) v. wracac
walk down ('ło:k,dałn) v. schodzic
walk in ('ło:k,yn) v. wchodzic

walk off ('ło:k,of) v. odchodzic; zniknąc; ulotnic się (z czyms)

walk out ('ło:k,aut) v. wyjsc; opuscic

walk over ('ło:k,ouwer) v. wygrywac łatwo; traktowac pogardliwie

walk up ('ło:k,ap) v. podejsc; wejsc na gorę

walker ('ło:ker) s. piechur

walkie-talkie ('ło:ky-'to:ky) s. przenosny, mały odbiornik- - nadajnik radiowy

walking (ło:kyng) s. chodzenie; marsz; wycieczka piesza; adj. chodzący; wędrowny

walking papers ('ło:kyn'pejpers) pl. zwolnienie z pracy na pismie

walking stick ('ło:kyng,styk) s. laska

walking-tour ('ło:kyng,tu:r) s. wycieczka piesza; zwiedzanie piechotą

walk-out ('ło:kaut) s. strajk

walk-over ('ło:k-over ('ło:k-ouwer) s. walkower (sport)

wall (ło:l) s. sciana; mur; przepierzenie; wał; v. obmurowac

wall in ('ło:l,yn) v. otaczac

wall up ('ło:,ap) v. zamurowac

wallboard ('ło:l,bo:rd) s. licówka (sciany)

wallet ('łolyt) s. portfel

wallop ('łolep) v. walic; łoic; prac; pobic na głowę; galopowac; łazic ciężko i niezgrabnie; s. wyrżnięcie (cios); galop; ruch ciężki i niezgrabny

wallow ('łolou) v. tarzac się; kłębic się; kołysac się; s. tarzanie się

wallpaper ('łol,pejper) s. tapety; v. tapetowac

Wall Street ('łolstri:t) s. osrodek finansowy (USA)

walnut ('ło:lnat) s. orzech włoski

walrus ('ło:lres) s. mors

waltz ('ło:ls) s. walc; v. tan-

czyc walca; (slang): ruszac się żwawo

wan (łon) adj. blady; wybladły; blednąc

wand (łond) s. laseczka; pałeczka; pręt; buława

wander ('łonder) v. wędrowac; błądzic; błąkac się

wanderer ('łonderer) s. wędrowiec

wane (łejn) v. zanikac; gasnąc; s. zanik

wangle ('łaengl) v. (slang): wycyganic; wyłudzic; sfałszowac; s. krętactwo; kant

want (ło:nt) s. brak; potrzeba; niedostatek; niedopatrzenie; bieda; nędza; v. pragnąc; chciec; brakowac; potrzebowac; pożądac

wanted ('ło:ntyd) adj. poszukiwany

wanting ('ło:ntyng) adj. brakujący; kiepski; niedokładny; pozbawiony; nie na poziomie; słaby na umysle; prep. bez; mniej;przy braku

want in ('ło:nt,yn) v. chciec wejsc

wanton ('łonten) adj. złosliwy; krzywdzący; bez powodu; bezmyslny; samowolny; bezczelny; nieokiełzany; wyuzdany; lubieżny; bujny; zbytkowny; s. lubieżnik; lubieżnica; v. oddawac się rozpuscie; używac sobie; swawolic; rosc bujnie; trwonic; psocic; figlowac; bawic się

want out ('ło:nt,aut) v. chciec wyjsc

war (łor) s. wojna; v. wojowac; zawojowac

warble ('łorbl) v. nucic; jodłowac; s. nucący głos; nucona piesn; guz od siodła na grzbiecie konia; guz wywołany larwą gza bydlęcego

ward (ło:rd) s. dzielnica; cela; sala; oddział; podopieczny; opieka; kuratela; postawa obronna; parada; straż; v.odparowywac (cios); odsuwac (niebezpieczenstwo);umieszczac na oddziale

ward off ('łо:rd,of) v. odpa-
rowywać cios; odsuwać (zagro-
żenie)
warden ('ło:rdn) s. dyrektor
więzienia; dozorca; nadzorca;
gatunek twardej gruszki
warder ('ło:rder) s. strażnik
więzienny; posterunek; buława
ward heeler('ło:rd,hi:ler) s.
naganiacz partyjny
wardrobe ('ło:droub) s. garderoba; szafa na ubranie
ware (łeer) s. towar; wyrób;
ceramika; v. uwaga na coś;
trzymać się z dala od czegoś;
excl.:strzeż się !
warehouse ('łeerhaus) s. magazyn; składnica; dom składowy;
v. magazynować; składować
warm (ło:rm) adj. ciepły; świeży (trop); bliski znalezienia;
zadomowiony (na posadzie);
zamożny
warm up ('ło:rm,ap) v. ożywiać
(się); podgrzewać (się); ogrze-
wać (się); rozgrzewać (się)
warmup ('ło:rmap) s. ćwiczenia
rozluźniające (przed zawodami
etc); zagrzanie się
warmth ('ło:rms) s. ciepło;
serdeczność; zapał
warn (ło:rn) v. ostrzegać;
przypominać; wzywać; zapowiadać; uprzedzać
warn against(ło:negejnst) v.
ostrzegać przed czymś
warning ('ło:rnyng) adj. ostrzegawczy; s. ostrzeżenie; przestroga; znak ostrzegawczy;
wypowiedzenie (posady)
warp ('ło:rp) v. wypaczyć (się);
zwichrować (się); wykrzywić
(się); spaczyć (się); przyholo-
wywać do miejsca utwierdzenia
liny lub łańcucha; użyżniać
(przez zalewanie osadem);
s. spaczenie; wypaczenie; osnowa; szew skośny; lina holownicza; osad
warrant ('łorent) v. usprawiedliwiać; uzasadniać; gwarantować; s. upoważnienie; gwarancja;

nakaz prawny (aresztu; rewizji,
etc). pełnomocnictwo dla ad-
wokatów; patent starszego pod-
oficera (USA)
warranty ('łorenty) s. gwarancja; poręka; rękojmia; podstawa; usprawiedliwienie; upoważnienie; dokument sądowy
warren ('łо:ryn) s. królikarnia
warrior ('ło:rjor) s. wojownik;
żołnierz; adj. wojowniczy
wart (ło:rt) s. brodawka; ku-
rzawka
wary ('łeery) adj. ostrożny
was (łoz) v. zob. be
wash (ło:sz) v. myć (się); prać;
prać (się); oczyszczać; zraszać; lekko barwić; lawować;
umyć się; sunąć; płynąć z
pluskiem; płukać (rudę);
s. mycie; pranie; płyn (czyszczący); fale; plusk; pomyje;
lura; wypłukane miejsce w ziemi; ględzenie; zaburzenie wody za statkiem; zaburzenie powietrza za samolotem; ziemia
na tacy zawierająca złoto; pod-
mywanie przez fale; mielizna;
kanał wyżłobiony przez wodę;
mielizna naniesiona wodą; la-
wowanie; cienka warstwa metalu;
kilwater; ślad wodny
wash away (ło:sze,łej) v. spłu-
kać; zmyć; unosić
wash down ('ło:sh,dałn) v. zmywać strumieniem wody; popić
jedzenie
wash off (ło:sh,of) v. odeprać;
wymywać
wash out ('ło:sh,aut) v. wypłu-
kiwać (się) (z pieniędzy etc,)
wash up ('ło:sh,ap) v. zmywać
naczynia; wymyć się
wash and wear ('ło:sz,end'łeer)
s. bielizna i odzież gotowa
do noszenia po praniu bez pra-
sowania
washbowl ('ło:sz,boul) s.mied-
nica; umywalka; umywalnia
washcloth ('ło:sz,clos) s. zmy-
wak; szmatka do zmywania

washer ('ło:szer) s. uszczelka; podkładka; maszyna do prania

washing ('łoszyng)s. mycie; pranie; przemywanie; woda z prania; popłuczyny; wypłukane złoto; wypłukany żwir; bielizna do prania

washing machine ('ło:szyng,me szi:n) s. pralka; maszyna do prania

washing powder ('ło:szyn'pałder) s. proszek do prania

washing up ('ło:szyng,ap) v. obmycie się

washleather ('ło:sz,ledzer) s. ircha; zamsz

washout ('ło:szaut) s. zapadnięcie się; podmycie; (slang): klapa; niepowodzenie

washtub ('ło:sztab) s. balia

washy ('ło:szy) adj. wodnisty; rzadki; blady; cienki; wypłowiały

wasn't = was not

wasp (łosp) n. osa; (slang): biały-anglosaksonin-protestant

waspish ('łospysh) adj. zjadliwy; cienki w pasie (jak osa)

wastage ('łejstydż) s. strata; zużycie

waste (łejst) adj. pustynny; pusty; nieużyty (ziemia); opustoszały; wyludniony; leżący odłogiem; zużyty; niepotrzebny; zbyteczny; odpadowy; v. pustoszyć; psuć; niszczyć (się); stracić (też zabić); zmarnować; ginąć; zużywac (się); zapuscic; zaniedbac; s. pustynia; marnowanie; trwonienie; zniszczenie; ubytek; zużycie; odpady; bezmiar (np. wody); zaniedbanie; marnotrawstwo

waste away ('łejst,e'łey) v. marnieć

wasteful ('łejstful) adj. rozrzutny; marnotrawny

wastepaper basket ('łejst-pejper-ba:skyt) s. kosz na śmieci

waste pipe ('łejstpajp) s. rura odpływowa; rura ściekowa

waster ('łejster) s. marnotrawca; zepsuty materiał; artykuł wybrakowany; nicpoń

watch (ło:cz) s. czuwanie; pilnowanie; czaty; czujność; wachta; zegarek; miec się na baczności; oczekiwanie na coś; wygladanie czegos; v. czuwać; oczekiwać; czatowac; pilnowac; opiekowac się; uważac; miec na oku; miec się na bacznosci; wyglądac czegos; obserwowac; szpiegowac; przyglądac się; patrzyc; oczekiwać sposobności; sledzic

watch out ('ło:czaut) v. uważać; strzec się; uwaga !; uważaj !

watchdog ('ło:czdog) s. pies podwórzowy

watchful ('ło:czful) adj. czujny; baczny

watchmaker ('ło:cz,mejker) s. zegarmistrz

watchman ('ło:czmen) s. stróż; dozorca

watchtower ('ło:cz,tauer) s. strażnica; wieża strażnicza

watchword ('ło:cze:rd) s. hasło; slogan

watch your step ('ło:cz,jo:r'-'step) exp.: uważaj !; pilnuj się !

water (ło:ter) s. woda; wysięk; przypływ; odpływ; pl. zdrój; wody lecznicze; ocean; morze; jezioro; rzeka; v. polewać; podlewać; pokropic; poić; isc do wodopoju; nawadniac; rozwadniac; rozcienczac; skrapiac; łzawic się; slinic się

water anchor ('ło:ter'aenker) s. kotwica dryfująca

water blister ('ło:ter,blyster) s. pęcherzyk z wodą

waterborne ('ło:ter,born) adj. przenoszony lub przekazywany przez wodę

water bottle ('ło:ter,botl) s. karafka; manierka

water brush ('ło:ter,brasz) s.    watering place ('ło:teryng-
zgaga                                plejs) s. wodopój; kąpielisko;

water but ('ło:ter,bat) s.          zdrojowisko
zbiornik na deszczówkę        waterless ('ło:terlys) adj.

water-cart ('ło:ter,ca:rt) s.     bezwodny; pozbawiony wody
beczkowóz                        water lily ('ło:ter,lyly) s.

water closet ('ło:ter'klozet)     grzybień biały; lilia wodna
s. ustęp                       water level ('ło:ter'lewl) s.

watercolor ('ło:ter'kaler) s.     poziom wody
akwarela                        waterline ('ło:terlajn) s.

water cool ('ło:ter,ku:l) v.      linia zanurzenia statku
chłodzić wodą                  waterlogged ('ło:ter,logd) adj.

watercourse ('ło:ter,ko:rs)      przesycony wodą
s. strumień; rzeka ; kanał      watermain ('ło:ter,mejn) s.

watercress ('ło:ter,kres) s.      główna rura wodociągów
rzeżucha wodna                waterman ('ło:termen) s. prze-

water-cure ('ło:ter,kjuer) s.      woźnik; wioślarz
kuracja wodna                watermark ('ło:terma:rk) s.

water-dog ('ło:ter,dog) s. pies    znak wodny; wodowskaz; v. ro-
myśliwski aportujący z wody;    bić znak wodny
(slang): amator pływania, etc)   watermelon ('ło:ter,melen) s.

water down ('ło:ter,dałn) v.      arbuz; kawon
rozwadniać                    water meter('ło:ter'mi:ter) s.

waterfall ('ło:ter,fo:l) s.        wodomierz; licznik wodny
wodospad                    water mill ('ło:ter,myl) s.

waterfowl ('ło:ter,faul) s.       młyn
ptactwo wodne              water mocassin ('ło:ter,mokesyn)

waterfront ('ło:ter,frant) s.      s. żmija wodna w USA
wybrzeże; doki; dzielnica       water motor ('ło:ter'mouter) s.
portowa                    motor wodny

watergap ('ło:ter,gaep) s.       water plane ('ło:ter'plejn) s.
przełom rzeki               hydroplan

water gate('ło:ter,gejt) s.       waterpower ('ło:ter'pałer) s.
śluza                      siła wodna; prawo do używania

water gauge('ło:ter,gejdź) s.     wody
wodowskaz; licznik wodny     water pot ('ło:ter,pot) s.ko--

water-glass ('ło:ter,gla:s) s.     newka; polewaczka
szklanka; naczynie; kubek;      waterproof ('ło:ter,pru:f)
szklany wodowskaz; przezier-   adj. nieprzemakalny; v. robić
nik podwodny              nieprzemakalnym

water hammer ('ło:ter,haemer)     water-rat ('ło:ter,raet) s.
s. silny wstrząs wywołany na-   szczur wodny
głym zatrzymaniem wody w ru-    water rate ('ło:ter,rejt) s.
rze                       opłata za wodę; cena wody

water hen ('ło:ter,hen) s. kur-    waterscape ('ło:ter,skejp) s.
ka wodna               krajobraz morski

water hole ('ło:terhol) s. sto-    watershed ('ło:ter,szed) s,
jąca woda (w suchym łożysku    dział wodny; (slang): ważna
rzeki); wodopój           granica

water ice ('ło:ter,ajs) s. sor-    water-ski ('ło:ter,ski:) s.
bet                      narta wodna

water spout('łó:ter,spaut) s.
trąba wodna; rynna pionowa
water supply ('łó:terse,plaj)
s. zaopatrzenie w wodę; sieć
wodociągowa
water table ('łó:ter,tejbl) s.
poziom (w ziemi) wody zaskór-
nej
watertight ('łó:ter,tajt)
adj. wodoszczelny
water tower ('łoter,tauer) s.
wieża ciśnień
water wave ('łó:ter,łejw) s.
ondulacja wodna
waterway ('łó:ter,łej) s.
droga wodna; kanał; rzeka
spławna
waterwheel ('łó:ter,hłi:l) s.
koło (młynskie) wodne
water witch ('łó:ter,łycz) s.
różdżkarz
waterworks ('łó:ter,łe:rks) s.
wodociągi; fontanna
watery ('łó:tery) adj. wodnisty;
zalzawiony; sliniący się; wro-
żący deszcz
watt (łot) s. (electr.) wat
waul (ło:l) v. miałczeć ostro
i przeciągle
wave (łejw) s. fala; falistość;
ondulacja; pokiwanie ręką;
gest ręką; v. falować; ondulo-
wać; machać do kogos
wave away ('łejwe'łej) v. odprawiac machnięciem ręki
wave back ('łejw,baek) v. przy-
woływać (spowrotem) machnięciem ręki
wavelength ('łejw,lenks) s.
długosć fali
wave meter('łejwmi:ter) s. falo-
mierz
waver ('łejwer) v. zachwiać(się);
zamigotać; być niezdecydowanym;
załamywać się; drzec; zawahać
się; kołysać się; trzepotac
się;schwianie (się)
wavy ('łejwy) adj. falisty; sfa-
lowany; drzący; migocący;
karbowany
wawl ('łó:l) v. wrzeszczeć jak
kot

wax (łaeks) s. wosk; adj. woskowy; v. woskować; stawać się
waxen ('łaeksn) adj. woskowy;
miękki jak wosk
wax paper ('łaeks'pejper) s.
papier woskowy
waxwork ('łaeksłe:rk) s. figura woskowa; v, modelować
z wosku
waxy ('łaeksy) adj. woskowy;
woskowaty; (slang): wściekły;
zły; okrutny
way (łej) s. droga; szlak;
trakt; przejście; wolna droga;
odległość; kierunek; strona;
sposób; zwyczaj; bieg; tok;
sens; stan; położenie
way back (łej baek) adv. dawno
temu; daleko w tyle; dawno
waybill ('łejbyl) s. list
przewozowy; fracht
wayfarer ('łej,feerer) s. podróżnik (pieszy)
waylay ('łejlej) v.zob. lay;
zaskoczyc kogos; czyhac na
kogos; czatować
way of life ('łej ow,lajf) s.
styl życia; sposób życia
way-out ('łej,aut) s. wyjście;
rozwiązanie; adj. (slang):
nadzwyczajny; nadzwyczaj;
dobrze zrobiony; nadzwyczaj
zdolny; (zob.: far-out)
wayside ('łej,sajd) s. skraj
drogi; adj. przydrożny
way station (,łej'stejszyn) s.
przystanek
-ways (łejz) (przyrostek)
w taki sposób (np:sideways)
wayward ('łejłerd) adj. przewrotny; uparty; kaprysny;
nieobliczalny; chimeryczny
we (łi:) pron. my
weak (łi:k) adj. słaby
weaken ('łi:kn) v. osłabiać;
słabnąć; rozcieńczac
weak-kneed ('łi:kni:d) adj.
słaby
weakling ('łi:klyng) s. sła-
beusz; cherlak; człowiek słaby; adj. słaby

weakly ('łi:kly) adj. słabowity; adv. słabo
weak-minded ('łi:k,majndyd)
adj. słaby na umyśle; słabe-
go charakteru
weakness (łi:knys) s. słabość;
słabostka
wealth (łelş) s. bogactwo; dobrobyt
wealthy ('łelşy) adj. bogaty
wean (łi:n) v. odłączać od
piersi; oduczać; odrywać
weanling ('łi:nlyng) s. dziecko świeżo odsunięte od piersi
weapon ('łepon) s. broń
wear; wore; worn (łeer; ło:r;
ło:rn)
wear (łeer) v. nosić; chodzić
w czyms; ścierać się; wycierać się; żłobić; zacierać się;
przechodzić; mijać; zdzierać;
nużyć; męczyć; wyczerpywać;
długo trwać; długo służyć;
s. noszenie; rzeczy noszone;
moda; zużycie; wytrzymałość
wear away ('łeer,e'łej) v.
zużywać; wlec się
wear off ('łeer,of) v. zetrzec (się); zacierać (się);
mijać
wear on ('łeer,on) v. wlec się
wear out ('łeer,aut) v. zdzierać (się); wyczerpywać (się)
wearing ('łieryng) adj.przezna-
czony do noszenia na sobie
wearisome ('łierysem) adj.
męczący; nużący; nudny
weary ('łiery) adj. zmęczony;
znużony; znudzony; męczący;
nużący; nudny; v. męczyć;
nudzić; naprzykrzać się;
uprzykrzać sobie
weasel ('łi:zl) s. łasica
weather ('łedzer) s. pogoda;
adj. atmosferyczny; odwietrz-
ny; pogodny; v. zwietrzać;
okrywać się patyna (śniedzią)
weather-beaten ('łedzer,bi:tn)
adj. zaharowany; skołatany
przez burze
weather-bound ('łedzer,baund)
adj. zatrzymany przez pogodę
(statek)

weather bureau ('łedzer,bjuerou)
s. instytut meteorologiczny
weather chart ('łedzer,cza:rt)
s. wykres meteorologiczny
weathercock ('łedzer,kok) s.
chorągiewka na dachu; kurek
na dachu; człowiek niestały
weather forecast ('łedz,fo:r-
ka:st) s. komunikat meteorologiczny
weather vane ('łedzer,wejn) s.
wiatrowskaz; chorągiewka na
dachu
weave; wove; woven (łi:w; łouw;
łouwn)
weave (łi:w) v. tkać (tkaninę);
knuć (spisek); układać (intry-
gę; opowiadanie) spleść; splatać; zajmować się tkactwem
weaver ('łi:wer) s. tkacz
weaving ('łi:wyng) s. tkactwo
web (łeb) s. tkanina; sztuka
(materiału); stek (kłamstw);
pajęczyna; błona (nietoperza);
tkanka łączna; usztywnienie
wed (łed) v. zaslubiać; łączyć
się; pobrać się; adj. zaslubiony
wedded ('łedyd) adj. zaslubiony; ślubny; oddany (sprawie)
wedding ('łedyng) s. ślub; wesele; adj. ślubny; weselny
wedding ring ('łedyng,ryng) s.
obrączka ślubna
we'd (łi:d) = we had; we would;
we should
wedge (łedż) s. klin; trójkatny
kawałek (tortu); golfowy kijek
z klinowym zakończeniem; v.kli-
nować; zaklinować; rozklinować;
łupać
wedge in ('łedż,yn) v. wpychać
(się); wcisnąć (się)
wedge off ('łedż,of) v. wypychać (się)
wedlock ('łedlok) s. małżeństwo
Wednesday ('łenzdy) s. środa
weed (łi:d) s. chwast; zielsko;
cygaro; (slang): chuchro; cherlak; mizerak; szkapa; v. pie-
lić; odchwaszczać
weeder ('łi:der) s. pielnik;
wypielacz

weed grown ('łi:dgroun)adj. zachwaszczony

weed out ('łi:d,aut) v. wypielac; usuwac

weeds ('łi:ds) pl. krepa załobna; strój żałobny

weedy ('łi:dy) adj. zachwaszczony; chudy; wysoki

weed killer ('łi:d,kyler) s. trucizna na chwasty

week (łi:k) s. tydzien

weekday ('łi:kdej) s. dzien powszedni

weekend ('łi:kend) s. niedziela oraz części wolne soboty i poniedziałku; v. spędzac weekend

week in-week out ('łi:k,yn-'łi:k,aut) adv. exp.: co tydzien

weekly ('łi:kly) adj. tygodniowy; adv. tygodniowo; s. tygodnik

weep; wept; wept (łi:p; łept; łept)

weep (łi:p) v. płakac; opłakiwac; zapłakac; lamentowac; cieknąc; wyciekac; ociekac; s. płacz; cieknięcie

weeper ('łi:per) s. płaczek; płaczka; welon żałobny; krepa żałobna

weep away ('łi:pe,łej) v. wypłakac się

weeping willow ('łi:pyng,łylou) s. wierzba płacząca

weep for joy ('łi:p-fo:r-dżoj) v. płakac z radości

weep out ('łi:p,aut) v. powiedziec z płaczem

weigh (łej) v. ważyc (się); rozważac; mierzyc; równoważyc; podnosic (kotwicę); s. ważenie

weigh in ('łej,yn) v. ważyc (boksera; dżokeja przed zawodami)

weigh out ('łej,aut) v. wyważyc człowieka przed zawodami

weigh up ('łej,ap) v. rozważyc

weigh upon ('łej,apon) v. przygniatac; ciążyc na kims

weight (łejt) s. ciężar; waga; obciążenie; ciężarek; odważnik; przycisk; grubość (odzieży); znaczenie; doniosłość; odpowiedzialność; v. obciążać; pogrubiac sztucznie tkaninę

weight lifting ('łejt lyftyng) s. (sport) podnoszenie ciężarów

weightless ('łejtlys) adj. lekki; bez ciężaru

weighted-with(łejyd,łys) adj. obarczony (np. wiekiem)

weighty ('łejty) adj. ciężki; ważki; doniosły; ważny; poważny; przekonywujący; rozważony; przemyślany

weir (łier) s. jaz; grobla

weird (łierd) adj. niesamowity; tajemniczy; nadprzyrodzony; dziwny; dziwaczny; s. los

welcome ('łekem) exp.: witaj ! witajcie ! s. powitanie; adj. mile widziany; mający pozwolenie; mogący korzystac; v. powitac; witac (z radością)

weld (łeld) v. spawać (się); spajac; zespalac; zgrzewac; s. spoina; spawanie; spojenie; miejsce spojenia

welder (łelder) s. spawacz; spawarka; przyrząd do spawania

welfare ('łelfeer) s. dobro; dobrobyt; powodzenie; pomyślność; szczęście

welfare-state ('łelfeer'stejt) s, panstwo o bardzo wysokich świadczeniach społecznych

welfare-work ('łelfeer,łe:rk) s. praca społeczna; społecznictwo; praca dobroczynna

well; better; best (łel; beter; best) adv. dobrze; lepiej; najlepiej

well (łel) s. studnia; otwor wiertniczy; odwiert; źródło; klatka (schodowa); adv. dobrze; należycie; porządnie; mocno; solidnie; szczęśliwie; całkiem; wyraźnie; łatwo; lekko; słusznie; adj. dobry; zdrowy; zadawalający; pomyślny; w porządku; exp.: dobrze ! a więc ?

well-balanced ('łel'baelenst)
adj. zrównoważony
well-behaved ('łelby'hejwd)
adj. dobrze wychowany
well-being ('łel'bi:yŋg)s.
dobrobyt; powodzenie; po-
myślność
well-born ('łel'bo:rn) adj.
dobrze urodzony
well-bred ('łel'bred) adj.
rasowy; dobrze wychowany
well-connected ('łel'konektyd)
adj. dobrze skoligacony
well-disposed ('łeldys'pouzd)
adj. życzliwie usposobiony
well done ('łeldan) exp.:
brawo ! dobrze zrobione !
well-fed ('łelfed) adj. dobrze
odżywiony
well-founded ('łelfaundyd)
adj. uzasadniony
wellhead ('łel'hed) s. źródło
well-heeled ('łel'hi:ld) adj.
slang): forsisty (ma forsę)
Wellingtons ('łelyŋtenz) s.
buty z wysokimi holewami
(też z gumy)
well-informed ('łel-ynfo:rmd)
adj. dobrze poinformowany;
wykształcony
well-intended ('łel-'yntendyd)
adj. dobrze pomyślany
well-judged ('łel-'dżadżd) adj.
rozsądny; roztropny; dobrze
pomyślany
well-knit ('łel'nyt) adj.
zwarty; dobrze zbudowany;
jędrny
well-known ('łel'nołn) adj.
dobrze znany
well-meant ('łel'ment) adj.
zrobiony w najlepszej intencji
well-nigh ('łel'naj) adv. nieledwie; o mało co; o mało nie
well-off ('łel'o:f) adj. dobrze sytuowany; zamożny
well point('łel'poynt) s. rura
do usuwania wody podskórnej
(przed kopaniem)
well-read ('łel'red) adj.
oczytany
well-sinker ('łel'syŋker)s.
studniarz

well-spoken ('łel'spouken) adj.
uprzejmy; pięknie mówiący;
dobrze powiedziany
wellspring (łel'spryŋg)s.
źródło
well-timed ('łel'tajmd) adj.
na czasie; odpowiedni
well-to-do ('łel-te'du:) adj.
zamożny; dobrze sytuowany
well-wisher ('łel'łyszer) s.
sympatyk
well-worn ('łel'ło:rn) adj.
wytrwały; wyswiechtany; oklepany; dobrze noszony
welsh (łelsz) adj. walijski;
s. wykręcanie się od płacenia;
v. uciekać nie zapłaciwszy
welter ('łelter) v. falować;
tarzać się; s. falowanie;
powódź; zamęt; kolos; silne
uderzenie
wench (łencz) s. dziewucha;
ulicznica; v. latać za dziew-
kami
Wendish (łendysz) adj. łużycki
went (łent) v. zob. go
wept (łept) v. zob. weep
were (łe:r) v. zob. be
we're (łier) = we are
werewolf('łe:rłuf) s. wilkołak
west (łest) s. zachód; adj.
zachodni; adv. na zachód; ku
zachodowi
westerly ('łesterly) adj. zachodni; adv. na zachód
western ('łestern) adj. zachodni; pochodzący z zachodu
westward ('łestłerd) adj. zachodni; ku zachodowi; na zachód
wet (łet) adj. mokry; wilgotny;
zmoczony; przemoczony; słotny;
deszczowy; dżdżysty; (slang):
w błędzie; s. wilgoć; wilgot-
ność; trunek; v. moczyć (się);
zwilżać; zraszać
wet nurse ('łet,ne:rse) s.
mamka; v. karmić
wether ('łedzer) s.skop (ka-
strowany baran)
wet through ('łet'tru:) v.
przemoczyć (na wylot)
we've (łi:w) = we have

whack (hłaek) v. walić; grzmocić; (slang): dzielić się
czyms; s. walnięcie; trzas-
nięcie; (slang): część; próba;
stan (rzeczy)
whacker ('hłaeker) s. kolor
whacking ('hłaekyng) adj. kolosalny
whale (hłejl) s. wieloryb;
rzecz wspaniała; v. polować
na wieloryby; (slang): bic
whale-boat ('hłejl,bout) s.
łódz do połowu wielorybów;
łódz straznicza; ratunkowa
whalebone ('hłejlboun) s, fisz-
bin
whale-fin ('hłejlfyn) s. fisz-
bin
whale-oil ('hłejl,ojl) s. tran
wielorybi
whaler ('hłejler) s. statek do
połowu wielorybów
whammy ('hłaemy) s. (slang):
urok (rzucony na kogoś)
whang (hłaeng) s. grzmotnięcie;
huczenie; v. walić; grzmocić;
huczec
wharf (hło:rf) s. przystań (wy-
ładunkowa); nabrzeże; v. cumowac do wyładunku; wyładowywać
w przystani
wharves (hło:rfs) pl. nabrzeża
wyładunkowe
what (hłot) adj. jaki; jaki
tylko; ten; który; ten...co;
taki... jaki; tyle.., ile;
pron. co; to co; cos;
excl.: co ? czego ? jak to !
what about ('hłote,baut) exp.:
a co z... ?; co powiesz o...?
whatever (hłot'ewer) adj.
jakikolwiek; pron. cokolwiek;
wszystko co; co tylko; bez
względu; obojętnie co
what for('hłotfo:r) s. (slang):
bura; lanie; exp.:za co ?
what next ('hłot,nekst) exp.:
co dalej ?
whatnot ('hłotnot) s. etażerka;
cacka; (slang): cokolwiek;
obojętnie co; wszystko

whatsit ('hłotsyt) s. jak się
to nazywa; ten (przedmiot)
whatsoever ('hłotsou'ewer) adj.
jakikolwiek by; cokolwiek by;
co tylko by; pron. wszystko
co tylko
wheat (hłi:t) s. pszenica
wheaten ('hłi:tn) adj. prze-
niczny
wheel ('hłi:l) s. koło; kółko;
ster; kierownica; v. obracac
(się); wrócic (się); prowadzić
taczki (rower); wozic taczkami
etc.
wheelbarrow ('hłi:l,baerou) s.
taczki
wheel chair('hłi:l,czeer) s. fotel na kołkach
wheeler-dealer ('hłi:ler,di:ler)
s. cwaniak; politykier
wheelwright ('hłi:lrajt) s.
kołodziej
wheeze ('hłi:z) v. sapac; s. sa-
panie; (slang); dowcip; komunał
wheezy ('hłi:zy) adj. sapiący;
zasapany
when (hłen) adv. kiedy; kiedyz;
wtedy; kiedy to; gdy; przy;
podczas gdy;
s. czas (zdarzenia)
whenas (,hłen'aez) conj. kiedy;
podczas gdy
whence (hłens) adv. & conj. skąd
whenever ('hłenewer) adv. kiedy
tylko; skoro tylko
whensoever ('hłensou'ever) adv.
skoro tylko; skądkolwiek
where (hłeer) adv. & conj. gdzie;
dokąd
whereabout ('hłeere'baut) adv.
gdzie ?
whereabouts ('hłeere'bauts) adv.
zwazywszy; gdzie; mniej więcej;
s. miejsce zamieszkania; (pobytu)
whereas('hłeer'aez) conj. podczas
gdy
whereat ('hłeer,et) conj. podczas
gdy
whereby ('hłeer,baj) adv. po
czym ? po kim ? po ktorym; za
pomocą którego? jak?którym

wherefore('hłeerfo:r) adj.
dlaczego; dlatego; z tego
powodu
wherefrom (hłeer'fro:m) adv.
skąd; z czego
wherein (hłeer'yn) adv. w czym;
w którym
whereof (hłeer'ow) adv. z czego; z którego
whereon (hłeer'on) adv. na
czym; na którym
wheresoever (,hłeersou'ever)
adv. wszędzie by; dokądkolwiek
by; gdzie tylko by
whereupon (,hłeere'pon) adv.
na czym; po czym
wherever (,hłeer'ever) adv.
dokądkolwiek; wszędzie; gdzie
tylko
wherewith (,hłeer'łyz) adv.
(z) czym ?
wherewithal (,hłeerły'so:l) s.
potrzebne środki (fundusze,
przybory)
whet (,hłet) v. naostrzyć;
zaostrzyć (też apetyt);
s. ostrzenie; zakąska
whether ('hłedzer) conj. czy-
czy; czy tak, czy owak
whetstone ('hłet,stoun)s. osełka; kamień szlifierski
whey (hłej) s. serwatka
which (hłycz) pron. który; co;
którędy; dokąd; w jaki (sposób)
whichever (hłycz,ewer) adj.
którykolwiek; jaki; każdy...
jaki; który tylko; pron.
którykowiek; każdy
whichsoever (,hłyczsou'ewer)
adj. pron. = whichever (z naciskiem)
whiff (hłyf) s. powiew; podmuch; tchnienie; zapach; dym;
lekki wybuch gniewu; v. dmuchać; dymić; palić; lekko
wiać
while (hłajl) s. chwila; pewien czas; po chwili; niebawem; wkrótce; conj. podczas
gdy; jak długo; dopóki; póki;
natychmiast; chociaż co prawda

while ago ('hłajl'egou) adv.
(nie)dawno
while away ('hłajle'łej) v.
spędzać czas; skracać sobie
czas
whim ('hłym) s. kaprys; zachcianka; fantazja; fanaberia;
kołowrót górniczy
whimper ('hłymper) v. piszczeć;
kwilić; skomleć; skowyczeć;
s. kwilenie; skowyt; skamlanie
whimsical ('hłymzykel) adj.
kaprysny; dziwaczny; cudaczny
whimsy ('hłymzy) s. kaprys
whim-wham('hłymhłaem) s. cacko
whine ('hłajn) v. skomleć; jęczeć; powiedzieć jękliwie;
s. skomlenie; jęk
whip (hłyp) s. bat; bicz; pomocnik; woźnica; naganiacz;
uderzenie biczem; bita śmietana; v. chłostać; zacinać (batem); ubijać (śmietanę); smagać; przyrządzać na prędce;
zwyciężyć; zakasować (kogoś);
owijać; windować; śmigać;
zbierać; wyjechać (pospiesznie)
whip in ('hłyp,yn) v. zapędzać
batem
whip off ('hłyp'o:f) v. zerwać
coś; czmychnąć z czyms
whip on ('hłyp'on) v. popędzać
batem
whip out ('hłyp,aut) v. wyciągnąć błyskawicznie
whip round ('hłyp,raund) v. odwrócić się znienacka
whip together ('hłyp te'gedzer)
v. zganiać batem; zwalać na
kupę; montować na gwałt
whipped cream ('hłypt'kri:m) s.
bita śmietana
whipper-snapper ('hłyper'snae-
per) s. chłystek; smarkacz
whipping boy ('hłypyng,boj) s.
kozioł ofiarny (chłopak chło-
stany za innego)
whipping top ('hłypyng,top) s.
bąk do podbijania
whippy (,hłypy) adj. giętki;
elastyczny

whipsaw (‚hłyp'so) s. wąska
piłeczka; v. ciąc piłką;
wygrac podwojnie; pobic podwojnie
whipstock (‚hłyp'stok) s. biczysko
whirl (hłe:rl) v. kręcic (się);
wirowac; zawirowac; porywac
w wir; s. wirowanie; ruch
wirowy; wir; (slang): proba
(czegoś)
whirlpool ('hłe:rl'pu:l) s.
wir
whirlwind ('hłe:rl'łynd) s.
trąba powietrzna; wir po-
wietrzny
whirlybird (hłe:rly'be:rd) s.
helikoper (USA)
whirr (hłe:r) v. furgotac;
warkotac; s. furgot; warkot
(maszyny)
whisk (hłysk) s. wiechec;
śmignięcie; trzepaczka (do
jajek etc.); miotełka;
v. otrzepac; odpędzac; porywac; szybko odwozic; przywozic; czmychac; wymachiwac;
smigac
whisk away ('hłyske'łej) s.
strzepnąc; przewiezc lotem
strzały; czmychnac
whiskers ('hłyskers) pl. baki;
bokobrody; wąsy
whisky ('hłysky) s. (wodka)
whiskey
whisper ('hłysper) v. szeptac;
mowic cicho; szmerac; szelescic; s. szeptanie; szmer
whistle ('hłysl) v. gwizdac;
swistac; zagwizdac; s. gwizdanie; gwizd; swist; gwizdek;
gardło
whistle away ('hłysle'łej) v.
pogwizdywac sobie
white (hłajt) adj. biały; bezbarwny; blady; czysty; niepokalany; uczciwy; rzetelny;
niewinny; s. biel; biały (człowiek); biało; białe wino
white coffee (hłajt'kofi) v.
kawa z mlekiem
white-collar('lajt,koler) adj.
zajęci biurowo(urzędnicy etc.)

white elephant (hłajt'elyfent)
s. towary wybrakowane; buble
white collar worker ('hłajt,ko-
ler łerker) s. pracownik
umysłowy
white frost ('hłajt'fro:st) s.
szron
white-headed ('hłajt'hedyd) adj.
siwowłosy
white heat (hłajt'hi:t) biały
żar
white lie (hłajt'laj) s. kłamstwo; wykręt towarzyski
white paper ('hłajt,pejper) s.
oficjalna publikacja wykazują-
ca, że rząd ma zawsze rację
(USA)
whiten ('hłajtn) v. wybielac;
pobielac; bielic; zbielec
whiteness ('hłajtness) s. biel
whitewash (‚hłajt'łosz) s.
wapno; wybielanie czegos lub
kogos; v. wybielac; wymywac
na czysto; uniewinnic; uspra-
wiedliwic; pobic na sucho
(na zero)
Whitsuntide ('hłajtsntajd) s.
Zielone Swięta
whittle down ('hłytl,dałn) v.
strugac; zestrugac; wystrugac;
obstrugac
whity ('hłajty) adj. białawy
whizz (hłyz) s. swist; (slang):
mistrz; rzecz wspaniała;
v. swistac; suszyc
who (hu:) pron. kto; ktory
whodunit (hu:danyt) s. (slang);
"kryminał"; powieść detekty-
wistyczna
whoever (hu:'ewer) pron. ktokolwiek
whole (houl) adj. cały; pełno-
wartosciowy; zdrowy; s. całosc
wholehearted ('houl'ha:rtyd)
adj. serdeczny; szczery
whole hogger ('houl'hoger) s.
człowiek idący na całego
whole length ('houl'lenks) s.
(portret) w całosci
wholesale ('houl,sejl) s. hurt;
handel hurtowy; adj. hurtowy;
masowy; adv.hurtem; masowo

wholesaler ('houl,sejler) s. hurtownik

wholesale trade ('houlsejl- ,trejd) s. handel hurtowy

wholesome ('houlsem) s. zdrowy; zdrowotny

whole-time ('houltajm) adj. pełno-etatowy (czasowy)

whole-wheat ('houl'hłi:t) adj. pełno-ziarnisty (chleb)

who'll (hu:l) = who shall; who will

wholly ('houly) adv. całkowicie

whoom (hu:m) pron. kogo ? zob. who

whoop (hu:p) s. okrzyk (wesoły np.)

whooping ('hu:pyŋg) adj.(slang): ogromny

whooping cough ('hu:pyŋ,kof) s. koklusz

whore (ho:r) s. wulg.: kurwa; dziwka; v. kurwic się; gonic za dziwkami

whorelet ('ho:rlyt) s. wulg.: kurewka

whose (hu:z) pron. & adj. czyj; czyja; czyje; ktorego

why (hłaj) adv. dlaczego; czemu; czemuż; dlatego; własnie; s. przyczyna; powod; exp.: jak to ! własnie ! patrzcie; no wiesz !;no to co !

why so ('hłaj'sou) adv. dlaczego

wick (łyk) s. knot; tampon

wicked ('łykyd) adj. niegodziwy; niedobry; frywolny; paskudny; złosliwy; zły; nikczemny

wickedness ('łykydnys) s. nikczemnosc; niegodziwosc

wicker basket ('łyker,ba:skyt) s, pleciony kosz

wicker chair (łyker,czeer) s. plecione krzesło

wicket (łykyt) s. furka; kołowrot; okienko kasowe; bramka; cel; drzwi na poł wysokosci (otworu)

wide (łajd) adj. szeroki; rozległy; szeroko otwarty; ob-szerny; wielki; pokazny; znaczny; duzy; daleki; szeroko otwarty; adv. szeroko; z dala (od czegos)

wide-awake ('łajde,e'łejk) adj. czujny; rozbudzony; bystry; z szeroko otwartymi oczami

widen ('łajdn) v. poszerzyc; rozszerzac

wideness ('łajdnys) s. szerokosc; rozległosc; bezmiar

wide-open (,łajd'oupen) adj. szeroko otwarty

widespread (,łajd'spred) adj. rozprzestrzeniony; szeroko rozpostarty

widow ('łydou) s. wdowa; v. wdowiec

widower ('łydouer) s. wdowiec

width (łyds) s. szerokosc

wife (łajf) s. zona; pl. wives (łajwz)

wig (łyg) s. peruka; v. zaopatrywac w peruke

wild (łajld) adj. dziki; dziko rosnący; gwałtowny; wściekły; szalony; burzliwy; rozwichrzony; pustynny;zdziczały; rozwydrzony; fantastyczny; nierealny; podniecony; s. pustynia; dziki teren; adv. na chybił trafił

wildcat ('łajld,kaet) adj. porywczy; awanturniczy; nadzwyczajny (np. pociąg); s. zbik; szyb naftowy na nowym terenie; awanturnicze przedsiębiorstwo; spekulacja; samotna lokomotywa; porywcza osoba; v. szukac nafty na niesprawdzonych terenach

wilderness (łajldernys) s. pustynia; puszcza; odludzie

wildfire (,łajld'fajer) s. błyskawicznie rozprzestrzeniający się ogień; ogień grecki; błędny ognik

willful('łylful) adj. rozmyslny; umyslny; zamierzony; swiadomy; samowolny; uparty

will (łyl) s. wola; testament; siła woli; v. postanowic; zarządzac; zapisywac (w testamencie) zmuszac; chciec

willing (,Ćylyŋg) adj. skłonny
(cos zrobic); chętny; pełen
dobrej woli
willow ('Ćylou) s. wierzba
willowy ('Ćyloćy) adj. smukły;
gibki; giętki; obfitujący
w wierzby
will power ('Ćyl,paćer) s.
siła woli
willy-nilly ('Ćyly'nyly) adv.
chcąc nie chcąc
will you ? ('Ćyl,ju:) exp.: czy
zrobisz; czy zechcesz ?;czy
obiecasz ?
wilt (Ćylt) v. więdnąc; opadać;
oklapnąć; powodować zwięd-
nięcie; opadac z sił; s. więd-
nięcie; osłabienie; depresja
wily (Ćajly) adj. chytry
win; won; won (Ćyn; Ćon; Ćon)
win (Ćyn) v. wygrywać; zwyciężać; zdobywać; zarabiac;
osiągać; pozyskać; przedostac
się; przezwyciężać; s. wygrana; zwycięstwo
win over (Ćynouwer) v. pozyskać sobie; przekonac
wince (Ćyns) v. skrzywic się
(z bólu) drgac; s. drgnięcie;
skrzywienie
winch (Ćyncz) s. korba; wyciąg; kołowrot; v. podnosic;
wyciągac kołowrotem lub korbą
wind; wound; wound (Ćajnd;
Ćaund; Ćaund)
wind (Ćajnd) v. nawijac; zwijać; zwinąc; owinąc (się);
wić (się); zakończyc
(Ćynd) s. wiatr; podmuch; oddech; dech; zapach; puste
słowa; gadanie; v. trąbic;
dąc w róg; przewietrzyc;
zwietrzyc; poczuc; zmęczyc;
dac wytchnąc
windbag ('Ćyndbaeg) s. czczy
gaduła
windfall ('Ćynd fo:l) s.
gratka; owoc zrzucony wiatrem
winding (Ćajndyŋg) adj. kręcony; kręcący się
winding-stairs (Ćajdyŋgsteers)
s. kręcące się schody

wind-instrument (Ćynd,ynstru-
ment) s. intrument dęty
windlass (Ćyndles) s. wyciąg;
kołowrot
windmill ('Ćynmyl) s. wiatrak
wind off(Ćajnd,o:f) v. odwinąc
(się)
wind up (Ćajnd,ap) v. nakręcac
(zegar); konczyc (mowę; zamykac zebranie)
window ('Ćyndou) s. okno; okienko
window dressing ('Ćyndou,dres-
syŋg) s. dekoracja wystawy
sklepowej
window pane ('Ćyndou,pejn) s.
szyba okienna
window shade ('Ćyndou,szejd)
s. żaluzja
window shopping ('Ćyndou-
szopyŋg) v. oglądac wystawy
(a nie kupowac)
window-sill ('Ćyndou,syl) s.
parapet
windpipe ('Ćynd,pajp) s. tchawica
windshield ('Ćyndszyld) s.
szyba ochronna (przednia) w
samochodzie
windshield wiper ('Ćyndszyld-
'Ćajper) s. wycieraczka
szyby ochronnej
windy ('Ćyndy) adj. wystawiony
na wiatr; wietrzny; gadatliwy
wine ('Ćajn) s. wino
wineglass ('Ćajngla:s) s. kieliszek do wina
wine-press ('Ćajnpres) s. wy-
tłaczarka do winogron
wing (Ćyŋg) s. skrzydło; ramię
kulisa; dywizjon; lot;
v. uskrzydlac; przewozić na
skrzydłach; przeleciec (przez
cos); leciec; szybowac
wing commander ('Ćyŋg-ke,ma:n-
der) s. dowódca dywizjonu
lotnictwa (podpułkownik)
wink ('Ćynk) s. mrugać (na kogos); przymykać oczy; s.mrug-
nięcie
winner ('Ćyner) s. zdobywca nagrody; człowiek wygrywający;
laureat

winning ('łynyŋg) s. otwór do
wydobywania węgla; adj. ujmujący; zwycięski
winning post ('łynyŋg,poust)
s. meta
winnings ('łynyŋgs) pl. wygrana
winsome ('łynsem) adj. ujmujący; pociągający
winter ('łynter) s. zima; adj.
zimowy; v. zimować
winter crop('łynter,krop) s.
ozimina
winterize ('łynterajz) v. dostosowywać, przygotowywać do
zimy
wintry ('łyntry) adj. zimowy;
chłodny; obojętny
winy ('łajny) adj. podchmielony; winny
wipe ('łajp) v. wycierać; ocierać; ścierać; wymazać; za-
machnąć się; s. starcie; wy-
tarcie; bicie
wipe away ('łejpę,łej) v. wycierać; wymazać
wipe off ('łajp,o:f) v. ze-
trzeć (plamę etc.)
wipe out ('łajp,aut) v. wytrzeć; wymazać; wyniszczyć;
zgładzać
wipe up ('łajp,ap) v. wytrzeć
(podłogę etc,)
wire (łajer) s. drut; przewód;
telegram; kabel; struna metalowa; sidła; v. drutować;
zadrutować; złapać (w sidła);
założyć przewody (w domu);
zatelegrafować; ciągnąć za
sznurki zakulisowe
wire cutter ('łajer,kater) s.
szczypce do cięcia drutu
wire haired ('łajer,heerd)
adj. ostrowłosy (pies)
wireless ('łajerlys) adj. radiowy; bez drutu
wireless set ('łajerlys,set)
s. radio
wire netting ('łajer,netyŋg)
s. siatka druciana
wire-pulling ('łajer,pulyŋg)
s. używanie protekcji; wpły-
wów

wire rope ('łajer,roup) s. lina
stalowa
wiry ('łajery) adj. twardy; żylasty; muskularny; druciany
wisdom ('łyzdem) s. mądrość
wisdom tooth ('łyzdem.tu:s) s.
ząb mądrości
wise (łajz) s. sposób; adj. mądry; roztropny
wiseacre ('łajz,ejker) s. mądra-
la; mędrek
wise after('łajz,a:fter) adj.
mądry po...
wisecrack ('łajzkra:k) s. dowcip-
na uwaga; v. robić dowcipy
wise guy ('łajzgaj) s. nadęta
wielkość
wise saw ('łajzso:) s. przysłowie
wish (łysz) v. życzyć (sobie);
pragnąć; chcieć; s. pragnienie;
życzenie; chęć; powinszowanie;
ochota; rzecz upragniona
wishbone ('łyszbojn) s. kość
widełkowa (ptaków)
wish for ('łysz fo:r) v. życzyć
sobie (np. pogody)
wishful ('łyszful) adj. pragnący
wishful thinking ('łyszful-
tynkyŋg) s. pobożne życzenie
wish well ('łysz,łel) v. dobrze
życzyć
wishy-washy ('łyszy,łoszy) adj.
bez treści; wodnisty; lurowaty
wisp (łysp) s. wiązka; garść;
pęczek; kosmyk; wstęga (dymu)
wistful ('łystful) adj. smutny;
zadumany; pełen tęsknoty
wit (łyt) s. umysł; rozum; dowcip; człowiek dowcipny; inteligencja; olej w głowie
witch (łycz) s. czarownica;
czarodziejka; v. zaczarować;
oczarować
witchcraft ('łycz.kra:ft) s.
czary; czarnoksięstwo
witch doctor ('łycz,dakter) s.
czarownik; znachor
witchery ('łyczery) = witchcraft
witch hunt('łyczhant) s. tro-
pienie czarownic; polityczne
głośne śledztwo (propagandowe)
w celu udowadniania działalności wywrotowej

with (łys) prep. z (kims; czyms)
u (kogoś); przy (kims); za pomocą); (stosownie) do; (cierpliwość) dla

withdraw (łys'dro:) v. zob.
draw; cofac (sie); wycofywac
(sie); odwołac (cos); ode-
brac (ze szkoły); odsuwac
(zasłonę)

withdrawál (łys'dro:el) s.
wycofanie

wither ('łydzer) v. powodowac
wiednięcie, usychanie; zabijac (spojrzeniem); usychac;
usuwac sie (w cien itp)

withers ('łydzers) pl. kłęby
(u konia między łopatkami)

withhold (łys'hould) v.zob.
hold; wstrzymywac; odmawiac;
wycofac

within (łys'yn) adv. wewnątrz;
w domu; u siebie; w (czyms):
w duchu; do wnętrza; w obrę-
bie; w odległości (np. mili);
w ciągu (np..dnia); w zasięgu (wzroku); s. wnętrze

without (łysaut) prep. bez;
poza; na zewnątrz; adv. na
zewnatrz; pozá domem; s. strona zewnętrzna

withstand (łys'staend) v. zob.
stand; opierac sie; przeciwstawiac sie; byc wytrzymałym;
wytrzymywac

witling ('łytlyng) s. dowcip-
niś

witness ('łytnys) s. świadek;
widz; świadectwo; v. byc
świadkiem; świadczyc (też
podpisem)

witness box ('łytnys,boks) s.
miejsce dla świadka w sądzie
(USA)

witness stand ('łytnys,staend)
s. miejsce dla zeznawania
w sądzie (USA)

witticism ('łytysyzem) s. złośliwy dowcip; dowcipkowanie

witty (łyty) adj. dowcipny

witty at someone's expense
('łyty et'somłans,yks,pens)
exp.: dowcipny cudzym kosztem

wives (łajwz) pl. żony; zob.
wife

wiz (łyz) s. (slang): znawca;
mistrz; rzecz wspaniała

wizard ('łyzerd) s. czarownik;
czarodziej; adj. czarodziejski;
(slang): wspaniały

wo (ło:u) exp.:prrr (na konia,
żeby stanął)

wobble ('łobl) v. chwiac sie;
ruszac sie chwiejnie; chodzic
chwiejnie; jechac kołysząc sie;
mowic drżąco; grac drżąco (me-
lodię); drgac; wahac sie; byc
niezdecydowanym

wobbler ('łobler) s. człowiek
chwiejny

wobbly (łobly) s. chwiejący
sie; chwiejny

woe (łou) s. nieszczęscie

woebegone ('łoubi,go:n) adj.
nieszczesny

woeful ('łouful) adj. bolesny;
żałosny

woke (łouk) v. zob . wake

woken (łoukn) v. zob. wake

wolf (łulf) s. pl. wolves
(łulvz); wilk; (slang): kobieciarz; v. żrec; pożerac; połykac jak wilk; polowac na
wilki

wolf down ('łulf,dałn) v. pożerac jak wilk

wolfcall ('łulf,ko:l) s. (slang):
gwizdanie na kobietę (z po-
dziwem, zaczepką etc.)

wolf-cub ('łulf,kab) s. wilczek;
wilczę; młodszy harcerz

wolf-dog ('łulfdog) s. wilczur

wolfhound ('łulfhaund) s.
wilczur rosyjski lub alzacki

wolfish ('łulfysz) adj.wilczy

wolf skin('łulf'skyn) s. wilcza
skóra (na podłoge etc.);
wilczura (okrycie)

wolf whistle('łulfhłysl) =
wolfcall

wolverene (,łulve'ri:n) s.
rosomak; mieszkaniec stanu
Michigan

woman ('łumen) s. pl. women
('łymyn); kobieta; baba; żona; v. mówić per "kobieta";
umieszczać między kobietami
woman doctor ('łumen'dakter)
s. lekarka
womanhood ('łumenhud) s. kobiety; kobiecość (dojrzała)
womanish ('łumenysz) adj. bab-
ski; zniewieściały
womanize ('łumenajz) v. ba-
bieć; niewieścieć; gonić za
kobietami
womankind ('łumen,kajnd) s.
kobiety; ród niewieści
womanlike ('łumen,lajk) adj.
kobiecy
womanly ('łumenly) adj. kobiecy
womb (łu:m) s. macica; łono;
żywot
women ('łymyn) pl. zob, woman
womenfolk ('łymynfouk) =
womankind
won (łan) v. zob. win
wonder ('łander) s. zdumienie;
cud; v. dziwić się; być cie-
kaw; zastanawiać się
wonderful ('łanderful) adj.
cudowny
wonderland ('łanderlaend) s.
kraina cudów (czarów)
wonderment ('łanderment) s.
zdziwienie; zdumienie
wondering ('łanderyng) adj.
zdumiony; niedowierzający
wonderwork ('łanderłe:rk)
s. cud
wonder-worker ('łanderłe:rker)
s. cudotwórca
wonder-working ('łanderłe:rkyng)
adj. sprawiający cuda
wondrous ('łandres) adj. cudowny; adv. cudownie
wont; wont; wonted (łont;
łont; łantyd)
wont (łant) v. przyzwyczajać;
mieć zwyczaj; s. zwyczaj;
przyzwyczajenie
won't (łount) = will not
wonted ('łantyd) adj. zwykły

woo (łu:) v. zalecać się (do
kobiety): umizgać się; ubiegać
się; namawiać do czegoś
wood (łud) s. drzewo; drewno;
lasek; pl; lasy; puszcza;
v. obsadzać drzewami; dostarczać drzewo
woodbine ('łudbajn) s. powój
wonny; wiciokrzew pomorski
woodblock ('łudblok) s. drzeworyt (do odciskania)
wood carving ('łudka:rwyng) s.
drzeworytnictwo
woodchuck ('łudczak) s. świstak
wood coal ('łudkoul) s. węgiel
drzewny
woodcock ('łudkok) s. słomka
woodcraft ('łudkra:ft) s. znajomość lasu
woodcraftsman ('łudkra:ftsmen)
s. myśliwy; traper
woodcut ('łudkat) s. drzeworyt
woodcutter ('łudkater) s.
drwal; drzeworytnik
wooded ('łudyd) adj. lesisty;
zalesiony
wooden ('łudn) adj. drewniany;
tępy
wood engraver (,łudyn'grejwer)
s. drzeworytnik
wood engraving(,łudyn'grejwyng)
s. drzeworytnictwo
wooden head ('łudn,hed) s. głupiec
woodland ('łudlaend) s. las;
lesisty okręg; adj. lesisty
leśny
woodman ('łudmen) s. drwal;
leśnik
wood notes('łudnouts) s. dźwię-
ki lasu
woodpecker ('łud,peker) s. dzię-
cioł
wood pulp ('łud,palp) s. miazga
drzewna
woodruff ('łudraf) s. marzan-
na (wonna)
woodshed ('łud,szed) s. drwal-
nia; drewutnia
woodsman ('łudsmen) s. mieszkaniec lasu; drwal

wood sorrel('łudserel) s. szczawik zajęczy

woodsy (łudzy) adj. leśny

wood wind ('łud,łynd) s.(dęty) instrument drewmiany

woodwork (łudłe:rk) s. wyroby drzewne; częsci drewniane (np. ramy okien etc.); drewniana częsc budowy; budowa drewniana; stolarka; ciesiołka

woody ('łudy) adj. lesisty; drewniany

wooer ('łu:er) s. zalotnik

woof (łu:f) s. wątek

wool (łul) s. wełna (czesana, strzyżona, zgrzebna); czupryna; włosy (wełniste); owcze runo; wełniane rzeczy

wool-bal ('łulbo:l) s. kłębek wełny

woolen ('łuln) adj. wełniany; s. wyrób wełniany

wool fat ('łulfaet) s. lanolina

woolfell, ('łulfel) s. baranica; skóra owcza

woolgathering ('łul,gaedzeryng) adj. głupio rozmarzony (roztargniony); s. głupie marzycielstwo

woollen ('łulyn) adj. wełniany; pl, tkanina wełniana

woolly ('łuly) adj. wełnisty; oschły (głos); mętny umysł; nie soczysty; mączasty; włókniasty (owoc); zamazany; (slang): surowy i niekulturalny; s. wełniana odziez; (slang): owca

wooly ('łuly) = woolly

woozy ('łu:zy) adj. (slang): wstawiony; otumaniony; niezdrów

word ('łe:rd) s. słowo; wyraz; słówko; komplement; przechwałka; obelga; mowa; wiesc; rozkaz; adv. ustnie; słownie; adj. słowami wyrażony; v. wyrazic; redagowac; sformułowac; ubierac w szatę słowną; przybierac w słowa

wordage ('łe:rdydż) s. ilosc słów

word-blind('łe:rd,blajnd) adj. niezdolny do rozumienia pisma

wordbook ('łe:rd,buk) s. słownik

wording ('łe:rdyng) s. ujęcie, wyrażenie słowami

wordplay, ('łe:rd,plej) s. gra słów

word-splitter('łe:rd,splyter) s. pedant słowny

word-splitting ('łe:rd,splytyng) s. sofistyka; dzielenie włosa na czworo

wordy ('łe:rdy) adj. rozwlekły; gadatliwy; słowny (wojna słów)

wore (łó:r) v. zob. wear

work ; worked; worked (łe:rk; łe:rkt; łe:rkt)

work (łe:rk) s. praca; robota; zajęcie; energia; zadanie; dzieło; utwór; uczynek; pl. fabryka; huta; fortyfikacje; ozdoby; v. pracowac; działac; funkcjonowac; skutkowac; oddziaływac; wywoływac; sprawiac; wykonywac; kazac robic; prowadzic; obsługiwac; poruszac (motor); posuwac (się); przesuwac (się); wprawiac w (pasję); nadawac kształt; przeprowadzac przez cos; obrabiac; urabiac (się); wyszywac; robic robótkę; (slang): wykorzystywac (znajomosci); drgac; burzyc; falowac; fermentowac; trzeszczec (statek); zle działac (maszyna); wyczerpac się; odrabiac; wypracowac; wytwarzac; uzyskiwac z trudem; podniecac (się) stopniowo; zaznajamiac się z czyms; mieszac w całosc; dokazywac (cudów); wywierac (wpływ); urabiac; fasonowac; exploatowac (kopalnie itp.)

work away, ('łe:rke,łej) v. pracowac zawzięcie

work in ('łe:rkyn) v. pasowac; wprowadzac cos

work off ('łe:rko:f) v. pozbywac się czegos

work on ('łe:rkon) v. pracować dalej

work out ('łe:rkaut) v. przeprowadzac; realizowac; obliczac; rozwiązywac; wyczerpy-
wac; wyeksploatowac; skończyć; wynosic (w sumie)

work up ('łe:rkap) v. pod-
niecać(się); doprowadzać
(się); opracowywać; wyrabiac;
rozwijac; wspinac się; podnosić (się)

workable ('łe:rkebl) adj.
możliwy (do obróbki, uprawy
etc.); opłacalny; wykonalny;
realny; możliwy do przeprowa-
dzenia; w stanie używalności

workaday ('łe:rkedej) adj.
codzienny; roboczy; powszedni

work-basket ('łe:rk,ba:skyt)
s. koszyk z robótką

workbook ('łe:rk,buk) s. podręcznik ze wskazówkami;
dziennik pracy

workbox ('łe:rkboks) s. pudełko z przyborami do szycia

workday ('łe:rkdej) adj.
dzień roboczy; dzień powszedni

worker ('łe:rker) s. pracownik;
robotnik

workhouse ('łe:rk,haus) s.
dom poprawczy; przytułek

working ('łe:rkyng) adj. pracujący; pracowniczy; roboczy;
praktyczny; działający; czynny; ruchomy; powszedni;
s. praca; robota; działanie;
ruch; roboczodniówka; obróbka

working capital ('łe:rkyng -
kaepytl) s. kapitał obrotowy

working knowledge ('łe:rkyng-
'nolydż) s. wiedza praktycz-
na

working-class ('łe:rkyng'-
kla:s) s. klasa robotnicza

working day ('łe:rkyngdej)
s. dzień pracy

working hours ('łe:rkyng,au-
ers) s. godziny pracy

working load ('łe:rkyng,loud)
s. ciężar użyteczny; nosność

workingman ('łe:rkyng,men) s.
robotnik

working pressure ('łe:rkyng,pre-
szer) s. ciśnienie robocze

workless ('łe:rklys) adj. & s.
bezrobotny

worklike ('łe:rklajk) adj. dobrze wykonany; dobrze nasta-
wiony do pracy

workman ('łe:rkmen) s. pl.
workmen ('łe:rkmen); robotnik
(fizyczny); fachowiec

workmanship ('łe:rkmanszyp) s.
wykonanie; jakość wykonania;
faktura; twór

work of art ('łe:rk-ow,a:rt) s.
dzieło sztuki

workout ('łe:rkaut) s. trening;
zaprawa; danie komus szkoły

workroom ('łe:rk'rum) s. pracownia

works council ('łe:rks'kansl) s.
rada zakładowa

workshop ('łe:rkszop) s. pracownia; warsztat; zakład; posiedzenie

workshy ('łe:rkszaj) s. próżniak

worktable ('łe:rktejbl) s.
biurko

workup ('łe:rkap) s. podniecenie (się); powalanie podczas
druku

workwoman ('łe:rkłumen) s. pl.
workwomen ('łe:rkłymyn) ; robotnica; pracownica fizyczna

world (łe:rld) s. świat; ziemia; kula ziemska; sfery; masa; mnóstwo; zatrzęsienie czegoś; bezmiar; wielka ilość
adj. światowy

worldling ('łe:rldlyng) s.
człowiek oddany sprawom doczesnym

worldly ('łe:rldly) adj. światowy; ziemski; doczesny

worldminded ('łe:rld'majndyd)
adj. oddany sprawom doczesnym

world old ('łe:rld,old) adj.
stary jak świat

world power ('łe:rld'pałer)
s. potęga światowa; wielkie
mocarstwo
world-series ('łe:rld'sieri:z)
s. mistrzostwa palanta
(baseball) USA
world-war ('łe:rld'łor) s. wojna światowa
world-weary ('łe:rld'łeery)
adj. zmęczony życiem
world-wide ('łe:rld,łajd) adj.
światowy
world wise ('łe:rld,łajz) adj.
obyty; doświadczony
worm (łe:rm) s. robak; roba-
czek; glisda; dżdżownica;
gwint; zwojnik; śruba (nie
ostra); wężownica; v. wkra-
dac się; wykradac; czołgac
się; wyciągać(tajemnicę z
kogoś); czyscic (zwierzę)
z robaków; czyscic (grządkę)
z robaków
wormcast ('łe:rm,ka:st) s.
gleba wydalana przez dżdżow-
nicę
worm-eaten ('łe:rm,i:tn) adj.
robaczywy; stłoczony przez
robaki; (slang); przestarzały
worm-fishing ('łe:rm,fyszyn)
s. łowienie ryb na robaki
worm gear('łe:rm,gier) s.
przekładnia ślimakowa
wormhole ('łe:rm,houl) s.
dziura wygryziona przez roba-
ka
wormseed ('łe:rm.si:d) s.
rosliny stosowane przeciw
robakom
worm wheel ('łe:rm,hłi:1) s.
koło przekładni ślimakowej
wormwood ('łe:rm,łud) s. pio-
łun;(też) przykrosc
wormy ('łe:rmy) adj. robaczywy
worn (ł0:rn) v. zob. wear;
adj. używany; noszony; pomarszczony
worn-out ('ł0:rn,aut) adj. zużyty; zniszczony; wynoszony
worried ('łe:ryd) adj. zatros-
kany; zaniepokojony

worriment (łe:ryment) s. zmartwienie
worrisome (łe:rysem) adj. tra-
piący; lubiący się martwic
worry (łe:ry) v. dręczyc (się);
martwic (się); trapic (się);
zadręczac; zamartwiac; naprzykrzac (się); narzucac (się);
napastowac; kąsac; szarpac zębami; s. zmartwienie; troska;
kłopot; kąsanie (zdobyczy przez
psa)
worry along ('łe:rye,long) v.
uporac się z trudnosciami
worry dawn ('łe:ry,dałn) v. połykac łapczywie
worry out ('łe:ry,aut) v. rozwiązac z wysiłkiem (np. problem)
worse (łe:rs) adj. gorszy (niż:
bad; evil; ill); podniszczony;
słabszy; bardziej chory;
s. cos gorszego; to co najgor-
sze; najgorszy stan; najgorszy
wypadek; v. pogarszac się;
adv. gorzej; bardziej
worsen ('łe:rsn) v. pogorszyc
(się)
worship ('łe:rszyp) s. czesc;
kult; uwielbienie; nabożeństwo;
bałwochwalstwo; v. czcic;
wielbic; uwielbiac; brac udział
w nabożenstwie
woshipful ('łe:rszypful) adj.
pełen czci; czcigodny
worship(p)er ('łe:rszyper) s.
czciciel
worst (łe:rst) adj. najgorszy;
s. cos najgorszego; najgorszy
wypadek; adj. najgorzej; najbardziej; (slang) : bardzo
v. pokonac; wziąc nad kims górę; zadac klęskę; pobic
worsted ('łustyd) adj. czesan-
kowy; s. kamgarn; przędza wełniana czesana; czesanka
worth (łe:rs) s. wartosc; cena;
adj. wart; opłacający się
worthless ('łe:rslys) adj. bez-
wartosciowy
worth reading ('łe:rs'ri:dyng)
adj. wart czytania

worth seeing ('łe:rş'si:yng)
adj. wart widzenia
worthwhile ('łe:rşhłajl) adj.
wart zachodu; opłacający się
worthy ('łe:rşy) adj. godny;
wartościowy; poczciwy;
s. godny człowiek; wybitny
człowiek (też żartem)
would (łud) v. zob. will
(forma warunkowa)
would be ('łud,bi:) adj. rzekomy; niedoszły; adv. rzekomo;
niby to
wound (łu:nd) s. rana; v. ranić; zob.: v. wind
wounded ('łu:ndyd) adj. ranny;
urażony
wove (łouw) v. zob.: weave
woven ('łouwn) v. zob.: weave
wow (łau) (slang): s. szlagier;
świetna rzecz; v. mieć powodzenie; wywoływać zachwyt
excl.: au !;cudownie !
wrack (raek) s. = wreck (age);
chwasty morskie wyrzucone na
brzeg; używane na nawóz
wraith (rejs) s. sobowtór;
cień (duch)
wrangle ('raengl) s. kłótnia;
burda; v. kłócić się; (slang):
pilnować koni
wrangler ('raengler) s. kłótnik;
pastuch koński (kowboj)
wrap; wrapt; wrapt (raep;
raept; raept)
wrap (raep) v. zawijać; owijać;
zapakowywać; spowijać; otulać
się; okrywać (się); zachodzić
na siebie; s. szal; chusta;
okrycie
wrap up ('raepap) v. owijać
(się); pakować
wrapper ('raeper) s. opakowanie; opaska; obwoluta; bande-
rola; papierek; bibułka; osłona; podomka (damska); pako-
wacz
wrapping ('raepyng) s. opakowanie
wrapping paper ('raepyng pejper) s. papier do pakowania

wrapt (raept) v. zob. wrap
wrasse (raes) s. (ryba) wargacz
wrath (ra:ş) s. gniew; oburzenie
wrathful (ra:şful) adj. gniewny
wreak (ri:k) v. wywierać (zem-
stę); dawać upust; wyładować
(gniew)
wreath( ri:ş) s. wieniec
wreathe (ri:z) v. wieńczyć; wić
się; splatać; spowijać; pleść
się; kłębić się (dym etc.)
wreck (rek) s. ruina; wrak;
rozbicie się (np.statku); katastrofa; szczątki (np. na wodzie); zniszczenie; rozbitek
życiowy; kaleka; wypadek;
v. rozbić (pojazd); zniweczyć
(nadzieje); burzyć; być roz-
bitym; spowodować rozbicie;
zrujnować; mieć wypadek
wreckage ('rekydż) s. rozbicie;
szczątki; gruzy
wrecked ('rekt) adj. rozbity;
zniszczony; zepsuty
wrecking company ('rekyng'kampeny) ş. przedsiębiorstwo
rozbiórki budynków
wrecking service ('rekyng'se:r-
wys) s. przewóz zepsutych samochodów
wrecker ('reker) s. sprawca wypadku; ciężarówka (z dźwigiem)
do przewozu zepsutych samochodów; kierowca przewożący ze-
psute samochody; przedsiębiorca rozbiórki budynków; przedsiębiorca wydobywania zatopio-
nych statków; człowiek kradnący
szczątki statku; szkodnik; roz-
bijacz małżeństwa
wren (ren) s. strzyżyk
wrench (rencz) s. gwałtowne
skręcenie; ukręcenie; szarpnięcie; wykręcenie; zwichnięcie; przekręcenie (faktów);
ból (rozstania); klucz maszynowy; klucz nasadowy; klucz
nakrętkowy; v. szarpnąć;
skręcić; wykręcić; zwichnąć
(nogę); przekręcać(fakty);
ukręcać

wrench open ('rencz'oupen) v.
odkręcić; otwierać; odsrubo-
wywać

wrench off ('rencz,o:f) v. wyrywać; wykręcić; ukręcić
(głowę)

wrest (rest) v. wykręcać; wyrywać; przekręcać (fakty);
wydobywać zeznania; s. wykręcanie; wyrywanie; klucz
do strojenia (harfy)

wrest from ('restfrom) v. wyrwać komuś

wrestle ('resl) v. mocować
się; zmagać się; borykać się;
walczyć; s. zapasy; walka

wrestler ('resler) s. zapaśnik

wrestling ('reslyng) s. za-
paśnictwo

wrestpins ('rest,pynz) pl. koł-
ki na struny fortepianowe

wretch (recz) s. nieszczęśnik;
biedaczysko; biedak; nędzarz;
łajdak; łotr; nikczemnik

wretched ('reczyd) adj. nieszczęśliwy; pechowy; biedny;
nędzny; marny; fatalny;
ochydny; wstrętny; nadzwyczajny (łotr)

wrick (ryk) v. lekko zwichnąć;
nadwyrężyć; s. zwichnięcie;
lekkie naderwanie

wriggle ('rygl) v. wić się;
wkręcać (się); kręcić; wy-
winąć się; s. ruch wijący
się; wicie

wriggle along ('rygle'long)
v. posuwać się wijąc

wriggle in ('rygl,yn) v. wkręcać się

wriggle out ('ryglaut) v. wykręcać się

wright (rajt) s. robotnik;
twórca

wring; wrung; wrung (ryng;
rang; rang)

wring (ryng) v. wyżymać; wykręcać; ukręcić (łeb); przekręcać (słowa); ściskać (serce); uściskać (rękę); wymóc
(coś na kimś); zniekształcić;
s. wyżymanie; uścisk; ścis-
kanie; wyżęcie; wyciśnięcie;

wringer (rynger) s. wyżymaczka

wrinkle ('rynkl) s. zmarszczka;
fałda; zmarszczenie; (slang):
ciekawy pomysł; rada
v. marszczyć (się); być pomar-
szczonym; zmiąc (się)

wrinkle up ('rynkl ap) v. po-
marszczyć

wrinkly (rynkly) adj. pomarszczony

wrist (ryst) s. przegub; ruch
ręki w przegubie

wristband ('rystbaend) s. mankiet u koszuli

wristwatch ('ryst,łocz) s.
zegarek na rękę

writ (ryt) s. nakaz pisemny;
prawny

writ for ('ryt,fo:r) s. rozpi-
sanie (wyborów)

write; wrote; written (rajt;
rout; rytn)

write (rajt) v. pisać; napisać;
zapisać; wypisać; komponować;
wstawiać (czek); spisywać;
sławić (piórem)

write back ('rajt,baek) v. odpisywać (komuś)

write down ('rajtdałn) v. spisywać; notować; określać (ujem-
nie)

write home ('rajt,houm) v. pisać do domu

write-in ('rajt,yn) v. wpisywać; dopisywać

write-off ('rajt,of) v. odpisywać (na straty); pisać na
prędce

write out ('rajt,aut) v. wypisywać; sporządzać

write-up ('rajt,ap) v. zapisywać; opisywać; przesadnie szacować; pochwalić

writer ('rajter) s. pisarz;
niżej podpisany; powieściopisarz

writhe (rajs) v. wić się (z bólu); cierpieć (zniewagę);
skręcać się (ze wstydu)

writing ('rajtyng) s. pismo;
utwór; artykuł; pisanie;
pismiennictwo; sztuka pisania;
praca literacka; napisana rzecz

writing desk ('rajtyng,desk)
s. biurko; pulpit
writing ink ('rajtyng,ynk)
s. atrament
writing paper ('rajtyng,pej-
per) s. papier listowy; papier do pisania
writing table ('rajtyng,tejbl)
s. biurko
written ('rytn) v. zob.: rite;
adj. pisany
wrong (ro:ng) adj. zły; niewłaściwy; błędny; nie w porządku; mylny; niekorzystny;
niesprawiedliwy; s. zło; wykroczenie; krzywda; wina; pomyłka; grzech; strata; nie-
sprawiedliwosc; v. skrzyw-
dzic; niesłusznie posadzac;
byc niesprawiedliwym;
adv. mylnie; niewłaściwie;
błędnie; źle; zdrożnie; nie-
korzystnie
wrongdoer ('ro:ng'du:er) s.
krzywdziciel; grzesznik;
winowajca
wrongdoing ('ro:ng'duyng) s.
nadużycia; wykroczenia;
grzechy; przestępstwa
wrongful ('ro:ngful) adj.zły;
krzywdzący; niesprawiedliwy;
bezprawny
wronghead ('ro:ng'hed) v.
przekręcać (słowa etc.)
wrongheaded ('ro:ng'hedyd)
adj. uparty; przewrotny
wrote (rout) v. zob. write
wroth (ro:g) adj. gniewny
wrought (ro:t) v. zob. work
wrought iron ('ro:t'ajern)
s. kute żelazo
wrought-up ('ro:t,ap) adj.
napięty; zdenerwowany
wrung ('rang) v. zob. wring
wry (raj) adj. krzywy; okrzy-
wiony
wryneck ('rajnek) s. zastrzał
szyi ; kręcz karku
wynd (łajnd) s. (kręta) uliczka
x (eks) dwudziesta czwarta litera angielskiego alfabetu;
rzymska cyfra 10; niewiadoma

xenon ('zenon) s. ksenon
xenophobia (,zene'foubje) s.
ksenofobia
Xmas ('krysmes) = Christmas
x-ray ('eks'rej) adj. rentge-
nowski; v. prześwietlać; robic
zdjęcie rentgenowskie
x-ray diagnosis ('eks'rej,da-
jeg'nouzys) s. rozpoznanie
rentgenowskie
x-ray examination ('eks'rej-
yg'zaemynejszyn) s. badanie
rentgenowskie
x-ray picture ('eks'rej'pykczer)
s. zdjecie rentgenowskie
x-rays ('eks'rejs) pl. promienie rentgenowskie
xylem ('zajlem) s. drewno
xylophagous (zaj'lofeges) adj.
drzewożerny
xylophone ('zylefoun) s. ksylo-
fon
y (łaj) dwudziesta piąta litera
angielskiego alfabetu
yabber ('jaeber) v. gadac
yacht (jot) s. jacht; y. płynąc
jachtem; urządząc wyscigi jach-
towe
yachting ('jotyng) s. sport
żeglarski
yak (jaek) s. jak; (slang): gadanie; śmiech; v. gadac; smiac
się
yap (jaep) v. ujadac; (slang);
paplac; s. ujadanie; paplanina;
krzykacz; jadaczka
yard (ja:rd) s. jard (91.44 cm);
podwórze; dziedziniec; v. umieszczac w ogrodzeniu
yarn (ja:rn) s. włókno; przędza;
historyjka; v. opowiadac histo-
ryjki
yawn (jo:n) v. ziewac; ziąc; zionąc; s. ziewnięcie; ziewanie
ye (ji:) pron. wy (biblijne)
yea (jej) adv. tak; s. głosowanie "tak"
yeah (jej) (slang): tak; excl.:
tak ! nie wierzę !
year (je:r) s. rok
yearly (je:rly) adj. roczny;
coroczny; adv. corocznie;
s. rocznik;adv.raz na rok

yearn (je:rn) v. tęsknić
yeast (ji:st) s. drożdże; ferment; piana; v. fermentować;
pienić (się)
yell (jel) v. wrzeszczec;
s.wrzask; dopingowanie
yellow ('jelou) adj. żółty;
(slang): tchórzliwy; zawistny;
żółty z zazdrości; n. żółty
kolor; żółtko; v. żółknąć;
powodować żółknięcie
yelp (jelp) s. skowyt; v. skowyczeć
yeoman ('joumen) s. podoficer
marynarki; (dawniej) wolny
chłop
yep (jep) adv. (slang): tak
yes (jes) adv. tak; v.potakiwać
yesterday ('jesterdy) adv. &
s. wczoraj
yet (jet) adv. & conj. dotąd;
jeszcze do tej pory; na razie;
jak dotąd; jednak; ani też;
mimo to
yew (ju:) s. cis
Yiddish (jydysz) s. język żydowski
yield (ji:ld) v. wydawać; dawać; rodzic; przynosić; oddawać (się); porzucać; ustępować; s. plon; zysk; wydajność
yielding(ji:ldyng) s. wydajność; adj. ustępliwy
yogurt ('jouguert) s. jogurt
yoke (jouk) s. jarzmo; v. zaprzęgac; nakładać jarzmo;
(slang): zaskakiwać (przechodnia) w celu rabunku
yolk (jouk) s. żółtko; rodzaj
łoju
yonder ('jonder) adj. & adv.
tam dalej; tamten
you (ju:) pron. ty; wy; pan;
pani; panowie; panie
you'd (ju:d) = you would;
you had
you'll (ju:l) = you shall;
you will
young (jang) adj. młody; młodzieńczy; młodociany

youngster ('janster) s. dziecko;
młodzik
your (ju:r) adj. twój; wasz;
pański
you're (jo:r) = you are
yours (juers) pron. twój; wasz;
pański (z poważaniem)
yourself (,juer'self) pron. ty
sam
yourselves (,juer'selvz) pron.
wy sami
youth (ju:s) s. młodość
youths (ju:dz) pl. młodzież;
młodzieniec
youthful ('ju:sful) adj, młody;
młodzieńczy
youth-hostel ('ju:s'hostl) s,
schronisko młodzieżowe
you've ('ju:w) = you have
Yugoslav ('ju:gou'sla:w) adj.
jugosłowiański
z (zi:) dwudziesta szósta litera alfabetu angielskiego
zany ('zejny) adj. pocieszny;
błazenski; s. błazen; głupek
zeal (zi:l) s. gorliwość
zealous ('zeles) adj. gorliwy
zebra ('zi:bre) s. zebra;
(slang): mulat; adj.pręgowany
zebra crossing ('zi:bre'krosyng)
s. pasami znaczone przejście
jezdni dla pieszych
zenith ('senit) s. zenit; szczyt
(sławy)
zero ('zierou) s. zero; v. ustawiać na zero; brać na cel
zest (zest) s. smak; pikanteria;
rozkosz; zamiłowanie; v. dodawać pikanterii
zigzag ('zygzaeg) s. zygzak;
adj. zygzakowaty; adv. zygzakiem
zinc (zynk) s. cynk; v. cynkować
zip (zyp) s. świst; wigor;
v. śmigać; gnać; zapinać zamek
błyskawiczny
zip code ('zyp,koud) s. numeracja pocztowa miejscowości
zipper ('zyper) s. zamek błyskawiczny

zippy ('zypy) adj. żywy; zgrabny

zloty ('zlouty) s. złoty (pieniądz polski); adj. golden

zodiac ('zoudjaek) s. zodiak

zombie ('zomby) s. bóg-pyton; (slang) bałwan; tuman

zone (zoun) s. strefa; zona; v. opasywać; dzielić na zony

zoo (zu:) s. ogród zoologiczny

zoology (zou'oledży) s. zoologia

zoom (zu:m) v. buczec; wzlatywac; wzbijac się szybko; śmigac; s. poderwanie (samolotu); soczewka zbliżająca w aparacie do filmowania oraz w aparacie do fotografowania

340

## ABBREVIATIONS – SKRÓTY

| | | |
|---|---|---|
| a. | – attribute | – przydawka |
| adj. | – adjective | – przymiotnik |
| adj. f. | – adjective feminine | – przymiotnik żeński |
| adj. m. | – adjective masculine | – przymiotnik męski |
| adj. n. | – adjective neuter | – przymiotnik nijaki |
| adv. | – adverb | – przysłówek |
| am. | – American | – amerykański |
| chem. | – chemistry | – chemia |
| conj. | – conjunction | – spójnik |
| constr. | – construction | – budowa |
| etc. | – and so on | – i tak dalej |
| excl. | – exclamation | – wykrzyknik |
| expr. | – expression | – wyrażenie |
| f. | – substantive feminine | – rzeczownik żeński |
| gram. | – grammar | – gramatyka |
| hist. | – history | – historia |
| hyp. | – hyphen | – łącznik |
| indecl. | – indeclinable | – nieodmienny |
| inf. | – infinitive | – bezokolicznik |
| m. | – substantive musculine | – rzeczownik męski |
| m.in. | – among others | – między innymi |
| n. | – substantive neuter | – rzeczownik nijaki |
| num. | – numeral | – liczebnik |
| part. | – particle | – partykuła |
| pl. | – substantive plural | – rzeczownik liczba mnoga |
| poet. | – poetry | – poezja |
| polit. | – politics | – polityka |
| p.p. | – past participle | – imiesłów czasu przeszłego |
| prep. | – preposition | – przyimek |
| pron. | – pronoun | – zaimek |
| s. | – substantive | – rzeczownik |
| sb. | – somebody | – ktoś |
| slang | – slang | – gwara, żargon |
| v. | – verb | – czasownik |
| vulg. | – vulgarity | – ordynarność |
| wg | – according to | – według |
| W.W. II | – World War II | – druga wojna światowa |
| zob. | – see | – zobacz |

CZĘSTO UŻYWANE PRZEDROSTKI I CZŁONY WYRAZÓW ZŁOŻONYCH
COMMON PREFIXES, SUFFIXES AND COMPONENT WORDS

| Polish | English |
|---|---|
| a- (a-) | = no- (nou-); non- (non-) |
| anty- (anti-) | = anti- ('aentaj-) |
| arcy- (ar-tsi-) | = arch- (a:rcz-) |
| auto- ('aw-to-) | = auto- (,o:te'-) |
| bez- (bez-) | = -less (-lys) |
| beze- (be-ze-) | = -less (-lys) |
| bi- (bee-) | = bi- (baj-) |
| centy-, (cen-ti-) | = centi- (senty-) |
| ćwierć- (ćhvyerćh-) | = quarter- ('kło:ter-) |
| daleko- (da-le-ko-) | = far (fa:r-) |
| de- (de-) | = de- (dy-) |
| długo-(dwoo-go-) | = long- (long-) |
| do- (do-) | = to- (tu-) |
| | till- (tyl-) |
| drobno- (drob-no-) | = small- (smol-) |
| dwu- (dvoo-) | = two- (tu-) |
| eks- (eks-) | = ex- (eks-) |
| ekstra- (eks-tra-) | = extra- ('ekstre-) |
| gorzko- (gosh-ko-) | = bitter- ('byter-) |
| hetero- (khe-te-ro-) | = hetero- (hetere-) |
| homo- (kho-mo-) | = homo- (houmo-) |
| hydro- (khi-dro-) | = hydro- (,hajdre'-) |
| inno- (een-no-) | = other- (odzer-) |
| | else- (els-) |
| jasno- (yas-no-) | = fair- (feer-) |
| | clear- (klier-) |
| | light- (lajt-) |
| | bright- (brajt-) |
| jedno- (yed-no-) | = single- (syngl-) |
| | one- (łan-) |
| kilko- (keel-ko-) | = some- (som-) |
| | - few- (fju-) |
| kilku- (keel-ku-) | = some- (som-) |
| | = few- (fju-) |
| ko- (ko-) | = co- (ko-) |
| kontr- (kontr-) | = counter- (kaunter-) |
| kontra- (kon-tra-) | = counter- (kaunter-) |
| krótko- (kroot-ko-) | = short- (szort-) |
| | curt- (ke:rt-) |
| lewo- (le-vo-) | = left- (left-) |
| mało- (ma-wo-) | = few- (fju-) |
| | little- (lytl-) |
| między- (myań-dzi-) | = between- (by'twi:n) |
| | amont- (e'mang-) |
| | inter- ('ynter-) |
| mili- (mee-lee-) | = milli- (myly-) |
| multi- (mool-tee-) | = multi- (malty-) |

| | |
|---|---|
| na- (na-) | = on- (on-) |
| | onto- (ontu-) |
| | up- (ap-) |
| nad- (nad-) | = over- (ouver-) |
| | above- (e'bav-) |
| | on- (on-) |
| nade- (na-de-) | = over- (ouver-) |
| | above- (e'bav-) |
| | on- (on-) |
| naj- (nay-) | = most- (moust-) |
| neo- (ne-o-) | = neo- (ni:e-) |
| neuro- (neu-ro-) | = neuro- (nju'rou-) |
| niby- (ńee-bi-) | = as if- (es yf-) |
| | would-be- ('łud-bi:-) |
| nie- (ńe-) | = no- (nou-) |
| | non- (non-) |
| nisko- (ńees-ko-) | = low- (lou-) |
| nowo- (no-vo-) | = new- nju:-) |
| o- (o-) | = un- (an-) |
| | re- (ry-) |
| | de- (dy-); (de-) |
| ob- (ob-) | = off- (of-) |
| obco- (ob-tso-) | = foreign- ('foryn) |
| obe- (o-be-) | = off- (of-) |
| od- (od-) | = from- (from-) |
| | since- (syns-) |
| ode- (o-de-) | = from- (from- ) |
| | since- (syns-) |
| ogólno- (o-gool-no-) | = wide- (łajd-) |
| około- (o-ko-wo-) | = about (e-baut-) |
| ostro- (os-tro-) | = sharp- (szarp-) |
| pan- (pan-) | = pan- (paen-) |
| paro- (pa-ro-) | = couple- (-kapl) |
| | two- (tu:-) |
| pełno- (pew-no-) | = ful- (-ful) |
| pierwszo- (pyerw-sho-) | = first- (fe:rst-) |
| płasko- (pwas-ko-) | = flat- (flaet-) |
| po- (po-) | = after- ('a:fter-) |
| pod- (pod-) | = under- (ander-) |
| pode- (po-de-) | = under- (ander-) |
| poli- (po-lee-) | = poli- (poly-) |
| polsko- (pol-sko-) | = Polish- (poulysz-) |
| ponad- (po-nad-) | = above- (e'bav-) |
| post- (post-) | = post- (post-) |
| poza- (po-za-) | = out- (aut-) |
| pół- (poow-) | = half- (ha:f-) |
| prawo- (pra-vo-) | = ortho- (orgo-) |
| | right- (rajt-) |
| | law- (lou-) |
| pre- (pre-) | = pre- (pry-) |
| pro- (pro-) | = pro- (pro-) |
| | (pre-) |

| | |
|---|---|
| prosto- (pros-to-) | = straight- (strejt-) |
| proto- (pro-to-) | = proto- (proute-) |
| prze- (pzhe-) | = across- (e'kros) |
| | over- (ouwer) |
| przeciw- (pzhe-cheev-) | = counter- ('kaunter-) |
| przed- (pzhed-) | = before- (by'fo:r-) |
| przeszło- (pzhe-shwo-) | = over- (ouwer-) |
| przy- (pzhi-) | ▬ by- (baj-) |
| | near- (nier-) |
| pseudo- (pseu-do-) | = pseudo- ('sju:dou-) |
| psycho- (psi-kho-) | = psycho- ('sajke-) |
| radio- (ra-dyo-) | ▬ radio- ('rejdjou-) |
| roz- (roz-) | = de- (dy-) |
| | ex- (y'gs-) (,egz-) |
| roze- (roze-) | ▬ de- (dy-) |
| | ex- (y'gs-), (,egz-) |
| równo- (roov-no-) | = equi- (,i:kły'-) |
| różno- (roozh-no-) | = many- ('meny-) |
| s- (s-) | = over- (ouwer-) |
| | off- (-of), etc. |
| samo- (sa-mo-) | = self- (self-) |
| słodko- (swod-ko-) | ▬ sweet- (słi:t-) |
| spektro- (spektro-) | = spectro- (spectrou-) |
| staro- (sta-ro-) | = old- (ould-) |
| stereo- (ste-re-o-) | = stereo- ('stjery,ou-) |
| sub- (soob-) | = sub- (sab-) |
| super- (soo-per-) | = super- (super-) |
| szeroko- (she-ro-ko-) | = wide- (łajd-) |
| szybko- (shib-ko·) | = quick- (kłyk-) |
| srednio- (shred-no-) | = average- (aewrydż-) |
| | tolerably- (tolerebly-) |
| środkowo- (shrod-ko-vo-) | = center- ('senter-) |
| | middle- (mydl-) |
| | mean- (mi:n-) |
| sród- (shrood-) | = center- ('senter-), etc. |
| tele- (te-le-) | = tele- (tely-) |
| termo- (ter-mo-) | = thermo- (ṭe:rmo-) |
| trans- (trans-) | = trans- (traens'-) |
| trój- (trooy-) | = three- (ṭri:-) |
| u- (oo-) | = at-(et-) |
| | de- (dy-), etc. |
| ultra- (ool-tra-) | = ultra- (altre-) |
| w- (v-) | = in- (yn-) |
| wąsko- (vown-sko-) | = narrow- ('naerou-) |
| wczesno- (vches-no-) | = rearly- ('e:rly-) |
| we- (ve-) | = in- (yn-) |
| wice- (vee-tse-) | = vice- (wajs-) |
| wielko- (vyel-ko-) | = great- (grejt-) |
| wodo- (vo-do-) | = water- (ło:ter-) |
| wolno- (vol-no-) | ▬ free- (fri:-) |
| wpoł- (vpoow-) | = half- (ha:f-) |

| | |
|---|---|
| ws- (vs-) | = co- (kou-) |
| | (ko-) |
| wspól- (vspoow-) | = co- (kou-) |
| | (ko-) |
| wy- (vi-) | = out- (aut-) |
| wysoko- (vi-so-ko-) | = high- (haj-) |
| wz- (vz-) | = up- (ap-) |
| z- (z-) | = out- (aut-) |
| za- (za-) | = behind- (by'hajnd-) |
| zeszło- (zesh-wo-) | = past- (pa:st-) |
| zielono- (źhe-lo-no-) | = green- (gri;n-) |
| złoto- (zwo-to-) | = gold- (gould-) |
| żółto- (zhoow-to-) | = yellow- ('jelou-) |

| GEOGRAPHIC NAMES | NAZWY GEOGRAFICZNE |
|---|---|
| Abyssinia (,aeby'synje) | – Abisynia (a-bee-si-ña) |
| Adriatic (,ejdry'aetyk) | – Adriatyk (ad-ryá-tik) |
| Africa ('aefryke) | – Afryka (áf-ri-ka) |
| Alabama (aele'baeme) | – Alabama (a-la-bá-ma) |
| Alaska (e'laeske) | – Alaska (a-lás-ka) |
| Albania (ael'bejnje) | – Albania (al-ba-ña) |
| Albany ('o:lbeny) | – Albany (al-ba-ni) |
| Alberta (ael'be:rta) | – Alberta (al-bér-ta) |
| Algeria (ael'dźierje) | – Algeria (al-gér-ya) |
| Alps (aelp) | – Alpy (ál-pi) |
| Amazon ('aemezen) | – Amazonka (a-ma-zón-ka) |
| America (e'meryke) | – Ameryka (a-me-ri-ka) |
| Arabia (e'rejbje) | – Arabia (a-ráb-ya) |
| Argentina (,a:dźen'ti:ne) | – Argentyna (ar-gen-ti-na) |
| Arizona (,aery'zoune) | – Arizona (a-ree-zó-na) |
| Arkansas ('a:ken,so:) | – Arkansas (ar-kán-sas) |
| Armenia (a:'mi:nje) | – Armenia (ar-me-ña) |
| Asia ('ejsze) | – Azja (áz-ya) |
| Atlanta (et'laente) | – Atlanta (at-lán-ta) |
| Atlantic (et'laentyk) | – Atlantyk (at-lan-tik) |
| Auschwitz ('ouszwyc) | – Oświęcim (osh-vyáñ-cheem) |
| Australia (os'trejlje) | – Australia (aws-trál-ya) |
| Balkans ('bo:lkens) | – Bałkany (baw-ka-ni) |
| Baltic ('bo:ltyk) | – Bałtyk (báw-tik) |
| Baltimore ('bo:lty,mo:r) | – Baltimore (bal-ti-mó-re) |
| Belgium ('beldźem) | – Belgia (bél-gya) |
| Belgrade (bel'grejd) | – Belgrad (bél-grad) |
| Benelux ('beny,laks) | – Beneluks (be-ne-looks) |
| Berlin (be:r'lyn) | – Berlin (bér-leen) |
| Bermuda (be:r'mju:de) | – Bermudy (ber-moó-di) |
| Birmingham ('be:rmynem) | – Birmingham (beer-meéng-ham) |
| Black Sea ('blaek'si:) | – Morze Czarne (mó-she chár-ne) |
| Bolivia (be'lywje) | – Boliwia (bo-leév-ya) |
| Brazil (bre'zyl) | – Brazylia (bra-zíl-ya) |
| Britain('brytn) | – Brytania (bri-ta-ña), |
| British Isles ('brytysz'ajlz) | – Wyspy Brytyjskie (vis-pi bri-tíy-skye) |
| Bronx (bronks) | – Bronx (bronks) |
| Brussels ('braslz) | – Bruksela (broo-ksé-la) |
| Budapest ('bju:de'pest) | – Budapeszt (boo-dá-pesht) |
| Bulgaria (bal'geerje) | – Bułgaria (boow-gár-ya) |
| Byelorussia (by,elou'rasze) | – Białorus (bya-wó-roosh) |
| Cairo ('kaje,rou) | – Kair (ka-eer) |
| California (kaely'fo:rnje) | – Kalifornia (ka-lee-fór-ña) |
| Cambodia (kaem'boudje) | – Kambodża (kam-bó-ja) |
| Canada ('kaenede) | – Kanada (ka-na-da) |
| Caribbean Sea (,kaery'bjen'-si:) | – Morze Karaibskie (mó-zhe ka-ra-eéb-skye) |
| Carolina (,kaere'lajne) | – Karolina (ka-ro-leé-na) |
| Carpathians (ka:r'pejtjenz) | – Karpaty (kar-pá-ti) |

| | |
|---|---|
| Caspian Sea ('kaespjen'si:) | – Morze Kaspijskie (mó-zhe kas-peéy-skye) |
| Caucasus ('ko:keses) | – Kaukaz (káw-kaz) |
| Chicago (szy'ka:gou) | – Chicago (chee-ká-go) |
| Chile ('czyly) | – Chile (cheé-le) |
| China ('czajna) | – Chiny (kheé-ni) |
| Cincinnati (,synsy'naety) | – Cincinnati (tseen-tseen-ná-tee) |
| Cleveland ('kli:wlend) | – Cleveland (kle-ve-land) |
| Colorado (,kole'ra:dou) | – Kolorado (ko-lo-rá-do) |
| Congo ('kongou) | – Kongo (kón-go) |
| Connecticut (ke'netyket) | – Connecticut (kon-nek-teé-koot) |
| Copenhagen (,koupn'hejgen) | – Kopenhaga (ko-pen-khá-ga) |
| Corsica (ko:rsyke) | – Korsyka (kor-sí-ka) |
| Cracow ('kraekou) | – Kraków (krá-koov) |
| Crimea (kraj'mje) | – Krym (krím) |
| Croatia (krou'ejsze) | – Chorwacja (khor-váts-ya) |
| Cuba ('kju:be) | – Kuba (koó-ba) |
| Czechoslovakia ('czekou-slou'waekje) | – Czechosłowacja (che-kho-swo-váts-ya) |
| Dakota (de'koute) | – Dakota (da-kó-ta) |
| Dalmatia (dael'mejszje) | – Dalmacja (dal-máts-ya) |
| Danzig ('daentsyg) | – Gdańsk (gdáńsk) |
| Delaware ('dele,łeer) | – Delaware (de-la-vá-re) |
| Denmark ('denma:rk) | – Dania (dá-ña) |
| Detroit (dy'troit) | – Detroit (de-tro-eet) |
| Drezden ('drezden) | – Drezno (dréz-no) |
| East Prussia ('i:st'prasza) | – Prusy Wschodnie (proó-si vskhód-ñe) |
| Edinburgh ('edynbere) | – Edynburg (e-din-boorg) |
| Egypt ('i:dżypt) | – Egipt (e-geept) |
| Eire ('eere) | – Irlandia (eer-lánd-ya) |
| England ('ynglend) | – Anglia (áng-lya) |
| Europe ('juerep) | – Europa (e-oo-ró-pa) |
| Eurasia (jue'rejzje) | – Eurazja (e-oor-áz-ya) |
| Finland ('fynlend) | – Finlandia (feen-lánd-ya) |
| Florida ('floryda) | – Floryda (flo-rí-da) |
| France (fra:ns) | – Francja (fránts-ya) |
| Gdansk (gdaensk) | – Gdańsk (gdańsk) |
| Geneva (dży'ni:wa) | – Genewa (ge-né-va) |
| Georgia ('dżo:rdżje) | – Georgia (ge-órg-ya) |
| | – Gruzja (groóz-ya) |
| Germany ('dże:rmeny) | – Niemcy (ńem-tsi) |
| Great Britain ('grejt brytn) | – Wielka Brytania (vyél-ka bri-tá-ña) |
| Greece (gri:s) | – Grecja (gréts-ya) |
| Hague (hejg) | – Haga (khá-ga) |
| Haiti ('hej-ty) | – Haiti (khá-ee-tee) |
| Hamburg ('haembe:rg) | – Hamburg (khám-boorg) |
| Havana (he'waena) | – Hawana (kha-vá-na) |
| Hawaii (ha:łai:) | – Hawaje (kha-vá-ye) |
| Helsinki ('helsynky) | – Helsinki (khel-seén-kee) |

Himalayas (,hyme'lejez)    – Himalaje (khee-ma-lá-ye)
Holland ('holend)    – Holandia (kho-land-ya)
Hollywood ('holyłud)    – Hollywood (kho-leé-vood)
Honolulu (,hone'lu:lu:)    – Honolulu (kho-no-loó-loo)
Hungary ('hangery)    – Węgry (váń-gri)
Iceland ('ajslend)    – Islandia (ees-lánd-ya)
Idaho ('ajde,hou)    – Idaho (ee-da-kho)
Illinois (,yly'noj)    – Illinois (ee-lee-nó-ees)
India ('yndje)    – India (eénd-ya)
Indiana (,yndy'aena)    – Indiana (een-dya-na)
Indianapolis (,yndje'naepolys) – Indianapolis (een-dya-no-pó-lees)
Iowa ('ajoue)    – Iowa (ee-ó-va)
Iraq (y'ra:k)    – Irak (eé-rak)
Ireland ('ajerlend)    – Irlandia (eer-lánd-ya)
Israel ('izrejel)    – Izrael (eez-rá-el)
Italy ('ytely)    – Włochy (vwó-khi)
Jamaica (dże'meike)    – Jamajka (ya-máy-ka)
Japan (dże'paen)    – Japonia (ya-pó-na)
Java ('dźa:wa)    – Jawa (yá-va)
Jericho ('dżery,kou)    – Jerycho (ye-ri-kho)
Jersey ('dźe:rzy)    – Jersey (yér-sey)
Jerusalem (dże'ru:selem)    – Jerozolima (ye-ro-zo-leé-ma)
Jordan ('dżo-rdn)    – Jordania (yor-da-ña)
Jugoslavia ('ju:gou'sla:wja)    – Jugosławia (yoo-go-swáv-ya)
Kansas ('kaenzes)    – Kansas (kán-sas)
Kentucky (ken'taky)    – Kentucky
Kiev ('ki:ew)    – Kijów (keé-yoov)
Klondike ('klondajk)    – Klondike (klon-deé-ke)
Korea (ko'rje)    – Korea (ko-ré-a)
Laos (lauz)    – Laos (la-os)
Latvia (lat-wja)    – Łotwa (wot-va)
Lebanon ('lebenon)    – Liban (leé-ban)
Leipzig ('lajpzig)    – Lipsk (leepsk)
Leningrad (,lenyn,graed)    – Leningrad (le-ñeen-grad)
Libya ('lybje)    – Libia (leéb-ya)
Lithuania (,lytju'ejnje)    – Litwa (leét-va)
Lodz (lodz)    – Łódź (woodżh)
London ('landen)    – Londyn (lón-din)
Los Angeles (los'aendży,li:z) – Los Angeles (los án-ge-les)
Louisiana (lu,i:zy'aena)    – Louisiana (loo-ee-syá-na)
Lublin ('lablyn)    – Lublin (loób-leen)
Lvov (lwow)    – Lwów (lvooy)
Madrid (me'dryd)    – Madryt (má-drit)
Main (mejn)    – Men (men)
Maine (mejn)    – Maine (ma-eé-n)
Manhattan (maen'haetn)    – Manhattan (man-kha-tan)
Maryland ('meerylaend)    – Maryland (ma-ri-land)
Massachusetts (,maese'czu:sets) – Massachusetts (ma-sa-choó-sets)
Masuria (me'sjuerje)    – Mazury (ma-zoó-ri)
Mediterranean (,medite'rejnjen)– Śródziemne (śhrood-żhém-ne)

Memel ('mejmel)            – Kłajpeda (kway-pé-da)
Mexico ('meksy,kou)      – Meksyk (mék-sik)
Miami (maj'aemy)        – Miami (mya-mee)
Michigan ('myszygen)     – Michigan (mee-chée-gan)
Milwaukee (myl'ľo:ky)    – Milwaukee (meel-wó-ki)
Minneapolis (,myny'aepelys) – Minneapolis (mee-ne-a-pó-lees)
Minnesota(,myny'soute)   – Minnesota (mee-ne-só-ta)
Mississippi (,mysy'sypy)   – Mississippi
Missouri (my'suery)      – Missouri
Montana (mon'taena)     – Montana (mon-ta-na)
Montreal (,montry'o:l)    – Montreal (monʇ-ré-al)
Moravia (mo'rejwje)      – Morawy (mo-rá-vi)
Morocco (me'rokou)      – Maroko (ma-ró-ko)
Moscow ('moskou)       – Moskwa (mós-kva),
Nebraska (ny'braeske)   – Nebraska, (ne-bras-ka)
Neisse ('najsy)         – Nysa (ní-sa)
Nevada (ne'wa:de)      – Newada (ne-vá-da)
New England (nju:ynglend) – Nowa Anglia (nó-va áng-lya)
New Hampshire (nju'haempszier)– New Hampshire
New Jersey (nju:'dże:rzy) – New Jersey
New Mexico (nju:'meksy,kou) – Nowy meksyk (nó-vy mék-sik)
New Orleans (nju:'o:rlienz) – Nowy Orlean (nó-vy,or-le-an)
New York City (nju:'jo:rk'- – Nowy Jork (nó-vy york)
syty)
Niagara(naj'aegere)    – Niagara (ńee-a-gá-ra)
North Carolina ('no:rt,kaere'-– Karolina Północna
lajne)                  (ka-ro-lee-na poow-nóts-na)
North Dakota ('no:rt-de'koute)– Dakota Północna
North Sea ('no:rt'si:)    – Morze Północne (mó-zhe poow-nóts-ne)

Norway ('no:rłej)      – Norwegia (nor-vég-ya)
Oder ('ouder)          – Odra (ód-ra),
Odessa (ou'dese)       – Odessa ,(o-dés-sa)
Ohio (ou'hajou)        – Ohio (ókh-yo)
Oklahoma (,oukle'houme) – Oklahoma (o-kla-khó-ma)
Ontario (on'teery,ou)    – Ontario (on-ʇar-yo)
Oregon (o'rygen)       – Oregon (o-ré-gon)
Oslo ('ozlou)          – Oslo (ós-lo),
Ottawa ('otele)        – Ottawa (o-tá-va)
Palestine ('paelys,tain)   – Palestyna (pa-les-ti-na)
Panama (,paene'ma:)    – Panama (pa-na-ma)
Paris (paerys)         – Paryż (pá-rizh)
Peking ('pi:kyɲ)       – Pekin (pe-keen)
Pennsylvania (,pensyl'venje) – Pensylwania (pen-sil-vá-ña)
Persia ('pe:rsze)       – Persja (pér-sya)
Pittsburgh('pytsbe:rg)   – Pittsburg (peéts-boorg)
Podolia (pe'doulje)     – Podole (po-dó-le)
Poland (,poulend)      – Polska (pól-ska)
Pomerania (,pome'rejnje) – Pomorze (pp-mó-zhe)
Pos.en ('pouzn)        – Poznan (póz-nan)
Prague (pra:g)         – Praga (prá-ga)

Prussia ('prasze)        - Prusy (proó-si)
Quebec (kźy'bek)       - Quebek (ke-bek)
Red Sea ('red'si:)       - Morze Czerwone (mo-zhe cher-
                              vo-ne)
Reykjavik ('rejkje,wi:k)    - Reykjawik
Rhine (rajn)           - Ren (ren)
Rhode Island ('roud,ajlend)   - Rhode Island
Riga ('ri:ga)         - Ryga (ri-ga)
Rockies('rokyz)      - Góry Skaliste (goó-ri ska-
                              leés-te)
Rome (roum)         - Rzym (zhim)
Rumania (ru'mejnje)     - Rumunia (roo-moó-ña)
Russia ('rasze)       - Rosja (rós-ya)
Salt Lake City ('so:lt,lejk'- - Salt Lake City
  syty)
San Francisco (,saen-fren'- - San Francisco (sán-fran-tseés-
  syskou)              ko)
Saskatchewan (ses'kaeczy,źan) - Saskatchewan
Saudi Arabia ('saudy-e'rejbje)- Arabia Saudyjska (a-rab-ya
                              saw-diy-ska)
Savannah (se'waene)     - Savannah
Saxony ('saekseny)      - Saksonia (sak-só-ña)
Scandinavia (,skaendy'nejwje) - Skandynawia (skan-di-náv-ya)
Scotland ('skotlend)     - Szkocja (shkóts-ya)
Seattle (sy'aetl)       - Seattle
Serbia ('se:rbje)       - Serbia (seŕ-byą)
Siberia (saj'bierie)     - Syberia (si-beŕ-ya)
Sicily ('sysyly)        - Sycylia (si-tsil-ya)
Silesia (saj'li:zje)     - Śląsk (shlównsk)
Sinai ('sajny,aj)       - Synaj (si-nay)
Slavonia (sle'wounje)    - Sławonia (sla-vo-ña)
Slovakia (slou'waekje)   - Słowacja (swo-váts-ya)
Slovenia (slou'wi:nje)   - Słowenia (swo-ve-ña)
Sofia ('soufje)        - Sofia (sóf-ya)
South Carolina ('sous,kaere'- - Karolina Południowa (ka-ro-leé-
  lajne)               na po-wood-ñó-va)
South Dakota ('sous de'koute) - Dakota Południowa (da-kó-ta
                              po-wood-ñó-va)
Soviet Russia ('souwjet'rasze)- Rosja Sowiecka (rós-ya so-
                              vyéts-ka)
Spain (spejn)         - Hiszpania (kheesh-pa-ña)
Stettin ('stetyn)       - Szczecin (shché-cheen)
Stockholm ('stokhoulm)   - Sztokholm (sztók-kholm)
Sudetes (su:'di:ti:z)    - Sudety (su-dé-ty)
Suez ('su:yz)          - Suez (soó-ez)
Sweden ('słi:dn)        - Szwecja (shvets-ya)
Switzerland ('słytserlend)   - Szwajcaria (shvay-tsár-ya)
Syria ('syrje)         - Syria (siŕ-ya)
Tahiti (ta:hyty)        - Tahiti (ta-khee-tee)
Taiwan (taj'źaen)       - Taiwan (táy-van)
Tallin ('taelyn)        - Tallinn (tá-leen)

| | |
|---|---|
| Tangier (taen'dżjer) | – Tanger (tán-ger) |
| Tannenberg ('taenen'be:rg) | – Stębark (stań-bark) |
| Tatra ('ta:tre) | – Tatry (tát-ri) |
| Teheran (te'ra:n) | – Teheran (te-khé-ran) |
| Tel Aviv (tel'a:wyw) | – Tel Awiw (te-la-veev) |
| Tennessee (,tene'si:) | – Tennessee |
| Teschen ('teszn) | – Cieszyn (ćhé-shin) |
| Texas ('tekses) | – Teksas (tęk-sas) |
| Tibet (ty'bet) | – Tybet (ti-bet) |
| Tyrol ('tyrel) | – Tyrol (ti-rol) |
| Tokyo ('toukj,ou) | – Tokio (tók-yo) |
| Toledo (to'lejdou) | – Toledo (to-le-do) |
| Toronto (te'rontou) | – Toronto (to-ron-to) |
| Transylvania (,traensyl'-wejnje) | – Siedmiogród (śhed-myo-grood) |
| Trieste (try'est) | – Triest (trée-est) |
| Tunis ('tju:nys) | – Tunis (toó-ñees) |
| Turkey ('te:rky) | – Turcja (toór-tsya) |
| Turkestan (,te:rkys'ta:n) | – Turkiestan (toor-kyés-tan) |
| Ukraine (ju'kreyn) | – Ukraina (ook-ra-eé-na) |
| Ulster ('alster) | – Ulster (oóls-ter) |
| Union of Soviet Socialist Republics ('ju:njenew'-souwjet'souszelyst-ry'-pablyks) | – Związek Socjalistycznych Republik Radzieckich (zvyówn-zek sots-ya-lees-tich-nykh re-poób-leek ra-dzhets-keekh) |
| United Kingdom of Great Britain (ju'najtyd'kyndemew'-grejt'bryten) | – Zjednoczone Królestwo Wielkiej Brytanii (zyed-no-chó-ne kroo-lés-tvo vyél-kyey bry-ta-ñee) |
| United States of America (ju'najtyd,stejts,owe'meryka) | – Stany Zjednoczone Ameryki (sta-ni zyed-no-chó-ne a-me-ri-kee) |
| Upper Silesia ('apersaj'li:z-je) | – Górny Śląsk (goór-ny shlównzk) |
| Ural ('juerel) | – Ural (oó-ral) |
| Utah ('ju:ta:) | – Utah |
| Vancouver (waen'ku:wer) | – Vancouver (van-koó-ver) |
| Varna ('wa:rna) | – Warna (vár-na) |
| Vatican ('waetyken) | – Watykan (va-ti-kan) |
| Venezuela ('wene'zuejle) | – Wenezuela (ve-ne-zoo-é-la) |
| Venice ('wenys) | – Wenecja (ve-néts-ya) |
| Vermont (we:rmont) | – Vermont |
| Versailles (weer'saj) | – Wersal (ver-sal) |
| Vienna (wy'ene) | – Wiedeń (vye-deñ) |
| Vietnam (wjet'na:m) | – Wietnam (wyét-nam) |
| Vilna ('wylne) | – Wilno (veél-no) |
| | Wilnius (veél-noos) |
| Virginia (wer'dżynje) | – Wirginia (veer-żeé-ña) |
| Vistula ('wystjule) | – Wisła (veés-wa) |
| Volga ('wolga) | – Wołga (vów-ga) |
| Volhynia (wol'hynje) | – Wołyń (vo-wiñ) |

| | |
|---|---|
| Walachia (łe'lejkje) | - Wołoszczyzna (vo-wosh-chíz-na) |
| Wales (łejlz) | - Walia (vál-ya) |
| Warsaw ('łó:rso:) | - Warszawa (var-sha-va) |
| Washington ('łószynten) | - Waszyngton (va-shíng-ton) |
| Waterloo (,łó:ter'lu:) | - Waterloo (va-ter-lo) |
| West Virginia ('łéstve:r'- | - Wirginia Zachodnia (veer-gee- |
| dżynje) | ña za-khód-ña) |
| White Russia ('łájt'rasza) | - Białoruś (bya-wó-roosh) |
| Winchester ('łynczyster) | - Winchester |
| Winnipeg ('łyny,peg) | - Winnipeg |
| Wyoming (łah'oumyŋg) | - Wyoming |
| Yalta ('jaelte) | - Jalta (yáw-ta) |
| Yellowstone ('jelou,stoun) | - Yellowstone |
| Yugoslavia (ju:gou'sla:wje) | - Jugoslawia (yoo-go-swáv-ya) |
| Yukon ('ju:kon) | - Yukon |
| Zagreb ('za:greb) | - Zagrzeb (zág-zheb) |
| Zakopane ('za:kop ane ) | - Zakopane (za-ko-pa-ne) |
| Zealand ('zi:lend) | - Zelandia (ze-lánd-ya) |
| Zurich ('zjueryk) | - Zurych (zoó-rikh) |

| CHRISTIAN NAMES | IMIONA WŁASNE |
|---|---|
| Abel ('ejbel) m. | – Abel (á-bel) |
| Abraham (ejbre,haem) m. | – Abraham (ab-rá-kham) |
| Ada ('ejde) f. | – Ada (á-da) |
| Adalbert ('aedel,be:rt) m. | – Wojciech (vóy-chekh) |
| Adam ('aedem) m. | – Adam (a-dam) |
| Adela ('aedyle) f. | – Adela (a-dela) |
| Agnes ('aegnys) f. | – Agnieszka (ag-ñesh-ka) |
| Albert ('aelbert) m. | – Albert (ál-bert) |
| Alec ('aelyk) m. | – Lech (lekh) |
| Alexander (,aelyg'za:nder) m. | – Aleksander (a-lek-sán-der) |
| Alfred (aelfred) m. | – Alfred (ál-fred) |
| Alice ('aelys) f. | – Alicja (a-leéts-ya) |
| Alois (e'louys) m. | – Alojzy (a-lóy-zi) |
| Andrew ('aendru:) m. | – Andrzej (ánd-zhey) |
| Ann (aen) f. | – Anna (án-na) |
| Antony ('aenteny) m. | – Antoni (an-tó-ñee) |
| Antonia (aen'tounje) f. | – Antonina (an-to-ñeé-na) |
| Arnold ('a:rnld) m. | – Arnold (ár-nold) |
| Arthur ('a:rter) m. | – Artur (ár-toor) |
| Augustine (o:'gastyn) m. | – Augustyn (au-goós-tin) |
| Avis ('aewys) f. | – Awia (áv-ya) |
| Barbara ('ba:rbere) f. | – Barbara (bar-ba-ra) |
| Benedict (benydykt) m. | – Benedykt (be-né-dikt) |
| Benjamin ('bendżmyn) m. | – Benjamin (ben-yá-meen) |
| Bernard ('be:rnerd) m. | – Bernard (bér-nard) |
| Bill (byl) m. | – William (veél-yam) |
| Blanch (bla:ncz) f. | – Blanka (blán-ka) |
| Bob (bob) m. | – Robert (ró-bert) |
| Boris ('borys) m. | – Borys (bó-ris) |
| Bridget ('brydżyt) f. | – Brygida (bri-geé-da) |
| Camilia (ke'mylje) f. | – Kamila (ka-meé-la) |
| Carlotta (ka:r'lote) f. | – Karolina (ka-ro-leé-na) |
| Carol ('kaerel) f. | – Karolina (ka-ro-leé-na) |
| Casimir ('kaesymjer) m. | – Kazimierz (ka-zheé-myezh) |
| Catherine ('kaeteryn) f. | – Katarzyna (ka-ta-zhí-na) |
| Cecil ('sesl) m. | – Cecil (tsé-tseel) |
| Cecilia (sy'sylje) f. | – Cecylia (tse-tsíl-ya) |
| Charles (cza:rlz) m. | – Karol (ká-rol) |
| Charlie ('cza:rly) m. | – Karolek (ka-ro-lek) |
| Christina (krys'ti:ne) f. | – Krystyna (kris-tí-na) |
| Christopher ('krystefer) m. | – Krzysztof (kzhísh-tof) |
| Clara (kleer) f. | – Klara (kla-ra) |
| Claud (klo:d) m. | – Klaudiusz (klawd-yoosh) |
| Claudia ('klo:dje) f. | – Klaudia (klawd-ya) |
| Clement ('klement) m. | – Klemens (klé-mens) |
| Clementine (,klemen,tajn) | – Klementyna (kle-men-tí-na) |
| Conrad ('konraed) m. | – Konrad (kón-rad) |
| Cyprian ('syprien) m. | – Cyprian (tsip-ryan) |
| Cyril ('syryl) m. | – Cyryl (tsí-ril) |

| | |
|---|---|
| Damian ('dejmjen) m. | – Damian (dám-yan) |
| Daniel ('dejnjel) m. | – Daniel (da-ñel) |
| David ('dejwyd) m. | – Dawid (da-veed) |
| Dennis('denys) m. | – Dionizy (dyo-ñée-zi) |
| Denise (dy'ni:z) f. | – Dioniza (dyo-ñée-za) |
| Dick (dyk) m. | = Richard |
| Dominic (do'mynyk) m. | – Dominik (do-mée-ñeek) |
| Dorothy ('dorety) f. | – Dorota (do-ró-ta) |
| Edmund ('edmend) m. | – Edmund (éd-moond) |
| Edward ('edłerd) m. | – Edward (éd-vard) |
| Edwin (edłyn) m. | – Edwin (éd-veen) |
| Eleanor ('elyner) f. | – Eleonora (e-le-o-nó-ra) |
| Elias (y'lajes) m. | – Eliasz (él-yash) |
| Elvira (el'wajere) f. | – Elwira (el-vée-ra) |
| Emily ('emyly) f. | – Emilia (e-méel-ya) |
| Eric ('e:yk) m. | – Eryk (e-rik) |
| Erica ('eryka) f. | – Eryka (e-ri-ka) |
| Eugene (ju:zejn) m. | – Eugeniusz (ew-ge-ñoosh) |
| Eugenia (ju:dzi:nje) f. | – Eugenia (ew-gé-ña) |
| Eva ('i:we) f. | – Ewa (e-va) |
| Evan ('even) m. | – Jan (yan) |
| Eve ('i:w) f. | – Ewa (e-va) |
| Felicia (fy'lysie) f. | – Felicja (fe-leéts-ya) |
| Felix ('fi:lyks) m. | – Feliks (fé-leeks) |
| | – Szczęsny (shcháńs-ni) |
| Frances ('fra:nsys) f. | – Franciszka (fran-chéesh-ka) |
| Francis ('fra:nsys) m. | – Franciszek (fran-chée-shek) |
| Frank ('fraenk) m. | = Francis |
| Frederic ('fredrik) m. | – Fryderyk (fri-de-rik) |
| Gabriel ('gejbrjel) m. | – Gabriel (gáb-ryel) |
| George (dżo:rdż) m. | – Jerzy (ye-zhi) |
| Gervase ('dże:rwes) m. | – Gerwazy (ger-vá-zi) |
| Gregory ('gregeri) m. | – Grzegorz (gzhé-gozh) |
| Gustavus (,gus'ta:wes) | – Gustaw (goós-tav) |
| Guy (gaj) m. | – Wit (veet) |
| Harold ('haereld) m. | – Harold (khá-rold) |
| Hedwig ('hedlyg) f. | – Jadwiga (yad-veé-ga) |
| Helen ('helyn) f. | – Helena (he-le-na) |
| Henrietta (,henry'eta) f. | – Henryka (hen-rí-ka) |
| Henry ('henry) m. | – Henryk (hén-rik) |
| Herbert ('he:rbert) f. | – Herbert (hér-bert) |
| Hilary ('hylery) m. | – Hilary (hee-lá-ri) |
| Hubert ('hju:bert) m. | – Hubert (hoó-bert) |
| Ian ('yen) m. | = John |
| Igor ('i:go:r) m. | – Igor (ee-gor) |
| Irene (aj'ri:n) f. | – Irena (ee-ré-na) |
| Isabella (,yze'bele) f. | – Izabella (ee-za-bé-la) |
| Isidora (,yzy'do:re) f. | – Izydora (ee-zi-dó-ra) |
| Isidore ('yzy,do:r) m. | – Izydor (ee-zi-dor) |
| Ivan ('ajwen) m. | = John |
| Ivo (ajwou) m. | – Iwo (eé-vo) |
| Ivor (ajwo:r) m. | = Ivo |
| Jack (dżaek) m. | = John |

| | |
|---|---|
| Jacob ('dźejkeb) m. | - Jakub (ya-koob) |
| James (dźejmz) m. | = Jacob |
| Jane (dźejn) f. | - Janina (ya-ńee-na) |
| Jeane (dźi:n) f. | = Jane |
| Jenny (dźeny) f. | = Jane |
| Jerome ('dźerem) m. | - Hieronim (khye-ro-ńeem) |
| Jill (dźyl) f. | - Juliana |
| Jim (dźym) m. | - James |
| Jimmie ('dźymy) m. | - James |
| Joanna (dźou'aene) f. | - Joanna (yo-án-na) |
| Joe (dźou) m. | - Joseph |
| John (dźon) m. | - Jan (yan) |
| Jonas (dźounes) m. | - Jonasz (yo-nash) |
| Joseph ('dźouzyf) m. | - Jozef (yoo-zef) |
| Josepha (,dźou'zefa) f. | - Jozefa (yóo-ze-fa) |
| Julia (dźu:lje) f. | - Julia (yoól-ya) |
| Julian (dźu:ljen) m. | - Julian (yoól-yan) |
| Kate (kejt) f. | = Catherine |
| Keith (ki:s) m. | - Keith |
| Kenneth ('kenys) m. | = Kenneth |
| Laura ('lo:re) f. | - Laura (láw-ra) |
| Laurence ('lo:rens) m. | - Wawrzyniec (vav-zhi-ńets) |
| Leo ('liou) m. | - Leon (lé-on) |
| Leonard ('lenerd) m. | - Leonard (le-o-nard) |
| Leopold ('lje,pould) m. | - Leopold (le-o-pold) |
| Lewis ('luys) m. | - Ludwik (loód-veek) |
| Lily ('lyly) f. | - Lilia (leél-ya) |
| Lilian ('lyljen) f. | - Lilianna (leel-yán-na) |
| Louisa (lu'i:ze) f. | - Ludwika (lood-vée-ka) |
| Lucas ('lu:kes) m. | - Łukasz (woó-kash) |
| Luther ('lu:ter) m. | - Luter (loó-ter) |
| Lydia ('lydje) f. | - Lidia (lýd-ya) |
| Marian ('meeryen) f. | - Marianna (mar-yan-na) |
| Mark (ma:rk) m. | - Marek (má-rek) |
| Martha ('ma:rte) f. | - Marta (már-ta) |
| Martin ('ma:rtyn) m. | - Marcin (mar-cheen) |
| Mary ('meery) f. | - Maria (már-ya) |
| Mathilda (me'tylde) f. | - Matylda (ma-til-da) |
| Matthew ('maetju:) m. | - Mateusz (ma-te-oosh) |
| Maurice ('morys) m. | - Maurycy (maw-ri-tsi) |
| Maximilian (,maeksy'myljen) | - Maksymilian (mak-si-mil-yan) |
| Michael ('majkl) m. | - Michał (mee-khaw) |
| Monica ('monyke) f. | - Monika (mo-ńee-ka) |
| Moses ('mouzyz) m. | - Mojżesz (móy-shesh) |
| Natalia (ne'ta:lje) f. | - Natalia (na-tál-ya) |
| Natalie ('naetely) f. | - Natalia (na-tál-ya) |
| Nathan ('nejten) m. | - Natan (na-tan) |
| Nicholas ('nykeles) m. | - Mikołaj (mee-kó-way) |
| Nicola ('nykele) f. | - Michalina (mee-kha-lee-na) |
| Olga ('olge) f. | - Olga (ól-ga) |
| Olivia ('olywje) f. | - Oliwia (o-leew-ya) |
| Ophelia (o'fi:lje) f. | - Ofelia (o-fél-ya) |

Oscar ('osker) m.     - Oskar (oś-kar)
Otto ('otou) m.     - Otton (ót-ton)
Pamela ('paemyle)     - Pamela (pa-me-la)
Patricia (pe'trysze) f.     - Patrycja (pat-ríts-ya)
Patrick ('paetryk) m.     - Patrycy (pat-rí-tsi)
Paul ('po:l) m.     - Paweł (pa-vew)
Paula ('po:le) f.     - Paulina (paw-leé-na)
Pepe (pi:p)     = Joseph
Peter ('pi:ter) m.     - Piotr (pyotr)
Philip ('fylyp) m.     - Filip (feé-leep)
Rachel ('rejczel) f.     - Rachela (ra-khe-la)
Ralph (raelf) m.     - Ralf (raif)
Randolph ('raendolf) m.     - Randolf (rán-dolf)
Raphael ('rejfel) m.     - Rafael (ra-fá-el)
Ray (rej) m.     - Ray (raj)
Rebecca (ry'beka)     - Rebeka (re-bé-ka)
Ricarda (ry'ka:rde) f.     - Ryszarda (ri-shár-da)
Richard ('ryczerd) m.     - Ryszard (rí-shard)
Robert ('robert) m.     - Robert (ro-bert)
Roberta (rou'be:rte) f.     - Roberta (ro-bér-ta)
Roger ('rodżer) m.     - Roger (ro-dżer)
Roland ('roulend) m.     - Roland (ró-land)
Rolf (rolf) m.     - Rudolf (rú-dolf)
Rose (rouz) f.     - Róża (roó-zha)
Rosemary ('rouzmery) f.     - Róża Maria (roó-zha már-ya)
Samuel ('saemjuel) m.     - Samuel (sa-moó-el)
Sean (szo:n) m.     = John
Shane (szejn) m.     = John
Sigismund ('sygysmend) m.     - Zygmunt (zíg-moont)
Simon ('sajmen) m.     - Szymon (szí-mon)
Sophia (se'faje) f.     - Zofia (zóf-ya)
Stanislaus (staenys,lo:s) m.     - Stanisław (sta-neés-wav)
Stephana ('stefene) f.     - Stefania (ste-fáń-ya)
Stephen ('sti:wen) m.     - Stefan (ste-fan)
Teresa (te'ri:ze) f.     - Teresa (te-ré-sa)
Thaddeus ('taedjes) m.     - Tadeusz (ta-de-oosh)
Theodore ('tje,do:r) m.     - Teodor (te-ó-dor)
Theophilus (ty'ofyles) m.     - Teofil (te-ó-feel)
Thomas ('tomas) m.     - Tomasz (to-mash)
Titus ('tajtes) m.     - Tytus (ti-toos)
Tobias (te'bajes) m.     - Tobiasz (to-byasz)
Ulric ('ulryk) m.     - Ulrych (oól-rikh)
Ursula ('e:rsele) f.     - Urszula (oor-shoo-la)
Valentine ('vaelen,tajn) m.     - Walenty (va-lén-ti)
Valerian (ve'ljerjen) m.     - Walerian (va-lér-yan)
Vera ('vjere) f.     - Wera (vé-ra)
Victor ('vykter) m.     - Wiktor (veék-tor)
Vincent ('vynsent) m.     - Wincenty (veen-tsén-ti)
Virginia (ver'dżynje) f.     - Wirginia (veer-geé-ña)
Walter ('ło:lter) m.     - Walter (val-ter)
Will (łyl) m.     - Wiliam (veél-yam)

William ('ʎyljem) m.            - Wilhelm (veél-khelm)
Winston ('ʎynsten) m.          = Winston
Xavier ('zaevjer) m.           - Ksawery (ksa-vé-ri)
Yve (i:w) m.                   = Ivo
Yves (i:w) m.                  = Ivo
Yvonne (y'won) f.              - Ivona (ee-vó-na)
Zach (zaek) m.                 = Zachariah
Zachariah (,zaeke'raje) m.     - Zachariasz (za-khár-yash)
Zenobia (zy'noubje) f.         - Zenobia (ze-nób-ya)

| CARDINAL NUMBERS | - | LICZEBNIKI GŁÓWNE |
|---|---|---|
| 0 | nought, zero, cipher | - zero |
| 1 | one | - jeden, raz |
| 2 | two | - dwa |
| 3 | three | - trzy |
| 4 | four | - cztery |
| 5 | five | - pięć |
| 6 | six | - sześć |
| 7 | seven | - siedem |
| 8 | eight | - osiem |
| 9 | nine | - dziewieć |
| 10 | ten | - dziesięć |
| 11 | eleven | - jedenaście |
| 12 | twelve | - dwanaście |
| 13 | thirteen | - trzynaście |
| 14 | fourteen | - czternaście |
| 15 | fifteen | - piętnaście |
| 16 | sixteen | - szesnaście |
| 17 | seventeen | - siedemnaście |
| 18 | eighteen | - osiemnaście |
| 19 | nineteen | - dziewiętnascie |
| 20 | twenty | - dwadzieścia |
| 21 | twenty-one | - dwadzieścia jeden |
| 22 | twenty-two | - dwadzieścia dwa |
| 23 | twenty-three | - dwadzieścia trzy |
| 24 | twenty-four | - dwadzieścia cztery |
| 30 | thirty | - trzydzieści |
| 40 | forty | - czterdzieści |
| 50 | fifty | - pięćdziesiąt |
| 60 | sixty | - sześćdziesiąt |
| 70 | seventy | - siedemdziesiąt |
| 80 | eighty | - osiemdziesiąt |
| 90 | ninety | - dziewięćdziesiąt |
| 100 | one hundred | - sto |
| 101 | one hundred and one | - sto jeden |
| 110 | one hundred and ten | - sto dziesięć |
| 200 | two hundred | - dwieście |
| 777 | seven hundred seventy seven | - siedemset siedemdziesiąt siedem |
| 1,000. | one thousand | - tysiąc |
| 1,500. | fifteen hundred | - tysiąc pięćset |
| 1978 | nineteen hundred and seventy eight | - tysiąc dziewięćset siedemdziesiąt osiem |
| 500,000. | five hundred thousand | - pięćset tysięcy |
| 1,000,000. | one million | - milion |
| 3,000,000. | three million | - trzy miliony |
| 1,000,000,000. | one billion | - miliard |

| ORDINAL NUMBERS | - LICZEBNIKI PORZĄDKOWE |
|---|---|
| 1st first | - pierwszy |
| 2nd second | - drugi |
| 3rd third | - trzeci |
| 4th fourth | - czwarty |
| 5th fifth | - piąty |
| 6th sixth | - szósty |
| 7th seventh | - siódmy |
| 8th eighth | - ósmy |
| 9th ninth | - dziewiąty |
| 10th tenth | - dziesiąty |
| 11th eleventh | - jedenasty |
| 12th twelfth | - dwunasty |
| 13th thirteenth | - trzynasty |
| 14th fourteenth | - czternasty |
| 15th fifteenth | - piętnasty |
| 16th sixteenth | - szesnasty |
| 17th seventeenth | - siedemnasty |
| 18th eighteenth | - osiemnasty |
| 19th nineteenth | - dziewiętnasty |
| 20th twentieth | - dwudziesty |
| 21st twenty-first | - dwudziesty pierwszy |
| 22nd twenty-second | - dwudziesty drugi |
| 23rd twenty-third | - dwudziesty trzeci |
| 24th twenty-fourth | - dwudziesty czwarty |
| 30th thirtieth | - trzydziesty |
| 40th fortieth | - czterdziesty |
| 50th fiftieth | - pięćdziesiąty |
| 60th sixtieth | - sześćdziesiąty |
| 70th seventieth | - siedemdziesiąty |
| 80th eightieth | - osiemdziesiąty |
| 90th ninetieth | - dziewięćdziesiąty |
| 100th (one) hundredth | - setny |
| 101st (one) hundred and first | - sto pierwszy |
| 102nd (one) hundred and second | - sto drugi |
| 103rd (one) hundred and third | - sto trzeci |
| 104th (one) hundred and fourth | - sto czwarty |
| 200th two hundredth | - dwusetny |
| 500th five hundredth | - pięćsetny |
| 1,000th (one) thousandth | - tysięczny |
| 3,000th three thousandth | - trzytysięczny |
| 1978th nineteen hundred and seventy eighth | - tysiąc dziewięćset siedemdzie-siąty ósmy |
| 500,000th five hundred thousandth | - pięćsettysięczny |
| 1,000,000th millionth | - milionowy |
| 3,000,000th three millionth | - trzy milionowy |

FRACTIONAL NUMBERS, ARITHMETIC EXPRESSIONS AND TIME
UŁAMKI, WYRAŻENIA : DZIAŁANIA ARYTMETYCZNE I CZAS

$\frac{1}{2}$ one half, a half — pół, połowa
   half a mile — pół mili
   half way — pół drogi, w połowie

$1\frac{1}{2}$ one and a half — półtora, jeden i pół

$3\frac{1}{2}$ three and a half — trzy i pół

$\frac{1}{3}$ one third, a third — jedna trzecia, trzecia część

$\frac{1}{4}$ one fourth, quarter — jedna czwarta, ćwierć

$\frac{3}{4}$ three fourths, three quarters — trzy czwarte, trzy ćwierci

$1\frac{1}{4}$ one and a quarter — jeden i ćwierć, jeden i jedna
     czwarta
$\frac{1}{5}$ one fifth, a fifth — jedna piąta

$2\frac{4}{5}$ two and four fifths — dwa i cztery piąte

.3 point three — 0,3 zero przecinek trzy
3.5 three point five — 3,5 trzy przecinek pięć
result in 100% — wynik stuprocentowy
single — pojedyńczy
double
twofold — podwójny
      — dwukrotny
threefold — potrójny
treble — trzykrotny
triple — trzykrotny
fourfold — poczwórny
quadruple — czterokrotny
fivefold — pięciokrotny
quintuple — pięciokrotny
sixfold — sześciokrotny

once — raz
twice — dwa razy
three times — trzy razy
twice as much — dwa razy więcej

first(ly) — po pierwsze
secondly — po drugie
thirdly — po trzecie
fourthly — po czwarte
in the first place — po pierwsze

3 x 3 = 9 three times three — trzy razy trzy równa się
     make nine, — dziewięć
     three multiplied
     by three are (make)
     nine

2 + 3 = 5 two plus three are — dwa plus trzy równa się pięć,
        five                 dwa dodac trzy równa się pięć

7-- 4 = 3 seven minus four — siedem minus cztery równa się
        are three           trzy,
                                     siedem odjąc cztery równa się
                                     trzy

8 ÷ 2 = 8 : 2 = 4 — osiem podzielone przez dwa
        eight divided by         równa się cztery
        two make four

TIME   —   CZAS

| | |
|---|---|
| an hour | godzina |
| half an hour | pół godziny |
| a quarter of an hour | kwadrans |
| a minute | minuta |
| what time is it, please? | Przepraszam, która godzina? |
| it is exactly three o'clock | punktualnie trzecia |
| it is only two o'clock | dopiero druga |
| it is past seven | po siódmej |
| it has struck five | piąta wybiła |
| it is a quarter to one | za kwadrans pierwsza |
| | za piętnaście pierwsza |
| it is a quarter past two | kwadrans na trzecia, |
| | piętnaście po drugiej |
| it is three minutes before one | pierwsza za trzy minuty |
| it starts at six a.m. | zaczyna się o szóstej rano |
| it ends at one p m. | kończy się o pierwszej |
| | kończy się o trzynastej |
| at eight p.m. | o ósmej wieczór |
| | o dwudziestej |
| the morning | rano , przedpołudnie |
| noon. midday | południe |
| the afternoon | popołudnie |
| the evening | wieczór |
| tonight | dziś wieczorem |
| the night | noc |
| midnight | północ |
| a day | dzień |
| a week | tydzień |
| a month | miesiąc |
| a year | rok |
| a leap year | rok przestępny |
| a century | wiek, stulecie |
| today | dziś |
| tomorrow | jutro |
| the day after tomorrow | pojutrze |
| yesterday | wczoraj |
| the day before yesterday | przedwczoraj |
| a year and half | półtora roku |
| good night | dobranoc |
| good morning, sir | dzień dobry panu |

# POLISH WEIGHTS AND MEASURES
## MIARY I WAGI

1. Lineal measure - miary długości

   1 mm milimetr - millimeter
   = 0.039 inch
   1 cm centymetr - centimeter
   = 10 mm = 0.394 inch
   1 m metr - meter (metre)
   = 100 cm = 1.094 yards =
   3.281 feet
   1 km kilometr - kilometer
   = 1000 m = 0.621 mile

2. Square measure - miary
   powierzchni
   1 $mm^2$ milimetr kwadratowy -
   - square millimeter
   = 0.002 square inch
   1 $cm^2$ centymetr kwadratowy -
   - square centimeter

   1 $m^2$ metr kwadratowy - square
   meter
   = 10,000 $cm^2$ = 1.196
   square yards
   = 10.764 square feet
   1 a - ar = 100 $m^2$
   = 119.599 square yards
   1 ha - hektar - hectare
   = 100 a = 2.471 acres

3. Cubic measure - miary
   objętości
   1 $cm^3$ centymetr sześcienny -
   cubic centimeter
   = 1000 $mm^3$
   = 0.061 cubic inch
   1 RT tona rejestrowa -
   register ton
   = 100 $feet^3$
   = 2,832. $m^3$

4. Measure of capacity -
   miary pojemności

   1 l litr - liter (litre)
   = 1.760 pints
   = 1.057 U.S. liquid
   quarts
   = 0.906 dry quarts

   1 hl hektolitr - hectoliter
   = 100 l
   = 2.75 bushels
   = 26.418 U.S. gallons

5. Weights- wagi

   1 g gram - gram
   = 15.432 grains

   1 kg kilogram - kilogram
   = 1000 g
   = 2.205 pounds ardp
   = 2.677 pounds troy

   1 q = kwintal
   = 100 kg
   = 1.968 hundred-
   weights
   = 2.204 U.S. hundred-
   weights

   1 t tona - ton
   = 1000 kg
   = 0.984 long ton
   = 1.102 U.S. short
   tons

AMERICAN AND BRITISH  WEIGHTS AND MEASURES
AMERYKAŃSKIE I BRYTYJSKIE WAGI I MIARY

1. Measures of length - Miary długości

   1 mile (majl) = 1760 yards (ja:rdz)    = 1609,3 m
   1 yard (ja:rd) = 3 feet (fi:t)      = 91,44 cm
   1 foot (fut) = 12 inches ('ynczyz)   = 30,48 cm
   1 inch (yncz)                      = 2,54 cm

2. Measures of surface - Miary powierzchni

   1 square mile (skłeer majl) = 640 acres ('ejkerz)
                                       = 258,99 ha
   1 acre ('ejker) = 4840 square yards (skłeer ja:rdz)
                                       = 0,40 ha
   1 square yard (skłeer ja:rd) = 9 square feet (skłeer fi:t)
                                       = 0,836 m²
   1 square foot (skłeer fut) = 144 square inches
                        (,skłeer'ynczyz) = 929 cm²
   1 square inch (skłeer yncz)      = 6,45 cm²

3. Measures of capacity - Miary pojemności

| | BR. | AM. |
|---|---|---|
| 1 quarter ('kło:rter) (BR.) | | |
| = 8 bushels (buszlz) = | 290,94 1 | - |
| 1 bushel (buszl) = 8 gallons | | |
| ('gaelenz) = | 36,368 1 | 35,238 1 |
| 1 gallon ('gaelen) = 4 quarts | | |
| (kło:rts) = | 4,546 1 | 4,405 1 |
| 1 quart (kło:rt) = 2 pints (paints) = | 1,136 1 | 1,101 1 |
| 1 pint (paint) = | 0,568 1 | 0,5306 1 |

4. Weights (avoirdupois) - Wagi
           (and apothecary)

| | | |
|---|---|---|
| 1 pound (paund) = 16 ounces ('aunsyz) | = | 453,59 g |
| 1 ounce (auns) = 16 drams (draemz) | = | 28,35 g |
| 1 dram (draem) = 3 scruples (skru:plz) | = | 4,00 g |
| 1 scruple (skru:pl)= 20 grains (grejns) | = | 1,33 g |
| 1 grain (grejn) | = | 64,7989 mg |

   1 ton (tan) (U.S.) = 20 hundredweight ('handredłejt) (U.S.)
                  = 2000 pounds (paundz)   =  907,185 kg
   1 hundredweight (U.S.) = 100 pounds (paundz) =   45,359 kg
   1 ton (tan) (Br.) = 20 hundredweight ('handredłejt) (Br.)
                  = 2240 pounds (paundz)   = 1016,047 kg
   1 hundredweight (Br.) = 112 pounds (paundz) =   50,802 kg

NOTE: Metric system in Poland since 1918, now is gradually
      introduced in the United States and in Great Britain

UWAGA: System metryczny jest obecnie stopniowo wprowadzany
      w U.S.A. i w Anglii.

AMERICAN, BRITISH AND POLISH CURRENCY

PIENIĄDZE W OBIEGU W U.S.A., ANGLII I POLSCE

American coins – monety

$ 1 dollar ('doler)      = 100 cents (sents)
1 half dollar ('ha:f,doler)= 50 cents
1 quarter ('kło:ter)    = 25 cents
1 dime (dajm)           = 10 cents
1 nickel (nykl)         = 5 cents
1 ₵ penny ('peny)       – 1 cent (cent)

Banknotes:one dollar and up (1; 2; 5; 10; 20; 50; 100 etc.)
Banknoty: jednodolarowe i wyższe.

British: 1 pound sterling – funt
(,paund'ste:rlyŋg) = 100 pence (pens)

coins (koynz)          50 pence
monety (mone⁴ti)       10 pence
                        5 pence
                        2 pence
                        1 penny ('peny)
                        $\frac{1}{2}$ halfpenny ('hejpny)

Banknotes: 1 pound notes and up.
Banknoty: jednofuntowe i wyższe.

Polish: zl. złoty (zwó-ti) = 100 groszy (gróshi)

coinz (koynz)          20 zł – złotych (zwo-tikh)
monety (monéti)        10 zł
                        5 zł
                        2 zł
                        1 zł. – złoty (zwó-ti)

                       50 gr. – groszy (gró-shi)
                       20 gr
                       10 gr

Banknotes: 50 zł; 100; 200; 500; 1000; 2000 etc.
Banknoty: pięćdziesiąt złotowe i wyższe.

# -NOTES-

–NOTES–

# —NOTES—

# -NOTES-

# -NOTES-